"An excellent overview of the first ten centuries of Christian history. Unsurpassed in its thoroughness, clarity, and organization. This belongs in the library of anyone interested in the history of Christianity."

**Justo L. González,** historian and theologian, author of *The Story of Christianity* and *The Mestizo Augustine*

"This is probably the best single-volume account of the history and key themes of the undivided Christian church through the first millennium and beyond available today. Its scope is both broad and focused, covering all geographical areas and epochs of that period, yet also introducing particular key figures and providing thoughtful analyses of important topics such as the relationship between church and state or the understanding of human sexuality. It also provides well-chosen selections of primary texts for further reading. It is sure to become a standard textbook and reference work for all students of that period."

**John Behr,** dean, professor of patristics, St. Vladimir's Orthodox Theological Seminary, Crestwood, New York

"In this massive introduction to the history of Christianity's first millennium, John Anthony McGuckin has succeeded in producing a work of great scholarly depth that is easy to read. Although, given the vast scope of this book, he has to move relatively quickly over the numerous theologians of the fourth and fifth centuries, who have been well treated elsewhere, McGuckin is at his brilliant best in rehabilitating the theologians of the second and early third centuries—theologians whose fundamental importance for all later forms of Christianity he demonstrates in definitive fashion. When he turns to particular themes of Christian faith and practice, he combines a master historian's attention to differences between epochs with a master theologian's open willingness to take sides in controversies. A marvelous achievement!"

**Matthew Levering,** James N. and Mary D. Perry Jr. Chair of Theology, Mundelein Seminary

"This is a monumental work that wonderfully synthesizes a dazzling array of virtues. It is vastly comprehensive, but also enlivened by a judicious selection of concrete detail; deeply learned, yet written with elegant lucidity; it takes the reader on a brisk march through Christian history while also offering historically situated contemplations of perennial Christian themes and preoccupations, such as philanthropy and sexual morality. John McGuckin's prodigious talents as a scholar and teacher, honed over decades, here achieve a brilliant and widely accessible distillation."

**Khaled Anatolios,** professor of theology, University of Notre Dame

"To attempt a study of this kind of historical, geographical, prosopographical, literary, and theological scope for a period as massive as the first ten centuries of the Common Era is as ambitious as it is daring. To actually do so, not only with comprehensiveness but with real depth of insight, is an extraordinary achievement. John McGuckin is one of the most learned and energetic historians of early Christianity in the world, and this fine work may be the capstone of his many distinguished studies. From Christian polity to liturgy, from perspectives on war to practices of healing, from views of slavery to views of art, this spectacular volume covers themes largely untouched in earlier macrohistories of the early church."

**Paul M. Blowers,** Emmanuel Christian Seminary at Milligan College

"John McGuckin has already provided several comprehensive guides to Eastern Orthodoxy. In this book, he discusses the history of the whole church during the first millennium, when there was yet no schism between East and West. He discusses not simply the public story of the institutional church, as is customary, but pays careful attention to what it was like to be a Christian in this period: how Christians prayed and worshiped, and how they dealt with wealth and poverty, not to mention slavery. Fr. John tells his story with immense erudition and insight, but simply and directly. The result is a rare achievement of immense value to all Christians as they seek to understand their past—and their future."

**Andrew Louth,** professor emeritus of patristic and Byzantine studies, Durham University UK, honorary fellow, faculty of theology, Vrije Universiteit, Amsterdam, author of *Modern Orthodox Thinkers*

# THE PATH OF CHRISTIANITY

## THE FIRST THOUSAND YEARS

JOHN ANTHONY McGUCKIN

An imprint of InterVarsity Press
Downers Grove, Illinois

InterVarsity Press
P.O. Box 1400, Downers Grove, IL 60515-1426
ivpress.com
email@ivpress.com

©2017 by John Anthony McGuckin

All rights reserved. No part of this book may be reproduced in any form without written permission from InterVarsity Press.

InterVarsity Press® is the book-publishing division of InterVarsity Christian Fellowship/USA®, a movement of students and faculty active on campus at hundreds of universities, colleges, and schools of nursing in the United States of America, and a member movement of the International Fellowship of Evangelical Students. For information about local and regional activities, visit intervarsity.org.

All Scripture quotations, unless otherwise indicated, are the author's translation.

Cover design: David Fassett
Interior design: Jeanna Wiggins
Images: Christ Pantocrator, Byzantine School, Monastery of Saint Catherine, Mount Sinai, Egypt /
    Photo © Zev Radovan / Bridgeman Images

ISBN 978-0-8308-4098-4 (print)
ISBN 978-0-8308-9952-4 (digital)

Printed in the United States of America ∞

 As a member of the Green Press Initiative, InterVarsity Press is committed to protecting the environment and to the responsible use of natural resources. To learn more, visit greenpressinitiative.org.

**Library of Congress Cataloging-in-Publication Data**

Names: McGuckin, John Anthony, author.
Title: The path of Christianity : the first thousand years / John Anthony
    McGuckin.
Description: Downers Grove, IL : InterVarsity Press, 2017. | Includes
    bibliographical references and index.
Identifiers: LCCN 2017000167 (print) | LCCN 2017000761 (ebook) | ISBN
    9780830840984 (hardcover : alk. paper) | ISBN 9780830899524 (eBook)
Subjects: LCSH: Church history--Primitive and early church, ca. 30-600. |
    Church history--Middle Ages, 600-1500.
Classification: LCC BR165 .M35 2017 (print) | LCC BR165 (ebook) | DDC
    270--dc23
LC record available at https://lccn.loc.gov/2017000167

| P | 23 | 22 | 21 | 20 | 19 | 18 | 17 | 16 | 15 | 14 | 13 | 12 | 11 | 10 | 9 | 8 | 7 | 6 | 5 | 4 | 3 | 2 | 1 |
|---|---|---|---|---|---|---|---|---|---|---|---|---|---|---|---|---|---|---|---|---|---|---|---|
| Y | 37 | 36 | 35 | 34 | 33 | 32 | 31 | 30 | 29 | 28 | 27 | 26 | 25 | 24 | 23 | 22 | 21 | 20 | 19 | 18 | 17 | | |

To my beloved Eileen

# CONTENTS

| | |
|---|---|
| Prelude | xvii |
| Abbreviations | xix |

## PART ONE: THE CHURCH'S PILGRIM PATH

### 1 The Fertile Second Century — 3

The End of the Apostles and the
Beginnings of Apostolicity — 3

A Proliferation of Christian Schools
and Teachers — 4

    Jewish Christian groups — 4
        *Encratites*
        *Nazarenes (Nazoraioi)*
        *Ebionites*
        *Elkesaites*

    Montanism — 14
    Asia Minor Quartodeciman communities — 22
    Christian gnosis — 26
        *A context*
        *Valentinus (fl. 120–160)*
        *Bardesanes (c. 154–222)*
        *Basilides (fl. 135–161)*

    Marcionism — 41
    Irenaeus of Lyons (c. 135–200) — 48
    The apostolic fathers — 54
        *Clement of Rome and the pseudo-Clementines*
        *Ignatius of Antioch (c. 35–107)*
        *Hermas (active 90–150)*
        *Polycarp (c. 69–156)*
        *Papias of Hierapolis (active early second century)*
        *The Letter of Barnabas*
        *The Didache*
        *The Letter to Diognetus*

    The second- to third-century Monarchian movement — 73
    The anti-Monarchian early Logos school — 89
        *Justin Martyr (d. c. 165)*
        *Tertullian (c. 155–220)*
        *Hippolytus (c. 170–235)*
        *Novatian of Rome (c. 200–258)*

Early Orthodoxies and Heterodoxies — 104

A Short Reader — 106

Further Reading — 111

## 2 | Blood in the Arena: The Age of Persecutions and Resistance: Second to Third Centuries — 117

Christians in the Roman Imperial Sightline — 117
- Nero's persecution — 122
- Domitian's persecution — 122
- Trajan's persecution — 124
- The Severan interlude — 125
- The persecution of Maximinus Thrax — 126
- The Decian persecution — 127
- The persecution of Valerian — 128
- The Diocletianic persecution — 128
- The memory of a persecuted community — 131

Roman Ideas on Law and Religion — 134
- The principate and dominate (27 BC to AD 313) — 134
- A Christian response to Roman oppression: Tertullian's social theology — 136

Hellenistic Attitudes to Christianity: The Case of Celsus — 146

Rival Non-Christian Orders — 150
- Mithras — 150
- Isis, queen of magic — 156
- Cybele — 162
- Manichaeism — 166

Early Christian Relations with the Jews — 174

The Christian Apologetical Tradition — 183
- Justin Martyr (d. c. 165) — 185
- Tatian — 187
- Athenagoras of Athens (c. 133–190) — 189
- Melito of Sardis (d. c. 180) — 190
- Clement of Alexandria (c. 150–215) — 191
- Theophilus of Antioch — 194
- Tertullian (c. 155–240) — 195
- (Marcus) Minucius Felix (later second century) — 197

A Short Reader — 199

Further Reading — 207

## 3 | Coming of Age: Christianity in the Third Century — 210

The Establishment of Christian Polity — 210

Rome and North Africa: Aftermaths of Persecution: Cyprian and Stephen — 212

The Christian Schools at Alexandria and Caesarea — 223

| | | |
|---|---|---|
| | The Alexandrian catechetical school | 223 |
| | *Origen of Alexandria: Master theologian and philosopher* | |
| | *Origen's biblical theology of salvation* | |
| | *Origen's heritage: Dionysius of Alexandria* | |
| | The school of Caesarea | 259 |
| | Christianity and the Philosophers | 261 |
| | A Short Reader | 271 |
| | Further Reading | 275 |
| **4** | **The Gospel on the Throne: Christians in the Fourth-Century East** | 278 |
| | Diocletian and the Constantinian Revolution | 278 |
| | The Arian Crisis and Its Resolution | 282 |
| | Arius and Alexander in conflict | 282 |
| | The Council of Nicaea 325 | 296 |
| | Searching for commonality and consensus | 304 |
| | *The Synod of Serdica 343* | |
| | *The Synod of Alexandria 362* | |
| | Athanasius's opponents | 310 |
| | *Eusebius of Nicomedia* | |
| | *Aetius and Eunomius of Cyzikos* | |
| | The Cappadocian Theological Synthesis | 315 |
| | Basil of Caesarea (330–379) | 316 |
| | Gregory of Nazianzus (329–390) | 320 |
| | Gregory of Nyssa (c. 331–395) | 323 |
| | The Councils of Constantinople 381 and 382 | 327 |
| | Christianity's Fourth-Century Ascendancy and Its Protestors | 336 |
| | A Short Reader | 342 |
| | Further Reading | 354 |
| **5** | **Reconciling the World: Christian Ascetical and Penitential Imperatives** | 357 |
| | Repentance and Reconciliation in Early Christian Theory and Action | 357 |
| | Eastern penitential canons | 361 |
| | *The Synod of Ancyra 314* | |
| | *Monastic influences on penance* | |
| | Western penitentials and the system of confession | 371 |
| | Feudal ideas of restitution and expiation | 375 |
| | *Purgatory as posthumous expiation* | |
| | *Feudal atonement theory in the West: Anselm's* Cur deus homo? | |

| | | |
|---|---|---|
| The Christian Monastic Movements | | 383 |
|     The emergence of varieties of Christian monasticism | | 383 |
|     Syrian monasticism | | 389 |
|         Aphrahat the Sage | | |
|         Macarius the Great | | |
|         Mar Isaac of Nineveh | | |
|         Symeon Stylites | | |
|     Egyptian monasticism | | 394 |
|         Tales of Antony | | |
|         Tales of the desert: The Christian fayyum | | |
|         Pachomian federated monasticism | | |
|         Other notable Egyptian monastic centers: Gaza and Sinai | | |
|     Monasteries in Palestine and beyond | | 404 |
|         Euthymius | | |
|         Mar Saba | | |
|     Early monasticism in the West | | 406 |
|         Martin of Tours | | |
|         John Cassian in Marseilles | | |
|         Irish monasticism | | |
|             Columba | | |
|             Columbanus | | |
| A Short Reader | | 414 |
| Further Reading | | 422 |

# 6 | Remaking Society: The Church in the West in the Fourth to Sixth Centuries

| | |
|---|---|
| | 425 |
| The Church in a Troubled Imperium | 425 |
| The Western Nicene Leaders | 432 |
|     Hilary of Poitiers | 432 |
|     Ambrose of Milan | 434 |
| The Donatist Controversy | 436 |
| Augustine and His Social Vision | 436 |
|     Augustine's *City of God* | 445 |
|     Augustine and the Donatists | 448 |
| Friends and Opponents of Augustine in the West | 450 |
|     Pelagius | 451 |
|     Caelestius | 454 |
|     John Cassian | 456 |
|     Jerome and his agenda | 456 |
| The Early Medieval Papacy and the Acacian Schism | 459 |
|     Pope Damasus | 459 |
|     Popes Felix and Leo | 463 |
|     The Acacian schism | 464 |

|   | Christianity in the Barbarian Kingdoms | 467 |
|---|---|---|
|   | The Vandal kingdom | 467 |
|   | Boethius among the Ostrogoths | 467 |
|   | A Short Reader | 469 |
|   | Further Reading | 477 |
| 7 | **A Church of the Nations: Ancient Global Christianity** | 479 |
|   | The Latin and Greek Foci of Classical Church History | 479 |
|   | Syria | 482 |
|   | China | 489 |
|   | Arabia | 491 |
|   | India | 495 |
|   | Armenia | 497 |
|   | Georgia | 499 |
|   | Nubia | 501 |
|   | Ethiopia | 502 |
|   | Slavia Orthodoxa | 505 |
|   | A Short Reader | 506 |
|   | Further Reading | 515 |
| 8 | **The Rise of the Ecumenical Conciliar System in the Fifth to Sixth Centuries** | 519 |
|   | The Christian Patriarchates | 519 |
|   | John Chrysostom at Constantinople | 527 |
|   | The Origenistic Crisis | 532 |
|   | The Christological Controversy of the Fifth Century | 539 |
|   | The clash of Antioch and Alexandria | 539 |
|   | The reform campaign of Nestorius at Constantinople | 542 |
|   | Cyril of Alexandria's countercharge | 547 |
|   | The Council of Ephesus 431 | 553 |
|   | Ephesus II 449 and its aftermath | 557 |
|   | The Council of Chalcedon 451 and Its Aftermath | 560 |
|   | The Council of Constantinople II 553 | 567 |
|   | Byzantine Platonism at Athens and Palestine | 570 |
|   | Damascius of Athens and the neo-Platonic school | 571 |
|   | Dionysius the Areopagite | 577 |
|   | A Short Reader | 580 |
|   | Further Reading | 601 |

| 9 | **The Emergence of Christian Byzantium in the Sixth to Ninth Centuries** | 604 |
|---|---|---|
| | Justinian the Great | 604 |
| |     The *Digest* (or *Pandects*) of Justinian | 609 |
| |     The *Institutes* of Justinian | 613 |
| |     The *Novels* of Justinian | 614 |
| |     Justinian's *Corpus Iuris Civilis* | 615 |
| | The Emergence of the Monophysite Church | 616 |
| | Heraclius and the Exaltation of the Cross | 619 |
| | Monoenergism and Monothelitism | 623 |
| | The Council of Constantinople III 680–681 | 629 |
| | Islam and Its Impact on Eastern Christianity | 631 |
| | The Byzantine Iconoclastic Crisis | 637 |
| | Photius the Great (c. 810–897) | 640 |
| | The Byzantine Slavic Missions | 643 |
| | A Short Reader | 645 |
| | Further Reading | 658 |
| 10 | **The Flourishing of Medieval Rome in the Seventh to Tenth Centuries** | 661 |
| | Benedict and Benedictinism | 661 |
| | Gregory the Great and His Successors | 666 |
| | The Carolingians and the Holy Roman Empire | 669 |
| | The Medieval Papacy | 676 |
| | A Short Reader | 681 |
| | Further Reading | 689 |
| 11 | **The Formation of Christian Liturgy** | 691 |
| | Earliest Origins of Liturgy | 691 |
| | The Classical Patristic-Era Formulations of Liturgies | 695 |
| |     Eucharistic | 695 |
| |     Baptismal rites | 699 |
| |     Penitential rites | 703 |
| | The Liturgical Cycle of Feasts | 708 |
| | Latin Styles of Liturgy | 709 |
| |     The African rite | 710 |
| |     The Ambrosian rite | 710 |
| |     The Mozarabic rite | 711 |

| | | |
|---|---|---|
| | The Gallican rite | 712 |
| | The Celtic rite | 713 |
| | The Eastern Rites | 713 |
| |    The Antiochene liturgical family | 714 |
| |    The Alexandrian liturgical family | 715 |
| | A Short Reader | 717 |
| | Further Reading | 725 |
| **12** | **The Great Parting of Ways: Greek East and Latin West in the Tenth to Eleventh Centuries** | 727 |
| | Byzantine Monastic Renewal: Symeon the New Theologian and Hesychasm | 727 |
| | Byzantine Intellectual Life | 733 |
| |    John Mauropous | 733 |
| |    Constantine (Michael) Psellus | 735 |
| |    John Xiphilinus | 738 |
| |    Constantine Leichoudes | 738 |
| | Apologia and Conflict: Michael Cerularius and the Great Schism | 739 |
| | The Rise of the University Schools in the West | 746 |
| | A Short Reader | 749 |
| | Further Reading | 758 |

## PART TWO: A WINDING ROAD: SELECT THEMES AND IDEAS

| | | |
|---|---|---|
| **13** | **The Bible and Its Interpretation in the Early Church** | 763 |
| | Old and New Biblical Interpretation | 763 |
| | Relativism and the Ecclesial Mind | 766 |
| | The Principle of Consonance | 769 |
| | The Principle of Authority | 774 |
| | The Principle of Utility | 776 |
| | A Short Reader | 781 |
| | Further Reading | 788 |
| **14** | **The Church and War** | 790 |
| | Conflict as Blessing or Bane? | 790 |
| | Is Christianity a Peaceful Religion? | 792 |
| | Struggling with Conflicting Sources on Religious Violence | 795 |
| | Constantine and the "Christ-Loving Armed Forces" | 797 |

| | Major Christian Theorists | 798 |
|---|---|---|
| |     Pre-third-century writers | 798 |
| |     Origen | 798 |
| |     Lactantius | 800 |
| |     The fourth-century Fathers | 800 |
| |     Augustine | 803 |
| |     Byzantine attitudes | 804 |
| | A Short Reader | 806 |
| | Further Reading | 813 |
| **15** | **The Development of Christian Hymnography** | 815 |
| | Origins of the Greek Christian Hymns | 817 |
| | Religious Hymns Among the Pre-Christian Greeks | 819 |
| | Pre-Nicene Christian Hymnody | 822 |
| | Hymns of the Heterodox-Orthodox Struggles | 824 |
| | Hymnography After the Arian Crisis | 827 |
| |     Latin hymns | 827 |
| |     Pre-sixth-century Syro-Byzantine hymns | 829 |
| | A Short Reader | 834 |
| | Further Reading | 857 |
| **16** | **Ways of Prayer in the Early Church** | 860 |
| | Gathering for Prayer | 860 |
| | The Heart as Sanctuary in the Old Testament | 865 |
| | The New Testament Doctrine of the Heart | 867 |
| | Prayer in the Early Christian Monastic Movement | 869 |
| | Syriac Christian Tradition on the Prayer of the Heart | 876 |
| | A Short Reader | 885 |
| | Further Reading | 889 |
| **17** | **Women in Ancient Christianity** | 891 |
| | Greek Silence | 891 |
| | Women in the First Centuries of the Church | 895 |
| | Women in Ancient Christian Epigraphy | 900 |
| | Women in the Age of Persecutions | 901 |
| | Christian Women in the Patristic and Byzantine Era | 904 |
| | Women in the Later Byzantine Hagiographies | 911 |
| | A Short Reader | 916 |
| | Further Reading | 921 |

| | | |
|---|---|---|
| **18** | **Healing and Philanthropy in Early Christianity** | 923 |
| | Healing in Ancient Hellenism | 923 |
| | Healing in Early Christian Perspectives | 925 |
| | *Philanthropia* in Classical Greek Thought | 934 |
| | Philanthropy in the Byzantine Divine Liturgy | 943 |
| | The Hospital as Symbol of the Church | 945 |
| | A Short Reader | 948 |
| | Further Reading | 952 |
| **19** | **The Exercise of Authority in the Church: Orders and Offices** | 955 |
| | New Testament Polity | 956 |
| | Authority in Hellenistic and Christian Usage | 956 |
| | Ordination and Offices in Early Christianity | 965 |
| |     Apostles | 965 |
| |     Christian prophets | 971 |
| |     Presbyters | 975 |
| |     Bishops | 982 |
| |     Deacons | 991 |
| |     Widows | 994 |
| |     Virgins | 996 |
| | A Short Reader | 1000 |
| | Further Reading | 1005 |
| **20** | **Christians and Magic** | 1008 |
| | Antique Fears of Black Magic | 1009 |
| | Magical Amulets | 1012 |
| | Exorcists and Magi | 1015 |
| | A Short Reader | 1019 |
| | Further Reading | 1023 |
| **21** | **The Church and Wealth** | 1025 |
| | Classical Greek Inheritances | 1025 |
| | Christian Attitudes to Wealth | 1030 |
| |     Scriptural evidences | 1032 |
| |     A tradition rooted in eschatology | 1035 |
| |     Wealth in the earliest centuries of the church | 1041 |
| |     The patristic-era teachings | 1043 |
| | A Short Reader | 1045 |
| | Further Reading | 1054 |

| 22 | **Church and Slavery in an Age of Oppression** | 1056 |
|---|---|---|
| | Slavery in Ancient Social Structures | 1056 |
| | Scriptural Approaches to Slavery | 1065 |
| | A Short Reader | 1076 |
| | Further Reading | 1088 |
| 23 | **Attitudes to Sexuality in the Early Church** | 1090 |
| | Philosophical Renewals of Interest | 1090 |
| | Greek Love | 1093 |
| | Some Nonphilosophical Greek Attitudes to Sexuality | 1097 |
| | Greek Medical Notes on Sexuality and Gender | 1097 |
| | Hellenistic Jewish Approaches to Sexuality | 1101 |
| | The New Testament Evidence on Sexual Morality | 1103 |
| |     The Jesus tradition | 1104 |
| |     The Pauline and Pastoral Letters | 1107 |
| |     The patristic era: The triumph of renunciation theory | 1110 |
| | A Short Reader | 1114 |
| | Further Reading | 1119 |
| 24 | **A Brief Account of Ancient Christian Art** | 1121 |
| | Early Christian Egypt and the Origins of the Icon | 1121 |
| | Earliest Christian Art Theory | 1123 |
| | Symbols and Practices in Early Christian Art | 1129 |
| | Iconoclastic Opposition to Sacred Art | 1134 |
| | Conflicted Attitudes to Christian Art | 1136 |
| | A Short Reader | 1137 |
| | Further Reading | 1145 |

| Epilogue | 1149 |
|---|---|
| Appendix 1: The Seven Ecumenical Councils: A Brief Guide | 1150 |
| Appendix 2: List of the Roman Popes to 1054 and the Patriarchs of Constantinople to 1453 | 1158 |
| Appendix 3: List of the Roman Emperors to 1453 | 1168 |
| Index of Persons and Places | 1177 |
| Index of Subjects | 1195 |
| Index of Biblical Citations | 1203 |

# PRELUDE

THIS INTELLECTUAL AND SOCIAL HISTORY of the early church in its first thousand years has been designed from the outset as a textbook. I hope it will be useful to a wide range of readers: clergy, seminarians, a diverse array of students of Christian thought and culture, and also to the general reader who has an empathy for this great culture-building religion and who might wish to know how the church got to be the way it is. Most important things were settled by the fifth century. Much of what we now see as characteristics of the Christian movement are variations on the foundations, reactions to it, reactions to the reactions, and so on. One thing is abundantly true of Christianity: it was born of an eschatological philosophy that looked to the past and from which it took its bearings for the future. It has remained, ever since, a profoundly conservative force even when, as often was the case, it was being socially and religiously radical and proleptic. The church's history, accordingly, is like a vast antique emporium, where very little has ever been thrown away and some archaic things are, most surprisingly, still being pressed into daily use. An understanding of how the church in the first millennium got to be the way it is will not only offer the reader a fascinating gallery of stories in their own right, but might also explain much about the contemporary church: why some parts of it seem so slow to acknowledge change of any kind, and why other parts seem not to be able to change fast enough; why some aspects of Christian pastoral practice have been, and remain, moving and admirable, and why other aspects seem less than attractive in a modern age that values individual freedoms and responsibility.

Many programs of advanced study of Christian history follow a twelve-week semester plan and often devote two class sessions a week to a major-credit course, ranging from two to three hours. It was for this reason I conceived the book in two parts. The first section follows the historical line of development of the first millennium in a synchronous way. It looks at the different protagonists and crises in the various centuries as they temporally unfold. The opening chapter, devoted to the second century, is one of the most extensive in the book. This is so because the second century was the nurturing womb for the embryonic international Christian movement. If the second-millennium church is deeply dependent on the first, then the first millennium certainly grows organically out of that second century. The first part of the book allows one to follow a predictable linear progression. The second part of the book plays a different note. It suggests that real life rarely follows such a straightforward, linear movement as the recorded formal narrative might suggest. Accordingly, part two takes a diachronic approach to the story. It leaves the account of mainline developments and instead investigates key structural ideas: themes and obsessions of the Christians that might throw a different kind of light on our study: a light that might give different dimensionality and new perspectives.

In the course of my teaching of this material, for more than ten years in England and then twenty years in New York, I offered two classes on first-millennial history each week in the fall semester. In the first of those meetings we made a linear progress through the centuries, with my lead lecture underlining salient episodes and protagonists. In the second class we spent more time collectively reading and discussing key primary texts, and considering "issues" and themes as they cut across the centuries. I have tried to reproduce this in the structure of parts one and two of the present volume. In each part, however, I have had the luxury in the book, which was not always possible given the pressures of the classroom, to offer a wide range of primary texts for each chapter. My advice to the reader is to take chapters in sequential order from part one, and then alternate them with reading of chapters (not necessarily in sequence) from part two. This way the long, thousand-year road will not be too daunting.

If the book is used as a class text, therefore, it lends itself immediately to a linear presentation, followed by a seminar discussion: synchronic and diachronic at the same time.

I hope it proves useful. It has certainly been illuminating putting it all together so as to serve as a clear and honest exposition of an extraordinary and often extremely beautiful set of phenomena, which I have tried to expound with a clear historical eye, yet also with a view to the spiritual and radiant character of the church's inner life: the soul in the body that gave it vitality, which it always claimed was the spirit of its risen Lord, still inhabiting its concerns despite the very human fallibility it often showed on its long earthly pilgrimage.

# ABBREVIATIONS

| | |
|---|---|
| *ANF* | Ante-Nicene Fathers |
| *ANRW* | Aufstieg und Niedergang der römischen Welt: Geschichte und Kultur Roms im Spiegel der neueren Forschung. Part 2, *Principat*. Edited by Hildegard Temporini and Wolfgang Haase. Berlin: de Gruyter, 1972– |
| c. | circa |
| CSEL | Corpus Scriptorum Ecclesiasticorum Latinorum |
| d. | died |
| fl. | flourished |
| *JEH* | *Journal of Ecclesiastical History* |
| *JTS* | *Journal of Theological Studies* |
| OECT | Oxford Early Christian Texts |
| PG | Patrologia Graeca [= *Patrologia Cursus Completus*: Series Graeca]. Edited by J.-P. Migne. 162 vols. Paris, 1857–1886 |
| PL | Patrologia Latina [= *Patrologia Cursus Completus*: Series Latina]. Edited by J.-P. Migne. 217 vols. Paris: 1844–1864 |
| r. | reigned |
| SC | Sources Chrétiennes |
| *StPatr* | *Studia Patristica* |
| *VC* | *Vigiliae Christianae* |
| *ZNW* | *Zeitschrift für die neutestamentliche Wissenschaft und die Kunde der aälteren Kirche* |

# PART ONE

# THE CHURCH'S PILGRIM PATH

# THE FERTILE SECOND CENTURY

## THE END OF THE APOSTLES AND THE BEGINNINGS OF APOSTOLICITY

The second century is an extraordinarily fertile time in Christian history. It is a period that often "falls between the gaps" in common knowledge: being too late for those focused intently on the New Testament and too early for those who wish to see the classically formulated shape of post-Nicene ecclesiality. The period was often studied by theological historians chiefly for what it might adumbrate of the shape of things to come, rather than what it had to say for and of itself. But like the study of all embryology, this foundational era in Christian post–New Testamental development can tell us so much, as long as we are willing to listen to the stories, however odd they might strike us at first, and put a rein on our desire to address them primarily in terms of what came before or what was to follow after. Of course, most of what we find in the second century found itself in a similar dilemma of self-classification. Much of the time the writers of this era were making explicit claims among themselves, sometimes in sharp disagreement, to represent the authentic lineage of the apostolic era. So many conflicting claims to be the genuine continuation of the teaching and direction of the first-generation disciples, however, led to an inevitably growing sense that not all such claims could possibly be true, and not all visions of the central thrust of Christian consensus were compatible. This led much of the controversy of this era to be focused around the issue of tradition and traditioning: the *paradosis* of the church (what was handed on as core and definitive).

Apostolicity and what it meant came to be a crucial issue. It is one that is reflected even today in the power of the notion of the apostolical canon (what can be regarded as fundamental and authoritative New Testament Scriptures) and apostolic succession of authority from the first generations to the successive ones. These twin notions of what is the new scripture of the new community and who speaks for it (in other words, apostolic canon and who the ordained officers of the liturgical assembly are, who speak for that canon in exegesis and preaching, as successors to the apostles) are the dominant masterthemes of this whole century. By the end of this formative period, central things have come into shape that will mark Christianity for millennia to come: the nature of ordained authorities; the central core of what can be regarded as the Christian holy books, and not least how to interpret them; whether or not the church is bound to the Jewish laws if its accepts the Jewish holy books; what is the nature of fundamental Christian hopes; what is the status of the person of Jesus, or the Holy Spirit; whether the Christian God was monist, binitarian, or trinitarian in form; and how disputes might be resolved across the growing Christian world. The church expanded out from Jerusalem very quickly. It followed trade routes by sea and land, first into Asia Minor and then to all the great Roman sea ports. Its international coherence was not a given thing at first. It seems, to me at least, to have developed by the spread of good practice watched and copied by communities who had an eye to one another's doings and who were also encouraged toward greater commonality across the second century by the church leaders of the larger city communities who could boast of a greater accumulation of skilled and learned leaders in their assemblies. This is much the same way that religious communities develop even to this day: strong locally, but also internationally aware by personal connection and historical respect.

Our story in this chapter will progress by looking at the remarkable range of people, events, controversies, and developments that occurred in this important period. If the New Testament is the true embryology of the Christian church, then this century was its infancy. Learning is imprinted as much as consciously acquired in such formative times. Likewise, patterns laid down here endured for centuries to come as fundamental charter structures. Our story begins by looking at some of the leading movements and individual teachers, claiming attention as the continuators of the Christian story in the larger Roman world after the destruction of the Jerusalem temple.

## A PROLIFERATION OF CHRISTIAN SCHOOLS AND TEACHERS

*Jewish Christian groups. Encratites.* Encratites are regarded as a secessionist sect by the later heresiologists, but it is probable that they never existed in this concrete form, that is as a polity or church group as such. Rather, their attitudes were part of a much wider ascetical, world-denying "spirit of the age," which by the late second century had come to mark them out as secessionist from the mainstream Christian communities, who were less radical in their attitudes to asceticism than these others and who, accordingly, came to regard the ascetical practices as specific identity markers for these different communities. So the attitude to *encrateia* (undoubtedly a commonality among such factions) was probably elevated in the second century as a catchall to identify groups that might have been much more variegated in terms of the broader charter of identifying doctrines they sustained. The term *encrateia* means "self-mastery" in the philosophical literature, the ability to control the forces of body and spirit in a disciplined way, to permit the sophistic life.[1] A second-century compilation of sophistic aphorisms (that had some currency among Christian readers) was the *Sentences of Sextus*.[2] It is a clear example of sophist asceticism seen as first of all a detachment from materialist and bodily desires to allow for contemplation, but also a form or "way of life" (*politeia*) that could easily turn toward a certain "despising" of common human values.

Among the Christians the term *encrateia* soon came to mean "continence," and when allied to dietary observances (common to both Jewish and pagan groups of the time) such ascetical disciplines could easily become group identifiers. The "Encratites" the later heresiologists object to seem to have been radical ascetic groups among the Syrian churches of the first three centuries, some of whom overlapped in unclear ways with Gnostic and, later, Manichaean tendencies. A specific litmus test for distinguishing Encratism from mainline Christian asceticism (especially as this became prevalent in the later monastic movement) was the belief among the radicals that sexual activity was deeply unspiritual and inimical to the liberation of the soul, conceived of as a struggle to escape from fleshly bonds.[3] Among Encratite circles marriage was thus frowned on, even forbidden to the élite of the communities. The movement was also recorded as being strictly vegetarian and non-wine-drinking. Pythagorean ascetics had long inculcated vegetarianism, since vegan foodstuffs had less "animate matter" in them to keep the souls of the consumers who so "trapped them," themselves tied in to this sublunar region.

The movement was often allied with a strongly dichotomous worldview of the "two ways" (ever-warring poles of light and darkness, good and evil) that held the cosmos to be profoundly corrupted by material forms; and it understood the church, in a defining and circumscribing way, as the body of pure elect withdrawn from that wicked cosmos.[4] Some have seen connections between the epistle to Titus (especially

---

[1] Aristotle, *Nicomachean Ethics* 7.4.4.
[2] H. Chadwick, ed., *The Sentences of Sextus* (Cambridge: Cambridge University Press, 1959); see online "The Sentences of Sextus," translated by Frederik Wisse, *The Gnostic Society Library*, http://gnosis.org/naghamm/sent.html, accessed May 25, 2016.
[3] Hugo Koch compiled a fine survey of Encratite sources serving as a prelude of influences on the later monastic movement. See *Quellen zur Geschichte der Askese und des Mönchtums in der alten Kirche*, part 1 (Tübingen: Motor, 1933).
[4] By "in a defining and circumscribing way" I mean that if the church is by definition seen as the body of the pure elect, it cannot tolerate the presence of the impure within it—so it is by that fact a highly exclusionist ecclesiology.

the admonitions of chapter 2) and the Encratite movement: but there is a world of difference, the ascetical advice in Titus being reflective of the very common and widespread sense of ascetical morality (the "Roman household code"), which was a kind of democratized form of Hellenistic sophism for the masses.[5] That kind of ascetical advice does not begin to approach the radical dualism of flesh and spirit we find characteristic of Encratism properly understood. It was among Encratite circles that the large body of apocryphal writings of the first three centuries seem to have originated, most of which are marked by these ideological tendencies, even if they are not yet hardened into a common doctrinal ideology.

Syrian Christian theologian Tatian is usually elevated as a concrete example of such an Encratite. Irenaeus was the first to see him as the "patriarch" of the Encratites, though he was probably just a more severe form of the ascetical tendencies prevalent throughout much of Syrian Christianity of the first three centuries, a church that struck Greek and Latin external observers as increasingly out of step with the mainline communities of the Mediterranean.[6] Among the Syrians, for example, it has been thought that baptism, until well into the fourth century, was thought also to be a solemn invitation to profess lifelong chastity, which meant from earliest times the clergy of the Syrians were celibate, baptism being a requirement for clerical orders. The larger majority of the worshiping faithful would be catechumens who never received the sacraments until late in life, when they were either on their deathbeds or chose baptism and a life of celibate old age thereafter. According to Irenaeus the Encratite movement saw procreative sex as responsible for transmitting the stigma and stain of damnation from Adam through to the whole human race. It is highly reminiscent of ideas that later influenced Augustine from his time among the Manichaeans. Irenaeus traces this idea to influences from Valentinian Gnosticism. Indeed, it has "hung around" Christian attitudes toward sexuality from time immemorial, appearing regularly from the Messalians of the fourth century to the Bogomils of the eleventh and after.

A string of Christian theologians in the early patristic mainstream regularly denounce the Encratite movement.[7] In many cases it is a cultural tendency they strike against. One notices, nevertheless, that the overall deeply reverential bow Christianity of the second century makes toward sophistic asceticism prevents the same

---

[5]Cf. G. Sfameni Gasparro, "L'Epistula Titi discipuli Pauli De dispositione sanctimonii e la tradizione dell' enkrateia," *ANRW* 2.25.6, 4551-64.

[6]See Irenaeus, *Adversus Haereses* 1.28.1; A. Voobus, *History of Asceticism in the Syrian Orient*, vol. 1 (Louvain: Peeters, 1958).

[7]Irenaeus, *Adversus Haereses* 3.23; Clement of Alexandria, *Paedagogus* 2.2.33; *Stromateis* 1.15.71.6; 3.17.101.1-2; 7.17.108.1-2; Hippolytus, *Refutations* 8.20.1-4; Eusebius, *Ecclesiastical History* 4.29; Epiphanius, *Panarion* 45-47.

writers from ever penning a celebratory encomium of the sacramental holiness of sexual union blessed by Christ, or from noting just how extensively the desire for a wholly celibate leadership, and the setting of virginity as the highest ideal of Christian virtue, are established as unremarkable tropes by the very fourth-century writers who find the Encratite "school" disturbing. Perhaps the closest we can come to finding a typical text of Christian Encratites themselves (apart from the apocryphal acts of the apostles)[8] is the cited fragment of the dialogue of Jesus and Salome in the Gospel of the Egyptians.[9] Fourth-century historian Eusebius, describing the situation of the third century, says that one Severus, whom he classes as a Gnostic, was a leader of such a Christian radical ascetic sect.[10] The latter accepted the Old Testament but rejected the writings and authority of Paul (making him redolent of the Ebionites as described by Irenaeus). Epiphanius argues that this radical ascetic movement was still alive in Christian Phrygia and Pisidia in the fourth century.[11]

Encratism would eventually be swamped, overtaken by larger Christian orthodoxy in the very act of its merging with mainstream forms of Christian life, when the fourth century brought the monastic movement into its heartland: insisting then, as it made it mainstream, only that such ascetical trends did not despise the sacramentality of marriage, or the holiness of procreation, and the virtue possible in the ordinary lay life. The overwhelming character of fourth-century ascetical Christianity, however, meant that while these niceties were observed, the theology of marriage, or reflections on the positive spiritual value of human physical experience, were massively neglected by Christian writers even into the modern age.

*Nazarenes (Nazoraioi).* Fourth-century heresiologist Epiphanius of Salamis (never wholly reliable in his historical judgment, unfortunately) gives us the information that the Jewish-Christian community of Jerusalem that survived the Roman war of AD 70 fled to Pella in the Decapolis.[12] This was the region of the "Ten Cities" across the Jordan. This much is undoubtedly true. Epiphanius then derives the

---

[8] Ascetical Syrian apocrypha such as Acts of Thomas, Acts of Paul, Acts of John, and Gospel of Thomas. See further Y. Tissot, "L'encratisme des *Actes du Thomas*," ANRW 2.25.6, 4415-30.

[9] Quoted in Clement of Alexandria, *Stromateis* 3.9.63.2–66.1; Clement of Alexandria, *Excerpts from Theodotus* 67.1-4.

[10] Eusebius, *Ecclesiastical History* 4.29.4-5.

[11] Epiphanius, *Panarion* 47.

[12] Ibid., 29.7.7; 30.2.7; *On Weights and Measures* 15. Eusebius speaks of this in *Ecclesiastical History* 3.5.3, suggesting the move to Pella came just before AD 70: "But the people of the church in Jerusalem had been commanded by a revelation, vouchsafed to approved men there before the war, to leave the city and to dwell in a certain town of Perea called Pella. And when those who believed in Christ had come there from Jerusalem, then, as if the royal city of the Jews and the whole land of Judea were entirely destitute of holy men, the judgment of God at length overtook those who had committed such outrages against Christ and his apostles and totally destroyed that generation of impious men."

"Nazarene" (*Nazoraioi*; thus also *Nazorean* or *Nazorene*) Jewish-Christian sect from that original remnant community of the Jerusalem church and chronologically lists them as flourishing near the time of Cerinthus the Gnostic: hence mid-second century. Epiphanius lists them in his chronicle of secessionists and so obviously has issues with them. What emerges from his treatment is first and foremost that they did not call themselves Christians like everyone else (as by his day had become the universal practice as established at Antioch) but rather Nazarenes (which was also an antique Semitic way of referring to Christians in the Roman Orient—as he also admits). He says they also referred to themselves as Jesse-ans (after the biblical ancestor Jesse, father of king David) and goes on to give a scriptural discourse on the nature of Jesus' claim to the kingly and priestly status of the house of Jesse. Epiphanius makes the point here that with Herod the ruling house of Israel lost all claim to priestly kingship in the line of Jesse (since Herod was a Gentile) so that after Jesus it clearly passed on as a common heritage to the church.[13] This can be read, between the lines as it were, as manifesting Epiphanius's chief bone of contention with the *Nazoraioi*: how important were bloodline and belonging to the church? A Jewish-Christian heritage might well have different views on that (as well as attitudes to the law's continuing relevance or not) from Gentile communities. The *Nazoraioi* seem to have laid some abiding stress on the importance of the physical heritage of Jesus, and when we recall that the very first structuring of the Jerusalem church was based on the first-generational leaders related most closely to Jesus (James the brother of the Lord, and Mary his mother) we might see the point of this.

Epiphanius notes that their Gospel was Matthew in Hebrew. Since this, we remember, begins solemnly with the genealogy through Jesse, and since Epiphanius later complains that the group has excised the genealogy in the Hebrew version they read, it is now generally thought that Epiphanius has come across a Hebrew text of "a Gospel" that they used that was actually not the same as Matthew, and concerning which he simply makes confused identifications. It is now called the Gospel of the Ebionites, from fragments reassembled in Epiphanius's work.[14] It is thought to have been a Gospel synopsis (similar to Tatian's *Diatessaron*—a pastiche of texts used in their worship, a Gospel "harmony"). Irenaeus attested the existence of this work, but if he discussed it, these sections of his work are now lost. Apart from cutting the genealogy, the text portrays Jesus and John the Baptist as vegetarians (probably a cultic mark of adherents), emphasizes hostility to the sacrificial cult, and includes the summation of the law in the writer's own teachings. The text is generally thought

---

[13] Herod was a Nabatean Arab of Edomite descent, raised as a Jew—but never seen as pure enough by the rabbis, who held just as jaundiced a view of him as did the Christians.

[14] For the text see M. R. James, *The Apocryphal New Testament* (Oxford: Clarendon, 1924), 8-10.

by commentators to have been composed in the mid-second century as a harmony of Matthew and Luke, to reflect the school's particular doctrines.[15]

The wider issues with the Nazarenes as Epiphanius understands them might also be placed in the context of the spreading influence of Pauline Christianity as a norm in the Gentile communities of the second century, a norm that had been taken for granted since its establishment (by the third century) but that was certainly not a fait accompli, in Palestine at least, in the second. The wider issue, of authority and identity, is akin to the problem that Paul himself had with the dominance of the Jerusalem leaders, especially James, and with what happened when the Gentile Christian communities outside Palestine no longer cared to follow the cultic or dietary prescripts of the law. Bishop Epiphanius, possibly a former Jew himself, writing from a very established fourth-century perspective that looks back on these Jewish Christians as retro minority relics of another age, wants to undermine this Nazarene theology decisively. He insists that Jesus has the priestly kingship of Melchizidek, while James of Jerusalem had the high priesthood after Aaron. James was also Joseph's son, he notes, not Mary's. It was Mary's son who held the Jessean lineage, and the Melchizidekian priesthood and passed this on to the *ekklesia*, not to members of his immediate family.[16]

At *Panarion* 29.5.1, however, Epiphanius seems to tell his readers that he is basing his knowledge of the Nazarenes on Philo's account in his book *The Jesseans* and his admiration of their ascetical lifestyle at Mareotis in Egypt.[17] This part of his narrative, then, seems to be conflated with Philo's account of the Therapeutae, whom Epiphanius evidently thinks (following Eusebius) were Christian monks, and it is partly lifted from a reading of Eusebius's *Ecclesiastical History* 2.17.16-18; 2.17.21-22. One wonders, therefore, how much of Epiphanius's treatment at this juncture is grounded at all.[18] Some scholars have jaundiced views of his worth, but Ray Pritz has recently argued that he cannot be dismissed wholesale.[19] At *Panarion* 29.7.2, however, Epiphanius's focus seems to become sharp once more. He speaks of a sect calling themselves Nazarenes who definitely identify as Christian while

---

[15] Rejection of the virgin birth, rejection of Pauline elements, and so on.
[16] *Panarion* 29.3.7; 29.4.5.
[17] Actually in Philo's *De vita contemplativa*, not *The Jesseans*. See Eusebius, *Historia ecclesiastica* 2.17.
[18] He describes the Nazarenes with terms derived, it would seem, from Irenaeus's account of the Ebionites. *Adversus Haereses* 1.26.2; Hippolytus, *Haereses* 7.34.1; Eusebius, *Ecclesiastical History* 3.27.5.
[19] Such as H. Schaeder in *Theological Dictionary of the New Testament*, ed. G. Kittel and G. Friedrich (Grand Rapids: Eerdmans, 1942), 4:879, who imagines Epiphanius to be making up the whole thing out his own misconstrued patristic reading. R. A. Pritz's careful study (*Nazarene Jewish Christianity: From the End of the New Testament Period to Its Disappearance in the Fourth Century* [Leiden: Brill, 1988]) shows this is not the case. In the midst of some of his confused deductions, there is also solid line of historical reminiscence.

maintaining all the Jewish customs (to Epiphanius's annoyance), who use the New Testament alongside the Law, the Prophets, and the Writings, in the rabbinic manner of interpretation; except that they are messianists, who proclaim the resurrection of Christ, upholding the unity of God and that Jesus is his Son.[20] They observe, he says, the practice of circumcision and the maintenance of the sabbath. Epiphanius admits that he does not know the details of their Christology: whether they affirm the godly status of the Christ born of the virgin by the Holy Spirit.[21] He implies that they were still present in his own day and resident in the town of Berea of Coelesyria, and the town of Bashanitis or Khokhabe, both near Pella in the Decapolis region.[22] Jerome, later in the fourth century, lived as a hermit near Berea and also seems to suggest the movement still had adherents in Palestine in his own time. Jerome's treatment of the Nazarenes depends to some extent on his teacher Apollinaris, who had a close knowledge of the movement from his own home base in Laodicea and Antioch, near Berea.[23]

Epiphanius seems to launch his attack against them chiefly for having the audacity to maintain a Jewish desire to maintain an observance of the law as Christians, when Paul and the apostolic council of Jerusalem (recorded in Acts) had removed the burden of the law for the church and when God himself had made the law after Jesus' ascension impossible physically (given the end of the temple) since it had been spiritually fulfilled in the Christ. Nazarenes, then, largely seem to be a straw man for Epiphanius's supersessionist theology. But the way he treats them, despite being dubiously sourced, does seem to indicate that notable Jewish Christian communities still existed in his own time in the Decapolis region, which means communities still observing large elements of the Torah, not just Aramaic-speaking communities. After the fourth century there seems to be no further mention of them. Epiphanius separates them out from the Jewish-Christian Ebionites (whom he deals with in his next section of the book), though he claims the latter sect was founded by a man called Ebion who had formerly been a Nazarene.[24] R. A. Pritz thinks that the term *Christian* might well have been used to designate Gentile followers of Jesus, with the title *Nazarene* being preferred to designate the remaining Jewish disciples resident in Palestine.[25] Justin, in his

---

[20]Presuming that they included the Pauline materials, unlike the Ebionites, according to Irenaeus.
[21]*Panarion* 29.7.6.
[22]Jerome, *De Viris Illustribus* 3; Eusebius, *Ecclesiastical History* 1.7.14. Kefar Sechaniah was also known as a "town of the Nazarenes" in rabbinic literature, with one Jewish Christian, Jacob, mentioned in the Talmud *Avodah Zarah* 16b-17a; Pritz, *Nazarene Jewish Christianity*, 96.
[23]Pritz, *Nazarene Jewish Christianity*, 49-51.
[24]Epiphanius, *Panarion* 30.1-2; this error shows from the start his lack of historical grounding, since the term is not a personal name but a Semitic reference to the movement as the "poor ones."
[25]Pritz, *Nazarene Jewish Christianity*, 13.

mid-second-century *Dialogue with Trypho* had, long before Epiphanius, indicated that there were two groups of Jewish Christians in Palestine, one of which tried to make Gentile converts keep the law, the other which did not; one of which did not accept a divine status of Jesus, and one of which did, and which Justin claims were just like himself (as a Christian) except for their continued observance of matters of the Jewish law.[26] His term of division, we can notice, is again a christological one; and the sense of the nondivine Christology operative among some of the Jewish Christians of his time seems to align this group with what is referred to by several other Christian writers as characteristic of the Ebionites. Jerome also implies that the Nazarenes "Believe in Christ, the Son of God, born of Mary the Virgin, and they confess about him that he suffered under Pontius Pilate and rose again."[27]

Some, such as Origen in *Contra Celsum*, who speaks of "both types of Ebionites," are possibly confusing Nazarenes (whose only "distinctiveness" from more standard Christian communities of the Diaspora was their desire to honor the law as continuing Jews) with Ebionites, who were a more radically divergent movement in terms of Christology.[28] If we take the evidence of Epiphanius and Jerome as including personal knowledge of Palestine in the fourth century, then the Nazarene movement can be seen to have endured until the fourth century (when it gives way to the expansion of imperial Byzantine Palestinian church foundations, which push it out). If we are more skeptical of the latter testimony, the rest of the patristic witnesses accumulate to show that they were still in existence up to the end of the third century: a body of Jewish Christians who observed the law, kept the Old Testament equally authoritative alongside the New, and were not regarded as being theologically dissident in any other way. This was not the case with the patristic descriptions of the Ebionites, however.

*Ebionites.* The name derives from the Greek transliteration of the Aramaic word for the "poor ones." It is also used in patristic literature to refer to a distinct group within the surviving remnants of Judeo-Christianity, again in an apparently geographically restricted area of Palestine before the virtual refounding of the church there in the Constantinian age. Irenaeus is one of the first to mention them, and Origen explains the significance of the Semitic name correctly but cannot resist the pun that the poverty concerned refers now to their "intellectual penury."[29] It might well have been originally a self-designation of the Palestinian church as the *anawim* of God, the "poor saints" (see Mt 5:3; Jas 2:5). Later antiheretical writers such as

---

[26]Justin Martyr, *Dialogue with Trypho* 47-48 (PG 6.577, 580-81).
[27]Jerome, *Letter* 112.13 (to Augustine).
[28]Origen, *Contra Celsum* 5.61 (PG 11.1277).
[29]Irenaeus, *Adversus Haereses* 1.26.2; Origen, *On First Principles* 4.3.8; *Against Celsus* 2.1.

Hippolytus and Tertullian, and Epiphanius in the fourth century, all falsely imagined they were a sect founded by a person called Ebion (by then a heresy had to have a heresiarch inventing it).[30] According to Irenaeus their movement was distinguished by their rejection of the writings of St. Paul, whom they regarded as an apostate Jew who illegitimately separated the gospel from the Torah. In relation to the universally emerging canon of Scripture, they seemed to have accepted only the Gospel of Matthew, retained all the observances of the law, and denied the virginal birth of Christ, generally regarding him as Messiah, but prophetic and human, not divine.[31] Origen adds that they observed Passover as the ultimate liturgical festival and that at least one group among them did accept the traditions of the virginal birth (though implying that many among them did not).[32] This suggests that they were known to him, in Alexandria and perhaps Caesarea, as a real body of Christians.

Eusebius's information about them is also confident, sometimes excessively so. Some of it seems to derive from Irenaeus via Hippolytus and Origen. It is Eusebius who makes the connection between them and the church of Jerusalem, which fled to Pella, thus connecting them with the Nazarenes in some way and implying that their christological dissidence was a falling away from the more antique group that retained the fuller Christian traditions (that is, both Testaments).[33] He also notes that there were "two types" of Ebionites, whom he distinguishes christologically. One group, he says,

> understood Christ to be a plain and ordinary man who had achieved righteousness by the advancement of his character; and who had been born in the natural manner from Mary and her husband. They insist on the complete observance of the law and do not consider that they would be saved by faith in Christ alone, and by a life in accordance with faith. . . . But there were others besides these, who bear the same name, and have escaped the absurd folly of the first group, and who did not deny that the Lord was born of a virgin and the Holy Spirit, but even so agreed with them in not confessing his preexistence as God, insofar as he was Logos and Wisdom. And so they shared in the impiety of the former group, not least insofar as they were zealous in insisting on the literal observance of the law.[34]

---

[30]*Refutation of Heresies* chaps. 7, 10; *On the Prescription of Heretics* 4.8. See further G. A. Koch, "A Critical Investigation of Epiphanius' Knowledge of the Ebionites: A Translation and Critical Discussion of *Panarion* 30," PhD diss., University of Pennsylvania, 1976.

[31]Tertullian, *On the Flesh of Christ* 14.

[32]Origen, *Contra Celsum* 5.61; *De Principiis* 4.3.5. Symmachus, whose version of the Scripture Origen used as one of his columns in the *Hexapla*, was an Ebionite, and similarly the Theodotion version of the LXX came from another Jewish Christian.

[33]Eusebius, *Onomasticon*, ed. P. De Lagarde (Gottingen: A. Rente, 1870), 138, 24-25.

[34]Eusebius, *Ecclesiastical History* 3.27.2-6.

Epiphanius of Salamis provides further information, including excerpts from their writings that include what has since, and recently, been identified as the Gospel of the Ebionites.[35] Generally speaking, it is difficult to know whether they were a continuation of the earliest circles of the Jerusalem church, dating back to James the brother of Jesus, who were cast into obscurity by the aftereffects of the Roman-Jewish war and were later seen as an isolated (and by then apparently "odd") group once the wider church caught up with them again (as Bauer imagines); or whether they were simply one of the more "unusual" groups among a wider body of Jewish Christians in Palestine, who by the third century had already become "curious" in the eyes of the vastly Gentile church and who caught the eye of church commentators first for their Jewish customs (which by now were regarded as archaic among Christians) and then more acutely (in the context of the larger Gnostic struggles) because of their secessionist Christology, which seemed akin to "psilanthropism" (Christ was a "mere man").[36] The Clementine Homilies and Recognitions are aware of two of the books belonging to this sect: the Periodoi of Peter and the Anabathmoi of James. Epiphanius has come across these references in the Clementines.[37]

*Elkesaites.* Another Jewish group, called the Elkesaites, is also recorded as impinging on the life of the Christian church in the early second century: but they were more a late Jewish revelatory movement that had many elements of pluralist religious fusion in it. They are mentioned by Origen as having tried to evangelize Christians at Caesarea in the third century, preaching universal forgiveness; and by Hippolytus, who records that their teacher Alcibiades of Apamaea came to Rome in the time of Pope Callixtus (pope 218–223) and preached, on the basis of their secret revelation, the need for a second baptism.[38] He tells us they stressed the utility of Jewish observance, practiced exorcisms, and valued astrology. Jesus was taken by them as one of a series of holy sages sent into the world to preach repentance. A. F. J. Klijn regards them as originating in Jewish-Christian communities of eastern Jordan who were gathered together around a special revelatory book, the core holy text of their prophet, which demanded conversion of lifestyle in the face of an impending apocalyptic judgment.[39] There is no real reason, however, to think they were Christian Jews as such, but more a kind of apocalyptic Jewish fusion movement of the post–Bar Kokhba

---

[35]Epiphanius, *Against the Heresies* 30.16.7-9.
[36]On James, cf. Eusebius, *Onomasticon*, ed. De Lagarde, 138, though Eusebius opines the same about the Nazarene sect. See W. Bauer, *Orthodoxy and Heresy in Early Christianity* (Philadelphia: Fortress, 1971); Tertullian, *De Carne Christi* 14.
[37]See Epiphanius, *Panarion* 30.15.1; 30.16.6-7.
[38]Eusebius, *Ecclesiastical History* 6.38; Hippolytus, *Refutation* 9.13.1-17.
[39]A. F. J. Klijn, "Elkesaites," in *Encyclopedia of Ancient Christianity*, ed. A. di Berardino (Downers Grove, IL: InterVarsity Press, 2014), 1:797.

period, which when it arrived in Rome found the Christian community there a natural target for its preaching (along presumably with the Roman synagogues and the general populace). Christian commentators later presumed their prophet-founder was a man named Elxai, but scholars have recently argued that this is projection (a heresy needing a heretic to go with it) and that the name derives from a Greek mishearing of the Hebrew name for their actual book of revelations itself, *ksh hyl* or "Book of Hidden Power." They will be mentioned in the following chapter for the influence they had on the Manichaean movement.

**Montanism.** Montanism is the name opponents gave to the movement that its own protagonists called "New Prophecy."[40] Montanus seems to have been an early Christian prophet who began a charismatic revival movement in Phrygia (Asia Minor) between 155 and 160. We know about the movement now through a few fragmentary remains of their teachers cited in early synods of bishops who quickly gathered to contest their claims to be teaching the core gospel, and their (imputed) claims to supreme authority—that prophets speaking in the name of Christ acted in the church *in persona Christi*. This was one of the first times that the early Christian communities really had to face up to their authority structure: what were the rankings of offices and orders within the communities; what were sedentary and what were nomadic? The earliest Christian prophets seem to have been transitory missionaries rather than sedentary community leaders, and this nomadic character seems to attach to the Montanist prophets. The issue raises the question of what manner of authority can ever be held by a single Christian leader (bishop, prophet, presbyter, wonderworker, whatever) in any given community: whether such claimed authority can ever "stand in for Christ," whether it is ever additional to the record of Scripture, or independent of (and standing over) the consensus of the Christian community. After the Montanists, Christian communities in the main resisted ecstatic prophetic leaders who claimed the authority of Christ, and they tended to move in the direction of synodical, conciliar, group consensus, obedient to prior traditions, texts, and practices, as a way of regulating authority claims in the postapostolic generations. Whenever this has given way, in later history, to claims for any inspired leader or supreme authority in the Christian polity, it has usually been a prelude to a dramatic reaction and rejection.

Although the Montanists' own voice has been diffracted, later historians did assemble their archive, especially church historian Eusebius of Caesarea in the fourth century, whose record includes accounts from the contemporary synods gathered to discuss them, which actually quote the Montanist leaders (albeit partially).[41] Eusebius

---

[40] Or opponents called it the "Phrygian heresy," from the Asia Minor province where it originated.
[41] Eusebius, *Ecclesiastical History* 5.14-19; also Epiphanius, *Refutation of All Heresies* 48-49.

lifts up the "Phrygian heresy" as an example of how the discipline of church history itself develops as a constant attempt to mark off true faith from secessionism.[42] Attempts have been made recently to restore their archive as it survives without the context of condemnation prevalent in these synodical accounts.[43] It might well be the case that the clerical resistance to Montanist ecstatic and charismatic approaches to Christian teaching led to the creation of that process of bishops gathering in larger-than-local councils, something that in the next century would be an established church protocol of episcopal provincial synods as a key aspect of international polity.

Appearing suddenly as a traveling Christian preacher (some versions of the story say that he had only been recently converted from paganism), Montanus moved around the towns and villages of central Asia Minor with two female prophets, Maximilla and Prisca (Priscilla), associated in his mission. Eventually he would organize collections of money so that his disciples could receive a salary for their preaching travels.[44] It has usually been assumed that he was the leader. But this is by no means certain: it is what later hostile critics presume from the vantage point of two centuries later.[45] The existence of the female prophets is significant (though little actually is known about them), as they are striking representations of female leaders of the early Christian movement. We can of course discern female leadership in the earliest levels of the New Testament texts, but it come to be increasingly rare in text evidence at the end of the first century as Christian communities become established, settled, and more and more subject to what is known as the Roman household code, in which women are expected to have a domestic role and be seen but not necessarily heard.[46] The change in tone, elevating this domestic code (prevalent in secular Greco-Roman society of the age), can be seen in the Pastoral Letters of the New Testament. It is also witnessed in writings from the earliest episcopal leaders of settled communities, such

---

[42]"The enemy of God's church, who is so emphatically the hater of good and lover of evil, who never leaves untried any form of trickery against human beings, was again active in causing strange heresies to spring up against the church of this time. For some persons, like venomous reptiles, crawled over Asia and Phrygia, boasting that Montanus was the Paraclete, and that the women who followed him, Priscilla and Maximilla, were prophetesses of Montanus." Eusebius, *Ecclesiastical History* 5.14.

[43]See R. E. Heine, ed., *The Montanist Oracles and Testimonia* (Macon, GA: Mercer University Press, 1989); W. Tabbernee, *Fake Prophecy and Polluted Sacraments: Ecclesiastical and Imperial Reactions to Montanism* (Leiden: Brill, 2007).

[44]Eusebius, *Ecclesiastical History* 5.16.7; 5.18.2.

[45]See further A. Jensen, "Prisca—Maximilla—Montanus: Who Was the Founder of 'Montanism'?," *StPatr* 26 (1993): 147-50.

[46]On female prophets see F. C. Klawiter, "The Role of Martyrdom and Persecution in Developing the Priestly Authority of Women in Early Christianity: A Case Study of Montanism," *Church History* 49, no. 3 (1980): 251-61; C. Trevett, *Montanism: Gender, Authority and the New Prophecy* (New York: Cambridge University Press, 1996).

as the Clementine letters from the Roman church, or the letters of Ignatius of Antioch. By the beginning of the second century the concept of traveling female evangelists, or missionary prophets, seems "scandalous" to the settled church.

Because of the centrality of the female prophets to any understanding of the Montanist movement, recent works discussing them have sometimes elevated them as symbols for a renewed call for ordained female leadership in the church and isolated their antique rejection as a symbol of patriarchal oppression. Others have seen that connection as more to do with feminist theology and more recent church polity than historically grounded analyses. Much of the argument about them as symbols of relevance rises, on both sides, as *argumenta e silentio*.[47] Even so, the aspect of female leadership, which remained prevalent in the later Montanist communities (where there were even female presbyters) but not in the catholic communities, has been scrutinized by some recent commentators as a revealing window onto a once-wider pattern of authorities and offices in earliest Christianity that was increasingly narrowed down in Asia Minor and elsewhere after, and partly because of, the Montanist controversy.

Montanus claimed that he was the mouthpiece of the Holy Spirit and that the Paraclete who had been promised in John 14:26; 16:7 was now incarnate in him. Some of the characteristics of the church of Philadelphia as described in the Johannine Revelation can perhaps be seen in the Montanist movement, and it might well trace its origins to aspects of early Asia Minor ecclesial traditions (powerful revival movements, visionary claims, eschatological expectations). The precise context of what Montanus thought his mission was about might well be connected with such foundational apocalyptic elements of the book of Revelation. He probably represents a protest against the declining apocalyptic expectation among the early Christian communities and a corresponding adjustment of organized church life to a sedentary urban environment, where authority was more and more passing away from nomadic prophets and missionary exorcists, to (perhaps less charismatic) local councils of presbyters and bishops.

His critics who accused him of being too recent a convert to be a real missionary were implying that his sense of ecstatic enthusiasm (*enthousiasmos*) was less a genuine vocation of the divine Spirit, and more a carryover from his pre-Christian adherence to pagan oracular cults, and that this was the context in which they needed to see his reliance on female prophetesses, needing them as a channel to deliver oracles, as with pagan *magoi* and soothsayers.[48] Apollinaris of Hierapolis, one of Montanus's

---

[47] "An argument from silence"—stitching together large theories on the basis of little (if any) evidence; presuming you know what the evidential silence means.

[48] The word *enthousiasmos* derives from being "filled with the god" and describes praxis common in pagan cults.

contemporary episcopal opponents, recounts that his frenzied style of prophecy led some in the churches to fear he was demonically possessed and says he was forbidden from speaking in the assembly.[49] Montanus himself claimed that the imminent presence of the end time (*eschaton*) had impelled the need to preach an urgent sense of repentance, so the church could renew itself under the impetus of the Spirit. He encouraged speaking in tongues (*glossolalia*) and other manifestations of *enthousiasmos*.

The three inner-circle prophets claimed no less than the direct authority of God. They habitually spoke *in voce dei*, as if they were the mouthpiece of God, who talked unmediatedly through them. Hostile witnesses claimed to be shocked by this, as if the prophets were claiming for themselves divine status: but it was probably no more than a customary form of Christian prophetic witness in the earliest assemblies, where prophets spoke "in the name of Jesus." Anyone questioning their utterance, therefore, was questioning God himself. This was why they allowed bishops the authority to organize communities (worship, finances, and so on) but as having no dominion if they withstood the message of the prophet: and the bishops generally regarded this as unacceptable arrogation of rights to the prophet as having supreme governance over the churches. Montanus claimed that his utterances had superior authority over "older" Scriptures.

Part of their teaching that the end times were imminent was the call to moral reform. To ready themselves for the final cataclysm, Christians had to adopt a rigorously ascetic lifestyle. Marriage was banned among their adherents. Only later was this relaxed to become a ban on any remarriage, including that after the death of a spouse. Regular and severe periods of fasting were encouraged, and so too was substantial almsgiving. Martyrdom, as another eschatological virtue, was also encouraged. Any flight from persecution was forbidden as tantamount to apostasy, and this was perhaps another reason urban bishops disliked Montanists so, their eagerness to advance themselves for martyrdom being an endangerment to many other Christians in local communities under stress. When the end came, the early Montanist teachers claimed, the New Jerusalem promised in the Scripture (Rev 21:1-10) would physically descend from heaven to the little Phrygian village of Pepuza (or sometimes Timione). Pepuza

---

[49]Eusebius, *Ecclesiastical History* 5.16.7-8, abridges Apollinaris of Hierapolis, a contemporary source: "A recent convert, Montanus by name, through his unquenchable desire for leadership, gave the Adversary an opportunity against him. He became beside himself and was suddenly in a sort of frenzy and ecstasy, and he raved and began to babble and utter strange things, prophesying in a manner contrary to the constant custom of the church handed down by tradition from the beginning. Some of those who heard his spurious utterances at that time were indignant and rebuked him as if he were a man possessed and under the control of a demon and led by a deceitful spirit, who was thus distracting the multitude. They forbade him to talk, remembering the distinction drawn by the Lord and his warning to guard carefully against the coming of false prophets (Mt 7:15)."

was Montanus's hometown and later center of operations. To this holy place true believers were called to gather together before the Lord's coming. The failure of Pepuza to develop as the great eschatological locus was one of the chief reasons the steam went out of the movement in Phrygia, but not before the little town had been greatly expanded by Montanist investment.

Montanism, however, seems to have been a movement largely uninterested in "doctrine" as such. It is, to this extent, somewhat unique among early Christian secessionist movements. Montanism did fully accept the idea of the resurrection of the flesh (a notion that was usually in contention among more Gnostic-flavored secessionist Christian groups of this era), and it interpreted many points of Scripture with a very simple directness (one supposes this was a style not too far removed from the majority among the contemporary Christian communities). This too, of course, made their leaders very open to criticism from current and later theologians that they were simplistic. One of the chief things that emerged in later Christian pneumatology, after the fading of Montanism, was that the possession of the Spirit of God in the church is not witnessed first and foremost by ecstatic possession and nonsensical utterances but rather by a progressive clarity of the mind, a refinement and focus of the intellectual and spiritual gifts for teaching.[50] Ecstasy gave way, in a profound way in subsequent Christian experience, to the elevation of human gifts and awareness as part of the spiritual task of "discerning the Spirit." Montanists' increasingly hostile reception in Asia led them to denounce the communities there as "slayers of the Spirit." The charge rankled.

The Montanists also seem to have gloried in their heroic resistance to persecution, claiming the crown as a martyr community. The mainline communities also found this a little hard to stomach. Bishop Apollinaris of Hierapolis, for one, made a count of who among them had actually suffered execution and claimed it was a zero sum total.[51] But he contradicts himself after this (Eusebius, as a later archivist, consistently wishes to underestimate the martyr lists of the heretics), because in another passage from his treatise (which Eusebius also records) Apollinaris makes a point of saying that whenever the catholic martyrs were imprisoned, they did not make

---

[50]The word *ecstatic* is derived from the Greek *ekstasis*, meaning "being outside oneself," not in possession of one's faculties; being dispossessed, as it were.

[51]Eusebius, *Ecclesiastical History* 5.16.12: "And so, since they called us slayers of the prophets because we did not receive their babbling prophets, whom they claimed to be the ones the Lord promised to send to the people (Mt 23:34), let them answer before God's own presence: Who is there, my friends, of all of those who began to talk, from Montanus and the women down to the present, who was ever persecuted by the Jews, or killed by lawless men? Not one. Have any of them been seized and crucified for the sake of the name? Indeed, not one. Well, has a single one of these women ever been scourged in the synagogues of the Jews, or stoned? No, never; anywhere."

common fellowship with the Montanist or Marcionite confessors present in the same prisons.[52] Other first-generation opponents of Montanism were named by Eusebius as Alcibiades, who wrote a treatise on how the Spirit of God would never disrupt a person's senses, and Miltiades, who argued that the ecstatic manner of prophesying was contrary to the custom of the church and not represented in the original apostolic generation, such as the family of Philip or Agabus in the New Testament period.[53]

The writer Apollonius also left notes on the movement, forty years after Montanus first started preaching.[54] He claimed that Prisca and Maximilla were induced by Montanus to leave their husbands after they received the spirit of prophesying. He mentions this disapprovingly and also wants it placed on record that their disciples' claims that Prisca and Maximilla were "virgins" is a false one.[55] The anti-Montanist critics also were quick to point out that the custom of earlier prophets had been not to receive gifts of money and not to stay resident in one place.[56] This embracing of poverty is one of the few "signs of a real prophet," such as were commonly accepted and survived in the Didache, for example.[57] The anti-Montanist charge is that they have proved themselves false by accepting money, but the real issue is probably that their collecting of money from the preaching tours had allowed them to try to establish a hierarchy of prophets in a nonnomadic environment for the first time.

Not everyone in the church found them objectionable. Some of the Asian bishops supported them as a revivalistic and sincere body of believers and did not think they had made themselves into a breakaway sect. One of the leading minds of the era, Irenaeus, who was himself a native of Asia Minor but now leading the community in Lyon in Gaul, found them to be an admirable spiritual group, and he defended their cause at Rome. His own form of chiliastic millenarianism might reflect the Asia Minor tendency toward apocalyptic prophecy.[58] In the end, by the late second and third centuries, when the Montanist movement had moderated its eschatological

---

[52]Ibid., 5.16.22 (citing Apollinaris of Hierapolis): "When those called to martyrdom from the church for the truth of the faith have met with any of the so-called martyrs of the Phrygian heresy, they have separated from them and died without any fellowship with them, because they did not wish to give their assent to the spirit of Montanus and the women."
[53]Ibid., 5.17.1-3.
[54]Ibid., 5.18.12.
[55]Possibly an attempt to make them resonate with the four virginal daughters of the evangelist Philip mentioned in scripture (Acts 21:8-9), who prophesied and in whose house the prophet Agabus met Paul.
[56]Eusebius, *Ecclesiastical History* 5.18.4, 7.
[57]Didache 11: "But whoever says in the Spirit, give me money, or something else, you shall not listen to him. But if he tells you to give for others' sake who are in need, let no one judge him."
[58]Irenaeus, *Adversus Haereses* 5.

message (after their prophesied end time failed to happen), they were eventually folded back into North African church traditions. But the Asia Minor bishops remained ever suspicious of them. This might be the reason the book of Revelation was never popular in the Eastern church. Not until it was passed back to the Greeks in the fourth century as a part of the "Western" canon of Scripture, which they were expected to acknowledge (the Greeks insisted the West should accept in return the letter of James), did Revelation enter the canon of accepted Scriptures. Even then it is noticeable that to this very day it is given the silent treatment in the liturgies, prayers, and offices of Eastern Christianity: the book is still never cited in church.[59]

The lack of big-picture objectionable doctrinal elements caused church authorities considerable difficulties in deciding what, if anything, was wrong with Montanism. The movement spread to the West, where for a time in 177 and 178 important Roman church communities were thinking of recognizing it as an admirable movement but eventually did not. From Rome it moved to North Africa, where it enjoyed a longer and more sedentary second life (we might call it stage-two Montanism) and, as mentioned above, was eventually absorbed into the wider community traditions. Indeed, in this later form of North African Montanism, in the late second and early third centuries, many of the original highly charged apocalyptic elements were smoothed out. The function of ecstatic prophecy was then given a lighter stress, and the urgency of the imminent parousia seemed to have receded. The rigorist African theologian Tertullian passed from being a stern critic to an enthusiastic adherent late in his life. It is thought by some that leading Monarchian theologian Theodotus the Tanner was also closely associated with the Montanist movement, although Tertullian tells us that Monarchian church leader Praxeas (perhaps a code name for Pope Callixtus) was instrumental in having Montanist ideas and assemblies banned at Rome.[60] Pope Aniketos earlier had also been hostile to them there (pope c. 157–168).

Many have thought that the Montanist movement was clearly involved in the production of the Passion of Perpetua and Felicity, that classic martyr narrative in which dream-vision and prophetic apocalyptic themes play dominant roles. The strong advocacy of martyrdom as the supreme Christian glory remained characteristic of Montanism to the end and flavored the Christianity of North Africa. But the movement's most hallowed text was undoubtedly the book of Revelation itself, which also emanated from Asia Minor and probably represents the archaic traditions of the church

---

[59] See further J. A. McGuckin, "The Book of Revelation and Orthodox Eschatology: The Theodrama of Judgement," in *The Last Things: Biblical and Theological Perspectives on Eschatology*, ed. C. E. Braaten and R. W. Jenson (Grand Rapids: Eerdmans, 2002), 113-34.
[60] *Against Praxeas* 1. *Praxeas* can be translated as "busybody." Callixtus was pope at Rome c. 218–223.

of that area, which took a particularly sharp form in the rise of Montanism, perhaps serving to bridge the Semitic patterns of visionary martyr resistance in Revelation with Gentile patterns of ecstatic worship.

The movement dwindled away almost everywhere by the fourth century, except in the village of Pepuza, which endured now as Montanist sectarian headquarters. Its long-term effects on Christianity were mainly in the form of the reactions it caused. It probably served to push apocalyptic ways of thinking to the side after the fourth century, allowing Christian thought to become more spaciously metaphysical. It turned Christian pneumatology away from the inspiration of ecstasies and visions, toward scriptural exegesis, reflective intellect, and moral endeavor. It had a long-term effect in sharpening the attribution of episcopal authority, especially as this was witnessed in bishops of many churches gathering together in synods whenever large problems affected the peace of the churches.[61] The synodical reaction to Montanism is probably the first time that episcopal councils (which would soon become a standard way of organizing all the mainline churches) is witnessed in Christian history. One record of such a synod gathered to discuss Montanism survives in the writings of the Asia Minor bishop Apollinaris of Hierapolis (d. c. 175). Excerpts from his notebooks survived to be Eusebius's main source in *Ecclesiastical History* 5.16. As a worked-out example of "good practice" in governance, this pattern of crisis leadership through synods established itself internationally in Christian communities by the end of the next century. Very quickly the synodal "mind of the bishops" would claim the prophetic authority that had been wrested from the Montanists and define prophetic insight as being necessarily vindicated by more than a single prophet's claim for authenticity: resting, in other words, in the communal acclamation of that prophetic voice by a discernment that was lodged in the collective.[62] The resolution of this crisis, as a side effect, marked the rapid retirement of the ancient office of Christian prophet in favor of an ascendant role for bishops and presbyters, who absorbed many aspects of that role (missionary preaching, scriptural interpretation, moral encomium) into their own functions.

Here below are several Montanist prophets' original oracles, which have been preserved by heresiologists, generally unsympathetically, though Tertullian (for once) is a more charitable source:[63]

---

[61] See Eusebius, *Ecclesiastical History* 5.16.10.
[62] The idea that all the bishops gathered together in prayer could not fail to be inspired by the Holy Spirit becomes a dominant concept in synodical theory.
[63] See further J. Laporte, *The Role of Women in Early Christianity* (New York: Mellen, 1982), 57; and P. de Labriolle, *La Crise Montaniste* (Paris: Leroux, 1913), 34-105.

Maximilla said: "After me there will no longer be any prophetess. The end will come."[64]

Maximilla said: "I am chased like a wolf from the sheep; but I am not a wolf; I am Word, and Spirit, and Power."[65]

Maximilla said: "Do not listen to me; listen rather to Christ."[66]

Maximilla said: "The Lord sent me as a sectarian, and a revealer, an interpreter of this labor and announcement and covenant. I am compelled, whether I want to or not, to learn the gnosis of God."[67]

Prophetess Prisca said that a holy minister knows how to administer sanctity, for: "Purity is harmonious and they see visions, and turning their face downward, they even hear manifested voices, as salutary even as they are secret."[68]

[On those who deny the resurrection of the flesh] Prisca said: "They are carnal, and yet they hate the flesh."[69]

The Cataphrygians (Montanists) say that in the town of Pepuza, Quintilla, or was it Priscilla, was sleeping, and Christ came and slept with her: "Under the appearance of a woman, in a beautiful dress, Christ came to me. He made me wise and declared that this place was sacred, and that there the heavenly Jerusalem would descend from heaven."[70]

***Asia Minor Quartodeciman communities.*** The life of the communities of Christians in Asia Minor in this period is further illumined by another dispute that the later heresiologists wish to record; they name it Quartodecimanism, as if it were a dissident movement, when it was more a matter of the larger Mediterranean Christian

---

[64] Epiphanius, *Against All Heresies* 48.12. This might be the end of the prophetic movement or the end of the world. Montanist: *Oracle* 11.
[65] Eusebius, *Ecclesiastical History* 5.16.17. Montanist: *Oracle* 12.
[66] Epiphanius, *Against All Heresies* 48.12. Montanist: *Oracle* 13.
[67] Epiphanius, *Against All Heresies* 48.12. Montanist: *Oracle* 14.
[68] Tertullian, *Exhortation to Chastity* 10. Montanist: *Oracle* 15. In *De Anima* 9, Tertullian speaks also about a woman in his own pro-Montanist community in Africa who had similar spiritual experiences.
[69] Tertullian, *On the Resurrection of the Flesh* 11. Montanist: *Oracle* 16.
[70] Epiphanius, *Against All Heresies* 49.1. Montanist: *Oracle* 17. One sees the hostile way this dream-vision (Christ's visitation in sleep) is turned into a salacious wink-and-nudge sexy story to discredit it. There are some instances of pagan incubation temple rituals that involved sacred sex with the god (priests dressed up as the god), but the concept of incubatory divine dream oracles was well established in the ancient world (one thinks of the Aesculapian cult or the Isiac cult). Later Byzantine Christianity came to a much more positive view of it, as can be seen even in learned Christian writers such as Gregory of Nazianzus. See further J. Pettis, ed., *Seeing the God: Ways of Envisioning the Divine in Ancient Mediterranean Religion* (Piscataway, NJ: Gorgias Press, 2013).

communities noticing that things were not all neatly aligned in the growing international consensus of Christian praxis. The thing that was out of alignment in this case was not any matter of doctrinal behavior but a question of how different Christian communities should rate traditionalism when it came to their liturgical practices, and from that issue of tradition keeping (since all the communities aspired to "keeping the tradition") what issues of authority emerged. If keeping the passed-down traditions was the primary concern of the churches, then this surely took priority over any other claim to authority that might be advanced against it. Or, perhaps, if an "authority figure" in the church who claimed to be a high authority precisely because he was the guardian of tradition intervened and demanded a change of local traditions that did not seem to be in alignment with larger traditions elsewhere, did his authority triumph over the local? This is what seemed to be the issue with the Quartodecimans' case, and this too is why it was kept in the registers for later centuries, as it was an early paradigm of how Christianity might set precedents in terms of setting a resolution principle for clashes between local and more international understandings of Christian identity.

The word *Quartodecimans* derives from the Latin for "fourteenth" and refers to the custom in some of the Asian churches of following the Jewish liturgical calendar and observing the Christian Passover (in other words, Pascha or Easter) on the fourteenth day of the month of Nisan (April), regardless of what day of the week that fell on. By the end of the second century, many other Mediterranean churches had appointed the festal celebrations of Pascha to the nearest Sunday after the date of the Jewish Passover. This insistence that the Pascha of Christians should always be after the Jewish Passover had taken place was to be confirmed as international established practice for all the ancient churches at the Council of Nicaea (in its canons) two generations later.[71]

At first it did not much matter what local differentiations there might be in liturgy. Not many people traveled much. But port cities, of course, showed up differences quite strikingly, and news traveled back quickly to that key hub of seafaring trade in the empire, the city of Rome. Its bishop thus became highly informed of international affairs and, seated within this ancient and prestigious church (with its many theologians, martyrs, and archivists), he emerged as the second century progressed as a leading arbiter of internationalized "good practice" in the Christian communities. This also meant that he increasingly felt it his duty to secure common standards and

---

[71]The departure from that observance is one of the reasons today that Eastern and Western Christians observe different dates for Pascha (as well as a thirteen-day calendrical difference). The East still observes the Nicene canon on the matter of never preceding or falling over the same time as the Jewish Passover.

advise when they were not being observed. In the middle of the second century a large-scale disparity of liturgical practice would become a matter of critical concern, and nothing would bring that to common notice more quickly than pilgrims from one church (seafarers or merchants) finding themselves locked out of Pascha celebrations because of an odd local calendar in operation in a remote spot. By the middle of the century the elaboration of a *triduum*, a three-day solemn observance of severe fasting and prayer for Great Friday and Holy Saturday preceding the festivities of Pascha Sunday, was becoming common. How strange it seemed to visitors, therefore, that the Asian custom was to observe the Christian Pascha on whatever day of the week it fell on Nisan 14. It would be like having Good Friday on a Monday.

One suspects that increasing numbers of merchant travelers made complaints to their bishop(s) when they returned home. Equally, one imagines, the Asia Minor bishops were annoyed that visitors would not follow their ancestral practices, especially if they believed this was ancient Christian tradition, and so they stood against pressure from other communities (especially the Roman) to fall in line with Sunday Paschal observance, distance from the Jewish calendar, and admitting a Lenten *triduum*. Eusebius of Caesarea, first mentioning the cause of the controversy, attributes it to an anxiety over the timing of fasting rituals.[72]

The first time this controversy broke the surface was on the occasion of a visit by a famous Asia Minor theologian to Rome in 155. On that occasion Polycarp, the bishop of Smyrna, himself disturbed by the liturgical disparities, tried to make the Romans conform to the Asia Minor customs. The Syrian Pope Aniketos of Rome refused at that time to make any changes, albeit commending Polycarp for the antiquity of his own observance.[73] In the next generation, however, Rome decided that it ought to take the lead in arguing for a greater international uniformity in the observance of Pascha, and the then-incumbent Pope Victor (189–198) summoned a synod of bishops at Rome and wrote widely to ask other synods to convene in other large churches to

---

[72] Eusebius, *Ecclesiastical History* 5.23.1. "A question of no small importance arose at that time. For the parishes of all Asia, as from an older tradition, held that the fourteenth day of the moon, on which day the Jews were commanded to sacrifice the lamb, should be observed as the feast of the Savior's Passover. It was therefore necessary to end their fast on that day, whatever day of the week it should happen to be. But it was not the custom of the churches in the rest of the world to end it at this time, as they observed the practice that, from apostolic tradition, has prevailed to the present time, of terminating the fast on no other day than on that of the resurrection of our Savior."

[73] Aniketos's (Greek) name means "unconquered one." He was the first pope to notice the increasing presence of the Montanist movement at Rome and took action against them there. Eusebius tells us, on the authority of Irenaeus, who was personally involved in the later discussions with Pope Victor, that this controversy had first started between Polycarp and Aniketos. See Eusebius, *Ecclesiastical History* 5.24.

discuss the issue.[74] Polycrates, the bishop of Ephesus and leader of the Asia Minor episcopate, reported back that his synod had met at Rome's request but refused to be cajoled into what Rome wanted and was not afraid by Rome's threats of cutting off communion if the common order was not implemented. Eusebius records much of Polycrates's report and reply.[75]

Pope Victor pressed the case and announced the Asia Minor excommunication (bishops must not communicate with Polycrates's synod until such time as they conformed but rather treat them as secessionists and dissidents). His "firm stand," however, backfired to some extent, as many of the synods that had been glad enough to follow his guidance over common standards thought that applying a penalty to the Asian traditionalism was rather out of order. Polycrates's report had stressed that they followed an antique local custom, and also that Pope Aniketos had venerated Polycarp and allowed him to preside over the Eucharist at Rome when he visited, even though they could not agree on the liturgical matters. Irenaeus of Lyons was one of the priest delegates sent from the church of Lyons (where there were many migrant communities of Asia Minor workers) to register official protests at the harshness of the Roman measure, and it seems that the Asian churches retained their local custom for some time longer. Eusebius attributes the reconciliation to Irenaeus's arguments that since the differences had existed among great and holy elders of the past, they ought not to be taken now as grounds for breaking communion. In the fifth century there was still a Quartodecimans sect in Asia Minor, though by this period it had become a separate, schismatical community (cut off from the Asia Minor churches around it that now followed the international pattern), a group that had taken its allegiance to old traditions as a do-or-die stand as being the last exemplars of true orthodoxy.[76]

There have been many similar groups since them, usually taking small issues of internal church development as crisis points of faithful resistance and exemplifying an understanding of tradition as synonymous with "no change." Calendrical and liturgical changes often initiate such crises. In ancient times the Paschal liturgies were especially prone to such anxiety, for it was a widely held belief that Christ

---

[74]Eusebius lists the one at Rome and also says he has archives from his own Palestinian church of these meetings. He also mentions synods to the same effect at Pontus, Gaul, Syria, Corinth, "and many others" who came "to a unanimous decision." It is one of the earliest examples of how, through synodical episcopal process, international standards of "good practice to be observed collectively" were established among Christians in the name of "apostolic tradition." See Eusebius, *Ecclesiastical History* 5.23.2-3.

[75]Ibid., 5.24.

[76]*Schismatical* (from the Greek for "split," *schisma*) is increasingly used in antiquity to denote a secession that takes place for a reason that is not substantially affecting any doctrine of the faith but arises from a disciplinary matter or a refusal to accept legitimate authority. A secession for doctrinal reasons now is clearly labeled a heresy (*hairesis*).

would return to earth in judgment at the Paschal vigil—and if one part of the church was in prayer and the other part was in bed, the issue of when the vigil took place was indeed a critical one for all Christians. The issue has an enduring interest not only for what it reveals about the history of liturgical observance and the growing pattern of province-wide episcopal synodical guidance of the churches, but also for the light it throws on the emergence of a sense, at Rome, that the papacy had a special presidential responsibility for international church order. This issue would henceforward rise up as an ever increasingly significant factor in Christian affairs, sometimes to the good of establishing a highly respected court of international appeal, and sometimes detrimentally as a cause of protest and dissension. As the third century opened, and certainly by the fourth, it was operative (at Rome at least) as a tradition that Rome had a special and "superapostolic" tradition that gave it the right to be heard everywhere. In the Arian disputes of the fourth century (and in many later controversies), often Rome felt it only needed to issue a statement and everyone else only needed to fall into line accordingly. This growing expectation would eventually cause no end of new disputes.

**Christian gnosis.** *A context.* Up until the early decades of this century Christian historical commentators (who were often as much theologians in disguise as they were historians) largely thought that they knew what Gnosticism was—a single "thing": mainly a deviant external and quasi-parasitic sect of loosely related eccentric teachers who mythologized Christian teachings, a movement that sprung up in the early second century and was widely rejected among Christian churches by the early fourth century, setting in place, in the course of that reaction to it, the fundamental rules of the "orthodox-catholic" definitions of Christianity. In some sense, then, they approached Gnosticism as a precipitating agent for early catholicity with its organization around a closed canon of agreed Scripture and a fixed sense of demonstrable apostolic tradition held up as a yardstick lineage. The anti-Gnostic impetus was seen to grow out of an ecclesial desire to stick to common-sense, liturgically grounded (creedal) statements of faith in preference to speculative mysticism of various types.

In this (a classic synopsis of the "gnostic problem") the commentators were predominantly following the very negative assessment of Irenaeus of Lyons, the second-century bishop-theologian who first set out to rebuke a Lyonnais group of Valentinians (loose disciples of Valentinus of Rome) whom he regarded as attacking important premises of his own local church. Irenaeus's sights in his *Adversus Haereses* ("Against the Dissidents") were raised higher than usual, more globally, as it were, because of his knowledge of the work of Valentinian teachers at Rome. But even though his work sets out to amass a great range of details and charges about the Gnostic movement, above all else Irenaeus was a local teacher. He was moved to pen a devastating critique of Gnosticism as a pernicious enemy of Christian authenticity because of the damage he saw it inflicting on his own traumatized Lyonnais congregation as it was just emerging from a severe and fatal persecution. As time moved on, and the good ideas that Gnostic teachers had offered were quietly absorbed (as is often the case with movements that are at first attacked as pernicious) while the "more dubious things" they represented were noisily denounced, Irenaeus eventually came to be the chief spokesman for the whole anti-Gnostic movement, and his architecture of ideas represented the substance of what came to be classed as the catholic system of self-identity. It was the anti-Gnostic reaction that indeed did much to bring this into a crystalline shape in the mid-second century.

Texts were expensive to reproduce in antiquity and amounted to much labor as well as the cost. Defeated intellectual movements tended not to have devotees to keep their literature in circulation. And so by the fourth century Gnostic authors were more or less sent to the "remaindered" pile, the fate that attends most inactive literature: falling out of print and out of mind. Paradoxically, it was the very Christians who rejected Gnosticism who were mainly responsible for keeping the memory of the movement alive. The Gnostics lived on, preserved for a long time in the aspic of Irenaeus's text, precisely as examples of radical heresy. Eventually most historians within Christianity accepted Irenaeus's version of events as the sole context of approach and took his synopses of what Gnostics taught as the primary account. That changed, and "Gnosticism" as a lump category began to be dismantled after new discoveries of so-called Gnostic texts from the late nineteenth century onward and especially in the mid-twentieth century, above all the Nag Hammadi collection of cached literature from Chenoboskion discovered there in 1947. The latter was in all probability a dump from the nearby Pachomian monastery that was clearing out its library collections. Some have made much of this, imputing it as an example of censorship, but there is no serious evidence whatsoever to think that the dump of this (already antique) literature was anything other than the normal exercise of a library discarding unwanted materials. Fourth-century Pachomians, and Christian ascetic devotees in general, were interested in other literature than this, and this other corpus they have extensively kept, recopied, and protected over two millennia as the vast collections of ascetical and mystical theology we have today. If a corpus of literature has an audience that values it (short of natural disasters), it will survive. The kind of theosophical metaphysics represented in the Gnostic treatises rapidly lost its core audience after the very early fourth century. In short, it was not so much suppressed by anyone; it just died a natural death until being forcibly resuscitated in modern times, by new devotees, often investing it with significances it did not originally have.

The find at Nag Hammadi, however, started a veritable explosion of reassessments of what Gnosticism was in the latter part of the twentieth century. Indeed, this has run on even today into popular religiosity (heavily influenced by latter-day conspiracy theories, especially in the United States, where publishers can make a lot of money out of that genre) to account for the unusual phenomenon that many people in North America today know little about ancient Christianity other than the "secret lost gospels" that are alleged to have been much more fun than the publicly retained Gospels everyone has heard of. Over many decades I have met the excited expectations of college freshmen wishing to major in Gnostic literature with the advice to go read the primary materials first, only to see crestfallen faces when they come back to confess that they are not at all as exciting as they had been led to believe by some commentators and indeed were at times positively incomprehensible. Irenaeus pulled no punches when he argued that "to refute such literature it is only necessary to describe it," but between his view that heresy has nothing to offer except corruption and the inflated view of a few scholars that here is a viable alternative to hyperdogmatic Christianity, there is perhaps a middle way: namely that this literature, now that one can approach it without the intellectual commentary of hostile witnesses, has somewhat widened our understanding of the conditions of the church in the second century and opened up our concept of what a private school led by a philosophical-religious *didaskalos* might look like in the second century.

More than this, perhaps, we gain here a deeper perspective on how this style of speculative religious metaphysics stood in relation to mainline Christian metaphysics. Some scholars have begun to argue (in an excessive reaction to Irenaean apologetics) that probably there never was a "Gnostic" movement other than a made-up heresy of heresiologists. This seems to me, at least, to be a massive overstatement of the evidence, since it was not only the Christians who shouted out against "Gnostics" (naming them as such—from their own self-designation, but adding on that as far as they were concerned it was "pseudo-gnosis," or false wisdom), but it was also the ancient established schools of Hellenistic philosophy that found them intellectually odious.

In the *Enneads* of the great third-century Platonic commentator Plotinus, he has a specific anti-Gnostic section, where he takes them to task for a radically pessimistic view of the relation of the divine to cosmology, accusing of them of having a "contempt for the creation," and refutes their tendency to multiply cosmological principles (or hypostatic archons).[77] In his hands, as was the case with the second- to fourth-century

---

[77] *Enneads* 2.9; 2.9.5.

Christian fathers, the projection of the divine Triad was a view of divine outreach to the cosmos that was at the same time a fundamental curtailing of Gnostic speculative metaphysics.[78] Plotinus regarded them, one suspects, as theosophists who had only superficial confluence with his own metaphysical agenda. Origen (who had much respect for Plotinus, though it was not returned) felt much the same. His attitude toward Gnostic thought would represent the other end of the spectrum from Irenaeus. He too was an opponent of most of the core ideas of Gnostic theory, but he was able to recognize and respond to problems of theodicy and divine revelation that the Gnostics had raised in a serious manner. If the second-century thinker found nothing good to say, intellectual theologians of the third century such as Clement of Alexandria or Origen, then, found much that was good to absorb, quietly and judiciously, so that it could be "reclaimed" for the mainline church (we might start calling it the "great church" at this era). So it would be fallacious to think that all major Christian theologians were unanimously hostile to the Gnostic agenda. They were hostile to much of it, and to almost all of its methods and metaphysical premises. They wished to test its more mystical apprehensions (the sense of the inspired initiate and the wide metaphysical panorama of salvation many Gnostic texts evoked) by conformity to common-sense biblical, historical, and liturgical precedents: things that could be weighed and measured alongside things that could only be intuited. That element of conforming personal illumination to community experience and guidance is the quintessential difference.

It is important to recognize, also, that the mainline church certainly did not suppress or censor the Gnostic movements. The second century is too soon to imagine any bishop with censorship power—other than the simple force of argument. Most ancient apologetics are robust in a way that shocks the modern reader (who also forgets how brusque our own apologetic will sound to later ears). The ancients were not in the business of listening to different "schools of thought" with irenic pacifism. They were trained as win-all controversialists. We do not need to adopt their methods here but can review the evidence in a more detached spirit (perhaps!) while holding to two premises: that this was a sideline movement as far as the mainstream development of Christianity was concerned (even though it gave the long-term church great depths of reflection in mystical insights), and that while Gnosticism was not all of a piece, or even a particularly coherent movement across the centuries of late antiquity, when it had some vogue (especially the second to third centuries, when it most significantly affected the Christians), nevertheless there were some discrete schools that can be observed in relation to the history of the church. This is

---

[78]Ibid., 2.9.2-3. Some of the cosmic emanational schemes of the Gnostics ran to 365 divine emanations.

why the concept Gnosticism still has force of significance, but also why this section will concentrate on Valentinus, Bardesanes, and Basilides as its most significant points of attention. How to describe them and their intent, therefore?

The ancient Gnostic movements (there was never just one) were given what coherence they had by a shared axiomatic principle that salvation was the experience of enlightenment (*gnosis* can be best translated as "wise enlightenment") and that this enlightenment grew out of the fundamental realization that this present cosmic material existence was an imprisonment of true spiritual (*pneumatikos*) and intellectual (*logikos, noetikos*) life, in material (*hylic*) darkness, suffering, and blindness. For me this fundamental approach to metaphysics defines what I regard, still, as "Gnostic material" proper, as distinct from "sophianic" material, which abounds in all ancient philosophy and religion (including Christianity in its many forms). If we mix up "sophianic" with the issue of the light captured by the darkness, we do run the risk of losing our grip on the meaning of *Gnostica*, so I would advise we reserve the term *Gnostic* for those materials where we see the war myth of light and dark actively engaged as a cosmological principle—not simply references to that idea or theme, which are antique commonplaces, but rather substantive metaphysical "arrangements" of life around the idea of a fall into darkness and an introduction to illumined enlightenment (by a Savior figure) as the exact dynamic of salvation.[79] So for our purposes here Valentinus and his system (which is exactly what Irenaeus was originally attacking) still remain archetypal for what one might sensibly mean by "Gnostic Christianity."

Several Gnostic movements at the time of the early Christianity leaned on the myth of the preexistent soul as given by Plato. Here the concept of the soul's "unawareness" that its present life (in the world) is one of illusion and deceit is conveyed graphically by his famous story of the prisoners in the cave (they see shadows on the back wall of the cave and are under the illusion that these shadows are reality—not knowing that the real world is elsewhere, outside the cave, and needing a heroic effort of discernment to "turn around" and grapple with it).[80] The sad state of being trapped in matter and ignorance (the antithesis of wisdom-gnosis) is regarded by some Gnostic movements as the "fall" of the spirit into flesh, and the primeval fall is witnessed (in many varied elaborations of that tale, especially in the forced birth of spiritually aware—that is, sentient—beings in the hybrid life of material consciousness). In short, the very existence of the suffering human race exemplifies the fall—our existence is our sin. Our sin is

---

[79] The word *sophianic* is from Sophia or "wisdom traditions," a manner of theologizing that depicts insight as light and ignorance as darkness. Sophianic thought includes Gnostic as one subcategory but is much larger than this, prevalent throughout Scripture, and central to the evangelical tradition too.

[80] *Republic* 514a-520a.

ignorance and existential sorrow. Our salvation is our liberation from the terms of such an existence. The heavenly and earthly Savior(s) who feature in Gnostic systems are those who will teach us to be free of the waltz floor of ignorance, suffering, and death.

Gnostic styles of metaphysics preexisted Christianity, and many of these themes can be witnessed in second-century Manichaeism.[81] Earlier works, such as those by Hans Jonas and Kurt Rudolph, tended to think the origin of Gnostic ideas could be found in ancient Near Eastern religions. Indeed, some scholars posited an Iranian origin for it (especially its strong belief in the cosmic struggle of two primeval powers: Dark and Light, Good and Evil, Saviors and Oppressors). But there are no pre-Christian instances of clearly Gnostic texts extant, and it seems rather to have been a profoundly Hellenistic movement reaching its zenith in the second century of the Christian era. It should not simply be regarded as a "parasitic" form of Christianity, Judaism, or Manichaeism, for it was equally at home in various "readings" of Hellenistic philosophical lifestyles, independent of any "Christian" element at all. The Nag Hammadi texts, for example, have some Christian *Gnostica* among them, but other materials are straightforward classical philosophical and ethical treatises, making it impossible to call Nag Hammadi a Gnostic collection at all. Adolf von Harnack, the great Protestant church historian of the late nineteenth and early twentieth centuries, defined Gnosticism (in its Christian guise) as an example of the "extreme Hellenization" of the Gospel tradition.

This desire sharply to distinguish "biblical truth" and "Greek philosophical religiosity" was once prevalent in theological writing of the last century but is no longer seen as defensible. Several of the earliest Christian so-called Gnostic elements are actually in the New Testament itself and are manifestations of late Jewish apocalyptic genre. Moreover, the Judaism of the time of Jesus was heavily influenced by Hellenistic cultural currents. Harnack's black-and-white categories do not work. Later work by Michael Williams and Karen King has warned afresh about the overcategorization involved in drawing too tight a description of Gnostics understood primarily as Christian dissidents, a perspective that follows the rhetorical drive of the patristic apologists too closely.[82] It is also a good thing, perhaps, to remember that this does not mean that they "were not" Christian dissidents, or that their dissidence is the very reason we remember them, for good or ill, for what possible alternatives they might have offered to Christian structures or for what structures the great church set in place to counteract their potential influence.

---

[81] Hans Jonas, *The Gnostic Religion: The Message of the Alien God and the Beginnings of Christianity*, 2nd ed. (Boston: Beacon, 1963); and Kurt Rudolph, *Gnosis: The Nature and History of Gnosticism* (San Francisco: Harper & Row, 1983), treat these matters of origins very well.

[82] Karen King, *What Is Gnosticism?* (Cambridge, MA: Harvard University Press), 2003; Michael Williams, *Rethinking Gnosticism: An Argument for Dismantling a Dubious Category* (Princeton, NJ: Princeton University Press, 1996).

So, there were clearly "Christian" Gnostics who taught in schools that regarded themselves as independent of the control of Christian *episkopoi* and not much subject to guidance or hedging by the issues of Christian communitarian traditions. The Jesus stories they inherited and wished to allegorize were to them base material for metaphysical storytelling, far more than historical narratives relative to Old Testament covenant theology adapted by Jesus' sophianic teachings.[83] These Gnostic *didaskaloi* (or masters) opened their own private rhetoric schools (*daskaleia*) in the great Hellenistic cities, such as Antioch, Alexandria, Rome, and Edessa. Chief among the most overtly Christian of these *didaskaloi* were Valentinus of Rome, Ptolemy his disciple, Theodotus, Basilides of Alexandria, Bardesanes the Syrian, and Hermogenes. This core group can be safely considered as centrally significant and as giving us solid historical data important to the development of early Christianity.

*Valentinus (fl. 120–160).* Christian Gnosticism of the Valentinian type was a form of knowledge that was thought intrinsically to give salvation to the elect redeemed—usually leading to mystical union with the divine principle. This was an experience that was closely related to spiritual afterlife and personal salvation, and thus its reformulation as a doctrine might have resulted from Gnostic *didaskaloi* attempting to attract adherents of the pre-Christian Greek mysteries. Valentinian Gnosticism was hostile to the principle of materiality and often used a highly allegorized, spiritualizing set of symbolic interpretations of sacred texts or material phenomena—in harmony with the loosely Platonic idea that material reality is actually "unreal" and more of an illusion and an entrapment than a wholesome and empirically dependable "real existence." Among them this was often related to heavily intellectualist rereadings of the ancient religions or myths (so to some extent pluralist), and in some cases it was based on readings of Christian stories that set out to harmonize them with Hellenistic myths of descending and ascending saviors. Highly allegorical symbolistic readings of Scripture at once kept the shape of traditional texts but freed the interpreter from any subordination to the original meanings.

This allegorical way of reading (and being liberated from) a text was, it seems, first popularized among Christians by the Valentinian Gnostics. It was already widespread among the Hellenists as a way of reading classical literature. This manner of biblical exegesis was a trend that at first greatly alarmed the great church, before

---

[83]That is, they took the proclamation of Jesus as God's Son and interpreted it to present Jesus as a universal cosmic savior in the manner of a Greek *Soter-Theos*, often laying little stress on the material historical reality of Jesus—some versions of the Gnostic Christology regarded the man Jesus as simply a shell the divine force inhabited temporarily—thus causing the first known major argument about Christology in the ancient church, the Docetic crisis (was Jesus real or merely an appearance [*dokesis*] of a divinity?), since a true divinity could not really be somatic flesh.

such readings came to be standard in the third and fourth centuries. Indeed, the first inventor of "Christian biblical commentary" in an allegorical form was Valentinian exegete Heracleon. His work was purged by the much greater biblical critic Origen, who set out to render the allegorical method of interpretation "appropriate" for catholic orthodoxy in the third century by refuting most of the "principles of dogma" that Heracleon and Valentinus were able to spin from their allegorical reading of the scriptural narratives about Jesus. Allegory, it should be noted nonetheless, tones down the historical voice involved in textual reading and turns up the volume on metaphysical speculations. The church has always been wary of the tension involved in that process: the difference between an enslaved scriptural literalism and a free-ranging myth making of the witness of the past.

Valentinus himself was famed in his lifetime for his brilliant intellectual and rhetorical skills. His rejection by the church at Rome and soon after by other major Christian communities was the spark that started the process of distinctly clarifying the difference between orthodox and Gnostic theologies (even though there was, of course, still a wide variety at that time in both the ideas of catholicity and Gnosticism). Valentinus is thus the catalyst of the whole concept of the apologetic tradition of orthodoxy, regardless of the interest his own ideas have in their own right. He was a native of Alexandria who took up a teaching position at Rome sometime between 136 and 140.[84] He seems to have left for Cyprus in 160, according to Eusebius and Tertullian, largely because of the hostility toward him generated by the Roman church authorities. He became identified as the arch-heretic in the Christian apologetic literature, and very little of his original work remains, although his system was described (chiefly to be ridiculed) by several hostile witnesses, especially Irenaeus of Lyons.[85] But there are others of the Fathers who had also read and commented on him and who preserve some of his actual fragments.[86] The discoveries of Gnostic

---

[84]Epiphanius, *Panarion* 31.2.3; Irenaeus, *Adversus Haereses* 3.4.3; Eusebius, *Ecclesiastical History* 4.11.1.
[85]The extant Valentinian fragments can be found in M. Simonetti, ed., *Testici gnostici in lingua greca e latina* (Milan: Fondazione Lorenzo Valla, 1993) (with Italian translation). Also see C. Markschies, *Valentinus Gnosticus? Untersuchungen zur valentinianischen Gnosis mit einem Kommentar zu den Fragmenten Valentins* (Tübingen: Mohr, 1992). Markschies's thesis is that Irenaeus's account of Valentinianism is not in harmony with the extant fragments, if the latter are studied without his overwhelming apologetic intent in mind. But while one might readily admit Irenaeus's hostile marshaling of evidence in the manner of much other ancient apologetics, both Christian and non-Christian, about rival schools of thought, it is nevertheless another matter altogether to dismiss him as making it all up from whole cloth. He was, and remains, a major witness to Gnostic teaching as it devolved to him from Roman and Lyonnais sources of the contemporary teachers. See also F. M. Sagnard, *La gnose valentinienne et le témoignage de Saint Irenée* (Paris: J. Vrin, 1947).
[86]Clement of Alexandria, *Stromateis* 2.36.2-4; 2.114.3-6; 3.59.3; 4.89.1-3; 4.89.6–4.90.1; 6.52.3–6.53.1; Hippolytus, *Refutation* 6.42.2; 6.37.7; 10.13.4.

literature at Nag Hammadi in the twentieth century were important for bringing him further out of the shadows, as many scholars now believe that the Gospel of Truth contained in the Nag Hammadi cache is a work by him, or at least reflecting his teaching in a substantial way.[87]

At the core of his school's program is the myth of restored gnosis, a salvation narrative of fallen spiritual powers and their rescue.[88] Valentinus's theology teaches that the divine world, or Pleroma, is a summation of thirty powers or Aeons. From the primordial creative pair (a male-female—androgynous—syzygy called Ineffable Depth [*Bythos*] and Silence [*Sige*], which is the ultimate principle of being), a second syzygy emanates (*Nous* and *Aletheia*). This second syzygy is the creatively fecund firstborn of the Original, and by this self-reflection God can generate and manifest his/her true being to God's-own-self, as well as reflect it outward. It is thus the archetype of true revelation, which shall now be emitted in a cascading series of emanations toward the lesser entities. From this original four comes a second set of four, making the eight primary principles that constitute the First Ogdoad.[89] Eleven pairs of male-female Aeons now emanate in turn out of these eight primordials, and this system of emission-declination produces the completion of the full cycle of the thirty Aeons. The youngest and last of them all is Sophia (Wisdom). As the lowest emanation out of the Primordial Ogdoad, she is defective, lacking balance, and is restless. Her wandering error (especially her inordinate desire to comprehend the Supreme Father) produces the (disaster of the) material cosmos. Sophia's great weakness was her lust to know the Ineffable Fathering. Her excessive pride tries to imitate this divine generativeness of the primordial first pair independently, but it is done in ignorance and produces only sin and error. The result is the cosmic mess (the sources describe it as a cosmic abortion instead of true generative birth) that we know as our material world. Valentinus believes that in the process of Sophia's disastrous production of the material cosmos some true spirit-existence became entrapped in matter. The fundamental "problem" and "error" of this chaos is the entrapment of spiritual light in material darkness, or the collision of spirit within a fleshly environment, which becomes an ontological source of ultimate distress and ignorance for all sentient being.

In Valentinian mythology, one of the lowest and most wicked of all spiritual principles falls to this earth and poses as the Demiurge, or lord of the world. This

---

[87]There are now believed to be eight texts in the Nag Hammadi corpus that are "Valentinian": Prayer of the Apostle Paul, the Gospel of Truth, the Tripartite Tractate, the Letter to Rheginus, the Gospel of Philip, First Apocalypse of James, Interpretation of Knowledge, and a Valentinian Exposition.

[88]For a reconstitution of his dogma see C. Markschies, "Valentinian Gnosticism: Toward the Anatomy of a School," in *The Nag Hammadi Library After Fifty Years*, ed. J. Turner et al. (Leiden: Brill, 1997), 401-38.

[89]Four pairs of male-females: Ineffable-Silence; Nous-Truth; Word-Life; Humankind-Church.

wicked spirit is the one called God by the Old Testament texts, who generally mistake his power for goodness. It is also the spiritual force behind the gods of the Hellenistic religions and the biblical God of simple Christians who unthinkingly follow the Jews in blind traditionalism. The worship of the Demiurge, however, is meant to enslave men and women and stop them from seeing the light. The God of the Scriptures is thus a false God. Jesus comes as a liberator to tell humankind about of a new divine force—the salvation of the true Father. As Marcion would also insist, the Father and the Old Testament "Lord" are two very different beings. The Demiurge masquerades as (a) beneficent god(s), so as to keep mortals believing there is something good about the material environment, and all they need to do to achieve righteousness is worship, be kind, persevere, endure cosmic suffering, and so on. He takes particular care to kill off true spiritual teachers (such as Jesus and other prophets) who might let out the news that this is all religious illusion. The ultimate religious error, for the Gnostics, is to confuse the good God (who despises this world but wants to free souls from its corruption) with the evil god, who wishes to enslave psychic spirits within this world and offers earthly benefits and apparent earthly blessings to enslaved worshipers.

For Valentinus, the Supreme God was so appalled that this pseudo-creative Sophic mess has resulted that, even though the ultimate divine power is transcendently removed from all earthly concerns, it determined to heal them and sent heavenly "emanations" from the lower ranks of the Aeons to repair the broken cosmic structure. The good God also inspires earthly "correspondences" to those heavenly patronal beings—great Gnostic teachers (such as John the Baptist, Jesus, Mani, and so on) who will declare the saving truths of enlightenment. One of the higher Aeons, the compassionate heavenly Christ, sent down the Savior Jesus to liberate spiritually inclined souls from their material, earthly imprisonment. Those who comprehend the message of truth (the *gnostikoi*) are enlightened and saved. Those who cling to material forms (the *hylikoi*) continue their enslavement to the Demiurge in a sorrowful and broken world that is robbed of spiritual significance and devoid of the potential for psychic progress. The believers are classed, according to their level of enlightenment (*gnosis*), as materials, psychics, or spirituals (*somatikoi*, *psychikoi*, *pneumatikoi*). The spirituals are those who enshrine the ultimate secret of the final ascent to reunion with the higher Aeons after death. *Pyschikoi* are learners. This latter category was, it would seem, an "ecumenical outreach" to the members of the great church, encouraging them to advance their spiritual ascent (faster than the episcopal church rituals would promise them) by subscribing to Valentinus's version of Christian spirituality.

For the Valentinians, because sin is ignorance, so is salvation enlightenment. Those spirituals who recognize the ultimate state of their psyche's entrapment are liberated to become true Gnostics and will be freed from material evil. Meanwhile, the Demiurge, true to his character as the wicked and perverted *daimon* of this earthly domain, tries all he can to keep humans trapped in darkness. He regards the liberation of souls from his domain as a loss of prestige and dominion. The war of light and darkness continues throughout the cosmos. Just as the divine light emanated in creative pairs from the primordial Ogdoad, and unity was symbolized in the syzygies, just so it can be broken by sin. This is symbolized in the sexual separation of Adam and Eve (the breaking of the androgyny and the origin of lust) as recounted in Genesis. The spiritual human being must henceforth seek to be united to his or her corresponding heavenly partner.

The whole layout of the myth might seem bizarre at first sight (and the great church apologists certainly seized on this as an argumentative tool, ridiculing it), but basically the whole narrative is a moral call to salvific action for its hearers: ascent away from materiality to a sophic wisdom. What jarred most with the great church was that such a scheme basically cut the line that tied in Jesus with a real history: one in which flesh mattered as a sacramentally holy thing; one in which the world mattered, and in which it was a good world and one that God loved and wished to redeem by healing. The reaction that the great church set up against these fundamental Gnostic principles was twofold and can be simply stated. First, it is most succinctly expressed in the anti-Gnostic sophiology of the Johannine prologue in that resonant statement "And the Logos became flesh" (Jn 1:14). Second, it was encapsulated in a creedal refutation of the principle of Aeonic emanations: "We believe in One God, the Father Almighty, Maker of Heaven and Earth, of all that is seen, visible and invisible." Indeed, although the creeds are later elevated in the fourth century to be bulwark statements of belief, they undoubtedly originated in the early second century to offer a simple statement of fundamental belief to offset Gnostic theo-cosmology.

If we stand away a little from the details of the macronarrative and consider its larger form or type, it is clear enough, perhaps, that Valentinus's cosmological system is a strongly Middle Platonic expression of the problem of the one and the many, using religious motivations and philosophical archetypes and envisaging a descending hierarchy of emanations to mediate between the High God (the One) and the daimonic powers and entities of the material world (the many). Valentinus, however, is distinct from the run-of-the-mill philosophical theosophists of his time in that he combines a Platonic metaphysic with major elements of the Christian salvation story and in the process gives his understanding of the life of Jesus a profoundly cosmic significance. The orthodox opponents of his scheme resisted him chiefly on the grounds that he had disconnected the Jesus story from history and wrenched it away from the seamless context of the Hebrew Scriptures, but they were also deeply influenced by the majestic way Valentinus had explained the metaphysical and universal implications of the Christian message of salvation. When one speaks of the ultimate rejection of the Gnostic systems in the mainline or great church, this belies to a considerable extent the way in which so many insights of the Gnostic movements were tamed and incorporated into mainline Christianity of a mystical type.

The Valentinian elevation of mysticism over history, however, was something the great church never accepted, though it would increasingly look favorably, from this time onward, on the concept of expressing the *kerygma* of evangelical salvation through the lens of cosmological narratives beyond those of Semitic apocalypticism. A profound sense of cosmic alienation is fixed within all the Gnostic schemes and becomes increasingly visible in wider forms of late second-century Christianity. The tension produced when early Christianity in some parts replaced its first, apocalyptic sense of "alienation" with a more universalist sense of cosmological collapse has been thought by some scholars to be at the root of a growing trend to present Christianity as an ascetic and world-denying religion.

Dualism in some form is central to many Gnostic patterns of thought, especially that of Valentinus: light and darkness are perpetually at war, as are spirit and matter. In some form, of course, one could say that this was also true of all religious systems in late antiquity—but the Gnostic movement brings the conflict to the fore more noticeably and elevates it as more of a metaphysical, even a theological, principle. This the great church reacted against consistently. The mythic scheme of salvation for Valentinus works by means of these dynamic oppositions—a confrontational set of opposites that to a significant degree sets it against the current of much earlier popular Greek religious thought, which had often tended to presume a close connection between the deities and the world order. Judaism also presumes a close sense of world as blessed by a single covenant-father God. Since this premise of God's close bonding with his earth and his covenant people on the earth was also the *fundamental* insight behind Jewish scriptural theology, as well as behind the first interpretations of the life and death of Jesus, it was inevitable that a strong battle would be waged over Gnostic tendencies in the Christian church, and also that it would quickly be seen as a matter of the "correct interpretation of the Scriptures." Valentinus's greatest disciple, Heracleon, is fundamentally an exegete. So too is the church's greatest anti-Gnostic, Origen of Alexandria.

Valentinus left behind him two schools (*didaskaleia*) of disciples.[90] The first was the so-called Western school, including Ptolemy and Heracleon.[91] This Italian group taught that Christ had a psychic body, which the Spirit entered at the baptism. Ptolemy authored the *Letter to Flora*, which has been fully preserved by Epiphanius.[92] It offers a version of the teaching in a simple form for a beginner. It holds the Demiurge to be a creature midway between God and the devil: neither wholly good nor evil but rigidly obsessed with justice. The *daimon* who composed the Hebraic laws of vengeance proves himself to be defective, and Paul, who informs us we must treat these things allegorically, helps us toward insight in this matter of the role of the Bible. Ptolemy seems, in this work, to have been aware of Marcion's work. The chief work of Heracleon was his renowned *Commentary on John*. He was, indeed, the first Christian known to compose a complete biblical commentary, and its extensive fragments are preserved in Origen's *Commentary* on the same Gospel. Clement of Alexandria called him "the most famous of the school of Valentinus."[93]

The second faction of the school was the Eastern *didaskaleion* presided over by Marcus and Theodotus, whose writings are discussed and argued against by Clement of Alexandria in his treatise *Excerpts from Theodotus*. They held to the opinion that Christ had a spiritual body that simply passed through Mary as through a water pipe, without having any real physical contact with her. Theodotus gave perhaps the most famous simple synopsis of Gnostic soteriology. His questions of salvation (quasi-creedal ways to demonstrate enlightenment) were threefold: Who are we? Where did we come from? Where are we hastening to? The work of Marcus is more difficult to comprehend, and Irenaeus gathers together a lot of caustic hearsay about his loose morals: performing magic, seducing rich women, and so on. It would seem, nevertheless, that theurgy, astrology, and numerology played a significant part in his teachings and that women had a cultic role in his rites. Irenaeus does not so much call him a philosopher as much as a leader of a cultic society (*thiasos*).[94] Marcus describes a deathbed ritual of release (*apolytrosis*) wherein the dying person is given the secret words to transition from this world safely to the spiritual realm, a form of rite comparable to some of the Greek mysteries.[95]

---

[90]Hippolytus, *Refutation* 6.35.
[91]Irenaeus, *Adversus Haereses* 6.35.5-7.
[92]Epiphanius, *Panarion* 33.3.1–33.7.10.
[93]Clement of Alexandria, *Stromateis* 4.7.1.
[94]Irenaeus, *Adversus Haereses* 1.13.4.
[95]Ibid., 1.25.5. The dying person listened to the ritual and had to recount it to the Demiurge so as to gain freedom from his power: "I am a child of the Father, the Pre-Existent Father. . . . I am returning to my own, form whence I came. . . . I am a precious vessel, more precious than the female who made you. . . . I know myself and know from whence I came, and I invoke the Incorruptible Wisdom, who is in the Father, and who is Mother of your mother, who had no father and no male consort."

This battle of the great church with Gnostic schemes was fierce in the second century and continued in lesser forms until the fourth. It has flared up again in various later centuries in Christian history (some see the medieval heresies of Bogomilism or the Cathars/Albigensians as Gnostic related, at least in conceptual form). Gnosticism has marked the whole Christian movement in positive and negative ways ever since the second century. Almost every aspect of Christian doctrine (salvation, anthropology, canonicity, preferred authority patterns, forms of liturgy) has been deeply and clearly shaped by the Gnostic movement. Most important of all, perhaps, was the Logos theology that came to underpin the whole of subsequent christological reflection. It can be said, therefore, that this first great international crisis that hit the early Jesus movement gave it its classical architecture by forcibly sharpening its mind on fundamental categories and transformed the movement from an overwhelmingly Semitic to a predominantly biblically Hellenistic religion. As an example of this, one also observes that each and all of the seminal Christian documents are no longer in Aramaic/Syriac but Greek.

*Bardesanes (c. 154–222).*[96] Also known as Bar-Daysan or Bar Daisanes, this Syrian teacher is the first known Christian poet in that language, and he set a standard for generations of Syrian poetic theologians who followed him. None of this work survives except for some titles in Ephrem's reference to him in his *Hymns Against the Heretics* (55).[97] Fragments of his prose are preserved by later writers, who censure him (from the perspective of fourth-century Nicene orthodoxy) for allegedly holding Gnostic ideas. His system is represented in a surviving work, *The Dialogue of Destiny* (or *The Book of Laws of Countries*). Some scholars think that the apocryphal Acts of Thomas was written in his larger school. Astrology was important to his system, and he probably served as court astrologer and counselor. He wished, in his role as an important state philosopher, to discuss how personal freedom could be understood in the light of destiny. He argues against the common fatalism of the classical astrologers that Christ has counteracted the overwhelming force of the planets. He seems to be heavily dualist in tone—but a dualism that is predominantly moral rather than metaphysical: evil is profoundly mixed with the good in this world, a theme he describes, in Semitic form, as a battle between light and darkness. Ephrem the Syrian in the fourth century claimed that Bardesanes understood Christ's incarnation as merely an appearance of human nature (Docetism). But this might have been his anachronistic importation into Bardesanes of what was by then a common belief about the generic Docetism of Gnostics in general. All in all he was an interesting

---

[96]In this section I draw extensively on my previous article, "Bardesanes," in *The Westminster Handbook to Patristic Theology* (Louisville: Westminster John Knox, 2004), 44.

[97]*Bar* is the Syriac term for "son of."

early example of a palace theologian, a Christian philosopher-astrologer in the court of King Agbar VIII at Edessa.

Recent work by Hilaria Ramelli has drawn intellectual connections between Bardesanes and Origen, both men being early exemplars of thinkers who took seriously the issues involved in connecting their new Christian faith with age-old problems of cosmological philosophy.[98] The connections between the two are perhaps most frequently provided by common reliance on Middle Platonic interests in providence, theodicy, and revelation theory, via readings of Plato's *Timaeus* and elements of Stoic cosmology. Some Christian sources remember Bardesanes not only as a philosopher and courtier but also as being a deacon or a presbyter of the liturgical assembly and as having written refutations of Marcion and Gnostic principles, and even as having suffered for the defense of his faith in a time of persecution.

*Basilides (fl. 135–161).* Nothing has directly survived of the work of this Syrian theologian who was the leading teacher of a Gnostic-type school at Alexandria during the reigns of Hadrian (117–138) and Antoninus Pius (138–161) and who composed some of the earliest Christian biblical commentary, including *Twenty-Four Books on the Gospel* and a *Book of Odes*.[99] He might even have composed an (apocryphal) gospel of his own.[100] Two text traditions about his writings give significantly different pictures. In Irenaeus's account, Basilides's doctrine seems to be roughly akin to the Valentinian system.[101] The deity is beyond description, beyond existence, and emanated a series of intellective powers (*Nous, Logos, Phronesis, Sophia,* and *Dynamis*). The last two created the first heaven, initiating a series of other dyads making other descending hierarchies of heavens until the perfect number of 365 is completed, thus offering some form of metaphysical answer to the ubiquitous philosophical problem of reconciling the One and the many. Angels in this final and lowest heaven (led by the rebellious one the Jewish Scriptures mistakenly proclaimed as god) made the material cosmos, a work dominated by evil and oppression. Christ, embodying the heavenly spirit of Nous, was sent to effect liberation of souls from this gloomy bondage. Having been arrested and condemned to death by the machinations of the evil Demiurge, this Christ-power "shifted shape," assuming the features of Simon of Cyrene, who was helping him carry the cross, leaving Simon to be crucified while he ascended free. Irenaeus finds this passage scandalous in the extreme (and delights in

---

[98] H. Ramelli, *Bardaisan of Edessa: A Reassessment of the Evidence and a New Interpretation* (Piscataway, NJ: Gorgias Press, 2009).

[99] Clement of Alexandria, *Stromateis* 7.106.4; Origen, *Commentary on Job* 21.11; Eusebius, *Ecclesiastical History* 4.7.7.

[100] Origen, *Homily 1 on Luke*.

[101] Irenaeus, *Adversus Haereses* 1.24.

recounting it so as to shock his readers), but it probably signified originally the symbolic differentiation of the psychic "foolish" disciple who lives a mimesis of Simon by a path of endurance and discipline, as distinct from the Gnostic (Christ-like) disciple who seeks after Nous and realises the essential insignificance of the material body and its affairs. It gives, nevertheless, a clear example of the kind of christological Docetism among the Gnostics that the wider church found troubling.

In the other text tradition presented in Hippolytus and supported by some references in other Christian writers, the story comes across with some differences.[102] Basilides is said to have taught the cosmos existed as the high God's own all-inclusive "world-seed." Three sonships, in a descending hierarchy (light, heavy, and defiled) derive from the seed. The first is an ascentive power; the second ascends with power from the Holy Spirit; the third is purified by assisting human souls to ascend. Two archons also derive from the seed, and both are accompanied by their sons. The first son leads his father and his realm (the perfect eight—or Ogdoad) to repentance, while the second son mirrors this process and teaches truth to his father and the realm of Seven (the Hebdomad). The salvific light of the Ogdoad and Hebdomad was what inspired Jesus, the enlightened one, who calls the elect back to God, healing the essential sinfulness of certain souls. Origen later tells us that Basilides had taught the doctrine of the transmigration of souls. The essential impact of his system seems to have been a principle of soteriological mediation, one that tried to meld the Christian *kerygma* with Hellenistic philosophical systems of cosmological mediation. Basilides is one of the first Gnostic teachers who shows a reaction to the great church apologetic that apostolic succession is critically important for Christian authenticity. According to Hippolytus, he claimed to have derived his teaching from the secret initiations that came from the school of the apostle Matthias and said that he was the student of Glaucias, who had served as the apostle Peter's interpreter.[103]

**Marcionism.** Another window onto the diverse schools of Christian Rome is opened for us by Marcion of Sinope (c. 85–160). He was a thoughtful Christian, very rich and thus well educated, and one of the few at this time to be raised in the faith from childhood, by a leading clerical family of Pontus.[104] His reading of the Hebrew Scriptures appalled Marcion as much as it edified him. Moses the great hero and prophet of God, who speaks to God and leads the redeemed people, for him was

---

[102]Hippolytus, *Refutation* 7.20-27.
[103]*Refutation of All Heresies* 7.20.1-5. Obscure New Testament characters who left no public record to consult were always a good target for pseudepigraphers and psychopomps of secret traditions.
[104]His family wealth came from shipping, and he extended it greatly by military trading. He was the son of the bishop of Sinope, a Black Sea community. His own father is said to have excommunicated him from his local church.

equally the warlord who commanded his soldiers to go back and vindictively slaughter the Midianite mature women and children after their military victory (when the soldiers themselves wished to spare them), keeping only the young virgins alive as their own sexual spoils. How could a text containing such scriptures be considered wholly sacred when it represented so many ambiguous, not to say downright immoral, episodes in parts? Was God truly genocidal in character, or so patently unstable in temper, as many of these ancient stories indicated? Or were they historically conditioned (Bronze Age war tales, like those of the Greeks in Homer's hands) and needing a radical sifting and sorting before they could be safely brought in on board the Christian religion as religious and ethical authorities? But if they were in need of such drastic interpretative sorting (judging the very standard of judgment), how could they be afforded global authority or canonical authority over Christians as the unmediated "Word of God"? Could the religion of mercy and forgiveness such as Christ represented survive its marriage to the whole of the Hebrew Scriptures, or would they swamp the canoe and pull down the coherence of early Christian theology and morals?

These are sets of questions that, externally, continue to exercise wider society when it looks at the moral criteria of religious communities, and internally still challenge thoughtful Christians today. Evidently the Christian church today commends the totality of Scripture—it is just that often the church cites it in a very piecemeal way, is very careful about what to read in church or what not to read, and has sophisticated historical canons for deciding what is "edifying" (and eternally valid) or "disedifying" (and historically time bound). Christianity's extensive developments of sophisticated textual interpretation in the late third and fourth centuries gave a set of answers to some of these questions that Marcion found troubling, and they served to distance the church from "the letter" of the Old Testament, affording it authority but not in an absolute sense.[105] Paul the apostle had, of course, already started wrestling with such issues, and Marcion, if nothing else, was a close reader of Paul.[106] Of Marcion's works only seven short Latin prologues to the Pauline epistles have survived.[107] But Marcion began the discussion of the question of the enduring significance of the Old Testament from a largely Gentile perspective, different from that

---

[105]Except for (what is historically speaking) a minority of "fundamentalist" theoreticians who might still argue that every line of the Old Testament is equally significant as every line of the New and that every line of each bears an absolute authority over the community. Such views are, however, not found in antiquity, as both are early modern in character and held by very small factions of the larger Christian family, even when that larger family sustains traditions of biblical inerrancy, infallibility, and supremacy.

[106]See R. J. Hoffmann, *Marcion, on the Restitution of Christianity: An Essay on the Development of Radical Paulinist Theology in the Second Century* (Chico, CA: Scholars Press, 1984).

[107]From the hand of a close disciple. See J. Wordsworth and H. J. White, *Novum Testamentum Domini Nostri Jesus Christi Latine*, vol. 2 (Oxford: Clarendon, 1913).

of Paul, and his answers to it rose to an order of significance to serve as a watershed for subsequent generations. Having articulated this problem, he thereby caused a permanent fork in the road for anyone who came after. Even though he and his theory of Bible were ultimately rejected, his influence lived on in many ways for centuries after him. The community he founded as an alternative church remained a popular alternative to mainstream Christianity until well after the year 200 in Asia, when it was more or less absorbed into the Manichaean movement. In the Latin West it was still in evidence up to the end of the third century; and in Syria it had its longest survival into the fifth century, as can be seen by Syrian theologians as late as Rabbula and Theodoret writing refutations of it.[108]

After Marcion was expelled from the mainline community at Rome, he preserved the rituals and forms of Roman Christianity in his own churches, leading the fourth-century bishop Cyril of Jerusalem, who has left us his instructions to the newly baptized, to warn his new converts to make sure they were in the catholic, not the Marcionite, church when they traveled abroad.[109] Later Christian fathers, following Epiphanius, characterized him as one of the earliest "seducers" of the virgin that was the church, thus listing him as one of the early arch-heretics in what would emerge later as the symbolic heretical *quincunx* of Simon Magus, Mani, Valentinus, Marcion, and Arius.[110]

His works are now dissipated, and only fragments can be reconstructed from his very active list of opponents, which includes some of the most significant writers of the second century: Tertullian, Justin Martyr, and Irenaeus. Later Christian writers speaking about Marcion are recycling the works of these earlier theologians. The chief source of our knowledge about him still remains Tertullian's treatise *Against Marcion*.[111] Justin was a contemporary of his and spoke of him extensively in his (now lost) *Syntagma Against All Heresies*.[112] Irenaeus is responsible for many previous generations

---

[108] G. May, "Markion/Markioniten," in *Religion in Geschichte und Gegenwart*, 4th ed. (Tübingen: Mohr Siebeck, 1998–2007), 5:834.

[109] This was 250 years after Marcion's death. See Cyril, *Catecheses* 4.4.

[110] *Refutation of All Heresies* 42.2. Hostile accounts of his life report that his father allegedly excommunicated him for having an affair with a Christian virgin in Sinope; and thus he came to Rome to develop his studies and set up, effectively, his own church-*schola* there.

[111] *Adversus Marcionem*. See E. Evans, *Tertullian: Adversus Marcionem* (Oxford: Oxford University Press, 1972) (Latin text and English trans.). See also E. P. Meijering, *Tertullian Contra Marcion: Gotteslehre in der Polemik: Adversus Marcionem I-II* (Leiden: Brill, 1977).

[112] It is possibly the first time (anticipated, however, in the third letter of John) that the concept of heresy (*hairesis*), which had up until that point signified a division of opinion between various philosophical schools (and thus was something that continued to be discussed), shifted its weight to the ecclesiological meaning prevalent from then among Christians—that is, referring to a conceptual differentiation or divergence that fractures the possibility of continuing mutual recognition as being part of the same family of faith.

regarding him as a Gnostic. Irenaeus probably oversystematizes his views of heresy by tracing them to single roots of teachers. In Marcion's case he claims that he was taught by the Syrian Gnostic Cerdo (*Kerdon*), disciple of Simon Magus at Rome after 135, from whom he took his ideas that the god of the Old Testament was radically different from the God and Father of the Lord Jesus Christ, and also that evangelical accounts had to be read in a wholly spiritual (nonmaterial or Docetist) manner.[113] This Gnostic connection has come under question of late. Marcion certainly knew Gnostic teachers in Rome and elsewhere, but his real intellectual program derives from his desire to systematically and severely epitomize the corpus of sacred Christian texts by means of imposing a radical Paulinist ideology as an interpretative lens.

Marcion's own chief writing was the *Antithesis*. Adolf von Harnack described it as a kind of very early "Introduction to the New Testament" for Christians.[114] It seems that most of his writing was concerned with exegesis and establishing a much smaller authoritative corpus of sacred literature. Even though his work would be fundamentally rejected by the larger body of Christians, it is undoubtedly the case that Marcion was the single most influential force in making Christians think seriously about their attitude toward the sacred texts of Judaism and propelling them toward clarifying their concept of a canon of Christian Scripture.

Marcion came to Rome and studied there, settled down, and became part of the larger community of Roman Christians. One needs to imagine a nexus of house churches, leading presbyter-bishops, and some notable Christian philosopher-theologians setting up *scholae*. At this period double belonging was not either impossible or unheard of. The growing stress with Gnostic *didaskaloi* was soon to make the issue a fraught one. When Marcion arrived in Rome, he donated a very large sum to the finances of the catholic Christian community: two hundred thousand sesterces.[115] In 144, when the Roman bishop (possibly Hyginus) excommunicated him for his teachings, his money was returned to him in full. There are indications in the accounts that Marcion was not happy about his separation, though Tertullian's version that he sought reconciliation at the end and was prepared to renounce his doctrines to effect it (though was prevented from so doing by death) is probably wishful thinking. He died in 160, having left Rome and probably returned to Asia Minor.

Marcion refused to reconcile the god of the Old Testament (whom he concluded

---

[113] Irenaeus, *Adversus Haereses* 1.27.1.

[114] He discusses the work in his monograph *Marcion: The Gospel of the Alien God*, trans. J. Steeley and L. Bierma (New York: Labyrinth, 1990), 53-63; see also his *History of Dogma*, trans. N. Buchanan (Boston: Little, 1901), 1:266-81.

[115] A loaf of bread in Rome cost half a sestertius, and a half-liter of good wine twice that. In the first century a legionary's army pay was nine hundred sestertii per annum. On that basis his gift was near enough a four-million-dollar donation in today's values.

was a vindictive and petty tribal god of the Jews) with the Father spoken of by Jesus. He took Jesus as the figure who first revealed the "true God" to the world and elevated Paul as his chosen apostle after he had seen, from glory, that the other apostles had made a disastrous job of passing on the teaching. He deduced this from Jesus' teachings about the universal love of his Father, compared to the bloodiness of the god mentioned in the Old Testament. He made lists of incidents where this god was clearly manifested as vindictively wicked. In Isaiah, for example, this god says, "I am the Creator of evil."[116] Marcion added philosophy to his exegetical razor and concluded that the Old Testament god was none other than the *Demiourgos*, the shaper-maker of this visible cosmos, who had charge of all sublunar activities (the "prince of this world" whom Jesus referred to as the enemy of the kingdom), but who was deeply hostile to human beings and did not want them to have spiritual knowledge (as he already revealed in the episode of Adam and Eve in the garden). He went on in a systematic way: the Demiurge is to be classed as a lesser but powerful *daimon*, not the real God; his character clashes with the essential benignity of the God Jesus reveals as philanthropic. Accordingly the whole of the Old Testament revelation, celebrating this Demiurge, this God of Israel, must be rejected root and branch from the Christian revelation: rooted up as weeds from the new wheat field. The apostles of Jesus had not understood this fundamental task, the radical message that the true God wishes to liberate the world from enslavement to the Demiurge, who, since he has made humanity, regards it as his slave property. Humankind was made for divine insight, but the carelessness of this cosmic god allowed the race to fall away into ignorance and sin, and his malice condemned them to punishment and death. The God revealed by Jesus, however, though not the creator of the flawed cosmic order or of humanity that is part of it, is a most merciful deity who sees the plight of humans under the tyranny of the Demiurge and so sends his beloved Son to announce a rescue: for spiritual liberation and ascent to a new service of a newly revealed deity of love. Points of contact can be seen here, of course, between Gnostic cosmological teachings and Manichaean theological dualism.

For Marcion the realization of this staggering insight means that even the New Testament texts already emerging in his day as "apostolic" have to be purified. Jesus is the radically new apostle of the true, merciful God, wholly different from the creator god spoken of in the old literature, an idea still seducing the Jewish-influenced minds of several of the early disciples of Jesus, who have mistakenly thought that his Father was the old god of Israel. The Old Testament texts, therefore, must not be read allegorically in an attempt to reconcile the law with the gospel of grace, but always read literally. Nothing in the New Testament is a fulfilment of

---

[116] Is 45:7 LXX (*ktizon kaka*). See Tertullian, *Adversus Marcion* 1.2.

any Old Testament types or traditions. Because of this exegetical literalism, Marcion was often an object of ridicule for later Christian writers.[117] The only one who understood the radical separation of law and grace, Marcion argued, was Jesus' chosen and most enlightened apostle Paul. It is Paul's corrective teachings that must be used as the sieve that sifts out demiurgic pollution that has crept in to the new *kerygma* as part of the ongoing hostility of the Demiurge, who was trying yet again to lead humankind's spiritual instinct astray and back to enslavement by encouraging Christians to adopt Jewish ideas. So it was that Marcion set about cutting large passages even from the New Testament corpus. His main work in Rome was to be concerned with producing a defense of these ideas, along with a definitive version of the "authentic canon" of Christian sacred teaching: his own version, that is, of the apostolic tradition.

Marcion had a very small Bible left to him then. He sees fools, corrupters, and Judaizers as responsible for the mess that is the literary corpus of early Christian teaching. He has no other exegetical method apart from this ideological construct (the Demiurge craftily raising up tares in the wheat); but, I suppose, it is a little like the Jesus Seminar of the late twentieth century: a set of theological premises about Christology dominates the "method" elected, to produce basically a much smaller canon of literature accepted as only authoritative, which ultimately supports the ideology and so (not surprisingly!) justifies the method in a closed hermeneutical circle.

For Marcion, when Jesus descended to earth he assumed a body that only looked material. The evil minions of the god of the world crucified him to stop the liberative message being preached to mortals but did not realize he himself was not mortal, and so his death was their undoing, since it allowed him to descend into the Demiurge's psychic prison of Hades and announce even there that he would bring spiritual rescue. He tells them the gospel that his divine forgiveness does not require postdeath punishment—that it is in fact merely a character failing of the evil god to wish to do this to psychic beings. Marcion's moral message was based on the teaching that to understand the force of the loving-kindness and forgiveness offered by the God and Father of Jesus leads one to long to live in love and peace, and to rise up from the corruptions of this world to join with the Savior in a new heavenly kingdom. One needed in this material cosmos, then, to live as little under the sway of the evil god as possible. Marcion advocated the abandonment of marriage and sexual activity (procreation keeps up the supply of spiritual slaves to the god of this cosmos). Concepts of a fleshly resurrection and eternal condemnation

---

[117]Irenaeus, *Adversus Haereses* 1.27; 4.8, 34; Tertullian, *On the Prescription of Heretics* 30-44; Clement of Alexandria, *Stromateis* 3.3-4; Origen, *Against Celsus* 6.53; and especially throughout Tertullian's dedicated apologia *Against Marcion*.

are foolish, an example of how the old ideas of the materialist Demiurge have corrupted Jesus' message of spiritual liberation.

What shaped the Marcionite canon was probably the liturgical demands of the early eucharistic celebration. His move toward the full abandonment of the Old Testament meant, liturgically speaking, relatively less of a "shock tactic" than if we approach the matter exegetically. In liturgical practice it meant that he replaced the Psalter as a source of antiphons and hymns. The extent of reading Old Testament passages at the Eucharist must have varied at this period. In some places Old Testament readings were located in the vigil service of the evening before Sunday dawn. Marcion thus presented his effective canon as a two-volume corpus: *Evangelikon* and *Apostolikon*. The Gospel account cuts out the references to Jesus' birth and childhood (simply a playacting to avoid the attention of the Demiurge). His final text is a highly edited version of a single Lukan core.[118] Marcion's *Apostolikon* consisted of ten letters of St. Paul, again with his own edits. He either does not know, or rejects, the Pastoral Epistles. This focus on two liturgical volumes is still the liturgical practice of the Eastern church—Scripture in the liturgical mode is not so much iconically presented to the church as bound Bible containing Old Testament and New Testament (only in later post-Reformation praxis), but as two bound volumes of Apostle and Gospel. The Old Testament readings are not rejected, of course, in this liturgical lectionary process toward canon, but in Byzantine practice, for example, are located chiefly in the evening service of Vespers before Sunday.

Marcion's overall theories represented a potent mix of simple and charismatic messages of love and freedom; no divine judgment; no need to take the things of this world as serious except as dangerous illusions; Christ a spiritual symbol and his message a matter of enlightenment; the church fundamentally a community of spiritual fellowship. It was a movement that retained all the external iconographic forms and ritual of the mainline church but was a theosophical simplification of it. One imagines (though Marcion does not speak about it in his remains other than to suggest many "corruptions" have been admitted into the ecclesial system) that Marcion would probably think that systems of authority (such as leadership offices in the early church) were not valid if they were oppressive: and to this extent one wonders whether he had a cavalier attitude to the episcopal and presbyteral teachers of the liturgical communities. Certainly they regarded themselves as having real authority over him to adjudicate his doctrine, not to have him adjudicate them in terms of his doctrine. The most startling aspects of his teaching, of course, were the wholesale sinking of the Old Testament Law and Prophets because of his daimonic

---

[118] A process of simplification he based on Gal 1:8-9.

theology, and the Docetic Christology he presumed, that Christ only seemed human and came to bring a purely spiritual message of escape. Tertullian, for one, began to wrestle seriously with the christological implications of this in his treatises, not least his anti-Docetic arguments in *On the Flesh of Christ* but also across all his large corpus of dogmatic works on theology, trinitarianism, Christology, pneumatology, ecclesiology, heresiology, and sacramentalism.

Even when they are not mentioning Marcion by name, the furious sounds issuing from the workshops of second-century major Christian theologians (and indeed on throughout the third) demonstrate how dramatically Marcion had stirred the pot. As with his views on Scripture, revelation, and canon, his ideas were not admitted by the larger body of the church. But he was the catalyst that set the system in its most important ferment and so caused the later nexus of solutions. Likewise, he can be regarded on a much wider front as the thinker who perhaps more than any other (and this because he was so much more "in the church" than the Gnostics or the Manichaeans) moved Christianity away from the dominating genres of Semitic poetry toward a more philosophical and cosmologically based systematic presentation of the sources of its faith. After Marcion we see the birth of Christian systematics. The Monarchian controversy, extending from multiple late second-century churches across to the early part of the third century, exemplifies this most distinctly.

**Irenaeus of Lyons (c. 135–200).** Irenaeus is an immensely important theologian of the second century. He came from Smyrna and tells us that he had known Polycarp (though he was very young and Polycarp was very old) when Florinus, the Roman presbyter to whom he was writing, was already a person of substance in the Smyrnaean church.[119] He studied first at Rome before becoming a presbyter of the church at Lyons. In 177 that church sent him on a mediating mission to appeal to Pope Eleutherius for tolerance of the Montanists, and while he was there a savage persecution broke out at Lyons, claiming the life of bishop Pothinus, whom Irenaeus succeeded on his return from his mission.[120] In the year 190 Irenaeus returned to Rome to plead with Pope Victor (189–198) on behalf of the Quartodeciman Asia Minor bishops who wished to safeguard their local custom of celebrating Easter on the fourteenth of the spring month of Nisan, who had been censured by a recent encyclical letter of Pope Victor, calling on all

---

[119]Eusebius, *Ecclesiastical History* 5.20.5-7.
[120]Eusebius knew the letter of recommendation that Irenaeus carried to Rome and cites it: "If we had known that rank can confer righteousness on anyone, we should first of all have recommended him as being a presbyter of this church [of Lyons], for that is his position." Ibid., 5.4.2.

synods of bishops to break with this practice.[121] Later Christian tradition suggests Irenaeus was martyred.[122]

Irenaeus is one of the major voices opposing the Gnostic Christianities of his time, especially the Valentinian and Sethian schools, which one presumes he knew best from experience at Lyons and Rome. His style of apologia established patterns of thought (a focus on christologically centered, historical, antispeculative theology) and administration (a focus on the authority of the bishop to teach, exegete, and control the books read in the churches) that became constitutive for later catholic orthodoxy (core theories of apostolic succession and canonicity of Scripture). He is an interesting, if somewhat prolix, theologian who influenced Origen and the later Alexandrian tradition in significant ways and thus shaped the mainstream of developing catholicity.

His major work is the five-volume tractate *Against All Heresies* (*Adversus Haereses*).[123] He uses his own knowledge of dissident teachers at Rome and Gaul, as well as the works of the apologetic writers before him: chiefly Justin Martyr, Theophilus of Antioch, and Papias. It is difficult to discern where these borrowings are in his work, since the corpus of these same writers has largely been lost. In the first book (on the detection of false gnosis) he reviews the Gnostic theological systems, especially that of Valentinus's school, and he makes a list of the chief Gnostic teachers. He makes the line start with Simon Magus (to demonstrate his principle that the heretical teachers began resisting the apostles from the outset and continue to the present day) and continues it from Menander in this order: Satornil, Basilides, Carpocrates, Cerinthus, the Ebionites, the Nicolaites, Cerdon, Marcion, Tatian, and the Encratites. It is clear from this that we have here a mix-up of Tatian, Marcion, and Jewish-Christian groups whom we would not call "Gnostics" today along with Gnostics proper. For Irenaeus they were all "pseudo-Gnostics," according to his taxonomy. In other words, all of these teachers represented, for him, systems or schools led by false teachers (so isolated and named by him as heretics) who gave the church their own doctrines instead of the truth of the apostolic tradition. In other words, it is not that Irenaeus has got Gnosticism wrong somehow, but rather that his definition of what pseudo-Gnosticism is does not derive from a systematic analysis of the content of the "Gnostic" literature but from a prior theological conception of what constitutes apostolic truth: a consonance of the faith of the churches (guarded by the commonality of *episkopoi*), which they clearly depart from. Consonance, *harmonia*, is his key to the catholic tradition that is heir to apostolic teaching.

---

[121]Eusebius (Ibid., 5.24.17) says that he lived up to his name (*Irinaois* means "man of peace") by the way he appealed to both sides to come to agreement.

[122]Gregory of Tours, *Historia Francorum* 1.27.

[123]Its full original title was *Detection and Overthrow of the Pretended but False Gnosis*.

Book two of the *Adversus Haereses* focuses on the Valentinian system and the Marcionites. It still remains important evidence as to what was held by both schools, though it is overly formalist in many respects and always ready to cast moral aspersions. Valentinianism, apparently, was not very fixed even in its transmission from master to immediate disciples. Even so, Irenaeus had firsthand knowledge; he is the most important witness of the movement (albeit an enemy), and his testimony cannot be dismissed as wholly irrelevant. He sets himself up in his own volume as the voice of reason (the Logos of God is the fountain of *logos* or rationality in humans), refuting erroneous doctrines about Wisdom and its nature. This is why he clearly stresses the unreasonable nature of his opponents at every step. Book three turns to refute the false systems from the basis of the church's traditions about God and Christ. Book four does it from the basis of an exegesis of the sayings of Jesus himself. Book five is dedicated largely to the catholic concept of the resurrection of all flesh, which he lifts up as a core doctrine guaranteed to annoy Gnostics of all stripes, whom he is certain will find the idea of flesh being so valued by God as philosophically objectionable. He thus pushes this doctrine forward as a chief test case, as it were, for how to flush out a Gnostic sympathizer. His writing is rather sprawling in character. Like many other rhetoricians (and he is certainly a learned man with deep theological reflections at his command) he foresaw he would attract criticism for his writings and tries to disarm the reader (and does so in a charming way).[124]

Until the Nag Hammadi discoveries of 1947 (a cache of abandoned literature, including several lost and original Gnostic treatises along with other nonecclesiastical literature), Irenaeus was one of the most comprehensive sources for knowledge of what Christian Gnosticism was. Discovery of some of the originals shows that while he is unfailingly a hostile witness, and frequently a distortive quoter (as were almost all the ancients, it needs to be noted), his characterization of the (mainly Valentinian) Gnostic system was not wildly inaccurate. Some recent scholars wishing to rehabilitate Gnosticism as a viable "road not taken" for the Christian church, one that was allegedly more urbanely ecumenical, have caricatured him as a narrow episcopal censor and someone who did not understand what he was fighting against. Ancient apologetic, however, never (from any side one approaches it) believed its task was to represent its opponents fairly. It only gave itself the duty of isolating the dangers and errors it could see in the opposing system. Accordingly, if one could

---

[124] *Adversus Haereses* 1, preface 3. "Do not expect from me, resident as I am among the Celts and accustomed for the most part to use a barbarous dialect, any display of rhetoric, which I have never learned, nor any excellence of composition, which I have never practiced, nor any beauty or persuasiveness of style, to which I make no pretension. But please accept in a kindly spirit that which I write to you in similar spirit, simply, truthfully, and in my own homely fashion."

deduce false premises from out of a system under criticism (even if the adherents had not actually set out those premises) this was fair game: for such premises, if legitimately deduced, were reckoned to be part and parcel of any philosophical school. Irenaeus deduces many such *sequiturs* from his review of Gnostic schools. He sees them as falsifying history, encouraging elitism in the community, and reducing the central force of revelation of the life and death of Jesus, all of which needed to be withstood by the pastoral care of the local *episkopos*. He is not best understood as a censor (for he had no coercive power at his disposal over the opposing groups, other than rhetoric and logical argument), but rather as a leader of a school of thought (early catholicism, as it was clarified in his hands) fighting against alternative schools of thought: one orthodoxy asserting itself over others who claimed a more esoteric mantle of truth.

A chief way Irenaeus sees of doing that is to assert the episcopal office: it is the head of the liturgical assembly, bringing out not only extensive rhetorical arguments against the Gnostic teachings but more precisely elevating the baptismal creeds as the simple rule, or canon, of truth that has to be sustained and affirmed in all simplicity and fidelity against all manner of "explaining them away." Irenaeus has little time for speculative cosmologists who weave the story of Jesus into a larger Hellenistic myth of decline and ascent of souls. His context, that of a church leader who has returned to find a congregation devastated by fatal persecution, explains much about his conservative call for obedience and liturgical discipline: like many other leaders in the aftermath of persecution, he wishes to protect and build up again what has been traumatized. Although he is an interesting intellectual in his own right, and one of the best of the early generation of "weavers" of Scripture, it is perhaps in his demonstration of how the office of *episkopos* had evolved so significantly in the context of second-century conflicts and political troubles that he most gains our attention as a witness to the church of his times.[125]

His hostility to pseudo-gnosis, in short, is expressed in the mindset of a benign pastoral authoritarian. He does not wish to set up an alternative "orthodox gnosis" in the way Clement of Alexandria and Origen, shortly after him, would deal with the issue, but he seeks to apply "common-sense rules" (canons or *regulae*) to prevent his community from being led astray by lay teachers whose popularity clearly threatened the administration of the early Christian bishops and their status as the authoritative theologians in the local Christian community. To this end Irenaeus emphasized the unity of God and his profound involvement with the material order as the dynamic principle of salvation understood in an orthodox way. It follows from

---

[125] *Episkopos* means "overseer/bishop."

this that he saw as one of the root flaws of all the Gnostic systems he disliked, their hostility toward materiality, their suspicion of it always as a root of evil. Gnostic specialists have recently complained that this is not a fair analysis of the varieties of all the Gnostic schools, but Irenaeus is not interested in reproducing Gnostic teachings accurately: he wishes to put his finger on a pervasive flaw in Hellenistic religiosity as a whole (which he claims the Gnostic schools fan into flame), which is its overwhelmingly pessimistic attitude to material being and a desire to transcend it in a Platonizing manner. In this he actually gets it right. The second century was awash with theosophies that lamented the natural world order and regarded it as the tomb or prison of the spirit. For Irenaeus the incarnation of the divine and eternal Logos descending into the heart of material creation in the person of Christ elevated materiality into a sacrament of salvation, endorsing the theology of creation in Genesis: "And God saw that it was good" (Gen 1:10). For him, the church continues faithfully the biblical witness of the prophets that the one God, the supreme Father, is the good maker of heaven and earth.

It is likely that the initial clauses of the creeds ("I believe in One God, the Father Almighty, Maker of heaven and earth, all that is visible and invisible") were formed at this same era to refute a core Christian Gnostic premise of the difference between the "Father" of Christ and the wicked Demiurgic god of this material cosmos (the false god spoken of in the Old Testament, such as Marcion advocated). As part of his overarching vision of the sacredness and revelatory character of this cosmos, Irenaeus sets out a theory, based on Paul, of the recapitulation (*anakephalaiosis*) of human destiny in the person (and body) of Christ. As Christ sums up the whole cosmos in his divine and human person, so humankind is liberated from sin and death and restored to a divine destiny. His system is a major patristic elaboration of the theology of deification (*theosis, theiopoiesis*) that will be so important to the Greek systematic theologians of the fourth century. It is notable in his work how Irenaeus's cosmology becomes seamlessly integrated with his soteriology. Such is his primary, and most impressive, argument against Gnostic dissidents. He also used as many other anti-Gnostic arguments as he could muster. Chief among them was a ridiculing of their ideas of multileveled cosmic mediation. Like many ancient rhetors, he delighted in pressing the implications of his opponents' positions until they yielded nonsense, for which he then berated them.

Irenaeus believed that the intellectual heritage of the Jesus tradition was best protected by the authority of the bishop, and to this end he greatly developed on Ignatius of Antioch's ideas of single presidential episcopate. For Irenaeus, the bishop is the linear, didactic successor of the apostles and the embodiment of the direct continuing tradition of a simple apostolic faith (as distinct from the pseudo-sophisticated theosophically esoteric doctrines of the Gnostics that innovate major elements hostile to the tradition). The tradition of apostolic Christianity, deriving immediately from Jesus' teachings, is demonstrated in the whole corpus of the Scriptures, according to Irenaeus. He strongly asserts the fundamental unity of the Old and New Testaments and their constant Christ orientation. Christ is the center of time and the focal point of all revelation, the axial point of all that has been and all that is to come. He also sees the tradition of faith as manifested clearly in the traditional liturgical practices of the congregations, especially creeds and prayers of the church, all of which make up a rule of faith (*regula fidei*). It is this rule that can be used to test bishops (to demonstrate their harmonious fidelity and mutual consonance), as well as being elevated as a yardstick against which to assess the variety of Gnostic professors (*didaskaloi*) who, he says, contradict the tradition and diverge wildly from one another. Irenaeus is a major figure developing the idea of the Scriptures as a normative theology of consonance, and he insists that they are a closed canon, thus ruling out the many Gnostic apocrypha that were being produced in his day.

In 1904 a lost work of his was rediscovered in Armenian translation, the *Demonstration of the Apostolic Preaching*.[126] It relates the Old Testament texts to the coming of Christ. Further, acting as a major apologia against the Gnostic separation of the testaments, it also serves as a handbook he intended to be used in the ongoing instruction of the faithful. Chapters one to three discuss the motives for his composition. His first part (chaps. 4-42) presents the basic and core doctrines of catholic Christianity (Trinity, creation, fall of humankind, incarnation, and redemption in the panoply of salvation history). The second part (chaps. 42-97) offers a series of "easy proofs" of Christian teaching from the Old Testament prophecies. Their ethos, Irenaeus argues, turns around the announcement of Jesus as the Son of David and our messianic hope. The biblical doctrine once again underscores the apostolic tradition of the church:

> If the prophets thus predicted that the Son of God would appear on this earth, and if they announced where on earth, how, and in what manner he would reveal himself; and if the Lord took on himself all that had been foretold about him, then our belief in him is truly established in all firmness. And the tradition of our preaching must be true. In other words the testimony of the apostles is true, they who were sent by God and who preached over the face of the world, about that sacrifice that the Son of God made by enduring death and resurrection.[127]

---

[126]Published by the discoverer Ter-Mekerttschian in 1907. It had been known by repute from Eusebius, *Ecclesiastical History* 5.26.
[127]*Proof of the Apostolic Preaching*, chap. 86.

*The apostolic fathers.* This is a later and collective title for the earliest writers of the Christian church, coming immediately after the New Testament period (and in some cases coterminous with the last books of what came to be the complete New Testament canon). They are immensely important for a larger understanding of the formation of the earliest Christian communities, but they were relatively neglected by the post-Nicene church because they were so very different in form and style from their own contemporary interests in theology, mainly because they did not possess the authoritative status of the scriptural writings, and also because they often had a more generic concern for church "order" rather than any clear and precise agenda in doctrinal or liturgical matters. They belong to the world of the house church or the incipient rise of the monarchical bishops, and their overarching focus on moral encouragement in a markedly eschatological context or outlook gives us a sense of what most of the earliest episcopal preachers must have sounded like in their own time. The main writers of the group are Clement of Rome, Ignatius of Antioch, Hermas, Polycarp, Papias, and the anonymous authors of the Letter of Barnabas, the Letter to Diognetus, and the Second Epistle of Clement. The Didache is also traditionally included in this group. The two books known as the Apostolic Church Order (Egypt, c. 300) and the Apostolic Constitutions (Constantinople, late fourth century), which claimed to be part of this group, are really fourth-century texts pretending to be antique. Several Christian writers of the third and fourth centuries, therefore, were already deliberately archaizing so as to be included in this early group, partly for theological reasons, but especially concerning matters of church organization and ritual, where they wished to gain the moral heights of antique precedence—even if they had to invent it!

A review of these writers once more shows how richly diverse the second century actually was. They have little commonality and no great stress on deep theological content. For the most part the apostolic fathers are scriptural in a mainly diffuse way (not the very focused exegetical kind of arguments and systematics we find later in the Logos school), and they are highly "traditional" in character. The latter is of course an interesting concept for an infant church, which must have seemed so novel to its main religious contemporaries, both Jews and pagans. What does emerge as a common characteristic of these writers who are elevated as the ancestors of mainline Christianity is their conservative and morally down-to-earth character, so highly contrastable with the cosmologically speculative writings of many of the Gnostic schools that slightly postdate them. These apostolic fathers were often younger contemporaries of the original apostles of Jesus and to later Christian eyes were seen to make that vital link between the first generation and the structures of ecclesial organization (and authority) that rose up in the second and third generations. This is why authority, both as a theoretical concept and a practical issue, was important within these texts: either explicitly focused on as a topic or implicitly presumed as in the manner they give out ordinances. It is also why the following generation looked back to them as conservative forces in a time that seemed so often to be dominated by relatively wild speculations that had few precedents in any agreed canon of Scripture. Their authority was afforded charismatically: that they had been eminent churchmen and significant saintly witnesses. Their "weight" as authorities consisted in this adjoining of saintly character and observance of respectable traditional continuity with the earlier generation that preceded them.

In many instances what this continuity was might not be precisely iterated. It was enough to point to a charismatically sober lineage of church leaders, "fathers" of the community, who passed on the faith that could be recognized in its liturgical confession. Their apostolic charism, therefore, was predominantly seen in terms of preservation of order within their own lifetimes, and of being authoritative linkages to the first generation, historically speaking, for Christian theorists of later generations. What they represent chiefly is simplicity of prayer and moral behavior, obedient discipline, close community order. They are not markedly agitated by competing Christian groups (such as we see in some of the apologists, such as Irenaeus objecting to Gnostics, or the African apologists objecting to pagan persecutors). Their focus is not so much on the outside, but rather on the internal life of the communities: acutely aware of the need to establish polities that would work, yet would also (at least seem to) have precedence from a generation of greater leaders.

*Clement of Rome and the pseudo-Clementines.* Clement was a renowned leader of the Roman churches, operating some time at the very end of the first century and in the early decades of the second. Eusebius fixes his term of office from the twelfth year of Domitian to the third year of Trajan (92–101). He is normally placed a few years earlier than that today. He has thus entered the lists of the church as one of the very first "popes" of Rome, but that is, perhaps, to fix him too much in the perspective of later times.[128] He certainly was a pope, when that title meant "father" or liturgical president, rather than the idea it can suggest of papal monarchy from later times. He was a learned man, steeped in Jewish theological attitudes, well-read in the Scriptures, and possessed of an elegant (if perhaps somewhat surface) classical education, insofar as he demonstrates the fusion of Stoic ideas of cosmological balance and ethics with a universalist sense of God's guiding providence. According to Irenaeus Clement knew both Peter and Paul personally, and according to Origen he was that same Clement

---

[128]Irenaeus lists him as the third successor there of St. Peter (*Adversus Haereses* 3.3.3). Tertullian says he was consecrated by Peter himself (*De Praescriptione Haereticorum* 32) as his immediate successor (ignoring Linus and Anacletus, who normally figure as predecessors).

whom St. Paul praised as his collaborator in his epistle to the Philippians, though this might simply be a matter of exegetical name collating by this stage.[129]

Clement shows us some very early evidence of the movement of the Christians generally (given that Rome is usually a marker and harbinger of things happening elsewhere in ancient Christianity) from various house-church organizations (such as witnessed still in the time of Paul's letters) to larger, city-based ideas of *ekklesia*. One of the chief interests of his writing, apart from the early shape of the doctrinal construct he manifests, is the argument he puts forward about the authority structure of an original apostolic generation preparing for a succeeding generation of "apostolical" bishops and diaconal leaders who would carry on their authority: standing in the Christian community and being part of it, but never wholly subordinate to it because of this elevation to authoritative and supervisory office.[130] Clement, like Ignatius, gives some concrete organizational teeth to the idea of apostolic succession.

Clement's one authentic *Letter to the Corinthians* is an important piece of evidence for this polity in the early catholic communities (excerpted in the reader at the end of this chapter). It was possibly composed during the persecution of the emperor Domitian and seems to have still been read out, alongside the Pauline letters, at the church of Corinth in 170, showing in a sense that it was afforded a quasi-scriptural authority well into the second century.[131] The text was occasioned, as so much else in this period, by particular controversies. The Corinthian community had decided to oust an ineffective board of leaders. Clement (who probably has received a plea for support from the same ousted *presbyteroi*) pleads for the restoration of peace in a divided community and supports the leaders who have been ejected. If God has appointed them, he says, it is not in the power of the community (even if that community elected them) to replace them at its own whim. Their elevation is marked by that

---

[129] Clement's *Letter* is the most reliable source for Peter's stay at Rome in the time of Nero, for Paul's journey to Spain, and to the martyrdom of both leading apostles. Relating to Philippians, see Origen, *Commentary on John* 6.36; Eusebius, *Ecclesiastical History* 6.3.15. As part of his legendary development Clement was also later elevated to become Domitian's own cousin, Titus Flavius Clemens, the consul who is said to have been executed in 96 for religious reasons (Dio Cassius, *History of Rome* 67.14). In the fourth century a largely legendary Martyrdom of St. Clement was produced with little historical value. There is more possibility in the theory that he was a freedman of the clan of Flavius Clemens, whose patronymic he therefore assumes.

[130] Clement presents us in his own reflection with a pattern of bishops and deacons, yet refers to the ousted leaders of Corinth as presbyters (plural) with an implication of *episkopos* already beginning to have the association of a single presidential abstraction from the plural council of elders, with deacons associated as assistants of the bishop, not of the presbyter. When he speaks of *episkopoi* in the plural, it is in the context of a succession of them. So, while the nomenclature of offices is still fluid here, the eventual clearer distinction of *episkopos* and *presbyteros* is indicated.

[131] Bishop Dionysius of Corinth reports this to Pope Soter of Rome (Eusebius, *Ecclesiastical History* 4.23.1). Eusebius mentions elsewhere that the reading of the "long and wonderful Epistle of Clement" had spread to other churches too (*Ecclesiastical History* 3.16).

apostolical (authoritative and inspired) character the first apostles wished to transmit to the churches by instituting a system that would move from their own guidance of the interprovince communities of the first age to the direction of "approved men," "bishops and deacons," in the second and subsequent ages. His work in this *Letter* became the classical exposition of the theology of apostolic succession in Christian orders, one that is also developed significantly by bishops Ignatius of Antioch and Irenaeus of Lyons.

Clement's thought world is decidedly akin to that of the late antique Roman household code: established order is not to be ruffled by rebels. From Scripture he deduces several arguments against the sin of envy (to which he attributes the revolt against authority) and demonstrates the importance of humility, obedience, and good hospitality in the communion (*koinonia*) of the church. Clement even appeals to the good example of discipline offered by the Roman army. On higher theological ground he alludes to the hierarchy so evidently established in the Old Testament, but more immediately to the patterns of authority laid down by Christ's conferral of his own authority on the apostles and how they arranged a succession of it in the churches.

*A Second Letter to the Corinthians* was also attributed to Clement in the fourth century. It is not authentically his and comes from a slightly later period, but it still has great interest as perhaps the earliest surviving example of second-century Christian homiletic emerging from a liturgical context and based around Isaiah 54:1. This text turns much on the idea of the election of the church and the need for repentance.[132] Its Christology is that of the divine and merciful Savior:

> Brethren, we ought to think of Jesus Christ as of God, as of the Judge of the living and the dead. . . . He had great pity on us, and in his mercy he saved us. He saw the great error and the destruction that was in us, and he saw that we had no hope of salvation, except through him alone. . . . Christ the Lord saved us, and if he, though originally spirit, was made flesh and in this way elected us, then so also shall we receive our reward in this very flesh. (1.1-2; 9.5)

Clement's name carried cachet in the early church of this period: an episcopal figure of apostolical weight. Accordingly, his legend became almost as big as his person. Soon he began to be a pseudepigraphical receptacle for much other literature from this energetic period that was seeking an authoritative home. Chief

---

[132]"As long as we are in this world, let us repent with our whole heart of whatever evil we have done in the flesh, so that we may be saved by the Lord while we still have time for repentance. For once we have departed form this world, we shall no longer be able to confess our sins or repent of them." *Second Epistle of Clement* 8.2-3. "Brethren, let us repent here and now. Let us learn to be sober for our own good, for we are very full of madness and evil. Let us wipe off our former sins, and let us be saved by repenting with our whole hearts." Ibid., 13.1.

among this corpus of so-called Clementine literature are the Clementine Homilies and the Clementine Recognitions. This literature shows marked relations with early Jewish-Christian thought, Clement's authentic writing less so. Both treatises (as Epiphanius attests) use the apocryphal books the Periodoi of Peter and the Anabathmoi of James. In these sources, contact between Christians and "Gentiles" should be avoided, ritual purifications should be carefully observed, the prophets do not carry high authority, and Christ made several epiphanic appearances across history before this latest one. These apocrypha and their pseudepigraphical relaunching under Clement's name perhaps testify to a continuing Jewish-Christian presence at Rome (Trastevere was a very strong Jewish quarter in the ancient city when Christianity first took root). Clement seems to stand as a bridging figure in the now-mixed Jewish-Gentile Christian churches. In his legendary development in this early romance literature, Clement became seen by the third and fourth centuries as a major theologian (and even a martyr) whom the apostles used to transmit their teaching to the orthodox catholic churches.[133]

*Ignatius of Antioch (c. 35–107).* Ignatius also allows us a chance to look more closely at the character of the early Christian *episkopos*. He was the bishop of the Antiochene church. Late in Trajan's reign (98–117) he was arrested for his profession of Christianity, selected as a high-profile leader of the movement, and taken to Rome (at his own expense) under a guard of ten soldiers. On the way to his trial he composed a series of letters to the leaders of the Christian churches he was passing by, implicitly seeking support in the form of food, lodging, and expenses (otherwise the guards became very nasty indeed), and explicitly using the opportunity of his passage (as a confessor for the faith) through a wide international swath of Christian communities to offer pastoral and organizational advice. He was received at Smyrna by Polycarp, who arranged his reception by a larger group of leaders of the local Asia Minor churches. From Smyrna, Ignatius wrote letters of encouragement to the churches of Ephesus, Magnesia, and Tralles, and one to Rome, asking them not to prevent his chance of martyrdom (presumably by bribery of the magistrates). He was then taken by his guards to Troas, and while there he wrote another three letters: to the churches of Philadelphia and Smyrna, and to Polycarp personally. Other letters than these seven were apocryphally added to the corpus in the fourth century (some attribute these forgeries to the author of the Apostolic Constitutions).

It is generally presumed that his journey to the capital ended in his execution (so Origen and Polycarp presume), for his reputation as a martyr was very high in the

---

[133] Trajan is supposed to have had him exiled to a quarry in the Crimea, and after his performance of a miracle there, he was tied to an anchor and thrown into the sea. The Clementine anchor (or mariner's cross) thus became his sign.

ancient church. Hagiographical accounts (*acta*) concerned with the details of his death were composed later without much historical foundation. Ignatius's letters, first collated by Polycarp and preserved archivally by Eusebius of Caesarea in the fourth century, are a major source for the state of the church at the beginning of the second century. They demand comparison with the manner in which the collection of Paul's letters was assembled, but they also reflect (and greatly assisted the establishment of) a monarchical (that is, single-presidential) model of episcopacy governing the council of presbyters in the international Christian communities. Ignatius, along with the deutero-Pauline letters, is a strong advocate of the single bishop of the community holding the status of Jesus in the church. The bishop is elevated as the efficient symbol (the sacrament) of the unity of the church and is the chief legitimator of the sacraments of baptism, Eucharist, and marriage. His authority devolves directly from Christ. As the second bishop of the great church of Antioch, Ignatius shows signs of some dissensions there. He gives a word in the ear to the younger bishop Polycarp in Smyrna to beware of the Christian virgins, who, as a collective, surely seem to have given him some grief in his ministry, probably by asserting a degree of independence he did not countenance. Ignatius also warns more solemnly against doctrinal dissidents who were at Antioch, but he also wishes to warn the other churches against their spread. These seem to be of a "spiritualist" type that saw little value in the flesh. Accordingly, the incarnation of Christ was not a significant reality or perhaps even a permanent reality. He only "seemed" (*dokeo*) to suffer. For Ignatius this Docetic Christology that denied Jesus' fleshly reality inevitably disconnected him from history, and thus from the Gospel tradition, and thus from us. He says,

> If, as some of these atheists and unbelievers say, Christ's suffering was only make-believe (but in truth it is they who are the make-believers), then why do I now stand in chains? Why should I bother to pray that I might contend with the beast?[134] If they are right I would die in vain, and my witness would be only a lie about the Lord. No. Shun these wild grafts, which can bear only a deadly fruit, one taste from which spells our doom.[135]

Ignatius is a strong advocate of Jesus' divinity coterminous with his humanity, referring to the Savior as "our God, Jesus the Christ." He loves to elaborate his thought in balanced antitheses: "There is only one physician, both fleshly, and spiritual, born and unborn,[136] God become man, true life in death, sprung from Mary

---

[134] To fight with Satan, who instigates persecution, and as a martyr do so in the form of contending with the beasts in the Roman arena.
[135] *To the Trallians* 10-11.
[136] *Gennetos kai agennetos*. The former term is a synonym of *Son*; the latter is an ancient title and definition of the Godhead.

and from God; subject first to suffering and then incapable of it, Jesus Christ our Lord."[137] He writes tersely, doubtless partly because his scope is limited in a traveling letter, but also reflective perhaps of a creedal concept of the statement of his faith: "Jesus is truly of the lineage of David, according to the flesh, and is Son of God by the will and power of God. He was truly born of a virgin, and baptized by John, in order to comply with every ordinance."[138] His eucharistic theology is dynamic and realist. He calls the Eucharist "that flesh which suffered for our sins" and elsewhere "that medicine of immortality" (*pharmakia tes athanasias*).[139] He sketches the mystical connection between the believer and Christ as established in the Eucharist, not least when he refers to his own impending martyrdom in the image of himself being ground (like bread) in the jaws of the lions, just as Jesus was eucharistically the sacrifice of salvation. All of this shows his implicit understanding of Christianity from the context of a presiding eucharistic *episkopos*, a testimony also to how much the ancient liturgy must have shaped the patterns of christological thinking.

As confessor-martyr and as bishop, Ignatius both sees and designates himself as God-bearer (*Theophoros*). In the next generation Irenaeus would bring his sketch of monarchical episcopate to complete fruition in his theology of the apostolic succession. Ignatius's key text advocating the duty of all to obey the ruling bishop implicitly and without question became a tidal marker of the move toward single episcopal presidency in the churches.[140] It is reproduced in the short reader at the end of this chapter. Even so, prophet of unity though he might be, Ignatius's recurring stress on the absolute importance of harmony, symphony between all the leaders and members of Christian communities, and commonality of doctrine and discipline must surely also indicate that he felt he needed to stress such themes in the face of many troubling disparities and divergences in the communities he knew. He advocates that seriously dissident theological thinkers (such as the Docetists, who stayed away from the Eucharist)[141] ought to be treated as intellectual and not merely liturgical excommunicates:

> Those who have questioned the gift of God perish in their contentiousness. They should have had love, so as to have profited in the resurrection. The right thing, therefore, is not to have association with such people, and not to speak about them either in private or in public. Instead, study the Prophets closely, and especially the Gospel, in which the passion is revealed to us, and the resurrection shown in its fulfillment.[142]

---

[137] *To the Ephesians* 7.2.
[138] *To the Smyrnaeans* 1.1.
[139] *To the Ephesians* 20.2.
[140] Ibid., 4.
[141] Possibly as being too "materialist" a sacrament of the Lord's presence in the church.
[142] *To the Smyrnaeans* 7.

*Hermas (active 90–150).* Hermas is another highly interesting, and significantly "different," member of the apostolic fathers. He is the writer of The Shepherd, a treatise that at one stage was considered for inclusion in the New Testament canon. The work gains its title from the character of the angel of repentance, who appears in the guise of a shepherd to guide Hermas's understanding of God's message to the church. Another figure, an old woman who becomes progressively younger, is one of the first female characterizations of the *ekklesia* or church. The oldest part of the work is a freestanding apocalypse written circa 90 (Visions 1-4), making it a Christian eschatological narrative almost as old as Mark 13. The apocalyptic character is never far absent from all the later materials in his work too.

Hermas was a slave in Rome who rose to high prominence because of his spiritual gifts in the Roman Christian community. He probably came from Roman Palestine and possibly was one of those brought in captivity to Rome after the fall of the temple. Some have hypothesized that he was formerly a Jewish priest (*kohen*).[143] He is contemporary with Clement of Rome, the author of the *First Letter of Clement to the Corinthians*, and Hermas tells us in one of his visions that the heavenly *ekklesia*, appearing to him as an ancient woman, instructs him to make two copies of his revelation and give one of them to Clement.[144] This interesting contemporaneity gives us a slightly different perspective as to the conditions of the Roman church(es) at this time. The figure of the heavenly *ekklesia* as an old crone (who grows progressively younger and more radiant in his work) is an interesting sidelight on his elevated ecclesiology.[145]

Hermas's Roman slave owner was the wealthy matron Rhoda, who was a Christian and who eventually freed him and set him up with property on the road from Rome to Cumae. Later we learn that he was financially ruined in a persecution raised against Christians at Rome, which was probably that of Domitian. Hermas was denounced to the authorities by his children, who apostatized. He complains much about his personal life, especially about his wife, and one suspects they separated

---

[143] His Greek text is full of Semitisms and Latinisms. Cf. A. Hilhorst, "Semitismes et latinismes dans le Pasteur d'Hermas," *Revue de l'histoire des religions* 184 (1973): 25-48.

[144] Shepherd of Hermas 4.3. This relation is to be preferred to the evidence of the Muratorian canon (end of second century), which makes Hermas the (familial) brother of Pope Pius of Rome (pope c. 140–155). J. Quasten thinks both statements might be true (*Patrology*, vol. 1, *The Beginnings of Patristic Literature* [Westminster, MD: Newman Press, 1972], 92-93) by arguing the Vision section of the Shepherd dates to Clement's time and the final putting together of the work came under Pius's papacy. Origen thought the author was the Hermas mentioned by Paul in his Letter to the Romans (Rom 16:14).

[145] An angel visits him and asks who he thinks the old woman is who has given him the book of instruction. He corrects Hermas's misapprehension that it was the sibyl and tells him that it is the church, who is presented as so old because "she was created first of all things, and for this reason she appears old, and for her sake the world itself was established." Shepherd of Hermas Vision 2.4.1.

soon after the persecutions had ruined him, as he tells us that he had determined, in the course of receiving revelations, to adopt a penitent and ascetical life.

The Shepherd was composed over a considerable period and has something of a ragbag literary character. Pierre Nautin thought that Hermas was the author only of Visions 1-4, and the rest of the book (Vision 5 and Mandates) was from an anonymous author of the same era, but this seems an excessive way to account for the fact that the Shepherd as a whole lacks literary cohesion.[146] It is clear enough that as a visionary charismatic prophet his primary ministry was preaching, not necessarily writing; and seen as a paraenetic document, the whole things holds together very coherently as an extended set of homilies on repentance. It begins with a series of visions Hermas received that serve as vehicles for his teaching to the wider church community. The work as a whole is now divided triadically: five Visions; twelve commandments, or Mandates; and ten parables, or Similitudes.

Theologically speaking, the writer is grappling with the problem of postbaptismal sin among Christians at a time when it was predominantly thought that the *ekklesia*, the church of Christ, is the pure community of the elect. Holiness is its raison d'être, its fundamental charism. In such an ecclesiological model, sin has no place. It simply cannot be accounted for. In the aftermath of the persecutions (when perhaps as many might have denied the faith to save themselves as ever offered themselves for martyrdom), Hermas and his contemporary church leaders were vexed with the issues of postbaptismal sin and possibilities of repentance. Indeed, this was a subject that later obsessed most synodical canons of the *episkopoi* through to the early fourth century. These worrying concerns, in fact, turning around the axes of unity, holiness, apostolicity, and universal communion, eventually come to sum up the whole theology of the period in the famous sentence that concludes the baptismal creed and comes down to contemporary Christianity. Here, one remembers, the definition of church is given as "one, holy, catholic, and apostolic." Hermas is focused on the first two of those issues, whereas Clement concerns himself chiefly with the latter two.

The Shepherd represents one of the first solutions to the problem of evident sin among the worshiping community: a theology and protocol of repentance. Hermas's solution reveals to us his function in the Roman church—as one of the "prophets" such as those we meet in the Didache. He tells us that through his visions and special revelations he has learned that God has permitted new possibilities of repentance after baptism. He announces that a second, postbaptismal repentance is permitted in the church, and even a final repentance (probably meaning a deathbed confession),

---

[146]"Hermas," in *Encyclopedia of Ancient Christianity*, ed. A. Di Berardino (Downers Grove, IL: InterVarsity Press, 2014), 220.

but it is not to be taken lightly. His text does not so much invent the notion of postbaptismal repentance but seeks to clarify it, as can be seen in the text in the short reader at the end of this section, which represents his teaching. He seems to be writing in the pastoral context of encouraging the church not to delay baptism until the deathbed, which was the effective result of the earlier Christian belief that baptism was a once-for-all and thus completely unrepeatable purification of sins. He is optimistic, though rigorous. Fasting is essential, but Christians should not put faith in it that it will automatically earn them God's forgiveness (he has in mind the communal "stations" or fasting periods the Roman church had instituted, like early forms of Lent). In his eighth Similitude he tells us that the church is like a robust willow tree. The branches that have been torn from it and seem to have dried up will still be able to blossom again if they are once again rooted back into the moist earth. Just so, those who have fallen away must return by repentance. The tone of the work is rigorist throughout, despite its advocacy of a theology of reconciliation. Even so, it was not nearly rigorist enough for Tertullian, who denounced it as the "Shepherd of adulterers" (since it allowed the rehabilitation of serious postbaptismal sins such as adultery and also permitted Christians to contract a second marriage after the death of a spouse, which Tertullian held to be tantamount to adultery).[147]

Hermas has another striking image of the church in his third of the Visions. Here the old lady shows him a tower under construction. It is the church presently being built up into its ideal, finished condition. As work progresses, not every stone is found to be fit for its purpose, and so some are rejected. Similarly, he learns, every Christian who does not embrace repentance shall be cast out from the communion. A ready response is needed here and now, as the time remaining is not long. This idea of the shortness of the window of repentance is revisited later, in the ninth Similitude.

The light the book throws on the character of the Christian prophet in the ecclesial structures at Rome is that the office seems to be predominantly concerned with moral paraenesis.[148] His twelve Mandates are a synopsis of Christian moral teaching such as would be useful for catechetical instruction: how to live in faith and sobriety, how to conduct oneself in the married or widowed condition, who are false and true prophets, whom one should believe or not believe, how to deal with sadness and doubts in the mind and heart, how to root out evil from the heart and fill it with joy and goodness.

In his second Similitude Hermas gives an allegory of the vine and the elm tree. The one is sturdy and strong and allows the vine, weak and feeble in its own branch

---

[147]Shepherd of Hermas Mandates 4.4.1-2.
[148]Exhortation, encouragement, warning, and correction. An early kind of spiritual ascetical father.

structure, to climb up it and eventually make the elm itself offer a rich fruit that it could not offer on its own account. This, he says, is the way God wishes the rich and poor to interact in the Christian community: the rich supporting the wretched out of their own substance so that they can bear fruit in God's eyes.[149] His Christology is of an archaic type. He identifies the Holy Spirit with the preincarnate Son, a form of binitarian equation of the two as "Spirit" that is witnessed in a few other early writers, and he suggests that the Trinity came into being after the ascension. Although not a Monarchian as such, Hermas's christological scheme is rather crudely elaborated and has elements akin to some of that inchoate monarchianism the Logos theologians would come to resist at Rome in the time of Tertullian and Hippolytus:

> God made the preexistent holy spirit, which created all things to dwell in a body of flesh chosen by himself.[150] This flesh, in which the holy spirit dwelt, served the Spirit well, in all purity and sanctity, and never inflicted the least stain on it.[151] After the flesh had conducted itself so chastely and so well, after it had assisted the spirit and worked in all things alongside it, ever showing itself to be strong and courageous, God admitted it to share with the holy spirit. This was because the conduct of this flesh pleased him in so far as it was never defiled while it bore the holy spirit on earth.[152] And so he consulted his Son and his glorious angels, in order that this flesh which had so blamelessly served the spirit, might obtain a place of habitation and might not lose the reward of its services. Just so, there is a reward for all flesh that shall be found to be without stain on account of the indwelling of the holy spirit.[153]

The progressive moving back of the charismatic prophets from the leadership of the communities (one can contrast his visionary "feeling his way forward" with the calm orderliness of the Clementine letter) allied with his undeveloped theology compared with the Logos theologians meant that his work commanded respectful interest in the second century but very quickly lost its relevance in the next.[154] The first quarter of his book is still bound up with the New Testament literature in the Codex Sinaiticus, probably one of those great Bibles prepared for the Constantinian churches by the scriptorium of Caesarea in the early fourth

---

[149] See further J. A. McGuckin, "The Vine and the Elm Tree: The Patristic Interpretation of Jesus' Teachings on Wealth," in *The Church and Wealth*, ed. W. J. Sheils and D. Wood, Studies in Church History 24 (Oxford: Blackwell, 1987), 1-14.
[150] He is not clear whether this is the Holy Spirit or the creative Logos "through whom all things came into being" (see 1 Cor 8:6).
[151] Again indeterminate as to whether it should be *spirit* or *Spirit*.
[152] Again not discriminating whether the flesh (of Jesus?) was personal or mindless. Was it simply a vehicle of flesh adopted by the Son of God, or a person so honored with elevation beside the Lord? These were all the problems the Logos theologians demanded the monarchians should resolve.
[153] Shepherd of Hermas Similitudes 5.6.5-7.
[154] He never uses the title *Logos* even once in his work.

century, but other writers of this period are at pains to point out it ought not to be given scriptural status at all.

*Polycarp (c. 69–156).* Polycarp is another of the apostolic fathers; he served as *episkopos* of Smyrna and assisted Ignatius of Antioch when the latter was traveling as a prisoner through Asia Minor. When Polycarp was an old man, he was an inspiration to Irenaeus of Lyons as a child and became for him a living example of a venerable and wise apostle of the second generation, thus influencing Irenaeus's mature theory of the apostolic succession (the transmission of authority from the apostles of Christ through to the bishops of the early catholic communities). Irenaeus tells us that Polycarp was himself a disciple of the apostle John and was appointed to his episcopal duties by the apostles themselves, thus serving personally to demonstrate the transmission of the apostolical charism of authority to episcopal hands.[155] It was Polycarp who probably collated and published the writings of Ignatius. His own letters to Ignatius and to the church at Philippi survive, an example of how the structure of episcopal government of the church was evolving in that period, and how bishops were keeping in touch with other communities in terms of their doctrines, liturgical practices, and general well-being by means of letters to fellow bishops. These letters were soon to be called *eirenika*, "documents of peace." He visited Rome to speak personally with Pope Aniketos there about matters of concern over the Quartodecimans controversy, and he was held in high regard, even though the two churches could not come to an agreement over whose liturgical usage ought to be followed concerning the dating of Pascha.

For Irenaeus, Polycarp was a great rock of faith to whom the later second-century church looked back, counting its great men of the second generation as comparable to those of the first. His writing shows many concerns similar to those evidenced in the Pastoral Epistles of the New Testament. When Polycarp writes to the church of Philippi, he does not speak of a bishop there, only a council of presbyters, whom he depicts in a cameo of the ideal presbyter:

> The presbyters should be tenderhearted, merciful toward all, turning back [the sheep] who have gone astray, visiting all the sick, not neglectful of the widow or the orphan or the poor man, but always taking thought for whatever is honorable in the sight of God and man, abstaining from all anger, social snobbery, unrighteous judgment, holding far from love of money, never hastily believing the worst against anyone, not stern in judgment, knowing that we are all debtors on account of sin.[156]

As with the Clementine Letter to the Corinthians, there seems to have been at this period still operating a double system of a single *episkopos* with deacons, and

---

[155] Recounted in Eusebius, *Ecclesiastical History* 5.20.5; Irenaeus, *Against the Heresies* 3.3.4.
[156] Polycarp, *Epistle to the Philippians* 6.1.

councils of presbyters, which eventually was to be resolved as a protocol formed by the mechanisms adopting each other to become a more widely standardized pattern of a single presiding *episkopos*, heading a council of presbyters, with deacons. Irenaeus tells the story that Polycarp once met with Marcion and was not going to speak until Marcion stopped him and said, "Do you recognize me?" to which Polycarp is reported to have replied, "I do indeed. You are the firstborn of Satan."[157] This was an extension of the selfsame phrase from Polycarp's *Letter to the Philippians*, where he castigates the Marcionite and Docetic heresies, saying, "For everyone who shall not confess that Jesus the Christ is come in the flesh is antichrist. And whoever will not confess the witness of the cross is of the devil. And whoever distorts the words of the Lord to fit his own desires, and says that there is neither resurrection or judgment, such a one is the firstborn of Satan."[158]

The dramatic account of Polycarp's arrest, trial, and martyrdom (Martyrdom of Polycarp), recorded in 156,[159] is probably the first-ever Christian narrative of a martyr's death, excepting the Acts account of Stephen, and gives witness to the powerful rise of the cult of the holy martyrs in the early church.[160] It contains other bons mots, such as his final words when the proconsul Statius Quadratus, taking pity on his old age and venerable appearance, offered to let him go free if he would renounce his faith: "Swear that you renounce Christ, and I shall release you." And he replied, "I have been serving him these eighty-six years past, and he has never done me any wrong. How then could I now blaspheme my King who has saved me?"[161] His martyrdom account ends with Polycarp making a fine extempore prayer, as if at the eucharistic anaphora (presiding as he would as *episkopos*), and this time the offering was of his own flesh. It is recorded in the reader at the end of this section. Its final doxology gives strong indications that the liturgical formulae were strong factors in processing a primeval trinitarian systematic in the form of glory offered to God the Father through the priestly mediation of the Son in the grace of the Holy Spirit. This liturgical awareness will also explain why it is precisely the *episkopoi* and *presbyteroi* (who knew the anaphora prayers by heart at this period, before they were ever written down) who were generally the class of theologians who were most articulate against alternative theologies (such as those of Marcion, the Docetics, or the Gnostics), which generally speaking were not so liturgically rooted.

---

[157] Irenaeus, *Against the Heresies* 3.3.4.
[158] Polycarp, *Epistle to the Philippians* 7.1.
[159] *The Life of Polycarp* by Pionius is not authentically contemporaneous. It is a fourth-century hagiographical extension of the original second-century texts.
[160] After his burning at the stake the Christians of Smyrna carefully gathered up his ashes, "more precious than costly gems," and buried them, marking his annual memorial as a great festival.
[161] Martyrdom of Polycarp 9.3.

*Papias of Hierapolis (active early second century).* Papias was another of the apostolic fathers, said to be a companion of Polycarp and held in high regard by the later church as one of the "great ancients." He was a bishop of a community in Asia Minor. His writings seem to have represented a highly physical sense of millenarianist eschatology (namely chiliasm, a thousand-year rule of the saints of Christ on earth after the defeat of the antichrist). The way that later church generations came to regard this apocalypticism as archaic, odd, even disturbing, accounts for the fact that by the fourth century Papias's reputation survives, but his writings have been quietly forgotten, so that only small fragments were felt worthy of being recorded and archived. Eusebius, in his *Ecclesiastical History*, records most of what we now have extant from him but cannot hold back from noting that he did not think much of Papias's intelligence, even when he uses him as an authority for ancient affairs.[162] It was the chiliast millenarianism that chiefly offended Eusebius's own Origenian traditions.

There are also fragmentary quotations of Papias in other later authors. For Eusebius he was a main source for very early traditions about the composition of the Gospels. Papias seems, therefore, to have been a very ancient exegetical commentator. He gave his opinions about the formation of the Gospels in his (now lost) treatise in five books (*tomoi*): *Exegeses of the Sayings of the Lord*. This seems to have been written circa 130 and had significant influence on both Hippolytus and Irenaeus. The latter thinks of him as an "ancient" witness of apostolic traditions. Papias's views of the order of Synoptic composition (a Hebrew-original Matthew, and then Mark as the written record of a direct disciple of Peter) had much subsequent influence on ideas of biblical transmission until the modern era, which has largely dismissed his views as being based chiefly on his own deductions rather than firsthand historical knowledge. He also held to and taught a form of the doctrine of apostolic succession among bishops, and the significance of the "living tradition of the elders," themes that can also be seen in Ignatius and Polycarp and came to a focused form in Irenaeus, all of whom also shared roots in the Asia Minor church at a similar time.

*The Letter of Barnabas.* The letter of Barnabas gained high authority in the ancient church, so much so that the fourth-century Codex Sinaiticus binds it in with the New Testament books immediately after the Apocalypse of John. It did not manage to keep its place in the New Testament canon, but it has always been regarded from early times as written by Barnabas, the apostolic companion of St. Paul. It was part of the Codex Hierosolymitanus, written in the year 1056, which was rediscovered by Metropolitan Bryennios in the library of the Jerusalem patriarchate in 1875: the

---

[162]Eusebius, *Ecclesiastical History* 3.39.3.

same codex that contained the Didache and first letter of Clement, and whose publication in 1875 threw new light and interest on this ancient material.[163]

The text is not really a letter, only formally pretending to be so, but is rather a theological tract composed in apocalyptic genre. Its author sets out to teach "perfect knowledge" (*gnosis*) and faith. It falls into two parts: one apologetic (against the Jews), the other concerned with setting out a guide to Christian moral living. Its main purpose at first is to show how the Jewish interpretation of the Old Testament in literal and historical emphases is completely wrong: the revelation needs to be understood in spiritual and typological forms, requiring not the circumcision of flesh to be part of the elect but the circumcision of our hearing so that the mind might understand truth in the symbols. This exegetical understanding leads to *teleia gnosis*, or perfect knowledge of the faith. For example, the unclean animals spoken of in the law are no longer unclean and forbidden: rather, they represent sinful attitudes that Christians must now avoid (chaps. 9-10). The author sets out allegories of revelation: for example, the 318 servants of Abraham whom he had circumcised was a prefiguring of how salvation comes through the cross of Jesus. In Greek mathematics, three hundred is written as *T*, and eighteen is *IH*; in other words, the cross followed by the first two letters of Jesus' name. The author argues that the law was intended for Christians from the beginning in God's foreknowledge, knowing that the Jews would prove unworthy of it: "Moses received the law, but they were unworthy of it. . . . Moses received the law, but it was the Lord himself who gave it to us, as the people of the inheritance, by suffering for our sake." Jewish rabbinic exegesis has been misled by an evil angel, Barnabas argues.[164]

The text speaks of the destruction of the temple in Jerusalem and looks forward to a time when the temple might be rebuilt, but it stresses (very unusually for early Christian writing) how current forms of Jewish worship resemble pagan idolatry, since both the Jews who look to a reconstructed temple and the pagans who build them everywhere think that they can worship God in an exterior shrine, rather than in the heart.[165] There is a current attempt to rebuild the temple, he says, but not by the Jews: "For so things came to pass, for through their wars [the temple] was destroyed by the enemies, and the servants of their enemies build it up at present." "But God, indeed, dwells in our own house: namely in us."[166] The second part of the letter is very similar to the Didache's moral paraenesis.[167] It adopts the theme of the "two

---

[163] Adolf Hilgenfeld used Bryennios's manuscript for his edition of the letter in 1877.
[164] Barnabas 14.4; 9.4.
[165] Ibid., 16.2.
[166] Ibid., 16.3-4, 9.
[167] Ibid., 18–21.

ways." In the Didache they are life and death: here they are light and darkness. The way of light is depicted with many moral instructions derived from the Decalogue, and the way of darkness is illustrated as a catalogue of vices and sins to be avoided.

The date has been argued over variously because of internal clues prised from the writing with varying levels of success. The reference to a possible rebuild of the Jerusalem temple is a key indicator. This seems to refer to general speculations current in the early second century that a temple could be rebuilt on the temple mount. The Bar Kokhba revolt of 132–135 certainly put an end to any possible reconciliation between Jewish and Roman state authorities. Such dreams evaporated then and were only revived in the time of Emperor Julian. Hadrian (117–138) eventually built a temple to Jupiter on the site of the temple mount to symbolize the ending of the Jewish nation's independence,[168] as well as a temple to Venus (a functioning brothel) over the site of Jesus' tomb, then the most important Christian place of worship. It would seem, therefore, that the letter of Barnabas can be firmly placed between AD 70 and its citation by Clement of Alexandria in 190, with a midway date seeming most plausible, that is, around 130, before the Bar Kokhba revolt occurred. Scholars are undecided whether to locate it in Alexandria or Roman Palestine: both sites had large contingents of Jews and observant Jewish Christians.

It is clear that the main issue facing the author was conflict he was receiving from rabbinic theologians. This tension had accelerated the splitting of the ecclesial communities from the synagogues. Both posttemple rabbinic Judaism and Christian house churches were claiming to be heirs of ancient Judaism: the "true inheritors" of a way of life and worship that had gone under before the Roman conquest of AD 70. Rabbinic Judaism was claiming that the reading of the Torah in the synagogue would be the way forward to keep faith with the tradition. The writer of the letter of Barnabas is arguing for a more radical sense of a new covenant made in the blood of Jesus. It is one of the first clear doctrinal signs of the separation of the ways. It is evident too that the author had little time for circles of observant Christian Jews such as the Nazarenes and Ebionites.

The Christology of the letter is very early but elevated. It stands in marked contrast with that of the Ebionites. Christ is the incarnated heavenly Son of God who existed before the ages and is the agent of the Father's creation of the world and humankind within it. "Let us make man in our own image and likeness" was a plural, the author says, used by the Father addressing his Son.[169] The crux of the incarnation

---

[168]Harnack sees this in the letter's allusion to rebuilding a temple and thus dates the whole to 130–131. Lietzmann thought it might refer to the Roman destruction of a temporary temple, constructed under Bar Kokhba's short dominion.
[169]Barnabas 5.5.

was the "filling up of the measure of the iniquity of those who had persecuted the prophets, and killed them." Christ's passion is the core of a new covenant made with the church. The author of the letter departs from Pauline tradition at several instances. Whereas Paul saw the law as a preordained pedagogue to the truth, the author sees it as a diabolical deception.[170]

*The Didache.* Parts of the Didache have been found in a fourth-century Oxyrhynchus parchment, with several other fourth-century documents, notably the Syrian-originated Apostolic Constitutions, which incorporates almost all of it, as well as in a fifth-century Coptic manuscript in the British Museum (Papyrus 927) and third-century Latin manuscripts. So it was obviously already well known in earliest times, but after the fourth century it fell into disuse and was eventually forgotten by all except a few liturgical historians. The oldest complete manuscript in which it is found is that of the notary Leo of Constantinople (dated 1056).[171] And yet, it was so highly venerated in the earliest times of the church that the writers of the fourth century had to insist, even at that date when it was increasingly regarded as obsolete, that it should not be considered a part of the canon of sacred Scripture.[172] It caused a sensation when the Didache was found intact in a manuscript in Jerusalem and republished in the nineteenth century.[173] It was like rediscovering a magical photograph of the early second-century church, and much attention was given back to it.

The Greek word *didache* means "teaching" and is the abbreviation of the original title: The Teaching of the Lord Through the Twelve Apostles to the Nations. It was composed between AD 100 and 150, possibly in Syria (though some locate it in Egypt), and is more in the style of a compilation of practices for a group of churches than the work of a single theologian-author. It has sixteen chapters. The first part of it (chaps. 1-10) consists of liturgical instructions, and the second part of disciplinary rules for community life. Whoever put it together (and we might presume the hand of an *episkopos*) seems to have collated rather than composed the discipline rules for a nexus of communities. Chapters one through six, which speak of the "two ways" of living, have a close parallel with chapters eighteen through twenty of Barnabas, but it is not agreed which way the relation of dependence runs. The two ways is such a generic trope of this era that both texts might independently show dependence on

---

[170]Ibid., 9.4.
[171]He lodged it in the library of Hospice of the Anastasis at Constantinople, whence it came to the library of the Greek patriarchate in Jerusalem. See Quasten, *Patrology*, 1:37-39.
[172]Eusebius, *Ecclesiastical History* 3.25.4; Athanasius, *Festal Epistle* 39; Rufinus, *Commentary on the Creed* 38.
[173]The learned Greek metropolitan Philotheos Bryennios published Leo's eleventh-century codex in 1883.

an earlier Jewish text.[174] Sections 1.3-2.1 of the Didache, as well as chapters six and fourteen, are often thought to have been later inserts, meant to keep the text up to date at a later time.

One thing is certain, that overall this is one of the most primitive Christian texts from the postapostolic era. It shows a church composed mainly of Gentiles, who are in the process of abandoning many practices of the old law. It reflects a community where baptism by triple immersion has been adapted to allow for the (more practical) baptism by triple infusion, but only as a tolerated exception. The great reverence in which prophets were held in an earlier time seems to have given way, so that the author of the texts has to stress again that these are missionary officers of the church who have the highest precedence when they visit. These itinerant "apostles and prophets" are still designated as "your chief priests." The local ministers are commanded to give way to the prophets for a short time, but the prophets are not to linger in one church for more than a few days. While resident they should be the chief celebrants of the Eucharist. But already the stress on their exceptional but temporary authority suggests that the prophetic office is on the wane in the face of the growing sedentary nature of the ecclesial communities with their correspondingly fixed boards of officers and established polities. It also suggests very strongly that the apostolic office is being discontinued, with the idea of apostolicity being pushed back to a closed set of first-generation high leaders belonging to a different order. The book offers the reader one of the first glimpses into the conduct of the Christian liturgy: a very simple, childlike form of thanksgiving, or eucharistic, prayer (excerpted in the reader at the end of this chapter). Before taking communion the church is admonished always to make confession of sins.[175]

As a text that was afforded the highest antiquity, the Didache's regulations for church order were very influential and marked most subsequent liturgical books as having something of an antiquarian character.[176] Even in the ninth century when the

---

[174] The two ways are the way of life (virtue) and the way of death (vices). This style of moral catechesis had been used before the Christians applied it in the synagogues of the Hellenists for instructing proselytes. "There are two ways; one of life and one of death; and there is a great difference between the two ways. Now the way of life is this: first, love the God who made you. Second, love your neighbor as yourself. Do not do to another what you do not wish done to yourself. . . . But the way of death is this: first of all, it is wicked and altogether accursed: murders, adulteries, lustful desires, fornications, thefts, idolatries, magical arts, sorceries, robberies, perjuries, hypocrisy, duplicity, fraud, pride, malice, surliness, covetousness, dirty language, jealousy, immoderation, snobbery, pretentiousness, lack of the fear of God." Didache 1.1-2; 5.1.
[175] Ibid., 4.14.
[176] The *Apostolic Tradition* of Hippolytus of Rome, the Syriac Didascalia, and the (fourth-century) Apostolic Constitutions. The latter reproduces much of the Didache's ordinances in its own chapter seven.

scroll (as a book form) had become as obsolete as a gas lamp might seem to us now, the texts of the great cathedral liturgies at Constantinople were written on scroll rather than in a codex: a little evocation of antiquity, preserved most carefully of all in the liturgy. The disciplines represented in the Didache were repeated in several later liturgical handbooks even into the fourth century. St. Athanasius in Alexandria, at that time, tells us that the text of the Didache was still being widely used as a manual for the instruction of catechumens. His relegation of its utility to the catechumenate, however, was also coded text for it being now regarded as "very basic" material.

Chapters seven through ten give instructions on baptism, prayer, and fasting, as well as the *agape*, or common meal. The church's fast days are set as Wednesday and Friday. Prayer is to be offered in the form of the Lord's Prayer three times every day. The eucharistic prayers in the book (chaps. 9-10) are based on Jewish table blessings. It is still not universally agreed among scholars whether these reflect a "real-world usage" (as distinct from specimen texts drawn up as examples), and if so whether they reflect the Christian *agape* (love feast) or a Eucharist proper, or a combination of both. In chapter fourteen the *synaxis* of the Lord's Day is mentioned, and reconciliation among the community is given a high priority as the proper eucharistic preparation. Chapter fifteen gives a very early instruction on the election of deacons (*diakonoi*) and bishops (*episkopoi*). Presbyters are not mentioned, but the authority structure seems to be deacons and bishops in the plural, possibly comparable to a council of elders (*presbyteroi*) that is mentioned elsewhere. So most likely this text is on the cusp, regarding the rise of the presidency of a single *episkopos*, with texts such as the letters of Ignatius representing the other side, where such presidency is already established (at Antioch, and Rome above all), though at this stage it would be excessive to call it "monarchical episcopate." The Didache ends in chapter sixteen with a warning about the coming of the antichrist and the parousia, which it envisages as now imminent.

*The Letter to Diognetus.* This so-called letter is really an anonymous mid- to late second-century Greek apology for Christians in time of persecution.[177] It is addressed to someone called Diognetus. Some scholars have thought him to be either the tutor of the Emperor Marcus Aurelius (161–180) or a high-ranking Alexandrian magistrate mentioned in other papyri (c. 167–203). Because of its opening address, it was mistakenly thought, when it was rediscovered in modern times, to be an epistle. It had survived from antiquity, apparently, in only one thirteenth-century manuscript, which itself was afterward destroyed in Strasbourg in 1870.[178] The text begins (chaps. 2-4) with arguments for why Christianity is superior to paganism and

---

[177]The author makes allusive reference to the works of Irenaeus.
[178]The Strasbourg library was burned in the Franco-Prussian War.

Judaism (the one being idolatrous, and the other being excessively ritualistic). Its most famous section is chapters five and six, which give a very eloquent encomium of the Christian faith (Christians live spiritually detached in the world as its very soul). Chapters seven and eight argue that the new religion has appeared so late in time because God wished to demonstrate the unarguable need of salvation to the human race, which had utterly gone astray. The text ends with chapter ten, inviting Diognetus himself to become a Christian. The final sections in the manuscript (chaps. 11-12) seem to be from a separate treatise, written by one of the early Logos theologians. They have an interesting ecclesiology, describing the gathering together of the church of God as the reconstitution of paradise.

**The second- to third-century Monarchian movement.** The earliest of the Monarchians at Rome (early to middle second century) do not really represent a discernible movement or secession in the church as such (though heresiologists from a later date will always be ready to brand them as an early heresy because of later perspectives); rather, is it the case that in the middle part of the second century they are more a tendency of very early Christian theology to articulate its sense of the Godhead in a particular way: not so much wondering whether it was monotheist (which few would ever wish to contest) but worrying exactly "how" it was monotheist and yet could simultaneously offer Jesus divine honors (titles of acclamation, prayers for salvation) in its worship. These earliest Monarchians were most likely, then, a group of traditional thinkers who disliked the developing Logos theology represented by some of the leading intellectuals of the Christian community. It is, after all, Tertullian who first named the movement in this way; he flushes them out, as it were, as his own opponents, and brands them as archaic and uninformed. They were probably chiefly a foil of the Logos theologians, who were sharpening their wits against a more inchoate set of older theologians who did not use their terms and felt uneasy with them, but who could not exactly find alternatives to use to erect against them.

The earliest level of the movement is probably best understood as a highly traditionalist, Semitic (scriptural) way of thinking about God that had not "thought through" the *problemata* that occupied the more intellectual theologians of the Logos school and needed the initial stimulus of the Logos apologists to bring it into focus as a real movement. If this is the case, we might imagine that the thinkers whom Tertullian classifies as Monarchians were actually only Christians who had not fully elaborated what the christological imperative of divine honors ascribed to Christ involved metaphysically. They were possibly content to give Jesus divine titles and functions (agent of creation, Savior) such as those indicated in the later Pauline epistles without feeling the need to worry about explaining how these things sat with

Jewish monotheism. Or perhaps it was the case that in some of these communities, at this stage, these early Monarchians had not yet accepted the Pauline epistles as properly canonical Scriptures and instead sustained a highly subordinationist Christology of Jesus as the earthly servant of the Father.

The third-century Monarchian schools were of a different ilk to this, however. Far from being representative of undifferentiated and vague, scripturally rooted Christology, the later protagonists have all the hallmarks of consciously projected school theories, and we start to find precise names attached to the leaders of the movement. It was then that the "Monarchian" designation of the older generation of Logos theologians was felt to be a good and recognizable handle to be applied to these new opponents as a collective disparagement; and they were attacked for what the Logos theologians wished to present as their defective understanding of Christology and Trinity. The diffused and inarticulate theology of the second century had now become the heresy of the third. The "opponents" who are unnamed for reasons of discretion in that earlier period can now be named and dissected as leaders of schools in the later generation.

This act of naming and critiquing represents, in many ways, the dawning of systematic theology among Christians as they increasingly adopted Greek patterns of logical and metaphysical thinking and overlaid them onto Semitic scriptural imagery about God. Monarchianism is, therefore, at first probably not more than a nonintellectual traditionalism. However, by the middle and end of the third century, many theologians had indeed organized their thoughts against the early Logos school, and by that stage we can draw up varieties of Monarchianist theories on one side and Christian Logos theories on the other. The early Logos school was represented especially by Justin (c. 100–165), Irenaeus (d. 202), Tertullian (c. 160–225), Hippolytus (c. 170–235), and Novatian (c. 200–258); and along with its exalted Christology initiated its prototrinitarian ideas to explain the issue of God's unity in diversity, exceeding the limitations that monist theology placed on the doctrine of God.

By the third century the names of several of the Monarchian teachers can also be listed:[179] Theodotus the tanner, Theodotus the banker, Paul of Samosata, Noetus of Smyrna, Artemon of Rome, Beryllus of Bostra, Epigonus, Cleomenes, and Sabellius,

---

[179] The second-century Praxeas, who is usually listed first, because Tertullian erects him as the archetypal monarchian in his *Adversus Praxean*, is quite possibly a stage name used to hide who the real target was. The term means "busybody" and might have been a rhetorical "cover" for an attack by Tertullian on Pope Callixtus of Rome, who had enraged Tertullian by his anti-Montanist strictures in the Roman church and by his moves to relax sacramental discipline in certain cases. It might have been this wider animus that stimulated this full-scale attack on conservative opponents of Logos thought.

from whom came the heresy named Sabellianism, a classical way later thinkers had of referring to the Monarchian movement as a whole (in an extreme form). Not all these names formed part of a single school by any means (though some of them certainly regarded themselves as scholastically linked). By the middle of the third century, when the greatest of all the Logos theologians was operative, Origen of Alexandria, the Monarchian opposition was more and more being regarded as a side issue. Monarchianism's refusal to adopt the complexly metaphysical trinitarian thought scheme and language of the Logos school was one thing (the latter's weakness was its inability to lay its hand on a large variety of simple biblical proof texts), but Monarchianism's own Christology of an exalted man, as often advocated by the later protagonists, was also widely seen as "irreverent" by large sections of the church. It seemed to jar with the cultic practices and liturgical honor given to Jesus in the churches. The school was sidelined because it could not properly embrace the *lex spiritalis* of Christians at large.[180]

Later Christian systematicians have separated the Monarchian group into two major streams (on the basis of an imposed history of ideas): those of modalist Monarchianism and those of dynamic Monarchianism. The modalists (such as Sabellius) were seen as the school that tended to think the three persons of the Godhead, Father, Son, and Spirit, were simply alternative names for the selfsame God who operated in different modalities within history, and thus the "persons" were not really distinct entities per se, only revelatory modes of the same single divine entity—in other words, nominal distinctions. The modalist theology turned around the concept of the coherence of the divine being. The dynamic Monarchians (such as Paul of Samosata) again saw God as a single divine entity reaching out in acts of spiritual power (*dynamis*) to make revelatory aspects of itself in history. These schemes turned chiefly around the concept of Christology and its coherence and generally saw the (indeterminate) divine Spirit adopting the man Jesus of Nazareth and lifting him up by an act of divine power (transforming human limitations—hence the term *dynamic*) into the divine ambit for the purposes of revelation (temporarily or permanently). For this reason the latter school was also called adoptionists.

The early concept of Monarchianism derives from the chosen key term of the movement: the idea of the monarchy of God as the expression of a single power that gives consistency of being to his own self. It is a term that is lifted out and named by one of the most acute of the early Logos theologians, Tertullian, who assiduously

---

[180]The "spiritual law" of theology, or the principle of *lex orandi lex credendi* ("the rule of prayer is the rule of belief"), which argues that theology is ultimately the articulation of right worship (*ortho-doxia*), not right speculation (*ortho-logia*).

dissected and critiqued his Christian opposition.[181] When he was being less kind, Tertullian called them Patripassians, a made-up word signifying "those who make the Father suffer." The attribution of suffering to the Deity being the greatest single mistake an ancient theologian (of any kind) could ever make, this title of mockery was his way of arguing that the Monarchians were one step up from being incompetent idiots. This classical schoolroom denunciation of one's opponents as having nothing sensible to say at all has often led later readers astray, forgetting that Tertullian is at one moment setting up the arguments of his opponents and then knocking them down, so one needs to put his rhetorical absolutes into some form of abeyance if one is to hear their own voice. This is difficult, of course, because even in his *Adversus Praxean*, the voice is generally that of Tertullian all the time. Even so, we can perhaps sum up the earliest Monarchian sentiments as being a stress on the complete unicity of God. Unity is presumed to preclude diversity on a simple logical ground. In other words, the concept of complex unity is not envisaged.

This monism seemed to the earliest monarchians a view of God consonant with the Bible: the one God, who is the Father, and no other god beside him. But the extension of the biblical stories of the "one God" into the domain of metaphysics in this way actually meant that the Christians who so "simply" connected the two did not realize that they had read into the Bible stories of God a metaphysic of mathematical unity derived from the Greek philosophers. The Logos theologians, on the other hand, tended to argue that the acts and appearances of God in the Old Testament were acts of "God as revealed in the cosmos," that is the Logos of the Father, who was the agent of creation (as the New Testament already indicated): and thus all divine acts *ad extra* (of God to the world) were de facto manifestations of the Logos or Son, not the Father himself.[182] The Father was the supreme absolute who remained ever invisible and inconceivable to humanity, except as revealed in and through the divine Logos. On this basis, to identify the God of the Old Testament as Father and assert that the Son was wholly other than him was a logical fallacy that gave priority to earthly concepts (mathematical ideas of unity) instead of divine revelation. Posing as a simple, fundamental, and straightforward reading of the Scriptures, it was, in fact, shown by Logos critics to be a tendentious exegesis (often called a "Judaizing" reading) because it gave no allowance for the radical way Christians had of interpreting the scriptural texts christocentrically.[183]

---

[181] *Adversus Praxean* 10.1.
[182] Tertullian sets out this case, working toward his doctrine of God "economically" (that is, from the account of God's manifestation of his saving works and revelations) from Old Testament proofs in ibid., 14.
[183] See, for example, ibid., 31.

The Logos school argued that in the revelation as given to Christians, the entire Old Testament theology was radically changed perspectivally: the Father is shown to have revealed himself fully "only" in the Son, and to have given himself fully only in the Spirit, through the Son. The Son and Spirit were thus in the divine being, as the very energy of salvation, not apart from it, as mere servants of a monist God's will. The unity of God was thus a complex relational idea, not an undifferentiatedly monist one. The issue still stands today as a dividing line between Jewish and Islamic ideas of God's single undifferentiated being on the one hand (unicity), and Christian ideas of complex relational unity on the other (trinity).

What made the issue even so much more complicated in the second century, however, was that such a radical realignment of biblical perspectives had not been fully established as yet in exegetical practice. It would be one of the major achievements of the Logos school to bring this exegetical theory into play to underpin their theology of God, but it would not be established with common procedures, techniques, and terminology until the mid-third century. Moreover, the very idea of a "complex unity" was a neologism that the philosophical schools of the day could not accommodate, and so any steps Christian theorists took in this direction at this period were made without a preexisting semantic foundation. It would take another two centuries before trinitarian language terms could be internationally established and recognizable across the Christian world. In many senses this earliest level of engagement between the Logos and Monarchian theologians in the mid-second century was like a "feeling the way forward."

Tertullian's treatise *Adversus Praxean* is a major step up for Christian theological systematics. It is a masterly example of thinking through one's theological logic. In the course of it he invents the neologism *Trinity*. It would have a very long-term influence. It is a conflation of two Latin words, *one* and *three* rendered into an abstract noun, "Three-One-ness." It now seems a Christian commonality. It must have sounded very strange to its first, and unsympathetic, hearers. But to explain the idea of complex unity Tertullian presents a large-scale accumulation of scriptural texts, very closely argued as examples of how to exegete the Bible properly. His overarching idea is that God is one in terms of substance or essence and three in terms of person; one in power and energy, three in the forms of that outreach. He is one (implicitly three) in his divine immanence, and three (implicitly one) in his divine economy (or outreach of salvation). He is thus "one in three" and "three in one," but never to be considered one, nor three, in abstraction.

For Tertullian, absolute (monist) unicity is either the God of the pagan philosophers or the world of Old Testament shadow theology. The latter monism does not demonstrate the deity who is the God and Father of our Lord Jesus Christ, the sender of the Spirit; and the former ideas of divine unity in plurality (which the philosophers argue about) come from the world of pagan polytheism. Christian revelation, on the other hand, teaches the economy of the Holy Trinity. Tertullian's term *economy* signifies the manner in which the divine omnipotence, which is unapproachable in itself, reaches out as Father, Son, and Holy Spirit, toward the creation to both make and renew it. His oneness in himself comes to the world as his tri-unity in the dynamics of salvation. This will later be refined into the concepts of the immanent Trinity (God in himself) and the economic Trinity (God as revealed).

Tertullian sums up this argument right at the beginning of his work, presenting the whole Monarchian position as monumentally "wrongheaded." Those who insist only on the monarchy of God, he says, and cannot introduce any distinction into such unicity

> believe it is impossible to confess God's oneness except by affirming that the Father, the Son, and Holy Spirit are one and the same thing. As if the one [reality of God] were not all [of these things]. So we explain it in this way: that they are all one in virtue of the unity of substance, while even so we protect that mystery of the economy which disposes the unity into trinity, showing Father, Son, and Spirit as three. But these are three, not in quality but in sequence; not in substance but in aspect; not in power but in the manifestation [of power]. For they are of one substance and one quality and one power, because it is one God from whom those sequences and aspects and manifestations are reckoned, in the name of the Father and the Son and the Holy Spirit.[184]

His logic is precise and laser-sharp against his opponents, who have argued that unity cannot be anything other than unicity. The idea cannot be sustained, Tertullian argues, if trinity is seen to be an extension or administration (*oikonomia*) of the unapproachable divine unity so as to make it revealed and gifted to the cosmos.[185] The Monarchians who accuse the Logos school of being heretical innovators have in fact shown that it is they who are not authentically in line with received Christian faith: "They put it about that we are preaching one, two, and even three gods, while they claim to be worshipers of only one God. As if their thoughtless synopsis of unity was not itself a heresy, and our trinity, so logically set forth, did not constitute the truth."[186] In *Adversus Praxean* 2 he even cites an early creed to demonstrate that his position is in line with the baptismal formularies, while the Monarchians' not-thought-out positions are innovatory.

---
[184]Ibid., 2.
[185]Ibid., 3: "The [Monarchians'] claim that the plurality and ordinance of trinity is a division of unity, although a unity that derives from itself a trinity is not destroyed but rather administered by it."
[186]Ibid.

Tertullian gives away some of the wider context of this argument when he justifies his Logos theology as being quite distinct from the Gnostic teachers at Rome and elsewhere, who have argued about divine emanations (*probolai*) from the Godhead, or divine aspects (*epinoiai*), of which Word and Wisdom were but two among many. It seems that some of the early leaders of the Roman church were as leery of the Logos theology as they were of Gnostics in general. In his exposition, which was soon to be classical, the Son or Word or Wisdom of God is a divine extension (salvifically sent out to the world) of a single divine substance, and for this very reason of singleness of essence is personally distinct from God the Father but never separate. Tertullian makes the relational bond of unity a grounded ontological one, in famous images of root and branch, sun and radiance, fountain and stream:

> Therefore the Word is always in the Father, as he says, "I am in the Father"; and always with God, as it is written, "And the Word was with God"; and never separate from the Father or other than the Father, because, "I and the Father are one." This is the true sense of *probole* and is the guardian of truth, whereby we confess that the Son was sent out from the Father but never separated. For God sent out his Word, as even the Paraclete teaches, just as a root sends forth a shoot, and a spring the river, and the sun its radiant beam. And these manifestations are also projections of those substances from which they proceed.... In this way the Trinity, proceeding by intermingled and connected degrees from the Father, in no way whatsoever challenges the monarchy, while it ever conserves the quality of the economy.[187]

Faced with such a monumental theological barrage, one feels sorry for Praxeas, whom Tertullian characterizes as a conservative influential confessor of the Roman church, obviously very cautious about resisting Gnostic influences by clever teachers at Rome and wishing only to preserve the simple faith of a Bible reader. Tertullian certainly did not feel sorry for him, however. In a most famous dismissal (referring to the former's arrogant censuring of Tertullian's beloved Montanist colleagues at Rome and his unthought-out conflation of Father with Son), Tertullian dismisses him as an incompetent teacher, someone who is memorable only for doing "two pieces of the devil's work" at Rome: "He drove out prophecy and introduced heresy: he put to flight the Paraclete and crucified the Father."[188] It is surely a devastating epitaph for a theologian he despised.

The later Monarchians of the third century were certainly more intelligent opponents of the Logos theologians. They do not form a coherent group as such, so they are best discussed briefly in terms of the main teachers whose names and doctrines

---
[187]Ibid., 8.
[188]From which he derives the ridiculing nickname for them of Patripassians (father-sufferers).

have been recorded. Collectively they represent that very fluid state of Christian *didaskaloi*, that is independent, adult-level school teachers who attracted attention (chiefly of disapproving bishops and liturgical presidents in the larger communities) because they became prominent as Christian-inspired philosophers or sophists. The larger cities had an abundance of such schools, ranging from large and serious establishments where the wealthy could engage in classical philosophy and rhetoric down to the very common "self-improvement" schools where paying clients could learn deportment and basic skills and more practical educational background. The "heads" of these schools (who, like today, could range from internationally known professors down to independent tutors of very modest establishments) laid claim to a very old tradition among the sophists that they represented the "throne of the city." In its origins this meant the throne of rhetoric. The idea was that the greatest and most prestigious of the sophistical teachers of a given city would be the ones who "spoke for" the city in any dealing it had to have with the imperial authorities. Such rhetorical displays were part decorative and part deadly serious (when it came to dangerous political negotiations in times of civil unrest). On the larger front, however, the concept of "throne of the city" spread democratically, almost like the use of the title *Professor* today. It could be claimed by a dean of an Ivy League school, or (as in Continental tradition) by anyone who teaches small children. Bishops started to claim the concept of occupying the "throne of the city" by the third century and into the fourth. The term survives today in the designation of the episcopal central church—the cathedral. The word derives from the Latin *cathedra*, or "throne." But originally this was not a royal throne, rather the rhetorical throne; since the bishop was regarded as the one who had the supreme right to preach and teach in the Christian liturgical assembly.

This is the context in which the early third-century Monarchian *didaskaloi* stood up and become identifiable out of the mists. It is clear that they, like the Gnostic *didaskaloi* of the similar time period, also claimed the right to teach around the Christian faith. Since Christianity was the core of their "philosophy," they did not see the need to respect the claim that *episkopoi* alone ought to be Christian teachers. Indeed, the increasing stress (in the fourth century) on restricting doctrinal teaching to bishops alone probably emerged from this period as a reaction to the independent (thus less controllable) *didaskaloi*. So it is, then, that several Christians, especially lay ones, start to appear as teachers in schools (*scholae*) separate from the liturgical assembly, in the late second century and into the third. Their audience base was probably the increasing number of socially ascendant Christians who wanted an improving education but not one that was steeped in pagan mythology or the camaraderie of cultic meals that often accompanied it. What these teachers had to tell their paying clientele, of course, soon got back to the larger liturgical assemblies and was quickly a matter of wide reportage. Conflicts were inevitable, especially if the more sophisticated and speculative teachings clashed with a more conservative, restricted, intellectual agenda as manifested by a local liturgical president.

This certainly became the case with the Gnostic teachers and their very early clashes with Christian *episkopoi*. Our present group of early third-century *didaskaloi* attracted the global term *Monarchian* largely because it was a handy term already established in the previous generation (after Tertullian) to compact together thinkers who had already projected monist views. But the ones we know about actually come in two quite different "schools" of thought. Both of them are variations on a common theme of how to sustain devotion to Jesus as divine agent without harming a more fundamental monotheistic imperative. Both trajectories were felt to stretch in radical and alarming ways the more simple biblical faith of the earlier generations. As these teachers pulled the focus more and more sharply and demanded the Christian faith be more exactly articulated, the reaction they caused also pushed forward the agenda of sharpening and clarifying and seeking a more specific, universally recognized semantic for the faith of the international communities, a *koine* or common tongue, as it were, for the "catholic" communities.[189]

This step-by-step, unwanted zig-zag advance, as if two people had accidentally tied their right shoelaces together, is something that became characteristic of the later formative centuries of the church: clashing teaching from speculative schoolrooms sharpened the articulation of the larger Christian consensus. It is a pattern that was soon phrased as heresy sharpening orthodox responses, and thus in a real sense it determined what orthodox formularies would be, for by and large it is a conflict that set the intellectual agenda of the early centuries and the narrow terms of reference of the early conflicts that have to be represented (embraced and encompassed) by the orthodox answers. This dialectic of heresy-orthodoxy might have made it no longer possible to presume and prove the idea of a universal harmony of ancient times now challenged by a few reckless dissidents (though this remained forever a favorite theme of the orthodox), but it did push the idea of universal consensus to the fore in

---

[189]*Katholike* meaning, originally, what was accepted across the wider Christian world—the international consensus. At this period we should use the word *catholic* always with a small *c*. By the fourth century the term emerged as a key notion in defining the position that the consensus belief of the liturgical communities is the "true faith," or the authentic tradition, of core Christianity. At this time the word took on a new significance as *Catholic* with a large *C*. It always is meant to evoke the core central tradition of the universal church, in the way that *evangelical* or *orthodox* will also serve to do. In this sense, the proprietary claiming of the word by post-Reformation-era local traditions (such as "Roman Catholic," as if it were the only meaning of the term *catholic*), is a very innovative (denominationalist) use of an important (antidenominationalist) notion.

a very conscious way, by no means invalidating it. If the universality was no longer to be that of a presumed geographical conformity,[190] then it emerged instead as a qualitative accuracy: what has been held and passed on regarding the core elements of the faith. This form of "catholicism" as qualitative discernment became a most important quality-control mechanism for the mainline church in assessing schools of thought and controversies until the middle of the fourth century, when a larger complex of formal mechanisms to establish and protect orthodox teaching were put in place. The Gnostic and Monarchian *didaskaloi*, therefore, were not just significant for what they had to say individually but also for how they serve to set in place this odd, rhythmical relationship between heresy and orthodoxy as a process of the development of Christian doctrine.

The first group of Monarchian teachers to consider were the so-called modalists. Apart from Tertullian's straw man, Praxeas, they are represented by those whom Tertullian called Patripassians: "those who made the Father suffer" in the sense that they so confused the persons of the Trinity that the Son was also the Father and the Spirit. From this Tertullian derived the "implication" of their school that the Father suffered on the cross. This manner of logically deriving idiotic results from the premises of one's opponents (however fair or unfair it was) was a standard form of ancient philosophical apologetics. The more ridiculous the conclusions you could deduce, the clearer you could make the point that there was something radically wrong with the core teachings. Tertullian set the argument in this way, of course, to make the idea of the Father suffering theologically repugnant to every Christian who heard it.

The teacher who can be first associated with this theological tendency to register language about the persons of God as modes of divine being, not substantively distinct realities, was Noetus of Smyrna. From Asia Minor his school transferred to Rome, where in the early part of the third century it gained some purchase with the teachings of Epigonus, Cleomenes, and Sabellius. It is the latter who, ever after, found his name attached to it as the heresy of Sabellianism. Noetus, active in the latter part of the second century, was the teacher who served as the foil of the Logos theologian Hippolytus of Rome, who gives us most of our information about him.[191] Noetus was opposed, at an early stage, by a body of presbyters in Smyrna, giving one of the earliest concrete indications of the clash between theological *didaskaloi* and liturgical presidents. Twice they summoned him to account for his conflation of the Father and the Son, and on the second time they expelled him from the eucharistic community, at

---

[190]"What everyone in every place has always thought," a rather banal notion that Vincent of Lerins will later try to foist on the West as a definition of orthodox tradition.
[191]*Against Noetus*; *Refutation of All Heresies* 9.7-10. (The first book of the refutation was also known as the *Philosophoumena*.)

which point (Hippolytus says) he set up a separate school. One imagines he already had a school, but after his excommunication he set it up in rivalry to the Smyrna church, at which point, as far as Hippolytus is concerned, it then emerged into the light as a heresy as such, whereas before that it was merely a mistaken idea. When Noetus demanded to know from the presbyters why they objected to his glorifying Christ as the one God, they replied by citing the (baptismal) creed as a way of exegeting monotheism in distinction: "We too, in truth, know but one God. We know Christ. We know that the Son suffered even as Christ suffered, and died even as he died, and rose again on the third day, and is at the right hand of the Father, and shall come to judge the living and the dead. And these things which we have learned, we also teach."[192]

Noetus seems to have made his foundation of all theology the concept of the unicity of God as taught in the Scripture: "You shall have no other God beside me" and also "I am the first and the last, and besides me there is no other" (Ex 3:6; 20:3; Is 44:6). Hippolytus quotes Noetus as deducing from this, "If I, therefore, acknowledge Christ to be God, he must be the very Father if he is God at all. And if Christ suffered, since he was God; consequently the Father must have suffered, for Christ was the Father himself."[193] Noetus made the claim that Christ was divine and personally the suffering God so as to be able to explain how his suffering was salvific and redemptive: having a divine value as exemplarist and liberative. Hippolytus complains against him that he has been immensely selective in his choice of scriptural passages, assuming that monist unicity is the only mode of unity possible.

Hippolytus, judging from numerous fragmentary remains of his exegesis, was probably the most important biblical thinker of this era, with the exception of Irenaeus and later Origen. His chief anti-Monarchian point is that the "principle" of monism is being used against the common-sense flow of the meaning of scriptural passages that speak of the Son and Spirit as distinct persons in the plan of salvation. In *Contra Noetum* 4 he accuses the Monarchian school of consistently quoting the Bible passages out of context. "In this way they mutilate Scripture," he complains. His reply is based on the plain sense of the word, but as seen in the context of the economy of salvation:

> It is of the Son that the Father says, "I have raised him up in righteousness." And that the Father did raise up his Son in righteousness, the apostle Paul also bears witness, saying, "But if the Spirit of him who raised up Christ Jesus from the dead dwell in you, he who raised up Christ Jesus from the dead shall also quicken your mortal bodies by his Spirit that dwells within you" [Rom 8:11].[194]

---

[192]*Contra Noetum* 1.
[193]Ibid., 2.
[194]Ibid., 4.

Texts such as John 20:17 ("I go to my Father and your Father, my God and your God"), Hippolytus says, make it clear Noetus is teaching "senselessness." One wonders whether Hippolytus, who clearly has texts of the movement at hand, has missed something of the larger context here: namely whether the Monarchian refuses or not to admit the canonicity of Paul or the Gospel of John at this period. Hippolytus's larger argument against the school is that they have no sense of the taxonomy of salvation. *Taxis* is the Greek word for "order" or "process." Hippolytus introduces as core to his anti-Noetan argument here the idea of the "mystery of the economy" (*mysterion tes oikonomias*). It will become the central distinction of Christian trinitarianism: God as immanent in his own single being; God as economically reaching out to the creation in his extrapolated distinct persons; singularity of being and power and majesty; plurality of outreach, persons, conditions. He puts it this way: "As far as regards the power, therefore, God is one. But as far as regards the economy there is a threefold manifestation."[195]

Against two other teachers, Beron and Helix, Hippolytus goes further to defend the integrity of the Logos school against the core Monarchian premise that they alone represented a coherence of monotheist theology. He argues here that the Son is at one and the same time infinite God and finite man, supremely powerful, and yet passible.[196] One can see why Monarchians might be dissatisfied by this placing of paradox so centrally in the core dogmatic profession. Hippolytus explains that the solution to what seem to be contradictory statements is the context of the economy of salvation. The Word is infinite God in the bosom of the Father, from the Father's own being, and is thus indivisible from him in power and nature and rank. But when we consider him as Son, the concept refers us to the incarnation. He is sent forth out of the Father as obedient Son to be incarnate within history for the salvation of the world. The birth of the Son from the Father thus teaches the distinction of persons, while the single sameness of divine being and power and honor (given by the Father to the Son) ever maintains the unity of the divine nature.

Hippolytus had close contact with the Monarchian school of Noetus, for the latter's close disciple Epigonus brought the school to Rome in the time of Pope Zephyrinus (pope 199–217) and initiated his own disciple Cleomenes to teach there. Hippolytus

---

[195]Ibid., 8.
[196]*On Theology: Against Beron and Helix* (fragment 1). He describes Beron as having abandoned the Valentinian school and starting to teach that Christ was divine flesh in a way that suggests he had become Monarchian: "But how will they conceive of the one and the same Christ, who is at once God and man by nature? And what manner of existence will he have according to them, if he has become man by a conversion of the deity, and if he has become God by a change of the flesh? For the mutation of these realities, such that one becomes other, is a total subversion of both." *On Theology: Against Beron and Helix* (fragment 5).

has little love for Pope Zephyrinus or his successor, Callixtus (pope 218–223), regarding them as "fellow champions of these wicked tenets," although it is more likely that the two church leaders were conservative "old style" Monarchians, who found more to fault with Logos theologians. For Hippolytus, the popes were at fault for allowing such ideas to gain hold at Rome. For his part, Zephyrinus found Hippolytus's regularly voiced objections irritating and even accused him of teaching two gods, something that he in turn found immensely annoying.[197]

About Sabellius very little is known. None of his works survive even in quoted fragments. He was probably active at Rome in the time of Pope Callixtus. St. Basil the Great said he was a Libyan by birth.[198] Be that as it may, he now gives his name to the whole modalist Monarchian position. This is because, following the work of the heresiologists, after the fourth century a heresy had to have a heretic who founded it, and he founded it always as an act of sinful pride. In this way all orthodoxy was attributed to the inspiration of the divine spirit; and all heresy was attributed to the single inspiration of the "father of lies" (Jn 8:44). Finding a heretic in every heresy has now become a central part of the ongoing history of dissident ideas in the church as not simply a history of opinions, but rather an eschatological struggle. Epiphanius suggests that Sabellius's teaching was a refinement of modalist Monarchianism, taking on board some of the critiques of the Logos thinkers: namely that the names Father, Son, and Spirit were three distinct modes of the being of the single God.[199] In other words, they had adopted some aspect of economic salvation theory. The Son died, the Father did not. But Son, Father, and Spirit were not separately substantive realities: they were not three beings so named, but rather three aspects of the same being in different modes of revelation and operation. To Sabellius is sometimes ascribed the earliest use of the term *homoousion* to denote how God is a single and indivisible reality or substance. Later, in the Arian crisis of the fourth century, this would be a rock lying to hand to throw against the Nicene party, who favored this word in a different context, so as to associate them with reviving an antique and discredited heresy. What seems to have been the base point of Sabellius's argument, however, was that the modes of God's revelation were not substantive in themselves.

At this point of time, the Christian theologians generally had come nowhere near the clarification of the necessary terms of the theological argument about divine substance and separate "instantiation" of characters. At this period *substance* (underlying

---

[197] *Refutation of All Heresies* 9.2, 6.
[198] Basil, *Epistle* 210; Eusebius, *Ecclesiastical History* 7.6.26. Dionysius of Alexandria, around 260, complained that the Pentapolis of Libya was a place where the Sabellian ideas still thrived (Athanasius, *On the Opinions of Dionysius* 26; *Discourses Against the Arians* 3.23.4).
[199] Epiphanius, *Panarion* 62.

essence or being) and *instantiation* (concretely real instantiation of that being, qua individual) were actually used as synonyms in Greek. It would not be until the semantic differentiation of *ousia* and *hypostasis* (Latin *substantia* and *persona*) that this argument could be resolved. Tertullian went a long way toward settling this matter by attributing definitions to the key terms (*substantia* and *persona*), but the Greeks took longer to arrive there and always suspected the Latin doctrine of God of being too monist in character. These suspicions would run on into the classical trinitarian debates of the fourth century.

According to Epiphanius, Sabellius preferred the term *prosopon* (plural *prosopa*), "face" or "mask," to connote the three aspects of God. Like Tertullian, he used the image of the sun and its radiant beams to describe the doctrine of God: the figure or form of the sun itself was the Father; the sun's radiant heat was like the warmth of the Holy Spirit; the sun's radiant light was like the Son, who brings illumination. While his opponents clearly stressed his "confusion" of the three "persons" (the Latin term *persona* being the semantic equivalent of the Greek *prosopon*) such that it resulted in "obfuscation," Sabellius was probably more insistent on not making out the divine persons to be substantially separate, yet without having a sufficiently developed concept of how to represent the distinct realities of Father, Son, and Spirit, other than as nominal (and thus "insubstantial") terms. To have left the central core of Christian theology (doctrine of God) in the domain of the insubstantial was a serious weakness, for it implied the divine being (source and energy of all substantiality) was revealed in insubstantial categories.

The dynamic school is the other group of Monarchians, so distinguished largely by subsequent systematicians. These are also known as adoptionists. They tended to resolve the problem of the unity and diversity of God with a razor slice through the center of the knot, but from a very different angle from that of the Sabellians. The former wished to elevate Christ as God. Since God was the Father, Christ had to be Father too if he was God. What is prevalent in this is the "high" or divine Christology that motivates it. With the dynamic monarchians, God's unity and unapproachability cannot be compromised by involving them in the day-to-day goings-on of earthly life. So, they argued, when Christians call Jesus God, they do so by attribution. The supreme Godhead catches up the earthly man Jesus into the ambit of divine energy and fits him for the task of divinely inspired preaching or witnessing. Jesus is divine in the sense of being elevated, or exalted by God: given divinely graced powers and honors, but never God in himself. He can be seen to be adopted by God (hence adoptionism) or given divine graces and powers (hence dynamic modalism) for a time when he acts as revealer of God's teachings on earth.

To the school's orthodox opponents it was easy enough to seize on the central most objectionable premise and elevate this as the core reason it was a heresy: and that was the basic implication that Jesus of Nazareth was simply a man lifted up by God to perform a holy task. It was a Christology one stage removed from the view of the prophets. However much he was a unique agent of God, the orthodox opponents argued, he was still only a man. From this they derived the term *Psilanthropism* (the "merely-a-man" school) and used it as a catchall for anyone associated with such tendencies. For this reason several members of this school come to be associated when there was probably no historical link between them originally. The main thinkers here are the two Theodoti at Rome, and especially two Eastern thinkers, the third-century Paul of Samosata and the fourth-century Photinos of Sirmium, whose names (as happened with Sabellius) come to be used as a synopsis of the whole movement and for anyone thereafter who denigrated the full divine stature of Jesus.

Theodotus the leatherworker was a native of Byzantium (later to be the site of Constantinople).[200] Epiphanius recounts that when he arrived in Rome as teacher there, he founded his theological school on a nexus of texts represented by Isaiah 55:3 ("he was a man of sorrows"), Jeremiah 17:9 ("the heart of man is corrupt"), and John 8:40 ("I am a man who told you the truth I heard from God").[201] He is said to have deduced from his reading of the scriptural evidence that Jesus was a most holy human being who was born of a virgin by special dispensation of God the Father; he lived a pure and holy life and was elevated by God as his chosen messenger when the divine power descended on him in a most profound way at his baptism in the Jordan. Adopted into the divine ambit at this moment, Jesus was then able to represent divine graces and divine teachings on earth; but he was essentially a human being, elevated as a chosen and grace-endowed messenger by God's goodwill and favor. Pope Victor (pope c. 189–199) was moved to censure him as not representing the church's belief. Hippolytus adds the detail that Theodotus claimed that it was the "higher Christ" that descended on Jesus at his baptism. Only after his reception of the spirit of the Christ was Jesus empowered to perform miracles. Some of Theodotus's later disciples said that the baptism was the moment of Jesus' exaltation, while others said it this came after the resurrection. His opponents accused Theodotus of being one of the lapsed who had denied Christ in the persecutions at Rome and who subsequently taught he was a mere man to mitigate his sin of denial. It is difficult to tell how accurate this hostile testimony was.

---

[200] Or "tanner" instead of "leatherworker." Known in earlier British circles as "Theodotus the cobbler."
[201] Hippolytus, *Refutation of All Heresies* 7.24; 10.20; Epiphanius, *Panarion* 54; Eusebius, *Ecclesiastical History* 5.28.

Theodotus the banker was a wealthy second-century Roman Christian teacher who was a follower of Theodotus the leatherworker. He and his associate Asclepiades were strong critics of Pope Zephyrinus, accusing him of departing from the "old tradition" of the church that had prevailed until the time of his predecessor, Victor.[202] He prepared a bowdlerized edition of the New Testament to demonstrate what he thought the old tradition actually was, according to notes from a book that was drawn up against him at the time and that is referred to by Eusebius.[203] His school was said to have had dissensions in it from an early stage, arguing over what exactly it was that comprised the old tradition. His addition to his teacher Theodotus's school was the emphasis on the Melchizidekian tradition he employs. Here he argues that Melchizidek was a higher divine spirit than Christ, and the heavenly Christ was formed as a lesser image of it, an idea he possibly derived from Hebrews 5:6. Common to all the schools was the sense that Jesus was a human being given an exaltation and so "said to be" lifted up into the Godhead: but nominally so, as a grace, never God in himself or by nature. Most of the ancient critics, because of this human Christology, classified Roman adoptionism as a "Jewish" heresy, associating it with the Ebionite tradition of regarding Jesus as simply a man among men. The adoptionist teachings never seem to have caught the mainstream of Christian belief and seem rather to have attracted a smaller elite and intellectualist group in antiquity. The clashes that brought them to notice were in the larger cities, with bishops censuring local scholars who worked independently of their authority. In later centuries adoptionism became a clichéd concept: *Psilanthropism* or "mere-man-ism" for orthodox thinkers to use as a brick to throw at all manner of opponents whose theology they found objectionable.

In the third century the movement gained a brief surge of notoriety once more in the case of Paul of Samosata, a speculative philosophical teacher with powerful political friends who was elevated to the role of local Christian bishop because of his fame as a master of his school. His adoptionist views, once preached from the pulpit, caused the local church quickly to seek international help in ousting him. His views were a more sophisticated form of those of Theodotus and will be considered in the next chapter. But he did not make any large school from among Christian followers and indeed was more useful to the larger mainstream of Christian opinion to help it clarify the reasons for its instinctual dislike of such a Christology. And again, in the fourth-century Arian crisis, to appear to be an adoptionist was an accusation (resurrecting an antique heresy to rule opponents out of order) that was often leveled by the Nicene party against the Arians. At that stage bishop Photinos of Sirmium was

---

[202] Hippolytus, *Refutation of All Heresies* 7.24; 10.20; Epiphanius *Panarion* 54-55.
[203] Eusebius, *Ecclesiastical History* 5.28.

haled as a resurrecter of ancient adoptionism, and the movement was then renamed as Photinianism.[204] One of the weaknesses of the adoptionist position is that it accounts well enough for Jesus' authentic doctrine, and satisfactorily for his miracles of exorcism and healing, but is less than useful for explaining his dramatic acts of salvation in his cross and resurrection: how they could possibly have salvific power to forgive sins and cleanse the world. In the adoptionist scheme the resurrection appears simply, and reductively, as a reward to Jesus for fidelity, rather than being faithful to the New Testament manner of seeing it as the dawning of the covenant of the new age as forged in the salvific passion.

As with the Gnostic schools, the Monarchianist-Logos clash opens up for us one of the most important intellectual crises of the late second and early third centuries and serves as our bridge into the issues of that important period of consolidation for a more global sense of Christian orthodoxy in terms of commonly agreed doctrines. We shall follow up that era more fully in the following chapter. It was a century that, compared to the one that preceded it, can certainly be called "a coming of age."

**The anti-Monarchian early Logos school.** *Justin Martyr (d. c. 165)*. Justin is one of the few second-century masters of the numerous schools of *paideia* who did not become classed as a dissident, and indeed he set himself to be a champion of Christian theology against its intellectual critics. He was from early times classed as one of the leading Christian apologists, that group of earliest authorities whose works the church held up as examples of useful dialectical theology (and hence was willing to reproduce across the generations until they assumed the status of classics). Because of this his work has been preserved and archived as a highly important witness to the ordinary life, theology, and worship of the church in the second century.

Justin was a Palestinian from Nablus. He seems to have been a pagan who made a restless tour of the various philosophical schools (he speaks of Stoics, Peripatetics, Pythagoreans, and Platonists) until as a mature adult, in about the year 132, he discovered the teachings of the Christians through an encounter with an old sage. This *didaskalos* became a mentor of his and represented to him the Christian doctrines as the fulfilment of all the aspirations of the ancient world's many seekers after truth. Thereafter Justin became a fervent convert, and even after his baptism he continued to wear the philosopher's cloak in church and outside it, the sign of the sophist-rhetorician; and so garbed he began to teach Christianity alongside the other itinerant sages typically found in the agora of the ancient Hellenistic cities. He was explicitly saying (a thing that must have struck many Christians of the time as a novel idea) that his new religion was a

---

[204]The term *adoptionism* has also been applied to a (relatively obscure) eight-century Spanish controversy over the nature of the sonship of Christ: whether it was true or adoptive. The latter is addressed in Alcuin's *Seven Books Against Felix*.

coherent philosophy. He had been deeply impressed by the courage he had seen from Christians who held to their wisdom and way of life (a good enough definition of a philosophy, one supposes) despite any threat to their lives. He records how his old sage showed him the meaning of the Old Testament texts and their fulfillment in the life and teachings of Jesus. Justin describes the experience in words reminiscent of the disciples on the road to Emmaus (Lk 24:32): "Immediately a fire was kindled in my heart ... and I embraced Christianity as the only safe and wholesome philosophy."[205]

Justin moved to Ephesus around 135, during the time of the Bar Kokhba revolt, and engaged in debate with a Jewish rabbi named Trypho, who wished to impress on Justin the errors of his interpretation of the Hebrew Scriptures. The dialogue, a public disputation lasting over two days, was later written up by Justin in a literary form and became one of the first opportunities to address why Christian exegesis departed from early rabbinic styles; the matter, of course, centering on the unrelenting christocentric focus of how the church read the Bible. Fulfillment of prophecies is a recurring and strong argument that Justin brings forward for the defense of Christian doctrines, both in the *Dialogue* and his *Apologies*, and he marshals his evidences to present a heavy database, probably representing the manner of literary process that was customary in his schoolroom. Justin then traveled on to open a school at Rome, where the Syrian Christian Tatian was one of his pupils.[206]

Justin flourished during the reign of Emperor Antoninus Pius (138–161), publishing *The First Apology* (c. 155) to make a case for the defense of Christians being persecuted by unjust laws. At this time he also published an account of his Ephesian debate, titled *A Dialogue with Trypho the Jew*. Soon after Marcus Aurelius assumed imperial power (161), Justin issued a *Second Apology* addressed to the senate of Rome. It is thought (from his references to the jealous rivalry of his enemies) that one of his philosophical rivals, the Cynic sophist Crescens, denounced him to the prefect of Rome, Junius Rusticus (163–167), along with several of his students. When they refused to offer sacrifice, they were scourged and beheaded. The record of their trial was taken down by eyewitnesses and still survives.

Justin is one of the most intellectual of the group of Christian apologists.[207] He not only refuted the usual charges made against the earliest Christians (immorality, seditious intent, hatred of humanity) but also set out to show to open-minded hearers the

---

[205] *Dialogue with Trypho* 8.
[206] Tatian was later a leading Encratite teacher and composer of a Gospel harmony called the *Diatesseron*.
[207] The group usually includes, as its chief members across the second to early fourth centuries, Justin, Tatian, Irenaeus, Tertullian, Athenagoras, Aristides, Theophilus, Hippolytus, Novatian, Minucius Felix, Arnobius, and Lactantius. There were others whose works have been entirely or largely lost: Quadratus, Miltiades, Aristo, Apollinaris of Hierapolis, and Melito of Sardis.

essential character of the new movement. He describes the church as the community of those devoted to the Logos, or reason of God. The creative Logos had put a germinative seed of truth (*Logos spermatikos*) in all human hearts as their deepest conscience and religious instinct, and, in the person of Jesus, the supreme Logos had personally incarnated within history to reconcile all lovers of the truth in a single school of divine sophistry, designed to bring all men and women of good faith into the common affirmation of truth. For Justin, Christianity is therefore the summation and fulfillment of all prior human searching for truth (both pagan and Jewish). Christians are monotheists and believe that the Logos is God, in second place to the supreme God. His ideas about the relationship between the supreme God and the divine Logos are heavily colored by subordinationism, which is how he maintains the duality within the framework of monotheism. His treatise *Dialogue with Trypho* is one of the first texts to advance the argument (one that soon became a dominant motif among Christians) that the Christian Gentiles were elected as the "new Israel." Justin approaches and interprets the Old Testament in a thoroughly christological and Logos-centric way. His *First Apology* is one of the earliest and most authoritative accounts of the primitive Christian liturgies of baptism and Eucharist, all the more precious because it seems that many bishops of the same period did not wish to speak publicly of the celebration of these sacred mysteries. Justin gives us, as it were, the lay view of what went on and what it meant, as if explaining it to a non-Christian friend in church.

Justin's intellectual confidence began a much more open trend among Christian thinkers to believe they could adopt Jewish theology and Hellenistic philosophical wisdom in a judiciously balanced manner to serve as a vehicle for Christian preaching. The fear of Greek thought and terminology that the Gnostic teachers had spread among many in the church was allayed by the success of Justin's work, conducted in a spirit of faithful and orthodox confession. His martyr's death also sealed his reputation positively for future generations. To this extent he was an important bridge between the exegetically based theologians, the Logos thinkers, and the cosmological-metaphysical teachers. The reconciliation of all of them was to occur in the mid-third century with Origen of Alexandria. But Justin, Hippolytus, and Irenaeus proved to be important stepping stones to that ultimate resolution that set the term for Christian theologians to be much more expert synthesists than they had hitherto been. This openhearted confidence of Justin can be clearly seen in a distinctive passage from his *Second Apology*:

> I confess that I am proud to be called a Christian, and with all my strength I strive to be one. Not because the teachings of Plato are so different from those of Christ but rather because they are not in all respects similar. The same is true with regard to all the others;

the Stoics, the poets, and historians. For each man among them spoke well according to the degree that each one had a share in the spermatic Logos, and so could recognize all that pertained to it [Logos]. But the [teachers] who contradicted themselves on the more important points appear not to have possessed that heavenly wisdom and the knowledge that cannot be refuted. And so, whatever correct teachings all men have promulgated, these are the property of us Christians. For next to God, we worship and love the Logos who is from the unbegotten and ineffable God, since he also became man for our sakes, so that, becoming a partaker of our sufferings, he might even bring us healing.[208]

*Tertullian (c. 155–220).* Quintus Septimius Florens Tertullianus (Tertullian) was another leading member of the early Logos school and is perhaps its greatest literary advocate. He was also one of the finest Latin apologists the early church produced, as well as one of the best early systematicians. His work in apologetics led him to take on the might of the Roman legal machinery, which was then being applied violently in state persecutions that had classified all manner of Christian religion as illicit and had thus attached fixed state penalties of treason against it. He writes passionately and with powerful élan (often in a most pugnacious way). His style and cultural rigorism can put off modern readers, and his tirades against the immodesty of women in church (dress codes and so on) have led to his being the early Christian theologian modern feminists most deeply despise. He is a man of his time in maintaining the patriarchal bias of the Roman household code. But, even so, his intellectual insights gave the early church a profound basis for future development. In his legal fights with Roman authority he elevates the issue of how justice must take precedence in law, because law is the servant of justice, not the other way around. It is an idea the world still has not fully absorbed, it might seem. And he is a dramatic defender of religious freedom: "It is the right of every human being to choose their own religion."[209] In his systematic reflections on Trinity, Christology, and salvation theory, he established the terms of much of the earliest Latin theological vocabulary of Christians.

Later in life he apparently moved to join the Montanist movement in Carthage and became a stout defender of a group that was increasingly being sidelined. His rigorism seems to have been exacerbated by this move. He eventually defended the position that it was not right for a Christian to try to avoid a martyr's death, even by fleeing from the authorities. Despite this, Tertullian's reputation as one of the founding minds of orthodox Latin theology was maintained by all his Latin literary successors in the church, including Cyprian, Lactantius, and Augustine. His great work, the *Apologeticum* (*Apology*), even when the old social conditions no longer

---

[208] *Second Apology* 13.
[209] *Ad Scapulam* 2.

applied to a now imperially protected Christianity, stood as a monument to them of how noble his spirit had been and how trenchant his criticism of pagan society.[210]

Tertullian was the son of a pagan centurion serving in Roman Africa and as a young man pursued a successful legal career at Rome.[211] In middle age (circa 193) he was converted to Christianity, probably in Carthage. The courage of the Christian martyrs seemed to have deeply impressed itself on him: "Everyone in the face of such prodigious endurance," he writes, "feels himself struck as if by doubt and ardently longs to find out what there is at the root of all this. From the moment that he discovers the truth, he straightway embraces it himself."[212] Jerome, in the fifth century, is the sole witness who says he eventually became a presbyter, but the extent of his subsequent teaching ministry between 195 and 220 and the intimate knowledge of church processes he demonstrates make it not unlikely.[213] His knowledge of both Latin and Greek enabled him to make a study of the international Christian tradition: a factor that enriches his work and also served to tie together the Greek and Latin Christian intellectual tradition at a crucial period. His style in apologetic is terse and often relies on caricature and ridicule (a standard element of law-room argument in his day). It is not usually safe to deduce his opponents' real positions from Tertullian's way of dragging them around the intellectual arena to show their ridiculous "conclusions." Sometimes his preference for the terse aphorism leads to aspects of his thought having an unnecessary obscurity. A later Latin commentator criticizes his style in this regard.[214]

But when he was not engaging in an explicit denunciation (of foes outside or inside the church), Tertullian regularly shows himself to be a deeply reflective theologian. Like many other great orators, he had a gift for the telling summative phrase, and many of his aphorisms still have resonance in the church. Warning the pagan authorities that their persecution policy was futile, he famously said, "The blood of martyrs is seed [for the church]." Speaking of the mystery of why God would reveal himself in the crucified and resurrected Christ, he argued back against detractors who were trying to ridicule Christian faith as "wholly unbelievable": "I believe it precisely because it is absurd," implying that God's truth is not to be judged on the standards of human, linear logic.[215] Again, scornfully dismissing the ridicule of contemporary philosophers, he replied

---

[210] "Consider this, then: how the charge of irreligion may be laid against you by virtue of the fact you destroy freedom of religion, forbidding a person their choice of god, so that I may not worship whom I would, since I am forced to worship whom I would not; when surely no one, not even a man, would ever wish to receive reluctant worship." *Apologeticum* 24.6-7.

[211] Quasten thinks he can be identified with the jurist Tertullianus, whose opinions are excerpted in the Roman *Corpus Civilis*. See J. Quasten, *Patrology*, vol. 2 (Antwerp: Spectrum, 1975), 246.

[212] Tertullian, *Ad Scapulam* 5.

[213] Jerome, *De Viris Illustribus* 53.

[214] Vincent of Lerins: *quot paene verba, tot sententiae*: "Almost his every word stands for a proposition."

[215] And echoing Paul, of course: 1 Cor 1:25.

with a wholesale sweep of his own arm: "What has Athens to do with Jerusalem?" And in his treatise *On the Witness of the Soul*, where he argued that natural life is an instinctual witness to the divine presence, he made a bold apologetic statement that has given rise to generations of Christian reflection on the gospel as the root of culture, saying, "The soul is naturally Christian" (*anima naturaliter christiana*). In this work he demands that the sophistries of philosophers must give way before the simple and unadorned truths of the witness of a human conscience:

> I appeal to you, soul, but not when you are belching forth sophistries in the style of a schoolmaster, or a person trained in libraries, or fed in Attic academies and porticoes. No, I address you [soul] as simple, untutored, uncultured, and unlearned: qualities they have who have only you as their possession: that very experience of the road, the street, the workshop, all integral. It is your very inexperience I want, since no one seems to have any confidence in your so small experience. But what I expect from you is those very qualities that you yourself introduce into a man, and which you know either out of yourself, or from your Author.[216]

A lot of his fierce intellectual freedom and boldness derived from his passionate desire to find the truth, tell it, and expose the false claimants to truth. To this extent his motto was *veritas non erubescit nisi solummodo abscondi*: "Truth will blush for one reason only: when it is hidden away."[217] He constantly advocates truth telling but sees its results as generally fatal for the truth teller. It is the truth that stirs up the hatred of demons for the church and moves them to move the wicked to assassinate the Christian as a witness to truth. "Truth," Tertullian says, "persuades by teaching, but does not teach by persuading."[218]

Tertullian enriched the Latin theological literature by his knowledge of ecclesiastical customs and controversies from the East, not least by raising the Logos theology to prominence in his theological schema. He was an early and caustic critic of the Monarchian movement at a time when it was held to by some of the Roman leaders as a "safe conservatism." From around 205 his writings show an increasing respect for Montanist ideas, but the style of Montanism as it was then influential in North Africa was a much moderated form of the original Asia Minor movement, and there is no clear indication that he ever broke from the catholic community. His major works include the *Apology* (written c. 197), in which he makes a passionate appeal for legal toleration of Christianity. In a series of moral works addressed to Christians (*On*

---

[216] *De Testimonio Animae* 1. For Tertullian, the very simple nature of the soul, of even the most unlearned people, testifies, if it is clean, to the presence of God, the immortal condition of human destiny, and the universal ethic of love. The soul naturally knows it is the image of God.
[217] *Adversus Valentinianos* 3.2.
[218] Ibid., 1.4.

*Attending the Theater, On Military Service, On Idolatry, On Penance*) he severely warns them of the dangers of assimilation to the corrupt standards of contemporary pagan society and warns against adopting a military profession (largely because of the requirement to worship the imperial genius, though also with a conviction that such a life is contrary to the irenic gospel).

He wrote a work arguing (from the legal principle of prescription as a "preliminary ruling out of order" of certain arguments offered to a court) that heresies could not be considered part of the Christian world at all (*On the Prescription of Heretics*). He followed Irenaeus in setting the principle of the apostolic succession as the proof of where catholic Christianity resided de facto. It was to have the effect of massively reinforcing the importance of catholic (that is, "international") orthodoxy in the definition of the church. He composed a series of works attacking the ideas of the Gnostics and Marcion (*Against Marcion, Against Hermogenes, On the Resurrection of the Dead, On the Flesh of Christ*), taking up the central theme that Christ's incarnation was a true physical reality that vindicated the goodness of the material world and gave the promise of true resurrection to believers. Much of his knowledge of the Gnostic systems derives from Irenaeus and the lost works of Justin, Miltiades, and Proculus, but in his preface and early chapters he gives an overview that is distinctively his own, that the varieties and divergences of Gnostic systems demonstrate the constant characteristic of all human sophistries: arrogant speculation into mysteries beyond their capacity and wide wandering away from the truth as a result.

His major attack (*Against Praxeas*) on the Monarchians is addressed to a certain Praxeas (or "Busybody"). This is probably not a real name but might conceivably be an ironic way of ridiculing Pope Callixtus of Rome, his contemporary, whom Hippolytus (a Logos theologian he greatly respected) had also accused of Monarchianism. In this work Tertullian sets out the foundations for what would become the Latin doctrine of the Trinity. He demonstrates how modalism is unscriptural, despite its protestations to be biblically anterior to Logos theology, and he sets out to explain how the Word and Spirit emanate as distinct persons (*personae*) from the Father, all possessing the same nature (*natura*). His approach to Christology understood natures in the sense of legal possessions, which set Latin thought on long path: Christ possesses two natures but is only one person.

Tertullian's treatise *Adversus Judaeos* is a record he made of a daylong disputation between a Christian convert and a Jewish proselyte in North Africa.[219] He felt that the argument had confused more things than it had clarified, so he determined to make a written investigation and set down conclusions for the church. In this work

---

[219] Only the first eight chapters are authentically his.

he sets a tone of radical separationism that had immense influence over later Latin thinking about Judaism. The Jewish people, he argues, rejected God in rejecting his Christ, and thus rejected his grace, thereby departing from it. Because of this the Old Testament no longer has any force and must only be interpreted spiritually, not literally, by the church, who has inherited it as of right, since the Gentiles were called by God as his new chosen. Jewish law does not have any spiritual precedence anyway. The primordial law was already given by God to all humankind, enacted for Adam and Eve in paradise, and this "natural law" of God inscribed invisibly in human hearts is the divine basis from which all other laws derived, including that of the Jews. The written Torah prescripts were inferior to it. Circumcision, sabbath observance, and sacrificial cult have all been abolished, and the law of retaliation has fallen before the love of mutual love. The true priest of the new sacrifice is Christ. The treatise ends with proofs of the Lord's coming foretold in the prophets, using arguments he quarried mainly from Justin Martyr.

Tertullian's treatise *On Baptism* gives interesting illumination about early third-century liturgical practice. He clearly dislikes infant baptism, which was becoming more common. His work *On the Soul* introduces the idea of Traducianism, the concept that the soul was handed down along with all other aspects of life (color of eyes and so on) from parent to child. It was a door that led to the concept of the transmission of "original sin" like a stain of guilt permeating the race. It would be developed significantly by another African theologian, Augustine, in his later argument with Pelagius, and the idea would come to cast a certain pessimistic shadow over all subsequent Latin thought. In his final years the renewed interest in eschatology and an increasing strain of rigorism mark what have been called Tertullian's "Montanist"-period works (*On Monogamy, Exhortation to Chastity, On Fasting, On Modesty*). This latter treatise was written circa 200 in anger at the bishop of Carthage's intention (like that of Pope Callixtus) to allow even the forgiveness of serious sexual sins to lapsed Christians as part of the developing system of Christian penance, meant to deal with the large number of lapses following after the age of persecutions.

*Hippolytus (c. 170–235).* Hippolytus is another, and significant, Logos theologian, though one less speculatively important compared with Tertullian, Clement of Alexandria, or Origen, who were more masterly systematists in the range of their thinking. By comparison Hippolytus is more of a churchman: interested in matters of polity and liturgy, and a controversialist who sees in philosophy more a source of many errors than a microsystem of ideas that could be pressed into ecclesial service. He was a rhetorician, perhaps, more than a philosopher per se, a leading presbyter of the Roman church, though he was, quite possibly, like other great intellectuals in Rome in this era, a migrant from the East. His mastery of the Greek language and his intimate knowledge of the doctrine of the mystery religions all point to a specialist religious knowledge of long standing. He straddles the second to third century and is a significant weathervane of what kind of theological concerns would mark the church of the next century. His international renown was such that the great Origen traveled to Rome to hear him lecture. Several Eastern sources describe him as the bishop of Rome. If this is accurate, he must have broken away from the communion of Pope Zephyrinus (198–217), or (more likely) Callixtus (217–222), whom Hippolytus regarded as doctrinally dubious for his Monarchianism and morally lax for his relaxation of canonical strictures against public sinners and his revision of the marriage laws.

It is often thought that Hippolytus thus became one of the first antipopes. Because of this history, and also because he wrote in Greek (common among the theologians of Rome at that period), his reputation and his text tradition suffered neglect until the modern era.[220] Compared to Tertullian, for example, he was more or less overlooked. The early Roman tradition was that both Hippolytus and Pope Pontianus (230–235) were arrested in 235 and condemned to be worked to death in the salt mines of Sardinia (the "island of death," as the church called it). In their exile they were reconciled, and Pope Fabian (236–250) had both their bodies brought back to Rome as revered martyrs and located them in the cemetery on the Via Tiburtina. In 1551 excavations in the same area brought to light a statue of Hippolytus as rhetor and teacher, prepared in his own lifetime, which is now in the Vatican museum collections. It has engraved on the back of the base his Paschal table and a list of his *opera*.

His chief work (though a minority does not attribute it to him) was the *Philosophoumena* (or *Refutation of All Heresies*), which derives all Christian heresies from the corruption of mystery religions or Hellenistic philosophy prioritized over the gospel.[221] Hippolytus here depends on Irenaeus's *Adversus Haereses* for much of his knowledge of the Gnostic systems, but he also seems to have access of his own to other Gnostic literature, and of course he forms his own opinions, which makes him a distinct and valuable witness as to what the Gnostic movement was about. Like Irenaeus, Hippolytus elevates the church's scriptural tradition, historically rooted, and the tradition of its teacher-saints (apostolic tradition) as the main arguments to offset Gnostic speculations claiming to represent Christian traditions. He tells his readers in the prologue that his work will require extensive research to investigate

---

[220] In a time when the later Latin tradition became increasingly obsessed with obedience to the Roman pontiff to be the be-all and end-all of ecclesiology.

[221] It is not listed in any of the ancient tables of his works, either that on the statue or in Eusebius (*Ecclesiastical History* 6.22) or Jerome (*De Viris Illustribus* 61). But the author of the work refers to known writings of Hippolytus as his "earlier treatises."

the origins of the various theses, but that he will demonstrate convincingly that in each instance of the heresies he will discuss the various philosophers have advanced their own theories, not the tradition of the church. He lists some thirty-three variations of Gnostic school and relates each one to the type of Greek philosophical schools he has outlined in his preamble in the first book. His books five through nine are regarded as the most distinctive and personal part of his writing.

A short work titled *Syntagma* (also known as *Against All Heresies*) is lost but seems to have been a source for Tertullian's work *De Praescriptione* and is perhaps summarized in chapters forty-eight through fifty-three of the latter. Epiphanius made a wide use of Hippolytus's original in his own work on a similar theme (*Panarion*). The doctrinal work *On the Antichrist* has survived intact. It was composed around the year 200 and addressed to a certain Theophilus.[222] It is a text written with the book of Revelation in mind and standing at an angle to it. Many members of the Christian congregations at Rome were highly eschatologically conscious at this period of persecutional savagery. Politically expressed, their eschatology often equated Roman imperial power with the antichrist's arrival (most recently with Septimius Severus's persecution). Hippolytus shows a careful reading of the texts to argue (from the book of Daniel) that Rome is only the fourth power described in Daniel's vision, and so the antichrist is still to appear in the future. His *Chronicle*, or universal history of the world, subsequently argued there were at least two hundred more years to go before the expiry of the determined six thousand years of the creation. Later Hippolytus wrote a specific *Commentary on Daniel* (surviving complete in its medieval Slavonic edition), which refers back to this work. He shows himself to be an Alexandrian in his allegorical style of interpretation, though significantly less mystically profound than his younger contemporary Origen. He takes the story of Susanna in the garden, spied on by two lecherous elders who try to seduce her under a compulsion of fear, as an allegory of how two peoples, the Roman pagans and the Jews, have consistently tried to lead the pure maiden church astray from her paradise of being with her husband (Joachim-Christ):

> For when the two peoples conspire to destroy any of the saints, they watch for a suitable time and then enter the house of God and seize some of them and drag them off and imprison them and say repeatedly: Come and agree with us and worship our gods. But if not, we shall bear witness against you. And when they refuse, they drag them before the court and accuse them of acting contrary to the decrees of Caesar and condemn them to death.[223]

---

[222] If (as with the *incipit* of the book of Acts) this is a real person and not simply a cipher for "god-loving reader."

[223] *Commentary on Daniel* 20.

His extant *Commentary on the Song of Songs* seems to be a collation of church homilies he gave.[224] It follows the same lines as Origen would in his own masterwork. The king in the song stands for Christ, and the bride is the church. The image also doubles as an allegory of the love between the Logos and the individual soul, which God loves and to which he gives the inherent desire to long for him. St. Ambrose used Hippolytus's work in his own exposition of Psalm 118. The idea launched a whole tradition of Western medieval mystical devotion. Hippolytus's other biblical writings, such as *Benedictions of Moses* and *Benedictions of Isaac and Jacob*, are also extant.

Hippolytus also composed a highly influential *Apostolic Tradition*, a discussion of how the community's worship ought to be conducted, with examples of liturgical prayers that the presiding bishop ought to offer. It marks the moment when presiding bishop-presbyters were moving away from spontaneous prayer in the sacraments to standardized ritual forms. Scholars have recently been able to abstract this writing from the various later liturgical collections in which it was incorporated. It now stands as one of the earliest and most important sources for knowledge of early Christian ordination rituals, the ordering of various ministries, the catechumenate, baptism, and the praxis of the early Eucharist. An excerpt from the baptismal ritual is given in the reader at the end of this chapter. In the description of the immersion ritual one sees how the entire creedal structure of the Roman church of his day is passed on almost accidentally. As a theologian Hippolytus stood for a vision of the church as the community of the pure elect and strongly resisted the trend he deplored in Callixtus, to advance a theology of reconciliation (a pastoral polity of a church of sinners following the path of repentance).

Hippolytus's attack on Sabellian Christology as represented by the Symrnaean teacher of Christian philosophy Noetus (*Contra Noetum*) served not only to isolate this tradition of Christology and marginalize it but also to set out the major parameters of the Logos school's development. The *Contra Noetum* has caused controversy as to whether it was originally part of a previous work (Tillemont says a fragment of the *Syntagma*)[225] or a freestanding treatise (as Butterworth convincingly argues) that is simply another of those works not listed in the extant table of Hippolytus's *opera*.[226] This work is in diatribe style and falls into two parts. The first refutes Noetus of Smyrna's version of Monarchianism as a fallacious "common-sense" view

---

[224]Completely preserved in Georgian, and partially in Greek, Slavonic, Armenian, and Syriac, showing how highly Hippolytus was regarded in the later Eastern churches.

[225]See discussion in A. Brent, *Hippolytus and the Roman Church in the Third Century: Communities in Tension Before the Emergence of a Monarch Bishop* (Leiden: Brill, 1995), 117-19.

[226]R. Butterworth, *Hippolytus of Rome: Contra Noetum*, Heythrop Monographs (London: University of London Press, 1977).

of Scriptures. The second goes on to expound the personal distinction of the divine Logos from the Father on the basis of biblical exegesis, being careful to show how the very texts Noetus relies on are capable of significantly different interpretation. Discussing the favored Monarchian "proof-text" from John, Hippolytus says,

> If, again, Noetus alleges his [Christ's] own teaching when he said, "I and the Father are one," let him attend to the facts and learn that he did not say "I and the Father am one" but said rather "are one." For the word are is never spoken in reference to one person only, but here it refers to two persons and one power. [The Lord] has himself made this clear, when he spoke to his Father concerning the disciples, "The glory which you gave me I have given them, that they may be one, even as we are one: I in them, and you in me, that they may be made perfect in one; that the world may know that you have sent me."[227]

Like the earlier apologists (such as Theophilus of Antioch), Hippolytus argues that the Logos was emitted from God the Father to serve the purpose of creating the material order and for its salvation in latter days.[228] The Logos was at first immanent in the Divine Monad, then became the emitted Word in the process of creation, and finally was the incarnate Word in the economy of salvation.[229] The Logos is "God

---

[227] *Contra Noetum* 7.

[228] "God, subsisting alone, and having nothing contemporaneous with himself, determined to create the world. And conceiving the world in his mind, and willing and uttering the Word, he made it; and straightway it appeared, formed as it had pleased him. For us, then, it is sufficient simply to know that there was nothing contemporaneous with God. Beside him there was nothing; but he, while existing alone, yet existed in plurality. For he was neither without reason, nor wisdom, nor power, nor counsel. And all things were in him, and he was the All. When he willed, and as he willed, he manifested his Word in the times determined by him, and by him he made all things. When he wills, he does; and when he thinks, he executes; and when he speaks, he manifests; when he fashions, he contrives in wisdom. For all things that are made he forms by reason and wisdom—creating them in reason and arranging them in wisdom. He made them, then, as he pleased, for he was God. And as the author and fellow counselor and framer of the things that are in formation, he begot the Word; and as he bears this Word in himself, and that, too, as (yet) invisible to the world which is created, he makes him visible; (and) uttering the voice first, and begetting him as Light of Light, he set him forth to the world as its Lord (and), his own mind; and whereas he was visible formerly to himself alone, and invisible to the world which is made, he makes him visible in order that the world might see him in his manifestation and be capable of being saved. And thus there appeared another beside himself. But when I say another, I do not mean that there are two Gods, but that it is only as light of light, or as water from a fountain, or as a ray from the sun. For there is but one power, which is from the All; and the Father is the All, from whom comes this power, the Word. And this is the mind that came forth into the world and was manifested as the Son of God. All things, then, are by him, and he alone is of the Father. Who then foolishly adduces a multitude of gods brought in, time after time?" Ibid., 10-11.

[229] "Thus a man, however unwillingly, shall be forced to acknowledge God the Father Almighty, and Christ Jesus the Son of God, who, being God, became man, to whom also the Father made all things subject, himself excepted, and also the Holy Spirit; and that these, therefore, are three. But if he desires to learn how it is shown still that there is only one God, let him know that his power is but one. As far as regards the power, therefore, God is one. But as far as regards the economy there is a threefold manifestation." Ibid., 8.

from God" (*theos hyparchon ek theou*), in which terminology he predates the Nicene Creed by a century.[230] The Logos is the very expression (revelation) of the unapproachable and infinite and unknowable God, who by nature (in his immanent being) resists the approach of all creation; and thus the Logos is the high priest of the creation, its mediator before the Godhead. The Word is distinct from the Father but is not a second god alongside the Father, for there is but one single power of the divinity: and it is in the Word from the Father.

Hippolytus goes on also to discuss the distinct roles the three persons of the Trinity continue to play in the process of salvation. Both of these major ideas, the Logos as revelatory high priest of creation and the Trinity as the economic revelation of the immanent life of God, would be developed extensively in the centuries to follow. Hippolytus's relatively undeveloped sense of the significance of the Holy Spirit (it led to an accusation from Pope Callixtus of his being a ditheist) and his lack of precision (as compared to Tertullian, or later Origen, for example) show a significant thinker standing at a very early stage of the rise of trinitarian controversies at Rome.[231] This lack of semantic precision in his work was a key factor in making him a theologian who was held in reverence more for things other than his dogmatic construct in later generations.

Nevertheless, in his spacious understanding of soteriology, Hippolytus follows Irenaeus's concept of salvation as recapitulation (*anakephalaiosis*), whereby Christ assumes flesh to reverse the damage caused by Adam and restore immortality to the human race. This would be taken up throughout the third century by Origen and his followers and run on into the fourth century mainline patristic tradition to become the dominant strand of all Logos theology: a theme and emphasis that we might thereby characterize as dynamic soteriological incarnationalism. Photius, the Byzantine early medieval scholar who had read some of his lost work, says explicitly that Hippolytus was a disciple of Irenaeus.[232]

*Novatian of Rome (c. 200-258).* With Novatian we come decidedly into the third century, but in many respects he is already an antique figure within that century, as compared, let us say, with Clement of Alexandria and Origen. Novatian continues the older tradition of Hippolytus as a Logos theologian; and in this respect his treatise *On the Trinity* is most revealing and deserving of attention, but even so very clearly a work

---

[230]In *Contra Noetum* 10 he also speaks of "Light from Light."
[231]"I shall not indeed speak of two Gods, but of one; of two persons, however, and of a third economy, namely the grace of the Holy Ghost. For the Father indeed is one, but there are two persons, because there is also the Son; and then there is the third, the Holy Spirit. . . . For it is through this Trinity that the Father is glorified. For the Father willed, the Son accomplished, the Spirit manifested." Ibid., 18.
[232]*Bibliotheca* codicil 121.

that shows its mind was on the relation of the Son and Father rather than on the issue of the Trinity as such. The pneumatology is still relatively embryonic and understated. In his life story Novatian was as much as controversial character as Hippolytus seems to have been before him, but this time we have much more data recorded about Novatian. He was said to have been a disciple of Hippolytus who was baptized on his sickbed by aspersion, not immersion (then regarded as an impediment to orders). He later rose to prominence in the Roman church and was elevated to the presbyterate, but is then said (by Cornelius, his chief rival, who assumed the papal office and was a very hostile witness) to have been disappointed not to have been elected to the vacant papacy and so started a rival movement at Rome by soliciting ordination from some Italian suffragan bishops as a papal claimant. Cornelius, who was a distinguished Roman aristocrat and seemed to have commanded the large majority of the Roman church throughout Italy, regarded his rival as a treacherous schismatic.[233]

Novatian positioned his school as a defense of ancient traditions and rigorous standards: a rigorism that gave no opening to the growing sense of pastoral accommodation to sins and lapses that had previously been regarded as meriting no post-baptismal forgiveness at Rome. The rigorist school he represented endured for many generations after him. Even in the fifth century the historian Socrates has a lingering respect for the conservative Novatianists he knew in the region around Constantinople. Even so, Novatian was the first theologian at Rome to write in Latin. In his *De Trinitate,* which he wrote before 250, he is conscious of Tertullian's *Adversus Praxean,* but he adds to the tradition and is one of the first theologians to demonstrate an advance by careful reading of predecessors: a conscious development of a literary tradition, something that would become a norm for theologians of the next century.[234] His prose is elegant, and his level of reflection is deep. He tries to systematize the work of the main thinkers before him in regard to the central doctrine of God (Theophilus, Irenaeus, Hippolytus, and Tertullian). He approaches the idea through the three cardinal clauses of the Roman baptismal creed: belief in God the sole Creator of heaven and earth (chaps. 1-8); the confession of faith in the divine Son, present to the world in two natures united together (chaps. 9-28); and the life and work of the Holy Spirit within the church, raising gifts of spiritual graces within the bride of Christ (chap. 29). In his christological section Novatian sums up the dissident teachings of the Docetics, Ebionites, adoptionists, Monarchians, and modalists and argues against them. He concludes the work (chaps. 30-31) demonstrating the unity of the Godhead and how the divinity of the Son does not weaken that essential oneness.

---

[233]Cf. Eusebius, *Ecclesiastical History* 6.43.2.
[234]Jerome, in his *De Viris Illustribus* 70, says he made "a kind of epitome of the work of Tertullian."

Novatian seems to wish to make a bridge in his theology between the Monarchians and the adoptionists. He therefore carefully avoids the word *Trinity* (*trias*), which his predecessors in the Logos school had used, and stresses the divine unity, laying emphasis too on the subordination of the Son to the Father and that of the Spirit to the Son.[235] Following Tertullian, Novatian calls the Son "the second person after the Father" (*secundam post patrem personam*) but does not follow his mentor in designating the Spirit *tertiam personam*, which Tertullian had done quite clearly.[236] For Novatian the Son is divine, but less than the Father, who is his origin and who alone is without origin: "He proceeded from the Father, at whose will all things were made, as most truly God proceeding from God, constituting the second person after the Father, as the Son, but never robbing the Father of the unity of the Godhead." The divine unity is preserved by the complete submission of the Son to the divine will of the Father—ideas that found their resurgence a century later in some of the Arian thinkers. For Novatian the divinity of the Son is a "received one," which in a sense runs back to its source: the oneness of the divinity of the Father:

> Thus all things are placed under his feet and delivered to him [the Son] who is God; and the Son acknowledges that all things are in subjection to him as a gift from the Father. In this way he refers back to the Father the entire authority of the Godhead. The Father is thereby shown to be the one God, true and eternal; because from him alone does this power of divinity issue; and though it is transmitted to the Son and centered on him, it runs its course back to the Father through their communality of substance. Thus the Son is shown to be God, since divinity is manifestly delivered and granted to him; yet equally the Father is here proven to be the one God, since step by step the selfsame majesty and Godhead, like a wave folding back on itself, is sent forth from the very Son and returns to find its way back to the Father who first gave it.[237]

So he gives a fine presentation of the economy of salvation in the Trinity but weakens some of the force of his Logos theology predecessors by regarding the Son's divinity as almost an imputed *energeia*.

His pneumatology similarly approaches the Spirit as the source of divine grace, the distributor of prophecy, holiness, miracles, virginity, and martyrdom in the church—virtues and charisms that make it shine as the bride of Christ in the world:

> [The Spirit] makes the church of the Lord perfect and complete in all places and in all respects. In apostles he gives witness to Christ. In martyrs he shows the unyielding

---

[235]"The Paraclete received his message from Christ, and if he so received it from Christ, then Christ is greater than the Paraclete. . . . This inferiority of the Paraclete at once proves that Christ, from whom he received the message, is God." *De Trinitate* 18.
[236]Tertullian, *Adversus Praxean* 11.
[237]*De Trinitate* 31.

faith of religion. In the breast of virgins he locks the wondrous continence of a sealed chastity, and in the rest of humankind he protects the laws of the Lord's doctrine, keeping them incorrupt and unspoiled. He it is who destroys heretics, corrects the errant, convinces the faithless, exposes imposters, and corrects the wicked. He keeps the church incorrupt and inviolate in the sanctity of perpetual virginity and truth.[238]

In theologizing about the union of natures in Christ, Novatian sets out, in addition to Tertullian's terms based on the possession and correlation of two natures, graphic terms of union such as *concretio permixta*, conjunction of Word and flesh, and concordance (*concordia*) of divinity and humility.[239] He also speaks of an incarnation into *kenosis* as an economy (disposition) for salvation. In his work we can at once see how much Logos theology needs to refine its thinking and at the same time how much it has clarified its reflections considering the work of intellectuals from the beginning of the century. The great thinkers of the third century, particularly Origen, took the story to much more precise heights based on the work of their predecessors.

## EARLY ORTHODOXIES AND HETERODOXIES

The range of teachings and commentators across the second century is almost bewildering. Tantalizing, too, since we have always a sense that we never quite know enough of the larger context to their thought. There seems already a significant distance at work between the Semitic idioms and sophianic Torah teachings that are witnessed in Jesus own' midrash and haggadic interpretations of Scripture in the Gospels, and idioms of Hellenistic philosophy that are constitutive of the base educational formation of many of the most literate teachers of the second-century communities. The disparate Christian groups seem stretched in a living and obvious tension between the worlds of Scripture and metaphysical philosophy. Many historical commentators of the past have characterized this period as a tug of war between scriptural literalizers (such as the radical Jewish schools with which we began the chapter) and the extreme Hellenizers (as Harnack described the Gnostic teachers). Could Greek philosophy be used as a harmonizing tool, interpreting the scriptural narratives in a wider, more metaphysical manner and giving the Jesus story its properly universal setting? Or did the very importation of Greek philosophical constructs and speculations profoundly falsify and corrupt the springs of Christian revelation?

Tertullian had famously asked (as if expecting an affirmation of his negative skepticism), "What has Athens to do with Jerusalem?" But in truth, the story is not so polarized as this rhetoric might lead us to think. Just as the ancient Jewish world

---

[238]Ibid., 29.
[239]Ibid., 11, 14, 16.

of the time of Jesus was not hermetically sealed from Hellenism (and Jesus himself might even have known and spoken some Greek), so too fundamental categories of Jewish religious thought had already been suffused by Greek metaphysical interests centuries before the appearance of Jesus. The cultures were themselves entwined in considerable and deep-rooted tension before ever the Christians woke up to find this problematic persisted into their own communities. The second-century church, therefore, did not so much betray Jesus into the hands of the philosophers as much as it tried seriously and energetically to reexpress the essential idiom of the Gospels, considered as a basic interpretation of the *ethos* and *telos* (fundamental gist and moral end) of the Old Testament, in terms it could itself comprehend metaphysically, for only then could it pass it on to the Hellenistic world as the coherent missionary narrative of cosmic salvation. This evangelistic imperative so highly valued in the church was why new categories of theology were required and new semantics of precision were constantly called for throughout the second century: Was Jesus an angelic servant of the good Father, or a hypostasis (substantial presence) of God's own being? Was he thus an exalted creature servant, or an exalted and inseparable part of the uncreated Godhead? Such questions of Christology seemed at once novel yet part of the familiar presuppositions of ancient worship rituals. Once "noticed" as *problemata* they stood out luridly, of course, as fundamental questions of Christian identity. Each and every one of these testing questions that occupied the second century was, in its own different way, all about manners of interpreting the scriptural and historical evidences: what weight and relative balance to give them.

The welter of different answers that were being regularly offered throughout this century produced schools of thought that caused the wider church (what some have called the great church or "early catholicism") to set up a furious resistance to dissidence it considered had transgressed the boundaries of toleration on fundamental matters of Christian identity. It started to call these sects and schools *haeresis*, or heresy: no longer in the old schoolroom sense of a recognized difference of opinion, but in the newer sense of a set of stated beliefs that put the holder outside the core of ecclesial belonging. To this extent, it is possible to see more or less the entirety of the second century as a prolonged battle about belonging and exile, core identity and secessionist deviation. Who, or what, was the core? Where were the boundaries?

Out of this struggle came the classic definitions of how one might recognize that central ethos of Christian belief. It is classically set out in the rule of faith, or creed, which Irenaeus puts forward in *Adversus Haereses* 1.10.1-2.[240] This is itself little more than a digest of the Christian Scriptures, but set out in a common-sense reading and

---

[240] The text is offered below in the reader.

offered in a liturgical setting (a hymn before one entered the baptismal waters—and thus also an oath of allegiance)—a response, that is, such as might be expected from one of the early community's bishops. This commonality of accepted belief in apostolic standards across the world was elevated by Irenaeus as a panacea against excessive deviations in the Christian body. He appeals to the image of one heart and one mind (the creed remains to this day, claiming Christian unity as a core value)[241] and says that the churches of his time as far afield as Germany and Asia Minor all testify to this unanimity. His rhetorical image might blindside us a little to the real diversity of his times, but what emerges out of his work, taken as a whole, is that he is not a solitary casuist, seeking to impose a unity that does not actually exist or create "apostolicity" out of thin air. His work is shadowed by a number of others who share his sense that apostolic catholicity means precisely this middle way of a scripturally based faith (neither literalist nor wildly speculative) that is rooted in the historical memory of Jesus, who was himself given to the community's memory and its present life in material sacraments, and treasured teachings, enshrined in liturgy as perennially regnant Lord of the community: not a cipher to be reexpressed according to anyone's intellectual or moral whim, but a standard against which to judge the fidelity of the community that bears his name and that celebrates his progressing work of divine revelation and healing forgiveness.

From this energetic diversity emerged a notion of universal harmony under a liberal idea of catholic apostolicity, which we might translate intellectually as a broad-based scripturalism seeking universal significance. How the Christians set these foundations up in the second century was a work that went forward into several centuries to come, but to them belongs the achievement, after the great achievements of the New Testament foundation literature, of making foundations for a universal church polity. It was marked by canon, creed, liturgy, spiritual mysticism, close attentiveness to the Scriptures, and allegiance to specific leaders whose works were tried and tested as having both spiritual value and respect for the consensus of the tradition of the saints who had preceded them. It was no mean accomplishment.

## A SHORT READER

***The eucharistic prayer, in Didache 9 (late first century).*** Concerning the Eucharist; give thanks in this way: First of all, in relation to the cup: "We give thanks to you, our Father, for the holy vine of your servant David, which you have made known to us through your servant Jesus. To you be glory for evermore." Then, concerning the broken bread: "We give thanks to you, our

---
[241]"And we believe in . . . one holy catholic and apostolic church."

Father, for the life and knowledge you have made known to us through your servant Jesus. To you be glory for evermore. As this broken bread was scattered over the hills and then, once gathered, became one portion, so also may your church be gathered from the ends of the earth into your kingdom. For yours is the glory and the power, through Jesus Christ, for evermore." Let no one eat or drink of your Eucharist except those baptized in the name of the Lord.

**Eucharistic instructions for the Lord's Day, in Didache 14 (late first century).** On the Lord's own day, assemble in common so as to break bread and offer thanks. But first of all confess your sins, so that your sacrifice (*thusia*) may be pure. And yet, no one quarreling with his brother may join your assembly until they are reconciled. Your sacrifice must not be defiled. For as regards this we have the Lord's own saying: "In every place and time offer me a pure sacrifice; for I am a mighty king, says the Lord, and my name spreads terror among the Gentiles" (Mal 1:10).

**Clement of Rome, 1 Clement 42; 44.1-3; 47.6 (late first century).** The apostles preached to us the gospel they received from Jesus Christ. Jesus Christ was God's ambassador. In other words, Christ comes with a message from God, and the apostles come with a message from Christ. Both of these orderly arrangements, therefore, derive from the will of God. Accordingly, after receiving their instructions and being convinced because of the resurrection of our Lord Jesus Christ, as well as confirmed in faith by the Word of God, the apostles went out possessed of the fullness of the Holy Spirit and preached the good news that the kingdom of God was close at hand. From country to country, therefore, and from city to city they preached. Out of the number of their first converts, they appointed men whom they had tested in the Spirit to act as bishops and deacons for the sake of believers to come. This was no innovatory thing, for long before Scripture had spoken about bishops and deacons; for somewhere it says "I will establish their overseers in observance of the law, and their ministers in fidelity."[242] . . . Likewise, our apostles were given to understand by our Lord Jesus Christ that the office of the bishop would give rise to intrigues. This was why, since they were endowed with a perfect foreknowledge, they appointed the aforementioned men and subsequently laid down a rule once and for all to this effect, that when these men die other approved men should

---

[242]LXX *episkopoi* and *diakonoi*. Possibly reminiscent of 2 Chron 34:17, but Clement does not specify where he gets this citation from. See also Acts 20:28.

succeed to their sacred ministry. And this is why we consider it an injustice to throw out from the sacred ministry the persons who were appointed by the apostles, or in later times by other men in high repute, with the consent of the whole church. It would indeed be no small sin on our part if we were to throw out those who have offered the gifts of the bishop's ministry in an unblameable and holy manner. . . . It is shameful, dearly beloved, yes, utterly shameful and unworthy of your standing in Christ that the news should go abroad that the very steadfast and ancient church of the Corinthians has instigated a sedition against its presbyters for the sake of one or two persons.

**Ignatius of Antioch, To the Ephesians *4 (late first century)*.** And so it is proper for you to act in agreement with the mind of the bishop. And I know you do this. Your presbyters are a credit to their name, and it is certain too that it they are a credit to God, because they are in harmony with the bishop as totally as the strings are with a harp. This is why the praises of Jesus Christ are sung in the symphony of your concord and love. And you, the rank and file, should also form a choir, so that, joining the symphony by your own concord, and taking your key signature from God himself, you too may sing a song to the Father with one single voice through Jesus Christ. In this way he will listen to you, and because of your good life he will recognize in you the melodies of his Son. It is to your advantage, then, to continue in your flawless unity, so that you may at all times have a share in God.

**The Shepherd of Hermas, Mandate *4.3.1-6 (late first century)*.** I have heard, sir,[243] from certain teachers that there is no other repentance other than the one offered when we descended into the water and received remission of our former sins. He said to me, "You have heard correctly, for so it is. Whoever has received remission ought not to sin again but rather live in purity. But since you inquire diligently about all matters, I will explain this also to you: not so as to give an excuse to those who shall come to believe in the future, or to those who already have believed in the Lord. For those who have already believed or are about to believe have no repentance of sins but have remission of their former sins. As for those who were called before these days, the Lord appointed repentance, for the Lord knows the heart, and knowing all things in advance, given the weakness of humankind and the sly cunning of the devil, he knew that he would do some evil to the servants of God and would treat them wickedly. And so, since the Lord is full of compassion, he had mercy on his creation and established this repentance, and to me was given

---

[243]The angel of repentance, who appears to him in the guise of a shepherd.

the power over this repentance. But I tell you," he said, "After that great and solemn calling, if someone should be tempted by the devil and sin, he has one repentance. But if he should sin repeatedly and repent, this would be of no profit for such a person; for it will be very difficult for him to find life." I said to [the angel], "I achieved life when I heard the accurate presentation of these things from you. For now I know that if I do not further add to my sins, I shall be saved." "You shall be saved," he told me, "As will all who do these things."

***Pseudo-Clement, Second Letter to the Corinthians 16.4 (early second century).*** Almsgiving is good even as a penance for sin. Fasting is better than prayer. But almsgiving is better than both. Love covers a multitude of sins, but prayer rising from a clear conscience delivers a soul from death. Blessed is every person who is found rich in these things, since almsgiving removes the burden of sin.

***Valentinus the Gnostic, Fragment 2, from the Epistle on Attachments (mid-second century).*** "There is only one who is good" (Mt 19:17). This free expression of his is the manifestation of the Son. Through him alone can a heart become pure, when every evil spirit has been expelled from the heart. For the many spirits dwelling in the heart do not allow it to become pure. Instead, each one of them acts in its own way, polluting the heart in diverse manners with improper lusts. In my opinion the heart experiences something to that which often happens in a public inn. One finds many holes dug there that are often backfilled with excrement by indecent guests who have no consideration for the building, since it does not belong to them. In the same way, a heart that is indwelt by many *daimons* is also impure until it starts being cared for. But when the Father, who alone is good, visits the heart, he makes it holy and fills it with light. And so a person who has such a heart is called blessed, for that person "will see God" (Mt 5:8).

***Polycarp of Smyrna, quoted in Martyrdom of Polycarp 14 (mid-second century).*** O Lord, Almighty God, Father of your beloved and blessed Son Jesus Christ, through whom we have received the perfect knowledge of you, God of angels and hosts and of all creation, and of the whole race of the saints who live under our eyes: I bless you, for you have seen fit to grant to me, on this day and in this hour, a share of the chalice of your anointed one in the company of your martyrs, that I may so rise to eternal life in both body and soul, in virtue of the immortality of the Holy Spirit. May I be accepted among them in your sight this day, as a rich and pleasing sacrifice, such as you, our true God who can never utter falsehood, have foreordained, revealed in advance, and brought to perfection. And so I praise you for all things. I bless you and glorify you, through the eternal and heavenly high priest, Jesus Christ, your beloved Son, through whom be glory to you, together with Him, and the Holy Spirit, both now and for the ages to come. Amen.

***Irenaeus of Lyons,*** **Adversus Haereses *1.10.1-2 (mid-second century).*** The church, though dispersed through the entire world, even to the very ends of the earth, has received from the apostles and their disciples this very faith: that she believes in one God, the Almighty Father, the maker of heaven, and earth, and the sea, and all things that are contained therein; and in one Christ Jesus, the Son of God, who was incarnate for our salvation; and in the Holy Spirit, who through the prophets proclaimed the dispensations of God, and his advents, and the birth from a virgin, and the passion, and the resurrection from the dead, and the ascension into heaven in the flesh of the beloved Christ Jesus, our Lord; as well as his revelation from heaven in the glory of the Father when he will "gather all things into one" (Eph 1:10) and will once more raise up the flesh of the whole human race, so that, as is the will of the invisible Father, "Every knee shall bow, of things in heaven, and things on earth, and things under the earth," before Christ Jesus, our Lord and God, our Savior and king (Phil 2:10-11). "And that every tongue should confess" him; and that he should execute just judgment toward all; and thus send "the wicked spiritual powers" (Eph 6:12) and the disobedient apostate angels into the everlasting fire, in the company of the ungodly, the unrighteous, the wicked, and profane among men; but may also, as the exercise of his grace, confer immortality on the righteous, the holy, and those who have kept his commandments, and persevered in his love; some from the beginning, and others from the time of their repentance, so that he may surround them with everlasting glory. As I have already observed, the church, having received this same preaching and this faith, although scattered throughout the whole world, even so, as if occupying only one single house, she carefully preserves it. She also believes these doctrines just as if she possessed only one single soul, in one and the same heart. These things the church proclaims and teaches and hands down with perfect harmony, as if she possessed only one mouth. For, although the languages of the world are dissimilar, even so the import of the tradition is one and the same.

***Hippolytus of Rome,*** **Apostolic Tradition *12-20 (late second century).*** And when the person who is to be baptized goes down into the water, let the one baptizing him lay hands upon him and say this: Do you believe in God the Father

Almighty? And he who is being baptized shall answer: I do believe. Then let him immediately baptize him once with his hand laid upon his head. And after this let him say: Do you believe in Christ Jesus the Son of God, who was born of the Holy Spirit and the Virgin Mary; who was crucified in the days of Pontius Pilate, and died, and was buried, and rose on the third day, living, from the dead; and ascended into heaven, and sat down at the right hand of the Father; and will come to judge the living and the dead? And when he answers a second time: I believe; then let him be baptized a second time. And then once more let him say: Do you believe in the Holy Spirit in the holy church? And in the resurrection of the flesh? And he who is being baptized shall say: I do believe. And so let him baptize him a third time. And then when he comes up out of the water he shall be anointed by the presbyter with the oil of thanksgiving; who shall say: I anoint you with the oil of thanksgiving in the name of Jesus Christ. And then each one shall dry themselves with a towel and put on their clothes again, and after this let them come together in the church assembly.

## FURTHER READING

### *General Concepts*
Baus, K. *From the Apostolic Community to Constantine.* London: Burnes & Oates, 1965. Pages 159-216.

Marjanen, A., and P. Luomanen, eds. *A Companion to Second Century Christian "Heretics."* Leiden: Brill, 2005.

Quasten, J. *Patrology.* Vol. 1, *The Beginnings of Patristic Literature.* Westminster, MD: Newman Press, 1972.

### *Encratism*
Barnard, L. W. "The Heresy of Tatian: Once Again." *JEH* 19 (1968): 1-10.

Cecire, R. "Encratism: Early Christian Ascetic Extremism." PhD diss, University of Kansas, 1985.

Grant, R. M. "The Heresy of Tatian." *JTS* 5 (1954): 62-68.

### *Jewish Christian Groups*
Bagatti, B. *L'Église de la circoncision.* Jerusalem: Franciscan Print Press, 1965.

Bauckham, R. "The Origin of the Ebionites." In *The Image of the Judeo-Christians in Ancient Jewish and Christian Literature*, ed. P. J. Tomson and D. Lambers-Petry, 162-81. Leiden: Brill, 2003.

Bauer, W. *Orthodoxy and Heresy in Earliest Christianity.* Philadelphia: Fortress, 1971. Pages 241-85.

Keck, L. E. "The Poor Among the Saints in Jewish Christianity and Qumran." *ZNW* 57

(1966): 54-78.

Klijn, A. F. J., and G. J. Reinink. *Patristic Evidence for Jewish-Christian Sects*. Leiden: Brill, 1973. Pages 19-43.

Pritz, R. A. *Nazarene Jewish Christianity: From the End of the NT Period to Its Disappearance in the Fourth Century*. Leiden: Brill, 1988.

**Montanism**

Aune, D. E. *Prophecy in Early Christianity and the Ancient Mediterranean World*. Grand Rapids: Eerdmans, 1983.

Barnes, T. D. "The Chronology of Montanism." *JTS* 21 (1970): 403-8.

Butler, R. D. *New Prophecy and New Visions: Evidence of Montanism in "The Passion of Perpetua and Felicitas."* Washington, DC: Catholic University of America Press, 2006.

Fischer, J. A. "Die antimontanistischen synoden des 2-3 jahrhunderts." *Annuarium Historiae Conciliorum* 6 (1974): 241-73.

Frend, W. H. C. "Montanism: A Movement of Prophecy and Regional Identity in the Early Church." *Bulletin of the John Rylands University Library of Manchester* 70 (1988): 25-34.

———. "Montanism: Research and Problems." *Rivista di Storia e Letteratura Religiosa* 20, no. 3 (1984): 521-37.

Heine, R. E., ed. *The Montanist Oracles and Testimonia*. Macon, GA: Mercer University Press, 1989.

Jensen, A. "Prisca—Maximilla—Montanus: Who Was the Founder of 'Montanism'?" *StPatr* 26 (1993): 147-50.

Klawiter, F. C. "The Role of Martyrdom and Persecution in Developing the Priestly Authority of Women in Early Christianity: A Case Study of Montanism." *Church History* 49, no. 3 (1980): 251-61.

Labriolle, P. de. *Crise Montaniste*. Paris: Leroux, 1913.

Massingberd-Ford, J. "Was Montanism a Jewish Christian Heresy?" *JEH* 17 (1966): 145-58.

Soyres, J. De. *Montanism and the Primitive Church: A Study in the Ecclesiastical History of the 2nd Century*. London, 1878.

Stewart-Sykes, A. "The Original Condemnation of Asian Montanism." *JEH* 50, no. 1 (1999): 1-22.

Tabbernee, W. *Fake Prophecy and Polluted Sacraments: Ecclesiastical and Imperial Reactions to Montanism*. Leiden: Brill, 2007.

———. *Montanist Inscriptions and Testimonia: Epigraphic Sources Illustrating the History of Montanism*. Macon, GA: Mercer University Press, 1997.

Trevett, C. *Montanism: Gender, Authority and the New Prophecy*. New York: Cambridge University Press, 1996.

Tyler, E. "Tertullian and Montanism." MA diss., Columbia University, 1917.

Vokes, F. E. "Penitential Discipline in Montanism." *StPatr* 14, no. 3 (1976): 62-76.

### *The Quartodecimans Controversy*

Brightman, F. E. "The Quartodecimans Question." *JTS* 25 (1923–1924): 250-70.

Dugmore, C. W. "A Note on the Quartodecimans." *StPatr* 4 (1961): 411-21.

Talley, T. J. *The Origins of the Liturgical Year*. New York: Pueblo, 1986. Pages 5-33.

### **Christian Gnosis**

Drijvers, H. J. W. *Bardaisan of Edessa*. Studia Semitica Neerlandica 6. Assen: Van Gorcum, 1966.

———. *The Book of the Laws of Countries: Dialogue on Faith of Bardaisan of Edessa*. Assen: Van Gorcum, 1965.

Frend, W. H. C. *Saints and Sinners in the Early Church*. London: Darton, Longman, and Todd, 1985.

Gartner, B. E. *The Theology of the Gospel of Thomas*. London: Collins, 1961.

Grant, R. M. "Place de Basilide dans la théologie chrétienne ancienne." *Revue des Études Augustiniennes* 25 (1979): 201-16.

Jonas, H. *The Gnostic Religion: The Message of the Alien God and the Beginnings of Christianity*. 2nd ed. Boston: Beacon, 1963.

King, K. *What Is Gnosticism?* Cambridge, MA: Harvard University Press, 2003.

Layton, B., ed. *The Rediscovery of Gnosis*. Proceedings of the International Conference on Gnosticism at Yale March 28-31, 1978. Leiden: Brill, 1980.

Löhr, W. A. *Basilides und seine Schule: Eine Studie zur Theologie- und Kirchengeschichte des zweiten Jahrhunderts*. Tübingen: Mohr, 1996.

Pelikan, J. *The Christian Tradition*. Chicago: University of Chicago Press, 1973. Vol. 1. Pages 68-97.

Quispel, G. "The Original Doctrine of Valentine." *VC* 1 (1947): 43-73.

Ramelli, I. L. E. *Bardaisan of Edessa: A Reassessment of the Evidence and a New Interpretation*. Gorgias Eastern Christian Studies 22. Piscataway, NJ: Gorgias Press, 2009.

Robinson, J. M., ed. *The Nag Hammadi Library in English*. New York: Harper & Row, 1977.

Rudolph, K. *Gnosis: The Nature and History of Gnosticism*. San Francisco: Harper & Row, 1983.

Stead, C. "The Valentinian Myth of Sophia." *JTS* 20 (1969): 75-104.

Williams, M. *Rethinking Gnosticism*. Princeton, NJ: Princeton University Press, 1996.

### *Marcion*

Bianchi, U. "Théologien biblique ou docteur gnostique?" *VC* 21 (1967): 141-49.

Blackman, E. C. *Marcion and His Influence*. London: SPCK, 1948.

Gager, J. G. "Marcion and Philosophy." *VC* 26 (1972): 53-59.

Harnack, A von. *Marcion: The Gospel of the Alien God*. Translated by J. E. Steely and L. D. Bierma. Durham, NC: Labyrinth, 1990.

Hoffmann, R. J. *Marcion, on the Restitution of Christianity: An Essay on the Development*

of Radical Paulinist Theology in the Second Century. Chico, CA: Scholars Press, 1984.
Johnson, M. D., ed. *From Paul to Valentinus: Christians at Rome in the First Two Centuries.* Minneapolis: Fortress, 2003.
Marjanen, A., and P. Luomanen, eds. *A Companion to Second Century Christian "Heretics."* Leiden: Brill, 2005.
Wilson, R. S. *Marcion: A Study of a Second Century Heretic.* London: Clarke, 1933.
Wordsworth, J., and H. J. White. *Novum Testamentum Domini Nostri Jesus Christi Latine.* Vol. 2. Oxford: Clarke, 1913.

**The Apostolic Fathers**

Andriessen, P. "The Authorship of the Epistula ad Diognetum." *VC* 1 (1947): 129-36.
Aune, D. E. *Prophecy in Early Christianity and the Ancient Mediterranean World.* Grand Rapids: Eerdmans, 1983. Pages 299-310.
Barnard, L. W. "The Epistle Ad Diognetum: Two Units from One Author?" *ZNW* 56 (1965): 130-37.
———. "The Shepherd of Hermas in Recent Study." *Heythrop Journal* 9 (1968): 29-36.
———. *Studies in the Apostolic Fathers and Their Background.* Oxford: Blackwell, 1961.
Bowe, B. *A Church in Crisis: Ecclesiology and Paraenesis in Clement of Rome.* Philadelphia: Fortress, 1988.
Clarke, W. K. L., ed. *The First Epistle of Clement to the Corinthians.* London: SPCK, 1937.
Connolly, R. H. "Ad Diognetum 11-12." *JTS* 37 (1936): 2-15.
———. "The Date and Authorship of the Epistle to Diognetus." *JTS* 36 (1935): 347-53.
Donfried, K. P. *The Setting of Second Clement in Early Christianity.* Leiden: Brill, 1974.
Giet, S. *L'Enigme de la Didache.* Paris: Ophrys, 1970.
Grant, R. M., ed. *The Apostolic Fathers.* New York: T. Nelson, 1964.
———. *Ignatius of Antioch.* Philadelphia: T. Nelson, 1985.
———. "Papias in Eusebius' Church History." In *Mélanges H.C. Puech,* 209-13. Paris: College de France, Ecole pratique des Hautes Etudes, 1974.
Jefford, C. N. *The Sayings of Jesus in the Didache.* Leiden: Brill, 1989.
Kleist, J. A., trans. *The Epistle to Diognetus.* ACW 6. Westminster, MD: Newman, 1948. Pages 125-47.
Kraft, R. A. *Barnabas and the Didache.* The Apostolic Fathers: A New Translation and Commentary. New York: T. Nelson, 1965.
Lawson, J. *A Theological and Historical Introduction to the Apostolic Fathers and Their Background.* London: Macmillan, 1966.
Lightfoot, J. B. *The Apostolic Fathers.* London, 1890.
Meeks, W. A. *The Origins of Christian Morality: The First Two Centuries.* New Haven, CT: Yale University Press, 1993.
Munck, J. "Presbyters and Disciples of the Lord in Papias." *Harvard Theological Review* 52 (1959): 223-43.
Osiek, C. *Rich and Poor in the Shepherd of Hermas: An Exegetical-Sociological Investigation.*

Washington, DC: Catholic Biblical Association of America, 1983.
Schoedel, W. R. *Polycarp, Martyrdom of Polycarp, Fragments of Papias.* Camden, NJ: T. Nelson, 1967.
———. "Polycarp: Witness to Ignatius of Antioch." *VC* 41 (1987): 360-76.
Snyder, G. F. *The Shepherd of Hermas.* Camden, NJ: T. Nelson, 1968.
Sparks, J. N. *The Apostolic Fathers.* Nashville: T. Nelson, 1978.
Tugwell, S. *The Apostolic Fathers.* Oxford: Geoffrey Chapman, 1989.
Vokes, F. E. "The Didache: Still Debated." *Church Quarterly* 3 (1970): 57-62.
Voobus, A. *Liturgical Traditions in the Didache.* Stockholm: Stockholm, 1968.

### *Monarchianism and Adoptionism*

Kelly, J. N. D. *Early Christian Doctrines.* London: A&C Black, 1958. Pages 115-19, 158-60.
Simonetti, M. "Sabellio e il sabellianismo." *Studi Storico Religiosi* 4 (1980): 7-28.
Uribarri-Bilbao, G. *Monarquia y Trinidad: El concepto teológico 'monarchia' en la controversía monarquiana.* Madrid: University Pontificia Comillas de Madrid, 1996.

### *The Logos Theologians*

Barnard, L. W. *Justin Martyr: His Life and Thought.* Cambridge: Cambridge University Press, 1967.
Barnes, T. D. *Tertullian: A Historical and Literary Study.* Oxford: Clarendon, 1971.
Bery, A. *Saint Justin: sa vie et sa doctrine.* Paris: Bloud, 1901.
Butterworth, R., trans. *Hippolytus: The Contra Noetum.* London: Heythrop College, University of London Press, 1977.
Chadwick, H. *Early Christian Thought and the Classical Tradition.* Oxford: Clarendon, 1966. Pages 1-30.
Dix, G., trans. *The Treatise on the Apostolic Tradition of St. Hippolytus of Rome.* London: SPCK, 1968.
Goodenough, E. R. *The Theology of Justin Martyr.* Jena: Frommann, 1923.
Holmes, P., and J. Morgan. *The Importance of Tertullian in the Development of Christian Dogma.* London: K. Paul, Trench, Teubner, 1928.
Holte, R. "Logos Spermatikos: Christianity and Ancient Philosophy According to St. Justin's Apologies." *Studia Theologica* 12 (1958): 109-68.
Lawson, J. *The Biblical Theology of St. Irenaeus.* London: Epworth, 1948.
Nielsen, J. T. *Adam and Christ in the Theology of Irenaeus of Lyons.* Assen: Van Gorcum, 1968.
Osborn, E. *Tertullian: First Theologian of the West.* Cambridge: Cambridge University Press, 1977.
Osborne, C. *Rethinking Early Greek Philosophy: Hippolytus of Rome and the Pre-Socratics.* Ithaca, NY: Cornell University Press, 1987.
Papandrea, J. L. *The Trinitarian Theology of Novatian of Rome: A Study in Third Century*

*Orthodoxy.* New York: Mellen, 2008.

Powell, D. L. "The Schism of Hippolytus." *StPatr* 12 (1975): 449-56.

Roberts, R. *The Theology of Tertullian.* London: Epworth, 1924.

Thelwell, S., trans. *Works of Tertullian. ANF* vols. 3-4. Edinburgh, 1885.

Trakatellis, D. *The Pre-Existence of Christ in Justin Martyr.* Missoula, MT: Scholars Press, 1976.

Wingren, G. *Man and the Incarnation: A Study in the Biblical Theology of Irenaeus.* Edinburgh: Oliver and Boyd, 1959.

# BLOOD IN THE ARENA

The Age of Persecutions and Resistance:
Second to Third Centuries

### CHRISTIANS IN THE ROMAN IMPERIAL SIGHTLINE

That one so readily associates images of the early Christians with martyrs fending off wild beasts in the Roman arenas, or believers undergoing horrendous tortures in prisons, is a testimony not only to the savagery of life in the ancient world, generally speaking, but also to the propaganda machine that was the church's literary effort in the domain of martyrology.[1] The word *martyrology* means the study or chronicles of the martyrs: a concept that Christianity elevated to a highly visible point in its projection of a self-definition over and against the larger society of its time. *Martyr* is the Greek term for witness, and if a believer was forced to choose between execution and faith, it was regarded as the highest eschatological testimony if that faith endured to the death.[2] This was why martyrs and martyrdoms caught the attention of the Christian communities across the world, perhaps even more than they caught the attention of oppressive authorities who instigated persecutions. To the latter this perseverance was merely a political annoyance, demonstrating the mental instability or social misanthropy of this new group of zealots. To the church, however, endurance to the death became a focal point of theological self-articulation.

The sufferings of the martyrs demonstrated to the surviving community members the fundamental character of Christians as the eschatological community of the eighth day.[3] The blood of the martyrs (as is sketched out in the book of Revelation) was thought by many in the second and third centuries to be that last sacrifice that

---

[1] Arenas were so named because of the sand strewn on the display floors to absorb blood and animal waste.

[2] *Martyr* was the language the early Christians used habitually even when in Italy. The Roman liturgy was celebrated in Greek until the fourth century.

[3] The seven days of creation were regarded as consummated by the "eighth day" of the impending new age, or kingdom of God.

called to the God of heaven to come in vindication of his suffering elect and end the course of world history dominated by evil powers. But not all those Christians challenged to deny their faith, of course, chose the thorny way of martyrdom. Many (and the numbers become increasingly problematic for church authorities in the early fourth century) chose the path of least resistance and argued that a little conformism here and there (a grain of incense offered to the divine genius of the emperor, perhaps) was "not too bad"; "not really idolatry," if all things were considered. Those who were brought to trial and agreed to renounce their faith in times of oppression were called the *lapsi* or the *sacrificati*, depending on whether they had merely "fudged" their Christianity or had actually volunteered to sacrifice to the old gods in order to prove their renunciation of the Christian religion. Persecution in the early era, as has happened in many ages since, devastated the unity and coherence of the community. It does not just simply produce a floral bouquet of inspiring martyrs; it sets family against family, house against house, and leaves in its aftermath a wake of distrust and resentment. So it was with the early church. The darker side of the reverential cult of the martyrs is the tormented process of reconciliation that the church had to instigate to cater to its more frightened members who failed their test. Keeping a lively and proud focus on those who had accepted death freely, for the sake of the gospel, the Christian apologists and martyrologists deliberately used rhetoric to turn the propaganda of the oppressors back against themselves and try to rally a spirit of resistance and bravery among ordinary Christians under immense duress.

Their rhetoric on this score, however, was fascinatingly powerful. In terms of simple numbers of martyrs that Christianity can show, for example, the martyrs of the twentieth century alone probably outweigh the number of Christian martyrs of all the preceding nineteen centuries put together. That we do not customarily think this way and instead see the second and third centuries as the great ages of resistance throws some light on the strength of that magnifying lens of the early Christian theology of martyrdom, as well as the way the church in its later centuries has generally stepped away considerably from the eschatological matrix of its self-definition. In short, then, persecutions were a powerful force in shaping the early Christian movement, both in real-political and in ideological terms.

The word *persecution* derives from the early Roman legal concept of "prosecuting" (*persequi*) those dissidents who were regarded as especially dangerous to the stability of the state. From the viewpoint of official authorities, Christians were first and foremost a local problem to be dealt with by the normal methods of suppression invoked throughout the empire's large extent. There were many ways of social control available to the extended Roman government in antiquity. In local towns governance was largely devolved. The upper classes formed the political council of governance, responsible for tax matters and enforcement of social stability. The large extent of the slave class, who were governed by harshly repressive laws, was of necessity held under control by readily available recourse to military might, if necessary. Usually it was not necessary, the ever-present readiness to resort to extreme violence being enough not to have to call on it. If necessary, the military governor could be called on to back up any especially violent or organized tumult that the normal governance by magistrates could not handle with its own militia.

The law courts would predominantly deal with affairs of dispute between the upper classes, who received "special treatment" under law. Those who were lowborn (and that included the majority) were held in legal (and social) contempt most of the time, and physical punishments such as whipping, chaining, beatings, and imprisonments would be widely and vigorously applied, as being particularly fitted to them. Low birth, low educational status, and rough social manners were regarded as innate character showing through. Slaves and the vulgar uneducated were not made so: they were born so. Even among Christian writers this Greco-Roman sense of the innate quality of human beings emerging in their predestined social rank was hard to shift. There was little sense visible in antiquity (hardly any in extant writings) of social privilege being a self-referential circle. Imprisonment was at the expense of the one imprisoned and was a dire threat not only because of the financial and social ruin it always caused or the threat of enslavement it brought with it, but also because of what horrors could casually be inflicted on one in prison.

But religion was always a different matter in the ancient world. Crimes against religion fell into a special category in the Roman Empire. They carried an automatic death penalty. Offenses committed against Roman state religion were doubly indemnified: as well as being regarded as blasphemy against the gods and disruptions of the bond of religion that was supposed to underlie society (for Roman antiquity was anything but a secular state), crimes against imperial religion were evidently treasonable, as they defied the sacred authority of the emperor himself, the supreme pontiff (*pontifex maximus*) of Roman religion. Sacrilege against the monarch was by definition *lèse majesté* (that is, a crime against the dignity of the the sovereign) and attracted an immediate penalty of death by the most excruciating and public manner possible (to discourage others), as well as needing nothing more in terms of a trial than to establish that the defendants were indeed religious dissidents (by virtue of their refusal to conduct rites of honor to the divine emperor). Much literature about the trials of the martyrs has survived because of the careful archiving work of the Christians themselves.[4]

These varied methods of punishment of dissidence were applied with varying degrees of enforcement depending on the hostility of the local community (and the character of the provincial governor and local magistrates). In most sources up to the fourth century (when imperial authorities really did become conscious that the Christian movement represented an international force that had to be contended with), the Roman authorities seem to have been simultaneously bewildered by the tenacity shown by Christians in their refusal to offer conformist state sacrifices and angered by their antisocial "misanthropy." The general attitude was that everyone knew that state religion was a formality—and so why would anyone not want to take part in it alongside the private devotional religion that they might wish to adopt personally?

The stubbornness of the Christians in refusing to honor any other god than the one Father and his kingly Son who would soon come to judge the wicked struck the upper-class authorities in a wide swath of Roman culture, from great city to small town, as a distasteful fundamentalism in a world that called for pluralisms. Paradoxically, therefore, the authorities regarded their suppression of the Christians as an exercise in favor of religious tolerance, while the Christian themselves saw it as a supreme example of religious intolerance. What had happened, almost without them noticing it at first, was that Christianity had brought into social discussion the concept of freedom of religion: that the devotion one followed should not to be determined by the state. This was a new idea altogether, and it seemed contradictory to fundamental views of ancient religion: that the duty of the religious believer was to worship the gods for the sake of petitioning social stability. Religious governance in the cause of pursuing conformity to traditional values was thus the first duty of the wise ruler. This charge of misanthropy that was leveled against the church led to the earliest Christian communities suffering a large degree of local mob resentment across a wide range of territories, which often spilled out in periods of officially endorsed persecutions.

From the viewpoint of most Christians, however, these state persecutions were not primarily a local or merely a legal matter, not even fundamentally about freedom of worship, but were rather an eschatological sign of the end times. The sufferings they called down on their heads for their worship of Christ were for them a manifestation of the rage of the prince of the world, the evil spirit, against the elect bride, the church, which was the community of salvation in the last age. Persecutions sponsored by the Roman state, which Scripture had already identified as the great beast, the

---

[4] Later martyr narratives become more and more rhetorically "staged" as moral tales among the Christians, but the first martyrologies are clearly based on actual note taking of the trials themselves.

agent of the satanic "dragon" (Rev 13:1-10), were thus taken as an apocalyptic sign of the end times, foretold as such by Jesus (Mk 10:17, 39; Jn 15:17-21), who thus, in the passion narrative, became the archetype of all Christian martyr resistance.

This theological perspective explains why the church carefully recorded the "acts" of the martyrs, the instances of each church community contending with apocalyptic evil, and was very conscious of the importance of having martyrs in each community to validate its powers as a congregation of the new age. Martyrs were widely believed to pass immediately from this world into the proximity of the supreme martyr, Christ, and to be able to exercise a powerful ministry of intercession on behalf of their local churches. All their sins were forgiven in the shedding of their blood, and they were given a throne of glory, reigning alongside Christ until he came again in glory. This is why the recording of the persecutions was precise and (generally) accurate from the outset of Christianity (beginning with the account of the protomartyr, Stephen, in Acts 7:60, and the execution of James and arrest of Peter in Acts 12:2-3).

The theological attention given by the church to the eschatological nature of the persecutions, of course, gives them a "priority" and a significance in ecclesiastical sources that they did not necessarily have in, for example, a broader view of the history of the period. Paul is described by the writer of Acts as being "persecuted from city to city" (Acts 17:10-13), which really means little more than he caused hostile resentment among the local Jewish congregations by his preaching visits there, and sometimes that blew over into street disturbances that caught the attention of the local council. It is unclear at times whether he has to leave town quickly to avoid arrest by council officials or by local thugs employed by his enemies, or even if these two things overlapped. Of course, if the disturbance threatened the city's peace and public order, then the formal Roman governmental machinery would come into play. Paul's case was different from many that followed in the next generation, as the Roman administrators clearly had wind of the large donations he had brought to the Jerusalem church before he was arrested, and they were undoubtedly motivated by venal interest.

Several of the early state persecutions were intent on forcing the rising Christian middle class to conform by threatening against them loss of property and civic rights rather than compulsory capital charges. Others focused only on leading Christian teachers, or recent converts, clearly to set an example against conversions. But for the church they were all the same, and in its perspective these persecutions were always addressed against "the church of Christ" indiscriminately, thus giving the notion of "Roman persecutions" a historical continuity and coherence that they often did not have, being in many cases merely ad hoc responses and tentative policies, or even just examples of the kind of random mob violence or official callousness that was a daily commonplace in ancient cities.

***Nero's persecution.*** The first of the imperial persecutions was that of Nero, the executioner of Peter and (probably) Paul, and always regarded ever after by Christian memory as the archetypal evil genius of a long series of "wicked emperors" to follow. The idea of that series of the wicked kings is brought out brilliantly by fourth-century writer Lactantius in his treatise *On the Deaths of the Persecutors*, in which he demonstrates (in parallel to the books of Maccabees) how the evil emperors (as defined more or less entirely by their persecution policies) were cast down by God in violent deaths, whereas the good emperors flourished, most notably Constantine**,** who abolished all persecution of the church and so was rewarded by God with supreme power. Nero's persecution in AD 64 was stimulated by a desire to be seen to be doing something in response to the disastrous fire of Rome. As a highly unpopular, foreign, and non-common-worshiping group, the Christians were an easy target and were treated with spectacular cruelty by the emperor. His choice of this minority group was partly designed to placate the anger of the gods (whose ire had obviously resulted in the great fire), while cathartically purging the anger of the city populace and serving to distract it away from the imperial palace.

This violent pogrom was restricted to the city itself, but it left a sharp memory for generations to come because it affected a Christian community that was both highly visible to other Christians and had thought itself relatively safely established. It is quite possibly reflected in Mark's Gospel, where the parable of the sower is adapted to apply itself to a community under oppressive pressure and threat (see Mk 4:13-17). In the course of this Peter died in Nero's circus on Vatican Hill and was buried in the wall of the adjacent cemetery, the "Red Wall," which was long remembered in the community and where a century or so later a modest memorial was placed around his *loculus*.[5] In the fourth century, when Constantine occupied the capital and gave his favor to the church, the great basilica church of Saint Peter's was raised as a martyr memorial directly over the spot. The Red Wall *loculus* still exists today, many feet directly under the high altar of the present-day (Renaissance) church.[6]

***Domitian's persecution.*** Christian commentators list Domitian as the second persecutor, in AD 95.[7] His repressive measures were more focused than Nero's attempt to divert mob anger. The Christian movement in his time seemed to have truly

---

[5]The niche in the wall where his bones were placed in accordance with Jewish and Christian custom. Pagan funerals centered on cremation and an urn that contained ashes.
[6]For a lively account of the archaeological search for the *loculus*, see J. E. Walsh, *The Bones of St. Peter* (New York: Doubleday, 1985).
[7]Eusebius, *Ecclesiastical History* 4.26.8; Tertullian, *Apologeticus* 5.4.

become more socially mobile. The emperor Domitian was chiefly concerned not with local proletarian types who had converted to the faith but specifically with members of the Roman nobility who were showing a degree of attraction to what was called "Jewish ideas" in morality and worship. Domitian despised this movement as eroding traditional Roman values and traditions among the very class who were supposed to uphold them as the guardians of Roman culture. Domitilla, the emperor's niece, was possibly a Christian and in this period was exiled to the island of Ponza, where her "cell" became a church cult center in the fourth century.[8] Her husband, Flavius Clemens, was executed for (among other things) "Jewish sympathies." He has been, for a long time past, conflated with and identified as Clement of Rome, one of the greatest early leaders of the Roman Christians. Now it is generally thought that Pope Clement was more likely related to the clan of Flavius Clemens the aristocrat, perhaps as a freedman client.

Domitian's desire to deify himself confirmed the worst suspicions of Christians of his time: once again that this persecution was no mere political accident but related to the ever-present hostility of the demons, who hated the church because it led society to true worship and denied the evil spirits (for so the Christians defined the gods) their cultic rites in the temples. Domitian's persecution is reflected in several Christian sources, and not least in the New Testament book of Revelation (Rev 2:13; 20:4), which it brought into being as a reactive apologia.[9] It was the cause of the apostle John's exile to Patmos and the curious case of the summoning of the last known relatives of Jesus to Rome for legal examination, according to Hegesippus.[10] At this period at Rome, Christianity was lumped in together with the blanket descriptor "Jewish practices," though by the end of the first century Roman law would start to make a clear distinction between them—one greatly to the detriment of Christianity, since it lost any claim it previously had for special consideration. Jewish religion was given favored status under pagan Roman law: it was held to be antique, morally refined, and sufficiently reverential in so far as it prayed for the well-being of the emperor. Christianity, on the other hand, was increasingly regarded as a religion of the lower classes, advocating the worship of a condemned criminal who had taught a revolutionary idea of equality of love and freedom: dangerous ideas that had no regard for traditional religious rites, the divine authority of kings, or the sustenance of the status quo. It was something to be decried and if necessary put down violently.

---

[8] Eusebius, *Ecclesiastical History* 3.18.4; Jerome, *Epistle* 108.7.
[9] 1 Clement 7.1; 59.4; Shepherd of Hermas; Tertullian, *Apologeticus* 5.4; Melito of Sardis, in Eusebius's *Ecclesiastical History* 3.17-18; 4.26.9.
[10] See Eusebius, *Ecclesiastical History* 3.19-20.

***Trajan's persecution.*** The next significant state persecution was that recorded under Trajan, whose legate in Bithynia, Pliny the Younger, brings it before our eyes dramatically when he asks for special instructions sometime between AD 112 and 113.[11] Exercising his role as provincial governor in an enlightened and judicious way, he reported to his imperial master that he was unhappy at the way locals were vindictively taking the occasion of the generic state censure of Christianity to denounce a list of their social and business enemies out of mere pettiness. He tells the emperor that he has conducted investigations of his own, torturing a lower-class woman of the Christian movement in prison, whom he says was called a "deaconess," who had revealed to him enough about the movement to show that it was a fairly harmless sect.[12] Pliny clearly thinks the enlightened emperor will be equally uncomfortable with what is being done in his name by local thugs. His letter poses the question to the court whether Christians should be executed simply for "profession of the name" or only on account of demonstrable crimes.

The imperial reply is to the effect that capital punishment is certainly merited if the accused person refuses at an official tribunal to retract his exclusive devotion to Christ and would not "worship our gods," but that Christians ought not to be sought out (*conquirendi non sunt*) like common criminals. Crimes against religion were not to be considered matters of local discretion. But as long as they did not fall under the spotlight and become obviously a challenge to state religion, the Christians could be ignored. This position left Christians vastly exposed, of course, and wholly sails around Pliny's point: that it left the denunciation of Christians all too frequently in the hands of local enemies who might have much to gain from securing the deaths of their neighbours. Trajan's successor, Hadrian, similarly instructed the proconsul of Asia in AD 124–125 not to pander to local mob outcries against the Christians and to prosecute them only if they committed crimes proven under trial. Hadrian went so far as to give to the Christians the right to cross-examine those who denounced them and even prosecute their detractors under the laws of calumny.

This rescript calmed the local tendency to denounce Christian groups under vague charges of misanthropy or magic, but local outbreaks of hostility or mob violence still accounted for several other "persecutions," and in the face of these the Roman law was of no utility.[13] Some of them stood out vividly in the Christian memory, such as the

---

[11] Pliny the Younger, *Epistle* 10.96.2.
[12] Roman law did not regard a confession of the lower classes to be valid unless it had been extracted by torture.
[13] Half-heard reports of what the Christians did in their (closed) worship meetings circulated among the townspeople and emerged as suspicions of sexual orgies (probably from news of the liturgical kiss of peace) and ritual murder (eating the Eucharist as the flesh of Christ, as Christian theologian Minucius Felix suggests in his *Apology* [*Octavius* 9] to the outraged pagan Caecilius; or perhaps a

execution of Justin at Rome in 165, or Polycarp at Smyrna at the same time, and also the martyrs of Lyon in 177.[14] Marcus Aurelius, during whose reign these things happened (161–180), is thus credited as the fourth of the "persecuting" emperors. It would have been a strange thing for this philosopher-ruler who imagined himself laying down a reputation as a model of sagacity and balance in his rule to have seen how the Christians classed him. His own tutor, however, Cornelius Fronto, who by all accounts was a kindly and most reasonable man, had himself denounced the Christians in the strongest terms he could think of (literally drawn from the denunciation of the Catiline conspirators) as subversive and dangerous elements: as "a sect that fled the light and conspired in the shadows" (*lucifuga et latebrosa natio*).[15]

During this same period (c. 178) pagan philosopher Celsus decided to write a strong apology for traditional Hellenistic values and composed a treatise called *The True Word*, in which he argues that the common people's hostility against Christians is well justified and based on their mutual association taking secret oaths to support one another, and not least because they undermined Roman values by negating the gods and refusing public service while advocating irrational myths of their own confection. For Celsus, the Christians were a society that ought to be sought out and eradicated for the common good.[16] In religious terms he thought they had turned back the clock, replacing an increasingly refined sense of abstract pluralism in religious philosophy that had matured out of prehistoric anthropomorphic myths, and in deifying Jesus, a crucified Jew, had betrayed all common sense and ethics. His work is among the first of the anti-Christian apologetics that takes them seriously enough to do basic research. Celsus read some of the sacred texts and offers witheringly sarcastic remarks against the Jesus tradition. It is interesting to note how the Christians of his day subjected his treatise to a judgment of silence, even though much apologetic writing took place in response to pagan attacks. It was not until a generation later that Origen took up the pen to refute his book point by point, in the process preserving it for the historical record.

***The Severan interlude.*** In 193, when the Severan dynasty occupied the imperial throne, the pressure against Christians was again eased in a more relaxed policy

---

misunderstanding of the custom of eating ritual funeral meals in the Christian sections of the cemeteries). See further A. McGowan, "Eating People: Accusations Against Christians in the Second Century," *Journal of Early Christian Studies* 2, no. 3 (1994): 413-42. Child murder was part of the darkest forms of necromantic magic in antiquity and was a capital offense, so the misinformation was extremely dangerous to Christians, as even if it was fallacious it could serve to bring them before the tribunal anyway, where their very refusal to worship the emperor could be legally construed as a capital offense.

[14]Eusebius, *Ecclesiastical History* 4.15.26, 29; 5.1; 5.2.1-8; Martyrdom of Polycarp.
[15]Minucius Felix, *Octavius* 8.4.
[16]Origen, *Contra Celsum* 8.69.

toward oriental religions in Rome. At this time Christianity resumed its missionary efforts more openly, and clearly with considerable success, for paradoxically a new wave of popular hatred against the church was soon in evidence between 197 and 212, and a series of violent local outbreaks against Christian communities occurred at Rome, Alexandria, and Latin North Africa.[17] At Carthage, Perpetua and Felicity were among the casualties. A recent convert to the church, the African lawyer Tertullian, witnessed this violence and was moved to write against it, some of the church's first considered political theology. Without it being a formal state persecution, as such, the officials where such mob violence was prevalent put in place the customary repressive laws against religious dissidents. Perpetua and Felicity, a well-born lady and her domestic servant, demonstrate a common element in the violence of this time in that it seems especially to have been directed against recent converts to the movement who came from the upper and middle classes.[18] Christian writers retrospectively attached much of the symbolic guilt for this to the emperor Septimius Severus, who in 202 had issued a rescript forbidding conversions to either Judaism or Christianity, classing him as the fifth of the persecuting emperors. Even so, between 212 and 235 there was another period of peace, culminating in the reign of Alexander Severus (222–235), who seems to have consciously tolerated the urban spread of the church and to have had Christians present in his court. It is from this period that the first recognizable Christian buildings (such as the decorated Christian *refrigeria* in the Roman catacombs and the decorated baptistery and church at Dura-Europos) are witnessed.[19]

**The persecution of Maximinus Thrax.** The Severan dynasty was violently overthrown in March 235 by Maximinus Thrax (235–238), with a concomitant purge of Alexander's Christian palace supporters.[20] This bloodletting soon spilled over into a purge of other leading Christians at Rome, including noted intellectuals and clerics. At Rome, the theologian Hippolytus and Pope Pontianus were sentenced to (a fatal) exile to the salt mines in Sardinia and perhaps also in Palestine.[21] Maximinus was himself overthrown by the Gordian dynasty in 238, and although in that year Origen (*Commentarium in evangelium Matthaei* 24.9; *Homiliae in Matthaei* 39) gloomily prophesied a future worldwide pogrom against the church, this period proved to be another brief interlude of peace. The Syrian general Philip the Arab, who rose as a warlord in this turbulent era to the status of emperor from 244 to 249, has been thought by some to have been a Christian himself. He was, at the least, a

---

[17]Tertullian, *Adversus Nationes* 1.14; *Apologeticus* 18.4.
[18]See also Eusebius, *Ecclesiastical History* 6.3.
[19]*Refrigeria* are Christian ritual rooms where memorials for the dead were celebrated.
[20]Eusebius, *Ecclesiastical History* 6.28.
[21]Origen, *Exhortation to Martyrdom*.

sympathizer. According to Eusebius and John Chrysostom, the Christian bishop of Antioch, Babylas, welcomed him to the church but made him stand among the penitents to hear the Paschal liturgy (on account of his killing).[22] Eusebius also records that Philip and his wife received letters from Origen.

***The Decian persecution.*** The assassination of Philip in 249, which brought Decius, the seventh persecutor, to the throne (249-251), also brought with it another strong public reaction to the visibly growing extent and power of Christians and a determined attempt to kill off the church. Christians had again become visible in the highest political circles as well as commonly known in the cities and towns. Decius found it convenient to lay the blame for Rome's military and political decline at the door of the blatant Christian rejection of traditional Roman values, and in January 250 he ordered that the annual sacrifice on the Capitoline Hill to the gods of Rome should be solemnly observed in all the provincial capitals too. To mark the occasion he arrested many prominent Christian leaders. Bishops Fabian of Rome and Babylas of Antioch were martyred because of their refusal to sacrifice, and the intellectual bishops Dionysius of Alexandria and Cyprian of Carthage had close escapes. After the first wave of repressions, Decius established religious commissions in many places to oversee the observance of regular and traditional sacrificial rites and to ensure that the local citizens were required to take part in them. This was designed partially to root out Christian objectors, and the legal possession of certificates (*libelli*) became a necessary proof for an individual that the mandated sacrifice had indeed been offered. Christians who conformed, either by offering incense or sacrifice (called *sacrificati* in the penitential literature) or by bribing officials to sell them a certificate (then called *libellatici*), were regarded by the church as equally guilty of apostasy.

For all the church's bravado of resistance, however, Decius's policy clearly had a considerable impact on the larger number of converts to the church. It cowed and frightened off many. It was certainly the most systematically organized of the persecutions to date. Cyprian of Carthage gives much information about the period and the disruption it caused to the life of the church. In its aftermath the Christian clergy had to institute a whole new formal ritual of penance. The rigorism of the "old days," when it was thought that baptism had once and for all wiped away all sins and there would be no need for any further forgiveness, fell before the pastoral necessity of arranging some manner of reconciliation for the lapsed. Emperor Decius was killed in battle with the Goths in 251, and his successors, Gallus and Volusianus, at first tried to continue his religious policy, but it soon ran out of steam, and the church quickly reestablished itself, as can be seen from notable advances in theological literature and

---

[22] Eusebius, *Ecclesiastical History* 6.34.

organizational matters in this period.[23] Reconciliation and a tightening of standards for clerical leaders become a key part of the lessons learned after Decius.

***The persecution of Valerian.*** The emperor Valerian (253–260), fighting a losing battle with Persia, tried once more to insist on religious devotion to the Roman gods and in 257 became the tenth of the persecuting emperors when he issued an edict that demanded Christian conformity in religion. In the following year he published an even stronger policy of suppression. According to its terms, Christian clergy would be arrested and summarily executed; Roman senators and knights who professed Christianity would thereby lose rank and property; matrons would suffer confiscation of all goods and be exiled; civil servants would be reduced to slavery and sent to labor camps.[24] In 258 Cyprian of Carthage, an aristocrat who had recently converted and been elevated as clerical leader, was brought out of his house arrest and condemned to die for the crime of sacrilege and for "posing as an enemy of the gods of Rome." The Valerian persecution was not regarded by the Christians as anything like as terrible as those of Decius or later Diocletian, but it probably was one of the most severe the church ever suffered, though not of long duration. It was aimed at shattering the church's leadership and at frightening off upper-class membership: a testimony to how successful the Christians must already have been in attracting intelligentsia to their ranks.

Valerian was captured by the Persians while fighting at Edessa in 260. He would be kept as a fattened hostage for the rest of his life, but after death his body was flayed and the skin stuffed and dyed imperial purple to hang, swinging, in the temple of the Persian gods as a triumphant votive offering. It was a particularly merited punishment as far as the Christians were concerned. His son Gallienus (253–268) issued a rescript for toleration of the church in 262, more or less as soon as he had stabilized the throne. For the next forty years the church enjoyed political stability and made great advances.

***The Diocletianic persecution.*** The next time of crisis, therefore, struck with particular force and so earned the name of "Great Persecution."[25] This lasted in the Western half of the empire from 303 to 305, and in the Eastern empire from 303 to 312. Diocletian introduced a policy of conservative religious reform as part of a larger package of measures he introduced designed to stabilize the empire. It has been argued that members of his own family were probably Christian sympathizers, and that may be why his own attitude was ambivalent in regard to a violent persecution; but his immediate deputy, the Caesar Galerius, was more overtly hostile to the Christian cause and persuaded Diocletian to demand religious conformity by an empire-wide edict in February 303. Once this was published, refusal to obey became, as usual, a capital

---

[23]Cyprian, *Epistle* 59.8.
[24]Cyprian, *Epistle* 80.
[25]Eusebius, *Ecclesiastical History* 8.6.10.

offense. The terms of the edict still avoided mentioning the death penalty but ordered the destruction of Christian churches, the burning of all copies of the Scriptures, the social degradation of upper-class believers, the reduction to slavery of civil servants, and the general loss of legal rights by stubbornly professing Christians. An additional edict soon demanded the widespread arrest of the clergy, but the prison system was then so overloaded that this was amended to require them all to offer sacrifice and then be set free. Many were tortured to ensure their conformity. Some became heroic martyrs at this time (celebrated in Eusebius's *On the Martyrs of Palestine*), though many lapsed out of fear, and the destruction of the clerical infrastructure, along with the burning of the churches, proved devastating.

Early in 304, following Diocletian's sickness and temporary retirement, Galerius stepped up the measures more strictly and issued an edict of his own demanding that all citizens offer a sacrifice and a libation to the gods under pain of death. This caused turmoil among the Christians in North Africa and resulted in a large number of public executions: something that burned the episode into the larger Christian consciousness. In 305 Diocletian and his senior colleague Maximian resigned as regnant emperors in the West as part of a planned retirement system he had initiated to stabilize the imperial succession. It was intended to avert the recurrence of civil war fought over the throne, but it caused one. The new officially designated leaders were soon distracted by a number of rival claimants marshaling armies. This was the time in which Constantine rose to preeminence, not accidentally tying his fortunes to his self-positioning as a protector of Christians. In all likelihood his mother, Helena, had been Christian. Constantine himself had been tutored by the Christian theologian-politician Lactantius when the latter was chief rhetorician of the capital city, and he himself was held hostage in Nicomedia by Diocletian to secure his father Constantius's good behaviour as junior caesar in the West.

In the eastern provinces, where Galerius was now the senior emperor, the persecution continued. In spring 306 his new junior, Maximin Daia, issued an edict requiring all provincial governors to ensure their people sacrificed. In Palestine this was heavily enforced (producing a famous cluster of early Palestinian martyrs), but elsewhere it was sporadically observed through 309, after which it became increasingly obvious to all concerned that it was an ineffective policy. In 311 Galerius fell mortally ill and, convinced that he had unwisely angered the Christian god, decided to rescind the policy. He now demanded merely that Christians should pray for the welfare of the state and for the healing of himself, and he allowed them to rebuild their churches.[26] Six days later, this twelfth of the persecutors died. His successor,

---

[26]Ibid., 8.17.3-10.

Maximin Daia, took over the command of his territories and, without specifically voiding Galerius's edict, made it clear that he himself encouraged local authorities to assault Christian communities and target any significant leaders they could find. This "half-official" violence accounted for more outbreaks of persecution in Nicomedia, Tyre, and Antioch.[27]

At this time there was an even more violent episode of oppression in Egypt, during which renowned theologian-bishop Peter of Alexandria was martyred.[28] The last victim of this pogrom was the internationally famous theologian Lucian, bishop of Antioch, who died in January 312. Emperor Maximin Daia himself died in 313, just as Constantine had finally conquered his last Western rival, Emperor Maxentius, at Rome, and was now free to turn his armies toward the East. In that same year a formal reconciliation of Constantine and Licinius, the latter of whom was now augustus of the whole East, brought a formal end to the Great Persecution. This decree, known now as the Edict of Milan, raised the hopes of Christians throughout both of the empire's halves and signaled widely that Constantine was to be their significant protector. It has been hailed as the first great rescript of official religious toleration in European civilization. In the Western provinces under his direct control, Constantine now clearly encouraged the Christians. Many served in his army, and he already saw (which became his explicit policy later on) that the bishops among them fulfilled the function of democratically accessible local magistrates. Constantine has traditionally been regarded as the champion and savior of the Christians in the early fourth century. While his gifts to the church of protection, political favor, and financial restitution cannot be underestimated, it should equally not be forgotten what Constantine himself got from the Christians: widespread political support and soldiers serving in the army that had permitted his ascendancy.

As Constantine's aspirations to supreme power became more and more obvious, Licinius, the augustus of the Eastern provinces, decided to fall back once more on the alternative power bases of the old religion and its traditional supporters. He encouraged a policy of sporadic incidents of hostility to the Christians of the East. This Constantine seized on, in 324, as justification to topple Licinius from power as the last of the persecutor emperors, leaving his own way clear to supreme monarchy over the empire's Eastern and Western divisions. He and his dynasty were, from that point onward, intimately associated with the Christian movement, and in the later fourth century the church enjoyed unparalleled peace and growth. There was a brief but halfhearted effort to hinder the church's cause by the emperor Julian (361–363),

---

[27]Ibid., 9.7.10-11.
[28]Ibid., 9.9.4-5.

but the latter's death (possibly by the hands of Christian assassins in the army) effectively spelled the end of pagan emperors ordering persecutions against the church.[29] In the West there would be a considerable number of further persecutions in the fifth and sixth centuries, as invading Gothic Arian kings made their power felt over native Nicene Catholics, and in Byzantium, zealous Christian emperors imposing their varieties of orthodoxy in later centuries would equally be designated by many sources as "wicked persecutors," but all of this was strictly "by analogy" compared to what had happened between the late first and early fourth centuries.

***The memory of a persecuted community.*** This extraordinarily fast and popular emergence of the Christian movement in Roman society had clearly worried not only official authorities but even ordinary townspeople, who saw in their very midst a new kind of "belonging" emerging radically, which frightened them into violent reaction. The Christian martyr accounts generally try to show the martyrs as supremely reasonable in their attitudes: defenders of the rights of humanity, free speech, and freedom of spirit. But there were some who simply appeared to the persecuting authorities as dangerously mad zealots with a death wish.[30] Most of the intellectual commentators who took any notice of the Christian martyrdoms regard them with great distaste. Tacitus the historian thought that their refusal to conform to the laws manifested only a "resolute hatred for the human race."[31] Pliny the Younger saw Christian resisters only as an example of "rebelliousness and invincible obstinacy."[32] Marcus Aurelius, aware of the resolution with which they faced death, did not find it a badge of courage but rather of "vulgar audacity."[33] The Roman writers unanimously speak (as their philosophy had taught them) from a lofty superiority that regarded the common man as little more than a brute waiting for an opportunity to cause unrest and constantly needing the suppressive guidance of his betters. But the Christian accounts, perhaps with a view to more common attitudes even though they are educated, indicate that while there was much mob hostility,

---

[29]Julian is denounced in Gregory of Nazianzus's *Orations* 4-5, *Contra Julianum*. These are the finest philippics written in Greek since the time of Demosthenes. Their style is ostentatiously brilliant, to give mocking lie to the emperor's insistence that Christians, having renounced the gods the Hellenistic literature celebrates, had thereby lost the right to that literary tradition. "O most foolish of men," Gregory says, "to think he could deprive the Christians of their Logos [divine Word/discourse]."

[30]And Tertullian himself, a great advocate for martyrs' courage, is aware that some zealots were worrying in their hatred of the pagan authorities and in their determined zeal to offer themselves up for martyrdom, something that must have been a nightmare for the clerical leaders of the church, who also had a duty to protect their flock as much as possible. See Tertullian, *Ad Scapulam* 5; *Apologeticus* 50.1.

[31]Tacitus, *Annals of Imperial Rome* 15.44.6.

[32]Pliny the Younger, *Epistle* 10.96.3.

[33]Marcus Aurelius, *Meditations* 11.3.3.

sometimes the courage of the martyrs had an effect in softening some people's hearts, winning their admiration, and on occasion even inducting them to the church. Tertullian made much of this and coined his famous aphorism that the "blood [of the martyrs] is the seed of the Christians."[34] Even Tacitus, annoyed though he was about it, admitted this happened in his account of Nero's persecution.[35]

Issues of an appeal to freedom of religion struck the ancient authorities as disingenuous in a world where all parties sensed that the favor of the gods was what determined the rise or fall of nation-states. Rome had flourished because of the favor of its own gods. To despise those gods was to work against the empire as drastically as to take up arms. The Scriptures of the Christians taught them the same truth: those who worshiped the true God would be blessed, and those who venerated idols would be cast aside by God. In the early fourth century theologian-rhetor Lactantius would make this claim very explicitly on behalf of Christians, basing his evidence on the book of Maccabees, drawing a direct parallel between the church and the Maccabean warriors in revolt and listing all the scriptural instances where God cast down wicked kings into the dust. By then, of course, he had thrown off the need for caution in the light of the persecution by Galerius, and he used the book, *The Deaths of the Persecutors*, to propagandize the ascent of Constantine as the church's defender.

Neither the Romans on the one side or the Jews and Christians on the other had any real confidence, therefore, in the argument that there was any such thing as a secular state that would, or should, permit complete freedom of religion. We cannot interpolate this modern value into late antiquity. Christians across the ranks of the church regarded martyrs as exemplifying the church's role as eschatological precipitator. The church was the shining witness to divine truth in an age of demonic worship, in their minds. Accordingly, the violent rage they roused against themselves was not merely a political affair but a manifestation of the rage of the demons who had been thwarted by Christ and an attempt to stop the work of his Spirit on earth. The political violence, in other words, was a continuing of the machinations of Satan that had caused the passion of Christ in the first place and now still thought it could overcome the grace of the resurrection by slaughtering the church and wiping it off the face of the earth. For Christian believers, Christ's words of apocalyptic encouragement were vividly real (Mt 16:18), and it was commonly taught within the communities that martyrs would ascend directly to heaven, to sit with Christ, not waiting in some form of peaceful Hades until the last day.[36] Their blood

---

[34]*Apologeticus* 50.13; *To Diognetus* 7.7-9.
[35]In the short reader below.
[36]Irenaeus, *Adversus Haereses* 4.33.9; Hippolytus, *Commentariem in Danielem* 2.37.3; Tertullian, *The Scorpion's Sting* 10.12; *On the Resurrection* 43; *On the Soul* 55.

shed for Christ was a mimesis of Christ's own passion, and it was imbued with some of his divine grace, causing the remission of all their sins and winning reconciliation for penitents for whom they advocated in heaven.[37] Gaining immediate admittance into paradise meant for the church that these great saints would continue actively working as intercessors for the church on earth.

The cult of the martyrs grew apace in the age of persecutions, and when that era had passed, it remained the custom to build churches in honor of the martyrs and eventually to bring their relics inside the churches (a revolutionary change of social attitude toward death) to bring the martyr cult in close parallel to the eucharistic celebration. Relics, first of the martyrs and then of other categories of Christian saints, became a very real and potent encapsulation of the sense of divine presence among the early Christians. The very bones were regarded as imbued with divine grace and intercessory power. From the third century onward those who were arrested and suffered for the faith but had not been executed were given high honor in the community as "confessors."[38] Their prayers were felt to carry great power before God, and many Christians approached them asking for intercession for the forgiveness of sins.

In the layout of ancient cemeteries the graves are generally speaking set out haphazardly, without pattern. But taking a bird's-eye view of the plan, one can see immediately where an early Christian martyr has been laid to rest: for suddenly all the graves adjacent to it start being laid out in parallel and crowding as near as possible. The church vividly believed that these were living intercessors, and on the day of judgment people wished to be near them as their bodies were resurrected. This graphic belief was no mere trope. Ordinary Christians passionately wanted to be near their heavenly patrons. The prominent cult of the martyrs, though it is perhaps not something that immediately speaks to contemporary Christian experience, is one way of seeing how the early church organized its view of the world in the time of political distress.[39]

The age of persecutions, then, served to temper the new movement in extraordinary ways. It hardened the church's sense of not wishing to compromise in any pluralist way with pagan ritual. It gave the Christians a very tightly drawn community sense. If the second century had offered a very "fertile" and "varied" set of Christian profiles, the age of persecutions drew the boundaries of ecclesial belonging much more tightly. Out of it emerged a much stronger sense of Christian polity and

---

[37]Tertullian, *On Baptism* 16; *To the Martyrs* 1; Origen, *Exhortation to Martyrdom* 30; *Apostolic Tradition* 19; *Commentarii in evangelium Joannis* 6.281-283; Cyprian, *Epistle* 23.
[38]Eusebius, *Ecclesiastical History* 5.2.3-4.
[39]See further J. A. McGuckin, "Martyr Devotion in the Alexandrian School (Origen to Athanasius)," in *Martyrs & Martyrologies*, Studies in Church History 30 (Oxford: Blackwell, 1993), 35-45; reprinted in *Recent Studies in Church History*, ed. E. Ferguson, vol. 5 (Hamden, CT: Garland, 1999).

an enhanced role for the executive presidency of the *episkopoi*, who had, by and large, come out of their immense pastoral challenges with increased prestige and governance skills. In its ever more expanding liturgical calendar the church kept the memories of its many martyrs alive, by doing so also underscoring its highly eschatological interpretation of political society, something that can be seen in fourth- and fifth-century political theologians Lactantius and Augustine.[40] The church had been born into persecution and emerged as a powerful force of resistance through four centuries of difficult circumstances. Ever afterward that memory became for it a kind of archetypal encouragement for its (many) later troubles.

## ROMAN IDEAS ON LAW AND RELIGION

*The principate and dominate (27 BC to AD 313).* The Roman legal system was an ancient one, rooted in religious rites. It was part and parcel of Roman religion. Law codes had first arisen in Roman prehistory as ways of securing oaths between people and having them witnessed by priests in the temples of the gods. *Lex*, or law, was thus a binding of people socially under the eye of the Roman gods. Obviously, as the Latin empire spread out by conquest to become first an international and then a global reality, trade with foreign peoples at great distances pressured Roman law to become something far more universal in its turn, and the legal system started to develop extensively. For our concerns here, in relating Roman law to the church in its early centuries and seeing why so much conflict occurred, we can turn our attention to the later stages of that story: the impact of the system of emperors and how their acquisition of monarchical power affected law.

Because of Augustus's pretense that he would never assume monarchical power, this period has been called the principate (derived from the emperor's claim to a status merely as "first citizen" or *princeps*). Of course Augustus made sure that the two bases of the real monarchical power he needed were secured in his person (1) in terms of political control of the law (and thus he became the chief magistrate and appellate adjudicator), and (2) in terms of his assumption of the role of commander-in-chief of the armies of Rome *imperator* (commander or emperor). Controlling the political aspect of law and being able to back up his claims with might enabled Augustus to continue the pretense of a historic republic and allowed him to make radical changes in the name of traditional reforms. His self-portrayal was as "restorer of the republic." So it was that from 27 BC onward the personal role of the emperor became more and more the central crux in the issue of making and promulgating Roman law. He managed the change to monarchical domination quietly,

---

[40]In the former's *Divine Institutes* and *Deaths of the Persecutors*, and in the latter's *City of God*.

by using a clever collection of republican offices. He allocated to himself the proconsular power, which meant he had charge of all the armies of Rome in the frontier provinces; the consular power, which gave him supreme authority in the city of Rome itself; the powers of the tribunate, which meant he assumed direction of the law, personally approving all the traditional magistracies; and the headship of all religious affairs in assuming (after 12 BC) the office of pontifex maximus.[41]

Augustus and the senate clung to the illusion that he was merely the "first citizen" for a long time. He did not wish to supplant the established processes of lawmaking by assuming legislative powers based solely on his personal force of dominion (as winner of the civil war). This remained a principle of the early principate until the emperors after Diocletian cast aside the illusion and acted for what they were, the absolute monarchs now using the law and the senate as their instruments. By this time we call the imperial era the dominate. It is the principate and dominate that led into the Christian revolution under Constantine, which in turn paved the way for a more thoroughgoing revision of the terms and principles of Roman law under the Christians.[42] Nevertheless, the emperors personally assumed significant and increasing magisterial powers, which expanded over time into the Byzantine system of the emperor having supreme command over the issuing of law as its *fons et origo*. He became the law personified. Popular assemblies that once had the capacity to issue binding legal statutes under the purview of the praetor were abolished by the principate. By 125 the praetor's control of legal administrative matters was also abolished. Hadrian set the seal on this in 131 when he decreed that all previous praetorian decrees were now to be codified with no further additions permitted. Henceforth the emperor would fulfill all the praetor's ancient legal duties by personal edict.

Despite such centralizing momentum, of course, the enforcement of law was not universally equitable in all parts of the empire. Much depended on the zeal (or bigotry) of local governors. The further one got from the ambit of the capital, the more uneven things became. The often-repeated demands in the law codes for the same rulings to be observed suggests that Roman legislation was neither absolute nor assured everywhere. The patchy application of penal laws against Christians in various provinces also testifies to this quite clearly. But the intent was there, nevertheless, to establish the law as a uniform pattern of "good standard" throughout the empire's provinces.

One result of this centralizing movement, and also one that started to look to legal rescripts more as a universal charter than a simple record of precedence cases, was the shifting of the whole Roman legal system, by the end of the third century,

---

[41]The great majority of Rome's armed forces were located in the frontier provinces.
[42]See further J. A. McGuckin, *The Ascent of Christian Law: Patristic and Byzantine Reformulations of Antique Civilization* (Crestwood, NY: St. Vladimir's Seminary Press, 2012).

away from the formulary system that had earlier been in use and toward a new system of *cognitio extraordinaria*. Most private Roman law before the third century had been essentially a common form of "witness to disputes," in which two disputants had agreed with their lawyers what the essence of the conflict was and had left it to the resolution of a third party on the basis of their agreed formulary. Now, the state (in the person of the emperor as supreme personification of law) assumed greater powers in its own right. In place of the older, system-based adjudication, the state itself now assumed the right to prosecute cases from beginning to end. The emperor's honor and dignity as the personification of the state became a cipher for that kind of social protection of the commonwealth and its peace, which he saw as his duty of office. This was why it became a key part of imperial administration to extend a massive oversight of the legal system through imperially appointed magistrates. Magistrates were embodied icons of the majesty of the emperor.

The change in the system not only continued the centralization aspects of the imperium but also underlined that it was now the state's duty, not that of individuals within it, to prosecute justice. What this meant in terms of reference to Christian dissidents is that the law was not first and foremost about the preservation and defense of matters of justice. It was primarily a protection of the dignity of the emperor, considered as a cipher for the well-being of the commonwealth. Christians appealed to issues of justice. Their refusal to adopt the simple pluralism of worship that underlay the divine genius of the emperors acting as *pontifices maximi* of the state religion meant that the emperors saw only the disobedience. That disobedience was a far more immediate and pressing matter than theories of equity and justice, or the niceties of worship theology, for it told the imperial officials that here was a group that did not share a belief in the invincible right of the emperor and his state. This, in short, was why Christian dissidence over matters of worship was regarded as high treason and carried the death penalty. Instead of being a universal social protection, the very law had become deadly to Christians. Some of the lawyers among the church had much to say on this topic, and their opinions would grow in later centuries to be the basis for a new Christian polity of civilization based on rights. But for the time being they were simply concerned with an urgent self-defense.

**A Christian response to Roman oppression: Tertullian's social theology.** Tertullian's legal cast of mind is woven throughout all his work. He is a classically trained rhetorician and has inside knowledge of the principles of Roman jurisprudence.[43] To this he added a sharp skill in literary apologetics and a solid grounding in ethical philosophy.

---

[43] A biographical and literary consideration of Tertullian as a Christian apologist appears later in this chapter.

He is one of the first who robustly turns against the church's upper-class opponents that charge of barbarism that they have been using to suppress Christianity violently. The bloody refusal to listen to reason, Tertullian argues, is proof positive that it is the rulers who are barbarous, not the Christians they are slaughtering without sufficient cause. As he was one of the leading Christian orators of the second century, it is natural that the legal and moral issues involved in state persecution for religious reasons would occupy his mind, and accordingly Tertullian is one of the chief witnesses to how thinking Christians responded to political oppression in this era. His central reflections on law, justice, and society appear predominantly in his *Apologeticus*, which he wrote in 197, a few years after his conversion and during the reign of Septimius Severus. Here he sets out to make the case for the toleration of the church.

He knew his primary task was to reverse the legal principles of *praescriptio*. He himself had used it to good effect in his argument in his treatise *De Praescriptione Haereticorum*. Now it had to be dismantled in reference to charges of criminal treason by virtue of refusal to worship the divine genius of the emperor. Prescription worked in Roman law by ruling "out of court" certain large arguments. Whatever their logic or apparent validity, prescription meant that they were irrelevant in the legal process. The concept still applies today extensively. When Tertullian applied it to the (Christian) heretics, he made the case that the extent of the dissident opinions these various secession groups held made them unsuitable witnesses to represent Christianity when considered as a corporate body. Their dissidence had become so extensive as to make them lose title to the name *Christian*. By applying such a "prescription," he felt their arguments could be globally synopsized and rejected from the corporate body of Christian self-definition. Now his problem was that the same argument was being used against him. However much he argued that Christians ought to be given a hearing, the juridical position of the state was that certain crimes against religion were inherently so monumentally outrageous that they de facto deprived the criminal of normal rights of due process. The same argument is often invoked today in reference to terrorism offenses.

Tertullian protests that Christians, by virtue of their religion alone, which has induced them to resist Roman religious rites, had not forfeited the protections afforded to them by law and natural justice. The contrary argument arose from the sacral character still attached to classical Roman law. Ancient Roman law regarded crimes of religion in the category of sacrilegious offenses having been committed against the order of justice established by the gods. To offset the outlaw's breaking of these sacred obligations, an expiation had to be made, a religious sacrifice of some kind to repay the debt. At first, for great crimes, the sacrifice in antique Roman society was required to be the life of the offender. Later this severity was reduced and substituted for exile and confiscation of goods. Such an exile was literally an "outlaw." He was outside the scope or protection of Roman law. He stood as an *homo sacer*, and anyone finding him on Roman soil was regarded as having fulfilled a religious duty to avenge the sacrilege committed.

In Tertullian's day this religious character still attached itself to Roman law, albeit in an extended sense. The root of the imperial persecutions of the Christians (however politically motivated in particular cases, such as Nero's reaction, or explicable on the grounds of ethnic scapegoating, such as the martyrs of Lyons) always demonstrated a profoundly religious character to the authorities and the people. The Christians had, by refusing honor to the gods who supported Rome, definitively set themselves apart from Rome. The mobs at Christian executions are genuinely outraged by the "atheists" who "hate society." The general population feared that by living in the midst of the empire yet offending the Roman gods day by day the Christians were a threat to Rome's continuing greatness and were thus a cancer that had to be extirpated. Their similar refusal to honor the divine genius of the emperor was simply a particular example of the overall and relentless dishonor the Christians offered to the gods (whom they regularly called wicked demons). By virtue of this fundamental character of their religion (the refusal to worship any but the Christian God), had not the Christians declared themselves to be de facto outlaws? It was against this type of prescriptive argument that Tertullian was forced to make one of the church's first philosophically considered legal cases.

The Christians actually learned from this the hard way that their persecutors were correct in their major premise. The way a society worships determines the moral character of the body politic. This experience of suffering persecution at the hands of a self-righteous state machinery led the Christians to articulate a major departure from the ancient religious attitudes of Roman and Near Eastern society. It can be seen clearly in the writings of Tertullian, amounting to one of the first appeals for freedom of conscience in all matters relating to religious practice and belief. This was a monumental departure from the usual theology of divine providence that applied in ancient societies (it applies alike to Jewish or pagan sources), namely that the people's veneration of the electing deity (or deities) covenantally secured the protection and flourishing of the state. Religion thus mattered politically and militarily: there could be no such thing as private devotion. The Christians in the time of Tertullian are one of the first ever groups in history to argue strongly for a certain disconnection between divine providence (let us say, as discerned in this case as the manifest will of God for a nation) and fidelity to the cult. The fuller implications of this disconnection of political favor and the sustenance of divine cult took some centuries longer to elaborate more fully. It was spectacularly written up in Augustine's *City of God*, in the fifth century, in which he demonstrates the religious fallacy of self-identification as the god-favored nation without a concomitant sense of moral scrutiny and repentance. But Tertullian certainly began that revisioning of political theology. Lactantius, in the fourth century, took it to a higher pitch in his *Divine Institutes*, in which he argues that the new *politeia* of the Christians could serve as just that freshening of moral philosophy that could regenerate Rome's aspirations for a truly world-class civilization as well as liberate it from its present delusions that military conquest and financial oppression constituted the true global civilization the world was grateful to them for bringing.

Since Tertullian could not secure a hearing in the courts, he wrote special appeals in literary form. Against the Roman claim that Christian refusal to honor the gods of Rome was fittingly a capital charge because it cosmically undermined the divine honors on which account the gods had granted Rome's political ascendancy, Tertullian answered with the acerbic response: Rome never flourished on this earth because it was religious; it gained the world precisely because it was irreligious, always ready for war and rapinage.[44] It was not the gods of Rome who dealt favors to Italy, but, on the contrary, it is the supreme God of all history, the one God of all humankind, who allots and takes away kingdoms.[45] Tertullian often comes back to this insistent setting of earthly history into an apocalyptic frame of reference. It gives much of his work an interesting sociopolitical edge. In this instance he implies that if one is to read history aright, one cannot simply read it as a story of this or that particular nation's rise to dominate others and then claim divine permission to continue the dominance. On the contrary, the evidence of a truly global religion argues that the oneness of the Deity who is the sole Lord of history makes of human culture both a search for harmony and fraternity and also a moral test: What did one society do with their moment of ascendancy: extend their brutal rapinage while they held the upper hand, or seek to raise the common good?

Because of his dislocation of simplistic providence theology, it followed that Tertullian could make what would have appeared to his ancient contemporaries as a very startling conclusion. Religion, he says, is a mater of private conscience. He is one of the first Christian theologians to argue that the peace of a diverse society demands that every human being has an inalienable right, by virtue of being a rational and moral creature, to freedom of worship. It is a privilege of our nature, he

---

[44]*Apologeticus* 25.
[45]Ibid., 26.

says, that each one must worship according to their deepest conviction. He goes on to say that legal compulsion of religious matters is therefore counterrational and contrary to morals: "It is, assuredly, no part of religion, to compel religion, to which free will alone must lead a rational being."[46]

His position owes a lot to Stoic theories of natural law, which he has seamlessly blended with evangelical principles on holiness and justice (*tsedaqah*) as the innate character of the one God. Tertullian makes the Stoic sense of "natural law" into the power that underlies the bond of human society. For him it is synonymous with "conscience."[47] It is this foundational energy of harmony and consensus that keeps human society working. Law is merely the element that binds it together on the surface. If the underlying fundament of rational consensus should disappear, law would not be enough to sustain human society. It is imperative, therefore, that law should foster and sustain the springs of this natural moral harmony and due order in society. In Tertullian's hands, and in those of later Christian theorists of law, this idea of the moral consensus behind society, of which law is the external face, is more potently charged with individual religious overtones of grace and sinfulness than ever it was in the Stoics, and much more religiously rooted in both than it is in modern appeals to the social utility of natural law. But the idea of this appeal to natural law that he uses undoubtedly served in the ancient world as a commonly recognized lingua franca among those who, for many centuries past, had been arguing that law was the servant of justice and equity, not a slave of the political and financial status quo. Tertullian commends the progress of Roman law through the ages precisely on this basis, that law conforms itself more and more to justice as society matures.[48]

Tertullian's argument would have been easily recognized by any well-educated jurist of the day and would have evoked a certain sympathy, echoing some classical sources of their own such as Ulpianus, Paulus, and Cicero, who had made similar cases.[49] The real problem with Tertullian's position, however, is illustrated in his claim that the ferocious determination of the Christian martyrs not to make any compromise at all with Roman authority was simply a manifestation of the calm determination of the Stoic sage.[50] This "no compromise: no conformity" (because religious cult was involved) was unquestionably hard for most of the local magistrates to swallow as anything remotely like the exercise of reason, when religion for

---

[46] *To Scapula* 1.
[47] "Neither God nor nature lies." *On the Soul* 6.1. Conscience is the "primordial gift of God to humankind." *Against Marcion* 1.10.3.
[48] See J. C. Fredouille, *Tertullien et la conversion de la culture antique* (Paris: Etudes Augustiniennes, 1972), 246.
[49] See A. D'Alès, *La théologie de Tertullien* (Paris: Beauchesne, 1905), 407.
[50] *Apologeticus* 49.6, 50.

the ordinary Roman was probably comparable to no more than a civic saluting of the flag. They could not see why devotion to the new god, Christ, ruled out any reverence at all for state rites, unless those rites were hateful to the new religion on political grounds. Moreover, the legal convention of distinguishing the classes into *nobiles* (propertied classes who merited different punishment and kinder treatment) and *vulgares*, or common folk, who merited only burning or throwing to the beasts if they demurred from the values of their betters, meant that much (if not all) of Tertullian's argument was destined to fall on deaf ears.

The Christian martyrs were removed from normal due process because of the nature of the charge that put them into the category of criminals by sacrilege, *lèse majesté*, illicit political association, or the practice of magic.[51] The charges of *lèse majesté* and sacrilege were the favored ones, and these two foci (which are very closely associated in Roman legal thought)[52] thus become the governing argument structure of Tertullian's *Apologeticus*.[53] Crimes of this nature were instructed to be dealt with by summary expedited process, before a judge without the need for other representation, and they carried with them automatic capital penalties.[54] What we read, in later Christian history, as the extraordinary (sometimes romanticized but generally horrendous) tortures of the martyrs were simply the second- and third-century standard penalties for dealing with what was seen as systematically organized opposition to the state. Antiquity was a brutal age. The acts of the martyrs, in holding up the sufferings of the righteous criminals for public pity and respect, are all about changing the social perception of justice and that of compassion. But in regard to Tertullian's problem in posing a legal defense of the church that got around the fence of *praescriptio*, his great difficulty was how to mount the argument for religious freedom without convicting himself in the first sentence.

He sets out a case that Christians deny the existence of the gods of Rome, certainly, but do not deny the existence of a supreme God who rules the affairs of humankind.[55] Nor are they alone in denying the existence of many gods, as they share this skepticism

---

[51] Illicit political association was closely associated with armed rebellion and occupation of a temple (hence sacrilege) and given the same legal penalties. *Digest* 47.22.2; Ulpian 1.6; *On the Office of Proconsul*. Cf. D'Àles, *La théologie de Tertullian*, 385.

[52] *Digest* 48.4.1; Ulpian 1.7. *On the Office of Proconsul*: "What is called treason is very close indeed to the concept of sacrilege. Lèse-majesté is that crime committed against the Roman people, or against its security, and they are guilty of it who have initiated matters by malicious counsel, or actual association." D'Àles, *La théologie de Tertullian*, 385.

[53] "Let us deal with the charges of sacrilege and treason; for this is the chief accusation against us; indeed the sole charge." Tertullian, *Apologeticus* 10.

[54] *Pauli Sententiae*, 5.29.1. "The lower classes are to be thrown to the animals, or else burned alive; and the nobler classes are to be decapitated." D'Àles, *La théologie de Tertullian*, 385.

[55] *Apologeticus* 11.

with many of the educated classes who are condemning them for it.[56] He thus raises the shibboleth that if everyone who denied the reality of the Roman pantheon were guilty of treason, there would be few people left safe. Thus, to apply the legal prescription brutally, that all deniers of the gods are worthy of execution, is a scandalous abrogation of reason, which any rational discussion (should the Christians ever be allowed time in court to set out their religious beliefs) would be able to dispel.[57]

So if belief in the gods is not at issue, really, he argues, there remains the question of the political loyalty of the Christians. "A Christian," Tertullian says, "is an enemy to no one, and least of all to the emperor of Rome, whom every believer knows to have been appointed to that place by God, and whom he thus cannot but love and honor."[58] The Christian duty to love and obey the emperor does not mean, however, that the Christians do not have the rights of citizens to criticize or correct abuses. (He was on dangerous ground here.) The Lord's command to "give to Caesar what is Caesar's" also means that they are duty-bound to withhold from him what is not his.[59] But the emperor, if he is a true emperor of the Romans, will himself recognize the limits of what is just and right. God, Tertullian says, has appointed him to power in order to enforce just laws. This is his primary duty, his very raison d'être.[60] He must preserve the peace and punish the wrongdoer.[61] If he should ever reverse this divinely appointed natural order and, instead, punish the just and reward the wicked (as the persecutions demonstrate), then he would preside over a major revolution in good order. Law must sustain the foundation of all society, which is reason. Persecution of the innocent Christians is, therefore, counterrational.[62] But if the emperor fulfills his true function, then he deserves the obedience of all citizens, and in this respect the Christians will not be lacking in showing their loyalty.[63]

In this, of course, Tertullian (an African himself) departed knowingly from a certain tendency in earlier North African Christianity that had glorified the martyr's resistance precisely because it spurned the earthly city and all pagan rulers. Such an attitude can be found in the stark "otherworldliness" of the *Passion of the Scillitan Martyrs*, written after their executions in 180. Here there is little common ground between Christianity and empire, little awareness of any Christian expectation to do

---

[56]Cicero is a prime example in his *De natura Deorum*.
[57]*Apologeticus* 11.
[58]*To Scapula* 1.
[59]*Apologeticus* 32.
[60]Ibid.
[61]*The Scorpion's Sting* 14.1.
[62]*On the Military Crown* 4.5. He goes further, of course, and demonstrates to what extent Christian morality and philanthropy have benefited the state: *Apologeticus* 36; 37.8; 39.
[63]*Apologeticus* 30–32; 33.1; 36.2.

much more in this cosmos than witness to its passing away, and certainly little civic religiosity such as Tertullian is appealing to.[64] But such texts as the Passion of the Scillitan Martyrs probably represented the simpler village mentalities of men and women who had never looked beyond the boundaries of their small holdings, never felt the need to articulate a wider Christian social vision in the way Tertullian did. He had his sights set on much wider horizons. He was sensing the winds correctly. In less than 150 years Christians would not only be heard but would have governing sway in imperial affairs.

The persecutions serve as litmus tests for the record of the individual emperors, Tertullian argues. They divide the rulers into two types: wise and brutal.[65] One can either choose to be like a Nero or like an Augustus, who was diffident about receiving divine honors.[66] At the local level, he points out, many magistrates demonstrate their humanity and wisdom by summarily dismissing cases brought against Christians, simply out of their own love for justice and law.[67] Why should the law's master be any less clement? To press his point he gives particular attention to Trajan's rescript to Pliny, who had investigated the Christians in Asia Minor and declared them basically innocent. By officially recorded rescript, Tertullian argues, Emperor Trajan declared that Christians ought not to be sought out any longer on the basis of their name, but those who had already been brought to the attention of the authorities ought to be punished. But what legal inconsistency was this, Tertullian concludes? If they are innocent, why should they be punished at all?[68] Even when Tertullian is promising the Romans his loyalty, there is always the important and necessary caveat that underlies all Christian judgment on social polity. The allegiance is never to be absolute or unthinking; social obedience always depends on the giving of allegiance to a God-appointed authority whose duty it is, pagan or Christian, simply to sustain that which is right. Accordingly, the root of the Christian social duty is always to remind the leaders of this limit of their authority: and this is surely why they will so rarely be thanked for it.

---

[64] On July 17, 180, a group of twelve Christian youths was brought before Proconsul Publius Vegellius in the African town of Scillium. One of them, Speratus, spoke for all of them, and his dialogue in court was written down. The proconsul asked them to "come back to their senses" so as to receive clemency from their lord the emperor. Speratus replied, "We have never done anything wrong or committed any crime. Even when people mistreated us we gave thanks, because we honor the emperor." When the proconsul asked them to swear before the divine genius of the emperor, Speratus went on, "I do not know the empire of this world. The one I serve belongs to God."

[65] *Apologeticus* 1.5.

[66] Ibid., 5; 34.1.

[67] There was wide latitude for local judges in hearing cases. Once they were initiated, however, the results were predetermined. Cf. *To Scapula* 4.

[68] *Apologeticus* 2.9.

The role of reason underlies all his wider thought on legal polity, and it derives directly from his deeply rooted theological anthropology. For Tertullian, God has established an order in society, which is an apex of that which he has established as the rational system underlying all creation.[69] Humankind is the high point of that creation and emerges as Lord of the creation in mimesis of the Father Creator, to the extent that humankind demonstrates *Logos* on earth; that is a way of life that is consciously lived out in accordance with the dictates of reason and order.[70] Moral order is chief among these aspects that put human social systems in harmony with the natural orders of the creation. The rational life of society is, in short, the highest manifestation of natural law, not something opposed to it. It can be perverted, however, and when humankind acts out a lifestyle that is disordered, given to selfish and immoral activities rather than philanthropic social care, then not only is society disrupted, but the whole creation is unbalanced, since its God-appointed head, the human race, has lapsed into subhuman irrationality. A reasonable and mutually philanthropic lifestyle brings about social harmony and the peace of society, which allows all civilized art to flourish. This is precisely why, Tertullian says, the emperor has been set up by God to preside over the administration of reasoned justice on earth,[71] and this is why he commands the allegiance of the Christians.[72]

Tertullian consistently argues throughout his writings that, of all forms of human social systems, it is that of the Christians who will most effectively bring peace into the heart of the human society, since it is a revelation of a lifestyle built on the premise of love. Within Christianity, Tertullian says, love is for the first time ever in history elevated as the supreme rule of society, the highest vision of social communion.[73] It is both the perfection of an individual life and the perfect flowering of God's desire for society. This law of love is the universal law established as a natural order within humankind, though it has struggled to emerge, first growing in the social code of ancient Israel, which was set by God to teach the world—but never belonging solely to Israel, since the law of love was set in the heart of that first law God gave to Adam and Eve

---

[69] The empire of Rome has a part to play in that evolving system. Despite many who have (perhaps carelessly) read Tertullian as innately hostile to Roman politics, more recent careful analysis has demonstrated that the pagan cults and their embeddedness in the political system are his constant target. He envisages the system of imperial government itself as a cultural force that has been God-blessed with immense potential for human good. His political theology is set within a biblically rooted apocalyptic vision of God's overarching judgment of human affairs. See R. Klein, *Tertullian und das romische Reich* (Heidelberg: C. Winter, 1968); A. Z. Ahondokpe, *La Vision de Rome chez Tertullien*, 2 vols. (Lille: A.N.R.T, Université de Lille, 1991).

[70] *On The Soul* 17.11; *Apologeticus* 4.5.

[71] *Apologeticus* 30.2; *To Scapula* 14.1.

[72] *Apologeticus* 30–32.

[73] *On Patient Endurance* 12.8; *On Flight* 14.2.

from which the law of Moses later developed.[74] The way Christianity has gone on to bring this natural law to its divine perfecting within society is, for Tertullian, a major revelation of truth to the world of his time. The law of universal love is taken, in Jesus' command, to the pitch of loving even against the grain: "Our perfect and unique form of goodness," Tertullian comments, "is not something that is shared with any others. All love their friends. Only Christians love their enemies."[75] But all the laws of humankind, for Tertullian, insofar as they are explicit attempts to lead society to virtue, devolve directly and divinely from the law of God as their ancient model.[76]

The higher standard of the Christians' moral lives in the empire, and their reasonable and peaceful behavior, he says, is the new movement that will lift the empire to a purer standard of culture. But it is exactly this higher standard that has, in his current era, annoyed the Christians' neighbors, who clearly prefer to live a brutish life and thus wish to annihilate the Christians from their midst. His argument here returns full circle, insisting that the persecution is the perfect example of social disorder: a profoundly irrational movement, initiated at a simplistic level by unthinking and socially destructive mobs, yet sustained at a more damaging level by Roman legal officials, who ought in all conscience to have seen that the Christian lifestyle is deeply attached to reason and morality and de facto ought to be protected as society's benefactor. It is only the prayers of the Christians, Tertullian argues, that restrain the anger of God from bursting out on the corruptions of Roman life. It is their prayers that have often secured Roman victories in times of war.[77]

Even though so much of Tertullian's writings and reflections were produced under duress, as occasional answers to direly pressing problems, it is extraordinary how wide-ranging his reflections on theological polity are. He sets out, in the course of mounting an immediate claim for legal equity, reasonableness, and moral balance for the benefit of his suffering coreligionists, a deeper understanding and a broader vision of what would constitute a truly just society. Although he is deeply rooted in Stoic moral philosophy, his vision is far more than that; it takes social polity beyond the generalities of a sophistic appeal to "natural law" as a putative societal bond. Such an appeal still sustained the basic Roman distinctions of class, benefitting the elite and oppressing the poor. Tertullian is able, by appealing to a rationally elaborated theology of Christian love, to set in place a truly equitable vision of a commonwealth, in which the supreme leader is an adjudicator, not a tyrant—someone who must rule in accordance with a system of agreed equitable values and whose

---

[74] *Against the Jews* 2.4.
[75] *To Scapula* 1.3.
[76] *Apologeticus* 45.
[77] Ibid., 4.2; 5.4; *To Scapula* 4.1.

task it is to elevate and protect those values as widely as possible. More than this, we find for the first time in a serious Christian theologian a profound defense of the value of individual conscience and freedom of religion. Tertullian gives to all subsequent Christian reflection on law and social theory a significant benchmark. To his immediate Latin successors Lactantius and Augustine, he set a bar and determined an agenda that they both recognized had to be elaborated extensively in the new era of the Christian ascendancy of the *Pax Constantina*.

## HELLENISTIC ATTITUDES TO CHRISTIANITY: THE CASE OF CELSUS

Second-century philosopher Celsus gives us a very different window onto the church of this period. He hated Christianity with a passion that is reflected in a very hostile work he composed in the year 177, during the reign of Marcus Aurelius and his son Commodus, against the church and several aspects of Judaism, titled *Logos Alethes* (*A True Discourse*).[78] This in all probability was using a play on the several meanings of *logos* as "word," "treatise," "reason," or "speech," knowing full well that Christian intellectuals were beginning to claim the idea as a designation of the incarnate Word in Jesus. The treatise was so acerbically mocking of Christ and his religion that the church met it with silence for more than a generation: perhaps something of a *damnatio memoriae* against a popular intellectual who took advantage of a time of persecution to supply alleged moral reasons why that violence was justified.[79] It was not until the time of Origen of Alexandria in 248 that a Christian intellectual made a systematic reply to its charges, though some have seen intimations of a reply in the anonymous Christian text Diognetus.

Celsus's work itself has been lost (the Christians would not preserve it for their part) except for the many quotations Origen gives in his refutational treatise *Contra Celsum*, which allows us to see the substance of its attacks.[80] It is possible, however, that Origen has only turned his attention to that part of Celsus's writing that had a direct relevance to Christian affairs. So we cannot presume from Origen's fragments that we have the whole treatise. It has some interest, nevertheless, as the first time ever a pagan intellectual bothered to look into the new movement (he has read the Scriptures to do his basic research) and make a sustained critique. The conflict between schools this represents might well have taken place in Rome or Alexandria and is another aspect of that regular clash of city schools that one finds within the Christian movement in

---

[78] Origen, *Contra Celsum* 8.71, suggests a joint imperium.
[79] Ibid., 8.69.
[80] J. M. Vermander ("De quelques répliques de Celse dans l'apologétique de Tertullien," *Revue des Etudes Anciennes* 16 [1970]: 205-25) has thought to see answers to various charges by Celsus given in the apologists without naming him: Tertullian, *Apologeticus* 21; Minucius Felix, *Octavius* 10-12; Theophilus, *To Autolycus* 3.

the second century (and after) between catholics and heretics, and also outside it among the various rival philosophies and religious cults (of which there were many).

Origen calls Celsus an Epicurean,[81] but it is chiefly from the standpoint of an eclectic form of Middle Platonic metaphysics and theology that he comes at the church, and he might well have been aware of claims by such intellectuals as Justin Martyr, Athenagoras, or the early Logos school that the church was the fulfillment of the aspirations of human schools of wisdom.[82] He replies that he finds Christianity full of the ignorant, who give more weight to blind faith than to learning or judgment, though there are, he admits, some few intellectuals among the movement who are tolerably educated and skilled in allegorical interpretation of texts. But overall he finds the texts and the doctrines insufferably barbarous and thinks that Christianity is a major step back in the development of religion, on the grounds that for centuries philosophy has been refining the vulgar idea of gods assuming human forms and trying to lead souls to the heights of divine transcendence by ascetical reflection on the truth. Now here comes a religion that deifies a crucified Jew (he has all the social and racial prejudices of his class), claiming that this tawdry execution is the core focal point of all the philosophical, moral, and cultural tradition of the human race. The incarnation of the Logos was a scandal to the late antique philosopher (as the Evangelist well knew in penning Jn 1:14), and Celsus is very much offended by the thought of developing Christian metaphysics and morals out of the basis of evangelical Christology. Its materially grounded particularity and exclusiveness are what shock him most. As a result he offers a systematic dismantling of Christian claims.

Christians, he says, merit the public censure they receive because their assemblies are illegal.[83] The love (*agape*) that they boast of so much is nothing other than the corollary of a group that holds together under external threats. The teaching is barbarous, completely arbitrary, and ethically speaking does not offer the world anything at all that is new: just a measure of recycled concepts.[84] Christ himself was a simple man, born in the natural way from the Jewess Mary, possibly by means of an illegitimate birth, as some of his sources recount, and was wretchedly put to death and gained a following only in very recent times by using methods of sorcery to falsely convince people he had divine powers.[85] The magic deeds that he did were no better than Egyptian magicians, from whom he probably learned his trade, and

---

[81] Origen, *Contra Celsum* 1.8; Eusebius *Ecclesiastical History* 6.36. He probably means it as shorthand for "atheistic kind of skeptic."
[82] Origen refers to the neo-Pythagorean commentator Numenius four times: *Contra Celsum* 1.15; 4.51; 5.38, 57.
[83] Ibid., 1.1; 8.17.
[84] Ibid., 1.2-5.
[85] Ibid., 1.6.

they accumulate only to folktales to convince the simpleminded. Indeed, the church is full of the ignorant and prejudiced.[86] The adherents of this new cult prefer blind faith to reasoned reflection and are rigid in that attitude. The doctrine of the resurrection is a corruption of the purer Hellenistic doctrine of the immortality of souls.

The Christian scheme might, after all, he admits, have some value in serving to instruct the uneducated in basic matters of moral behavior, but what a disaster that the whole movement follows the Jewish style of exclusive disconnection from the Hellenistic mainstream, or the wisdom of the Persians, where pluralist worship demonstrates that all great truths have a common root in human society.[87] Their narrow misanthropy leads Christians to become bad citizens, unpatriotic, not willing to undertake the defense of the homeland, and overall politically untrustworthy. Only by adopting Hellenistic liberalism can they make an ascent from the narrow pit into which they have dug themselves.

Celsus in a sense is making a kind of evangelical outreach of his own to the Christians. His chief desire is to see the ways of the ancestors respected and the rites of the gods honored in a pluralistic ecumenism that will allow them to serve as patterns of the deeper (philosophical) truth that the more educated have already perceived. It is the separatism that most annoys him, however: an attitude he finds more objectionable since he argues that Moses, who stands behind the whole Christian system, more or less stole all he had of merit from the traditions of other nations and other sages. The latter argument is something that the Christian philosophers will particularly focus on to reverse the very terms of it: that Moses' revelation was more ancient than the Hellenes. Antiquity mattered in this era as a fundamental character of the truth, and the startling novelty of Jesus was, to Celsus, a simple testimony as to how the religion was *res novae*: the words literally mean "new things," but for late antique Romans they were actually the term for "revolution." Celsus represents much of Marcus Aurelius's attitude, that of Julian the (apostate) emperor in the fourth century, and the Roman senator Symmachus, whose similar critiques Augustine was moved to answer in his *City of God* in the fifth century.

Origen started off his book at the request of a Christian patron, Ambrosius.[88] At first he decided to answer point by point, but as he realized this would enslave him to Celsus's agenda and end up with a mammoth tome, he started using Celsus more as a

---

[86] Ibid., 1.26-27.
[87] Ibid., 8.42.
[88] Ibid., 6.8; Eusebius, *Ecclesiastical History* 6.34-36. Ambrosius funded several of Origen's literary projects. He was a Gnostic adherent whom Origen had converted back to the great church, and for whom Origen would later write his *Exhortation to Martyrdom*, a short time before his own arrest and torture.

soundboard to develop his own more general sets of principles, envisaging how Christianity "fits" into the history of culture. It is interesting to see his mind develop on this. He is clearly a more spacious and learned philosopher than the (dead) critic he sets out to refute. Where Celsus is a scintillating apologist, ready with a telling phrase and an acerbic putdown, Origen thinks about the grand scheme of truth. Origen regards Celsus as a very clever man, but not at all a wise one. Truth has a character, he argues, that is consistent with itself. For all the ancient traditions Celsus boasts of, supposedly held together in a bond of society provided by common cult of the gods, the fact is that the Hellenes adhere to ridiculous mythic religions whose gods are not worthy of any respect, let alone veneration. Their religions and their wisdom traditions are in serious conflict with each other. The mystical and ancient wisdom of the Persians, which Celsus so alluringly points up, for example, while he mocks Christology, amounts in the end to alleged sages who worshiped fire, making the observer very skeptical about the quality of this so-called spiritual wisdom that cannot tell the difference between the creations of God and the God who creates them.

The patriotism Celsus calls for, Origen says, is not witnessed in a blind adherence to the "might is right" argument that Roman imperialism tends to presuppose as natural, but rather refined in a society that appeals to justice as the true bond of societal cohesion. God used Rome as an evangelical instrument. The system of roads that first crossed the entire globe in the time of the Romans became the means for the evangelization of the world, Origen argues. Christ Jesus appears as a humble, unprepossessing teacher of virtue and chooses no earthly glorious trappings to make his doctrine spread across the world. He is the fleshly agent of the eternal Wisdom of God, who indwells him. His truth, which is loving, humble, courageous, and rational, reaches out to humankind by virtue of its own divine charism of clarity. That charism of freshness of truth and inherent authenticity remains in the Christian message to his own day, he says, renewing its force of conviction generation after generation. Using Paul, as he so often does, Origen argues that the Logos assumed flesh as a hidden mystery of wisdom. And, as Paul teaches, the wisdom of God can indeed seem like foolishness to the wise of this world, who stand outside the grace of revelation (1 Cor 1:25).

For Origen, Celsus's arrogance (that he can arrive at the truth by the light of human reason unaided) has blinded him. Humanity cannot rise to the divine. The divine has to stoop down to the human spirit and cleanse it from the darkness in which it has veiled itself and its religious sensibility. It was this commission to answer Celsus's work, along with his own desire to found a university-level school in Caesarea that would be open to all seekers of the truth and would use scriptural revelation as a primary method for assessing the merit and worth of philosophical systems, that made Origen one of the great minds of the third-century church.[89] He was able to put together as a system of the metaphysics of salvation the more piecemeal and random aspects of the earlier Logos theologians and apologists and to consider the Christian schema as it related to both philosophy and biblical doctrine. He is the first truly great philosopher the Christians could boast of. In his *Letter to Theodore* Origen was one of the first (of many followers) who took the story of the Jews in Egypt being instructed by God to "despoil the houses of the Egyptians" (Ex 3:22) before they left on their exodus as an allegorical indication of how the church ought to move from its sure basis in scriptural revelation to a certain plundering of all that was of value in the Hellenistic traditions of philosophy and culture: accepting and valuing what was truly useful for human culture and being able to reject and set aside what was harmful. This became a veritable navigational chart for the church of the fourth century and afterward in creating a theology of Christian civilization.

Although it had taken almost a generation to think about it, Celsus had not simply shocked the church of his day by his questions but eventually stimulated it to realize it had a significant mission to the intelligentsia. One of the main differences, perhaps, between the second and the third century church is the increasing range of socially elevated and more highly educated people it attracted. This obviously meant that a greater number of its leaders would be of the educated classes too. For the first time in the third century we start to see evidence of this in the larger number of episcopal and presbyteral writings that start filling out the church's cabinet of Christian literature.

## RIVAL NON-CHRISTIAN ORDERS

*Mithras.* The cult of the Iranian god Mitra has deep and ancient roots in Persia. The god is mentioned also in the Indian Rig Veda. The Roman cult of Mithras, however, while once thought to have close associations with Iranian religion, from which it was once exegeted, is now considered to have been a particularly discrete phenomenon of the globalization of the Roman empire and a relatively late arrival on the Roman imperial scene.[90] The cult is called the "mysteries of Mithras" or sometimes the "mysteries of the Persians" by the ancients, but probably in much the same way

---

[89]His curricular design included astronomy, philosophy, and textual analysis: it is described in the *Address of Thanks by Theodore* (*Panegyric*).

[90]In particular Franz Cumont, the founder of modern Mithriac studies, explored the supposed Iranian connection in his two-volume work: *Textes et monuments figurés relatifs aux Mystères de Mithra* (Brussels: H. Lamertin, 1894–1896). His introductory volume is now regarded as superseded, but the second volume collects the ancient data (see the text online at https://archive.org/details/textesetmonument02cumouoft). See further R. Beck, "Mithraism Since Franz Cumont," *ANRW* II.17.4, 2002-2115.

as the Hermes Trismegistus cult adopted the mantle of "ancient and mysterious" Egyptian religious rites to give itself an alluring antique heritage, or the Greco-Egyptian cult of Serapis tried to position itself as antique. Novelty was fatal for any religion in the ancient world, and Christianity paid dearly for its openly acknowledged recent, proletarian, and scandalous character. Mithraism appeared at the same time as Christianity, the first century AD, and rivaled the church as a very fast-growing cult before it faded away in the fourth century, more or less completely. In the formative Christian centuries, however, Mithraism had much more open popularity than Christianity, although it most likely was a "man's religion"; and while that might have been its strength in one sense, it was also its severe limitation in another.

Earlier commentators often paired the Christian and Mithraic movements together (looking for parallels and mutual borrowings), but it was not a fruitful approach, and most likely there were no explicit mutual reliances at all. The Mithraists were happily unconcerned with details of doctrine and creeds or historical roots and interpretative traditions. They were more interested in practical bonding ceremonies and archetypal attitudes. This very large-scale disinterestedness in dogma and moral precisions made it ideal as a syncretistic form of bonding among many other cults. Mutual religious belonging was not only possible but encouraged. And yet, looking at the great attractive power Mithraism obviously had can perhaps throw some light on the qualities and characters that accounted also for the rapid spread of the Christian religion. Both were religions of liberation and the victory of the good, with heroic redeemer figures central to the cult. They had things in common, though the disparities were numerous. Some Christian commentators, such as Justin Martyr, Minucius, and Tertullian, found the similarities in ritual (sacramental meals in particular) to be the devil's deliberate mockery of the church.[91] But all of the parallels cited are most likely commonplaces of Hellenistic life and religiosity rather than deliberate mimicry from either side.

Adopting many characteristics of the archaic mystery religions, the Mithraic cult was immensely secretive. It did not propagate its doctrine openly. As a result it is necessary to reconstitute what was being taught and how the rituals were conducted from the many surviving ritual artifacts (statues and friezes) that survive from all over the empire but especially Italy. There are no surviving literary sources that recount the doctrine, no extant scriptures. Porphyry, a neo-Platonist philosopher of

---

[91] See Justin Martyr, *First Apology* 66. "For the apostles, in the memoirs composed by them, which are called Gospels, delivered unto us what was commanded of them, namely that Jesus took bread, and when he had given thanks, said, 'Do this in remembrance of me, for this is my body,' and in the same way, having taken the cup and given thanks, he said, 'This is my blood,' and gave it to them alone. Now this, the wicked devils have imitated in the mysteries of Mithras, commanding the same thing to be done. For as you know, or can learn, bread and a cup of water are placed with certain incantations in the mystic rites of one who is being initiated."

the third century, tells us that accounts of the Mithraic faith once did exist, as composed by Euboulos and Pallas, but they have not survived.[92] The interpretation of the cultic exterior (fabric) remains is thus the chief manner of reconstituting the *mythos*, or sacred narrative, of the religion.

Crudely put, it has this format: The god is born from a rock. He is identified as a young hero with a Phrygian cap.[93] He hunts down and then slays a great bull in a cavern. Wrestling it to the ground and stabbing its neck (*tauroctony*) is one of the chief ritual symbols of the cultic places. He encounters the sun god (Helios), who kneels before him. The two gods shake hands and dine together on the remains of the bull. Other divine figures are sometimes associated with the divine hero.[94] A fairly frequent appearance is the naked youth with the head of a lion. He has a snake entwining his winged corpus, which rests its head on the lion's head. The lion face has a grim appearance. This youth sometimes stands on a globe bearing a key and a scepter in his hands. In some depictions four zodiacal animals are present. A scorpion attaches itself to the bull's testicles.[95] A dog and a snake approach the outflow of the bull's blood, and there is a raven also.

The Roman cult was especially based around the capital city and spread across the empire, chiefly through the military, from there. The ritual places of meeting were called caves (*spelaia*). They were vaulted like caves and had stone benches down each side, where the members reclined for the ceremonies. These underground places of meeting (appropriate for the rock-born deity and the locus of his victory over the bull) were usually inserted into public buildings, not private homes. It was, therefore, an "open-closed-mystery," if we can call it that, never having to hide itself as the church once did. Mithraism never became any official part of Roman state religion, but it was a welcomed personal cult, seen as solidarity building.

In the initiation ceremony the initiate was presented by a sponsor to the celebrant, who was dressed as Mithras, in the Phrygian cap and a short (military-type) cloak.

---

[92] Porphyry, *De Antro Nympharum*.
[93] A distinctive Persian garb, a floppy, pointed cap and short cloak.
[94] His torchbearers are Cautes and Cautopates. Along with the sun and the moon, other zodiac figures appear in the sacred meal frescoes.
[95] In the Great Mother mysteries at Ephesus, the remarkable cult statue there used to be called the "many-breasted Artemis" (*polymammaeal*), from the pomegranate-like clusters all over her chest. These are now thought by commentators not to be breasts at all but rather multitudes of bulls' testicles (*vires*) from the animals sacrificed to her. In the Mithras cult the zodiacal Scorpio shares in the triumph over Taurus. What it means is highly obscure (and probably meant to be). Once, after teaching an undergraduate course on the mystery religions, I read an exam essay that recounted the details of the *tauroctony*, culminating with a note on the detail of the scorpion pinning the bull's genitalia. The student commented, "This, as we can see, is very similar to Christian baptism." I am still trying to exegete what that comment meant.

The mystagogue holds out some kind of rod to him (it is probably a sword). He kneels like a condemned captive with his hands tied behind his back. The figure of the god symbolically liberates him by cutting his bonds. There are several initiation frescoes in the Mithraeum of Santa Maria Capua Vetere in Italy. In some of the panels it seems the god figure is standing on the captive's calves behind him. It is difficult to reconstruct all of this—as nigh impossible if we could imagine the Christian religion to have lost all its earliest texts, and a few surviving frescoes from the catacombs were all we had to go on: with old men carrying sheep, three female figures at a monument, and a woman with upraised hands, for example. How would we know these were Christian iconic symbols of the afterlife, the resurrection, and the church at prayer? We gain the clues from the texts of course. It is not until the late fourth century that we start seeing explicit iconic references to Jesus and the evangelical narratives in Christian iconography, and even then the images are deliberately ambivalent: meant to be recognizable for those "in the know" more than for outsiders. But working in the form of a Greek mystery—the root of the word is the verb "to keep silent"—the Mithras initiates did not disclose what happened in their rituals to outsiders and made all promise to guard their secrets jealously within the initiate community.

But putting various clues together is one effort at exegetical interpretation. True religion is about salvation from this world of numerous evils. The divine Mithras is the force of liberating light and goodness. He overcomes the primal force of brute strength, the bull, who is the symbol of cosmic darkness and ignorance. His might is proven as liberator, a savior in the sense of a conqueror of darkness and barbarism, more than a forgiver of sins or purveyor of revelation (as far as we know). The sun god, who was a popular generic cult among soldiery (and whose cult would run on into the early Christian era as the favored cult of Constantine himself in his early stages), himself comes to acknowledge the invincible might of Mithras the god and kneels before him, since he himself could rule only in the day and could not overcome the darkness entirely (see Jn 1:5). But having accepted the homage of Helios, Mithras embraces him as a brother divinity (the two cults could be combined happily), and they share a sacramental meal of bonding fellowship. In numerous epigraphic testimonies from the fourth century the symbiosis of cults is proven: Mithras is now *sol invictus*. He is first and foremost a victor, the personification of the conquest of evil.[96]

---

[96] So too did the fourth-century church interpret the cross of Jesus fundamentally as a symbol of his resounding victory over death: never in the form (that later sprung up) of a motif of compassionate sorrow for the suffering Jesus. The cross for the early church was always called a "trophy" of conquest. See further J. A. McGuckin, "Soter Theos: The Patristic and Byzantine Reappropriation of an Antique Idea," in *Salvation According to the Church Fathers*, ed. D. V. Twomey (Dublin: Four Courts Press, 2010), 33-44.

The winged lion-headed figure is more obscure but probably an attendant daimon: hostile to all enemies (manifold spirits of evil) and shown to be godlike and beneficent to cult devotees by his wings. His vague similarity to the figures of Mercury, Aesculapius, Aion, even the Great Mother (with her lions, for there is a considerable amount of syncretism at play here, as would be suitable to a deliberately pluralist cult), means, perhaps, that he is the quasi-angelic go-between of the god for the benefit of his worshipers. He holds a scepter promising exaltation and a share in the divine victory to Mithras's devotees. The keys he holds might also symbolize admission to the superlunar world of a blessed afterlife for those who honor Mithras's victory over barbarism. The attendant zodiacal figures (Scorpio, Canis Minor, probably the snake and raven, as well as Helios and Luna) demonstrate Mithras's sovereignty over the heavenly spheres: liberator of souls who wish to escape the sublunar oppressions of wicked spirits and rise to the heavens (as Mithras himself does after his killing of the bull, when he ascends on high in a chariot).

In the initiation ceremonies of other mysteries the believer comes before the god figure and is made to experience a frisson of the divine terror that he (in Mithraism it was a "he" because the cult was predominantly masculine) is sharing with the god, with whom he is being merged. So, for example, the subterranean rites of the Eleusinian mysteries seem to have made the initiate be buried underground (along with Kore in the Underworld) and then liberated into the light (the symbol of the ear of grain that is shown to the initiate, which sprouts once more when Ceres regains her lost daughter from the kingdom of Hades). By analogy I suspect that the initiate to Mithras is brought as a war captive before the mystagogue who is dressed like the god. He advances toward the initiate and mimics the ritual of the execution of a captive, the cutting of the throat perhaps, but at the last minute changes this into the ritual cutting of all the bonds and setting the captive free, raising him up from the ground as a brother of the god. The courageous initiate (now proven manly and on the side of enlightenment) finally shakes hands with the god (as once did Helios) and is thus known as a *syndexioi* (a man to whom one could give the right hand in greeting). The ultimate test of bravery (the initiate might not have been told of the secret rituals and so might well have been alarmed as the mystagogue came toward him with a sword) was the last in a series of tests of character that the Mithraic candidate was put through before his final initiation.[97] The death of the great bull being the once-for-all victory over darkness, the god no longer permits evil to be triumphant and elevates his devotees into the heavenly banquet, where they sacramentally eat the flesh of the beast together.[98]

---

[97] St. Gregory of Nazianzus refers to this in *Oration* 4.70.
[98] It is reminiscent of the theology of victory in the fundamental New Testament narrative, in which the kingdom of God triumphs over the rule of the evil prince of this world.

Other ritual elements related to water (the god Oceanus is often present in the frescoes), and Mithraea were often sited near rivers or springs. Bread with water was ritually consumed. The regular assembly, where the brethren ate together, was a main feature of the Mithraic mysteries: a sacred banquet club of brothers sworn to advance each other's cause and who would together fight the forces of evil and darkness (again particularly relevant to the imperial armies). There we have a salvation myth being practically worked out in a mutual-help society.[99] It is no wonder it appealed to soldiers, who needed to know they were ready to protect one another's backs, and also businessmen, who thus cooperated together.

One knows also that the tight community sense of the Christians was very attractive. Liberation from the earthly realm, where evil often seemed to triumph, to the heavenly kingdom of God, where God's dominion would be manifest in majesty and true judgment, was also critical to the central belief system of the church. Jesus' resurrection and heavenly ascent were not merely a personal triumph but taken as a foretaste of the spoils of victory he had won for his followers, to whom he promised the mysteries of life after death.

The church had many distinctive differences, of course. Where Mithraism was open to all cults, multiple belonging being a factor that commended it to the imperial rulers, Christianity was so hostile to religious multiple belonging (categorizing all foreign gods as malevolent demons) that it earned the (often deadly) hostility of most of the other religions of the day. Whereas, as far as we know, Mithraism was not much concerned with details of history and tradition (turning instead around large archetypal concepts of astrological patterns and cosmic liberation), Christianity was rooted from the outset in sacred text: bearing on its back an ambivalent heritage of the Testament of the Jews and interpreting this through the highly particular lens of the narrative of the teachings, works, and death of its founder, Jesus. There was, then, much more particularity of the moral tradition and the issue of fidelity to the life and example of the founder in the Christian case. One point of interesting comparison is the important place close bonding took among the worshipers in the form of ritual meals together. The barring of women's presence from the Mithraic sacred meals stands in noted contrast to the Christian practice of larger cross-gender and cross-generational gatherings. There is also little to suggest that Mithraism was so open to class fluidity as the church seems to have been.

---

[99] Mithras is not predominantly titled a savior figure in the extant references (certainly not a savior figure in the way Jesus was depicted), but the form of the liberation narrative, the contrast of darkness and light, the struggle of heroism and brutalism—these give to Mithraism clearly all the forms of an archetype of salvation myth for its devotees.

**Isis, queen of magic.** The Isiac religion was another extremely popular cult in early Christian times.[100] This was more firmly rooted in some form of traceable prehistory, probably running back to the Fifth Dynasty (c. 2500 BC) in Egypt. Our focus here will be chiefly on the form of the religion in the early Christian period, when it had undergone many mutations and indeed emerged as a truly global phenomenon in the Roman imperial world, with cultic evidence of Isis's presence ranging from Portugal to Afghanistan and from northern England to the Sudan.[101] Her cult was one of the last to survive in a popularly practiced form. Her great cult temple at Menouthi along the Canopic Way from Alexandria (near modern Aboukir) was still seen as a scandalous remnant of paganism by Cyril of Alexandria in the fifth century, and her other great temple at Philae remained active until closed by Emperor Justinian in the sixth.[102] There was hardly a port in the empire that did not have a shrine to Isis in its harbors, so that sailors could pray to her for safe passage as they ventured across the seas.

Isis was the mother goddess of love (more homely than the lascivious and fickle Aphrodite). She was even to rival the Great Mother and assume her attributes in her paradoxical acclamation as mother and virgin. Isis was the great worker of magic and the patroness of all who wished their magic to do good and bring beneficent results to their prayers. This focus on love, hearth, and home made it a religion particularly appealing to mothers and young women in the late empire. She was the royal goddess, giver of the *ankh* of life, consort to the lord of the underworld, mother of the living monarch, protector of souls in death. Once again the sacred narrative (*mythos*) of the religion can be a starting point to interpret its theological contours. Isis was the consort of the Pharaoh Osiris. In several accounts they were a prehistoric royal couple who taught the arts of civilization to their people. Isis's name (*Aset*) means "throne." Her *mythos* ended up in the early Christian period as a result of many conflations, particularly with her and the roles of the goddess Hathor, and her son Horus with Ra. Plutarch made an account for Greek cosmopolitan consumption that rationalized the many variants of the story.[103]

One simplified form of the *mythos* is that the Pharaoh's beneficent rule is envied by his wicked brother Seti. The latter is god of the wild places and all wild things, especially the wilderness outside the reach of the life-giving floods of the Nile. He

---

[100] Still the best overview is R. E. Witt, *Isis in the Ancient World* (London: Thames and Hudson, 1971).
[101] By the Roman era she had absorbed the cultic attributes of Demeter, Artemis, Astarte queen of heaven, Cybele, and Aphrodite, as well as other, lesser deities.
[102] See further J. A. McGuckin, "The Influence of the Isis Cult on St. Cyril of Alexandria's Christology," *StPatr* 24 (1992): 191-99. Cyril designates her as "a demon in the desert."
[103] D. S. Richter, "Plutarch on Isis and Osiris: Text, Cult, and Cultural Appropriation," *Transactions of the American Philological Association* 131 (2001): 191-216; C. Froidefond, ed., *Plutarch: Isis et Osiris: texte établi et traduit* (Paris: Belles Lettres, 1988).

tricks his brother Osiris into a coffin-like chest and murders him to seize dominion. Osiris, weeping extravagantly for her lost husband, eventually finds him, but Seti has dismembered the corpse and scattered the pieces far and wide. Disheveled, she searches and gathers the parts of her dead husband together again.[104] She finds everything except the phallus, which has been consumed by a wild beast. Then by great magic arts she revivifies Osiris, making for him a phallus of clay, by which she is able to conceive a legitimate heir for him, their son Horus, thus reasserting their dominion. Osiris descends to rule the underworld as its pharaoh, and Isis serves as the living throne of Horus. The child is given to a wet nurse to be fed but shrivels away and appears to be dying. Realizing that a god cannot be fed on mere mortal's milk, Isis feeds him herself, and he revives and grows strong. She thus is often depicted as *Isis lactans*: in sitting position, breastfeeding the divine ruler, in such a way that she herself is the throne on which he is installed.[105] She is not only the giver of life but the constant source of healing and renewal.

The Christians of the third century onward stole several of her titles and actively used the Mary cult to try to subvert her popular appeal. Isis, for example, was known as the "mother of the god" (Horus), and Egyptian Christians applied that title to Mary as *Theotokos* (god-birther).[106] In sixth-century Egypt it also became common to depict Mary breastfeeding Jesus as an icon of the Eucharist. As Isis's ambrosial milk gave life to the divine Horus, now Mary shows that Christ, flesh of her flesh, is the life giver who gives his own divine flesh to the church as the source of its spiritual life in the Eucharist.[107] Mary enthroned holding the Christ-child on her lap became a standard icon in later times. It was known then as the *Platytera* (wider than the heavens), signifying (as in the case of the original Isis iconography) that Mary's powerful intercession with her divine Son was part and parcel of his regnant glory.[108]

---

[104]This becomes a central ritual in the Isiac Passion Week rituals, when devotees would go around houses symbolically disheveled and weeping, searching for clay figurines of parts of the god, a ritual sardonically mocked by apologist Minucius Felix, who witnessed it in North Africa.

[105]See further V. T. Tinh, trans., *Isis Lactans: Corpus des monuments gréco-romains d'Isis allaitant Harpocrate* (Leiden: Brill, 1973).

[106]First seen in the time of Origen of Alexandria but becoming a dogmatic confession (Mary is the mother of God because Jesus her son is God incarnate) at the Council of Ephesus in 431. See further J. A. McGuckin, *St. Cyril of Alexandria and the Christological Controversy: Its History, Theology, and Texts* (Leiden: Brill, 1994).

[107]See further L. Langener, *Isis lactans—Maria lactans: Untersuchungen zur koptischen Ikonographie* (Altenberge: D. Rayen, 1996); E. Gebremedhin, *Life-Giving Blessing: Inquiry into the Eucharistic Doctrine of Cyril of Alexandria*, Studia Doctrinae Christianae Upsaliensia (Uppsala: Upsala universitets årsskrift, 1978).

[108]From the line in the Psalms that addresses God as "him who cannot be contained by the heavens." Since Mary's womb contained him (as incarnate God), the church argued, she must be "wider than the heavens."

None of these parallels are substantive ones in the sense that they demonstrate the church was heavily influenced by the Isis cult in any formative period. They are, rather, examples of later Christian missionary strategy in the patristic period, along the strategic lines of using the aspects of the alternative system one wishes to disrupt in a newly angled way. At the end of the day, it has to be said, Mary the mother of Jesus might have been given a title and an iconographic stance from the Egyptian environment; but there remains a world of difference between the virgin of Nazareth and the erotic queen of magic. The Marian cult was meant primarily to disrupt Isiac devotion, not mimic it.

Isiac religion had a very developed liturgical sense. Many of the prayers and litanies addressed to her are extant.[109] She was the "goddess of a thousand names." Public street processions and elaborate ceremonies before a congregation made it a very attractive social religion, unlike the solitary rites of the ancient Egyptian temples, where the public was not admitted for most of the cult. A vivid example of this can be found in the often bawdy, always lively, novel *The Golden Ass: Or the Metamorphosis of Lucius*, written by fifth-century magus-philosopher Apuleius of Madaura. He writes of a character who is transformed into a donkey by black magic and has all kinds of adventures until, at the culmination of the novel, the donkey eats the festival roses of Isis on one of her street processions and is turned back into a human being once more. The moral is that Isiac devotion finally "transfigured him" into a true man.[110]

Priests carried *sistra* (rattles) that can still be found in Coptic and Ethiopic Christian ritual to this day. Holy water was sprinkled, and officiants wore white surplices over their clothing, sending up clouds of incense from thuribles. For the less-than-scholarly commentators on the Internet this of course "proves" a link to Catholic Christian ritual. But the connections are certainly peripheral. The priests of Isis would gather for the weekly celebration of her rites, and the question would be posed to the assembly: "Who has seen the Lady (*Kyria*)?" Those who had experienced visions of the goddess that week would be inducted as chief celebrants. Her temples were often used for incubational healing services (in the manner of the *aesculapia*), where the sick would stay overnight and be attended by healing clergy in the daytime but also expect to be

---

[109] See H. Kockelmann, *Praising the Goddess: A Comparative and Annotated Re-edition of Six Demotic Hymns and Praises Addressed to Isis* (New York: de Gruyter, 2008).

[110] Isis appears to him then and delivers the essence of her creed: "You see me here, Lucius, in answer to your prayer. I am nature, the universal mother, mistress of all the elements, primordial child of time, sovereign of all things spiritual, queen of the dead, queen of the ocean, queen also of the immortals, the single manifestation of all gods and goddesses that are. My nod governs the shining heights of heavens, the wholesome sea breezes. Though I am worshiped in many aspects, and known by countless names . . . the Egyptians who excel in ancient learning and worship call me by my true name, that is, . . . Queen Isis." Apuleius of Madaura, *The Golden Ass* 11.2.

visited by dream intimations of the divinity at night. Emperors Vespasian and Titus spent nights in the Iseum at Rome. Domitian built another temple for her there, too. On the arch of Trajan at Rome, the emperor is shown standing before Isis and Horus, presenting a votive offering of wine. Visionary experience was given a high role in this religion, and it attracted high-class devotees along with the poor.[111]

One night, in the late fourth century, a wandering Isiac priest on his way to the ceremonies in Alexandria got himself hopelessly lost in the desert to the south of the city.[112] Finding a light in the wilderness, he knocked on the door of what turned out to be a cave cell of Abba Olympius. Horrified to find that the visitor was a "priest of the idols" from Scete, he and his cell companion were nevertheless compelled by the rules of hospitality to offer him shelter for the night. Observing them at their prayers and admiring their ascetical way of life, he expressed the opinion that they must "see their god regularly" because of their devotions. Puzzled, they asked what he meant, and he told them of this practice of theirs. Abba Olympius said that he did not receive any visions when he prayed, and the pagan priest told him, "Then your heart must be impure." After he left them the following day, the story tells how Abba Olympios went to discuss this with the elders of the region, who enthusiastically endorsed the pagan's conclusion; and all agreed because the heart is impure the practice of prayer becomes all the more necessary. It is a deliberately humorous tale, a Christian deflection of the pagan critique of nonecstatic visionary experience, but one that gives testimony of what must have been regular encounters, especially in Alexandria, between Christians and Isis devotees. It shows that visionary, perhaps even ecstatic, cult was common in the latter and not in the former. The category of divine vision, so taken for granted among the Isiac priests, is a puzzlement to the Christian monks and something that clearly is being depicted for the less experienced as a trap to be avoided.[113]

In the fifth century, the Christian archbishop Cyril of Alexandria announced to his congregation that "a female demon has arisen in the desert called Menouthi." It turns out on closer investigation that this is code language for the great Isiac temple at Menouthi (a place, not a person's name). The temple, at the end of the great processional Canopic Way that led out of Alexandria, was the healing center for the Isis priests, where for a small fee healings were administered. The temple walls still bear the inscriptions of the cures effected there. In the seventh century, Patriarch

---

[111] Witt calls her the "darling of the emperors": Witt, *Isis in the Ancient World*, chap. 17.
[112] The story is in B. Ward, trans., *Sayings of the Desert Fathers: The Alphabetical Collection.* "Omicron" [Olympios] (Kalamazoo: Cistercian Publications, 1975), 160.
[113] See further J. Pettis, ed., *Seeing the God: Ways of Envisioning the Divine in Ancient Mediterranean Religion* (Piscataway, NJ: Gorgias Press, 2013); see especially my two articles in that volume, "The Ambivalences of Seeing in the Gospel Narratives," 105-27, and "Seeing Divine Things in Byzantine Christianity," 223-38.

Sophronios, exiled from his see of Jerusalem because of the Islamic invasion, visited the spot, because then there was a monastery there dedicated to saints Cyrus and John, and he presumed these healings were all those effected by the Christian saints.[114] What had happened was that two centuries previously Cyril, acting as Christian ethnarch and high priest of the great city, said that he had prayed because of his worries about the "female demon" who was luring souls to destruction in the desert. After his prayer he had a vision in the night, and a martyred soldier saint appeared to him, telling him that he was laid under the high altar of Cyril's church. If his relics were lifted, the saint said, he would go to the spot in the desert and battle with the demon and cast her out. One notes here the relatively rare occasion of matching vision for vision in the interreligious encounter.[115]

When Cyril ordered the altar to be excavated, he found, to his confusion, not one set of relics but two, and not knowing which one was the soldier saint, he did some research and found that one was Cyrus, a monk martyr from earlier times, and the other was John, a soldier martyr. He wrapped both sets of relics in cloth of gold and carried them down the Canopic Way (formerly used for great city ceremonial rituals of Isis and now commandeered by the Byzantine Christians) in a chariot accompanied by all the local church. When he got to the Isis temple, he built adjacent to it a *martyrium* (a shrine to the martyrs) staffed by monks and installed the relics for veneration, leaving the saints to unravel the power of the demon.

We see at one level a specific theological conflict: vision for vision; new saint versus old goddess; monks versus Isiac priests; Christian healing replacing temple healing. At another level we see the clash of civilizations in miniature, for the Isis cult was very like Mithraism in many respects. There was an encouragement of multiple religious belonging. One could worship Isis and other gods, could go to her rites and attend others without concern. For Cyril, however, the leakage of his Christian congregation to the festivals of the synagogue was something he warned against regularly in his Paschal sermons.[116] Even more anxiety provoking (though he will not mention it, as rhetorical prudence debars it from open discourse) was the leakage that must have been taking place in the Christian ranks to other religions' rituals.

Isiac cult must have been doubly attractive to ancients: first for its colorful ceremonies and then for its offer of easy access to healing services (especially important at a time when a city doctor would have charged a high fee). The Isiac cult was immensely liberal and open, but one thing it absolutely forbade, and that was recent

---

[114] Sophronios of Jerusalem, *Encomium on Saints Cyrus and John* (PG 87.3).
[115] McGuckin, "Influence of the Isis Cult."
[116] Written every Pascha for the church of Alexandria, when clearly many Christians were attracted also to the celebrations of the Passover in what was still a very Jewish city.

contact with the dead, anything dead, which was ritually defiling. The priests of Isis even had to shave off their bodily hair (it being considered as a dead thing) so as not to defile the holiness of the goddess's sacred sanctuary. Cyril has thought about this carefully. By installing the bones of his Christian martyrs, he has made it a sure thing that henceforth Christians coming to Menouthi to see the great temple would surely also pay their respects to the Christian shrine and kiss the holy relics. Now, when they presented themselves for Isis rituals, it would be the priests of Isis themselves who made sure those (Christians) who had "kissed the dead" would be strictly refused entry to the precincts. Cyril did not frighten off his believers from Isis by admonition; he used the vulnerable points of the Isiac system itself to effect his desired missionary strategy. In later centuries the Christian shrine of saints Cyrus and John itself became know as a center of the "unmercenary healers." The Isis shrine fell into ruin, and the monastic complex around the shrine became a replacement center of healing. Today the Egyptian place name (Aboukir) is a surviving Coptic reminiscence of it (*Abba Kyros*).

As with the Mithras cult, we again see Christianity in its early centuries somewhat dwarfed before the successes of this alternative religious system, in an age when the older cults were being clearly synthesized to produce new pluralist and open-ended religious rites. The church learned much strategy for its evangelization processes from this environment, but it clearly dug itself in on several key issues. First and foremost, it classed all the gods of other religions, Judaism excepted, as demons. It was because of this attitude that the Christians changed the very meaning of the word *daimon* from the original pluralistic sense of "helpful attending lesser divinity" into a cipher for dark and malevolent demon, servant of Satan, seeing them as spirits restless to seduce human beings to false cults, where these spirits could feed off the psychic reverence of devotees and stir them up to immorality as well as keep them from the true worship of the one God. The apocalyptic sense of the early Christians saw in these cults the demon hiding behind the temple statues who was delighted to encourage hostility to the Christians at every turn. Such an approach to cult made a chasm yawn between the rites of the various parties. Christian bishops would, without hesitation, debar from communion any Christian having anything to do with rites of the old gods after baptism. Before baptism the old religionists were solemnly exorcized before they could even approach the baptismal font.

In addition, the church is remarkable (and evoked much unfavorable criticism from its contemporaries for this point) for being a society seeking adherents (thus open to that extent) yet that was culturally closed on multiple moral and dogmatic levels. It put up a barrier between its ways and demands and those of the society around it. As a result, it stood out, not only attracting attention from those who found this way of life attractive because it was demanding, but also from those who in every age respond to such cultural difference by wishing to crush and destroy the other. The friction that we see between Christianity and Isiac religion went the church's way eventually, but for the early period it was certainly the other system that gained imperial approval and the support of the Roman intelligentsia.

**Cybele.** The cult of the mother goddess Cybele (*Kybele*) gives us another window through which to look at the wider Greco-Roman religious horizons in the early Christian period. According to Roman historians, the cultic *eidola* of Cybele was ordered to be brought (almost like a military hostage) to Rome during the crisis of the Second Punic War (218–201 BC), when the African general Hannibal was threatening the safety of Rome. The Sibylline books were consulted (Rome's collection of ancestral oracles that were regarded as the store of prophecies about all matters to do with the city's destiny), and an oracle was found that said the city's safety would be ensured by an Idaean mother.[117] This was taken to refer to the cult of the Great Mother in Asia Minor (Phrygia). The renowned temple *eidolon* (from which Christians rendered the concept of idol as a false god) that was worshiped at Pessina in Phrygia was a large piece of black meteorite (fallen to earth from heaven as a symbol of the goddess). In 204, therefore, the black stone was carried to Rome in triumphant procession and installed there in a shrine. Hannibal's retreat soon after, to fall back to the defense of Carthage, was widely seen as a fulfillment of the prophetic hope and led to the embrace of the cult of the Great Mother by virtue of Sibylline authority, giving her cult a formal status in the Roman pantheon, which otherwise such an Eastern cult (with numerous things the Romans continued to find socially distasteful in other foreign religious imports) would have found hard to achieve. A larger and more prestigious temple was built for Cybele on the important Palatine Hill in Rome in 191 BC. Finally, the Emperor Claudius (41–44 BC) acknowledged the cult as part of the official Roman religious rites. By the time of the Christian era, then, this religious system was a commonplace in Rome and regarded as "traditional." Her place in the pantheon was then often seen as interchangeable with Rhea, Demeter, and Artemis.

Cybele was acclaimed as the Great Mother (*Magna Mater*), or mother of the gods (*Mater Deorum*), protector of all things to do with womankind. She was healer as well as sender of disease. She presided over the fertility of things, not least the fields and harvests. She protected citizens in time of war. She was mistress of mountaintops and caverns, and queen of all wild things, especially bees and all wild beasts. At some indeterminate stage in ancient history her cult had subsumed that of the male Phrygian

---

[117]The "home" of Cybele was said to have been Mount Ida, near Troy.

god of vegetation, Attis. He was seen as a parallel to the Greek vegetative god Adonis, and so these two merged. The related cults were explained on the basis of a lover's relationship (some had Attis/Adonis as Cybele's son, which gave the whole thing an even tenser twist). Cybele was the divine goddess, the great mother, who loved a mortal. Distracted from this consuming divine passion, however, Attis fell in love with a young mortal woman and intended to marry her (some versions say it was the daughter of King Midas). Coming in immense wrath to the wedding ceremonies, Cybele scattered the guests and drove the terrified Attis out into the wilderness. On a mountain under a pine tree, Attis became frenzied (the cultic ceremonies were intended to induce an ecstatic emotional frenzy in the devotees in memory of this), and in this remorse of divine madness castrated himself and bled to death.[118] Cybele, now herself feeling remorse for the poor mortal lover, petitioned Zeus, the king of gods, to give him eternal life. This was how he was allowed to die yet return to life yearly, thus giving force and energy to the annual vegetational cycle as a dying and resurrected god. In his cult statues Attis as a youth is shown wearing the Phrygian cap (like Mithras), while the metamorphosized Attis is shown reclining peacefully, wearing braided hair and dressed as a woman. In later iterations of the Cybele cult, the life force the goddess offered was not merely agricultural but also passed over into a promise of personal immortality for her devotees, of which the resurrection of Attis/Adonis was the symbol, passing from fickle and suffering mortal to pacific deified being: an instance of the Roman concept of *apotheosis*, or divinization.

The priests of Cybele were a famous sight in the streets of Rome and elsewhere. Dressed in brightly colored women's robes, wearing long, oiled hair and heavy jewelry, and singing with cymbals and drums accompanying the statue of the Great Mother with dance, they begged for offerings in the street. All of them had to be male, and the initiation rite involved their castration. They were known as the Corybantes, but at Rome had the nickname *Galli*, or cocks. Other female devotees would share in this life-giving symbol of the blood by self-mutilation (cutting the body so that blood flowed profusely) when they too had danced themselves into a frenzied state. Such an ecstatic state was known as *enthousiamos*, which gives us the word *enthusiasm*, of course, but literally means "state of being filled with the god." Reaction against this explains the long-lasting Christian suspicion of religious frenzy and the preference of almost all the major Christian theologians for an understanding of the state of Spirit inhabitation that regards it as intelligence enhancing, rather than mind numbing, a state of joyful calm rather than a condition of agitated

---

[118] The pine became his sacred symbol. Pinecones, real or carved, were used in houses as amulets against evil.

exaltation.[119] The cultic ceremonies were known as the *orgiai*, from which we derive the concept of "orgies," once again from the opprobrium that the Christians attached to this form of ecstatic dance worship.

The statue of the goddess was that of a matron veiled and wearing a crown, the latter often in the form of a city wall. She is accompanied by lions. Sometimes the lions pull the chariot in which she rides. Often she carries a bowl and a drum. At Rome her chief festival was the Megalensia, held at the spring equinox: a fertility festival in which Attis's resurrection was celebrated. Games were held, and the main festivities passed from a day of mourning to a "day of blood," when Attis's passion was remembered and devotees would scourge themselves, to the Hilaria (the days of rejoicing), when street processions were held and anyone could dress up in masquerade. These events occured annually around March 25, and Christians would later choose this day to institute the feast of Mary's reception of glad tidings from the angel Gabriel, again using the cult of Mary to dislocate socially rooted pagan festivals at Rome.

From the second century onward there is increasing evidence that the ritual of *taurobolium*, a significantly elaborate ceremony of the sacrifice of a bull, was connected to Cybele's cult.[120] The one making the offering stood underneath the animal, which was stabbed in the heart, depositing the blood as a shower on the devotee, standing in a trellised trench beneath. This ritual baptism by blood was a very expensive rite, keeping it out of the range of the common person, and was believed to wash away all sins committed for at least twenty years. The devotee was now *renatus in aeternum*, given a heavenly rebirth. Fifth-century Christian poet Prudentius, being deliberately disrespectful of the mysterious rites by publicizing them, gave a famous (and hostile) account of one kind of *taurobolium*, expressing his disgust at the concept of the priest bathing his head in blood and opening his mouth to drink it. Prudentius concludes, "Defiled as he now is with such pollution, entirely unclean with this foul blood of the newly slain victim, the congregants afterwards make way for him and give him reverence and acclamations: and all because the useless blood of a dead ox has spilled over him while he hid himself in a filthy hole in the ground."[121]

In Prudentius's time the ritual and the rites of the Great Mother served as a rallying point for the last pagan aristocratic reaction against Christianity. At this period, at least, women seemed to have been able to serve in the priestly rites. One aristocrat, Aconia Fabia Paulina, in AD 384 composed a memorial for her husband, Vettius Agorius Praetextatus, that said, "As you looked on I was initiated into all the

---

[119] This can be seen very clearly in the struggle against Montanism, a Phrygian movement that several early bishops thought had brought over elements of Cybelean religiosity and prophetic frenzy.
[120] R. Duthoy, *The Taurobolium: Its Evolution and Terminology* (Leiden: Brill, 1969).
[121] Prudentius, *Peristephanon* 10, lines 1006-50.

mysteries. You who are my reverent partner in life honour me as the priestess of the goddess of Mount Dindymus and of Attis. It was you who ordained me with the blood of the bull."[122] The ritual was also performed for the health and protection of emperors. The last time a known artifact records it is when it was celebrated for the welfare of Diocletian. The Christian emperors banned this ritual as one of their first enactments. The cult carried on in many places until fifth-century Christian Western Emperor Valentinian II officially proscribed the entire Cybele religion; after Theodosios I, it was progressively suppressed in the East.

It is difficult to unravel all the psychological and sociological signals contained in this archaic set of rituals and belief systems. Cybele stands as a challenge to the modern imagination. It represents the deep, earth-rooted, and prerational aspect of religious cult in antiquity. The "correspondences" between this and Christianity, which positively hated the cult of the Great Mother, are predominantly negative. Christianity has several aspects that profoundly contrast it with such a cult: first, its deep emphasis on biblical morality (especially sexual morality) that looked on the Cybelean *mythos* with hostility; second, its refusal to advocate a frenzied form of worship (Christianity kept to the Jewish custom of reading sacred Scriptures and shared its eucharistic meal very soberly, from all accounts); third, there is a deep turning away in Christianity from animal sacrifice and bloodletting rituals, which were so prominent a feature of the Cybele cult. Last, noting the popularity of the festivals such as Hilaria, the church, once it gained a social ascendancy after the fourth century, did not so much seek to replicate them as fundamentally exchange them. As it did with the feast of midwinter Lupercalia, so too with the vernal equinox Hilaria: the popes at Rome first introduced the feast of Christ's nativity, and then, retrospectively to the spring, located the feast of his conception, the annunciation to the virgin, deliberately so to fall over the pagan celebrations to try to overshadow them.

Some have thought to discover deeper assonances, though none of these, I think, can be considered direct dependencies in any sense at all. Rather, they illustrate for us what ancient men and women of this time looked for as a religion to begin with. So, for example, Attis as a dying and rising god whose passion was celebrated in the springtime, and whose resurrection was marked by festivals, bears some resemblance to the passion and resurrection of Christ at Pascha (spring) time. The *mythos* narratives, of course, could not be more different. Although Attis did become a symbolic form of *apotheosis* (divinization) in later periods when extensive allegorization was applied to the ancient rites, it is not clear that the resurrection of Attis was originally understood much as a core paradigm of the individual resurrection of believers.

---

[122] Cited in M. J. Vermaseren, *Cybele and Attis* (London: Thames and Hudson, 1977), 110.

Likewise, the baptism by water into the death of the Lamb (Jesus) might seem to bear parallels with the entrance into the death of Attis by the *criobolium* rite (the offering of a ram). But again the rationale of the *mythos* here is radically different, the Lamb-Jesus parallel being supplied entirely from scriptural symbolism related to the Jerusalem temple, not from Hellenistic culture. Moreover, Christian thought about Jesus as a sacrificed lamb is actually code language in the church for arguing that animal sacrifice is now passé and redundant after the death of Jesus on the cross as a final, once-for-all sacrifice of atonement for the whole world. No twenty-year validity of forgiveness is offered by Christianity, but more a wholesale shifting aside of such rites of temporary lustration. Nothing in the Great Mother archetypes, either, corresponds to the Christian Marian cultus, except that the latter was obviously used in a missionary spirit to disrupt the former. What is common, of course, is the archetypal notion of what sacrifice was, what atonement might mean: how humanity suffered from its mortal limitations and how universal the aspiration was for ascent to the divine and elevation away from fickleness and sorrow toward a state of godly peace. These fundamental religious concerns can indeed be seen as commonalities. The answers as given by the two religions were radically different, though both religious systems grow out of the same sociopsychological soil.

**Manichaeism.** As a last example of (the many) rival cults and religious systems that operated at the same time as the early church, we can look briefly at the Manichaean religion. This is different in many respects from such things as Isis and Cybele, which were antique religions reinventing themselves in the later Hellenistic period, or Mithraism, a new religious revival clothing itself in antique forms. Mani was a real person, someone whose teachings were given to real audiences, collected by devoted disciples, and who was arrested for his theology and executed in a horribly tortured form. His *cultus* sprang up after his death and extended far and wide, demanding severe moral styles of obedience from followers. He was a moral and a metaphysical teacher who expected his message to impinge on daily life in a very personal way. Albeit two centuries after Christ, the pattern of the reception of this new doctrine has several parallels with Christianity, though in its doctrinal shape and in the form of the polity that it assumed Manichaeism takes a significantly different path from the early church. Even in the fifth century it was attractive to intellectuals such as the young Augustine, who spent many years of his life as a Manichaean before converting to the catholic Christians.

In previous generations very little was known about the movement, except for how it featured in Christian apologetics, though the first intellectual to complain in writing about Manichaeism as a movement was actually pagan philosopher

Alexander of Lycopolis.[123] The fourth-century Christian apologists who write against it include Ephrem of Nisibis and Titus of Bostra, both in Syria; Serapion of Thmuis in Egypt; Epiphanius of Salamis in Cyprus; and in the following century Augustine of Hippo in North Africa. Later apologetic exchanges show the movement carried on for a long afterlife in the Roman Orient, though in the Western Christian areas it more or less faded away after the sixth century.[124] In the Eastern church sixth-century Syrian theologian Severus of Antioch is engaged against them, and in the eighth century so too is Theodore Bar Konai.[125] Through the ninth to the eleventh centuries the Manichaeans crop up in Arabic Islamic apologias.[126] In the twelfth century they feature in Buddhist sources, too.[127]

In 1904, a series of original Manichaean documents was rediscovered, beginning a stream of subsequent documentary sources from their own circle, which greatly amplified and contextualized the understanding of the movement.[128] As a religion dedicated to religious fusion, the sources themselves demonstrate very great intellectual flexibility and variety. There is a still a lively subculture in existence debating the movement's precise relationship(s) to Christianity, Gnosticism, Persian religion, astrology, and Buddhism. Despite the obvious fact that this was a very open and absorptive system by design, there seems, nevertheless, to be a core of ideas that were common to most variant forms of Manichaeism across its large geographical and historical span.

Mani (which seems to have been a title of respect more than a personal name) was born on April 14, 216, in Parthia near the city of Seleucia-Ctesiphon, which had recently fallen under Persian military control.[129] In the Roman imperial domains his movement would never quite get over the association with Parthia, which was the great political enemy of Rome. In 220 his parents, Patik and Maryam, took him to live with an Elkesaite community, the Jewish apocalypticists who taught that the world had received a series of revelatory sages to teach it wisdom across the ages, of

---

[123] Alexander of Lycopolis, *Against the Teaching of Mani*.
[124] Several claims have been made that later dualistic heretical movements of the medieval period, such as Albigensianism or Bogomilism, are resurrected forms of Manichaeism—but any direct connection is no more than tenuous.
[125] A. Scher, ed., *Theodor bar Konai: Liber Scholiorum II* (Louvain: Brill, 1960).
[126] Wadih al Ya'qubi (ninth century); an-Nadim (tenth century); al-Beruni (eleventh century); and al-Sharastani (twelfth century).
[127] The histories of Tsung-Chien and Chich-p'an.
[128] See P. Mirecki and J. BeDuhn, eds., *Emerging from Darkness: Studies in the Recovery of Manichean Sources* (Leiden: Brill, 1997); I. Gardner and S. N. C. Lieu, eds., *Manichaean Texts from the Roman Empire* (Cambridge: Cambridge University Press, 2004).
[129] The modern region of Iraq. His biography can now be based more reliably on the late fourth-century Codex Manichaeus Coloniensis, discovered in 1969 in Upper Egypt, now lodged in Cologne.

which Jesus was a recent example. Mani's first language was Middle Persian, but he produced, in the end, most of his works in Syriac.[130]

When he was twelve he received a revelation from a heavenly twin companion (*syzygos*), who gave to him his fundamental systemic ideas: that the world was a battlefield for a perennial struggle of the two primal principles, light against darkness. The twin urged him to break with the Elkesaites. A second epiphany when he was twenty-four commanded him to become a messenger of light and salvation to the world. Accordingly, in 241, he journeyed to "India" (Afghanistan) and studied aspects of Buddhism there. When Shapur I became the shah of Persia (242–273), Mani presented himself at court to preach his mission and had a favorable reception. For thirty years the Persian court was a center of his mission. He took other journeys to Egypt and appointed his close disciples Addai, Thomas, and Hermas to lead his missionary endeavors.[131]

Close association with kings, however, can be a dangerous as well as a helpful thing for a missionary. After Shapur's death in 273 a violent reaction set in, with traditional Zoroastrian religion making a concerted effort against Mani and his whole movement. The new shah, Bahram I, had Mani arrested and executed in prison in 274.[132] His body was flayed, to remove the skin whole, which was then stuffed with straw, dyed, and hung off the walls of the city of Gundispur as a warning to all. His followers were savagely persecuted, which caused rapid movements eastward (to India and China) and westward to Egypt, North Africa, and Rome, where they now come into the Christian purview. At this same period, Diocletian's government, already persecuting the Christians, also regarded them as a dangerous and illicit religion.

Mani regarded his vocation as bringing about a universal religious syncretism. He certainly saw himself (modeling himself on Paul) as "an apostle of Jesus Christ," also calling himself both Paraclete and last of the Christian prophets. He probably also portrayed himself as a reincarnate form of Zoroaster and Buddha: last of the line of sages sent to the world by the powers of light to rescue souls fallen into the darkness of ignorance. His own followers paralleled his execution with the crucifixion of Jesus, a fate of the many sages of light, who were hunted down by the powers of darkness in this sublunar cosmos.

---

[130] His key writings are a *Fundamental Epistle*, which St. Augustine comments on closely; the *Shabhuragan*, written in Middle Persian, which he dedicated to the shah; *A Living Gospel*; the *Letter to Edessa*, contained in the Cologne Codex; and the *Book of Giants*. He is also said to have produced a book of illustrations of the creation called the *Arzhang*, which gave him the epithet in Islamic sources of "Mani the painter."

[131] Alexander of Lycopolis, *Against the Teaching of Mani* 4.20.

[132] Some sources have 277.

Manichaeism is essentially a cosmogony: an explanation of how the world originated and why it works as it does, especially why there is so much evil and suffering in it. To this extent it shows marked influences from Buddhism and the Four Noble Truths. According to Mani, Christians had some things right but had many corrupted sources. Chief among the mistakes was their adherence to the book of Genesis. Far from being a creation of a good God, this world is really a passing product of three phases of primordial development: former, present, and future.

In the former (time) we have the primeval, happy separation of spirit and matter, light and darkness, good and evil. There is no evil for the spiritual, no suffering. The good "God of Four Faces" (also the "Father of Greatness and Light") presides over the kingdom of light, which perennially sponsors all good energies and achievements and is composed of five elements of beatitude: the gentle breeze, the refreshing wind, the radiant light, the living fire, the limpid water. There are five dwelling places (mansions) in this beatific life: Intelligence, Knowledge, Reason, Thought, and Deliberation. The kingdom of darkness is situated to the south of the dominion of light, presided over by the monster whose head is a lion, whose rump is a dragon, whose wings are a bird's, and whose tail is of a fish.[133] The "prince of darkness" is fundamentally evil, presiding over all that is negative and hostile to the life of spirit and truth. All here is lust and conflict. His primordial domain of darkness is characterized also by five elemental forces.[134]

Second is the time of the present of middle moment. It consists of the painful mixture of both of these warring sets of principles in this current world. Spiritual forces (archons) of the darkness enter the domain of light accidentally. They lust after the energies they see and try to capture them. Materiality is one of the evil dominion's characteristic forces, bearing with it the source and root of all suffering. Seeing the light at its border, the principle of evil invades the spirit world to enslave its energy. To defend the peaceful and vulnerable kingdom of goodness from the assault of the archons, the Great Father creates out of the light a number of archetypal warrior Aeons.[135]

In the war that follows, the Great Spirit and Primordial Man invade the dominion of darkness and defeat the archons, but from their body parts the present material cosmos is formed by the Demiurge. He makes ten heavens and eight earths. This cosmos is unstable and begins the immense problem that is to follow (of the mixing

---

[133]On three sides the kingdoms reach out to infinity: on the fourth side, however, they are tangential to one another.

[134]The stifling smoke, the devastating fire, the destroying fire, the turbulent water, the obscurity of chasms.

[135]The mother of life, who is also the Great Spirit; she emits the Primordial Man and his five elemental sons (his weapons of the five elementals: air, wind, light, water, and fire).

up of light and darkness), but his intention was to imprison the evil archons. To keep the cosmos stable, the Great Spirit evokes from herself five sons.[136] The first and last hold the cosmos between them. When they shall finally cease to do so, the conflagration of the end will come, which is the third and ultimate moment, when light and darkness will once more be finally separated into their respective spheres (a cosmological and personal salvation). The warrior spirits are largely successful in trying to resolve the great evil of the polluting mixture of good and evil in the cosmos. They stabilize an unstable creation and also start to prepare the means of the future separation of light and darkness. Even so, throughout the cosmos multitudes of particles of the light remain trapped within the structures of darkness. In interpreting the world, therefore, both aesthetically and morally, all that we find good and gracious in it is on account of the particles of light; all that is evil and ugly is because of the darkness still present in it.

The Great Father's system of salvation works by means of his spiritual agents through the various heavens. Evil principles are either pinned to the heavens (if they have not been responsible for trapping light in this world) or else swept aside by the spiritual elemental forces. The aim is always to liberate light and spirit from the entrapment of dark evil. The Living Spirit (greatest of the warrior Aeons) makes two important salvific movements. First, she fashions the sun and moon out of purified light, to serve as safe zones and collecting stations for the pure light that remains entrapped.[137] Spiritual lights (including souls) once freed from the mixed cosmos would be saved here and then sent back via the Milky Way to the kingdom of Pure Light.[138] Second, she sent the hermaphroditic "Third Messenger" to battle the demons who still kept spirit-light imprisoned by force. The Third Messenger represented him/herself before each of them in the guise of an exquisitely desirable sexual partner. If their lust led them to embrace him/her, they were made to ejaculate the spirit-light within them, and then the Third Messenger sent it upward in liberty. The demons of darkness, however, grew wise to this strategy and reacted by making a counterfeit of the Primordial Man by employing the energy of sexual copulation among themselves. A great male and female demon was thus fashioned by the prince of darkness, and they captured all the light particles they could and then copulated with each other to make Adam, the first of terrestrial humans. He is the microcosm that contains in

---

[136] Splenditenens, the king of honor, the Light-Adamas, the king of glory, and Atlas.
[137] The spirit-lights proceed from the moon to the sun, which is why the moon waxes and wanes at various times.
[138] This is why astrology played an important role in the religion. The Milky Way was the Manichaeans' "column of glory." The zodiacal forces, however, were imprisoned archons and thus evil signs, having dark sway over sublunar life and hating one another.

himself the light of the soul and the darkness of the material body. The demons then repeated the process to make Eve. She was like Adam but had less light trapped within her and was meant to keep the soul-light repetitively trapped within matter by endless copulations among humanity, making them forget their greatest need is to escape material entrapment.

So the making of the human race, far from being a creation of the good God, was a work of demonic malignity designed to keep spiritual light in perpetual ignorance and thrall. To offset this disaster, however, the forces of light send the great Jesus the splendor to be a revealer to Adam. He allows Adam to glimpse the Great Father and his own glorious work as rescuer of light, and makes him eat of the tree of life, which is how knowledge of the state of imprisonment dawns among humankind. To assist this work of salvific revelation the great Jesus the splendor evokes from his powers of light the Light Mind (a great, cosmically beneficent being who has great powers to liberate light from darkness) and then the apostle of light. It is this latter spiritual principle who becomes incarnated across history in the great religious sages who beneficently teach humankind the *gnosis* of their spiritual imprisonment: sages such as Buddha, Zoroaster, or the historical Jesus. The forces of darkness, however, deliberately defile and corrupt the teachings of each of the sages, so in the end Mani has to come to give the full revelation of the paths of escape. He is the historical incarnation of the superior Light Mind. His, therefore, is the supreme "religion of light" and the greatest of all paths to salvation.

Mani's use of Jesus as a sage figure in his system, therefore, does not always refer to the historical Jesus. Augustine says the Manichaeans used the title of Jesus to refer to at least three entities who functioned as saviors: one stationed on the sun and moon (Jesus the splendor) one who sums up the light imprisoned in our universe (suffering Jesus, cross of light), and one who came among humans in the guise of a human being to teach truths of liberation (Jesus Son of God).[139] Even this Jesus the Son of God, however, is not to be identified with the historical Jesus of Nazareth who was crucified. The latter's very birth from Mary (whether virginal or not) proved that he was a material being and could not possibly have been a primeval Savior of the Great Father, only a teacher of truth. For this reason, the several Jesus hymns one finds in Manichaean worship books (while they might have appealed at first glance to Christians of the great church as comparable even to their own christological hymns) would soon be explained to them in a more "exact" manner by Manichaean catechists. Jesus among the Manichaeans is usually not referring to the Jesus the mainstream Christians imagined, but rather to archetypal principles of whom Jesus

---

[139] Augustine, *Contra Faustum* 20.11.

of Nazareth was merely a partial symbol, never an instantiation. An example of one of these Manichaean Jesus invocations is in the short reader following.

For the later Manichaeans, Jesus of Nazareth himself was in all likelihood only appearing to be human. Those who insist on his materiality, his physical birth and death, simply show their ignorance of the ways of the light. In this, the Gnostic-Docetic Christologies appealed to the Manichaeans considerably.[140] It is possible that this Manichaean aversion to the fleshly reality of Jesus influenced early Islam and made its way into the Qur'an, with its great aversion to the notion of the reality of crucifixion. When Mani calls himself "apostle of Jesus Christ," therefore, he did not intend this to mean he was a disciple of Jesus of Nazareth, in the way Paul might have done. He means it to refer to his status as soul vehicle of the great angelic being, Jesus the Light Mind, whom he will teach Christians, presumably, to replace in their devotion, should they turn to his greater truth.

True believers had to understand that their religious goal was now to detach themselves as much as possible from the entrapments of materiality and live for the light, hoping for its ultimate separation, when the soul could return to the kingdom of light. A descending set of ascetical practices was thus prescribed. The organization of the Manichaean community seems to have been (roughly) mimicking the early polity of the Christians. At the top of the hierarchy was the *archego*, the successor to Mani. Then there were the elect. First came twelve teaching apostles, major disciples and missionaries. After them ranked seventy-two bishops. Augustine's onetime mentor Faustus was one of them. Then there were 260 priests. Below them ranked the ordinary Manichaean faithful. These were called the auditors (catechumens).

Strict ascetical separation from material concerns was enjoined on the hierarchy, but the auditors were allowed to follow ordinary lifestyles and even to marry, although procreation was to be avoided in their sexual lives, as this simply made the problem of entrapped light even worse.[141] They could kill life if necessary (even harvesting grain was a life-killing activity), but they had to feed and care for the elect, who could own nothing, could kill nothing themselves, had to be vegetarian, and could not marry.[142] As a result, the elect tended to live nomadic lifestyles, depending on the support and care of the communities of auditors.

---

[140] See further E. Rose, *Die Manichäische Christologie*, Studies in Oriental Religion 5 (Wiesbaden: O. Harrassowitz, 1979).

[141] All those above auditors had to control their senses, live chastely, make the heart focused on only on light-filled spirit realities, and never kill life, either animal or vegetative, in order to live. They had to pray seven times a day and observe many fasts (about a quarter of the year).

[142] Their digestion of bright vegetables (containing most light) was a practical act of religion, since it liberated light from matter altruistically. See Augustine, *De Moribus Manichaeorum* 13.29–16.53; *Contra Faustum* 5.10.

Their meetings had holy days and fast days regularly. The death of Mani was commemorated by the Feast of Bema, when a portrait of the founder was venerated on a five-stepped raised platform (*bema*) and his *Living Gospel* was read out. New elect members were at that time initiated by a clasping of hands, a kiss of peace, and a laying on of hands. Auditors could hope, after death, to be reincarnated as elect, but only the male elect could pass from death to the kingdom of light (similar to the Buddhist doctrine of only monks entering Nirvana). This would be the way of salvation and endure until the final conflagration, when all this cosmic order would be destroyed and the two primal kingdoms would again be separated—after as much light as possible had in the interim been set free. Jesus the splendor will preside as last judge over this final conflagration and great separation.

Manichaeanism overlapped easily and extensively with Gnostic circles, with Marcionism, and with prophetic ecstatic movements. It was adaptable to many different systems, co-opting them, as it did with Christian doctrines, to its own overarching concerns. Portraying itself as a purer form of the original intent of Christianity, it explained the latter's alleged failures by corruptions. For the Manichaeans the importation into the Christian canon of the Old Testament was a serious error, and Paul should be given the lead in trimming the Gospel stories and their meanings (allegorically understood). The definite focal point of their system was the appeal to a metaphysical dualism of a strict order. By including materiality in the domain of evil and darkness, they offered the world of their time a striking moral imperative and motive. It was one that appealed to the religious and political pessimism that was extensive in the third-century empire, wracked by civil war and economic inflation.

Dualism has remained, if not a principle so starkly posed, a temptation of many religious systems ever since. Some have argued that Augustine of Hippo never really shook himself entirely free from his Manichaean upbringing, with its intrinsic distaste for sexuality and understanding of eroticism as a work of shameful evil, and that through him Manichaean tinges have survived in Western Christianity ever since. By and large, however, the church always saw Manichaeism as a hostile, piratical movement, which it fended off first by laying continued stress on the historicity of its founder, a living, breathing teacher who truly suffered and died; and second by holding fast to the canon of the Old along with the New Testament and teaching a continuity of prophetic witness fulfilled in the resurrection.

Because Manichaeism came along only in the middle of the third century, the church had already laid down most of its foundational governance structures and had already adopted the creedal system that allowed it to remain largely impervious to Manichaean influence. What dualistic metaphysics remains in

Christianity is more ascribable to Jesus himself, who taught the coexistence on earth of the kingdom of God and the dominion of the prince of this world, who constantly wars against the children of light and seeks to damage them. In this moderated form of dualistic metaphysic, however, the stress is firmly on the singleness of the divine power, an ultimate force of light and goodness, directly related to the cosmic order (not distantly mediated to it), which it regards as fundamentally good. In the New Testament doctrine (which comes from Jewish apocalyptic thought, as originally did Mani's borrowings) ultimate victory belongs to God, but the kingdom of God will be built out of the very fabric of the righteous use of the material world.

The Christian system, for all its appearances of dualism, does not share the fundamental Manichaean pessimism at all. It is at heart a highly optimistic system of a God who is not an ultimate principle of goodness, but a loving Father, who does not regather scattered cosmic principles of light as much as draw his family into himself by virtue of the exercise of charity and justice. It is ironic in some ways that this most adaptable, historically free-floating religious system did not so much absorb Christian religion as it hoped, but consumed so much of Christian ideas itself, though ultimately in a tangential way. Christianity's strong local polities of episcopal governance and tightly organized communities of worship gathered around Eucharist, gospel, and creed made this third-century threat to its coherence not critical at all. It makes no sense, by this stage, to talk about Manichaean Christianity or Christian Manichaeism in a way that, for example, a century earlier one might have done with the (equally adaptable and plastic) adjective *Gnostic*.

## EARLY CHRISTIAN RELATIONS WITH THE JEWS

This ought to be, one would think, a major section of any early Christian history. And one is probably right in that supposition to this extent, that relations and interreligious engagement, whether positive or negative, must have been extensive and on a daily basis between Jews and Christians. This especially must have been true in Roman Palestine, Rome, Antioch, and Alexandria, where we know definitively that large communities of Jewish intellectuals and merchants gathered at exactly the same time that Christianity was establishing itself as a distinct and urban phenomenon. But this is not going to be a large section of the book, for precisely the reason that the surviving accounts are extraordinarily slight. Was there some form of deliberate excision of each other from the accounts? Was it a case of embarrassment over the relationship? It is difficult to say because so much of the time one has to work out of a context of argument on the basis of silence.

This is not to say that "Jews" do not feature extensively, massively even, in references in early Christian literature. But even in the New Testament literature, which is the closest one suspects they ever get, the figure of the Jew is clichéd. Pharisees and scribes are relentlessly brought in as "opponents" of Jesus in the Gospels, establishing an impression that he faced relentless hostility, even though so much of his teaching (resurrection of the just, purity of heart as the key to the covenant observance, fundamental concern with exegeting the Scripture) would have resonated so positively with the Pharisaic movement, and even though we learn from the Gospels that several Pharisees were clearly out to protect Jesus from harm (Lk 13:31). The recurring way that the Gospels present the Pharisees as testing Jesus and contradicting his teachings is taken by (Gentile) Gospel readers (of most ages) to depict them as hardhearted and stubborn.[143] But the reality of being a first-century Torah teacher in Roman Palestine was that this is exactly how an ancient Jewish religious teacher operated—by mutual debate with other teachers in the presence of the teacher's respective disciples. Every dialogue, of course, was recorded by the respective school of disciples as a hands-down victory for "their rabbi." It was not a hostile and fractious clash, then, just the way ancient rabbis conducted themselves. The Gospel writers have been dislocated from this Semitic environment and have presumed, in the second Christian generation, that a dialogue between schools can be nothing other than a conflict between sophic teachers, as was the case when Hellenistic *didaskaloi* clashed in the larger cities—and used the occasion to try to poach disciples from one school to another. So the "hardhearted Pharisee myth" came to be born by lack of cultural understanding as the Christian message spread out to a Gentile audience outside Israel's geographical and intellectual borders.

This is not to say, of course, that Jesus had no areas of conflict with the Pharisaic party, for his idea of reconciliation was undoubtedly more radical than made them feel comfortable. But my point here is that even by the middle of the first century "the Jew" has become a stereotype, a two-dimensional figure in the literary apologetics of the church. And this set the tone for much to follow. Many Pharisees were surely among the first sympathizers of, even converts to, the Jesus movement after the first Pentecost, not just Paul (Acts 5:34; 15:5; 23:6-9; 26:5).

In considering the church's relation to Jews from the paucity of surviving texts one needs always remember the difficulty of drawing a large-scale picture from the indications we possess. It is like having three dots as distinct from a hundred dots that would

---

[143] A simple word search for *Pharisee* in the Gospel narratives presents this overwhelmingly negative façade, as do the results of a word search for *the Jews* in the Fourth Gospel. The latter term probably ought to be rendered in English as "the Judeans," not the Jews as such but rather the party of religious leaders in Judea in the generation immediately following Jesus, which was hostile to the first missionaries, as Josephus and Acts inform us.

make up a hidden picture if one joined them up. Since the 1939–1945 war, also, there has been a growing (long overdue) movement to reassess and dig out of the long and hostile relationship that had grown up between the church and the synagogue. The Nazi genocide shook the conscience of Europe and made Christians think again about the pernicious nature of hostile interreligious rhetoric. This is a healthy and positive thing, but it has, to a certain extent, led to a certain amount of looking for "happy evidence" in the scholarly treatments of the theme of early Jewish-Christian relations, whose literature has been expanding since the late seventies of the twentieth century.[144]

One needs to make a division, in terms of the evidence of the relations between the two great communities, between Latin world, Greek East, and extraimperial borders. One then needs to make a division into five eras or stages. First of all, there are the first two centuries, where the New Testament literature and the earliest letters of the apostolic fathers give us the tone.[145] This then opens up into the early third century, when apologetics between communities show a sociological distance between Christians and Jews, when Gentiles now make up the majority of the church, and when battles over scriptural interpretation (and ownership) seem to be to the fore.[146] This is in some sense a time when the communities start to detach, covered by a cloud in the evidence. After 200 we do not possess any significant Jewish religious text in Greek. The tradition of such cultural bridge builders as Philo passes over solely to the Christians, and after this time one has to look for clues about interrelations in the rabbinic literature which, precisely because it has other agendas than bridge building, is nowhere as interested as the church is in making itself justified before another alien community. There are indications that rabbinic literature of the later third century starts to notice the Christian phenomenon more frequently as one of several factional secessions: the *minim* whom they think have lapsed from the covenant community.[147]

Third comes the latter part of the third century, when the larger Hellenistic cities became a locus of connection where larger numbers of Jews and Christians came into

---

[144] An excellent and succinct treatment can be found in A. S. Jacobs, "Jews and Christians," in *The Oxford Handbook of Early Christian Studies*, ed. S. A. Harvey and D. G. Hunter (Oxford: Oxford University Press, 2008), 169-85, with full bibliography.

[145] See further S. G. Wilson, *Related Strangers: Jews and Christians, 70–170 C.E.* (Minneapolis: Fortress, 1995).

[146] The chief question perhaps being, "Who is the legitimate heir to ancient Judaism?" Was it the rabbinate, who sought to make a new text-centered, synagogue-focused, and racially purist religion out of the ruins of the temple-centered covenant cult of ancient Judaism; or the Christians, with their deracinated, Gentile-centered, symbolic reinterpretation of the covenant rituals? Both inheritors were at a distance to the ancient Judaic practices (as can be seen, for example, by both traditions' desire not to reinstitute animal sacrifice as central to holiness practice), but both fought vigorously for the right to be seen as the legitimate heir to the title "Israel of God."

[147] J. Neusner, *History of the Jews in Babylonia* (Leiden: Brill, 1968), 3:12-16.

close intellectual contact, especially at Rome, Caesarea, and Alexandria. It was also a time when christological issues begin to take over the spotlight of "difference": from the Christian side interpreted that the Jews refused to acknowledge the fundamental issue of Jesus' divine status and thus his global role as world redeemer and sole mediator; and from the Jewish side interpreted that the Christians had apparently swept aside all other matters (law observance, historically grounded text interpretation) and deified a man, thus betraying the essence of monotheistic cult that was at the core of Jewish identity.

Fourth is the fourth to fifth centuries, when the patristic writers increasingly make "the Jews" into a literary two-dimensional opponent without much practical or personal connection—they simply serve as a theological foil (a covenant outmoded or sometimes even taken away by what is new). The way the Jewish people are treated in the hymns and comments of the fourth-century Ephrem the Syrian, for example, show a very marked loss of that "eirenic disputation" one can still find in his Syrian Christian predecessor of the previous generation, Aphrahat. The sermons of John Chrysostom, archbishop of Constantinople in the fifth century, and the exegetical commentaries of Cyril of Alexandria in the fifth century both show a sea change that has happened. A more caustic and dismissive tone is in place, along with the view that the Old Testament as a whole is as "shadowy" as the Jewish cause is outmoded. This large-scale theory of "placement" of the Jews in terms of salvation history was clearly not one shared by the Jews themselves, but it marks a deep disconnection religiously between the two peoples, and the rhetoric of "deicide" and supersessionism began a long road of mutual suspicion and alienation. From the later fourth century onward, Christian imperial legislation now started to turn the tide against pagans and Jews in terms of being equal citizens.

Fifth, and setting the tone finally as far as the first millennium is concerned, there is the sixth century and after, when Justinianic (and other) imperial pressure was increasingly applied legally against Jewish inhabitants of the empire—a sign of Jewish intellectual and cultural survival as still being robust within Byzantium. This pressure of legal disability started a move of Jewish cultural and religious forces further eastward and increasingly puts Jews out of the category they had inhabited for the first five hundred years of Christian life—that is, as a daily known reality. From this time onward Jews increasingly occupied the category of "the other" to the Christians. The frictions that had existed in the Judeo-Christian (dysfunctional) family since the beginning had by this stage really become a divorce, and the very idea of Judeo-Christian communality was not spoken of again for many long centuries to come.

The first of these periods, the first two Christian centuries, are dominated by the New Testament texts. Paul's letters provide a massively loud indication of how relations might be between established synagogues and wandering Jesus missionaries, and this material suggests quite clearly that disputation was the common language. It is only to be expected. From the standpoint of the missionaries for Jesus, only wholehearted and complete conversion was significant. Conversion was an apocalyptic choice: for or against God's Messiah. So the dialogue is presented from the outset in the starkest terms. The Gospel writers preserve Jesus' own instruction that whoever will not hear the Word of God, from the Messiah's messengers, is to be considered no longer a part of Israel. This is the meaning attached to the ritual of knocking the dust off one's clothes as one left a place (Mt 10:5-6, 14-15 and parallels). Now generally this was a custom of Jews who had traveled abroad and returned to the Holy Land; before entering its borders, they knocked off the dust of paganism so as not to tread it into holy ground. It was a graphic symbol of belonging and not belonging. Jesus attaches it to his own teaching by this instruction to his earliest missionaries to indicate to the villagers "within" the boundaries of Israel that covenantal belonging does not automatically attach to where one is resident (or even how one is born) but derives from "hearing the word of the Lord." In other words, it originates with Jesus' first missionary tours to stand as a major claim to prophetic status. Of course it was remembered in the Gospels in a second generation, when the missionary impulse of Christianity had largely moved out of the Holy Land proper, and then the instruction became more apologetically charged: who had the right to be regarded as Israel anyway?

Matthew's version of this story still relates it to the special ministry of Jesus as a prophet speaking only to the Jews. In Mark's hands, however, it is clear that this Evangelist scours all the Jewish foundational texts to find each and every example of how the rupture with the Jews would be prefigured. In his case it is not anti-Semitic attitudes that sponsor this literary *tendenz*, but rather the way that he finds the theme of the rejection of Jesus by his coreligionists to be the stimulus for God to pass the covenant gift on to the Gentile Christians. He has taken Paul's lead, for his is a thoroughly Pauline Gospel, and yet has sharpened it, forgetting (doubtless to Paul's chagrin, had he been alive to see it) the sense that the election of the Gentiles was not necessarily, or desirably, the deselection of the Jews (Jn 4:22; Rom 11:26, 28b-29).

One of the great powers behind the missionary expansion of early Christianity was not that it was different from Israel at all, but rather that it was the completion and fulfillment of Israel. We can even make that idea more precise: less theological, if one likes. It was not so much that earliest Christianity was saying it represented a fundamental break with Israel (this was to be argued later, when the church was predominantly Gentile and did not fully understand the profoundly Jewish matrix of thought the New Testament writings represented), more that it represented all that was best of Judaism, but for a more Gentile consumption: a universalized form of Judaism with a heavily curtailed application of food and ritual regulations.

At first the Christian missionaries such as Paul worked predominantly in the context of the synagogue Diaspora. We see such examples as Paul himself, Apollos, Barnabas, and several other named Jews and Jewesses who preached or sponsored missionary preachers. Paul's own career, as recorded in his letters and in Acts, focuses on successes and problems (rejections) with this bright apocalyptic lens of black and white reactions. But the historical reality must have been very different, with shades of opinion represented in the Jewish quarters of many ancient towns about how Jesus of Nazareth figured in the annals of Judaism. The writer of Acts plays the theme of the missionary preaching causing many disturbances in towns and the Jewish magnates of cities seeking the expulsion of the missionaries, like a recurring bass motif. But this is evidence that can be taken two ways, because the disturbances that did occur (apart from the times when pagan cult was disparaged) were surely internal Jewish arguments and community synagogue unrest and not (as later church imagination would have it) friction between Christians and Jews considered as two discrete religions. Paul can acutely sense a strong rejection in the synagogues where he preached of the very issue of the inclusion of Gentiles into the expanded Israel of God; but he sees this rejection by the Jews as no more than a temporary and local effect (Rom 11:11), something that could not possibly endure in God's scheme of things and certainly not a parting of the ways into two religions.

Flavius Josephus was a younger contemporary of Jesus himself. Arrested in the Jewish War, in which he served as a general, he gained the patronage of Vespasian, who employed him as interpreter. He was brought to Rome and liberated when Vespasian rose to imperial power, and then spent his time composing a retrospective history of the Jewish people. He gives a very early view of the Jesus movement from the side of a Jewish observer. Before his text was doctored, the reference to Jesus in his *Antiquities* suggested a certain disapproval that this teacher was a magus-like figure, a sorcerer (always a very bad thing in Jewish and Roman literature) who pandered to people's longing for works and wonders.[148] He does not think Jesus was a good thing in any way at all, more like one more of those disruptions that he

---

[148]Josephus, *Antiquities* 18.3.3, published in AD 93. It is the so-called *Testimonium Flavianum*. I would reconstitute the original (predoctored) text as having read something like this: "About this time there lived Jesus, a magus, who performed surprising acts and became a leader of such people as delight in such tricks. He won over many Jews and many of the Greeks, claiming to be the Messiah. After the accusation of the principal men among us, Pilate condemned him to a cross, but even then his followers did not disperse. The tribe of Christians, so called after him, endures even to this day."

chronicles that led to the great disaster of the Jewish-Roman war of AD 70. However, on the other hand, the several Jewish-Christian groups that survived (albeit as an increasing oddity in Christian perspective) well into the third century (*Nazoraioi*, Elkesaites, Encratites, Ebionites) each showed that the black-and-white model of conversion-rejection of the gospel, or the sarcastic reductionism of such as Josephus, was not one that corresponded with the larger reality. The Jesus movement proved very conducive to many Jews of the first century and was undoubtedly the seedbed of the spread of Christianity to Hellenistic cities, where it took root in the Diaspora synagogues after the fall of Jerusalem.

Instead of sharp lines between Judaism and Christianity, therefore, before the fourth century one must expect permeable areas. Even in the fifth century the regular Paschal messages of the Alexandrian archbishops, that Christians ought not to go to the liturgical celebrations of the Jews, suggests, does it not, that this was a pastoral problem that was addressed precisely because significant numbers of Christians enjoyed going to these Passover and other liturgies. There were points of conflict and friction, undoubtedly, as the core preaching of the Christians turned on issues of interpretation of the Jewish Scriptures in ways that challenged core areas (circumcision, legal observance, messianic expectation); and the record of second-century clashes such as those recorded in Justin's *Dialogue with Trypho the Jew*, or the way the pagan Celsus introduces to his *True Discourse* the figure of an acerbic Jewish critic to make his most caustic remarks about the stupidity of the Christians, all go toward supporting this. One also finds a few references (one notable one, for example, in the Martyrdom of Polycarp) in second-century persecution literature that complains that Jewish opponents were delighted at the arrest and execution of Christians. Jewish figures who join vociferously in with the accusations of the pagans are bitterly scorned in this literature, but there is also the sense here that somehow the Christians expected things to be different, that they ought not to have been treated as enemies by "the Jews." But in all this, it is important to remember the silent context as well, precisely because it is silent in comparison to the written record that observes the conflicts: namely, that the Christians grew up in the synagogue environment and must have done so quite happily until well into the second century.

The third century, as can be illustrated from the case of Origen of Alexandria, was a time when the two communities took stock of each other in a discernibly new light. They were aware of each other now as intellectually and culturally different: undoubtedly now as different *scholae*. The rabbis saw the Christians' claim to the Hebrew Scriptures in the same way that the Christians regarded the Gnostics' claim to represent the inner meaning of the Christian holy texts: with alarm. The rabbinic schools (Tannaitic, and then Amoraic rabbinism) of the early third century onward, which saw the birth of the Mishnah, moved Judaism out of a verse-based exegetical form and mentality (which Christians still held to) toward a subject-based system of close commentaries. This would ultimately sever its link with Hellenistic philosophy (though both Christians and Jews still used Hellenistic allegorical method extensively in this formative era). The Christians would retain a close relation to philosophical modes of analysis and discourse until well into the seventh century. This difference also sped up the distancing between them.

Origen's school at Caesarea was in close contact with Tannaitic sages, but the relationship between his *schola* at Caesarea and that of Rabbi Hoshaya, active at the same time, was like two sets of scholars devoted to the same library using very different methods of analysis and watching one another more than cautiously through binoculars from across the street.[149] Origen was a very close reader of the Scriptures. His *Prelude* to the famous John commentary is a masterly study on the nature of the call to be a (new) covenant people; but while he is deeply favorable to the Jewish religion, he is decidedly of the opinion that it missed the boat when the election of the Gentiles was delivered to it as a possibility for a new international future. Origen studied the Jewish master Philo closely, learning close allegorical technique from him, and it is probably due to Origen that Philo's works were preserved for posterity. He learned some elements of Hebrew himself and consulted with several Jewish scholars in Alexandria when he compiled his *Hexapla* Bible texts.[150] In many places he admits he has taken hints on exegesis from Jewish scholars.[151] He studied with a Jewish professor to advance his knowledge of Hebraic theology and was a personal acquaintance of the renowned Rabbi Hillel the Younger, the son of Jewish patriarch Gamaliel III.[152]

Even so, these encounters only underscored Origen's recurring teaching that it is only in Christianity that Jewish tradition attains its proper end.[153] He teaches

---

[149]See further N. R. M. De Lange, *Origen and the Jews: Studies in Jewish-Christian Relations in Third Century Palestine* (Cambridge: Cambridge University Press, 1976); P. M. Blowers, "Origen, the Rabbis, and the Bible: Toward a Picture of Judaism and Christianity in Third Century Caesarea," in *Origen of Alexandria*, ed. C. Kannengiesser and W. L. Petersen (Notre Dame, IN: University of Notre Dame Press, 1988), 96-116; J. A. McGuckin, "Origen on the Jews," in *Christianity and Judaism*, ed. D. Wood, Studies in Church History 29 (Cambridge, MA: Blackwell, 1992), 1-13.

[150]The six-columned versions of Scripture text and translations then available, which he used in Jewish-church dialogues over exegesis. See Origen, *Commentary on John* 6.212; *Commentary on Psalms* 3.2.

[151]*Peri Archon* 4.3.14; *Commentary on Matthew* 11.9; *Homilies on Genesis* 2.2; *Homilies on Numbers* 14.1; 27.12; *Homilies on Ezekiel* 10.3.

[152]Origen, *Homilies on Numbers* 13.5; *Homilies on Isaiah* 9; also see *Epistle to Africanus* 7; *Praefatio Commentary on Psalms* (PG 12.1056).

[153]See further the excellent synopsis of J. S. O'Leary, "Judaism," in *The Westminster Handbook to Origen*, ed. J. A. McGuckin (London: Westminster John Knox, 2004), 135-38.

that the special election of the Jews was given to the race because of the manner in which this people above all others raised its eyes to God and worshiped him in the purest of cults. But, for Origen, the special standing of the Jews (as firstfruits of peoples) was taken away because of their moral failures in latter times. And it is a fear he has for the church: that its zeal might cool and God might lose his special care for it.[154] He argues that the mistakes of Israel are moral examples the Christians must always remember and learn from.[155] Origen is a very close student of St. Paul, and he never forgets Romans 11:26, that God will never take back his promise from his chosen people.

But not everyone who followed him was as careful an exegete as he was. His is a highly philosophic way of moralizing, of course, and a long way away from a doctrine of God "taking away" election from one people and passing it on to another people. But one can see the stepping stones that could be taken to that later position. Origen's dominant exegetical theme of movement (in the advent of the church) "from shadows to reality" was taken up universally in Christian writing after him.[156] So those stepping stones were trodden, especially in Latin theological writing of the third and fourth centuries, which saw a flourishing of treatises titled "Against the Jews" (*Contra Judaeos*). This itself, of course, suggests that Jewish theological life remained strong in Italy and put up a robust defense of itself against a growing sense of supersessionism in the Latin church. The eras of the fourth century on into the fifth and sixth see the sense of supersession expanding and being reflected in imperial social and economic legislation against the influence of Jewish communities in the empire. In an ever uncertain political domain, where Jewish civil rights were protected or neglected according to how visible the community was, there came an ever clearer move of the intelligentsia eastward. Babylon, no longer Rome or Constantinople or Alexandria, became the focal center of Jewish life, and relations were frozen for many centuries in the aspic of the kind of supersessionist standoff visible in the late third century.

---

[154]Origen, *Homilies on Jeremiah* 4.3.
[155]Ibid., 4.5; *Homilies on Ezekiel* 7.1; *Homilies on Leviticus* 13.2; *Homilies on Psalms* 36.3.10.
[156]The "Old Testament" being understood as shadowy adumbrations of things that would only be clearly and perfectly revealed in the New Testament. For Origen, Christians were not only legitimate heirs of the Hebrew Scriptures, but more than this they were also the first people to have this old revelation fully opened to them, the first to understand the Hebrew Scriptures, since God's revelation was not a chronological mystery (first on the scene has legitimacy) but an eschatological one (the last to see sees the final truth most purely). See further J. Daniélou, *From Shadows to Reality: Studies in the Biblical Typology of the Fathers* (London: Burns and Oates, 1960).

## THE CHRISTIAN APOLOGETICAL TRADITION

The main thrust of "problems with enemies" that the church faced, however, was with the pagan society around it, and in assessing how it might deal with that threat the Christians learned much from ancient Judaism. Philo's work *Contra Apionem*, in which he gave a riposte to pagan philosophical critiques of Judaism, was in some sense a model for the Christians to follow, though it was not until the middle of the second century that they started to organize themselves to mount a literary defense against attacks from the pagan intelligentsia. Before that time it was mob violence and political denunciations that really were a more pressing issue to deal with.

For many pagan intellectuals, the racially specific and deeply exclusivist aspects of Judaism made it an object of attack, if not of derision, in late antique Greco-Roman society. Many of the earliest attitudes to Christianity carried on from this; even into the second century, many external commentators pile onto Christianity the selfsame anti-Jewish critiques, seeing it as simply an offshoot of Judaism that had retained its exclusivist mentality without adding much to the salvation narrative beyond scandalous tales of a resurrected criminal. This approach is clearly seen in Celsus's second-century *True Discourse*, in which he even uses the literary character of a Jewish intellectual to voice his worst criticisms of the Jesus movement. Other significant pagan critics were Lucian of Samosata (who found Christians simplistically naive) and court philosopher Marcus Cornelius Fronto of Cirta.[157] By far the most significant intellectual critic of the church, however, was Porphyry of Gaza in the next generation, whose eye was coldly fixed on Origen and his claims that Christianity fulfilled the aspiration of all the philosophies of the past. He was the most intellectual of all the ancient enemies of the church, and his Christian respondents knew that they could not bluff metaphysics in his company. This is in part why fourth-century Christian theology became rapier-like in its exactness.

In the second century, the persecutions in the time between Trajan and Marcus Aurelius stepped up the sense, both among pagans and Christians themselves, that they had emerged more clearly into the light on their own and now were not allowed any longer (by law or general belief) the subterfuge that they were just a pro-Gentile sect of Judaism. The legal persecutions that started to come on them thus stimulated the first wave of significant Christian apologists. The genre of apologia does not have in it any sense of our modern word *apology*. On the contrary, it signified "defense" or "justification" in the face of charges. The third century would see another wave of

---

[157]Lucian of Samosata composed a comedic novel recounting the adventures of the charlatan Peregrinus and ridicules the Christians by his account of how they honored him in his (short) period among them.

apologists whose thought about Christianity shows significant developments, more specifically rooted in an ecclesial environment. Then there were such men as Bishop Cyprian, Commodian, and the great Origen, who will be considered later. The fourth century too showed a significant alteration in the style and tone of the apologists writing at that period. The Diocletianic persecutions and the subsequent threats against the church by Julian then brought out mature Christian responses from theologians and philosophers who had read deeply in the earlier Christian tradition and who also enjoyed significantly more advanced educations than many of their predecessors. These fourth-century apologists are usually also "other things," such as historians, philosophers, and politicians: writers such as Lactantius, Athanasius of Alexandria, Gregory of Nazianzus, Apollinaris of Laodicea, and Eusebius of Caesarea. They have a lively sense that they are now in the ascendancy, socially as well as intellectually. Their apologias for the church are also meant as a detailed exposition of the spirit of Christianity so that the educated outsider can be attracted in.

But the second-century apologists, who shall be our chief focus here, are of a slightly different mode. Quadratus was the first known among them. By Eusebius's time in the fourth century he was almost legendary. Only one paragraph (as quoted by Eusebius) has survived of his work.[158] Tertullian stands out among them all as a whirlwind intellect and fierce writer. In those sharp times the church gained a curmudgeonly public intellectual who used his pen as a weapon of subversion and was caustic in his defense of his persecuted community and its integrity. His sharp tone and his puritanical style of manners have left him with far fewer sympathetic readers in this era. Feminist readers especially have often been shocked when they pick up Tertullian. Part of this is that he derives from the antique Roman context of social manners among the educated classes (his idea of social roles being determined by a large amount of the so-called Roman household code), but part of it is also that his very robust attacks on his enemies seem shocking to modern academic ears. Modern academics especially like to imagine that they are balanced and irenic in their attitudes and opinions. It is necessary to remember that several of those intellectual opponents in his day had served as state informers to make sure that

---

[158]We find mention of him in Eusebius's *Ecclesiastical History* 4.3.1-2. He addressed his *Apology* to Hadrian (emperor 117–138), probably at the time Hadrian visited Asia Minor, which would be AD 123–124 or 129. St. Jerome mistook him (*De Viris Illustribus* 19; *Epistle* 70.4) for Bishop Quadratus of Athens, who lived in the reign of Marcus Aurelius. He might have been that "prophet Quadratus" who was a disciple of the apostles mentioned by Eusebius in *Ecclesiastical History* 3.37.1; 5.17.2. The one surviving fragment reads, "But the works of our Savior were always present since they were true. For those people who were healed, and those who were raised from the dead, were not only seen when they were healed or raised up, but they were constantly present among us. And this not only when our Savior was still living, but even after he had departed, for they remained alive for a long time: so much so that some of them even survived into our time."

Christian intellectuals were arrested. This was the case with Justin Martyr, who was denounced to the state police by his colleague the philosopher Crescens and executed. Tertullian does not intend to go down quietly and has no love or respect for what he considers to be the enemies of truth and decency.

His literary disciple Minucius Felix, also a North African, shares that angularity. His apologia *Octavius* is full of ridicule of pagan rites, as well as protestations that Christianity is not the immoral cult the pagans have been brought up (from their own low level of religious expectations) to suspect. Neither Tertullian, nor Minucius, nor indeed any of the other second-century apologists can be accused of harboring tender thoughts of pluralist approachability. They wish to defend themselves; they intend to make a claim that legal proscription is unjust as well as unnecessary; and they also want to make a written encomium of their religion to attract to the church the well-meaning intelligentsia (the people who could read and might be expected to have social influence), in the first place to attract them enough to gain a toleration and peace, but also perhaps to convert them to the gospel. While the apologists usually exercise great reserve in offering close details of the Christian rituals, they nevertheless do provide some of the earliest information we have about the inner life of the church. But always it is that ecclesial life as chosen to be represented to the educated literary class. We see that family, as it were, posed for a formal photograph, not bantering around the dinner table. Almost all these first apologists come from an intellectual background themselves of Middle Platonic thought (a religious form of Platonism mixed with Pythagorean and Stoic ideas), and their depiction of the gospel is deeply moralistic in character.

**Justin Martyr (d. c. 165).** One of those leading apologists, and one who is also an important source for the life and worship of the church in the second century, was Palestinian philosopher Justin from Nablus. He was born a pagan and spent his early manhood making a dedicated tour across many places in the empire, studying the various philosophical schools that were available to him. In this educational journey, which coincided with his desire to find a philosophy to live by, not just something to study with academic detachment, he read the Stoics, peripatetics, Pythagoreans, and Platonists. Eventually, he tells us, as a mature professional philosopher (wearing all his life the cloak that signified his status as professor) about the year 132, he discovered the teachings of the Christians through an encounter with an old sage in the Holy Land and thereafter became a fervent convert to the gospel. He had been deeply impressed by the courage he had seen evidenced by Christians who held fast to their convictions despite being threatened with martyrdom.

Justin records how his Christian mentor showed him the meaning of the Old Testament texts and their fulfillment in the life and teachings of Jesus. Justin describes the experience in words reminiscent of the disciples on the road to Emmaus (Lk 24:32): "Immediately a fire was kindled in my heart . . . and I embraced Christianity as the only safe and wholesome philosophy."[159] He then began to teach Christianity as a way of life, alongside the other itinerant sages typically found in the agora of the ancient Hellenistic cities. Justin moved to Ephesus around 135 and engaged in debate there with a Jewish teacher named Trypho. One of his main writings was published after this as a stylized form of the record of that exchange: an apology dealing with Trypho's objections to the church's christocentric use of the Jewish Tanakh.

He then traveled on to open a school at Rome and set up a Christian school of philosophy there, where Tatian became one of his pupils. He taught during the reign of the Emperor Antoninus Pius (138–161), publishing his *First Apology* some time around 155, to make a case for the defense of Christians presently being persecuted by unjust laws. Soon after Marcus Aurelius assumed power, around 161, Justin issued a *Second Apology*, addressed to the senate of Rome. Cynic philosopher Crescens, who headed a rival school at Rome, denounced Justin to the authorities, along with several of his students. When they refused to offer sacrifice, they were scourged and beheaded. The record of their trial was taken down by eyewitnesses and still survives.

Justin is one of the most interesting of the Christian apologists. He refuted the usual charges made against the Christians (immorality, seditious intent, exclusivism manifesting hatred of humanity) but also set out to show to open-minded hearers the essential character of the new movement. He describes the church as fundamentally the community of those devoted to the Logos, or reason/Wisdom of God. The creative Logos had put a germinative seed of truth (*Logos spermatikos*) in all hearts, and in the person of Jesus the same divine Logos had incarnated within history to reconcile all lovers of the truth in a single school and communion of divine sophistry.[160] For Justin, Christianity is the summation and fulfillment of all human searching for truth. It is the archetypal truth brought to earth by the one who is God's own way and truth and life. Christians are monotheists, Justin explains to his audience, and believe that the Logos is God, like the *deuteros theos* spoken of by the philosophical tradition in reference to the Demiurgic world-maker. The Logos is in second place to the supreme God.

For later Christian tradition Justin's *Dialogue with Trypho* was a very important force in establishing a view of the Christian Gentiles as the new Israel. Like Irenaeus, he uses the Old Testament in a thoroughly christocentric way. His *First Apology* contains one of the earliest and most authoritative accounts of the primitive Christian liturgies of baptism and Eucharist. It is not a full version (and readers

---

[159]Justin Martyr, *Dialogue with Trypho* 8.
[160]R. Holte, "Logos Spermatikos: Christianity and Ancient Philosophy According to St. Justin's Apologies," *Studi e Testi* 12 (1958): 109-68.

thinking it is have been misled to think the ritual was very bare at this period, when it might well have been more liturgically ceremonial) because he only wishes to give his pagan readers enough knowledge to realize that the wild rumors prevalent about their initiation services are grossly exaggerated, and that the baptismal and eucharistic rites are deeply moral, concerned with cleansing of heart and loving communion: not naked orgies and cannibalistic magic. Justin's clarion call that Logos theology will be the dominant motif in linking together all roads of human wisdom and religion to Christ was something that soon became a core focus in all the theologians who followed. He, of course, undoubtedly followed the lead in this of the Evangelist John in his prologue who, using Sirach 24, merged Logos theory with the sophianic (wisdom) traditions of the Scripture to provide an overarching narrative of salvation history culminating in Jesus' incarnation.

**Tatian.** Tatian the Syrian seems to have been attracted by Justin's reputation when the latter was a Christian professor of philosophy at Rome. Tatian came there to study with Justin. When the arrest and execution of his teacher scattered the school he returned to the East, since he had been one of those the philosopher Crescens had threatened to destroy after they beat him in argument.[161] His chief works are an apologia titled *Discourse to the Greeks* and a four-Gospel compendium (the *Diatesseron*), in the latter of which he runs the discrete narratives into one (to make a single harmonized *evangelium*). Like Justin, Tatian says he had studied all the various schools of thought before he chanced on the sacred Scriptures of the Christians and was entranced by them.[162] This was some time around AD 155. The anti-heretical Christian writers of later times regarded him with suspicion as having too many leanings toward Gnostic-type thought. It became a tradition among them that it was only after Justin's death that his pupil started to go astray.[163]

Tatian structures his apology to the Greeks in four main sections. The work begins (chaps. 1-3) with a violent attack on Hellenistic culture as false, self-serving, and through and through corrupt. The philosophers particularly come in for a pasting. Then he offers a short "First Principles of Christian Theology" (chaps. 4-28). His topics are the spiritual nature of God, the creative role of the divine Logos, the Christian concept of resurrection, the nature of angels and their fall, the original humans and their lapse into the foolishness of idolatry and astrology, the pervasive force of demons, how the spirit works, how the mind and soul work, and how humankind finds salvation. It concludes (in chaps. 17-28) with a denunciation of so

---

[161]Tatian, *Discourse to the Greeks* 19.
[162]Ibid., 29.
[163]Irenaeus, *Adversus Haereses* 1.28.1; 3.23.8; Eusebius, *Ecclesiastical History* 4.29.1; Epiphanius, *Panarion* 46.

much in contemporary pagan life (gladiatorial games, drugs, political structures, sexual immorality) that is fostered and amplified by demonic deceits. The logic of all this curriculum strikes the modern reader as "strange" in its sequencing. But the topics were not far removed from a fairly standard "introduction to religious philosophy" of his day, and traces of this schema (moving from divinity to cosmogony, demonology to psychology) can still be seen in the way Origen structures his own *First Principles* in the next century. The remainder of his work (chaps. 31-41, prefaced by a short autobiographical section in chaps. 29-30) turns around two large themes: first (chaps. 31-35), the clear moral and intellectual superiority of the Christians, compared with the dissolute state of Hellenistic culture; and second (chaps. 36-41) the authentic tradition of wisdom demonstrated historically: namely, that the Greek traditions of wisdom are later, secondary, and thus show corruption of mind and morals. The earliest wisdom traditions are those given by God to Moses, which the church has inherited. In this way the church is far more ancient, rooted in the original streams of divine wisdom, than the Greeks, who falsely boast of their antiquity.

Tatian was a deeply ascetical person, and his teaching shows signs of leaning toward the Encratite position we have noticed earlier. His fierce hatred of the Greek culture in which he grew up is partly explainable by the savagery he encountered in the persecution, but also because he is deeply eschatological and sees the results of demonological corruption everywhere. Ascetical practice is necessary to withstand the relentless force. Later church writers regarded him as being quasi-Gnostic because of these tendencies. Clement of Alexandria read his now-lost work *Perfection According to the Savior*, which was an extended discussion on the Christian life. It seems to have continued his highly pessimistic tone about the conditions of life and the possibility of salvation. Clement, who is already a severe critic, says Tatian interpreted Paul's words in 1 Corinthians 7:5, "Do not refuse one another except perhaps by agreement for a season, that you may devote yourselves to prayer," to mean that only by celibate abstention from marriage and sex could one find union with God.[164] The continuance of marriage symbolized a continuance of enslavement to the devil.[165]

Tatian's doctrine is resonant with much of what would describe Syrian Christianity before the fourth century. For him, Christ is the model of all perfection because he is a poor man, a virgin celibate, a humble man. In this way of life he reverses (and redeems) the pride of Adam. This is one of the earliest ascetical elaborations of the core

---

[164]Clement definitely thinks Tatian was a Gnostic, attributing to him an interpretation of Gen 1:3 ("Let there be light") that read it as a plea from the Creator God to be the supreme God so that light may come into being. Clement of Alexandria, *Eclogae ex Scripturis Propheticis* 38.1. See also Origen, *Contra Celsum* 6.51.

[165]Clement of Alexandria, *Stromateis* 3.12.81-82.

"monastic" concepts of poverty, chastity, and obedience. Epiphanius of Salamis administered the deathblow to Tatian's posthumous reputation in the fourth century by classing him as a heretic who cut pieces out of the New Testament (not only the *Diatesseron* but also emendations he made to the Pauline letters) and who was so led astray by Encratite ascetical ideas that he banished wine from the Eucharist and drank only water. In his own time, however, Tatian offers an interesting glimpse of how a Christian *didaskalos* at Rome conceived his task. After his return to his native Mesopotamia, it is clear that his *Diatesseron*, before the fourth century ousted it, when Syrian church life came more in line with established Latin and Greek ecclesiastical practices, was for many generations the official liturgical Gospel of the Syrian churches.

**Athenagoras of Athens (c. 133–190).** Another learned Christian philosopher, Athenagoras of Athens, sometime around 176 composed a *presbeia*, or political embassy or petition,[166] to the emperors Marcus Aurelius and his son Commodus. He possibly wrote this for the occasion of the two rulers visiting Athens in September of that year. A treatise *On the Resurrection* is also extant (in one manuscript of the *Embassy*, which incidentally announces the theme in chap. 36, which attributes it "to the same author"). Athenagoras has a lively and clear style. The main purpose of his written work was to demonstrate to the literary emperor that the Christians were not the boorish underclass he might have been led to believe on hearsay. The prelude to the work (excerpted in the short reader below) asks for a hearing of the case of Christians, that they should not be condemned unjustly on mere hearsay but that the philosophical benignity the emperor is renowned for should be extended to them too as a matter of simple justice. Why, he asks, when all manner of people have the most ridiculous beliefs, deifying animals or even criminals, do Christians alone get marked out in imperial law and hunted to the death without even an investigation of their true positions? His apology then sets out to refute the most common charges of the mob against the church: that they are not atheists (chaps. 4-30) and that they do not worship with wild orgies and eat babies (chaps. 31-36).

His treatise on the resurrection is a considered philosophical defense of the rationality of belief in a resurrected body: a part of Christian doctrine that paddled against the entire stream of Platonizing sensibility in late antiquity. Athenagoras here does not appeal to scriptural arguments at all but addresses himself to the philosophical suitability of the biblical doctrine, as a philosopher among philosophers. He mainly addresses the force of the arguments that this is "ridiculous and unlikely," demonstrating several cases that illustrate his concluding theme of the preamble that "nothing is impossible to God." In the latter part of his argument he advances his own

---

[166]Known in Latin as *legatio*.

theory that since a human being is a synthesis of body and soul, the resurrected body is the fitting, completed vehicle of God's judgment on the life of that being: the resurrection being a formal part of restitutive divine justice, not an integral part of one aspect of humanity (such as the immortal soul the philosophers spoke of).

**Melito of Sardis (d. c. 180).** Melito was one of the leading Christian philosopher-bishops of Asia Minor in the second century. He was famed in his lifetime among the Christians as a celibate ascetic and prophet-philosopher, one of "the great lights of Asia," as he was called.[167] He was one of the Asia Minor leaders who held to the local custom of celebrating Pascha on the fourteenth of the month (Quartodecimans controversy). He composed about twenty different works that were read for generations after him, but in later centuries they were largely dissipated, and most are now lost. Eusebius gives a list of his compositions.[168] He also passes on to us some fragments of the *Apology* Melito wrote, addressed to Marcus Aurelius in the 170s.[169] Apart from this we have, more or less complete, a sermon he gave *On the Pascha*, which is a very rare and precious example of second-century liturgical preaching. It was rediscovered in 1936.[170] His sermon *On the Pascha* shows a lively conception of the divinity of Christ and is sharply focused against Jewish objections to Christianity, showing that in religious terms the local Jewish community was still his major discussion partner.[171] The work is a fine example of typological exegesis: a scriptural story being symbolically fulfilled in the life and work of Christ. This approach was to be become standard as a Christian way of appropriating the Hebrew Scriptures and demonstrating how all runs out of and back to the redemptive work of Christ, the alpha and omega of salvation history.

Melito's mind was steeped in scriptural symbolism. Many fragments of his remarks on Scripture have survived in what are known as the *Catena*, or fragments of exegetical observations from the ancients that were collated in later times as a quick guide for preachers. He composed a specific discussion on the book of Revelation, which of course refers to his own church in the very first generation (Rev 1:11; 3:1, 4). Melito went on pilgrimage to the holy places in Jerusalem (the first Christian known

---

[167] He was a celibate ascetic according to the testimony of Polycrates, cited by Eusebius in his *Ecclesiastical History* 5.24.2-8. He was called a prophet-philosopher by Tertullian, according to Jerome in *De Viris Illustribus* 24.
[168] Eusebius, *Ecclesiastical History* 4.26.1-4.
[169] Ibid., 4.26-27. The manuscript superscript titles it to Antoninus, but at a time when Marcus Aurelius was executively administering the empire.
[170] C. Bonner, *The Homily on the Passion by Melito Bishop of Sardis* (London: Christophers, 1940); O. Perler, *Sur la Paque et fragments*, Sources Chrétiennes 123 (Paris: Du Cerf, 1966); A. Stewart-Sykes, *The Lamb's High Feast: Melito, Peri Pascha and the Quartodeciman Paschal Liturgy at Sardis*, Supplements to Vigiliae Christianae 42 (Leiden: Brill, 1998).
[171] Based around Ex 12 and written between AD 160 and 170.

to have done so) in order to make notes so that he could explain the Scriptures more clearly to his congregation. He is also the first Christian known to use the term *Old Testament* to describe the Hebrew Scriptures, a concept Origen would popularize after him in the following century.

Melito's *apologia* to Marcus Aurelius, like that of Athenagoras, expresses a sense of disbelief that an emperor so renowned for philosophy and moderation, such as Marcus Aurelius, could really want to preside over a bloody persecution of an innocent community such as the Christians. He attributes the injustice to the emperor's local agents but calls for the ruler to take note of what is being done in his name and intervene. In the *Apology* Melito notes how the empire of Augustus and the appearance of Christ occurred at the same time and connects the two as collaborators in the civilization of the world. Origen will take this idea much further in his *Contra Celsum*, and it gave the church an increasing sense that the empire might well be the providential means that God would use to spread the gospel to the far corners of the earth, a missionary hope that is at the same time the dawning of a Christian theology of culture. Christianity, for Melito, is habitually called "our philosophy," a term that is used onward into the fourth-century Fathers (especially St. Gregory of Nazianzus) to underline not only the right of Christianity to take its place alongside the classical philosophical schools but even to claim a superiority over them. In Melito's case, he argues that the Christian way of life is a supremely practical philosophy of living, in whose close focus on morality it demonstrates its superiority over the classical schools because it can be spread among all classes and intelligences.

**Clement of Alexandria (c. 150–215).**[172] It was once thought that Clement was a presbyter of the Alexandrian church and head of its catechetical school, though the latter is no longer generally accepted.[173] It is far more likely that he was master of a private philosophical school, at a time when several other Christian philosophers (many of them Gnostics) were also teaching in the city. Clement began his studies in Greece and traveled to Italy, then through Syria and Palestine, before settling in Egypt as a philosopher. His encounter at Alexandria with Christian philosopher Pantaenus was decisive for him, and he was converted here to the Christian faith. He read extensively in Christian and Hellenistic sources. Clement's desire was to avoid the excesses of Gnostic speculation but still relate Christianity to the flow of Hellenistic philosophy. He spends time advising wealthy Christians on the right use of possessions and on

---

[172]Titus Flavius Clemens. Because he first speaks of beginning the travels that comprised his "quest for wisdom" in Athens (*Stromateis* 1.1.11), it has often been thought that he was a native of that city.

[173]He is thought to be a presbyter on the basis of *Pedagogus* 1.37.3; see Eusebius, *Ecclesiastical History* 6.11.6.

correct social behavior,[174] a sign perhaps of the type of student that the Christian church was now sending out for higher education as a result of its social and financial upward mobility.[175] His higher philosophy seminars presented Christianity as the true aspiration of all the ancient wisdom traditions of Hellenism, and in this respect he was one of the early and most original Christian employers of the Logos theology witnessed in the biblical Wisdom literature, in Philo, and in the Fourth Gospel.

His chief works comprise a trilogy (of sorts): *An Exhortation to the Greeks* (*Protreptikos*), *A Basic Instructor* (*Paidagogos*), and *Miscellaneous Pieces* (*Stromateis*, or *Stromata*). The contents of the three volumes present, in some form or another, an ascending curriculum for his students. The first attracts beginners to the philosophic life. The second advocates a standard of ethical behavior that is consonant with the pursuit of wisdom and that finds in Jesus the supreme guide to conduct and the midwife of wisdom as Logos incarnate. The final volume (symbolically named a "carpetbag") is a random set of aphorisms and teachings, highly enigmatic in nature, suggesting the curriculum that might be offered to advanced students of Clement who pursue the higher paths of esoteric seeking and are now fitted to be fed not so much with basic instructional materials but questions for further mutual discussion (a kind of list of suggestions for a symposium or advanced seminar). It is quite different in tone and conception from the other two volumes.

In later eras, beginning with his great successor, Origen, Clement had a powerful influence over some of the most mystical thinkers of the later Christian tradition; but his independence from many of the mainstream concerns of the church in succeeding generations (he is the last great Christian theologian to exist in an environment largely uncontrolled by episcopal scrutiny) also sidelined him. In ancient times he was called *makarios* (blessed) and *agios* (saint), but in the sixth-century West his supposed role in teaching Origen caused him to be seen (anachronistically) as a condemned Origenist, and in the ninth-century East Photius of Constantinople damaged his reputation for the medieval Byzantine world by claiming that his Christology was unorthodox.[176]

Clement's is a vision of Christianity that can use judicious philosophical training to absorb even some of the Gnostic ideas and synthesize them with the mainstream church in its mystical tradition (which is where the positive aspects of Gnosticism

---

[174]Advising them not to spit during dinners, and on how to choose a signet ring, and other such matters suitable for wealthy aspirants.

[175]See J. A. McGuckin, "The Vine and the Elm Tree: The Patristic Interpretation of Jesus' Teachings on Wealth," in *The Church and Wealth*, ed. W. J. Sheils and D. Wood, Studies in Church History 24 (Oxford: Blackwell, 1987), 1-14.

[176]Again on the basis of many anachronistic judgments—that second- and third-century theology did not use the terms of the Nicene faith.

are ultimately distilled and lodged by his and Origen's efforts). He is, in a sense, an anti-Gnostic Gnostic. He composed a treatise titled *Excerpts from Theodotus*, taking passages from the works of this Alexandrian disciple of the Gnostic master Valentinus and showing how the problems raised by that school ought to be understood by an intelligent person who was more in the mainstream Christian movement. He uses the method of dialogue so seriously and attentively that he is not simply giving a list of propositions to be condemned, rather ideas to be discussed. He affirms the value of the material world as a training ground given by God for humankind's good, and this overarching soteriological vision sees the Father-God drawing all humanity back to divine communion and ultimately angelic metamorphosis of the race, through initiation in the Logos-Son. The Logos is the pedagogue, the shepherd, or even the "breasts of God," giving the milk of psychic nourishment to the initiate soul.

Clement understands salvation as largely a cosmic ascent to truth, and in this sense his master scheme of salvation theology displaced some of the earlier Christian eschatology in favor of a transcendentalist metaphysic of communion. This was a movement that was to have a wider effect when taken up more systematically and extensively by Origen in the next generation. A similar attitude of open-minded discussions of "comparative wisdom," comparable to the *Excerpts from Theodotus*, is found in his biblical work *Eclogae Propheticae*. Here Clement collates the earlier Christian reflections on Genesis that he has at his disposal and relates them in a considered way to Hellenistic philosophical cosmogonies—Genesis, of course, being a friction point in the Gnostic-catholic controversies on the nature of God and the material world. Although Origen soon after him shows a similarly large imagination and expansive intellectual spirit, the latter was to attract the ire of leading bishops for his urging on Christian intellectuals to "go where reason (*logos*) took them."[177]

Clement's intellectual freedom and curiosity are rare in the annals of the church, and a certain closing of mind is inevitably witnessed in the later centuries when the bishops (such as Irenaeus) preferred simplicity of teaching for the masses in a liturgical setting, rather than advanced classes in theological philosophy for the educated elite. The friction between the Christian *didaskalos*, or professor, and the bishop hierarch (*episkopos*) is one that has remained warm even to this day, as of course has the gap between those who reduce the Christian faith to the simplest moral and historical levels, and those who see it, as Clement certainly does, as the fulfillment of all the aspirations of the world for wisdom and understanding.

---

[177] His motto was *hopou logos agei*: making a pun (reason/word) that reason's path would de facto be the way the divine Logos would lead the mind forward.

**Theophilus of Antioch.** Theophilus was bishop of Antioch between 169 and 183, according to Eusebius of Caesarea.[178] He was born near the rivers Tigris and Euphrates, and he became a Christian by choice, entering what he describes as a denigrated minority after being impressed by the reading of the Scriptures.[179] Of his four major writings only one now survives: a work of apologia titled *To Autolycus*, written at a time shortly after the death of Marcus Aurelius in 180.[180] Soon after, he was a source for several other Christian writers, notably Clement, Tertullian, and Irenaeus, who all studied him. His literary influence lasted longest in his later native Syrian church.

In his treatise *To Autolycus* Theophilus tries to demonstrate the superiority of the religion of Christ and its views on morality and the origins of the world, in contrast with the Olympian myths, which he argues taught only examples of immorality and idolatry. He addresses his work to a learned pagan inquirer who said he could not understand why any rational person would want to become a Christian. Theophilus devotes much attention to the profound immorality inherent in Hellenistic cult and religion. He also majors on the massive amount of contradictions one finds in Greek philosophical approaches to the nature of the world and God's involvement in it. Against this he places the teachings of the prophets, who have surety of truth about hidden matters because they were inspired by God, not simply relying on their own speculations.

His book contains an extended exposition of the book of Genesis as a creation theology. He also developed Logos theology more than many other Christian thinkers had before him and thus helped to set the basis for this school to become a standard way of theologizing in the third century church and after. In reference to the doctrine of creation Theophilus speaks of a time when God's Logos was immanent within him in an undifferentiated way (*Logos endiathetos*), but then sees the Logos as extrapolated, precisely for the purposes of the creation of the cosmos through the medium of holy Wisdom (an uttered wisdom: *Logos prophorikos*). Theophilus is thus an early exponent of trinitarian theology as a manner of conceiving the economy of God's

---

[178] Eusebius, *Ecclesiastical History* 4.20, 24; Jerome, *On Illustrious Men* 25; *Epistle* 121.6.15.
[179] Theophilus, *Ad Autolycum* 2.24; 1.24; 3.4; 1.4.
[180] The four major works include a treatise attacking the work of Hermogenes the Syrian (Eusebius, *Ecclesiastical History* 4.24), a dissident Christian philosopher who taught that matter was eternal and preexistent, that evil in the world was inherent in this matter (thus not ascribable to God), and that the soul also derived from it and not from God directly. Tertullian also wrote a refutation of the same in his *Contra Hermogenem*, using the work of Theophilus. Another significant work was *On History*, in which he recounted the history of the world and argued that the scriptural traditions were more ancient than any other, making the Hellenistic claims to antiquity less substantive than those of the church. Eusebius, again at *Ecclesiastical History* 4.24, says that he wrote powerfully against Marcion.

salvation of the world. In his works the term divine Triad (*trias*) first makes it theological debut to refer to "God, Word, and Wisdom."[181]

**Tertullian (c. 155–240).** Once again we encounter Tertullianus, for he towers among the apologists and was undoubtedly the major Latin thinker the Western church produced in its early creative period, that is, overlapping the end of the second well into the third. As we have noted earlier, his literary style is brilliant: pithy, sarcastic, and moving by turns, depending on his rhetorical intent. His scope of intellect moved the work of the Christian apologists out of the business of simply making answers to pagan charges (either of a political or philosophical nature) and into the matter of formulating a comprehensive systematic of their own. As this had already been adumbrated in the greater apologists such as Theophilus of Antioch and Clement of Alexandria, and would be brought to perfection in his Eastern contemporary Origen of Alexandria (in Greek), Tertullian shows the same development come to full fruition in Latin discourse. In this he was undoubtedly aided by his knowledge of the Greek language and his wide reading. Tertullian's *Apologeticus* is one of the most brilliant summations of the Christian countercharge to pagans. But his many other works also show the laying down of a technical Christian theological language of unparalleled precision. His influence on the later Latin Christian tradition has been inestimable. Until Augustine in the fifth century no one could challenge him.

Tertullian came from Carthage in North Africa. His was a brilliant and pugnacious legal mind set to the service of the church in the era of persecutions, as we have already noted; and despite what some thought of as a later leaning toward Montanism, his reputation as one of the founding minds of orthodox Latin theology was maintained by his successors, including Cyprian, Lactantius, and Augustine. He was the son of a serving centurion and as a young man pursued a legal career at Rome. In middle age he was converted to Christianity, probably in Carthage. St. Jerome says he became a presbyter in the church. His style in apologetic is terse and relies on caricature and ridicule (a standard element of law-room argument in his day—and after). It is not usually safe to deduce his opponents' real positions from Tertullian's way of dragging their ideas around the room, but when he was not engaging in an explicit denunciation (of foes outside or inside the church) he shows himself to be a reflective theologian. He had a gift for the telling phrase, and many of his aphorisms still echo in the minds of Christians. Speaking of the mystery of why God would reveal himself in the crucified and resurrected Christ, for example, he argues, "I believe it precisely because it is absurd." Scornfully dismissing the ridicule of contemporary philosophers for the Christian movement, he replies, "What has Athens to do

---

[181] Theophilus, *Ad Autolycum* 2.15.

with Jerusalem?" And in his treatise *On the Witness of the Soul*, where he argues that natural life is an instinctual witness to the divine presence, he made the bold apologetic statement, "The soul is naturally Christian."

Modern readers find the dramatic style, his cultural rigorism (again, not untypical of the general attitude in the African church) and his frequent misogyny (woman was the "devil's gateway") to be barriers when reading him today. Nevertheless, he enriched Latin theological literature by his knowledge of ecclesiastical customs and controversies from the East, not least by raising Logos theology to prominence in his theological schema. Putting this schema at the heart of his work and taking it into Latin meant it gained a great impetus to become the standard theological way of articulating soteriology in both the Eastern and Western parts of Christianity in the third century, thus making it an international Christian *Koine*.

From around 205 Tertullian's writings show an increasing respect for Montanist ideas, but the style of Montanism as it was then influential in North Africa was a much moderated form of the original Asia Minor movement, and there is no clear indication that he ever broke from the catholic community, so the oft-repeated assertions that "he became a Montanist later in life" are misleading. His major works include the *Apology* (*Apologeticus*, written c. 197), in which he makes a passionate appeal for legal toleration of Christianity. In a series of moral works addressed to Christians (*On Attending the Theater, On Military Service, On Idolatry, On Penance*) he severely warns Christians of the dangers of assimilation to the corrupt standards of contemporary Roman society and warns against adopting a military profession (largely because of the regular and standard requirement to worship the imperial genius, though also with a conviction that such a life is contrary to the irenic gospel).[182] He wrote a significant work on the Christian heresies that had a major influence on the church's readiness ever afterward to classify certain sects that departed doctrinally from the creed as having departed from the church altogether. He applied the principle of legal prescription (arguments heard before a case begins that made it clear that an agent did not have a right to be represented in a case, that is, a "preliminary ruling out of order") to make the case that heresies could not be considered part of the Christian world at all (*On the Prescription of Heretics*)—not that they were legitimately dissident Christians, but precisely that having departed from the church's teaching in a substantive manner, they had also lost the right to be called Christian in the first place.

He followed Irenaeus in setting the principle of the apostolic succession as the deciding matter of Christian authenticity, the proof of where catholic Christianity

---

[182] It was customary to reassert allegiance as a troop when picking up a soldier's pay by putting incense on the coals burning before the imperial image in the barracks. Tertullian says this is idolatry.

resided de facto. This centralizing of Irenaeus's argument would have the effect of massively reinforcing the importance of catholic orthodoxy in the definition of the church. He composed a series of works attacking the ideas of the Gnostics and Marcion (*Against Marcion, Against Hermogenes, On the Resurrection of the Dead, On the Flesh of Christ*), taking up the central theme in each of these works that Christ's incarnation was a true material reality, which vindicated the spiritual value of the material world and gave the promise of true resurrection to believers.

He wrote a major attack (*Against Praxeas*) on the Monarchians addressed to one Praxeas ("Busybody"), which was probably an ironic way of ridiculing Pope Callixtus of Rome, his contemporary, whom Hippolytus (a Logos theologian he respected) had also accused of Monarchianism. In this work Tertullian sets out important foundations for what would become the Latin doctrine of the Trinity (*trinitas*). He makes a close argument showing that the modalism of the anti-Logos theologians was unscriptural and set out to explain how the Word and Spirit emanate as distinct persons (*personae*) from the Father, all possessing the same nature (*natura*). His terminology became constitutive of Latin Christology after him. His own approach to Christology understood natures in the sense of legal possessions, which set Western Christian thought on long path: Christ possesses two distinct natures but is only one person. His treatise *On Baptism* gives interesting illumination about early third-century liturgical practice (he dislikes infant baptism, which was becoming more common in his day).

His work *On the Soul* introduces the idea of traducianism, the concept that the soul was handed down along with all other aspects of life from parent to child by a kind of genetic inheritance. It was a door that led to the concept of the transmission of "original sin" like a stain of guilt. It would be developed significantly in the fifth century by Augustine in his argument with Pelagius and would come to cast a certain pessimistic shadow over all subsequent Latin thought. In his final years the renewed interest in eschatology, an admiration for the strict morals of the Montanist movement, and an increasing strain of personal rigorism marked his late period works (*On Monogamy, Exhortation to Chastity, On Fasting, On Modesty*). The latter treatise was written circa 200 in anger at the bishop of Carthage's intention (following the example of Pope Callixtus at Rome) to allow the forgiveness of serious sexual sins to lapsed Christians.

**(Marcus) Minucius Felix (later second century).** Minucius Felix also came from North Africa, like Tertullian, and like him was a brilliant rhetorician. He is not the mach for Tertullian in the range of his work; but his apology, in the form of a dialogue, titled *Octavius*, is a brilliantly lively piece of literature that shows a Christian community emerging from the shadows and having a robust exchange with the pagan society around it. The quality of that exchange is at times mocking. He describes, for example, the passion week of the Isiac cult, with the female devotees with disheveled hair roaming the streets looking for pieces of Osiris (dismembered cult amulets ritually hidden by other devotees), and he sardonically remarks how careless they must be to keep on losing bits of their god year after year.[183] One can imagine that remarks like that won him no friends among his townsfolk and that many would have been glad to see an anti-Christian pogrom when it came (and when it did, it was usually savage in North Africa).

His book is a very lively window onto the religiosity of its time. It describes a conversation between a Christian, named Octavius, and a pagan respondent, named Caecilius, from the town of Cirta in Numidia. This is the town from which the great Latin apologist of the fourth century, Lactantius, would later come, and, perhaps not coincidentally, the town of origin of great anti-Christian rhetorician and politician Marcus Cornelius Fronto (100–160), the religious adviser to Marcus Aurelius.[184] Minucius starts the book by reminiscing about his great Christian friend Octavius and how, when he had been on a sea voyage with him in the company of Caecilius, the latter's bowing before an image of the god Serapis started a religious conversation that ended in Caecilius seeing the beauty of Christianity. At first he is disdainful: Christians have no intellectuals among them; they are socially scorned and hold stubbornly to exclusivist ideas beyond their intellectual ability. Above all they do not respect the customs of the empire, though it has clearly been blessed by the gods. Octavius replies that God has given the universal gift of reason to all humankind. Roman religion, however, blindly celebrates past custom and is merely a gross collection of irrational superstitions that even educated Romans laugh at. It is the single divine providence of God that governs all things. Rome has not gained its empire because of divine favor but because of its savage military oppressions. Octavius then goes on to explain how much of Caecilius's opinion about the church is based on faulty prejudices. The final books end with Caecilius admitting he has been convinced and seeking admission to his friend's religion.

Minucius's work was addressed chiefly to a broad, pagan, educated readership, assuming a mutual respect for Stoic moral values and universalist spiritual aspirations that could serve as a common ground with the church's ideas.[185] While Minucius avoids most references to Scripture or church practice (which one would not expect in a treatise dedicated to a pagan readership), he makes a strong case for the superiority of Christianity in terms of its rationality. Lactantius later took much of his attacks on the

---

[183] A little like the pious custom of searching for Hannukah gelt, or the tradition of hidden Easter eggs.
[184] Fronto was thought to have urged on the emperor to take a very hostile view of Christianity as a barbarism worth suppressing. He is mentioned in *Octavius* 9, 21.
[185] Minucius uses Seneca and shows a close reading of Cicero's *De Natura Deorum*.

absurdities of pagan cult from Minucius's work and adopted them in his magisterial *Divine Institutes*. For Minucius, the church's moral integrity, its universally held monotheism, its advocacy of divine providence, and its teachings on the immortality of the soul all demonstrate values that any intelligent and moral pagan ought to aspire to.

There is a long-running scholarly dispute as to whether Tertullian used the *Octavius* for some of the ideas in his *Apology* or whether Minucius himself borrowed from the *Apology* of Tertullian, but there is certainly a relationship of dependence between the writings.[186] At the end of *Octavius*, Caecilius declares himself to have been convinced of the arguments for the church and says that he wants to become a Christian. The work is an indication of the buoyant optimism that characterized North African Christianity at this period and an indication that the church felt it was poised to make a significant missionary expansion. The Decian persecution in 249, when Cyprian was the church's leader in Carthage, would shake that optimism but not shatter it. It would be Diocletian's persecution, however, that roused the last of the ancient apologists, among whom Lactantius was preeminent. The social conditions provided by the Christian emperors removed the primary stimulus for this genre of work. The fourth century required more consolidation from Christian systematicians in the manner of an Origen. The difference then would be that it was the *episkopos*, the hierarchy, who stepped forward as the litterateurs.

## A SHORT READER

***Publius Cornelius Tacitus (AD 55–117),*** **Annals of Imperial Rome 15.44.** But all human efforts, all the lavish gifts of the emperor, and the propitiations of the gods, could not banish the suspicion that the great fire of Rome was the result of a planned order. Consequently, to dispel that rumor, Nero fastened the guilt on a class hated for their abominations, who were called Christians by the populace, and inflicted the most exquisite tortures on them. Chrestus, from whom the name took its origin, had suffered a capital penalty during the reign of Tiberius at the hands of one of our procurators, Pontius Pilatus, but a most mischievous superstition, thus momentarily checked, broke again not only in Judea, the primal source of the evil, but even at Rome, where all things hideous and shameful come from every part of the world to run to the center and become popular. Accordingly, an arrest was made, first of all those who pleaded guilty;

---

[186] I favor the view of P. Monceaux that it was Minucius who borrowed ideas from Tertullian. See *Histoire littéraire de l'Afrique chrétienne depuis les origines jusquà l'invasion arabe* (Paris: E. Leroux, 1901), 1:316-46. J. Beaujeu, *Minucius Felix: Octavius* (Paris: Belles Lettres, 1964), gives a list of all the parallel passages.

then, as a result of their informing, an immense multitude was convicted, not so much of the crime of setting fire to the city as of hatred against humankind. Mockery of every sort was added to their deaths. Covered with the skins of beasts, they were torn by dogs and so perished, or were nailed to crosses, or were condemned to the flames to be burnt, and to serve as a nightly illumination when daylight had passed. Nero offered his own gardens for the spectacle, as if he were exhibiting a show in the circus, and all the while he mingled with the people dressed like a charioteer or standing aloft on a chariot. Accordingly, even for these criminals who deserved extreme and exemplary punishment there arose a widespread feeling of compassion; for it was not, as it seemed, for the public good that they were being destroyed, but rather to glut one man's cruelty.

**The Martyrdom of Polycarp 9-16 (AD 160).** Just as Polycarp was entering into the stadium, a voice came to him from heaven, saying, "Be strong and show yourself a man, Polycarp!" No one saw who it was that spoke to him, but those of our brethren who were present heard that voice. As he was brought out in public, the crowd grew very noisy, hearing that Polycarp had been captured. When he came near, the proconsul asked him whether he was indeed Polycarp. When he admitted that he was, the proconsul tried to persuade him to deny [Christ], saying, "Have respect for your old age," and the other similar things they usually try, such as, "Swear by the genius of Caesar," or "Repent and shout out 'Away with the atheists.'" So then Polycarp turned to look with a stern appearance at the large crowd of the wicked pagans then present in the stadium, and waving his hands at them, with deep groans he raised his eyes to heaven and cried out, "Away with the atheists." But the proconsul continued to press him, saying, "Swear and revile Christ, and I will set you free." Polycarp answered him, "I have served him for eighty-six years, and never has he done me any injury. So how could I possibly blaspheme my king and my Savior?" When the proconsul pressed him again, saying, "Swear by the genius of Caesar," he answered, "Since you seem so pointlessly to insist that I should swear by the genius of Caesar, pretending to be unaware of who and what I am, let me tell you quite plainly. I am a Christian. And if you wish to learn what the doctrines of Christianity are, fix an appointment, and I will tell you about them." The proconsul replied, "Persuade the people." But Polycarp answered, "I considered it only right to offer you an account [of the faith], because we have been taught to give all fitting honor to the powers and authorities that are ordained of God as long as this does not entail injury on ourselves. But as regards those others. I certainly do not consider them worthy of receiving any account from me." . . .

While he spoke these and many other similar things, he was filled with confidence and joy, and his face shone with grace.... The proconsul was astonished and sent his herald to proclaim three times in the middle of the stadium, "Polycarp has confessed to being a Christian."... Then the whole multitude, both the pagans and the Jews living at Smyrna, shouted out with uncontrollable rage, "This is the teacher of Asia, the father of the Christians, who tries to overthrow our gods and has been teaching many not to worship or offer sacrifice to the gods." Shouting out in this way, they called on the asiarch Philip to set loose a lion on Polycarp. But Philip answered that it would not be lawful for him to do this, since the beast shows were already finished. So then it seemed the best idea to them to shout out with one voice that Polycarp should be burned alive. This was necessary so as to fulfill that vision that had been revealed to him earlier ... when he said to the faithful who were with him, "I must be burned alive." This was carried into effect almost as soon as it was spoken, because the crowd immediately gathered together piles of wood out of the shops and bathhouses, and the Jews noticeably, as usual, were glad to assist them in this matter. And when the funeral pile was ready, Polycarp set aside all his garments, ... and immediately then they piled around him all those things that had been prepared for the funeral pile. They were also about to fix him with nails, but he said, "Leave me as I am; for he who gives me strength to endure the fire will also enable me to stand still in the pyre without you having to secure me by nails." So they did not nail him then but simply tied him. With his hands placed behind him, he was tied like a distinguished sacrificial ram from the flock, made ready to be an acceptable burnt offering to God. And he looked up to heaven, and said, "O Lord God Almighty, the Father of your beloved and blessed Son Jesus Christ, by whom we have received the knowledge of you, who are the God of angels and powers, and of every creature, and of the whole race of the righteous who live before you, I give thanks to you for having judged me worthy of this day and this hour, that I should have a part in the company of your martyrs, and in the cup of your Christ, to the resurrection of eternal life, of both soul and body, through the incorruption given by the Holy Spirit. With the martyrs may I be accepted this day before you like a fat and acceptable sacrifice, according as you, the ever truthful God, have preordained, and have earlier revealed it to me, and now have brought it to fulfilment. And so I praise you for all things. I bless you and glorify you, along with the everlasting and heavenly Jesus Christ, your beloved Son, with whom, to you, and the Holy Spirit, be glory both now and to all coming ages. Amen." When he had pronounced this amen and so finished his prayer, those who were appointed for that purpose kindled the fire. And as the flames blazed up in great fury, we, to whom it was given to witness this, saw a great miracle. And we have been preserved safe in order to report to others what then actually took place. For the fire, shaping itself into the form of an arch, like the sail of a ship when it is filled with the wind, billowed around the body of the martyr like a circle. And Polycarp appeared within not like flesh that is burnt, but more like bread that is baked, or as gold and silver glowing in a furnace. Moreover, we experienced such a sweet odor as if frankincense or other precious spices had been smoldering there. Finally, when those wicked men perceived that his body could not be consumed by the fire, they commanded an executioner to go near and pierce him through with a blade. And when he did this this, a dove ascended, and a great quantity of blood issued, so that the fire was extinguished; and all the people were amazed that there should be such a difference between nonbelievers and the elect, of whom this most admirable Polycarp was certainly one, having in our own generation been an apostolic and prophetic teacher and a bishop of the catholic church that is in Smyrna. For every word that went out of his mouth either has been or shall yet be accomplished.

**Celsus the Philosopher, The True Discourse *(AD 177; fragment preserved in Origen, Contra Celsum 3.44).*** The following seem to be the rules laid down by the Christians. "Let no one come to us who has been formally educated, or who is wise or prudent—for such qualifications are deemed evil by us; but if there should be any who are ignorant, or unintelligent, or uninstructed, or foolish, let them come with confidence." By such words, acknowledging that these types of individuals are worthy of their God, they manifestly demonstrate that they really want, and are able to persuade, only the ridiculous, the wretched, and the stupid, along with women and children.

**Athenagoras the Athenian, An Embassy for the Christians *1 (AD 176).*** To the emperors Marcus Aurelius Antoninus and Lucius Aurelius Commodus, conquerors of Armenia and Sarmatia, and more than all else, philosophers.

In your empire, O greatest of sovereigns, different nations observe different customs and laws; and no one is hindered by law or fear of punishment from following their ancestral practices, however ridiculous these may be. A citizen of Ilium, for example, can call Hector a god and pay divine honors to Helen, identifying her with Adrasteia. The Spartans venerate Agamemnon as Zeus.... In short, among every nation and people, men offer whatever sacrifices and celebrate whatever mysteries they feel like. The Egyptians count even cats, crocodiles, serpents, asps, and dogs among their gods. And both you and the laws give permission to all these to act in this way, because you think that, on the one hand, to believe in no god at all is impious and wicked, and on the other, it is necessary for each individual to worship the gods of their choice, in order that through fear of the deity, people may be kept from wrongdoing. And so, with admiration of your mildness and gentleness, and your peaceful and benevolent disposition toward every man, individuals live in the possession of equal rights; and the cities share in like honor according to their rank; and the whole empire, under your intelligent sway, enjoys profound peace. Even so, for us who are called Christians you have not shown a comparable benevolence. Although we have committed no crime, indeed as this discourse will demonstrate in what follows, we are of all men most reverently and righteously disposed toward the Deity and toward your government; nevertheless, you allow us to be harassed, plundered, and persecuted. The mob makes war on us for our name alone. This is why we venture now to lay a statement of our case before you. You will learn from this discourse that we suffer unjustly, indeed contrary to all law and reason. We beseech you to bestow some consideration on us, so that we may no longer be slaughtered at the instigation of false accusers. The fines imposed by our persecutors are not aimed merely at our property, nor do their insults attack merely our reputations or damage our general interests. These things we hold in contempt anyway, though to the populace they appear matters of great importance; for we have learned not only not avoid returning blow for blow and not to go to law with those who plunder or rob us, but even to offer the other cheek to those who strike us on one side of the face, and to offer our cloak to those who try to take away our coat. However, even when we surrender our property, they still plot against our very bodies and souls, pouring out on us wholesale charges of crimes that we have never committed, not even in thought, but that more properly belong to these idle gossipers themselves and all the tribe of those who share their values.

**Tertullian, Address to the Martyrs *1-2* (*AD 202*).** First of all, blessed souls, do not grieve the Holy Spirit (Eph 4:30) who has entered with you into this prison. Indeed, if he had not entered there with you, you yourselves would not be in that place today. And so take care that he might remain there with you and so may lead you from that place to the Lord. The prison is also the house of Satan, and he keeps his own family there. But you have come into the prison to trample on him, in his own house. And indeed you have already trampled on him outside it. Do not allow him to say: "Now they are inside my own house I will tempt them with petty quarrels, failings, and mutual disputes." Rather, let him fly out of your sight and slink away into his own hole, coiled up and sluggish like a snake that has been charmed or smoked out. Do not allow him to gain an advantage in his own domain so as to set you at odds among yourselves. Rather, let him find you strong and armed with concord, because your peace is war to him. Some members of the church who have lost this peace have the custom of asking for it from the martyrs in prison. So all the more you ought to have this peace in yourselves, cherish it, and guard it, so that perhaps you can bestow it on others. Perhaps in like manner other difficulties of soul may have accompanied you to the prison doors, just as far as your relatives did. But from that point on, you were separated from the world itself. So how much more should you be separated from the spirit of this age and its concerns. It should not upset you that you have been separated from this world. For if we regard the world itself as a prison, we look on you as those who have escaped from prison, not who have gone into one. It is the world that has the greater darkness that blinds the human heart. It is the world that puts on the heavier chains that bind the very soul. It is the world that breathes the worse stench of human lust. In short, it is the world that ultimately contains the greater number of criminals, namely the entire human race. This is why it stands waiting for the judgment—not that of the proconsul but of God himself. From this prison, blessed ones, think that you have been liberated, as if into a safe house. It is full of darkness, but you yourselves are light (Mt 5:14; Eph 5:8). It is full of chains, but you have been set free by God (Gal 5:1). Its stench is evil, but you are an odor of sweet savor (Eph 5:3; 2 Cor 2:15). You are waiting on a judge, but you yourselves are destined to judge (1 Cor 6:2) these very judges. It may be gloomy for the one who sighs for the enjoyments of the worldly life, but a Christian, even outside the prison, has renounced the worldly life; and the same applies even when one is in prison. To you who are beyond the world, where you may be in it is of small importance. And if you now have lost some of the joys of life, it is no more than a good bargain to lose a little in order to gain a great deal more. And I say nothing at this moment of the reward to which God calls his martyrs. . . . The prison is to the Christian what the desert was to the prophets. The Lord himself often used to go into retirement to pray more freely and to withdraw from the world. It was in a solitary place that he showed his own glory to his disciples (Mt 17:1-2 ). So let us stop calling it a prison; let us call it a retreat. Even if the body is shut in and the flesh held fast, even so all things are open to the spirit. So in spirit walk abroad, in spirit roam free, but not as if setting before your eyes shady walks or long porticoes, but that path that leads to God. As often as you walk in spirit along this way you will no longer be in prison. Your ankles will not feel the chains when your mind is in heaven, for the mind carries with it the whole person and carries him wherever it wills. Remember: where your heart will be, there will your treasure be also (Mt 6:21). And so, let our hearts be in that place we would have our treasure.

***Origen of Alexandria,*** **Exhortation to Martyrdom *4 (AD 235).*** And so I appeal to you to remember in these present trials the great reward that is laid up in heaven for those who are persecuted and reviled for the sake of righteousness. And so be glad and leap for joy on account of the Son of Man (Mt 5:10-12; Lk 6:23), in the same way that the apostles once rejoiced when they were accounted worthy to suffer ignominy for the sake of his name (Acts 5:41). If you should ever feel your soul pulling back, have that "mind of Christ that is within us" (Phil 2:5) encourage it whenever it wishes to upset that mind, insofar as it can: "Why are you cast down my soul? Why groan within me? Hope in God, for still shall I give thanks" (Ps 42:11). But I pray that our souls may never be so troubled. Even more than this, I pray that even in the tribunals, or when the unsheathed swords are drawn against our necks, our souls may be kept safe in "the peace of God that passes all understanding" (Phil 4:7) and may find rest in the thought that they who are aliens in the body are yet at home with the Lord of all (2 Cor 5:8). And even if we are not that strong that we keep peaceful all times, at least let us not allow the sorrows of the soul to pour out in the presence of strangers, for then we shall have grounds for our apology to God when we say to him: "O God, my soul is troubled within me" (Ps 42:5, 11; Mt 26:38). The Word also exhorts us to remember too what is said in Isaiah, namely: "Do not fear the reproaches of men, and do not be dismayed before their contempt" (Is 51:7). For God is undoubtedly the master of all that moves in heaven and within it, and by his divine care rules over all that is accomplished both on earth and on the seas: over everything that is born, takes its origin, eats and grows, all the different kinds of animals and plants. So it would be foolish to close our eyes and not look to God (Is 6:10; Mt 13:15; Acts 28:27). Rather, let us turn our eyes toward that fear they must have who will soon die and then be handed over to the judgment that is fitted to their deeds.

***Manichaean Liturgy, Psalm: A Hymn to Jesus the Splendor*** **(third to fourth century).**

> We would fill our eyes with praise, and open our mouths to invoke you.
> Honor and majesty we offer you . . . ,
> To you, Jesus the Splendor, Liberated ruler and New Dispensation.
> You are the garment of blessing, beloved brother.
> Come for salvation, for you are all salvation.
> Come for graciousness, for you are all grace.
> Come to bring love, for you are all love.
> Come as Healer, for you are all healing.
> Come to bring peace, for you are all peace.

Come as victor, for you are all victory.
Come as Lord, for you are all lordship.
Come for redemption, for you are all redeemer. . . .
Welcome, First One and primeval First-Born.
Welcome, good Mediator . . .
Mediating between us and the Father.[187]

**Eusebius of Caesarea, On the Martyrs of Palestine 1 (AD 303).** Concerning the confession of Procopius: In the first year [303] of the persecution appearing in our own days [of Diocletian]. The first of all the martyrs who appeared in Palestine was named Procopius. He was truly a man of God, for even before his confession he had dedicated his life to great asceticism, and from the time that he was a little boy he was noted for his pure habits and strict morals. By the force of his mind he had so brought his body into such subjection that, even before his death, his soul seemed to dwell in a body that was completely mortified. He had strengthened his soul by the word of God so much that even his body was sustained by the power of God. His food was simple bread, and his drink only water; and he would take nothing else apart from this. On some occasions he would eat only every other day, and sometimes every third day. Often he would spend a whole week without food. But never, by day or night, would he leave off from the study of the word of God. He was ever careful as to his manners and modesty of conduct, so that he was a source of edification in his humility and fervor to his own community. Although his main focus of attention was to divine subjects, he was also significantly learned in the natural sciences. His family came from Baishan, and he exercised a threefold ministry in the church. First, he was a scriptural reader; second, he translated from Greek into Aramaic; and third (which is even more excellent than the preceding), he opposed the powers of the evil one, and the devils trembled before him [as an exorcist]. Now it happened that he was sent from Baishan to our city of Caesarea, along with his brother confessors. And at the very moment that he entered the gates of the city they brought him before the governor. As soon as he appeared in court, the judge, whose name was Flavianus, said to him: "It is required that you should make sacrifice to the gods." But he replied with a loud voice: "There is no God but one alone, the Maker and Creator of all things." Feeling stung by the martyr's words, the judge took up arms of a different kind to fend off the truth and, disregarding his first injunction, then ordered him to

---

[187]See further C. R. C. Allberry, ed., *A Manichaean Psalm Book* (Stuttgart: W. Kohlhammer, 1938).

sacrifice to the emperors, who were then four in number. The holy martyr of God laughed even more at this remark and repeated the words of the greatest of the Greek poets, where he says that "the rule of many is not good: let there be but one ruler and one sovereign." It was on account of this answer, which was deemed insulting to the emperors, that he was delivered over to death (though he was truly alive in his behavior). The head of the blessed man was struck off, and an easy passage was thus afforded him along the road to heaven. All this took place on the seventh day of the month Heziran, in the first year of the persecution in our days [303]. This confessor was the first who was perfected in our city of Caesarea.

## FURTHER READING

### The Persecutions

Barnard, L. W. "Clement of Rome and the Persecution of Domitian." *New Testament Studies* 10 (1963): 251-60.

Barnes, T. D. "Legislation Against the Christians." *Journal of Roman Studies* 58 (1968): 32-50.

Boyarin, D. *Dying for God.* Stanford, CA: Stanford University Press, 1999.

Delvoye, C. *Les Pérsecutions contre les chrétiens dans l'Empire romain.* Brussels: Les Cahiers Rationalistes, 1967.

Frend, W. H. C. *Martyrdom and Persecution in the Early Church.* Oxford: Anchor Books, 1965.

Jannsen, L. F. "*Superstitio* and the Persecution of the Christians." *VC* 33 (1979): 131-59.

Keresztes, P. "The Jews, the Christians, and the Emperor Domitian." *VC* 27 (1973): 1-28.

———. "Marcus Aurelius a Persecutor?" *Harvard Theological Review* 61 (1968): 321-41.

Musurillo, H. *The Acts of the Christian Martyrs.* Oxford Early Christian Texts. Oxford: Oxford University Press, 1972.

Pellegrino, M. "Le sens ecclesial du martyre." *Revue de Science religieuse* 35 (1961): 151-75.

Sherwin-White, A. N. "The Early Persecutions and Roman Law—Again." *JTS* 3 (1952): 199-213.

St. Croix, G. E. M. de. "Why Were the Early Christians Persecuted?" *Parola del Passato (Rivista di Studi antichi)* 26 (1963): 6-38.

Workman, B. W. *Persecution in the Early Church.* Oxford: Oxford University Press, 1980.

### The Church and Roman Law

Barnes, T. D. *Approches de Tertullien.* Paris: Institut d'Études Augustiniennes, 1992.

———. *Tertullian: A Historical and Literary Study.* Oxford: Oxford University Press, 1971. Pages 57-66, "Christianisme et pouvoir impériale d'après Tertullien."

Fredouille, J. C. *Tertullien et la conversion de la culture antique*. Paris: Etudes Augustiniennes, 1972.

Klein, R. *Tertullian und das romische Reich*. Heidelberg: C. Winter, 1968.

McGuckin, J. A. *The Ascent of Christian Law: Patristic and Byzantine Reformulations of Antique Civilization*. New York: St. Vladimir's Seminary Press, 2012.

**Rival Religious Systems**

Allberry, C., ed. *A Manichaean Psalm-Book* II. Stuttgart: W. Kohlhammer, 1938.

Beck, R. *The Religion of the Mithras Cult in the Roman Empire*. Oxford: Oxford University Press, 2007.

Clauss, M. *The Roman Cult of Mithras*. Edinburgh: Edinburgh University Press, 2000.

Coyle, J. K. "Mani." In *The Encyclopedia of Ancient Christianity*, ed. A. di Berardino, 2:661-65. Downers Grove, IL: InterVarsity Press, 2014.

Dunand, F. *Isis: Mère des Dieux*. Paris: Errance, 2000.

Lane, E. N., ed. *Cybele, Attis and Related Cults: Essays in Memory of M. J. Vermaseren*. Religions in the Graeco-Roman World 131. Leiden: Brill, 1996.

Neusner, J., ed. *Judaism and Christianity in the First Century*. New York: Garland, 1990.

Ries, J. "Jésus-Christ dans la religion de Mani." *Augustiniana* 14 (1964): 437-54.

Rose, E. *Die Manichäische Christologie*. Studies in Oriental Religion 5. Wiesbaden: O. Harrassowitz, 1979.

Solmsen, F. *Isis Among the Greeks and Romans*. Cambridge, MA: Harvard University Press, 1979.

Takács, S. A. *Isis and Sarapis in the Roman World*. Leiden: Brill, 1995.

Turcan, R. *Mithra et le mithriacisme*. Paris: Presses Universitaires de France, 2000.

Ulansey, D. *The Origins of the Mithraic Mysteries: Cosmology and Salvation in the Ancient World*. Oxford: Oxford University Press, 1989.

Van der Horst, P. W. *Hellenism, Judaism, Christianity: Essays on their Interaction*. Leuven: Brill, 1998.

Vermaseren, M. J. *Cybele and Attis*. London: Thames and Hudson, 1977.

Wilson, S. G. *Related Strangers: Jews and Christians. 70–170 C.E*. Minneapolis: Fortress, 1995.

Witt, R. E. *Isis in the Ancient World*. London: Johns Hopkins University Press, 1971.

**The Apologists**

Barnard, L. W. *Athenagoras*. Paris: Beauchesne, 1972.

———. *Justin Martyr: His Life and Thought*. Cambridge: Cambridge University Press, 1967.

Barnes, T. D. *Tertullian: A Historical and Literary Study*. Oxford: Oxford University Press, 1971.

Baylis, H. J. *Minucius Felix and His Place Among the Early Fathers of the Latin Church*. London: SPCK, 1928.

Chadwick, H. *Early Christian Thought and the Classical Tradition.* Oxford: Oxford University Press, 1966.

Clarke, G. W. "The Historical Setting of the Octavius of Minucius Felix." *Journal of Religious History* 4 (1967): 267-86.

———. "The Literary Setting of the Octavius of Minucius Felix." *Journal of Religious History* 3 (1965): 195-211.

Cohick, L. H. *The Peri Pascha Attributed to Melito of Sardis: Setting, Purpose, and Sources.* Providence, RI: Brown Judaic Studies, 2000.

Goodenough, E. R. *The Theology of Justin Martyr.* Jena: Philo, 1923.

Grant, R. M. *Theophilus of Antioch. Ad Autolycum.* Oxford: Oxford University Press, 1970.

Hall, S. G. *Melito of Sardis: On Pascha and Fragments.* Oxford: Oxford University Press, 1979.

Hunt, E. J. *Christianity in the Second Century: The Case of Tatian.* London: Routledge, 2003.

Lilla, S. R. C. *Clement of Alexandria.* Oxford: Oxford University Press, 1971.

Méhat, A. *Études sur les Stromates de Clément d'Alexandrie.* Paris: Editions du Seuil, 1966.

Osborn, E. F. *The Emergence of Christian Theology.* Cambridge: Cambridge University Press, 1993.

———. *Justin Martyr.* Tübingen: Mohr Siebeck, 1973.

———. *The Philosophy of Clement of Alexandria.* Cambridge: Cambridge University Press, 1957.

———. *Tertullian: First Theologian of the West.* Cambridge: Cambridge University Press, 1977.

Rogers, R. *Theophilus of Antioch: The Life and Thought of a Second-Century Bishop.* Lanham, MD: Lexington Books, 2000.

# COMING OF AGE

## Christianity in the Third Century

**THE ESTABLISHMENT OF CHRISTIAN POLITY**

In the second century so many developments took place in the Christian world that had long-lasting impacts that it is almost like observing the phenomenal growth rate of a young child: from tiny infant to hulking adolescent in so short a time that if the growing continued at the same rate indefinitely, the child would end up as a giant. But of course growth does not follow on at the same rate as the early period. In church history, there are often, so it seems, eras of immense foundational energy, followed by longer periods of consolidation and settlement: a sideways spread, if you like, where movements are more carefully assessed and filtered. The third century is like this: a time of deepening consolidated reflection, when the alternative schools have largely been named, categorized, and often rejected; but some of their agendas, and indeed several of their best insights, have had time to be taken on board and sifted.

What, in my opinion, characterizes the Christian church's developmental process in the third century is not so much the use of censorial concepts such as episcopal authority determining agendas, or orthodox suppression of heresy (in any case, who had the power to enforce such dictats in this era? though it is a concept that delights conspiracy theorists of our time) but rather the seeking after of good practice: the common-sense approach to what was in conformity with "apostolic doctrine," by which I mean (as the majority of the earliest Christians writers mean) the New Testament literature's embrace and exegesis of the Hebrew Scriptures broadly understood as a type of the Christ events proclaimed in the Gospels. Of course, this process toward agreed good practice was shaped and accelerated by polity, or structures of church organization, and polity was instantiated by local prophets, bishops, and presbyters.

It is also clear that while the Christian intelligentsia of the second century had set the pace, it still remained the case that it was pastoral and liturgical custom that was used both as a sea anchor to stabilize the ship and as some form of rudder for its governance. Second-century bishops were mere embryonic forms of what they would become in the fourth century, when, by collaborating in province-wide synods, given weight under imperial law, they assumed a dominant voice over church affairs; but already they were showing a way forward, making a structure of polity in a time that needed it. Irenaeus is an indicator of much that was to come. The Asia Minor synods that assembled to adjudicate Montanism were another. Presbyter-theologians such as Hippolytus, Clement, or Tertullian show how deep reflection on the implications of the Gospels, when allied with basic philosophical and rhetorical training, could make the Christian cause missionarily viable. Persecutions reaching into the very heartland of Christian worship focused the mind dramatically and served to sharpen Christian self-identity rather than dissipate it in forms of more generic pluralism.

All of these factors—this immense ferment of ideas clashing and reacting against one another, being rejected and yet still partially influencing even the mainstream that objected to them—all of this "agenda remaining to be resolved" served to make the third century a time of consolidation, when doctrinal and polity patterns were more broadly established that by the next century would hardly be challenged again for centuries to come.

Our first place to look more particularly would be the issue of Christian orders and offices. This is such a revelatory and significant aspect that it worth devoting particular attention to it in one of the chapters in part two of the book. So here we will treat the matter only insofar as it relates to the literary episcopate and presbyterate. It is not that theologians and clergy are the leaders of the church in a vacuum. Far from it; each such leader has been initiated and formed in a preexisting tradition-culture (dominated by forms of worship and scriptural preaching) that eventually they too wish to propagate and preserve. The leadership role is not so much creative, in most instances, as preservative. But the third century sees the significant rise of the number of intelligentsia among the church's leadership, many of whom in its earliest centuries would have been chosen to lead prayers and to prophesy on the basis of their spiritual charism and personal holiness, not on the size of their villas or the quality of their oratory. But things change by the third century. Education was seen to matter as the church took its place in Hellenistic society.

As well as the new emergence of an intelligent and literary governing class of clergy, we have in this century the appearance of the first real genius the Christian movement produced since the time of Jesus (and arguably the apostle John/Evangelist of the Fourth Gospel): and that was Origen of Alexandria. After him, almost everything that he touched became constitutive architecturally in Christian thinking, even when his views were set aside with major amendments by theologians of the fourth through sixth centuries. His monumental impact on the church that followed him demands that his system be treated with attention.

The manner in which educated Christian bishops (*episkopoi*) start taking over the intellectual agenda of the church and shaping an increasingly international polity in the third century is quite noticeable and sets a pattern for the fourth century, when this becomes standard practice. Then the authority of the bishops to govern churches and discipline the congregations was much more significant, and Constantine's elevation of Christian bishops to the status of parallel local magistrates also gave them a legal stature as head of the local "church corporation," which consolidated their authority and gave it a social force for the first time. The generic way this development of orders worked, from a variety of charismatic offices in ancient Christianity toward a more restricted and authoritative set of clerical and teaching ranks and governances, is set out in chapter nineteen of this book and can be seen in overview there. Here it will enough to look more closely at some of those leading-edge bishops, see how they communicated with each other, and note what agendas were in primary play, remembering that this century too, like its predecessor, was one in which being a visible Christian was a dangerous matter. The pastoral context of the church, therefore, was a troublesome one of keeping together a traumatized community, but no longer a simple, zealous sect that felt the present troubles were adumbrations of the final age and a last call to keep purity before the coming of the Messiah. Now, rather, it was an increasingly sophisticated and more educated set of linked international communities who, since the time of Marcus Aurelius, were much more ready to defend their corner intellectually and politically and wanted leadership from their theologians that went further than mere exhortations to endure.

## ROME AND NORTH AFRICA: AFTERMATHS OF PERSECUTION: CYPRIAN AND STEPHEN

One illustrative case of episcopal governance in this era is the way the leaders of the communities dealt with the crisis of persecution in the third century and how it affected their ideas of polity organization. The correspondences of Stephen of Rome (pope 254–257) and Cyprian bishop of Carthage (c. 200–258) can illustrate this for us, for we see two eminent leaders who eventually are both targeted and executed by the Roman authorities but who do not allow the threats hanging over them to deflect them from the pressing duty of keeping the churches in good order.

Caecilius Cyprianus (Thascius) was probably born in Carthage around the year AD 200 and came from a rich and highly respected family of the Carthaginian pagan upper class. He rose to prominence in his city as a leading rhetorician-lawyer. Jerome tells us that he was attracted to the Christian movement because of its purity of morals, and under the influence of a leading presbyter in the city called Caecilius, whose name he took at baptism, he was initiated into the community.[1] He gives a moving account of how the gospel moved him to a very different lifestyle after baptism from the one he had beforehand:

> When I was still lying in bondage to darkness and the gloom of night, I used to think it was nigh impossible, excessively demanding, to do what God's mercy was suggesting to me. . . . You see, I was held in chains by the innumerable mistakes of my previous life, and I did not believe that I could possibly be delivered from them, and this was why I was disposed to acquiesce in my stubborn vices and indulge my sins. . . . But after that, by the help of the waters of new birth, the stain of my former life was washed away, and a light from above, a light serene and pure, was infused into my reconciled heart. . . . A second birth restored me to the state of a new man. How wondrously, then, every doubt began to fade away. . . . I clearly understood that what had first lived within me, enslaved as it was by the vices of the flesh, was that which was earthly, and that what the Holy Spirit had worked within me to replace it was divine and heavenly.[2]

Shortly after his baptism he was, unusually, elevated to the presbyterate, a sign of his elevated social rank and possibly an acknowledgment of his very large charitable donation to the church for the relief of the poor. Jerome says he gave away "all his fortune." Not long afterward, about 248 or early 249, the episcopal seat became vacant, and the lay church members shouted out for his election to the see, a popular acclaim that carried weight with it against some of the votes of the presbyteral council of the church. Several of the older presbyters, led by one Novatus, did not wish to see this rapid ascent continue. The popular lay majority, doubtless feeling the constant threat of a new outbreak of persecutions against them, surely felt that for the first time they could have a well-placed political leader, an educated lawyer and member of the intelligentsia, who might do much to help them in any times of distress. One wonders how well Cyprian was trained in the practices and theology of the Christian movement.

Jerome tells us (reading the biography Cyprian's secretary, his deacon Pontius, left behind) that each day the bishop called for "the master" to read, which was in fact his copy of the works of Tertullian.[3] His own writing shows a massive theological dependence on that writer, but he moderates most of the abrasive points of his teacher and puts all the prose into a more exquisite and refined Latin style. He also has left under

---
[1] Jerome, *De Viris Illustribus* 67.
[2] Cyprian, *To Donatus* 3-4.
[3] R. E. Wallis, trans., *ANF* 5.

his own name a book called *Testimonia Ad Quirinum*. But this is not a work of his, but rather an antique (and very significant) Christian document that collates together biblical texts in one column and shows how they were "fulfilled" in the New Testament in another. In short it is a vade mecum for whoever wants to preach their way through the Scriptures (the bishop's fundamental liturgical role alongside his public prayers) and allows more or less anyone to demonstrate apparently advanced scriptural cross-referencing skills even when they do not know the texts well. Both this reliance on Tertullian and the Scripture handbook he kept very close to him suggest that Cyprian's rapid ascent left him "catching up" considerably.[4] This is why he is not so significant a voice for theological ideas or biblical insights; but he does bring a Roman lawyer's acuity to his role as church administrator, and in marrying this skill with the episcopal office he points out the way that office would develop in the next century.

Even with his fast learning abilities, Cyprian was still caught unawares, for in 250, as the opening act of his episcopacy, and with an immediate circle of senior presbyters around him who were still conflicted about his leadership, the Roman authorities launched the Decian persecution. The emperor, who had ascended to the throne on the occasion of the assassination of the pro-Christian Philip in late 249, ordered in the January of the new year a radical turning back to the traditional gods of Rome. He thought that this religious traditional reform should stanch the series of alarming military reversals the empire was having. Christians were a chief target of interest, and after large-scale sacrifices conducted on the Capitoline Hill in Rome, Decius ordered the executions, as traitors, of significant Christian dissidents who had denounced the sacrifices as pointless. Bishop Babylas at Antioch and Pope Fabian at Rome died at this time, and the order to observe the patriotic sacrifices spread out to the provinces. The Christian leaders were to be the first to be forced to comply, but all leading citizens had to procure a certificate to give legal proof, if required, that they too had conformed.

Cyprian decided to go into hiding, suspecting that this policy would have a short duration and would not affect his laity. He kept in regular touch with the Christian congregation at Carthage through his friends on the council of presbyters, but many felt he had been a disappointment (both in failing to advocate for them and in failing to demonstrate grit like the bishops of Rome and Antioch), and his opponents on the presbyteral council were stirred against him once more. The North African ec-

---

[4]In the end he left a very respectable body of short treatises: *On the Lord's Prayer*; *Apology to Demetrianus*, in which he refutes the idea that calamities such as plagues and lost battles are the cosmic fault of the Christians; *On Mortality*; *On Works and Almsgiving*; *That Idols Are Not Gods*; *On the Advantage of Patience*; and *On Jealousy and Envy*, as well as numerous epistles, several of which are dogmatic treatises in nature.

clesial tradition of gladly welcoming the opportunity of a martyr's death was still high in memory: and besides, Cyprian's solution was not one that the majority of believers could practically adopt.

When the persecution was soon ended, following Decius's death in battle in 251, Cyprian returned to a church that had been much disrupted by the pressure to sacrifice to the old gods. Many had not been able to embrace martyrdom with the same eagerness of their heroic narratives of earlier times. Some had sacrificed, under heavy compulsion, or simply out of fear of pain, and were designated the *sacrificati*. The wealthier and more politically connected Christians had used their networks to bribe false certificates out of officials that said they had sacrificed. The presbyters determined that both categories had effectively sinned deeply, lapsed from their baptismal vows, were ritually defiled, and so could not approach the Eucharist. The execution of Pope Fabian was announced by letter to Cyprian and the church at Carthage, and the council of presbyters and deacons at the capital took the opportunity to express a degree of surprise at the news they had heard (certainly from his own dissident colleagues in Carthage) that Cyprian's own response had been to disappear from view. In reply Cyprian published a treatise in defense of the principle of flight from persecution (based on Jesus' words in Mt 10:23). And he sent to Rome accounts to show he had not run away; rather had "tactically withdrawn" so as not to be a focus of persecution dragging down others around him:

> I think it necessary to write this letter to you all to give an account of what I have been doing, what my discipline was, and how diligent I have been. In accordance with the teaching of the Lord, as soon as the first outbreak of the disturbances against us rose up, and the mob was violently and repeatedly shouting for me, I did not so much consider my own safety as rather have a lively fear for the public peace of the brethren. This was why I withdrew for a short while, so that I would not further provoke the tumult that had already started by maintaining a public profile. But even though I was absent in body, I was not deficient in spirit or activity or advisement and did not neglect any benefit I could give the brethren through my counsel.[5]

From his Roman correspondence we learn a lot about this period and see in practical detail the polity of one large church "overseeing" another: the remit and limits of such a relationship. The international sense of awareness of the Christians and the readiness of the episcopate to sustain relations between churches is notably more advanced than ever before.

Cyprian still needed to offset criticism at home of his right to adjudicate in the matter of the excommunicates when he had not been personally present for the torture

---

[5]Cyprian, *Epistle* 20.

trials themselves. Some of those who had resisted and either had been racked (and survived) or imprisoned for the faith (and thus were ready to embrace execution) gained great prestige at this time and were widely regarded as *confessores*, living martyr-equivalents whose prayers carried great weight with Christ and the angels in heaven. Their intercession was seen as specially powerful.[6] Many ordinary believers among the lapsed went to them and begged their intercession, and indeed several of the confessors exercised charismatic pastoral care to assure them that their sins had been forgiven. Cyprian took this as an illegitimate intrusion into the rights of the bishop and presbyters to determine who would be communicate and who would be penanced as an excommunicate until the hour of death. When the confessors had instructed the penitents to return to the practice of their faith, the bishop stood in their way, insisting that this lapse from baptismal purity set them apart from eucharistic communion.

One of Cyprian's deacons, Felicissimus, gathered a group of confessors together and led them into breaking with the bishop. Soon the five presbyters who had been most opposed to Cyprian's election also joined with them. The presbyter Novatus became their leader and went off to Rome to seek supportive endorsement. He got no encouragement from the newly elected aristocrat Pope Cornelius, so he attached himself and his party as supporters of the dissident rival bishop at Rome, the theologian Novatian, who had been administering the Roman church in its interregnum after Fabian.[7] By this means the issue of the African church's question about possible readmission for the lapsed was immediately tied in with the question of what are the principles of unity and authority within the universal church. Here Cyprian's undoubted gifts as legal advocate became manifest, and he has left behind a dominant influence on the longer-term concept of "catholic church unity."[8] Two of his letters became immensely authoritative, the first *De Lapsis* (*On Those Who Have Lapsed*), on the question of how to administer reconciliation, and the other *De Ecclesiae Unitate* (*On the Unity of the Church*), concerning the issue of schism in his own and other churches.[9] The dissident party in Carthage meanwhile arranged for a rival African bishop, Fortunatus, to lead them. This secession, based as it was on a matter of church discipline in the main (rather than on a point of significant doctrinal difference), was classed as a schism.[10]

---

[6]See further J. A. McGuckin, "Martyr Devotion in the Alexandrian School (Origen to Athanasius)," in *Martyrs & Martyrologies*, ed. D. Wood, Studies in Church History 30 (Oxford: Blackwell, 1993), 35-45.

[7]Cyprian, *Epistle* 55.8-9.

[8]See further P. Hinchcliff, *Cyprian of Carthage and the Unity of the Christian Church* (London: Geoffrey Chapman, 1974).

[9]Text in M. Bevenot, ed., *Cyprian: De Lapsis and De Ecclesiae Catholicae Unitate* (Oxford: Clarendon, 1971).

[10]The term is from the Greek for "split," as in a ripping of a cloth. The image derived from the notion of the "seamless robe" of Christ, which was his church. See Cyprian, *De Unitate Ecclesiae* 7.

Cyprian was set to maintain, on a legal basis he had learned from Tertullian's *De Praescriptione*, that those who had departed from the communion of the church no longer had any right to the assets of the church. Since the corporate function of the church was to administer the grace of salvation, for him this meant that schismatics no longer had access to grace. His adage became "outside the church, no salvation."[11] Another famed saying of his was, "Whoever does not have the church as their mother cannot have God as their Father."[12] His thought marks a significant movement toward tightening the definition of belonging or not belonging to the Christian community. It also opened up a major way of thinking about the salvation possibilities of those who were not in the Christian congregation. Several key points of Cyprian's theology of church (his "ecclesiology") would be relaxed later by the time of Augustine. But Cyprian's teachings impressed themselves on the Eastern churches too, and Augustine's later, more liberal adaptation of the argument in his own conflicts with fifth-century dissident schismatics at Carthage (the Donatists) was then not observed by the Eastern church. This has led to a set of varying strictnesses of approach within Christianity, existing to this day (and largely responsible for the fact that Christianity's internal divergent movements have been very difficult to resolve over the centuries) in the face of the basic question: if members of the Christian community break communion with the local bishop, can they retain communion in the grace of the sacraments with any larger concept of the Christian communion? That is: what does "church" mean, theologically speaking?[13]

Cyprian's basic view that secessionists do not just leave a local communion but depart from all Christian communion (since the universal Christian communion is

---

[11] *Extra ecclesiam nulla salus.* It can also be translated (less drastically) as "Outside the church there is no safety (in one's salvation assurance)."

[12] Cyprian, *De Unitate Ecclesiae* 6. "The spouse of Christ cannot commit adultery. She is uncorrupted and pure. She knows one home; she guards the sanctity of one bed with chaste modesty. She keeps us for God. She prepares the children whom she has born for the kingdom. Whoever is separated from the church and unites with an adulteress is separated from the promises of the church. No one who forsakes the church of Christ can receive the rewards of Christ. Such a one is a stranger; such a one is profane; such a one is an enemy. No one can have God for his Father who does not have the church for his mother."

[13] The Roman church would take this argument and extend it with special reference to the role of the bishop of Rome as personally assuring sacramental communion (to the point that if one was not in communion with the bishop of Rome, one could not claim full membership of the church of Christ). This would eventually develop into full-scale papal theory. Even in Cyprian's time, of course, the argument he had outlined about the episcopal role as paradigm of church communion was used against him by Pope Cornelius to pressure him to conform to Rome's international polity about other matters. Maurice Bevenot, in his edition of Cyprian's *De Unitate*, has noticed the two versions of his text available in antiquity and has posited that Cyprian himself made these editorial changes so as to reduce that aspect of his argument that seemed to exalt the "Petrine" role in church unity, since Pope Cornelius was using it against him in a dispute about baptismal practices that differed between Rome and Carthage and suggesting that in matters of difference obedience to Peter was what counted most.

instantiated in the local assembly) is based on his reading of 1 John 2:19, allied with his reading of the promise of Christ to the apostle Peter (standing in his mind as a paradigm for all apostles) that he would be the rock on which the church was built and on which it would be sustained (Mt 16:18-19).[14] His argument sets the cap on the concept, seen in such early episcopal writers as Ignatius of Antioch or Irenaeus of Lyons, that the bishop is the present-day ecclesial equivalent of the apostle and in his own person is the sign and surety of ecclesial unity.

Knowing that his local problem with his own dissidents had spread to an unavoidable engagement with the Roman authorities, Cyprian was forced to a clarification of his mind. Novatian at Rome had clashed with Pope Cornelius over the question of the enduring efficacy of baptism, arguing that the lapsed who had denied Christ had also voided their baptism. Several other bishops at this time (synods at Spain, provincial bishops in North Africa, and the bishop of Antioch chief among them) also held to the "Novatianist" position that reconciliation could only be given to the lapsed by God alone, and probably not until the last judgment. Cornelius, Cyprian, and Dionysius of Alexandria, however, held to the position that baptism was a unique and unrepeatable event. Reconciliation would have to be effected by repentance alone, acknowledged and administered by the church authorities.

After peace was restored, Cyprian adopted a more moderate position with regard to the question of the lapsed, one that reflected Pope Cornelius's preferred pastoral stance.[15] Denial of the faith after baptism was traditionally seen as an "unforgivable" sin. Cyprian holds that no one in the church, not even confessors, had the right to declare such a sin simply "forgiven and forgotten." All those who had sacrificed or obtained certificates by lying (*libellatici*) had to be placed, he insisted, under a formal (temporary) ban from communion so as to stand as penitents in the porticoes of the church to hear the liturgy from the fringes of the community they had renounced. Depending on the seriousness of the fall, whether torture had been applied, or whether Christians had run forward to volunteer conformity on the grounds of a mere threat or simply to protect their property, the term of penance would be assigned, longer or shorter. At the point of death anyone could be reconciled who showed sincere sorrow. In 251, signs that the emperor Gallus was considering a new round of persecutions changed Cyprian's mind again. He then decided to accelerate the reconciliation for all who were repentant. In spring of that year Cyprian consolidated his position in advance by convening a synod of local African bishops who

---

[14]Cyprian, *De Unitate Ecclesiae* 9.
[15]Cornelius's rival pope, Novatian, represented a more hardline position, which the African dissidents had at first complained of when Cyprian adopted it but now had lined up with to secure Roman support.

endorsed this polity collectively and also formally excommunicated the rival bishop Fortunatus, the presbyter Novatus, and his associate dissidents.

Having established his position in Africa (since Carthage was the main city-church of the region) Cyprian was now able to turn his attention to the "larger implications" of the experience. In his work *On the Unity of the Church* (*De Unitate*) Cyprian looked further afield, to the schism of Novatian at Rome, paralleling that of Fortunatus in his own church of Carthage. This text became a classical exposition of Christian ecclesiology for later centuries both in the Orthodox East as well as the Latin West. It is the one area in which Cyprian goes theologically beyond his teacher Tertullian. Leaning heavily on Tertullian's legal concept of a move that legally invalidates a claimant's right to be heard in court (a "prescription"),[16] Cyprian invokes the fourfold core definition of "church" that is found in the ancient baptismal creed: that it is one, holy, catholic, and apostolic. Where Irenaeus's emphasis had been on the catholic and apostolic aspect, in his struggle with Gnostic dissidents, Cyprian turns to the issue of the church's oneness. How can someone who is "not in unity" with the local church claim to be still a member of it, if the essence of the church is unity as well as apostolicity? Whereas Tertullian had been using that argument of prescription against heretics, Cyprian now shifts its emphasis toward "schismatics," that is, dissidents whose raison d'être is not so much a doctrinal disagreement on any core matter but a rift that has come about over a matter of church discipline (moral or liturgical or authority issues). Such became the classic distinction, ever after, between heresy and schism.

His argument is twofold: first, that the bishops are, in this era, what the apostles were in the primitive generation of the church. To this extent he manifests the same argument as Irenaeus: that of the apostolic succession of the bishops. Their role as the primary teachers of the churches continues the function of the apostles, who bore witness to the authentic teachings of Jesus in the Gospels. They are thus themselves the key arbiters and guarantors of apostolicity of Christian doctrine—not presbyters, professors, theologians, or any other Christians, who all can (of course) manifest the charism of truth in their Christian teaching; but the bishops alone have this duty as the core aspect of their ordained office. The harmony of the body of bishops thus manifests and defends the deposit of faith across the ages.[17] This is an extension of their liturgical role of teaching the faith to catechumens and neophytes, literally "teaching the church its creed."

---

[16] On that basis Tertullian had argued that heretics had no right to speak for the Christian church since their fundamental divergence from its standards in core doctrines had invalidated their claim to belonging.

[17] Cyprian, *De Unitate Ecclesiae* 5. "You cannot separate a ray of light from the sun, because its unity does not allow division. You can break a branch from a tree, but when broken, it will not be able to bud. Cut a stream off from its source, and it dries up."

Second, Cyprian argues, in being such a bastion of faith personified, the episcopal charism also emerges as chiefly to manifest the unity of the church in its local realization. This is the aspect of argument that Cyprian now draws out most dramatically. The bishop will do this by presiding over the Eucharist. If he is not the sole celebrant (a church with a single cathedral), then he will do so by presiding over all other presbyters who celebrate under his leadership. Following the lead of Ignatius of Antioch, who had so strongly stressed the need for obedience to the bishop as the liturgical symbol of Christ's unity, Cyprian notably moves the idea forward in legal terms: that disobedience to the bishop becomes a crime against the unity of the church, a sinful lapse from the core doctrine of the creed that the church must manifest unity in Christ. And so, for Cyprian, the act of schism is no longer "not a doctrinal matter" but rather an ecclesiological lapse that puts the dissident outside the communion of the church.[18] Schism can be readily assessed: is the person in or outside the communion of the local church, as guaranteed by the bishop? In other words, is the individual in communion with the bishop or not?

This is a dramatic moment of the ultrasharp focusing of the claims to authority of the local *episkopos*. It will later be tempered (and probably already was so tempered in Cyprian's time) by the fourth-century insistence that the local bishop is not an absolute monarch but is himself assessed, monitored, and guided by his own need to stand in harmony with the other local bishops around him, who will form a synod and work with a strong degree of collegiality toward a common consensus of faith and practice. But this structural theology will be more fully explicated in the fourth- and fifth-century development of conciliar theology.

In Cyprian's argument, Christ so wanted unity to be known as the charism of his church that he symbolically fastened the notion of ecclesial coherence to the singular person of Peter, and only then did he extend Peter's rights and duties to all the apostles. The other apostles all had what Peter had, but Christ deliberately chose to give Peter the promise of the church's coherence to indicate the significance of unanimity (Mt 16:18-19). This showed, for Cyprian, that collegial unanimity is at the heart of what being an apostolic bishop is all about. For Pope Cornelius (d. 253), and Pope Stephen (254–257), who succeeded him, who were working on another concept of what "Peter" represented, one that saw him as the apostolic founder of the great church of Rome and a martyr whose tomb in the city meant he still had a mystical presence among the Romans, the Lord's promise to Peter meant something else: not a symbol of the collegial unity of the episcopal body, but rather the special preeminence of the see of

---

[18]Cyprian, *De Unitate Ecclesiae* 4. "So how is it possible for anyone to think they keep the faith if they break the unity of the church?"

Rome.[19] To this day the Cyprianic view and the Roman view of the Petrine office continue to clash in the catholic conceptions of papacy. When Stephen clashed with Cyprian over points of liturgical order, their differing ideas over episcopal authority came out into the open.

Between 255 and 257 Cyprian was involved in a war of letters with Pope Stephen concerning the question of whether or not sacraments administered by heretical and schismatic clergy were valid. Cyprian took the conservative view (consistent with his notion that someone who departs from the church has no further entitlement to any of its "assets" and therefore that there is no grace in any of the dissidents' sacraments) that they were not valid or potent. This being the case, Cyprian insisted on having anyone who came to the church from a schismatic or heretical body rebaptized. In fact, it would be more accurate to say he insisted on them being baptized before approaching the Eucharist (as he did not accept their prior baptism in the sect as at all valid). On this point, however, Rome had adopted a more liberal view, that grace remained in the sacraments of the church even when administered by schismatics, by virtue of a form of "ecclesial memory" (the closer the administrators were to the ecclesial tradition, the more they still coinhered to some degree in the energy of the church's sacramental life).[20]

The Roman position was that the sacraments of schismatics were illicit but not invalid. Cyprian regarded them as both illicit and invalid: containing no grace and having no salvific effect when administered outside the communion of the church catholic. The Roman clergy, who were currently still resisting the Novatianist rigorism at home, censured Cyprian for holding this hardline position but, feeling that the traditional customs, maintained immemorially in Africa, were being overturned, Cyprian was outraged, defending his cause robustly against Roman disapproval. It was at this time that he probably revised the text of his *De Unitate Ecclesiae* to tone down his high praises of Peter being the symbol and focal point of episcopal unity.[21] Stephen was leaning on the Petrine office theory to advance his claims that the Roman church not only had a symbolic role in standing for church unity but even enjoyed a juridical function in assuring church unity, and so he was expecting to have his advice obeyed by provincial bishops. Cyprian wanted to make it clear that he had not meant a theory of papal

---

[19]For a long time the Roman pontiffs described themselves as the "vicars of St. Peter." They later changed the title (and the papal claim) to "vicars of Christ."

[20]Something that Basil the Great would set out in a canonical epistle for the Eastern churches a century later.

[21]Two ancient text traditions exist for the work, the later one being clearly less an encomium of the Petrine office. Cf. Bevenot, *Cyprian: De Lapsis and De Ecclesiae Catholicae Unitate*.

supremacy by his elevation of the symbol of Peter as chief of the apostolic band (papal primacy not necessarily including juridical authority). For him, all the bishops were equally apostles, held equally the same authority, though some held a symbolic role in addition.

This conflict has remained alive to this day within catholic Christianity in the manner the Orthodox churches and the Episcopalians interpret Petrine primacy in a significantly different (nonjuridical way) compared to Roman Catholicism. The issue of whether Christians coming into the church catholic from other ecclesial bodies require (re)baptism or a simple confession of faith and conversion has also remained conflicted. The Roman tradition after Augustine's time followed Stephen's lead universally. The Eastern Orthodox churches represent both positions and some compromises in between. Those who baptize such Christian converts, however, are universally of the strict position that Christian baptism can never be repeated, and thus they deny the validity of any prior baptismal ceremonies, effectively denying that other Christian movements are really Christian at all (though they might express it as "fully Christian"). The third-century argument, in other words, has never really gone away from the present ecumenical scene. Today some see the church as the sole locus of grace, what Cyprian called the "ark of salvation." In this sense being "outside the church, where there is no salvation," means being outside Noah's ark, where there was no alternative to drowning; or outside Christ's mystical body, thus apart from him, devoid of his Spirit. Others see the church as a less all-encompassing medium of grace. Cyprian clearly invested his ecclesiology with deep eschatological significance. Many contemporary ecclesiologies now exist with little or no eschatological dimensions.

In 257 the emperor Valerian issued a new edict demanding public sacrifice from eminent citizens. The churches knew that the persecution would be renewed strenuously, and Cyprian expressed to his followers that he had a premonition of death. This time he was sought out by the authorities and sent into exile. It was a gesture that recognized his high social standing as a Roman gentleman and was designed to give him time to recant. A year later he was brought back to Carthage and confessed that he would not accept any of the terms of the new religious laws. He was then tried in Carthage in 258 and, confessing his faith, was publicly beheaded under the proconsul Galerius Maximus. His personal holiness allied with his martyr's death left a high reputation behind. His letters were lively and remain a fountain of detailed information about the state of the developing church of the third century, and how important the role of the upper-class, educated *episkopos* was in that process.

## THE CHRISTIAN SCHOOLS AT ALEXANDRIA AND CAESAREA

*The Alexandrian catechetical school.* Alexandria in the third century shows us another aspect of Christian theological and organizational development at this time, for here we notice the emergence of a strong episcopal catechetical school. The ancient process of preparing candidates for baptism has by this time been organized in many different churches. We see examples of it in Alexandria, Rome, and Jerusalem. The fully developed aspect can be seen very clearly in the *Catechetical Homilies* of Bishop Cyril of Jerusalem in the fourth century, in which he addresses his candidates for baptism in the course of Lent, and we learn that they have received various rites and ceremonies from the hands of presbyters who, with the church's deacons, have been teaching them. These preparations were conducted all through the course of their period of catechumenate, a trial space where their allegiance to old ways and moral practices of paganism was tested so as to give way to new customs and habits as Christians. Various categories of people were strictly excluded: actors (then synonymous with part-time prostitutes), sex workers, soldiers, and obviously active devotees of the rites of the gods. Renunciations had to be made to become a catechumen.

Once admitted to prepare for baptism, the name of the "convert" was written into the rolls of the church membership, and they were signed on the brow with olive oil in the form of a cross, and hands (of the bishop or presbyters) were laid upon them to signify their turning toward the Lord.[22] Throughout this period of preparation the candidates were put through "scrutinies," in which the clergy would question them about their moral attitudes and practices, inviting them to deeper self-knowledge and ongoing repentance.[23] Exorcisms were performed on them. As we have seen, the early church regarded the cult of the gods not as something that was vacuous and empty but rather as a spiritually energized cult, geared to the worship of evil and powerful entities who had sought the moral dissolution of their devotees so as to lead them away from God. To prepare for baptism, therefore, the presbyters of the church exorcised the candidates several times from demonic possession. The remnants of these lengthy prayers of exorcism still endure to this day in the Eastern church's baptismal ritual.

Toward the end of Lent, which preceded the Pascha (Easter), at which they would be initiated, the bishop of the church would take a more engaged role in the

---

[22]*Convert* is so named for the *conversio morum*, or "conversion of morals," that was demanded of them.
[23]*Candidates* are named because the catechumens would be required to dress all in white on the occasion of their initiation, that is, be *candidatus*, as a symbol of their resurrection though the sacrament of baptism.

preparation of the catechumens.[24] To him would be instructed the higher levels of initiation-teaching: matters dealing with the theology of the church, its liturgical symbolism, the higher meaning of Scriptures (beyond their moral pedagogy), the significance of sacraments, the ways of prayer, and the doctrine of the Holy Spirit. These things were regarded as *arcana*, hidden mysteries that ought not to be spoken of freely among pagans.[25] To this day those receiving communion in the Eastern churches have to say a prayer of promise before approaching the altar: "I will not speak of your mysteries to your enemies." The candidates were required to keep all these things hidden from pagans and the nonbaptized catechumens and to reflect on them in their hearts, as the interior core of the church's commitment was not a matter of mere external belonging but rather a process of "belonging to the Lord" that was bonded in the internal spirit, which was made one in Christ by the Holy Spirit through the action of the sacraments.

In this higher stage of episcopal catechising, the ongoing life of the believer "in Christ" was the focus of attention. The teaching stressed that the bonding with the Lord had to be deepened through the Eucharist, through reflection on the Scriptures, and by assiduous prayer. This was why attention was given first of all to scriptural exegesis. In the ancient eucharistic celebrations, a massively important place was given to the reading and exposition of the Scriptures—not for any historical rationale but always primarily for what these sacred writings had to say about the Christ mystery that was currently being celebrated in the church's sacramental life. The bishop or a senior presbyter he had designated would be the single agent of this instruction. It was highly regarded, as one of the chief functions of the episcopate: breaking the bread of Scripture was seen as a sacred priestly task.

In Alexandria that task had led to a specific development of polity by the third century. We see in this great church a series of highly educated bishops. Even at Rome, where we have other significantly elevated social leaders by this time (such as the aristocrat Cornelius), they are not always very highly educated. At Alexandria, however, we seem to have a preference to elect to the episcopal office educated theologians: a sense that the bishop is the head of the Christians' school of catechesis and

---

[24] Early Christianity always called "Easter" *Pascha*. Not until the encounter with the Saxon nations did the term *Easter* come in to replace it among the English-speaking nations (from *Yeostre*, the goddess of spring, whose name was also attached to the season). Baptisms in the ancient church were also carried out on Pentecost day. They were collegial (numbers admitted at the same ceremony) in character and involved the threefold element of initiation as baptism of water for cleansing of sin, anointing with chrism for initiation into the gifts of the Spirit, introduction to communion (at the Eucharist) for full joining with the body of the Lord.

[25] The word *mystery* derives from the Greek *muein*, "to keep silent." The devotees of the ancient mystery religions were prohibited by vow from ever telling outsiders about their rituals.

that this is no small task, but rather the essence of all that Christians stand for. Other significant theologians have turned up by this period, such as Novatian at Rome or Tertullian at Carthage, but it is at Alexandria that the tradition of theologian-bishops starts to become paradigmatic for a large metropolitan center. It is no accident, then, that it is at this time and in this university city that we see the first signs of clashing between theologian-presbyters and bishops as to who has the higher calling by virtue of office: in other words, whose official charism to teach ranked higher than the other's: the bishop as preacher and ecclesial organizer, or the theologian-*didaskalos* as inspirational professor? It is another form of the earlier tension between prophet and *episkopos* that was resolved in favor of the *episkopos*. This time the church at large does not give its teaching role away so readily to one charismatic officer. The greatest exemplar of this is the theologian Origen of Alexandria.

In older books it has been often presumed that the catechetical school of Alexandria was something like an institution, with buildings and employees. Pantaenus, the renowned presbyter-theologian, was one of the early leaders of the "school," and Dionysius, later bishop at Alexandria, was another. We also know that Pantaenus inducted Clement of Alexandria into the church, and his teachings were primarily addressed to converted laity, so he was a luminary of this "school." Origen began life teaching doctrine and practice on behalf of the bishop Demetrius before ending up as the Christian world's greatest intellectual. Origen's colleague Heraclas, another theologian, succeeded to his post when he left it to devote himself more fully to philosophical teaching and would also succeed Demetrius as bishop. Two of Origen's pupils at Alexandria went on to become bishops in Palestinian Caesarea and Jerusalem (and would later invite Origen to teach there as a presbyter). But rather than putting all this evidence together to imagine a single "school" at the city, to rival the alternative schools of the Stoics, or Platonists, or the academicians of the Great Library, for example, it is perhaps better to imagine that this great Christian city had already accumulated an intellectual tradition and a succession of leaders who had established a style of theology that was read and developed across several generations. The "school of Alexandria," therefore, is a real enough thing, but more in the form of a tradition of theologizing than a discrete building. It is also something that is partly under the direct control of the bishop (in terms of early-level catechising of baptismal candidates) but not entirely so (in terms of higher level philosophical teachings given to paying, private pupils—such schools as Clement and Origen established).

In the earlier generation of the church, the clash between the catechetical teachings given by the *episkopoi* to convert candidates for baptism and the kind of speculative religious-cosmological instructions given by *didaskaloi* in the private establishments of further education (the ancient schools) was witnessed in the so-called Gnostic crisis. As a result of that first clash the bishops of the main church established a line of doctrine characterized by the basic points of salvation history narrated in the creed (a liturgical prayer in origin for those being baptized, to make an oath of allegiance to what they believed) and by straightforward "common-sense" exegesis of the scriptural narratives. In the middle of the third century that context is still present, but there is a greater sense of distance between the mainline "creedal" teachers and the cosmologically sweeping vistas of the Gnostics—but also a growing acceptance among some of the Christian intelligentsia that the speculative questions that the Gnostics had posed, about a cosmically scaled sweep of salvation and its implications, were serious ones that the church's tradition needed to embrace.

Following from that there was also a growing acceptance of the principles of allegorical interpretation: the reading of the Scripture that allowed an interpreter to approach an event not in a straightforward literalist sense but in a symbolic way that could argue that "this really stands for that." The Gnostic interpreters had heavily used allegorical reading techniques, so much so that many of the earlier generation of bishops had shied away from it as an heretical tendency. But the technique did not so much belong to the Gnostics as such, but rather to the Hellenistic academy in a larger sense. Alexandria was the world center of such an approach. At the Great Library there, a deliberate attempt was being carried out in Origen's time to accumulate an example of every text in existence and collate the commentaries on it.[26] If ever a ship or a caravan arrived in the city or the docks, the law demanded it be searched and every book surrendered until it was copied in the library. Then only the copy was returned and the original kept in the archives.

The schools at Alexandria were, therefore, in the forefront of the academic enterprise. Several Christians of this period saw the need for the church to be heavily vested in this project for the success of the church's social mission. This represented a turning away from earlier exclusionist mentalities, perhaps encouraged by periods of regular persecution at times when the literary intelligentsia did not feature highly in the Christian numbers, and manifested instead the dawning of the church's sense of social theology, not so much representing a duty to endure in this world until the end times, but rather a destiny to make an alternative society, to create a Christian culture and baptize Hellenism itself. Origen represents this awareness more than any other, and it is to him we can now turn. He was, without question, the first truly international intelligence the church had yet produced, and he remains arguably the most important

---

[26]See further J. A. McGuckin, "Origen as Literary Critic in the Alexandrian Tradition," in *Origeniana Octava*, ed. L. Perrone (Leuven: Peeters, 2003), 121-35.

theologian of the Christian church after the Evangelist John and the apostle Paul. Even those who consciously rejected his conclusions often followed his agenda.

*Origen of Alexandria: Master theologian and philosopher.* Origen's fame in the Christian world, already notable in his own lifetime, ensured that his personal history was very well charted in antiquity, even if the nature of the sources for that life have brought some degree of confusion into the interpretation—or rather, the sequencing—of some of the events.[27] His own writings provide important and primary information, and other major sources include a *Letter of Thanksgiving* or *Panegyric* dedicated to Origen by Theodore, one of his students at the school of Caesarea, whom Eusebius the church historian tells us later became a great luminary in the Cappadocian church, none other than St. Gregory Thaumaturgos.[28] The *Panegyric* gives us priceless information about Origen the scholar and about the curriculum he offered at this advanced Christian *schola*, his own foundation and brainchild.[29]

The single most important secondary source about him is the fourth-century church historian Eusebius, who dedicated the large part of his sixth book of *Ecclesiastical History* specifically to his hero, Origen. Eusebius demands close attention, even when one suspects his versions of events, for he was himself (as bishop of Caesarea) the successor of his teacher Pamphilus, who was one of the most dedicated "Origen disciples" of his age. As Pamphilus's protégé, Eusebius was the second-generation keeper of the library archives at the Caesarean church that Origen had founded. So it was that he had unrivaled access to Origen's own books and correspondences, which are now otherwise lost.[30] Eusebius constructed his small *Life of Origen* from his own readings of the primary text as well as from reliance on a now-

---

[27]Cf. P. Nautin, *Origene: Sa Vie et son Oeuvre* (Paris: Beauchesne, 1977), who made an extensive source-redactional study of the materials and has a justified suspicion of Eusebius's ability, in his *Church History* bk. 6, to have synthesized correctly all the disparate sources he uses for constructing a life of Origen. Not all of Nautin's theories have gained the same degree of hearing among scholars, but he successfully demonstrated the difficulty of taking all the literary evidence "straightforwardly," and this certainly accounts for modern divergences on the details of the sequencing of Origen's *vita*. There is a clear and cogent presentation of all the historical data collated from all the ancient sources in H. Crouzel (*Origen* [Edinburgh: T&T Clark, 1989]), though the latter proceeds so confidently in his chronological narrative only by virtue of having dismissed many of the source-critical problems (p. 2).

[28]Or "wonderworker": so named from the tradition of his many miraculous wonders performed in the course of his preaching ministry. He was a spiritual guide for Basil the Great's grandmother and was highly influential in the shaping of Cappadocian patristic theology, which itself took Origen's work to a wider international audience through the *Philocalia of Origen*, collated by Basil and Gregory of Nazianzus.

[29]For how Origen conceived this as a missionary endeavor see J. A. McGuckin, "Caesarea Maritima as Origen Knew It," in *Origeniana Quinta*, ed. R. J. Daly (Leuven: Peeters, 1992), 3-25.

[30]Eusebius tells us (*Ecclesiastical History* 6.36) he had collected together more than one hundred letters of Origen, now all dispersed.

fragmentary treatise composed by Pamphilus.[31] His *Life of Origen* is one of the earliest hagiographies we have of someone who was not a martyr-saint.

Eusebius also had access to the complete text of an important letter Origen wrote to defend himself against episcopal charges (leveled against him by the bishops of Alexandria and Rome) of irregularity soon after he had moved to Caesarea. This otherwise lost text, known as the *Autobiographical Letter*, is embedded now throughout the text of Eusebius, unrecoverable, of course, except through the redactional use made of it by both Pamphilus and Eusebius in turn—both of whom have urgent reason to defend Origen from any charge of unorthodoxy, because in so doing they were also defending their own reputations as churchmen and theologians dedicated to his memory and his school.[32] Other lists of Origen's writings, or notes about his life, can be found in various litterateurs, such as the fourth-century and highly unreliable Epiphanius of Salamis, as well as Jerome and Rufinus, who both preserved sections of his partly autobiographical *Letter to Friends in Alexandria* but who were at war about his enduring importance.[33] Other witnesses were fifth-century historian Socrates Scholasticus and the late but very important testimony from learned ninth-century patriarch of Constantinople, Photius, who was head of a scholarly book reader's circle of close friends before his accession to the patriarchate and who published his notes on the various books they studied.[34] This work, titled *Bibliotheca* (*The Library*), has one chapter (118) that concerns Origen and his writings.

Eusebius tells us that Origen was "not yet quite seventeen" when the persecution by the Emperor Septimius Severus broke out in 202 and hit the Egyptian church very severely.[35] This gives his birth date as 185/6. Eusebius also gives the information that Origen died, "having completed seventy years less one," about the time that Gallus became emperor after Decius's assassination.[36] These two details conflict historically, and preference ought to be given to Eusebius's note of his age of

---

[31]Pamphilus, *Apologia for Origen*. Text in PG 17.521-616. Eusebius was the research assistant in writing this work.

[32]Cf. Eusebius, *Ecclesiastical History* 6.19.12-14. This is possibly the same as the letter Origen wrote to Pope Pontianus of Rome to defend himself against charges (by Demetrius of Alexandria) of irregularity of ordination and unorthodoxy in doctrine. It is mentioned by Jerome in *Epistle* 84.9, *To Pammachius and Oceanus*.

[33]Epiphanius, *Panarion* (*Medicine Chest Against All Heresies*), c. 64. Rufinus, *De Adulteratione librorum Origenis* 8; Jerome, *Apologia Contra Rufinum* 2.18-19; also *Epistles* 33, 84. Some of Origen's works are now lost not only because of the ravages of time but also because there was a concerted campaign to burn his books, especially after his posthumous condemnation by church authorities in the fifth and sixth centuries.

[34]Socrates, *Ecclesiastical History* 5.

[35]Eusebius, *Ecclesiastical History* 6.2.12.

[36]Ibid., 7.1.

sixty-nine at death.[37] So, if Origen was born in 186, he died in the reign of Valerian, in 255, a victim of the anti-Christian persecutions begun under the emperor Decius, which had seen him severely tortured.

When Origen was a young man at Alexandria, the theologian Clement was active as a noted Christian professor. Origen's father, Leonides, was his colleague and also active as a Christian teacher of literature and rhetorics. Origen's given name (a thoroughly Egyptian populist one, derived from the Greek for "child of Horus"[38]) suggests he was the child of a mixed marriage between one of the *honestiores* and a woman from the class of *humiliores*.[39] At that period not everyone in the empire had the universal right to citizenship, and children of such mixed-class marriages were excluded from the political rights and privileges of their fathers. This surmise is borne out by his ability in later life to attend, unharmed, the executions of his disciples who had been condemned for their profession of Christianity.[40] He did this so as to encourage them to persevere to the end despite the fury of the crowd that this practice raised against him. It is an indication that he did not have citizenship rights. The persecution of Severus was directed solely against citizens who had adopted the Christian religion.[41] Origen's father, Leonides, however, was a marked man and was decapitated as a martyr.[42] The impact on his family was financially devastating, since the whole estate of those executed was confiscated to the treasury. As Origen was the eldest of seven sons, the support of the family fell onto his shoulders.[43]

Probably to help his family financially in the aftermath of the execution, the local bishop Demetrius appointed Origen when he was eighteen to the task of giving

---

[37]The conflict creates a divergence of two years in the chronology that Eusebius himself has set up for the reader. It is an internal conflict that is by no means uncommon throughout Eusebius's history. Crouzel notes the preference (*Origen*, 2).

[38]Horus was the child of the goddess Isis by Osiris. The Isis movement was the most powerful of the pagan religions of Egypt in Origen's time.

[39]Cf. A Rousselle, "The Persecution of the Christians at Alexandria in the Third Century," *Revue historique de Droit francais et étranger* 2 (1974): 222-51 (esp. 231-33). Origen's mother, according to Jerome (*Epistle* 39.22), was either a Jewess or a Christian. He tells us that she taught the young child to recite the Psalms from an early age.

[40]Eusebius, *Ecclesiastical History* 6.3.4-5; 6.4-5.

[41]The *Historia Augusta* (*Severus* 17.1) says that this persecution was aimed at those who proselytized for Christianity. Crouzel (*Origen*, 5) takes it as an indication that Leonides might have been an important figure in the catechetical school of the church (into which office Origen seems to have been later inducted). It might be so, but suppositions about the episcopal school of catechesis in Alexandria often elide the important difference between a *schola* belonging to a private *didaskalos*-philosopher (such as Origen was) and a teacher of catechesis under the direction of the bishop (as Origen also seems to have been for some time). That Origen was not simply a catechist under Demetrios but a powerful and famous *didaskalos* in his own right is the real source of all the friction between them.

[42]Leonides's execution by beheading denotes his class rank as citizen.

[43]Eusebius, *Ecclesiastical History* 6.2.12.

catechetical direction for the Alexandrian church—not to be head of some prestigious and official school of theology, but rather that he was given care of the basic preparation for catechumens.[44] Origen was here basically being inducted by the bishop into the lower orders of the paid ministers of the church. Simultaneously he also extended his private teaching and turned more and more to the self-designation of a rhetor-philosopher rather than a grammaticus. He adopted the characteristic "simple lifestyle" and behavior of the sophist. Eusebius describes this in a way that highlights its Christian ascetical character, and it became an iconic picture of the sleepless student of the sacred Scriptures who embraced poverty, celibacy, and the disciplines of prayer and fasting in such a way that it more or less co-opted Origen into the role of founding father of the monks, who were becoming more and more a feature of life in the fourth-century church when Eusebius was writing.

In his early twenties, he found wealthy patrons who were willing to help him in his career.[45] One of them was a wealthy Valentinian Gnostic named Ambrose, whom Origen brought back into the communion of the great church and who would soon commission several major works from Origen's pen, such as the *Treatise on Prayer* and the magnificent *Commentary on John*.[46] At this time Origen sold his father's extensive library for a small pension that allowed him to become a full-time philosopher.[47] Ambrose also supplied stenographers to make multiple copies as Origen discoursed. Another of his unknown supporters was the wealthy woman who took him into her household as a scholar and tutor. She was a *patrona* also of renowned Gnostic theologian Paul of Antioch, who used her household as a base for his lectures and was highly successful as a teacher in Alexandria.[48] Eusebius is at pains to tell his fourth-century readers that while Origen studied in the same house, he never once "prayed in common" with a Gnostic.[49] But the close association started to raise the suspicions of the Alexandrian bishop Demetrios against his precocious catechist. While Origen was taking advanced classes at the schools of Alexandria, his own teachers included the famous Platonist Ammonius Saccas, who was also (a few years later) the teacher of Plotinus. The latter, now

---

[44]Ibid., 6.3.3.
[45]The amount of money he received (four obols) was less than the regular wage of a poor laborer. It signals, I think, not his inability to command a good price, but more his determination to live in voluntary poverty under the "dole" of a *patronus* or *patrona*.
[46]Eusebius, *Ecclesiastical History* 6.23.2.
[47]The library was the one part of the patrimony that seems not have been confiscated by the state after Leonides's execution. Cf. Eusebius, *Ecclesiastical History* 6.2.13.
[48]Paul of Antioch is a teacher of whom nothing else is known. He is typical of the independent Christian *didaskalos* of Alexandria in the third century, who attracted the hostility of the Alexandrian bishops, then rose in their power and their control over the whole Christian affairs of the city.
[49]Eusebius, *Ecclesiastical History* 6.2.13-14.

regarded as the founder of the neo-Platonist school, was twenty years Origen's junior. This influential movement of thought marked a new epoch of forging a very close association of the philosophic and religious quests. Origen himself, though technically more of an eclectic in his own philosophic tradition and having close relations with the Middle Platonists whom Ammonius had introduced to him, can also lay claim to having at the heart of his life's work the same weaving together of the philosophic and mystical imperatives that neo-Platonism also demonstrated.[50] He is not a "Platonizing Christian," however, for he retains always a critical eye on all that he adopts to explain Christian thought to the Hellenists. The very conflict between the Plotinian school and the Christian heirs of Origen is a sign of how close were the agendas between the leading Hellenist and Christian intellectuals of the day.[51]

Eusebius's statement that Origen had been taught by Clement of Alexandria is probably not accurate (he thinks the catechetical school of third-century Alexandria was like that of Caesarea in the fourth).[52] Origen himself shows no signs of a close relation with Clement, and though he does refer to Clement's ideas on a few occasions, it is as much to correct as to follow him.[53] His associate in Christian teaching at that time, and possibly also an assistant in his own house school for philosophy, was Heraclas, brother of his pupil Plutarch, who had recently been martyred.[54] Heraclas too was an avid disciple of the Alexandrian philosophers. He would be ordained a priest at Alexandria and eventually became bishop there. In later years, when Bishop Demetrios of Alexandria was prosecuting him for irregular ordination, Origen ruefully pointed to the manner in which Heraclas still wore the cloak of a philosopher, even as an Alexandrian presbyter, and mused why he alone seemed to draw criticism because of his philosophical work.[55]

---

[50] He is technically a Christian Middle Platonist: much influenced by Plato, Numenius, Albinus, and others. But equally marked on him is the influence of Aristotle and Pythagoras. Into the rich soup of this kind of eclecticism we cannot forget that he was driven, perhaps above all else, by his close reading of the Scriptures and his faithful adherence to the ecclesial tradition mediated to him in his time not only through prior theological patterns but through the liturgy and through his belief in the ongoing inspiration of the preacher/teacher in the church assembly. Cf. J. A. McGuckin, "Origen's Doctrine of the Priesthood," *Clergy Review* 70, no. 8 (August 1985): 277-86; *Clergy Review* 70, no. 9 (September 1985): 318-25.

[51] Porphyry, the leading disciple of Plotinus, attacked Origen for betraying the neo-Platonist cause by his "Christianizing" agenda (cf. *Ecclesiastical History* 6.19.4-8), much to the outrage of Eusebius. In this passage Eusebius seems to confuse Ammonius Saccas with Ammonius of Thmuis, a Christian author whose works he knows.

[52] Eusebius, *Ecclesiastical History* 6.6.

[53] In the *Commentary on Matthew* 14.2. Origen refers to the exegesis of Mt 18:19-20, which Clement offers in his *Stromateis* 3.10.68.1.

[54] Eusebius, *Ecclesiastical History* 6.3.2, 15.

[55] Ibid., 6.19.12-14.

Eusebius tells his readers that the young philosopher lived a highly ascetic life, fasting and abstaining from wine as well as choosing to live in simple poverty.[56] He also reports that Origen took an extreme step to ensure his reputation and respectability as a private instructor of young men and women. He allegedly paid to be castrated by a doctor. Eusebius explains this away as evidence of his immaturity, because he had taken the words of Jesus in Matthew 19:12 (being a eunuch for the kingdom's sake) in a literal way. Eusebius commends him for his zeal, if not for his wisdom. The story features in the *Ecclesiastical History* as the chief explanation (along with implied episcopal jealousy) of why his bishop wanted to prosecute Origen at episcopal courts in Rome, Palestine, and his own diocese of Egypt. Eusebius tells his readers that Demetrios was told of the castration by Origen in secret and approved of it but later publicized it when he had fallen out with Origen and used it to attack the validity of his ordination.

The story, though lurid enough to ensure that it is the one thing most people remember about Origen, is hardly credible.[57] We have no indication that the motive of castration for respectability was ever regarded as standard by a teacher of mixed-gender classes in antiquity. Female disciples (of whom Eusebius knows and is sufficiently surprised to list some of their names) in Alexandria in Origen's day would certainly have been members of the higher class and would naturally have had several attendants. More to the point, when Origen turns his attention to Matthew 19:12, he himself mockingly derides the literalist interpretation of the eunuch pericope, saying it was something only an idiot would put into literal effect.[58] Origen's own text ought always to be preferred as a historical source over and above Eusebius, whose motive at this juncture was evidently to cover over (with ascetical zeal that would appeal to a fourth-century monastic readership) the undoubtedly real reason Origen got into trouble with the bishop—and that was doctrinal: a reason fourth-century monastics would not

---

[56]Ibid., 6.3.9-13. While this is a picture drawn by Eusebius to relate Origen of the third century to the ascetics of the late fourth century, for whom he was writing, there is no reason to doubt the accuracy of his remarks. The asceticism he speaks of was commonly seen to be a charism of the philosophic life—*sophrosyne*—the sobriety and simplicity that demonstrates the willingness of the teacher to live out the implications of their doctrine. Origen, though not a monk, was in fact influential on the developing patterns of Christian monasticism.

[57]Crouzel (*Origen*, 9n32), who says Origen writes with "apparent" firsthand knowledge about eunuchism, does not realize he is drawing this entirely from the medical treatise of Galen. Already in the nineteenth century, F. Boehringer (*Kirkengeschichte* [Zurich: 1869], 28) saw through the castration tale. It has become increasingly suspect in modern historiography and ought now to be laid aside. Postinfantile castration debilitates massively, and Origen was a very robust and energetic individual all his life until his final torture.

[58]*Commentary on Matthew* 15.1-5.

like to hear about. The cause of the dissension was surely the publication of his treatise *De Principiis*, which contained many speculative elements that alarmed Demetrius because of their surface "Gnostic" character. Origen's interest in celibate living, then, did not come to him from Matthew 19:12 but from his preference for Paul (1 Cor 7:5-9). Like Paul, Origen's celibacy was a directing of his energies dramatically into the service of the Word. Several other patently false stories, such as the tale that he had offered incense to the gods in time of persecution, were put out about Origen in later times. Such slanders were designed to damage a reputation that was growing, alarmingly so for many hierarchs of the fourth century. Epiphanius is a prime example of such a gatherer (and creator) of dubious tales in his *Panarion*.[59]

As Origen turned more and more away from the identity of a grammarian to that of a rhetor-philosopher, he seems to have passed on his church catechetical duties to his younger colleague Heraclas while he himself began to set up more publicly as a Christian professor (*didaskalos*). This also set him apart more independently from the bishop (the ancient curriculum was not only about religion, but astronomy, cosmology, and mathematics too—and what would a cleric necessarily know of such things?). So began his collision course with Bishop Demetrios. The latter was one of the most energetic church administrators of the third century and responsible for elevating the episcopal office into a new institutional primacy in Egypt. This was not just because he was a dominant personality; rather, it was an aspect of his pastoral instinct to keep the church under a tight rule through one of the most bitter and bloody persecutions that had ever fallen on a Christian congregation. Up until his day the presbyters of the Alexandrian church seem to have elected one of their number to represent them, but after the time of Demetrios the strict separation of presbyteral and episcopal "identities" is enforced. Egypt was also unique in terms of Christian polity organization in that its one great city in the entire country (Alexandria) so dominated the appointment process of all other Egyptian bishops that for many centuries to come they almost functioned collectively as suffragan bishops to the metropolitan hierarch, rather than as independent church leaders in a national synod.

Origen's emergence as a professional and quasi-independent head of his own "Christian" school of metaphysics meant that he was bound to clash with this monarchically minded bishop, who instinctively saw himself as the single head of the Christian school of the city. We learn that Origen started to travel to hear other teachers in other cities and gather books (at Athens and Rome) as well as conduct some royal-command

---

[59] Epiphanius, *Panarion*, c. 64.

tutorials.[60] He also brought out his own first major *opus*, an introduction to Christian thought, a systematic "First Principles" called *De Principiis* or *Peri Archon*.[61] This manual of Christian philosophic instruction was something radically new in Christian writing. Not only was it a coherent attempt to start from the beginning and connect all the aspects of Christian thought from creation, cosmology, and anthropology onward (the nature of God, and the origins and destiny of angels, planets, and humankind), but it also demonstrates a driving and coherent inner vision.

The whole work (and all else he wrote after it) revolves around one of Origen's basic principles, that the pursuit of reason (*Logos*) is an inherently divine task. For him, all human reflection, conducted in purity of mind and heart, is a holy and sacred quest, God-inspired, and leading to an ascent of the spirit of the creature back to union with the God who made him such a seeker. For Origen, the footsteps and fingerprints of the Creator are left abundantly in the cosmos and especially in the mental capacities of humans. Accordingly, the professor is the high priest of Christian mysteries: the new prophet who scrutinizes the sacred writings and reflects profoundly on them to offer treasures of deeper mysteries to the faithful who are prepared to receive them. His book represented a far-reaching and ambitious project, but its newness and some of the ideas it taught about the pretemporal origin of souls rang alarm bells in many Christian circles. His doctrine of incorporeal resurrection bodies and the other speculations that must have been contained in his *Stromata* (book of lecture notes), as well as many of the unusual points of doctrine still extant in the *De Principiis*, would have been enough to give Demetrios grounds for complaint.

Returning to Alexandria, Origen ran into the riots surrounding the unfortunate occasion of the state visit of Emperor Caracalla to Alexandria.[62] It was this close shave with danger, along with growing tensions with Demetrios, that probably induced him to leave the city and settle in Palestine, where two of his students were

---

[60] According to Eusebius (*Ecclesiastical History* 6.14.10), the Roman governor of Arabia sent letters to the prefect of Egypt asking him to send on Origen, accompanied by official bodyguards, so that he could hear more of the Christian movement from one of its leading intellectuals. This was probably in the reign of Antoninus (Caracalla) rather than Septimius Severus. Eusebius also tells us (*Ecclesiastical History* 6.14.10) that Origen visited Rome at the time Zephyrinus was pope (198–217), probably in 212. One of the lecture rooms he attended at that time was that of the Logos theologian Hippolytus, who, as Jerome reports (*De Viris Illustribus* 61), drew the attention of his audience to the presence of the distinguished Origen among them. Later in his life he would receive an imperial summons to lecture before Julia Mammaea (Eusebius, *Ecclesiastical History* 6.21.3-4).

[61] In Latin the title reads *About First Things*, which is a pun meaning "introductory matters" and "elementary guide"; but in Greek it also has the dubious quasi-Gnostic resonance of *On the Archons*.

[62] In the winter of 215–216, when Caracalla made a state visit to Alexandria, students there publicly mocked him with the title of "Geticus" (implying he got his throne by the murder of his brother Geta), and he ordered his troops to ravage the city, execute the imperial governor, kill all protesters, and exile the faculty who were teaching in the schools.

the leading bishops, at Caesarea and Jerusalem.[63] They too wanted to establish a church that would be renowned for its learned institutions and, like Origen, were keen to construct a library and academy at the center of all Christian enterprises. This new vision for the nature of the Christian church was one that Origen came to build at Caesarea (the first-ever Christian university), and he was surely commissioned to do it by the hierarchs of Palestine, who also asked him to give some preparatory discourses in the churches.

This preferment roused the fury of his bishop Demetrios, who complained that it was unheard of to allow laymen to teach doctrine in church in the presence of bishops.[64] Origen returned to Alexandria for a short time after this but soon moved permanently to Caesarea, where he was ordained to the priesthood. Demetrios constantly complained of him afterwards, but his opposition was largely ignored, except at Rome, where the hierarchs had reason to dislike Logos theologians, as can be seen by the hostility Hippolytus roused. The suspicion of the bishops of Rome and Alexandria, however, is not simply a matter of "jealousy," as Eusebius will later have it. The rapid ascent and development of Logos theology in the third century, accompanied by the great flowering of allegorical exegesis, which accelerated that rise, were, of course, two of the most distinctive marks of the career of Origen as a thinker. Many conservative bishops still associated allegorical exegesis with either the myth-making of the Hellenist pagans or the antihistoricism of the Gnostics, and few were then able to see that it spelled a new future for Christian exegesis, as Origen claimed.

Origen's devotion to the Scriptures was lifelong. In an age before computer word searches or concordances, he was able to match verse by verse according to word pairs and idea associations. Those who accuse him of not having much respect for the literal meaning of the text can never have read him carefully. He knew the text backward and forward. He is immersed in it, textually, historically, and above all mystically. It is the secret navigational chart for all his thinking: about the world and its origins as well as the nature and destiny of humankind. He regards Scripture as a mystical map of how to be conformed to Christ. Approaching the Scriptures, Origen begins with grammatical and historical studies of its meaning. But he does not think that its significance ends there. As a divinely inspired text, for Origen, the Scripture contains many hidden levels of meaning, opaque to the spiritually uneducated or the morally coarse, but opening up, like locked levels giving way to perception, in accordance with the spiritual growth and fidelity of the disciple.

---

[63]Theoctist of Caesarea and Alexander of Jerusalem. Another leading bishop, Firmilian of Cappadocia, was one of Origen's passionate supporters (Eusebius, *Ecclesiastical History* 6.26-27).

[64]"It has never been heard of and never happens even in this day that the unordained should preach in the presence of bishops."

At Alexandria and Caesarea he studied with Jewish sages[65] and tried to learn at least enough Hebrew to recognize words—even though his sense is that the Greek Septuagintal text (LXX) is the "real" Christian version to be used in the churches.[66] He put this knowledge to work in collating the *Hexapla*, a six-column set of versions of the Bible beginning with the Hebrew and continuing with the available Greek translations. This was surely prepared to correlate scriptural exegesis between Jewish and Christian schools, but also designed from the perspective of the Great Library's project of a universal academic collation of literary texts. It can claim to be the church's first critical-methodological work of biblical scholarship.

Origen's knowledge of the New Testament betrays a deep preference for Paul and the Gospel of John, but all the literature has been closely studied by him. He is one of the earliest and greatest of the church's Pauline theologians. Paul was more than a mere systematist of the Christian tradition; as far as Origen was concerned, he was especially that theologian carried off in rapture to the third heaven (2 Cor 12:2), whose special revelation afforded him a profound mystical insight into the mystery of Jesus that often escaped the other disciples, with the exception of the great apostle John. Time after time the source of Origen's particularly nuanced biblical interpretations of the Old Testament text can be explained on the basis of the Pauline or Johannine text through which he is reading the old narratives.

His whole approach to biblical interpretation is to read the lesser and more obscure through the resolving lens of the greater and more radiantly clear. This means in practice that he draws up a list of those texts that contain more of the prophetic message of the divine Word to the world (as distinct from a moral or ceremonial message meant for a people at a certain time in history) and sets them in order: a taxonomy of importance of revelatory character, in short. First come Paul and John, then come the Psalms (seen as the direct communication of the Word of God), then the Synoptic Gospels, then the greater Prophets and Song of Songs, and then other New Testament "apostolic" writings and other Scriptures. The whole significance of a scriptural text has to be located in its larger context of revelation (not atomistically

---

[65]*De Principiis* 1.3.4 (*Hebraeus magister*); 4.3.14 (*Hebraeus doctor*). Origen's Hebrew master at Alexandria might well have been Judeo-Christian, for the interpretation he gave of the seraphic cry of thrice holy, in Is 6:3, is very much in line with early Christian trinitarian tradition. When Origen was resident in Palestine he consulted on several occasions with famous rabbis. He tells us in the preface to his *Commentary on the Psalms* that some of his ideas came from a consultation with the rabbinic patriarch Ioullos. Talmudic texts also depict Origen in discussion with Caesarean Jewish scholar Hoschaia Rabba.

[66]The Eastern churches retain this view to the present. Only the Protestant Reformation restored the Hebrew text to pride of place liturgically in the churches and the academy.

considered in a way that modern commentaries often approach it), that is, in terms of what it has to say in the harmony of consideration of all the other Scriptures.

The books of the Bible, then, are not simply separate historical creations of disparate authors, for Origen, but insofar as they are "Holy Scripture," they are all part of a "seamless robe," like the robe of Christ, the clothing of the eternal Word of God, speaking about his descent to earth for the purposes of salvation. The Scripture as a whole leans toward the Christ-incarnation mystery, and its purposes are fully explicated within it: like a fruit growing toward completion in the fullness of time. The books and their message are not ultimately historical, but eschatological, transhistorical, reaching out to a mystery that is revealed more fully in the incarnation event, but still reaching forward to that timeless posthistory, when all human souls will be restored to archetypal unity with God. That vast scope of Origen's transhistorical vision does not so much despise the historical message of each of the books (rooted in their own time, as it were) but continues to process that message in terms of its eternal, metahistorical significance.

In a famous analogy in his *De Principiis*, and one that would determine the church's exegetical method for the next two millennia, Origen describes the Scriptures as also being characterized by three different levels of meaning, comparable to when Christ gives some of his teachings in valleys, some on plains, and some on mountaintops. Some valley texts, he says, are meant for the simple moral instruction of those who are not very advanced. Some (the plains) are meant for more advanced disciples who wish to go beyond simple morals and see deeper spiritual mysteries. Some (symbolized by those elite instructions given to specially chosen apostles on mountaintops) are out-of-the-ordinary mystical revelations of deep truths only meant for spiritually advanced disciples, who have already received prior initiations from the Spirit of God and whose souls have been assiduously prepared by asceticism and study so as to become pure enough to recognize the voice of the Word of God when it speaks, quietly and intimately, to the receptive soul.

Eusebius lists the main works Origen composed while still resident in Alexandria as the *De Principiis*, the first five books of the *Commentary on John*, the first eight books of his *Commentary on Genesis*, a *Commentary on Psalms 1–25*, a *Commentary on Lamentations*, *Two Books on the Resurrection*, and *Ten Books of Stromata* (*Miscellaneous Notes*). After settling in Caesarea he completed his *John Commentary* (one of his greatest masterworks) and his *Commentary on the Song of Songs* (one of the most influential books of Christian spirituality ever written). He would write a very moving *Exhortation to Martyrdom* later in life, when his own reputation had made him one of the most wanted Christians in the world when the emperors reintroduced persecution.

His jailers would then protract his torture over many months to try, in vain, to force his apostasy. By the end of his life he had made detailed commentaries and liturgical homilies on nearly every book in the Christian canon of Scripture.[67] It was an unrivaled accomplishment that seized the imagination of the church and set a standard for ages to come. St. Gregory the Theologian challenged the fourth century to admit that Origen was still "the whetstone that sharpens us all."

Origen's early duties as presbyter in Caesarea went hand in hand with his other vocational task, which was to establish the church of that city as a major center of intellectual activity. The establishment of a Christian "school of Caesarea" at this period parallels what we know of Caesarea as a center of Hellenistic philosophical activity, and more particularly a center of the rabbinic movement that was to produce that body of Torah philosophy and commentary that was later to be known as the Mishnah. Origen's commission was to found a Christian *schola* that would revolve around him as its leading professor and the president of a major new archive and library. It was designed from the outset as a missionary endeavor: setting up the Christians as a cultural force in the city to rival the pagans and Jews. The site appears to have been near the city harbor, adjacent to the Augustus Temple.[68] Only small ruins survive today, but his work in his lifetime successfully established an important library, a rival to the archives of the church of Alexandria, and this university experiment is the first exemplar of how the church ought to invest itself in education as part of its essential "mission" to the world. The Caesarean library attracted a series of learned bishops down until the fifth century. Even after the seventh century invasions of the Holy Land, when the importance of Caesarea as a center of Christian learning was only a distant memory, the achievement of Origen was not lost, for the principle had been established throughout Byzantine Christianity—that the church leadership ought to base its cultural mission around a nexus of higher-education services. It is largely to Origen and his later disciples that Christianity owes this insight and its practice for centuries following.

His transition to Palestine was, therefore, a stormy one and marks a time when he had to engage in some serious self-justification before the ecclesiastical court of Rome as well as in his native Alexandria (to his friends, if not to the bishop), and we might presume to his new patrons in Palestine. The strength of the opposition raised against him by Alexandria, in his early years in Palestine, can be seen in his preface to the sixth book of the *Commentary on John*. Here he compares himself to an Israelite who

---

[67] A listing of the complete works of Origen along with numerous articles interpreting the various books in greater detail can be found in J. A. McGuckin, ed., *The Westminster Handbook to Origen of Alexandria* (Louisville: Westminster John Knox, 2004).
[68] See further McGuckin, "Caesarea Maritima as Origen Knew It."

has escaped the perverse persecution of Egyptians. But he soon seems to have settled down in Caesarea, supported by encouraging hierarchs, and this became a period of his greatest literary activity. He was increasingly used by his hierarchs as a theological expert in several Palestinian and Arabian church synods. Whatever the charges raised against him, they more or less failed with the death of Demetrios, which took place a few years after he had left Alexandria.

As a presbyter, Origen was called on to perform an array of services and orations that involved him in working with a greater range of educational ability than hitherto had been his custom as a professional teacher. One of the ways this affected his output was the genre of the preached church homily. Every Wednesday and Friday, as well as the Sunday synaxis, the church gathered for preaching and prayer, sometimes in the context of a eucharistic offering and sometimes not.[69] Some of his orations on the Scripture were delivered extempore. His *Homily on the Witch of Endor* shows that he did not always know which reading would be required for comment on the day.[70] The *Homily on the Witch* begins with a request for bishop Theoctist to choose which of the four readings he will speak about. Origen then evidently spoke extempore. Eusebius tells us that Origen refused to allow anyone to transcribe these church sermons until he was over sixty—a moral to all preachers that high inspiration never excuses the task of preparation.[71]

As Crouzel points out, this means that his surviving *Homilies* generally represent the preaching of his last decade of life. An exception to this is the series of *Homilies on Luke*, which were delivered early in his time at Caesarea and show signs of having been written down before their delivery.[72] Generally speaking, Origen's surviving *Homilies*—as distinct, for example, from his *Commentaries* or *Treatises*—are simpler and more to the point in highlighting a moral or spiritual message for a general congregation. One of his important works from Caesarea shows the influence of his newly achieved presbyteral status: the *Treatise on Prayer*. It was a work asked for by his old patron Ambrose, who was now a deacon at Nicomedia. Origen begins the work with a systematic consideration of forms of prayer and petition as they are listed in the Bible, and he considers the question of whether or not prayer interrupts the plan of divine providence. So far it is classically Origenian in its systematic intent. But in the middle of the book there is a section devoted to the exegesis of the Lord's

---

[69]Socrates, *Ecclesiastical History* 5.22, says that Origen preached every Wednesday and Friday.
[70]1 Sam 28:3-25. It is one of the few *Homilies* to have survived in the original Greek. Select translations of the *Homilies* can be found in R. B. Tollinton, *Selections from the Commentaries and Homilies of Origen* (London: SPCK, 1929).
[71]Eusebius, *Ecclesiastical History* 6.36.1.
[72]Crouzel, *Origen*, 30.

Prayer.[73] This seems to have been part of the lecture series he offered to the baptismal candidates of his own church who were preparing for initiation at the end of great Lent, in the early thirties of the third century. As such it is an important and early example of liturgical preaching, with a direct and forceful pastoral style.

One of the pupils he attracted soon after his arrival in Caesarea was a wealthy young man who was en route with his brother to study law in Beirut. They were delivering their sister to the safekeeping of a family member who was in the imperial administration at Caesarea when they stopped to listen to Origen lecturing. They abandoned the idea of going to Beirut and became his dedicated pupils. The student, Theodore, vividly describes the impact Origen made:[74]

> It was like a spark falling in our deepest soul, setting it on fire, making it burst into flame within us. It was, at the same time, a love for the Holy Word, the most beautiful object of all that, by its ineffable beauty, attracts all things to itself with irresistible force, and it was also love for this man, the friend and advocate of the Holy Word. I was thus persuaded to give up all other goals. . . . I had only one remaining object that I valued and longed for—philosophy, and that divine man, who was my master of philosophy.[75]

Theodore published his graduating address, a panegyric in praise of Origen, and it is a revealing glimpse into the curriculum of Origen's school. Studies began with Socratic-style exercises in logic and dialectic.[76] Cosmology and natural history followed.[77] Theodore demonstrates how Origen made the study of the natural order a foundational exercise for the contemplation of God's design for and providence in the world.[78] After that came ethics, and finally theology proper, which Origen taught as the summit of philosophic wisdom, the fourth of his major divisions of Christian philosophy.[79] Theodore was much impressed by Origen's open and eclectic attitude to his teaching.

Unlike many other sophists of the age, Origen seems to have encouraged a wide curricular reading of different philosophic traditions.[80] Porphyry, the neo-Platonic

---

[73] *Treatise on Prayer*, cc. 18-30.
[74] Theodore probably assumed the name Gregory at his baptism—which, it can be presumed, Origen arranged at Caesarea. He became known to later Christian tradition as St. Gregory the wonderworker (Thaumaturgos), one of the most important theologian-hierarchs of Cappadocia. Cf. Eusebius, *Ecclesiastical History* 7.14. Theodore's brother Athenodorus also became a leader of the Christian communities of his region.
[75] Gregory Thaumaturgos, *Panegyric on Origen* 6.
[76] Ibid., 7.
[77] That is, physics, geometry, and astronomy. A good example of this style of cosmological-theological speculation has been provided by the recent study of A. Scott, *Origen and the Life of the Stars* (Oxford: Clarendon, 1991).
[78] Gregory, *Panegyric on Origen* 8.
[79] Ibid., 9-12, 13.
[80] Ibid., 14.

philosopher who had once gone to hear this most renowned teacher of the Christians, raises this against him when he accuses Origen of having betrayed the insights of philosophy by subjugating them to the exegesis of the tawdry Christian Scriptures.[81] But what for Porphyry stood as a fault was, for Origen, the glory of the Christian philosophy: that divine revelation as given in the sacred texts should be harmonized with philosophical searching, through the medium of spiritualizing exegesis.

Porphyry tells us some of the authors Origen studied, apart from his evident dependence on the writings of Plato, Aristotle, and Pythagoras. They include the main academic thinkers of his era: Numenius, Chronius, Apollophanes, Longinus, Moderatus, Nichomachus, Chaeremon, and Cornutus—a roll call of antiquity's major Platonist, Pythagorean, and Stoic intellectuals. What made Origen's eclecticism specifically focused, of course, was his strong advocacy of the Christian tradition as he had received it. The tradition of the faith was something Origen set himself to maintain and defend. For him that meant not only a complete christocentric, or soteriological, focus in all his thought, but more precisely that the plan of cosmic meaning was given to the inspired commentator primarily in the text and subtext of the sacred books.[82]

For Origen, as the Scriptures of the Old and New Testaments spoke at first level about patterns of historical salvation, so too at a deeper level they drew the pattern of a vast cosmic illumination to which souls were called and which enlightened souls could recognize as their call to divinization. The exegesis of the Scriptures was all important for him and made Origen's whole eclectic philosophical stand, however much it might be indebted to the Hellenists, entirely and unarguably a Christian, and a biblicist, enterprise, as we shall note below.

Soon after Origen settled in Palestine the emperor Alexander Severus, whose court had proved so hospitable to Christian and other religious philosophers, was assassinated, and his military commander Maximin the Thracian took the throne and instigated a widescale purge of the old party and their supporters. This revolt occurred in 235 and would last for three years. During this time the pogrom was extended to include well-known Christian leaders. In Rome Pope Pontianus and the theologian Hippolytus were sent into exile in 235, and Origen must have known he was in considerable danger. He seems to have gone into hiding while continuing to

---

[81]Eusebius, *Ecclesiastical History* 6.19.1-11.
[82]The concept that all the world's history, and all its meaning, longing, and sense of direction, was summated in the rescue from the collapse into ignorance and alienation that the Logos of God provided. Chief among the instances of the Logos's determination to recall the wandering souls back to himself was the incarnation of Jesus. This recalling, or cosmic vision of salvation (known as soteriology), is very typical of all Origen's thought and serves as an organizing principle for him.

write.[83] His patron, Ambrose, was arrested in Nicomedia, and Protoctetus, the archpriest of Caesarea, was also arrested. This was the time Origen composed for them an *Exhortation to Martyrdom*, which has ever after been received as one of the church's major pieces of resistance literature. It is also known that Origen traveled extensively through the Holy Land, specially seeking out the places associated with the ministry of Jesus.[84]

The historian Palladius, when passing through Caesarea in the late fourth century, found a book in the library there with a marginal note inside, written in Origen's own hand. It reads, "I found this volume at the house of the virgin Juliana, at Caesarea, when I was hiding there. She said she had got it from Symmachus himself, the Jewish commentator."[85] Theoctist, the bishop of Caesarea who was a devoted follower of Origen's teaching, also avoided imprisonment during the persecution of 235 and went on to rule over the church for another twenty-five years. Theoctist took Origen with him on numerous synodal occasions and so brought him to the attention of another leading theologian of that period, Firmilian, bishop of Caesarea in Cappadocia. Firmilian "urged Origen to come to his own country (Cappadocia) for the benefit of the churches there."[86] On the basis of this, many commentators have presumed a visit of Origen to Cappadocia, but we do not know this for certain.

Conciliar episcopal conferences had been established even by the second century as a preferred way of establishing an international standard of orthodoxy. When the news of the famous Bishop Beryllus of Arabian Bostra reached the ears of the Palestinian hierarchs, they knew that sensitive action was required.[87] Beryllus was one of the most energetic and outstanding bishops of Arabia, but his thinking on many aspects of biblical theology was out of harmony with the increasingly international standard of Logos theology. Origen was called in by his hierarchs to convince Beryllus of the error of his ways in a public disputation in Arabia. Beryllus seems to have denied the preexistence of the Lord (presumably indicating that he was not a

---

[83]Palladius thinks this was in Cappadocian Caesarea (he himself was from Cappadocia), but it is just as likely that Origen went into hiding in his own town of Palestinian Caesarea.

[84]Epiphanius tells us how he preached in Jerusalem on Ps 50:16 and had the congregation in tears. It is a text particularly apposite for a time of persecution (cf. Epiphanius, *Panarion* 64.2). He also went to Jericho (Origen, *Commentary on John* 6.24) and Sidon, where he stayed some time (Origen, *Homilies on Joshua* 16.2).

[85]Eusebius, *Ecclesiastical History* 6.17.1. Symmachus was one of the leading Jewish-Christian Ebionite theologians in Palestine. Origen knew him chiefly as one of the famous early translators of the Bible and one of the earliest Christian writers of exegetical commentary.

[86]Ibid., 6.27.1.

[87]Jerome, not easily impressed, described him as a bishop who "ruled his church most gloriously." *De Viris Illustribus* 60. Eusebius tells us that he left behind many elegant treatises (but does not detail them) in *Ecclesiastical History* 6.20.

Logos theologian) and went on to argue that the divinity attributed to Jesus was simply and solely an indwelling of the deity that properly belonged to the Father. In other words, he sounds like a typical old-fashioned Monarchian theologian.[88] After his ideas had gained notoriety among the local hierarchs, the metropolitan of Caesarea was summoned to adjudicate. He asked Origen to lead a public disputation. According to Eusebius, this was so successfully resolved that Beryllus agreed to abide by Origen's interpretations of Logos theology henceforth.[89]

Eusebius also tells of another synod in Arabia that concerned the refutation of local ideas concerning the death of the soul with the perishable body. Origen again was invited to the local church to lead the disputations in a local synod. His arguments on the immortality of the soul were so successful that Eusebius says, again, that "the opinions of those who had formerly fallen were once more changed."[90] The disputation was probably the same as the record of a synodical debate involving Origen that was discovered in the Toura papyri finds of 1941; synonymous, that is, with Origen's treatise *Dialogue with Heracleides*. The latter was an Arabian bishop who maintained an ancient Judeo-Christian attitude that the soul was synonymous with the blood of the living being. As such, again according to the rules of ancient debate summary, he could be designated "a denier of the immortality of the soul." On a wider canvas it may also be thought that this was an instance of a formal occasion when Monarchian attitudes were being set aside in church preaching in favor of the terms of Logos theology. Both synods mentioned above seem to have taken place during the reign of the Emperor Philip the Arab (244–249), who, if he was not Christian himself, was certainly a protector of the Christians of Palestine and a patron of Origen as a significant rhetorician.[91]

Sometime between 238 and 244 Origen journeyed once more to Athens, and his stay lasted some time, as Eusebius tells us he completed in that city the *Commentary on Ezekiel* he was working on and started his great *Commentary on the Song of Songs*.[92] Again, sometime before 244, according to Eusebius's chronology,[93] Origen received a letter from a Christian scholar Julius Africanus,[94] who had gone to study

---

[88] Eusebius, *Ecclesiastical History* 6.33.1.
[89] Ibid., 6.33.2-3. "Origen was invited to discuss and went there for a conference in order to discover his true opinions. When he had understood Beryllus's views and saw that they were erroneous, he persuaded him by arguments and convinced him by demonstrations, and so brought him back to the profession of true doctrine and restored him to his former soundness of mind."
[90] Ibid., 6.37.
[91] Eusebius thinks he was Christian. Cf. ibid., 6.34.
[92] Ibid., 6.32.2, sets the visit only within the reign of Emperor Gordian III.
[93] Ibid., 6.31.1-3, tells the story of the *Letter to Africanus* before announcing the end of Gordian's reign in 244.
[94] Julius was one of the most learned textual critics of his age, a Christian who occupied the imperially sponsored post of librarian archivist at the pantheon in Rome.

with Heraclas in Alexandria and sent on to Origen critical points of biblical exegesis.[95] Origen replied to this letter, noting that he was in Nicomedia with Ambrose. If (and I lean that way myself)[96] "Origen the philosopher" mentioned by Porphyry is one and the same as our Christian Origen, then he also made a visit (either to Antioch or to Rome) to see the only other philosopher of that age who could rival him in importance, another former student of Ammonius Saccas in Alexandria, the greatest of the neo-Platonists, namely Plotinus.[97]

After the assassination of the Emperor Philip, all those associated with him were in double danger, and the succeeding emperor, Decius, began another pogrom against Christians, during which the leading bishops and theologians of Palestine suffered considerably. Pope Fabian was martyred at Rome, and Origen's patron, Alexander of Jerusalem, was arrested and thrown into prison in Caesarea, where he died as a confessor. A similar fate befell Babylas, the great martyr-bishop of Antioch. Origen was a marked man. He had evaded previous persecutions by hiding in the villas of his friends and congregants. This time he was deliberately sought out as the leading Christian intellectual of the age, and his arrest was specially designed to bring him to a public recantation of the faith. He was tortured with special care, so that he would not die under the stress of his pain. He was chained, set in the infamous iron collar, and stretched on the rack—four spaces no less—as Eusebius tells his readers who knew exactly what degree of pain that involved and how many dislocations of bones and ripping of sinews it brought with it.[98] He who had encouraged others in his time now received a gracious encouragement himself in the form of an "exhortation to martyrdom" written by his admirer Dionysius, who had risen to episcopal office in Alexandria and had rehabilitated Origen's memory there.[99]

---

[95] Africanus argued that the Susanna story had clear syntactical evidence within it indicating it did not belong to the book of Daniel as a whole. Origen would not accept his opinion, one that is now universally accepted by modern text critics.

[96] Scholarly opinion is still divided. The earlier belief that the "Origens" were the same as the Christian teacher has of late been considerably qualified.

[97] Porphyry, *Vita Plotini* 14. The issue of identification is conflicted as Porphyry, in his own *Vita Plotini*, speaks of Origen as if he were entirely a Hellenist philosopher with a range of works apparently different from his familiar "Christian" corpus, whereas the Porphyry of Eusebius's text points unmistakably to the Christian writer, but in a passage in which the Christian historian confuses the identity of Ammonius Saccas. The existence of two famous Origens, both with similar interests to Plotinus and not distinguished by Porphyry, seems to contradict Occam's basic principle of the razor.

[98] Eusebius, *Ecclesiastical History* 6.39.6. Some translations misstate this as having his legs stretched "four paces," which is ridiculous. The four spaces refers to the ratchet divisions of the Roman torturer's racking machine and is a near-fatal amount that leaves the victim permanently crippled, if not paralyzed.

[99] Ibid., 6.46.2. Eusebius specifically claims Dionysius as Origen's pupil, though the association has been questioned in modern times. Dionysius is, however, the first clear "Origenian" Logos theologian of Alexandria.

Eusebius clearly recognizes the martyr's heroism in Origen's endurance. He was saved time after time, only because the governor of Caesarea had commanded he should not die under the torture before he had publicly denied the faith. This was why he suffered throughout all the two years of persecution and was liberated only by the death of the persecutor Decius, assassinated with his children in 252. Origen's health had been broken by his ordeals, however. He was, by the standards of his age, an extremely old man already at sixty-nine and died from the accumulated sufferings of his martyrdom shortly afterwards. That he died as a confessor, not as a martyr under the rack, was instrumental in the loss of so much of his work in later centuries, when he was censured for unorthodox opinions and a saintly martyr status could not serve to protect his reputation.

He died, probably, a year or so after Gallus, that is, early in the reign of Valerian (253–260), and most likely in the year 254. Jerome tells us that he was buried (and so presumably was also resident at the time of his death) in the Palestinian city of Tyre.[100]

So it was that the greatest Christian of the age passes out of our notice quietly and without fuss. Even from his deathbed he was concerned to console those who had been scarred, both psychologically and physically, by the latest time of torture. It is a sign of advanced spiritual greatness that his heart's desire, even in his own excruciating posttraumatic context, was to offer "sweet words of consolation" to the faithful who were grieving after surviving the cruel tyranny against them, as Eusebius describes the last work he composed, which was dedicated to consoling the confessors of his church. It is regrettable that this text has not survived.

*Origen's biblical theology of salvation.* Origen's thought, even at its broadest metaphysical and speculative levels, is dominated by his reading of the Bible. It was his fundamental belief that the gift of divine revelation and the innate human quest for enlightenment would meet together, harmonized in that moment (*kairos*) of the gift of salvation, which was the encounter of the soul with God in the divine Logos. This theoretical marriage of heaven and earth he saw as mystically, yet concretely, witnessed in the incarnation of the Christ-Logos within history. The eternal Word here assumed an incarnate manifestation precisely for the purpose of enlightening humanity, as its pedagogue, but the Word also left an enduring monument to the energy of this once-for-all revelation in the form of the Word's "extended body," which is the corpus of Scripture: the "word" of the Word, so to speak, or in other terms, Scripture as the sacrament of the Word's creative work as maker and redeemer of the world. So we see from the outset not only the vast scope of his horizon but also that all of Origen's biblicism is driven by his Christology, and all of the latter is elaborated with a soteriological intent:

---

[100]Jerome, *De Viris Illustribus* 54.

that is, the whole story (as he sees the Bible and the interpretative task of theology) is one of the Word's relentless seeking after the souls that were lost to him on earth.

Origen tells that story with a vast sweeping brush, in which he tries to reconcile Semitic eschatological thinking (dominant in the biblical records) with patterns of Greek metaphysical thought (determining his contemporary culture). For Origen, the story of salvation begins pretemporally, eternally, with God the Logos (*deuteros theos*) creating, on behalf of the supreme God the Father (*autotheos*), the array of spiritual beings (*noes*), which will be his chorus of praise. This is the spiritual creation (which long predates the material creation, as we shall see). All the beings within it are perfect, immortal, and pure spirit. Each one is *nous*, spiritual intellect, having nothing material in them. It would not be far off the mark to call them the archangelic beings. They are the primeval, intended creation of unalloyed beauty and harmony with the Creator-Logos. They each relate, preeternally, to God the Father through the medium of the radiance of the divine Logos. They form a circle around the Logos, together contemplating his beauty, and in so doing make up the heavenly church (*ekklesia*) in all its unity and holy perfection.

But something starts to disrupt that perfection over countless aeons. Origen calls it an unaccountable appearance of wilfulness and sin: a turning away from God's beauty as the source of life and happiness to the contemplation of the created self, which does not contain within it the source of being. In any case, some *noes* start to be distracted from the eternal contemplation of God in the Logos, and Origen calls this a process of ontological "cooling down." They find that they are immediately distanced from God because of this loss of contemplation. Their contemplation of God, he teaches, was what kept them in being. Origen thus roots Plato's epistemological metaphysics (consciousness is ontology) in a Christian framework. Losing the contemplation of the Logos, they progressively lose their stability of being and their beauty. Now, with varieties of closeness to the Logos inherent in it, the pure circle of the first creation's ontological union with God is broken. Some of the *noes* remain close to the Logos, as his great angels, but others have fallen away, in relative degrees. Some have even rebelled against him and been exiled from heaven as wicked spirits.

Those *noes* who have fallen, but not utterly, are unable in their now-damaged condition to receive with any clarity the spiritual *paideia* of the Logos, who still reaches out to them to bring them back into communion but who now finds their spiritual receptivity to his presence and message is drastically limited. This is a serious problem, since this *paideia* is, in itself, the revelation of God that gives life. Accordingly, as part of their rehabilitation (not their punishment), Origen teaches, the Logos changes the terms of their existence: he makes for these *noetic* creatures a material environment to serve as a new school of training, repentance, return, and ascent. This is the making of the material world we now call the creation. It is meant as an environment for noetic spirits who have declined from ontological purity to assume the status of souls (*psychai*) who can now best be helped to ascend to God once more through a partly material medium of salvific teaching. The history of humankind within this material environment is a story of the long struggle of our race to relearn purity of heart and spiritual acumen: the "ascent of man" to the original spiritual, angelic capacity of our souls' being.

For Origen it is this salvific motive on the part of the Logos that explains why it is we have the present salvation order, that peculiar condition of embodied souls. This intimate juxtaposition of soul (*psyche*) and body (*soma*) is not a natural condition, certainly not the condition God intended for us. Our place on earth is nothing other than a suffering environment, a testing ground. He wishes those *noes* or spirits who have been placed in this state to realize this and desire more earnestly to ascend out of it and back to spiritual communion with God (and with the other *noes* who wait for our return), a communion that will eventually mark a reversion to the primeval beauty of the intended creation of God, when all will be spiritually realized at the *eschaton*.

Knowing how much the souls (*psychai*) on earth are now deaf and blind to spiritual pedagogy, the divine Word relies on the fact that there remains a great deal of *logos* still prevalent in the consciousness of the human being, in their soul's instincts and their moral aspirations. So throughout long ages he sends holy prophets and angels to teach humankind. He elevates the Jewish people to be the leaders of the world's spiritual ascent. In the fullness of time the Logos prepares his own descent to earth as the supreme pedagogue and leaves behind himself a hidden—and an open—record of salvific teachings: clear doctrines of moral improvement for the less perceptive (those who had fallen further) and hidden mysteries of advanced spiritual wisdom for the more spiritually acute (those who had not fallen as far and can still remember their former spiritual greatness).

Origen's approach to this salvific *paideia* of the Logos, which he operated in countless myriads of fashions (*epinoiai*), was governed by the notion that the Scripture was a single reality, a coherent corpus emanating from one mind, that of the divine Logos himself.[101] Its apparent multiplicities were but the masking of the

---

[101] The *epinoiai* (aspects) of the Logos were manifold—the various ways he changed (metamorphosed) himself, like a good teacher coming down to the level of a recalcitrant pupil so as to get his message of reconciliation across to souls of all different conditions and capacities. He appeared to his creation, therefore, in terms of deep structures of existence (mathematics, world order), wisdom, beauty, morality, and other such elevating energies. His direct revelations are contained in the consciousness of the *ekklesia* and in the Scripture, and in human reason (*logos*), where the main image of the divine Logos still resides.

eternal revelation under the illusory appearances of history and relative conditions. A biblical text, therefore, had several layers of meaning. It had a historical import (such as Israel taking possession of the promised land), a moral meaning (the story of the fight for the promised land "more significantly" connoted the individual's constant battle for control of his or her own *psyche* in the face of passionate desires), and a mystical meaning (the "real meaning" or the highest significance of the entry to the promised land would be the soul's communion with God in the kingdom that is to come after this earthly cosmos passes away). For Origen, those who stayed only with the literal meaning of the biblical text were unenlightened souls who had not realized that Jesus gave some of his teaching in the valleys and some on mountaintops. Only to the latter disciples, those who could ascend the mountains, did Jesus reveal himself transfigured (cf. Mk 9:1-8).

For Origen, Scripture is a coherent whole. It has a single revelatory author, not the historical writers so much as the metahistorical Spirit of God teaching about the Logos, using the media of (historically located) saints who are illumined by the Word and who communicate truth according to their level and capacity to receive (and thus retransmit) the revelation through the vehicle of material symbols.[102] This implies from the outset that historical method cannot capture the full reality of the scriptural medium, since it is only partly rooted there in the first place, and its overwhelming "ethos" is rather the *afflatus* (breath) of the Spirit connecting the Logos to the inspired interpreter.[103] This revelatory capacity (how the Logos is mediated in different degrees to those who seek for him) is matched, then, by a corresponding need, at the other end of the hermeneutical line, to have an interpreter who is capable of receiving—that is, seeing—the illumination of the Logos. The Logos emits the Spirit, as it were, but the media at both ends also require correct tuning to transmit and receive; and, as Origen understands the matter, this is profoundly correlated to the degree of their soul's illumination, which in turn depends on the degree of the soul's prior purity and clarity.[104]

From this it follows (since all Scripture comes from the single divine author, who has a singular *skopos*, or overarching intentionality, which he wishes the sacred text to accomplish) that all parts of the Scripture have mutual self-reference. Whatever their time of composition or their apparent disparity as a large library of works, for Origen they all coinhere with a collective and connected message. In order to understand an

---

[102] *Peri Archon* 1, praef.4; 1.3.1; 4.1.6; 4.2.2; 4.2.7; 4.3.14; *Against Celsus* 3.3; 5.60; *Commentary on Matthew* 14.4; *Homilies on Genesis* 7.1; *Homilies on Exodus* 2.1; *Homilies on Numbers* 1.1; 2.1; *Homilies on Joshua* 8.6; *Homilies on 1 Kings* 5.4.

[103] *Ethos* means the larger purpose and intent of a text.

[104] Origen's closely attentive reader, St. Gregory the Theologian, expounds this clearly, for the benefit of later orthodoxy, in his *First Theological Oration* (27).

obscure part, therefore, one might legitimately turn to a clearer part elsewhere to elucidate, even a different book. This is where Origen actually underlines a fundamental and ancient Semitic principle of revelation theology: only Scripture interprets Scripture. This runs counter to most post-eighteenth-century biblical hermeneutics, but it is in full accord with many of the fundamental principles of ancient Greek and rabbinic text interpretation. For the first time, arguably, a Christian intellectual had given the church a macrotheory of christological biblical interpretation.

In Origen's hands, the single *skopos*, or divine authorial intent, which allows this internal cross-referencing and sense coherence over large distances of time and editions—between Chronicles and Revelation, or Malachi to Matthew—is quintessentially *soteria*, a salvation to be effected by divine illumination, which leads to our growing understanding (enlightenment) about the single fundamental fact of existence. Namely, this fact is that the soul has been alienated from God across time and space and must turn again (*metanoia*, repentance) in order to ascend back to union with God (the prelapsarian *status quo ante*). The Scripture contains a living soteriological force. In this regard Origen compares Scripture to the body of the Logos; it is sacramentally charged, similar to the Eucharist.[105] All the books are designed by God as acts of revelation to time-bound and fallen creatures, created specifically for their rescue by first impressing them with the fuller time scape of their plight as fallen souls, then uplifting them morally by examples and commands, and then giving them the dawning glimpses of a deeper initiation that the Logos wishes them to recall, a concept of possible communion with the Logos as source and meaning of their being. This is the ideological root of Origen's threefold sense of ascending exegesis: literal-historical meanings, moral meanings, and mystical senses.

Though all the biblical texts are sacred and illuminative, Origen thinks that they act soteriologically in differently nuanced manners. Most basically: the Old Testament adumbrates the New. The New Testament explains and interprets the Old. The meaning does not clarify or progress according to chronology, that is, historical sequencing or unfolding, but rather by radically discontinuous eschatological priorities. The scriptural texts are metaphysical maps for pedagogically turning the mind of the initiates around with fuller awareness, always a matter of repentance. These core notions of repentance (*metanoia*) and revelation (*apokalypsis*) are fundamental to all of Origen's thought, in every instance. His hermeneutic is thus fundamentally a metaphysical soteriology, and we might legitimately classify it as a deep form of eschatological metaphysic. Scripture therefore exists as one of the major ways or *epinoiai* the

---

[105]Indeed, he regarded the Scripture as being more soteriologically charged with grace than the Eucharist, a position that the later church reversed.

Logos uses to save his fallen world, as pedagogue and illuminator. The contextual location of a scriptural text "in its own day," which has become such an overriding demand within all modern "critical" approaches to the Bible in our time, would therefore strike Origen as a mismatched method: for if a text is fundamentally eschatological, it requires an eschatological method to address it, not a historical one. For him, history can only be a methodological footstool toward the eschatological analysis, where the Logos's fuller soteriological intent is lodged. This is not merely a matter of hermeneutical method, as if it were a sideshow to something else. It is the fundamental basis to all his philosophical system. To put it in another way: divine illumination, and the communion it confers, are not merely moral or mystical refinements of the created order, for Origen; they are rather its core ontology.

We might call this aspect of ascentive soteriological psychology the first plane of a double axis to Origen's fundamental hermeneutical theory. Ben Blosser's recent book on Origen's psychology sets this out elegantly and persuasively.[106] When Origen talks of a psychic or moral sense to a text, he does not mean simply finding a morally edifying message in the Scriptures; more than this, he intends his readers to seek for the navigational key back to God, from whom they have lapsed through time and space. The psychic or moral sense is mainly, in Origen's hands, what we should properly call a symbolic reading, that is, a higher-than-face-value literal exposition, and is explicitly related to the mysteries of the faith. Time and again he approaches the text in this "iconic" way: as if it were a sacramental, painted icon that does not give all its hidden mysteries away to the casual observer but rather prefers to keep its fuller symbolism reserved for those who already know the mystical language of the icon. Mysteries are, after all, he implies, meant for the initiated.

But there is there is another macrostructural axis at play in how Origen conceives of Scripture, overlying and fleshing out this primary axis of metaphysical ascent. For within his overview of the new revelation reversing time's flow eschatologically in order to interpret the old (the narrative is historically backward; the Christ key unlocks the ancient true sense of the old covenant), there cuts across all of this that important fact that not all the sacred books are equally weighted.[107] The uninitiated who think that they are will be radically confused by their mistake. A few of the Old Testament texts have greater revelatory power than some of the New.

---

[106]B. P. Blosser, *Become Like the Angels: Origen's Doctrine of the Soul* (Washington, DC: Catholic University of America Press, 2012).

[107]On that principle alone, Origen (who invents the terms Old and New Testaments) radically differentiates the Tanakh and Torah of the Jews from the Old Testament of the Christians. They are not the same thing by virtue of the "key to the significance" being withheld from those the Logos has not yet initiated.

Some parts of Old Testament texts that are generally not as significant as New Testament books have partial episodes that are more symbolically revelatory than several sections of the New. If we were to try and draw up a list of prioritized texts (those containing more of the revelatory power of the Logos, who leaves his symbolic revelations hidden in the scriptural symbols), then we would need to do it by reference to how Origen regularly makes up his own lists of "authorities" in various arguments deduced from the Scripture. We can definitely perceive a pattern of his relative weightings, as previously mentioned: first John, then Paul, then the Psalms, then the remaining Gospels, then the greater prophets, then the remaining apostolic writings, and then the historical and legal books of the Law—but all the while remembering that for him certain Logocentric episodes within different books contain "mountainous" symbols that can individually carry more weight than the remainder of those books. So, for example, the narrative of Sinai, or the account of the temple sanctuary, can carry greater weight in themselves than the rest of the books in which they first appear. Origen does not argue this as a specific theory. This is just how he sets about things in his own exegetical process: the theory emerging from the *praxis*. The Synoptic Gospels can fall below the level of Johannine and Pauline authority (the one who is initiated as he leans on the bosom of the Logos, and the other who is lifted up into the third heaven), as their apostolic authors, generally, appear rather lower down the scale of illumination, and often in the accounts they appear as being spiritually slow-witted.

If we try to envisage the model of this hermeneutical system that the great Alexandrian elaborates, we need to imagine this double axis operative in his thought. It is almost like a three-dimensional astrolabe. One plane of his axis of approach is atemporal, vertical, from the Logos to the illumined soul (in varying degrees of which historic interpreters can claim more brilliance of illumination from God). And the other plane is provided by the complexities of a historical axis where the past is opened only by the future, and history has to give way to eschaton in any attempt to understand what is at stake in the narrative relations.

It is not simple to keep this in mind, and most Origenian critics of earlier generations singularly failed to recognize its constant presence in Origen's theological imagination. But it does resolve to a relatively simple base theory: all is coherent and unified in pedagogical soteriological intent. All Scripture is a sacrament of the Logos's illuminations to recall fallen souls to their former state of (pre- and postcosmic) union with the Word. Union brings illumination. Illumination brings ascent. This double axis of his hermeneutic, the psycho-soteriological, and the metaphysical-eschatological, is most strongly welded together as two aspects of a single theology of divine *energeia*: the Logos seeks to reconstitute the wholeness of the creation by restoring the psychic integrity of his world of fallen souls.

Over the centuries Origen's exegesis has been subject to many criticisms of being overly symbolic, not tied in enough to the text, or being allegorically too fanciful. But a reading of the primary texts closely shows at each instance how Origen was a serious and exacting *grammatikos* and is always, without exception, deeply aware of the primary text: its grammar, syntax, and context.[108] He is, more than this, however, a symbolist poet: he simply believes the primary text rarely, if ever, exhausts itself with its immediate literal signification, and neither is he of the opinion that history is the highest level of meaning.

Criticisms that he is "fanciful" have also generally ignored the greater axes of his *theoria* as we outlined earlier. Why are there three levels in a text? Because there are three levels within the psychic ontology of the individual: whether we call that body, soul, and spirit, with Paul; or lower soul, upper soul, and *nous* along with the Origenists (developing the epistemology of late Platonism in a distinctly Christian direction). Or, to take a slightly different angle, because there are also a symbolic three levels of initiation within the church, which is given the text as a sacrament of salvation. As Paul said, milk is necessary for babies, solid food for those more grown up: and the Logos is ultimately sustenance enough for the perfected.

These, then, are the grander structures of his biblical theology. There are other rules and processes that he gives to his students in the course of his many writings. Some of them are images designed to help in the application of the theory, such as the notion that the Scripture is to be imagined as a series of locked doors in a tower, with keys lying outside each door, but that are not necessarily the keys to that particular door. The wise interpreter has to pick up the key and find the correct lock it matches. The only way to wise interpretation is a gift of light from the Logos. Meaning is not simply given; it has to be sought for ascetically and intellectually. Another rule is his famed axiom *opou logos agei*, namely, "We must go wheresoever the Logos leads us." It is, of course, a deliberate pun on the triadic level of semantic meanings contained in the Greek word *logos*, as divine Word, rationality, and systematic method. So his axiom means that exegesis is always an encounter with the Word, and therefore intellectual insight, acuity, and spiritual depth of hermeneutic

---

[108] We remember that this was his first professional trade, the *grammatikos* being a careful and systematically trained pedagogue in the meanings of a specific text (usually Homer). After his father's martyrdom in the Severan persecution, Origen sold his books of grammar and launched himself as a philosopher-rhetor: but his early training remains acutely present, as can be seen, for example, in his careful (and exhaustive) textual work on the *Hexapla*.

are an integral part of the very sacramentality of that standing on holy ground. What a forward-looking and courageous view of Christian civilization that amounted to.

Another axiom Origen brings forward is that of the *defectus litterae*, those places where the literal sense of a biblical passage leads to odd or scandalous things, or simply the impossible geographical details we can find there. These are "stumbling blocks," Origen says, left there for us by the Logos. They are not proofs that the text is unreliable or crude, but rather they are left like red flag markers in a Google map—signs for the acute, to realize that all this is symbol, too, and to test us to discover what is the "fitting" theology behind them.[109] The test is to ensure that we will never interpret the odd things as if they had literal authority. For example, the phrase "Happy is the man who shall take your infants and dash their brains against a rock" (Ps 137:9) is not be a jihadist's excuse. The psalm text advocating the murder of babies, he argues, is a symbolic reference to other things: in this case the children are what Scripture specifies elsewhere as the "children of Amalek," that is, the typological symbol of Satan and evil, and they (that is, the vices) are the things that need to be savagely dashed from the soul of each one who wishes to ascend the path of psychic purification.[110]

Too fanciful for us today? Well, in this stress on symbolic exegesis Origen did an inestimable service for the church. He cut clean through the hawser of holy war doctrine that would continue, arguably, to anchor deeply the canonical theology of Judaism and Islam. Later Christian biblical fundamentalism would swim down, unadvisedly, to retrieve its leaden weight once more, and even in our own time we still hear voices using the Bible to justify violence in the name of religion: a Bronze Age text here shoring up a Stone Age mentality. Origen's symbolic reading gave a system to set the ancient texts in a process of ascentive enlightenment that protected the church (inoculated it, in fact) against wooden fundamentalism.

His notion of "fittingness" in all exegesis (*theoprepes*) demands that the teaching text must never corrupt, and if it seems to inculcate a foolish (*alogon*) or impossible (*adynaton*) view of God, the true exegete must show how this cannot be so by reference to other, clearer passages. This view of navigating ancient texts was first set out in Hellenistic literature by Xenophanes and was heavily used in the philosophical rereading of Homer before it was picked up by Philo to rework the consistency of the Old Testament narratives, using a macrotheory of Logos theology. This principle, that each and every scriptural exegesis must reflect the merciful goodness and honor of God, allied with Origen's reminder to us that we must read the Old Testament through the resolving lens of the New, is one of the most characteristic aspects of

---

[109]*Peri Archon* 4.2.9.
[110]An instance of how Scripture itself must be used to unveil Scripture (by word association and assonance in this case of the commonality of the term *children*).

what was widely accepted after his lifetime as the church's overall approach to biblical process, and it has endured even to this day.

Another of his minor principles was that Origen expected his students to "complete the action" when reading a text. This was another common technique in the Hellenistic *scholae*. The *magistros* set out the broad premises and principles in an exposition, and then the students (to prove they had grasped the point) were expected to be able to add the conclusion themselves. This explains why so many of Origen's exegeses are left incomplete or seem tentative in nature, and often why he leaves books incomplete, such as the magisterial *Commentary on John*, which ends at the Last Supper. Many of these Origenian rules of exegesis would have been widely recognized in the schoolrooms of antiquity.[111] But he was the first to systematically lay them at the disposal of the Christians, and his architecture thus became constitutive for the church for centuries to come, even if (after the fourth century) many adaptations to its particular architecture were forced on it.

Origen left behind him a tidal wave force of ongoing theological energy that ran on in the Alexandrian school and through it to the wider Christian world, a school that was, more accurately, Origen's intellectual legacy, for more or less every significant doctrinal argument that arose for the next three hundred years in the Greek- and Latin-speaking Christian world was a working out, often a heavily conflicted one, of principles that Origen had established when he set up his great systematic architecture of Christian soteriology.

*Origen's heritage: Dionysius of Alexandria.* One of Origen's notable successors at Alexandria was Dionysius, who became the bishop there in 248, dying around 265. Dionysius was a highly intellectual and well-placed civil servant in Alexandria before entering on his ecclesiastical career.[112] Eusebius gives us the information that he was a disciple of Origen (I think this means he was probably one who had actually studied with him) and worked with Heraclas (Origen's colleague in the catechetical school of Alexandria, before the former became bishop of the city after Demetrios's death). Dionysius succeeded Heraclas. Almost as soon as he became the bishop, a persecution broke out against the Christians of Alexandria. Dionysius remained in the city, hiding from the authorities, who issued a warrant for his arrest. In the following year a civil war broke out in which eventually Decius, an emperor who hated

---

[111]Cf. K. J. Torjesen, *Hermeneutical Procedure and Theological Method in Origen's Exegesis* (Berlin: De Gruyter, 1986), 23-26, 124-29; K. J. Torjesen, "Influence of Rhetoric on Origen's OT Homilies," in *Origeniana Sexta*, ed. G. Dorival and A. Le Boulluec, Bibliotheca Ephemeridum Theologicarum Lovaniensium CXVIII (Leuven: Peeters, 1995), 13-25; J. A. McGuckin, "Origen as Literary Critic in the Alexandrian Tradition," in *Origeniana Octava*, ed. L. Perrone (Leuven: Peeters, 2003), 121-35.

[112]See Eusebius, *Ecclesiastical History* 7.11.18.

the Christians, assumed power, in autumn 249. In Alexandria the war was exacerbated by a plague that struck the city in the early part of that year. These troubles are reflected in Dionysius's letters.

As was the case with Cyprian, his governance of a church under such crisis was made difficult not only by pressures from hostile outsiders but even more so from within. When Decius issued his imperial decree that Christian leaders must be forced to sacrificed to the gods of Rome, Dionysius left Alexandria and took to hiding in the marshes around lake Mareotis, in the wilderness regions outside the city. This triggered a section of the Christians of his congregation to accuse him of cowardice and a refusal to accept the call to martyrdom. Like Cyprian, he took the stance that flight in time of persecution was advocated by Jesus himself (Mt 10:23), and he refused the argument of the more zealous that devoted Christians should be willing to hand themselves over.

He was active in hiding, with letters and regular instructions to the church, and the persecutions at Rome came to his attention, and thus he was drawn into the conflict there between Novatian and Cornelius. The latter's election to the episcopate was attacked at Rome on the grounds that he had bought a certificate that attested to his having conformed to Decius's decree (a way around the Decian edict that several wealthy Christians had used). Novatian was preaching a strict attitude to all who had "lapsed" in the persecution, whether by actual apostasy or by this subterfuge of bribing one's way to safety. Dionysius immediately put his support behind Cornelius and argued that Novatian's severity was dangerous and excessive. Cornelius's successor, Pope Stephen, was later drawn into a controversy with the African church under Cyprian, concerning the issue of how to admit "Novatianists" back into the communion of the great church. As we have seen earlier, Cyprian took the hardline position that as schismatics, the baptism that these Novatianists had received was one that was devoid of grace, invalid in all respects. They needed, thus, to be baptized (not rebaptized) to be joined to church communion. Pope Stephen (254–257) was disturbed by this rigorous view and argued (successfully, because it later became the church's wider position) that schismatics could be reconciled instead by a simple presbyteral "laying on of hands." It was, in effect, a recognition by the Roman church that the Spirit's grace still operated in the sacraments of a schismatic movement. Cyprian appealed personally to Dionysius and gained his support: a position he took in his several surviving letters to Pope Stephen and his successor Sixtus II (257–258).

Dionysius did not succeed in budging the Roman position, though it would not be a commonly held one in the Western church until Augustine definitively moved African theology away from Cyprian's theology of grace in the sacraments, in the fifth century, and adopted the Roman position, which thereafter became the standard view for admitting schismatic movements to communion (qualified by the position that "other" significant sacraments of schismatics were usually held to be of questionable validity, namely, Eucharist and ordination). The Eastern churches remained conflicted much longer about the question of whether a schismatic break from the church's communion necessitated an immediate loss of validity of all its sacraments, including baptism (the root that, if defective, would certainly invalidate all the others). Significant heretical movements, involving conflicts of doctrine and morals, were widely held, in both East and West, to involve such a catastrophic loss of grace and sacramental potency, and to require baptism to admit former secessionists into larger communion. Dionysius and Cyprian's disciplinary letters (canons) remained authoritative and influential for a very long time. They are still cited as authorities in matters of church theology and practice in Eastern Christian circles to this day.

Toward the end of his life Dionysius was drawn into another theological controversy, one that prepared the way (a generation later) for the clarification of the Christian theology of the Trinity. Dionysius had closely read Origen's concept of trinitarian relations, as evidenced in the *De Principiis* and other writings of his teacher. Origen's concept of the relation of the three persons (hypostases), Father, Son, and Holy Spirit, was one that privileged Logos theology in the sense that the Father was conceived as having "issued" (generated, birthed, sent, or several other related ideas) the Son-Logos into the world for the cause of salvation. In the trinitarian relations Origen had stressed the descending hierarchical nature of this economy of salvation (*oikonomia*). He called the Father "God himself" (*autotheos*) and called the Logos "subsidiary deity" (*deuteros theos*). These were technical terms used by some of the neo-Platonists of the time to designate God's outreach to the world as a process that did not involve his essential inner transcendence (thus salvation outreach to material creation was an act of God's energy, not an alteration of his being), but they did not have any foundation in the New Testament texts and were regarded by many nonphilosophical Christians of Origen's age as highly speculative and disturbing. As we saw earlier in our discussion of the Logos school and the Monarchians in chapter one, each side used such different terminology to connote the mystery of God's being that they tended to hear one another with deep alarm, as teaching out and out nonsense or, worse, blasphemy.

Logos theologians stressed the personal distinctness of the three persons in the Divine Triad. They used the concept of hypostasis to insist on real distinctness of personhood. To Monarchians, this sounded like a confession of three gods and a betrayal of monotheism. The latter could not quite grasp the Logos theologians' relation of threeness of hypostatic entity (Father, Son, and Spirit) with the idea of specific representations of the selfsame substance. Thus the Godhead was not three, and not one, but rather tri-unity, or Trinity. The Monarchians, on the other hand, insisted so strongly on the unicity of God (the Father) that all differentiation of persons was reduced to phenomenal or temporary significance. They tended to be monist in their approach to the divine being and could not take on board the "problem" of ascribing divine stature to the Son of God (or the Spirit, whom they tended to ignore) except by regarding terms such as *Son*, *Logos*, *Spirit* as synonyms for God the Father, different "modes" of his revelation of himself in history. For this reason they are often called modalists.

Dionysius of Alexandria was mired in the middle of this semantic trouble. Tertullian, as we have seen, was a robust defender of Logos theology and capable of sarcastic but memorable denunciations of Monarchian modalism as untenable and unfaithful to the New Testament christological evidence. But it was Dionysius's involvement in the trinitarian controversy that served as the benchmark for the later Greek East, and which established a common technical trinitarian language there of three subsistences (*hypostases*) and one being (*ousia*) in the divine triad. After the controversy with Dionysius, which was more or less all about misunderstood semantics across the Greek and Latin churches, the Western church agreed to accept the East's terminology as equivalent to its own trinitarian schema of one nature (*natura*) and three persons (*personae*).[113]

The conflict had been occasioned because in Dionysius's own ecclesial territory, as supervisory archbishop, the bishop of the small Libyan town of Ptolemais had caused a large scandal by his theological preaching. His local episcopal colleagues on the southern Mediterranean littoral accused him of Monarchianism, reviving the heresy of Sabellius, which had already been discredited. Their local synod appealed to Dionysius, who supported their analysis and censured the Sabellian teaching so severely that his enemies at home in Alexandria took the occasion to accuse him to Pope Dionysius of Rome (259–268) of upholding the opposite fault of tritheism. The literal Latin translation of Dionysius's key Greek term *hypostasis* was *substantia*. Obviously, with the hindsight of the twenty-twenty vision that time and space afford us, it is perfectly clear that Dionysius of Alexandria used the term *hypostasis* in reference to

---

[113] It was not the same, philosophically speaking, of course; for the Greeks meant the being of God was one and the same in that it was the Father's own being gifted by him eternally to the Son and Spirit, whereas the Latins meant the divine nature was a common substrate shared by three persons all inhabiting it. But this is not the time to unearth that complexity here. It can wait until the great trinitarian theologian of the fourth century, St. Gregory the Theologian (Nazianzen), realizes he has to clarify the matter more fully in the fourth-century Arian crisis, which we deal with in the following chapter.

the persons of the Trinity, to mean "something that subsists in" another. But his enemies had slanted the reading of his letters to give it a wooden rendition in Latin as the hyperliteral "sub-stantive" (*sub-stantia* being a semantic cipher for *hypo-stasis*). And so Dionysius of Rome, having a Latin digest of his colleagues' work before him, heard him as teaching three divine substances and one divine nature. This is not only self-contradictory (since trinitarian theology used *nature* as an equivalence of *substance*) but fundamentally heretical in that it gives more than lip service to three discrete divine principles, and so monotheism falls. Dionysius of Rome accordingly wrote a censorious letter to his namesake in Alexandria, and the latter replied with a serious and seminal study of Christian trinitarianism in four very forceful books.[114]

When the two senior bishops had stopped berating each other, and it was clear as day that Dionysius of Alexandria was someone who knew his theology very well indeed, it became commonly agreed that the Latin and Greek formularies of the Trinity were "substantially" the same, and each side could acknowledge the other's good faith. From that time onward, although there remained subtle differences in the trinitarianism of each set of churches (which remain significant to this day), a widespread agreement was reached that churches could express the same faith in slightly different language.[115] This would be an important principle established, as it was increasingly realized in the fourth and fifth centuries, as churches far and wide became more literarily connected, that different local traditions (Syrian, Coptic, Armenian, Ethiopian, Latin, Irish, and so on) all had quite distinct emphases and different favorite analogies in the way they chose to articulate the gospel and its philosophical implications. In the Dionysius affair (very public in that involved one of the first large clashes between two leading theological schools, which were also leading churches of the international Christian communion) the church as a global factor had taken a large public step in moving toward an internationally agreed set of language rules about its core doctrine of God's Fatherhood, Christ's divine status, and the nature of the Trinity as God's salvific outreach to the world—and that movement as from out of his own hypostatized being (as Logos inhominated), not simply as an "external" act of condescension through grace.

In his old age Dionysius was regarded as one of the most learned theologian bishops alive in the Christian world. This also indicated that the following century would expect more of its bishops to be learned men, at least if they governed the

---

[114]Dionysius of Alexandria, *Refutation and Apologia*. Fragments of the work are cited, as important authorities, by fourth-century archbishop Athanasius of Alexandria in his work *De sentential Dionysii* and so entered into classical trinitarian debate in the Arian crisis.
[115]Early Latin thought generally tending to stress the unicity of Godhead; Greek thought trending to stress the differentiation of the one.

churches of important imperial cities. At the beginning of the third century most bishops had probably been simple, relatively unlearned men, common folk leading in piety and ritual a common congregation. By the end of the third century the expectation had certainly arisen that the bishop should be socially important, highly educated, and an articulate apologist for the traditions of Christianity as exemplified by the local church he represented. At this period this meant above all the super-churches of Rome, Antioch, and Alexandria, whose episcopal theologians come to dominate the landscape of fourth-century Christian thought. At this time, somewhere around 264 or 265, Dionysius received an invitation to come to Antioch to be the chief judge of the ecclesiastical trial of Paul of Samosata, one of the last significant modalist philosopher-bishops. He declined the invitation on account of failing health. Among his other works, now mainly lost, are a Paschal canon that he composed and some biblical commentary.[116] His insightful and analytical judgment is apparent, even though the work is no longer extant, in the opinion (Eusebius records) that in his treatise *On the Promises* Dionysius argued that the book of the Apocalypse was clearly not from the same hand as the apostle and Evangelist John.

**The school of Caesarea.** Although Origen had removed himself from Alexandria to seek a more peaceful base of actions in Palestinian Caesarea, his reputation was soon restored in his native city after the death of the hostile bishop Demetrios, and his disciples often formed the elite group of clergy from which future bishops of the city were chosen. Dionysius is a prime example, but so too were learned Alexandrian bishops throughout the third, fourth, and fifth centuries: Theognostos, Alexander, Athanasius, Peter, Theophilus, and Cyril. Even when these bishops sometimes protested they had distanced themselves from the "errors of Origen," their theological writings and their exegeses clearly show that their continued dependence rises out of a close working knowledge of the antique master, so powerfully did his legacy endure there.

But after Origen's actual move to Caesarea Maritima, he set up a new school and built a considerable library in that ecclesiastical capital of Roman Palestine. In his own time it has claim to being the very first Christian university (or institute of higher learning). In the following centuries this school was headed by a series of very learned bishops. Its prestige as a center for Christian learning attracted many Christian intellectuals to study there and confirmed the bishops in a policy of presenting their city as a kind of intellectual lighthouse for the development of Christian tradition. Some tension grew up, especially in the fourth century, over the various interpretations of Origen's intellectual agenda, especially in relation to Christology and the Trinity, and to what extent his original teachings should be moderated. This

---

[116]Eusebius, *Ecclesiastical History* 7.20.

friction would be at the heart of what emerged as the great Arian crisis in the fourth century, as we shall see.

Caesarea in the lifetime and immediate aftermath of Origen nevertheless became a great intellectual center: a considerable library collected together that became one of the first Christian archives (along with the churches of Alexandria and Rome) that were used to document the past and use precedents and agreements as basic building blocks toward agreed international ecclesiastical polity. Origen's two theological disciples had first invited him to work alongside them in Palestine, namely bishop Alexander of Jerusalem and Theoctist of Caesarea (216–258). They not only encouraged his missionary work (for the enterprise of building a Christian school there to rival the pagan Alexandrian academy and the rabbinic Tannaitic school based in Caesarea was certainly envisaged by them as a missionary strategy aimed at converting pagans and Jews to the church) but also involved him closely in their episcopal work at local synods.[117] He appears at several of these in Arabia and Palestine in the guise of a priestly theological expert.

After them several other Caesarean bishops kept the library and archive up to standard, making it a renowned place of Christian learning until the middle of the fourth century. Some of those Origenian leading lights in the school of Caesarea were Acacius the One-Eyed (340–366) and Gelasius (367–372, and again 380–395). The presbyter and martyr Pamphilus was a famous and most dedicated follower of Origen there. He was the mentor of Bishop Eusebius of Caesarea (260–340), the great church historian who used the archives of the church to produce one of the first (certainly most prestigious) accounts of Christian history written since the days of the Acts of the Apostles.

The school Origen founded was located next to the Augustus temple in the center of the Caesarean docks. It had a prestigious reputation until the fourth-century Arian crisis. At that point many of its bishops fought so strenuously against the Alexandrian tradition of Alexander and Athanasius, and that of the Roman and Spanish churches[118]—that is, against the Nicene tradition of the *homoousion*—that they became widely suspect as Arian sympathizers.[119] After the ascent of Nicaea as the

---

[117]The rabbinic Tannaitic school based in Caesarea was working on the text that finally emerged as the Mishnah.
[118]Bishop Hosius of Cordoba (c. 256–237), the imperial agent at Nicaea, and Pope Sylvester (314–345).
[119]*Homoousion* here is shorthand for the doctrine in the creed of Nicaea (325) that the divine logos was *homoousion* or consubstantial (same in being) with the Father. Eusebius of Caesarea did not deny the concept's essential force (namely that the Logos was divine, and God form God) but rather resisted the importation of the word *homoousion* into centrally agreed dogmatic language (that is, as an international standard) because (1) it was not scripturally warranted and (2) Origen had criticized the term as being a materialist conception (stuff and compositions), which was unfitting in its application to God as immaterial being. His philosophical niceties were overran

standard of catholic faith, by the end of the fourth century, the reputation of Caesarea as a leading school of Christian science was fatally damaged. It was more or less ruined as a center of influence, therefore, long before the seventh-century Persian invasion of Palestine physically destroyed it.

## CHRISTIANITY AND THE PHILOSOPHERS

The bishops of the second-century church do not seem to be great intelligences by and large. One supposes their churches were filled with people much like them: of the poorer classes in the main, expecting piety and scriptural teaching when they came to church, not learned discourses about metaphysics. The bishops of the third century, however, are clearly beginning to be a different order of creature. The Gnostic schools had challenged the churches' complacency. A great deal of ridicule had come from these Gnostic schools concerning the fideist character of many Christian communities: their reluctance to engage in speculation and the way they wanted a simple faith narrative tied to the scriptural literal meanings. The first wave of anti-Gnostic church responses, excepting Irenaeus, tended to come from learned presbyters. But by the third century this had established a pattern. In significant churches it was felt necessary to have an episcopal leader who was a well-educated person, very able in apologetics, to stand up for the Christian faith in a world full of critics—pagan, Jewish, and philosophical—and above all someone who had a strong sense of politics and could advocate for the church rhetorically in times of trouble. These factors conspired across the third century to the phenomenon of the birth of the highly learned rhetorician-bishop, a phenomenon that would only be accelerated in the fourth century under the Constantinian peace.

But now that learned presbyters and bishops were becoming much more common in the churches, and ordinary Christians were more regularly seen from the middle classes, eager for rhetorical education that would make them fitted for social ascendance in Greco-Roman society, it followed that both church leaders and church faithful came face-to-face much more frequently than before with philosophical issues. It began what would run on for two millennia as the story of the church's long and deep engagement with (and at times ineffectual "turning its back on") philosophy. In this era of antiquity, rhetoric was the staple of the educational curriculum and was seen as an extension of politics, law, and philosophy, all run through the resolving lens of poetry and literary appreciation. What this meant for Christian leaders, all educated as they were under the terms of ancient rhetorical forms, was

---

at Nicaea, and Eusebius himself was forced to recant his opposition to the word being inserted at a critical juncture in the creed.

that they began to see things in stereoscope: both as Christians looking at the world through a lens of scriptural promise and typological fulfillment, and through the lens of the dominant classical philosophies of the day—Aristotelianism, Platonism, and Stoicism. There were many other schools extant, of course, but it was these three that dominated the Christian imagination in ancient times and were all formative influences on the shape of doctrinal thinking in the postapostolic period.[120]

From Platonism the church gained a large vocabulary about metaphysics. The Christian intellectual tended to regard Plato as the most religiously inclined of the ancient thinkers. In some Greek churches to this day one sometimes finds the iconographic representation of Plato in the church entrance porch, as a kind of prophetic forebear of the gospel (similar to the way the sibyl is sometimes regarded in the Christian West).

Plato (428–346 BC) was a Greek aristocrat and student of Socrates. The state-mandated suicide of his teacher and mentor stimulated him to abandon a career in politics and dedicate himself to the life of philosophy, especially as that was concerned with the creation of an ideal society, a new order of state. Between 389 and 367 BC he organized his own school in the grove of Academus near Athens, which gave Platonism its alternative name of "the Academy." "Academic" enterprises still take their name from this. His treatises are often set in the form of *Dialogues*, where Socrates appears as a major character, setting questions to the reader, who looks in over the shoulders of the discussants. These questions raised about the basic meaning of such concepts as piety, friendship, or love are meant to probe the individual's understanding of core values and to shed the large amount of unthought-out cliché that attends much of our intellectual attitudes. Socrates in these dialogues successfully refutes most of the definitions offered by the various characters until bafflement (*aporia*) sets in among them (and the reader). This is a deliberate pedagogical method, meant to bring the reader to a state of clarified unknowing, the point of this being that truth can only start to be approached once falsehoods have been eliminated from one's thinking.

A common conclusion of these often "inconclusive" dialogues is that the individual needs to embark on a life of more serious study and thoughtfulness, given that so much of our common attitudes are built on flimsy and insupportable opinions. This educational method Plato called the *maieutic* (midwifery), since it was fundamental to the philosophic task to allow the individual agent "to emerge," not to be dominated by imposed opinions. His early dialogues (such as *Euthyphro* or *Lysis*) are particularly

---

[120]The topic is a vast one. Recommended further reading is H. A. Wolfson, *The Philosophy of the Church Fathers* (New Haven, CT: Yale University Press, 1956); J. Pelikan, *Christianity and Classical Culture* (New Haven, CT: Yale University Press, 1993); F. C. Copleston, *A History of Philosophy*, vol. 1, *Greece and Rome: From the Pre-Socratics to Plotinus* (London: Search Press, 1946).

concerned with establishing a moral basis for human reflection. The good is seen to be that which is truly beneficial; evil is defined as ignorance; virtue is knowledge. The Gnostic movement was much influenced by this basic metaphysics of epistemology and the equation of virtue with knowing awareness (*gnosis*), which is seen to be liberative. For Plato, the quest for the ideal is that which will direct an ethical life.

In his middle-period dialogues (*Phaedo*, *Symposium*, *Republic*) Plato sets out the character of the ideal society in greater detail and speculates on the nature of true reality as such. His thinking turned to more metaphysical and grandiose vistas. These metaphysical canvases were highly attractive to Christian intellectuals in the third and fourth centuries, who tried in various ways to reconcile their great scope with the more "folksy" schemes of the Hebrew Bible. In these middle works Plato posited that ideals such as Beauty, Truth, or Justice exist as real entities, in and of themselves, subsisting outside all material or relative conditions, and are not themselves susceptible to variations imposed by time, context, or culture. They are absolute standards, always the same. These ideals he called the Ideas, or Ideal Forms, and he saw them as the prototypes that cause their individual manifestations in the world of materiality. Absolute Beauty (Ideal Beauty) is thus the exemplar and root, or common factor, of whatever is beautiful here in our human, earthly, and multivaried experience of "beautiful things."

Plato taught that human beings apprehend the Ideals through intellectual perception (the *nous* as the organ of spiritual perception). This latter idea was very much taken to heart in the Christian ascetical movement. It underlies much of the Christian sense of prayer as the ascent of the spiritual intellect to God, human *nous* rising to communion with Divine Logos, who emanates it in the material world to begin with. The greatest of the early spiritual writers, such as Origen, Evagrius, Macarius, Gregory of Nazianzus, Gregory of Nyssa, Dorotheus of Gaza, and Dionysius the Areopagite, all form a long-lasting school of mysticism that took that insight from Plato and moved on ahead of him, adding in to his generic schemes the biblical sense of personal communion with the divine principle.

For Plato, understanding comes from the fact that in a prematerial existence (before the soul was imprisoned in a bodily form) the intellect recognized the Ideal Forms directly, and even now the human mind has some "recollection" of them through reminiscences and evocations (*anamnesis*) provided by material copies (*mimesis*) of the various absolutes. The theory of the Ideas was not so much emphasized in the later writings of Plato, leading some historians to speculate that he moved away from the notion as it attracted more and more criticism from his disciple Aristotle and his school. The concept of Ideal Forms was taken by many Christian writers and bent to a more biblical conception of metaphysics by personalizing it in the theory of the divine Logos, who created the world of material forms by placing within them evocations of his own likeness. Christian thinkers fastened together the biblical doctrine of humanity as the image of God (from Genesis) with this loosely adapted idea of Ideal Forms embedded in the world like signposts to the hand of the Maker.

Some significant Christian theologians, such as Origen and Evagrius, also were impressed by the theory of a knowledge of truth running on in humans from a previous disincarnate life (Wordsworth returned to this idea in his own mystical poetry). But the condemnation of Origen and Evagrius posthumously for holding such biblically unsanctioned ideas more or less steered the church away from preexistence speculation. Plato's later successors as heads of the Academy, especially Albinus in the mid-second century AD, also developed the old notion in new ways and partly synthesized it with aspects of later Aristotelian thought. Albinus, for example, giving rise to the movement of Middle Platonism, argued that the Ideas were thoughts in the mind of a supreme good, or God. It was particularly this form of late Platonic theory that affected and influenced the Christians after the time of Origen.

Plato himself developed his theory of Ideas with an increasing emphasis on the manner in which material reality misled the mind from true perception, offering only a (frequently illusory) reflection of reality. In the *Republic*, he used what became a famous image of a fire that prisoners in a cave could see, insofar as it cast shadows of their forms on the wall before them as they sat facing the back of the cave. They were so distanced from the "true world," the world of reality outside the cave, that they finally came to think that the shadows were real things and made their deductions about reality from these insubstantial illusions. Plato thus made a strong contrast between material instability and the permanence of the "true and ideal world." Christian thinkers were much attracted by this idea, especially the ascetical philosophers of the early monastic movement. They substituted *spiritual* for *ideal* and made a sharp distinction between the spiritual realities one could not see and the material realities that all too frequently led believers astray into physical sensuality. This was to cause a marked change in tenor of Christian spiritual thought from ancient Jewish and pagan spiritual attitudes, which celebrated the body more openly. It was, however, not simply a Greek philosophical influence but also something that had come to Christianity through its reliance on aspects of Jewish apocalyptic thought, which stressed the impermanence and suffering aspect of the material dimension.

Several of Plato's important dialogues (*Phaedo, Phaedrus, Republic, Timaeus*) speak about the soul in its relation to the body. The soul was envisaged as partly separable from the body in its rational dimension (*To Logistikon, Nous*) and intrinsically immortal, whereas the body was rooted in the material cosmos and subjected to flux and illusion. In the *Republic* Plato describes a tripartite soul consisting of a higher part of reason, a "spirited" aspect, which is motivated to the good and creative, and then the "desirous" part, which is motivated by acquisition. The last requires the guidance of reason and the discipline of the "spirited" soul, otherwise it falls into dissipation. Philosophy, according to Plato, can give right order to the soul, orienting it away from earthly illusions and toward intellectual (noetic) truth. Such an orientation is no less than an ascent to the good (*To Kalon*), or the spiritual world of the Ideas. In the treatise *Gorgias* Plato spoke of a salvific (soteriological) and quasi-religious (or certainly metaphysical) scheme wherein the righteous soul ascends through a cycle of reincarnations by virtuous living to an eventual escape from material subjugation in a blessed existence.

Not all of this amounted to a system, properly so called, but it certainly made for a coherent view of reality that later generations of Platonists developed extensively. Christian theologians too were highly influenced by Platonic soul theory. They adapted it to the Pauline concepts of soul and psyche, which Paul speaks about only occasionally in his letters, and in their adaptation made for the birth of a genuine Christian psychology (soul-theory) that taught a threefold ascentive consciousness of the human being as creature of a transcendent God. The lowest level was physical consciousness (*sarx, soma*); the next level (related to it and rising out of it) was psychic or soul awareness (*psyche*); and the highest level was noetic awareness (*nous*), which was the spiritual intelligence of a human being who was able to sense communion with the divine Logos who had placed his own divine image into the heart of the mortal being—giving it the gift of immortal transcendence. The theory of soul, the concept of divine creator using the Demiourgos (second god, *deuteros theos*) to make material reality, and the concept of an epistemological ascent to God driven by a life of virtue were formative influences Platonism gave to the church, helping it to take its biblical worldview out into the wider marketplace of ancient world culture.

Aristotle, who had been one of Plato's own brightest pupils for a time, made extensive revisions to the Platonic schema, but he did not ultimately divert the Academy from its goals. Platonism was perhaps the most dominant form of ancient philosophy, while Aristotelianism was the most extensively "absorbed" into many other schools, chiefly because its methods were so well thought out. Both forms would make a major impact on Christianity in the patristic era. Aristotelian methodology would be of great importance in Christian logic and anthropology, but

Plato's ideas on the moral ascent to the good had dramatically captured the imagination of some of the earliest and most important Christian intellectuals, who thought they could find here a "friend" of their religion.

Throughout all the periods when Christianity was actively in dialogue with Platonism, notably the second century through the sixth (after that point Platonism became merely a textual reality), none of the Platonists themselves were happy about the manner in which their school had been absorbed and re-presented by Christians. They felt their core ideas had been hijacked and mixed with unproven assumptions and despicable tales (what the Christians would call divine revelation, the incarnation of Christ, and the stories of the Scriptures). Great third-century neo-Platonist teacher Plotinus fought bitterly with Gnostics, castigating them in his *Enneads*. Porphyry, his disciple, attacked Origen and wrote a bitter denunciation of the Christian religion. Proclus (the last leader of the Academy in the fifth century) lamented the manner in which Christianity had so overshadowed the school that Greek culture had been overthrown (he had witnessed the final closing of the Academy by order of a Christian emperor).

Christian intellectuals, however, proved more than ready to take building materials from anywhere they thought would be useful, and much of the Platonic thought world was adapted for use in theology. Hardly anything of Plato's original architecture was left untouched, so thoroughly did Christian thinkers subordinate it to the overall prescripts of their biblically inspired religion and their sense of the personal presence of the Savior as enduring Lord of the church, but it is certainly possible to see the major impact "Christian Platonism" made on the history of theology in the antique period. Some apologists claimed Plato as a Christian before his time. That approach was brought to a climactic head in Eusebius's *Preparation for the Gospel*, in which he argues that ancient philosophy (especially Platonism) had served as an evangelical catechesis for the world of the pagans (in a manner comparable to the Old Testament serving as a *propaideusis* of the gospel for the Jews), and now the intellectual and spiritual aspirations of both the Greek world and the Jewish world could be fulfilled in the advent of Christianity, which was their harmonious synthesis under the command of God to bring the world together in a universal monotheism.

Plato's understanding of the transcendent nature of divinity, resolving into a unicity beyond material forms, was certainly a strong influence on Christians as they too began to describe God's existence in terms that were not merely dependent on the anthropomorphisms of the biblical account. Origen has been often described as the most blatant "Platonizer" of the patristic era, but a close study of his works shows that he was a careful and critical synthesist. Some aspects of Plato's work were important to him (he particularly emphasizes the metaphysical "map" of the soul ascending to the supreme good as a moral *katharsis*), but in other instances he radically departs from Plato when he considers the teacher is not compatible with the Scriptures. So, for example, Origen insists on a worldview involving a creation from nothing (*ex nihilo*) to reinforce the biblical understanding of the supremacy of God, over and against the Platonic view of divinity as an agency within a more determinist and eternally preexisting cosmos.

The Platonic idea of philosophy as a training of the soul to ascend to the good was also heavily used by other Christians, through the medium of the theory of the Ideas. Plato's sense of the natural immortality of the soul was also much referred to, although Christians generally did not advocate this concept of a natural immortality of the soul in the early period. More thoughtful theologians taught instead that the soul was conditionally immortal, that is, human beings had been given a transcendent destiny they could either accept or reject. If they accepted it, they rose out of their mortal natures enslaved to death and entered into the resurrectional life of Christ. If they rejected it, they stayed locked within a nature saddled with death and decay.

In the Latin world Marius Victorinus and Augustine were enthusiastic advocates of the beneficial effect neo-Platonism could have on Christian self-expression. For the East, Origen, Gregory of Nyssa, Pseudo-Dionysius**,** and Maximus the Confessor especially represent the new Christian Platonism of Byzantium. Plato's view of philosophy as a moral discipline, whereby the soul could rise to true perception, was highly influential on the early Christian monastic movement, who regarded themselves as "true philosophers," using ascetical techniques to distance themselves from material illusions in the cause of advancing noetic insight. As we have noted, in the fourth to sixth centuries Platonism itself took on a deepened religious character of its own in the form of neo-Platonism, but in many senses the Christian monastic movement as represented by its Origenian advocates (such as Evagrius and Maximus) was an authentic heir to the earlier Platonic movement. Platonism as a whole, in its profound and indigenous suspicion of material reality, was never quite able to be digested in the generic Christian schemata, which, through the foundational medium of the Scriptures and the primacy given to the incarnation of the Logos, actually elevated materiality to a sacramental status in a way that was, and remained, wholly alien to core Platonic values.

From Aristotelianism the church gained an equally large set of insights on anthropology. It also offered a method of thinking, terms of analysis and process, that many Christian intellectuals valued (and still do). Aristotle (384–322 BC) challenged Plato for domination of the Greek and Hellenistic philosophic traditions.

Since the first century (beginning with the Middle Platonist teacher Albinus), Hellenistic philosophy eclectically combined elements from the Aristotelian system within a broad matrix of Platonic thought, producing the synthetic intellectual context into which Christianity was born. Aristotelianism had always emphasized empirical method. Its major methodological procedure was classification: the taxonomic identification of the variety of species and their respective inherent *teloi* (or ontological goals) based on close observation of the natural order and its related phenomena. The idea of natures containing the principles of their destinies, which subsequently unfolded in the pattern and the dynamic of their life courses, was important to the system. So too was ethical reflection (beginning with Aristotle's own *Nicomachean Ethics* in the fourth century BC). The system was also identified with structures of syllogistic reasoning and gave a prime place of importance to correct deductive method.

In the church fathers Plato was generally regarded as more conducive to reflection on the divine mystery, and Aristotle as more of an empiricist concerned with the material order, but this belied the massive amount of Aristotelianism that was quietly adopted by the early apologists in their meditations on the order of the created world and how it manifested the hand of God within it. Arguments in the church about how the natural order manifested the handiwork of God are as often as not heavily cribbed from Aristotelian literature, adding in a much more explicit sense of a personal creator's involvement. Chief among the Aristotelian ideas assimilated by the church were the concepts of form and matter, the metaphysical preeminence of the good, the idea of first cause, and the notion of balanced ethics as the median and reasonable position from a set of alternative possibilities. Origen of Alexandria was one of the first Christians to make a dramatic synthesis between Aristotelianism and Platonism in his own systematic theology. He began the rigorous classification of various types of literature and literary method, thus giving birth to the first (more or less) "scientific" Christian exegesis. Origen's system had many Platonic features in its metaphysical aspects, of course, but its rational substructure was provided by biblical exegesis first and foremost, and that in turn sat on Aristotelian interpretative principles that he learned from the example of the Alexandrian Academy and Great Library.

Origen's disciple Gregory of Nazianzus, in the fourth century, was even more explicitly indebted to Aristotle. He and other Cappadocian friends such as Basil the Great and Gregory of Nyssa prepared a wholesale assault on the neo-Arian teachers Eunomius and Aetius, who had elevated Aristotelian syllogism to center stage in their theological method (thus arguing the Son's nondivinity, since the category of "Son" is inherently different from that of "Father"). Gregory painstakingly used Aristotelian method in his *Five Theological Orations* (27-31) to demonstrate the strengths and limits of the various syllogistic forms of reasoning and to argue for the Nicene doctrine of the full deity of the Son (based on the premise that titles such as *Father* and *Son* were accidental, or relational, not substantive categories). After Gregory's authoritative example of the value of Aristotelian syllogism in the service of theology, the use of explicit Aristotelian method was "blessed" by high patristic authority.

After the fifth century many of Aristotle's works were translated into Syriac and would exercise a strong influence on Syrian Christian philosophy. Among the Latins, the foundational work of Tertullian was very aware of Aristotle and blended some of his work with Stoic attitudes to ethics. Most of the major Latin intellectuals after him had a good working knowledge of Aristotelian principles, something that gave to Latin Christian thought, in general, a distinctly empirical, down-to-earth character. In Byzantium, Aristotle's idea of humankind's telos, the inherent natural drive that unfolded in an anthropologically defining manner, was refined into a Christian spiritual philosophy that saw assimilation to the divine image (communion with God) as the fundamental human telos, and in this sense Aristotelian ideas became constitutive of the Byzantine mystical and theological writers, especially Maximus the Confessor, Leontius of Byzantium, and John of Damascus. Through the latter, especially his theological "handbook" (*On the Orthodox Faith*), Aristotle's influence came back (though mainly in the medieval period) into the Western church. Aquinas used John as a major source in forming his influential *Summa theologiae*.

From Stoicism the church borrowed much of the intellectual framework of its earliest ethical forms of analysis, at those times when it was not being specifically biblically led. Stoicism was a school of ancient Greek philosophy that derived from Zeno (c. 333–262 BC). It took its name from the "painted colonnade" (*stoa poikile*) at Athens, where Zeno first taught. Its major figures apart from its founder were Chrysippus, Panaetius, Posidonius, and Seneca (the Roman tutor of Nero). Stoicism evolved considerably over its long existence but was one of the dynamic influences on early Christian thinkers; it was one of the most highly respected philosophical systems at the time of the appearance of the church. The Stoic metaphysical view that the world was infused with divine sparks from the ultimate Logos, the immanent principle of divine order and reason that indwelt the souls of rational human beings, was an idea that almost all the Christian Logos theologians adapted enthusiastically to their own ends. So too was the extensive system of Stoic ethics. The Stoics taught that order and conformity to the laws of nature were primary ethical imperatives. The theory of natural law (also adapted to biblical prescripts) became of immense value to Christian thinkers. The pervasiveness of Logos as a common bond (a divine principle) marking our "common humanity" was a distinctive mark of the Stoic school, which was thus one of the few philosophical movements in antiquity to speak openly about the equality of all rational human beings and the inconsistency of social distinctions (not least slavery). Friendship was highly emphasized among the Stoics as the bond of charity that underpinned society. Such ideas also found a strong resonance among Christians, who had elevated the notion of love (*caritas, agape*), on the authority of Jesus, as chief of the virtues.

The Stoic school was deeply interested in logic and syllogistic argument, like the Aristotelians. In the fourth century many of the Christian theologians used Stoic and Aristotelian logical rules to develop a systematic approach to major doctrines such as Trinity and Christology. Tertullian and Lactantius are among the Latin fathers who demonstrate the most overt influence of Stoicism in their works. The comparisons between Christian values and Stoic ethical ideals were so marked that later Christians forged a set of letters purporting to be a correspondence between St. Paul and his contemporary the Stoic philosopher Seneca.

The Stoic cosmology, which envisaged the world as proceeding from one great fiery conflagration to another, with divine sparks of Logos scattering after each conflagration into souls and finally being drawn back together, is really like some vast panentheist system. In its totality it was wholly opposed to Christianity, and not one of the Fathers adopted Stoic elements without substantively revising them. Nevertheless, in this philosophical system, as with much of Platonism, several of the patristic thinkers (especially Justin Martyr, Clement of Alexandria, Origen, and Eusebius of Caesarea) found here a form of propaedeutic of the gospel message—if not an anticipation, at least a friendly element in Hellenistic society that could be positively adapted for the purposes of the Christian evangelistic mission. They merged "resonances" of the widely pervasive view of the world-end order with their own teachings from the Scriptures about apocalyptic judgment and used the Stoic substrate to serve as a missionary tool for approaching intellectuals with the Christian message.

In their approach to all the main schools of Greco-Roman philosophy we find this common denominator: the Christian intellectuals are highly eclectic. They take and mix and match. They are rarely in awe of any "pagan" philosopher, however elevated his reputation before them. For the Christians, the biblical authority and the traditions of the church remain predominantly important. But the Christian thinkers are always ready to use philosophy as a tool of communicating their ideas, expecting thereby a wider audience to their message and a more approachable context of understanding to their theology. Lactantius uses much of Stoicism,

Aristotle, and Plato, but when he turns to the overall value of the philosophers as guides to truth and morality he is little short of caustic.[121] Plato he criticizes most of all, for not living up to his own promise.

In a brilliantly memorable apothegm Lactantius shows the difference of mindset between a Christian theologian who knows he stands on the basis of revelation married to reason as distinct from a human speculative thinker, either transcendentalist or materialist, who places all his faith in reason. He says, "Plato, it is true, spoke many things respecting the one God, by whom he said that the world was framed. But in regard to true religion he spoke nothing, for he only had dreams of God; he had never known him" (*non cognovit deum solum somniavit de eo*).[122] Lactantius was a lay theologian. He saw himself as a rhetorician-philosopher-theologian first and foremost. He stands on the bridge between the third and fourth centuries, a victim of persecuting emperors and yet also the tutor and eventual political adviser of Constantine the Great. He is symbolic in many ways of how much the church had learned in its first three hundred years among the philosophers and scholars. It had stocked its libraries, solidified its traditions, and cherished (in the main) its intellectuals. Now it was poised for the great adventures facing it in the fourth century: perhaps the most dramatic and formative time it had known since the age of the apostles themselves. To this we now turn.

## A SHORT READER

***Cyprian of Carthage*, On the Mortality 20, 24, 26 (AD 252).** Our brethren who have been freed from this world by the Lord's own special summons should not be mourned for, because we know that they are not lost but rather have been sent on ahead of us. . . . Let us demonstrate to others that this is our true belief and so not mourn over even the death of our dearest ones. When the day of our own summons comes, let us gladly, and unhesitatingly, come to the Lord, hearing his invitation. . . . Let us reflect, dearly beloved brethren, that we have renounced this world and are only living here in the meantime as guests and strangers. When that day comes that snatches us from here and reassigns us to our proper home, let us greet it with gladness because it delivers us from the snares of this world and puts us back in paradise and the heavenly kingdom. Who is there who, having been exiled in foreign lands, would not hurry to return to his own homeland? Who, hurrying on his way back to his friends, would not gladly welcome a prosperous gale, so that he might all the more

---
[121]Lactantius, *Divine Institutes*, book 3.
[122]Ibid., 5.15.

quickly embrace those he loves? Since we look on paradise as our homeland and can already look on the patriarchs as our parents, then why should we not run and hurry along so that we can look on our homeland and there greet our parents? Already there are a great number of loved ones waiting for us to come: a dense crowd of parents, brothers, children, all longing for us to be there, already certain of their own safety, but anxious for our salvation. What a joy for both them and us to come into their presence and embrace them once more. What delight there is in that heavenly kingdom, beyond the fear of death. How exalted and endless is its happiness in everlasting life.

**Cyprian of Carthage, On the Unity of the Church 4 (c. AD 258).** There is no need for lengthy arguments about this [matter of church unity], since the truth is obvious, as you will see from this synopsis. The Lord says to Peter, "You are Peter, and on this rock I will build my church, and the gates of hell shall not overcome it. I will give to you the keys of the kingdom of heaven, and whatever you bind on earth shall be bound in heaven, and whatever you loose on earth shall be loosed in heaven" (Mt 16:18-19). Then, after his resurrection, he says, "Feed my sheep" (Jn 21:15). He then gives equal power to all the apostles: "As the Father sent me, so I send you. Receive the Holy Spirit. If you forgive anyone's sins, they shall be forgiven, and if you retain anyone's sins, they shall be retained" (Jn 20:21). But, to demonstrate just how important unity was, Christ ordained that it should start with one apostle. The rest of the apostles were just the same as Peter, evidently, partners with him in dignity and power, but the source of things was in the unity. In the Song of Songs, the Holy Spirit describes this same church in the person of our Lord: "My dove, my spotless one, is but one. She is the only one of her mother, the elect of her who bore her" (Song 6:9). So how is it possible for anyone to think they keep the faith if they break the unity of the church? The blessed apostle Paul teaches this same sacrament of unity when he says: "There is one body and one spirit, one hope, one Lord, one faith, one baptism, one God" (Eph 4:4). Those who fight and resist the church, do they really believe that they still remain within it?

**Cyprian of Carthage, Epistle 17.** I too suffer and grieve for our brethren who lapsed and fell beneath the violence of the persecution. They tore away part of our own heart with them, and their wounds have inflicted a like pain on us. But this the divine mercy can indeed repair. But I think we must not be too hasty, or do anything inadvisedly in a rush, in case a rash grasping of reconciliation should provoke the divine displeasure even more. The blessed martyr-confessors have written to me about certain persons, requesting that their desires should be considered. When peace is finally given back to us all by the Lord and we can return to the church, then each case shall be examined in your presence and with the aid of your counsel. Nevertheless, it has come to my ears that some of the presbyters, unmindful of the gospel, nor considering what the martyrs have written to me, nor even reserving to the bishop the honor due to his priesthood and his chair, have already begun to restore the lapsed to communion, to offer the oblation for them, and to give them the holy Eucharist. But they should have come back to this by due process. For even in lesser offenses, those that are not high blasphemy, penance is performed for an appointed time, and confession is made, with an inquiry instituted into the life of the one who is doing penance; and none of them may come to Communion until the bishop and clergy have laid hands on them. This being so, how much more, in the case of these extreme and most grievous sins, should all process be observed with caution and reserve, according to the discipline of the Lord. Our presbyters and deacons surely ought to have advised you on these matters, as part of their duty to tend to the sheep that were committed to them, and to instruct them in the path of achieving salvation in the ways God has established.

**Origen of Alexandria, On First Principles, preface 2.** Nevertheless, because there are many believers in Christ who today differ from each other, not only in small and trifling matters but also on subjects of the highest importance, such as those questions relating to God, or the Lord Jesus Christ, or the Holy Spirit; and not only about these matters but also in relation to other created existences, such as the heavenly powers and the holy virtues; then for these reasons it seemed to me to be necessary first of all to fix precise definitions and lay down a clear rule regarding each one of these questions before passing on to the investigation of other points. For my part, after I came to believe that Christ was the Son of God, I stopped looking for the truth among those who claimed their false opinions enshrined it, and so I disregarded the many claims of Greeks and barbarians to make it known. For I was convinced that we ought to learn the truth only from the Lord himself. And yet there are many who think they hold the opinions of Christ, even though some of them think very differently from their predecessors. But the teaching of the church is transmitted in orderly succession from the apostles and endures in the churches to the present day. This is why that alone is to be accepted as truth that differs in no respect from ecclesiastical and apostolical tradition.

***Origen of Alexandria,*** **On First Principles,** *preface 4, 8.* The particular points that have been clearly delivered in the apostolic teaching include the oneness of God . . . and, finally, the fact that the Scriptures were written by the Spirit of God, and have such meaning, not only that which is apparent at first sight, but also another, which escapes the notice of most people. For the scriptural words are written down as the forms of certain mysteries and icons of divine things. In relation to this, there is one opinion that prevails throughout the church, namely that the whole law is indeed spiritual; but that the spiritual meaning which the law conveys is not known to all, but only to those on whom the grace of the Holy Spirit has been gifted in the word of wisdom and knowledge.

***Origen of Alexandria,*** **On First Principles 2.7.** Just as an act of the will proceeds from the understanding but does not thereby divide its understanding or become separated or isolated from it, so after some such fashion should we envisage that the Father has begotten the Son, who is his very image. Just as the Father himself is invisible by nature, so he also gave birth to an image that was invisible. For the Son is the Word, and thus we should understand that there is nothing in him that is graspable by the senses. He is Wisdom, and in wisdom there can be no suspicion of anything corporeal. He is the "true light which enlightens every man that comes into this world," but he has nothing in common with the light of this present sun. Our Savior, therefore, is the image of the invisible God. And when considered in relation to the Father himself he is the truth: and when considered in relation to us, to whom he reveals the Father, then he is that image by which we ourselves come to the knowledge of the Father, whom no one knows except the Son and whomever the Son has been pleased to give that revelation. And his method of this revelation of God is through the understanding. For whoever understands the Son himself accordingly understands the Father also, as he himself has told us: "Whoever has seen me has seen the Father also."

***Origen of Alexandria,*** **On First Principles 8.4.** It is not from want of discrimination, or from any other accidental cause, that the principalities hold their dominion and the other orders of heavenly spirits have obtained their respective offices. Rather, it is from the fact that they have received their rank on account of their merits, though we have not been privileged to know or deduce what those meritorious acts were by which they earned their place in any particular spiritual order. It is enough for us only to know this much, so that we can demonstrate the impartiality and righteousness of God, that (as St. Paul tells us) there is no favoritism with him. Rather, he disposes everything according to the merits and moral progress of each individual.

This is why the angelic office does not exist except as a consequence of the merits of these powers. And the powers themselves do not exercise power except by virtue of their individual moral progress. Those who are called thrones in Scripture, who have the power of judging and ruling, likewise administer their powers only by virtue of their merit. Dominions likewise exercise their rule out of merit. Indeed, all that great and distinguished order of rational creatures comprising the celestial existences is set out in a glorious variety of offices. The same opinion should be held concerning those dark opposing influences that have given themselves up to places and offices appropriate to them; namely, that they derive the property by which they are made into principalities, or powers, or rulers of the darkness of the world, or spirits of wickedness, or malignant spirits, or unclean demons, not as a result of any essential nature, nor from their being created in that form, but rather that they have ended up in these degrees of wickedness in proportion to their individual conduct and their own decline into evil. So they have made up a second order of rational creatures, those who have devoted themselves to wickedness in so precipitate a fashion that they are unwilling, rather than unable, to pull themselves back from it on their own account. With them the thirst for evil has already turned into a passion and gives them pleasure. But there is also a third order of rational creatures, namely those who have been judged fit by God to replenish the human race, namely the souls of men. These too can be assumed into the order of angels by virtue of their moral ascent. So, for example, we can see some of them who have been made the sons of God, or the children of the resurrection, those who have abandoned the darkness, and have loved the light, and have been made children of the light. And there are those who have proved victorious in every struggle who, becoming men of peace, have become the sons of peace and the sons of God. There are those also who, having mortified their members on earth and risen above their corporeal natures, and even above the faltering movements of their very souls, have found union with the Lord and have been made wholly spiritual. These will be one spirit with him for ever, discerning all things in him until they arrive at a condition of perfect spirituality, when they will discern all things by the light of their perfect illumination, in all holiness through the word and wisdom of God, and will themselves become altogether undistinguishable (from him) by any other.

## FURTHER READING

### Cyprian of Carthage

Bevenot, M., ed. *Cyprian: De Lapsis & De Ecclesiae Catholicae Unitate.* Oxford: Clarendon, 1971.

Brent, A. *Cyprian and Roman Carthage.* Cambridge: Cambridge University Press, 2010.
Burns, Patout J. *Cyprian the Bishop.* London: Routledge, 2002.
Fahey, M. A. *Cyprian and the Bible: A Study in Third Century Exegesis.* Tübingen: Mohr Siebeck, 1971.
Hinchcliff, P. *Cyprian of Carthage and the Unity of the Christian Church.* London: Geoffrey Chapman, 1974.
Sage, M. M. *Cyprian.* Cambridge, MA: Philadelphia Patristics Foundation, 1975.

### Origen of Alexandria

Bertrand, P. *Mystique de Jésus chez Origène.* Paris: Aubier, 1951.
Crouzel, H. *Origen.* Edinburgh: T&T Clark, 1989.
Daniélou, J. *From Shadows to Reality.* London: Burns and Oates, 1960.
Dively-Lauro, E. *The Soul and Spirit of Scripture Within Origen's Exegesis.* Leiden: Brill, 2005.
Hanson, R. P. C. *Allegory and Event.* 2nd ed. Louisville: Westminster John Knox, 2002.
Knauber, A. "Das Anliegen der Schule des Origenes zu Casarea." *Munchener Theologische Zeitschrift* 19 (1968): 182-203.
Lewis, G., trans. *The Philocalia of Origen.* Edinburgh: T&T Clark, 1911.
McGuckin, J. A. "Origen as Literary Critic in the Alexandrian Tradition." In *Origeniana Octava*, ed. L. Perrone, 121-35. Leuven: Peeters, 2003.
———. "Structural Design and Apologetic Intent in Origen's *Commentary on John.*" In *Origeniana Sexta: Origen and the Bible*, ed. G. Dorival and A. Le Boulluec, 441-57. Bibliotheca Ephemeridum Theologicarum Lovaniensium CXVIII. Leuven: Peeters, 1995.
———, ed. *The Westminster Handbook to Origen of Alexandria.* Louisville: Westminster John Knox, 2008.
Origen. *Commentary on the Gospel According to John: Books 1-10.* Translated by R. E. Heine. Fathers of the Church 80. Washington, DC: Catholic University of America Press, 1989.
———. *Contra Celsum.* Translated by H. Chadwick. London: Cambridge University Press, 1980.
———. *On First Principles.* Translated by G. W. Butterworth. New York: Harper & Row, 1966.
Rahner, K. "The Spiritual Senses in Origen." In Karl Rahner, *Theological Investigations*, vol. 16, *Experience of the Spirit*, 82-103. New York: Crossroad, 1979.
Shin, D. "Some Light from Origen; Scripture as Sacrament." *Worship* 73, no. 5 (1999): 399-425.
Torjesen, K. *Hermeneutical Procedure and Theological Method in Origen's Exegesis.* Berlin: de Gruyter, 1986.
Trigg, J. W. *Origen: The Bible and Philosophy in the Third Century Church.* London: Routledge, 1983.

### Third Century Christian Culture and Thought Generally
Griggs, C. W. *Early Egyptian Christianity: From Its Origins to 451 CE*. Leiden: Brill, 1989.
Kelly, J. N. D. *Early Christian Doctrines*. London: A&C Black, 1980.
McMullen, R. *Christianizing the Roman Empire AD 100–400*. New Haven, CT: Yale University Press, 1984.
Pelikan, J. *The Christian Tradition*. Vol. 1, *The Emergence of the Catholic Tradition (100–600)*. Chicago: University of Chicago Press, 1975. Pages 27-120.
Prestige, G. L. *God in Patristic Thought*. London: SPCK, 1975. Pages 1-176.
Quasten, J. *Patrology*. Vol. 2, *The Ante-Nicene Literature After Irenaeus*. Utrecht: Spectrum, 1975.

### Christianity and the Philosophers
Arnou, R. "Platonisme des Pères." In *Dictionnaire de théologie catholique*, 12:2294-2392. Paris: Letouzey et Ané, 1903.
Gerson, L., ed. *The Cambridge History of Philosophy in Late Antiquity*. 2 vols. Cambridge: Cambridge University Press, 2010.
Ghellinck, J de. "Quelques appréciations de la dialectique d'Aristote durant les conflits trinitaires du IV-ième siècle." *Revue d'histoire écclesiastique* 25 (1930): 5-42.
Lilla, S. "Platonism and the Fathers." In *Encyclopedia of the Early Church*, ed. A. di Berardino, 2:689-98. Cambridge: Clarke, 1992.
Norris, F. W. *Faith Gives Fullness to Reason: The Five Theological Orations of Gregory of Nazianzus*. Leiden: Brill, 1991. Pages 17-39.
Ricken, F. *Philosophy of the Ancients*. London: University of Notre Dame Press, 1991. Pages 123-81.
Rist, J. M. *Platonism and Its Christian Heritage*. London: Variorum, 1986.
———. *The Stoics*. Berkeley: University of California Press, 1978.
Ross, W. D. *Plato's Theory of Ideas*. Oxford: Clarendon, 1951.
Runia, D. T. "Festugière revisited: Aristotle in the Church Fathers." *VC* 43 (1989): 1-34.
Spanneut, M. *Le Stoicisme des pères de l'église: de Clément de Rome à Clément d'Alexandrie*. Paris: Editions du Seul, 1957.
Tatakis, B. *La Philosophie Byzantine*. Paris: F. Alcan, 1949.
Wenley, R. M. *Stoicism and Its Influence*. New York: Cooper Square, 1963.

# THE GOSPEL ON THE THRONE

## Christians in the Fourth-Century East

**DIOCLETIAN AND THE CONSTANTINIAN REVOLUTION**

If one looks at the regnant dates of the Roman emperors of the third century, it is very clear soon enough that something was terribly wrong with the empire.[1] Generals fighting to assume the purple plunged the Roman world into a series of disastrous civil wars that weakened an empire already seriously sick from economic problems that saw inflation running at rampant, seemingly uncontrollable rates.[2] After Alexander Severus's assassination by his own troops in 235, there followed a fifty-year period that saw no less than twenty-six senatorially recognized claimants to the throne. Plague followed the steps of the legions.[3] The coinage that paid them collapsed in value, robbing them of the "retirement future" for which they committed their long years of military service. Landowners and small farmers were left with crops that won them less than their costs, even before tax imposts were demanded by a harried administration. Flights from farms were not uncommon. Even civic honors and offices were resisted by the wealthier classes as carrying too much burden to offset the traditional honor; for even their wealth, of course, was vested in the land. The much-vaunted political unity of Rome split at this era into three fractured Roman zones: the Gaulo-Brittanic, the Palmyrene, and Italian. It was only Aurelian (270–275) who managed to reunite them before his own assassination. His work prepared the way for Diocletian and the great reform movement that set Roman imperial administration on a more secure footing for the future.

---

[1] See appendix 3 for a list of emperors.
[2] See further O. Hekster, *Rome and Its Empire, AD 193–284* (Edinburgh: Edinburgh University Press, 2008); A. H. M. Jones, *The Later Roman Empire*, vols. 1-2 (Oxford: Blackwell, 1964); A. Bowman, P. Garnsey, and A. Cameron, eds., *The Cambridge Ancient History*, vol. 12, *The Crisis of Empire, AD 193–337* (Cambridge: Cambridge University Press, 2008).
[3] The Antonine or Galenic plague of 165–180 (probably smallpox) decimated the population of the empire. It was carried back to Rome by troops serving in the Near East.

Diocletian was one of the greatest practical administrators the empire had ever seen. In governance and military matters he replaced the (allegedly) republican-democratic systems of the emperor consulting with a senate, from whose ranks the major governorships were selected, with a more overtly autocratic structure of a single imperial ruler centralizing most of the important forms of control and policy direction with himself and an advisory consistory. He realized that much of the instability of previous generations had been because of the lack of a regulated system of the transition of power in the imperium. Accordingly, he instituted the system of the tetrarchy to ensure that a regular and peaceful handover of power would be effected from one emperor to the next. This was his hope, in any case. It did not materialize, as we shall see.

Diocletian had the vision to see that the territorial extent of Roman dominions now made it nearly impossible to govern from one center. But if power was devolved too far, the fringes equally became unmanageable. He therefore instituted the concept of the Eastern and Western empires, with a college of rulers. He made the old governorships smaller but more numerous, reducing the risk of using them as a launching pad for civil war. He doubled the old system of administrative provinces from fifty to one hundred. He took away military roles from the governors, creating a new class of dukes who had charge of the armed forces under the imperial oversight. In the two respective parts of the new empire a senior emperor, titled an augustus, would reign, and have as his associate a junior emperor titled the caesar.

Diocletian selected as his Western colleague his longstanding military companion Maximian, making him caesar in 285 and promoting him to augustus in charge of the West the following year. His own legal workload was so heavy (previous emperors had neglected the legislative role) that he consulted with Maximian, and they agreed that the system of appointing caesars for both East and West would be beneficial. Galerius was appointed to assist Diocletian in the East, and Constantius Chlorus, another old companion in arms and father to Constantine, was appointed to assist in Maximian's western territories. Diocletian was based at the capital in Nicomedia, Galerius at Sirmium, Maximian at Milan, and Constantius Chlorus at Trier. This system of four rulers has given rise to the name of the tetrarchy. Diocletian's presumption was that on reaching a suitable age of retirement (twenty years of regnant service), the two senior *augusti* would together voluntarily abdicate and the caesars would assume the title of augustus and appoint their own caesars. This peaceful system of renewal would, it was hoped, obviate the recurring problem of civil war. Diocletian was happy enough to retire to his fortified palace in Split, in 305. Maximian had to be coaxed into it, but he remained restless and insecure. Constantius and Galerius thus were promoted. Severus II was then appointed caesar of the West, and Maximinus Daia in the East.

But while this was happening Constantius Chlorus lay dying, stationed at York in Britain, in 305. His son Constantine, who was then being held as a high-ranking "hostage" at Nicomedia, heard the news and fled the Eastern capital at the same time that Galerius, with Diocletian's approval, was instigating a large-scale persecution against the Christians and a purge of their party at court. It might already indicate that Constantine's sympathies lay with the church (his tutor for several years in his time in Nicomedia was the Christian philosopher-rhetorician Lactantius, who followed him to the West and for some years became an adviser). But on his flight to Britain he knew well enough that when he arrived at York the gauntlet had been thrown down. It was in effect a rebellion and instigated the last great Roman civil war.

Constantius Chlorus's troops rejected the imposition over them of Severus and acclaimed Constantine, their general's son, as new augustus of the West. Maximian's own son, Maxentius, seeing Constantine's maneuver, also decided to act. He defeated and soon after killed Severus II and proclaimed himself co-augustus with his father, whom he had "persuaded" out of retirement. Galerius demanded a meeting with Maximian at Carnuntum on the Danube in 308. Here they set up a new arrangement. Licinius was to be appointed augustus of the West; Constantine could keep office as caesar, assisting him; Maximian must retire permanently once more; and Maxentius would be declared an outlaw if he did not resign his claims. All this did was set all the protagonists on a course for civil war. The "caesars" Maximinus Daia and Constantine refused to accept Licinius as their overlord. Maxentius, meanwhile, militarily conquered Italy and Africa and settled in to his base at Rome. In 309 Galerius was forced to recognize both Constantine and Maximinus Daia as his fellow *augusti*. Now there were four of them, as Maximian, freed from constraint, reappeared to support his son's claims. The Diocletianic idea was evidently in tatters. From this point onward it had to be resolved by force of arms.

Constantine made a strong campaign south aimed at Rome. He required Maximian's suicide in 310. Galerius died of disease at Nicomedia in 311, on his deathbed expressing remorse for his persecution of the Christians and reversing his suppressive policy. In 312 Constantine arrived at Rome and in a decisive engagement outside its gates (the battle of the Milvian Bridge) he defeated and panicked the army of Maxentius, which ran as a mob across the previously weakened bridge over the Tiber.[4] The crush of troops unhorsed the heavily armored Maxentius, and the bridge

---

[4]Famous in Christian history as the locus of the time when Constantine claimed a vision of the cross in the sky (alternatively a dream of Christ's voice instructing him to paint the sign of the cross on his troops' shields, according to variants in Eusebius of Caesarea or Lactantius). Maxentius's sappers had mined the bridge in case it needed to be destroyed in the case of an advance of the assaulting troops.

supports gave way, toppling the crowds into the river and drowning the emperor. Constantine walked into the city as its master. The Christians ever after attributed the startlingly "easy" conquest of Rome to the "new god" who had instructed Constantine to draw on the cross as the new palladium of Rome.

The augustus Maximinus committed suicide in 313 at Tarsus in Syria after being defeated by Licinius. This left Licinius in the East and Constantine in the West. In 313 Constantine arranged a meeting, and they both issued from Milan the famous edict of 313 that granted toleration to Christian subjects in both parts of the empire. Constantine's sister Constantia was married to Licinius in a show of fraternity, but relations were not as they seemed, and the civil war eventually progressed to its inexorable result when in 324 Constantine defeated Licinius, and having first spared his life, later required him to commit suicide, thereby becoming the undisputed monarchical ruler of the single empire.

The reason for instigating his final act of arms against Licinius was the latter's assumption of punitive policies against the Christians of his eastern dominions. Licinius had good reasons to suspect that the Christian soldiery of his eastern army looked to Constantine as their natural protector. Licinius's sporadic persecutions of the church indeed proved to be the last of the violent Roman imperial moves against the Christian faction. With Constantine they would rise to great ascendancy in both parts of the empire. Constantine undoubtedly had already envisaged this. The legends of the dream/vision before the battle of the Milvian Bridge were an acknowledgment of the significance of the Christian faction in his army. His cause had favored the Christians since early days; they had replied in kind with political support. His mother, Helena, was probably a Christian from her youth and had opened to Constantine the inner life of the communities, which he admired for its monotheism and practicality of morals. As an imperial hostage in Nicomedia, he had studied closely with Christian intellectuals and throughout his career would offer high patronage to Christian intellectuals and would eventually raise the Christian bishops to the rank and status of local magistrates, one of the most significant ways that the fourth century-church expanded its mission.

After defeating Licinius he determined to move eastward and set up his base in a new camp he called Victory City (Nicaea), where he had a large palatial villa built with a great meeting hall adjoining a beautiful lake (modern-day Iznik in Turkey). He started to plan for the stabilization of the eastern provinces: drawing up large plans for a new capital at the mouth of the Black Sea, on the site of a little colony on the Bosphorus called Byzantium. He would rename it, when it was finally completed in 337, as Constantine's city, Constantinople.

However, all was not going smoothly on the administrative front. Disturbing reports were brought to him that the Christian episcopate in the East might not be as helpful as he had hoped: they were in great disarray over internal matters of belief. It was something that caught his attention immediately. It became something of an immense moment in the history of the church and is forever associated with the little lakeside camp he had set up as a temporary mark of his victory over Licinius: Nicaea.

## THE ARIAN CRISIS AND ITS RESOLUTION

*Arius and Alexander in conflict.* The dispute, into which Constantine was drawn at a very early stage, was the so-called Arian crisis. Arius (c. 256–336) was a Christian priest of the city of Alexandria. His name, Areios, derives from Ares, the Greek god of war. He had charge of the dockland district of Baucalis in the city, and from what we can discern, he was popular there as a Christian leader of a congregation, a theologian and preacher with a lively flair for poetry and rhetoric. He was able to put his doctrine into verse form, the *Thalia* he called it, and even teach it to dock workers when he felt he needed the people's support for his cause. Moreover, he enjoyed a high local reputation for his ascetical lifestyle. His opponents in the Nicene movement, from whom we learn most of what we know of what he taught, had never a good word to say about him. So bitter was this controversy and so long running that when it was finally over, and "Arianism" was generally admitted in the chief international churches as a heretical "ism" that derived from his teachings (and so to be banned), the moral opprobrium of "archheretic" was heaped on him. This was a dogmatic issue—derived from the late New Testament letters such as Jude and John, where dissidence in doctrine was laid as the door of satanic impulses in the heresiarchs who manifested them (1 Jn 2:18-19; 2 Jn 7, 9-11; Jude 4, 19).

Following this biblical precedent allowed the apologists who fought against Arius and his school to level all manner of hard judgments against him. This is unfortunate, perhaps, to the modern reader, who might expect Christian clergy at odds with one another to have some degree of irenic moderation. But this was the nature of general debate in antiquity. Ad hominem attacks were part and parcel of how different sides characterized each other. Similar sharp judgments can be seen in the way dissident opponents were treated in the cases of the Gnostics and the Monarchians in the second and third centuries. Theological conflicts of a serious nature were seen, in the ancient church, to be of monumental importance: difficult for us to imagine in a modern age used to pluralism and relativism in most matters of philosophy and moral lifestyle and certainly doctrinal positioning. It was not so in antiquity. Then, serious dispute over religion was (if not a bloody matter of fatal strife) at least an all-out war of words in which bricks were thrown without a second thought, in accordance with rules of rhetorical diatribe established many centuries before in Greek literary tradition. The church writers, by and large, use the styles of Greek rhetoric, diatribe included. For this reason, and also because many of the judgments recorded against Arius come from a later period of hindsight, it is often difficult to arrive at a clear historical picture. We know little about him, but what little we know more or less is assured and confirmed from several angles, not least his own surviving fragments.

What brought him into the limelight was a fight he had with his local hierarch. It was Alexander's custom, once he had succeeded to the role as archbishop of this important city, to show his leadership of the theological school, for which the city was also renowned, by offering an advanced seminar on theology on regular occasions, expecting his clergy and local intelligentsia (lawyers, philosophers, rhetoricians, and the like) to be part of it and to share his hospitality in a forum akin to a symposium. These were a halfway house, one imagines, between episcopal sermonizing and philosophical lecture, where the archbishop stood as one theoretician addressing others. It is an interesting moment that happens with Arius, because that older, broader model of the bishop of a leading "school" acting as a professor (*didaskalos*), and perhaps positing speculative developments of Christian thought or novel clarifications of perceived problems, all comes crashing down. Arius had trained in rhetoric and theology at the school of Antioch under the renowned thinker Lucian.[5] The latter's works have not survived. He was a victim of the persecutions, and so his reputation was high as a martyr, but his style of thinking was critical of many of the suppositions and approaches of Origen of Alexandria, who remained the ghost behind the scenes of all of this in the city of his origins.

Arius contradicted Alexander on a major point: a critical principle of metaphysics, on which the two could not see any possible rapprochement. After that instance it was clearly no longer possible to say that Christians all hold the same thing on basic matters of faith here in this local church. And since Arius thought Alexander was drastically wrong on a substantial matter of faith, and Alexander similarly thought Arius was, the two parted company, refusing each other's communion. In effect Alexander suspended Arius from priestly service for what he judged was a lapse from the traditional faith of the church. Arius felt he had been treated unjustly, that Alexander had condemned him for upholding the traditional theologies and dissenting from the novelties he himself wanted to teach. Once this

---

[5]See further G. Bardy, *Recherches sur Saint Lucien d'Antioche et son école* (Paris: Beauchesne, 1936); H. C. Brennecke, "Lukian von Antiochien in der Geschichte arianischen Streites," in *Logos: Festschrift für Luise Abramowski* (Berlin: De Gruyter, 1993), 170-92.

priestly suspension occurred, church law (canon law) was now advanced to the point that Arius was able to appeal to another episcopal court for judgment, and he did so to his acquaintance the bishop Eusebius of Nicomedia, who was also a learned rhetorician who had himself valued Lucian's school and teachings. Eusebius found nothing wrong in Arius's approach and criticized Alexander's judgment and doctrine. Now the matter had suddenly gone viral, involving highly placed political bishops, larger geographical areas, and long-established Christian schools, all claiming that they represented the essential faith of the church.

What was at stake in the Arius matter, however, seemed shocking to most of those involved, because it came down, in the end, to two simple questions of the greatest magnitude: Was the divine Logos, whom the church revered as the Son of God, really divine or just notionally "divine"? Was the Logos God? Or was this term *God* something that ought only to be used, in all strictness, about the one and only Father? The other question flowed from it as its "example," as it were: Was the Logos eternal or time bound? That is, was he uncreated (as God is and must be, simply to be God) or created (made by the Father) and thus a creature (and thus not God, properly speaking)?

These were questions that had never been voiced before in the larger salons of the church. But it also seemed a very late time, the fourth century no less, for the Christians to be explicating such very basic questions as to the divinity of the Son, whom they had worshiped as divine for so many prior generations. An outsider (one with the benefit of hindsight!) might have commented, seeing the furor this debate caused, that perhaps the Christians had not yet clarified the basic terms of their metaphysics of the divine. How many gods did they believe in? Did they hold a semimythical view of Christ, ascribing a "kind of divinity" to him and full divinity to the Father?

The questions only seemed to deepen and get more problematic the more one picked over the issues: For example, what were the implications of this view in relation to Jesus of Nazareth? Was he God walking on earth for our salvation? Or was he a sign of the presence of the Logos among us, a Logos who was "like an angel" more than a deity exactly: for how could God turn into a human being? And if all of this made for ever-denser problematics: What was the status of the church's Scriptures? Did they give any clear solution to the problem of the deity of the Logos? Could we find there clear evidences for or against any particular doctrinal position?

Most of these questions had been the base matter of the conflict between Monarchians and Logos theologians in the previous two centuries. Given that the Logos school had enjoyed the undisputed victory in that development, the Arian dispute can also be seen as a pressing of the implications of Logos theology: forcing it to clarify the extent of its applicability, especially how it conceived the Logos's eternal relation to the Father and how the Logos entered into relation with the humanity of Jesus in the incarnation (could one say, for example, that the "Logos" and "Jesus" were two synonymous personal subjects?).

In reference to the divine Logos, the church had long before equated titles such as *Word*, *Son*, and *Wisdom* as referring to the eternal Son of God, making *Logos* a synonym for the Son. The Alexandrians were quick to point out that the creeds of the earlier times (especially the Nicene Creed, which they would rally around) all began by speaking of the eternal Son of God but continued without qualification to speak about this very Son's incarnation, virginal birth, crucifixion, and resurrection. But the problems remained unclarified: namely, that the Logos preexisted all time, and Jesus of Nazareth definitely had a beginning in time. It would make no sense to speak of Jesus being present in the Stone Age, for example. So what was the precise relation between the Logos as personal subject and Jesus as personal subject? Very little existed in any of the earlier writers to clarify this, and so it became a key point of contention in the Arian dispute.

Yet, even if the church's general reading of the Old Testament titles such as *Wisdom* and *Word* had been harmonized to refer to the same Son, nevertheless a cursory look at the key texts showed problem upon problem still unclarified. Arius turned frequently to a favored text of Proverbs (Prov 8:22), where Wisdom (*Sophia*) describes its position vis-à-vis deity as follows: "The Lord created me at the beginning of his work, the first of his acts of old." Arius applied a theory that claimed that all Scripture speaks directly about divine realities and used this (rather bare) exegetical strategy to conclude that Scripture taught clearly enough that the Logos was a creature of God. It might be an exalted one ("first of all creation") and one that was used to serve as the medium of salvation for the rest of creation, but, nonetheless, the Logos was a creature, was not God in the strictest sense of being uncreated, and was "called divine" in Christian prayer and worship only in an attributed, honorific sense. But while Arius deduced all this from his text, at the same time his opponents (who found all of this blasphemous and held to the insight that Christian tradition had clearly ascribed divine honors to Jesus, Logos inhominated, from the very beginning) turned to the New Testament prelude to John and found this written: "In the beginning was the Logos, and the Logos was with God, and the Logos was God." These texts seemed to indicate opposite directions on the same thing.

Not only had metaphysics come to a grinding halt for Christian theologians internationally (for news of this controversy electrified the church from Britain to Africa), but so too its sense of reliance on Scripture for clarity of preaching, and both things raised immense challenges for what the church had so laboriously erected over the preceding centuries in its conflicts with Gnostics and other sectaries as a growing sense of its core traditions. At the dawning of a new age of toleration, with the Constantinian peace promising so much around the corner, it now seemed that Christians could not even decide on the one question that any pagan asking for admittance to baptism would ask them: Do I believe Jesus is God, or is he a godly man? Do I have to believe the Logos is God (and then how many gods do I believe in?), or do I hold that the Logos is one of God's great angelic powers?

Once opened, this debate could not be pushed under the carpet. Arianism has rightly been called the watershed conflict that would determine the shape of core Christian tradition for centuries to come. For many generations past it has also been described as the "archheresy" of the Christian religion. If the clash with Gnostics and pluralists in the second century definitively conditioned the church's ways of attaching itself to scriptural authority, it was Arianism that decisively shaped Christianity's attitude to philosophy and metaphysics: ultimately demanding clarity in doctrine even when theologians appealed to the notion of mystery. For Christianity, henceforth, mystery could never again be mystification exalted by simple authority over pious ignorance. In the Arian dispute the church decisively committed itself to a rational faith, however much tension the juxtaposition of those two words generated (and still does generate).

Bishop Alexander had set out to teach in his seminar an aspect of theology that Origen had left as a "query" for his advanced students. Of course, now, Alexander was a fourth-century bishop, not a third-century philosopher, so the implications of his teaching, whatever it was, were far more public and authoritative than ever Origen's university seminar statements ever were. But by this stage Origen had himself been transmuted into a significant theological master of antique standing. Alexandria wanted to claim him. But so did the school of Caesarea Maritima and its learned bishop Eusebius of Caesarea, who disagreed with several of Alexander's presuppositions. Other Christian traditions, such as the school of Antioch (Lucian and others), had deeper divisions. Arius and Eusebius of Nicomedia become key dissident figures for us in this regard.

Alexander's point was that Origen had left his students with a conundrum: Was the Logos eternal or temporal? That the Logos was "within the divine being" was never at question in Origen's theology. He had taught the equality of divinity between Son and Father.[6] He had even defended (partially, to be sure) the applicability

---

[6]He teaches that the Son and the Father share an indissoluble oneness and that it is this oneness of being that makes the Logos what he is: God from God, outside and above all creation. Cf. *De Principiis* 1.2.1. Origen taught there never was a "when" when the Logos did not exist (*Commentary on Hebrews* 1.8).

of the word *homoousion* as long as it was not understood to be a materialist subdivision of the indivisible Spirit of God.[7] It was more the manner of "how so?" that was at stake with the antique theologian. In accordance with others of his day, Origen had tended to lean toward a theory of divine declension. Put crudely, this would be that the Father was supreme God, the Son-Logos was god of this God but ontologically dependent or derivative, and to connote this he used Platonic resonances of the Demiourgos, the divine principle used in the making of the material world order. For the Platonists the key distinction to be made in metaphysics was this: the differentiation of the One from the (world of) the many (that is, the differentiated manifestations of cosmic order, including materiality). The sublime Transcendent (absolute divine being and source of all order) could not be involved in any way with the created material domain. If there was any involvement, the former would obviously cease de facto to be absolute Transcendent.

Origen thought that using terms like *deuteros theos*—secondary divine being, a title of the Demiurge in Platonic thought—might help clarify the complex relationships of the Trinity.[8] But, one remembers, precise Christian terminology for the doctrine of the Trinity was still a long way off. Indeed, it was only as a result of the Arian crisis that such a thing was quickly brought to the front of the theological agenda. The doctrine of the divine Logos, clarified and explained in relation to the supreme Godhead, and the doctrine of the Trinity are one and the same thing described in two different ways. So when many scholars say that Arianism was essentially the clarification of Christology, they are not entirely right. Arianism is about the doctrine of the Trinity. But when Arius first disagreed with Alexander, the wider church did not yet have in place a commonly agreed semantic to appeal to and would not be in that position until the end of the fourth century, which is exactly why the Arian controversy was so drawn out and so confusing to all its participants.

Alexander wanted to bring some of that clarity to Christian metaphysics so as to advance Origen's legacy in Christology. His starting point was that the Logos is truly God—not some "honorary" being who has a title to divine status that he does not actually hold in and of himself. For, to make no bones about it, surely worshiping a creature as God who is not God is tantamount to idolatry. He further pressed the points of the aporia or problematic: if the Logos was not eternal, as God the Father is, then he cannot be God, as God is essentially (inescapably, we might say, as part of the definition of terms) eternal. He does not come into being or go

---

[7] Cf. M. J. Edwards, "Did Origen Apply the Word Homoousios to the Son?" *JTS* 49, no. 2 (1998): 658-70.

[8] He was the theologian who established the language of the three distinct hypostases in the Trinity in the single *ousia* of the unbegotten Father. *Commentary on John* 2.10.75.

out of being, as a creature might do. But if he is eternal, then how can he be said to come "from out of the Father"? Does not this affirmation of priority and subsidiarity (the Son is "of" the Father) imply two things inescapably?—namely, that the Son had a time when he came into being, when before that he was not in being, and that the Son is inferior to the Father since he is "from him." This is an aporia, a metaphysical puzzle Alexander thought well worthy of a seminar because if one affirms either of those conclusions (there was a time when the Son-Logos did not exist, or that the Son is inferior qualitatively to the Father), then of course the Son-Logos cannot possibly be God in the same sense that one might apply that word to the Father. In short, the Son would logically be inferior, and thus not absolute God, and in no way equal to the Father.

Such problems seeking resolution were staples of ancient scholastic reasoning and served to stimulate the group's philosophical discussion. But this is the point where Alexander's philosophy seminar and his role as episcopal teacher of the handed-down tradition of faith came into conflict. Alexander's conclusion, following other leads Origen gave in his work, was that the Son-Logos derived from the Father "before all time began." Therefore, the issuing of the Son from the Father was not a time-bound, temporal, that is, "creational," event at all. It preceded all creation and had its context in God's own timeless being. It was, then, an internal act of the single divine being of the timeless Father, an ontological part of God's self-existence.

So, the Son who proceeded (was born, begotten, issued, or whatever other verb one used) from the Father's own being was possessed of all the selfsame attributes as the Father, who begot him out of his own inner singularity of being (for there are not two instances of being between Father and Son). The church's habitual (traditional) use of the verb *begot*, signifying intimate familial relationality, was taken as the indication that such an eternal begetting was something far different from a creation or a making. The Son of the Father's own being thus had the Father's own glory, eternity, omnipotence, and so on. Everything, that is, that could be attributed to the Father as supreme God could also be attributed to the Logos, who had no other being than that of the Father, with all the qualities of that single being, except now as instantiated in a different hypostatic (subsistent) form: namely, the person of the Son-Logos, who was sent from the Father for the purposes of making the world and saving it.[9] Alexander summed it up aphoristically: "God is eternally a Father. The Son, thus, is everlastingly Son." The Alexandrian theologians took up here all the earlier christological images: light from light, stream from spring,

---

[9]For classic instantiations of this Logos Christology in the New Testament see Jn 1:1-3; Col 1:15-16, 19-20.

radiance from sun, and pressed them all to insist on the selfsameness of being and differentiation of personal instantiation of that being (as Father, Son, and Spirit in the single Godhead: one *ousia*, three *hypostases*).

The Arians rejected the concept of selfsameness of being, mutually shared (being unable to imagine how God the Father could share his own being, since they saw the divine unicity as a nontransferable monadic state). Alexander and Athanasius (and especially the Nicene Cappadocians at the end of the century) understood that the Christian God was not the monad of Judaism and not the polytheistic plurality of paganism, but a Trinity of mutuality composed by the gift of the complete single being of the Father to his Son and Spirit. Those who cannot understand the logic of Trinity, therefore, cannot begin to unravel the Arian controversy. As Origen had long ago indicated, the affirmation of the singleness of divine being, and the intimate oneness of the Son within the being of the Father, had also to be balanced by the profession of the three hypostases of the divine persons: Father, Son, and Spirit. It was Arius's tendency to insist on the former aspect alone and press Origen's complex idea of unity in relationality into an undifferentiated unicity. This generic Arian refusal to develop a trinitarian language is openly manifested in the way the Arian school has a massively undeveloped doctrine of the person of the Spirit (pneumatology). For them, if the complete divinity of the Son was a step too far, that of the Spirit of God was a mistake built on a mistake. For the greater church, the clarification of trinitarian logic was the ultimate stepping into the light and professing that the God of the Christians was indeed a new revelation: a radical new theology that approached the divine being, not simply the divine economy, through the life and ministry of Jesus taken as nothing less than a sacrament of God and far more than a witness to a godly, obedient life.

In Alexander's theology, then, the Son was certainly the agent of the Father, obedient to him in all things, yet coequal to him in glory and all the attributes of his being, since his being was that of the Father. By the midpoint of the long controversy that would follow from this, after the events of the Nicene Council, the Alexandrian school would fasten on a tightly wound word that would express this succinctly like a lapel badge: *homoousion*, the state of possessing "the same being, or substance, or nature, as something else." Thus the confession that the Logos was *homoousios*, consubstantial, with the Father became a keystone of Alexandrian theology. We shall see how this played out at the Council of Nicaea in 325. But at the early moments of the controversy, Alexander and his young assistant, Deacon Athanasius, certainly did not prefer this word or project it as a cardinal term of their argument. It had bad precedents. It had been used by Monarchian theologian Paul of Samosata in a way that clumsily suggested the Father was simply the Son in another form.[10] It also had no biblical precedent behind it. Moreover, it had already been criticized as a potentially misleading theological term by Origen himself, who had had to justify himself from appearing to apply "same-substance" language to speak about the God of all things who is beyond all (material) substance and untrammeled by the very notion of it. Some of his hostile contemporaries had taken his theology of the Son sharing the Father's selfsame being as tantamount to resuscitating Manichaeist ideas that envisaged "parts of divinity" located in the created orders. It was Origen's leeriness of this idea that made his closest disciples in later times, such as Pamphilus and Eusebius of Caesarea, always hostile to the word *homoousios*, even though the likes of Eusebius were not inimical to the essential claims of the Nicene party, that Christ was God from God.[11]

For many reasons, then, the Alexandrians preferred at the outset to use the phrase *tautotes tes ousias* (the Son-Logos is of the *selfsame essence* or being as the Father) to connote the ontological relation of Father-Logos. Even so, when it became clear to them (after the council in 325) that their opponents were rewriting their script in several instances and attributing different definitions to key terms, they settled on the phrase *homoousion* (consubstantial) as constitutive of their position, a term that had the advantage of being something the Arian party wholly despised, which served, therefore, to be a marker of clear space between them, and one that the Latin church was willing to endorse alongside them.

Arius answered Alexander's argument with the claim that the prior Christian tradition did not call the Son-Logos equal to the Father and only acclaimed him with divine honors because of his exaltation by the Father for his faithful service. The Logos was inferior to the Father. As a subsidiary "deity," he was dependent on the Father for his very existence and thus is clearly not "God" in the proper sense of that word. He is "said" by the church to be divine in terms of acknowledging that he is lifted into God's glory by the Father because of his faithfulness and good service. But he is best considered as one of God's greatest angelic agents: a high priest of his creational and salvific work. The Scriptures ought to be read in a way that makes this dependency clear. Philosophically it ought to be made clear by insisting that the Son-Logos did not exist eternally, as only the Father can be said to be eternally. This means he had a beginning of his existence. It might not have been a beginning in the cosmic, material time sequence we know, but it was a beginning of existence

---

[10]Whose thought had been brought to the attention of the Alexandrians in the third century when Dionysius of Alexandria was asked to serve as his trial judge.

[11]This inner conflict between various forms of Origenists in the Nicene anti-Arian parties led to a great deal of internal conflict among the opponents of Arius until the latter part of the fourth century.

nonetheless, and so there was a conceivable state when he did not exist and God was all in all. This means that God the Father is the sole absolute self-originating One, and the Son-Logos, therefore, stands within the creation (even if he is before it temporally) as the "firstborn of all creatures," but a creature nevertheless, because he does not emanate from God's own being but from God's choice (will and energy) to make him from the nothingness that his divine Creator's energy shapes into being for all of creation.

When Arius wrote to appeal to Bishop Eusebius of Nicomedia, he summed up the points of Alexander's doctrine that he disagreed with, presenting them to Eusebius as clearly unreasonable propositions:[12]

> The bishop [Alexander] is ravaging and persecuting us terribly, and moving against us in every bad way.[13] In short, he drives us out of every city as if we were godless men, all because we will not agree with his publicly affirmed teachings that "There was always a God, and always a Son," or that "As soon as the Father was, so the Son was," or "The Son coexists with the Father: unbegotten, ever-begotten, begotten without begetting,"[14] or "God does not precede the Son, either in aspect or in a moment of time," or "There is always God, thus always a Son, since the Son is from God himself."

He will not listen to such impieties, Arius tells Eusebius, whom he is anxiously seeking to become his new episcopal protector. His own teaching is, in summary form, that

> the Son is not unbegotten, nor a part of an unbegotten entity in any way, nor from anything in existence, but rather he subsists in will and intention before time and before the ages, full of grace and truth, God, the only begotten, unchangeable. Before he was begotten, or created, or defined, or established, he did not exist, for he was not unbegotten. Even so, we are persecuted because we have said the Son has a beginning while God has no beginning. We are persecuted because of that, and also for saying he came from nonbeing. But we said this since he is not a portion of God, nor of anything in existence. This is why we are persecuted. You know the rest of the story.[15]

---

[12] The *Letter of Arius to Eusebius of Nicomedia* survives. It can be found in Theodoret, *Ecclesiastical History* 1.5.

[13] He deprived Arius of his right to function as a presbyter in the city.

[14] Here he deliberately tries to make Alexander sound illogically stupid in thus presenting him. But his presentations of the rest of the arguments are clear and accurate. Here Alexander meant that the Logos's "being born" from the Father was by no means the same as "being made" by the Father (even though the Greek verb *begotten* could bear those meanings).

[15] Arius sent this letter of appeal to Eusebius by the hand of the cleric Ammonius, and he also names the wider party of supporters of his in the Eastern provinces who, he implies, also look to Eusebius (of Nicomedia) for support against Alexander. He names Eusebius of Caesarea, Theodotus, Paulinus, Athanasius (not of Alexandria), Gregory, and Aetius. The first of that list would renounce any allegiance to the Arian position. The last in the list became the most radical upholder of the creaturely status of the Son of God active into the next generation as head of the radical heterousiast Arian party.

A notable aspect of Arius's teaching that can be clearly seen from this summa he presents is its scholastic nature. It starts a tradition that is prevalent in the fourth century (and has come to characterize much of Christian theology afterwards) of approaching metaphysical matters syllogistically.

Arius has thus distilled down many pages of Origen's complex soteriological schema into a few tight propositions, which he wants to make razor sharp and to serve as arbiters of the faith. His chief argumentation is this: (1) The Logos is not unbegotten (*agenetos*), thus he is begotten (*gennetos*), and since being unoriginate (*agenetos*) is definitively constitutive of deity, the Logos is not God in the sense that God (the Father) is God.[16] (2) The Logos is begotten from the Father: it follows that there must have been a state "before begetting" when the Logos did not exist and God was solitary. It was soon to be distilled into the famous Arian syllogism "there was when he (the Logos) was not" (*een pote hote ouk een*). The whole thing hammered into this syllogism could be, and was, taught to his parishioners and painted on walls in the city as part of his protest against his treatment. It was meant to show Alexander was incapable of understanding logic—if he maintained the Logos was begotten and did not affirm his sometime nonbeing.

(3) The Logos subsists (has his existence from) the will and choice of God the Father. This in stark contrast to the school of Alexander, which argued he has his being from the Father's very being. No, Arius argues, the Logos derives (like all created things) from the choice (and power or energy) of the Father to bring things into being from nothingness. The Logos is thus a creature—a perfect creature (*ktisma*), admittedly, but a creature like all other creatures. (4) Unlike other creatures, Arius affirms his special nature in some respects. The Logos is "unchangeable" (*atreptos*). This means he is not fallible like other creatures, capable of sin or disobedience. He affirms the Logos's supreme holiness, his proximity to God, and his great power as agent of salvation. All of this accumulates to allowing the church to affirm that the Logos is divine—a title of honor. But this is never to be understood as affirming his deity is the same as the Father's or coequal to that of the Father. He certainly cannot understand or comprehend the Father (something the Nicenes took as one of the great blasphemies of their opponents).[17] Rather, the Logos is a great

---

[16]In his *Thalia* Arius says, "The Father in his essence (*ousia*) is a foreigner to the Son, because he exists without beginning." Cf. Athanasius, *De Synodis* 15. Athanasius lists his positions as "the blasphemies of Arius."

[17]In the *Thalia* he says, "In brief, God is inexpressible to the Son. For he is in himself what he is, that is, indescribable, so that the Son does not comprehend any of these things or have the understanding to explain them. For it is impossible for him to fathom the Father, who stands by himself. For the Son himself does not even comprehend his own essence (*ousia*), for, being Son, his existence is most certainly at the will of the Father. What logic would allow that he who

spirit, the highest angelic power of the Father. The church's worship of him as divine acclaims that: nothing more. To say more would be a denial of monotheism. The Arian sense of monotheism ultimately depended on a view that God was a "monad."

Arius and his companions who had been deposed by Alexander wrote a letter to the bishop setting out their theology publicly.[18] In it they repeated that the Logos was a creature (*ktisma*), albeit perfect and morally unchangeable, and they compromised (of sorts) in allowing that he was "created at the will of God, before time and before the ages, and came to life and being from the Father, and the glories that coexist in him are from the Father." In this they partially allowed Alexander's point that "there was no time when he did not exist," since he was begotten before time began. But their insistence on his creaturely status fundamentally denied Alexander's point that the Logos's divinity was essential to him (conatural), since it derived from his being begotten "out of the being of the Father" (*ek tes ousias tou Patros*), not out of the will or creative power of the Father, and thus his divinity was coequal and coeternal with that of the Father.

For the Arians the linear logic of priority and subsidiarity, of before and after, of superior and inferior, made it clear that the Logos was inferior to God and that Christian monotheism ought to be defending divine unicity.[19] Alexander and Athanasius (who would take this argument into the future) found that logic to be entirely bound in with materialist presuppositions: temporal order, earthly senses of power and authority, and wholly unable to grasp that the divine generation of the Son from the very heart of the Father's own incomprehensible being was a mystery that could not be pressed into material forms. It was, they said, the church's tradition, manifested in the clear ascription of divine honors it had always given to Jesus, that the Son had the Father's own being and thus was all the Father was, except that he was the Father's hypostasis of creation and salvation: distinct in his hypostasis as Son, totally the same in his being as God, since his being was the selfsame being as the Father's, no other being, which was exactly why the Trinity safeguarded, and did not compromise, monotheism.

---

is from the Father should comprehend or know his own parent? No, clearly that which has a beginning is unable to conceive or grasp the existence of that which has no beginning." Text in Athanasius, *De Synodis* 15.

[18]The text is preserved in Athanasius, *De Synodis* 16. Arius headed it, cosigned by the priests Aethales, Achilles, Carpones, Sarmatas, and another Arius; also the deacons Euzoios, Lucius, Julius, Menas, Helladius, and Gaius. The bishops Secundas of Pentapolis, Theonas of Libya, and Pistus were also listed as supporters. The latter was eventually set up by the Arian party as rival bishop in Alexandria.

[19]In the *Thalia* Arius writes, "So there is a triad, but not of equal glories. Their hypostases are not mixed together among themselves, and as far as their glories go, one is infinitely more glorious than the other."

Why did all this matter? Was it not a very finely tuned debate about pretemporal metaphysics, something akin to that medieval argumentation among scholastic theologians allegedly debating how many angels could dance on the head of a pin? The Enlightenment sophists laughed about it, and the historian Gibbon mocked that there was hardly an iota of difference between the *homoousians* and the *homoiousians*. Well, yes and no. A lot hangs even on an iota sometimes, just as it does on the little signs + or -. To think otherwise relativizes all divine philosophy to the status of private opinion. All this is certainly a complex debate and takes some following even today, when we have much better access to primary-text evidences. It must have been very hard for the majority of bishops in the early fourth century (not those few specialized theologians who make most of the running at the Council of Nicaea and its aftermath) to have kept up with the terms of what was happening, to have adjudicated what in this was in harmony with the older ecclesial traditions and what, if anything, was innovation and dissonance.

Many relatively uneducated bishops who would soon assemble at Nicaea to adjudicate this matter would undoubtedly be glad they did not have to take the floor and expound the whole matter themselves. And yet, on the other hand, beyond all the complexities and details, this theological dispute seemed to be turning around a very simple set of issues: Was the Logos, properly speaking, God? Was he one in the Father's own being, or was he an alien (albeit exalted) creature of God, sent for the service and sanctification of the world? Many common believers were puzzled and confused by the complexities of the metaphysics of the Alexandrians, who talked about the selfsame being shared between Father Son and Spirit. They could appreciate the idea but not necessarily reconcile it with the concept of distinct hypostases in the Trinity. To this day, as the twentieth-century theologian Karl Rahner once put it, most of those who profess the orthodox Trinity doctrine still act as if they were, practically speaking, tritheists in their common beliefs. Arius's doctrine was much simpler to take in. It was special pleading, nevertheless, to keep calling the Logos "divine." And this was where the traditional faith of the earlier communities came into play.

Was it not the case, many felt, that from the Gospels onwards the Son-Logos's communion with the Father meant that he had always been seen as intimately one with the Father's divinity, not simply as a blessed or holy man? Those who had, earlier on, confessed him to be solely a holy man had been decisively rejected as heretics. The latest famed example had been Paul of Samosata, and he had received no hearing at all. So, if the Son-Word was not merely a man, and it was not possible to conceive of a halfway house between Godhead and creaturehood (if one wanted to step out of polytheistic myths), then was it not the case that Arius's highly logical approach clashed with traditional pieties of the Christian communities? One thing was clear enough, that when his chief propositions were taken out and held up as syllogisms (something he had laid himself open to) they sounded very "foreign" to Christian ears: the Logos is not equal to the Father, the Logos is alien to God and cannot comprehend him, is ultimately an exalted creature. The Alexandrian theologians carried much weight internationally when they listed these things as "the blasphemies of Arius."

More than simple traditionalism, however, both sides in the debate knew that the argument mattered in a very precise way. Both sides agreed that the Logos was sent by God to save the world. Salvation was at stake in this controversy. For Arius, if the Logos were wholly divine and bore the undiluted characteristics of God himself, then how could he possibly enter into human life and act as the personal subject Jesus of Nazareth and still be called God? For Arius, it was obvious that Jesus was a man of limited knowledge and experience, time bound, and capable of suffering and change. The terms of ancient theology (from the Greek philosophers onward) meant that it was impossible to attribute suffering and change to the Godhead. Since Jesus evidently suffered, how could he be the unchangeable Logos? Arius thought that if one equated the personal titles *Logos-Son* and *Jesus Christ*, it could only be to the detriment of theology: one would be defiling the notion of God, dragging divinity down into the dirt of time and space.

For Alexander, Athanasius, and the later Nicene theologians, this was the whole point of the theology of the incarnation. If the Son-Logos were not divine, then his lifting up of humanity into his own ambit of life would have no more value for salvation that that of a good man standing as an example of godly life. If the Logos were not God, his acts in the flesh would have no universal salvific value. If he were not God, one ought not to talk about an incarnation of the divine on earth, but instead it would be a kind of temporary habitation, an epiphany among humanity. At best this would be like an angelic visitation, as described in the Old Testament, and at worst it would be a relapse to the polytheistic ideas of pagans, with gods visiting the world on occasions. Christian incarnational thought, on the other hand, stood for the very Word of God himself assuming human nature, in the form of a human body, to effect works of salvation in that suffering body, works that would have an impact on the whole of the human race, precisely because the subject who suffered in the earthly body was the eternal Son and Word of God. Only if the Logos was God could he give to flesh a sacramental and divinized value. Athanasius expressed this with a brilliant syllogism (reusing terms of Irenaeus): "He (the Logos) became man, so that man might become divine."[20]

---

[20] Athanasius, *Contra Arianos* 1.39; 3.34; *De Incarnatione* 54.3; Irenaeus, *Adversus Haereses*, book 5, preface.

For those who defended the divine status of the Logos directly assuming human life (contrary to the Arians, who held the divinity at arm's length from such involvement in history), incarnational thought became the very mechanism of salvation. Salvation emerged thus not as a simple sacrificial forgiveness of sins of the race, as exemplified in Jesus' faithful obedience; rather, it became the Logos's direct engagement with human life in person, refashioning a human life so that it could be intimately united with the divinity, making the flesh ascend into the divine presence. What he established in his own body he was seen to have granted to the church as a grace. It was this aspect of soteriological thought that came to dominate the Arian-Nicene controversy in its second stage. If the argument with Arius himself had largely been a metaphysical one, the argument that evolved after Nicaea in 325 was predominantly a soteriological one. The Council of Nicaea began that process.

***The Council of Nicaea 325.*** Once Arius and his colleagues had appealed their deposition and claimed that their bishop was misguided in his exposition of the faith, not them, it was inevitable that some form of larger synod would have to be assembled to adjudicate this matter more internationally. How that could happen was not at all clear, for the church was suffering in its Eastern provinces in the course of the latest Roman civil war, which had been inaugurated when Diocletian's tetrarchy had been pushed aside and Constantine had been acclaimed as emperor in Britain in 305, commencing a long military campaign that had brought him to victory at Rome and a shared dominion with the Eastern emperor Licinius. But the alliance was an uneasy one. When the Arian crisis was in progress, Licinius was already arming himself against Constantine and was applying political pressure and penalties to the Christians of the East, whom he suspected of being Constantinian sympathizers. In the last act of the civil war that followed, Licinius was decisively beaten in 323 in a way that left Constantine as sole monarch of the whole imperium, East and West.

Constantine had recognized across the course of his long march to monarchy that the Christian religion could be of great service to him. His theological aims overlapped with it in many ways: he wished to abolish animal sacrifices and rally all the peoples of the empire around the notion of one God in heaven and one God-blessed ruler on earth. In practical terms he also saw great advantage in using the system the Christians had already instituted of local bishops having the respect and trust of local communities. One of the great strides forward in his polity was to endow these bishops with quasi-magisterial rank and allocate to their episcopal courts a parallel validity to civil courts. This meant that poorer people could for the first time feel confident about having access to Roman law, with a chance of receiving equity and justice from someone who possibly knew them and their family and was committed to pastoral care and moral values, without desire for a corrupt profit. Constantine's arrival in the East displaced the imperial center of Nicomedia. He did not intend to occupy it, suspecting (as he had at Rome) that it was too full of the supporters of his enemy. So he established a base by a lakeside in Bithynia, calling it "Victory City" (*Nikaia*), while he planned a large-scale dream of having a new Rome built on the Bosphorus (Constantinople).

The Eastern church immediately sensed its relief from oppressions under Constantine and had expectations of the new ruler, which were confirmed by reports from the Roman clergy, that he had proven to be a friend. It soon became apparent to the emperor, however, that his hopes of using the episcopal chancery system as a new form of democratized justice dispensing, part of the *Pax Constantiniana*, was going to be difficult, because the church itself was rent with divisions and suspicions after many years of regular and bitter persecution under Diocletian's successors. The internal life of the churches was broken. He also discovered that the sharp intellectual dispute of the Arian crisis was presently taking its oxygen away. It called to his mind a comparable problem of church unity in the West that had marked his debut in involvement with internal Christian affairs. He had occupied Northern Africa in the winter of 311, and the issue had immediately been presented to him. He thought he had dealt with that fairly well; it had gained him a large-scale reputation for fairness among the Western bishops, and it surely colored his view on how to treat the resolution of the Arian dispute that now loomed before him. The Western problem had been the early form of the Donatist schism, and it will be worthwhile to make a little detour to look at how Constantine acted here, for it was surely a precedent in establishing his dynasty's protocol in dealing with the church. We see here a careful set of decisions to follow up a wide appeal to international Christian sentiment, with legal sanctions.

The disruption in Africa took its origin immediately after Diocletian's Great Persecution (303–305) and divided the African church, off and on, for the next four centuries. The schism first arose because many clergy during the persecution handed over sacred books to the authorities. These *traditores* (or "hander-overs"—the word is the origin of *traitor*) were denounced by a group of imprisoned confessors who declared (with the great spiritual authority then afforded to confessors in the African church) that only those who acted bravely in the persecution would be given a heavenly reward.[21] Their zealous attitude, however, was censured by the archdeacon of Carthage, Caecilian, who was (later) said to have punished them by reducing their dole of prison food paid for by the church. He did this chiefly to offset the motion

---

[21] *Acts of Saturninus* 18.

from the zealots that all Christians ought to volunteer themselves for martyrdom, but it cost him a great deal of grumbling in the church community afterward. In 311 Caecilian was elected as bishop of Carthage in a contested consecration, and in the following year the primate of Numidia held a council of seventy bishops at Carthage, which deposed Caecilian and elected another. Caecilian refused to give way.

That same winter Constantine's armies occupied North Africa, and Caecilian was accepted into Constantine's administration as bishop and chaplain, serving as the emperor's representative in Africa. Constantine gave moral weight and a large income to Caecilian, and he threatened his rivals with legal penalties if they did not come around to his communion. After many continuing protests, when he learned the niceties of Christian synodical process, Constantine referred the dispute between Caecilian and the Numidian bishops to the hearing of Pope Miltiades at Rome, who once again decided in favor of Caecilian. The rival party was now led by Bishop Donatus, who arranged another appeal to the emperor, alleging that one of Caecilian's consecrators was a *traditor* and thus Caecilian's whole ordination was invalid, as it had been performed by an apostate who lacked sacramental grace.

Constantine decided to refer the matter once more to a larger, internationally constituted episcopal synod to adjudicate it, which took evidence about the circumstances of Caecilian's original consecration. The council met at Arles in 314. The decision again went against Donatus, and this ecclesial decision was reaffirmed in secular law by imperial decree in 316. In 320 a separate trial before the imperial governor of Numidia revealed that many of Caecilian's opponents in the Numidian hierarchy had themselves been *traditores* in the persecution. Even with this revelation of mass hypocrisy, the movement did not lose momentum. The Donatist protest gained its greatest allegiance in those provinces of North Africa that were the least Romanized (Numidia and Mauretania Sitifensis), suggesting its popularity was closely related to anticolonial protests. One of Donatus's most celebrated remarks was "What has the emperor to do with the church?"[22] The Donatist communities were generally rural, radical in their anticolonial attitudes, and seen as revolutionary in their often-violent attempts to smash the structures of colonial slavery affecting them.

By the latter half of the fourth century, Donatism probably represented the majority of rural churches in North Africa, but it was always regarded as a very "local" schism, with very provincial views on theology and a very closed and narrow conception of church as the elite body of the pure. The rest of the Christian world looked to Caecilian as the true bishop. After his death the "Caecilianist party" disappeared, and the issue became seen as a schism between the "Catholics" and the Donatists. In

---

[22]Optatus of Milevis, *Against the Donatists* 3.3.

the fifth century Augustine and his fellow bishops persuaded Emperor Honorius to apply more pressure on them to disenfranchise them, but they still continued as a dissident presence in African Christianity down to the Arab invasion, always suspicious of the attitudes of emperors, whether or not these now claimed to be Christian.[23]

In relation to the Arian dispute this Donatist episode, ten years earlier, although not entirely successful, had shown Constantine a way to proceed. He would try first of all a personal intervention, demanding a cessation of the problem.[24] He would follow the advice of a trusted court bishop. He would involve the leading authorities of the great Christian cities, who were educated men, which meant especially Rome and Alexandria. He would call a widely representative international group of bishops together to debate and resolve the conflict, and then he would add the seal of legal support to the conciliar decisions. There would be some problems in applying this pattern of a protocol, of course, and these conspired to make the Nicene process something even more hit-and-miss than his Donatist decisions. His choice of a court bishop was conflicted between the Spanish bishop Hosius of Cordoba, whom he had brought with him from the West as adviser, and a court favorite, Eusebius of Nicomedia, whom he had confirmed as bishop of the Eastern imperial capital.[25] Hosius was an ardent supporter of the Alexandrian bishop's Christology, whereas Eusebius, as we have noted, was one of the leading enemies of Alexander. Likewise, Constantine tended to lean by default toward accepting the views of the bishops of the great cities. But in this case the dispute involved the leader of one of the primary sees of the Eastern church, not simply in a clash with a local priest but now in a clash with the bishop of the former imperial capital.

By the end of 324, however, Constantine had made up his mind. He would arrange for the grand celebration of his twenty-year anniversary since being acclaimed as emperor in York in 305, his *vicennalia*; and as part of the jubilee festivities that this event would involve, following also in the aftermath of his undisputed victory over Licinius in the East and his unquestionably enhanced reputation as protector

---

[23]For more on Donatism see W. H. C. Frend, *The Donatist Church: A Movement of Protest in Roman North Africa* (Oxford: Clarendon, 1952); R. A. Markus, *Saeculum: History and Society in the Theology of St. Augustine* (Cambridge: Cambridge University Press, 1970); M. Tilley, *Donatist Martyr Stories: The Church in Conflict in North Africa* (Liverpool: Liverpool University Press, 1996).

[24]Constantine indeed sent a letter to Alexander and Arius in 324 demanding that they leave off "foolish disputations" that were peripheral to Christian affairs. He censured Alexander for raising such quibbles about silly metaphysics in the first place and rebuked Arius for being disobedient to his superior. The letter, of course, revealed he had no idea what he was talking about theologically, and it basically had no effect whatsoever. The dispute had already spread to larger churches and needed a synodical resolution. His courtiers were soon able to advise him of this need, Hosius of Cordoba playing the leading role in the preconciliar arrangements.

[25]See further V. C. De Clerq, *Ossius of Cordova: A Contribution to the History of the Constantinian Period* (Washington, DC: Catholic University of America Press, 1954).

of Christians across the world, he was confident he could effect peace in the Eastern Christian provinces and then, on the basis of this harmony, move on with his plans to advance the bishops to status as local magistrates and so bring about his larger scheme for changing the face of imperial administration. He would bring the Christian bishops to peaceful concord even if he had to drag them there. The date would be 325, his actual anniversary, making Nicaea an integral part of his official celebrations of victory. The setting for calling together a large group of bishops would be his own summer palace at Nicaea (modern-day Iznik in Turkey). From the start the council was thus invested with the air of a quasi-senatorial legislative. All the bishops were afforded free use of the imperial post stations for their travel (though very few Western sees were represented: only eight delegates in all), and they were given other privileges and gifts that dramatically marked their emergence from the era of persecutions.

Hosius came to Antioch in 324 and held a preliminary synodical meeting there to make investigation as to the cause of disagreements in the East. As a result of this, several leading clerics, Eusebius of Caesarea among them, were put on suspension until a fuller meeting could be held. This synod in 324 largely determined that when Nicaea opened its sessions in the following year, Hosius and Alexander would be the leading protagonists. All of this, one suspects, was surely done with the agreement of the imperial court and after consultation with the papal see, which had expressed clear confidence in Alexander. The council opened, therefore, at Nicaea on June 19, 325, after several weeks of symposia in the town, when the floor had been laid open, so to speak, for rhetorical presentations by various speakers, philosophers, rhetoricians, and clerics, all setting out the specific claims of their different parties. Later tradition, following Athanasius of Alexandria, says that three hundred or 318 bishops were in attendance for the formal session of the synod, but this figure is probably exaggerated because of biblical-typological rhetoric.[26] Two hundred and fifty is probably a truer figure.

As the meeting opened, Constantine took his place on the imperial throne and greeted his guests.[27] He spent the opening session accepting scrolls (secret petitions for favors and for redress) from the many bishops in attendance, and then startled them all the next day by bringing in a large brazier and burning the whole pile of scrolls before them—with the enigmatic words that in this way the debts

---

[26] Athanasius, *Epistle Ad Afros* 2. He is probably thinking of the symbol of the 318 in Gen 14:14. The number 318 in Greek symbology is the letter tau (which is also the cipher of the cross) followed by *I* and *H* (which is the abbreviation of the name *Jesus*).

[27] For a fuller analysis of the intellectual concerns of the synod see J. A. McGuckin, "The Council of Nicaea," in *The Seven Oecumenical Councils*, ed. S. Trostyanskiy (Piscataway, NJ: Gorgias Press, 2016). The conciliar decrees and letters are represented in the short reader at the end of this chapter.

of all had been canceled. By this he implied that most of the petitions from the bishops had been aimed at one another, and rather than put many on trial, he had given a common amnesty.

But one case was crying out for attention, and that was the appeal Eusebius of Caesarea had made against his deposition in 324. Constantine made it very clear that he expected Eusebius to be exonerated as part of the amnesty (he always tended to support and encourage learned bishops, possibly in fond memory of his own childhood tutor, the Christian theologian Lactantius). So, when Eusebius offered his church's baptismal creed as an example of the faith, he held it was deemed enough and he was rehabilitated. The council was quick to forestall and reject without much debate a blatantly pro-Arian creed that was then offered by Eusebius of Nicomedia. Eusebius of Caesarea's creed was also refused as the one the council would adopt as its *ekthesis*, or official statement. The statement they finally settled on was probably one built out of a matrix of the Jerusalem church's confession of faith (its baptismal creed) without the Origenian glosses Eusebius of Caesarea wished to attach. But to this framework the conciliar fathers were careful to add specific glosses of their own. These can be seen in the form of several emphatic repetitions of clauses and stressed insertions of clarification, all to the effect that the Son's divinity was not a nominal one but derived from his substantive relation to the Father, such as was not shared by anything in the created order. The council was firm on the issue that it would not rehabilitate those who resisted its creed: chiefly Arius and his Libyan episcopal supporters, as well as Eusebius of Nicomedia, who offered a strong and unwavering resistance. It was only his high rank that saved Eusebius of Nicomedia from the punishment inflicted on the lesser Libyan bishops, Theonas and Secundus, who were deposed and condemned to hard labor in the salt mines of Sardinia.[28] Eusebius was sent off in disgrace but bounced back soon enough and returned to imperial favor.

At Constantine's insistence, following Hosius's influence, the Nicene Creed contained the technical term *consubstantial* (*homoousios*) at a critical juncture, to describe the Son of God's relationship to the Father and thus his full divine status. It was a term that decisively vindicated Alexander's doctrine that the Son was born "out of the being/essence of the Father" (*ek tes ousias tou Patros*) and thus was "God from God" in every sense of what that concept meant. Into the basic creedal structure that had existed for several centuries beforehand, the bishops inserted several specific anti-Arian annotations and appended five specific anathemas (or denunciations) to proscribe all the major points of Arian teaching.

---

[28] More, one suspects, for obstinately refusing Constantine's command for *concordia* and rapprochement at his *vicennalia* than for the niceties of the theology they represented. This was a secular sentence levied against them. The ecclesial sentence was simply deposition from active ministry.

By such means the council affirmed a realist hermeneutic of the biblical analogy of Sonship and Fatherhood. It clarified that the traditional phrase "begotten from the Father" meant "from the essence (*ousia*) of the Father." It also turned to make specific clarifications of older, traditional statements about the Son's manner of procession from God. To avoid any lingering subordinationist hermeneutic of "a (secondary) god from (a higher) God," or "a (smaller) light from the (great) Light," it added the force of buttressing synonyms: "God from God, light from light, true God from true God," the repetitions serving to pile on emphasis. To leave no room for any Arian revisionism or retranslation of its intent, it also appended five specific sentences of condemnation (*anathemata*) of the cardinal points of Arian theology. In this way it was thought the Arian dispute could be definitively laid to rest.

This, of course, proved to be a hopelessly optimistic position. Partly this was Constantine's fault. The emperor (as can already be seen in his *Letter to Alexandria* in 324) positively discouraged any clarifying debate on the meaning of key terms.[29] Even the decisive term, *consubstantiality*, which he agreed to introduce as the primary emphasis of the synodical meeting, he wished to leave vague enough so that it could serve as a generic rallying point for the majority. Many there heard the word in different resonances. Some intended it as confessing the Son and Father shared the selfsame being. Some interpreted it as meaning the Son and Father had the same kind of nature, which was a much looser notion and which grew, in the years after Nicaea, when the council seemed to be a source itself of ongoing controversy, into the very broad church position of the Father and Son being "like one another" (homoianism) or even "substantially like one another" (homoiousianism).[30] In the post-Nicene era the party of Alexander, soon to be headed by Athanasius his disciple, regarded the homoians as out-and-out Arian recidivists. On the other hand, they eventually felt they could deal with the party of the homoiousianists, with whom they would come to some form of ecumenical agreement after a reconciliation synod held in Alexandria in 362.

Constantine himself had only one desire at the council, to get the largest harmony that he could, and so finding that only a rump of hardline supporters of the Arian concept would refuse to endorse the homoousian insertion, he pressed on with it. Accordingly, several bishops present there that day signed with varying understandings of core matters of christological detail, a factor that contributed to the doctrinal confusions that would follow in the Nicene aftermath for the next fifty years. In the years after Nicaea it is clear enough that Constantine drew away from Hosius of Cordoba as a religious adviser and gave his ear to Eusebius of Nicomedia,

---

[29] Cited in the short reader below.
[30] *Homos* being the Greek for "same" and *homoios* being the Greek for "like."

who would eventually baptize him as he lay dying just over a decade later. His dynasty, following after him and sustaining a policy that lasted until the death of Valens in 378, more or less supported a "soft Arian" position that allowed for a lot of vagueness in what was meant by Jesus' or the Logos's divinity.

After the formal sessions of Nicaea concluded, the *vicennalia* celebrations for the emperor began in earnest. The bishops received gifts of gold to accompany them home and were guests of honor at the festive banquets. Some returned as local heroes. Alexander and his deacon Athanasius went back in triumph to their city. Others fumed in exile (Eusebius of Nicomedia) and planned their revenge (which would not be long in coming). Eusebius of Caesarea worried and fretted as his carriage rattled back to Palestine, for he had told his local church that he would rather die than accede to any compromise pushed on him by the Alexander party, and now he had some explaining to do for having signed the creed with the *homoousion* in it.

Across the Christian East generally, the sustenance of the exact terms of the Nicene Creed became a matter of hard resistance, often in the face of imperial disapproval, suppression of sees, and enforced exiles of Nicene supporters. The caucus of the major Nicene theologians was Athanasius (succeeding Alexander) of Alexandria, Eustathius of Antioch, Eusebius of Samosata, Apollinaris of Laodicea; and (a younger caucus) Basil of Caesarea in Cappadocia, Gregory of Nazianzus, and Gregory of Nyssa. In the West indefatigable defenders of Nicenism were represented by the successive popes and by apologist theologians such as Lucifer of Cagliari, Hilary of Poitiers, and (the younger caucus) Jerome and Ambrose of Milan.

Some time later, after the accession of Theodosius I, the Nicene Creed was reaffirmed at the Council of Constantinople in 381, and then state support of Arian alternatives was withdrawn abruptly, and the Nicene Creed became the basis for the rapprochement of the Western and Eastern churches in a common statement of faith. Then it was preferred to remember Constantine the Great as the architect and proponent of Nicaea, not the emperor who chose to be baptized by an Arian sympathizer. He was then elevated as the supporter of true faith, and only his sons and successors were denounced as betrayers of the Nicene cause.

Despite the importance of the Nicene Council, a detailed record of proceedings (if there ever was one) does not survive. Historians now have only a random collection of letters, indirect testimonies, and later accounts of what went on. A *Synodical Letter* survives (announcing the council's decisions in Alexandria to interested parties there), and twenty "canons" or laws are also attributed to the council.[31] Their common theme is that of raising standards among the clergy and bringing order back into

---

[31] The synodical letter is in the short reader below.

church practice after times of persecution.[32] Some eyewitnesses wrote about the council many years afterwards, but several of our histories come from even later periods. Athanasius's and Rufinus's versions of the council events focus on the synod as a general assembly of bishops seeking consensus in the faith. Eusebius of Caesarea's account depicts it as being run closely by Constantine the Great, and it is often a detailed and vivid picture he presents, but one that is also careful to leave out details he did not like to dwell on. The later historian Philostorgius, in his own history of events written from a radical Arian (Eunomian) viewpoint, describes the conciliar agenda as being overdetermined by Hosius and Alexander of Alexandria. So the "neutrality" of these accounts from various sources is something of a problem. Evidently the history of such a momentous and divisive event still was tendentious many years afterwards.

Of course, after 381 Nicaea was elevated by the larger catholic church as the great watershed "council of all councils," the very standard of faith and the definition of catholicity henceforth. So it is no surprise that it attracts legends to it and amplifications. In its historical context it is more than likely that many bishops who attended did not affix to it the same "epoch-making" significance it assumed in hindsight. This was something the Alexandrian school of Athanasius fought hard to achieve, and that he did so was testimony to the often unspoken but solid support of the Latin church, especially the see of Rome, which refused to budge from the standard of Nicaea despite the later Constantinian dynasty's wavering on the issue of the *homoousion*, the consubstantiality of the Son with the Father.

**Searching for commonality and consensus.** Athanasius had been a young deacon in attendance on Alexander, and so privy to the preliminaries to the Nicene Council as well as, so tradition says, one of those attending the council itself, though not one who took an active part in any presentation there. In 328 Athanasius succeeded Alexander in a highly contested election. For many years afterward he had difficulties keeping a united front in the ecclesial affairs of his own church and attracted a growing number of international "enemies" to his person and doctrines, not least Eusebius of Nicomedia, who was determined to orchestrate Athanasius's political downfall in any possible way. His elevation to the see of Alexandria coincided with the period when Constantine and his sons were increasingly abandoning the anti-Arian policy that the Nicene doctrine of the *homoousion* of the Logos was meant to represent. Because he refused to allow the Nicene settlement to fall into obscurity, Athanasius soon became a prominent symbol of opposition to imperially sponsored consensus theology in the

---

[32]For a more detailed discussion of the legislation of Nicaea, see J. A. McGuckin, *The Ascent of Christian Law* (Crestwood, NY: St. Vladimir's Seminary Press, 2012), 193-203.

East and was deposed by ecclesiastical enemies at the council of Tyre in 335. He returned from exile and resumed his claims to governance of the Alexandrian church on the death of Constantine in 337, but he was soon forced to flee again and took refuge in Rome, where he was received as a champion of orthodoxy.

*The Synod of Serdica 343.* From this time onward Athanasius gained the constant support of the Western churches, who encouraged his resistance as a renowned "confessor." This was dramatically expressed in a synod held at Serdica in 343.[33] Athanasius had taken his case to the adjudication of Hosius, whom he had first met at Nicaea 325, and Hosius in turn arranged a large gathering of Western bishops to publicly try his case (since he had been deposed by Arianizing synods in the Eastern church) with a view to rehabilitate him. Pope Julius I successfully lobbied both the emperors (Constans in the West and Constantius II in the East) to hold this council to attempt a general reconciliation of all the parties divided over the Arian question. It largely turned on the issue of whether or not Athanasius himself, and all he stood for theologically, could be brought back into communion with the Eastern bishops who had several times anathematized him (and thus the Nicene doctrine he stood for) in the previous years, while at the same time he had also been exonerated and praised by leaders of the Western church. The emperors (vaguely) hoped that a formula could be arrived at Serdica that would, once and for all, settle the doctrinal divisions that had been running on for so long after Nicaea 325. What was really wanted was a reconciliation of East and West. It was felt important, therefore, to secure the heavy attendance of many Greek bishops.[34] These arrived, however, and old enmities resurfaced quickly.

Many of the Easterners were determined that Athanasius should not be rehabilitated on any grounds and passionately protested at the decision of Hosius to allow Athanasius to sit in the council itself. Their position was that he could not attend any episcopal meeting as a deposed cleric, certainly not one that considered his case. There were also sharp tensions between Athanasius and his former friend Marcellus of Ancyra.[35] Hosius tried to make backstage negotiations, attempting to move the animosity

---

[33]Serdica is now Sofia, the capital of Bulgaria.

[34]Hosius presided over affairs, and Pope Julius I was represented by the priests Archidamus and Philoxenus and the deacon Leo. According to Athanasius, bishops attended from Italy, Spain, Gaul, Africa, Britain, Egypt, Syria, Thrace, and Pannonia. Ninety-six Western bishops attended, with a lesser number of Easterners.

[35]See further J. T. Lienhard, *Contra Marcellum: Marcellus of Ancyra and Fourth Century Theology* (Washington, DC: Catholic University of America Press, 1999). Both he and Athanasius had been declared orthodox defenders of faith in the Synod of Rome in 340. They were being presented for rehabilitation at Serdica together. But Athanasius had come to realize that Marcellus was everything that the anti-Nicenes had cause to suspect. His "sameness of being" between the Father and Son was actually based on an archaic Monarchianist way of thinking; that is, he tended to think of the term as affirming a divine monad. Athanasius realized that unless he distanced

away from the figure of Athanasius himself and toward the greater plan of East-West unity, but his efforts were in vain. Fearing the Latin majority would outvote them, the Easterners vetoed the conciliar proceedings on the grounds that one council of the church could not contradict another (though this is exactly what had been happening in relation to the several synods held in the East bent on reversing Nicaea and ruining the careers of its defenders). They therefore left the council and decamped to the city of Philippopolis (in modern Bulgaria), where they brought out their own creedal statement. The Latin bishops were more determined to proceed when they saw this and quickly moved for the exoneration of Athanasius and two other bishops who had been deposed and who now presented their defenses. Athanasius was not asked for a defense: all charges against him were declared invalid. The Eastern bishops were then censured for their attitude, and some of their leaders were declared excommunicated.

The end result, therefore, was a significantly failed attempt at first reconciliation, but the Serdican synod made a significant statement by refusing to publish its own creed or any further amendments to that of Nicaea. This was a decisive underscoring of the enduring significance of the Nicene Creed of 325 and a loud indication to the East that it would be on these terms of faith alone that reconciliation could be effected in the future.

The final act of the Serdican council was to make several changes to church (thus state) legislation concerning bishops. These were aimed at putting an end to the turmoil caused in the preceding decades by conflicting synods and antagonistic bishops preaching across different sees, activities that were causing more confusion than settlement. The main Serdican canons, or laws, forbade wandering bishops, appeals of clergy direct to the emperor (short-circuiting synodical process), theologians being promoted to bishoprics in small villages (again a cover for nomadic bishop-theologians) or professors or rich people being advanced to the episcopate without many years prior service in the church so that their faith could first be assessed. The council concluded its work by sending two letters, one to the city of Alexandria and the other to the bishops of Libya and Egypt, announcing in the clearest terms that Athanasius and the faith he stood for had been exonerated. The Eastern emperor, Constantius II, responded negatively by confirming the order of the governor of Egypt that if Athanasius dared to appear once more in the city, to try to take up possession of his see, the soldiery should kill him on sight.

In the light of this stalemate, the Western emperor Constans, who had agreed to support the Western church's general support of Nicene doctrine, in 346 demanded

---

himself from Marcellus he could not explain to the many orthodox theologians (who agreed to the anti-Arian thrust but did not feel happy with the Nicene semantics) that the *homoousion* did not necessarily mean the implications witnessed in Marcellus.

Athanasius's rehabilitation from his Eastern imperial colleague. Reluctantly, Emperor Constantius allowed Athanasius to come back to Alexandria, but after Athanasius showed great energy in reconstituting the Nicene opposition (after a series of imperially nominated pro-Arian bishops there), Constantius lost patience with him after only a few months and he was once more ordered into exile, where he could be closely watched. To avoid these restrictions, he disobeyed the imperial decree (thereby again becoming an outlaw in the East) and fled to hide in the Egyptian desert. This was a time when he fostered his relations with the growing monastic movement, whose hero he publicized in his widely read text *The Life of Antony*.

He also began to sketch out a highly influential work explaining why a Christology of the divine Lord Jesus mattered as the central pillar of the church's evangelization of pagans. Here he thinks through the central logic that if the Word is truly God and personally assumed human life in the incarnation, it is primarily because he wishes, as the Logos who first made humankind for life, to convey to dying (mortal) humanity the divine and reparative gift of immortality. Athanasius sees the Word graphically wanting to do this in his own human body first of all, but then using this as a paradigm to work it through the rest of the human race. The Logos's divinization of his own flesh (making it rise from the dead, for example, or making it an energized source of miracles) was "natural" to him, Athanasius argues, because that flesh could only be energized by so close a presence of the divinity within it. But in the case of the rest of the human race, he goes on to argue, what the Logos incarnate is "by nature," he offers to the world "through grace." In other words, his personal immortal union of Godhead and humanity becomes the paradigmatic source of grace for how humans can be reconciled to God and in that restored communion find heavenly life.

This is essentially the great insight Athanasius added to the Nicene debate on metaphysics. He brings it down more closely into the working mechanisms of salvation theology, and he connects it more precisely to the sacraments. For example, he points out that if the Word is not truly God and does not wholly identify with a human life in the incarnation (as many Arians had argued) then the sacraments of Eucharist or baptism would simply be commemorative acts of remembrance. But traditionally, Athanasius counterargues, Christians have never looked at them in that light, seeing them instead as powerful graces that divinize their recipients. Only if the Logos is truly God and personally assumes humanity can the Eucharist be the flesh of God. If the Arians were correct, such a sacrament would not be worthy of adoration as the abiding presence of God on earth. Again, Athanasius takes theology out of the abstract and connects it with the actuality of sacramental, liturgical life in the churches. His message had a wide appeal. In his time in Egyptian internal exile he drafted up two treatises that depict this soteriological theology very simply and persuasively. For centuries afterward they remained popular as early "classics" of Christian spirituality. They are the *Contra Gentes* (*Against the Pagans*) and the *De Incarnatione* (*On the Incarnation of the Word of God*).

*The Synod of Alexandria 362.* On hearing of the death of the implacable Constantius II, in 362, Athanasius came out of hiding and once more returned publicly to Alexandria. Soon afterward, however, he was exiled once more by Emperor Julian, who did not want such a powerful figure to become a Christian rallying point when he was trying to sideline the church in a new return to pagan practices. But Julian did not live long enough to see his anti-Christian policy take any root at all. On that emperor's sudden death in Persia in 363, Athanasius was able to return to his followers in Alexandria in the following year under the more tolerant dominion of the Christian emperor Jovian. With the exception of another short exile in 365–366, this time Athanasius was able to stabilize his ecclesiastical administration of his church and so start to use the great city of Alexandria as a leverage in harmony with Rome and as the disseminating point for a massive effort to rehabilitate the Nicene doctrine in both parts of the empire.

The Nicene party had been so broken up in the Eastern Roman provinces over the previous forty years after the council (it had cost a lot to stay faithful to Nicaea) that the most pressing need for anyone to give Nicenism second wind was to effect reconciliation among theologians who were deeply suspicious of one another. In his later years, and using his reputation as a confessor of the Nicene faith who had endured much personal hardship for the cause, Athanasius worked hard to assemble a coherent international group of Eastern "Nicene" theologians who would finally start to work with one another. In a synod in Alexandria in 362 he made a striking move to harmonize the different parties of the larger anti-Arian alliance (especially the *homoiousian* party) by agreeing that precise vocabulary (were you for or against the *homoousion*?) was not as important as the reality of consensus in a Christology organized around the idea of the full deity of the Logos as the personal subject of Jesus. If theologians would confess these two fundamental principles—that the Logos was God of God in every sense of that (eternal Son of the eternal Father, coequal in glory to his Father) and that this divine Logos was the direct and personal subject of the Lord Jesus, who was God incarnate among humankind for its salvation—then the precise way of expressing that did not matter so much as the unity of faith it manifested.

This reconciliation activity was a major step forward to ensuring that the Nicene faith took hold in the East as much as it already had in the West. At stake was that a group of younger theologians were already making great strides in developing the full implications of Nicene Christology and trinitarian thought in powerfully conceived treatises. Some of the leaders of this movement came from Cappadocia. They have been known since collectively as the Cappadocian fathers, Basil the Great, Gregory of Nazianzus, and Gregory of Nyssa chief among them. But that whole Cappadocian area of the church had also committed itself to honoring the memory of St. Gregory Thaumaturgus, one of the first founders of Christianity there, and he had been a disciple of Origen when he was alive. So that whole church's tradition tended to entertain a dislike for "substance" language to describe spiritual divinity, seeing it as a hypermaterialist term ill fitting to a spiritual and immaterial reality. It was for such reasons that they had not liked the Nicene *homoousion* when they first heard it, and in the decades after Nicaea had preferred throughout the Cappadocian territories to speak about the Logos being "substantively like the Father" (*homoiousios*).

At first Athanasius had regarded them as just one more type of "defaulter" from Nicaea and had little time for them. Older textbooks relating to this period tended (wrongly) to call them "semi-Arian," but they were certainly not as enamored of the Nicene language as the Latins and the parties of Athanasius and Eustathius of Antioch were, not until it dawned on them that the decades of division and dispute they had lived through could really only be laid to rest by a common affirmation of what Nicaea had quintessentially stood for.[36] In his older and calmer stage of life, Athanasius also realized it was time to lay aside his suspicion of theologians who were not his closest allies: men like Eustathius of Antioch and the younger Cappadocians. He came to realize that if one added "like the Father in all things," as many of them already did, these others were more or less confessing exactly what he wished to defend in the Nicene theology. So he compromised and called a large meeting of theologians to Alexandria in 362, and there they set out the terms of a new Nicenism that would affirm the basics without worrying about the precise terms being used.

Paradoxically, this had the effect of gathering around him a much larger school of Eastern theologians that finally agreed that his understanding of the *homoousion* was the best and simplest technical term to rally round, as well as being a refined interpretation of Nicaea and its creed that met all the objections that "those of the same faith" had raised against it. Moreover, it was useful, as Athanasius continued to point out, because it was a term that flushed out all Arians of all sorts. Those who would not confess the central faith that the Logos was God and that he was also the personal subject of Christ, the God-Man, were all remarkable for refusing to admit the legitimacy of the *homoousion*. So the term and

---

[36]Those who were only willing to call the Logos *homoios* (like God) were, properly speaking, Arian. So too the more radical party using the term *anhomoios* (the Logos is unlike the Father).

the Nicene creed it was embedded in actually gained a new lease of life after the synod of 362. The way was set toward a final push to lay Arianism aside from the central faith confessions of the Eastern empire, though it would take another twenty years. The final push would come when the last of the emperors attached to the Constantinian dynasty would pass away. This took place with the death of Valens in 378.

Athanasius's late *Letters to Serapion* were also of major importance in the developing doctrine of the Trinity, a systematic that was the final elaboration of the Nicene faith. His work in creating a more widely based "Nicene party" was taken to its pitch by the Cappadocian theologians who came after him, especially the triad previously mentioned, who will be looked at more closely in due course. Athanasius's policy of reconciliation came to fruition with the accession of the Spanish general Theodosius as emperor in the East; he summoned the Council of Constantinople in 381 and established Nicene orthodoxy as the subsequent standard for the churches of the eastern and western Roman empire. Athanasius had spent his life in this cause, but he gave up his soul eight years before he could see the final fruits of his labors. He died in Alexandria on May 3, 373.

**Athanasius's opponents.** *Eusebius of Nicomedia.* If Athanasius was seen as the public face of Nicenism, it was Eusebius of Nicomedia (d. 342) who was the personification of the early (and bitter) opposition.[37] He had shared a common teacher with Arius in the person of Lucian of Antioch. He was a highly placed aristocratic bishop, first of Beirut but then transferred at the invitation of the emperor Licinius to preside over the new imperial metropolis of Nicomedia in Bithynia. He had many friends in the new Constantinian court and wider administration because of his enduring friendship with Constantia, Constantine's sister and former wife of Licinius. When Constantine arrived in the East, Eusebius gained his ear very quickly and soon supplanted Hosius as his closest adviser for religious and philosophical affairs. When the emperor was dying, in a camp during army field exercises, it was Eusebius he chose finally to baptize him into the Christian faith. In 339 Constantine invited him to transfer once again to be first bishop of the new capital at Constantinople, and he ensured that the imperial city, with few exceptions, would be governed by anti-Nicene bishops for many years to come.

---

[37]The other "grand defenders" of Nicaea were less notorious, perhaps: Hosius of Cordoba and Hilary of Poitiers for the West, as well as a succession of the Roman popes. For the East: Eustathius of Antioch and Eusebius of Samosata, who was the mentor of the younger Cappadocian fathers. For many years the energetic ascetic bishop Eustathius of Sebaste was also a key defender of Nicenism and trained the young Basil of Caesarea in that cause. But Basil decisively broke from him over his unwillingness to explicate the theology of Trinity, which the younger Nicenes saw as the ultimate logic of Nicene faith.

When Arius's trial and deposition were first reported to him, Eusebius knew immediately that if Arius was to be condemned for such a theology, he himself would face trouble soon enough, and so he went on the offensive. He made it clear, even before Nicaea opened, that he was not in the business of giving allegiance to a presbyter's personal opinions (though he remained a steadfast and loyal supporter of Arius, defending him to the end of his life). What was at issue was a whole way of conceiving of the divine being. Christianity had to apply logic to its conception of Godhead and limit the "excesses," as he saw them, of both the Monarchian tendencies still prevalent in the church and the tendency of the Logos school to speak of coequality or "full deity" in reference to the Word of God, which he saw to be biblical code for the subservient agency of God working in the creation.

At the Council of Nicaea Eusebius reluctantly accepted the *homoousian* creed but refused to subscribe to the condemnation of Arius himself, for which Constantine deposed and banished him. He was recalled within two years, however, and was ever after the emperor's close confidant. Constantine wished to move to a consensus theology that could be established in the East, and Eusebius argued strongly that the best chance he had of this would be to abandon the strict reliance on the Nicene *homoousion* (which the West stood by) and move instead to a vaguer type of Logos theology that was more open to a subordinationist Christology. Realizing that Eusebius was a prime mover in the unraveling of Nicaea and that he was using synodical process to have his chief opponents tried for defective teaching or incompetence in administration and deposed from office, the Nicene party turned against him as its chief enemy. Eusebius scored a victory in managing to secure Athanasius's deposition at the Arianizing Synod of Tyre in 335.[38] He also secured the deposition of other leading Nicene opponents, including Eustathius of Antioch and Marcellus of Ancyra.

In 341, the year before his death, Eusebius presided over the Dedication Council (*In Encainiis*) at Antioch, an event that marked the ascendancy of official Arianism

---

[38]Constantine was furious with Athanasius for refusing to admit Arius back to communion in Alexandria, which he had occupied as bishop since 338. In 338 Athanasius was summoned for trial (on specious charges of black magic and murder) to a synod at Caesarea, where Eusebius of Caesarea and Eusebius of Nicomedia would be present. He refused to come for it. The emperor made it clear to him that if he did not attend the synod to be held at Tyre he would be brought forcibly. Athanasius brought with him forty-eight Egyptian bishops in support, but the 310-member synod condemned him for the charges and ordered his deposition. A personal appeal to the emperor at Constantinople gained him more justice. He was cleared of all ecclesiastical charges, but the emperor convicted him (through his spy system) of having rashly threatened to cut off the grain supply to the capital from Africa if he were removed from his city. On the basis of this charge, which he could not deny, he was exiled to Trier in the West and could not return to Egypt until Constantine's death in 337.

for the next generation in the East.[39] The council issued a creed that explicitly censured some of the more "extreme" tenets of Arius's thought (aspects currently being stressed by his more radical followers Aetius and Eunomius), to the effect that the Son of God "came from nothing" or "came from a different essence than God" (*heteras ousias*) or that "there was when he was not." These classic aspects of Arian subordinationism were held up for condemnation. So while it looked on the surface that this was a certain kind of anti-Arian ecumenism, one did not have to look too hard to see the hand of Eusebius of Nicomedia present. For the statement of faith quite carefully takes out from the creed all reference to the *homoousion* and to the idea of the Son's true, or full, divinity, leaving it to vaguer biblical titles to give a sense of honor, without explicating the central point Nicaea stood for. It calls the Son the "firstborn of every creature" rather than the quite different meaning of the biblical term "firstborn of all creation." The Son here is an "exact image" (*eikon*) of the Godhead. In regard to the coequality of being and the Spirit's divinity, this creed is deliberately vague. But vagueness before an argument is one thing; vagueness after having had it clarified abundantly is another thing and amounts to the rejection of an argument.

The Dedication Creed, then, was heavily censured by Athanasius, who regarded it as no more than a soft version of Arianism for wider consumption. Eusebius's political acumen orchestrated this compromise so as to give the imperially favored "theological vagueness" a chance to spread widely in the East. Characterizing the Nicene party on the one side and the radical Arian party on the other as unacceptable extremes gave a coherence to the Arian movement, more so than Arius himself ever provided through much of its early development. The movement Eusebius set in motion would endure after his death for another forty years. Knowing his central importance in setting the tone of Constantius's religious policy, his posthumous followers were often called the "Eusebians" by their Nicene opponents.

*Aetius and Eunomius of Cyzikos.* Aetius (c. 300–370) was one of the most radical of the late Arian theologians. He was originally a metalworker trading at Antioch (his opponents called him a "tinker") who through native ability rose from humble origins to the position of renowned sophist and logician at Alexandria. He attracted imperial patronage as a scholar and educator, and he served as tutor and mentor to Caesar Gallus (later executed by Constantius in 354), who gave him the revenues of the island of Lesbos in recognition of his oratorical gifts. Aetius was ordained deacon by 345 but was implicated in the downfall of Gallus and exiled in 354. Councils at Ancyra (358) and Constantinople (360) condemned his teachings, but through the patronage of

---

[39] *In Encainiis* was so called because it was summoned together for the dedication ceremony of the new golden basilica at Antioch. Emperor Constantius was present for it, with one hundred bishops from the East.

Caesar Julian (Gallus's brother) he was rewarded with episcopal rank as a "roving bishop." His devoted secretary, Eunomius, became the most energetic spokesman of the school and looked after Aetius in his old age at Constantinople. After his death Eunomius wrote a hagiography ascribing miracles to his mentor and spurring the Nicene side to balance this out with claims for sanctity among their own party, too.[40]

Aetius pressed the implications of Christian doctrinal statements to their semantic limits. He was leader of the school that asserted ingeneracy (*theos agenetos*), or self-origination, as divinity's fundamental definition and argued that while the Nicene party who asserted the essential identity of the Father and the Son-Logos (*homoousians*) was mistaken, so too was the anti-Nicene majority, which had fallen into two camps, one affirming the essential likeness of the Father and Logos (*homoiousians*), and the larger school, which banned essentialist language and argued for the vaguer idea of the likeness of the two hypostases (*homoians*). As a result these radical Arians, who called themselves *heterousians* (because they professed that the Son-Logos was of a wholly different essence [nondivine] to that of the divine Father), were positively detested by Arian and Nicene factions alike.

Aetius was, then, a philosopher who specialized in logical semantics (he is reminiscent in some ways of early Wittgenstein). His chief and only surviving work is the *Syntagmation* (*Tractatus*), which demonstrates this logical syllogistic method of theological progress very strongly. Brief excerpts from it are in the reader below. If Self-Origination (*autogenes*) is a synonym for deity, he said (as most Hellenistic philosophical schools of his day would have agreed), then that the Son-Logos is not self-originate but rather "originates from the Father" means that he is not God. His bold way of stating logical syllogisms and affording them an absolute character of truth led him to the famous assertion of his school: that one could say all that there was to say about God, no mystery necessary. He defended the axiom that words (especially scriptural ones) revealed essences, not relations. On this basis he went on to argue that that the relation of the Son to the Father was one of complete dissimilarity (*an-homoios*). If the Father was quintessentially the Ingenerate, then the Son, being generate, was radically unlike the supreme Godhead. The Father was "essentially" Fatherhood, Aetius argued. The Son was "essentially" Sonship. They were two different things. God was God in himself. The Logos-Son was a creature, a servant of salvation honored by God.

Aetius's party called down the fury of all sides against it and was classed by opponents as the Anomoians (the "unlikers": also *anhomoians*, *anomoeans*), though

---

[40]Gregory of Nazianzus composed *Oration* 18 in 379, in honor of the blessed Athanasius, basically as a first great theological hagiography to solemnize the figure of the famous but often stormy Nicene stalwart of the first generation. By the next generation all the Nicene theologians of note were canonized as saints.

their own preferred self-designation was *heterousiasts* ("different essencers"). The moderate Arian party, such as that manifested at the Synod of Tyre, were annoyed that Aetius had resurrected the most objectionable aspects of Arius's original position, with a strong stress on the creatureliness of the Word. The Nicenes, on the other hand, found his position so polar opposite to their own that in refuting it they were able to marshal a whole set of reflections that led them through to the completion of their own system. It is in dialogue (often a hostile and tumultuous one) with these radical Arians that the Cappadocian fathers perfected their trinitarian theology. Aetius's work (and that of his close disciple Eunomius) stimulated Basil of Caesarea to compose his important defense of the deity of the Holy Spirit (*De Spiritu Sancto*) and spurred on Gregory of Nazianzus to compose his monumental defense of Nicene theology in his *Five Theological Orations*.[41]

In that refutation of central aspects of the neo-Arian agenda, Gregory argues that biblical words do not reveal essences, only relationalities, and this was an important influence in the Cappadocian development of trinitarian doctrine: taking paternity, sonship, and procession (of the Spirit, according to Jn 15:26) as descriptive of hypostatic relationality within a single essential being (*ousia*) of the Father's own Godhead. Thus the Son was originated from the Father: hence not Unoriginate (*agenetos*), but certainly still fully God, because unoriginateness was not definitive of God's being (*ousia*) but rather only of the Father's person (hypostasis). Likewise with the Spirit: the Spirit and Son both possessing no other divine essence other than that single divine essence that belonged to the Father (as unoriginate hypostasis) but that was freely gifted to both Son and Spirit to have as their being. And so all three hypostases were coequal and singular in all respects of being: entirely one and the same in essence (*ousia*) and honor (*time*) and powers (*energeia*), and three in their distinctive communion of hypostatic relations. This accounted for different roles in the economy of salvation, the Son and Spirit bringing all creation in atonement and sanctification to the unity of God the Father. Gregory described the process, or economy of trinitarian salvation, as to the Father, through the Son, in the Holy Spirit. It is arguable that without the spur of Aetius's radical reductionism in theo-logic (Gregory certainly preferred the language of poetic mysticism to set against his school), the classic neo-Nicene position might not have been elaborated so concisely or so well.

It was Eunomius who more or less ensured this would happen; when hearing that Gregory of Nazianzus had moved to Constantinople on hearing of the death of Valens, he too hired a building in the city, and both theologians started a preaching

---

[41] *Orations* 27-31. See text and commentary in F. W. Norris, *Faith Gives Fullness to Reasoning: The Five Theological Orations of Gregory Nazianzen* (Leiden: Brill, 1991). See also J. A. McGuckin, *St. Gregory of Nazianzus: An Intellectual Biography* (Crestwood, NY: St. Vladimir's Seminary Press, 2001).

campaign aimed at offering their versions of the faith to the capital's public. Gregory used his cousin's villa near the Hippodrome, consecrating it as a little church because the anti-Nicene bishop of the city refused to allow him to celebrate in any of the churches there. Eunomius made sure that Gregory's lectures were filled with hecklers (until Gregory got wise and himself hired Egyptian sailors as bouncers). Knowing that it was likely that a pro-Nicene emperor would be appointed shortly (as indeed Theodosius I was) and would remove the state oppression of Nicenism, Gregory was spurred, by Eunomius's many attempts to convict him of obfuscation, to provide a strong defense of the necessity to use more than logical syllogism in addressing the great mystery of God: to use the idea of mystery as a starting ground of wonderment, but to follow logic properly and in attentive reverence to the deeper sense of Scripture (not merely elevating a series of dislocated proof texts). Eunomius's *Apology* survives, as does his *Confession of Faith* and numerous sections of his *Apology for the Apology*, which are cited in Gregory of Nyssa's defense of Basil from Eunomius's very bitter personal and posthumous attacks. Theodosius exiled Eunomius to the Cappadocian countryside after the pro-Nicene council of 381.

## THE CAPPADOCIAN THEOLOGICAL SYNTHESIS

In many ways this council of 381 can be seen as the final victory of the older Nicene party, put in place by the younger generation of Cappadocian theologians, who provided its theological text. The later Christian tradition, retrospectively recognizing Nicaea 325 as the first of the great "ecumenical" councils, calls the Council of Constantinople 381 the second of that line.[42] Thereby the catholic tradition sets to the side all the false starts and dead ends of the many synods that littered the fourth century between Nicaea and Constantinople. In a clean line it redraws the topography of the fourth century—not in a historical or linear manner, but in a theological manner: from this council to this council only. This is the line of development of the classic catholic and orthodox Christian faith.

To this extent, then, those present at Constantinople in 381 had a distinct sense of knowing that they were about the business of reconciling the Western and Eastern parts of Christendom on the basis of the Nicene Creed. The additions the later council makes to the original statement are few but significant, for they underscore how it is the trinitarian doctrine of one *ousia* and three hypostases that finally gives logical coherence to the understanding of how the Son Logos's relation to the Father can be conceived. This giving of a trinitarian home to christological doctrine, casting

---

[42]The word *ecumenical* comes from the Greek *oikoumene*, which means "worldwide": that is, having international importance and authority for the great church tradition. It has no relation to the modern use of the term *ecumenical* to connote charitable interchurch relations.

it as fundamentally a soteriological process, was the achievement of the Council of 381. But to get there it took a lot of effort, which the Cappadocian fathers demonstrate in their theological works.

**Basil of Caesarea (330–379).** Known even in his lifetime as "Basil the Great," he was the most dynamic and politically active of the Cappadocian fathers, if not the most original thinker among them. He was the son of a rhetorician, from a wealthy Christian family. He studied in Cappadocia (where he first met Gregory of Nazianzus, one of the most learned men of his age, equally dedicated to the defense of Nicene faith), then in Constantinople, and finally for six years at Athens, where his friendship with Gregory of Nazianzus was deepened into a lifelong alliance. In 355 he returned to Cappadocia and taught rhetoric for a year before he made his way (probably in the company of Eustathius of Sebaste, an early mentor) to tour the ascetical communities of Syria, Mesopotamia, Palestine, and Egypt. Basil was baptized on his return to Cappadocia and embraced the ascetical life under the influence of Eustathius and his own sister Macrina, who had already adapted their country estate at Annesoi in Pontus as a monastic retreat. Here he invited Gregory of Nazianzus, though the latter found the style of organized egalitarian monasticism not to his taste, preferring a more scholarly seclusion on his own estates.

Gregory and Basil collaborated in producing the *Philocalia* (a first edition of selected passages from Origen) as well as writings about the monastic life. This early work of writing manuals for the ascetics gathered around them (especially Basil's *Asketikon*, though some see the latter as a work of Eustathius) had a historic impact in the form of the "monastic rules" that later gave Basil the title of "father of Eastern monks." The *Moralia* came first in 358 (largely traditional ascetical maxims attached to their biblical proof texts) and was followed by the *Asketikon* circa 363 (which is what most refer to as the "rule of Basil").

Although Basil has traditionally been associated with monastic withdrawal, he was in fact a very energetic churchman, politician, and apologist. He traveled widely with Eustathius of Sebaste in tours that were meant to offset the rising influence of Arianism in the east, and he was the main speaker at several events attached to synodical and other large church assemblies. In this early activity he gained a reputation for himself as one of the leading anti-Arian disputants of the age. Growing dissatisfaction with the theological position of Eustathius put a distance between Basil and his mentor, and from that time onward he begins to see that his rootless ascetic's life of traveling around might be less useful, if he wanted to influence church affairs, than a solid base somewhere. The chief metropolitan see of Cappadocia at Caesarea was the obvious choice.

Ordained a reader in 360, Basil's first public appearance was as a newly ordained deacon, attacking the *Syntagmation* of the neo-Arian theologian Aetius in a public debate held between the two of them at Constantinople in 360. His very cold reception at the capital encouraged him to settled back at Caesarea, and he was ordained priest for the cathedral church there in 362. His encounter with Aetius and Eunomius in 360 made him realize that they were the systematicians of Arianism that he most wanted to deconstruct. Their robust insistence that the *homoousion* doctrine was blasphemous had led at that council to an imperially aided policy to depose homoiousianist bishops (those who were close in faith to the Nicene party) in many key cities of the East.

This unhappy experience at Constantinople in 360 led Basil to focus much of his anti-Arian arguments thereafter on the heterousiast school. In his resulting mature work *Contra Eunomium*, he begins his attack on the heterousiasts with a denial of their major premise: that God is defined as the Ingenerate One (*agenetos*). If the Son is generated as Son of the Father, they had argued, then he cannot be God from God but in terms of logic must derive out of the deity as a generated being and therefore be a creature of the single God-Father. Basil applies Aristotelian categories against Aetius and Eunomius (who prided themselves on their Aristotelian logical methods) to argue that ingeneracy is an aspect of a conception of God (an *epinoia*), not a substantive definition of deity.[43] Ingeneracy (*agennesia*), he explains, describes the "how" of God's being, not the "what" of it.[44] We might know "that" God is, but to know "what" God is remains beyond our limited human conception. In other words, it is fundamental for Basil that we can know God only from his revelations to us, and this knowledge lies along the pathway of his external energies or activities in the world (*ek men ton energeion*), not his unapproachable and ineffable essence.[45]

Early in his *Contra Eunomium* Basil addresses the Arian refusal of the *homoousion* directly. They cannot accept it, he says, on the specious grounds that it smacks of Sabellianism, that is, as if it necessarily and unavoidably connoted that the Father and the Son were one and the same reality, an indistinguishable essence considered as a "thing," a *res materialis*. A more refined understanding of philosophy and logic

---

[43] *Contra Eunomium* 1.7.

[44] Ibid., 1.11: "Our reasoning shows us that the concept of unbegotten does not occur in relation to the 'what' of the divine nature (*en te tou ti estin anereunesei*) but rather, as I am somewhat straining to say, in the 'how it is' (*en te tou opos estin*)." In short, for St. Basil: "The essence of God is unbegotten, but unbegottenness is not his essence." See also 1.15.

[45] "We can say that we know the greatness of God, his power, his wisdom, his goodness, his providence over us and the justness of his judgments; but we do not know his essence.... We say rather that we know our God from his activities (*ek men ton energeion*) but do not presume to approach his essence. His activities (*energeiai*) descend to us, but his essence (*ousia*) remains inaccessible." Ibid., 1.12.

(again he deliberately accuses them of being inconsistent in their reasoning), he insists, would have allowed them to see that terms referring to the divine essence are not de facto conferring material limitations on it.[46] Basil's central point is that *homoousion* primarily means that whatever is properly referred to the divine essence of the Father is referable also to the divine essence of the Son, the essence being a common and shared one (*to tes ousias koinon*).

He concludes that the Father and Son are related both substantially and hypostatically, giving at once unity and differentiation: "For the divinity is one," he says, "and we can clearly see the unity as being according to the principle of the essence. Which means that the differentiation lies in the number, and in the properties that characterize each one; while in the principle of divinity, we see the unity."[47] This is clearly a reference to the full *homoousion* doctrine without naming it, without affirming it as the be-all and end-all of Nicene orthodoxy, which, he implies, can be sustained in parallel ways beside it for the wider Syro-Cappadocian church.

At home in Cappadocia, serving as the theological priest-adviser to his more easygoing bishop, Eusebius, Basil was actively involved in resisting the encroachments in his archdiocese of the heterousiast and homoian Arian parties.[48] Through his literary work he gained the wider renown of Nicene sympathizers, but also the enmity of many clergy in the outlying parts of this large ecclesial see. At first attached to the homoiousian party, which was the dominant position in Cappadocia, he increasingly aligned himself with the defense of the Nicene creed (and the homoousian party). He was an early advocate of the position that the Son being "substantially like the Father in all things" was a (better) synonym for the *homoousion* of Nicaea that had caused so much dissension. Soon, however, he fell out (a mix of philosophical and personality conflicts) with his local bishop and retired to his estates until, in 364, the threat of an installation of an Arian bishop of the entourage of the visiting emperor Valens, intended to spread pro-Arian polity by ousting local hierarchs not attached to the cause, panicked Eusebius sufficiently to petition Basil to return to his clerical staff. Gregory of Nazianzus mediated that return, and the threat from Valens was deflected, though Basil's new ascendancy earned him several more enemies among the local Caesarean clergy.

In 368 Basil administered the church's relief effort for a great famine in the region and won the lively support of the common people. In 370 he was elected bishop of

---

[46] The *Syntagmation* had been published in the style of a treatise on logic, and Eunomius made the attack on Basil very personal by caricaturing him as incapable of logical thought: "a mere provincial farmer."
[47] *Contra Eunomium* 1.19.
[48] Eusebius here being the incumbent of Cappadocian Caesarea, not to be confused with the learned bishop Eusebius of (Palestinian) Caesarea.

his city, despite the opposition of the town curia and many regional bishops. Shortly afterward, his great metropolitan diocese of Cappadocia was divided in two by imperial decrees (Basil decried it as a pro-Arian ploy meant to weaken his influence), and to offset the growing influence of the parallel metropolitan, Anthimus of Tyana, Basil desperately tried to fill small towns with new episcopal ordinations drawn from his circle of friends. It elevated Gregory of Nyssa and Gregory of Nazianzus to episcopal status (in insignificant villages) but also caused rifts even among his immediate circle, who felt his machinations were chiefly squabbles about revenues dressed up as theological conflicts. As he moved more and more to become the public face of the Nicene party, Basil stood in alliance with Meletius of Antioch, one of the old Nicene stalwarts. This alliance (which brought him into conflict with Athanasius and Pope Damasus, who profoundly distrusted Meletius) he saw as fundamental for the Nicene cause in the East, and he was faithful to it, even though it definitively alienated his old friend and mentor Eustathius of Sebaste, who more and more openly espoused the pneumatomachian doctrine, denying the deity of the Holy Spirit.[49] The public breach with Eustathius was marked by Basil's publication of a highly influential work: *On the Holy Spirit* (books 1-3), in which Basil affirms the deity of the Son and Spirit and paves the way for the full neo-Nicene confession of the Trinity, which Gregory of Nazianzus would elaborate at the Council of Constantinople in 381.

Basil died, worn out with his labors, in 379. His letters are major sources of information about the life of the church in the fourth century. His *Hexaemeron*, or interpretation of the creation through the Genesis account, is a masterpiece of early Christian scriptural theology and shows him as a moderate Origenist, with a fine feel for the moral power of Scripture. His treatise *Against Eunomius* was a major force revitalizing the Nicene resistance, and he did much in his time to persuade the homoiousians that their position was in substance reconcilable with that of the homoousians, a key element for the long-term success of the Nicene cause. His work in his church as teacher and public defender of his town (he instituted the building of one of the first major hospital sites staffed by Christian monks—an innovation whereby he subordinated the monastic impulse to solitude to the church's missionary needs) made Basil a model for all future Eastern bishops, and in Byzantine times he was designated along with Gregory of Nazianzus and John Chrysostom as one of the "three holy hierarchs," the most important bishop-theologians of the ancient period. Their corpus of works became the fundamental source for all trainee theologians in the Eastern Christian world afterward.

---

[49]The word *pneumatomachian* was invented by the Cappadocian Nicenes and means "fighters against the Spirit of God" (because they denied the hypostatic distinctness, as God, of the Holy Spirit).

***Gregory of Nazianzus (329–390).*** Gregory was the son of a wealthy landowning bishop in Nazianzus, Cappadocia (also named Gregory). He received the finest local schooling and then (with his brother Caesarios) was sent to Alexandria, and finally to Athens, where he spent ten years perfecting his rhetorical style and literary education. He was, without doubt, the finest Christian rhetorician of his day and is certainly the most learned bishop of the early church.[50] His sea journey to Athens in 348 was interrupted by a violent storm and, fearing for his life, Gregory seems to have promised himself to God's service, a vow he fulfilled by accepting baptism at Athens and beginning his lifelong commitment to the ascetical life. It was a dedication he saw as entirely consonant with the commitment to celibacy required of the serious philosopher (*sophrosyne* being an academician's virtue in the ancient tradition before it was appropriated by monastics). Gregory did much to advance the theory of early Christian asceticism, but always with the stress on seclusion in the service of scholarly reflection.

He regularly describes Christianity as "our philosophy." At Athens he shared lodgings with his friend Basil of Caesarea. Returning to Cappadocia in 358, Gregory's plans to live in scholarly retirement on his family estate were rudely interrupted by his father, who forcibly ordained him to the priesthood in 361, intending to utilize his talents in the day-to-day administration of the Nazianzen church. Not having that lifestyle in mind, Gregory fled in protest to Basil's monastic estates at Annesoi, where he edited the *Philocalia of Origen*, an edition of the works of the great Alexandrian that abstracted "the very best of" as a guide to preachers who wanted exegetical theory and method lessons.[51]

He soon returned to assist in the administration of his local church, and in 363 Gregory led the literary attack against Julian's imperial policy of barring all Christian professors from holding educational posts in the empire (*Invectives Against Julian*) on the grounds that if professors did not believe in the gods the literature celebrated, they must be forbidden from teaching that subject. In the *Invectives* he models himself on the *Philippics* of Demosthenes and castigates the emperor as one of the stupidest men ever to have held high office. In 364 he negotiated Basil's reconciliation with his bishop and eventually, in 370 assisted him to attain the episcopal

---

[50]For a much fuller treatment see McGuckin, *St. Gregory of Nazianzus*.
[51]Already Origen's metaphysical speculations were causing some damage to his posthumous reputation. Gregory's edition, for which he called Basil to his aid, protected and disseminated Origen's principles of allegorical exegesis for centuries to come. The *Philocalia* is more or less an anthology from Origen's works, focused on biblical interpretation and removing some of his wilder speculative elements.

throne at Caesarea. Thereafter began their long alienation. Basil accused him of pusillanimity, and Gregory regarded Basil as having become too high and mighty.

In 372 Basil and Gregory's father conspired, against his will initially, to appoint him as bishop of Sasima in a project designed to reduce the influence of Basil's rival Anthimus of Tyana. Accordingly, Gregory found himself dropped in a miserable frontier town at the center of an argument over local church politics, and, deciding it had nothing to do with doctrinal substance, he refused to occupy the see. He assisted his father as suffragan bishop of Nazianzus instead and began his series of episcopal homilies, all of which were taken down by scribes and edited at the end of his life for publication as a basic dossier of "sermons on every occasion" for a Christian bishop. In this guise they enjoyed an immense influence throughout the later Byzantine centuries.

From the outset Gregory stood for the Nicene cause of the *homoousion* and advanced it to the classic neo-Nicene position of demanding that the *homoousion* of the Holy Spirit (namely, that the Spirit is consubstantial with the Father just as the Son is) should also be recognized. His famous defense of this, in *Oration* 31, is presented in excerpt in the reader at the end of this chapter.[52] In this he thereby became the primary architect of the classical doctrine of the coequal Trinity, wherein the Son and the Spirit each received from the Father the gift of the single and selfsame being of the Father and thus were one in essence, though three in person.[53] His theology of the incarnation is equally impressive. Against Apollinaris of Laodicea he advocated the thesis that "what is not assumed is not saved," to insist that the Logos incarnate in Christ was truly human in all respects, except sin (which was not, in his book, an integral part of humanity but a lapse from it).[54]

Gregory also took the idea of God's merciful humility and self-emptying (*kenosis*) as the major rationale for a theology of the incarnation. He describes the incarnation as God's self-humbling before the altar of sacrificial love.[55] His argument with the heterousian theologians Eunomius and Aetius is most particularly on this point: that they find the ascription of suffering and death to Christ, if he is considered as divine and consubstantial with the Father, a terrible "injury" to the

---

[52]For an Engish translation (with commentary) of the full text of Gregory's masterwork, the *Five Theological Orations* (*Orations* 27-31), see F. W. Norris, *Faith Gives Fullness to Reasoning* (Leiden: Brill, 1991).
[53]See further J. A. McGuckin, "Perceiving Light, from Light, in Light: The Trinitarian Theology of St. Gregory the Theologian," *Greek Orthodox Theological Review* 39, nos. 1-2 (1994): 7-32.
[54]"What the Logos has not assumed he has not saved." Gregory took the phrase from Origen's *Dialogue with Heracleides* and extended it to teach that it implied the incarnate Logos must have had a human soul since it was this, primarily, he came to heal and sanctify.
[55]*Oration* 37.3 (PG 36.285B).

dignity of the Godhead. For Gregory this alleged "cause of dishonor" is actually the cause for the greatest wonderment and praise of God. The humility of God is not a shame but a source of glory and divine salvation, that the Lord himself should stoop so mercifully to repair the pains of death so prevalent in a corrupted human nature.[56] Gregory himself expresses wonderment how the Arians can have missed the central mystery of salvation, according to the teaching of the apostle in Philippians, that it is Christ's very *kenosis* that is the cause of his exaltation to glory.[57] Basing himself on the apostolic text that the cross remains to his day "a scandal to the Jews and mere folly to the Gentiles" (1 Cor 1:23-24), Gregory adds in a third party of offense, adding, "And let the [Arian] heretics too, talk on until their jaws ache; but even so," he insists, it is the passion of the Christ that "justifies us, and effects our return to God" (Eph 2:16; Rom 4:24–5:1).

Over the years they were clerical colleagues together in Cappadocia, Gregory constantly pressured Basil to make his own position on the divinity of the Holy Spirit clear and led him, eventually, to break with Eustathius of Sebaste and declare openly for the deity of the Spirit of God. On his father's death in 374 Gregory retired to monastic seclusion, putting the local church under the care of a caretaker presbyter, Cledonius, but he was summoned out of his retreat in Seleucia, after Valens's death gave new hope for a Nicene revival, by the leaders of the Council of Antioch (379).[58] This key Nicene power group directed him to assume the task of missionary apologist at Constantinople, where he had high-ranking family in residence. He began, in 379, a series of lectures in Constantinople on the Nicene faith (*The Five Theological Orations*) and was recognized by the leading Nicene theologians—Meletius of Antioch, Eusebius of Samosata, and (initially) Peter of Alexandria (though not by Pope Damasus)—as the true Nicene bishop of the city. When Theodosius took the capital in 380, his appointment was confirmed when the incumbent (Arian) bishop Demophilus was exiled.

In 381 the Council of Constantinople was held in the city to establish the Nicene faith as standard in the Eastern empire, and when its first president, Meletius, died suddenly, Gregory was formally elected in his place, publicly announcing his right to govern the capital as archbishop. His mild and reasoned leadership (and also probably his prosecution of the doctrine of the *homoousion* of the Spirit) soon brought the council into crisis, and he concluded that resignation was his only way

---

[56]*Oration* 37.4 (PG 36.285C).
[57]*Oration* 38.14 (PG 36.328B).
[58]Especially Meletius of Antioch and Eusebius of Samosata, who wanted Gregory to "soften up" the capital with a preaching campaign since, from its foundation, it had been notoriously pro-Arian in sentiment, and not one of its churches professed a Nicene doctrine.

out (though he was surprised that the emperor acceded to it—he felt Theodosius should have had more backbone and supported him).[59]

Gregory retired to his estates in Cappadocia and composed a large body of apologetic poetry, which gives crucial information on the controversies of the time. In his final years he issued large amounts of poetry (some of it very good) and prepared his *Orations* for publication. In the Byzantine era Gregory was the most studied of all the early Christian writers. His theological works against Apollinaris were cited as authorities at the Council of Chalcedon (451), where he was posthumously awarded the title "Gregory the Theologian."[60] His writing on the Trinity was never rivaled for conciseness and depth, and he is the undisputed architect of the church's understanding of how the divine unity coexists in three coequal hypostases as the essential dynamic of the salvation of the world. It is a position we shall look at shortly, when we consider the doctrine of the Council of Constantinople 381.

**Gregory of Nyssa (c. 331–395).** This Gregory was the younger brother of Basil of Caesarea and friend and supporter of Gregory of Nazianzus, his elder contemporary. He had studied rhetoric in the villa of Gregory of Nazianzus and worked alongside the older man in many important episodes, not least the Council of Constantinople in 381, when he first sent the older Gregory his own deacon Evagrius of Pontus to assist him scribally and then came himself to the capital in 381 to offer his support to Gregory's preaching of the Nicene faith. The younger Gregory was before the 381 council somewhat overshadowed by his elder brother's work, and that of Gregory of Nazianzus, but after 381 he emerged as the leading Nicene advocate in the East. He had a high reputation as theologian and orator in his lifetime, but after his death his very philosophical style of writing (and some of his Origenian views, which were less diluted than those of his mentor Gregory of Nazianzus) caused his work to be quietly set aside in favor of the "three holy hierarchs."

In recent decades that neglect has been itself overturned, and the true brilliance of Gregory Nyssen's mind has more clearly emerged from scholarly analysis of the same. His theology of personhood, for example, was so developed that it brought him to be one of the only patristic theologians of this period who demanded an end to slavery on the grounds that it was an indefensible sacrilege (most others of his time advocated only that deep Christian charity should move God-fearing Christian owners to

---

[59]Gregory refused to press for civil criminal charges against those who had differed in faith, wanting instead to let all old scores be forgotten in the hope that it would accelerate a general reconciliation.
[60]Especially *Letters* 101-2 *To Cledonios*, and *Oration* 22.

manumit their slaves voluntarily).[61] He has intrigued a new generation because of his interest in apophatic mystical theology as, for example, in his *Life of Moses*, where he depicts the achievement of divine communion in the manner of entering a dark cloud of unknowing. His exegesis, particularly seen in such works as *Commentary on the Song of Songs, On the Christian Manner of Life*, and *On Virginity*, is deeply influenced by Origen's sense of the human soul being always innately driven onward to seek communion with the Logos. He is the most openly "Origenian" of all the Cappadocians, teaching that souls preexisted and that even souls in hell would eventually return to God.[62] His disciple and deacon, Evagrius of Pontus, later did much to disseminate Origen's influence on the Christian theory of prayer and asceticism.

Gregory was brought up and educated by his sister Macrina, who tried in vain to enroll him as an ascetic in the monastery she had founded on their familial estates in Pontus. Macrina was more successful in her influence over her brother Basil, who committed himself decisively to the ascetical life. Though Basil never admitted her influence, Gregory the younger brother always looked to Macrina with deference and eventually composed a *Life of Macrina*, depicting her in the manner of the dying Socrates, who discourses on her deathbed on the subject of the immortality of the soul.

Gregory was pulled into church politics by Basil, who ordained him in 371 to the newly created, tiny episcopal see of Nyssa (now Nevsehir in Cappadocia). In 376 the Arian faction in Cappadocia targeted him for his Nicene preaching and orchestrated his dismissal from his see on the grounds of financial mismanagement. He regained control of Nyssa following the death of Valens in 378, when the state-supported Arian incumbent was forced to flee. After Basil's death in 379, Gregory took up the literary cause against the Arian movement with renewed force, especially in his attacks on Eunomius, who continued, with particular spleen, to denigrate Basil posthumously. His own works *Against Eunomios* stand alongside Gregory of Nazianzus's *Theological Orations* as a classic exposition of the advanced Nicene thought on the sophisticated doctrine of *homoousion*: namely that it does not signify that the Father and Son (and Spirit) have "the same kind of composition" as one another (three members of the same class or genus, for example) but rather that the Father gifts his own single and selfsame being to them, to be their own being, instantiated in their respective hypostases as Son and Spirit.

---

[61] Especially see Gregory's *Fourth Homily on Ecclesiastes*, trans. S. G. Hall and R. Moriarty, in *Gregory of Nyssa: Homilies on Ecclesiastes: An English Version with Supporting Studies*, ed. S. G. Hall (Berlin: De Gruyter, 1993), 72-84. See also D. F. Stramara, "Gregory of Nyssa: An Ardent Abolitionist?," *St. Vladimir's Theological Quarterly* 41, no. 1 (1997): 37-60.

[62] Here he followed Origen's concept of the final *apokatastasis*.

After the Council of Constantinople in 381, it was Gregory of Nyssa who was commissioned by the emperor Theodosius to be the chief arbiter of Nicene orthodoxy for bishops in the region of Pontus. It was his role to ensure that Arianism was no longer professed by any active bishop there. Favored by the imperial court, he was specially called for to deliver the state orations for the funerals of Princess Pulcheria and Empress Flacilla. Apart from his works on asceticism and anti-Arian apologetic, Gregory also wrote on the full humanity of Jesus. He attacked Apollinaris's view that there was no need for a human mind or soul in Jesus Christ since the divine Logos inhabited him from birth and more or less replaced his human mental faculties. He rejected this theory as something that destroyed the very sense of the Logos assuming a real human life, and which also made nonsense of the theology of salvation, which understood the Word to have entered all aspects of human life (especially the mental and moral) so as to purify and sanctify them by his incarnate inhabitation.

Gregory became one of the early church's greatest expositors of the mystical power of the incarnation understood as a regeneration of human ontology. The divine incarnation, and especially the transaction of ontological power that this manifests in the fabric of the human being, is for him the core and central locus of human redemption. Gregory speaks of the act of incarnation as almost like a massive magnetic presence of God in Christ that "draws to himself" all of humanity. He says in one treatise,

> Mankind was led back to the true and living God, and those who through the adoption followed the Son were not cast out or banished from their paternal inheritance. Thus, the one who had made himself the firstborn of the good creation among many brothers (Col. 1.15) drew to himself the whole of that Nature which he had shared in through the flesh that was mingled with Him.[63]

For him, the incarnation was a uniquely bright locus of the overwhelming generic presence of God in the created order:

> For who, when they survey the universe, can be so simple-minded and uneducated as to fail to believe that there is Divinity in everything, penetrating it, embracing it, and seated within it? And this is because all things depend on He Who Is, and there can be nothing whatsoever that does not possess its being in He Who Is.[64]

This brightest point of all, however, is effectively the radiant light of the restoration of a perfect divine-human union, which is recreated by the divine Logos in his incarnation as the Christ:

---

[63] *On the Three Days' Interval*, in *Gregorii Nysseni Opera*, ed. E. Geberhardt (Leiden: Brill, 1967), 9:305.
[64] *Catechetical Oration*, c. 25.

Why, then, are people scandalized to hear of God's plan of revelation when it teaches that God was born among humanity? This same God, whom we are certain even now does not stand outside of humankind? Because although this last form of God's (incarnated) presence among us is not the same as that former presence, even so his existence among us is equally manifested in both; except that now the One who holds together in being all of nature is transfused within our nature, just as in earlier times he was transfused throughout our nature, and this in order that by this very transfusion of the divine our nature might itself become divine: being rescued from death in this way and set beyond the caprice of the antagonist. For his return from death [in the resurrection] became for our mortal race the beginning of our own return to immortal life.[65]

Gregory approaches the incarnational theology of redemption as a cosmic mystery. His favorite image for this is the cosmological cross that the Logos sketches over the whole world in the figure of his crucified self: the figure of a cross embracing the upper (heavens), the lower (depths of hell), and the wide horizons of the middle world (East and West). In this figure of the cosmic cross, Gregory argues that the incarnation in history was effected as an act of power, not a demonstration of weakness (as Arians had argued), since this divine humility was meant to regenerate a dying nature by giving it the power of life (the principle of resurrection). Here Gregory exegetes the Pauline theology of the mystical body of Christ:

> Since, then, what the whole of our nature needed was a lifting up out of death, he stretches forth a hand, as it were, to humanity, who lies prostrate, and stooping down to our fallen corpse he came so far within the grasp of death as to touch a state of deadness himself, and then in his own body to bestow on our nature the principle of the resurrection, raising along with himself the whole of humanity, as he accomplished by his power. But his own flesh, which was the receptacle of the Godhead, had come from no other source than the physical mass of our nature, and it was this that was raised up in the resurrection together with the Godhead. Following from this, then, we can see how, just as in the case of our bodies the working of one of the organs of our senses is felt immediately throughout the entire bodily system, which is thus united with that member, so also the resurrection principle of this single member of humankind [Christ] passes through the entire human race, as if the whole of humankind was a single living entity, and it is passed on from this single member to the whole body by virtue of the continuity and oneness of the nature.[66]

Gregory left behind numerous other works setting out the inner logic of the Nicene faith, but this previous treatise, his *Great Catechetical Oration*, was designed to serve as a guide for the deacons who instructed baptismal candidates. It is a

---

[65]Ibid.
[66]Ibid., c. 32.

fascinating introduction to sacramental theology and basic doctrinal themes from the fourth-century Nicene perspective and has since his time served many generations of Christians as an approachable summation of the Nicene faith.

## THE COUNCILS OF CONSTANTINOPLE 381 AND 382

The doctrinal settlement that the Constantinian dynasty preferred was one that clashed with the preferences of the Western churches and that of the church of Alexandria. The latter wished to hold hard and fast to the terms of Nicaea 325, where Arianism was seen as the arch-heresy denying the full divinity of Christ and the *homoousion* was seen as the only hope to preserve the faith of the church. But in the Eastern provinces, not all the various churches were convinced that the Nicene *homoousion* was such a good way forward. Because of the radical Arians, who continued to propagandize (led by Aetius and Eunomius in the heterousiast school), and their out-and-out teaching that Christ and the Logos were by no means to be considered as divine, being wholly and substantially "other than God" (*heteras ousias*), most of the Eastern bishops had definitively moved away from the stark postures of early Arianism that wanted to call the Logos a created servant of God. Traditional terms of liturgical reverence also moved them and their congregations this way.

But in that larger body of Eastern bishops there was a wide range of theology current. Some, such as the so-called homoiousian party, had a very similar faith to the Nicene party. They believed that Christ and the Logos were "substantially" akin to God. As Basil the Great would argue, if one added "in all things" to that confession, it was surely a synonym of the high Nicene confession of faith in the divinity of the Logos, and the Logos as personal subject of Christ incarnate. But a large body of other bishops, typified perhaps by the late Eusebius of Nicomedia and his settlement at the Dedication Council in Antioch in 341,[67] were content with a vaguer Christology of subordination that more and more abandoned the straightforward position "the Logos is not God" for a set of reverential statements about Christ that were meant to express his high honor. The Dedication Creed, nevertheless, insisted that the Logos was the "firstborn of the creatures," applying that to denote his pretemporal state qua Logos, not (as the Nicenes argued) denoting his primary position of honor as incarnated Christ within history and creation in his economy of salvation. The Dedication Creed tried to compromise, saying, "If anyone say that the Son of God is a creature like any one of the creatures . . . let him be anathema." But only to careless ears could this be taken to imply anything other than he was a creature and thus not divine.

---

[67]The synod *In Encainiis*. Text from Athanasius's *De Synodis* 23. English version in H. Bettenson, *Documents of the Christian Church* (Oxford: Oxford University Press, 1974), 41-42.

In succeeding years, after Eusebius's death, a set of variations was made from this basic broad Arian confession to try to make it more palatable in terms of honoring the Christ-Logos. In 345 another synod at Antioch brought out a new edition of the same, with a longer set of commentary notes, trying to reconcile Western opinion. It gained the nickname in the West of the "Long-Winded Creed" (*makrostitch*). It projected the catchphrase that the "Logos is like the Father" (*homoios to patri*) in the hope that this broad church might shelter both Nicenes and anti-Nicenes. It was to no avail. The West, and the Eastern Athanasian-Nicene party, began to realize how much it was in the interest of the wider Arian clerics to mask their stark syllogisms by vague language. The more they sensed this, the more stubborn they were on insisting there could be no replacement for the Nicene Creed. Bishops such as Ursacius, Valens, and Germinius wanted to keep up the stress on a more radical kind of Arianism, but not so stark as that of Aetius. They headed up a synod at Sirmium in 357, which was castigated by the Latin Nicene theologian Hilary as "the blasphemy of Sirmium," a nickname that stuck.[68] At their synod Ursacius and his colleagues tried to veto all mention of "substance," whether same substance (*homoousion*) or like substance (*homoiousion*), and then worked to apply state sanctions against any bishops who insisted on using these terms.

Another compromise move was made by the bishop of Palestinian Caesarea, Acacius, who gathered a second synod at Sirmium two years later in 359. He intended to soften the position of Ursacius and present a creed that could command a wider acceptance even in the West.[69] This was a product of the *homoian* party (the Son is "like the Father"). This followed the lead of Ursacius in some senses, removing all reference to substance because all matters concerning the generation of the Son "are beyond the understanding of humankind, and no one can explain the birth of the Son." The Acacian creed began by signaling that it saw itself as a universal statement of the catholic faith. Its preface started, "The catholic faith was published . . . on May 22." Athanasius poured ridicule on this opening: as if it could claim that it alone was the catholic faith and derived from the fourth century, instead of having been from the outset of the church's life and vested in its Scriptures, its liturgy, and the consensus of the believing people. For this reason he nicknamed it "the dated creed." Acacius described the Son of God begotten "before all substance," and went on, "And we decided to do away with all reference to the term substance, and no use must be made of it in future as a descriptor of God because the divine scriptures nowhere use it in reference to the Father and the

---

[68]The synod is described in Socrates Scholasticus, *Ecclesiastical History* 2.30.
[69]Described in ibid., 2.37; Athanasius of Alexandria, *De Synodis* 8.

Son.[70] But we say that the Son is like the Father (*homoios*) in all things, as the holy scriptures say and teach."[71]

A synod at Constantinople propagated this as the faith of the church. When this creed was published in the West, in Latin translation, the editors carefully removed the phrase "in all things" and reverted back to the simper *homoian* position of Ursacius and Valens (the Son is like the Father). It was this version that the Nicene theologian Jerome famously described in the following terms: "The world gave a groan, and woke, marveling, to find itself Arian."[72]

By dint of a policy of removing reference to "substance" terms, the various Arianizing parties used imperial legislation to have many senior pro-Nicene clerics deposed from office and replaced by adherents of their own parties. The Nicenes tried some tactics of appointing a "Nicene" bishop in sees that had Arians they wanted to oust but could not sustain it as a serious policy, since the Arian bishops had state support. Apollinarius of Laodicea instructed several of his younger ascetical followers to police episcopal elections in sees that were vacant and make sure that a Nicene candidate agitated for the post. The pope supported a rival Nicene candidate at Antioch to counter Meletius (who was also a supporter of Nicaea but no friend of Athanasius), and this caused years of internal rivalries among the Nicene party of the East. These exiles initiated by the Synod of Sirmium, however, were instrumental in bringing together in closer solidarity the Nicene party and the larger *homoiousian* supporters in the East. And this became a large group biding its time, waiting for better political climates, when it could oust the state-supported Arianism and its adherents in the episcopate.

That moment happened when the emperors of Constantine's immediate family had died out and Valens occupied the throne in the East. He vigorously pursued the pro-Arian policy. His bishop in the capital was Demophilus. Large-scale demographic movements beginning in the far East had put nomadic pressure of extraordinary severity on the banks of the Rhine, the northern frontier of the Empire. As tribes migrated westward, from the Far East, others were forced closer and closer to Roman borders. In the end the Goths were massed on the banks of the river, and in the particularly severe winter of 378, starving and freezing, they crossed over into the imperial territory in Thrace (modern Bulgaria) intent on marching to Constantinople to petition for the right to settle.

Valens decided that a ragged bunch of refugees posed no serious problem, but he was determined to scatter them away from the capital and punish their leaders. He

---

[70] He argued that this was because it had been largely misunderstood, it was not in the Scriptures, and "had given offense."
[71] English version in Bettenson, *Documents of the Christian Church*, 43-44.
[72] Jerome, *Dialogue Against the Luciferians* 19.

led out his armies from the capital for what he thought would be a short and uneventful campaign. But he took things too lightly. Commandeering a farm house, he and his senior military staff settled down one night for some heavy eating and drinking and did not notice that their camp guards had been assassinated by an advance group of Gothic warriors. Recognizing who was in the building, they quietly piled tons of brushwood up against it, setting light to a great bonfire that incinerated the entire senior staff along with the emperor.

The armies of Rome were in great disarray on discovering what had happened and fell back to the capital to defend it. The emperor of the West, Valentinian, ordered the immediate sending out of a punitive and defensive army from the West, and he elevated the Spanish general Theodosius to the imperial purple, instructing him to round up the Goths, who had by now disseminated across Thrace and into Greece, and then secure the capital at Constantinople. Theodosius began as most Christian emperors had, by being careful not to confuse his military career with ecclesiastical laws and requirements. For this reason, although he was a devoted, Nicene catholic when he set out, he was not yet baptized. Political and military life, requiring many violent deeds, was best felt to be set aside in advanced old age, when a baptism would render the soul innocent enough to prepare for its final end. In short, he was a catechumen. But passing through Greece, he was taken seriously ill with typhus, and being told that he was dying he sought and received baptism at the hands of a Nicene catholic bishop. He recovered soon after. But from that point onward, the realization that he was a baptized Christian emperor was not lost on him. His religious policy changed. He was now set on establishing the Nicene faith as the catholic creed everywhere, and in simplest terms he announced that he expected his loyal subjects in the East to adopt that faith represented by the bishops of Rome and Alexandria and all those in communion with them.

It would take him two years, until 380, to arrive at his capital. In those two years the Arian parties of the East suspected they were living on borrowed time as the new emperor made his way toward Constantinople. In 379 the Nicene party of the East sent word to Bishop Gregory of Nazianzus, living in retirement in Seleucia and renowned for his eloquence, to go quickly to the capital and begin a pro-Nicene preaching campaign. When he arrived there, all the churches were barred to him. His family, however, were high-placed aristocrats who owned property near the imperial palace and the Hippodrome.[73] The large villa was placed at his disposal, and he took it over, consecrating it as a church called the Anastasia, the "Resurrection Chapel," from where he preached his series of evening lectures on the real meaning of the Nicene faith. These

---

[73] Possibly the site of today's Mehmet Sokollu Pasha mosque in Istanbul.

have gone down in history as the *Five Theological Orations*, and at the later Council of Chalcedon in 451 they were recognized as sufficient exposition of the Nicene faith, making them, throughout the Middle Ages of both Eastern and Western Christendom, the primary theological reading of all those training for ordination.

During his delivery of those orations Gregory's villa was several times invaded by "hearties" sent from Eunomius, who was lodging nearby and mounting his own preaching campaign for the heterousiast position. Demophilus, the incumbent bishop, wished a plague on both their houses. After Gregory was heckled and had stones thrown at him ("the only banquet any bishop there offered me was pebbles," he recalled afterward) he co-opted a body of Egyptian sailors from the Constantinopolitan docks to act as bodyguards, and things proceeded more smoothly. In their presence he delivered *Oration* 18, a praise of the life and virtues of Athanasius of Alexandria that signaled widely that he was the one true defender of the Nicene faith. It secured the initial acceptance of Peter, archbishop of Alexandria, but the Roman pope was suspicious of him because of his known connections with Meletius of Antioch, whose reputation Athanasius had blackened (unnecessarily) at Rome. Gregory's work was very important in preparing for what everyone now knew would have to be a new "great council" held in the capital city shortly after Theodosius arrived.

Preparations for this became energized. Nicenes began to come back from exiles imposed on them by Valens. In preparation for the council (to be held in 381) Gregory asked for assistance from Gregory of Nyssa and received from him Evagrius of Pontus, a brilliant young theologian, to serve as his temporary deacon and scribe. In the advance guard of the council Jerome and Cyril of Jerusalem attended, as did the young protégé of Meletius of Antioch, Diodore of Tarsus, who was there to ensure the rights of Meletius to resume his see at Antioch, as the rightful Nicene incumbent, were safeguarded.[74] Gregory of Nyssa in his letters of this period says that when he arrived in the capital and asked for a loaf of bread, all the baker could talk about was the generation of the Son. This has sometimes been taken as evidence that the ordinary Byzantine was extraordinarily well versed in theology, but it is really meant as a wistful comment on how heated the population was at the thought of having to change official religious policy. The capital had, after all, had as its episcopal founder no less than Eusebius of Nicomedia, and almost all its successive bishops had been Arians to that point.

Gregory of Nazianzus was now insisting that not only should Nicaea be confirmed, with the *homoousion* of the Son and Father clearly stated as essential elements of the faith, but also that the last sixty years of reflection also had to be taken

---

[74]The Western church had established a rival there, Paulinus, to be their recognized Nicene hierarch.

into account, and the doctrine of the Holy Trinity had to be proclaimed as the only logical context for understanding the generation of the Son from the Father. His solution for a permanent "Nicene" settlement at Constantinople in 381, therefore, was a sophisticated and advanced statement that went beyond the creed of 325. In particular Gregory demanded that the council should declare the personal (hypostatic) divinity of the Holy Spirit of God and not leave this as vague and nebulous as the Arian parties had wished to leave the doctrine of the Son. For Gregory the Son was God from God: the Spirit equally was God from God. "Is the Spirit *homoousion*?" he asks, quite openly, and answers, "If he is God he is certainly *homoousion*."[75]

What Gregory taught was the classic doctrine of the Trinity. God the Father gifts his own being to the Son. The Son receives it by generation (*gennesis*), as Scripture calls it, that is, by filiation from the paternity of the Father. The image of "generation," Gregory insists, has nothing to do with material procreation (substance is being used analogously, not literally with reference to the eternal and wholly spiritual generation of the Son, he repeats many times), but it does connote that the relation of the Son and Father is not accidental or peripheral. It is like a Father's relation to his own flesh and blood. In the case of God it means that the Son comes out of the very being of the Father (*ek tes ousias*). But the Father is the single and sole *arche*, that is, the principal and cause, of the Godhead. In this role he is the sole God (*monos theos*) who "causes" his Son. This causality does not make the Son inferior, or secondary, or later in time, however, because the causing is eternally acted from God's own being and is nothing other than the gifting of the Father's being across to his Son, so as to be the very own being possessed by the Son too. In other words, the Son is God of God because he has his Father's being, not his own (separate) being. And the being of the Son is thus coequal, coglorious to that of the Father. All things that can be said of the Father can be said of the Son, with this exception: the one causes (begets), and the other is caused (begotten), and this causing or begetting is for the sake of the economy of salvation; for the Son will be the Lord of the world, bring it into being, and work for its restoration after it falls into alienation and thus mortality.

In regard to the Spirit, Gregory teaches also that the Spirit receives the same being of the Father, but not by filial generation; rather, as Scripture says (Jn 15:26), by "procession" (*ekporeusis*). So the Father "begets" the Son and "processes" the Holy Spirit out of his own single being, eternally and wholly, which means that all his divine characters and glories are equally gifted to the Son and Spirit. The Son is God of God, true God of true God, and so is the Spirit. The Son and Spirit are united together because the Father is the sole source of both of their respective beings, and their relation

---

[75]*Oration* 31 (excerpted in the reader below).

to the Father is their common bonding. In fact the mutual relationship of the three divine hypostases (persons) is based around the constant movement within the single divine being: to the Father, through the Son, in the Holy Spirit. This movement is the rationale of God's own (incomprehensible) eternal being. But it is also imprinted as the rationale of all the created order, too. All things, especially angels and humans, are meant to move to the Father, through the Son, in the Holy Spirit. For mortal beings, the Trinity is identical with the energy of salvation: it is the process of deification (*theosis*), Gregory says, being rendered like to God and thus saved. As to what the Trinity's life is from the viewpoint of God, eternally, one cannot say; except that it is constituted by great generosity, mercy, and all-embracing love.

Where had this been taught before? his critics asked. God has revealed it in all clarity in this last generation, Gregory answered, because only who is inspired by the grace of the Holy Spirit can preach the things of the Spirit. God only reveals the secrets of theology to those whose lives have been ascetically purified and manifest refined virtues. Gregory boldly proclaims himself, in *Oration* 31, to be the bright herald (*kerux*) of the Spirit for this last age of revelation. His opponents were enraged.

When the emperor arrived in the capital he appointed Gregory to be the administrator of the see, with the expectation of confirming his appointment as archbishop when the great council could be called together. And so Gregory started to instruct the candidates for baptism, that Pascha of 380, about the mystery of the Holy Trinity, into which the gift of the Spirit would initiate them. His deacons assisting him, however, were muttering so much that Gregory had to dismiss them. They were all that was left of the Arian clergy that had been installed in the cathedral, for Bishop Demophilus had fled (taking with him all the account books, as Gregory wryly remarked). The deacons were scandalized that Gregory should interpret baptism in this trinitarian way. As Arians they had been used to a form of baptism "in the name of Jesus" only, not in the threefold divine name of Father, Son, and Spirit.

Gregory's remarkable homilies *On the Lights* depict this monumental theology in the form of sacramental practice. Many other orations he gave after his occupation of the Cathedral of the Holy Wisdom began to set out this classic doctrine in simple forms the people could appreciate. In all, his doctrine clearly leaves behind the archaic suspicions of Nicene homoousianism. He showed that the "substance" involved here was not a kind of material substrate in which all the divine persons shared, as if they were members of the same special genus of god-substance. For Gregory what mattered was the singleness of the Father's being, which all three persons of the Triad instantiated (hypostatized) in a different energy of being that brought the transcendent divine presence out into the world of immanent realities.

One needed to be quite intelligent, however, to understand what Gregory was getting at. Not all the bishops who started to come to the council of 381 qualified in that regard. Many of them sensed that it was the time to get revenge on generations of Arian oppressors. They wanted lots of names to be struck off the register of bishops and sent into exile. Gregory wanted reconciliation, so as to give the council a real chance of taking root as a common statement of agreed faith. The Antiochene party wanted Meletius to be reappointed in charge of Antioch. He was the last surviving "great old man" of the earlier Nicene movement.[76] When he arrived in Constantinople, Gregory ceded to him the presidency of the council. But on the sudden death of Meletius in the middle of proceedings, Gregory himself assumed the leadership of the synod. The emperor stressed that he wanted the outcome to be "reconciliation of all parties," a rather optimistic hope. He especially wanted Gregory to make alliance with the party of thirty or so bishops who had firmly refused to add anything in the creed about the divinity of the Holy Spirit.

Athanasius, long before Gregory, had already dubbed this party the "pneumatomachians" (those who attacked the Spirit), and the Nicenes knew that their reconciliation was hardly likely. Gregory simply pressed, then, for the admission of the *homoousion* of the Spirit, as well as that of the Son, in the final synodical creed; and it brought the house down around his ears. The bishops, even those who were close to him, thought he had pressed the envelope too far: a more delicate use of language might be better, they believed. For Gregory this was exactly what had been happening for too long in vaguely worded Arianizing creeds: now was the time for clarity. The emperor also wanted to know what he thought he was doing: what had happened with the reconciliation of the party of Bishop Macedonius (the pneumatomachians)? They were all threatening to walk out (which they did eventually anyway).

Gregory had also pressed for a general "forgetting" of past troubles and grievances, especially at Antioch. The council could start its work of reconciliation by laying aside all strategies of revenge and displacements. Now that Meletius had sadly passed away, why could not the rival Nicene factions recognize the alternative (pro-Latin) incumbent Paulinus? This caused roars of anger from the large Syrian faction of Nicenes at the council led by Diodore of Tarsus. All points now seemed to be massing against Gregory's leadership. And so he approached the emperor and offered him his resignation if he thought it could help rescue this reconciliation council. He probably expected the emperor would see what he was trying to do and ask him to stay, give him

---

[76]Hosius had died in 359, Athanasius in 373, and Eusebius of Samosata, an indefatigable exile who had traveled around the empire even in exile dressed as an army officer so as to ordain Nicene bishops in defiance of imperial policy, had been fatally struck on the head by a roof tile thrown down on him by an Arian sympathizer in 379 in the town of Dolikha.

his more obvious support, for he expresses some surprise in his later accounts of these events that Theodosius "seemed to agree too rapidly to accept my resignation."[77] Gregory did not hold him in very high regard after that point. And so he made his way back to Cappadocia in retirement. But he was determined to write a detailed account of what had happened at the council. For him that meant one thing: what essentially did it do to profess the Nicene faith? He recorded this theology in great detail, and it is this record that came down to posterity, for apart from the creed the council finally promulgated in 382, there were few other records apparently kept. It is Gregory's version of events and theological meanings, therefore, that has become the widespread accepted interpretation of the meaning of the council. And here it is Gregory's theology that Gregory records, not necessarily that his theology was argued against.

The council ended obscurely. It was looking as if it all might have been a damp squib, not a great fireworks of reconciliation. But a year after events the emperor instructed Gregory of Nyssa to assist at a second synodical meeting at Constantinople that would issue a creed that would be the standard henceforth across the Eastern empire. As might have been expected, this reasserted the primacy of the creed of Nicaea in 325. But there were some additions, along the lines Gregory of Nazianzus had indicated were necessary. The *homoousion* of the Son was placed centrally once more as the basic christological statement, but in the reiteration creed of 382, the clauses about the Holy Spirit were expanded significantly from the creed of 325. Then it had been said only "And we believe in the Holy Spirit"; now in 382 was added a series of riders: "The Holy Spirit, the Lord and Life-Giver, who proceeds from the Father, who with the Father and the Son is coworshiped and coglorified, who has spoken through the prophets." If one reads this through the lens of Gregory of Nazianzus, it is clear that this teaches the full divinity of the Spirit. The West certainly read it in this way and was content with it. Most of the East took it in the same way, and eventually it came to have the meaning Gregory assigned to it. No one cared any more that "coworship" and "coglorification" had, until then, been the key terms that the soft Arians had used to try to describe the relationship between (a nondivine) Logos and the Father. Timidity of theology had caused the council to pull back from a hearty endorsement of Gregory's teaching on the *homoousion* of the Spirit of God. That did not make it, at least verbally, into the creed.

That the church universally, after the fourth century, has indeed interpreted the Constantinopolitan creed exactly as if it did proclaim the *homoousion* of the Spirit

---

[77]Especially in his long autobiographical poem *De Vita Sua*, trans. C. White, *Gregory of Nazianzus: Autobiographical Poems* (Cambridge: Cambridge University Press, 1996).

of God is a testimony to the enduring power of Gregory of Nazianzus's work of teaching and interpreting, even after he had been more or less forcibly removed from the council he was trying to lead. As was the case of Athanasius in his lifetime, Gregory himself personally exemplifies the catholicity of faith that the conciliar system tries to articulate by committee. The Council of Chalcedon, recognizing this, gave him posthumously the title of "Gregory the Theologian."

## CHRISTIANITY'S FOURTH-CENTURY ASCENDANCY AND ITS PROTESTORS

It has been estimated that from a small Jewish sect in the first century, Christianity grew slowly but steadily in the port cities across the empire to stand in the third century at (as a rough approximation) something between 7 and 10 percent of the imperial population. This is a remarkable growth in itself. Christians were being noticed as a social factor in the third century. They were then first seen to be climbing the social registers, and this is of course the period when Christians enter the higher educational system and thus leave more extensive literary remains, not to mention their absorption into the armies of Rome, a factor that triggered much alarm among third-century statesmen and accounts for the quite ruthless attempts to purge them. It is also a factor that can also be seen to apply, even more so, in Diocletian's persecution of the early fourth century.

But the fourth century sees an even more remarkable spurt of growth. It is in this century (where we also witness another distinct step forward in the sophistication of the Christian literature and the widening remit of its theology) that we can begin to talk about the "ascent" of the church as a dominant social factor. It was a century in which the old religions and antique ways of structuring the social order still held great sway, but the Christian movement was starting to make its voice, its attitudes, its wider culture felt in the fabric of Roman society. This is, without question, related to the advent of Constantine and his adoption of Christianity as a broad example of what he considered as "good religious and moral practice" for the new empire he was modeling. It also had particular relation to his decision to elevate the Christian episcopate, especially in the smaller cities and hinterland of empire, as a parallel magistracy, one that increasingly democratized the legal system of appeal and had the inevitable result of making the application of justice more equitable among the poorer classes, which thus found the church to be a helpful protector of their interests.

Modern historians have accounted for the growth of the early church in several ways, especially looking at social phenomena that the church encouraged (strong bonds among small local communities and an ethic of mercy, for example).[78] Theologians, then and now, have traditionally used other arguments (doctrines of God's providence and the moral superiority of the Christian message). It is no great "advance" to suggest that the approaches might be complementary rather than ruling each other out. The Christian doctrine of fraternity and mercy must have had strong appeal socially among the dispossessed. Equally, the theological underpinning of that anthropology (that all humankind were brothers and sisters because of the elevation of the human being to iconic status as having an immortal soul and standing among the creatures of the earth as the unique icons of God) gave credence and weight to a working concept of democratization on the basis of the principle of subsidiarity.

At the very least this divine anthropology deeply undermined the widespread belief of the rulers of the day in the divine right of the upper classes to hold dominion. All of the church's internal power structures stressed conciliarity rather than monarchy, and though Christians such as Eusebius of Caesarea were quick to point out to the likes of Constantine himself that the Christian theology of one God corresponded with the divine election of one just ruler such as himself, the clear teaching of the church even in relation to emperors was that no single person was above the law. This directly contradicted what Roman political theory had explicitly taught about the emperor, that he himself was the *fons et origo* of all law. Christians would never cede that role to a mortal man, however elevated. Destroying the late antique theory of kingship and offering a more deeply emphasized anthropology of the infinite value of each immortal soul, Christians had, in fact, from a simple, religious starting point radically revolutionized the basic premises of ancient society.

It was only a matter of time that these attitudes broke the social surface. This seems to have been decisively in the fourth century. The first public signs of it are in April 311, when Galerius stopped his persecution and issued in his name, along with those of Licinius and Constantine, an edict of toleration. After his death Licinius and Constantine made an alliance together, of sorts, issuing the famed Edict of

---

[78]Historian Rodney Stark (*The Rise of Christianity: How the Obscure, Marginal Jesus Movement Became the Dominant Religious Force in the Western World in a Few Centuries* [Princeton, NJ: Princeton University Press, 1996]), for example, argues that if, in time of plague, instead of running for the door, as was a common custom in antiquity—and thus taking the plague with you on crowded transport systems to wreak its greatest possible havoc—one stayed at home instead and cleaned and fed the sick of one's household (as Christian charity advocated), even using these simplest hygiene rituals the survival rates for Christians in times of plagues must have been higher than those of pagans. He finds in such examples a sociological correspondence for the theological (providence-based) and moral arguments that the church apologists used to account for its spread.

Milan in 313, which finally gave Christianity legal status and rights in the universal empire of Rome.[79] The successive Christian emperors gave more than toleration. Beginning with Constantine, restitutions of money and buildings were made to compensate the church for what it had suffered in the past. This has often been seen as excessive favoritism, but it is unlikely that the restitutions amounted to more than a fraction of what had been sequestered in the times of persecution. But Constantine did give very public and visible buildings over to the service of the church, not least the Lateran Basilica at Rome, which has ever since been the official seat of the popes. He also built some prestigious churches across the East de novo and made special commissions for them of pandects of the Bible.[80] Of these churches only the basilica at Bethlehem still stands intact, though the footings of the church on Vatican Hill can still be seen in the crypt of St. Peter's in Rome, and the oddly shaped sections of the church of the Holy Sepulcher are due to Constantine's builders. The twenty biblical pandects, made out of Eusebius of Caesarea's scriptorium, might have surviving exemplars in the codices Sinaiticus and Vaticanus.

Even in the Christian ascendancy, of course, pagan culture and attitudes thrived, alongside and even inside the church in many respects. Old, indeed archaic, customs and attitudes tended to die hard. We, the English-speaking heirs of the Saxons, can witness this through the lens of the Christianization of the Saxon tribes, who still (and even to the day) wanted to keep the old names for the days of the week instead of the new Christian terminology (*Dominica* for the Lord's Day, and then enumerating every other day out from this). So it is that the long-standing English-speaking Christian world still calls its days after the "old gods."[81] The culture was not allowed to wither, not only because it still had many passionate adherents but also because the state subsidized many significant religious and cultural aspects of the old religious system.

The Latin West was generally seen as more willing than the Eastern provinces to hold on to the old pagan ideas and values. This was especially true in the upper classes, who held to their ancient literary tradition, enshrining stories of the gods in an elevated poetic and literary corpus that they guarded with an almost religious zeal. Constantine had decided to move his capital to the Byzantium as early as his victory in the battle of the Milvian Bridge (312) because he realized how stuck were the senators and leading families of Rome in the old way. He set out the planning of Constantinople

---

[79] Recounted in Christian political commentator Lactantius's *On the Deaths of the Persecutors* and in Eusebius of Caesarea's *Ecclesiastical History* 10.2.
[80] These were total copies of the Old and New Testaments: a massive undertaking (and expense) in terms of scribal effort and animal skins used in the making.
[81] Moon-day, Tiw's day, Wodin's day, Thor's day, Frega's day, Saturn's day, and Sun-day. Western Christians even still call the Holy Pascha "Easter," after the Druidic goddess of spring, Yeostre.

from its earliest foundations as a "new city" where Christianity would thrive, and the very art he established in the city streets was, deliberately so, a massive secularization of the ancient cultic statues and cultural icons, which he "liberated" from the Roman world's most important classical temples and sacred precincts and set up on his street corners: nakedly deracinated for the poorest street cleaner to gaze on.

In 341 the Christians turned the law punitively against pagan sacrificial rites. Constantine himself had tried to banish animal sacrifice from the empire as a whole earlier in his reign, attempting to turn pagan ritual to a more intellectualist, moral, and symbolic form of religion—akin to his own favored cult of the sun god. Julian had tried ineffectively to turn back the clock and offered many financial subsidies for those who would reopen the temples and offer sacrifices to the gods. The decay that had set into the old cults, however, was not reversible. The story goes that when he went to Antioch, the priest of Apollo could only muster a goose to offer as sacrifice when the emperor called for a state occasion.

Julian did not wish to act punitively against Christians (though the church fathers record several hostilities he initiated) but hoped that the "Christian superstition" would wither away once imperial patronage was withdrawn. When this did not happen as he hoped, he issued his Edict on the Professors in 362, which forbade the presence of Christian teachers in state-supported academies of learning.[82] His rationale was that those who scorned belief in the gods ought not to teach the literature that took its root in the praises of those gods. It was a body blow to Christian intellectuals that they felt, more of a scorning than a real challenge to the church, though it alarmed many Christian intellectuals to feel that they might be exiled from the institutes of higher learning. In response to it Gregory of Nazianzus composed his philippics against Julian (*Contra Julianum*), declaring boldly that the emperor must be a fool if he ever thought he could deprive the Christians of their *logos*.[83]

Christian apologist Firmicus Maternus shows the sentiment at the middle of the century among Christians, how bitter were their memories of pagan supremacy and how deeply they had come to hate the old rituals. Firmicus, of course, was not a cradle Christian but a convert to the church from the pagan upper classes (he was a notable astrologer in his former life and probably a practicing court augur). His treatise, written in 346 and dedicated to the emperors Constans and Constantius II, *On the Errors of Profane Religions*, is a withering attack on the immorality and stupidity of

---

[82] It did not come out with force of punitive law, being more in the form of an "encouragement" to fire such professors. See further N. McLynn, "Julian and the Christian Professors," in *Being Christian in Late Antiquity*, ed. C. Harrison (Oxford: Oxford University Press, 2014).

[83] A pun, since the word signifies three concepts equally: divine Logos (Christ), rationality, and literary discourse.

the old religions.[84] There is no ecumenical common ground here, and little to suggest that at street level it was any different in the lower strata of society, either.

Yet, even in 381, the state Roman religion, with its veneration rituals of the historic gods of Rome, received (Christian) state subsidy for its priesthood. It was not until Gratian, emperor of the West in 382, that the lands belonging to the pagan temples were confiscated to the state and all social privileges for the pagan priesthoods and the vestal virgins were finally withdrawn.[85] Alaric, who sacked Rome in 410, drew withering complaints from the many pagan senators still active in Rome, who publicly laid the blame for Rome's decline on Christian values, which had sapped the imperial military vigor. It is a charge that Edward Gibbon was still repeating into the eighteenth century, with his recurring (and much overdone) contrasts of "virile" Roman men at arms with "effeminate and hysterical" Christian ascetics and bishops. The setting up, however, of dedication stones to Jupiter and other official Roman gods, as well as the oriental cults, such as Cybele and Isis, radically tailed off in the latter part of the third century.[86] This demonstrates that some things were sickening and dying in upper-class attitudes to the old cults.

One imagines, however, that at a more simple, peasant level, the old rituals, which were more domestically based (for the old temples did not assemble ritual congregations inside them like the Christian churches and Jewish synagogues), must have carried on for a longer time. It is indeed for this very reason that Christians invented the pejorative term *paganism*. *Paganus* signified a country bumpkin and the kind of old religion rituals that they were accustomed to keep up (now seen by Christians as "superstitions"). It is ironic in many ways that this pejorative view of the old religions as bumpkin cult was hung on everyone still attached to the old religions, from simple peasants in the fields to sophisticated philosophers and senators such as Symmachus in the fourth century, the very leader of the (pagan) senatorial party who was accusing the Christians of having lost the ethos of Roman imperial values by abandoning the cult of the gods of Rome.

Symmachus's impassioned petition to Gratian to countermand his order in 382 focused on stopping the new Christian majority there from throwing out the altar of victory that had stood in the senate from time immemorial. He repeated the memorial in 384, addressed to Valentinian II. His speech was dedicated to the idea of multiple religious tolerance. It fell on deaf ears. The Christian senators forwarded a counterpetition in support of the emperor's action and demanded to have the

---

[84]English translation: C. A. Forbes, *The Error of the Pagan Religions* (New York: Newman Press, 1970).
[85]Codex Theodosianus 16.10, 20.
[86]See C. H. Moore, "The Pagan Reaction in the Late Fourth Century Author(s)," *Transactions and Proceedings of the American Philological Association* 50 (1919): 122-34.

famous altar of incense removed as an offensive sight in their eyes.[87] They, who remembered so many recent persecutions by the state, were not impressed then by pleas for toleration, and on the contrary wished to express the "new wave" quite defiantly. Bishop Ambrose of Milan wrote in no uncertain terms to Valentinian II to remind him that he had a duty as Christian emperor to prevent these hypocrites from succeeding.[88] The pagan senatorial party did not forget their grievance, however, and it was a repetition of Symmachus's claims in the aftermath of Alaric's sacking of Rome that called forth the Christian senators to petition Augustine of Hippo to write a long refutation of the charge that the church had wrecked the empire. It was a call that resulted in Augustine's monumental work of apologia, the *City of God*. It is worthy of remark, nevertheless, that Augustine keeps very quiet (if indeed he knew it in the first place) that Alaric was a Christian warlord.[89]

The running argument between pagans and Christians in the fourth century came to a symbolic end when Theodosius, the first emperor to be baptized from the outset of his reign, acted to proscribe public ceremonial of pagan rites. From the time of his taking up his capital at Constantinople in 381 he forbade pagan rituals, which had been part of the city life even under former Christian rulers. He reiterated Constantine's ban on animal sacrifice and made the taking of auguries from animal entrails a crime punishable by death. Between 389 and 391 he moved to enshrine this proscription in law, and a series of edicts in the Theodosian Code amounted to a wholesale ban on pagan lifestyle.[90] Pagan magistrates who tried to protect pagan ritual from the force of the laws were actively prosecuted. Temples were closed and demolished. The "eternal" vestal fire at the Roman forum was forcibly extinguished, and the vestal virgin sisterhood was terminated and dispersed. In 391 in Alexandria a Christian mob, sensing the tide had turned, took advantage of the legislation and

---

[87]Constantius ordered its removal in 356 when he visited Rome, but Julian had deliberately restored it.
[88]Ambrose, *Epistle* 17.3-4: "And so, most Christian emperor, since the true God expects his due from you in terms of faith and zeal, care and devotion for the faith, I wonder how the hope has risen up in some hearts that you should feel it your duty to restore by imperial command altars to the gods of the heathen and even to furnish the funds requisite for profane sacrifices; for surely in regard to such things that have long ago been sequestered by the imperial or city treasuries you would be volunteering from your own funds, rather than restoring anything that belongs to them by right. But they are complaining of their losses, the very ones who never spared our blood and who destroyed the very buildings of our churches. And they petition you to grant them privileges, the very ones who by the last Julianic law denied to us the common right of speaking and teaching." Ambrose's *Epistle* 18 replies to Symmachus's petition to Emperor Valentinian and argues against the latter's claim that recent famines have been caused by allowing the rites and honors of the old gods to lapse.
[89]He was a Gothic Arian tribal chief.
[90]Codex Theodosianus 16.10.11.

ransacked the city for busts of Serapis, smashing them and painting the cross over the lintels of buildings instead. The great Serapeum was torn down to its foundations.

After 392, when Theodosius became emperor of the Western provinces also, his suppression of pagan shrines spread there more widely too. Although the Western provinces remained more actively pagan in many parts for longer than the East, it was the reign of Theodosius that effectively spelled the death of classical Mediterranean paganism in the Roman provinces. It was another matter, of course, with the Slavic and Germanic tribes of the northern barbarian lands. Christianity would continue to encounter polytheistic cult innumerable times thereafter. It would rarely, if ever, show toleration of the polytheistic instinct, adopting from its reading of the late prophets an enduring suspicion and downright hostility to nonmonotheistic worship.[91]

Older textbooks, however, which tended to speak in simpler ages about a definitive Christianization of society at any given moment (be it fourth century or fourteenth) need to be taken with advisement. The transition to Christian values across a wider scale of society than ever before certainly happened from the fourth century onward. To what extent was it the Christianizing of society at large? Well that is a more debatable matter. Formal paganism remained active throughout this century, and on into Byzantium and the Middle Ages in many diverse attitudes, if not so much in cultic practices. The transition to the dominance of the church was a much messier affair in late antiquity than has hitherto been thought to be the case. To baptize the local culture has always been the church's social aim. It is surely still attempting to put into effect that aspiration.

## A SHORT READER

***Arius of Alexandria, cited by Athanasius of Alexandria,* Contra Arianos 1.5-6.**
And so God himself, as he really is, is inexpressible to all. He alone has no equal, no one similar (*homoios*), and no one of the same glory. We call him unbegotten (*agenetos*), in contrast to him who by nature is begotten (*gennetos*). We praise him as without beginning in contrast to him who has a beginning. We worship him as timeless, in contrast to him who in time has come to exist. He who is without beginning made the Son a beginning of created things. He produced him as a Son for himself by begetting him. He [the Son] has none of the distinct characteristics of God's own being (*kath' [h]ypostasin*), for he is not equal to, nor is he of the same being (*homoousios*) as, him. God is wise, for he himself is the teacher of Wisdom. Sufficient proof that God is invisible to all: he is invisible both to things that were made through the Son and also to the Son himself.

---
[91]Cf. Is 45:20; Ps 115:4-8.

***Arius of Alexandria,*** **Letter of Arius and Clergy with him to Bishop Alexander,** ***in Athanasius,*** **De Synodis *15.2-5.*** Our faith from our forefathers, which also we learned from you, blessed Father [Alexander], is this: We acknowledge one God, alone unbegotten, alone everlasting, alone without beginning, alone true, alone having immortality, alone wise, alone good, alone sovereign, judge, governor, and provider of all, unalterable and unchangeable, just and good, God of the Law and the Prophets and the New Testament; who begot an only begotten Son before time and the ages, through whom he made both the ages (Heb 1:2) and all that was made; who begot him not in appearance, but in reality; and that he made him subsist at his own will, unalterable and unchangeable, the perfect creature (*ktisma*) of God, but not as one of the creatures; offspring, but not as one of the other things begotten; nor as Valentinus pronounced that the offspring of the Father was an emanation (*probole*); nor as the Manichaeans taught, that the offspring was a one-in-essence-portion (*meros homoousion*) of the Father; nor as Sabellius, dividing the monad, speaks of a Son/Father (*uiopator*); nor as Hieracas speaks of one torch taken from another, or as a lamp flame divided into two; nor that he who existed before was later generated or created anew into a Son, as you yourself, O blessed father [Alexander], have often condemned both in church services and in council meetings; but, as we say, he was created at the will of God, before time and before the ages, and came to life and being from the Father, and the glories which coexist in him are from the Father. For when giving to [the Son] the inheritance of all things (Heb 1:2), the Father did not deprive himself of what he has without beginning in himself; for he is the source of all things. Thus there are three subsisting realities (hypostases). And God, being the cause of all that happens, is absolutely alone without beginning; but the Son, begotten apart from time by the Father, and created (*ktistheis*) and founded before the ages, was not in existence before his generation, but was begotten apart from time before all things, and he alone came into existence (*hypeste*) from the Father. For he is neither eternal nor coeternal nor co-unbegotten with the Father, nor does he have his being together with the Father, as some speak of relations, introducing two unbegotten beginnings. But God is before all things as monad and beginning of all. Therefore he is also before the Son, as we have learned also from your own public preaching in the church. Therefore he thus has his being from God; and glories, and life, and all things have been given over to him; in this way God is his beginning. For he is over him, as his God and being before him.

But if the expressions from him [Rom 11:36] and from the womb [Ps 109:3 LXX, i.e., Ps 110:3 RSV] and I came from the Father, and I have come (Jn 16:28), are understood by some to mean that he is part of him [the Father], one in essence or as an emanation, then the Father is, according to them, compounded and divisible and alterable and material, and, as far as their belief goes, the incorporeal God will endure a body.

***The Creed of the Council of Nicaea 325,*** **Proem** ***of the*** **Acts of the Council of Ephesus 431.** The synod at Nicaea set forth this creed. We believe in (*pistevomen*) One God, the Father, All-Powerful Master (*Pantokrator*), the Maker of things that are visible and invisible; and in One Lord Jesus Christ (Mt. 23.10; cf. Jn. 10.30; Rom. 5.17-21; Rom. 10.8-13; 1 Cor. 8.6), the Only Begotten (*Monogene*) Son of God, begotten of the Father, that is, of the being (*ousia*) of the Father; God from God, Light from Light, True God from True God, begotten (*gennethenta*) not made (*poiethenta*), the same in being (*homoousios*) as the Father; and through him all things came to be (*egeneto*) (1 Cor. 8.6; Jn. 1.2; Coloss. 1.15), things in Heaven, and things on earth. For us humans (*anthropous*) and for the sake of our salvation (*soterian*) He came down (*katelthonta*) and was incarnate (*sarkothenta*). Being made man (*enanthropesanta*), He suffered, and on the third day he rose up (*anastanta*), and he ascended (*anelthonta*) into heaven. He is coming to judge (*krinai*) both the living and the dead. And [we believe] in the Holy Spirit. Whosoever shall say that "there was a time when he was not" (*en pote oti ouk en*); and that "before he was begotten he was not" (*prin gennethenta ouk en*); and that "he was made of things that once were not" (*ex ouk onton egeneto*); or that he is of a different hypostasis or essence (*heteras hypostaseos e ousias*); saying that the Son of God is either subject to change or alteration (*trepton e alloioton*); such people the Catholic and Apostolic Church anathematizes.[92]

***Eusebius of Caesarea,*** **Life of the Emperor Constantine 3.10-13.** Now, when the appointed day arrived on which the council met for the final solution of the questions in dispute, each member was present for this in the central hall of the palace, which seemed to exceed the other rooms in its capacity. On each side of the interior of this room were many seats disposed in order, which were occupied by those who had been invited to attend, according to their rank. As soon, then, as the whole assembly had seated themselves with becoming orderliness, a general silence prevailed, in expectation of the

---

[92] Text and translation in N. P. Tanner, *Decrees of the Ecumenical Councils* (London: Sheed and Ward, 1990), 5.

emperor's arrival. And first of all, three of his immediate family entered in succession, then others also preceded his approach, not of the soldiers or guards who usually accompanied him, but only friends in the faith. And now, all rising at the signal that indicated the emperor's entrance, at last he himself proceeded through the midst of the assembly, like some heavenly messenger of God, clothed in raiment that glittered almost as if with rays of light, reflecting the glowing radiance of a purple robe, and adorned with the brilliant splendor of gold and precious stones. Such was the outward appearance of his person. But in regard to his inner mind it was evident that he was distinguished by reverence and godly fear. This was indicated by his downcast eyes, the blush on his countenance, and his gait. For the rest of his personal excellencies, he surpassed all present in height of stature and beauty of form, as well as in majestic dignity of appearance, and invincible strength and vigor. All these graces united in a delightful and serene style of deportment appropriate to his imperial station and declared the excellence of his mental qualities to be above all praise. As soon as he had advanced to the upper end of the seats, at first he remained standing, and when a low chair of wrought gold had been set for him, he waited until the bishops had beckoned to him, and only then he sat down, and after him the whole assembly did the same. The bishop who occupied the chief place in the right division of the assembly[93] then rose and addressed the emperor with a concise oration on the theme of offering thanksgiving to Almighty God on his behalf. When he had resumed his seat, silence ensued, and all regarded the emperor with fixed attention. He looked around the assembly most serenely with a cheerful aspect and, having collected his thoughts, in a calm and gentle tone gave utterance to the following words. "It has been my chief desire, dearest friends, to enjoy the spectacle of your united presence; and now that this desire is fulfilled, I feel myself bound to render thanks to God the universal king, because, in addition to all his other benefits, he has granted me a blessing higher than all others, in permitting me to see you not only all assembled together, but all united in a common harmony of sentiment. I pray therefore that no malignant adversary may interfere from this point onward to mar our happy state. It is my prayer, now that the impious hostility of tyrants[94] has been forever removed by the power of God our Savior, that the spirit who delights in evil may devise no further means for exposing the divine law to

---

[93] Most likely Hosius of Cordoba.
[94] The persecuting emperors Diocletian, Galerius, Maximian, and Licinius, who have preceded him.

blasphemous calumny; for, in my judgment, internal dissension within the church of God is far more evil and dangerous than any kind of civil war or conflict. And our differences here thus appear to me more grievous than any outward trouble. Accordingly, when, by the will and with the cooperation of God, I had been victorious over my own enemies, I thought that nothing more remained but to render thanks to him, and sympathize in the joy of those whom he had restored to freedom through my agency. As soon as I heard of that intelligence that I had least expected to receive, I mean the news of your internal dissension, I judged it to be of no small importance, but with the earnest desire that a remedy for this evil too might be found through my agency, I immediately sent word to require your presence. And now I rejoice in looking on your assembly. Even so, I feel that my desires will be most completely fulfilled only when I can see you all united in one judgment, having that common spirit of peace and concord prevailing among you all that, as consecrated ministers of God, it is your duty to commend to society. Delay not, then, dear friends. Delay not, you ministers of God and faithful servants of our common Lord and Savior. Begin from this moment onward to cast off the causes of that disunion that has existed among you, and remove the perplexities of controversy by embracing the principles of peace. For by such conduct you will at the same time be acting in a manner most pleasing to the supreme God, and you will confer a most gracious favor on me, your fellow servant." As soon as the emperor had spoken these words in the Latin tongue, which someone translated, he gave permission to the presidents of the council to deliver their opinions. At this juncture some began to accuse their neighbors, who defended themselves and offered recriminations in turn. So it was that innumerable charges were set forth by each party, and a violent controversy arose at the very outset of affairs.[95] Nevertheless, the emperor gave a patient hearing to all alike and received every proposition with steady attention, and, by occasionally assisting the argument of each party in turn, he gradually disposed even the most vehement disputants toward reconciliation. At the same time, by the affability of his address to everyone, and his use of Greek (for he was not unacquainted with the language), he was seen by all in a truly attractive and amiable light. He persuaded some, convinced others by his arguments, praised those who spoke well, and urged all to unity of sentiment, until at last he succeeded in bringing them to one mind and judgment respecting every disputed question.

---

[95] Including charges laid against Eusebius himself, which he glosses over.

***Sacra [imperial rescript] of the Emperor Constantine, announcing Nicaea (325).*** I believe it should be obvious to everyone that there is nothing more honorable in my sight than the fear of God. Though it was formerly agreed that the synod of bishops should meet at Ancyra in Galatia, it seemed to us for many reasons that it would be better for the synod to assemble at Nicaea, city of Bithynia; and this because the bishops from Italy and the rest of the European lands are coming, also because of the excellent climate there, and in order that I myself may be present as a spectator and participator in those things that will be accomplished. And therefore I announce to you, my beloved brothers, that all of you should promptly assemble at the said city, that is, at Nicaea. Let every one of you, therefore, as I have said previously, keep the greater good in mind and be diligent, without delay in anything, so as to arrive speedily, so that each may be physically present as a spectator of those things that will be accomplished. God keep you, my beloved brothers.

***Synodical Letter of the Council of Nicaea Announcing Its Decrees (325).*** [Text preserved in Gelasius, *History of the Nicene Council* 2.33; Socrates Scholasticus, *Ecclesiastical History* 1.6; Theodoret, *Ecclesiastical History* 1.9.] To the church of Alexandria, by the grace of God, holy and great; and to our well-beloved brethren, the orthodox clergy and laity throughout Egypt and Pentapolis, and Libya, and indeed every nation under heaven. The holy and great synod, of the bishops assembled at Nicaea, sends its wishes for health in the Lord. Insofar as the holy and great synod, which was assembled at Nicaea through the kindness of Christ, and that of our most reverent lord Constantine, who brought us together from our several provinces and cities, has considered matters that concern the faith of the church, it seemed to us to be necessary that certain things should be communicated from us, to you, in writing, so that you might have the means of knowing what has been discussed and scrutinized, as well as what has been decreed and established. First of all, then: In the presence of our most reverent lord Constantine, investigation was made of matters concerning the impiety and transgressions of Arius and his party. And it was unanimously decreed that he and his irreverent opinion should be anathematized, along with the blasphemous words and speculations in which he indulged, as when he blasphemed the Son of God, saying:

> that he is from things that are not,
> and that before he was begotten he was not,
> and that there was a time when he was not,

and that the Son of God is by his own free will capable of doing wrong or doing good;[96]

and saying that he is a creature.

All these things the holy synod has anathematized. We do not even want to hear this irreverent doctrine of his, or his blasphemous words, or his mania. You have already heard all the particulars of the charges that were made against him, and the results of those charges. If not, you will soon hear all about them—because we do not want to appear to have been oppressors of a man who has, in fact, received a fitting recompense for his own sin. His irreverence has spread to such an extent that he has even destroyed [bishops] Theonas of Marmorica and Secundus of Ptolemais, for they too have received the same sentence as the rest.[97] Nevertheless, when God delivered Egypt from that heresy and blasphemy, and from the persons who had dared to make disturbance and division among a people who had previously been at peace, there still remained the matter of the insolence of Meletius and those who had been ordained by him.[98] And now, beloved, as to that part of our work also we wish to inform you of the decrees of the synod. The synod was disposed to treat Meletius leniently (in strict justice, he deserved no gentleness), and so it decreed that he should remain in his own city but have no authority either to ordain or to administer affairs or to make appointments. He is not to appear in the countryside or in any other city (than Alexandria) for this purpose, but he should enjoy the simple title of his rank (as bishop). Those who have been put into position by him ought, after they have been confirmed by a more sacred laying on of hands should, on this condition only, be admitted to communion. Then they shall have their rank and the right to officiate, but they shall altogether be the subordinates of those who have been enrolled in any church or parish and were appointed by our most honorable colleague Alexander. This is so that these men are to have no authority to make appointments of persons who are pleasing to them, nor to make nominations; in fact, to do nothing whatsoever apart from the consent of those bishops of the catholic and apostolic church who are serving under our most holy colleague Alexander. On the other hand, those who by the grace of God and through

---

[96] Arius explicitly denied this in his teaching.

[97] Theonas and Secundus were bishops deposed at Nicaea and subjected to state sentences. Eusebius of Nicomedia was also censured, but his imperial rank saved him from penalty, and he soon regained the initiative so as eventually to unravel the entire pro-Nicene stance of the court.

[98] Meletius of Lycopolis was a conservative rival bishop in Alexandria who had claimed he had the true episcopal succession, not Alexander.

your prayers have been found to be in no schism at all, and on the contrary are of immaculate standing in the catholic and apostolic church, are to have authority to make appointments and nominations of worthy persons among the clergy, and in short to do all things in accordance with the laws and regulations of the church. Now, if it should happen that any of those clergy who are currently over the churches should die, then those who have but recently been received are to succeed to the office of the deceased—always providing that they shall appear to be worthy, and that the people should acclaim them, and that the bishop of Alexandria shall concur in the election and ratify it.[99] This concession, therefore, has been made to all the rest; but because of his disorderly conduct from the outset and the rashly precipitate nature of his character, the same establishment was not conceded for Meletius himself. Since he is a man capable of committing these same disorders again, no authority or privilege should be allowed to him.

These are the particular decrees that are of special interest to Egypt and to the most holy church of Alexandria; and if in the presence of our most honored lord, our colleague and brother Alexander, anything else has been enacted by canon or decree, he himself will inform you of it in greater detail, since he himself was both a guide and a collaborator in what was done here. We further proclaim to you the good news of the agreement concerning the Holy Pascha, that this also has been properly settled because of your prayers, and now all our brethren in the East who formerly followed the Jewish pattern will henceforth celebrate this most sacred festival of Pascha at the same time as the Romans, and as yourselves, and all those who have celebrated Pascha from the beginning.[100] And so—delighted by these happy outcomes, and in our common peace and harmony and in the excision of all heresies, we wish you to receive with greater honor and increased love, our colleague your bishop Alexander, who has gladdened us by his presence, and who at so great an age has undergone such immense fatigue in order that peace could be established among you and among us all. Pray for us, too, that the things that have seemed right in their accomplishment may stand fast. These things have been done, as is our belief, that are well-pleasing in the sight of God the Almighty, and of his only begotten Son, our Lord Jesus Christ, and of the Holy Spirit: to whom be glory forever. Amen.

---

[99]Namely, the clergy appointed by Meletius in various towns in Egypt as counterpriests and chorbishops who are willing to be reordained under Alexander's obedience.

[100]Setting Pascha (Easter) at the same time as Passover, on the same calendar: this meant the old Quartodecimans groups observing Pascha on the fourteenth of Nisan regardless of the day.

***Athanasius of Alexandria,* Against the Arians *1.15-16.*** When you Arians assert that "the Son was made out of nothing" and that "he did not exist before he was begotten," you imply that the titles of Son, God, Wisdom, and so on, are given to him in virtue of participation (*methexis*). . . . But participation in what? . . . In the Spirit? Surely not, for the Spirit "takes from what is the Son's" (Jn 16:14). . . . Therefore, it is from the Father that he "partakes," for this is the only remaining possibility. But what exactly is it that he partakes of? Where does it come from? If it is something external, offered by the Father, he no longer partakes of the Father. No longer can he be called the Father's Son. And so what he partakes of has to be "of the substance of the Father" (*ek tes ousias tou Patros*), for if it is something other than the Father's own being . . . something intermediate would have been posited between this that is of the Father, and the being (whatever that might then be) of the Son. . . . Thus we are compelled to conclude that the Son is entirely that which is "of the substance of the Father."

***Acts of the Synod of Serdica (343), in Theodoret,* Ecclesiastical History *2.8.42-43.*** If the Logos ever had a beginning he could not have existed always. But the ever-existent Logos does not have a beginning. God will never have an end. We do not say that the Father is the Son or that the Son is the Father: but that the Father is Father, and the Son is the Son of the Father. We confess that the Son is the Logos of God the Father and that beside him there is no other. We believe the Logos to be true God, and Wisdom, and Power. We affirm that he is truly Son, but not in the way that people are generally said to be children, for they are called "sons of God" on account of their regeneration or their merit, but not on account of their being of one hypostasis with the Father, as is the case with the Son.[101]

***Acts of the Synod of Alexandria 362, in Athanasius,* De Synodis *7.*** Since certain people seemed to be at odds concerning the economy of the Savior in the flesh, we made inquiry of both parties and found that what the one side confessed, the others also agreed to; namely, that the Word did not dwell in a holy man, as he did in the prophets, but that at the consummation of the ages, the Word himself became flesh, and "though he was in the form of God, he took the form of a servant" (Phil 2:7). From Mary, after the flesh, he became man for us. Accordingly, in him the human race was perfectly and entirely delivered from sin, and brought to life from its death, and brought to the kingdom of heaven. And they also confessed that the Savior did not possess a soulless

---

[101]The synod here uses the term *hypostasis* in an antique sense as a synonym for *ousia* or being.

body, or one that was devoid of sense and intelligence. For it was not possible, when the Lord became man for our sakes, that his body should be without intelligence. Nor was that salvation achieved in the very Word a salvation of the body only, but of soul also. Being Son of God in very truth, he also became Son of Man. Being God's only begotten Son, he also became at the same time "firstborn among many brothers" (Rom 8:29). And so there was not one Son of God "before Abraham" (Jn 8:58) and another after Abraham. There was not one who raised up Lazarus and another who made inquiries as to his state. But it was the same one who said, as man "Where does Lazarus lie?" (Jn 11:34) who, as God, raised him up to life. He who was bodily man spat in the dirt, but it was in a divine manner, as Son of God, that he then opened the eyes of the man born blind (Mk 8:22). As Peter says (1 Pet 4:1), in the flesh he suffered, and as God he opened the tombs and raised the dead. For these reasons, understanding all that is said in the gospel in this way, they were able to assure us that they held same truth about the Word's incarnation and his becoming man, as we do.

**Basil of Caesarea, Epistle 9.3 (360).** If I can express my own personal opinion, I would be prepared to accept the phrase [the Logos is] "like in substance" (*homoiousios*), provided that one adds to it the qualifier "without any difference." Then I would accept this as being the same as consubstantial (*homoousios*), according to the sound interpretation of that term. This was the opinion of the fathers at Nicaea when they gave to the only begotten such titles as "Light from Light" and "true God from true God" and then added on consubstantial as a corollary.

**Aetius, Excerpts from the Syntagmation 1-41 (370).** I take as my starting point the problem of ingenerate deity. Can the ingenerate deity make the generate ingenerate? If the ingenerate deity is superior to all cause, he must for that reason be superior to origination. Being superior to all cause clearly includes being superior to origination, for he neither received existence from another nor conferred it on himself. How could anyone sustain that the nature that is set forth (Son) could be exactly the same as the one that sets it forth (Father) if he did not confer existence on himself, being completely transcendent of all cause and of such a nature as admits no origination? If the deity abides eternally as ingenerate nature, and the offspring abides as eternally offspring, the perverse doctrines of *homoousion* and *homoiousion* are demolished. Each nature abides always in the rank proper to its nature, and each is completely different (heterousiast).

***Gregory of Nazianzus,*** **Poems (On the Son)** *1.2.18-35 (380).* If time certainly precedes my human existence, time is not prior to the Logos, whose begetter is timeless. When there existed the Father, who is without beginning (that Father who left nothing beyond his own Godhead), then also there existed the Son of the Father, having that Father as his timeless beginning, just as light emanates from that beautiful orb of the sun (though all images fall short here of the greatness of God), for we must not interpose anything between Father and Son, both of whom are everlasting beings, in case we sever the royal Son from the royal father. For whatever is prior to God, whether you conceive of it as time or will, is to me tantamount to a division of Godhead. As God, as progenitor, he is a mighty progenitor indeed. So if it is a great thing for the Father to have no point of origin for his own noble deity, it is no lesser glory for the revered offspring of that great Father to come from such a root. And so, do not sever God from God. You cannot discern the Son apart from the Father. The expressions "ingenerate" (*agenetos*) and "generation from the Father" (*gennetos*) do not define two different forms of deity (whoever came up with such an idea?). Rather, both these things are externals around the Godhead.[102] To my mind, the nature of Godhead is indivisible.

***Gregory of Nazianzus,*** **Fifth Theological Oration (Oration 31.2-4), On the Holy Spirit.** Now the subject of the Holy Spirit presents a special difficulty, not only because when these [Arians] have become weary in their disputations concerning the Son, they struggle with greater heat against the Spirit (for it seems to be absolutely necessary for them to have some object on which to give expression to their impiety, or life would seem to them no longer worth living!), but more so because we ourselves, who are worn out by the plethora of their quibbles, are in something of that same state as men who have lost all appetite—who, having taken a dislike to some particular kind of food, shrink from all food. Just so, I have come to have an aversion to all theological argumentation. Nevertheless, may the Spirit grant it to us, and then the discourse will proceed, and God will be glorified. Well, then, others have worked on this subject for us (as well as for themselves, just as we have worked on it for them), and I shall leave to them the task of examining carefully and analyzing how many senses the word *Spirit* or the word *holy* is used and understood in Holy Scripture, bringing that evidence forward that is

---

[102] Gregory argued that they were modes of being, relational (hypostatic) categories, not substantive ones. They did not argue that the Son's nature was quantitatively and qualitatively different from the Father's, as Arians concluded, simply that the Son related to the Father differently from the way the Father related to him—which was the dynamic of the three hypostases of the divine Trinity.

suitable to such an inquiry.[103] And I leave it to them to show how in addition to that evidence, those two words, I mean of course *Holy Spirit*, are used in a quite specific sense. Thus I will apply myself to the remainder of the subject. Now, those who are angry with us on the grounds that we are introducing a strange or interpolated God, namely the Holy Spirit, and who fight so very hard for keeping to the letter, should know that they are being timid when there is no need for fear. But I would have them clearly understand that their love for the letter is nothing more than a cloak for their impiety, as I shall demonstrate shortly when I will refute their objections with the greatest force I can muster. But we have so much confidence in the divinity of the Spirit, whom we adore, that we will begin our teaching concerning his divinity by ascribing to him the names that belong to the Trinity, even though some persons may think us too bold. The Father was the true Light that enlightens every man coming into the world. The Son was the true Light that enlightens every man coming into the world. The other Paraclete (Jn 14:26) was the true Light that enlightens every man coming into the world (Jn 1:9). You see: was and was and was, but was one thing. Light is thrice repeated; but it is one Light and one God. This was what David long ago signaled to himself when he said, "In your Light we shall see Light" (Ps 36:9). And now we have both seen and proclaim concisely and simply the doctrine of God the Trinity, comprehending Light (the Son), out of Light (the Father), in Light (the Holy Spirit). He who rejects this, let him reject it; for whoever wishes to commit iniquity can do so. For our part we shall proclaim that which we have understood. We will ascend into a high mountain (Is 40:9) and will shout it out, and even if we will not be listened to below, we will still exalt the Spirit. We will not be afraid, or if we are afraid, it shall be of keeping silence, not of proclaiming the news. If ever there was a time when the Father was not, then there was a time when the Son was not. If ever there was a time when the Son was not, then there was a time when the Spirit was not. If the One was from the beginning, then the Three were so too. If you throw down the One, I am bold to assert that you do not set up the other Two. For what profit is there in an imperfect Godhead? Or rather, what Godhead can there be if it is not perfect? And how can that be perfect that lacks something of perfection? And surely there is something lacking if the Godhead does not possess the Holy, and how would it have this if it were without the Spirit? For either

---

[103]"Them" referring to St. Basil of Caesarea and St. Gregory of Nyssa, with whose works in defense of the Spirit he was closely involved.

holiness is something different from him, and if so let someone tell me what it should be conceived to be; or if it is the same, how is it not from the beginning, as if it were better for God to be at one time imperfect and apart from the Spirit? If the Spirit is not from the beginning, he must stand in the same (creaturely) rank as myself, even though he may be a little before me, for we are both parted from the Godhead by time. And if he is in the same rank as myself, how can he possibly divinize me or join me with Godhead?

## FURTHER READING

*Arianism and Nicaea*

Anatolios, K. *Retrieving Nicaea*. Grand Rapids: Eerdmans, 2011.
Bardy, G. "L'héritage littéraire d'Aétius." *Revue d'Histoire Ecclésiastique* 24 (1928): 809-27.
———. *Recherches sur S. Lucien d'Antioche et son école*. Paris: Beauchesne, 1936.
Barnes, T. D. *Athanasius and Constantius*. London: Harvard University Press, 1993.
Beeley, Christopher A. *Gregory of Nazianzus on the Trinity and the Knowledge of God: In Your Light We Shall See Light*. Oxford: Oxford University Press, 2008.
Behr, J. *The Nicene Faith*. 2 vols. Crestwood, NY: St. Vladimir's Seminary Press, 2004.
Gavrilyuk, P. L. *The Suffering of the Impassible God: The Dialectics of Patristic Thought*. Oxford: Oxford University Press, 2006.
Gregg, R. C., and D. Groh. *Early Arianism: A View of Salvation*. Philadelphia: Fortress, 1981.
Hanson, R. P. C. *The Search for the Christian Doctrine of God: The Arian Controversy 318–381*. Edinburgh: T&T Clark, 1988.
Kelly, J. N. D. *Early Christian Creeds*. 3rd ed. London: Longmans, 1972.
Kopecek, T. A. *A History of Neo-Arianism*. 2 vols. Cambridge, MA: Philadelphia Patristic Foundation, 1979.
Lonergan, B. *The Way to Nicaea*. London: Darton, Longman, and Todd, 1976.
Luibheid, C. "The Arianism of Eusebius of Nicomedia." *Irish Theological Quarterly* 43 (1976): 3-23.
———. *The Council of Nicaea*. Galway: Galway University Press, 1982.
Lyman, J. R. "Arius and Arianism." In *The Oxford Handbook of Early Christian Studies*, ed. S. A. Harvey and D. G. Hunter, 237-57. Oxford: Oxford University Press, 2008.
McGuckin, J. A. "The Council of Nicaea." In *The Seven Oikoumenical Councils*, ed. S. Trostyanskiy, 9-46. Piscataway, NJ: Gorgias Press, 2016.
———. "St. Basil the Great's Exposition of Nicene Orthodoxy." In *Cappadocian Legacy: A Critical Appraisal*, ed. D. Costache, 49-62. Sydney: St. Andrew's Orthodox Press, 2013.
Norris, F. W. *Faith Gives Fullness to Reasoning: The Five Theological Orations of Gregory Nazianzen*. Leiden: Brill, 1991.
Stead, C. G. "Arius in Modern Research." *Theological Studies* 45 (1994): 24-36.

———. *Divine Substance.* Oxford: Clarendon, 1977. Pages 223-66.

Vaggione, R. P. *Eunomius of Cyzicus and the Nicene Revolution.* Oxford: Oxford University Press, 2001.

———. *Eunomius: The Extant Works.* Oxford: Clarendon, 1987.

Wickham, L. "Aetius and the Doctrine of Divine Ingeneracy." *StPatr* 11 (1972): 259-63.

———. "The Date of Eunomius' Apology. A Reconsideration." *JTS* 20 (1969): 231-40.

———. "The Syntagmation of Aetius the Anomoean." *JTS* 19 (1968): 532-69.

Williams, R. *Arius: Heresy and Tradition.* London: Darton, Longman, and Todd, 1987.

Young, F. *From Nicaea to Chalcedon.* London: SCM Press, 1983. Pages 65-83, 339-41, 362-67.

**The Cappadocian Fathers**

Balas, D. F. *Metousia Theou: Man's Participation in God's Perfections According to St. Gregory of Nyssa.* Rome: Libreria Herder, 1966.

Balthasar, H. U. von. *Presence and Thought: An Essay on the Religious Philosophy of Gregory of Nyssa.* San Francisco: Ignatius, 1995.

Clarke, W. K. L. *St. Basil the Great: A Study in Monasticism.* Cambridge: Cambridge University Press, 1913.

Conway-Jones, Ann. *Gregory of Nyssa's Tabernacle Imagery in Its Jewish and Christian Contexts.* Oxford: Oxford University Press, 2014.

Costache, D., ed. *Cappadocian Legacy: A Critical Appraisal.* Sydney: St. Andrew's Orthodox Press, 2013.

Dumitrascu, N., ed. *Cappadocian Theology.* Basingstoke: Palgrave Macmillan, 2015.

Fedwick, P. J. *Basil of Caesarea, Christian, Humanist, Ascetic.* Toronto: Pontifical Institute of Medieval Studies, 1981.

Harrison, V. E. F. *Grace and Human Freedom According to St. Gregory of Nyssa.* Lewiston, NY: Edwin Mellen, 1992.

Holman, S. R. *The Hungry Are Dying: Beggars and Bishops in Roman Cappadocia.* Oxford: Oxford University Press, 2001.

Jackson, B. *St. Basil: Letters and Select Works. NPNF* second series 8. Reprint, Grand Rapids: Eerdmans, 1989.

McGuckin, J. A. "St. Basil the Great's Exposition of Nicene Orthodoxy." In *Cappadocian Legacy: A Critical Appraisal*, ed. D. Costache, 49-62. Sydney: St. Andrew's Orthodox Press, 2013.

———. "St. Gregory Nazianzen: On the Love of the Poor (Oration 14)." In *Cappadocian Theology*, ed. N. Dumitrascu, 139-58. Basinstoke: Palgrave Macmillan, 2015.

———. *St. Gregory of Nazianzus: An Intellectual Biography.* Crestwood, NY: St. Vladimir's Seminary Press, 2001.

Meredith, A. *The Cappadocians.* London: Geoffrey Chapman, 1995.

---. *Gregory of Nyssa: Writings with Commentary.* London: Routledge, 1999.
Musurillo, H., ed. *From Glory to Glory: Texts from Gregory of Nyssa's Mystical Writings.* New York: Scribner, 1961.
Rousseau, P. *Basil of Caesarea.* Berkeley: University of California Press, 1994.
Ruether, R. *Gregory of Nazianzus: Rhetor and Philosopher.* Oxford: Clarendon, 1969.
Winslow, D. F. *The Dynamics of Salvation: A Study in Gregory of Nazianzus.* Philadelphia: Philadelphia Patristics Foundation, 1979.

**The Church in Fourth-Century Transitional Society**

Fletcher, R. *The Barbarian Conversion: From Paganism to Christianity.* New York: Holt, 1999.
McMullen, R. *Christianity and Paganism in the Fourth to Eighth Centuries.* New Haven, CT: Yale University Press, 1999.
---. *Christianizing the Roman Empire: AD 100–400.* New Haven, CT: Yale University Press, 1984.
Stark, R. *The Rise of Christianity: How the Obscure, Marginal Jesus Movement Became the Dominant Religious Force in the Western World in a Few Centuries.* Princeton, NJ: Princeton University Press, 1996.
Wilken, R. A. *The Christians as the Romans Saw Them.* New Haven, CT: Yale University Press, 1984.

# RECONCILING THE WORLD

## Christian Ascetical and Penitential Imperatives

### REPENTANCE AND RECONCILIATION IN EARLY CHRISTIAN THEORY AND ACTION

The writings of the apostle Paul demonstrate two chief aspects of early Christian thought on reconciliation. The one is global or metaphysical: the manner in which God has worked out the reconciliation of a fallen or alienated world. The other is personal, focused on the issue of the sin (or redemption) of the individual member(s) of the church communities. The first could be called the christological aspect of reconciliation. It is, technically, called *soteriology* in Christian thought: the doctrine of salvation as worked by God on the cosmos. The second, more personally focused aspect of the doctrine of salvation can be described as how the individual seeks forgiveness: repentance and purification from sin; what are the protocols of reconciliation an individual can find between the self and the divine, and between the self and the community.

Paul speaks to the first aspect of reconciliation throughout his work.[1] He is most distinctive (and influential on later generations) in his theological style, introducing the specific concept *katallasso/katallage* to convey his meaning.[2] The clearest example of his wide-ranging, cosmic sense of reconciliation is given in his redolent statement "God was in Christ reconciling the world to himself" (2 Cor 5:19).[3] In Colossians the

---

[1] See further R. Martin, *Reconciliation: A Study of Paul's Theology* (Atlanta: John Knox, 1981); J. Fitzmyer, "Reconciliation in Pauline Theology," in *No Famine in the Land: Studies in Honor of John L. McKenzie*, ed. J. W. Flanagan and A. W. Robinson (Missoula, MT: Scholars Press, 1975), 155-77. Key passages are 2 Cor 5; Rom 5:6-11; Eph 2; Col 1:11–4:6.

[2] *Apokatallasso*: Eph 2:16; Col 1:20, 22; *katallage*: Rom 5:11; 11:15; 2 Cor 5:19; and *katallasso*: Rom 5:10; 2 Cor 5:18, 19, 20.

[3] In his Torch Bible Commentary on 2 Corinthians (London: SCM Press, 1961), R. P. C. Hanson calls this passage "one of the charters of the Christian ministry in the New Testament." See further D. L. Turner, "Paul and the Ministry of Reconciliation in 2 Cor. 5.11-6:2," *Criswell Theological Review* 4, no. 1 (1989): 77-95; C. Constantineanu, *The Social Significance of Reconciliation in Paul's Theology: Narrative Readings in Romans* (London: T&T Clark, 2010).

Pauline theology moves explicitly from a cosmically scoped vista of the reconciliatory work of Christ to the specific way this works itself out in a demonstrable moral change in the believer's life. Paul, for example, teaches that as the suffering Lord has achieved victory over the forces of evil, through the sacrificial offering of his own body, and has gained God the Father's mercy for his new people (the church, which is his extended body), so too the community of the faithful that is "in Christ" (mystically associated with him in his sufferings and glorification) is called out of the old manner of unregenerate living (sinful and selfish) into a new life of spiritual freedom and communion with God and with the other parts of Christ's mystical body. This anthropological and social teaching was set in a very spacious metaphysical horizon.

But Paul can be very precise on the same matter, too. He can equally speak to the more individual, moral aspect of reconciliation, as when he (regularly) offers specific advice and admonition to the churches he regards as under his supervisory remit. These moral injunctions are either exhortatory in his letters (paraenetic material) or else they come in the form of rebukes, commands, or insistences, where he lays down the law (apodictic material) for the earliest Christian communities. A few examples might suffice to illumine the style of Paul's pastoral reconciliation ethic for us. In 1 Corinthians 11:18-22, for example, he alerts us to problems of order in the Corinthian church. Instead of celebrating a "common meal" at eucharistic celebrations, the community there seems to have split into factions (class distinctions, one senses he means) and subgroups bringing their own food without wishing to share it and eating separately from others.[4] "Shall I commend you in this?" says Paul. "No, I will not." When such practices debase the commonality of the meal, he says, "It is no longer the Lord's supper that you eat" (1 Cor 11:20). It is, on the other hand, an act that "despises the church of God and humiliates those who have nothing" (1 Cor 11:22). So whoever eats and drinks in this unworthy and selfish manner "profanes the body and blood of the Lord" (1 Cor 11:27). He goes on: "This is why many of you are weak and ill, and some have died" (1 Cor 11:30).

Here, reconciliation with the community members (horizontally, as it were) has a direct effect on the possibility of reconciliation with God (vertically). The sacrament of the Eucharist is the social expression of the reconciliation anticipated with the divine, through the medium of the body of the suffering and glorified Lord. The horizontal and vertical axes are by no means the same (one a social ethic, the other an eschatological-theological hope of divine communion), but for Paul they transect within the praxis of the sacramental life of the church. Charity is the core. As the philosopher

---

[4] The earliest eucharistic celebrations of Communion in the body and blood of Jesus were set within the context of a larger communal meal (*agape*), where members of the church brought food and were also supposed to be conscious of the needs of poorer members.

Cornel West has put it, "Justice is the public face of love."[5] The failures of an ethic of charity among the Corinthians, for Paul, actually render ineffectual the very sacrament of reconciliation, which is the Eucharist.

Another example of his approach to reconciliation is given in the (somewhat "occasional") judgment he is asked to pronounce on a man in the Christian community at Corinth who has transgressed the laws surrounding marriage: "It is actually reported that there is immorality among you, and of a kind that is not found even among pagans; for a man is living with his father's wife. . . . Let him who has done this be removed from among you" (1 Cor 5:1-2). The man seems to have married his stepmother: possible under Roman law but contrary to Jewish cultic regulation. Paul here calls for the forced expulsion of the guilty man (even if for a specific time until he shall conform to the requirement to set his wife aside). What is operative in his mind here is that the one guilty of a serious moral lapse endangers the right of the whole community to claim reconciliation with God and the peace of communion that flows from that (the security of salvation). For Paul, by harboring the sinner, the entire community of the pure elect risks radical defilement.[6]

Once again the small aspect of individual act (the praxis of the one man thinking he could observe Roman marriage customs since he was [presumably] a Gentile Christian, not a Jew) has large-scale communitarian and cosmic implications. He is not simply "sent to Coventry"; he is, more precisely, solemnly and cultically "handed over to Satan" (regarded as henceforth a pagan excluded from the protection of the ark of the church's salvation). Paul adds a note that he hopes this condemnation will cause the man's repentance and (presumably) reconciliation to the community afterward. In practice this would mean that the individual is excluded from the eucharistic assembly (excommunication) and not readmitted until his behavioral change demonstrates a new mind (*metanoia*, repentance). This sanction soon comes to be the specific responsibility of the president of the local eucharistic assemblies, that is, the bishop; and from early times we can note a strong link between moral supervision and the instinct to protect the sanctity of the altar and its sacraments.

Again, in Colossians 1:20-23, Paul (or his Pauline disciple) expresses the same sense that the axes of vertical and horizontal reconciliation transect in Christ when he says, "[Christ] has now reconciled in his body of flesh by his death, in order to present you holy and blameless and irreproachable before him, provided that you continue in the faith, stable and steadfast, not shifting from the hope of the gospel which you heard, which has been preached to every creature under heaven, and of

---

[5]Part of a speech by Cornel West at a John Coltrane tribute in New York, Oct. 6, 2013.
[6]1 Cor 5:6: "A little yeast leavens the entire lump," he says, here meaning yeast as a symbol of corruption spreading.

which I, Paul, became a minister." The cosmic work of Christ, conquering the aerial and terrestrial daimons and establishing peace on earth and allowing communion with God to be reestablished "in Christ," is once more shown here to be not merely a cosmic act of the Lord's but something that is also sustained, even developed, by the Christian community's ongoing efforts to live stably, steadfastly, and in accordance with the "hope of the gospel you heard."

In the generations after Paul, his moral advice becomes increasingly invested with high "apostolic" authority for the internationally spreading churches. Paul's corpus of letters was widely known by the later second century, and it set terms of reference for the way morality is deeply connected with theological proclamation (*kerygma*) in the early Christian mindset. The church community that sees itself as redeemed, bought from evil powers by the price of the blood of the Messiah, as Paul instructed them, also sees itself as the pure body, the unspotted bride.[7]

The Pauline letter to Titus (especially Tit 1:4–2:13) gives us a snapshot of how the mid- to late first-century Christian communities are at one and the same time breaking off from the "circumcision party" (which seems resistant to the Paulinist message) and establishing what has come to be known as the Romano-Christian household code as its charter of ethical conduct. In this, "respectable procedure" is preached as a high goal. Titus's admonition, for example, argues that for the sake of keeping the peace (an important aspect for a community that rightly had cause to fear persecution if noticed), even Christian slaves are to be encouraged to give obedience to their masters (the idea of resistance to unjust oppression is not even discussed in regard to the institution). Women are not to be drunk in public. Moderation is the golden mean in respectable behaviour. This accumulates to a set of ethical injunctions that would not really be out of place in many comparable social groups, Jewish or sophistic.[8]

The household code can also be seen in the writings of the apostolic fathers, which derive from about the same time as the late Pauline epistles. The moral injunctions of Clement of Rome, for example, could easily be mistaken for generic moral writing of the late antique period, and it is in other details that we have to look for significant "Christian" markers. The Titus catalogue of good behaviors (Tit 2:1-10) is, however, surely a massively idealized picture. Early Christian communities undoubtedly set high standards of moral performance before themselves, but evidences about troubled internal social relations, even in the New Testament era, suggest that there were problems in regard to living up to the vision of a "pure community" in the day-to-day

---

[7] 2 Cor 11:2; Eph 5:5; Phil 1:10. Other New Testament indications of this quest for purity are numerous: Jas 1:27; 1 Pet 2:9-11; 1 Jn 3:3-8; Rev 19:7-8.
[8] Stoic associations were also renowned for offering moral encomia of this kind to their adherents.

reality.[9] The Johannine letters are exercised with the issues of how sinners can still claim to be the pure elect. They come up with the solution (clearly thought about over a long time): that believers are redeemed in Christ and have expiation of sins in his blood; nevertheless, they still need to confess their sin and repent in all humility (1 Jn 1:6–2:17) so as to stay faithful to the way. It is this moral realism that comes to be more and more distinctive of standard procedures in the church as the second century progresses. We can see the evidence for it mounting in the number of "canons" or regulations that Christian clergy issue, especially when the bishops of various ecclesiastical provinces come together in synods.

**Eastern penitential canons.** The canons are attached to episcopal synodical process from a very early date.[10] They are a mark of a church that is some way down the road of establishing a standard polity organized around clerical leadership of presbyters and bishops, the latter meeting in provincial consultations to establish common disciplinary processes and standards of good practice across a wide domain of church communities.[11] What provided a spur to the formation of this process was the issue of liturgical purity: a theological and psychological impetus perhaps related very closely to Christianity's origination in Jewish circles where the purity laws dominated ethical thinking in a striking manner. When Christians abandon so many (not all) aspects of the external purity regulations of the Torah, they tend not to abandon the sense of the primacy of the cultic regulations. The strictures attached to laws of worship in the Old Testament become symbolically transferred in the way the churches come to look on their cultic rituals of baptism and Eucharist. Purity of heart and lifestyle is given so high a relevance that even to this day Christian rituals of taking Communion are prefaced by rites of penance and confession (even in those churches where the formal sacrament of confession of sins has been set aside).

What particularly pressured this development was the repetitive incidence of anti-Christian persecutions. These externally applied oppressions did not merely produce a body of heroic martyrs and confessors of the faith; they also produced a considerable number of those who ran away, fudged issues by bribing local officials, or simply agreed to become involved once more in the cults of the Roman gods and

---

[9]Internal dissensions are apparent from the outset between the "Judaizers" and Paul. Paul's letters express shock about the reports of Christian men visiting prostitutes in Corinth (1 Cor 6:15-18), along with many other examples of encouragement to stay away from decadent lifestyles: paraenetic rhetoric that would hardly be felt necessary if all had lived exemplary lifestyles in the first century. Paul's moral realism is summed up in his advice: "Therefore let anyone who thinks that he stands take heed, lest he fall" (1 Cor 10:12).

[10]The name *canons* derives from the Greek for "rule" or "measure": in this case a measurement of discipline and good order, or simply put, ecclesiastical laws.

[11]See further chap. 19.

the imperial *genius* (even if they did rationalize it to themselves on the grounds that these idols "were not gods really").[12] In the aftermath of bloody persecutions, when Christian communities could count members of their immediate families who had paid the ultimate price for their faith, it was not always easy to speak about reconciliation in regard to those who had "lapsed" or paid their way out of trouble.

Early attitudes had established a rule of thumb that baptism could never be repeated. It was a once-for-all event in a believer's life: a personal assumption to oneself of the cleansing power of Christ's death and resurrection conveyed in the sacramental washing and anointing. It made no sense to the earliest Christians to ask, "And what happens if I sin after baptism? How do such sins become forgiven?" But the late Pastoral Letters already show that this question was indeed becoming a common one. About the same time as the late Pastorals, the Shepherd of Hermas had given a prophetic word that a second, postbaptismal reconciliation "might conceivably be possible," but only once in a person's life.[13] The pastoral relaxation had called down on the author's head the denunciations of Tertullian, who branded the book the "Shepherd of Adulterers." Despite this, he followed Hermas's general recommendation and argued in his own treatise *On Penance* that one occasion of postbaptismal forgiveness might be sought after, never two.[14] His own church's penitential process at Carthage in the second century was one that involved the harshest of mortifications imposed punitively on public sinners. It consisted of severe fasts and ritual prostrations before the presbyters of the church, eventually leading to the laying on of hands in prayers that called on the community to beseech God's forgiveness on the fallen individual. This was a system of penance that marked a person off definitively and permanently, so it seems, for the rest of their Christian life. Their role in the church henceforward was to be "as a penitent" seeking a "very difficult forgiveness" from God because it had been theologically defined as an "impossible forgiveness." This dramatic entrance into the penitent state would hardly be done voluntarily. It was a matter of dealing with large-scale and public lapses.

But to defend the principle of the once-for-all-ness of baptism as a forgiveness of sins, the very early church also adopted a strategy that there were two distinctions of penance to be made. There were, on the one hand, an array of petty sins of the ordinary type that might be called regular domestic failings. Eventually these were designated as *venial* sins. Origen addressed, in the early third century, how a Christian might take on a more focused effort at moral rehabilitation by dint of prayer, fasting, and

---

[12]The title of *martyr* (witness) was given to those who died; the title *confessor* was given to those who were made to suffer for the faith but survived.
[13]Shepherd of Hermas, Mandates 4.1.8.
[14]Tertullian, *De Paenitentia* 7.9.10.

almsgiving. This spiritual practice of repentance would stand in as the typological fulfilment of the more externalized rites of purification spoken of in the old law.[15]

But there are also moral lapses of far greater weight. These would later be called *mortal* sins, insofar as it was felt they had the potential to definitively end the indwelling presence of the Holy Spirit within the soul. Three of these serious sins were also seen to be unforgivable. To commit them would effectively and permanently remove the person from the community of the elect church. These were apostasy (the blatant denial of Christ in times of stress, or the assumption of idolatrous worship after baptism) along with murder and adultery. The early Christian principle that the pure bride of Christ just did not commit sin was sustained in theory by this "reservation" of three unforgivable sins.

Setting these up as a hedge served to emphasise the economy of penance, a kind of pastoral relaxation of the rules, that could serve to work backward for the disciplining and reconciliation of those who had committed lesser faults. It was an "economic," or compromising, way the church leaders had to become more realistic about the extent of sinful behavior in their communities.[16] They had to manage this reality on a daily basis, and so they turned their focus, especially, on who was allowed to have access to the Eucharist and when. In this process they at one and the same moment acknowledged the moral realities of the daily lives of believers, yet acted to protect the old principle that the church was only the pure bride of Christ, by effectively protecting the sacral purity of the altar. This was to be done not only by setting up an ever greater set of rules to govern when Communion might be taken (after prior fasting and so forth) but also by making the disciplinary rules of the clerical orders ever more explicit.

It was the persecutions, of course, that started to erode even the symbolic position of projecting three unforgivable sins, and also the theological principle that serious postbaptismal sin was unforgivable. The postpersecution environment, when many Christians survived, was what tempered the earlier rigorism. By the third century, confessors, that is, those who had been tortured and mutilated but had not denied their faith, were widely believed to be invested with specially elevated spiritual powers by Christ the Lord of martyrs.[17] One of those spiritual powers was the ability to intercede for earthly sinners and call down from heaven the forgiveness of sins. The persecutions produced not only a cluster of martyrial graves as

---

[15] Origen, *Homilies on Leviticus* 2.4.

[16] *Economic* (*kat' oikonomian*) is used in Christian literature to designate a dispensation from the rules, less than strictly appropriate but offered so as to accommodate human weakness.

[17] See further J. A. McGuckin, "Martyr Devotion in the Alexandrian School: Origen to Athanasius," in *Recent Studies in Church History* 5, ed. E. Ferguson (Hamden, CT: Garland, 1999).

pilgrim foci, but also a lively attachment in local churches to the confessors to whom the less heroic faithful went, seeking the laying on of hands in prayer so that they might find a "kind of" second baptism of reconciliation. As we have already seen, in third-century Carthage this friction between the role of the confessors in assuring the faithful forgiveness of postbaptismal sins and the bishop's rights in determining whom he would admit to the sacraments (sinners excluded) came into sharp conflict.[18] This was why bishops had long been concerned with setting up common rules for guidance. These disciplinary canons of the Eastern church, therefore, are certainly a place where moral reflection moves after the New Testament era, but the origins of the development are rooted in liturgical and cultic motives.

A closer look at a few select synods of the early Eastern church can serve as short examples of how the canons grew in significance at the dawn of the fourth century, when records started to be kept in earnest. The pre-Nicene Synod of Ancyra can stand as our chief example.

*The Synod of Ancyra 314.* Ancyra was the capital city of Roman Galatia (now Ankora in Turkey). The episcopal gathering here was convoked very soon after the persecuting emperor Maximin had been killed, and Licinius (then partner to Constantine) had declared peace for the church. The bishops thought that this peace would be definitive, but Licinius shortly after turned against them, as part of his struggle for power with Constantine, and the real *Pax Christiana* would not be established until Constantine ended the civil war in 324 and called the Council of Nicaea to mark it. But in 314 the bishops took the opportunity of an end to hostilities to address the chaos that had come about in Christian affairs in the times when they had to function as hidden dissidents. Bringing coherent and visible order into the Christian communities was not only a desideratum of the bishops, of course, but was also civilly legally required so that the Christian religion could be formally constituted as a Roman legal corporation, which followed from its recognition as *religio licita*: a formally acknowledged religion within the imperium's protection.

The synod needed to make many repairs. In the latest wave of persecutions specifically wealthy Christians had been targeted as well as higher clerical leaders. The latter had been singled out for exemplary punishments meant to break the spirit of the others. Many of the laity had bribed officials to give them false certificates stating that they had fulfilled the imperial requirement to offer incense to the gods of Rome. These were known among the scandalized church faithful as *libellatici*. While it was not the same as having offered sacrifice to the gods, it was widely regarded as a matter of publicly lying in the very core of one's baptismal confession and as such meriting

---

[18]In this case the bishop was Cyprian of Carthage.

exclusion from the sacraments. The clergy who had suffered particularly heavy attack had also won their share of martyrs and their share of lapsed. Some had fallen because they could not endure the sophisticated and sustained tortures for which Rome was notorious. They had resisted at first and then had been broken. Some others had taken fright and broken quickly. Others still had run to the authorities scared out of their wits and conformed to their demands even before the first torture had commenced. The canons of the council clearly tried to establish a considered process of graded reconciliation, where the point could be made that some "did better than others" in the times of stress, where the need for repentance could be underlined, but also where a system of face-saving degrees of penance might be established, so that everyone could feel the church was moving forward again and not continuing the evil work of the oppressors either by indulging in destructive self-recriminations or by a blasé forgetfulness of the sacrifices that had been made.

The Ancyran canons, therefore, are among the first formal Christian regulations to deal with how penance can be practically regulated. The first rule stated (giving it a clear sign of importance) instructs that presbyters who lapsed can retain their places of honor in church but can never again offer the oblation (preside over the Eucharist) or preach, both of which were their fundamental liturgical functions. This sounds like a non sequitur, but in the standard liturgical context of the day it was a genuine face-saving solution, for the presbyters generally sat in the apse around the bishop, and the latter always offered the oblation as single president in any case. With discretion one would not notice the lapsed presbyter "stood out" Sunday by Sunday, and the ruling allowed the minister to continue serving the church in other capacities (teaching, administration, singing, and so on). Those who had broken only after extensive torture were treated even more compassionately. Deacons who had lapsed under torture were also allowed to retain their rank but not their functions in church. In this instance the bishops are allowed individually to have leeway in cases where this debarment from liturgical service "causes distress of mind." It could not be clearer: the honorable who broke in the torture rooms should be rehabilitated. The dishonorable (who caved in without pressure) should be relegated. The bishops should have discretion to test the character and caliber of the clerical leadership in the light of the cessation of persecutions to see who should continue to hold a function of spiritual leadership in prayers.

The second synodical canon allows laity who had been literally carried to the altars of pagan sacrifice and physically forced to offer incense to the gods (there were many such cases, the pagans having an idea from the Christians themselves that sacrifice to the gods "washed out" the baptismal initiation) restitution to communion immediately. It was noted that even if they had been forced to make pagan offerings, the worthy among these laity could still be ordained in the future, for such forced worship could not be counted as having "sacrificed to the gods of Rome," which would be a permanent debarment from orders. This regulation seems to mark out a new class of those from whom replacement leadership might be forthcoming. Other Ancyran canons regulate the penance and readmission process in differing grades of severity for laity in different circumstances: whether they had volunteered to the authorities to betray their faith or whether they had only been cowed into it by torture or severe threats. In each case the bishops were given discretion to look to the "general character of their lives," not just their performance in the time of stress (canon 7).

Great discretion is given to the bishop, apart from the instance that ministers of the altar should not offer the oblation again if they had sacrificed to idols. Only the laity are to be admitted to degrees of penance, which seem to be initiated or at least highly developed at this time. Clerics can never be formally enrolled as penitents. The two roles are incompatible. If a cleric is a notorious sinner, he must be deposed from office. As for the laity who enter the system of penance, we see in these canons the differentiated classes of sinners, listeners, kneelers, standers, and communicants. In later times, when the church buildings had porticoes, the "sinners" had to remain in the lobby when the Eucharist was in process. They were still part of the community but not admitted to its inner circle of sacramental mysteries. They had been symbolically returned to the status of an inquiring pagan as a penance, even though some hope of final restoration is held out to them (often after seven years of enduring this public loss of status).

The listeners were believers who had lapsed and had been symbolically restored to the status of prebaptismal catechumens. The latter were allowed to stay in the worship service until the Gospel had been read, and then before the eucharistic anaphora was started they were ushered out of the room by the deacons so as to remain in the portico until the Communion had been administered to the faithful. So once again we see a "degraded rank" being the punishment for lesser offenses than offering pagan sacrifice. The kneelers were those who were readmitted to the body of the church for the whole of the service but were not allowed to go to Communion yet. The Christians of the fourth century (and before) did not kneel to pray on Sundays. Kneeling was taken as a sign of penitent sorrow, appropriate only for times when one confessed one's sins to God. The canons of Nicaea 325 explicitly forbid anyone to kneel on a Sunday ever again (thus declaring a jubilee). To make a believer kneel when most of the community was standing in prayer was thus also a sign that they had to do some period of seeking forgiveness of their lapses, though the next stage after kneeling was to be readmittance to full communion with the assembly. Depending on the severity of the lapse, the time spent in this penitential process, slowly moving back into the interior of the church building and its community, could take two, three, even seven years.

One suspects that the legislation was more harsh in script than in practice. Such discretion was given to the episcopate that if the community peace was successfully reestablished (though such a system might be useful in assuaging wounds and resentments in the immediate aftermath of bloody persecutions where community members lost those near and dear to them) one suspects the bishop might have dispensed of its full rigors. Certainly the Nicene regulation dismissing the practice of kneeling at Sunday Eucharists is a clear sign that it wished to move away substantially from this system. The full process of moving from sinner to communicant through the various grades was definitively abandoned in the late fourth century, when the penance arrangement was put more or less entirely under episcopal discretion and celebrated by the sinner confessing misdeeds to the presbyters and being reconciled with a laying on of hands and instructions how to perform private penance before readmittance to Communion, a system that has endured to this day in the Catholic and Orthodox churches.

*Monastic influences on penance.* Monastic circles especially developed this middle stage of the system of penance, so as to make of it a meeting of the younger monk with his or her spiritual teacher or elder (*geron, starets*). In such a meeting the younger monk was expected to reveal all the secrets of the heart: not just major sins but minor failings and distractions. It is this monastic context of spiritual direction that transformed the Christian system of penance from a punitive legislative affair, into an issue of psychological and emotional guidance. Later monastic leaders, writing out of this context of self-scrutiny and self-revelation, would give birth to a new form of literature: the searching of the soul. Christian mystical literature is among the most advanced forms of ancient writing about self-awareness as a ground for perceiving the presence and work of God in the world. Some of these notable ascetic writers, such as Evagrius of Pontos, Dorotheus of Gaza, and Cassian of Marseille, actually stand in history as the true inventors of introspective psychological literature as a medium of metaphysics.

The Ancyran canons are not just concerned with the aftermath of involvement in pagan rituals, however. As can also be clearly seen, the sexual mores of the Christian community started to become a matter of explicit episcopal concern. One can contrast this with the almost total silence of church leaders in the New Testament texts. Even though the late Pastoral Letter*s* speak volumes about decency, good order, and being respectable, they pass over in silence the realities of first-century Christian worship in regard to sexual matters. Many of those worshipers, who were admitted freely to the

Eucharist, one presumes, were slaves, both men and women. At this period, Roman slaves were routinely used by their masters or mistresses, if they desired, as sexual objects. It is passed over in discretion. It is not a debarment from being a member of the pure bride of the church, and surely this was a powerful appeal of the early church in such a social system of endemic oppressions. But by the end of the third century, sexual circumstances were becoming more and more heavily legislated.

Canon 11 of Ancyra is an interesting reflection of the social disorder that occurs in the aftermath of war. It represents a compassionate move to assert the rights of women, who were (and are) so regularly victimized in time of civil unrest. The bishops at Ancyra legislated that, as far as the church was concerned, a virgin who was already betrothed to a Christian remained contractually bonded to her fiancé even if she had been carried off in time of war and suffered ravishment before she could be married. The church asserted, therefore, the permanency of betrothal as a sacramental bond (a rule that still applies to the betrothal rite of the Eastern churches). This strongly suggests that the bishops were concerned in their legislation to protect the honor of women returning from war captivity in a social environment where, presumably, many fiancés were trying to break the engagement on the pretext of their own honor because their former fiancées were no longer virgins.

Later church lawyers and commentators started, in Byzantine times, to weaken the force of this canon. Then the context was no longer war (we ought instead to imagine early medieval abductions in a village scene, family feuds, and so on), and the later canonists started to add the caveat "provided the fiancé was still willing to receive her." But the original draft and intent of this legislation here at Ancyra was a signal defense of the honor of women, according to terms of the setting of "standards of honor according to the heart's intent," not the forced circumstances of dishonor falling on the innocent. This, one remembers, was legislation issued in a Greek society that was heavily conditioned by principles of honor and shame (*time kai aischyne*). The legislation surely rubbed very much against the social grain, as can be seen in its progressive "relaxation" where the honor of the man is given higher value than the honor of the woman.

But many other of these early Greek canons are clearly focused on more personal, domestic matters of sexuality.[19] The canons of the near-contemporary Synod of Neo-Caesarea are even more obsessed with them.[20] So too can a similar obsession with

---

[19] Canons 16, 17, 19, 20, 21, and 25 of Ancyra. Text in H. R. Percival, *The Seven Ecumenical Councils of the Undivided Church: Their Canons and Dogmatic Decrees*, NPNF 14 (Oxford: James Parker, 1900), 63-75.
[20] Held certainly before Nicaea, probably some time around 315, in Pontus by the Black Sea. Texts in Percival, *Seven Ecumenical Councils of the Undivided Church*, 79-86.

sexual purity, especially in relation to cultic matters, be seen in the canons of the Synod of Gangra from 340, and particularly Elvira in Spain (306).[21] Such regulations are all apparently set on establishing a sexual moral code within the church that is distinctly higher than that prevalent in the external society. Some commentators have focused on this as revealing the increasing attempt by bishops to extend the remit of their power more and more into the domain of laity. But it is something that is seen as a characteristic of all of Constantine's new empire deal. He (regardless of the church, so it seems, but glad to affirm its efforts) was determined on setting higher and better standards of sexual ethics across the empire at large, believing that such a thing would call down the protection of heaven on his reign. Like Diocletian before him, Constantine was a puritan, not a cavalier.

Scholars who see the development of these canonical regulations of sexuality in rather simple terms of episcopal power flexing miss this historical moment in which the empire (emerging from generations of civil chaos and war) was changing its ethos. Rome always had a puritanical social dimension, but one that was regarded as "appropriate" for the middle classes more than the class of laborers or the superwealthy. The decadence of some of the Roman upper classes was, of course, a matter of much prurient reflection, even in antiquity.[22] It has become a cliché of modern filmic treatments of the Roman imperial past from De Mille to Fellini. What Constantine wished to do, however, was very traditional in antique terms. He wanted to return society generally, back to its simpler, rural, golden age, and he wanted to use the Christian church as a vehicle to perform that very precise restoration of *Romanitas* that he has in mind. The rise of Christianity itself is also a sign of this "change of times." The more externalized rituals of purification that were conducted before engaging in Roman religious ceremonies, however, were seen to be more internalized in the Christian

---

[21]Gangra was called by bishops alarmed by the spread of radical ascetical bands of men and women, under Eustathius of Sebaste's leadership, who had demanded an apocalyptic standard of chastity, almost expecting celibacy as a standard of normal Christian lifestyle. Although the Gangran episcopal sexual regulations appear strict, they are concerned nevertheless with asserting the legitimacy of sexually active marriages within the Christian community, something that the Syrian church had in the previous two centuries tended to discourage actively. To arrive at a censure of Eustathius, the synodical fathers made a rather extreme synopsis of his "tendencies" (rather than an accurate digest of his views). They condemn the views that the sexes are equal; that marriage is to be despised (canon 1); that virginity is to be the only true spiritual path; and that familial and spousal authority can be flouted in the name of Christ. The extraordinary attack on women wearing men's clothes in these canons turns out only to be a disapproval of women adopting gender-neutral monastic garb under Eustathius's guidance and thereby claiming the right to the itinerant life of the sophist community he led. Texts in ibid., 91-101. On Elvira, see further S. Laeuchli, *Sexuality and Power: The Emergence of Canon Law at the Synod of Elvira* (Philadelphia: Temple University Press, 1972).

[22]Suetonius's *Lives of the Caesars*, like an ancient *People* magazine, is not going to lose any chance to let the reader in on it.

approach to morality. Sexuality was here brought into focus as simultaneously a moral and a religious activity: something attached to the soul, not simply the body. This proved to be a momentous change of attitude in terms of human history.

What the increasing moral injunctions of such synods as Ancyra reflect, therefore, is not simply a matter of professing higher moral standards than the prevailing societal norm: it is perhaps also governed by the sense, in the time of the dawning Constantinian victory, that the larger numbers that started to fill the churches in times of peace had to be reminded of the ancient Jewish-Christian moral customs, which were significantly different from Roman lower-class attitudes (where more or less every corner bar sold the waitresses alongside the beer). The canons try to give a compassionate response to those who had spilled blood (most acutely aware of the many who had been guilty of killing in time of war). They are classed as being capable of rehabilitation with repentance. Christian sorcerers, soothsayers, and the like are also penanced at Ancyra with a ban from Communion for three years. This is clearly meant as an attempt to draw a sharper line between church and secular society, where such practices were part of the standard fabric of daily life. One remembers Firmicus Maternus, a noted convert to the church who had been a Roman augur beforehand and who continued to write works on astrology. But that was an earlier era. Now the bishops were deliberately targeting the professional (Christian) fortunetellers more so than the (presumably) even larger circle of laity who had recourse to them. The canon tries to show up the profession as incompatible with life in the church. It would take a long time indeed for the notion to bear general weight. Even Augustine, in the fifth century, admits (as an older bishop) that as a newly baptized Christian he still was popular among his *collegium* friends for casting good horoscopes.[23]

In the East (quite distinct from the Western churches, where the old penitential systems had a much longer run) the formal system of penance reflected in the synodical canons had a relatively short lifespan of just over two centuries. It was primarily a reaction to massive lapses in times of persecution. After the persecutions it grew increasingly redundant, though some of the principles of establishing penitential *epitimia* (a penance or proper corrective response for varied levels of sins) remained as permanently established via the synodical decrees and the so-called canonical epistles of the Fathers (especially those of Dionysius of Alexandria and Basil of Cappadocian Caesarea).[24] By the seventh century penitential practices of confession in the East had become private, chiefly administered by presbyters, and

---

[23]*Confessions* 4.3.4; 7.6.8. See L. Ferrari, "Augustine and Astrology," *Laval théologique et philosophique* 33 (1977): 241-51.
[24]See further J. A. McGuckin, *The Ascent of Christian Law: Patristic and Byzantine Reformulations of Antique Civilization* (Crestwood, NY: St. Vladimir's Seminary Press, 2012), esp. chaps. 4-5, 7.

more concerned with reconciling sinners than punishing them.[25] Nectarius of Constantinople, the archbishop who succeeded Gregory of Nazianzus in the capital, publicly abolished the clerical office of grand penitentiary, the person who had supervised the church's systems of penance. Already by that stage, at the end of the fourth century, the whole formal approach must have seemed obsolete.

**Western penitentials and the system of confession.** The Western church canons of the fourth-century synods, especially the Spanish ones, are noticeably stricter, not to say harsher, than those of the East. This is an attitude to penitential practice that can be traced from the very beginning of Western church practices, as manifested in Tertullian's writings, who continued to have influence in the Latin West (never in the Greek East). The Western system is described in its later stages (almost at a time when the ancient procedures are becoming outmoded) by Augustine of Hippo and Caesarius of Arles, and also by synodical acts of the synods of the bishops of southern Gaul. The sources suggest a common form of three moments of the process: entrance into penance (*accipere paenitentiam*), the endurance for several years of this status (*ordo paenitentium*), and the solemn readmission to the status of communicants, which took place through the imposition of hands by the bishop on Maundy Thursday of Holy Week (*reconciliatio*).[26]

The requirements to observe perfect continence in this process made it an "order" that many lay Christians decided to defer until late in life. Indeed, from end of the third century onward, baptism itself was increasingly deferred until late in life because of the anxiety of keeping all the moral code in the face of such penalties. At times between the third and fifth centuries a large majority of Christian communities might be composed of catechumens who did not communicate or attend all of the eucharistic service. The ritual is still present in the anaphora of the Eastern Orthodox liturgies, where the deacon comes out to address the congregation and demand that all catechumens should leave the building while the mysteries are about to be celebrated.

In the West the high status of this ancient system of penance, enduring some time after it had disappeared in the East, made it a model of rigorous standards. It also fell more and more into the hands of the individual bishops, who could apply discretion to the manner in which it was applied in various provincial churches. This was how it was migrated (when it was eventually abandoned in its primitive form)

---

[25]See further I. Hausherr, *Penthos: La Doctrine de la Componction dans l'Orient Chrétien* (Rome: Pont. Institutum Orientalium Studiorum, 1944); L. Ligier, "Dimension personnelle et dimension communitaire de la pénitence en Orient," *La Maison Dieu* 90 (1967): 155-88; F. van de Pavel, "La penitence dans le rite byzantine," *Questions Liturgiques* 54 (1973): 191-203.

[26]See further C. Vogel, *Le pecheur et la penitence dans l'Église ancienne* (Paris: Editions du Cerf, 1966); A. Fitzgerald, *Conversion Through Penance in the Italian Church of the Fourth and Fifth Centuries* (Lewiston, NY: Edwin Mellen, 1988).

into becoming a spiritual symbol more than a real canonical process universally acknowledged. The formal practice of penance, in other words, evolved to becoming a confessional system of spiritual penance, practiced privately, without the need for dramatic social excommunication that had characterized the ancient procedures. This, at first, made it also much more popular among the faithful at large.

This movement was taken up by Western monastics from the seventh century onward, who drove the penitential system even more deeply into the personal psychological forum. Beginning in the private devotions of the monastic (missionary) communities, where ascetics laid bare their spiritual states to their elders, a parallel system to that of the public churches became popular in the cause of seeking forgiveness for regularly committed sins. The theological focus shifted from being a church of the pure elect (the "saints" of the New Testament) to being a community of sinners seeking reconciliation in tears and lamentation. These two trajectories still continue to mark internal divisions within Christian ecclesial practice to this day. But the Western ascetical communities, being highly penitential in character and also very rigorous, tipped the balance. The Latin monks were also, much more than ever the case in the East, in the vanguard of the church's expansion into pagan tribal territories of the further West. Accordingly, they used their penance system as a missionary tool and thus introduced it to the new territories being evangelized, which had customarily been used to harsh tribal laws and fairly low moral standards. The monastic system came to be known as "tariffed penance" and had a long-lasting influence up to the twelfth century in the West. It is the invention, so it would seem, of Irish monastics and Anglo-Saxon church communities.

Tariffed penance gained its title from the principle of applying a specific penitential exercise, to express remorse, to each type of sin. From the clergy's point of view this became a pastoral tool in regulating the moral discipline of the congregations. There was no need for refined spiritual discretion anymore: one could simply look up in a book what appropriate punitive penance was for any given sin that was confessed. Such books were indeed written and came to be called the penitentials. From the people's point of view, sin was classified alongside civic crimes. As the latter offended against society and drew immediate and systematic penalties, so too it could be understood that God applied reasonable penalties in the spiritual domain for sins committed against him. He was rendered into a kind of super-Lord of feudal society. In an odd way, it seemed to be comforting to the Christians of the Dark Ages' West so to domesticate God.

The penitential system also passed on the administration and supervision of the whole affair to the hands of presbyters in parishes. It thus gained even more momentum by becoming localized in the smaller village societies of medieval Europe. If a sinner confessed to really serious sins (such as murder), the ecclesiastical penalty might be exile (the civil penalty could still be death, of course). But the larger amount of lesser sins were now usually dealt with by imposing an act of penance on the person confessing to the priest: a certain number of days to spent in fasts of varied severity. When the prescribed period of fasting had been completed the penitent would return to the priest and receive a blessing that permitted them to return to Communion.

After the ninth century one starts to see formal prayers of absolution being entered into the rite of confession; and from this point onward the confessional practice became a more commonly celebrated sacramental rite of the parishes. This new combination of the ancient ritual of receiving a laying on of hands to signify reconciliation, with this new extended form of fasting repentance, gained much popularity; so much that even clergy now started to request it. It was at this early medieval period that the mathematics of the system started to be realized.

Of course, if one kept repeating various sins that had a fixed number of days (or months) of fasting attached to them as a tariff, then it might not take long for a person not to be able to fulfill the fasting requirements even in the course of a whole lifetime. To offset this, dispensations were applied. These gained the name of ransoms or redemptions. Soon they would come to be called "mercies," though we know them more commonly by their Latin name of indulgences. These worked by negotiation with the confessor. A long fast of moderate proportions might be exchanged, for example, for a shorter fast of great severity. The Irish regarded self-imposed exile from one's home village as one of the greatest penances possible. A fast could be given greater power with additional elements of asceticism, such as flagellation. It is on record that some penitents were made to spend the night in the local cemetery (something the ancients hated with great fear and revulsion), which must have served as a public ridicule as well as an effective preventative. Some of the flagellations were self-imposed, but often they were composed of a beating administered by the confessor. A third party could be induced to perform the fast on one's behalf: monks, for example, could do this in return for gifts of land or such given to the monastery. Masses, performed again by monks who were priest-confessors, could wipe away much more sinfulness than fasting could ever hope to do. So making a Mass offering (again land, livestock, or money to the church) became bound up at the heart of the penance system.

To us moderns the idea of priests beating up their dissident congregation members might sound very dubious, but physical beatings were a very common part of the civic administration of justice in this era, and corporal punishments such as beatings for sins committed had long been established as part of regular internal monastic practice. To early medieval contemporaries it must have seemed as if the church's "new" system of penance had at last caught up with modern social practices. It is, nevertheless, an epochal moment in the history of the church when it moved into the domain of overseeing the punishment of its members and into the business of policing moral progress by means of tight social constraint, rather than an episcopal withdrawing of access to the chalice in cases of notorious wrongdoing.

Not everyone at this time thought the change was for the good. In the Carolingian court, for example, more literate and classically trained theologians there protested at the way such a tribal system had displaced the old urban-episcopal formularies of the church under the Roman Empire. But despite their attempts to turn back the clock to the antique system, it was clear that it would never regain the position it had in more classical times. As a result of their work, however, the Celtic-Saxon system was significantly checked and mitigated; and in the wider take-up of the penitential system under the aegis of Rome (meaning, at that early stage, Rome's great power as a central disseminator of liturgical practices and theological opinions in the Western Christian world), a tariffed approach was eventually adopted for serious private sins, and a public penance on the old (exclusionary) system for grave and public offenses.[27] This was the origin of the Western penitential (and eventually moral) distinction of "private forum" and "public forum": a sin was held to be more significant if it came to light than if it remained in the private sphere (because of the grounds for scandal it could induce). This compromise stayed in place until the beginning of the thirteenth century in the West.[28]

In 1204 the Fourth Lateran Council made it a canonical requirement for all Western Christians to attend sacramental confession at least once a year and receive absolution from a priest before taking Paschal communion. By that time the formal ancient system of exclusion was only used in the West for rare and scandalous events (infanticide, incest, large-scale arson, and so on). Even this eventually gave way to sins reserved for their absolution to the papacy. For clerics who committed grave public sins, a penance of pilgrimage was imposed, leading to the several cases of wandering student-clerics of the Middle Ages. It was a hardship imposed as a discipline, but also a way of removing such clergy from regular pastoral care of local churches. The practice of pilgrimage as a penitential exercise became common in the

---

[27]See P. Saint-Roch, *La pénitence. Dans les conciles et les lettres des Papes des origines à la mort de Grégoire le Grand* (Vatican City: Pontificio Istituto di archeologia cristiana, 1991).
[28]See further C. Vogel, *Le pecheur et la penitence au moyen age* (Paris: Editions du Cerf, 1969); G. Picasso, G. Piana, and G. Motta, eds., *A pane ed acqua. Peccati e penitenza nel Medioevo* (Novara: Europia, 1986).

Middle Ages even for laity as well. In the Eastern churches the penitential motive for pilgrimage was significantly less to the fore. For cases of serious hidden (private forum) offenses, the tariffed system was retained in the West, and eventually this grew into the system of regular auricular confession administered by clergy that lasted into modern times in the Catholic and Orthodox churches. It was a particular target of the Reformation divines, who were especially drawn to its destruction because of the whole machinery of commutations, displacements, and indulgences, which had laid the system open, for so many centuries beforehand, to innumerable abuses.

***Feudal ideas of restitution and expiation.*** The rise of the indulgence system in the penitential ideas of Western Christianity was clearly influenced by concepts already prevalent in the tribal law of the newly evangelized peoples, and those more remote from the influence of Mediterranean Roman civilization. It was an echo of the old idea of "an eye for an eye a tooth for a tooth" (Ex 21:24). Despite the fact that such an application of law universally would leave the world toothless and blind, it had an attractiveness for the Western church as it expanded in the tribal areas and faced a rougher and ruder set of peoples to whom it had to teach the gospel authoritatively. A tariff for this and a tariff for that was some comfort to monastic missionaries embarking on the often lonely task of church planting.

At the same period Old Testament law was gaining higher status in Latin theology. Origen's allegorical approach to the old law (how it had been overshadowed by the light of the new) was not held in such high esteem as it was in the Greek-speaking churches. Renowned Latin theologian Jerome had consistently attacked the great Alexandrian's reputation in the early fifth century and damaged it severely in the Western church.[29] Augustine had little to no knowledge of Origen at all, and so the Latin exegetical tradition, while not ignorant of his work, had definitely sidelined him more extensively than had the East. Origen's view, therefore, that the texts of the Bible had to be interpreted in a strictly ascending hierarchical order, with those of the New Testament having much greater significance and weight than almost anything found in the Old Testament, was not so well observed in the Western church. Here, on the contrary, there was tendency to regard a text from any part of the Bible as "authoritative" and applicable to ordinary church life—if not the ceremonial aspects of the law, then certainly its moral injunctions.

So it was that Western Christendom elevated many of the Old Testament moral regulations (and prescripts) far more highly than did the theologians of the Byzantine world, who tended both to allegorize them more freely and always to subordinate them

---

[29]Despite being so heavily indebted to the great Alexandrian that several of his own biblical works are paraphrastic renditions of the older writer.

to the insights of the Gospels, broader traditions of patristic sages, and dictats of Roman law.[30] Both contexts of thought, the tribal background of many of the new Germanic missions and the renewed stress on religion as "forensic law" in the West, made for developments in this late patristic period, from the seventh century to the tenth, that were distinctive of the Latin churches and that to some extent formed a buildup to several of the later medieval tensions that would, in the end, give rise to the doctrinal disputes of the Reformation period. Two examples will be taken as illustrative of the case here: the doctrine of purgatorial afterlife as evidenced in Pope Gregory the Great in the seventh century and onward, and the concept of expiatory atonement as found in the works of Anselm of Bec, the archbishop of Canterbury at the end of the first millennium. Neither of these positions gained universal acceptance in Christendom. The East generally stood against them, thus making them emerge as special *theologoumena* of the Latin tradition; but they had a very definite and widespread influence over all the Western churches of the latter part of the first millennium.[31]

*Purgatory as posthumous expiation.* The word (*purgatorium*) is the Latin Christian term for a place of cleansing (from the root *purgo*) and refers to the concept of a putative "middle state" between heaven and hell, reserved for those souls that at the time of death are judged not to deserve final damnation into the pains of hell but whose sins are such that they are not considered fit to enter immediately into the joys of paradise. Purgatory was thus envisaged as a place of penitential postdeath purification. The inhabitants of purgatory would one day, when their sins had been sufficiently purified (often it was envisaged that purgatory was composed of cleansing flames analogous to hell's punitive flames), be liberated and admitted to paradisial joy. The doctrine as sketched out above, and especially with the imagination that purgatory was a kind of middle metaphysical geography between heaven and hell, did not assume clear form in the Western church until the eleventh century

---

[30] Marriage legislation is a typical example of this. In the Latin church divorce was strictly forbidden (and remains so in Catholic practice). Some obfuscation was made around royal marriages that needed to be sidelined, with a papal declaration usually being invoked that the prior marriage was "invalid." But in the Christian East, (civil) Roman law was honored within canon law, which allowed the possible dissolution of a marriage by episcopal adjudication and up to two more marriages celebrated in church (with increasing marks of liturgical censure). See further J. A. McGuckin, *The Orthodox Church* (Oxford: Wiley Blackwell, 2008), chap. 5, 309-23; McGuckin, *St. Gregory of Nazianzus: An Intellectual Biography* (Crestwood, NY: St. Vladimir's Seminary Press, 2001), 332-36, for a consideration of how this issue was first treated when it was brought to the attention of the archbishop of Constantinople in 380 by the (Spanish) Emperor Theodosius, puzzled by the disparity of marriage law in the two halves of the church.

[31] *Theologoumena* refers to doctrinal traditions that are locally held as significant in some places but do not impose themselves as of central importance on the universal church. In these two cases the Western tradition claimed universal significance for them well into the twentieth century, which was a cause of conflict with Byzantine-traditioned churches throughout the Middle Ages.

(in the works of Hildebert of Tours), although the idea of some kind of after-death purification being necessary for the soul makes an early embryonic appearance even in the second-century works of Tertullian.[32] He deduced, in an influential treatise on the nature of the soul, that any spirit of the deceased that needed cleansing must be made to stay for a short time in "Sheol."[33] For him this would seem to apply to all souls, except those who were able to fly up straight to God on account of their martyrdoms, the willing acceptance of the pains of martyrdom being widely seen in the ancient church as admitting the person immediately to the joys of paradise.

Several other significant patristic writers, Origen, Cyprian, Gregory of Nazianzus, and Ambrose among them, also speculated that the ordinary believer's soul after death would probably need to be cleansed by some form of purgative fire.[34] How this fire was envisaged ranged from a more materialist conception to a purely spiritual symbol of cleansing by means of advanced psychic reeducation at the hands of angels. This theory of the soul's postdeath purification probably developed among the theologians on the basis of the words of St. Paul (1 Cor 3:11-15) that "fire shall try every person's work"; he goes on to the effect that those who have built on shoddy foundations "shall be saved, yet saved through fire." This doctrine of some kind of postdeath purification period was certainly known by other parts of the early rabbinic movement (cf. 2 Macc 12:38-45). The tendency to populate the afterlife in this way was not so much motivated by a desire to depict a fuller map of the geography of heaven as much as part of the pastoral care of the dead. In other words, from the beginning of their organized existence, both the synagogue and the early Christian church prayed extensively for their dead, and many of the most ancient prayers to this effect are still found in the liturgies of the Greek and Latin churches.

Purgatory was an idea that in the West received a massive boost by the endorsement given to it by Augustine.[35] It was Pope Gregory the Great in the seventh century, however, who elevated what he called the "opinion" of earlier thinkers into a more or less formulated doctrine with the prestige of the papacy behind it. He taught in a very popular and influential work that "purgatorial fire will cleanse every elect soul before it comes into the last judgment."[36] After that moment the Latin church took the idea

---

[32]Hildebert of Tours was also known as Hildebert of Lavardin (or even Gildebert, or Adelbert), circa 1055–1133. His work on this subject is in PL 171, col. 741. See further J. Le Goff, *The Birth of Purgatory* (Chicago: University of Chicago Press, 1986).
[33]Tertullian, *De Anima* 58.
[34]Cf. Origen, *Homily on Numbers* 15; Cyprian, *Epistle* 55.22; Ambrose, *On Psalms* 36.26.
[35]*De Civitate Dei* 21.26; *Enchiridion* 68-69; *Ennarratio in Psalm* 37.3. See R. R. Attwell, "From Augustine to Gregory the Great: An Evaluation of the Emergence of the Doctrine of Purgatory," *JEH* 38 (1987): 173-86.
[36]Gregory the Great, *Dialogue* 4.41.[39].

more and more into its official preaching, while the Eastern churches continued to regard it as a speculation, a *theologoumenon* that was not part of the central doctrinal tradition. The Eastern Christian world generally retained a simpler doctrine of the afterlife in which the souls of the elect, even those who were not particularly holy, would be retained in "a place of light, a place of refreshment, a place from which all sorrow and sighing have been banished."[37] This view reflected the statement in Revelation 14:13 that "those who die in the Lord rest from their labors." In short, the state of the afterlife as it was envisaged in the early Eastern church was generally a happy and restful condition (developing out of 1 Thess 4:13, which spoke of a state of rest) in which the departed souls of the faithful were not divorced from God but waited on the last judgment with hopeful anticipation, as the time when they would be admitted to a transfigured and paradisial condition in proximity to God.

Some traditions from pre-Christian Egypt (the weighing of the souls in various "tollhouses") formed part of popular Byzantine speculations about the state of the soul in the immediate stages after death, and liturgically these were partly reflected in the funeral rituals of the East, where memorials held in church on the first, eighth, and fortieth days after death were regarded as particularly beneficial to assist the soul's transition.[38] After forty days it was popularly thought the soul would cease visiting its earthly haunts and definitively leave the sublunar regions. But Origen's theological influence stopped such speculations being a formal part of Eastern tradition. He had argued forcefully that Christ's descent into hell (part of the early creeds) was a definitive liberation of the souls of the just, and his resurrectional glory spread abroad in the church accounted for the Pauline idea of the saints being "with the Lord." It was this view that began to account for Eastern Christian opinion moving toward a belief that the souls of the just entered, soon after death, into the very presence of Christ, while the wicked were definitively cast away from his presence in a gloomy Hades.

From the seventh century onward, therefore, the doctrine of purgatory only continued as a *proprium* of the Latin catholic world. But both churches, in the ancient period, maintained the position that envisaging of the souls in their afterlife condition was first and foremost about the encouragement of their earthly relatives to pray for their happy estate. In both East and West the primary place to ensure such prayers would be heard, even at God's judgment seat, was held to be the eucharistic service, and special diptychs, memorials specifically naming the dead, formed part of liturgical rites in Latin and Greek from early times. Because of the prestige of Pope

---

[37] Litany for the dead from the Eastern Orthodox Liturgy of Funerals.
[38] At these tollhouses, dues (taxes) had to be paid when angels demanded an account of how the soul had fared in regard to the specific virtue represented by each tollhouse. This shows the influence of Egyptian religion quite notably.

Gregory's name attached to the doctrine of purgatory (and Augustine behind him), the status of the doctrine became a cause of contention when the Latin and Byzantine Christian worlds grew apart in the early second millennium. For the Latin world, the councils of Florence (1438+) and Trent (1545+) endorsed the concept as part of official church dogma.[39] The insistence of the East that such a teaching was merely a *theologoumenon* of the Latins, without any universal authority, whether or not the pope or a Western council endorsed it, caused much annoyance and remained for Latin theologians a charge of "departure from tradition," which they leveled against Byzantine theologians thereafter (and had it laid back against them in return).

*Feudal atonement theory in the West: Anselm's* Cur deus homo? Another example of how various *theologoumena* grew up and assumed the status of enduring marks of division between parts of Christendom can be taken from the case of early medieval Latin atonement theology. Anselm de Bec, the archbishop of Canterbury of the Norman King William II, might serve to illustrate it for us. Between 1097 and 1098 Anselm composed a treatise that was designed to refute a theory that had been first mooted by Gregory of Nyssa in the fourth century and had some popular currency in his day.[40] He finished it in the same year he attended the Council of Bari, where he was one of the skilled Latin theologians called by the pope to refute Byzantine theological claims that the Western doctrine of the double procession of the Spirit (another significant Western *theologoumenon*) was a fundamental corruption of the doctrine of the Trinity.[41] He titled his treatise on redemption *Cur Deus Homo?* or "Why Did God Become Man?"

Anselm's general intent was to demonstrate that the church should not give credence to lurid ideas that the devil had any rights over God, such that the divine Word "had to" suffer and die in the flesh so as to pay a set price of ransom for the souls of humankind. He wanted instead to place the emphasis, in theories of the incarnate redemption, on the notions of the justice and mercy of God. However, his context of argument for approaching those ideas of justice and mercy was decidedly feudal and thus significantly constricted. Anselm thought that as a commentator on the redemptive process he was simply reflecting a clarified meaning of key terms such as *expiation*, *sacrifice*, *justice*, and *mercy*, as recorded in the scriptural writings. But already, by his time, the nuances of Hebraic liturgical concepts such as sacrifice, expiation, and atonement, which Paul

---

[39]See paragraph 1030 of the *Catechism of the Catholic Church* (2015).
[40]In Gregory's *Great Catechetical Oration*, in which he develops on an idea floated by Origen of Alexandria in the third century. See further J. A. McGuckin, "St. Gregory of Nyssa on the Dynamics of Salvation," in *The T&T Clark Companion to Atonement*, ed. A. Johnson (Cambridge: T&T Clark, 2016).
[41]Namely that "the Spirit of God proceeds from the Father and from the Son" (*filioque*).

and other New Testament writers were using analogously of the death of Christ on the cross, had slipped away from the still-living resonance they had for the early apostolic authors and had come to mean something else in the consciousness of the medieval mind.[42] So when Anselm elevated the concept of "satisfaction" as a key to explaining the reasons for the passion and death of Jesus it was a very different meaning from the more joyful sense that cultic worship based around the sacrifice (and common eating) of animals had in ancient temple worship.

Anselm's idea of satisfaction theory worked in this way. If, in contemporary feudal society, it was abundantly evident that an act of disrespect or some more grievous offense between people of the same rank demanded some kind of equally weighted satisfaction to be made before honor could be restored (dishonor assuaged) and thus reconciliation could be effected—then so it was with spiritual matters, too. For example, if a serf insulted another peasant in a local village dispute, arrangements for mediation could surely be made without resort to violence, but an apology of a weight consonant with the original insult would alone be enough to make satisfaction. Only this could allow reconciliation to be effected. And yet, if a serf stole another serf's pig, satisfaction could not consist of only an apology, for in addition the restitution of the (or another equal) pig would be essential. And so on in each case, taking regard for the respective ranks of those who had come in need of reconciliation. A one-sided forgiveness offered from one party to the other was not sufficient on its own: for then the requirements of justice would not be met (the offending serf or other ranking member of society would not have had his wickedness addressed). What was required, Anselm theorized, was that mercy (forgiveness) had to be balanced with justice.

But consider the case of a serf insulting and wounding a member of higher, aristocratic, feudal society, or even the king himself. In such a case there is surely nothing the serf could do to "atone" for his crime. He would pay for it in blood. The differentiation of rank made such a crime nonatonable by the peasant. If he had poached a deer, then he could not repay it. And even if he could, he could never repay the dishonor he had done, as a mere serf, so disrespecting his liege lord as to steal from him in the first place. The dishonor to the rank (innate dignity) of the king was even greater than the theft of the deer. And, Anselm implies, if things stand so between a serf and an earthly king, then "how much more" was that gap between a human being and God.

Sin, Anselm argues, even though it might appear of relative smallness, or even reaching up to greater offenses, was all of a piece when it was considered in the light

---

[42] See further J. A. McGuckin, "Sacrifice and Atonement: An Investigation into the Attitude of Jesus of Nazareth Towards Cultic Sacrifice," in *Remembering for the Future* (Oxford: Pergamon Press, 1988), 1:648-61.

of its essential nature: human slaves offending against the infinite dignity and majesty of God the most high King of kings. Even the smallest offense bore an infinite charge (lese majesty) when considered, in its essential nature, as unbounded ingratitude and blasphemy. In short, for Anselm, there was no way that humanity could ever hope to atone for its sins. It fell, therefore, to the mercy of God to initiate reconciliation that was otherwise hopeless. This mercy reached out from the heart of the Trinity in compassion to the human race. It was, and had to be, entirely God's initiative. It could not be a simple act of forgiveness from God's side, since such act of merciful wiping away of all offenses would itself mar the great justice and dignity of God, would itself be an offense against divine justice. The impasse could only be resolved if God himself decided to make atonement on behalf of the human race and supply his own satisfaction.

So it was, Anselm argued, that the divine Logos, second person of the Trinity, came down to earth, assumed flesh, and suffered in the flesh for the sake of humanity, so as to offer his life as an atonement. That the Son offers this atonement of deeply punitive suffering (the cross) in his human flesh, as a constituent representative of humanity, and offers it freely to his Father, in expiation of the sins of humanity against divine dignity: this makes it possible for God the Father (the high King) to stoop down in pity at the suffering of the Son and accept his loving mercy for the human race, take it as his own. Thus the satisfaction having been made, expiation is allowed and reconciliation is reestablished in and through Jesus, who thus serves as the mediator. Now, this is a very ingenious scheme and certainly spoke to the medieval mind, which understood society to work in this way: with satisfactions of honor integral to the manner in which the peace of the land could be kept. But it clearly does not work well anymore. Whether it ever captures the essence of (the much more joyous) ancient Hebraic sacrifice theology is debatable. But what is clear enough is that the Eastern patristic tradition did not approach redemption theology in this manner.

Anselm accurately represents (and here symbolically embodies) an ancient Latin Christian trend to become more and more forensic in its imagination. Such a tendency was present in Latin thought from the time of Tertullian and was underscored by Cyprian and Lactantius (in the third and fourth centuries) who were, like him, forensic lawyers, long before the time of Augustine. The Greek theologians, in marked distinction, approached the issue of Christ's redemptive action with a much greater range of analogies. They did not press the forensic theory of sacrificial expiation as directly or emphatically as the West. The fourth-century Fathers adapted and clarified many of the approaches of Origen of Alexandria to this theological issue, and they envisaged the entrance of the Logos into the flesh at the time of the incarnation as itself a major energy of "re-creation" of the human race (not just its repair). Athanasius, following Irenaeus from the second century, brought to the classical redemption theories of the fourth-century East the central notion that the incarnation of the divine Logos (the en-hominization or *enanthropesis*, as he called it) was a divine transaction whereby the two natures (divinity and humanity) entered into a new and dynamic synthesis, forged by divine and creative energy.[43]

In his widely read treatise *De Incarnatione* Athanasius summed this approach up in a memorable aphorism that dominated Eastern Christian redemption theology: "For the Son of God became man so that we might become God."[44] This theology was taken up by the great Fathers of the fourth and fifth century after him, especially the Cappadocians, Gregory of Nazianzus and Gregory of Nyssa, and Cyril, the fifth-century archbishop of Alexandria, to become a very central manner of conceiving the incarnation (enfleshment) of God as the deification (*theopoiesis*) of the human race.[45] It meant, in all the Greek Christian writers, a profoundly strong theology of transformative grace (not a revival of pagan Roman apotheosis theory as in the deifying of the emperors or demigods). What he (the Logos) was by nature (namely, God) his race is made by grace, as part of that same transaction whereby he drew humanity to himself: in order to afford it the qualities of his divine nature (purification, immortality) that it so badly needed to restore its ontological stability. The sacraments of the church, especially the ongoing formative influence of eucharistic communion, were seen in this Greek patristic tradition as the primary locus of this energized transaction of the process of salvation, the incarnational "deification principle" in the church's life and in the life of each individual within it.[46] Into this macro concept of the incarnation of God as deification of humanity, therefore, all the other analogies (expiation, sacrifice, atonement, ransom) were subsumed.

---

[43]Irenaeus, *Adversus Haereses*, book 5, preface: "[God] became what we are in order to make us what he is himself." And again: "If the Word became a man, it was so men may become gods." In *Adversus Haereses* he says (4.11.2), "For man receives progression and increase toward God. But as God is always the same, so also man, when found in God, shall always progress toward God."

[44]Athanasius of Alexandria, *De Incarnatione* 54.3. His concept here was *theopoiesis*: being divinized. See also *Contra Arianos* 1.39; 3.34. See further J. A. McGuckin, "Deification," in *The Oxford Companion to Christian Thought*, ed. A. Hastings et al. (Oxford: Oxford University Press, 2000).

[45]Gregory of Nazianzus, *Oration* 29.19; 30.14; Gregory of Nyssa, *Great Catechetical Oration* 37. See further J. A. McGuckin, "Deification in Greek Patristic Thought: The Cappadocian Fathers' Strategic Adaptation of a Tradition," in *Partakers of the Divine Nature: The History and Development of Deification in the Christian Tradition*, ed. M. Christensen and J. Wittung (Teaneck, NJ: Farleigh Dickinson University Press, 2006), 95-114; J. A. McGuckin, *St. Cyril of Alexandria and the Christological Controversy: Its History, Theology, and Texts* (Leiden: Brill, 1994); *St. Cyril of Alexandria: On the Unity of Christ (That the Christ Is One)* (Crestwood, NY: St. Vladimir's Seminary Press, 1995).

[46]See further the treatment of Cyril of Alexandria's sacramental theology of deification in E. Gebremedhin, *Life-Giving Blessing: Inquiry into the Eucharistic Doctrine of Cyril of Alexandria*, Studia Doctrinae Christianae Upsaliensia (Uppsala: University of Stockholm, 1978).

Deification theory had little time for satisfaction and expiation analysis in such forensic terms, as occupied the West. It was, even by late antique times, singing a very different melody from that of the Latin churches—laying emphasis on the glorious mysteries of the transfiguration and the vivifying power of the resurrection, rather than on the blood and the cross as primary engines of sacrificial atonement. Arguably, the theological "tendencies" of Eastern and Western Christianities, to this day, demonstrate the selfsame "crack line" in terms of theological approach to "redemption" theory. So once again a major line of thought that the Western church extrapolated as a basic way to conceive of a fundamental profession of faith was seen, rather, as a *theologoumenon* by the East: a particular (even peculiar) stress by one part of the church that did not have sufficient weight to command itself as the uniquely authoritative road of theology for the church universal.

By the time of Anselm, indeed for some centuries before him, the Latin West and Greek East had become uncomfortably aware of how much they had diverged in patterns of thought and in spiritual instincts since the end of the fifth century, when theologians of the two great traditions and language zones were no longer willing (indeed, no longer able, in most cases) to read one another's works. Anselm had already been drawn in by the pope as a heavyweight theologian to refute many of the claims of the Byzantine apologists. From the second millennium onward the refusal to acknowledge key elements of one another's insights bedeviled the relations between the Latins and Greeks. The Byzantines put into the category of peculiar *theologoumena* the Western theory of papal primacy and Petrine distinctiveness, the permanent existence of ordained character (even after deposition), and many other matters. Unwilling to see its special traditions sidelined in this way, the West increasingly came to attribute the Greek dissidence as a cause for serious schism emerging in the unity of Christendom. It prepared the great rift that would come at the end of the first millennium between the Eastern and Western traditions of the church: a fracture that has not yet been resolved.

## THE CHRISTIAN MONASTIC MOVEMENTS

***The emergence of varieties of Christian monasticism.*** Both churches, however, from the end of the third century onward, showed a very marked similarity in their attitudes to the ascetical imperative that was increasingly marking Christian communitarian life in this era. It would soon enough grown into particular observable institutions that we now call by the common descriptor of *monasticism*. The Reformation, especially in its northern territories, would strive very successfully, for ideological as well as social reasons, to smash this aspect of Christian polity. Nevertheless, from the time monasticism appeared as a dynamic force in the life of the churches of late antiquity, even into modern periods, it is clear that it has been a major factor in shaping the culture of the Christian religion—so much so that without an understanding of the phenomenon, the Christian religion makes little sense. Monastics transmitted more or less its entire culture across the ages: copying the Scriptures, annotating and exegeting them, forming and reformulating rules of conduct in the churches, setting standards of zealous observance of Christian moral discipline, and producing almost the entirety of the church's vast (and still largely unread!) literature on prayer and mysticism.

The term *monk* (*monachos*) essentially and semantically means the "solitary one" (*monos*). At the heart of the monastic experience there has always been such a gravitation to solitude and the stillness (*hesychia*), or inner concentration, that it can foster. This is so, even though (paradoxically) monasticism soon came to have predominantly a communitarian aspect. The entire spirituality of the Christian world in the first millennium and a half has been shaped and guided by the monastic experience, which time and again has provided for the church (especially in periods of duress and persecution) centers of continuance, endurance, and spiritual renewal across centuries of fluctuating political conditions. Monasticism has given the church innumerable writers and teachers and many of its greatest missionaries and leaders.

At first, that is, between the second and early third centuries, the ascetical imperative in Christian life was not channeled into the more communitarian monastic lifestyle as such, but more in the elite higher educational system, which Christians started to enter in greater numbers after the third century. In this system philosophical sobriety (*sophrosyne*) was inculcated as a primary ascetical ideal. Monasticism, technically speaking, would only derive from this, by extension, after the end of the third century. The ascetical imperative in ancient sophistic education was a fundamental part of the pre-*paideia* of the schools. Askesis was, at first, simply the pre-Christian word for "exercise": the kind of exercise that was undertaken on a regular (required) basis in the Greek *gymnasia*, where the youths of ancient society were trained in the arts of war alongside their other, more cultural pursuits. The ascetic (*askete* or athlete), in this context, underwent the rigors of physical exercise and training (like a modern suffering the pains of a visit to the gym) so that the goal of excellence (*arete*) could be achieved (Greek arts of war such as javelin or discus throwing eventually being symbolically transmuted into sports).

Stoic theorists in the pre-Christian era, following Aristotle's lead, used this motif of "suffering for the refinement of one's art" in a morally analogous way to denote the way that righteous people had to exercise themselves to acquire virtue. To live the moral life, in other words, was a habitus that did not come easy. One had to test and refine the body, mind, and soul to make it instinctively wish to follow the good in spite of the many temptations to follow the easy path to hedonism and selfishness. The philosophic tradition of Greek culture, in the time of the early church, was well aware of the significance of soul guides, mentors in this path.[47] They took the form of older sage-teachers (*didaskaloi*) guiding a small body of elected disciples (a small *schola*, as it were).[48] In this philosophical school culture the sage-mentor inducted the student-disciple into a way of life, not simply a body of philosophical or textual knowledge. As Hadot would describe it, this form of ancient ascetical philosophy was first and foremost seen as a way of life (*manière de vivre*), not an academically detached set of educational exercises.[49]

The relationship between the soul guide and the disciple was about formation, not just information. The goal (*telos*) of the sage was to teach his followers how to sustain a stable attitude to existence (the cultivation of the self) by means of understanding humanity and its place within the cosmological structure. This cultivation of the soul demanded a practical training for all the *schola* in the arts of combating the passions that distracted and led astray the soul and mind because of the unstable vitalities of the body. Plato's famous image of the formation of the soul as like the troubles of a charioteer in a chariot driven by twin horses reflects this generic philosophical ideal.[50] When the soul was trained not be led anywhere the bodily passions desired (or our customary mental illusory habits dictated), then the individual could become a true philosopher: acquiring *sophrosyne*, that is, sobriety of lifestyle, and the more acute mental awareness that flowed from it. Only such a person (purified and sanctified) could "ascend to the realms of the gods" in late Hellenistic thought. This kind of late antique religious philosophy was the intellectual seedbed for the origins of Christian ascetical theory and the polity of monasticism that developed from it. Indeed, monasticism took over the earlier Greek philosophical quest and would democratize it from the fourth century onward.

Asceticism, then, was a wider antique intellectual culture that the church understood and felt happy to apply in its own moral reflections, as can be seen from the very beginnings. The idea of askesis as a form of spiritual athletic exercise is first used by

---

[47]Cf. J. A. Francis, *Subversive Virtue: Asceticism and Authority in the Second Century Pagan World* (University Park: Pennsylvania State University Press, 1995); P. Brown, *Society and the Holy in Late Antiquity* (Berkeley: University of California Press, 1982), esp. 103-52, "The Rise and Function of the Holy Man in Late Antiquity"; G. Fowden, "The Pagan Holy Man in Late Antique Society," *Journal of Hellenic Studies* 102 (1982): 33-59.
[48]A classical book on this subject is P. Hadot, *Philosophy as a Way of Life* (Oxford: Blackwell, 1995).
[49]See D. Arnold, "Spiritual Exercises and Ancient Philosophy: An Introduction to Pierre Hadot," *Critical Inquiry* 16 (Spring 1990): 475-82; and R. Valantasis, *Spiritual Guides of the Third Century* (Minneapolis: Fortress, 1961).
[50]Plato, *Phaedrus* 246a-254e.

Paul in 2 Timothy 4:7, to signify the need of true Christians to train themselves by rigorous observances (sexual renunciation, fasting, and deprivations) to observe the commandments with exceptional zeal. Other parts of the New Testament literature develop apocalyptic themes by contrasting the sober life lived in accordance with the kingdom's values to the (dangerous) ease of a worldly existence.[51] The biblical theme of the "two ways" is another example of this.[52] The ascetical message resonated well with Hellenistic philosophical ideas about the "sober life" of the wise man or woman (*sophrosyne*), and much of late first- and second-century Christian literature such as the Didache, the Clementine letters, or the Shepherd of Hermas began to stress the need for ascetic sobriety as a fundamental character of Christian discipleship.

The encouragement to the ascetical life is a powerful impetus in the second-century writings of Tertullian, who already reports that there were large numbers of male and female lay ascetics in the Carthaginian church of his day.[53] Syrian Christian circles from the second century onward also laid great stress on the ascetical lifestyle as appropriate for all Christians, not merely a section of zealots. The Syrian Thomas traditions are among the earliest texts that rhetorically elevate virginity and freely adopted celibacy as among the preeminent Christian virtues. But it is Origen of Alexandria who set the theory of asceticism on its strongest Christian systematic foundations in the third century. In his treatise *On First Principles*, written in Alexandria between 220 and 230, Origen sketches out a dramatic account of why we occupy an ambivalent space between spirit and matter in the small compass of our earthly bodies. God the Logos, according to Origen, created the original plan of the cosmos as an entirely spiritual reality. It was only after the fall (considered as a pretemporal declination of pure spirits from God in a quasi-angelic state) that the divine plan extended toward a salvific aspect in creating the material world.[54] Earthly bodies with which the fallen spirit (*noes*) were endowed so as to work out their salvation through suffering and repentance thus became the media of the salvific path of repentance. In and through the body the believer must now struggle to resist the deceits of evil spirits, which try to prevent the ascent of the soul back to God, and the illusions and distractions caused when the body's material concerns try to establish a superior dominance (*hegemonikon*) over the affairs of the soul: thus reversing the intended soteriological order, where the body is made subservient to the requirements of the soul and the spirit.[55]

---

[51] The parable of the sower and seed in Mk 4:1-20 is an example (especially in the exegesis of the tale that the Evangelist gives in Mt 4:15-20), or the two roads (ways) in Mt 7:13-14.
[52] 2 Sam 2:22-24; 2 Kings 17:13; 21:21-22; Ps 1:1-2, 6; Prov 15:19; 21:8; Didache 1-6.
[53] Tertullian, *On the Dress of Women* 2.9; *To His Wife* 1.6; *On the Resurrection of the Flesh* 61.
[54] Origen, *De Principiis*, book 2.
[55] Ibid., book 3.

By the early third century Greco-Roman intellectual life was dominated by the merging of Platonic metaphysics and Pythagorean ascetic piety. For Christian circles Origen had refocused this to be the issue of how the soul's destiny was no less than mystical union with the Logos of God. The bringing of the body into subjection, for the sake of repentance and obedient attentiveness to God, is Origen's primary Christian rationale for the ascetical imperative. The spiritual task given to disciples now in the earthly condition is "to see God in the heart . . . and know him with the mind," which stands in a living tension against the dullness and deathlike state of material embodied existence, which is subject to physical collapse at every turn.[56] Origen regarded his mental, academic labors as an engine of asceticism. He modeled for his own disciples how the zealous Christian must freely choose to bring order and discipline into his own bodily existence so as to cooperate with the spiritual salvation the Logos is working within him so to achieve his perfection.[57] The ascetical theory is a point that historian Eusebius of Caesarea picks up in his fourth-century hagiography of his hero, in which he clearly intends to draw a line of connection between Origen understood as the ascetical philosopher seeking moral purification and mental clarity through his contemplative lifestyle, and Origen reclassified as a leading presbyter-theologian who is also a model protomonastic.[58] After Origen, the properly Christian notion of askesis was essentially allied with the idea of the soul's striving for union with the divine.

This theological redefinition of askesis as the path of repentance, which opened up the purified soul to the possibility of the divine vision, was widely accepted in the church after the third century, and is classically expounded in Gregory of Nazianzen's *First Theological Oration*, composed in 380.[59] By this time many of the leading bishops of the day, like Gregory, had embraced the single ascetical lifestyle and explicitly self-identified as "monastics." But monasticism in its first impetus seems to have been more of a movement among the commoner level of believer. Christian Syria and Egypt are two crucibles of the earliest monastic formations. Palestine between the fifth and seventh centuries became a place of new syntheses. The Western churches were a little slower to enter the monastic race, but once in they produced a flourishing of monastic lifestyles that endured with remarkable success across many centuries.

The original heartlands of the Eastern Christian monastic movement were the deserts of the Roman empire (Egypt, Syria, and Palestine), but soon the problems of defending the communities against barbarian tribal raids became acute, and

---

[56]Ibid., 1.1.8; 3.4.2.
[57]Ibid., 1.5.5-7.
[58]Eusebius, *Ecclesiastical History* 6.3.
[59]Gregory of Nazianzus, *Oration* 27.

monasteries began to appear in the outer suburbs of great cities such as Rome and Constantinople. As such cities spread, the suburbs soon became an integral part of the city landscape; and thus the Byzantine notion of the city monastery was born and flourished, particularly in the Eastern empire from the sixth century to the end of Byzantium's long political existence.

In describing themselves as "living the life of the angels," the early Christian monks evoked their sense that they were anticipating the age to come. In this way, the apocalyptic impetus was reappropriated for the fourth-century church by the ascetical movement, and it is notable that this coincides with the Constantinian era, when persecution is largely past and the church has come into higher social favor. Several commentators have interpreted monasticism as an attempt to recreate a new age of "spiritual martyrdom" for a church in danger of losing its fervor.[60] Although the monks did describe themselves as undergoing a "white martyrdom," this explanation of the origins of the movement is overly simplistic in sociological terms. There were also several strong political reasons why flight to the desert would be appealing to many at this period. The general collapse of the economy of the Roman Empire, witnessed in the third century, and the crippling obligations laid on many small holders, as well as punitive financial demands falling on the more intellectual members of the curial class, all conspired to make the prospect of private or communal subsistence lifestyles more attractive. There was, for some, a genuine sense of freedom gained by living on the fringes of imperial society, away from the excessive demands of sustaining city life in late antiquity. In a very short period the economic potential of these new Christian communities laboring together for a common purpose and with a simple lifestyle became amply demonstrated, and although later many monasteries were founded by generous aristocratic or imperial benefactions, from its early origins monasticism proved itself to be more than capable of earning its own living and generating surplus wealth.

For female ascetics, particularly those of an aristocratic background such as Macrina the Great in Cappadocia or the two Melanias in Rome and Palestine, monastic life could offer possibilities of self-determination, leadership, and intellectual development not otherwise available in contemporary society.[61] It was this paradox of the quest for a simple and poor life dedicated to God allied with the capability for successful social and economic expansion that was to dog the heels of monasticism throughout its history, threatening its authenticity both in the East and West whenever monasteries came to hold extensive possessions in the name of holy poverty.

---

[60]Eusebius, *Ecclesiastical History* 6.42.
[61]See E. A. Clark, *Ascetic Piety and Women's Faith* (New York: Edwin Mellen, 1986).

***Syrian monasticism.*** Ascetical associations of a more organized character than merely individuals attracted to ascetical lifestyles existed in Syrian Christian life from an early stage. This is one of the first places where orders of virgins (male and female) seemed to have congregated around the local church building (later making their own church buildings) for regular prayer and a more zealous life of poverty.[62] In the early Syrian tradition, before the fourth century, which saw a greater assimilation of Syrian church customs with those of the wider Roman Empire, the ascetical life of celibacy was especially encouraged for all those who wished to take up the challenge of baptism.[63] These baptized ascetics (protomonastics) were called the "sons and daughters of the covenant" (Syriac *bnay qyama*) and were given high local authority by reputation, since they were ready to adopt the single, celibate life as solitaries.[64] *Ihidaya* is a Syriac wordplay on single one/only begotten. In the first sense it is comparable to the Greek term for single person, *monos*, which gives us the term *monasticism*. In the second sense it draws the closest line possible between the witness of the celibates' lifestyles and that of the only begotten Son of God, who was himself a "virgin, Virgin-born." The earliest context of this very heavy stress the Syrian church laid on asceticism as a prerequisite for approaching baptismal consecration can be seen elsewhere, in the Thomas literature and in the Encratite movement.[65] Because of the high premium placed on celibate commitment in Syrian Christianity, it developed from the outset as a church where the majority of clerical leaders were monastic.

***Aphrahat the Sage.*** One of the earliest ascetical writers in Syria was the early fourth-century Aphrahat the Sage. He is also called Afrahat or Aphraates, and sometimes known as the "Persian sage," though he is one of the most important early writers in Syriac. He was an ascetic himself and wrote exhortatory spiritual works for his colleagues in the ascetical life. He was certainly a cleric and possibly a bishop (he wrote a synodical letter to the clergy of the whole region), whose "monastic" community gathered around him was also overlapping the Syro-Christian ecclesiastical leadership.

---

[62] C. Stewart, "The Ascetic Taxonomy of Antioch and Edessa at the Emergence of Monasticism," *Adamantius* 19 (2013): 207-21; S. Ashbrook Harvey, "Revisiting the Daughters of the Covenant: Women's Choirs and Sacred Song in Ancient Syriac Christianity," *Hugoye: Journal of Syriac Studies* 8, no. 2 (2005): 125-49.

[63] W. S. McCullough, *A Short History of Syriac Christianity to the Rise of Islam* (Chico, CA: Scholars Press, 1982); R. Murray, *Symbols of Church and Kingdom: A Study in Early Syriac Tradition* (London: Cambridge University Press, 1975); W. Wright, *A Short History of Syriac Literature* (London: A&C Black, 1894).

[64] Cf. G. Nedungatt, "The Covenanters of the Early Syriac-Speaking Church," *Orientalia Christiana Periodica* 39 (1973): 191-215, 419-44; H. M. Hunt, *Clothed in the Body: Asceticism, the Body, and the Spiritual in the Late Antique Era*, Ashgate Studies in Philosophy & Theology in Late Antiquity (Farnham, UK: Ashgate, 2012).

[65] E.g., Acts of Thomas.

His most important work is his *Twenty-Three Demonstrations*.[66] The first ten were composed in 337 as a set of dialogues for the guidance of ascetics, the next twelve in 344 mainly concerned with easing the local Christian-Jewish relations through dialogue, and the last one in 345, which is an extended essay on biblical history and the end of times based on the idea of the "the berry" (Is 65:8). The *Demonstrations* show a church that was still in regular communication with the synagogue, exchanging different perspectives without that climate of hostility that later characterized much of the interaction between the synagogue and church.[67] As is typical of the ascetical writers, Aphrahat has deep insights to offer on the practice of prayer. *Demonstration* 4 is particularly famous in this regard. He is speaking on prayer to an audience of ascetics who have made prayer the reason d'être of their apostolate and vocation. He characterizes the mystical life as a priesthood of the inner heart, where the zealot believer can offer the incense of prayer to the divinity. Ideas of peace and loving forgiveness are central to his thought. Later his writings became very influential in developing the East-Christian school of the "prayer of the heart."[68]

In the fifth century Theodoret, the learned bishop of Cyrrh, composed a *History of the Monks of Syria*, in which he catalogued the extent to which ascetical communities had accumulated an almost legendary record of heroism and holiness in his church.[69] Because Theodoret himself caused much controversy in the fifth century (one of the great opponents of Cyril of Alexandria) and as a result had his posthumous reputation overshadowed to some extent, this record never made as much impact on the later churches as that of the Egyptian church, because of such widely disseminated works as the *Apophthegmata Patrum*. Only in recent decades has the importance of the foundational role of Syrian asceticism in the earliest origins of monasticism been more fully recalled. The geography of the Syrian church also partially caused this overshadowing. It was a sprawling patriarchate gathered around Antioch. But the fortunes of Antioch fell after the mid-fifth century as the Monophysite and Nestorian schisms sundered church relations both within the mountainous and desert country itself and also without, that is, between Syria and the wider international churches, especially Egypt, Rome, and Constantinople, who were increasingly separated from it.

---

[66] Available in English translation: J. Gwynn, *Selections Translated into English from the Hymns and Homilies of Ephraim the Syrian and from the Demonstrations of Aphrahat the Persian Sage*, NPNF (second series) 13.2 (New York: James Parker, 1898).

[67] J. Neusner, *Aphrahat and Judaism* (Leiden: Brill, 1971).

[68] See further J. A. McGuckin, "The Prayer of the Heart in Patristic and Early Byzantine Tradition," in *Prayer and Spirituality in the Early Church*, ed. P. Allen, W. Mayer, and L. Cross (Queensland: Australian Catholic University, Centre for Early Christian Studies, 1999), 2:69-108.

[69] R. M. Price, trans., *A History of the Monks of Syria by Theodoret of Cyrrhus* (Kalamazoo: Cistercian Publications, 1985).

Islamic advances as well as the continuing use of Syriac as the ecclesiastical language all served to isolate the Syrian traditions, but the monastic practices lived on in a new form in the synthesis made of them (and other Egyptian ideas) in the crucible of the new archdiocese of Constantinople. As the latter capital grew in international importance after the end of the fourth century, the Syro-Constantinopolitan ideas of monastic life had a very large dissemination. Even so, it is a paradox that in this present era, the translations made of Syrian ascetical literature (on prayer and monastic life) are gaining for that tradition perhaps the largest-ever audience it has had in history. Great spiritual teachers are being revealed to the wider Christian world, almost as if for the first time. Two of the greatest of them are the fourth-century author of the *Fifty Spiritual Homilies* and the *Great Letter*, Pseudo-Macarius, and Mar Isaac of Nineveh (seventh-century bishop from Qatar).[70]

*Macarius the Great.* Macarius the Great is the pseudonymous name attached to this important Syrian monastic writer. It is a sad irony that he could only continue to be read when the wider church accepted him as an Egyptian master. He was an important monastic leader of a circle that had earlier been criticized for certain excesses in its spiritual theology. Some have identified him as Symeon of Mesopotamia (named as the group leader by Theodoret), and he is now often known as either Macarius-Symeon or Pseudo-Macarius.

The criticism of his monastic heritage begins to be discernible from the 370s onward. Sources call the movement Messalians (a corruption and misunderstanding of the Syriac word for "people of prayer"—*MshLni*). In some Greek sources they were known as the Euchites, but later heresiologists add to the confusion by thinking they were founded by a certain person called Messalius (who never existed). Even the objectionable element of the movement was not clearly understood by those criticizing it, and Epiphanius of Salamis, who attacked the Messalians in his *Refutation of Heresies* in 377, can only find their "lack of discipline" as grounds for censure. Other critics claimed they held that baptism was not sufficient for a Christian life and had to be constantly supplemented and sustained by deep interior prayer, a doctrine that could be heretical or not, depending on how it was received, by enemy or friend. The larger "Messalian" movement was condemned at a session of the Council of Ephesus 431, which cites passages from a key work called *Asceticon*. It is clear that elements of this text were taken from the homilies of Pseudo-Macarius.

---

[70]G. A. Maloney, trans., *Pseudo Macarius: The Fifty Spiritual Homilies and the Great Letter*, Classics of Western Spirituality (Mahwah, NJ: Paulist, 1992); cf. P. Hagman, *The Asceticism of Isaac of Nineveh* (Oxford: Oxford University Press, 2010); D. Miller, trans., *The Ascetical Homilies of St. Isaac the Syrian* (Boston: Holy Transfiguration Monastery, 1984); S. P. Brock, "St Isaac of Nineveh and Syriac Spirituality," *Sobornost* 7, no. 2 (1975): 79-89; *The Syriac Writers of Qatar in the Seventh Century*, ed. M. Kozah (Piscataway, NJ: Gorgias Press, 2014).

There are, however, certain themes that, whether "Messalian" or not (and the relationship of Pseudo-Macarius to any precise Messalian movement is still a dubious contention), do seem to be constitutive for the circle of Syrian ascetics for whom he was writing.[71] These include the idea that sin dwells in a human heart like a serpent and that the human being has a tendency to spiritual dissolution that needs to be offset by constant prayer and inner attentiveness. The school also advocated the abandonment of traditional monastic ideas of hard labor as a form of askesis, advocating instead a wandering lifestyle that focused more on spiritual withdrawal and recollection (which is probably why sedentary local bishops disliked them). Another typical theme of the writing seems to be the strong stress on the necessary sensible consciousness (*aesthesis*) of the working of the Holy Spirit in the innermost heart. This monastic family taught that if a person were not deeply conscious of the Spirit's presence, then the person was clearly unregenerate. Those possessed of the Spirit would express how they felt that presence as a vision of light or a sensation of consoling warmth.[72]

Pseudo-Macarius himself shows signs of all these elements; indeed, the spirituality of the attentive heart and the constant invocation of *penthos* ("joy-making mourning") are major contributions that he makes to the development of an international Christian monastic spirituality. There is little indication that he takes any of these ideas to an objectionable extreme. His work, chiefly the *Great Letter* and the *Fifty Spiritual Homilies*, influenced Gregory of Nyssa's ascetical theology and went on in later Byzantium to be a major source of the Hesychastic renewal from the eleventh century onward.

*Mar Isaac of Nineveh.* Mar Isaac was a monk of the Chaldaean church from Beit Quatraye on the Persian Gulf and had a high renown as a solitary.[73] He was appointed bishop of Nineveh sometime before 680, but after a few months in the position resigned his charge and returned to the solitary life. In later life he became blind from his scholarly labors. His spiritual authority and the beauty of his writings on prayer and mystical experience made his works cherished by both the rival Monophysite and Nestorian factions of the Persian church of his time. In the ninth century they were translated from the Syriac into Greek and Arabic versions and came to Byzantium shortly afterward, where they had a large impact on the developing Hesychastic spiritual theology of the early Middle Ages. Isaac lays great stress

---

[71] J. Meyendorff, "Messalianism or Anti-Messalianism: A Fresh Look at the 'Macarian' Problem," in *Kyriakon: Festschrift J. Quasten* II (Munster: Aschendorf, 1971), 585.

[72] The texts had a deep influence on the young John Wesley when he came across them at Oxford University.

[73] The Syriac word *mar* means "Lord" originally (as in *Mar anatha*: "Lord, come!"). By later times it was used by Syrian Christians to designate a saint.

on the sensibility of the grace of God in the heart (following Pseudo-Macarius) and wishes to teach his ascetical readers the skills necessary in discerning the movements of the heart and the spirit by introspection: skills he regarded as utterly necessary elements of discernment for those who wanted to advance in the life of prayer. Of all the ancients, Isaac is one of the most mature and gentle authors offering advice on the spiritual and ascetical life. In recent years lost works of his have been rediscovered, and by virtue of new English translations he is once again becoming known as one of the great masters of early Christian spirituality.[74]

*Symeon Stylites.* One of the most dramatic of all Syrian monks, however, did not write a word. He was an icon visible from a long way off. Symeon the Stylite (390–459) draws his name from the architectural pillar (*stylos*) on which he sat, in all weathers, for the most part of his life. Symeon was the first and most famous of a series of Syrian stylite ascetics, who lived exposed to the elements in a life of ascetical penance on top of columns. They were attended by disciples, who sent up food for the recluse and controlled the people who came to seek his advice and prayers. Symeon began as a Syrian monk in monasteries near Antioch and eventually, after the last ten years there living as an enclosed hermit, took to a form of eremitical life in the open air. After 423, he occupied a column drum and sat there in fixed meditation. It was about four feet off the ground. But soon he progressively raised it, adding more and more fallen drums from the ruined site of a Roman temple in order to avoid the press of crowds who came to him for spiritual intercession. He spent more than thirty years without leaving this restricted space, open to all the elements. His great fame, even in his own lifetime, classically exemplifies the rise of the cult of the holy man in the near East.[75] Western authors and monastics (especially Benedict) tended to disapprove of the sensationalism of these dramatically ostentatious Syrian forms of askesis; but they became favored in Constantinople and thus were made part of the general monastic memory in later Byzantium.

Symeon certainly impressed his example on the church and imperial authorities of his time. His objections prevented Theodosius II from restoring their synagogues to the Jews of Antioch, and he influenced Emperor Leo I to support the Chalcedonian cause in Christology. He is said to have converted, in one visit, the massed tribes of Arabia, when they camped around his column, causing them to have a mass burning of their tribal idols. Extensive ruins of his pillar and surrounding monastery

---

[74]A significant number of homilies were reclaimed only as recently as 1983: cf. S. Brock, *Isaac of Nineveh (Isaac the Syrian): The Second Part, Chapters 4-41,* Corpus Scriptorum Christianorum Orientalium 555 (Louvain: Peeters, 1995).

[75]See P. Brown, "The Rise and Function of the Holy Man in Late Antiquity," *Journal of Roman Studies* 61 (1971): 80-101.

(of more earth-bound disciples) still survive, including the base of his pillar, at Qal'at Sim'an. Symeon's pupil, Daniel the Stylite (d. c. 493), set up his own column in Constantinople and exercised a similarly influential ministry there. There was later another ascetic called Symeon the Stylite ("Symeon Stylites the Younger," d. c. 596), who set up his column to the west of Antioch and became a cult figure for later Byzantine hagiography. Such figures were very significant as iconic models more than as teachers. Their hagiographic biographies focus more on their deeds than their apothegmatic tradition as such.[76]

**Egyptian monasticism.** *Tales of Antony.* Antony has become elevated as the symbolic "father of monks" in Christian tradition. He lived between 251 and 356. His *Life*, written by Athanasius of Alexandria soon after Antony's death, became one of the most popular Christian texts of antiquity and was responsible for making him paradigmatic for later monastic theory, both in regard to the solitary life and that of the small community. He belonged to a Coptic merchant family in Alexandria. By the age of twenty he inherited his father's wealth and became head of his household. He experienced a dramatic conversion while hearing the Gospel read in church: "Sell all and follow me" (Mt 19:21), and taking it personally to heart, he dispossessed himself for the benefit of the poor, broke his familial ties, and left Alexandria for a life of ascetical seclusion in the semidesert lands around the Nile, near Fayyum.[77] He began his ascetical life near small village settlements (and from this period come the stories of Antony's famous "wrestling with demons" that are so popular in Quattrocento painting).

By 285 he moved deeper into the Egyptian desert, seeking a more solitary lifestyle at a place called Outer Mountain (Pispir). The monastic style of solitary life took from this the title *eremite* (later "hermit"), which is based on the Greek term for "desert" (*eremos*). At Pispir Antony organized a colony of disciples under a loose form of early communal rule. This in turn came to be called "cenobitic" monasticism, from the Greek term for "shared lifestyle," or "common life" (*koinos bios*). In 305, desiring a greater solitude in his lifestyle, he moved even farther into the wilderness, to a place called Inner Mountain (now Deir Mar Antonios) by the Red Sea. Here he presided over an association of more senior monks living in a loose collective as hermits.

So it was that he traditionally came to be associated with the foundation of the three basic types of later Christian monastic structure: (1) communes (*koinobia*) under the direction of a senior monk (*abba* or father); (2) *lavras*, from the Greek word for

---

[76]R. Doran, trans., *Symeon Stylites: The Biographies* (Kalamazoo: Cistercian Publications, 1988); S. Ashbrook Harvey, "The Sense of a Stylite: Perspectives on Simeon the Elder," *VC* 42 (1988): 376-94.

[77]He was hardly the first "inventor" of Christian monasticism, as later legend describes him. We are told that when leaving the city for the desert he placed his sister in the care of a Christian female ascetic community already established in Alexandria.

"back lane," or track that linked the separate caves of a valley to the common church, where scattered groups of individual hermits would meet for weekly worship under the spiritual authority of an elder (*geron*); and (3) the eremitical life proper, where a monk would live more or less in complete seclusion or live secluded with one or two junior attendants (*synkelloi*), whom he would direct. Antony's writings, not very extensive (as he was and remained illiterate), focused on the need to acquire freedom in the inner life so that the vision of God could be sought with a focused heart. His reputation as a holy man, counselor, exorcist, and thaumaturge, even in his own lifetime, was such that the fourth-century bishop of Alexandria, St. Athanasius, called on his assistance and used the power of his reputation to combat the Arian movement.

The *Life of Antony* recycles for Christian readers many themes that reflect how ancient Egyptians regarded the desert as the home of demons. It hovers between the depiction of Antony, on the one hand, as a man who commands the devils and is proved victorious after terrible struggles that nearly leave him dead, and, on the other hand, as a philosopher whose greatest fight is against the passions of his own fallible heart. In the Fayyum, at the early stage of his career, Antony retired to an ancient tomb (publicly braving pagan dread of the dead) and found there the demons ascendant in all manner of animal guises. We can read this, of course, as his audacity as a Christian to inhabit a tomb that bore on its walls the depictions of the old gods of Egypt—which to the Christians were now equated with demonic forces. This modeling of Antony's triumph is based also on Jesus' temptation in the desert. In this apocalyptic arena the force of the cross is manifested.

Athanasius's *Life of Antony* is thus very clearly an apologetic document aimed at showing how the new faith does two things above all: first, it gives to the disciple a power of protection against all demonic forces and thus a living proof that the church venerates the true God; and second, it gives to the believer an indwelling power of the Spirit, which purifies and strengthens the inner life. In the few epistolary texts that Antony himself left behind the purificatory aspect is elaborated. One of his most famous attributed sayings is "Whoever sits in solitude and is quiet has escaped from three wars: the wars of hearing, of speaking, and of seeing; and then there is only one war left in which to fight, and that is the battle for your own heart."[78] Another famous aphorism is this: "I no longer fear God. I have come to love him, for perfect love casts out fear."[79]

Antony's many different exempla in the *Life* and the sayings attributed to him in later monastic manuals taught Christian monks to balance their lives in the desert with a pattern of prayer and psalms through the night and the dawn, then rest in the

---

[78] *Sayings of the Elders* (PL 73.858).
[79] Based on 1 Jn 4:18. *Apophthegmata Patrum. Abba Antony* (PG 65.85).

morning with eating and labor, followed by sleep in the afternoon, then study, prayer, and dinner at dusk, and prayers again in the coolness of the night. This formula of daily variety between oral and mental prayer, physical labor, and rest, was said to have been revealed to him by the visitation of an angel since he had no one else to show him standards of "desert polity."

*Tales of the desert: The Christian fayyum.* After Antony's time the making of Christian ascetical settlements in the desert lands adjacent to Alexandria became more extensive. Antony's disciple Amun is specially credited with the first organization of the growing settlements in the Fayyum. This is the area of the inner desert associated with Antony's first stage of monasticism. It is also known as the Desert of Nitria, which is near Alexandria to the west of the mouth of the Nile. There are three central sites that became important here: Nitria, Kellia, and Scete. Each of them developed a form of monastic spirituality particular to the place and the spirit of their respective local founders.

Nitria (the modern El Barnugi) was the site where intending monks were inducted into desert, living in small communities designed to supervise them and test their vocations. It grew in the second generation, by the 390s, to become the intellectual center of nearly all the monastic communities of Egypt. Having started as the "first base" of desert monastic life, nearest the city, and modeling a very simple style of life, it changed its character toward the end of the fourth century as an influx of highly educated monastics made it a locus of intense reflection on theology and spirituality. Nitria was first associated with Antony and Amun but, as we have seen, Antony kept moving into deeper solitude toward the Red Sea area, and soon Amun himself would take off to found Kellia, which specialized in an even simpler, more rigorous, and more reclusive style of monastic life.

So it was that Nitria later became especially famous for its "second-generation founder" Ammonius, one of the so-called tall brothers. These were a group of leading intellectuals who stressed the monastic life as a philosophical pilgrimage toward integrity of vision. They were deeply influenced by the writings of Origen of Alexandria. Ammonius also came to exercise leadership over the nearby settlements at Kellia. The great ascetical scholar and mystic Evagrius of Pontus entered monastic life under the guidance of Ammonius, living first at Nitria, from 383 to 385, and then afterward settling permanently at Kellia. Evagrius is perhaps the single greatest representative of this monastic intellective spiritual school, which ran on directly into the greater Byzantine tradition. His writings, and those of Origen, suffered a posthumous condemnation at the Second Council of Constantinople in 553. That event was the culmination of more than two centuries of earlier conflict in the desert communities, from Egypt to Syria, as the simpler *fellahin* practices of the apothegmata (simple tales meant for a more peasant audience) generated friction against the more complex Evagrian mystical tradition. Yet, in many instances both traditions of monastic ascesis could be present in the same people, the same places, and sometimes the same houses: rarely cohabiting easily, however.

Kellia was the second of this trinity of the inner desert monastic settlements.[80] The name of the place is a Greek form of the Latin word for "poor hovel" (*cella*) or "storage cave." It was a loose association of monastic settlements covering many square miles of the desert, founded by Amun in 338. The word for the place, *cells*, gave to European language the basic term for a monastic dwelling and, incidentally, any penitential place, such as a prison "cell." It originated because Amun and some of the more advanced monks began to find the pressure of newcomers too irritating and wanted to return to the quieter and more severe days of the early foundation. Amun and Antony himself, so it is said, after dinner one evening both walked off into the desert until sunset, at which time they planted a cross and founded the new settlement in that greater solitude. It was twelve miles from Nitria. This lavriotic foundation numbered about six hundred monks in the 390s, and by the fifth and sixth centuries, it is thought to have numbered in the thousands. By that time the settlements extended over forty-eight square miles.

The poverty was very strict there, and only those experienced in desert living were encouraged to settle. Most of the time the monks lived in solitude, gathering only for the common weekly eucharistic services. Individual dwellings were placed far apart so that no sound from a neighbor could be heard and no sight of activity seen. This is a locus most associated with the "sayings of the desert fathers," which were later disseminated for international edification once the original communities had been scattered and reduced by barbarian raids.

These collections of the legends and sayings of the desert fathers have a simple aphoristic style of experiential wisdom. They are apophthegmatic: gnomic and pithy in character. There are also stories that are composed of short vignettes concerned with

---

[80] Today it is Al-Muna. It had its golden age in the fifth to sixth centuries; it suffered decline in the seventh and eighth centuries because of the doctrinal disputes affecting Egypt and also because of nomadic raids from the eastern (Libyan) desert. It remained inhabited up to the ninth century, but only archaeological remains survive today. Antoine Guillaumont began the excavations in 1964, and they have continued for many decades. Over forty-eight square miles, more than fifteen hundred structures were found, ranging from single hermit cells to clusters where two or three lived together, and a fewer number of larger complexes grouped around a defensive tower, which usually had a small chapel. There was also a central church site where the brethren gathered for worship in common (*qasr Isa*), a site for common care services (*qasr waheida*), and a commercial center (*qasr al-Izeila*). See Roger S. Bagnall, ed., *Egypt from Alexander to the Early Christians: An Archaeological and Historical Guide* (Los Angeles: Getty Publications, 2004), 108-12.

the "mighty deeds" of the founding fathers: great ascetical feats and domestic miracles are recorded. The monks are seen as earthly angels, returning through prayer and fasting to a state of childlike simplicity where even the wild animals come to trust them. They are soul guides and intercessors for their fellow Christians before God. Great stress is placed on constant prayer, focus on the control of thoughts, and relentless endurance. Some of the aphorisms of this tradition have become monastic commonplaces to this day: "Keep to your cell so that your cell may keep you." The monks prayed through the night, ate at sunrise and at dusk, maintained a balance of physical work that was deliberately mindless (gardening, rope making, basket weaving, for example) along with mental prayer interwoven with recitation of the Psalter.

After Evagrius's arrival Kellia became associated with the mystical Origenian tradition, as he quickly became its single most renowned inhabitant. Parts of the apothegmata tradition remark how many of the brethren found Evagrius's practices unsettling. For his part Evagrius drew his disciples around him closely in a conscious modeling of an ancient philosophical *schola*, where intellectual labor, study, deep meditative reflection, and the development of the states of inner peace and wordless prayer were given a higher priority over the traditional forms of ascetical labor and vocal prayer services (psalms and exclamations) favored by the earlier, less intellectual monks.

Scete was the third great center of monastic life in the inner desert. This place name, too, has survived in modern monastic usage as a descriptor of a form of lifestyle that blends the cenobitic life with the quietness of a semihermit existence. The term *skete* today usually means a small monastic house inhabited by a few more advanced disciples gathered around their elder. The original place was a desert area with several salt lakes to the west of Alexandria. It was south of and near Kellia. Today it can be found on the map halfway between Alexandria and Cairo. The salt lakes were used in ancient times for quarrying natron used in mummification rituals, and the place to day is called Wadi El Natroun (which has led many to confuse it with Nitria, which actually lay to the east). This was where the famous desert teacher St. Macarius of Alexandria settled in 330 and there attracted numerous monastic followers. From that time onward Scete was one of the most important spiritual centers of Egyptian monasticism, until the time of the barbarian devastations of the fifth century. Four monasteries of ancient foundation still survive in the area at the present day.

Macarius the Egyptian was the spiritual elder at Scete, while Macarius the Alexandrian was serving as a priest at Kellia. Both men had a formative influence on the desert tradition and especially on Evagrius. The Egyptian's reputation as an advanced ascetic won him the title of "Macarius the Great," but very little actual textual tradition survived from his hand. He is spoken about by travelers to the desert, who spread his fame in the capital cities, and so appears as a significant character in the collection known as the sayings of the fathers (*apophthegmata patrum*).[81] Being famous with empty bookshelves, as it were, he was a major target for the ancient practice of pseudepigraphy; that is, he was a refuge where other writings could be hidden in critical times. Accordingly, when the writings of a major Syrian theologian from the region of Cappadocia (probably named Symeon) were censured for aspects of apparent dualism in the early fifth century, the monastic school of this founder, which rightly regarded them as generally being misunderstood masterpieces of the inner life, rebranded them as works of Macarius the Great.[82] The issue is resolved by scholars nowadays calling the latter Pseudo-Macarius.

For the church of the fifth century onward, however, this subterfuge meant that Syrian spirituality, in a fifth-century literary conflation, was merged symbolically and practically for later ages with Egyptian desert traditions. The original Egyptian Macarius represented the continuance of the Antonian tradition of a radically simple lifestyle, along with dedication to regular prayer and physical labor. Pseudo-Macarius, on the other hand, is a master Syro-Greek rhetorician and theologian, with doctrines related to the theme of the heart as the throne of the indwelling Spirit. His *Great Letter* and his *Spiritual Discourses* are among the greatest writings on prayer ever produced by the early Christians.

*Pachomian federated monasticism.* Pachomius has also been called the "father of monks" and vies with Antony to be the symbol of basic inspiration behind common-life monasticism in its Christian forms. He lived c. 290–346, was based in Upper Egypt near ancient Thebes, and was an exsoldier who brought community-organizing skills to monastic life in Upper Egypt.[83] Being led in chains down the Nile as a pagan conscript for the armies of the late civil war, Pachomius was converted to Christianity in 313 after receiving kindness and mentorship from Christians as he passed through

---

[81]He is described, for example, by Palladius in his *Lausiac History* 17, and Rufinus in his *History of the Monks* 28.

[82]The school stresses the two principles of good and evil permanently warring in the heart. This could be read as a moral trope or a form of dualistic anthropology, depending on the perspective of the viewer; but it was one of the things that alarmed its episcopal critics when these spiritual teachers began propagating the view in the Syrian deserts. The inhabitation of an "evil spirit" in the soul sounded superficially like a resurgence of Manichaeism. This is clearly not what Symeon/Macarius was propagating. The earlier Syrian tradition has similar nuances (as does the Latin), but the Greek tradition was not as pessimistic in its view of the state of humankind's soul after the fall.

[83]He was a pagan conscripted into the Roman army, and the kindness of the Christians at Chenoboskion during his enforced service served to convert him. Baptized in 313, he served the ascetic Apa Palamon until 320, when he recounts that he heard a heavenly voice instructing him to build a monastery to receive many disciples.

Chenoboskion village. Here he had been comforted by advice from an old Christian ascetic (Abba Palamon) and so he later returned, after completing military service, to be trained in ascetical desert life by him.

Pachomius's own settlements after Palamon's death were composed of groups of ascetics living in a fortified compound under the supervision of a *higumen*, or abbot, who was the "father" (abba) of the community and had high authority over all aspects of the commune's life. The ethos of the movement was "work and prayer." Western Benedictine monastic orders emulate this pattern most closely. Up to Pachomius's time monasticism was both individualistic and rather disorganized. Pachomius brought system to the movement, and with that system came financial and military (protective) stability, which allowed his work as a founder to flourish. It was once thought he made foundations of his single "order" in many different places, but this is to invest his work retrospectively with more coherence than it might have had in its earliest stages. Even so, he founded two houses very shortly after each other, at Chenoboskion and Pbow, between 320 and 326. The second eventually became the headquarters of a string of eleven Pachomian houses along the Nile below Thebes in the region of Tabennisi (near modern Nag Hammadi), two of which were for women only. Modern scholarship suggests that the Pachomian monastery complexes were more in the manner of separate institutions entering into a kind of federation, something like a modern franchise.

Pachomius's military background is often said to have shaped his ideas of group organization, though some recent scholarship has pointed to the possible influence of Manichaean communities in the area. Pachomian settlements were characterized by a strict insistence on communal poverty, and the discipline in the houses sometimes bordered on what modern readers might regard as excessive, though in comparison to others such as Shenoute of Atripe, Pachomius was positively moderate. Antique monastic communities, however, seemed to have been extremely disciplined places, with many physical punishments appointed for infractions of order. Like Shenoute, Pachomius seems to have been a charismatic and visionary personality. Coptic sources suggest that visionary experiences and heavenly intuitions were a regular part of how he perceived the inspired Christian leader to function in the elect community. The Greek sources clearly underrepresent this aspect of Pachomius's life, playing down the charismatic visionary elements in the process of spreading his fame and example further afield in the international Greek-speaking Christian community.

In 345, Pachomius was censured by a synod of Egyptian bishops meeting at Latopolis. The ecclesiastical attack on him and the (obviously growing) power of his "parallel" ecclesial organization (then largely out of the control of local episcopates) had little effect, mainly because his death was soon to ensue but also because his supporters were sufficiently strong to be able to rebuff it directly. It is an interesting indication, one among several others from this period, of the growing tension between ascetical forms of the configuration of Christianity and the traditional power of village and city bishops. Similar issues are at stake in the Synod of Gangra in Asia Minor (340). It is reported that St. Athanasius was a constant supporter of the Pachomian ideal. When one considers that the Nag Hammadi Gnostic finds of the mid-twentieth century all most likely emanated from the library of a Pachomian settlement, deliberately buried rather than being burned, the exact nature of the relation between these ascetic houses and the established structures of Christian village communities, with their episcopal and priestly hierarchy, becomes an interesting source of speculation.

In 346 Pachomius died in a severe plague that ravaged the settlements along the Nile. At that time he had nine male and two female monasteries under his authority. Palladius the historian, writing circa 420, estimated that three thousand monastics belonged to Pachomius's federation in his lifetime.[84] By the fifth century the federation had entered into a process of dissolution, accelerated by divisive christological controversies affecting the Egyptian church in the aftermath of the Council of Chalcedon (451). Pachomius's modeling of cenobitic life, however, had by that time left an indelible mark on the consciousness of monastic organization elsewhere in the Christian world, such as at Sinai, Palestine, and Cappadocia, and was to have long-lasting effects.

The "rules" of Pachomius are highly practical and based on common sense and an active concept of the common good. They were perhaps not written down until after Pachomius's death, but they represent the essential tenor of his system. They not only influenced Basil of Caesarea and Shenoute of Atripe but, translated into Latin by St. Jerome, were a strong influence on John Cassian, Caesarius of Arles, and Benedict of Nursia, and thus indeed played a role as something of an archetypal guide to cenobitic founders both in the Eastern and Western churches, giving to many forms of monasticism the idea of a written "rule" to enshrine ethos, conduct, and values of various houses.[85] In Byzantine monasticism of the fifth century and

---

[84]See Palladius, *Historia Lausiaca* 26.18-20. Basil (330–379) was one of the major fathers of the church, and his writings had an enduring importance. His ascetical works included a reediting of the monastic treatises of Eustathius of Sebaste, a major ascetic of Cappadocia. Under Basil's name the *Asketikon*, issued in 363 (also known as Basil's "rule"), is a loose set of biblical aphorisms for the guidance of monks. It became very widespread and earned for Basil the title "father of monks."

[85]Shenoute of Atripe (c. 350–466) was also known as Sinute, or Shenoude; he was the first to demand of monastics written "profession." In 88 he became leader of his uncle's White Monastery in Upper Egypt. He radically applied the many monks at his disposal for purposes of the (often violent) supersession of the old Egyptian religion. He expanded the White Monastery to almost two thousand monks and had a women's foundation of almost the same size. He led a strict regime in which

onward, different houses could compose their own *typika* (rules), and one notes a fairly wide diversity until the ninth century brings a greater sense of settlement on standard forms.[86] The West followed a more static set of archetypes from an early date until, again in the ninth century, the rule of St. Benedict became of overwhelming significance in determining the ethos of Western monastic houses.

*Other notable Egyptian monastic centers: Gaza and Sinai.* Brief mention ought to be made of two other important exemplars of the Egyptian style of monastic life: Barsanuphius and John, the noted elders of Gaza; and John Climacus, representing the (many) Sinai elders congregated for many generations around the great monastery at the foot of Mount Sinai.[87]

Barsanuphius and John were two renowned elders who lived in the mid-sixth century and were regarded as an example of the last of the classical tradition of desert saints, since by that time Roman frontier security had deteriorated and barbarian raids had decimated the number of surviving settlements in the wilderness. Barsanuphius was an Egyptian by birth who lived as solitary ascetic in Gaza. His younger contemporary, John the Prophet, was a hermit who lived near him. Between the two men a series of literary exchanges took place that were later collected and disseminated under the title *Questions and Answers*. The book became a bestseller manual for the ancient monks. It was a series of queries posed to the elder, by John and other monks, possibly through John's mediation, that sought to elucidate the deeper meaning of the ascetical life, and practical ways to avoid common problems. The pithy dialogues sum up the desert tradition of the

---

floggings for infractions were common. For more on this figure who is regarded as a great leader of the early Copts, see D. N. Bell, trans., *Besa: The Life of Shenoute* (Kalamazoo, MI: Cistercian Publications, 1983); A. Grillmeier and T. Hainthaler, *Christ in Christian Tradition*, vol. 2, part 4, *The Church of Alexandria with Nubia and Ethiopia After 451* (London: Mowbray, 1996), 267-57; J. Limbi, "The State of Research on the Career of Shenoute of Atripe," in *The Roots of Egyptian Christianity*, ed. B. A. Pearson and J. E. Goehring (Philadelphia: Fortress, 1986), 258-70.

John Cassian (360–433) was the founder of important monasteries in the West, where he brought many Eastern ideas into the mix and composed an influential treatise on asceticism titled *The Conferences*. For further reading see C. Luibheid, *John Cassian: The Conferences*, Classics of Western Spirituality (New York: Paulist, 1985); P. Munz, "John Cassian," *JEH* 9 (1960): 1-22; P. Rousseau, *Ascetics, Authority and the Church in the Age of Jerome and Cassian* (Oxford: Oxford University Press, 1978).

Caesarius of Arles (468–542) was an important episcopal monastic organizer before the Benedictine era. He left behind a significant set of rules in Latin for male and female monastics: *Regula ad Monachos* and *Regula ad Virgines*. See further W. E. Klingshirn, *Caesarius of Arles: The Making of a Christian Community in Late Antique Gaul* (Cambridge: Cambridge University Press, 1994).

Benedict of Nursia was the so-called father of Latin monasticism, and we shall study his career shortly.

[86]*Regula* in Latin, *typikon* in Greek. The writings of monastic reformer St. Theodore Studite became a widely used rule for houses.

[87]Today called St. Catherine's, in Justinian's time (in the sixth century) called the Church of Transfiguration.

early Nitrian period, but edited so as to represent the sayings of the fathers (*apophthegmata*), as highly practical, nonspeculative teachers.

This edition of the tradition came at a time when parts of the monastic world in Egypt and Palestine were reacting strongly against Origen's speculative theology, and they had a profound impact on the later ascetical tradition during two important times of synthesis.[88] First of all, the works influenced the important monastic teachers of the seventh century, John Climacus and Dorotheus of Gaza.[89] And second, in a later period they would also enjoy a great revival at Byzantium, affecting such influential medieval mystics as Symeon the New Theologian and Paul of Evergetinos.[90] So it was that this book by Barsanuphius and John preserved, in the wider tradition of Eastern Christian ascetical theology, a classic image of the ancient desert monks. However, in its later adoption it became an image of monastic values that was not just a reiteration of the simpler apothegmatic school but one that added to it a quiet rehabilitation of the Origenian-Evagrian mystical traditions that focused more directly on the need to quieten the soul and rise from purity of heart to the sense of the mystical presence of God. The later Gazan teachers, in short, actually serve to synthesize the varied traditions of their monastic predecessors.

John Climacus (c. 575–650) takes his name from the title of the highly influential manual he wrote to advise trainee monks: *The Ladder of Divine Ascent*. *Climacus* means "of the ladder." He was for more than forty years of his life a strict recluse in the Sinai desert, but toward the end of that period he had become a much sought-after counselor for monks. Around 635 he was elected to be the *higumen* of the great fortified monastery at Sinai. Conscious that in his lifetime the many communes of the desert were passing away, he wrote a manual of spiritual guidance to capture the old practices and customs. It achieved immense fame in the early church and to this day is regarded as the classical introduction to a monastic lifestyle. It is a very practical book, set in the form of a "ladder to heaven" of thirty ascending rungs. The first twenty-three of them outline the dangerous vices that beset the radical disciple, and the last seven speak eloquently of the higher virtues, ending on the topmost rung, which is dedicated to the love of God. John's work is a clear and simplified synthesis of the Gaza elders' teachings and went on to be a major formative influence on

---

[88]Origen's speculative theology was defended by Evagrius and the tall brothers.
[89]C. 505–565 (some place his death in the early seventh century). A disciple of the two elders, he became an *higumen* of his own monastery in 540 and wrote books of spiritual counsel to monastics that had a large influence.
[90]Symeon the New Theologian (949–1022) was an important medieval Christian mystic and monastic teacher at Constantinople. Paul of Evergetinos (d. 1054 in Constantinople) was head of a major monastery there (the Evergetinos), and he compiled a large collation of monastic tales and aphorisms (*Evergetinon*) that had an extensive influence over the Eastern Christian church.

Athonite monasticism in the medieval Byzantine period. John Climacus has a special focus in his work on the monastic's need for simplification, concerning both life and inner prayer habits.[91] To this day the book is given to novices entering Eastern Christian monasticism as the first "go-to guide" for a new monastic aspirant.

**Monasteries in Palestine and beyond.** There are two standout teachers in the ancient Palestinian tradition of monastic life: Sabas and Euthymius. Cyril of Scythopolis (Beth Shan in Israel) became their later hagiographer, and his account in his book *Lives of the Palestinian Monks* is a classic source for the story.[92] Palestine under the Byzantine emperors flourished greatly between the fifth and seventh centuries as a central locus of the Christian world, looking to pilgrimage to Jerusalem and the holy places. Ascetics settled in the Palestinian deserts, in isolated caves, tiny *skete*-like families of three or four, and also in much larger fortress-like cenobitic houses. But above all the Palestinian monks favored the Lavriotic lifestyle, in which a valley would be taken over by a loose community of hermits living secluded lives for most of the week and coming together for a weekly liturgy on Saturday evenings and Sundays under the governance of a commonly revered elder and spiritual sage. Sabas and Euthymius were two such famous leaders. Palestinian monasticism was marked by the special geography of the region. The wilderness of the Judean desert was not so desolate or lonely as the Egyptian wilderness, and most of the desert houses here were close enough to the city of Jerusalem that the ascetics were able to enjoy an active pastoral life with significant influence over the affairs of the urban churches.

*Euthymius.* Euthymius (377–473) is regarded in the Eastern Christian tradition as one of the greatest ascetics of monasticism's history. He came from Melitene in Lesser Armenia, was ordained priest as a young man there, and held a high clerical office in the administration of the diocese. Though likely to have become a bishop, he came to Jerusalem seeking disconnection and solitude in 405. He lived as a solitary monk in several places near the holy city, but in 426 he finally established a *lavra* at a place called Khan El Ahmar (it is now covered over by one of the settlements on the West Bank). In the troubled aftermath of the Council of Chalcedon, he was one of the few high authorities in the desert who remained unwavering in his support of the council. His was a powerful voice in international monastic affairs in his time.

---

[91]The quieting down of nature was to be the root of later hesychasm (a term derived from this process of "quietening"). His stress on the utility of simple biblical expressions, repeated many times over, led also to the prevalence of the Eastern Christian tradition of the Jesus prayer.

[92]Cyril of Scythopolis (525–557+) entered monastic life aged eighteen, and a year later, 544, transferred to the *lavra* of Euthymius, where he stayed for eleven years. He then took over the leadership of the "New Lavra" after the expulsion of the Origenian monks who had founded it. See R. M. Price, *Cyril of Scythopolis: Lives of the Monks of Palestine* (Kalamazoo, MI: Cistercian Publications, 1991).

His teachings brought about a general and long-standing acceptance after him that the disparate cenobitic and Lavriotic lifestyles of monks could be combined. A young trainee ought to begin in the cenobitic houses and persevere there, learning spiritual discipline, before moving on to Lavriotic styles of life when he had gained some seniority and stability, and eventually, if he desired, claiming a lifestyle of great solitude as a hermit. So, if desired, a zealous monk might move through all three forms in his career and even return (as John Climacus did) to cenobitic life at the end. Or a monastic could stay for all his career in a cenobitic house if it suited his temperament better. This system allowed in Eastern Christian monasticism a much greater flexibility than was ever common in the West. After Benedictinism became widespread there, so did Benedict's insistence that a good monk should prefer the common life and once admitted to a monastery should never desire to leave it and wander around elsewhere.

*Mar Saba.* Sabas (439–532) was a native of Cappadocia (from the town of Mutalaska, near Cappadocian Caesarea) and spent time as a monk in the Flavian monastery in Caesarea before setting out, aged seventeen, for the holy places in Palestine. Once there he decided to stay and was briefly a monk in the monasteries of Abbas Passarion, and then Euthymius, and then (for a longer stay) in the community of Abba Theoctistus. He stayed with the latter mentor until he was thirty-four years old, in 473. Then he moved out of the cenobium for five years of solitary cave dwelling. In 478 he moved to a new cave on the bank of the river Kidron, near Bethlehem, a gorge in what is now the Wadi en-Nar. Here he started to attract many monastic disciples to his *schola*.

The austerity and size of the community soon made it renowned. The steeply sided gorge made the usual *lavra* design (a long valley housing many separate caves) impractical, so from earliest times the locally gathered cells became walled together, and the houses, so compacted, were fortified into the gorge walls. This house, now called Mar Saba (St. Sabas's) monastery, is one of the oldest continually inhabited monasteries in the Christian world. It survives like an impregnable fortress clinging to the rocks. In his day it was known as the Great Lavra. It is positioned in the very rugged desert between Jerusalem and the Dead Sea. In 490 Sabas reluctantly accepted ordination to the priesthood (at a time when that was most unusual for monks), and in 492 he was made the archimandrite of Palestine (single head of all monastics of the diocese) by the patriarch of Jerusalem.

Sabas featured strongly in the late fifth-century crisis that pitted two parties of monastics against each other: those who delighted in Origen's spiritual philosophy and those who wanted his influence purged from the church. He himself stood against the "Origenist" monks, but he had to work hard to make sure he kept control of his own house, and he could only do so by forcing the exit of many dissidents.

Like Euthymius, he was a powerful conservative force for the theology of the Council of Chalcedon and against Monophysitism. His monastic *typikon* (rule of the Great Lavra) became an important exemplar and model for later Byzantine monasteries.

He himself had a reputation as a very strict and dominant leader, and his rule aroused the opposition of many, especially among the educated literati and theologians opposed to Diphysitism, who did not appreciate the manner in which he sought to use his authority to close down debate. The disputes were so bitter at one stage that Sabas himself was ejected from his own monastery and had to seek imperial support in several visits to Constantinople when Justinian was regnant. His house was returned to him, and the Origenistic monks in turn left to found the "New Lavra." He died in Constantinople in 532 while on a mission there.

In the ninth century his Great Lavra became perhaps the most single important center for liturgical and theological writing in the Eastern world. It started another great force of synthesizing Syrian, Egyptian, peasant, and Origenian-Evagrian traditions of ascetical mysticism that had a long-lasting influence over subsequent forms of Byzantine monastic writing. To the forms of public liturgy already influenced by imperial court ceremonial, it added a strong "edit" to give prominence to the monastic style of the use of extensive psalms, prayers, and vigils. The liturgical structures of the Eastern Christian world are, to this day, strongly marked by the synthesis that first happened in the fifth-century Palestinian monasteries.

**Early monasticism in the West.** *Martin of Tours.* Martin (316–397) was a transitional figure bridging the twilight of the late antique classically resonanced world and the dawning of the early Middle Ages. He founded a very charismatic type of monastic asceticism in the West, using it in the cause of furthering an aggressive missionary expansion of the Christian faith into the rural hinterlands, where pagan cult was still strong in this period, with many functioning temples and shrines. Beginning as a monk, he would use the monks when he was elevated as a bishop as part of his episcopal arsenal in the cause of deconstructing paganism by any means at his disposal.

Born in the Roman imperial province of Pannonia (today straddling Austria, Hungary, Serbia, and Croatia), Martin was the son of a legionary officer and was brought up in Italy at Pavia. There, at the age of ten, he was attracted to the Christian community, and he asked to be enrolled as a catechumen in 326. In 331, when he was fifteen, he was required by law to follow his father into the armed forces and so became a cavalry officer in the armies of Emperor Constantius and then under Julian. He was part of the heavily armed horse guards (*cataphracts*). Sulpicius, who wrote his hagiographical *Life,* tries as much as he can to minimize this military phase of his life—and today Martin has even become a symbol of the conscientious objector.⁹³ But he undoubtedly served more time in the army than would appear from the text. What finally ousted him from military service was probably the ascendancy of Julian, who was by no means as welcoming to Christian officers as Constantius had been.⁹⁴ When Julian began his imperial policy of sidelining Christianity, it signaled to many Christians it was time to withdraw from the court. At this same time Gregory the Theologian wrote to his brother Caesarios, court physician to Julian, that it would be a good time to come back into private life. At this time, in 356, Martin himself would have been forty years old and would have fulfilled the required legal term of twenty-five years for an army officer.

At Worms, after he left the army, he met and joined the party of Hilary of Poitiers, the famous bishop-theologian, and assisted him in the spreading of ecclesial missions for the pro-Nicene party in the region of Illyricum—now the Albanian and Croatian coastal area. He clashed with the leading Arian bishop of Milan, Auxentius, and was banned from the city. Soon after this setback he became a hermit at Liguria on the island of Gallinara (off the northeastern coast of Italy, near Genoa). A few years after this, in 361, he resumed a public ministry at Ligugé, near to Poitiers. It coincides with the time when Hilary himself was restored to his see and his dignities. From this time Martin appears as a monastic superior leading a community on land that was probably given to him out of Hilary's own family estates. This was a historic moment, for it thereby became the first monastic foundation in the Western church that can be properly dated. Martin was increasingly pressed by the Nicene party to become the bishop of Tours and in this role spent the rest of his life, applying monastic forces to evangelize the still heavily pagan countryside areas of the mid-Loire region in (contemporary) France.⁹⁵

---

⁹³One story tells how he refused to fight a battle at Worms and was accused of cowardice. To this he replied he would gladly lead the troops into battle, but unarmed. Before his commanding officers could make him do this, the war is said to have ceased. The famed narrative of his splitting his military cloak with his sword to give half to a poor, cold man at the gate of Amiens (*Life of St. Martin* chap. 3; in the short reader below) was tantamount to an act of treason in that day, comparable to burning the flag in ours. It is a sign that politically he was bidding adieu to Julian. The *Vita* recounts this (and a subsequent vision) as the decisive moment for his baptism (when he was eighteen years old), but there is reason to suppose Sulpicius has foreshortened the episodes of the *Vita* so as to highlight Martin's preference for pacifism as the reason he left military service.

⁹⁴Julian was elevated as caesar in the West by Constantius, in 355, and his troops proclaimed him augustus in 360, thus initiating the civil war between himself and Constantius.

⁹⁵He is said (a trope of this kind of hagiographical literature) to have hidden in a barn to avoid episcopal consecration, but the farmer's geese betrayed his presence, and the common people forcibly demanded his consecration. The Gallic upper classes remained very dubious about him and his style of behavior, not only because of the ragged clothes of a peasant that he insisted on continuing to wear but also because of his rough-and-ready manners, which they thought were hardly suitable for a bishop.

For this he used two headquarters, including his episcopal place in Tours, where he set about organizing the clergy in a quasi-monastic manner of hierarchy. They were, not surprisingly, most reluctant to accept his episcopal authority. His other headquarters were based at the monastery he directed at Marmoutier (the French is a corruption of *maius monasterium*, or "great monastery"), which he founded in 372, two miles upriver from his episcopal city. As missionary bishop he was no pluralist. He advocated destroying temples and cutting down sacred groves of trees.[96]

He became a highly charged political figure and eventually gained much support from the provincial Roman aristocracy, who now saw the church as the best chance for the continuance of a classically based "Gallo-Romano" civilization in a declining political climate. The aristocracy supported him because they too sensed the need for the conversion of the Celtic pagan peasantry so as to fix the Romanization process in the face of the increasingly slight hold Roman imperial forces had over the Western provinces. A *conversio morum* was necessary, so it seemed, rather than a military occupation that could not be sustained in the longer term. But Martin had his own agendas too. He regularly appears as a bishop *philoptochos*, or friend of the poor, such as he had seen represented in the Eastern provinces by bishops of his time such as Basil of Caesarea or Gregory of Nazianzus. He defended the rights of the poor townsfolk against powerful governors such as Count Avitus, who had arrested many citizens of his region for nonpayment of taxes. He also appealed (unsuccessfully) to the usurper Emperor Maximus to stop the execution of Priscillian for heresy (the first Christian dissident to be burned by Christian secular powers).

Martin's missionary activity was very widespread and ranged over the northern and central areas of modern France. He used the monastics to head the missionary endeavors, something Hilary had probably suggested to him, but that was in contrast to the usual way of regarding monastics as withdrawing themselves from church affairs for the sake of contemplation. In the *Life* that his biographer Sulpicius presents, there is a profound stress on the visionary and the miraculous. The zealous monastic missionary is being modeled here, in the figure of Martin, as a charismatic exorcist and destroyer of demons, whose deep holiness inspires a powerful ministry of preaching, reconciliation, and conversion. His monks were given considerable freedom in the collective life, a marked contrast with the kinds of control we can see

---

[96]Sulpicius, in chapter 13 of the *Vita Martini*, shows how the locals preferred their own sacred trees to the Romanized surface cults represented by the classical temples: "When in a certain village he, Martin, had demolished a very ancient temple, and had set about cutting down a pine tree that stood close to the temple, the chief priest of that place and a crowd of other heathens began to oppose him vigorously; and, though, under the influence of the Lord, these people had been quiet while the temple was being overthrown, they could not patiently endure the tree to be cut down."

applicable over monks in the Pachomian and other Egyptian cenobitic establishments. Sulpicius's hagiography in his honor effectively canonizes Martin before his death (for it was written while he was still alive). Sulpicius makes out Martin to be a learned man, but the historical evidence suggests he was very much a rough-and-ready soldier, with a great force of personality and a powerfully elevated sense of holiness.

After Martin's death in 397, his cult (and his monastic polity, by extension) was actively propagated both by the *Vita Martini* of Sulpicius and later by Gregory of Tours, both of whom filled the narrative with miraculous stories (his fights with the devil, his visions, his avoidance of death when he stood under the falling [druidic] tree, his averting of flames issuing from his destruction of a Roman temple that threatened townspeople's houses, and so on).[97] He is clearly presented as a miracle-working figure to best any local shaman the pagan villages can throw up against him. Soon after his death the figure of Martin was taken up as a Christian symbol for the Merovingian dynasty, who advanced their cause under his special patronage. Their kings after the seventh century (when the practice is first attested) wore the relic of Martin's half-cloak (*cappa*) into battle as their *palladium*. The priest who had charge of the *cappa sancti martini* was called the *cappellanus*, and from this it spread to a title for priests who served the military, and even today it has survived as the word *chaplain*. The mosaic masters of San Apollinare in Nuovo in Ravenna put the figure of St. Martin at the very head of their depiction of the procession of martyrs to Christ's throne (even though he wasn't a martyr at all). Saint Benedict would also consecrate a chapel dedicated to his honor on top of Monte Cassino, where there had been a pagan temple. But notably Benedict turns to Cassian, not Martin, for ideas on monastic organization. Later, the Carolingians, following Benedict's indication, would advocate strongly for the Benedictine form of more ordered monastic polity.

At this period, toward the end of the ninth century, Martin's legend, and the idea of a charismatic missionary ideal of monastic wandering it advocated, had moved out of the Gallic region but was enthusiastically taken up in Ireland. Martin's old monastery at Marmoutier became a favored place of training for Celtic monks who intended to work as missionaries on the Continent. Columbanus stopped there for a while. Some Irish ecclesiastical legends even tried to make out that St. Patrick was Martin's nephew. Later Western medieval Christianity held his feast day, on November 11, in high honor,

---

[97] On Sulpicius (c. 363–425) see further C. Stancliffe, *St. Martin and His Hagiographer: History and Miracle in Sulpicius Severus* (Oxford: Oxford University Press, 1983); S. Farmer, *Communities of St. Martin: Legend and Ritual in Medieval Tours* (Ithaca, NY: Cornell University Press, 1991). Gregory of Tours (c. 538–594), the chronicler of the *History of the Franks*, also wrote four books *On the Miracles of Saint Martin*. In his time the tomb of Martin in his cathedral church drew numerous pilgrims.

calling it Martinmas Day. It was an expansive day of carnival feasting and carousing that was followed by forty days of fasting (*Quadragesima Sancti Martini*), later to be known as the Advent fast preceding Christmas.

*John Cassian in Marseilles.* John Cassian (c. 360–433) was a Scythian (modern-day Romania) by birth, a Latin-speaking region bordering the Eastern church, at a time when the traditions of both parts of Christianity were still fluently crossing over with mutual influences. John himself was fluently bilingual in Latin and Greek. His extensive travels finally brought him to the West, where he brought his firsthand knowledge of conditions and practices of Egyptian monasticism and became quickly established as a very influential "translator" of the desert monastic life to Western conditions. He established important Latin-speaking monasteries and had a foundational influence on the theology of ascetical experience for all the Western theologians that came after him. His writing, for example, was a major influence on St. Benedict.

He had first adopted the monastic lifestyle himself as a young man at Bethlehem. A few years after his profession, he moved to Egypt to study asceticism firsthand there and was deeply influenced by his encounter with the great mystic and theologian Evagrius at Scete, whose thought he afterward moderated and disseminated widely through his own writings. In Egypt he spent more than a decade living the ascetical life, and observing and recording sayings of the great elders. Early in the 400s he was at Constantinople, pleading the cause of the Origenist monks who had been attacked by Theophilus of Alexandria. He was ordained as a deacon in the service of renowned patriarch John Chrysostom. After Theophilus, with imperial approval, orchestrated John's deposition at the Synod of the Oak in 404, Cassian went to Rome on a mission of appeal to Pope Innocent I. Here he met and became friends with the Roman Archdeacon Leo, who would later become pope himself.

John seems to have settled in the West from the early decades of the fifth century, founding two monasteries at Marseilles in 415. It was for these communities he wrote his most famous two books: *The Institutes*, which describes the eight chief vices that hinder monks, and in which he dictates the regimen (details about food, dress, and monastic times of prayer) that should govern a serious monk's lifestyle; and also *The Conferences*, which relates the many conversations he had with famed monastic elders in the East.[98] Both works had a deep impact on monasticism as it was beginning to expand in the Western church. His *Institutes* in particular affected the form of many later Western monastic rules and was adapted as a substructure to the monastic charter by the Benedictine family. John had a typical Greek dislike

---

[98] *Institutes of the Coenobia*; *Conlationes* or *Collationes patrum in scetica eremo* (*Conferences of the Skete Desert Fathers*).

for Augustine's ideas on grace, and in *Conferences* 13, he attacks Augustine's ideas by presenting the teaching of John Chrysostom (so earning for himself, in the posthumous Augustinian ascendancy, the rather dubious and censorious designation as semi-Pelagian in the Western church, though in the Eastern church he is regarded as a saint and a great teacher). In the course of the lead-up to the Council of Ephesus, in 430, Pope Celestine, on Leo's advice, asked Cassian to prepare an official adjudication on the doctrine of Nestorius, and so he made a study of incarnational theology that eventually issued in his *Seven Books on the Incarnation of the Lord*.

Cassian's *Conference* and *Institutes* were meant as a deliberate counterweight to the influence of Martin of Tours in southern Gaul and of the ascetical philosophy of his biographer, Sulpicius, who had so stressed the charismatic and wandering-missionary aspects of the ascetical life. Cassian wished, by contrast, to bring a sense of order to a more settled house of ascetics living under the guidance of a single abbot in the style of the classic Egyptian cenobitic houses.

*Irish monasticism.* Christianity might have come to Ireland before St. Patrick (some random archaeological Christian finds from the fourth century have certainly been recorded), but it is with the mission first of the Roman Palladius, and then Patrick, that the first formally recorded origins of the church in Ireland can be dated.[99] According to Prosper of Aquitaine, Pope Celestine sent one of his deacons to be a bishop "for the Irish believing in Christ."[100] This suggests that an existing church was already there, probably based in the south of Ireland, but further knowledge of Palladius and his activity is lost in obscurity. The various *Lives of St. Patrick* (which are basically concerned with pushing Palladius aside) speak either of his martyrdom or say that he went back to Britain (even though he had never come from Britain) and are generally not reliable for definite information. Nevertheless, as one of the personal deacons of the pope, the Palladian Irish mission is not insignificant.

The real apostle of Ireland, however, was indisputably Patricius. He was a Christian from the southern coast of Britain who had been captured and enslaved by Irish pirates and made to work as a shepherd. He escaped and shortly afterward entered the monastic life, finally returning to Ireland as a missionary bishop. His field of work was in the north of Ireland, and for more than thirty years he developed a dramatic and dangerous traveling mission among the pagan lords of the north, one resonant in some respects with the iconic image of Martin of Tours. The churches

---

[99] See D. O. Croinin, *Early Medieval Ireland: 400–1200* (London: Longman, 1995); J. F. Kenny, *The Sources for the Early History of Ireland*, vol. 1, *Ecclesiastical* (New York: Columbia University Press, 1966); L. de Paor, *St. Patrick's World: The Christian Culture of Ireland's Apostolic Age* (London: University of Notre Dame Press, 1993).

[100] Prosper of Aquitaine (c. 390–455), *Chronicle* (for the year 431).

that he founded all flourished and grew. He learned Irish, and the many stories associated with him suggest that he attacked pagan magic head-on with thaumaturgal acts that outdid the local Irish shamans.

His mission, however, not only met stiff pagan resistance but was also attacked by the mainland British clergy, who thought he had infringed their ecclesiastical rights; and in response to their charges that his episcopate was invalid, he produced his famed *Confessions* to justify his apostolate. His *Letter to Coroticus* the British king bravely threatened the Christian warlord with excommunication for having disregarded church canons by enslaving Irish Christians during a raid. Both writings are the earliest known church documents written in Ireland, and they present a vivid picture of a courageous man, filled with a sense of his apostolic destiny.

After Patrick there is a paucity of historical sources about the Irish church until the late sixth century, when a series of monastic holy men and women (Columba, Brigid, Brendan, and Columbanus) demonstrate the highly ascetical, militant, and penitential character of the Irish church, which remained characteristic of it even into modern times. During the seventh century there was considerable internal conflict in the Irish church between the conservators (who wished to retain the ancient Celtic characteristics of their church) and the "innovators" (who wanted to adopt liturgical and institutional forms that brought Ireland more and more into line with evolving continental and Roman traditions). The controversies led to the formation of numerous small colleges and were responsible for the rise of the reputation of Irish churchmen as among the most learned in Europe. The tensions were generally settled at the end of the seventh century by the Romanists succeeding in having the Roman computation of Easter adopted generally, and the Celtic party succeeding in retaining the monastic organization of churches rather than a metropolitan system of bishops, as elsewhere.

Only after the ninth century did cities come to play a significant part in Irish church organization. In the sixth and seventh centuries Irish scholars (rooted equally in the Celtic spirit and in the forms of Latin literature) wandered far and wide in Gaul, Germany, and Italy, taking their literary and artistic skills with them. Writers such as Sedulius Scotus (*scotus* being the original Latin word for "Irishman") took the Celtic influence into the heart of the Carolingian domain on the Continent. The Irish writers of the patristic period were chiefly important as transcribers of manuscripts and made numerous (often brilliantly illuminated) copies of the Scriptures as well as preserving the works of the Latin fathers for Western Europe in a period when the infrastructure of the Western Roman Empire had effectively collapsed. Irish Christian poetry is one of the jewels of early medieval literature. Two of the great monastic figures are Columba and Columbanus.

COLUMBA. The monastic leader Columba (521–597), Latin for "dove," was known as Colm Cille in Irish ("dove of the church"). He was the missionary abbot of the monastery of Iona, off the Scottish shores. He was of royal Irish lineage (which at that period meant a tribal chieftain's relative of an ascendant warrior clan), but from his early youth he showed a marked preference for religious life and so was set aside from warrior training and marked out for education. Sent to monastery schools, he was educated by some of the leading lights of his time, including Saint Finian. He was a renowned (and exceedingly fast) copyist of manuscripts, and in what is possibly the earliest case known of a copyright dispute, a great battle broke out between the clans because it was thought Colm Cille had been deprived of his rights in a dispute about ownership of a manuscript. The clans rose to contest the high kingship of the Irish, and a bloody battle ensued in 561 at Cul-Drebene. Feeling partly responsible for the bloodshed, Columba adopted the radical form of penance known as *xeniteia* (voluntary exile form the homeland) and sailed from Ireland to Britain to do a long penance as missionary "pilgrim for Christ's sake." This was eventually how he came to found his monastery at Iona, on land given to him by the Pictish king, Bride. In 574 Columba anointed Aedan MacGabrain as king of the Scots of Dalriada and in the following year attended the convention of tribal kings at Druim Cett in Ireland. He founded the Irish monastery of Durrow in 585 (or sometime after).[101]

Columba's monasticism is that of a parallel warrior clan. The monks are closely bonded to the abbot by clan bonds or kinship ties and have to give the utmost loyalty as to the liege lord. Disobedience is tantamount to treason. The discipline was rough and strict. Infractions of the rule would bring about immediate repayments in beatings. As with Martin's monastics, these tightly organized and highly disciplined brotherhoods of movable ascetics were highly efficient as missionary evangelizers of the rough and dangerous tribes people of the Celtic and northern English world.

COLUMBANUS. Columbanus (d. c. 615) was named "the little Columba" as a slightly younger contemporary of Columba. He too was an abbot and missionary. He began his ecclesiastical career at the abbey of St. Comgal in Bangor. Around 590 he left Ireland and sailed to Gaul, setting up monasteries with very strict rules at Annegray and Luxeuil in the Vosges region. He brought penance dramatically to the fore in monastic life, as its raison d'être, and introduced severe fasts into the monastic lifestyle to represent the spirit of daily penitential mourning as a dominant motif of Irish monastic spirituality. He encouraged the monastics to reveal all the secret thoughts of the heart to their spiritual adviser, thus popularizing the concept of regular confession of sins.

---

[101] Although Bede says it was before 565.

His monks were a strong force in reviving Christian missions in Gaul at this time. By fiercely propagating Irish church traditions of community penance he first alarmed, and then galvanized, heavy opposition from the Gallic bishops, who forced him to present a defense of his behavior at a synod of Gallic bishops in 603. To bolster support for his cause, he also wrote in appeal to the pope. At first he had the support of the local king, but he soon lost this when he denounced the king's polygamous concubinage. In 610 he was expelled from Gaul by royal decree, and then he went to Lake Constance, where he started missions among the pagan Alemanni tribe. Here too he was driven out by political fighting in 612. Finally, he and his companions settled at Bobbio in Italy, which eventually grew to become a great center of Irish-inspired monastic learning. His literary remains include letters, thirteen sermons, the monk's rule, the communal rule, and the penitential. The authenticity of his poetry is disputed. A brief extract of his monastic rule is given in the reader below.

## A SHORT READER

**The Precepts of Pachomius *1-8 (fourth century)*.** 1. If an unlettered man comes into the assembly of the saints, then the doorkeeper should introduce him, according to his rank, from the monastery gateway, and assign him a seat in the assembly (*synaxis*) of the brethren. He must not change that place of his assigned rank in seating until the monk in charge of each house (*oikiakos*) assigns him to the place that is right for him. 2. He should sit with all modesty and meekness. He must take his goatskin that hangs off his shoulder, down his side, and tuck it up under his buttocks, as well as carefully tying up his sleeveless inner linen tunic, the *lebitonarium*, in such a way that his knees are covered up. 3. As soon as the newcomer hears the sound of the trumpet calling the monks to the *synaxis*, he should leave his cell and recite phrases of Scripture until he reaches the door of the *synaxis*. 4. When he starts to enter that room, on his way to the place where he shall stand and sit, he must avoid treading on the rushes that are laid there, which have already been steeped in water to prepare them for being plaited into ropes, so that no loss may come to the monastery through a person's negligence. 5. At night, when the signal is given, do not loiter by the fire that is usually lit to keep off the cold and warm up bodies. And never sit idly in the *synaxis*. Instead, with eager hands, prepare ropes for the warp of the rush mats. Of course, exceptions are to be made for those who are infirm, and they must be allowed rest. 6. When the monk who stands on the podium reciting Scripture from his heart claps his hand to signal the end of prayers, no one shall delay in rising. All should stand up together. 7. And let no one look at anyone else twisting ropes or praying. Let each one be intent on their own work, with downcast eyes. 8. Such are the precepts of life that the elders handed down to us. And if it happens that during the recitation of the psalms, or the time of prayer, or during a reading, someone should speak out, or laugh, then that person shall immediately unfasten his belt and go to stand by the altar with head and hands hanging down, and there be rebuked by the superior of the monastery. He shall do the same in the *synaxis* of the brethren, and also in the refectory.

**The Systematic Series of the Anonymous Apophthegmata (early fifth century).**
1 (10): An old man said: "This is the voice that cries to humankind until the last breath: Repent this day."

18 (89): An old man was once asked: "What must the monk be?" And he said: "In my opinion he must be alone with the Alone" (*monos pros Monon*).[102]

19 (90): An old man was asked: "Why am I afraid when I walk into the desert?" And he answered: "Because you are still alive."

20 (91): An old man was asked: "What must I do to be saved?" He was making a rope at the time, and without looking up from his weaving he replied: "You are looking at it."

22 (93): An old man was asked: "What is the work of a monk?" And he answered: "Discernment."

24 (95): An old man was asked: "What must a monk do?" And he answered, "Practice everything that is good. Avoid all that is evil."

25 (96): The old men used to say: "The mirror for the monk is prayer."

26 (97): The old men used to say: "The worst thing in the world is to pass judgment on another."

27 (98): The old men used to say: "The crown of a monk is humility."

28 (99): The old men used to say: "Say to every thought which comes to you: Do you belong to us or to our enemies? And it will have to confess."

32 (103): An old man once said: "Do not do a single thing before you have asked yourself if what you are about to do is according to God."

37 (108): An old man said: "Just as the earth is incapable of falling down, so too is the humble soul."[103]

53 (124): An old man said: "Keep far away from those who love conflict in discussion."[104]

---

[102] "Stand alone before the One [Who Is]." A Greek pun weaving together the themes of being solitary (the word *monk* derives from the Greek term for solitary) and being in the presence of the divine unity (supreme Monad).

[103] A pun on the Latin root for "humility"—meaning "close to the earth."

[104] *Apophthegmata Patrum: Systematic Series.* Texts in C. Stewart, *The World of the Desert Fathers* (Oxford: SLG Press, 1986).

**The Anonymous Series of the Apophthegmata Patrum (early fifth century).**
5. A brother once asked an old man, "How does the fear of God enter the soul?" And the old man said: "If a person has humility and poverty and does not judge anyone, the fear of God comes to him."

6. A brother came to see an old man and asked him: "Abba, why is my heart so hard, and why do I not fear God?" And the old man said to him: "In my opinion, if a person bears in mind the reproaches they truly deserve, such a one will acquire the fear of God."

7. An old man once saw a brother laughing and said to him: "We have to give an account of our entire life in the presence of heaven and earth. How is it you are able to laugh?"

8. An old man said: "Just as we carry our own shadow with us everywhere, so ought we to have tears and repentance wherever we go."

15. A brother came to see a very experienced old man and said to him: "I am in trouble." And the old man said to him: "Sit in your cell, and God will give you peace."

17. One of the old men went to visit another old man, who said to his disciple: "Prepare a few lentils for us," which he did, "and soak some loaves," which he also did. And they stayed on talking about spiritual matters until midday on the following day. And the old man said to his disciple: "My child, prepare a few lentils for us." And the disciple said: "It was ready yesterday." So then they ate.

18. Another old man came to see one of the fathers, who cooked a few lentils then said to him: "Let us say a few prayers." And the first one recited the entire Psalter; and then the other brother recited the two great prophets by heart. When it was morning the visitor went away. They had forgotten all about the food.

22. Seeing some nuns coming towards him on the road, one of the brothers made a wide detour. The abbess shouted across to him: "If you were a perfect monk you would not have noticed we were women."

90. An old man was asked: "How can I find God?" He said: "In fasting, in vigils, in labors, in devotion and above all in discernment. I tell you this: many have burdened their bodies without discernment and have then departed form us earning nothing. Our mouths smell bad because of the fasting. We know the scriptures by heart. We recite all the Psalms of David. But we still do not have what God requires of us: charity and humility."

102. An old man said: "Do not agree with every word you hear. Be slow to give your assent. Be quick to speak the truth."

151. A brother went to see a hermit and as he was leaving said: "Forgive me,

father, for taking you away from your holy duty." And he said: "My duty is to refresh you and send you off in peace."[105]

**Barsanuphius and John, Questions and Answers 90 (mid-fifth century).** Question: Is it appropriate to put before the elders all the thoughts that are born in one's heart?

Answer: Brother! Never bother the elders about all the thoughts that rise inside you. For some of them pass away in a moment. Only bring to attention those that endure for a long time in a monk and cause him trouble and strife. For it is like the case of a man who is heckled by many foes, yet pours scorn on his enemies and pays them no attention. However, should any one of them ever rise and approach as if to attack him, surely he would immediately inform his commander about it.

**Augustine of Hippo, Letter 211, To a Female Monastic Community (fifth century).** The rules that we lay down to be observed by you as persons settled in a female monastery are these: First of all, in order to fulfill the end for which you have been gathered into one community, dwell in the house with unity of spirit, and let your hearts and minds be united in God. Do not call anything the property of any individual, but let all things be held in common, and let distribution of food and clothing be made to each member by the prioress: and not in equal measure to all, because not all are equally strong, but rather to every one according to her need. For you can read in the Acts of the Apostles: "They held all things in common: and distribution was made to every man according as he had need." So let those who possessed any worldly goods before they entered the monastery cheerfully desire that these now become common property. Let those who possessed no worldly goods never ask within the monastery for luxuries that they could never have enjoyed while they were outside its walls. Even so, let the comforts which the infirmity of any member may require be given to such, even though their poverty before entering the monastery may have been such that they could not have procured for themselves the bare necessaries of life. In such cases let them be careful not to reckon it among the chief happinesses of their present condition that they have found food and clothing within the monastery, such as was otherwise beyond their reach. What is more, let them not hold their heads high because they are associated on terms of equality with persons whom they would not dared to have

---

[105]*Apophthegmata Patrum: Anonymous Series.* Texts in B. Ward, *The Wisdom of the Desert Fathers* (Oxford: SLG Press, 1975).

approached in the world outside; but let them rather lift their hearts on high and not seek after earthly possessions, because if the rich are brought low but the poor are puffed up with vanity in our monasteries, then these institutions will become useful to the rich only and harmful to the poor. On the other hand, never let those who once held some position in the world look down on their poorer sisters with contempt. Rather, let them be careful to glory in the fellowship of their poor sisters, more so than in the rank of their wealthy parents. And let them not exalt themselves above the rest simply because they might have contributed out of their resources to the maintenance of the community. For in that case they will find in their riches an even greater occasion for pride, for sharing them in the monastery, than they would even have found if they had spent the wealth on their own pleasures in the world. For every other kind of sin finds its outlet in evil works and brings them to completion; but pride can lurk even in good works, and it brings them to destruction. What use would it be to lavish money on the poor, and even become poor oneself, if the unhappy soul is thereby rendered more proud by despising riches than it had been by possessing them? So I bid you all live in unanimity and concord; and give honor to that God whose temples you have been made in the persons of each other.

Be regular in your prayers at the appointed hours and times. In the oratory let no one do anything other than the duty for which that place was made, and from which it received its name; so that if any of you who have leisure and wish to pray at other hours to those appointed, they may not be hindered by other members using the place for any different purposes. In the psalms and hymns you use in your prayers to God, let that be pondered in the heart which is uttered by the voice. Do not chant except those things you find to be prescribed to be chanted. But whatever is not so prescribed is not to be chanted. Keep the flesh under control by fasting and by abstinence from meat and drink, so far as health allows. If anyone is not able to fast, do not let her, unless she is ill, take any nourishment except at the customary hour of the meal. From the time you come to the table until you rise from it again, listen in silence and without arguments to whatever things are being read to you. So do not give only your mouths exercise in eating, but let your ears also be occupied in receiving the word of God. . . . Let your form of dress be utterly inconspicuous. Aspire to edify others by your behavior rather than by your style of clothing. Let your headdresses not be so thin as to show the nets below them. . . . Let your hair be worn entirely covered over, and when you go outside the monastery, it should not be carelessly disheveled or too carefully arranged.

When you go anywhere, walk together as a group, and when you come to the place to which you were going, stand together. In walking, or in standing, in deportment, and indeed in all your movements, do nothing at all that might attract the improper desires of any man, but rather let everything you do be in keeping with your sacred character. Though a passing glance may be directed toward any man, never let your eyes gaze fixedly at any. For when you are walking out you are not forbidden to see men, but you must never let your desires go out to them, or wish to be the objects of desire on their part. . . . And so, when you are together in the church, or in any other place where men also are present, guard your chastity by watching over one another, and God, who abides within you, will thus guard you by means of yourselves. . . . But if anyone among you has gone on waywardly into so great sin as to receive letters or gifts of any description secretly from a man, let her be pardoned and prayed for if she confess this of her own accord. But if she is found out and is convicted of such conduct, let her be more severely punished, according to the sentence of the prioress, or the prior, or even of the bishop.

Let your clothes be washed, either by yourselves or by washerwomen, at such intervals as are approved by the prioress, in case the indulgence of undue care about very clean clothes produces inward stains on your souls. Let your washing of the body and the use of baths not be daily but at the usual interval assigned to it, that is, once a month. But if any illness renders washing of a person more necessary, let this not be delayed. But let this be done on a physician's recommendation, and done without complaint, even though the patient might be reluctant, for she must do at the order of the prioress whatever health demands. . . . Let manuscripts for reading be applied for at a fixed hour every day, and no one who asks for them at other hours should receive them. But at whatever time of day clothes and shoes are required by someone in need, let those in charge of this department never delay in supplying the want. Quarrels should be unknown among you, or at least, if they arise, they should as quickly as possible be ended, lest anger grow into hatred. . . . And so, abstain from hard words; but if they have escaped your lips, be quick to offer words of healing from the same lips by which the wounds were inflicted. . . . Obey the prioress as a mother, giving her all due honor, that God may not be offended by your forgetfulness of what you owe to her. Still more is it incumbent on you to obey the presbyter who has charge of you all. To the prioress most specially belongs the responsibility of seeing that all these rules are observed, and that if any rule has been neglected, the offense shall not be not passed over, but carefully corrected and disciplined.... May the Lord grant you loving submission to all these rules, befitting persons who are enamored of spiritual beauty and who diffuse a sweet savor of Christ by means of good conversation, not as slave women under the law, but rather as those established in freedom under grace.

***John Cassian,*** **The Institutes 3 (fifth century).** Concerning the trial by which a man who is to be received in the monastery shall be tested: Someone who petitions for admittance to the discipline of the monastery must never be received before he gives some evidence of his ability to persevere. This shall be by lying outside the gates for ten days or even longer. It will demonstrate the strength of his desire, his humility, and his patience. Making a prostration before the feet of all the brethren who pass by, he shall be deliberately rebuffed and scorned by them all: as if he were forced to enter the monastery, not on account of religious motives, but as if he were forced into it. And when he has given this practical proof of his stability, in the face of many insults and annoyances, and has given an indication by the way he has suffered this disgrace of what he will be like in time of trials, and only after this testing of the fervor of his soul, then he shall be admitted. Then they shall ask him with the utmost carefulness whether he has the defilement of even a single coin on his person of the possessions that formerly belonged to him. For they know that a man cannot stay for long under the discipline of the monastery, and can never learn the virtue of humility and obedience, or even be happy under the poverty and difficulties of life in the monastery, if he knows that even a tiny sum of money has been kept hidden away. In such a case, as soon as the first troubles arise, he will at immediately run away from the monastery like a stone shot from a sling, driven to this course of action because he has paced his trust in that sum of money.

***Sulpicius Severus,*** **Life of St. Martin of Tours 3, 15.** And so, at one time when Martin had nothing on his person except his arms and his simple military uniform, in the middle of winter, a season that had been even more bitter than usual so that the extreme cold was proving fatal to many, he chanced to meet at the city gate of Amiens a beggar destitute of clothing. He was pleading with the passersby to have compassion upon him, but everyone walked past the wretched man and took no notice of him. For this reason, Martin, that man full of God, understood that this creature for whom the others had no pity, was, therefore, left to him. But what should he do? He had nothing except the cloak in which he was wrapped, for he had already given away other garments on similar occasions. And so he took out the sword he wore and cut his cloak into two halves, and gave one to the poor man, while once more wrapped himself in the remaining half. Seeing this, some of the bystanders started to laugh, because he now looked ridiculous, someone half-dressed. But several of the wiser ones felt sad inside because they had not done likewise. And they felt it all the more because they owned much more than Martin and could have clothed the poor man without reducing themselves to nakedness. The following night, after Martin had fallen asleep, he had a vision of Christ wearing that part of his own cloak that he had wrapped round the poor man. He gazed at the Lord most closely and was asked by someone whether this was his own cloak. And then he heard Jesus speak in a loud voice to the surrounding angels: "Martin, who is still only a catechumen, clothed me in this robe." The Lord was indeed mindful of his own words, for he had said while he was on earth: "Insofar as you have done this to the least of these, you have done it to me." This was why he announced that in the person of that poor man it was he himself who had been clothed. And to confirm this witness he bore to so good a deed, he deigned to show him himself in that very garment that the poor man had received. After this vision the saintly man was not puffed up with human glory but rather acknowledged the goodness of God in what had been done. Being now twenty years of age, he now hastened to receive baptism. He did not, however, immediately then cease from military life. He gave in to the entreaties of his tribune, who was his close friend and tent companion, for the tribune had promised that as soon as his own period of office had expired, he too would retire from the world. Martin then was delayed by waiting on the fulfillment of that promise for two more years after his baptism, and so he continued (but only in name) to act the role of the soldier. I shall also tell you of something that happened in the village of the Aedui. When Martin was there overthrowing a temple, a multitude of rural pagans rushed on him in a frenzy of rage. And when one of them, bolder than the rest, ran up to strike him with a drawn sword, Martin threw back his cloak and offered his bare neck to the assassin. This did not put the pagan off; he quickly lifted up his right arm, but in the very act of lifting it up he fell to the ground on his back. Then, being overwhelmed by the fear of God, the man begged for pardon. Something else like this happened to Martin. A certain man had resolved to stab him with a knife when he was in the act of destroying some idols. But at the very moment of striking the blow, the weapon was knocked out of his hands and disappeared. It happened on many occasions that when the pagans were pleading with him not to knock down their temples, he so soothed and conciliated the minds of the pagans by his holy preaching that, once the light of truth had been revealed to them, they themselves demolished their own temples.

**The Monastic rule of St. Columbanus 10 (seventh century).** *Concerning the Monk's Perfection.* Let the monk live in a community under the discipline of one father and in company with many, so that from one he may learn humility, and from another patience. For one may teach him silence, and another may teach him meekness. Let a monk not do as he wishes; let him eat what he is given, keep as much as he has received, fulfill the sum of his work, be subject to one he may not like. Let him come weary to his bed as if walking in his sleep, and let him be made to rise again while he would still wish to go on sleeping. Let him keep silence when he has suffered any wrong. Let him fear the superior of his community as a lord, but love him as a father, and believe that whatever he commands is good for his soul. Let him never pass judgment on the opinion of an elder, because it is his duty to give obedience and fulfill what he is commanded, just as Moses says: "Hear, O Israel," and what follows.

## FURTHER READING

### Repentance, Reconciliation, Penitentials
Foley, G. C. *Anselm's Theory of the Atonement.* London: Longmans, Green, 1909.
Langstadt, E. "Tertullian's Doctrine of Sin and the Power of Absolution in the *De Pudicitia*." StPatr 2 (1957): 251-57.
Morris, L. L. *The Atonement: Its Meaning and Significance.* Downers Grove, IL: InterVarsity Press, 1983.
Turner, H. E. W. *The Patristic Doctrine of Redemption.* London: Mowbray, 1952.
Vogel, C. *Le pécheur et la pénitence dans l'Église ancienne.* Paris: Editions du Cerf, 1966.
Ward, B. *Harlots of the Desert: A Study of Repentance in Early Monastic Sources.* Kalamazoo, MI: Cistercian Publications, 1987.
Watkins, O. D. *A History of Penance.* 2 vols. London: Longman, 1920.
White, L. M. "Transactionalism in the Penitential Thought of Gregory the Great." *Romisch Quartalschrift* 21 (1978): 33-51.

### Asceticism and Monastic Culture
Abouzayd, S. *Ihidayutha: A Study of the Life of Singleness in the Syrian Orient. From Ignatius of Antioch to Chalcedon 451 A.D.* ARAM: Society for Syro-Mesopotamian Studies. Oxford: ARAM: Society for Syro-Mesopotamian Studies, 1993.
Anderson, G. *Sage, Saint & Sophist. Holy Men and Their Associates in the Early Roman Empire.* London: Routledge, 1994.
Athanassakis, A., trans. *The Life of Pachomius.* Missoula, MT: Scholars Press, 1975.

Breydy, M. "Les laics et les *bnay qyomo* dans l'ancienne tradition de l'Église syrienne." *Kanon: Jahrbuch der Gesellschaft für das Recht der Ostkirchen* 3 (1977): 51-75.

Brown, P. *The Body & Society: Men, Women & Sexual Renunciation in Early Christianity.* New York: Columbia University Press, 1988.

Charanis, P. "The Monk as an Element of Byzantine Society." *Dumbarton Oaks Papers* 25 (1971): 61-68.

Chitty, D. *The Desert a City.* Oxford: Blackwell, 1966.

Clark, E. A. *Ascetic Piety and Women's Faith.* Lewiston, NY: Edwin Mellen, 1986.

Cloke, G. *This Female Man of God: Women and Spiritual Power in the Patristic Age. AD 350–450.* London: Routledge, 1995.

Evelyn-White, H. G. *History of the Monasteries of Nitria and Scetis.* 3 vols. New York: Metropolitan Museum of Art, 1932.

Faherty Dunn, M. *The Emergence of Monasticism: From the Desert Fathers to the Early Middle Ages.* Oxford: Blackwell, 2003.

Fahey, W. *The Foundations of Western Monasticism.* Charlotte, NC: Tan Classics, 2013.

Farmer, S. *Communities of St. Martin: Legend and Ritual in Medieval Tours.* New York: Cornell University Press, 1991.

Fowden, G. "The Pagan Holy Man in Late Antique Society." *Journal of Hellenic Studies* 102 (1982): 33-59.

Fry, T., ed. *The Rule of St. Benedict in Latin and English with Notes.* Collegeville, MN: Liturgical Press, 1981.

Goehring, J. E. *The Letter of Ammon and Pachomian Monasticism.* Patristische Texte und Studien 27. Berlin: De Gruyter, 1986.

———. "New Frontiers in Pachomian Studies." In *The Roots of Egyptian Christianity*, ed., B. A. Pearson and J. Goehring, 236-57. Minneapolis: Fortress, 1986.

Gregg, R. C. *Athanasius: The Life of Antony.* Classics of Western Spirituality. Mahwah, NJ: Paulist, 1980.

Griffith, S. H. "Monks, 'Singles,' and the 'Sons of the Covenant': Reflections on Syriac Ascetic Terminology." In *ΕΥΛΟΓΗΜΑ: Studies in Honor of Robert Taft S.J.*, ed. E. Carr et al., 141-60. Studia Anselmiana 110. Analecta Liturgica 17. Rome: Pontificio Ateneo S. Anselmo, 1993.

Harmless, W. *Desert Christians: An Introduction to the Literature of Early Monasticism.* Oxford: Oxford University Press, 2004.

Keller, D. G. R. *Desert Banquet: A Year of Wisdom from the Desert Mothers and Fathers.* Collegeville, MN: Liturgical Press, 2011.

Kirschner, R. "The Vocation of Holiness in Late Antiquity.: *VC* 38 (1984): 105-24.

Lawrence, C. H. *Medieval Monasticism: Forms of Religious Life in Western Europe in the Middle Ages.* London: Longman, 2001.

Leclercq, J. *The Love of Learning and the Desire for God: A Study of Monastic Culture.* New York: Fordham University Press, 1982.

Lowther Clark, W. K. *The Lausiac History of Palladius.* London: SPCK, 1918.

Luibheid, C. *John Cassian: The Conferences.* Classics of Western Spirituality. Mahwah, NJ: Paulist, 1985.

Luibheid, C., et al. *John Climacus: The Ladder of Divine Ascent.* Classics of Western Spirituality. Mahwah, NJ: Paulist, 1982.

McGuckin, J. A., ed. *Orthodox Monasticism Past and Present.* Piscataway, NJ: Gorgias Press, 2015.

Munz, P. "John Cassian." *JEH* 9 (1960): 1-22.

Petersen, J. *Handmaids of the Lord: Contemporary Descriptions of Female Asceticism in the First Six Christian Centuries.* Kalamazoo, MI: Cistercian Publications, 1996.

Price, R. M., trans. *Cyril of Scythopolis: The Lives of the Monks of Palestine.* Kalamazoo, MI: Cistercian Publications, 1991.

Rose, S., trans. *Saints Barsanuphius and John: Guidance Toward Spiritual Life-Answers to the Questions of Disciples.* Platina, CA: St. Herman of Alaska Brotherhood, 1990.

Rousseau, P. *Ascetics, Authority and the Church in the Age of Jerome and Cassian.* Oxford: Oxford University Press, 1978.

———. *Pachomius: The Making of a Community in Fourth Century Egypt.* Berkeley: University of California Press, 1985.

Rubenson, S. *The Letters of Saint Antony: Origenist Theology, Monastic Tradition, and the Making of a Saint.* Bibliotheca Historico-Ecclesiastica Lundensis 24. Lund: Lund University Press, 1990.

Stancliffe, C. *St. Martin and His Hagiographer: History and Miracle in Sulpicius Severus.* Oxford: Clarendon, 1983.

Stewart, C. *The World of the Desert Fathers.* Oxford: SLG Press, 1986.

Talbot, A. M. "An Introduction to Byzantine Monasticism." *Illinois Classical Studies* 12 (1987): 229-41.

Veilleux, A. *Pachomian Koinonia.* 3 vols. Kalamazoo, MI: Cistercian Publications, 1980–1982.

Vivian, T. *Journeying into God: Seven Early Monastic Lives.* Minneapolis: Fortress, 1996.

Voobus, A. *A History of Asceticism in the Syrian Orient.* 2 vols. Louvain: Secrétariat du Corpus Scriptorum Christianorum Orientalium, 1958, 1960.

Waddell, H. *The Desert Fathers.* London: Sheed and Ward, 1936.

Ward, B. *The Sayings of the Desert Fathers: The Alphabetical Collection.* London: Penguin, 1975, 1981.

———. *The Wisdom of the Desert Fathers.* Oxford: SLG Press, 1975, 1986.

Wimbush, V., ed. *Ascetic Behaviour in Greco-Roman Antiquity.* Minneapolis: Fortress, 1990.

# REMAKING SOCIETY

## The Church in the West in the Fourth to Sixth Centuries

### THE CHURCH IN A TROUBLED IMPERiUM

If the ascent of Constantine to power had seemed like a gift of God to many Christians, in that it offered the prospect of religious toleration from the time of the Edict of Milan in 313, the sense of political elation must have been short-lived.[1] It was true that even Julian's attempt to turn the clock back and fight for the return to the rituals of the old gods of Rome had fizzled out in a very short time. He himself had (probably) been assassinated by his troops on the Persian border after a shambolic campaign there, and a new Christian warlord, Jovian, immediately took his place. Since Constantine there had certainly been no revival of the old style-state persecutions, and the church had grown quickly and demonstrably in that period of peace.

After the long period of the Eastern Arian crisis, the ascent of Theodosius to the throne of augustus of the East, following the death of Valens, led in 380 to the joint issuing by himself and Gratian, the Western emperor, of the edict *Cunctos Populos*.[2] This, while not in itself the making of Christianity as the official state religion of Rome, as many have read it, came as close to this as an emperor of this period would wish to. It signaled two things: first, that catholic Nicene Christianity would be the only legally tolerated form of Christian church organization from henceforth. This made it the legal prelude to the theological settlement of the same issue at the Councils of Constantinople in 381 and 382. Second, the religion of the Christians was the future of Rome. If Christian dissidents were reckoned to be "foolish madmen

---

[1] Edict of Milan, February 313: "When you see that we have granted these things to the Christians, your worship will understand that we have also conceded the right of open and free observance of their rituals to other religions, for the sake of the peace of our time, that all may have the freedom to worship as they please. This regulation is made so that we may not seem to detract from the dignity of any religion." Text in Lactantius, *On the Deaths of the Persecutors* 48.
[2] Given in the short reader at the end of this chapter.

and ignominious heretics" in the edict, what pagans were was left unsaid but nevertheless clearly implied. That implication was even more forcibly stated by succeeding emperors, who gave constant patronage to Christian bishops and scholars.

Justinian's much-vaunted (and criticized) closing of Plato's academy at Athens in 529 (often taken as the closing of the allegedly open mind of the ancient world by censorious church forces) is an example of cliché elevated to symbolic status. Some even take it as the "date" when the ancient world ended and the "Dark Ages" begin. Others elevate it as a rather dubious mark of the real ascent of Christianity as a dominant power. But there is no edict traceable in Justinian that closes the academy. There is a minor edict that advanced catholic orthodoxy and prohibits non-Christian teachers from drawing a public subsidy.[3] Procopius's *Secret History* blames Justinian for ordering state confiscations of private property but never mentions the Athens academy in this regard.

This generic idea that he wished to suppress Hellenic philosophy has been taken up recently by several writers who wish to depict Byzantine Christian culture as something monolithic, censorious, and intellectually closed, which it certainly was not, and least of all as regards its attitude to Greek philosophical and literary traditions. Syrian historian John Malalas is partly responsible for the confusion in the garbled way he reports this alleged edict.[4] But within those who try to make this "event" a turning point in history, an argument seems to be running on subliminally that is not so much about Christianity's real record in antiquity but rather about the situation of religious pluralism, specifically neopaganism, today.

Byzantine historian Agathias tells how the last seven pagan leaders of the Platonic academy moved to Persia under the guarantee of the Sassanid King Khosrau I and taught there, because they were protesting the Christianization of Rome.[5] He draws a

---

[3] "We wish to widen the law once made by us and by our father of blessed memory against all remaining heresies (we call heresies those faiths that hold and believe things otherwise than the catholic and apostolic orthodox church), so that it ought to apply not only to them but also to Samaritans [Jews] and pagans. Thus, since they have had such an ill effect, they should have no influence nor enjoy any dignity, nor acting as teachers of any subjects, should they drag the minds of the simple to their errors and, in this way, turn the more ignorant of them against the pure and true orthodox faith; so we permit only those who are of the orthodox faith to teach and accept a public stipend." Codex Theodosianus.

[4] Malalas, *Chronicle* (for the year 529). "The emperor issued a decree and sent it to Athens, ordering that no one should teach philosophy or interpret the laws." And again, "The emperor decreed that those who held Hellenic beliefs should not hold any state office." The sloppy recounting of history to an audience of Monophysite monks is typical of Malalas. See further E. Watts, "Justinian, Malalas, and the End of Athenian Philosophical Teaching in 529," *Journal of Roman Studies* 94 (2004): 1-15; A. Cameron, "The Last Days of the Academy at Athens," *Proceedings of the Cambridge Philological Society* 195 (1969): 7-29.

[5] Agathias, *Histories* 2.30-31. The leaders of the academy were Damascius the Syrian, Simplicius of Cyrene, Eulamius of Phrygia, Priscian of Lydia, Hermes and Diogenes of Phoenicia, and Isidore of Gaza.

sad picture of them carrying into Persia the precious scrolls—as if they were depriving Hellenism of its light of learning. The whole thing is nonsense, of course. What happened was that they were ousted from Athens by the growing pressure of the Christian population, seeking Christian teachers, who would not require archaic and compulsory acts of pagan cult to accompany philosophical and literary studies. The pagan professors were pushed to their move, taking only their personal libraries with them, by the state withdrawal of publicly subsidized funding for their chairs. This would now make them financially viable as scholars only if they could attract a body of students on their own merits (like the great majority of philosophy teachers in the ancient world), which they obviously felt they could not. It is rarely acknowledged in any popular lifting up of this tale as evidence of Christian boorishness that the philosophers did not like it in Persia and petitioned the emperor to return after only two years. He not only allowed them to do so but gave them freedom to reside anywhere in the empire and to continue their work. They seem to have gone back to Athens.

The edict in question, then, was precisely to prevent pagan teachers drawing a public subsidy in schools that had to be staffed, henceforth, by Christian professors, who alone could hold a state-funded appointment. This meant only Christians in high endowed chairs; it did not prohibit pagan professors from teaching or publishing. Academic work at the schools of Athens continued well after 529, presumably with mixed religion professors of philosophy, even up until the Slav tribal invasions wrecked the institutions there between 579 and 587.[6] Admittedly, the academy was no longer the place to go of choice, as it had once been in classical times. But then, it had not been internationally renowned since the time of Proclus anyway. It had long been in decline, and religious philosophy had moved its epicenter to Constantinople and was to be pursued by monastic writers as much as by Hellene professors. Five of the seven Athenian philosophers who moved to Persia from the academy when it was allegedly "closed" by Justinian were Syrian in origin. Hellenism had moved eastward long before.

Nor should we imagine these seven Persian exiles were the entire corpus of philosophers then active at Athens. Only Damascius and Simplicius among them were of any great renown as pagan sages, and we know this because it was their works of neo-Platonic commentary that were treasured, copied, preserved, and transmitted down the ages by Christian monastics, who published successive editions of them in Greek and Latin. Justinian made no move whatsoever to close the academies at Alexandria, where pagan teachers (taking money from private instruction in the age-old manner)

---

[6]Even then, we find that Theodore (602–690), who later became the archbishop of Canterbury, had studied philosophy at Athens in the seventh century, as did the philosopher Tychicus the Byzantine in the same period.

such as Olympiodoros were active well until the end of the sixth century. It was the fall of the latter city to the caliph's armies that spelled the end of that great center of philosophical learning. But even then the libraries there were shipped off in a one-year interregnum truce, along with relics and numerous other church artifacts, to the schools and churches of Rome and Constantinople (also giving the lie to the oft-repeated calumny that Islam itself was hostile to learning and burned the Great Library at Alexandria). What the edict of Justinian in 529 really witnesses is twofold: that orthodox Christianity is to receive full state patronage henceforward, and that the old style of Hellenic civilization, which was already fading, would continue in a Christian-exegeted form. The Byzantine world carefully preserved and studied its ancient Greek classics. The idea that its Christian civilization was hostile to pluralist understandings of beauty, science, and wisdom is a foolish one, running contrary to the evidence.

But if the old civilization was showing its age and wear already by the end of the fourth century, the political stability that emperors since Constantine had offered to the structures of the church was also starting to show worrisome signs of disintegration. The years 375 through 476 were critical for the status of the Christians, especially in the Western part of the empire, and have gone down in history as "the barbarian invasions." Others push the period even longer and limit it at the end with the accession of Pippin the Short as leader of the Carolingian dynasty in 751, which would shortly produce Charlemagne as new Holy Roman Emperor on Christmas Day 800. *Barbaros* originally meant "wearing a beard" but was quickly adopted as a nomenclature for "the other," the tribes who existed on the frontiers of the imperial borders, who were constantly seen in all Roman propaganda (pagan or Christian) as fearful tribal forces bent on destruction of civilized values. Their advent to Roman territory came about as a massive migration of peoples that occurred in this period and for many generations between the late fourth to the seventh centuries. The immense social and political disruption this caused ended the stability of political life in the Western empire. It has been seen, popularly, as the "end of the Roman Empire."

Of course, the Roman Empire continued in its administrative reach in the Eastern dominions, as what we now call the Byzantine Empire, and from Constantinople and Ravenna several effective campaigns were mounted into the seventh century to bring back the Western dominions, such as Gaul, Spain, and North Africa, under Roman control. In this sense Roman imperial dominion lasted until the fall of Constantinople to Islamic armies in 1453. But the arrival of tribal warlords so extensively in the West, many of whom wished to replace Roman practices with their ancestral law codes, did spell the rapid dissolution of Roman order in this period. It covers the ending of an independent Roman empire in the West, if not an end to Roman civilization. The latter was taken up by the church to a large extent; and the vacuum caused by the collapse of a dominant central authority that was also invested with sacral authority (such as the Roman emperor in Constantinople claimed to hold) was increasingly filled by the rise of the medieval papacy. Gregory the Great can be our *exemplum casi* in this regard. The church in the Western provinces at this period was increasingly seen by the Christian and pagan intelligentsia as the last hope for continuance of Roman civilized values, and it ended a long-standing hostility that the pagan upper classes had sustained against the ascent of Christian institutions for generations past.

What happened at first lay outside Rome's line of sight. In the further eastern steppes, a long way from the natural Roman border of the River Danube, tribes were migrating westward. Climate changes and military conflicts have both been posed as the reasons for this, but the larger issues are still disputed. Even so, a relentless westward pressure of migrating peoples moved less militarily capable tribes ever further westward in a series of staggered migrations. In 406 Roman legions were extensively withdrawn from Britannia, starting a series of migrations across the English Channel, with Angles, Jutes, and Saxon tribes settling the southeastern corner of what would become their new (medieval) and definitely post-Roman England (Angle-land).

Across the Danube, in 376, the Huns clashed with and defeated the Thervingi Gothic tribes under the leadership of two rival chieftains, Athanaric and Fritigern. It was a military loss that pushed a large number of Gothic refugees into Roman territory for the first time. In the winter of that year the Danube froze over, and massed tribes of Goths who had been camped on the far side were able to take the opportunity and cross en masse. Fritigern, losing ground to his rival, appealed for Roman help and converted to (Arian) Christianity as part of an alliance with the Emperor Valens that would absorb the civilian Goths and induct their warriors into battalions of the legions, with rights to citizenship. Athanaric would eventually be defeated and baptized by Gregory the Theologian, as godson (hence ally) to Emperor Theodosius in 381.

In 377, meanwhile, Fritigern and his people were settled in Thrace. The emperor first sent out his praetorian prefect Lupicinus to marshal and order them. But the severe weather caused a failure of the harvest in the following spring, and Lupicinus's treatment of the settlers was so severe (selling them spoiled grain at inflated prices) that the Gothic troops took to armed rebellion and wiped out Lupicinus's command, to the great shock of the Romans. In the face of this significant military disaster at the main border of the empire, Valens led out the legions from Constantinople in 378 to send the Goths back by force of arms. However, in the course of a disastrously bungled campaign, Gothic scouts discovered the farmhouse where the emperor and his generals were resting for the night, near Adrianople, and set fire to it, killing him and his high command and causing a hasty retreat of the Roman armies to the safety of the great walls of Constantinople. This more or less gave the signal for a rapid spread of the Goths, southward into Greece and westward. The Western emperor, Gratian, moved quickly to appoint the Spanish general Theodosius to assume the purple as eastern augustus, and he partly rounded up the eastern Goths in a campaign that had the effect of settling the civilians in southern Europe and admitting the military in significant numbers into special Gothic mercenary battalions of the Roman Empire. The decisive moral victory the Goths claimed after defeating the praetorian prefect and assassinating Valens at Adrianople allowed them to gain very favorable treaty terms.

The Visigoths, a fusion group of the original tribal migration, were at the same time moving westward and continued to disprove the legend of Rome's impregnable military might by invading Italy, devastating the crops, and even attacking and sacking the city of Rome itself. It had for some time been in a slow decline, politically and militarily, after Constantine had moved his capital eastward; but the sack of Rome in 410 by Alaric (a Christian chieftain) and his warriors sent shock waves through the Roman system. It would eventually inspire Augustine's considered reflection of his *City of God*, in which he responded to complaints by senators that Christianity had "let in the barbarians" in so short a time being in charge. The tribes moved ever westward after this, carrying the booty, and settled in Iberia (Spain), where their Visigothic kingdom increasingly co-opted Roman administrators, assuming more Romano-barbarian features than many other tribes, and where it would eventually endure for three hundred years. Ostrogothic warlord Theodoric also led a massed migration and invasion force into Italy and settled there. Eastern Emperor Zeno acknowledged him as a vassal, pretending he held the territories under the permission of the empire. Germanic warrior Odoacer, his rival, claimed the kingship in Italy for himself (476–493) and deposed the last puppet emperor of Rome, Romulus Augustulus, a move that is widely taken to be the "end of the Western Roman rule." Theodoric would eventually capture the whole of Italy and finally took Ravenna, where Odoacer was besieged. In seizing the city, he declared a truce and ordered a festive banquet of reconciliation, during which he had Odoacer murdered.

The Franks, a Germanic people, increasingly spread out in Roman Gaul (France) throughout the fifth century. In 486 their leader, Childeric, and his son Clovis won a decisive battle against the Roman general Syragius that established them as the de facto rulers of the whole northern province of what had formerly been Roman Gaul. This too was a decisive change that has been often seen as the "real end" of Roman rule in the West. After a crushing defeat, all Syragius could do was flee for refuge to the court of the Visigothic King Alaric II at Toulouse. Afraid of the Frankish ascendancy, the latter sent Syragius in chains to Clovis, who shortly after saw to it that he was murdered in prison.

Another tribe, whose name still recalls the fear they imposed on the conquered Roman territories, had much less regard for Roman systems and administrative order. Not for them, as it was with the Visigoths and Franks, the continued reliance on Roman civil servants in the court: these were the Vandals, and their name still carries all the associations of the terror and wreckage they originally caused. They were an East Germanic tribe in origin. Pushed westward in a losing campaign against the Huns, in 429 they successfully invaded North Africa under their king Genseric and within ten years had established a kingdom that included all of former Roman Africa, and in addition Sicily, Corsica, Sardinia, Malta, and the Balearic Islands. They fended off several military attempts of the Byzantine emperor to dislodge them and eventually attacked Italy and sacked the city of Rome for a second time in 455. Their dominion would last until 543–544, when Justinian would recapture the province (temporarily) for Rome.

A second wave of barbarian invasions took place overlaying this first one, initiating what has been called the period of the "Dark Ages," between 500 and 700. At this time many Slavic tribes moved south and settled in central and eastern Europe. Turkish tribes such as the Avars and the Bulgars also moved south and westward in the east Roman territories, beginning a relentless loss of territories to the Eastern empire that would progressively dwindle its landholdings up to the end of the first millennium, constantly weakening its ability to sustain a strong defensive army. In 567 the Avars and the Lombards, another Germanic tribe, settled in northern Italy (now known as Lombardy) and threatened face to face the continuing claims of the Byzantine emperors to rule from their Western capital of Ravenna.

The term *Dark Ages* suggests a time of great loss. It is reminiscent of the evocation of the gathering clouds of war in the autumn of 1914, when the British foreign secretary, Earl Grey, summed up his feeling as "The lamps are going out all over Europe."[7] Many continental (usually Catholic) historians have expressed similar sentiments over the influx of these massive waves of migration, lamenting the barbarism and turmoil that characterized this period. On the other hand, northern European historians or commentators (usually Protestant or agnostic) have tended

---

[7] In his memoirs Grey notes, "A friend came to see me on one of the evenings of the last week—he thinks it was on Monday, August 3 (1914). We were standing at a window of my room in the Foreign Office. It was getting dusk, and the lamps were being lit in the space below on which we were looking. My friend recalls that I remarked on this with the words: 'The lamps are going out all over Europe, we shall not see them lit again in our life-time.'" Viscount Grey of Fallodon, *Twenty-Five Years: 1892–1916* (New York: Frederick A. Stokes, 1925).

to see it as a time when a decadent Roman imperial system was finally pushed aside to a large degree and given fresh vigor by new Germanic blood. What is true in all this is that the church preceded its imperial patronage, and in the West it survived the demise of that system of patronage, still having learned enough to assume the fallen mantle of the emperors and adopting a significant political role of leadership in the concerns of government creation and management that followed in the rise of nation-states in Western Europe.

In the East the Byzantine emperor still exercised control over the legal affairs of the army, the government, and the church, allowing the bishops discretion in matters of doctrine but expecting their complete obedience in political and legal affairs. The lack of a single imperial focus in the West from the fifth century onward, however, made a vacuum that the church inevitably filled. From this time onward, especially with the episcopacy of Damasus of Rome, we see the rise of the papacy to become a superepiscopate. But before we tell that story, let us resume with some of the more significant ecclesiastical leaders who bridge that period from the late fourth century to the time of Augustine, who died with his disciple and successor, Possidius, reading psalms to him, even as the Vandal tribes were outside besieging the city gates of Hippo.

## THE WESTERN NICENE LEADERS

Two significant figures can serve to illustrate the spirit of Western ecclesiality in the earlier part of the fourth century: Hilary and Ambrose.

***Hilary of Poitiers.*** Bishop Hilary (c. 315–367) was the leading defender of Nicene theology in the fourth-century Western church.[8] He seems to have converted to Christianity as a result of being impressed by the lofty moral character of the Scriptures. He was a wealthy married man, with one daughter and estates around the city, when he was elected as the bishop of Poitiers around the year 350. He stood for the *homoousion* policy of the Nicenes, in harmony with the pope, and so began drafting what would become his main work, a large-scale defense of Nicene faith titled *De Trinitate*. Because he would not consent to the imperial condemnation of Athanasius of Alexandria, he was censured at the Synod of Béziers and exiled by the emperor Constantius a long way off in the East, to Phrygia, Asia Minor, where he became acquainted with many aspects of Eastern Christian life, not least the practice of antiphonal hymn singing, which he brought back to the Western church. In doing so he became one of the earliest Latin hymnographers (now only three fragments surviving).

---

[8]C. F. A. Borchardt, *Hilary of Poitiers' Role in the Arian Struggle* (The Hague: Marius Nijhoff, 1966); E. P. Meijering, *Hilary of Poitiers on the Trinity* (Leiden: Brill, 1982); P. C. Burns, "Hilary of Poitiers' Confrontation with Arianism 356–357," in *Arianism*, ed. R. C. Gregg (Cambridge, MA: Philadelphia Patristics Foundation, 1985), 287-302.

While he was in his Eastern exile, he finished the *De Trinitate* in twelve books, and from his acquaintances in the homoiousian movement (anti-Arian but also resistant to Athanasian Nicenism) he gained a deeper appreciation for how the issue of christological orthodoxy at stake in the late fourth century was a larger concern than a simple and wooden acceptance of the letter of the Nicene Creed. It was a lesson Athanasius himself would learn only much later, in 372. Seeing the need to present this case, as a Nicene but arguing for a broader conception of who were friends of Nicenism and who were bitter enemies (he intended to reconcile the homoiousian party), he completed an account (*De Synodis*) for Latin readers as to why so many conflicting councils had been held in the Eastern church. In this work he tried to set out as clearly as possible, for Western readers, why the term *homoousion* had proved to be so controversial for the Greeks. Hilary appeared with the homoiousian party at the Council of Seleucia in 359. He made his way back to Gaul (though he was not allowed to resume episcopal duties at Poitiers), and there he organized alliances of the anti-Arian party as a kind of roving bishop. At the Council of Paris in 361 he succeeded in having a theology promulgated that reconciled the homoousian and homoiousian interests. He last makes an ecclesiastical appearance in 364, with Bishop Eusebius of Vercelli, trying to expel the radical and famed Arian bishop Auxentius of Milan.

Hilary also produced an *Opus Historicum*, which is an important document in that it preserves the text of Arian creeds, and he wrote a blistering *Apology Against Constantius*, the pro-Arian Western emperor whom he designates in his book as the living antichrist. Two significant *Tractates* on Scripture are also extant from his hands, one on Matthew and one on the book of Psalms, which shows that Hilary had closely studied Origen of Alexandria, one of the benefits of his enforced Eastern exile, when he evidently learned Greek.

As a significant patristic theologian, in a time of lively controversy and party spirit, theologian Hilary emerges as an unusually thoughtful and irenic man. In trinitarian theology he emphasizes the distinction of the Father and the Son but conceives of their unity as a mutual interpenetration (*perichoresis*) in which no difference remains except the manner (or mode) of origination: the Father communicates his entire self to the Son, and the Son receives all that is the Father, except that the one remains Father and the other is the Son.[9] To meet Arian christological arguments that the sufferings of the Logos incarnate logically demonstrate his nondivine (relative) status, Hilary proposed a Christology in which Christ's body was indeed real, but also heavenly; in which Christ could feel the impact of the crucifixion, for example, but

---

[9]Which reflects Basil of Caesarea's conception of the mode of origination of the persons (*tropos hyparxeos*).

not the pain of it. It was a dead end that the writers of his time veered away from as undermining the salvific reality of the incarnation and the legitimacy of Christ's human condition.

Hilary's pneumatology is relatively undeveloped. He certainly thinks the Holy Spirit is divine, contrary to the Arians, but conceives it as a dynamic power of God more than a distinct person or hypostasis. Again, it would be Origen's clearer doctrine of one single *ousia* and three persons or hypostases that would carry the day at the Council of Constantinople in 381 and constitute the classical doctrine of Trinity. Hilary acts as a significant figure, a political bishop with some real flair for governance and political lobbying. It is no accident that he was an aristocrat with significant landed holdings of his own estates in Romano-Gaul. He was soon to turn over part of them for the mission and work of Martin of Tours and his monastic expansion of Christian missions in the West. Hilary is a bridge between the old world, governed by the *nobiliores* or upper-class, landed gentry, and the likes of Martin, the ascendant lower classes of highly skilled and charismatic leaders of a new age. In the church they both made a point of meeting. The church had become the new clearinghouse of talent for the making of a new world out of the closure of the antique Western empire.

**Ambrose of Milan.** Ambrose (c. 339–397) rose to fame in Christian memory as a powerful and learned aristocrat who, after his conversion, was elected as bishop of Milan between 374 and 397.[10] He was a scion of a leading noble family, son of the praetorian prefect of Gaul. Educated in rhetoric and philosophy at Rome, he took up a career in law and by 370 had risen politically to be the *consularis* (governor) of the provinces of Aemilia and Liguria in northern Italy, with an administration based in Milan. In 374 he acted decisively to bring order to street disturbances that had broken out between the Catholics and Arians fighting over the legitimate successor to the dying (Arian) bishop Auxentius. His successful intervention impressed the city enough to ensure his own acclamation to that see, and so he was hurriedly baptized and consecrated a bishop. That he was eager to accede to their demands shows that Ambrose too saw the church as the inheritor and best forward transmitter of the highest values of Roman civilization. He proved to be a forceful leader of his city as a bishop and a strong advocate of the Nicene faith: the Christianity of the Romans. His pastoral civic care became a model for many generations of bishops after him, and stories about his successful standoffs even with emperors (making them toe the line in terms of church doctrine and morals, and thus publicly witnessing that no

---

[10]F. H. Dudden, *The Life and Times of St. Ambrose*, 2 vols. (Oxford: Clarendon, 1935); N. B. McLynn, *Ambrose of Milan: Church and Court in a Christian Capital* (Berkeley: University of California Press, 1994); A. Paredi, *St. Ambrose* (Notre Dame, IN: Notre Dame University Press, 1964); D. H. Williams, *Ambrose and the End of the Arian-Nicene Conflicts* (Oxford: Clarendon, 1995).

man was above law or the charter of the gospel ethic) gave symbolic grounds for the later Western church's theory of the preeminence of the priestly office, an important element in the rise of the monarchical papacy.

Ambrose as a neophyte bishop set himself the task of learning theology and biblical exegesis from the foundations in order to fulfill his preaching obligations. He was fluent in Greek (rare for that time in the West), and his work shows an intelligent dependence on Origen and the Eastern patristic tradition for Christology and trinitarian thought. He became a conduit whereby the Greek tradition was rendered into Latin in abbreviated and simplified form, and this had an influence for many generations after him. His biblical work, such as his *Hexaemeron*, where he expounded the scriptural story of the creation was, like Basil the Great's, a carefully simplified overview designed to give the laity a biblically rooted consciousness. His work as an exegete greatly annoyed Jerome, the better specialist, who sharply took against him and lost few opportunities to denounce his rising reputation as a theologian by telling all and sundry that Ambrose was simply plagiarizing Origen. Ambrose's sermons, however, show a vigorous mind of his own. They include many strong moral appeals for social justice. After his elevation as archbishop of Milan, Ambrose embraced the philosophical-ascetical life and gave much prominence to the idea of consecrated virginity in his works and to the cult of the martyrs. His treatise on the sacraments gives an important insight into fourth-century liturgical practice. He is also credited with the popularization of communal hymn singing in the Western church (which he took over from Eastern Christian practices), and his own four surviving authentic hymns mark the first flowering of a subsequently great tradition of Latin Christian hymnody.[11]

Ambrose pressured the emperor Valentinian not to accede to pagan appeals for pluralistic religious toleration, and he stood for the ejection of the ancient altar of victory from the senate house. He also refused to allow Arians rights of free worship in his city, and the occupation of church buildings, which he orchestrated among his own people at Milan, forced the imperial policy of passive toleration to be reversed. In this he is largely responsible for the ascent of Nicenism as the standard Christianity of the West. Ambrose enunciated the principle for the first time that "the emperor is truly within the church, not above the church," thereby setting a new standard of

---

[11]Many other hymns were fathered onto him afterward pseudepigraphically. See further M. J. Roberts, "Poetry and Hymnography 1: Christian Latin Poetry," in *The Oxford Handbook of Early Christian Studies*, ed. S. A. Harvey and D. G. Hunter (Oxford: Oxford University Press, 2008), 628-40. The article in the same volume (641-56) discussing the origins and development of Greek Christian hymnography is by me; that on Syriac hymnody in the same volume (657-71) is by Sebastian Brock.

ecclesiastical polity. He continued in the same tenor with Valentinian's successor, Theodosius I, excommunicating the emperor for his armed assault on the city of Thessalonica (with many deaths in the streets resulting) as a punishment for earlier mutinous riots there. Theodosius eventually accepted public penance to atone for this act of bloodshed and soon afterward initiated a series of laws demonstrating the progressive outlawing of public pagan cults in the empire and disenfranchising the establishments of the old temples.

## THE DONATIST CONTROVERSY

The Donatist crisis, which shapes much of Latin Christianity in this period between the early fourth and late fifth centuries, takes its name from a leading protagonist bishop, Donatus of Casae Nigrae in Numidia (later bishop of Carthage). It was a direct outflow of the times of persecution but ran on into the fifth century, and in addressing it the Western church had to face up to deep questions about its own identity and mission. Augustine of Hippo, who addresses the larger issues of ecclesiology in the fifth century, passed on his solutions to the whole Latin tradition after him. Even despite increasing imperial pressure to disenfranchise the Donatists, legally labeled as "schismatics," the movement continued on in North Africa, especially in the rural regions, until the occlusion of the church there after the Muslim invasions of the seventh century.[12]

The schism first arose because many clergy during the persecution handed over sacred books to the authorities. These *traditores* (the word is the origin of "traitor") were denounced by a group of imprisoned African confessors who declared (with the great moral authority then afforded to confessors in the times of persecution) that only those who acted publicly with bravely and scorned the risk of death would be given a heavenly reward.[13] This robust and no-compromise attitude of theirs, however, was censured by the archdeacon of Carthage, Caecilian, who was annoyed that it gave no room whatsoever for "discretion in times of danger." He knew from his pastoral concerns in the wider church he administered that not everyone was called to martyrdom, that even the Lord himself had advocated flight from persecutors (Mt 10:23), and that it was acceptable to keep a very low profile and hope that one's family did not come to the attention of the authorities. In a later account Caecilian is said to have punished the confessors for fomenting trouble in the

---

[12]To label them schismatics was to say that they were not advancing serious theological differences that would make them guilty of heresy but rather offering significant dissidence in ecclesiastical polity (discipline and issues of communion that caused ruptures of organization in the surrounding regions).
[13]*Acts of Saturninus* 18.

church by reducing their dole of supplies he was in charge of sending to the prison for their support.

In 311 Caecilian became bishop of Carthage in a contested election, but in the following year the primate of Numidia held a council of seventy bishops at Carthage that deposed Caecilian and elected another in his place. Caecilian refused to give way. That same winter Constantine's armies occupied North Africa in the course of his campaign during the civil war. He took Caecilian into his administration as the leading local bishop to serve as his representative in Africa. Constantine gave great moral weight and a large income to Caecilian and threatened his ecclesiastical rivals with legal penalties if they did not come around to Caecilian's communion. This actually hardened the opposition and made them radically distrust the Christian emperors (as much as they had always distrusted the pagan ones). But because the protests went on for several years without abating, Constantine, who was now secure in his rule of the Western empire, referred the dispute between Caecilian and the Numidian bishops to the adjudication of Pope Miltiades. At a synod in Rome the case was again decided in favor of Caecilian's rights as bishop of Carthage.

The Numidian opposition to Caecilian was now led by Bishop Donatus, who arranged yet another appeal to the emperor, alleging that one of Caecilian's episcopal consecrators was a *traditor*, and thus the whole ordination must be seen as invalid. It is the first time that the issue of legitimacy of ordination is explicitly connected with the concept of the legitimacy, or invalidity, of the sacraments those clergy administer. It would soon grow to the acute question that would disturb the Latin churches: Does the moral worthiness of the minister determine the effectiveness and validity of the sacraments they dispense in the churches? Or do the sacraments work powerfully for the benefit of the Christian people, regardless of the holiness of the priest or bishop?[14]

When Constantine saw the pope's adjudication had not served to quieten the dispute, he decided to refer the matter once more to a larger synod of bishops, who could resolve it with an authoritative and universal judgment. His actions in this process surely served to give him the idea for the Council of Nicaea ten years later, when he entered the Eastern provinces and found ecclesiastical divisions there too. This council of Western bishops met at Arles in 314 and took detailed evidence about the circumstances of the original consecration of Caecilian as part of its investigations. The synodical decision again went against Donatus, and the exoneration of Caecilian was reaffirmed by imperial decree in 316. In 320 a separate trial of certain clerics before the governor of Numidia revealed that several of Caecilian's key op-

---

[14] The technical term became *ex opere operato*: the sacraments work, that is, out of their own energy, not depending on the minister being in a state of deep communion with God to make them active.

ponents in the Numidian hierarchy had themselves been *traditores* in the persecution, and there were widespread recriminations of hypocrisy. Even so, the oppositional movement did not lose momentum.

The Donatist protest clearly gained its greatest allegiance in those provinces of North Africa that were the least Romanized (Numidia and Mauretania Sitifensis), suggesting its popularity was closely related to anticolonial sentiment. By the latter half of the fourth century Donatism possibly represented the allegiance structures of the majority of the local (certainly the rural) churches in North Africa, but it was always regarded (by the wider catholic and city-based Western churches) as a very "local" schism, with provincial views on theology. The larger catholic West held to the decrees of the Synod of Arles and regarded Caecilian as the true bishop. After his death the "Caecilianist party" (versus the Donatist side) simply disappeared, and the issue became seen as a schism between the "catholics" and a local secessionist sect of rigorists led by Donatus. His "schism" became known as Donatism.

From the "Donatist" perspective, of course, their bishops had the majority of African sees and were the true continuing church. The imperially recognized church was a colonial overlay on Africa, and its clergy had lost validity of orders because of numerous irregularities of ordination and appointment in the aftermath of the persecution. They argued that once the so-called catholics had lost the communion of the Donatist party, since the latter were the true church, they had lapsed from the church and could no longer claim the sacramental grace for any of their deeds. So this was, all in all, a serious rupture of communion in an important Western province.

In the day-to-day administration of North Africa, by the end of the fourth century, the imperial authorities were slowly accepting the reality of the Donatist majority and increasingly readmitting them to civil rights, when some of the leaders of that party allied themselves with Count Gildo, who rebelled against the empire in 397–398 and sought after the throne for himself. His downfall once more brought about a long-term suspicion of the whole Donatist movement, and from that point on the moral influence of the Catholics far outweighed their numbers. It was really Augustine's arrival on the scene as an African bishop of the Catholics that turned the tide. Between 399 and 415 he wrote a series of treatises against the Donatists, which inestimably advanced the looser ecclesiologies that had hitherto been operating across the board in North Africa and Western theology in general.

Augustine isolated as the chief points of his argument first that the initial charge against Caecilian had been wrong; second, that the Donatist movement was a purely local sect, obviously not in communion with the rest of the Christian world, and thus could not lay claim to catholicity (universality), which was a fundamental mark of the true church; and third, that they had lapsed into heresy by insisting on the rebaptism of converts who came to them from the catholic church. This was a practice instituted by Donatus, who decreed that all clergy who had lapsed in the Great Persecution should be rebaptized. Augustine argued that the ancient tradition of the church was that baptism is unrepeatable, and Donatus's practice was not only denounced by the pope as unacceptable but was actually heretical in that it gave a false view of sacramental grace.[15]

In 405 Augustine, then bishop of Hippo, and his colleague Aurelius of Carthage succeeded in persuading Emperor Honorius to ban the Donatists as a heretical movement, and at this time strong political pressure began to be inflicted on them. Augustine made an exegesis of the parable of the wedding feast, in which the king's servants are told to go out and invite guests to the wedding. When they returned and there were still places not filled, he said to them, "Go out into the hedgerows and bring in any you find there" (Mt 22:9). Augustine glossed that passage as having the king command his servants, "Go out and compel them to come in" (*compelle eos intrare*). The Donatist leaders were forced to attend a conference at Carthage in 411 (286 Catholic hierarchs, and 284 Donatist were present), after which the imperial tribune issued a decree condemning them as a separate hierarchy not to be afforded legal rights. They dwindled in numbers dramatically after that point but never completely disappeared as long as North Africa remained Christian.

The Donatists generally regarded the church as the society of the pure elite that could not tolerate within it the presence of sinners. If serious sin was manifested in any member, this de facto denoted a lapse from membership of the church. Clergy who lapsed lost all their capacity for communicating grace (being devoid of it themselves), which rendered all their sacraments void. The Donatist movement relied heavily on the writings of third-century saint Cyprian of Carthage to illuminate their view on the rightness of rebaptizing heretics. Augustine, in attacking them, advanced the theory that the church is the ark of salvation that contains both saints and sinners. He used the illustration from the parable in which the field of God's church contained wheat as well as weeds growing alongside it (Mt 13:24-30), but God decreed that both should coexist until the last judgment. Augustine argued that the very idea of a "church of the pure" was a contradiction of the church Christ wished to institute, which was more in the nature of a hospital emergency room than an sanitized health farm.

His work was heavily influential on later Latin ecclesiology and sacramental theology. The manner in which Augustine needed to stress the communion with Rome and the internationality of his own catholicity, over and against the localized sense

---

[15]The wider Latin tradition "retired" such clergy.

of communion operative among the Donatists, had a long influence in the later Latin theology about catholicity as assured, almost in a legally demonstrative way, by actual communion with the Roman see. For many centuries the Donatists were considered in church history only as a schismatic group that the great Augustine overthrew. In recent decades it has become clearer that they were much larger than the catholics made out and had a greater hold on local sentiment than previously supposed.

They also were a strongly charismatic movement, deeply conscious of the inalienable sense of equality of all Christians. We have instances where Donatist laity (egged on by their rural bishops) attacked rural landowners in colonial North Africa and forced them to trade places with their slaves. This element of social disruption in the cause of radical justice hostile to the very institution of slavery was one of the reasons the imperial authorities hated them and sent in troops to put down and execute Donatist lay dissidents.[16] The Donatists also seem to have held high the ideals of martyrdom and voluntary poverty. The rigorism that characterized their views on ecclesiology was part of a general outlook of a "resistance" church that had little trust in the attitudes of the emperors, whether or not these now claimed to be Christian. One of Donatus's most celebrated remarks was "But what has the emperor to do with the church?"[17] The idea that the church is a pure society destined to become smaller and smaller as an elite, as time goes on, is to this day still constitutive of many sectarian and rigorist movements in Christianity and continues to clash with a more embracing view of the church as the leaven of a larger world, a society of saints and sinners making their pilgrimage together.

## AUGUSTINE AND HIS SOCIAL VISION

Augustine of Hippo is one of the best known of all Latin Christian theologians of the ancient period. His writings were renowned even in his own lifetime. He had been a prodigy child, possessed of remarkable feats of memory, a skill that served him well both as a rhetorician and later as a bishop in provincial North Africa, when he tried to encompass in his writings the previous Latin theological tradition while at the same time meeting new problems that the ancient Christian authors had not foreseen.[18] His life is quickly told; his intellectual legacy is not: it goes on to be one of the major constituent forces of the Latin theological mind (both in its Roman Catholic

---

[16]Conditions for rural slaves on colonial plantations in late Roman times were particularly harsh. The sight of Christian landowners abusing Christian slaves struck the Donatist bishops forcibly.
[17]Cited in Optatus of Milevis, *Against the Donatists* 3.3.
[18]His works can be found easily both in print and on the web: see P. Schaff, trans., *Works of St. Augustine, NPNF*. There is also an excellent array of studies and bibliographies devoted to his life and thought in A. D. Fitzgerald, ed., *Augustine Through the Ages: An Encyclopedia* (Grand Rapids: Eerdmans, 1999).

and Protestant iterations) to the present day.[19] He never exercised much fascination over the Greek Christian world, and what he did came only in the high Middle Ages; but his influence over Christianity in the West can be compared only to that of Origen in the East.

Augustine came from Thagaste, near Madauros, in Roman North Africa. His father, Patricius, was a pagan (until his deathbed), and his mother, Monica, was a catholic Christian who enrolled her infant son as a catechumen. Augustine's talent was noticed early, and a wealthy patron, Romanianus, sponsored his education. He studied rhetoric at Carthage, where at the age of nineteen he was powerfully attracted to the vocation of rhetor-philosopher by reading Cicero's (now lost) treatise *Hortensius*. His mother pressured him to enroll for baptism, but Augustine had already set up house with a concubine (whom he never names) to whom he was deeply attached, and he was not willing to threaten that relationship or to submit himself to the doctrines of the catholics, which he had increasingly come to regard as simplistic.

He attached himself to the Manichaean movement (as a "hearer") and belonged to them for the next ten years, until 387. His burgeoning rhetorical career took him from Carthage to Rome, and eventually Milan, where he occupied the position of rhetoric professor, won for him by Manichaean patrons. In Milan he became increasingly disillusioned with the Manichaean movement, and a series of personal crises shook his security, beginning with increasing asthmatic troubles (something of course that was disastrous for an ancient orator). At this same time he fell in reluctantly with his mother's plan to dismiss his partner of fifteen years' standing (the mother of his son Adeodatus) so that he could make a rich marriage to advance his prospects. His heartless agreement to her dismissal was soon followed by heartbreak at her loss, and his rapid employment of a sexual surrogate caused him to regard his philosophical aspirations (which were then thought to demand a high degree of detachment from all pleasures, especially sexual) with a depressed skepticism. However, his increasing contact with one of the leading rhetorical and philosophical circles in the city (the group of theologians associated with the priest Simplicianus and the bishop Ambrose) opened up new vistas for him. He was greatly impressed by Ambrose and began to consider the possibility of a similar career as ascetic philosopher. He describes his psychosexual and spiritual struggle in a famous autobiography titled the *Confessions*, which he wrote many years later, and here he depicts the turning point of his life as occurring dramatically in a quiet garden attached

---

[19]See further P. Brown, *Augustine of Hippo: A Biography* (Berkeley: University of California Press, 1967); H. Chadwick, *Augustine* (Oxford: Oxford University Press, 1986); F. van der Meer, *Augustine the Bishop* (London: Sheed and Ward, 1961); W. T. Smith, *Augustine: His Life and Thought* (Atlanta: John Knox, 1980).

to a villa at Cassiciacum outside Milan, when he abandoned his destiny to Christ and subsequently petitioned for admission to the church.[20]

For a while he stayed with Christian friends, who formed a scholarly college around him. Soon, however, he returned to Rome, where Monica died, and then he made his way back to Africa, in 388, where he intended to live (more cheaply) with his companions at Thagaste. One day in 391, while making a visit to the seaport of Hippo Regius, he was seized by local Christians and forcibly ordained priest by Bishop Valerius so that he could help the old bishop in the church administration. He and his companions accepted the forced initiation into church administration, and by 395 Augustine was consecrated as Valerius's episcopal assistant and soon afterward his successor. Local bishops in Africa regarded his promotion as canonically dubious, and even his baptism as somewhat irregular—for the news of his early life (both his sexual liaisons and his membership of the heretical Manichaeans) was common gossip in a church much troubled by the rigorist dissidents the Donatists. To defend himself, after his priestly ordination, Augustine composed treatises against the Manichaeans, and after his consecration as bishop wrote the *Confessions*, an exercise in how self-scrutiny can be a salvific reading of the story of God's providence in creation and in a human life. It was a brilliant answer to his episcopal colleagues who had criticized him for slipping through the rigorous baptismal "scrutinies" of the African church by enrolling in the more easygoing Milanese ritual.[21]

As bishop, Augustine made profound moves to resolve the schism of the Donatists, which led to his enunciation of important principles that would form the basic substructure of Western catholic ideas of sacramentality and ecclesial legitimacy. His works greatly developed the Latin church's understanding of itself as both a heavenly and earthly body (like Christ himself—whose body it was—a complete and perfect synthesis of flesh and divine spirit). He separates Latin ecclesiological thought from the binaries of Cyprian's ecclesiology (contrary to Donatist practice). Opposed, at first, to applying secular pressure on dissidents, he reluctantly came to a position by 411 that allowed for the partial legitimacy of such a policy. His immediate context was the lively Donatist threat of physical violence leveled against him and his clergy; but his authority seemed to have been placed behind the idea of religious compulsion when necessary, and it was an authority much evoked to justify forms of ecclesiastical

---

[20]Really only the second of this genre the Christians had attempted, the first being the great poem *On His Life* (*De Vita Sua*) by Gregory of Nazianzus. Both theologians took autobiography, the scrutiny of the soul, as a highway to insight into God, the human soul being taken by each as an iconic mirror (*imago Dei*) of the divine in the innermost heart of humanity.

[21]The "scrutinies" were a series of rigorous moral questions posed to baptismal candidates by the African presbyters during the Lenten preparations for baptism. The soul scrutinies here (and their accompanying exorcisms) were much more demanding than elsewhere.

oppression in the medieval period when he was evoked as an authority on everything.

The publication of his *Confessions* had caused some scandal in Rome, where a moralist preacher called Pelagius had been appalled by Augustine's apparently fatalist resignation of his salvation to God's grace. Pelagius called for a more robust personal commitment and moral effort, and so began a controversy that was to mark all of Augustine's later life and cause him to elaborate a careful doctrine of grace that would become determinative for Western Catholicism. Augustine regarded humanity as having nothing on which it could base its salvation: all was a free gift of God. Humanity left to itself could only slip into the slavery of sin and corruption. His ideas were set out as a theology of praise for God's merciful providence, but in some, more negative, readings of his legacy, the pessimistic tone predominated in an unbalanced way, and Augustine in a real sense has to be seen as the author of a tendency in Latin theology to focus on the notions of original sin and the corruption of the material world along with an ever-present tendency of the whole human race to depravity.[22] Most Greek writers never laid such stress on this pessimism and never adopted as elements of the faith (unlike subsequent Western Catholicism) what they regarded as peculiarities of Augustine's local church (*theologoumena*).

After the sack of Rome in 410 Augustine began a work of large-scale apologetic to answer those who laid the blame for the decadence of the Western empire at the door of the Christians. Between 412 and 427 he produced a massive treatise called the *City of God*, in which he elaborates the Western church's first systematically considered ethical and political view of what Christianity conceived of as civilized order, in distinction to pre-Christian ideas of culture and society. He stresses the earthly city's (human society's) radical dissociation from the true city of God (the eschatological realization of the kingdom) but makes a case for how the earthly city is informed and guided by heavenly ideals. For him, slavery is a prime symptom of the inherent corruption of the world's affairs. In the midst of endemic violence and disorder, the church has the destiny to represent mercy and reconciliation, guiding society to a perfection it might never otherwise attain but to which it is inexorably summoned.

To stand alongside the *Confessions* and the *City of God* in the triad of world classics he authored, we should add Augustine's monumental work of theology *On the Trinity*, composed between 399 and 419. In this he constructs a major anti-Arian apologetic around the Nicene faith in Christology and pneumatology. Here Augustine demonstrates from a wide variety of triadic cosmic patterns the reasonableness of the trinitarian doctrine of three divine persons subsisting in one

---

[22]Original sin is the concept that Adam's sin passed on to all the human race, person by person, as inherited guilt before God, so that no one is born innocent.

single divine nature. Much use is made of triple patterns within human psychology (that is, the soul considered as the image of God), and he emphasized a deep connection between self-scrutiny and theological method (something common to Augustine and the Platonic tradition).

His vast corpus of writings became, of course, his own form of ascetical exercise. The great extent of his work made him function as an encyclopedic theological authority for the next millennium in the West. His spiritual writings gave a great impetus to monasticism as the organizing structure of the Latin church (something Gregory the Great later picked up and developed). He particularly stressed the element of true faith leading to a deep desire of the heart for God, an affective spiritual tradition that made him an attractive and highly approachable Christian writer—aspects that still appear from engagement with his work.

Only a few of his extensive treatises can be singled out here: such as *De Doctrina Christiana*, which laid out his biblical hermeneutical philosophy, or *De Bono Conjugali*, which argued (somewhat reluctantly) for the intrinsic holiness of sexuality in marriage (against Jerome's contemporaneous and deeply hostile opinions). *De Peccatorum Meritis et Remissione* and *De Natura et Gratia* both demonstrate why he thought Pelagianism to be destructive of Christian religious experience. The *Enchiridion* is a summatic handbook of theology, composed for ready reference. His greatest exegetical works are perhaps his *Tractatus CXXIV in Joannis Evangelium* and *De Genesi ad Litteram* (commentaries, respectively, on John's Gospel and the book of Genesis). The *Commentary on the Psalms* (*Enarrationes in Psalmos*) demonstrates his deep love for them as prayers. There is hardly a sermon, however, that is not an exposition of Scripture or a serious theological reflection in the manner he approaches it. Augustine's friend and monastic companion Possidius wrote a biography soon after his death and made an invaluable list of all his writings, most of which are still extant. Augustine died on August 28, 430. One of his last instructions was to have his favorite psalms written in large letters around his walls so that he could read them as he died.

Soon after his death, Prosper of Aquitaine began a process to lobby for Augustinianism as the standard theological system of the Latin west, a movement that slowly gathered momentum, culminating in Pope Gregory the Great's enthusiastic endorsement of Augustine as preeminent Latin theologian in the late sixth century. This era of the marked closing down of the range of intellectual diversity in late antiquity has been seen by many as the beginning of the Middle Ages. One result was that there were simply no longer as many significant intellectuals and writers in the Latin Christian world. Compared to those who came after, Augustine looked like a giant. Moreover, it was much easier to reproduce his writings than it was to gather a whole library of selections from others. So, in a short space of time, Augustine's works started to become assembled together like an encyclopedia of reference for the theology of the early medieval Western catholic church.

Ideas that once had limited and local appeal (typical North African notions that Augustine endorsed, such as the contagion of sin as passed on through sexual desire, or the urgent need to baptize babies, who were defiled by an ancestral original sin) were thus picked up internationally. Because he had elaborated them, such originally localized notions were adopted and disseminated by the great clearinghouse of Rome. Pope Gregory the Great was an avid follower, yet also a massive simplifier, of Augustine's doctrines, and he passed on a much less nuanced form of his thinking to the whole Western Christian world. Through Gregory, Augustine became the most authoritative source of philosophical and religious thinking after the Bible, and although his mind was impressively lively and imaginatively charged, it was, in many senses, too narrow a gate for this to be entirely a healthy thing for the larger Western tradition.

One of his most enduring legacies was to be on the imagination of the political role of Christendom. Augustine's ideas on *politeia* were fashioned by two major stimuli in his lifetime: first, the events that were taking place in Rome after Alaric's siege and plundering of the capital in 410; and second, on the home front, the threat of physical violence that was regularly leveled at him and his clergy by the Donatist Christians, who regarded Augustine's circle as colonialists who had betrayed the faith in earlier generations and therefore had no right to episcopal or magistratial office. The events in Rome made him think about politics and society on a large canvas. The events at home, when several of his friends were pulled from their carriages and severely beaten in the countryside, made him think in a very focused way about law and order. He surely never imagined that his musings would be the last voice that was heard for a very long time and would actually be used as a steel skeleton for building the social order of the Western medieval church. For better or worse, his notes and sketches became a paradigm for Christian political theology in the West.

**Augustine's City of God.** The capture and sack of the ancient city of Rome in 410 was a passing thing as far as the Gothic warriors of Alaric were concerned. They simply wanted to take treasure and be on their way once more. But the damage to the psyche of the Roman Empire in the West was massive. The pagan critics of the new church were savage in their anger. In so short a time Christian leaders had lost the glory of Rome. As far as most voices went, in their shame in the aftermath of Alaric, the Christians had either weakened the empire by feeble pacifism and neglect of the armies or had alienated the ancient gods who ultimately gave Rome good luck. As a reply Augustine composed a political answer to the critics from the perspectives of the Bible. In his great book the *City of God* he tries to tell in a new way the biblical history of divine judgment over all the earth.

Augustine's monumental treatise is actually the archetypal "tale of two cities" incompatible in character, the city of God and the earthly city of human cultures.[23] All earthly attempts to mirror, let alone reproduce, the heavenly city, he says, will fail. All attempts to ignore it will result in the making of an earthly hell of social oppression. His intense pessimism and rather strict dualism had immense political implications within the Christian order.[24] Two in particular can be singled out.[25]

The first is the common medieval misreading of what he actually said. This resulted from a bad exegesis of his work, partly the fault of St. Gregory the Great, the dynamic seventh-century bishop of Rome. He started off what soon became a standard reading of Augustine's thesis of the two separate cities: namely, that the earthly city presided over by politicians was corrupt, and that a heavenly city advancing gospel precepts and presided over by Christian clergy ought to replace it. In short: the church is the kingdom of God on earth and is a superior institution (with far greater governing authority) than the secular system of politics that preceded it.[26] This political charter was especially promulgated under Rome's ecclesiastical leadership after the seventh-century collapse of Byzantine rule in the West, and it was largely responsible for advancing the later theory of papal monarchy; but it was also significantly resisted by civil leaders in Christendom. Nevertheless, it was widely preached that the church was

---

[23]This incompatibility is the substance of the second part, books 11-22, of the *City of God*. Books 11-14 discuss origins of the heavenly and earthly cities; books 15-18 give a survey of histories from the vantage point of biblical narrative, showing the perennial interweaving of the two cities in human and sacred history; books 19-22 present a summatic review and point to the final destinies awaiting the two cities.

[24]Perhaps he did carry over more Manichaean attitudes into the church after his conversion than he thought he had.

[25]Perhaps one of Augustine's greatest contributions to social theory, which we do not have time to expand on here, was one in which he was largely bypassed in all subsequent thought. The Byzantine Christian tradition had largely accepted, by his day, the position argued by Cicero that law was an extended set of principles based around natural rights, especially the rights of nations (*ius gentium*). The notion of the right of nations included issues such as private property and slavery. Augustine is not at all happy about canonizing law as the fundament of true society, as he says that law, most of time, simply reflects greedy human desires and ambitions and does not represent a true search for justice, to which God's gift of conscience calls us. Law, therefore, can frequently be far less than what God has commanded humanity to aspire to. Law represents a certain compromise with goodness that is bent in accordance with the unjust and ingrained habits of society (*On the Spirit and the Letter* 36.65). According to Augustine, to be part of the heavenly city, one must never mistake law for love or justice and always seek to live by a higher standard than that which is acceptable to the majority. This principle continues to show itself in lively ways today in the regular conflicts around issues intersecting law and morality.

[26]Augustine did not say that the church was the kingdom of God on earth, teaching instead that evil was mixed even into the body of the church, which contained always within it seeds of the good and seeds of corruption: saints living alongside sinners until the end of time.

itself, and in itself, the ideal heavenly society. All who failed to fit in (Jews, heretics, atheists, pagans) not only were to be, but ought to be, suppressed for the sake of the health of society. This was a legal, not merely a moral, good. If applied literally this would surely lead to a theocratic and totalitarian state; but it never was adopted in toto despite many attempts to advance the standing of the clergy as political leaders—and, after all, it was clearly a misreading of Augustine, though it did tend to become the determinative "Augustinianism" of the medieval era. It thus explains much of ecclesiastical culture and politics for more than a thousand years in Western Europe.

A second aspect to Augustine's thought on human society derives from two of his foundational premises in the *City of God*: namely, that all things on earth are corrupt (all human motives rising out of selfishness) and that there can be no compromise possible between the earthly and heavenly cities. This can be summarized as the doctrine of the necessity of "political realism" that he inculcated. It defines all politics and all social engineering as by definition the setting up of the least harmful compromises. As all idealist solutions are impossible on earth, since the human heart and conscience (even its grasp of the nature of the good itself) are perennially corrupted by self-will, then all that remains for human society is to draw up for itself a plan of communal living that hems in excessive wickedness and tries to appeal to a common level of the positive aspirations of the multitude.[27] Politics, therefore, is not in the business of idealist visions of what ought to be done; rather, it is in the business of establishing peace among citizens by regulating them according to a standard of what can reasonably be achieved.

This view of "Christian realism" has had a very wide take-up across history and runs on into the present. In relatively recent times it was associated with the social theology of Reinhold Niebuhr. As a powerful strain of classical Augustinianism it has been found, in more than trace elements, in cultures as widely divergent as neocon strategists, liberal Protestantism, and Catholic action.[28] Augustine's enduring influence is not always recognized in his modern successors.

This view of the constant tendency toward moral corruption of all individuals and all societies is (however depressing, in moral as well as political terms, it might be) something Augustine has bequeathed to the Western European world: a tone of moral gloominess that is common to his inheritors in both the Catholic and

---

[27]He is not ruling out the redemptive activity of God through transforming grace (indeed this, theologically, is one of his core messages), but he sets this drama more on an individual plane of the ascent of the individual to holiness through many temptations and failures, rather than imagining it as a social endeavor. Western Christianity has, therefore, until relatively modern times been much more eloquent talking about individual sin and holiness, rather than corporate (social) sin and virtue.

[28]See R. Niebuhr, "Augustine's Political Realism," in *The Essential Reinhold Niebuhr: Selected Essays and Addresses*, ed. R. M. Brown (New Haven, CT: Yale University Press, 1986).

Protestant traditions, for both worlds clung to him as a founding father. With his innate pessimism about human motivations and his moralist's desire to correct and improve, he had a drastic effect on politics because he applied these constructs to a large metaphysical canvas, and this massively amplified "projection" of his ideas not only heightened the effect of his moral rhetoric but magnified some of its drawbacks too. One of those was the manner in which the Augustinian system privileged coercion over inspiration.

**Augustine and the Donatists.** Augustine's close encounters with the Donatists were not only couched in theological terms. The reason he appeals for outside secular assistance to suppress them was set in terms of the social disruption their lay mobs were causing. These were known as the *circumcellions* (the roamers) and served as a force of local occupation of the rural areas. Augustine complains that when they saw bishops of the catholics, they attacked them, threw them out of their carriages, and beat them up. He describes the issue as a major "problem" for law and order in these terms:

> Demented flocks of wicked men disrupt the quiet of the innocent in various lawsuits. . . . Through fear of their clubs and their arson and threats of immediate death, the title deeds of the worst kind of slave were ripped up, so that even such as these were able to depart as free men.[29] . . . Whoever ignored their hard words was forced to do what they had ordered by means of the imposition of yet harder sticks. . . . Some heads of households, born to an honorable social position, and nobly educated were taken from the scene barely alive after the beatings they had received.[30]

We notice in this complaint he makes to Count Boniface, the Roman military commander, the putting together of physical unprovoked attacks on respectable citizens with subversive attempts to liberate slaves. What was going on here was the attempts of the Donatists to demand the end of slave factories in their area, collective farms that sent their produce outside the province, to feed Rome. The Donatist bishops seem to have encouraged their faithful to give warnings to slave plantation owners and if they did not heed them to burn down the plantations. The Roman authorities came in force to prevent this type of disorder. Now Augustine here seems, rather unsympathetically we might think, to be on the side of the slave owners: or rather, on the side of the Roman authorities who intervene on behalf of the owners. He cannot see the issue as something other than a wide-scale threat to social orderliness. For him this outweighs any considerations of morality in trying to alleviate the wretchedness of rural slaves in Numidia.

---

[29]Does he mean the *coloni*, the rough-and-ready field workers who might well have been socially crass and uneducated (the "worst type of person") because of how they had been compelled to live?

[30]Augustine, *Letter* 185.15.

Now, if Augustine does not emerge as very farseeing in this instance, we ought to restore some honor to him by recounting another incident that has come to light only recently in a new cache of letters that portray him in his part-time role as an auxiliary local magistrate, a power that had been extended to Christian bishops by the imperial administration after Constantine.[31] In this specific case, in 420, the local catholic laity at Hippo Regius, his own hometown, rioted at the docks because a slave ship was loading up cargo there. They liberated all the slaves and forced the outraged slavers to go to court to claim them back. Augustine does not tell us who planned the action of his own congregation. We might guess, but he (deliberately) does not tell us because the action was now sub judice. He does tell us that the local judge in question then reviewed each case of enslavement on a person-by-person basis, and when the slavers could not produce necessary documents for each of the individuals (hardly likely, as the judge would have known) he passed a legally binding judgment that they had all been illegally enslaved in the first place and were thus entitled to remain free.

We only learn definitively that the magistrate in question was Augustine himself when he rather sheepishly mentions in this letter that he had recently been sued by the slave-ship owner in the secular court because of his adjudication (clearly proslave this time) and that he was going to have to account for his judgments at the superior secular court.[32] Several of his individual magistrate decisions exist in the new letters, and they show Augustine to have had a special interest in protecting the dispossessed, especially widows and orphans, and in several cases intervening on behalf of slaves suffering harsh treatment. It is fairly obvious that if he had his own way he would have abolished slavery, but in a sense he clearly accepts it—because he sees the "law of good order" as more significant in scope and importance than the instance of individual injustices. The earthly city is at best a compromise, in his view.

When Augustine complained about the Donatists liberating slaves, he wanted to get them into trouble, and to do so he knew exactly which Roman legal buttons to press: for Roman law, even in this Christian imperium, did not care about appeals to the brotherhood of humanity, but it did care about a member of a lower class offering violence to a member of the upper classes, and any infringement of this fundamental rule was swiftly and brutally dealt with. This is why Augustine, ever so casually, drops in the exact degree of rank of the cleric who had been beaten by the Donatist common mob. He knows unerringly that the recipient of this letter, the imperial Count Boniface, will do his bidding with a garrison following his directions as local magistrate, over and against that rather incompetent and "suspect" Donatist

---

[31] Discovered a few decades ago by H. Divjak and now cited as *New Letters*.
[32] *New Letters* 10.8.

bishop who was in the shadows behind the ripping up of slave title documents in the countryside (just as he was in the shadows at the Hippo slave liberation). In this cameo of the two slave "riots," the one Donatist, the other his own at the Hippo Regius docks, we see Augustine's polity at work, and it is at once sensible and deeply troubling: work within the status quo, accept the solution that is best overall for the containment of seething human passions and selfish interests.[33] Sensible, because that is how politics largely works to this day; troubling, because of the apparent exiling of absolutes from the making of the earthly city.

## FRIENDS AND OPPONENTS OF AUGUSTINE IN THE WEST

Augustine would, within a century and a half, grow in stature from being one of the leading theologians of the African church to being the undisputed *magister* of Western catholicism. This story would unfold with the energetic publishing work of the later Pope Gregory the First. In his own lifetime, however, Augustine had several detractors as well as supporters. Not everyone in the Latin world loved him. Cassian of Marseilles would always hold him in great suspicion for his teaching on grace and free will. This opposition earned Cassian some obloquy in return in later centuries, when Augustine's fame had risen to great heights. Apart from the Donatist bishops who regarded Augustine as a colonial interloper, even some of his own episcopal bench also looked on him askance in some ways: for his former moral life, his practice of astrology, and his embracing of the Manichaeans, and even for the irregular way he was consecrated bishop at Hippo.

But there is no doubt that even from the early part of his episcopal career in Africa Augustine was a renowned star. His works were read and discussed far afield. His immediate college, of some long-standing friends and new ascetical recruits to his extended episcopal household (which he had reworked as a kind of intellectual monastery), carefully husbanded his literary remains and kept his memory alive in Africa. His larger international reputation (already present in his lifetime) brought him to the attention of another Latin theologian, who admired him but certainly with some vinegar mixed in to that recognition, for he regarded himself, not Augustine, as the preeminent theologian of the time, and that was Jerome (c. 347–420): a prickly and irascible correspondent. Another set of readers who became entangled in Augustine's works, and this time had a negative reaction like Cassian's, was the circle around the British ascetic Pelagius (350–425), who was active as a spiritual teacher in Rome.

---

[33]He dresses the riots up as worlds apart because his was carried out under the appearance of law and order (albeit speciously), whereas the Donatist ones were carried out in a spirit of rebellion against (an unjust) order.

**Pelagius.** Shortly after Augustine had published his *Confessions*, around the year 400, the book arrived in Rome and was eagerly taken up as reading by a circle of dedicated ascetics there. Several of them found the ideas troubling. Not only was this depicting a bishop who had a somewhat checkered past, but he seemed to be saying to his general readership that human will was not sufficient to live a good moral life: people always and inevitably fell away from their ideals and had to be caught up in God's prevenient grace in order to do anything good at all. To their ascetical ears this sounded like moral fudge. Surely a moral life had to flow from a firm and zealous commitment to strengthen the human will: teaching it to resist temptation by means of fasting, penance, and good works.

Pelagius was one of those who recognized in this, almost from the start, the twinned issues of the rationale of the moral struggle, but also how it evoked, yet again, Paul's New Testament doctrine of grace and redemption. Was our salvation a gift from God such that those who did not get saved demonstrated a kind of moral resistance that God had seen in advance (predestined to rebel?), or was it a gift of God that was sent to us in return for God seeing our strenuous "best efforts" to live the good life to which the gospel called us? If the latter (that grace was given in response to God seeing our efforts—something Augustine would not have argued with but a position he thought did not capture the mystery in its fullness), the Roman ascetics thought that the confessions gave a "bad example" to the faithful. It was hardly a story about a young hero of repentance who came to grace by dint of hard askesis. It was more like the hymn "Amazing Grace" (which celebrates Augustine's theory of grace-led repentance precisely because Augustine was the hero of the Reformation theologies of justification). His *Confessions* tell the story of a man wrestling with his moral impotence in the garden of a villa, until he found a miraculous text in the Bible telling him to "give no more thought to the flesh"; and then he became baptized; and then (according to the *Confessions*'s narrative anyway) "presumably" he never again had any moral struggles with sexuality or any other moral problematic. In so many respects it was not really believable as a spiritual vade mecum.[34]

---

[34]Perhaps it was not meant to be. As a literary masterpiece, the *Confessions* ends its narrative at a dramatic moment of the neophyte throwing all doubts aside, casting himself on God's mercy, accepting baptism and walking into the unknown with God. This theodramatic book, of course, was written by Augustine as an experienced bishop. There was an afterstory; it is just that he was not going to tell it publicly. The reader had to be "everyman" Christian and slot himself or herself into that position of the protagonist. In other words, the point of the book, for Christians of some standing, was to renew your moral life by remembering the zeal you had when first you started off and accepted baptism (the era presumes most of the baptized were adults, of course). It achieves its point like all drama, with an emphatic statement. Equally, the Pelagian circle at Rome was right in saying that this does not work as a real down-to-earth guide to a moral life in a decadent city environment.

In many ways this was a very strange story, and its familiarity to us today after centuries of being a spiritual classic should not blind us to this. To be any use at all as a catechetical text for those who were thinking of leaving a pagan lifestyle and adopting a more ascetical Christian one, it lacks (what surely Augustine would have himself supplied *hors-de-texte* as a bishop in his own church) an extensive set of catechetical instructions: How does one live chastely, honestly, and so on, in the daily world? How does one overcome the numerous other temptations to fall aside? The Roman ascetics felt let down by this new book they had chosen for their reading circle. It was not morally athletic enough for them; it did not give sufficient injunctions to get up and get fighting and train the will by self-denial exercises; it was all too much a reflection on the fallibility of the human heart and the need for utter reliance on God.

It was one thing, then, for fifth-century Christian readers to feel disappointed in their choice of self-help book. But Pelagius was not merely a spiritual director at Rome; he was also a significant biblical interpreter, and he felt that Augustine not only had a wrong emphasis in his preaching but had misinterpreted Paul's meaning in a dangerous way, and he was willing to say this in the capital of the Latin Christian world. Pelagius felt Augustine was theologically misguided; and that started a major controversy that would dominate Latin thought for a long time to come, enduring in the background long after Pelagius's ideas were discounted in favor of Augustine's. At Rome, Pelagius enjoyed a high reputation as spiritual guide, preacher, and biblical exegete. His surviving *Commentary on the Thirteen Pauline Epistles* gives a view of his general exegetical approach.

A typical aspect of Pelagius's moral teaching is that God has given the church specific commandments in the Scriptures about standards of virtue and the manner of life expected of those who are called to the church. Moreover, God had made these injunctions for pagans too, not only Jews and Christians, who have the advantage of the revelation contained in Holy Scripture. God has set the chief lineaments of the moral law into the natural conscience of humankind. It is the duty of the Christian disciple, therefore, to use both natural conscience and scriptural guidance to put these injunctions into effect. The first response of the believer, then, is faithful obedience. We might fail in our task as believers setting off on the "narrow road," but failure can be repaired by repentance. Moral responsiveness, always difficult, is never impossible, Pelagius says. God would never have commanded what was not within the ability of his disciples to perform. Accordingly, the difficulties in observing moral laws have to be met and answered at every step by significant ascetical training. Knowing the way is hard, and backsliding is easy; the faithful disciple will discipline his or her life by the supplements of prayer and ascetical self-guarding to offset the tendency to wander.

This progressive determination to keep the commandments is synonymous with true Christianity: the Christian religion is a way of life more than a set of doctrines.

Much of this was regarded as wholly unexceptional in many circles of the church of his day, but the growing Augustinianism would read it increasingly as self-reliance theology and pitch "Pelagianism" as an antithesis of Augustinianism, understood as the sense of God's graceful salvation that is God-inspired, God-initiated, and God-accomplished in a sinful human being. It was not necessary, perhaps, that the two approaches should be so contrasted, and thus one had to be condemned; but that is how it happened, for Pelagius's approach and Cassian's adjustments to Augustine's theology were sidelined in a way that did not occur in Eastern Christianity. Indeed, although Pelagius got into great trouble with the North African synods that were soon to be held to adjudicate this matter (and were dominated by Augustine and endorsed by Rome), much of what he had to say on this matter of athletic Christianity would not have disturbed the majority of the Eastern monastics of his day. And when Pelagius came to Jerusalem and was forced to answer ecclesiastical charges that the way he taught underestimated God's grace and placed too high a premium on human effort (saving ourselves by good works) the learned bishop John exonerated him there, finding nothing wrong with his ascetical teachings at all.

Eastern Christianity to this day senses that Augustine's clash with Pelagius was unnecessarily limiting, and that while all the initiative for grace and redemption, at every level and stage, lies with God, the same God expects each believer to do his or her part in responding to the divine assistance. For the East, grace was not simply an assistance of God in the soul, but more so the transfigurative indwelling of God: and the capacity of the soul for recognizing and desiring that presence was never understood (as much as it was in Augustine) to be so wholly corrupted and paralyzed by the effects of sin. The different emphases on this (very discernible in Christian redemption theory) remain in the Eastern and Western traditions to this day.

Regardless, the clash of Pelagius and Augustine became definitive for much of later Latin Christian thought and was the catalyst for Augustine's further and extensive reflections on the theology of grace and redemption.[35] When it became known to Augustine that Pelagius's circle regarded his biography as rather scandalous (the life story of a bishop who did not have the moral fiber necessary to demand a stern moral reformation in the lax conditions of the age), he was extremely annoyed and thought they had entirely missed the point. Augustine's phrase "Command what you will, O God, and give what

---

[35] See especially his treatises *De Natura et Gratia*, *De Gratia Christi et de Peccato Originali*, and *De Gratia et Libero Arbitrio*. See further J. Patout Burns, "Grace," in Fitzgerald, *Augustine Through the Ages*, 391-98; S. Duffy, *The Dynamics of Grace: Perspectives in Theological Anthropology* (Collegeville, MN: Liturgical Press, 1993).

you command" was felt by them to be particularly objectionable. Pelagius believed that this hopelessly confused the assistance God gave to the disciple with the moral power that God expected the disciple to supply (to reform and accept discipline). Pelagius believed that if a disciple persevered in strong discipline and regular prayer he or she would reach a state of stability (after possible initial waverings under the force of temptation) where even the desire for sin would progressively fade away, a condition of ascetic dispassion (*apatheia*). Augustine, always a realist, could only raise a skeptical eyebrow. What he knew of the passions of the heart and its prideful and resentful ways did not give him much grounds to put much faith in the ascetical doctrine of *apatheia*.

**Caelestius.** So much for the theory that, behind all the front-stage apparatus, profoundly turned on principles of the exegesis of Pauline theology, especially Romans 7.[36] The actual clash with Augustine first came about through one of Pelagius's followers, Caelestius, who came to North Africa, on Augustine's home turf, and introduced these critical ideas. Caelestius's challenge to the leading bishop of Africa could hardly pass unnoticed, and soon enough he was called for synodical examination at the Synod of Carthage in 411, which censured him. This in turn cast a deep shadow over the reputation of his teacher Pelagius. Caelestius had mostly been attacking Augustine's view of the transmission of sin through the human race as if it were some form of infection: the defilement brought into all creaturehood by original sin. Augustine would answer his charges in a treatise titled *On Merit and the Forgiveness of Sins*, which was a major step forward in making this theory of original sin (sin in the fabric of the entire human race since the fall of Adam, and transmitted through each generation by selfish concupiscence) a doctrine not only of North African theologians but eventually that of the entire Western church.

Caelestius made it known at the Synod of Carthage that his understanding of sinfulness saw it as wholly a question of conscious moral choices, individually attributable. There could be no collective guilt to which an individual had not personally given moral assent; such would be a contradiction of the personal nature of moral choice. Children, therefore, were born in the same state of innocence as Adam was. In this he unwittingly was touching on deep liturgical anxieties in North Africa, where infant baptism was becoming more and more common and the old traditions that baptism washed away all a person's sinfulness had come to be queried in the case of newborn infants being brought to the font. How had they sinned? In Africa it had been mooted that what was being washed away in their case was the collective guilt of Adam: the results of his fall away from divine grace, thus "original sin."

---

[36]W. Babcock, "Augustine's Interpretation of Romans (AD 394–396)," *Augustinian Studies* 10 (1979): 55-74.

Reacting to Caelestius's censure, and concerned in case this *theologoumenon* of original sin would spread abroad in Christendom, Pelagius wrote a treatise *On Human Nature* in 412 to elaborate these views more extensively. Augustine read this carefully and severely criticized it in his own treatise *On Nature and Grace*. By this stage it was clear a confrontation was brewing on an international level. Augustine summoned the assistance of Jerome against Pelagius, and Jerome (who had already met and fallen out with Pelagius) wrote his own critique, titled *Dialogues Against the Pelagians*, in which he attacked them for being more Stoic in character than Christian. Jerome had in mind their views on *apatheia* and their hypothesis that human beings could have remained sinless if they had proved faithful.

After Pelagius robustly acquitted himself of charges of heresy (over his views on the potential of human sinlessness) at the Palestinian synod of 415, Augustine ensured that he was condemned for exactly the same views by Pope Innocent I at a Roman synod in 417. The pope's death in that same year, however, led to the case being reviewed by his successor, Pope Zosimus. He was less in awe of Augustine and much more inclined to sympathize with Pelagius, sharing some of the latter's alarm in case this particular African theology of original sin might have a greater ascendancy. Zosimus retrospectively rehabilitated both Caelestius and Pelagius and censured those who were attacking them without proper cause.

In the meantime, however, the Africans had gained the support of the imperial court, where Augustine had supporters, and Emperor Honorius issued a state decree condemning both Pelagius and Caelestius, not as heretics but as agitators and disturbers of the peace. Political pressure made Zosimus endorse the imperial ban later that same year, and Pelagius then wandered eastward (perhaps dying in Egypt), where he was not heard from again. While there has been much scholarly debate on what treatises can actually be ascribed to the historical Pelagius, the heresy "Pelagianism" has generally been drawn up in reference to Augustine's theology of grace and what Augustine said were Pelagian implications, not to what Pelagius was actually saying. Pelagius believed that God gave grace to human beings, certainly, but his primary grace was the freedom to choose and respond. Those who chose the path of goodness would be given further encouragement by God to progress in the spiritual life. Augustine believed that such a view would render Christianity into a simplistic cult of moral self-improvement. He believed the human race's capacity for free moral choice was so damaged by the ancient (and continuing) fall from grace and enlightenment that even the desire to return to God has first to be supplied by God's prevenient grace. All desire for, and movement toward, the good was thus the gift of God, in Augustine's estimate.

***John Cassian.*** John Cassian, the Scythian theologian who had spent many years among the Egyptian ascetics and was now a recognized spiritual master in Gaul, fully versed in both Greek and Latin theological literature, was bemused by the whole controversy and suggested a compromise between the two positions: that human free will cooperated with divine grace (an ascetical theology predominant in the Eastern monastic theologians and in Origen of Alexandria). For the East this had always been received as a common wisdom, although Augustine's views on the priority of divine grace were also accepted (not in Augustine's every formulation, by any means, especially not in relation to his radical pessimism about the damage caused to the soul by the fall). In the West, Cassian was ever afterward tarred with the brush of "semi-Pelagianism," though it was a term his enemies threw at him. He was not in any sense a student of Pelagius's views and thought he was simply offering a moderation of Augustine's position, which had refused to allow Pelagius any meaningful insight.

The issue of Pelagianism was never a large-scale heretical movement at all, more of a manufactured controversy to advance the grace theology of the circle of Augustine. It has, for that reason, never been extensively received, from that day to this, as a fruitful discussion in the Eastern church traditions. In the West, however, the Augustinian, pessimistic views on the transmission of the contagion of sin through the race, radically damaging human freedom and spiritual capacity, became the standard wisdom and ran on through medieval Catholicism into the fabric of the classic Protestant churches. The Augustinian theology of grace was certainly a rhapsodic celebration of the prodigality of God, but by virtue of Pelagius's severe condemnation it was passed on through Latin Christianity at no small cost to more positive visions of human freedom and responsibility and more optimistic anthropologies.

***Jerome and his agenda.*** Jerome (Eusebius Hieronymus, c. 347–420) was one of the most argumentative ascetics of the fourth century: irascible, restless, and brilliant, he was perhaps the most important biblical scholar of the early Western church.[37] He was born to wealthy parents in the town of Stridon, on the Dalmatian border of the empire, and studied Latin grammar before coming to Rome around 360 to study rhetoric with Aelius Donatus, one of the leading littérateurs of the day.[38] Here he polished his brilliant Latin style. In 366 Jerome converted to Christianity and, after staying for a while in Trier, moved to Aquileia in the company of friends, including Rufinus, where he adopted the ascetic lifestyle. About 372 he decided to live as a hermit in the East, and so he advanced his study of Greek at Antioch before moving to the desert of Chalcis in Syria for about five years, where he also learned Hebrew.

---

[37]Among the more renowned bearers of his name was Geronimo the American Indian warrior chief.
[38]Stridon was destroyed by the Goths in 379, and its exact location is now disputed.

Bishop Paulinus, the Nicene bishop imposed on the church of Antioch by the Latin faction, ordained him priest at Antioch, but he is never known to have exercised that office in any precise pastoral setting, and his enduring and faithful alliance with Paulinus won him many enemies in the Eastern church, which generally regarded the latter as a schismatic intruder there. It was in Antioch at this period that he heard the lectures of Apollinaris and had a famous dream in which Christ appeared and denounced him for being "a Ciceronian, not a Christian," a psychic warning he took seriously, turning his attention thereafter to theology and biblical interpretation as the main focal points of his restless energies. Jerome came to Constantinople with Paulinus and Epiphanius for the council of 381, and there listened to Gregory of Nazianzus and Gregory of Nyssa, whom he admired.

Traveling to Rome to secure Pope Damasus's assistance for Paulinus's claims, which were set aside at the council of 381, Jerome stayed on and acted as private secretary to the pope between 382 and 385. In this period Damasus gave him the commission to prepare a good Latin version of the Gospels from the Greek, a project that eventually grew into the Vulgate, an attempt to make a fluent and accurate translation of all the Bible to replace the rather crude *Itala*, or Old Latin, versions that had been in use beforehand. During his time in the capital Jerome attracted a group of wealthy ladies to his side, acting as spiritual father to them. They included Marcella, Paula, and her daughter Eustochium, who subsequently became important and generous patronesses. After Damasus's death, the Roman clergy (among whom he was generally as unpopular as he had been in the East) actively encouraged him to leave, and so he returned to Antioch, visiting Egypt and eventually settling at Bethlehem, in the episcopal domain of John of Jerusalem. He very soon had antagonistic relations with John, barely acknowledging the latter's ecclesiastical rights, feeling that as an ascetic he could be a roving ecclesiastic—and (as he maintained) priests were as good as bishops anyway.

At Bethlehem, with the aristocrat Paula, who had followed him, with her daughter, he founded a double monastery of men and women. The women ran the women's institution, while Jerome was abbot of the men's monastery. But Bishop John's attachment to Origenian ideas allied the bishop of the city and region more to Melania and her colleague Rufinus (who had themselves established a monastery on the Mount of Olives), and from this time onward Jerome's previous literary and personal friendship with Rufinus turned to bitter resentment. From having been a devoted Origenian scholar and translator himself (as Rufinus still was), Jerome began to denounce Origen as a baneful influence on Christian theology (while still continuing to use vast amounts of unacknowledged exegetical material from Origen).

Throughout the 390s Jerome sought and gained the support of the Roman and Alexandrian churches, to offset his enemies in Antioch and Jerusalem. He was a most touchy character, but by no means unsuccessful in his political trafficking. Toward the end of his life, as we have already noted, he had a cautious encounter with Augustine, whom he seems to have gruffly admired (they shared a common hostility toward Pelagius). Jerome's greatest work is the translation of many sections of the Bible into elegant Latin, using Hebrew and Greek skills that were in his day almost unheard of in other Western ecclesiastical writers. He anticipated the Hebraic canon of the Bible (as later advocated by the Reformers) rather than the traditional Septuagintal standard used in the Greek East.

Jerome had made a thorough study of the corpus of all the earlier Latin theologians, although his own scholarly gifts lay elsewhere than in the creative application of a synthesis. He was passionately pro-Nicene, passionately pro-Western, and unfailing in his advocacy of an ascetical and scholarly lifestyle. His translations of Origen (before he changed to foe) ensured the survival of important materials after the Alexandrian's condemnation by the fifth ecumenical Council of Constantinople 553, and he (along with Ambrose) more or less established Origen's high influence over most of later Western exegesis.

Jerome spent years producing biblical commentaries, especially on Genesis, the Prophets, Psalms (the latter preserves Origen's lost *Selecta in Psalmos*), Matthew, and Mark, as well as Revelation and select Pauline letters. His reputation as exegete is possibly overstressed in the Western church (at least if we look for originality), but he certainly served to establish canons of good style and (often Origenian) subtlety in much subsequent Latin exegesis that constantly looked to him as a model. Jerome deliberately sought to continue the historical work of Eusebius of Caesarea, with a most important handbook that gives us priceless historical information. It was given the title *On Outstanding Men* (*De Viris Illustribus*), which gives important details of Christian writers up to his day (culminating in himself), whom he wished to present as a demonstration that Christianity lacked nothing in comparison to paganism for the cultured intelligences it could inspire.

Jerome's apologetic works against individuals sometimes lack moderation and charity in modern eyes. He follows robust classical traditions of apologetic disparagement that make us wince today. In later life he wrote several treatises in praise of ascetical virginity in which he heavily and almost sarcastically disparaged sexuality as defilement and spoke of marriage in a pessimistic and extremist fashion (*Against Helvidius* and *Against Jovinian*), thus setting a precedent that cast a gloom over subsequent centuries of Christian (predominantly clerical and celibate) attitudes toward marriage, sex, and family life. His numerous surviving letters show him to be a brilliant, witty, and extremely prickly correspondent.

## THE EARLY MEDIEVAL PAPACY AND THE ACACIAN SCHISM

*Pope Damasus.* Damasus (c. 304–384) rose to prominence in church affairs as one of the chief deacons of Rome, in which office he showed himself a wily political arbitrator and a consummate organizer. He became pope in 366 after a violently contested election at Rome. There were public riots in its wake, and on one occasion 137 people were left dead in the basilica of Santa Maria Maggiore. The violence occasioned wry observations from pagan critics such as Ammianus Marcellinus, who records the events and comments on the number of deaths with the remark, "See how they love one another." The fighting over the election, however unedifying, is nevertheless demonstrative of how significant the papal office had already become as a political prize in this period. The unrest was resolved only by imperial intervention, when Valentinian I endorsed Damasus as bishop, exiled his rival, and stationed troops in Rome to calm the dissident factions.

Damasus is symbolically important in several ways, not least for being one of the first incumbents of the papacy who used the potential of that leadership office to the full and marking a watershed between the earliest (often Greek-speaking) holders of the chair of Peter and the powerful leaders who started to expand the range of the papacy's Western ecclesial dominance at the end of late antiquity. Damasus stood for the establishment of the standard of Nicene doctrinal orthodoxy, both at home and internationally. He frequently invoked the help of the secular arm, expecting and generally receiving the assistance of imperial legislation to back up his synodical decrees. Presiding over a council in Rome in 382, he established an official "canon" of the recognized books of the Bible and also commissioned St. Jerome to produce a pure Latin text of the Scriptures, a "Vulgate," which was to have immense influence on the subsequent Latin world, remaining until the dawn of the twentieth century as the Catholic Church's official Bible throughout the world.

Damasus worked diligently to set in order the archives of the Roman church and to restore its ancient monuments and martyr shrines. The beautiful Latin engraving that adorns his restorations of the fabric of Rome is a clear indication of a turn in fortunes of Roman Christianity and is easily recognized as "Damasan script." He is acting as pope, like one of the great nobles of Rome. This is a pattern that will reoccur from this time onward. He was one of the first popes to use the designation of Rome as the "apostolic see."

His interventions in the affairs of the Eastern church, however, were less happy. He had an enduring suspicion of St. Basil the Great, thinking him not sufficiently enthusiastic about the *homoousion*, as he understood it, and he also refused to recognize the legitimacy of St. Gregory of Nazianzus as Theodosius's nominee as bishop of Constantinople. By supporting the claims of Paulinus in the divided church at Antioch (the rival bishop installed by Western support against Meletius of Antioch), Damasus added greatly to the confusion of the leading neo-Nicene theologians in the East. The *Tome of Damasus* was a synopsis of trinitarian and christological orthodoxy Damasus put together, and it tried to get Paulinus to establish in the East from his (insecure) base at Antioch. It anathematized the continuing disciples of Apollinaris of Laodicea, who taught a Christology in which the human aspects of Jesus were subsumed into the divine power, and the pneumatomachians, who did not wish to ascribe hypostatic deity to the Holy Spirit.

Damasus's sense of entitlement to dictate terms of theological "solutions" to all the churches prefigures a style of later interventions on the part of his successors in the papacy—not least that of the *Tome of Leo* at the Councils of Ephesus 449 and Chalcedon 451. When Theodosius assumed imperial control of the East in 380, he decreed from the outset that the faith of Damasus of Rome and Peter of Alexandria (which, practically speaking, meant the Nicene Creed) would henceforth be the official orthodoxy of the empire. What the emperor had done here was to use the old system that Alexandria was the leading see of the East and Rome was the preeminent see of the West; hence, these two creedal focal points would de facto represent universal Christendom's orthodoxy. But already this archaic system was giving way. Alexandria was becoming overshadowed by the ascent of Constantinople as imperial capital and, increasingly after 380, as theological center of excellence. Soon the continuing rise of the papacy at Rome would lead to regular clashes of authority with the bishops of Constantinople, who called more and more ecclesiastical territories under their jurisdictional remit as the Eastern empire ascended in power and significance far above the troubled West.

The beginning of the clash of sees was exposed in canon three of the Council of Constantinople (381–382), which elevated Constantinople as "new Rome," affording it prestigious ecclesiastical governance privileges. This canon was studiously ignored by the Roman popes for many centuries after, even when they endorsed the theology of the Constantinopolitan creed as a standard of shared faith. The canon read, "The bishop of Constantinople, however, shall have the prerogative of honor after the bishop of Rome because Constantinople is new Rome." It was left much unclear what "after" old Rome meant. Did it signify that once, when Rome was the capital of the

Christian world, it enjoyed preeminent ecclesiastical authority, and now new Rome shall take that place, following after Rome in the sequence of capitals, which are naturally the centers of jurisdiction (following the principle of the Nicene canons that established the chief centers of ecclesiastical organization as those of the civil dioceses)? Or did it mean (as Rome reluctantly would take it) that new Rome will take its place in the order of ecclesiastical authorities after old Rome, that is, coming second in place and rank to old Rome, which continued as the first in place? The two things were very different; and while Constantinople increasingly came to understand it to mean the first, Rome always thought it had an eternally established legal precedence in the international Christian charter. The conflicting expectations of jurisdictional significance and pecking order latent here would cause untold crises in the centuries ahead and would ultimately lead to the separation of the Eastern and Western forms of Christendom at the end of the first millennium.

Any disagreement about the interpretation of Constantinopolitan canon three was removed by canon twenty-eight of the Council of Chalcedon in 451, which made it clear that the see of Constantinople had "equal" privileges to that of old Rome: in other words, was independent alongside Rome as court of appeal and source of authority for all ecclesial matters of jurisdiction in the East. The canon now read,

> Following in all things the decisions of the holy Fathers, and acknowledging the canon, which has been just read, of the one hundred and fifty bishops beloved of God (who assembled in the imperial city of Constantinople, which is new Rome, in the time of the Emperor Theodosius of happy memory), we also do enact and decree the same things concerning the privileges of the most holy Church of Constantinople, which is new Rome. For the Fathers rightly granted privileges to the throne of old Rome, because it was the royal city. And the one hundred and fifty most religious bishops, actuated by the same consideration, gave equal privileges (*isa presbeia*) to the most holy throne of new Rome, justly judging that the city that is honored with the sovereignty and the senate, and enjoys equal privileges with the old imperial Rome, should in ecclesiastical matters also be magnified as she is, and rank next after her; so that, in the Pontic, the Asian, and the Thracian dioceses, the metropolitans only and such bishops also of the dioceses aforesaid as are among the barbarians, should be ordained by the aforesaid most holy throne of the most holy Church of Constantinople; every metropolitan of the aforesaid dioceses, together with the bishops of his province, ordaining his own provincial bishops, as has been declared by the divine canons; but that, as has been above said, the metropolitans of the aforesaid dioceses should be ordained by the archbishop of Constantinople, after the proper elections have been held according to custom and have been reported to him.

This notion of the equal status of Constantinople as ecclesial court of appeal rankled with Rome, which saw itself as the most ancient see of Christendom, with special charisms and graces because of its venerability, whereas Constantinople had been an Arian city for the first fifty years of its existence and had only come into being as an ecclesiastical entity in the fourth century, after the emperors had built their administration there. Christian Rome in the later fourth century was more or less being equated with the papacy and its special traditions. The popes were not seen as like other bishops. Their thrones were set in the cathedral church of St. John Lateran, but the real charism was demonstrated at the central pilgrim church of Rome, which was on Vatican Hill. Here in Constantine's basilica, the tomb of the martyred apostle was set directly under the high altar of the church, and it became the custom to refer to the bishop of the city as the "vicar of Saint Peter," his locum tenens, as it were, who was vested not merely in the *pallium* of an archbishop with jurisdictional authority over adjacent churches but even with the personal mantle of the martyr to whom Christ had promised the keys of the kingdom of heaven.

The Eastern churches, generally speaking, were aware of this tradition of a Petrine presence in the thinking of the Roman episcopate but did not give it a serious weight. They located it, therefore, in the domain of a *theologoumenon*, a position that could be legitimately held by a local church but which did to have any weight outside that church. All of the Eastern thinking on matters of jurisdictional authority in international Christian affairs, as one can see from the terms of the canons of the councils of 325, 381, and 451, was that it was to be in the churches as it was in civil affairs, under the presidency of the emperor, who would validate episcopal synodical decrees with the supportive force of civil legislation of necessary.

Rome had introduced a mystical element to the issue of jurisdiction, however, in this notion of Peter's charism being upheld in his successor on the throne of Rome. As this attitude rose to prominence, so too did the concept of the episcopal throne change. At first it had been a borrowing from late antique usage that referred to the occupant of the "throne of a city" as someone who was the preeminent philosopher, rhetorician, or teacher of that place. Increasingly it was coming to refer to the bishop of a city as its ecclesiastical ruler. This was a tendency regularly squashed in the Eastern Christian provinces, where the emperor was not ready to allow any cleric to assume governance duties in any quasi-monarchical way. But in the West, where Rome was a single patriarchal see isolated from the others and a natural source of focus and interest for the many scattered Western churches, which naturally looked to it after the collapse of imperial authority in the late fourth century, Rome's bishops increasingly assumed quasi-regal attributes. The "throne" was well on the way to being more than a rhetorician's chair.

***Popes Felix and Leo.*** If Damasus's imperial attitudes were an early sign of this papal theory, the Acacian schism manifests it clearly. Felix III was the first pope for whom this developing theory of "superiority" (it is too early to speak of papal "supremacy") set the Eastern and Western churches into formal and long-lasting schism between 484 and 519. What had happened was that the post-Chalcedonian crises of theology between the Miaphysite movement and the Chalcedonians had been dragging on for a generation and seemed irresolvable. It was never acceptable to Byzantium, however, simply to accept the loss of communion of the large part of the Alexandrian patriarchate, which continued to refuse to accept the validity of Chalcedon as an ecumenical council. So many post-Chalcedonian projects were launched by the royal court with the assistance of the Constantinopolitan patriarchate to try to effect reconciliation. Rome was always guarded against these moves, however, because one of the chief reasons for the hatred the Miaphysites harbored against Chalcedon was that it had included in its statements the very binary terms of the *Tome* of Pope Leo. Rome was determined at all costs to elevate Leo's *Tome* as the "last word" of Roman doctrinal teaching on the issue of the christological union, but both the Byzantine Chalcedonians and the Egyptian and Syrian Miaphysites thought it was a very poorly conceived document.[39] The Byzantines thought it was orthodox but excessively rigid in its distinction of the two natures of Christ, as if they were spheres of operation, while the Miaphysites thought it bordered on the heretical in its refusal to speak of a real and decisive union having taken place in those natures so as to make them a unitary reality. Most theologians in the East, therefore, wished to allow the dust to settle thickly on the Leonine *Tome*, whereas Rome continued to push for it to be the last word.

Any hope for a theological reconciliation between Byzantine Chalcedonians and the Miaphysites, it was felt, had to be done by some degree of sidestepping around Leo, and by not allowing the *Tome* to be the quintessential summation of the Chalcedonian decree, which, arguably, had even in its own day used the theology of Cyril of Alexandria as an offsetting counterweight to the archaic Roman Christology the *Tome* represented.[40] Rome was ever vigilant, however, to make sure the *Tome* was never pushed aside.

---

[39]Leo, *Epistle* 28 *To Flavian*, sent to the archbishop of Constantinople for inclusion in the doctrinal acts of the Council of Ephesus in 449, where it was furiously rejected by Dioscorus of Alexandria and sent back for inclusion at the Council of Chalcedon in 451.

[40]The *Tome* was not written de novo by Leo but was in fact a pastiche of christological opinions and phrases drawn from the second-century Tertullian and the early fifth-century Augustine, neither of whom had any sense of the mid- and late fifth-century argument their opinions were being pasted onto.

***The Acacian schism.*** In 475 the Byzantine emperor Zeno was forced to flee his capital by the usurper Basiliscus, who had partly posed as a defender of dispossessed anti-Chalcedonian party. Twenty months later Zeno recaptured his city but knew immediately that he had to set about more vigorously restoring the civil and religious peace in Egypt and the other provinces to make secure the Byzantine domains in the East. He called on his patriarch at Constantinople, Acacius, and asked him to make up a settlement that could end the schisms troubling the East in the aftermath to Chalcedon. Acacius drew up a relatively simple "memorandum of union" called the *Henotikon*. This letter he issued on his own authority as patriarch, announcing it also as the will of the emperor, and in it he established the decrees of the Councils of Nicaea and Constantinople as the centrally authoritative statements of faith of the universal church. In reference to recent christological divergences and disputes Acacius was broadly irenic. He took the two polar extremes, Nestorianism (representing the doctrine of two personal subjects in Jesus) and Eutychianism (representing the doctrine of a confused *krasis* or mixture of Godhead and manhood in Christ to make a single hybrid nature), and roundly condemned both of them, in terms that suggested he would adopt, instead, the royal middle way, as Aristotle had taught. This golden mean he presented in terms of endorsing the christological *anathemata* of Cyril of Alexandria, which the latter had offered to the conciliar fathers gathered in Ephesus in 431 but which they had set aside at the time.[41]

Acacius was offering an olive branch to the Miaphysite movement, and everyone in the East knew it and sensed the lively possibility that peace could be reestablished. However, Rome knew exactly what the new theological equation had left out: and that was Leo's *Tome*. No mention was made of Chalcedon, and none of Leo, and Rome refused to have anything to do with the *Henotikon*, going so far as to denounce it. One of the disaffected bishops opposing Acacius, John of Talaia, made a personal appeal to the pope, and so the whole matter came under the official scrutiny of the synodical court at Rome. In 482 Emperor Zeno published the *Henotikon* as law and on its basis began to depose bishops, both Chalcedonian and Miaphysite, who refused to accept the terms of his union of peace.

At Rome, Pope Felix III heard John Talaia's complaints officially, and his synod commissioned two Latin bishops to travel to Constantinople in order to present letters that summoned Acacius to Rome to answer the charges in a church court held under the pope's own presidency. It was hardly likely that Acacius would accept his right to synodical supremacy and, of course, when the Latin bishops arrived in

---

[41]Propositions attached by Cyril to his *Third Letter to Nestorius*. They would eventually be synodically endorsed at the Council of Constantinople in 553.

Constantinople, Acacius treated them kindly, held discussions with them privately, but sent them back empty-handed, whereupon the unfortunate bishops were severely censured by the pope as having failed in their commission. In 484 Felix convened another synod, which deposed and excommunicated Acacius for refusing to attend for his trial and for disrupting the canonical peace in the East. Hearing of this synodical act, Acacius removed the liturgical mention of Pope Felix in the liturgy of the great Cathedral of Constantinople (the names of the leading world bishops with whom the particular see was "in communion with" and for whom public prayers were read) and thus treated the pope publicly as a renegade from the faith.

These mutual acts, one synodical and one liturgical, caused the first great schism between Rome and Constantinople formally to occur, but cross-relations had now become so relatively few and far between that it did not really matter in the sense of disrupting anything of practical significance. Of course, the unification efforts of the *Henotikon* now seemed to have been launched in the cause of reconciling Egypt only at the cost of losing Rome. It was felt, nevertheless, that Rome might more easily be dealt with down the road, if only the prize of the restoration of Egypt could be secured. Acacius continued as patriarch until his death in 489, and Zeno himself died two years later.

His successor, Emperor Anastasius I, continued Zeno's policy of reconciliation and sent delegates to the new Pope Anastasius II, but to no result. Anastasius eventually applied political pressure to the papacy, which continued to stand against his policy of ecumenical rapprochement in the East, and when a rival (antipope) appeared contesting the validity of Pope Symmachus, the Byzantine court supported him in order to unsettle the incumbent, all the more underscoring in the Roman mind that the Byzantine ruler was not the bastion of orthodoxy but the Roman papacy was. The Byzantines simply regarded the papacy as recalcitrant. Symmachus's papal successor, Hormisdas, tried to end the schism on several occasions, but he could not negotiate a result with Anastasius. It was not until Anastasius died in 518 that his successor, Emperor Justin, realigned imperial policy and actively sought to bring the papacy and the patriarchates of the East back into communion with one another. By this time the reconciliatory hopes of Zeno's *Henotikon* had not proved to be all that effective. It was no longer seen worth the risk of alienating Rome to secure such a small payoff with the Egyptians, and policy turned the other way in the wind. Emperor Justin and his new patriarch, John of Cappadocia, entered into negotiations with Rome, and the pope authored an agreement called the *Formula of Hormisdas*, which was accepted at Byzantium. As part of the cessation of the schism Rome demanded, and received, the posthumous condemnation of the names of Acacius, Zeno, and Anastasius.

The reunion of the Roman and Byzantine churches was then announced on March 28, 519. It has remained in the minds of many historians and theologians not so much for any deep theological thinking that was in evidence here (for there wasn't much along that line) but more for what the episode indicated about how things might go for the health of the relationship between Rome and Constantinople in the future, and for what kind of presuppositions were in evidence in the respective chanceries of the two great sees, in terms of what duties they held to the wider churches of the international ecumene and in terms of what their respective views were about the jurisdictional powers they each claimed.

The "Acacian schism" hardly gives one evidence of creative thinking. Political affairs in the West were, from this point onward, to go from bad to worse. The age of migrations so disrupted the Western imperial provinces that more and more the papacy was left as one of the few ancient institutions standing that still had some moral authority and a vestige of political coherence and functionality. The view eastward, to the still-powerful Byzantine emperors, was one that was increasingly jaundiced. Byzantium spoke of a sacred emperor, whose duty it was to protect the church and aid its progress through the world by civil means.

To the West, however, it seemed as if the imperium had simply abandoned its Western dominions to their own fate, as long as it felt secure behind its own more secure borders and ramparts. It was even accepting the fiction that the invading Gothic kings such as Odoacer and Theoderic were simply consuls or viceroys of the Eastern emperor, ruling by his grace and favor. There was, accordingly, a serious lessening of devotion in the Western provinces, even among the old elite, to the notion of one single Christian imperium under one holy God-appointed and church anointed *autokrator* of the Romans. The papacy thought more and more to present itself as the throne that secured the stability of the church's tradition. This was sedition to the ears of the Byzantine emperors, and whenever they had a chance to lay hands on a Roman pope (as Justinian would do to Pope Vigilius), they treated him as exactly what they regarded him to be, civilly a vassal, though possessing sacred powers as part of the *collegium* of senior bishops.

Never did the Byzantine court accept the terms of the papacy's growing sense that it was uniquely superior to all other bishops and certainly to all kings. Never would the emperors give that particular *theologoumenon* credence, and rarely would anyone else in the Eastern church give it any weight except as a sign of arrogant departure from ancient practice. In the West, nevertheless, the reputation of Rome as custodian of all the sacred traditions and laws of the Christians gained increasing weight in the light of its actual isolation, and as it did turn into being a beacon of authority for wide-flung Western missions, so too did the theory of special papal supremacy become established as a datum of the transmitted tradition, and so too did the memory of the Byzantine church polity and its view of the ancient tradition recede into memory.

## CHRISTIANITY IN THE BARBARIAN KINGDOMS

*The Vandal kingdom.* The fortunes of the barbarian kingdoms were varied in this time in the West. The African bishops under Vandal kings found themselves in the peculiar position of having to fight the battles of a previous century all over again. For the Vandals were Christians, but their faith was ancestrally given to them by the Arian bishops, who had been driven out of office in Byzantium at the time of the Council of Constantinople in 381. Then, dispossessed from their sees, many senior clerics had moved northward across the border as missionaries to the tribes and evangelized them from the beginning in the Arian faith. As kings in northern Africa the Vandal rulers now regarded their Nicene subjects as heretics and in turn oppressed the Nicene establishment of the catholic church. In Africa numerous Nicene resisters gained the status of confessors at this period. One of the most eminent of them was Fulgentius of Ruspe (c. 462–527 or later), one of sixty African Nicene theologian bishops banished to Sardinia by the Vandal King Hunseric.[42] Facundus of Hermiane, who was a severe critic, even from exile, of Justinian's policy of the Three Chapters, was another.[43]

*Boethius among the Ostrogoths.* Among the Ostrogoths, who had taken over the rule of Italy, things were felt to be reasonably good, for the rulers here approved of Roman civil customs much more than their Vandal counterparts and had co-opted many leading Nicene churchmen and laity into the political administration. A renowned example of that comes to us in the person of Boethius, who in 510 became consul under Ostrogothic King Theodoric. Being a consul in the sixth-century West, however, was obviously something different in reality from what it had been in earlier times, when there were emperors still on the Western imperial throne. His two sons were also raised as consuls, a hitherto unheard-of honor and one that showed how Boethius was held in the highest regard both by Theodoric and the

---

[42]Fulgentius's works are found in Sources Chrétiennes 487: J. Fraipont, ed., *Fulgence de Ruspe, Lettres ascetiques et morales* (Paris: Editions du Cerf, 2004).

[43]Facundus's works are in PL 67.527-878. Concerning the Three Chapters: seeking to reconcile the Miaphysites, the emperor secured at the Council of Constantinople in 553 the retrospective condemnation of three theologians, Theodore, Theodoret, and Ibas, in whose works several Latins saw (1) the attack on some aspects of their own christological tradition and (2) a deliberate sidestepping of the centrality of Pope Leo's understanding of Chalcedonian orthodoxy as enunciated in his *Tome*.

Eastern emperor Zeno. His great achievement, however, would cause his terrible downfall, illustrating the saying that "no man can serve two masters."

Anicius Manlius Torquatus Severinus Boethius (c. 480–525) was a Roman aristocrat with a family of long and ancient lineage (the Anicia clan) when the Ostrogoths occupied Italy. His family tree already boasted several consuls, two emperors, and a pope. His father had been consul under the barbarian King Odoacer in 487 but had died when his son was still a child. Boethius's studies had taken him through the traditional pattern of rhetoric and philosophy, but his lively mind developed with some originality on his formal training in a subsequent writing career that tried, with striking results, to synthesize in a Christian fashion the three discrete philosophical systems of neo-Platonism (of the type represented in Plotinus and Proclus), Aristotelianism, and Stoicism. Boethius has been called "the schoolmaster of the Western world" for the massive way his writings dominated the medieval Western curriculum.[44] His Latin adaptations and translations of the Greek sources were highly influential in the cause of securing an ongoing tradition of Latin letters and Roman culture under the barbarians.

His philosophic career was interrupted when he entered into political service under King Theodoric. Having been appointed consul in 510, he was moved in 522 to represent Theodoric as his master of offices at the Byzantine court held by the imperial exarch at Ravenna. Soon after this move Boethius was accused of entering into traitorous dealings with the Byzantine emperor and was imprisoned at Ticinum (modern Pavia) and then executed after being tortured, sometime between 524 and 526. The catholic faith of Boethius allied to his symbolic value as a Roman patriot executed by an Arian king led immediately after his death to a local cult as a martyr-confessor, and he is actually remembered to this day at Pavia as St. Severinus.[45]

Boethius left behind treatises on the *quadrivium*—the medieval school curriculum of higher studies (music, arithmetic, geometry, and astronomy), which especially in the domain of logic had a pronounced influence on the medieval West's subsequent educational curriculum. His understanding of philosophy was that all the schools could be resolved to a central corpus of doctrine, under the guidance of Nicene Christian faith. The faith itself could then be illuminated by rational inquiry. His concern was to probe the particular domains of revelation and reason, and in this he predated the medieval scholastics, who took his intellectual agenda to greater heights of speculation.

---

[44] His treatise on music was on the list of core textbooks at Oxford University until the eighteenth century.

[45] The local diocese and the Sacred Congregation of Rites in Rome decreed the official recognition of this local cult on December 15, 1883. His grave is in the church of San Pietro in Cielo D'Oro in Pavia.

In his theological writing he commented on the Nicene faith in Christology and Trinity (a brave thing to do in an Arian Ostrogothic court), and he made an enduring mark with some definitions of key Latin Christian terms that were to become classical, particularly that of *person* (which he defined as "an individual substance of a rational nature") and *eternity* (which he defined as "the simultaneous and perfect possession of a limitless life"). His most famous work was the *Consolation of Philosophy*, written while he was in prison and wrestling very personally with the issue of social injustice in the light of a belief in God's unfailing providence. It became one of the most beloved books of the Latin medieval world, a Christianized reaffirmation of the Platonic ideal that through fidelity to a philosophical way of life, the soul is made coherent, stable, and prepared for the vision of God.

Through the witness of the theological as well as the high literary culture of these intellectuals who sustained the old Roman tradition (now thoroughly Christianized) under the difficult conditions of the new dominions, the ideal of the church as the continuator and preserver of Roman cultural standards was launched and nurtured by the papacy. In a few more decades, in the era of Justinian the Great, the Byzantine emperor would launch another major military campaign to draw the circle back once more around the Mediterranean and claim it as the Roman lake it formerly used to be: conquering the Western provinces and taking them back from the barbarian kings in Northern Africa, Italy, and Spain so as to reabsorb them into the one single dominion of the Christian Romans. But in many senses the old magic had been lost by the obvious new realities that political power and economic wealth had definitively passed eastward. The West was entering a long twilight, in which the lights of the papacy would glimmer ever more noticeably from afar. Justinian's reconquest added to the bankruptcy of the West, for it had to pay for the privilege of being liberated and reunited to an Eastern-centered Roman imperium that few in the West thought had its concerns or privileges much in mind.

## A SHORT READER

***Theodosius the Emperor,* Edict Cunctos Populos, *in* Codex Theodosianus**
***16.1.2.*** Emperors Gratian, Valentinian, and Theodosius, the augusti. Edict to the people of Constantinople: It is our desire that all the various nations that are subject to our clemency and moderation should continue to profess that religion that was delivered to the Romans by the divine apostle Peter, as it has been preserved by faithful tradition, and that is now professed by the Pontiff Damasus and by Peter, bishop of Alexandria, a man of apostolic holiness. According to the apostolic teaching and the doctrine of the gospel, let us believe

in the one deity of the Father, the Son, and the Holy Spirit, in equal majesty and in a holy Trinity. We authorize the followers of this law to assume the title of Catholic Christians; but as for the others, since, in our judgment they are foolish madmen, we decree that they shall be branded with the ignominious name of heretics and shall not presume to give to their assemblies the name of churches. They will suffer in the first place the chastisement of the divine condemnation and in the second whatever punishment of our authority that in accordance with the will of heaven we shall decide to inflict. Given in Thessalonica on the third day from the Calends of March, during the fifth consulate of Gratian Augustus and first of Theodosius Augustus.

**Augustine of Hippo, City of God 11.1.** The city of God that we are talking about is the same as that which Scripture bears witness to; that Scripture that, by virtue of its divine authority, far excels all the sacred texts of the nations. It has swayed all kinds of minds, and not by any accidental intellectual force but rather by the explicit providence of God. For there in Scripture it is written, "Glorious things are spoken of you, O city of God" (Ps 87:3). And in another psalm we read, "Great is the Lord, and greatly to be praised in the city of our God, in the mountain of his holiness, increasing the joy of the whole earth" (Ps 48:1). And, a little after this, in the same psalm, "As we have heard, so have we seen in the city of the Lord of hosts, in the city of our God, which God has established forever." And in another psalm: "There is a river there whose streams gladden the city of our God, the holy place of the tabernacles of the Most High. God is in the midst of her, she shall not be moved" (Ps 46:4). From these, and similar testimonies, which to cite all of them would become tedious, we have learned that there is a city of God, and its founder has inspired us with a love that makes us long for its citizenship. But instead of this founder of the holy city, the citizens of the earthly city prefer their own gods, not understanding that he is the God of gods. Not, that is, God of those false gods, the impious and proud ones,[46] who, having been deprived of his unchangeable and freely communicated light and reduced to a form of poverty-stricken power, wildly grasped after their own private privileges and sought after divine honors from their deluded subjects; but rather God of those pious and holy "gods,"[47] who are more happy to submit themselves to the one than to subject the many to themselves; those who would rather worship God than be themselves worshiped as gods. Now to the enemies of this city we have given an apologia in the ten preceding

---

[46] The rebel angels.
[47] The obedient angels.

books, according to our ability and by the help afforded to us by our Lord and King. Now, recognizing what is expected of me, and remembering my promise, and relying, too, on this same help, I will attempt to deal with the origin, and progress, and deserved destinies of the two cities (that is, the earthly and the heavenly), which, as we have said, are in this present world commingled one with another and, as it were, entangled together. In the first place I will explain how the foundations of these two cities were originally set down in the difference that arose among the angels.

**Augustine of Hippo, On Grace and Free Will 7.** Therefore, my dearly beloved, as we have now proved by our preceding testimonies taken from Holy Scripture that there is within man a free determination of will for living rightly and acting rightly, so now let us see what are the divine testimonies concerning the grace of God, without which we will not be able to do a single good thing. And in the first place I will say something about that very profession that you make in your (ascetic) brotherhood. Now your society, in which you follow lives of celibacy, could never hold together unless you held conjugal pleasure as of little worth. Well, the Lord was speaking about this same topic one day when his disciples answered him, "If this is how things are between a man and his wife, then it is not good to marry." He then answered them, " Not all men can receive this saying, only those to whom it is given." Again, was it not to Timothy's free will that the apostle appealed when he exhorted him in these words: "Keep yourself chaste"? He also explained the power of the will in this matter when he said, "Having no necessity, but possessing power over his own will, to keep his virginity." But even so: "Not all men can receive this saying, only those to whom the power is given." So those to whom this is not given are either unwilling or do not fulfill what it is they do will. Whereas those to whom it is given will in such a way as to accomplish what it is they will. In order, therefore, that this saying, which is not received by all men, may yet be received by some, there is both the gift of God and free will.

**Optatus of Milevis, Treatise Against the Donatists 7.2.** *That good and evil will be found in the church of God and must be borne with to the Day of Judgment:* This is why for such a long time now we have been longing to receive you (Donatists) back into our communion. For after all, it was not you who sinned at that time, but your fathers. No man should pass judgment on another man, as though he were himself wholly without sin, since it has been written in the Gospel that Christ says "Judge not, that you may not be judged." And this is above all else because it is impossible to find one who is absolutely holy. If there are any who claim to be unable to sin, then they are guilty of lying when they say the Lord's Prayer and unreasonably beg for pardon and say to God the Father: "Forgive us our trespasses as we forgive those who trespass against us." Moreover, the apostle John reveals the consciences of all people and discloses his own with these words: "If we shall say that we have no sin, we deceive ourselves and the truth is not in us," and this is a saying that we have explained more clearly in our fourth book. But let us suppose that there are indeed some who have been made perfect with a complete sanctity. Then even then it is not lawful for them to be without brethren, whom they are taught not to repel by the precepts of the Gospel, for there we find described a field that stands for the whole world, in which the church exists and Christ the sower, who gives us his saving commandments. On the other hand, there is an evil man, that is, the devil, who sows cruel sins, not in the light but in the darkness. Then different kinds of seeds come to fruit in the one field. It is likewise in the church, where there is not a mass of souls all alike. The field receives good seeds or bad, for the seeds are different. But there remains one Creator of all souls and one Lord of the field. There are two who sow seeds whence the weeds are born, but the field has only one Lord, the Lord God himself. His is the earth; his are the good seeds; to him also belongs the rain. Accordingly, we have consented to receive you back into unity you, who have been drawn to us; for it is not up to us to cast out or reject even sinners who have been born with us in one field [and] have received nourishment from one watering, namely our common baptism; just as it was not up to the apostles to separate the weeds from the wheat (since separation is impossible without destruction), in case when pulling up what ought to be pulled up that which should not be pulled up might be trodden flat. In like manner Christ has commanded that both his own seeds and those that belong to the other one should grow in his field throughout the entire world, in which there is the one church. Only after all have ripened together will the Day of Judgment come, which is the harvest of souls. On that day the Judge shall take his seat, the Son of God, who recognizes what is his own and what belongs to the other. It shall be up to him to choose what he will gather into his barn and what he shall hand over to the burning; whom he shall condemn to torments that know no end and to whom he will give the rewards that he has promised. Let us recognize that we all are but men; let no one usurp to himself the power of judgment that belongs to God. For if any bishop were to claim it all for himself, then I ask you, what will there be for Christ to do in judgment? It should be enough for a man not to be guilty of sins of his own without wishing to be judge of the sins of another. This is why we take the position that not only do we not reject you, but even that for the sake of peace we would not have rejected your fathers if it had come to pass in their day that unity was capable of being accomplished. For it would be a sin for us bishops to do in this time what had never been done by the apostles, for they too were not permitted to make distinctions among the various seeds or pluck out the weeds from among the wheat.

**Pope Damasus, Decree of the Synod of Rome 382: On the Canon of Scripture.** Now we must speak of the divine Scriptures, as to what the universal catholic church accepts and what she should set aside. The order of the Old Testament begins here: Genesis one book, Exodus one book, Leviticus one book, Numbers one book, Deuteronomy one book, Josue Nave one book, Judges one book, Ruth one book, Kings four books, Paralipomenon two books, Psalms one book, Solomon three books: Proverbs one book, Ecclesiastes one book, Canticle of Canticles one book.[48] Likewise Wisdom one book, Ecclesiasticus one book. Likewise the order of the Prophets: Isaias one book, Jeremias one book, and Ginoth besides, that is, with his lamentations, Ezechiel one book, Daniel one book, Osee one book, Micheas one book, Joel one book, Abdias one book, Jonas one book, Nahum one book, Habacuc one book, Sophonias one book, Aggeus one book, Zacharias one book, Malachias one book. Likewise the order of the histories: Job one book, Tobias one book, Esdras two books, Esther one book, Judith one book, Machabees two books. Likewise the order of the writings of the New and eternal Testament, which alone the holy and catholic church supports: Of the Gospels, according to Matthew one book, according to Mark one book, according to Luke one book, according to John one book. The Epistles of Paul [the apostle] are in number fourteen: To the Romans one, to the Corinthians two, to the Ephesians one, to the Thessalonians two, to the Galatians one, to the Philippians one, to the Colossians one, to Timothy two, to Titus one, to Philemon one, to the Hebrews one. Likewise the Apocalypse of John, one book. And the Acts of the Apostles one book. Likewise the canonical epistles in number seven: of Peter the apostle two epistles, of James the apostle one epistle, of John the apostle one epistle, of another John, the presbyter, two epistles, of Jude the Zealot and apostle, one epistle.

---

[48]"Kings four books" is conflating 1 and 2 Samuel and 1 and 2 Kings. Paralipomenon refers to Chronicles. Canticle of Canticles refers to Song of Songs.

**St. Jerome, Epistle 14.1-3, To Heliodorus.** Your own heart, aware of our shared love, surely knows with what loving zeal I once begged you to stay together with me in the desert. This letter, stained as you can see with my tears, again bears witness to the grief, the sobbing, the lamentations with which I accompanied your departure. On that day, like a spoiled child, you cloaked your contemptuous refusal of my pleas with soft words, and I, in my foolishness, did not know what to do. Should I have held my tongue? I could not conceal my burning desires under a cloak of indifference. Should I have pleaded with you more urgently? Ah, but you would not have listened, for you did not love me as I loved you. The affection you scorned that day has done the only thing it could. It was not able to keep you when you were present, but it now comes to seek you when you are far away. As you left me, you asked whether I would write you a letter of invitation when I finally took up my home in the desert; and I promised that I would do so. That letter of invitation I now am sending to you. Come, and come quickly. Do not think of your former ties, for the desert loves the naked. Do not be put off by the hardships of our former travels. As you believe in Christ, so also believe in his words: "Seek first the kingdom of God, and all other things shall be added unto you." You do not need to take purse or staff. The man is more than rich enough who is poor with Christ. But what am I doing? Why do I send you these foolish entreaties for a second time? I will lay aside prayers. I have had enough with soft words. It is the duty of offended love to show resentment. You once despised my request, so now, perhaps, you will listen to my rebuke? What business do you have, you pampered soldier, lodging in your father's house? Where now are the ramparts, the trench, and the winter spent under canvas? Listen! The trumpet is sounding from heaven! See, our general comes out amid the clouds, fully armed to subdue the world! See, from our king's mouth there comes a two-edged sword, which cuts down everything in its path! Come on out man, from your chamber to the battlefield, from the shade into the sun. A body that is used to a soft tunic cannot bear a suit of armor. A head that has worn a linen hood cringes when it wears a helmet. A hand that has been softened in idleness is blistered by the hard hilt of a sword. But hear your king's decree: "Whoever is not with me is against me, and whoever does not gather with me scatters." Remember that day when you enlisted as his recruit, when you were buried with Christ in baptism. For then you took an oath of allegiance to him, confessing how in his name you would not spare either father or mother. See now how the adversary within your own heart is trying even to slay Christ! See how the enemy's camp is lusting after the bounty that you received before your service began. Even though your little nephew should clasp his hands around your neck; even though your wild-haired mother should rend her clothes and show to you the breasts which gave you suck; even though your father fling himself down upon the threshold; trample your family underfoot and go your own way. Run with tearless eyes to the standard of the cross. In such matters as these, to be cruel is a son's duty. The day will come soon enough when you shall return in triumph to your true homeland; when, crowned as a mighty warrior, you shall walk the streets of the heavenly Jerusalem. On that day you shall share with Paul the citizenship of that place, and ask the same privilege for your parents. Yes, and for me too shall you intercede, for thus urging you on to victory.

**Boethius, The Consolation of Philosophy 4.6.** [Philosophy says:] It is because you human beings are in no position to consider the larger cosmic order that everything seems upset and confused in your view. But the truth is that all things have their own position, which directs them to the good and in this way governs them. There is nothing that can happen to this order, because of wickedness, or because of anything deliberately initiated by the wicked themselves. As we have already clearly demonstrated, the wicked themselves are simply deflected from their own search for the good by mistake and error. That order that issues out of the Supreme Good at the very center of the universe cannot deflect anyone from his beginning. Doubtless you will make an objection, to the effect that it is impossible to have a more unjust confusion among us than that which is present when the fates of good men and bad men equally oscillate between adversity and prosperity. But I ask you, do men have such soundness of mind as to be infallible in their judgment of who is truly good and who is truly bad? I think not, for human judgment conflicts in such matters, and some people think the same characters deserve rewards, while others think them worthy of punishment. But suppose we admit that a man may be able to judge between the good and the bad. This would hardly enable him to discern the inner hidden temperament of people's minds, to use the terminology of physics. Your surprise strikes me like that of a man who does not know why in the case of healthy people, some like sweet things, while others prefer bitter things. Or in the case of sick people, why for some gentle remedies are useful, but for others only stringent remedies work. But this is no surprise at all to the doctor who knows the difference between health and sickness in both its manner and temper. For instance, we all know that in relation to the human mind, health means goodness, and sickness means wickedness. And we know that the protector of the good is God, who is also the scourge of the wicked. He is also the guide and physician of the human mind. He looks out form his watchtower of providence, sees what is suitable to each person, and applies to each one whatever he knows to be suitable. And this is the outstanding wonder of the order of fate—that a knowing God acts, while ignorant people look on in amazement at his actions.

**Boethius, The Consolation of Philosophy 5.6.** [Philosophy says:] It is the common judgment of all rational creatures, then, that God is eternal. But let us consider the nature of that eternity, for it will make clear to us both the nature of God and also his mode of knowing things. Eternity, therefore, is the complete, simultaneous, and perfect possession of everlasting life. This can be made clear by a comparison with the state of creatures that exist within time. Whatever lives within time exists in the present and progresses from the past to the future, and there is nothing set in time that can simultaneously embrace the entirety of the extent of its life. It is, rather, in the position of not yet having command of tomorrow, but it has already lost yesterday. In this life of the present moment, one can not live more fully than in the fleeting and passing moment. So whatever suffers from the condition of being within time, even supposing it never had a beginning, and even supposing it would never have any ending and its life would extend into an infinity of time (as Aristotle conceived the case of the world to be), then such a thing still could not properly be considered to be truly eternal. Its life may indeed be long, but it fails to embrace and comprehend its whole extent of life simultaneously. It would, therefore, still lack the future, while it has already lost the past. Only that which embraces and simultaneously possesses the whole fullness of everlasting life, lacking nothing of the future or the past, can be properly said to be eternal. It is necessarily always present to itself, controls itself, and has present to itself the infinity of fleeting time. In short, the philosophers were wrong, when they were told that Plato believed the world had no beginning in time and would have no end, and concluded from this that the created world is coeternal with the Creator. For it is one thing to move forward through everlasting life, as the world does in Plato's theory, but another thing altogether to have embraced the whole of everlasting life in one simultaneous present. The latter is clearly a property of the mind of God. God ought not to be considered as older than the created world in extent of time, but rather prior to it in the property of the immediacy of his nature. The infinite changeableness of things within time is an attempted mimesis of this state of the presence of unchanging life. But since such infinity cannot depict or equal this state, it falls from sameness into changeability, and from the immediacy of presence into the infinite extent of past and future. Time-bound reality cannot simultaneously possess the entire fullness of its life, but even so, by virtue of the fact that its existence cannot ever come to an end, it does seem, in some way, to emulate that which it cannot either fulfill or express. It does this by attaching itself to some form of presence in this small and fleeting moment. And since this manner of presence bears some resemblance to that abiding present, it confers on in whatever possesses it the appearance of being that which it imitates. But since it could not endure, it seized on the infinite journey through time, and in this way it became possible for it to continue, by forward progression, that life whose fullness it could never embrace by standing still. And thus, if we want to give things their proper names, let us follow Plato and say that God is eternal, while the world is perpetual.

## FURTHER READING

*Roman Society in the Age of Migrations*

Cochrane, C. N. *Christianity and Classical Culture: A History of Thought and Action from Augustus to Augustine.* New York: Columbia University Press, 1944.

Geary, P. *Myth of Nations: The Medieval Origins of Europe.* Princeton, NJ: Princeton University Press, 2003.

Fouracre, P., ed. *The New Cambridge Medieval History*. Vol. 1, *c. 500–c. 700*. Cambridge: Cambridge University Press, 2006.

Halsall, G. *Barbarian Migrations and the Roman West, 376–568.* Cambridge: Cambridge University Press, 2008.

Noble, T., and W. Goffart. *From Roman Provinces to Medieval Kingdoms.* London: Routledge, 2006.

*Augustine and His Environment*

Barker, E., ed. *The City of God. St. Augustine.* London: Dent and Sons, 1945.

Bonner, G. *St. Augustine of Hippo: Life and Controversies.* London: SCM Press, 1963.

Brown, P. *Augustine of Hippo: A Biography.* Berkeley: University of California Press, 1967.

Cranz, F. E. "*De Civitate Dei* 15.2 and Augustine's Idea of the Christian Society." *Speculum* 25 (1950): 215-25.

Deane, H. A. *The Political and Social Ideas of St. Augustine.* New York: Columbia University Press, 1963.

Fitzgerald, A. *Augustine Through the Ages: An Encyclopedia.* Grand Rapids: Eerdmans, 1999.

Frend, W. H. C. *The Donatist Church: A Movement of Protest in Roman North Africa.* Oxford: Clarendon, 1952.

Markus, R. *Saeculum: History and Society in the Theology of St. Augustine.* Cambridge: Cambridge University Press, 1970.

Tilley, M. *The Bible in Christian North Africa: The Donatist World.* Minneapolis: Fortress, 1997.

———. *Donatist Martyr Stories: The Church in Conflict in North Africa.* Liverpool: Liverpool University Press, 1996.

Willis, G. G. *St. Augustine and the Donatist Controversy.* London: Dent and Sons, 1952.

### Friends and Critics of Augustine

Bonner, G. *Augustine and Modern Research on Pelagianism.* Villanova, PA: Augustinian Institute, Villanova University, 1972.

Brown, P. "Pelagius and His Supporters: Aims and Environment." *JTS* 19 (1968): 83-114.

Burns, J. P. "Augustine's Role in the Imperial Action Against Pelagius." *JTS* 30 (1979): 67-83.

Evans, R. *Four Letters of Pelagius.* London: A&C Black, 1968.

Kelly, J. N. D. *Jerome: His Life, Writings, and Controversies.* London: Gerald Duckworth, 1975.

Morris, J. "Pelagian Literature." *JTS* 16 (1965): 26-60.

Rees, B. R. *The Letters of Pelagius and His Followers.* Woodbridge, UK: Boydell, 1991.

———. *Pelagius: A Reluctant Heretic.* Woodbridge, UK: Boydell, 1988.

Sparks, H. F. D. "Jerome as Biblical Scholar." In *The Cambridge History of the Bible*, ed. P. R. Ackroyd and C. F. Evans, 1:510-41. Cambridge: Cambridge University Press, 1970.

### The Early Medieval Papacy

Norton, M. A. "Pope Damasus." In *Leaders of Iberian Christianity*, ed. J. Marique, 13-80. Boston: St. Paul's Editions, 1962.

Taylor, J. "St. Basil the Great and Pope St. Damasus I." *Downside Review* 91 (1973): 186-203, 262-74.

### Boethius

Barrett, H. M. *Boethius: Some Aspects of His Times and Work.* Cambridge: Cambridge University Press, 1940.

Chadwick, H. *Boethius: The Consolations of Music, Logic, Theology and Philosophy.* Oxford: Clarendon, 1981.

Gibson, M. T., ed. *Boethius: His Life, Thought, and Influence.* Oxford: Blackwell, 1981.

O'Daly, G. *The Poetry of Boethius.* Chapel Hill: University of North Carolina Press, 1991.

Patch, H. R. *The Tradition of Boethius: A Study of His Importance in Medieval Culture.* Oxford: Oxford University Press, 1935.

Watts, V. E. *The Consolation of Philosophy.* Harmondsworth, UK: Penguin Books, 1969.

# A CHURCH OF THE NATIONS

## Ancient Global Christianity

### THE LATIN AND GREEK FOCI OF CLASSICAL CHURCH HISTORY

The common access to the history of the church, as times go on and memories of the original events blur (or were never sharp in the first place), becomes ever more dependent on texts. But here is the problem. The early church was predominantly nonliterate. Those who wrote anything were the tiny minority of highly educated clerical theologians. Women do not feature predominantly: their patterns of church involvement were in other than literary fields, in the main. This is, of course, one of the reasons why their massive presence and importance in early Christianity was increasingly overlaid, neglected, and eventually overshadowed. The textual record gives us a slice. But even when one reads an important text, one has to interpret the modality of the discourse. We have papyri of the common people, for example, especially from Egypt, where such things managed to cling onto a palpable existence through a long history because of the unusual climate condition. We find small windows there into the lives of ordinary merchants (never the lowest classes of *fellahin*, by and large whose lives gets reflected merely by accident precisely because they were taken so much for granted), but the data they tend to gve us of church conditions is partial: and we would not expect anything else.

Even in our age of massive textuality, how much paper record would one find in the average person's house (or even in a devout person's house) that records their engagement with official or significant matters of the life of their local churches? Very little, if any, one would imagine. The records that exist from the early church tend to be the writings preserved of those the ancients themselves regarded as "great theologians"; they came to be known as the "fathers of the church," and their works were carefully preserved across centuries by a cadre of devoted followers, or else preserved because of the importance of their office or the controversies they were involved in—such as the chancery records of great ecclesiastical leaders such as the popes or patriarchs of the great sees, or the conciliar records.

Writers such as Gregory the Theologian, or Basil the Great, Athanasius, Jerome, or Augustine, have left behind a veritable mountain of information about theology and the church of their times. In times past this was read, on the authority of these figures, with a reverence almost approaching the reception of Scripture. And to that extent often historical commentators forgot the rules governing rhetorical interpretation in the ancient world: a world where exaggeration, manipulation of ideas, and often pronounced social "slant" (not to say bias) were prevalent on every line. Reading the Scripture and the Fathers literalistically, as was often done, and without much regard for social context and rhetorical redacting, often led to a naive view of the state of the times: where everyone an ancient authority denounced was truly a villain, as the authority implied they were, and no shades muddled the black and white of the official view of history. But even if a historian or theologian trod very carefully and was aware that the writings of the condemned heretics had to be scrutinized more carefully than simply reading their enemies' synopses of it, or that nontextual sources had to be kept in mind, it was inevitable, given the very weight of the recorded sources from the greatest of all the churches, those of Rome and Constantinople, that their version of events would dominate the Christian archive.

And so they did dominate. The twin sees of Rome and new Rome organized, reshuffled, repristinated across the years the story of the development of Christianity. They codified it, understood it, and made propaganda for it, from their respective viewpoints as "mother churches." Rome became the undisputed see of the Western Christian world, the one to which all other West Europeans tended to look, after the fifth century, as the model for good practice and organization. Constantinople became, after the eighth century, the one bright star in the Christian East, fully functional, actively archiving and arranging Christian affairs from a stable political basis. The rise of Islam in the East, and the fracturing of Roman ideas of unity in the West after the age of migration, meant that Rome and Constantinople's preservation power, as living sources of Christian memory, was boosted even more and assumed an overwhelming force in Christian historiography. And so, even before the second half of the first millennium, the story of Christianity was well on the way to becoming a story told in Greek, or Latin.

The signs were already there from the outset, of course. The first indication of this was the determined translation of all that Jesus had to say from Aramaic into Greek, for the cause of its transmission in the Greek cities of the Roman world. Even Jesus' name was rendered from "Yeshua" into the Greek "Jesus" for the adoption of his story. All the foundational Christian documents of the next two centuries were transmitted in Greek: creeds, apologias, exorcisms, prayers. The very popes of Rome spoke Greek until the end of the third century, and the liturgy at Rome was in Greek before passing into a dynamic translation into Latin in the fourth, when the vernacular needs of a new demographic demanded it. Rome and Constantinople (after the fourth century) were the powerhouses of the Christian story, and their long endurance meant that they were safe houses for an archive that could be passed on in a long continuum.

All this meant that the story of the church became predominantly a Latin and Greek one. Of course, the church was not restricted to these two sees or their respective missionary remits. Acts of the Apostles (Acts 8:27-39) tells us that right from the earliest Pentecost, a Jewish apostle, Philip, speaking Aramaic and reading Hebrew, evangelized and baptized an Ethiopian eunuch, a high official of the *kandak* of his country in the highlands of Africa. The *kandak* was his queen, as we would say. The word means, or is, the title of the ruler. It is not a personal name (Candace), as the writer of Acts has mistakenly misheard it—because to him, a fine Greek littérateur, the "foreign" word was "barbarous" and unmanageable. Likewise, the magi of the Gospel nativity story are transmuted into kings in popular retelling of the story, or at least "wise men," because the original deliberate Zoroastrian echoes of astrological wizards sounded so bizarre to Western ears that it was thought best to redefine it.

To be registered widely, all needed to be retranslated into Greek or Latin: not only the language, but also in terms of intellectual horizons. The more successfully Rome and Constantinople did this, the more they spread their versions of the tale as matrices for future telling. The more this happened, the more the "fringes" of the remits of Roman and Constantinopolitan Christianity passed into deeper and deeper obscurity. And yet, we know that the very first origins of the Jesus movement were conducted in Aramaic. And we know that the gospel message, even in the first generation, passed into Africa, Libya, Asia Minor, Syria, Parthia, and beyond: all with different languages and customs.

By the sixth century and after, Christianity had moved deep along the Silk Road and entered China and India to the East and Nubia to the South. It permeated the Nordic and Germanic tribes of the Western forests and fjords. It would eventually enter the tribes of the Slavs and there create a safe haven for Eastern Christianity when Roman Christian power was only a fading memory. None of these extra-Roman, extra-Constantinopolitan zones saw themselves or wanted to record their story from the central viewpoint of these cities. They had their own traditions, their own tongues and stories to tell. But their locality moved them to the side of historiography. Greek and Latin were the lingua franca of the age. Even today English- and Chinese-language books dominate the world market. But the interchange between the two systems is nonexistent. If one wants to get out a message to the world, one does not choose Brabantian Belgian, not even French perhaps, but English. This also means that the history of the English-speaking nations is much better known than that of the Belgians, who will appear in the prior records more or less only as they affect the English story.

The non-Greek and non-Latin Christianities of the ancient world, therefore, have their own stories: much of which has been overlaid and forgotten, and some of it entirely lost, to the universal church. To penetrate those stories, even now, demands linguistic and historical skills offering significant challenges. But from the very beginning the Christian story saw itself as a universal one, a catholic (*katholike*) one, embracing all languages and all cultures. Its message was to "go out and make disciples of all the nations" (Mt 28:19). Christianity in its "neglected" language vesture is rich and often surprising. A brief overview of some of the main zones other than Greece and Rome will be all that we can manage here.

## SYRIA

The ancient church of Syria was the cradle of Gentile Christianity. It was at the great city of Antioch (now Antakya), the capital of the Roman province, that Paul's ministry of preaching was first commissioned and financed, there that Peter took up residence, and there too that the Jesus movement was first called "Christian." It is most likely that the Gospel of Matthew was the liturgical book commissioned and produced by the Antiochene church. Syrian theology in the late first and early second centuries continued the highly charged apocalyptic character of the earliest Christian *kerygma*.

Syriac is a language closely related to the Aramaic of Jesus' time. It is, perhaps, the third most important of the early Christian tongues. Not only does it contain the records of very early forms of Christian polity and theological thought, before the Nicene settlement, but (at a later stage of the Syriac-speaking church's development) it also became the receptacle of many Greek treatises that it alone has preserved. In the time of Alexander the Great, it was Aramaic that was the official language of all the indigenous peoples of his empire, of that large region stretching from Asia Minor to Persia and from Armenia to the Arabian Peninsula. Syriac falls into two main dialects: the western, as used in Palestine and Syria by both Christians and Jews as well as Palmyrans, and Nabateans; and the eastern, as used in Babylonia by the Jews, the Mandeans, the Manichaeans, and the tribes of

Upper Mesopotamia. The literary Syriac language that developed and would eventually collate this Levantine form of Christian experience derived from the eastern Mesopotamian dialect.[1] The Syriac of the Christians later devolved into two distinct dialects, western (Serta) and eastern (Estrangela), the former belonging more to the Miaphysite (Jacobite) writers and the latter to the Assyrian church (Nestorian) theologians.

With the collapse of the Seleucid dynasty in the Middle East after 63 BC, smaller kingdoms grew up around the Euphrates. One of the most significant of these was the kingdom of Edessa, with its capital at Osrhoene. Nisibis was also a highly significant center. In the Christian era this kingdom, at first patronizing the church, long before Constantine, became a lively center of theological and ecclesiastical culture. Its Syriac liturgical style dominated the adjacent churches from the Mediterranean in the West to the heartlands of Persia in the East. With the conflicts caused by the Council of Ephesus in 431, when Nestorius the Syrian archbishop of Constantinople was severely censured for teachings that many of this region felt were "traditional," a progressive alienation began to set in. This was not only theologically motivated (fractures caused by the so-called Monophysite and Nestorian secessions) but also heavily conditioned by the varying level of hostilities in operation between the empires of Rome and Persia, whose tense borders fell over the Edessan region. Syriac-speaking Christians under Persian rule were looked on as a fifth column, simply for being Christians, and so their connections with Byzantium or further West were deliberately played down. Up until the Monophysite schisms of the fifth century, many of the important Syriac-speaking theologians were also skilled in Greek. After that time, the Greek language was heavily overshadowed and soon lost. In the time of John Chrysostom bilingual sermons were given in his cathedral, and yet his Greek is among the finest ever written. After him at Constantinople, we find only Greek, and never again a patriarch who has command of spoken or written Syriac.

Between the fifth and seventh centuries was the golden age of Syriac Christian literature. After the rise of Islam in the seventh century, Arabic made increasing headroads into the culture, and soon even the Christians preferred Arabic, leaving Syriac only a liturgical language, or a refined clerical language that would endure in a progressively dwindling way until the thirteenth century. Phonetically written out, a sense of Syriac (close to Jesus' own Aramaic original) can be given by the text of the Lord's Prayer as follows:

---

[1] J. B. Chabot, "Syriac Language and Literature," in *Catholic Encyclopedia* (New York: Robert Appleton, 1912), 14:408-13. Another global survey can be found in B. Harris-Cowper, "The Syriac Language and Literature," *Journal of Sacred Literature* 2 (1863): 75-87; see also S. Brock, *An Introduction to Syriac Studies* (Piscataway, NJ: Gorgias Press, 2006).

*Abouwn de bashmayore nethqadash shemork. teethe malkuwthork. nehwe tsevyornork: aykanor de bashmayor orph baror. hav lan akhmor de suwnkornan yormornor. Washbuwk lan hawbain aiqanor d'orph h'nan sh'baqn l'haiorbain. w'lor ta'lan l'nesyuwnor elor phatsorn men beeyshor. metul' de deelork heey malkuwthor we hailor' we teshbuw-hetor. 'Orlam orlmeeyn ameen.*

The early chief monuments of this literature are the translations of the Scriptures rendered into Syriac and now known as the Peshitta, the works of the Gnostic teacher Bardesanes (c. 154–222); the writings of Aphrahat the Sage (d. 350) and Ephrem (d. 373); Rabbula and Ibas of Edessa in the fifth century, along with James of Nisibis and Philoxenus of Mabbug; and later in that same century Barsauma of Nisibis and Narsai.[2] Most of the latter authors were embroiled in the controversies following after the Council of Chalcedon in 451, which split the Syrian church into two tensely opposed factions, the so-called Nestorians and the Monophysites, with the Chalcedonians (who were those Syrians still wishing to relate to Constantinople and Rome) standing uneasily in the middle. In the sixth century Sergius of Reshaina was active and notable as a translator of Greek classics (both pagan philosophic and Christian patristic). It was through the hands of Syriac translators that the Arab world came to have knowledge of the Greek scientific and philosophical tradition, which they would, in turn, hand on back to the West in the high Middle Ages after the Crusades.

In the seventh century there were very important ascetical writers working in Syriac, not least Mar Isaac of Nineveh, and Sadhona (Abba Martyrios). Their works are only today receiving the universal notice they deserve with translations into English. J. B. Chabot eloquently describes the rich array of ancient and early medieval writers in Syriac, hardly any of whose names are known in the standard history books of the church, their works still largely unedited and untranslated in a modern European language.[3] By the thirteenth century the language itself was becoming archaic, and creative theological work passed into Arabic. Almost all the writers were monastic clergy, and being caught up in the centuries-long dissidence the Syriac Christian world experienced after Chalcedon, the works are generally highly ascetic in tone and (except for the monastic writings on prayer) sharply apologetic in character.

The ascetical nature of the Syrian origins is reflected in the title of Thomas the Athlete, which in Greek derives from *ascetic*. The earliest of all the legends of the Syrian (*Suryaye*) churches relate their founding to the apostolic ministry of Thomas, who was the twin (*Didymos*) of Jesus. The Greek name is mirrored in the Aramaic

---

[2]*Peshitta* means "straightforward" (or "literal" in this context—suggesting it was an accurate rendition of the original, that is, non-Septuagintal, versions).
[3]Chabot, "Syriac Language and Literature."

word for "twin" (*toma*). The so-called Thomas literature, especially the Gospel of Thomas, the Book of Thomas the Athlete, and the Acts of Thomas, is a very important witness to the earliest stages of this church and gives it a highly ascetical character that stresses the importance of celibacy as an eschatological proof of commitment to the gospel. The Thomas traditions have in recent decades become a new focus of scholarly interest. After the time of Ephrem, who was concerned to bring his Syriac church traditions more into line with the developing Nicenism of the Greek and Latin West, their noncanonical character and their more speculative mystical style were troubling enough to allow them to fall somewhat to the side.

One important group of very early, pre-Nicene Christians in Syria was known as the Benai Qeyama (female *Benat*): the sons and daughters of the covenant, or perhaps "sons of the oath." This seems to have been the oath that they swore at baptism bonding themselves together in celibate communities of males and females, living as brothers and sisters and attempting to live lives dedicated to prayer and poverty. Aphrahat, the author of the influential treatise *Demonstrations*, was a member of these Benai Qeyama. They were quite unlike the later organizations of ascetics in the West, where community (cenobitic) living was the norm, for many of the Syrian ascetics lived relatively disorganized lives, traveling around as holy men or living in a wilderness area on the outskirts of villages. These "solitary ones" (*ihidaya*) were at one and the same time distanced from the affairs of the local communities and near enough to intervene as adjudicators, and they were regularly called on by the pagan and Christian communities to settle disputes or give authoritative words of guidance.

Some scholars of Syrian origins believe that at an early stage celibacy was required as a lived commitment before baptism was administered by some of these ascetical first founders, although this is also disputed. The "special covenant" of celibacy was probably held out as the ideal form of the baptismal ceremony. Whether celibacy was actually required of the baptized or simply encouraged, it probably had the effect of making the majority of pre-Nicene Syrian Christians catechumens for most of their lives, with the clerical elite entirely celibate. This typical Syrian severity of ascetic mentality is demonstrated in the Thomas literature, and in part in the slightly later Book of Steps (*Ketaba de Maskata* or *Liber Graduum*). In the latter source it is clear that Syrian Christianity is slowly moderating its severe asceticism, perhaps in the cause of distancing itself from the Encratite movement, at which wider Christianity looked askance, even from when it first encountered it in the person of the theologian Tatian. This Encratite movement we have already looked at in the chapter devoted to the second century. By the fourth century, Ephrem certainly wanted to move his church this distance: keeping an ascetical monastic tradition but leaving behind the implied denigrations of the married state and sexual life.

The Book of Steps concerns the duties of these two groups within the Syrian church, the covenanters and those who have not yet taken that commitment step. The first are called "the perfect" (*gmıre*), and the others are designated as "the upright" (*kene*). The book calls on the upright to live in a way that is worthy of Christ, while taking care to support the perfect financially, who are enjoined to live lives of absolute poverty, chastity, and constant prayer. Forms of Syrian asceticism always remained significantly different from the patterns established by Egypt, Palestine, and the later West, where issues of obedience and common order prevailed. In Syria the stress was on radical ascetical feats: apocalyptic witness and charismatic actions. The style is given in the records of Syrian monasticism that were collated by Theodoret of Cyr in the early fifth century in his volume *History of the Monks of Syria*.

Typical Syrian ascetical forms were the self-deprivation of sleep, binding the body with chains, wandering naked in the winter cold, living in caves, never cutting nails or hair. A renowned Syrian practice was sitting in immoveable prayer in one place. Fifth-century ascetic Simeon took up residence on a large drum of a fallen column and sat there, slowly adding drum upon drum to avoid the importuning of visitors until he was thirty feet above ground. He stayed there for decades, being fed by disciples in a large monastery that grew up at the base of his column. His fame was such that even an emperor wanted to consult him on matters of state.

The Syrian "memory" remained alive in Byzantium for many centuries to come, where it was synthesized with the more ordered forms of cenobitic monastic lifestyle. One such "Syrian" memory was the tradition of the holy fool that originated there. It is a continuation of ancient Cynic traditions of the wandering sage but was appropriated by the ascetics as a manner of showing how an apocalyptic lifestyle was disconnected from the affairs of this world. The "fool" adopted many of the attitudes of the wandering beggars who were mentally ill in the ancient world and drew to himself the opprobrium that usually accompanied this state in life. But the purpose was to hide the prophetic charism under a mantle of foolishness (following Paul's teaching about Christ's self emptying *kenosis* and the "folly" of the cross [1 Cor 1:18-23; 3:19; Phil 2:6-11]). The Byzantine faithful loved these tales of heroic (and odd) sanctity. The Byzantine abbots of monasteries made sure they were not widely emulated by actual monks.

Thomas's apostolic founding of the church remained a constant claim of the Syrians. The church legends also speak of Thomas commissioning his disciple the apostle Addai (Thaddeus), who had been one of the seventy apostles sent out on the first mission by Jesus. Addai was sent to Edessa, demonstrating that these traditions reflect local lore of that school, in order to heal the sick. The book that contains these stories, The Doctrine of Addai, is one of the earliest texts that evidently is trying to knit together the disparate and confusing traditions that were already in circulation concerning Christian origins in Mesopotamia. The stories in the Addai tradition were taken up by the Greek church historian Eusebius and tell a tale that the latter wants to see standardized over all the churches (charismatic foundation, followed by regular organization, secured by stable successions of bishops). He focuses especially on how Bishop Palut was consecrated around the year 200 as the first Christian bishop of Edessa, by bishop Serapion of Antioch. Ephrem later tells us that the Orthodox (Nicene) Christians in Edessa were not called catholics but Palutians, and it is possible that we see in the Addai story a kind of second retelling of the lineage of Syrian Christianity, described from the point of view of rising standards of international orthodoxy.[4]

Some of the earlier writers, such as the alleged Gnostic Bardesanes, or the Thomas literature struck the wider Nicene world that came into contact with them as very oddly variegated from the standard orthodox-heretic narratives as established out of the Greco-Roman "normative axis" of Christian Rome, North Africa, and Alexandria, which had shaped the international Christian tradition in sharp opposition to the second-century Gnostic movements. In this Syriac-speaking church, however, the movements of Ebionism, Mandaeanism, Encratism, Gnostic currents, and Manichaeism continued visible long after they had faded elsewhere. Even in the post-Nicene theologians a different style of theologizing is observable: less of the linear, abstract theologico-philosophical approach, and much more of a Semitic, poetic idiom of reference.

The Doctrine of Addai contains the celebrated story of King Abgar V Ukkama of Osroene in the kingdom of Edessa (already the kings are being placed in a patronage role for Christianity contemporary with Jesus). According to the story, King Agbar, a leper, heard rumors of Jesus' healing powers and sent a letter to Jerusalem asking Jesus to come and heal him and preach in his kingdom.[5] Jesus declined the invitation but sent his blessing to the king and promised that after the ascension he would send one of his disciples to fulfill the king's demands. Hannan, an agent of Agbar who had traveled to Jerusalem, tried to paint the image of Jesus so as to take it back to his master. A variant form of the story has it that he was unable to capture anything because of the flashing light. Seeing this, Jesus pressed a cloth to his face and handed it to Hannan. When the latter unrolled it before the king back in Edessa the image (the icon *acheiropoieton*: not painted by human hands) was perfectly present, and the

---

[4] Ephrem, *Against the Heretics* 22.6.
[5] Also in Eusebius, *Ecclesiastical History* 1.13.

cloth (the *mandylion* or face cloth of Edessa) became a source of many miracles.[6] The iconic version of the story is preserved in the Greek source *The Acts of Thaddeus* (*Addai* being the Syriac version of *Thaddeus*). The traditions shows how iconic theology and practice (use of religious wonderworking imagery) was important from the outset in Syrian Christianity, long before this was the case in Byzantium.

After the Council of Ephesus 431, where Nestorius (a Syrian theologian who had been preaching his christological tradition from the imperial capital as archbishop) was deposed, the Alexandrian and Roman church tradition came into conflict on a broad stage with Syrian christological ways of speaking ("two Sons" Christology) that had been regarded as "traditional" since the time of Theodore of Mopsuestia. He was the celebrated fourth-century Syrian exegete who taught Diodore of Tarsus and inspired Nestorius. In the late fourth century Gregory the Theologian censured Diodore for supporting a way of speaking about "two Sons" (Son of God and Son of Man) insofar as it suggested two unresolved centers of personal life in the Savior. After Ephesus in 431 the Syrian Christology was censured and sidelined in the Greco-Roman world, and internal affairs in the Syrian church itself split the community into pro-Nestorian and pro-Alexandrian ways of speaking. This fracture severely weakened the church's ability to relate to the wider Christian world, and this, together with the progressive loss of multiple-language skills that marked the Christian East after the fifth century, put Syrian Christianity into an even deeper separation from the international churches. Pressure from Islam coming from the East would turn this distancing into more marked isolation as time went on.

Right from the beginning of Syrian theology, the chief writers and theologians of the tradition, such as Bardesanes, Ephrem, or Jacob of Serug, among others, show a vividly poetic and imagistic character that other parts of the Greco-Roman Christian world did not equal. That influence came heavily into Byzantine Greek liturgical poetry through the medium of Syrian cantor Romanos the Melodist, who worked in Constantinople and wrote masterpieces of liturgical poetry. The Syrian influence was also strong at Byzantium, albeit in a Greek medium, because when Constantinople was first founded it was built as a see out of ecclesial territories belonging to the Antiochene patriarchate. After the seventh century the history of the Syrian church became one of relentless shrinkage under Islamic domination. In its powerful years, from the third to the sixth centuries, Syrian Christianity was a strongly evangelistic

---

[6]It was celebrated as a major relic in Byzantium, the cloth and letter being brought to the church of St. Mary Blachernae in 944 and then housed in the Church of the Virgin of the Pharos at Constantinople. See R. Janin, *La Géographie ecclésiastique de l'Empire byzantin. 1: Le Siège de Constantinople et le Patriarcat Oecuménique*, vol. 3, *Les Églises et les Monastères* (Paris: Institut Français d'Etudes Byzantines, 1953), 172.

church and sent out missionaries as far as China, Persia, Ethiopia, and India. In the ninth century many of the Syrian classical spiritual texts, for example the spiritual writings of Pseudo-Macarius, the great fourth-century master and author of the *Fifty Spiritual Homilies* and the *Great Letter*, with their stress on personal experience of the Holy Spirit as the touchstone of the Christian life, made their way in translation back to the imperial capital and had a strong renovatory effect on ascetical life and spirituality there, not least in the great works of eleventh-century Byzantine mystic Symeon the New Theologian.

Christian Syria was the first part of the church to have to live under Islamic domination. Alongside many sufferings and destruction of monasteries and institutions, there were also opportunities for peaceful exchange and mutual enriching. Timothy I, patriarch of the Christian Syrians at Baghdad, was one such figure who composed one of the first explicit Christian-Muslim dialogues. He was a native of Hazza (near Arbelles), and a disciple of the theologian Abraham bar Daschandad. Timothy was elected bishop of Beit Bagash, and when the patriarch Henanisho died he became patriarch in a controverted election, relying on the support of the governor of Mosul to take command of his throne in 780. Until his death in 823 he actively encouraged the Assyrian church's missionary work in eastern Asia and tried to introduce many reforms. His literary work was wide-ranging. Of much interest today is the account he kept of a court disputation in 781 concerning the essential nature of Christianity before the Islamic caliph Al-Mahidi.[7] Timothy acknowledges to the caliph that Islam has had a fine spiritual record in converting the tribes from paganism. He also wrote an astronomical treatise entitled *Book of the Stars* (now lost), two volumes of *Canonical Questions*, a *Commentary on the Works of St. Gregory of Nazianzus*, and a dossier of about two hundred letters, of which about sixty are extant. Timothy supervised the first collection of the post-Chalcedonian Assyrian ("Nestorian") church councils. It was entitled *Synodicon Orientale* and comprises the acts of thirteen governing synods convened by his predecessors between 410 and 775.[8]

## CHINA

The presence of Christianity in China dates back, in terms of its first records, to the seventh century. It is mentioned in some church traditions that the apostle Thomas preached the gospel there in the first century. This is an echo, as with the cases of India and Ethiopia, that the gospel probably came to China via the missions of the Syrian church, notably out of the Byzantine-era patriarchate of Antioch. Artifacts from this

---

[7] A. Mingana, trans., "Timothy's Apology for Christianity," *Bulletin of the John Rylands Library* 12 (1928): 16-90.
[8] *Synodicon Orientale*, ed. J. B. Charbot (Paris: Imprimerie nationale, 1902).

ancient missionary enterprise along the Silk Road (once part of a wider Antiochene outreach to Ethiopia, India, and Persia) can now only be found rarely, but there are indeed some still surviving, literally cut into stone, such as the famous stele of Xian, set up by Nestorian missionaries in the early eighth century to celebrate their missionizing in China of 635.[9] The stone's head inscription reads, "Stele marking the propagation in China of the luminous religion of Daqin." It notes, in a beautifully incised Chinese script, that Christian missionaries, under the leadership of the traveler Alopen, reached the Tang dynasty capital of Xian in the year 635 and were allowed by the governor to establish places of worship and to preach freely about their faith.

The Tang dynasty, however, enacted repressive measures against foreign religions in 845, during the course of the anti-Buddhist repressions. Along with Buddhist monks, Christian missionaries and Zoroastrian evangelists were banned by Emperor Wuzong, and all the assets of the respective religions were seized by the state. All the Christian Chinese missions must have suffered extensively then. In 986 one Christian monastic, reviewing the state of the Chinese mission, lamented, "Christianity is now extinct in China; the native Christians have perished in one way or another; the churches have been destroyed, and there is only one Christian left in the land." His words are surely an exaggeration, as isolated communities clung on for a long time; as evidence for this, Christian gravestones (with crosses engraved on them) survive from the later Song and Liao dynasties, but the condition of desolation described at the end of the tenth century must have been accurate enough in structural terms.[10] Christian fortunes would not revive again in China until the thirteenth-century era of the Mongol dynasty. Several of the Mongol tribes were already established as Nestorian Christians, and indeed some of the wives of Genghis Khan were Christian, so toleration was once more afforded the religion.[11] The popes established an embassy at the Mongol capital of Khanbaliq Beijing. In this period we also have an account of two traveling monks of the Assyrian (Nestorian) church: Barsauma and Marcus, who traveled through China. Marcus was elected patriarch of the church of the East, and Barsauma came to the West in 1287 and gave an account of Christian affairs under the Mongols, in the royal courts there throughout the following year.

It is not possible to be more descriptive of the place of this antique Syrian mission in China, because the written records that would have clarified how expansive this

---

[9]See further P. Pelliot, ed., *L'Inscription Nestorienne de Si-ngan-fou, Kyoti*, Scuola de studi sull'Asia Orientale, Collège de France, Institut des Hautes Études Chinoises (Paris: Persee, 1996), 349-73.
[10]See further J. Foster, *The Church of the T'ang Dynasty* (London: SPCK, 1939); L. Tang, *A Study of the History of Nestorian Christianity in China and Its Literature in Chinese: Together with a New English Translation of the Dunhuang Nestorian Documents* (New York: Peter Lang, 2003).
[11]See further P. Jenkins, *The Lost History of Christianity: The Thousand-Year Golden Age of the Church in the Middle East, Africa, and Asia; And How It Died* (New York: HarperOne, 2008).

Eastern mission was were extensively burned in a much later period when the Roman Catholic Renaissance-era mission arrived there. Finding indigenous Christians with Syriac traditions and dissident views (concerning the papacy and christological matters) already present, the Jesuit missionaries consigned the "heretical" materials to the flames and decided to "reevangelize" them. This profound loss to the history of Christianity in China leaves the issue of the more antique Syro-Chinese community, originally connected to Syrian Christian traditions along the Silk Route, now a matter of speculation and deduction from folk traditions and oral legends. Catholic iterations of Christianity's advent to China now usually begin with Francis Xavier and Matteo Ricci, the Jesuits, while Protestant versions of the story commence in the nineteenth century.

## ARABIA

Arabian Christians first appear in the New Testament in two distinct but dramatic instances. The first is in the account of the original Pentecost in the book of Acts, when Arabian Jews are caught up in the gift of tongues at Jerusalem (Acts 2:11), reminding us of the conversion process that might well have occurred in the earliest centuries of the Arabian church out of the Jewish settlements of Arabia. And the other is the obscure reference St. Paul gives to his long sojourn in Arabia, immediately following his dramatic conversion near Damascus, where he consolidates his new faith (among Jewish Christians, one supposes) and learns his craft as a Christian missionary (Gal 1:15-17).

The Greeks called Arabia "land of the nomads" and identified the Syrian province of Beth Arabayé as their "Arabia." This was the land centered around the town of Nisibis. Another area, comprising southern Palestine, the lands to the north of Sinai, and those east of Damascus, they called "province of Arabia." Pharan was an important monastery in this region before the year 330, on Jerome's witness, and remained so for two centuries. Finally, the Greeks also designated the lands around modern Aden and Yemen as Arabia Felix (and sometimes they called it India!). Eusebius, in his *Ecclesiastical History*, with his usual motive of wishing to connect the foundation of international churches to the direct ministry of various apostles, attributes the evangelization of the Arab peoples to the work of the apostle Bartholomew.[12]

But the first historical data he is really able to give about these Arabian churches is the case of bishop Beryllus of Bostra, whom Eusebius describes as a learned and elegant writer of the third century Arabian church, and the synod he occasioned,

---

[12]Eusebius, *Ecclesiastical History* 5.10.3.

which was attended by "many bishops" in his city, around 240.[13] Beryllus probably held Monarchian views, and the renowned theologian Origen of Alexandria (then resident in Caesarea Maritima in Palestine) was invited to speak to the synod of bishops, where he is said to have convinced Beryllus of the error of his ways. This is how Eusebius has knowledge of early Arabia, that is, through his access to the archives of Origen's school in his own episcopal see. Origen's invitation to the synod, as a presbyter, suggests that at this stage synods were still held in the antique manner, as public disputations on contested points. By the time of Eusebius in the mid-fourth century he reads the synodical acts more in the fashion of synods of his own day, that is, as trials of orthodoxy. The lately discovered treatise of Origen *That the Soul Is Not the Blood* might reflect some of the arguments he presented there that weaned Beryllus away from an overliteral reading of scriptural authorities and led him to undertake a more explicit position on the divinity of the Logos, personally present in the Christ, and distinct from the deity of the Father.

In the fourth century the Christian emperors sent resident monastic bishops with small missionary entourages to convert many of the Arabian tribal rulers or phylarchs and to tie them in with Byzantine Christian affairs. Several of the desert princes were Christian, though many remained nomadic polytheists. During the fifth and sixth centuries the Ghassanid tribes were converted to Miaphysite Christianity and were courted thereafter as allies of the Byzantine imperial administration. The empire valued their existence and patronized them as a buffer against the pagan tribes of Arabia. The last king of the Lakhmid Arabs, Nu'man III, who was a client prince of the Sassanid Empire in the late sixth century AD, also converted to Christianity, not to the Miaphysites but to the Assyrian (Nestorian) church.

One episode of the life of St. Symeon the Stylite (390–459) records how hundreds of Bedouin encamped at the foot of his pillar to hear the words of the saint and to look on him for a blessing.[14] After preaching to them, using his monks in the ground-level monastery as intermediaries, the saint converted thousands of the tribesmen to Christianity over the course of a few days. He commanded them to bring out of their tents their ancestral idols, which the monks then arranged in a great pile to burn them. Elders of the tribes were ordained as priests to serve the liturgy for the nomads as they returned to the desert, and, one presumes, some of the monastics went along with them to supervise. This nomadic aspect of Arabian Christianity was, therefore, still very much alive in the mid-fifth century. The sedentary settlements alone would encourage the building of churches. Even then they

---

[13] Ibid., 6.20.
[14] See R. Doran, trans., *Symeon Stylites: The Biographies* (Kalamazoo, MI: Cistercian Publications, 1988).

tended to be small; but there were many of them in the fifth and sixth centuries, and many still remain to be excavated.

Because Arabia, after the seventh century, became the very heartland of Islamic expansionism, the history of the church was occluded in a very dramatic way. Most of the archaeological work that has since tried to (literally) excavate the evidence of the life of the church in Arabia was only done at a superficial level of mapping the surface areas of suspected antique Christian churches and annotating where Christian architectural remains had been incorporated (after their demolition) into the structures of later Islamic buildings. This surveying work had a heyday in the nineteenth century, when licenses were more easily obtained from the Ottoman suzerains, but twentieth-century Middle Eastern politics did not encourage further stages of excavations to be done, and until this is the case a complete record cannot be produced. Nevertheless, the results of the older surveys were collated by several excellent studies (such as Waddington [1870], Butler [1929], Devreesse [1942]); and as Bagatti and Pappalardo (2014) have shown, this work is now being returned to in recent years with a series of exploratory studies.[15] The works of Fr. Sidney Griffith have done much to raise awareness of the extent and importance of Arabic-speaking Christianity.[16] The aftermath of the Syrian civil war, however, will undoubtedly set things back considerably.[17]

Christian Arabic literature from the ancient period was very extensive. It is more or less wholly unknown in modern times. Its influence on early medieval Islamic intellectuals was profound, and from the hands of Arabic Christians the works of the Greek philosophers passed to Islam. Arabic Christian texts have only rarely been rendered into a modern European language. Graf made a monumental study, in four volumes, of this literature between 1944 and 1951, which remains to this time the most important collation of sources.[18] It is clear from Graf's account in the 696 pages of his first volume that the literature in its early period covered biblical exegesis and patristic theology, as well as canonical, apocryphal, and pseudepigraphical materials.

Following the patristic era, in the early period under Islamic domination, Arabic Christians first start to leave behind translations and produce an apologetic literature of their own. The leading chronicler-historian of the church was Yahya ibn

---

[15] W. H. Waddington, *Inscriptions Grecques et Latines de la Syrie* (Paris, 1870); H. C. Butler, *Early Churches in Syria* (Princeton, NJ: Princeton University Press, 1929); R. Devreesse, "Le Christianisme dans le province d'Arabie," *Vivre et Penser* (1942): 112-13; B. Bagatti, and C. Pappalardo, "Arabia," in *Encyclopedia of Ancient Christianity*, ed. A. di Berardino (Downers Grove, IL: InterVarsity Press, 2014), 205-9.

[16] See, for example, his latest work: S. H. Griffith, *The Church in the Shadow of the Mosque: Christians and Muslims in the World of Islam* (Princeton, NJ: Princeton University Press, 2008).

[17] Beginning in 2014 and still causing chaos as this book is being written.

[18] G. Graf, *Geschichte der Christlichen arabischen Literatur*, 4 vols., in Studi e Testi 118, 113, 146, 147 (Rome: Bibliotheca Apostolica Vaticana, 1944–1951).

Yahya of Antioch (d. 1066: not to be confused with the Andalusian Muslim scholar of the same name). Hunain ibn Ishaq, who was born in 808, an Assyrian (Nestorian) church theologian, is said to have been an indefatigable translator of the ancient Greek scientific writers from Syriac into Arabic. And Miaphysite (Jacobite) philosopher Yahya ibn Adi (893–974) ran a school of philosophy frequented by Muslim and Christian intellectuals alike.[19] The wandering bishop known as George of the Arabs (or Giwargi; d. 724) was chief pastor of the nomadic Christian Arab tribes of Mesopotamia after 686. He was a leading theologian of the Miaphysite (Jacobite) church, a disciple of Jacob of Edessa. George gives the lie to the presumption that a wandering desert bishop following the tribes for liturgical services must somehow be a "primitive" of sorts. He was, in fact, one of the most learned philosophers of his age. He was a translator and commentator on Aristotle and the author of several volumes of critical notes (*scholia*) on the works of St. Gregory of Nazianzus and a large correspondence on liturgical matters with the monks of Aleppo.[20]

Archaeological remains show that the Byzantine pre-Islamic period was the one where the affairs of Arabian Christianity flourished mostly. The famous church of St. George at Madaba was completed in the sixth century and has a renowned mosaic floor that portrays the view of the Holy Land from Mount Nebo as Moses the prophet saw it. The bird's-eye view of the holy city itself has been of great interest to historians, showing as it does the ancient form of the Christian shrines there. Excavations in the city of Madaba have also revealed the list of the town's bishops. It is known that a center of Christian mosaic workers, a school in fact, operated out of Madaba and across Christian Arabia. Monasteries and churches were also grouped around Mount Nebo.

The affairs of Christian Arabia fell into obscurity for three principal reasons: first, the reliance on Semitic dialects, moving from Syriac to Arabic and thus facing away from the chief *koine* languages of Christian Greek and Latin; and second, because the church was rent, after the later fifth century, between Assyrian (Nestorian) and Miaphysite (Jacobite) Christian parties, neither of whom were in communion with each other or the wider Byzantine Chalcedonian communities of the East. Islam supplied the third reason, cutting off the independence of Arabian Christianity at a critical point in its development and expansion. The shape and character of this ancient church tradition will not be properly known until the task of rendering more of its theological and spiritual literature into modern languages has had time to proceed.

---

[19] Ibid, 2:239-49.
[20] A Voobus, "The Discovery of New Important *Memre* of Giwargi, Bishop of the Arabs," *Journal of Semitic Studies* 18 (1973): 235-37.

## INDIA

Several of the ancients used the term *India* to refer to what we would today call Ethiopia, and thus the first appearances of Christianity on what we generally mean today by the Asian Indian continent proper are not clearly known. The first solid reference in the patristic literature is that of the sixth-century Byzantine writer known as Cosmas Indicopleustes (the Greek word standing in as his surname means "the sailor to India"), who made trade voyages out of Alexandria to the East and recorded his observations in his treatise *On Christian Topography*. He remarked that the Christian church was established in India long before the mid-sixth century. There was an ancient presence of a strong community of Christians in the southwest of India. They later spread outward from this area, which seems to have been founded out of the southwest coastal strip (suggesting mercantile missions), to become a strong evangelizing movement. The precolonial Indian church, with many Syrian characteristics in its liturgy and practice, suggests that the patriarchate of Antioch was the missionizing origin (just as it was with Ethiopia in parts of its early history). If parallels are drawn with Ethiopia, the founding missions probably derive from the golden age of Christian Antiochene monastic evangelism, in the late fourth to sixth centuries, and thus place the Syrian missionary outreach to India sometime in the region of the fifth century, when the Antiochene monastic movement was still at the height of its power and energetic outreach.

The Christian communities of India have a lively tradition of their own that they were founded in the first century by the apostle Thomas (Didymus, Syriac *Toma*), who brought the gospel in the fifties of the first century to Kerala as part of his mission to Jewish communities resident there. But the figure of that apostle, as a symbol of Encratite teaching, was already rooted in the ancient traditions of the Syrian church, and so the Thomas traditions might well have come to India by means of Syria as well. Eusebius of Caesarea, in his *Church History*, tells of how Pantaenus, the scholar-theologian from Alexandria, went to "India" in the time of Emperor Commodus (161–192) and found Christians living there who used Matthew's Gospel "in Hebrew characters."[21] This could just as well refer to a trip to Nubia or Ethiopia as to a sea journey to India proper.

The thesis of a Hebraic Matthew still extant in very remote places (Ethiopia always figures as a literary symbol of extreme remoteness in Greek literature of all kinds) is a trope of Eusebius, namely that Matthew composed his Gospel first in Hebrew, and then a Greek translation was made of it. Remote ecclesiastic places, in Eusebius's imagination, preserved the supposed lost Hebrew original. Scholarly analyses of

---

[21]Eusebius, *Ecclesiastical History* 5.9-10.

Matthew, however, have in our time demonstrated beyond doubt that Greek was the original of the Gospel's composition. Eusebius also speaks of a mission to India by the apostle Bartholomew, as does Jerome, following him. Again, he is probably referring to sub-Saharan Africa.

The third-century Syriac text Acts of Thomas connects the apostle Thomas with the mission to two Indian kings in the north and south of India, respectively.[22] This does indeed seem to refer to the Asian continent, for Thomas is reluctant to go so far in the story, and Jesus (by means of a vision) makes him accompany Indian merchant Abbanes to his home region in northwestern India, where the apostle ends up in the service of Indo-Parthian King Gondophares. Robert Senior's work on Indo-Scythian coins and what they reveal about early Indian chronology lends weight to the supposition that Gondophares I ruled between 20 and 10 BC, and his name subsequently became a title for later kings (or *gondophars*).[23] So the Acts of Thomas material might authentically sketch a link between Syria and Indian Christianity, but it does not necessarily give any firm historiography. The subsequent mission, mentioned in the Acts of Thomas to the southern kingdom ruled by King Mahadwa, has been claimed by the Thomas Christians as the one that founded their churches in Kerala, along the Malabar coast, and up the Periyar river.

The Chronicle of Seert, an Arabic text interested in the affairs of Persian Christianity under Zoroastrian toleration, written no earlier than the ninth century by a historian of the Assyrian (Nestorian) church, speaks of a mission to India by David the bishop of Basra around the year 300.[24] Later traditions, first recorded in the Portuguese colonial period, also connect Indian Christianity with ancient Christian Syria via the figure of Thomas of Cana (claimed by the southern Indians as a founder of their churches). He is said to have led a migration of Syrian Christians from the Middle East to India sometime after the fourth century. The historicity of these accounts is unsure. The apostolic Thomas origins were emphasized by the Portuguese

---

[22] "The [apostles] divided the countries among them, in order that each one of them might preach in the region which fell to him and in the place to which his Lord sent him. And India fell by lot and division to Judas Thomas the Apostle. And he was not willing to go, saying: 'I have not strength enough for this, because I am weak. And I am a Hebrew: how can I teach the Indians?' And while Judas was reasoning thus, our Lord appeared to him in a vision of the night, and said to him: 'Fear not, Thomas, because my grace is with you.' But he would not be persuaded at all, saying: 'I will go wherever you want to send me, O Lord. But I will not go to India.'" W. Wright, ed., *The Apocryphal Acts of the Apostles* (London: 1871), 2:146-298.

[23] R. C. Senior, *Indo-Scythian Coins and History: Volume IV, Supplement: Additional Coins and Hoards; The Sequences of Indo-Greek and Indo-Scythian Kings* (London: Classical Numismatic Group, 2006).

[24] A. Scher, trans., *Histoire nestorienne inédite: Chronique de Séert. Première partie*, Patrologia Orientalis 4.3, 5.2 (1908, 1910); *Histoire nestorienne inédite: Chronique de Séert. Seconde partie*, Patrologia Orientalis 7.2, 13.4 (1911, 1919).

merchants of the Renaissance period, who thereby felt they had some form of link (historical and theological) with their own Western catholic traditions, but there is no reason to suppose that they created them. The early traditions of the Indian Christians demonstrate more the character of oral traditions, subsequently seeking linear coherence, and less the nature of a well-founded textual dossier.

## ARMENIA

Armenia was probably the first of all Christian kingdoms, predating the adoption and protection of Christianity by Constantine the Great. The Syrian church once more appears to have been the missionizing agency behind the earliest evangelization. Traditions say that Addai (Thaddeus), who was sent to cure King Agbar of Esessa, also evangelized southern Armenia. The first patristic theologian, known as the apostle of Armenia, was Gregory the Illuminator (c. 240–325), whose preaching campaign converted the Armenian King Tiridates (252–330) in the year 301. To his work we should impute a greater extension of that first presence of Christians in the country since the early third century. In 302, St. Gregory the Illuminator (*Grigor Lousaworic*) eventually was consecrated archbishop by his childhood friend Leontios, metropolitan of Cappadocian Caesarea. When he returned to Armenia it was as *catholicos*, or national patriarch.[25] For quite some time afterward, the clerical office of *catholicos* was passed down his familial descendants. He is said to have torn down many pagan shrines and ordained a great number of clergy, giving the church a structure that became classical. After his vision of Christ coming down to strike the earth with a hammer, he and the king built a great church in the capital Vagharhapat, renaming it Etchmiadzin, or "Place of the Descent of the Only Begotten." It is near Mount Ararat.

For a long time the churches of Armenia and Cappadocian Caesarea sustained a close relation, all the Armenian archbishops being appointed by the metropolitan of Caesarea until, after the death in 374 of St. Nerses the *catholicos* (or patriarch), that relationship was repudiated. The separation coincides with the growing division of the region between Roman and Sassanid power struggles. Great Armenian clerical scholars Mesrob Mashtots (362–440) and Sahak (Isaac) the Great (*catholicos* 389–439) subsequently invented an alphabet for the Armenians (a new language rising out of Persian, Greek, and Syriac influences), and the translation of biblical and patristic writings began in earnest. The first completed Bible was ready in 434. It was the presence of the Armenian language that now consolidated a distinct national Christian identity that would endure. The secluded and secluding nature of

---

[25]Later the office of patriarch was distinguished from (as lower than) the office of *catholicos*, and the catholicate splt into two families, one based in Armenia and the other in Lebanoan (the "House of Cilicia").

Armenia (a rugged, mountainous land), and its relative linguistic isolation, has resulted in this library of translated patristic works surviving intact in Armenian. Some works by Irenaeus and Ephrem the Syrian, for example, only exist today because of the Armenian versions that were made of them in the patristic era.

The Armenian church was not engaged in the controversies leading up to the Council of Chalcedon and was not represented there. While it accepted the first three ecumenical councils, therefore (sending letters of agreement to the decisions of Ephesus 431), it never agreed to the theology of the fourth, which it found to be offensive in its language of "two natures." At the Council of Vagharshapat in 491, and reiterated at the Council of Dvin in 527, the Chalcedonian decree was officially anathematized, and thus began the long ecclesiastical separation from the Byzantine and Latin traditions of theology, even though both these Christian cultures deeply affected the Armenian church throughout its history in terms of liturgical, political, and cultural developments.[26] St. Cyril of Alexandria became the great christological authority favored by the church, in a manner similar to the Syrian and Egyptian Miaphysites.

In the time of Heraclius in the seventh century there was a strong attempt on the part of the Byzantine emperor to reconcile the churches, and numerous colloquia were held, resulting in no substantive move forward. At the Council of Dvin in 609–610 the Armenian clergy censured the Georgian church for acceding to the Chalcedonian settlement and broke off communion with it. After the eighth century came a period of several centuries in which strongly dissident groups destabilized Armenian church affairs. Chief among the heretical movements were the Paulicians and the Phantasiasts, whose presence thereafter appears in medieval Byzantium in a minor way. The later history of the Armenian Christians has been one of intense oppression and suffering. Its Christian character has been sustained with great heroism to the present day. The liturgical forms of the church are akin to the old Antiochene rite (the precursor of the Byzantine liturgies) and mainly follow the liturgy of St. Basil. Armenia also has liturgical traditions derived from Jerusalem, with which it had strong medieval ties, and also Latinisms from the post Crusader period.[27] The Armenians use unleavened bread, distribute the elements under one species only, and do not mix water with the wine in the chalice. Apart from christological theology, the doctrines of the church are very close to Eastern Orthodoxy in most respects.

---

[26]See K. Sarkissian, *The Council of Chalcedon and the Armenian Church* (London: Armenian Church Prelacy Press, 1965).

[27]See further A. A. King, *The Rites of Eastern Christendom* (Rome: Tipografia poliglotta vaticana, 1948), 2:521-646.

## GEORGIA

Georgia (called *Sakartvel* in the Georgian language) corresponds to the two ancient areas (divided from each other by the ridge of the Surami Mountains) of Greek Colchis to the west and Iberia to the east.[28] It lies, therefore, between the Black Sea, Azerbaijan, Armenia, and Turkey. Colchis had already become incorporated into the Greek colonial expansion by the sixth century BC. The Iberian province became Romanized as an imperial protectorate in 65–64 BC. The eastern part of Georgia in the fourth century was under Sassanid influence and was often the scene of military clashes between them and the Roman imperial forces. It was the eastern Iberian territories where Christianity had an easier start. Georgian affairs in Iberia were strongly tied to Byzantium until the tenth century.

Fifth-century writer Rufinus gives us an account of Georgian ecclesiastical origins, which he heard firsthand from a member of the Georgian princely house named Bacurius, who was serving in the imperial administration in Palestine when he was there.[29] Rufinus's version of the Georgian evangelization relates it to the era of Emperor Constantine, when King Mirian (256–342) ruled over Georgia. It is possible that the Black Sea areas received missionaries first. Much later Georgian traditions claim that it was as a result of the missions of the apostle Andrew (though this is a tradition that might show dependence on the founding of the church of Constantinople, which claimed Andrew as their apostolic patron).[30] It is, of course, equally possible that missionaries came to Georgia from the adjacent regions of Syria and Armenia. Several aspects of particularized Georgian practice show a reliance on the liturgical traditions of the church of Jerusalem (which might of course simply denote an Armenian influence).[31] Precise facts about origins are difficult to discern.

The story of St. Nino the Illuminator was one the Georgian church treasured about its origins. Nino was one of those few female saints from antiquity given the title of "equal to the apostles." In her hagiographical *Vita*, dating to the fifth century, she was said to have been a refugee from the anti-Christian persecutions of the Armenian king Trdat and to have evangelized in Mtskheta, the royal city. "Casting

---

[28] In antique Christian sources, when one finds references to "Iberia," it has no reference to Spain.
[29] Rufinus, *Ecclesiastical History* 1.10-11.
[30] The eleventh-century chronicle *Kartlis Tskhovreba* (Life of Iberia) says this: "The holy apostle Andrew set off and reached Atskhuri, earlier called Sosangeti, which lies opposite Sakrisi. He stopped to rest at a place that was a sanctuary of idols and is now called the Old Church. The icon of the Holy Virgin was laid in a fortress there and gave off a great radiance that could be seen there." These Andrew traditions always relate how the apostle brought with him a miracle-working icon of the Virgin Mary and established it in a shrine at Samtskhe, the first Christian center.
[31] The church followed the (Jerusalemite) Liturgy of St. James until the tenth century, when the liturgies of Chrysostom and Basil started to predominate instead.

down idols" by her spiritual power, she converted the royal household to her faith, and the first Christian edifice was said to have been built in the grounds of the royal palace, the origin of one of the most venerated shrines in modern Georgia.

Bishop Patrophilos of Pityus (Georgian Bichvinta, in the northwest of Abkhazia) was present at the Council of Nicaea in 325. Rufinus tells us that bishop Ioane was consecrated for service in Georgia by Archbishop Alexander of Constantinople. Nevertheless, other leading bishops in Georgia, known as the *catholicoi* of Iberia, seem to have been consecrated by the patriarch of Antioch up to the time of *catholicos* Ioane III (744–760). The first *catholicos* known was present in the capital, Mcxeta, in the reign of King Vahtang (446–499), but the first Georgian-born *catholicos*, Saba I (523–552), is not witnessed until the sixth century. At the end of that same century the close relations that had hitherto obtained between the Georgians and the Armenians were severed over conflicting attitudes to the Council of Chalcedon. At first the Georgian and Armenian churches together agreed to accept and propagate the christological settlement of the *Henoticon* of Emperor Zeno. But in the time of *catholicos* Kirion II (595–610), Georgia sided with the Byzantine Chalcedonians and condemned the Monophysite party. A celebrated ninth-century tome in the early Georgian language, *On the Division Between Iberia and Armenia*, recounts the longstanding hostility that then followed between these Christian neighbors. Attempts to heal the divisions occurred at the Council of Grtila in 1046, and once more in the time of King David IV of Georgia (1089–1125), but they were unsuccessful.

Notable Georgian theologians include Gregory of Khandzta, who had a massive influence over Georgian culture and history, making a bond between the sense of nationhood and the monastic movement that still exists in this church. Monasticism had first come to Georgia after Syrian anti-Chalcedonian monks fled there from the purges inspired by the Byzantine Empire between 540 and 542. They found in Georgia a more tolerant and protective atmosphere, and monasticism took root, flourishing into a veritable golden age between the ninth and eleventh centuries. Gregory of Khandzta was a great reviver of monastic culture in the southeastern part of Georgia, around Tao-Klarjeti. He was a member of the princely house of Iberia, and having been ordained at an early age and destined for an episcopal office, he decided to flee instead and adopt the life of a hermit monk. The chain of monasteries that he founded is today known as the "Georgian Sinai." In the 830s Gregory was appointed archimandrite (head of all monks) of the twelve deserts of Georgia. He introduced to the Georgian monasteries the ascetical rule (*typikon*) of the St. Sabas monastery of Palestine, with elements mixed into it from the classical Constantinopolitan *typikon* of the Stoudium monastery.

It was partly due to Gregory's influence that the Georgian church started to consecrate its own *myron* instead of bringing it from Antioch (a sign of the independent or autocephalous status of the church).[32] A Georgian community of monks went to live on Mount Athos, the celebrated Byzantine monastic community in Greece, and there founded the "Monastery of the Iberians" (now called Iviron), which for many centuries, until 1343, was a renowned extension of Georgian ecclesiastic life but is now wholly Greek. In the sixth and seventh centuries Iberian ascetics possessed the monastery of St. Theodore the Tyro in Bethlehem. Between the eighth and tenth centuries many Iberian monks were active at the St. Sabas monastery, near Bethlehem, and also at the Great Lavra of St. Chariton. In the eleventh century the Iberian monastics, under the leadership of Prochorius, built the Monastery of the Holy Cross at Jerusalem. All of these Georgian monastic centers became powerhouses of Georgian theological and ascetical writing.

Many ancient churches from the fifth century onward survive in Georgia and comprise a collection of some of the finest Christian antiquities extant in the world. They often have a special form, with distinctive, horseshoe-shaped arches. The chief antique churches surviving are that of Bolnisi Sioni (fifth century), the Holy Cross at Mtskheta (sixth to seventh centuries), Tsromi and Bana (seventh century), Gurjanni and Vachnadziani All Saints (eighth to ninth centuries), and the Oshi, Khakhuli, Kumurdo, and Mokvi churches (tenth century).

## NUBIA

The ancient church of Nubia, which was once (excepting Ethiopia) the only sub-Saharan example of indigenous Christianity in the ancient world, is now more or less thoroughly forgotten. It is a sad example of a church that once flourished, in the patristic period, with a lively connection to both Byzantium and Ethiopia through the trade route of the Nile, by means of the gateway of Alexandria, but that collapsed in a short space of time and was wholly subsumed into an ascendant African Islam in the late middle ages. With Alexandria's fall to Islamic power in the seventh century, Christian Nubia was effectively cut off from easy communication with the wider Christian world, and its subsequent record was (as was the case with Ethiopia) one of constant battle for survival. The Nubians and Ethiopians both had an extraordinary number of warrior martyrs in their calendars, a testimony to the bitter experience of their church history. The Nubian church existed for some nine hundred years in all. It was composed of the three African Christian kingdoms of

---

[32] *Myron* refers to the sacred chrism required for major sacramental services and ceremonies such as consecrations of churches.

Nobatia, Makurrah (or Makuria), and Alwah (or Alodia) and occupied the fertile land around the Nile from the first cataract (Aswan) to the borders of Ethiopia. The territory is now largely located in northern Sudan.

The church's structured presence in Nubia began with a mission to Nobatia from Alexandria, sponsored by Empress Theodora in the sixth century. By 580 all three kingdoms had become extensively Christian, in line with their kings. The three kingdoms were allied with the Byzantine court of Justinian after their Christianization but belonged to the anti-Chalcedonian christological tradition, which Theodora herself seems to have advocated and patronized. The events of the mission to the Nobatian court in 542 are described by John of Ephesus the great missionary preacher (507–588). In the early eighth century the three kingdoms were united in the person of King Mercurius of Nobatia. The Arabic Christian text *History of the Patriarchs* describes the events briefly and also speaks of the Christian court's diplomatic relations with the Islamic caliphate at Baghdad and the emirate at Cairo. During this time Nubia served as an important political patron and defender of the Coptic Christians of Egypt, who were under Islamic rule. Between the ninth and tenth centuries the Nubian church enjoyed considerable peace and prosperity, but the encroaching power of Islam and its own vulnerable strategic position led to its invasion and rapid collapse in the fifteenth century. As quickly as it had arisen, so did it decline when its kings at Dongola adopted the Islamic religion.

In 1960, when the Aswan dam was going to inundate parts of northern Nubia, rapid excavations demonstrated the extent and quality of the Christian civilization that had once flourished there. Its main churches were at Dongola, Qasr Ibrim, and Fars (where wonderful tenth-century Afro-Byzantine frescoes have been discovered). Although its highest church leaders were appointed from Alexandria, the frescoes clearly show that they were sub-Saharan African archbishops, not, as had often been "presupposed," imported Coptic clergy from Egypt.

## ETHIOPIA

Ethiopia (sometimes called "India" by the patristic writers and "Abyssinia" by writers of the early twentieth century) is, like Armenia, one of the oldest of all Christian civilizations, but also one of the most remote and disconnected. Its geographical isolation, later exacerbated by the collapse of the Nubian church in the later Middle Ages (which cut it off from the corridor Nile passage down to Alexandria), was made even more critical by the relentlessly advancing pressures of Islam (moving into it from the immediate East). Eventually Islamic power would cut off the Ethiopians from their possession of the northeastern African coastal strip, forcing them into the highlands and in the process further "sealing off" their Christianity from the rest of the Christian world. The Byzantine forms are very important to the Ethiopians (who are generally classified today as one of the Oriental, that is, non-Chalcedonian, Orthodox churches), especially as these were mediated by the more or less constant presence of Coptic influence from the church of Alexandria (which provided Ethiopia's archbishops from the beginning until late in the twentieth century), but other influences marked the Ethiopian church in unique ways.

The pervasive influence of Jewish ritual practice in Christian Ethiopia has been much debated: whether it is an early medieval influence or represents an ancient and indigenous form of Christianity that never adopted the more stringent synagogue-church separation that entered Latin and Byzantine Christianity in the rest of the Mediterranean world. The Ethiopians, for example, observe both circumcision and baptism; both Shabbat and Sunday; and they also preserve books in their canon that were not only never accepted anywhere else but that more or less fell from existence everywhere else. The rediscovery in Ethiopia of the book of Enoch proved a major event for modern biblical scholarship.

The origins of the church are quite possibly traceable to the first century, although Ethiopian legends themselves place the foundation in the celebrated encounter between Solomon and the queen of Sheba, who is said to have brought the ark of the covenant back with her to the highlands of Ethiopia (these Solomonic legends tend to date only from the thirteenth century). The reference to the Ethiopian eunuch in Acts, however, is a more certain historical incident. The apostle Philip (Acts 8:26-39) is shown baptizing the chief eunuch of the administration of the Ethiopian *kandak*, or queen. The author of Acts inserts this story to symbolize the spread of the gospel to the farthest corners of the world. Already in Greek literature the Ethiopians had been classified as the gentlest but most remote people on earth. Philip's encounter however, is significant in that it suggests the first Christians of Ethiopia were constituted from the "God-fearers" who regularly traveled to Jerusalem and took part in the festal celebrations of the temple. The trade routes to the holy city from Ethiopia (the eastward, Indian, land, and sea route) were well traveled in antiquity, and there is no reason to doubt a historical connection from the earliest times, a connection that has remained a vital and dominant part of Ethiopian church life ever since: exemplified today by the manner in which they have retained, at Jerusalem, a small chapel at the rear of the Holy Sepulchre aedicule and a monastic community on the roof of the same church.

Historical traditions relate that the church was given a second foundation by St. Frumentius (c. 300–380).[33] Frumentius and his brother Aedesius had been Roman youths, trading in Ethiopia during a time of war, when they were captured and forced to serve the Ethiopian king Ezana. Their rise in the court led to the adoption of Frumentius by St. Athanasius the Great, who ordained him bishop when Frumentius visited Alexandria and commissioned him to found churches in Ethiopia and institute services in the Alexandrian manner.[34] In the late fifth century Ethiopian traditions also start to speak of the arrival of the "nine saints." These appear to have been wandering Syrian missionaries and monks. Their impact on the Ethiopian church was inestimable, giving it the strongly monastic, ascetical, and apocalyptic character it bears to this day. These "third founders" established Christianity in a way that coincided with the rise of the Christian king Caleb. He rose to power by destroying the armies of the African-Jewish king Dhu Nuwas, who had slaughtered Christians in his dominions. Caleb's dynasty instituted Aksum as a center of Christian civilization and inaugurated the first great period of the church's flourishing. During this era the Bible and many patristic writings were translated into Ge'ez. After that time the rising power of Islam overshadowed the church and pushed it into a slow retreat into obscurity. The numerous wars and raids that devastated Ethiopian Christianity played havoc with its written sources; but there was also always a preference for the oral tradition, which today makes ancient Ethiopian Christianity difficult to reconstruct around its many expansive legends.

Clearer knowledge of the church's history only becomes available again after the rise of the Zagwe dynasty of kings (1137–1270), one of whom (King Lalibela) is thought to have ordered the construction of the amazing rock-carved churches of Roha-Lalibela. In this later period of the thirteenth to fourteenth centuries, another period of Christian expansion, led by monastic missionary Tekla Haymanot, extended the church to the south and began a further period of translations of Christian texts from Arabic, a time when many Western sources entered the literature, most notably causing a great upsurge of devotion to the mother of God.

The church's later history was marked by a cycle of encounters with Portuguese Catholicism and destructive wars with Islam. Through the church's historic outposts at Jerusalem and Alexandria, the higher Ethiopian clergy always managed to keep an eye on developments elsewhere in the Christian world while maintaining the distinctive character of their ancient traditions. The Ethiopian church shares a profound patristic heritage with the Copts and the Orthodox. Like the Copts, it rejects

---

[33]Rufinus, *Church History* 1.9-10; Socrates, *Church History* 1.19; Sozomen, *Church History* 2.24; Theodoret, *Church History* 1.22.
[34]Cf. Athanasius, *Apology to Constantius* 31.

the christological tradition of the Council of Chalcedon in favor of the single divine-human reality of the Christ (Miaphysitism).

## SLAVIA ORTHODOXA

Christianity came late to the Slavic lands, at the end of the first millennium. Byzantine monastic missionaries started extensive preaching campaigns, ordinations, and church building between the ninth and tenth centuries. This was an establishment of the church that had been initiated by earlier missions inspired by the brother saints Cyril and Methodius (who had given the Slavs a language built out of Greek letters—so named Cyrillic) but that was greatly assisted and developed by the conversion of Prince Vladimir at Kiev in 988 and his ordering of his people to be baptized with him in the river Dnieper. This was an event that the Russian Orthodox church takes as its originating moment, though there are also older claims that the apostle Andrew first came here as part of his missionizing travels. Vladimir was adopted by the Byzantine emperors, and the church established under his control was first led by Byzantine Metropolitans, though Slavonic was used as the official liturgical language from the earliest times, and increasingly the higher and lower clergy all became Russified.

In the early eleventh century Athonite forms of monasticism (though with a particularly local stress on severe ascetical forms, such as immuring or self-entombment as a penitential practice among hermits) came to Kiev. The hermit St. Theodosius (Feodisy) of Pechersk laid the foundations of a massive colony of cave dwellers along the banks of the River Dnieper (now the Kiev Pechersky Lavra). It was further organized by his disciple Antony between 1062 and 1074. Monasticism among the early Rus spread quickly and vibrantly, giving the Slavic church a deeply monastic, disciplined, and mystical character. Russian monasticism recycled the spiritual traditions of the ancient desert, mediated through the medieval Byzantine mystical theologies, and developed a large body of later medieval spiritual practice of their own. By the twelfth century there were seventeen monasteries in Kiev alone.

The period of conflict with the Mongols, from the middle of the thirteenth century onward, produced many princely Christian martyrs and gave the church deep traditions of the holiness of suffering (princely passion bearers). Some of the great early saints of the country were Sergius and Germanus, who founded the monastery of Valamo, on Lake Ladoga; and St. Sergius of Radonezh (1314–1392), who founded the central monastery of the country, at Sergei Posad (Sergey's village) outside Moscow. When the Muscovite princes moved the center of Russian church affairs to their own princely capital, in the early fourteenth century, the Kievan foundations were sidelined in one sense, but actually thereby also rose to become the classical standard of all of "Holy Russia" and gave a national sense of identity as "Slavia Orthodoxa."

Russian church traditions were staunchly Byzantine in form and content. After the collapse of an independent imperium at Constantinople in 1453, the Muscovite princes, known as the tsars, declared Moscow to be the "Third Rome," and until the Russian revolution in the early twentieth century they stood as the main protectors of Eastern Christianity.[35] The archbishops of Moscow eventually assumed the title of patriarch and governed (as they do even to this day) massive numbers of the faithful.

## A SHORT READER

***Syrian Christianity 1: Acts of Thomas 27 (third century).*** And the apostle rose up and gave them the seal. And the Lord was revealed to them by a voice, which said: "Peace be with you brethren." And they heard his voice only, but his image they did not see, for they had not yet received the additional sealing of the seal.[36] And the apostle then took the oil and poured it upon their heads and anointed and chrismated them, and began to say:

> Come, holy name of the Christ, which is above every name.
> Come, power of the Most High, and perfect compassion.
> Come, charism of the Most High.
> Come, compassionate mother.
> Come, communion of Man.
> Come, she who reveals hidden mysteries.
> Come, mother of the seven houses, so that thy rest may be in the eighth house.
> Come, elder of the five members: mind, thought, reflection, consideration, reason;
> So as to communicate with these young men.
> Come, Holy Spirit, and cleanse their inner selves and their hearts,
> And give them the additional seal,
> In the name of the Father and Son and Holy Spirit.

And when they were sealed, there appeared unto them a young man holding a lighted torch, so that their own lamps became dim at the approach of its radiant light. But he then went ahead and could no longer be seen by them. And the apostle said to the Lord: "Your light, O Lord, cannot be contained by us, for we are not able to bear it. It is too great for our sight." And when the dawn rose and

---

[35] *Tsar* is a form of the Byzantine title *caesar*.
[36] Chrismation following baptism.

morning came, then he broke bread and made them partakers of the Eucharist of Christ. And they were glad and rejoiced. And many others, who also believed, were added to their number, and came into the refuge of the Savior.

***Syrian Christianity 2: Pseudo-Macarius,*** **Spiritual Homilies *1.2, 4, 12; 2.5; 4.13, 16.*** The soul that is found worthy to participate in the Holy Spirit and be illuminated by his radiance, and the ineffable glory of his beauty, becomes his throne and his dwelling place. Such a soul becomes all light, all face, all eye [as in Ezekiel's vision: Ezek 1:4–2:1]. The soul becomes entirely covered with the spiritual eyes of light; nothing in it is left in shadow. When the soul becomes totally radiant and covered with the ineffable beauty of the glory of the light of Christ, it comes to share in the very life of the divine Spirit to such perfection that it is changed into the very chamber and throne of God. The souls of the righteous become heavenly lights, as the Lord himself told his apostles: "You are the light of the world" (Mt 5:14). And it was he who first transformed them in light, that through them he might enlighten the cosmos. If you have become the throne of God, if the heavenly charioteer has ascended within you, and your soul has become as a single spiritual eye and has become completely luminous; and if you have been clothed in light ineffable, and fed from spiritual delights, and drunk from living water, and all your inner life has been tested and proven in hope; then in all truth you have started to live the eternal life, even in this present age, and your soul has found its rest in God. The Lord clothes his chosen souls in the garments of the ineffable light of his kingdom: the garments of faith, hope, love, joy, and peace; the garments of goodness and kindness and all comparable things. They are divine garments, pulsating with light and life, and they bring us peace that passes all description; for God is himself love and joy, and peace, and kindness, and goodness, and this is exactly how he renews our very being in his grace. When a soul is full of expectant longing, and full of faith and love, God considers it worthy to receive "the power from on high" (Acts 1:8; 2:1-3), which is the heavenly love of the Spirit of God and the heavenly fire of immortal life; and when this happens the soul truly enters into the beauty of all love and is liberated from its last bonds of evil. Let us strive to seek after that supreme good, which the Lord spoke to us about, and let us desire this with great longing so that we may enter into the ineffable love of the Spirit, which St. Paul advised us to strive after when he told us to "Seek after love" (1 Cor 14:1). In this way we shall be turned from our hardness of heart by the right hand of the Most High and be made worthy to come into the day, our spirits finding their rest, and their deepest delight, when they are wounded by the love of God. For the Lord greatly loves humankind and is deeply moved whenever a human being turns in their whole self, wholly to him.

***Syrian Christianity 3: Sadhona the Persian (Abba Martyrios),*** **The Book of Perfection *2.4.7; 2.4.9* (seventh century).** Those who possess love, that perfection of the commandments, become the dwelling place of the Trinity and can see within their heart the vision of God. Blessed is that heart that has deserved to see this sight; blessed is the heart that has become the home of love and in which the Godhead has come to dwell. Such a person, even in this present age, is living in the kingdom of heaven. Blessed are you, O heart that is lucid, the dwelling place of the deity. Blessed are you, O heart that is pure, and that beholds the hidden essence. Blessed are you, flesh and blood, the dwelling place of the consuming fire. Blessed are you, mortal body made from dust, home of the fire that sets the ages alight. It is truly a matter for wonder and astonishment that he, before whom even the heavens are not pure, and who fills even his great angels with awe, should think to take delight and pleasure in a heart of flesh, one that is filled with love for him and so has become large enough and pure enough to be his dwelling place. Let us embrace the burning fire of God's love within our hearts, for the heart's purity is born from our closeness to him. It is only by unfailing and focused gazing that the spirit gravitates to God, but when the luminous ray of the simple eye of the soul is flooded with those intense rays of light that flash down on us from on high, then it is that the fire of God flares up in a great blaze within our hearts.

***Syrian Christianity 4: Mar Isaac of Nineveh,*** **Spiritual Homilies *14* (seventh century).** I shall tell you something, and I do not want you to laugh at it, for I am speaking the truth. Do not doubt my words, for the ones who passed them down to me were true. So, even though you should hang yourself by your eyelids before God, do not think you have attained anything exceptional by your manner of life you have arrived at until you have accomplished tears. For until you have tears your hidden self remains in the service of the world; in other words, you are still leading the life of those who dwell in the world, and you perform the works of God with the outward man. But the inward man still remains without fruit; for his fruit only begins with tears. When you finally attain to the domain of tears, then know this—that your mind has left the prison of this world and has set its foot on the highway of the new age, and has begun to breathe that other air, new and wondrous. Once it has done this it shall begin to shed tears, for the birth pangs of our new, infant state are on you. Indeed, grace, that common mother of us all, has hastened to give mystical birth to the divine image in your soul, for the sake of the light of the age to come. And when the time of its delivery has arrived, the mind at once begins to be stirred by something of that other age, just as the tiny breath of a baby starts to draw inside its body when it is born. But since the human mind cannot bear what is strange and unusual to it, just so it straightway sets the body to lamentation: a weeping mingled with the sweetness of honey. To the extent the inner babe grows up, so too there is an increase in the gift of tears. But this form of tears I am speaking of is not the only one that happens to contemplative monks from time to time. This consolation, which comes to us at different times, also belongs to every person who dwells with God in stillness. Sometimes it comes when a person finds themselves in the divine vision of the mind, and sometimes it comes through the words of Scripture, and sometimes in the conversation of prayer. But what I am really speaking about here is that form of tears that belongs to the one who weeps without ceasing, day and night. Whosoever has discovered the truth of these things, in all accuracy and veracity, will have found it in stillness. The eyes of such people will become like fountains of water for a period of two years or more, for this time of transition—that is, the mystical transition. But after this they shall enter into a state of peacefulness of mind, and out of this peace of mind they shall come to that rest that the apostle Paul speaks of, but only in part, and to the extent that nature can endure it. From the basis of that peaceful stillness the Holy Spirit will begin to reveal heavenly things to that person, and God shall dwell within him, and raise up the fruits of the Spirit inside him. From this he shall perceive, however dimly, and albeit only in symbols, the change that his nature shall one day receive at the renewal of all things. So I have written these things down for you, as a memento, and as a source of profit for myself, and for every person who happens on this book. I have spoken about what I myself have understood from the divine vision of the Scriptures and from the mouths of those who spoke the truth, as well as a little from personal experience. I hope that these things will be of help to me through the prayers of those who can profit by them. Believe me, I have taken no little trouble in setting them down.[37]

### *Syrian Christianity 5: Patriarch Timothy I of Bagdad,* **Apology for Christianity *(781).*** And our caliph said to me: "How can the eternal one be born in time?" And I answered: "It is not in his eternity that he was born of Mary, O our

---

[37] Isaac went blind in his old age and wrote with great difficulty thereafter.

caliph, but rather in his temporality and in his humanity." And our caliph said to me: "In that case there must be two distinct beings, if one is eternal and God from God as you have said, and the other is temporal. And so, it must follow, the latter is just a simple man born of Mary." And to this I made reply: "Christ is not two beings, O caliph, nor is he two Sons, but the Son and the Christ are one.[38] There are in him two natures, one of which belongs to the Word, and the other that is from Mary, and it was this one that clothed itself with the divine Word." And the caliph answered: "Then they must be two; one that is created and made, and the other, which is uncreated and not made." And I said to him: "We do not deny the duality of natures, O caliph, nor their mutual relations, but we profess that both of them together constitute one Christ and Son." And to this the caliph replied: "If he is one he cannot be two; and if he is two, he is not one." And I replied to him: "A man is one, while in reality he is also two: one in his composition and individuality, and two in the distinction found between his soul and his body; the former is invisible and spiritual, and the latter visible and corporeal. Our own caliph, together with the insignia of his dominion, is also one king and not two, however great may be the difference that separates him from his uniforms. In the same way the Word of God, together with the vesture of humanity which he put on from Mary, is one and the same Christ, and not two, although there remains in him the natural difference existing between the divine Word and his humanity. So the fact that he is one does not preclude the fact that he is also two. The very same Christ and Son is indeed known and confessed as one, and the fact that he is also two does not imply confusion or mixture, because the known attributes of his natures are preserved in one person (*parsopa*) of the Son and Christ." And our caliph replied to me: "Even in this argument you cannot save yourself from duality in Christ." So I demonstrated the fact to him through another illustration and said: "The tongue and the word are one with the voice in which they are clothed, in a way that the two are not two words nor two tongues, but one word, together with the tongue and the voice, so that they are all together designated by one tongue along with the word and the voice, and in this matter we do not think of two emissions. This is also the case with the divine Word. He is one with his humanity, while preserving the distinction between his invisibility and his visibility, and that between his divinity and his humanity. Even so, Christ is one in his sonship, yet two in the attributes of his natures."

---

[38] Demonstrating that the so-called Nestorian church did not sustain the theory of two separate personalities in Christ, as it has often erroneously been caricatured as doing.

***Armenian Christianity: Gregory of Narek,*** **The Book of Lamentations**, ***Prayer 1.1-2 (951–1003).*** I offer to you the sounds of a sighing heart, its sobs and mournful cries, O seer of secrets, placing the fruits of my wavering mind as a savory sacrifice on the coals of my grieving soul to be sent up to you from the censer of my will. Compassionate Lord, breathe in this offering and look more favorably on it than on a more sumptuous sacrifice that could have been offered with rich smoke. Please find this poor string of words acceptable. Do not turn away your face in scorn. May this unsolicited gift reach you, this sacrifice of words from the deep, mystery-filled chamber of my heart, consumed in flames and fueled by the gift of grace I may have within me. As I pray, do not let these petitions be irksome to you, Almighty One, as once were the raised hands of Jacob, whose irreverence was rebuked by Isaiah, and do not let them seem like the impudence of Babylon the psalmist criticized (Ps 72). But let these words be acceptable in your sight, as once were the fragrant offerings in the tabernacle at Shiloh raised up by David on his return from captivity to be the resting place for the ark of the covenant, which is a symbol for the restoration of my lost soul. For your stern judgment echoes mightily in the valley of retribution; contradictory impulses in my soul brace for battle like clashing hosts. Crowds of thoughts strike each other, sword against armor, evil against good, ensnaring me for death, as in former times, when your grace had not yet rescued me—that grace of Christ, which Paul, chosen of apostles, taught was greater than the law of Moses. For as the Scripture says, "The day of the Lord is upon us," and in the narrow valley of Jehoshaphat on the banks of the River Kidron, those small battlegrounds foreshadow on this earth victory in the life to come. Thus, the kingdom of God in a visible form has come already, rightly convicting me of wrongdoing worse than the Edomites, Philistines, and other barbarians—wrongs that brought down the hand of God on them. And whereas their sentences were measured in years, my transgressions merit punishment without end. As the prophet and the parable teller warned, the dungeon and shackles are already at my threshold to show me here and now the state of my eternal disgrace. Only you, who are the atoner for all humankind, can work the miracle to make life possible again for a soul so cast down by doubt; you who are exalted beyond all telling in your infinite and exalted glory, forever and ever. Amen.

***Georgian Christianity: Life of St. Nino.*** One summer day, on July 20, the king went on a hunting trip towards Mukhran. On that day the invisible enemy, the devil, tempted him by reviving in his heart the love of fire-worship and idols. So the king said to four of his advisors: "We have behaved unfittingly towards our gods by standing idle in their worship, and allowing the Christian magi to preach their doctrine in this land, for their miracles are caused by sorcery. I have now decided to wipe out all those who believe in the cross unless they agree to venerate the victory-giving gods of Georgia. I shall urge my wife, Nana, to repent and abandon her faith in the cross. If not, I shall forget my love for her, and she shall perish along with the others." His companions, strongly prejudiced on this matter, applauded his decision. Now it came to pass that the king had passed out beyond the limits of Mukhran and came to the high hill of Tkhoti, from which he could see Caspi and Uplis-tsikhe. When he reached the top, at midday, the sun became darkened and it turned as black as deepest night. All the land was wrapped in darkness, and the members of the hunting party lost touch with one another. The king was left alone, anxious and afraid. He wandered around on the hill until in his fear and anxiety he decided to stand still in one place, devoid of hope of being rescued. Then he began to reflect within himself. "All things considered, I have called on my own gods and found no comfort there. Now I wonder if the crucified one, whom Nino preaches, could save me from my troubles? O God of Nino, light up this darkness for me and I will confess your name. I will set up a wooden cross and venerate it and build a place to pray in, and I shall obey Nino and accept the faith of the Romans." No sooner than he had said these words, than it became light, and the sun shone once more in all its splendour. Then the King got down from his horse and stretched out his arms to the east towards heaven and said: "You are a God above all gods, and Lord above all lords, you the God whom Nino proclaims. Now I have understood that you desire my salvation, and I am filled with joy, blessed Lord, to draw near to you. I will set up a cross on this spot so that your name may be praised, and this wonder commemorated forever."[39]

### *Ethiopian Christianity 1: "The Harp of Glory."*

> My Lady Mary, at night, and at the dawn of day, I bow before you,
> Offering praise to that womb which contained the awesome radiance of God.
> My Queen, humble in heart, and merciful of soul,
> Raise me up from the sleep of indolence, to be a herald of your name.
> Make me zealous and skilful in the cause of your praise,
> Cast down upon me the great radiance of the light of your loveliness,
> Let me never be cut off or exiled from your peaceful court.
> My Lady Mary,

---

[39] D. M. Lang, *Lives and Legends of the Georgian Saints* (Crestwood, NY: St. Vladimir's Seminary Press, 1976), 29-30.

Gate of Peace from which the perfume of the spirit of life issues forth,
Which no wintry wind or rust can ever mar,
You are the House of Shem, which fell to him by lot, before his other brothers.[40]
You are that in which his father Noah's blessing was made effective.[41]
You are the Oak of Mamre where Abraham dwelt as an old man [Gen 13:18]

And whose shade contained the threefold God,[42]
When he made covenant with him, and all his seed thereafter [Gen 13:15].

You are that Fragrant Mountain of Isaac
Which produced the ram caught by its horns in the thorn bush [Gen 22:13].

You are the Golden Ladder, on which the angels of the Most High ascended and descended, [Gen 28:12]

Which Jacob saw when he was in flight from his brother.
O Virgin, holy shrine of the heavenly God,
You are the Mount of Horeb in which his splendor appeared,
And on which His very feet were placed, [Deut 5:2, Ex 17:6][43]

When He made his law known to Jacob and his judgment to Israel [Ps 147:8].

You are the Field of Araunah[44] in which David offered a sacrifice of salvation to his Maker,
When all his people were laid low under devastating plague [2 Sam 24].[45]

You are the Temple of Solomon whose inner chambers were filled with the glory of God,
On that occasion when the priests were unable to perform their service [1 Kings 8:11].[46]

---

[40]Jubilees 8:10–9:15; Shem (in the ark) is a type of Christ in the Virgin's womb.
[41]Mary is the ark of salvation.
[42]The revelation of the three angels at the oak of Mamre in Genesis (who are alternately designated as "lords" and "Lord") is taken as a type of the revelation of one God who is three. Containing in her womb one of the Trinity, who is inseparable from the other divine persons, Mary is thereby (paradoxically) the one who contains the uncontainable Trinity. In Byzantine tradition this is referred to as the *Theotokos Platytera* (the Mother of God "Wider-than-the Heavens").
[43]The Sinai theophany is a type of Mary's overshadowing by the Holy Spirit and the incarnation within her of the Word of God.
[44]David bought Araunah's threshing floor to be the site of his sacrifice to God. It was outside the original city of David and later became the site of the temple of Solomon.
[45]After David's sacrifice the plague was lifted from Israel. The episode becomes a type of how Mary, as temple of the divine presence, brings salvation to the world in the incarnation.
[46]The cloud of glory is a type of Mary, *Shekinah* of the presence of the Word.

You are that Cluster of Figs that became a healing poultice for Hezekiah
[2 Kings 20:7]

When his days had come to an end, yet God added years to his life.
O beautiful lady, see how I have compared you to all manner of good and lovely things,
For the roots of the tree of your love are entwined within my heart.[47]

**Ethiopian Christianity 2: Liturgical Ektenie, Ethiopian Litany from Morning Prayers.** O you who are far removed from all anger, abundant in mercy and righteous in deed, accept our daily prayer and our supplication, and accept our penitence and our humility and our liturgical service before your holy and heavenly ark, and before your holy, heavenly, immaculate, and spotless altar. Make us worthy to hear the word of the gospel and keep your commandments and your law and testimony, and bless us so that we may bear fruit, remaining not as single but increasing thirty, sixty, and an hundredfold through Jesus Christ our Lord.

Remember, Lord, the sick among your people, and visit them in your mercy and heal them in your compassion.

Remember, Lord, our fathers and brothers who have traveled and who have gone far to trade, and bring them back to their dwellings in safety and peace.

Remember, Lord, the dew of the air and the fruits of the earth; bless them and keep them without loss.

Remember, Lord, the falling of the rains and the waters and the rivers, and bless them.

Remember, Lord, the plants and the seeds and the fruits of the fields every year, and bless them and make them abundant.

Remember, Lord, the safety of your own holy church and all the cities and countries of our orthodox fathers, the apostles.

Remember, Lord, the safety of humankind and of beast, and also of me, your sinful servant.

Remember, Lord, our fathers and mothers, brothers and sisters who have fallen asleep and gone to their rest in the orthodox faith.

Remember, Lord, those who have presented to you this offering, and

---

[47] Strophe 1 of an alphabetical hymn to the Virgin Mary from the Middle Ages. Full text in J. A. McGuckin, trans., *The Harp of Glory: Enzhira Sebhat* (Crestwood, NY: St. Vladimir's Seminary Press, 2010).

those from whom they have brought these gifts; grant them a good recompense in heaven and comfort them all in their distress.

Remember, Lord, the captives among your people, and bring them again in peace to their dwellings.

Remember, Lord, the afflicted and the distressed.

Remember, Lord, the Christian catechumens among your people; show them your pity and have mercy on them, and establish them in the right faith. Banish from their hearts all remnants of idolatry; confirm your law within their hearts and your commandments so that they may fear your righteousness and your holy ordinances; and so that they may know the power of the word in which they have been instructed. And in the appointed time make them all worthy of the new birth and for the remission of their sins, and prepare them to be an ark for the Holy Spirit.

Remember, Lord, your servants, the poor who are under oppression; have pity on them and establish them in the right faith, and make them a dwelling place of the Holy Spirit through spiritual joy and the love of their neighbor, through your only begotten Son our Lord and our God and our Savior Jesus Christ, through whom to you, with him and with the Holy Spirit, be glory and dominion, both now and ever, and world without end. Amen.

## FURTHER READING

### Syria

Baker, A. "The Gospel of Thomas and the Syriac Liber Graduum." *New Testament Studies* 12 (1965–1966): 49-55.

Brock, S. *The Luminous Eye: The Spiritual World Vision of Saint Ephrem.* Collegeville, MN: Liturgical Press, 1992.

———. *Syriac Fathers on Prayer and the Spiritual Life.* Collegeville, MN: Liturgical Press, 1988.

Brock, S., and S. A. Harvey. *Holy Women of the Syrian Orient.* Berkeley: University of California Press, 1987.

Klijn, A. F. J. *The Acts of Thomas.* Supplement to Novum Testamentum 5. Leiden: Brill, 1962.

McCullough, W. S. *A Short History of Syriac Christianity to the Rise of Islam.* Chico, CA: Scholars Press, 1982.

Murray, R. *Symbols of Church and Kingdom: A Study in Early Syriac Tradition.* London: T&T Clark, 1975.

Quispel, G. "The Syrian Thomas and the Syrian Macarius." *Vigilae Christianae* 18 (1964): 226-35.

Stewart, C. *Working the Earth of the Heart: The Messalian Controversy in History, Texts and Language to AD 431.* Oxford: Oxford University Press, 1991.

Voobus, A. *History of Asceticism in the Syrian Orient.* Louvain: Secrétariat du Corpus Scriptorum Christianorum Orientalium, 1958.

Wright, W. *A Short History of Syriac Literature.* London: A&C Black, 1894.

### China

Baker, K. *A History of the Orthodox Church in China, Korea, and Japan.* Lewiston, NY: Edwin Mellen, 2006.

Barrett, D., et al., eds. *World Christian Encyclopedia.* Vol. 1. 2nd ed. Oxford: Oxford University Press, 2001.

Jenkins, P. *The Lost History of Christianity: The Thousand-Year Golden Age of the Church in the Middle East, Africa, and Asia; And How It Died.* New York: HarperOne, 2008.

Bays, D. H. *A New History of Christianity in China.* Chichester, UK: Wiley Blackwell, 2012.

Foret, A. "The Edict of 638 Allowing the Diffusion of Christianity in China." In *L'Inscription Nestorienne de Si-ngan-fou, Kyoti,* ed. P. Pelliot, 349-73. Scuola de studi sull'Asia Orientale. Paris: Collège de France, Institut des Hautes Études Chinoises, 1996.

Foster, J. *The Church of the T'ang Dynasty.* London: SPCK, 1939.

Tang, L. *A Study of the History of Nestorian Christianity in China and Its Literature in Chinese: Together with a New English Translation of the Dunhuang Nestorian Documents.* New York: Peter Lang, 2003.

### Arabia

Bagatti, B., and C. Pappalardo. "Arabia." In *Encyclopedia of Ancient Christianity,* ed. A. di Berardino, 205-9. Downers Grove, IL: InterVarsity Press, 2014.

Butler, H. C. *Early Churches in Syria.* Princeton, NJ: Princeton University Press, 1929.

Devreesse, R. "Le Christianisme dans le province d'Arabie." *Vivre et Penser* (1942): 112-13.

Griffith, S. H. *The Church in the Shadow of the Mosque: Christians and Muslims in the World of Islam.* Princeton, NJ: Princeton University Press, 2008.

Shahid, I. *Byzantium and the Arabs in the Fifth Century.* Washington, DC: Catholic University of America Press, 1995.

———. *Byzantium and the Arabs in the Fourth Century.* Washington, DC: Catholic University of America Press, 1984.

Waddington, W. H. *Inscriptions Grecques et Latines de la Syrie.* Paris, 1870.

### India

Neill, S. C. *History of Christianity in India.* Vol. 1, *The Beginnings to AD 1707.* Cambridge: Cambridge University Press, 1984.

———. *The Story of the Christian Church in India and Pakistan.* Grand Rapids: Eerdmans, 1970.

### Armenia

Arpee, L. *A History of Armenian Christianity from the Beginning to Our Own Times.* New York: Armenian Missionary Association of America, 1946.

Grousset, P. *Histoire del Arménie*. Paris: Payot, 1947.

Sarkissian, K. *A Brief Introduction to Armenian Christian Literature*. 2nd ed. Bergenfield, London: Faith Press, 1974.

———. *The Council of Chalcedon and the Armenian Church*. London: Armenian Church Prelacy Press, 1965.

Thomson, R. W., ed. *Moses Khorenats'i: History of the Armenians*. Cambridge, MA: Harvard University Press, 1978.

### *Georgia*

Gigineishvili, L. *The Platonic Theology of Ioane Petritsi*. Piscataway, NJ: Gorgias Press, 2007.

Grdzelidze, T. "The Patriarchal Orthodox Church of Georgia." In *The Encyclopedia of Eastern Orthodox Christianity*, ed. J. A. McGuckin, 252-63. Oxford: Wiley Blackwell, 2010.

Haas, C. "Mountain Constantines: The Christianization of Aksum and Iberia." *Journal of Late Antiquity* 1, no. 1 (Spring 2008): 101-26.

Kekelidze, K. *History of Georgian Literature*. Vol. 1. Tbilisi: Tbilisi University Press, 1960.

Lang, D. M. *Lives and Legends of the Georgian Saints*. Crestwood, NY: St. Vladimir's Seminary Press, 1976.

Lerner, C., trans. *The Wellspring of Georgian Historiography: The Early Medieval Historical Chronicle, the Conversion of Kartli and the Life of St. Nino*. London: Bennet & Bloom, 2004.

Licheli, V. "St. Andrew in Samtskhe—Archaeological Proof?" In *Ancient Christianity in the Caucasus, Iberica, Caucasia*, ed. T. Mgaloblishvili, 1:199-212. Richmond, VA: Curzon, 1998.

Nutsubidze, T., C. B. Horn, and B. Lourié, eds. *Georgian Christian Thought and Its Cultural Context*. Leiden: Brill, 2014.

### *Nubia*

Adams, W. Y. *Nubia: Corridor to Africa*. Princeton, NJ: Princeton University Press, 1977.

Grillmeier, A. *Christ in Christian Tradition*. Vol. 2, part 4, *The Church of Alexandria with Nubia and Ethiopia After 451*, 263-94. London: Blackwell, 1996.

Shinnie, P. L. "Christian Nubia." In *The Cambridge History of Africa*, ed. J. D. Fage, 2:556-88. Cambridge: Cambridge University Press, 1978.

Vantini, J. *The Excavations at Faras: A Contribution to the History of Christian Nubia*. Bologna: Nigrizia, 1970.

### *Ethiopia*

Grillmeier, A. *Christ in Christian Tradition*. Vol. 2, part 4, *The Church of Alexandria with Nubia and Ethiopia After 451*, 293-392. London: Blackwell, 1996.

Harden, J. M. *An Introduction to Ethiopic Christian Literature*. London: SPCK, 1926.

Hastings, A. *The Church in Africa: 1450–1950*. Oxford: Oxford University Press, 1994.

Heldman, M., ed. *African Zion: The Sacred Art of Ethiopia*. New Haven, CT: Yale University Press, 1993.

Hyatt, H. M. *The Church of Abyssinia.* London: Luzac, 1928.

**Slavia Orthodoxa**

Pospielovski, D. *The Orthodox Church in the History of Russia.* Crestwood, NY: St. Vladimir's Seminary Press, 1998.

Zernov, N. *The Russians and Their Church.* London: SPCK, 1945.

# THE RISE OF THE ECUMENICAL CONCILIAR SYSTEM IN THE FIFTH TO SIXTH CENTURIES

## THE CHRISTIAN PATRIARCHATES

The imperial church demanded a revision of earlier, simpler patterns of governance. The earlier polity of Christian churches, more and more commonly visible after the late second century, gave to each bishop in his own diocese a qualified monarchical authority that could not be countermanded except by the collaborative vote of the other adjacent bishops of his region in the context of a specially assembled provincial synod.[1] These synods did meet, and indeed after the Council of Nicaea in 325 they were mandated as a regular part of worldwide Christian governance. At first they had met only for resolutions of crises. The principle of the bishop as highest ruling agent within the local diocese was maintained in order to defend the ecclesiological principle that local churches were not "part of a whole," such as limited branches of a corporation, but were in fact the whole in each local instance. The bishop with his presbyters, deacons, and faithful thus was held to represent the church of Christ in all its totality.

This was the first ecclesiological principle we find articulated in ancient Christianity, and the second, which flowed from it, was the manner of securing the communion of churches. This was seen to be a very lively concept, appearing in the creed of Nicaea as the formal affirmation that the church was "one, holy, catholic, and apostolic." Oneness and catholicity were the twin forces that represented its local completeness and its universal (*katholike*) communion. This communion was secured in the earliest stages of church history less by formal agreement than by the international observance of "good practice." Churches that were in contact with one

---

[1]This monarchial authority claimed a share in the authority of Christ himself over his church as a *proprium* of their office.

another (by visitations of clergy, appeals cases, or movements of merchants) sent back reports on what each had seen, and good practice spread in terms of sacred texts received (the growth of the canon of agreed Scriptures), forms of worship observed (the establishment of a common liturgical rite), and patterns of offices and administration. The local bishops also sent letters to one another from early times (*eirenika*, or letters of peace) to secure lines of communication and communion with neighboring sister churches. But soon the concept of the provincial synod became established, as much to deal with regular business as crisis management, and from that time onward the office of the chairman of the synod grew in importance.

The notion of the archbishop (*archiepiskopos*) had emerged, the one who had governance duties and therefore rights over the other bishops of his province. This system, rising up secondarily, never ousted the more ancient principle that the individual monarchical bishop was the ruler in all ecclesiastical matters of his diocese, but it certainly served to put common-policy delimiters around it. The antique idea of the primatial role of the *episkopos* appealed to special providential charisms given by God to his anointed leader, such that the bureaucracy of administration ought not to overrule them; and this is why in ancient times it was regarded as something scandalous for a bishop to resign his office or seek to retire; it was seen as a lifelong, total commitment to the church under God's eye.

Archbishops were at first chosen from the senior bishops of a region, or those who represented the highest reputation for holiness and learning. But soon enough the civil system of governance started to influence matters of such polity. This principle is already seen at work in the canons of the Council of Nicaea, where the governance zones of the churches are mandated to follow those of the Roman civil imperium, for simplicity's sake. Indeed, it is the civil political division of the empire, the "diocese," that determines what the local division into episcopal areas of governance should be. The word *diocese* now is a peculiarly ecclesiastical one, but it was a civil political term in its origins. The acting archbishop was soon established to be not the oldest or most venerable cleric of an area (that must have been problematic, insofar as the oldest and most pious person is not necessarily the most efficient leader of a conference) but rather the incumbent of the largest metropolis city of that province: the local capital, as it were. Hence he came to be called also the metropolitan archbishop.

Before this system came fully into place throughout the Eastern and Western churches, it was also the case that certain supercities, not just metropolises but real capital cities of vast areas of the empire, had risen to a great preeminence in imperial political and cultural affairs. It was natural, therefore, that the bishops who occupied these great sees came to possess a sphere of influence, far greater than any ordinary bishop or local metropolitan. These supercities, active from the very beginning of the Christian movement, were Rome, Alexandria, and Antioch. They were the pivots of imperial culture. One might also add in Beirut and Athens as great school cities (later also the Christian school at Caesarea Maritima in Palestine); but nothing could compare to the massive orbits of influence that the three great cities possessed. They also had a deeply formative influence on the shape of the emerging ecumenical (international) Christian tradition. The bishops of these supercities soon emerged as superbishops themselves. Their synods were often larger than anyone else's, and thus acting as metropolitan archbishops their formal sway was greater.

By the fourth century very large territories of the church looked to each of these cities as its cultural and theological "mother church." All of the West tended to look to Rome. Everywhere Latin was spoken would always hold up Rome as its last court of appeal and center of excellence in all ecclesiastical matters. All of the Syriac-speaking churches from as far afield as Mesopotamia and Arabia looked to the ancient church of Antioch, where believers were first called Christians and where Peter himself was believed to have been the first "apostolic bishop." All the great territory of Christian Africa, from the towns along the Nile to Nubia and Ethiopia, looked to the great church established in the city of Alexandria.

These great ecclesiastical centers attracted Christian talent from far and wide. They were the natural courts of legal appeal, and they inspired missions and resolved complaints from international petitioners. Their incumbents tended to be looked on by the Christian emperors as guardians and arbiters of the international Christian tradition. So it was that they started by the late fourth and into the fifth centuries to be looked on as "patriarchs" of the Christian world. It would be some time after the Council of Chalcedon that this title became regularized in the system of the pentarchy of patriarchal churches, which we shall come to in a moment, but from the late fourth century, more and more the title of patriarch was being applied to the bishops of the three supercities.

The word (Greek *patriarches*; Latin *patriarcha*) originally meant "father of a race" and appears first in the Septuagint version of the Bible to connote the chiefs of the tribes of Israel (1 Chron 24:31; 27:22 [*patriarchai ton phylon*]; cf. 2 Chron 23:20). In the New Testament the title is applied to Abraham (Heb 7:4), to David (Acts 2:29), and to the twelve sons of Jacob (Acts 7:8-9). Christian writers of the fourth and fifth centuries started to use it as a title of honor to the most notable Christian archbishops. St. Gregory of Nazianzus refers to the elder bishops of the church as patriarchally venerable figures.[2] Emperor Theodosius II calls Pope Leo

---

[2]*Oration* 42.23. His own father, a bishop, lived to over one hundred years.

(c. 400–461) a patriarch, and Evagrius the church historian designates the archbishop of Constantinople, Acacius (471–489), by this title.[3] It is used alongside the title archbishop. The case of Acacius is reminiscent of that of John the Faster (*Nesteutes*), another archbishop-patriarch of Constantinople in the sixth century (582–595). John greatly annoyed the pope in Rome by claiming for himself the honorific title of archbishop of Constantinople and "ecumenical patriarch." The Roman pontiff thought this was an attack on his own prerogatives of church governance.

What had happened as an "annoyance" in the old precedence order was the appearance of Constantinople on the scene, disrupting the more ancient pattern of three supersees, Rome, Alexandria, and Antioch. Rome had the normal arch-governance of all Christian Latin affairs. This largely meant serving as a final court of appeal in conflicted matters and exercising a supervisory role in terms of matters of significant doctrinal or disciplinary interest. It reserved to itself, also, the right of final court of appeal relating to matters rising in other international conflicts, in the sense of claiming the senior precedence over the other two Eastern cities. This latter claim was not always respected in practice, even if it was usually observed in etiquette. Rome was accustomed, therefore, to recognizing Alexandria as the second city in terms of ecclesiastical precedent, with Antioch coming after that.

Alexandria was really the only supercity in the whole of the region of Africa. It drew to itself a very large number of bishops of smaller towns (approaching three hundred in number) and in a peculiar way, given its historical development (with only a very few Greek towns and a large number of Coptic-speaking village bishops), the senior bishop of Alexandria more or less treated all his patriarchate's bishops as his suffragans. By the fifth century they were each one ordained personally by him and took an oath of allegiance to him. This was why, when their leader was censured (as at Chalcedon in 451), the entirety of the Egyptian episcopate withdrew in confusion. They had not developed the tradition elsewhere of each bishop having independent ruling authority.

The Antiochene patriarchate drew into its ambit a vast territory stretching from the Chinese borders to Sinai, but one that was composed of extensive desert areas and many mountainous regions. It was always difficult to organize this area, a hard matter to bring all its bishops together for any occasion. Its central area of influence ranged all over the East, the Roman province Orientalis, from Syria proper, to Greece, Asia Minor, Armenia, and Cappadocia. Its liturgical traditions had an equally large spread. Its theological traditions, however, had been quite variegated in the time of the Arian crisis, and there was not a natural focal center to its intellectual traditions—

---

[3]Mansi, *Acta Conciliorum Oecumenicorum* 6.68; Evagrius, *Ecclesiastical History* 3.9.

not, at least, until the time of Theodore Mopsuestia (350–428), whose works caused controversy in his own day, however, and for long afterward.

Into this archaic system came Constantinople dropping like a star. Nicaea had recognized these ancient sees as having a deserved precedence of honor, but in terms of realpolitik after the fourth century, Constantine realized, after seeing how easily Rome had fallen in the civil war, that the Italian city was hopelessly positioned to be a truly international capital.[4] In the early fourth century it was also deeply invested in old family senatorial paganism and highly resistant to the new Christian middle classes. Accordingly, Constantine decided to make a brand-new capital of Rome, called after himself, "Constantine's City" or Constantinopolis.[5] And he placed it in an area he had already noted from earlier campaigns that he felt was brilliantly positioned to be highly defensible yet also at the center of world affairs. This was the Bosphorus, between the Black Sea and the Mediterranean, on the site of a small colony called Byzantium (now Istanbul). The emperor dedicated the new capital in 337. He had created a new senate for it and beautified the city by bringing to it all the finest examples of Greek and Roman artistry: statues, books, talent. St. Jerome, with his usual laconic wit, remarked, "Constantinople dedicated: All the world denuded."[6]

The city, however, had been almost nonexistent before. The bishop of Byzantium had been a poor suffragan of the bishop of Heraclea and unknown in church circles. Now, of course, Constantine wanted it to rank in importance in the church as much as Rome had ranked in the West. He wanted the bishop of the royal city to have significant weight. Many bishops in the Eastern church also thought that the bishop of the supercity had to have prominence in church governance, too. The idea had, after all, been validated at the Council of Nicaea, which said that church organizational lines ought to coincide with civil ones. But those ecclesiastics who thought more in terms of old church precedents for episcopal sees were less willing to welcome the newcomer. It did not have an apostolic foundation that was well known, though it soon remedied that by finding stories of its original foundation by the wandering apostle Andrew. But even so, it could not compete with the ancient Christian traditions of Rome, Alexandria, and Antioch: cities with long lists of martyrs and confessors.

To Constantinople Constantine immediately transferred his sister's favorite theologian, the controversial bishop Eusebius of Nicomedia, who had much practice in serving the royal family. He more or less ensured that for the next fifty years there

---

[4]Council of Nicaea canon 6.
[5]The city's name was changed to Istanbul after the Greco-Turkish war of 1922.
[6]Jerome, *Chronicon ad annum* 330. *Constantinopolis dedicatur paene omnium urbium nuditate.*

would be a succession of Arian bishops in the royal city.[7] This further jaundiced opinion about it, both in the East and West, as a dubious potential center of Christian orthodoxy and good practice. Nowhere was that jaundiced view more to the fore than in Rome and Alexandria.

At Rome, because a new rival had appeared. As Constantinople's fortunes rose as a city and ecclesial center, so too did Rome's start to decline. The years between the fourth and tenth centuries are a period of significant social decline for Rome. The "new Rome," as Constantinople was called in the East, was always growing, avoiding the crises that overran the West in the age of migrations and ever establishing itself as the undisputed center of Christian operations from the fifth century to the eleventh. At Alexandria the Egyptians saw their former role as the leading center of Christian intelligentsia being snatched away from them as the schools of Constantinople simply outshone them. Constantinople melded more international Christian traditions (from Cappadocia and Syria, Asia Minor, and Palestine) than the Egyptians ever did, in its cosmopolitan intellectual clearinghouse.

Alexandria deeply resented this loss of role as the number one ecclesiastical center of reference in the Eastern empire. And in the first two centuries of Constantinople's existence it regularly looked to Rome to see how the upstart's influence could be checked. This rivalry between these two great Eastern cities caused a series of dangerous tensions in Greek Christian affairs at this period, especially as these would manifest in the great councils of the fifth century. Antioch was not happy about its overshadowing, either, for it slowly and progressively lost territory to Constantinople as the latter added to its direct jurisdictional remit sees that had formerly been under Antioch's ecclesiastical supervision in Palestine, Asia Minor, Thrace, and Greece. The loss to Antioch and the additions to the royal city coincided, however, with a steep decline in the political and cultural vitality of the Syrian capital. Constantinople actually rose up as a strong replacement for it, absorbing, as it already had done since its inception, extensive Antiochene traditions in its own liturgy and spirituality, and eventually disseminating them far and wide over the Greek-speaking Christian world. One often imagines Byzantium to be a wholly Greek phenomenon, but in truth it was from the outset a symbiosis of Syro-Greek ecclesiastical traditions in liturgy and Palestinian-Egyptian traditions in monastic culture. Like many a global city since, it was a great clearinghouse of multiple traditions and synthesized them in new ways in the course of disseminating them throughout the very wide arc of its cultural influence.

The new preeminence of Constantinople as the effective senior capital of the empire came into visibility ecclesiastically at the Council of Constantinople called

---

[7] With the exception of Paul of Constantinople.

in 381 by Theodosius I. In the canons this meeting produced the following year, the third of the canons was designed to formalize its primatial role in the East (superseding Alexandria and Antioch and moving alongside the privileges of old Rome): "The bishop of Constantinople shall have the primacy of honor after the bishop of Rome, because it is new Rome." Successive popes, including the contemporary Damasus but up to and beyond Gregory the Great, refused to endorse this legislation, but the rise of the eastern city in terms of ecclesiastical importance was unstoppable. At the Council of Chalcedon in 451, it canons once more underlined Constantinople's place as primatial see of the East and moved to give it formal annexation of supervisory territories in Thrace and Asia Minor.

Canon 28 of the 451 council ostensibly starts off repeating the terms of canon three of 381, but it clearly goes beyond it to define "coming after" old Rome, to mean equality of honor alongside old Rome; that is, comes after it in history but not necessarily in importance. The canon would cause endless controversies between the Greek Christian East and the Latin West, and this tension would eventually cause a major rupture of communion between the two churches at the end of the first millennium. The East saw Rome's primacy of honor as following from its (former) role as center of the imperial administration. Rome, on the other hand, saw its popes having a primacy of jurisdiction following from its particular charism as the see of saint Peter and home of the earliest Christian martyrs. Canon twenty-eight, as we saw above, notes how privileges were afforded to the throne of old Rome, and equal privileges were given to Constantinople at the Council of Chalcedon, so that it should hold rank over the churches of the East.

From this time onward Rome, Constantinople, Alexandria, and Antioch became the order of precedences, and each of these four great cities became more often designated as "patriarchates," not only serving as senior courts of appeal but also serving as cultural magnets for their surrounding regions, attracting many churches to their own traditions and practices. But Rome held sway across the Latin West, and Constantinople increasingly came to dominate the entirety of the Eastern Christian world. Pope Leo (440–461), contemporary with this ruling, refused to acknowledge it and complained that it had been enacted without the presence of his legates. For many centuries to come Rome pretended that Alexandria was still the second city of the Christian world.[8] In actuality Constantinople had become the first and would act as

---

[8] It was not until the time of the Fourth Lateran Council in Rome (1215) that the popes allowed the patriarch of Constantinople to assume this place, as an act of their own personal canonical jurisdiction; but that was only because the Latin armies of the Fourth Crusade had driven out the Greek patriarch and occupied the city in 1204. As part of the Ecumenical negotiations in 1439, the Council of Florence admitted the role, finally, to the Greek patriarch.

such throughout the latter part of the first millennium. All the great conciliar meetings that attempt to harmonize international Christian doctrine and practice take place in and around Constantinople, with Greek theological currents setting the tone.

Into this system of the four patriarchates, the international consensus of bishops was always aware that Jerusalem had a heritage that deserved some notice. The city, however, was a tiny place with no great schools. It was an urban center with biblical prestige and also (until the seventh century) a large monastic tradition. But it never served as a great intellectual or political center for the church. It was primarily, in Byzantine times, a pilgrim focus, and a church whose liturgical ceremonies impressed visitors immensely and led to their copying in a wide arc of other churches.[9] At first Jerusalem had been a subsidiary church, in terms of the organization of the Palestinian synod, to the metropolitan capital at Caesarea Maritima. The Council of Nicaea in 325 in its seventh canon had given the primate of Jerusalem an honorary role but had not elevated him above Caesarea (which was then a great school of learning). But in the fifth century the highly skilled political bishop Juvenal of Jerusalem (420–458) negotiated for his see to be raised to a more formal patriarchal level. At the seventh and eighth sessions of the Council of Chalcedon the provinces of Palestine and Sinai were eventually taken away from the supervision of Antioch (not without controversy) and transferred to Jerusalem, which then was referred to as the fifth patriarchate. This ranking of Rome and Constantinople, then Alexandria, Antioch, and Jerusalem, was legally confirmed by Justinian's 123rd novella in the sixth century, which asserted that each patriarch would serve as a court of last appeal for all internal church legislative and disciplinary matters of their regions.

From that time onward the Latin West still looked to the papacy as being its primary ecclesiastical court of appeal. The Eastern churches, however, increasingly saw the system of the pentarchy of patriarchates as being a collegial example of how to govern international Christian affairs. If truly significant matters arose, it was thought that the communion of the five patriarchates would ensure that all controversies were dealt with judiciously and with attentiveness to the truly international character of Christian tradition. The popes always believed they were, singly, the superior bishop whose views had to be accounted for in all matters of conflict. The Easterners regarded the pope as one of the five patriarchs, *primus inter pares*, a pentarchical college whose commonality had to be sustained.[10] This collegial view

---

[9]From Yorkshire in Saxon England (the undercrypt of Ripon Cathedral) to Ethiopia (the rock-cut Lalibela churches), Christians mimicked the ceremonies and layouts of the Jerusalem churches in their local religious rituals. Their feasts were adopted widely (the blessing of waters on January 6, the Exaltation of the Cross on September 14, and so on).

[10]Primus inter pares means "first among equals."

tended increasingly to clash with the Roman primatial view. As the advance of Islam sent the patriarchs of Antioch, Alexandria, and Jerusalem hastening to take up residence and refuge in Constantinople, and as the anti-Chalcedonian churches of Syria and Egypt set up new parallel hierarchies, the theoretical system of pentarchy often materialized as simply a binary system of Rome's influence set against that of Constantinople. Even so, all councils held in the East demanded a theoretical convening of the five patriarchal sees to ensure their validity. This implied that all bishops (though the popes continued to dispute this through the Middle Ages) were subordinate to the determinations of a general council.

## JOHN CHRYSOSTOM AT CONSTANTINOPLE

This tensile balance of the great sees can be seen clearly operative in the life of St. John "the Golden-Mouthed" (c. 345–407), who was the most important archbishop of Constantinople, following after Gregory of Nazianzen's brief period as ecclesiastical leader there at the time of the council of 381. The successful high points, and also the tragedies, of his ecclesiastical career graphically demonstrate for us the way Constantinople was negotiating its delicate path between imperial politics and international church mediations.

John received the sobriquet "Golden Mouth," or Chrysostom, because his posthumous career was even more renowned than his acclaimed lifetime reputation as one of the great orators of antiquity. In the long centuries of Byzantium his works, and those of Gregory of Nazianzus, were held up as exemplary literature in the schools of rhetoric. Chrysostom was felt to be a model for how a Byzantine bishop ought to make up a dossier of sermons for varied occasions; Gregory was regarded as the consummate expositor of doctrine; and a third was added, Basil the Great of Caesarea, as a magnificently eloquent defender of asceticism. The student factions of medieval Constantinople attached themselves to each of their three heroes passionately, and the church and state had to intervene so often to suppress street fighting that eventually it was decreed that all three figures should be depicted on an icon together, and their common feast would be instituted as the "Three Holy Hierarchs."[11] Their writings, in Latin translation, were equally appreciated in the West, making them some of the few Greek patristic theologians to exercise a universal influence. In John's case, his sermonizing was deeply ethical and exegetical, and for both sections of the church this made him into a model moralist and social reformer.

John was a native of Antioch and the son of a high civil servant in the administration of the military governor of the Syrian province. His mother, Anthusa, was widowed at

---

[11] By Patriarch John Mauropous in the eleventh century.

twenty, but she spent herself to secure the highest level of education for her son, who probably studied under the rhetor Libanius, the greatest sophist of the age. John also studied theology with Diodore of Tarsus, a leading Syrian biblical theologian who himself had been a disciple of Theodore Mopsuestia and who, together with his master, was a strong advocate of the distinctive Syrian (Antiochene) manner of interpreting Scripture, with less of a stress on highly charged symbolic meanings, a style favored at Alexandria in the Origenistic tradition propagated there. The Antiochene approach preferred to read the text in a simpler and more morally purposeful way.

He came forward as a candidate for baptism at the age of twenty-three, in 368, and seems from this time to have considered himself a dedicated ascetic-sophist. He attached himself to the Antiochene bishop Meletius, then in his old age. Meletius was the great defender of Nicaea, whose reputation as a confessor of the faith was very high. In this period Chrysostom also began a systematic study of the Scriptures with Meletius, which might well have had the effect of moderating the influence of Diodore and Theodore on him. The latter two represent the Antiochene school in its most radical form. In christological exegesis they sustained positions that seemed to many other commentators, especially those of the Origenian traditions, rather extreme. They discounted, for example, most of the traditional messianic-christological interpretations of the Psalms, and habitually approached the christological issue of "two natures" (divine and human) in terms of designating "two Sons," the divine Son of God and the human Son of Man. Both Theodore and Diodore often spoke about the two Sons in ways that suggested to their more critical hearers the scandalous position that these were two distinct persons (subjects). Already in the late fourth century Gregory of Nazianzus had criticized Diodore for this obscurity, and shortly after John's death this issue, still simmering in controversy, would boil over at the Council of Ephesus in 431.[12]

John's exegesis avoids the most radical aspects of the Antiochene style and simply puts it to work, making a lively and clarified rendering of the Scripture for the purpose of moral instruction at the liturgy. In 371 John was ordained lector and spent some time in seclusion learning the ascetical (monastic) lifestyle with an aged Syrian hermit. But his constitution could not support the rigors of the desert tradition as it was then lived, and from 373 to 381 he was forced to return home in poor health, where lived with his mother as a monastic recluse. His talents were known, however, and in 381 he was sought after by Flavian, the newly appointed archbishop of Antioch, who inducted him into his administration as a deacon and then ordained him priest in 386.

---

[12]Gregory of Nazianzus, *Epistles* 101-2.

After that point he was given the charge of preaching regularly in the cathedral at Antioch. From this period he began to collect his sermons, and today they constitute a very large dossier of works that have survived. Their brilliant Greek, synthesized with a lively, down-to-earth touch as pastor of a large Syriac-speaking congregation (he would give bilingual addresses, providing a synopsis in Syriac for his people of what he would declaim from the pulpit in classical Greek), won him great applause in the church whenever he spoke, and his reputation as a consummate orator spread far. At Antioch he engaged in a polemic to stop local Christians from attending Jewish religious festivals (still at that date, apparently, a common practice among the ordinary people), and his language against the Jews in this context is often harsh and combative. In later times, applied in different contexts, it provided a dangerous paradigm for anti-Semitic rhetoric among Christians.

In 387 the people of Antioch rioted in protest against tax impositions. In the course of the street fighting the mob destroyed and mutilated several statues of the emperor. This was a crime of high treason, punishable in theory by the destruction of the city. When the riots calmed down, a great sense of fear spread abroad; the people were terrified the emperor at Constantinople would send garrisons against them to burn their town in punishment. Into the gap moved John as mediator. He delivered a series of passionate rhetorical appeals for imperial clemency, saving the face of the emperor and the necks of his own people. These sermons have also survived as his *Homilies on the Statues*. This set of orations brought him to the close attention of the imperial court at Constantinople, and in 398 he was chosen by Emperor Arcadius to replace Nectarius as archbishop of Constantinople.

Coming in as a renowned preacher and highly ascetical churchman, his arrival was something of a shock to the ecclesiastical administration that had been left by Nectarius. The latter had been elevated quickly to church orders after the sudden departure of Gregory of Nazianzus in 381. Nectarius had been a worldly wise aristocrat who knew his way around the city's politics and how to control the senate. His appointment was entirely because Emperor Theodosius wanted a safe pair of obedient hands for his court theologian. But when John arrived he made it clear that he intended to stop running the archiepiscopal palace as an elite entertainment center and make it an observant house of prayer. He also found much to criticize in the way the royal city's church was being managed and felt the standards of the clergy needed raising in short order. This made him many enemies in a small space of time, because the use of aristocratic patronage had been part of the way the archbishops had managed the church's affairs. As Gregory of Nazianzus had found out soon enough, if one did not invite the great and good to a rich table with great frequency, then very little was done. And if one was not ready to offer many costly "blessings" (*eulogia*) to political subordinates between the royal palace and the church administration, it was apparent how soon messages got lost and contact could be disrupted.

We might see it all as graft and bribery today and imagine John was right to be annoyed, but antique society in general had worked like this for many centuries, and the patronage system was deeply entrenched at Constantinople, both in the court and the church. When Chrysostom reduced the scope of the patronage from his palace, it not only puzzled most of the capital's ecclesiastical establishment but also enraged many leaders within it. This did nothing to dampen John's zeal to reform the palace and the whole city. But although his rhetoric was much appreciated (Constantinople wanted to have the greatest Greek rhetoricians and philosophers gathered within its walls to enhance its reputation as the world's major center of culture) his ascetical habits and severe attitudes to morals alienated many of the court and clergy.

This was especially true of Empress Eudoxia, who took his remarks about the venality of the vacuous rich who would not lift a finger to help the poor as a personal affront to her extremely rich lifestyle as *basilissa*. She began to hound John and press for his dismissal. He did not help things by muttering about Ahab and Jezebel. Archbishop Theophilus of Alexandria had long been waiting for an opportunity to check the growing importance of Constantinople and to reassert the significance of his own see. The occasion to attack Chrysostom arose when John acted instinctively as the leading court of appeal in the Eastern church, agreeing to hear the appeal of a group of dissidents whom Theophilus had driven out of his Egyptian church. In opening up this case formally, he had declared that his ecclesiastical right to adjudicate was superior to that of Theophilus. John was moved to do so by sympathy he had for the rights of the ascetical movement. He thus gave shelter in his own quarters to the so-called tall brothers, monks whom Theophilus had censured and exiled from Egypt because of their Origenist doctrinal positions. Not only had Chrysostom challenged his judicial authority, but he had also given every indication he sided with the Origenists and against Theophilus's theological teaching that this was a dangerous *hairesis*. This divergence in doctrine Theophilus seized on as a cause to raise formal complaint against John. The imperial court, now tired of their protégé, thought this might be the ideal way to take him down a peg or two, and so the emperor allowed Theophilus to preside over a court of inquiry composed of John's own higher clergy, held in the Constantinopolitan suburb of Chalcedon.

Here Theophilus came, accompanied by his nephew, the theologian Cyril, who would shortly succeed him at Alexandria, and presided over the Synod of the Oak in 403. With full imperial approval he stage-managed John's trial for ecclesiastical irregularities and imposed the sentence on him of deposition from episcopal orders. The emperor endorsed the sentence, conscious of John's growing popularity with the ordinary people of the capital compared to his own and, to the delight of Empress Eudoxia, he exiled him. He certainly did not intend to allow Alexandria to cast his own imperial church into the shade or impose long-term humiliation on it, but he equally wanted to humiliate John for a short time, presuming that this show of power would be enough to ensure his future good behavior. Of course it would not. As with Ambrose's clash with Theodosius in the previous century, the capital would soon discover that it had a churchman of independent mind who did not reckon anything to monetary inducements or physical threats.

As soon as John was recalled he renewed his reform program and his caustic attacks on the idle rich of Constantinople with even greater zeal, earning the undying enmity of the empress. He was soon exiled again, this time on the specious grounds that he had resumed his see after synodical condemnation but without canonical authorization of a new synodal hearing. International appeals on his behalf from Rome, which was alarmed by the blatant imperial interference in church governance matters, proved to no avail. Sent back at first to Antioch, his punishment was increased when he refused to be silent by a second enforced winter march to the Black Sea. These forced marches of nonmilitary prisoners were intended to be death sentences, and this one in freezing conditions was one that John's physical constitution could not support, and he died in its process.

John's posthumous fame grew as a fearless martyr-bishop who saw his task as the defense of the poor against the depredations of the rich. His popularity at Constantinople forced the royal household in the next generation to bring his bodily remains back to the capital, where they were housed in a great shrine, and he was honored as a saint. As the years passed his writings assumed the status of Christian classics, and Byzantine seminarians were trained in Greek rhetoric as well as exegesis and theology by using this primary textual resource. Later oral tradition associated his reform movement with liturgical changes. He probably rationalized some of the observances of the offices and liturgy, bringing in Antiochene practices to Constantinople.

In later times it was widely believed that he composed a whole new liturgy of the Eucharist. Today it is widely used in the Orthodox world and is named after him, the Liturgy of St. John Chrysostom. In fact this form of eucharistic rite is mainly an abridgement of the liturgy of St. Basil; but as both a liturgical doctor and major exegetical writer the subsequent tradition of Chrysostom's reform lived on to make him one of the central patristic authorities of the Greek church. Historically he is of immense importance for ensuring the enduring impact of the Syrian theological tradition in developing Byzantium. His very large manuscript tradition became a ready depository over the later centuries for numerous works not actually written by him, not least several sermons by the disgraced Nestorius ("Sermon on the High Priesthood of Jesus").

## THE ORIGENISTIC CRISIS

Chrysostom's downfall had been triggered by his support for the tall brothers. This was far more extensive an issue than simply protecting some Egyptian ascetics against the disapproval of their irascible bishop. The tall brothers, along with their colleague Evagrius of Pontus, were some of the most renowned theologian ascetics in the Christian world of that time; but they were avid readers of the works of Origen of Alexandria, and many of the monks in the Egyptian desert were far from being intellectuals and looked on Origen's speculative and universalist-tending thought as dangerously at variance with biblical doctrines such as the eternity of hell, the reality of purgatorial fire, the physical resurrection of the body, and other matters where they opposed a straightforwardly literalist reading of the texts against the symbolic exegesis of the Origenians. Theophilus, wishing to keep the loyalty of the many monks who made up his Egyptian diocese, came out heavily on the side of the simpler ascetics and monks and was sharply critical of the "Origenists," whom he treated as doctrinal deviants, even though, behind the scenes, Theophilus used Origen's exegetical writings extensively in his own preaching.

The so-called Origenistic crises (there were several waves of the same thing across more than a century of struggle in this period between the fifth and late sixth centuries) are not so much a battle about precise doctrines as such (although a number of Origen's more controversial ideas were raised up as flags) but rather a clash of cultures between Christian intellectuals who were open to reflection, even speculation, about the nature of God and the state of the soul, and those who followed biblical paradigms very closely and deeply distrusted the open-ended philosophical ambience of late antiquity, when debate and discussion were often open-ended. Origen's reputation, already somewhat controverted in his own lifetime for ideas he raised as speculative discussion points, became critically attacked by certain sections of the church in the fifth century because no allowance was made for his original context. Critics of that period read an ancient text primarily in the light of their own contexts and did not seek to fit any more nuanced historical background to it.

In the post-Nicene era the doctrinal precision of the church was much more tuned up than ever it was in Origen's day: so many of his statements appeared to be implied contradictions of solemnly endorsed Christian doctrine. This had not happened to many other theologians for two chief factors: first, Origen's range of interests was so vast that he had left statements on so many subjects of interest to the monks, who were the main theology-reading public; and second because Origen was still being read so attentively and extensively two centuries after his death. Many other writers from the earlier period had just fallen into oblivion. Origen was still a bestseller, and his "divergences" started to shock more and more people. Questions he raised about whether the soul had a prior existence to this earthly one, whether the resurrectional body would be physical or not, whether God would restore all creation to a universal salvation and recapitulation (*apokatastasis*), and to what extent the soul of Jesus was different from the divine Logos that dwelt within him: all these things and more occasioned a growing and bitter clash between monastics, who thought he was the church's finest mind ever and a Christian of a pure and saintly lifestyle, and those who wanted his name and writings condemned posthumously for heresy.

Two clashes in particular are chief moments in the "Origenistic controversy." The first took place in the fifth century and the second in the sixth.[13] The fourth-century Arian crisis, when several homoian theologians appealed to his example to cast doubts on the utility of the *homoousion*, undoubtedly caused serious damage to his reputation as a guide to orthodoxy. But the school of Caesarea sustained his name and his library with great care. Pamphilus's lost *Apology for Origen* was probably the primary text on which Eusebius of Caesarea based his sixth chapter of the *Ecclesiastical History*, which is more or less a hagiography of Origen as superlative churchman. But Eusebius's long-sustained opposition to Athanasius cost him his own reputation in many respects. And the manner in which Origen's thought was developed by Evagrius Ponticus and Didymus the Blind caused a strong reaction to both of these speculative theologians, serving to cast further doubts over the Origen they claimed to be speaking for. It was growing dissatisfaction on this score that led Justinian's court to issue posthumous condemnations of Origen and his commentators, which were (later) added to the *acta* of the great synod of 553. It is interesting to note how all the sentences of Origen that are condemned by Justinian are actually phrases taken from Evagrius. But however much individual theologians or even the court might protest, Origen remained one of the chief writers being read in the East. His approach to Scripture and his overarching ideas about soteriology had entered into

---

[13] In his own lifetime, in the third century, Demetrius the bishop of Alexandria had been a vocal critic, so too Pope Pontianus of Rome. In the fourth century Methodius of Olympus, Eustathius of Antioch, and Peter of Alexandria had all been critics. Gregory of Nazianzen and Basil's collaboration to produce the *Philocalia Origenis*, a compendium of the best passages of his works on exegesis and theology (all objectionable elements edited out), also suggests that even his devoted friends were anxious to repair his reputation.

the macrocontext of most theological arguments after the beginning of the fourth century. It was no easy matter to try to put the horse back into the stable.

The fifth-century Origenistic crisis is the better documented of the two. It is recorded by Epiphanius of Salamis, Theophilus of Alexandria, Rufinus, Jerome, and the historians Sozomen, Socrates Scholasticus, and Palladius. It was a clash of attitudes that flashed around monastic circles and attracted the intervention of several dominant bishops. So it was not simply an intellectual matter but an issue of the episcopal control of wandering ascetics. It began at the very end of the fourth century, with Bishop Epiphanius naming Origen as a heretical writer whose views were noxious. He objected to excessive allegorization along with a number of distinct propositions, which he named in his two volumes designed to root out heresy, the *Ancoratus* (375) and the *Panarion* (376).[14] Epiphanius approached John the bishop of Jerusalem, knowing that he fostered in his diocese the ascetical house of Melania on the Mount of Olives, where copies of Origen's works were both made and commented on in her school—a school that also sheltered Evagrius and Rufinus at various times. Jerome joined with Epiphanius in making common complaint. But Bishop John was an avid Origenian himself and shrugged off both clerics as troublemakers.

From this time onward a great bitterness rose up between Rufinus and Jerome, who had formerly been great friends and co-commentators on Origen. Jerome from that time onward denounced Origen vociferously, while continuing to rely on his exegeses and often incorporating extensive passages of them in Latin translation in his own works. Rufinus was one of the monastic leaders in Palestine who, in 393, refused to endorse the petition of the monk Atarbius to ban the works of Origen from the monasteries of Palestine. After leaving Palestine for Rome, Rufinus countered by making a Latin translation of Origen's *Treatise on First Principles*, and in his preface made sarcastic remarks about Jerome's change of face. Jerome, knowing that he himself had earlier studied Scripture with Didymus at Alexandria, who was Origen's leading commentator of that era, took fright in case his own reputation might be damaged by association, and so he produced his own Latin translation of the *First Principles*, which took special care to highlight the theological elements in Origen's work held to be most objectionable in his time.

The controversy was speedily transmitted throughout all the monasteries of Palestine, and it was inevitable that in a short space of time it should migrate south to Egypt. So it was that by 399 it reached the attention of Theophilus the archbishop of Alexandria. Theophilus was a learned scholar who used Origen's works in his own

---

[14]His chief objections were that Origen was subordinationist in Christology, speculated too freely, and revived the Encratite notion of ancient times that human sexuality was inherently evil. The latter charge was wholly unfounded.

writings and who had also tried to moderate the dispute in Palestine, but on his own front door he had a diocese made up of an extraordinarily large number of monks in many prestigious ascetical houses. He had already written once, in his *Festal Letter* of 399, to describe some of the ideas of the uneducated monastics (whom he calls "simple souls") as excessively "anthropomorphic." The monks had taken against Origen's allegorical approach to the Bible and had seemed, so Theophilus thought, to read the text literally, as if God indeed were an irascible person (when the Bible speaks of God's anger), that the resurrection of the flesh would indeed be a physical reconstitution of the bones and dust of a person's grave, and so on. But he sensed that if he wished to continue to sustain his influence over the Egyptian monastics he could not alienate the majority. When his festal letter was read out many monks came from the desert to cause local riots around his episcopal place. It was a lesson he took careful note of.

At Nitria there was a large colony of intellectual monks looking to the leadership of the three siblings, called the tall brothers, disciples of Evagrius who had settled there and made a school. Theophilus knew that they had smaller regard for his authority than for their own spiritual customs and so thought that by exiling them he might kill two birds with one stone: ensure his reputation as strong orthodox leader among his monastics and remove a source of challenge to his ecclesiastical leadership. So in 400 he called a synod together and asked his bishops to condemn Origen's thought (and that of the disciples of Origen by implication) chiefly by attacking the theology of Evagrius. He secured Pope Anastasius of Rome's agreement to this. Evagrius had been the leading spiritual master at Nitria, whom Theophilus had treated with immense respect while he was alive.

After his synod Theophilus expelled the tall brothers from their monastery at Nitria in 402, along with many other "Origenist" monks, ensuring by this purge that the monasteries understood who was the chief ecclesiastical power in Egypt. They took refuge with John Chrysostom at Constantinople, asking for a review of their treatment, and this, as we have seen earlier, was the proximate reason Theophilus traveled to the capital in the summer of 403 and at the Synod of the Oak presided over a synod that deposed Chrysostom himself.[15] Having collaborated with the emperor in the downfall of Chrysostom and asserted his see's dominance in the face of the international episcopate, and having cowed the monks of his great diocese, Theophilus felt his position was sufficiently impregnable as to be able to relax. Accordingly, in the aftermath of all this, he relaxed his position, returned to his scholarly reading of Origen's works (which can be traced in all his writings), and

---

[15] The Oak was a district of Constantinople, part of Chalcedon, a rich neighborhood with many large villas that could serve as meeting halls, including those of the emperor.

resumed friendly relations with the "intellectual" monastics of Nitria, no longer accusing them of being "Origenists" at all. This allowed the first phase of the crisis to fade away without having been fully resolved.

For this reason it blew up again in a critical way, this time in Palestine, in the sixth century. The record of these events is largely given to us in two places: first, in the writings of Cyril of Scythopolis who, in his *Lives of the Palestinian Monks*, gives a detailed account of the troubles in the Great Lavra of Sabas, near Bethlehem, and who writes from an anti-Origenian perspective; and second, from the records emanating from the court of Justinian, who intervened in the dispute to bring peace to the Palestinian monasteries and assert a central Constantinopolitan solution by synodical action.[16] The court at this time was much exercised in bringing about a solution to christological divisions in the aftermath of the Council of Chalcedon in 451 and was determined that the so-called Origenist crisis in the Palestinian monasteries (which was already showing a tendency to exacerbate a fracture line between those monks who agreed with Chalcedon and those who did not) would not derail the process of reconciliation they were trying to achieve.

The argument about the significance of Origen's works on prayer and theology began again in Gaza first of all and then spread to the desert monasteries between Jerusalem and the Dead Sea. The storm center became the Great Lavra, where Saba presided. There were many highly intellectual monk theologians traveling the desert at this period. The ideas that were controverted seem largely to have been those of Evagrius, who in his *Gnostic Chapters* and other mystical writings had argued that the monk was a true philosopher whose ascetical life was not only a bodily asceticism (renunciation of sexuality and bodily comforts) but a fundamental sharpening of the intellectual senses so as to allow human consciousness to become refined enough to allow the dawning of divine consciousness: a transition from *logismos* (intellectuality) to *noesis* (precise awareness of God). As Evagrius had taught, the life of prayer was to reflect this ascent of the mind: rising from simple prayers and psalm recitation to a state of maturity in which the ascetic would abide in a stasis of imageless prayer, more truly reflective of the God who transcended all thought and speech.

Many of the desert monks, however, were far from being intellectuals of this type, and the Evagrian ideas frightened them. They had a simpler and more straightforward view, that feats of bodily asceticism were important in themselves, to allay the tendency to sin; and that the purpose of the monastic life was to live a hard regime dedicated to long periods of prayer (by which they meant liturgy and psalm recitation) along with

---

[16]Especially in his *Life of St. Saba*. See R. M. Price, *Cyril of Scythopolis: Lives of the Monks of Palestine* (Kalamazoo, MI: Cistercian Publications, 1991).

physical labor. Some of the intellectual followers of Evagrius turned the disapproval of their simpler colleagues back on their heads and began stressing the right of ascetics to indulge in profound metaphysical speculation. They raised once more the antique (philosophical) ideas of Origen about preexistence of souls, but now in a context of ecclesiastical life that was far removed from the scholastic environment of the third-century university cities where Origen first worked. Origen had argued that the first creation of souls was a pure spiritual creation of psychic beings (*psychai*) who were all equal and equally beautiful. The Logos had created this circle of primal souls at the will of the Father. First in that circle was the great soul Jesus, who in the fullness of time would descend to earth to be the vehicle bearing the Logos within him. This early Origenian Christology (distinguishing Jesus and Logos) had been radically set aside more or less straight after his time and had been basically rendered redundant by the solutions offered by the great councils, including Ephesus 431, which insisted on the singleness of the divine person of Jesus Christ.

The Palestinian intellectuals wished to revive that part of the Origenian architecture that spoke about the ascent of the fallen souls of human being to achieve an advanced spiritual status after death—when they would be readmitted to this elevated circle of spiritual beings. They suggested that such souls of the elect saints would have the same status the Christ had. Their enemies seized on this aspect of the notion of spiritual *anabasis* (otherwise noncontroversial, for it had been spoken about by many of the great Fathers) and summed them up as blasphemers who taught that human souls could be reckoned the same as the divine Christ. They so named them the Isochristoi.[17]

Another group of monks who were followers of Origen's thought but were also alarmed by the radical responses of the Isochristoi, thought it would be wiser simply to speak as Origen originally had done, about the soul of Jesus as the "firstborn" of the circle of spirits around the throne of God. They were using biblical language, evidently, about Jesus as the firstborn of many brethren, wishing to stress the Pauline doctrine that "in Christ" many souls would be elevated to the presence of God. Their enemies were no more receptive of them, however, and labeled them the Protoktistoi (first creationers), stressing by that designation the implication that the soul of Jesus, in Origen's schema, seems to have been created, which by that date was tantamount to Arianism. The anti-Origenian monks summed it all up as the Isochristoi were reducing Christ to the level of a created being, and the Protoktistoi were promoting a created being into the ranks of the divine Trinity. Both these claims labeled the

---

[17] The Greek term meant "same as Christ-ers," the implication being that by achieving unity with God they would also achieve the same divine intimacy Christ enjoyed with the Father.

Origenians as heretics: heretics, moreover, who had made fundamental mistakes in theology of a very basic kind (thus implying they were idiots).

So the nonintellectual circles turned the tables on the intellectuals. Tensions ran very high. It is, in fact, one of the early examples of the struggle for terms of intellectual freedom in an increasingly closed society. Ethnic lines and different patriarchal loyalties also ran through the dispute. The Isochristoi tended to favor the Alexandrian traditions of theology. The Protoktistoi were more versed in Syro-Antiochene traditions. The inevitable result was that the Origenian parties fell out with each other. The Protoktistoi appealed against the Isochristoi to the Emperor Justinian, using the agency of the papal apocrisarius Pelagius, the Roman see's ambassador at Constantinople. The anti-Origenians, meanwhile wished both parties to take themselves off. Saba, the leader of the Great Lavra near Bethlehem, was at his wits' ends trying to keep the houses of monks in a state of peaceful prayer while all this was transpiring.

The domestic synod of the patriarch of Constantinople agreed in 543 that there was a case for censuring Origen's thought that lay behind all of this. The analysis of that doctrine (taken largely by gobbets lifted from the *First Principles*) was far from accurate, it has to be said, but the standards of citation and critical analysis at that period were loose. The emperor agreed that a censure ought to be issued, and the domestic synod's resolutions were passed on for signature by the pope and the other Eastern patriarchs.

This was essentially the position restated ten years later (indicating the tensions had not died down), when Justinian convened the Second Council of Constantinople in 553. In the early part of this great synod, when Pope Vigilius had been summoned to the capital but refused to appear at the sessions, a letter (*homonoia*) seems to have been issued by the emperor's personal cabinet to the assembled bishops denouncing the Isochristoi who were being led astray by Origen. Fifteen objectionable items were drawn up, a list of things to be anathematized. Peculiarly, the anathemata are all taken from the works of Evagrius of Pontus. The *anathemata* did not get themselves attached to the official acts of the council of 553, but to strengthen the legal case against the Origenist "disturbers of the peace" the *anathemata* were quietly added to the synodal acts at a later date and have consequently been received as conciliar records from the end of the sixth century onward, a sleight of hand possible by those who held the key to the archives.

In anathema eleven Origen is named explicitly as a christological heretic. In Justinian's *Homonoia*, however, and in Pope Vigilius's copy of the *anathemata*, which has survived, he is not named in this explicit way, and contemporary scholars have strongly suspected that his name was also added retrospectively. The primary focus of the synod of 553, of course, was an attack on the Syro-Antiochene theology of Theodore, Theodoret, Nestorius, and Ibas of Edessa, while at the same time elevating Cyril of Alexandria's Christology as paradigmatic, in the (vain) hope that the Coptic Miaphysites would reconcile themselves to the theology of the Council of Chalcedon 451. Whatever the case, it is clear enough that Origen was censured in the guise of a figure who was agitating sixth-century dissidents, and the severity of the attack on him (albeit through the writings of someone else) resulted in a marked sidelining of his textual tradition. He was still used, extensively so, but few were now willing to admit where their thought had come from. It is a miraculous thing that so much of his text tradition survived into the modern era, given the level of opprobrium directed against it at this period. Perhaps the greatest mind of the early church had to wait until the early decades of the twentieth century before his theology could be read accurately and his monumental status appreciated properly.

## THE CHRISTOLOGICAL CONTROVERSY OF THE FIFTH CENTURY

*The clash of Antioch and Alexandria.* In the immediate aftermath of Origen of Alexandria's program for establishing a pattern of reading of the biblical texts allegorically (that is, reading the stories as symbols of deeper spiritual mysteries rather than just taking them at face value), his manner of exegesis spread quickly and rapidly in the international church. But there were decided pockets of resistance: not only among the Christians he and his disciples called the *simpliciores*, the less educated believers (not readers or writers, since they were mostly illiterate), who felt theologians were making too much of simple narratives, rendering the stories into philosophical ciphers; but even among the more educated classes. It was especially true that in the Syrian-speaking regions of the church, based in the great Roman "diocese of the Orient" (which is why the Christian Greeks called these theologians the "Orientals") and focused around the archiepiscopal see of Antioch, a theological tradition that was hostile to Origen's legacy was developing strongly after his death.

Eustathius was the bishop of Antioch, whose fight for Nicene Orthodoxy gave him a very high reputation in the church of his time (but also caused his deposition, brought on by his enemies in 330). He wrote publicly and critically that Origen's allegorical approach was "excessive." He advocated for a simpler return to straightforward biblical meanings.[18] Other followers of this Syrian-Antiochene tradition were John Chrysostom, later to become archbishop of Constantinople, and his own friends and colleagues, Theodore bishop of Mopsuestia (350–428) and Diodore of

---

[18]His only extant work is an attack on Origen's reading of the witch of Endor: *De Engastrimytho contra Origenem*, ed. A. Jahn, Texte und Untersuchungen 2.4 (Berlin: Hinrichs, 1896); ed. J. H. Declerck, Corpus Christianorum Series Graeca 51 (Turnhout: Brepols, 1989).

Tarsus (d. c. 390).[19] These four great theologians established a distinctive "school of Antioch" (Diodore was the chief agent in it, but Chrysostom and Theodore the most fluent writers), which began to rival that of the Origenian-Alexandrian tradition. Diodore and Theodore, however, developed distinctive christological views, which they justified out of their exegetical writings.[20] It became a tendency of their rhetoric to speak of the contrast in the life of Jesus, between the divine works he manifested and the humility he showed as a suffering redeemer. To connote this paradoxical juxtaposition of "almost opposite things," they spoke of the Son of Man and the Son of God, using the christological titles to describe the respective natures of divinity and humanity witnessed in the life and work of the Savior. Strongly to the fore in their Christology (and thus in their exegesis too) was the need to keep the "two natures" of Christ sharply differentiated.

In the final decades of the fourth century, Diodore and Theodore had both been appalled by the theological work of Apollinaris of Laodicea, a onetime friend of Athanasius of Alexandria, and they had had fought vigorously against Apollinaris's doctrine that the natures of divinity and humanity in Christ were so strongly united as to be fused into one. Apollinaris arrived at this theory of profound unification (*henosis*) of natures on the basis that two into one does not go: something has to cede. For him it was obvious that if the magnificence of the divine nature of the Logos entered into union with the human nature, then such a human nature (of Jesus) would hardly need the smaller, iconic things that reflected the divinity within human beings—namely the intelligence and the soul. The divine Logos itself, therefore, could stand in for, replace, the human mind and soul of Jesus. This was why he was not simply or merely a man: his mind was that of the Word of God; his soul was the second person of the Trinity. For Apollinaris this christological fusion theory seemed a good way to emphasize the strict unification that had been effected in the divine incarnation between the nature of humanity and divinity. Now, in Jesus, Apollinaris argued, there was only divinohumanity. The net result was that the defective human nature of the world (dying, limited, ignorant, sinful) was now "perfected," even divinized. Apollinaris liked to think of humanity now being "lost in the Godhead" in the model of the incarnate union. A popular image used at the time was the humanity being a drop of wine, still present but now dissipated in the boundless ocean of the Godhead.

---

[19] See Gennadius of Marseille, *De Viris Illustribus* 12. Mopsuestia was about forty miles from Tarsus on the Pyramus (Ceyhan) River. John Chrysostom, Diodore, and Theodore had been students together under the rhetorician Libanius and adopted the ascetical life as young men. All three were renowned biblical theologians of the Syrian school.

[20] See further F. A. Sullivan, *The Christology of Theodore of Mopsuestia* (Rome: Analecta Gregoriana, 1956).

Gregory of Nazianzus was alarmed by this model of thinking, enough to write two important letters denouncing it.[21] These became adopted as the classical exposition of why this was a dubious theory and would be studied later by Cyril, the fifth-century archbishop of Alexandria, and absorbed into his work. But in the meantime the attack on Apollinaris was left to the pens of Diodore and Theodore. Both theologians felt that such a view of humanity absorbed into divinity was not a good model for the redemption of the race at all. What was posited, they argued, was not a perfected, rather a destroyed, humanity. As Gregory of Nazianzus had argued, a mindless and soulless humanity had stripped it of its quintessential spiritual values. It was precisely to reorder the human intelligence and to stabilize the human soul that the divine Word had come to earth and assumed flesh. If he abolishes both those things in the process, how can that be seen as a plan of redemption? Gregory had placed his finger on the chief defect of Apollinaris, that in trying logically to "order" the theory of a christological union of natures he had destroyed the whole purpose of incarnational thought, which was to show how it was a soteriological dynamism on the part of God: assuming human life in all its fullness, in order to reconstitute it in God's own image and likeness.

Diodore and Theodore took another angle of approach for their attack on Apollinaris. They decided to stress the opposite to his theory of fusion, by laying all the stress on how God does not alter human nature when he adopts it in his incarnation but rather preserves it intact and leads it by example into the paths of salvation. In all their work they speak in binaries: the Son of God does certain things (miracles especially), and the Son of Man does certain other things (suffering, human weakness, limited knowledge, and so forth). In this way it would be easy to avoid the attacks of Arians and Apollinarists. Their whole manner of thinking and writing was determined by these twin poles of the "enemies" of the church, whom they felt were all around them. The Arian party used to mock the Nicenes by arguing that Jesus could not possibly be the divine, coequal Son of God because he demonstrated on many occasions (not least by his painful death) that he was not omniscient, not omnipotent, and not immortal.

In order to offset that critique the Syrians argued that as Son of God he demonstrated divine characteristics, but as Son of Man he showed all the appropriate characteristics of a human being. To offset both Arian divisionism, therefore, and Apollinarist fusionism, they thought they could adopt a "middle way" by speaking of a "profound association" between divinity and humanity in the person of the incarnate Lord. For them the Word had not become man in the sense of turning into a man or

---

[21] Gregory of Nazianzus, *Letters* 101-2, *To Cledonius*.

in the sense of having turned a human nature into a deified nature (metamorphosis theory), but rather had come down to earth as divine Word in order to associate himself most intimately with human life in the person of Jesus. The term *person*, of course, did not bear all the associations in Syria that it did in Alexandrian Greek, or for that matter in modern English, where it is a far more developed notion than it was in antiquity. In the Syrian world the exact term was *parsopa*. In Greek, for they were bilingual, they used the term *prosopon*. In both concept the word had a range of meanings, but the Syrian christologians habitually used it to mean "that which presented itself in a nature to observation"—if we wanted to be technical, we could call it an instantiation. But the main issue to highlight would be that they used *prosopon* remarkably close to signifying "nature," as this was used in the Alexandrian Greek world. Vast amounts of confusion were now made possible between Rome-Alexandria on the one side, and Antioch-Constantinople on the other, because the latter two language groups (Greek and Latin) used the term *persona/prosopon* to signify an individual subject, while the Syrians used it to connote the characteristics representing a subject of interest (an existential state). This confusion becomes very apparent, as we shall see shortly, in the misunderstandings arising between Cyril and Nestorius.

For Diodore and Theodore it was most important to follow the lead of the Scriptures in talking about this mystery of the incarnation. Since Scripture referred to Jesus frequently as Son of God and also Son of Man, it was evident (to them) that this was a demonstration that Christians ought to use these binaries as their own guide to incarnational theology. Their usage became more and more widely known across the fourth century and into the fifth. In 428 a younger disciple of Diodore's, a zealous monk-theologian from Antioch named Nestorius, was appointed as archbishop of Constantinople and brought this style of teaching into the heart of the international church. With him it came very much to the attention of the two other great sees of the day, Rome and Alexandria, and it was this form of the preaching of it that lit the tinder beneath what would become a great conflagration of controversy over what exactly the Christian ecumene believed about the incarnation. It was almost as large a controversy as the Arian crisis of the previous century. This time the fighting was not about whether the Word of God was fully divine or not. That had been settled at Nicaea. Now the issue was, how was Jesus God and man? How did two realities, divinity and humanity, find harmony within him, and how was this to be understood as the model of salvation for the human race? It was a question, really, about the coherence of the concept of divine incarnation.

**The reform campaign of Nestorius at Constantinople.** Like Diodore and Theodore, Nestorius wanted to make sure that theological language always emphasized the distinctness of the human and divine natures in the incarnate Lord. He felt he was simply repeating the "traditional" teaching of the Syrian church in this. He had no sense of himself as an innovator but strongly wished to pose as a reformer and pull up the many more "sloppy" versions of theology that were then operating in the church. Chrysostom, Diodore, and Theodore were regarded as the three jewels of the Syrian church. But in 404 Cyril of Alexandria had aided and abetted his uncle, Theophilus, the archbishop of Alexandria, in deposing Chrysostom on trumped-up charges and sending him into his exile. Now that Cyril had succeeded his uncle as archbishop, Nestorius knew well enough to be very careful about never trusting him. He was determined from day one that he would not listen to anything coming out of Egypt. When Nestorius did eventually come across Cyril's writings (in the context of a sharp apologetic), he also misheard it as a simple restatement of the thoughts of Apollinaris. So from the beginning he was hostile and attempted to refute Cyrilline thought. But Cyril was not a *repetiteur* of Apollinaris. He had absorbed the theology of Athanasius, a very moderated form of Origenian exegesis, much of Chrysostom's biblical writing (ironically enough), and the thought of Gregory of Nazianzus. In addition, he was a very sharp and acute theologian himself who spoke for a wide range of international bishops.[22]

When Nestorius came to Constantinople in 428 and immediately started a "reform" campaign there, he decided to insist on Syro-Antiochene terms of Christology. In this he unwittingly started a great intellectual war of traditions. The Alexandrian christological tradition, while admitting Apollinaris was misguided and excessive in his theology of christological fusion, nevertheless insisted that what was at stake in the incarnation was a veritable "union" of God and humanity in the person of the Word: that union he made in his own existence was, the Alexandrian theologians insisted, offered paradigmatically as a realized return to union between God and the whole human race. If he did not make the union in his own person, how could he, they argued, have passed on that unification between God and humanity to the world through his incarnation? As Athanasius had put it, very simply yet strikingly, a generation beforehand: "He became man so that we might become god."[23] When Cyril heard Nestorius's terms of preaching, it was probably the first time he had listened extensively to a Syro-Antiochene orator of the school of Diodore. Chrysostom was much more moderate in his language. Nestorius gave it straight from the shoulder, and Cyril immediately thought it was heretical.

---

[22] A much more detailed account of this great debate is contained in J. A. McGuckin, *St. Cyril of Alexandria and the Christological Controversy: Its History, Theology, and Texts* (Leiden: Brill, 1994); 2nd ed., Crestwood, NY: St. Vladimir's Seminary Press, 2004.

[23] Athanasius of Alexandria, *De Incarnatione* 54.

What Nestorius said began with a simple, and innocent enough, call for more precision in theological thought. He felt his new capital city had all the laxness of an international court and needed some tightening up. From his early days at Constantinople, therefore, he commanded the monks to stop roaming the streets and stay in their monasteries (earning their hostility); tried to put a stop to independent ladies' liturgies (led by aristocrats, thus earning their enmity); insulted the Empress Pulcheria by questioning her claim to consecrated virginal status because she enjoyed such a lively social life (thus accidentally impugning her honor and earning her undying opposition); forced the closure of the last remaining Arian church in the city (which also happened to be the last chapel where the Gothic troops of Constantinople worshiped, thus alarming all the military commanders); and cleaned out the troop of actors, dancers, strip-tease artistes, fortunetellers, and courtesans who inhabited the environs of the Hippodrome (earning the sullen resentment of many of the populace). In a word: within a few weeks he had alienated massive sections of the city's political, military, popular, and ecclesiastical establishments.[24] He had the support of Emperor Theodosius II, who especially liked the way in which his new archbishop had annoyed his very dominant elder sister, Princess Pulcheria. But when international complaints against him started to accumulate, this lack of general support would cost Nestorius dearly.

The spark that started the fire was the occasion when Nestorius instructed his Syrian chaplain Anastasius to begin a series of sermons in the Cathedral of Hagia Sophia on why many people were being ignorant and carelessly heretical in their theology. They chose the example of a Marian devotion they had heard voiced in the capital. People were actually praying to the Blessed Virgin and calling her "mother of God" (*Theotokos*). This had to stop, he said, because it was both silly and blasphemous. Suddenly Nestorius's series of evening sermons got a large attendance, and many mutterings were heard from the floor of the church, because the use of this title was a long-established custom of Christian prayer outside Syria. The great controversy had started.

The archbishop's logic was a restatement of Syro-Antiochene thought and ran something like this. Theology must be done in all strict accuracy (*akribeia*), not following the whims of piety. Mary is not, strictly speaking, the mother of God, since the Word of God has no beginning or end and thus can have no mother. She is the mother of Jesus, if you like, or the mother of Christ, but never the mother of God. When Cyril of Alexandria heard this he answered back immediately: If Mary, "strictly speaking," is not the mother of God, then "strictly speaking" the one who is

---

[24] See further J. A. McGuckin, "Nestorius and the Political Factions of 5th Century Byzantium: Factors in His Downfall," *Bulletin of the John Rylands University Library* 78, no. 3 (1996): 7-21.

born from her is not God. Thus, to deny the title Theotokos, not the use of it, is a major heresy. Cyril went on to justify the use of all manner of christological paradoxes (like the Theotokos title). Paradox was important, he felt, because it was able to suggest to the believer that the divine incarnation was a mystery that could not be wholly captured in a theologian's strict accuracy of language. Traditional pieties also were important in the life of the church because they expressed the ancient tradition of faith in ways that were not subservient to the written, intellectual tradition. If the faithful called Mary mother of God, it was because it expressed their deeper faith that Jesus was God.

Likewise, the traditional pieties that spoke of God's tears (at the death of Lazarus) or the death of God on the cross were equally not foolish affirmations, as the Arians had said and as Nestorius was again suggesting, because in a simple and straightforward way they expressed common belief in the divine agency of the incarnation. What was understood in all these things, nevertheless, was the unspoken "qualifier" that this was an appropriate outcome of the incarnate state. What was meant by God weeping, then, was that "God wept, in the flesh" or that God died on the cross (as incarnated one) even though he could not die. If preferred, it all meant God died in his humanity, and was immortal in his Godhead—and this was why the incarnate Lord both died and rose again as immortal. Cyril insisted that the clue to all these paradoxes was that the selfsame and single person of the divine Word of God in the incarnation now operated in the dual role of his adopted nature (humanity) and his "own nature" of divinity, making these formerly separated things (human existence and divine being) now a seamless unity in his own person.

Nestorius reacted to Cyril's critique in three ways: first, he (wrongly) thought that the insistence on unification of natures was what Apollinaris meant by it a generation before: a mechanical *krasis* or confused mixture of unmixable categories (divinity and humanity to make a hybrid); second, he thought that Cyril exactly personified someone who could not get his theology accurately sorted out—appealing to "mysteries" to cover up conundrums and confusions; third, that the best way to deal with this attack from a senior cleric of a major see would be to be forearmed and unyielding and to restate his message more and more forcibly the more it was criticized. He made the mistake either of thinking in all honesty that Cyril was a stupid man or rhetorically pretending that Cyril's theology was brainless.

From the beginning, therefore, we see a very unyielding mindset in Nestorius, who simply refused to see any nuance in anyone other than those who followed his own lead. This would cause him great troubles when he came to an international gathering of bishops that would soon be assembled to adjudicate the matter of Christology at

Ephesus in 431. Meanwhile, he decided to develop his own thought on Christology more abruptly. This took it out of the Theotokos controversy and into a dispute about christological titles as such.

Nestorius said that it was important to be very precise about Jesus statements. If one referred to the human aspect of the Christ (such as Jesus the man), one should use the title Son of Man as a subject reference. If one referred to a divine aspect (the divine Word), one should use the title Son of God. If one referred to a form of mixed reality (the Word acting among humankind in the incarnation), then one should use the subjectival title *Christ* or *Lord*. This was necessary to preserve strict accuracy (*akribeia*) in christological language. What he meant to stress was that one ought to apply a different subjectival "set" of characteristics for each aspect of the incarnate Lord's life and work: this was the traditional way the concept of *parsopa/prosopon* had been used by his teachers in the Antiochene school.

He also developed a new type of semantic usage himself. He used the adverb *prosopically* to speak of a voluntary association of natures that could not otherwise be conjoined. So humankind could "prosopically" relate to God, if the human being became morally obedient to God. He used terms to suggest that a human being could be saved only if it had the *prosopon* of God (that is, was united with the divine by a free and moral choice). To "possess the *prosopon* of God" meant to will what God wills. The *prosopon* of a human was to will and act as a human being. A prosopic union of God and a human signified a union of wills in which a human and God were in harmony. For Nestorius the harmony that Jesus demonstrated (prosopically joined with the divine Word) was equally a symbol of his own holiness and a paradigm of how humankind in general could be brought into union with God through his example. Jesus' prosopic union was the root of his holiness: in this the Son of Man was designated as Son of God and was seated at the right hand of the Father.

Now, given that the term *prosopon* most everywhere else signified the concept of individual person, all this was a usage on Nestorius's part that was bound to lead to immense confusion of his intent at Alexandria (which did not follow this moral usage of the [Syriac] term *parsopa*) and at Rome (which used the Latin term *persona*). What Rome and Alexandria "heard him say" by his prosopic terminology was that there were at least two different personal subjects (*prosopa/personae* in the Alexandrian Greek and Latin sense) in the incarnate one: presumably the divine Word and some man named Jesus.[25] This out and out mishearing was not resolved by Nestorius explaining that he did not teach "two Sons" in that way. Cyril remained adamant

---

[25] When Nestorius spoke of a third *prosopon*, that of Christ, the *prosopon* of unity, Cyril was genuinely puzzled and accused him of unnecessary obscurity—thinking he was unaccountably teaching "three persons" in the incarnate Savior.

that if he did not intend to teach two personal subjects in the Savior, he still ended up teaching the same implied subjectival binary because he had not secured any alternative reason for any real sense of unity.

This lack of centering in his ideas about "personhood" was compounded by his equally adamant insistence that all talk of "unification of natures" should be avoided at all cost, because this would be to revive the heresy of Apollinaris.[26] The natures, Godhead and manhood, were ontologically and utterly distinct. The incarnation had not united them; it simply brought them into "intimate association." Nestorius sought for words to clarify what he meant by this association and once again elevated terms that were traditional in Syria (but not accepted internationally). This was the concept of a "relational association" of Godhead and manhood in Christ (*synapheia kata schesin*), and the stress on the concept becomes very characteristic of his thought. This *schesis*, or relationality between divine and human in Christ, is for Nestorius purely a moral one, a voluntarist association: the divine Word chooses in mercy to stoop down to humanity to save it, and humanity chooses to live the obedient moral life and is morally uplifted to God. This moral movement, descent of the divine, ascent of humanity, was for Nestorius what the concept of incarnation really meant. It certainly "did not" mean a change of natures in any way or an alleged union of them, incompatible as divinity and humanity were. Moral union was wholly connoted under the figure of the concept of incarnation.

***Cyril of Alexandria's countercharge.*** Hearing these ideas and recognizing that his own cardinal insight into Christology was under attack (namely, that the incarnation was a veritable and natural union [*henosis*] of God and humanity in Christ), Cyril began a series of treatises and letters from 429 onward, determined to secure a wide international agreement that this new archbishop of Constantinople was introducing dangerous innovations into Christian doctrine. Cyril applies a wide range of images and analogies to support his theology of *henosis*.[27] He has the common touch and wishes to appeal directly to the experience of common Christian piety. For both reasons—first, that he regularly uses the word *henosis* (union), and second, that his imagery uses popular piety—Nestorius tended to dismiss him as a third-rate thinker.

---

[26] Clearly the very concept of individual, subjectival (spiritual) personhood was being heavily developed and extended by this discourse. It would emerge, finally, as connoted by the concept of hypostasis. At the time, however, the notion of personal, individual consciousness as a profound ontological category did not exist. At that period Greek philosophy looked on individuation (*to idion*) as an "accidental" category, not a substantive one (*upokeimenon*). It was Christian discourse on the personhood of Jesus that advanced the notion of person to the stability of ontological status—a great moment in the history of consciousness—but this was a clarity that had not yet been achieved by the protagonists in the fifth century.

[27] Again, a much fuller exposition of this world of thought is available in McGuckin, *St. Cyril of Alexandria and the Christological Controversy*.

In fact he was a brilliant rhetorician and philosopher, and his very flexibility of expression (unlike Nestorius's constant insistence that all theology has to be done precisely and linguistically correctly) allows him to present a complex set of ideas very easily and persuasively. When it eventually came to a great gathering of bishops at the Council of Ephesus, Cyril was the one they understood, not Nestorius.

Cyril's main idea is that the two natures of Godhead and manhood come together in the one Christ, in the ontological foundation of the single divine personhood of the Word; and what was formerly separated (Godhead and manhood) by all manner of chasms (ontological divides between creator and created, or moral divides such as between holiness and sinfulness, or between power and weakness) is now brought back into union. The incarnation is precisely God's omnipotent act to bring about a union of God and humanity in the most intimate form possible: in his own personal life as second person of the Trinity. There is no other reason for the incarnation except to produce this union out of natures that were formerly apart and unreconciled. In short, the incarnation is a divine act of healing, reconciliation, and restoration of the human race into the very life of God, from which it receives its life and ontological power in the first place. Falling away from God, it had fallen into death. Being returned into God by Christ, humanity now lives once more in immortal grace and shall live forever with Christ in the kingdom. The incarnation, therefore, is no myth, no mere symbol of a voluntarist closeness between God and humankind (such a thing would make the incarnation a mere myth, not the cardinal event that reconstituted human nature), but a real ontological change in the state of reality.

For Cyril, Christ's own humanity is the arena where this unification of divinity and humanity is worked out (what Paul calls the "firstfruits"). In his own divine, personal subject, the omnipotent Word who first had made humanity now remakes humanity *a radice* by adopting a human life. He takes to himself a human body endowed with a rational soul and now begins to live within history through its medium. He himself, as divine Word, is not "changed into" a human man or human flesh in all that this means. Rather, the Word chooses to live through the medium of the body, as well as remaining omnipotent in his own nature as eternal Word. But his choice of life in the flesh is a genuine one (not a mere phantasmal appearance or a mythological experience as an avatar). What Cyril means by this is that it is a choice of divine omnipotence as Word (the only subject of the incarnate life) to live passibly in the flesh, as is appropriate to the flesh.

So when the omnipotent Word was born, he also accepted to live the life that followed after that: with weakness, mental confusion, suffering, the need to learn, and all other things leading up eventually to his death on the cross. This was the *kenosis* (self-emptying) he had accepted so as to be able to experience all things human in the flesh, so that he might be the high priest of our race and offer himself as our supreme teacher and mediator. But this, while real, and acutely felt (for Cyril, Jesus did indeed feel the pains of humanity in his own body), did not obliterate what he remained, as divine Word, in communion with the Holy Trinity. Cyril sees the bodily life of the Word not as a playacting but as a genuine consecration of human life and suffering, so that it could be lifted up into the Godhead and given a sacred character, be made worthy of sanctification, and rendered into a path to heaven. Cyril sees the descent of the Word into human life as the divine consecration of flesh in the person of the God-Man.

In other words, Cyril sees the divine incarnation as real but transgressive. God has done the impossible: he has personally become man while remaining God. He suffers (in his human experience) while remaining impassible (as the Word). He dies (as man on the cross) while remaining immortal and so causes even his own flesh to rise once more from the grave. He cannot do other than walk from village to village (since he cannot fly), but if necessary for the works of salvation, he will walk over the sea to save his disciples. Cyril criticizes Nestorius's constant desire to "keep the categories clean" (the distinctions between the two zones of nature—what is appropriate for humans and what for God) because he says, time and time again, God himself, in Christ, has broken the grip of the categories. He has lifted up humanity to the highest heavens in himself and has brought down the highest Godhead into extremes of humility, all this while without "confusing natures" or mixing them up into hybrids. Christ, as the Word incarnate, has done this impossible thing because he has united the different natures, that is, strictly and precisely "made them one," not in the realm of nature as such, but rather in the domain of his personhood. When Nestorius keeps criticizing his "sloppiness" in theological thinking, Cyril regularly replies that it is not he that is to blame if God himself has chosen to live the scandalous life of extreme humility and suffering instead of regal glory: this is the message of the gospel he is simply exegeting!

To express this critical idea of the personal union Christ has made between God and man, Cyril presses a new terminology on his readers (one that the Syrians refused to accept): he brings forward the word *hypostasis*. The Word has personally (hypostatically) made the human and divine realities one in himself. In his own divine person (hypostasis) he has made the impossible possible. He has done this so as to be the paradigm for all humanity. Not only will humanity become one with him in his own incarnate life, but he will make all humanity one with him in his kingdom. Cyril points to the personal gift of his divine flesh (in the Eucharist) to all believers as the cipher and promise of this greater reality. So, the incarnation of the divine

Word, as God-Man (*theanthropos*), welds the separated natures together as one, a pure unity, not a mixed confusion of states of being (natures as characteristics), a personal unity, not a material or mechanical one. This bringing together was not for its own sake, of course, but precisely because the human nature was lapsing into death and needed the proximity of the divine to give it life once more: the union, in other words, is the act of divine salvation, which is what the incarnation is all about, understood soteriologically. Such a concept of the "union of natures" was far removed from Apollinaris's mechanistic views of unity. Sadly, Nestorius was not able to perceive the difference. All talk of this kind of *henosis*, for him, meant that Cyril was preaching fourth-century Apollinarist heresy again a generation too late.

What Cyril found most objectionable in Nestorius was that he had missed the central point of redemption theory: that God had lifted up humanity into his own bosom, when once it had been far removed from God because of sin and death. Nothing less than the concept of union (*henosis*) would do for Cyril to express the spiritual potency of this idea, which was the inner workings of divine salvation of the human race. Now, the bringing together of humanity and Godhead into union, while it is a matter of awesome humility on the part of God, is a matter of equally awesome exaltation on the part of weak humanity. For humans, Cyril says, it is no less than our "deification" by God's grace (*theiopoiesis*). The entirety of our nature, once weak and mortal, is now rendered in union with God, and thus afforded the graces of holiness and immortality. This is what he means by deification by grace: not an arrogant ascent to divine stature, as the Roman pagans had thought of it, but the very inner dynamic of why and how the incarnation happened as the redemptive force of God's action, basically re-creating the corrupted nature of Adam, in Christ. The entire language of deification escapes Nestorius entirely: he is not able to compute it, even though it had been elaborated not only by great theologians of previous centuries, such as Origen and Athanasius, but also by the Cappadocian fathers Gregory of Nazianzus and Gregory of Nyssa.[28]

This, above, is the primary reason Cyril finds Nestorian language defective: the way in which a theologian speaks of the incarnation without realizing it amounts to speaking about salvation processes. Many modern commentators have accused Cyril of missing Nestorius's point entirely. He does not miss this point. Here he is right on target. The secondary charge he has against Nestorius, however, was something of a mishearing. But it was one he was rightly concerned about. For he heard

---

[28]See further J. A. McGuckin, "Deification in Greek Patristic Thought: The Cappadocian Fathers' Strategic Adaptation of a Tradition," in *Partakers of the Divine Nature: The History and Development of Deification in the Christian Tradition*, ed. M. Christensen and J. Wittung (Teaneck, NJ: Fairleigh Dickinson University Press, 2006), 95-114.

Nestorius certainly denying the union of natures in Christ, rightly suspected he did not substantively believe in a natural union (a union on a level of natures, that is), and misheard him to be proposing a plurality of persons in Christ, though in terms of the latter Nestorius was most probably only advocating a voluntarist association (*synapheia*) between Godhead and humanity in Christ.

Cyril thought he was teaching a divine person alongside a human person, or at least could not see why, on his terms of analysis, he was not committed to teaching a nonunited, loose association of subjects (that was not much better than seeing Christ as an elevated prophet obedient to the Word who was his God). This human person could only be a Jewish man called Jesus; and in his turn Cyril caricatured Nestorius as reviving the old heresy of Paul of Samosata, who had taught that a human being was one day caught up into spiritual power when the Word of God elevated him to fill him with grace and preach the gospel. But this man, so exalted beyond any prophet before him, was only "called" God. He was not God really or in truth.

Cyril found Nestorius's prissiness of linguistic usage a kind of dance around the issue of whether Jesus was God or not. Nestorius allowed that the Word was God and that Christ could rightly be called God. But was Jesus God? Nestorius wanted to make qualifications and say it is not appropriate to use a human designator-title (Jesus) and refer it to divine things. So, for him, it would be "foolish" theology to speak of the Virgin Mary putting on a vest for her baby son, as "the mother of God puts a vest on her divine Son." He would cringe at such language. Cyril takes his cringe as a failure of theological nerve. Does he not believe that this little baby is God? Cyril says, "For I do!" Accordingly, Cyril delights in applying theological tests of faith in the form of incarnational paradoxes: "God weeps and suffers"; "Jesus is my Lord and God"; "the holy Virgin is the mother of God"; and so on. The paradoxes, he always understands, and so should we too, gain their potency from the constant frame of reference, which is, "that is, within the mystery of the incarnation." But he felt that to be so obvious it did not need to be stated at every instance.

So the paradoxical force of language "God wept" or "God died" was useful, for Cyril, in the sense that it reinforces the mystery that the single subject of all these experiences, whether divine or human, was none other than the eternal Word. In short, Cyril insists, Jesus is the eternal Word. And if one finds that illogical (since Jesus existed from a certain date in history surely?) then even so it stands as truth because he who is Jesus is none other than the eternal Word. The apparent paradox is explained by the inexplicable grace of the divine assumption of the body within time. To refuse to confess "Jesus is the eternal Word" or more simply "Jesus is God" is, for Cyril, to wholly fail to grasp the implications of the mysterious divine *kenosis*, which is the incarnation act of redemption. On the other hand, the more Cyril insisted on such a theological approach of paradox, the more Nestorius thought he had lost his mind and was breaking every rule of semantic precision.

The falling out was so severe and had become so public and bitter by the year 430 that Emperor Theodosius II knew he had to call a general council of the church's bishops to resolve it. Nestorius had secured the initial support of the emperor, but he had earned the hostility of the imperial court. Cyril had forwarded several of Nestorius's sermons to Pope Celestine at Rome and to his learned archdeacon, Leo. Both Latins had been glad to receive the works translated into Latin for their benefit, by Cyril's theologians, and both had been disturbed by the Syrian theology of apparent double subjectivity. A synod had been held at Alexandria and another at Rome, and both had formally censured Nestorius's thought and called for his immediate retraction of all he had said. Nestorius had taken this as another attempt to break the importance of his archepiscopal see at the capital and had persuaded the emperor that they should try Cyril for heresy instead, perhaps bring him to Constantinople, where Nestorius would preside over the discussion of the theological points at stake in a learned meeting of the best minds of the day. It seems that the emperor had agreed to that idea and sent out an invitation limited to learned bishops only. But it was the custom of the councils of the church to be open to all bishops. Cyril, as a result, demanded (and brought) a large number of his Egyptian hierarchy with him, and many monks.

The tipping point, however, seems to have been an unseen hand with great influence and subtlety (I have always suspected Princess Pulcheria did this) who somehow or other shifted the place of the conciliar gathering from Constantinople to the city of Ephesus. This made travel to that place from the capital and from all the Syrian archdiocese very difficult indeed. It also made Nestorius's presidency of the council no longer a guaranteed thing: in fact, it snatched away the presidency from his hands. Instead of Ephesus 431 being a trial of Cyril, it was rapidly developing into a trial of Nestorius: for he was now subject to two synodical condemnations, one from Rome and one from Alexandria in 430, and according to the canons of Christian usage Nestorius now could not presume to operate outside his own diocese until he had answered all charges against him. Moreover, Ephesus was like the Lourdes of the ancient world. Its main cathedral was called the "Mary Church," and the faithful of the city were outraged at any attempt to denigrate their patroness, the holy Virgin and mother of God. That Nestorius was widely seen as an attacker and impugner of the honors and virtues of the holy Virgin did not bode well for him at Ephesus. All was set, then for a great council to meet there in the summer of 431. Nestorius asked his friend, the aristocrat Count Candidianus, to bring a detachment of guards to police the city and afford him personal protection. As long as he had that very direct form of support, he felt he could be brave enough until his Syrian colleagues arrived from the far-flung diocese of Antioch, the few theological friends he knew he could count on to understand him.

**The Council of Ephesus 431.** The trouble at Ephesus was, however, that Memnon, the local bishop, had immediately allied himself with Cyril and had recognized the latter's right to act as president of all proceedings. Not only was Nestorius under censure and unable to attend except as defendant, but also Cyril had been given the personal mandate of Pope Celestine to stand in and act for him as vicar. So, presiding as both pope of Rome and archbishop of Alexandria, his right to preside was uncontested by the clergy present—except by Nestorius. The remainder of the Antiochene bishops, led by John, the patriarch of Antioch, simply had not turned up. They would not appear until many weeks had passed since the predetermined starting date of the council.

Modern scholars have accused Cyril of not waiting long enough for them to come, but this was a matter of more than a month's delay in the heat of an Asia Minor summer. I also think that Cyril eventually came to think that maybe they deliberately wanted to be "too late" because they did not wish to be present for what might prove to be the condemnation of one of their own. Whatever the case (they pleaded a long and hard journey, with some of their elder bishops dying en route), proceedings were opened and concluded before they were present; and when they did come and heard what had happened, they were furious, opened their own minority council separately, and condemned the other bishops of the majority party.

During the long wait the majority had for the "Easterners," dialogues were initiated. Nestorius was asked by many for his opinions, but he barricaded himself in his lodgings, using the guard of Count Candidianus, as he felt unsafe with so many monks in the city who were hostile to him. He made it clear that he would not appear in any disputation that cast him in the role of defendant. So, when the council did eventually proceed on June 22, it made three formal calls to Nestorius to present himself to answer charges, but when he ignored all three, it simply proceeded to depose him on the grounds of his recalcitrance. No great investigation was held of his theology. But the damning moment came when some visiting bishops who had been friends of his reported to the assembly that they had gone to his lodgings only days previously to beg him to be reasonable, and in the course of talking about the meaning of the incarnation, Nestorius had apparently lost his temper and said to them, "I refuse to call a baby of only two or three months' age 'my God.'" It was possible that he was reacting against Cyril's tendency to use paradoxes such as "God in swaddling bands," but this outburst sounded very bad indeed when reported in the cold light of the general assembly of bishops, and it cost him a massive amount of good will among the general assembly, as it underlined Cyril's claims that he did not really believe in the reality of the incarnation. He not only was clashing with Cyril here but was scandalizing the deeply felt piety of the majority of the other bishops, too, who recognized their beliefs in Cyril's version in a way that they simply did not in Nestorius's version."

Lacking a viva voce record for Nestorius's position, since he refused to attend, the Ephesine bishops allowed Cyril to present a dossier of damaging texts he had excerpted from his correspondences. Cyril also produced a large dossier he had previously made up from his church's archives, reproducing statements by a range of earlier "patristic" theologians who endorsed his opinion and contradicted that of Nestorius.[29] This impressed the bishops and is actually one of the first instances of what would be a common practice in subsequent church gatherings—assembling patristic evidences to demonstrate "traditional" theological doctrine. He also adduced the second and third formal letters he had written to Nestorius where, he explained, he had outlined the essential matters in dispute. The gathered assembly read them and endorsed them as accurate and orthodox expressions of the faith.

Although Cyril had attached a series of *anathemata* to the end of his *Third Letter* sent the year before, demanding that Nestorius should sign them or else be considered excommunicate by Rome and Alexandria, the bishops gathered in Ephesus seem to have drawn back a little at that point, perhaps considering the terms of the anathemas too sharp for their own taste. Cyril here had summed up his theology in its most radical and syllogistic form. One example is the anathema that demands all the orthodox should confess how "one of the Trinity suffered in the flesh." Rather than protract matters and make his own thought the subject of conciliar scrutiny, Cyril withdrew the appendix of the *anathemata* from his requested endorsement. So it was that the *Second* and *Third Letters* were officially endorsed, but not the anathemas. They would be revisited, however, in the Council of Constantinople II in 553, where a radically strong Cyrilline line was taken, and then the *anathemata* were added to the list of conciliar ecumenical official texts.

The summer night of June 22, 431, was drawing on when the business was concluded and the final word was written: no other faith than the creed of Nicaea would ever be allowed to be taught as Christian orthodoxy. When the clergy made their way out of the church to go home to their lodgings, they were met with an extraordinary

---

[29]These texts and an analysis of them are offered in McGuckin, *St. Cyril of Alexandria and the Christological Controversy*.

sight: the dockland area (for the church once abutted the harbor at Ephesus, though for centuries since then the sea has receded many miles) and all the plaza around the Mary Church was ablaze with torches waved by Christian women. They were making their voice heard. Had the bishops, they asked, upheld the honor of the Virgin Theotokos, or not? When it became clear that her title as Mother of God was acclaimed, and Nestorius had been deposed from his offices, there was general rejoicing among the torch-bearing crowd of women (how quickly it might have become a flame-bearing mob was not lost on anyone), and they broke up to escort the hierarchs back to their houses in processions of honor.

Nestorius still refused to leave his lodgings at Ephesus and complained to Count Candidianus, who had been given the task of keeping citywide order. He refused to allow any bishop to leave the gates of Ephesus. And when the Syrian delegation eventually arrived, he gave a report that was critical of the way he felt the majority of other bishops under Cyril's leadership had disregarded his right to keep order.[30] The Syrians, with a significantly lesser number than the majority council, met themselves and deposed Cyril and Memnon, censured the majority bishops for not waiting for them, and exonerated Nestorius. After that point the majority bishops met again and censured all the Syrian bishops as dissidents and also anathematized them as heretics insofar as they were endorsing Nestorius's condemned teachings.

Count Candidianus was frantic. He had been given the charge by the emperor to make sure all things went smoothly at the council and a general consensus was happily arrived at. The result must have been the worst result imaginable. Now, it seemed, everybody was excommunicating everybody else. Candidianus barred the gates, but an exodus of representative parties was allowed to make its way to Constantinople (though not the main agents, who were closely held under house arrest from this time onward). Candidianus also sent a political report of events. The Syrians and the Cyrilline party equally made representations. When they arrived at the capital, Theodosius kept his own counsel for some long weeks, hearing reports across the summer in his palace in the suburb of Chalcedon.

The emperor, who had formerly been a supporter of Nestorius, realized that the latter's position was now hopeless. A series of popular riots in the city streets, all baying for Nestorius's imprisonment, helped to fix his judgment, although many "gifts" were also distributed at the capital by Cyril to allow his party to access the

---

[30]The bishops under Cyril's leadership asked him to read the emperor's decree (*sacra*) convoking the council and then absent himself, since a layperson could have no further part in proceedings. He felt he should have been allowed much more of a say.

palace more regularly.[31] Theodosius eventually ordered that the bishops should be allowed to leave Ephesus and go home and that Cyril and Memnon should be released from house arrest. The decisions of the majority synod would be endorsed as the official church teaching. Nestorius would proceed under guard, straight back to his monastery in Syria, never to return to the capital again. He should resume the simple monastic life. He must not speak or write in public. Nestorius's refusal to observe the terms of this judgment caused a series of increasingly severe judgments against him. In the end the emperor exiled him to Petra in Jordan and then, when he still wrote in his own defense, to the farthest corner of the Byzantine world, the Great Oasis in Upper Egypt, where he spent his last years in the company of disgraced imperial officials, political prisoners, and courtesans who had fallen out of favor.

But the triumph of Cyril was not complete. The Syrians returned to the vast Antiochene patriarchal territories and spread the word abroad there that Cyril had been condemned at the "Council of Ephesus" (for years the report circulated there that the minority gathering had been the official conciliar event), and despite the imperial command, the entire Syrian church refused to enter into communion with Alexandria. Two years later, a reconciliation was moderated by the palace and the new archbishop of Constantinople, Maximian. As a result of the mediations Cyril and John of Antioch signed a joint agreement known as *The Formula of Reunion* that set out a christological statement combining elements of both the Syrian and Alexandrian confessions and agreeing to the personal unity of Christ.[32]

This formal rapprochement certainly did not end the smoldering resentment of the Syrians over the way in which Egypt had railroaded the recent conciliar events, and indeed all of Cyril's writings after he signed the agreement continued to denounce the greatest of the Syrian teachers, namely Diodore of Tarsus and Theodore of Mopsuestia, as "teaching the same thing as Nestorius," though uncondemned. He made no secret of his dislike of Syrian ways of speaking of prosopic union and such like. In their turn the Syrians made no secret about their dislike of him and especially his language of a hypostatic union of natures, which Cyril (overoptimistically) regarded as having been universally accepted.

---

[31] This style of bribing the court officials to allow access to the higher nobles of the palace seems to us out-and-out corruption—but it was a standard political process of late antiquity. Nestorius, of course, had lost all access to state funds on news of his deposition, but Cyril could still command great resources and put these *eulogia* to good effect in advancing his arguments at the capital. We know about it because Cyril kept receipts for everything.

[32] It is preserved in Cyril's corpus of letters as *Epistle* 39, "Let the Heavens Rejoice." Its core, with which Cyril agrees, with numerous asides clarifying his thought in the face of Antiochene criticisms (from Theodoret of Cyr), was not composed by him but sent to him, and this is his replying giving his own agreement and thus effecting some form of reconciliation.

The fragile reconciliation of 433 tended to mask the key issue that had not been settled in any significant way at the council, namely the manner in which the "two natures" were combined. Was Christ a single union "out of two natures" (Cyril's preference), or was he a single person existing "in two natures" (the preference of Rome and Syria)? Cyril was persuaded not to persevere in his attacks on the Syrian tradition, for the sake of international peace. But his own followers, not least his immediate successor, Dioscorus, tended to think the old man had given in too easily to intellectualist obscurantists in Syria. After he signed the agreement, John of Antioch also lost much credibility among his own supporters. The original dispute was clearly still smoldering in the undergrowth, and it would not take much to make it burst out into flame once more. The death of Cyril in 444 was a proximate cause for his own archdiocese to keep an eye open for any opportunity to intervene at Constantinople again and pull down to the foundations any attempt to restore Antiochene influence there.

Dioscorus of Alexandria thought he had found the ideal cause in 448 when news came to him that a highly respected Archimandrite, Eutyches of Constantinople, leader of more than three hundred pro-Cyrilline monks at the capital, had been charged with heresy by Domnus, the new archbishop of Antioch, and Eusebius of Dorylaeum, a lawyer turned cleric who had pressured Flavian, the archbishop of Constantinople, to try the old man and condemn his doctrine, thereafter deposing him from office. The archimandrite appealed to Dioscorus of Alexandria, who demanded to hear the appeal formally in a general council. The emperor, wishing to keep to his policy of supporting Cyril's majority council at Ephesus 431, declared that any new gathering should reassemble at Ephesus and be under the presidency of Dioscorus. The date was set for gathering there once more in 449.

**Ephesus II 449 and its aftermath.** This council has not been entered into the ranks of the key "ecumenical" councils. It has for many centuries been known instead, following Jerome's witticism, as the "Brigandage of Ephesus" (*Latrocinium*) or the "Robber Council." This report of it went out for two chief reasons, first because the input of Rome was ignominiously rejected by Dioscorus once he had read it, and second because security was poorly administered there. Many monks were present in the city, and mob violence flared up, with many passions hotly stirred between the theological antagonists, who were determined not to be pushed out of the proceedings this time round. In the course of one of these violent scuffles, the archbishop of Constantinople Flavian was manhandled and his entourage beaten. His death shortly afterward was widely held up (by Dioscorus's enemies) to be partly laid to the blame of his presidency, because he had encouraged the Egyptian monks excessively. His enemies began to moot this as a possible reason to seek for his impeachment and reopen the entire theological matter one more time.

What Eutyches had done at the capital was reopen the whole can of worms. He had preached a very strong form of Cyrilline theology, insisting on a natural union in such strong language (because he wanted to censure and suppress Syrian styles of speaking of two distinct natures in Christ) that it sounded as if he believed there was a fusion of natures into one. Eutyches spoke in terms of two natures before the union and one nature after it: the single divino-human nature of the God-Man. For the Syrians this was everything that they disliked Cyril for, the regular tendency to make union language work at a level of natures (a union of natures instead of a correlation of natures), and they were determined to secure his fall from grace as a heretic who had repeated the teaching of Apollinaris.

Unlike Cyril, Eutyches was more pious than learned. He spoke of the body of Christ that had come down from heaven (a heavenly body) and seemed to think that if he confessed Jesus' body was "like our own" he was committing some form of blasphemy against the divine Christ. At his trial, learned theologians tied him in knots, and he was easily convicted of a teaching (since somewhat falsely projected onto him as "Eutychianism"—a precursor of Monophysitism) that said out of two separate natures (Godhead and humanity) Christ had made a single heavenly nature for himself. After the union of the two there was now only one: or Christ was "one out of two." It would be irreverent to confess, Eutyches said, that Christ was "just like us" in humanity (consubstantial, that is, in his humanity with other humans) because his manhood was unique in all respects, being suffused with divine grace and elevated out of the category of ordinary humanity.

Dioscorus read this conflict not as a trial of some elderly theologian at Constantinople but more in the style of a wholesale attack on Cyril's memory. His presidency of the discussion at Ephesus in 449 meant that he had to receive the official contribution of the Roman church. In 431 Pope Celestine had simply allowed Cyril to represent him in all matters. The popes had come to regret that decision seeing the chaos that had resulted from Ephesus. Now Archdeacon Leo had succeeded Celestine, and Leo was no mean theologian himself. Seeing the gathering of 449 coming, he had commissioned the drawing up of an official Roman statement on Christology. This time Rome would speak from its traditional patristic sources and not rely on anyone else. It sent the letter, now called the *Tome of Leo*, in the hands of delegates. Dioscorus had presumed it would be more or less an endorsement of his position. It was an immense shock when he read it. Leo had acted conservatively, and so he had made up a text that was a pastiche of very traditional things the Latin theologians had taught about Christ.

The *Tome* is composed of lines drawn from Tertullian (second century) and Augustine (fifth century) and uses the very antique style of Latin statements about Christ "possessing" two natures. In short, it was traditional because it was archaic. Instead of addressing the issues at play in the late fifth century, it privileged philosophical terms and notions that were in circulation in the second century, and it advanced the very old Latin philosophical notion (from Tertullian) that the definition of the term *person* was "that which took possession of the properties of a nature." All sense, as had been developing across the church of the last generation, of personhood as an issue of spiritual subjectivity was held subordinate here. As a result, the Christology of Leo's *Tome* is extraordinarily binary in style. Christ is one single, divine person (in harmony with Cyril's insistence); but equally this one person presides over two quite distinct natures. This double presiding blows a hole in Cyril's insistence that what happens in the incarnation is a *henosis* of the natures once separate. Instead Leo speaks about how on the one hand, he does some things as God in his divine nature; and then on the other hand, he does some things as a man, in his human nature. The two sets of properties (actions) can be referred to the same person: so as God, Christ walks over the sea, and as man he weeps over his dead friend Lazarus.

This seemed eminently sensible to the Roman legal style of clarified theological discourse. But Dioscorus realized at once that it radically contradicted one of Cyril's chief insistences: that Christ did not do some things as man, some things as God, but rather did everything as God-made-man. He wept at Lazarus's tomb as God as much as man (for he wept as God-made-man), and it was his sufferings in the body also as God-made-man that invested them with infinite value as redemptive sacrifice. If he died in the body as man and rose from the grave as God, then clearly no "union" had been effected such as to ensure the deification of the human race by grace. Such ideas as "deification," of course, were not on Leo's horizons. When Dioscorus read Leo's *Tome*, he found it to his horror as alien as he thought Domnus of Antioch and Flavian were, and so he determined to take the *Tome* out of circulation, not least because if he had publicized it he felt he would have had to synodically condemn the Roman pope himself, which scandal he was eager to avoid.

To the fury of the Roman delegates, Dioscorus would not admit the *Tome* to the acts of the council. Flavian, Domnus, and Eusebius were all censured and deposed. As a result of his disgrace Flavian suffered the violence of the mob at Ephesus, including Egyptian monks who were involved. Once again the church of Antioch declared its refusal to give agreement to this debacle, and Constantinople had suffered yet another disastrous loss of its archbishop. Anatolius was chosen in place of the dead Flavian, a candidate recommended to the emperor by Alexandria, but who soon showed himself to be independently minded.[33] Despite the fury still held at Antioch, added to which was now the clamor rising from Rome for this synod to be set aside, Emperor Theodosius held firm to his policy of supporting Alexandrian theology and simply refused to allow another synod to redress the issues.

## THE COUNCIL OF CHALCEDON 451 AND ITS AFTERMATH

Things changed dramatically in 451, when this policy was quickly set aside following the unexpected death of Emperor Theodosius, who fell from his horse while riding and broke his neck. The throne was left without a male heir. As she had done many years before, to protect the minority of her royal brother, Princess Pulcheria moved quickly to stabilize the dangerous situation and formally arranged a marriage with the leading general of the capital, Marcianus. This marriage was a purely nominal affair (she had been dedicated to virginity since she was young), but she retained control of many aspects of internal policy while Marcian secured the military situation.[34] Pulcheria was not as fixed as her brother in the need to support Alexandria at all costs, and she and Marcian now endorsed a policy that the whole christological crisis had to be seriously and thoroughly revisited. This time the Roman views had to be heard. Equally, all the best of the Syrian views had to be admitted, if they were in harmony with the basic points of the *Formula of Reunion* of 433: two natures coming together in Christ, who was one single divine person. Such was the draft given to the imperial clerics who were charged with arranging a great synod at the suburb of Chalcedon.

There was a large imperial hall here, and it was thought better if the bishops could meet under the eye of an imperial garrison, which could ensure no riotous behavior on anyone's part could distract business affairs. Pulcheria made sure that great resources of imperial stenographers would be at hand: documents could be studied and adapted, and a consensus could be reached that would surely settle the matter definitively and bring peace to Rome, Alexandria, Constantinople, and Antioch. It was a brave hope; but there were now a lot of different voices on record that needed to be harmonized.

After he arrived with his numerous Egyptian bishops, Dioscorus was forbidden to attend as a regular member of the council until his case had been heard. He was charged with having bullied bishops into submission at Ephesus 449 and having mistreated Flavian. He was summarily deposed. His condemnation was meant to offer an early sacrificial victim to soothe the ruffled feathers of Rome and Antioch.

---

[33] Anatolius had been a deacon of Cyril of Alexandria and served as the delegate of the church of Alexandria at the imperial capital (*apocrisarius*).

[34] Her enemies in Egypt (Monophysites), who thought she had allowed Antiochene influence to gain too much sway, ever after pilloried her as a "lapsed virgin" and called her "the adulteress."

It had the unexpected effect, however, of making the entire Egyptian episcopate withdraw from the council proceedings, on the grounds that they could do nothing if their head was cut off. So the balance of events was skewed from the outset. The various sessions of the council that were then held (looking for a form of statement that all could have in common) threatened to come to a stalemate. The majority of bishops present seemed to have wished to endorse Cyril of Alexandria's theology as formalized by the Council of Ephesus in 431. Few wanted to elevate the relative complexities of the thought of Theodore and Diodore, from a generation before, and certainly not that of Nestorius, whose reputation was now completely lost.

But as they demanded Cyril's teachings should simply be repeated, especially his *Second and Third Letters* to Nestorius, the imperial chancery was equally adamant that the *Tome of Leo* should, in some sense or another, be admitted into the official conciliar acts. This was probably a sine qua non of the pope's recognition of the marriage of Pulcheria and Marcian, and his support for the new political order. The introduction of Leo's *Tome*, however, was as much a surprise to the Byzantine secretaries who were arranging the order of business at Chalcedon; and when they eventually, and apparently reluctantly, presented it to the whole assembly of the bishops there was no small degree of resistance.

The learned among them knew immediately that while the *Tome* was by no means Nestorian (insofar as it strongly endorsed the idea of a single divine person presiding over the two natures of Christ, and also made room for some form of mutuality in those natures in terms of "communion of properties"), this was a text that Cyril of Alexandria himself would have had great difficulty in swallowing, since it projected a very formalist and mechanistic sense of how those natures were united.[35] In its best reading it is a communion, not a union. Not "one out of two" but very much "two enduring in one person." When it became clear to all present that the imperial will would not permit them to sideline Leo yet again, the bishops started to shout out on the floor of the chamber. These shouts had been traditional parts of synodical assemblies. They were meant to be representative of how the episcopacy was "filled with the spirit" and acclaimed the truth under inspiration when it made concerted statements.

These acclamations were carefully recorded in the synodical minutes, but one suspects they were an attempt on the part of the bishops to resolve their dilemma; for the import of them (and recorded exactly in these words) was "Leo and Cyril think alike." Thus Leo's *Tome* could be accepted (however many misgivings the

---

[35] The *communicatio idiomatum*: namely, properties of one nature can be ascribed to the other by virtue of the sameness of personal subject. It is known in English as either the principle of the "communion of idioms" or the "exchange of properties."

Greek bishops had about it), but only insofar as it was in harmony with the statements of Cyril at Ephesus 431. The bishop here acclaim they they were willing to give it a generous reading in that regard. In other words, the *Tome* was accepted as a subordinate point of reference to Cyril.

Of course, this is not the way it was later read in Rome or the subsequent West. In Western tradition Chalcedon simply means Leo's *Tome* was victorious and allegedly represented a clarity none of the Greeks could have arrived at by themselves: once again Rome saves the day. But in terms of the real events at Chalcedon it seems evident enough that the *Tome* caused great disquiet (it would eventually cause the whole secession of Egypt and large parts of Syria from the Chalcedonian settlement). In acclaiming it as in harmony with Cyril, my reading of the Chalcedonian settlement is that the synodical bishops wished to present Cyril's thought as the leading edge of international Christian consensus, subordinating the Roman and Syrian traditions to this.

Even so, in the special documents they drew up themselves, the *ekthesis*, or formal dogmatic statement of Chalcedon, they passed beyond what Ephesus 431 had said to the effect that no new theological statement was necessary. They knew now that a clearer line had to be taken to give Roman and Syrian objections to the Cyrilline language some valid room for maneuver. This was why the union of natures was qualified with a set of four opposing and carefully balanced adverbs precisely outlining the "terms of union." The *ekthesis* also made it clear that Eutyches was a step too far: the human nature was consubstantial with general human nature. The Virgin was Theotokos. There was only one personal subject, and that the divine Word, who personally assumed human flesh endowed with a rational soul. All the old bases thus seemed to have been covered. It was only necessary to ensure that the Alexandrian sense of natures concurring to singularity of unity and the Roman/Syrian sense of continuity of distinctness of natures could be recognized and harmonized.

The whole text of this famous resolution is given in the reader below, but this was essentially the compromise formula that was adopted: "One and the same Christ, Son, Lord, only begotten, acknowledged in two natures that undergo no confusion, no change, no division, no separation; at no point was the difference between the natures abolished because of the union, but rather the property of both natures is preserved and comes together into a single person and a single hypostasis." We note that there is a leaning toward Antioch: one person "in two natures"; but also a leaning toward Alexandria: a veritable "union of the natures," where the properties are what is preserved distinct.

This solution was the latest and most heated of a series of theological positionings that had been taking place over the preceding generation. All of them, in a sense, were conciliar acts extending the range of meaning attributed to Nicaea. After Constantinople 1 of 381, which had set the entire christological debate into a metaphysical, trinitarian context, the last generation's arguments had turned around the issue of "how Christ" was a divine person possessed of a human nature like ours and the nature of his divine Father, as eternal Word. The high theology had become more and more elevated and refined. One feels that at Chalcedon dogmatics is in danger of passing out of the hands of the faithful and into the pens of the most learned and careful of stenographers.

In another place I have argued that these scribes at Chalcedon did their task diligently, trying to remain faithful; all the time they sought for an active harmony to the liturgical roots of Christian confession as it was rooted in the liturgical tradition.[36] What remained to see now was the big question: Would the reconciliation work? That was the anxiety of the imperial court: for Byzantine ecclesiastical division was not simply a small matter of religious options but a major rationale for the very continuance of the God-protected empire of the orthodox, under the aegis of the God-beloved orthodox emperor. If there was no religious union in Byzantium, the very concept of political unity was threatened.

The period that followed from Chalcedon in 451 to 553 is a complex one that is not much studied in the literature. I can sum it up here as a constant attempt by the emperors to readjust the terms of Chalcedon so as to move the pivot arm of the balance more toward a Cyrilline statement and more away from a Leonine reading of the two distinct natures. And equally there was a constant insistence by the Roman popes not to reduce the significance of Leo's presence at Chalcedon one iota—in fact, to read all of Chalcedon out of the lens of Leo, just as the Byzantines tried to real all of Chalcedon out of the writings of Cyril. All the while Egypt and large parts of Syria just turned their back on the Chalcedonian reconciliation or settlement, regarding it as no settlement at all, just a lamentable denial of truths established at Ephesus 431.[37] The quick synopsis would have to be that Chalcedon's ecumenical solution did not seem to be working, even in its immediate aftermath.

The emperors, of course, were deeply troubled by the religious divisions of the Eastern church that came about as a result of the Chalcedonian decree. It is a mistake to see them motivated only by political expediency, for they themselves saw the religious dimension of their rule as a critical charism of ensuring the unity of the body of the church. As the bishops at a great council propagated doctrine as high

---

[36] See J. A. McGuckin, "Mystery or Conundrum? The Apprehension of Christ in the Chalcedonian Definition," in *In The Shadow of the Incarnation: Essays on Jesus Christ in the Early Church In Honor of B. E. Daley*, ed. P. W. Martens (Notre Dame, IN: University of Notre Dame Press, 2008), 249-59.
[37] For greater detail concerning this complex period, see W. H. C. Frend, *The Rise of the Monophysite Movement* (Cambridge: Cambridge University Press, 1972).

priests, so too the emperors published those results as imperial law to guide the whole polity of the Christian empire. The refinement of ideas that developed just before and after Chalcedon in 451 was quite extensive, however. Monastic and clerical theologians were very well aware of what was at stake in the party catchwords that began to spring up, such as "in two natures" and "out of two natures." They were also versed in the major differences between the tendencies of the school of Alexandria and those of the school of Antioch under Theodore and Diodore. But there were many more simple believers, including monastics, who were confused as to what all this furor was about.

The imperial circle, led by the palace and the patriarchal chancery at Constantinople, realized that serious work had to be done behind the scenes, as it were, to bring back the significant party of Cyrilline theologians, in Egypt and parts of Syria, into communion with the Byzantine majority represented by Chalcedon. They knew too that it would be a far harder sell to make them ever happy with the binary nature of Leo's *Tome*, so they tended to be mediators. They represented themselves to the Egyptians as Byzantine Chalcedonians who were fundamentally on the same page as them as readers of the thought of St. Cyril of Alexandria, while representing themselves to the Romans as having a commonality of belief in the single-personed, two-natured Christ, as Cyril and Leo had articulated it at Chalcedon.

They did not involve Rome directly with their eastward ecumenical negotiations very much at all. One reason for this was that Rome continued to stress the binary nature of what Chalcedon taught, "Christ in two distinct natures," while the Byzantine Chalcedonians and the anti-Chalcedonian Cyrillines agreed that the stress ought to be placed on the sense of Chalcedon's *ekthesis* that these two natures before the union "ran together" to such an extent because of the union God the Word made with his own flesh, such that the differentiation of the two natures after that union could rightly be said to subsist only in a "mental acknowledgment" (*gnorizomenon*), as the *ekthesis* of 451 had said.

It seemed abundantly clear to the emperor and the patriarch of Constantinople that their job was to repair the damaged unity of the Eastern church and do it in a way that privileged Cyril's doctrine of an unconfused (unmixed) union of natures that was indeed a real union. As Cyril had argued in his lifetime, if one teaches there was a union of natures but then continues to speak of them as abiding distinct realities, in what sense does one really believe the semantic of union at all? What was needed, if the Chalcedonian terms, so elaborate in their distinctions and qualifying adverbs, were not acceptable? The emperor and patriarch, after seeing the post-Chalcedonian problems, were very worried that a separatist hierarchy would be created in Egypt and Syria.

This was exactly what did happen in the following century. After long agonizing about it, the Miaphysite Cyrilline clergy decided that the way forward was to advance a separatist, anti-Chalcedonian hierarchical structure.[38] Jacob Baradeus, in the time of Justinian, was one of the most energetic of these anti-Chalcedonian separationists, and from this, for a long time, the Monophysite church in Egypt and Syria was called "the Jacobites." But at first the idea of a schism of such magnitude was not on the horizon. Very few believed that the issue was not resolvable. No one would have imagined that it would go on in the Eastern Christian world for almost the next sixteen hundred years. The imperial court, therefore, had some grounds for optimism in the fifth century for thinking it could resolve matters. Best, they thought, not to call another great council again. The testimony of Ephesus 431, and 449, and even Chalcedon itself, showed that passions ran too high for cool thought to have a chance of winning the day. Would it not be better to work all this complexity out in the refinement of the patriarchal cabinet? So it was that two major initiatives were undertaken in this period.

The first was the encyclical of Emperor Basiliscus issued in 475. It was an attempt to bring about unity in the East on the basis of not mentioning Chalcedon or its *ekthesis* and trying afresh to find a common basis of confessional agreement. The draft document was composed by Paul the Sophist after close consultation with the Alexandrian patriarch Timothy Aelurus, one of the leading anti-Chalcedonian theologians of the day.[39] Acacius was the patriarch of Constantinople at the time, but Basiliscus wanted to portray himself more as a friend of the Egyptian Cyrilline Miaphysites. Yet Basiliscus was far from ideally suited to negotiate such a delicate matter. He was a usurping emperor whose own ability to hold the throne, after driving out Zeno, was widely doubted.

In fact, Zeno regained his throne twenty months later, in 476, and immediately buried all memory of Basiliscus, including his short-lived encyclical. He and Acacius issued a counterdocument, the *Anti-Encyclical*, which returned imperial policy to

---

[38] Miaphysite refers to those who elevated, instead of Chalcedon, Cyril's key phrase that the incarnation represented "one enfleshed nature of God the word made flesh" (*mia physis tou theou logou sesarkomene*). Cyril was using the term *physis* here in its antique sense of concrete subsistence, which he thought was a synonym of hypostasis. His sense in using the phrase (though he abandoned it in his later career when he saw how much confusion and argument it caused) was that the divine Word, in adopting the flesh as his own, made a radical unity: he was both one single person in the incarnation, and a divine one (one *physis*-hypostasis, that is), and also he lifted up the humanity into his divine power and energized it as life-giving flesh for the sake of the world's salvation. In the aftermath of Chalcedon, however, *physis* was being used by the radical adherents of Cyril in the sense of a synonym of *ousia* (a "nature" in the sense of "divine nature" and "human nature"). In this latter context the issue had shifted to be a test of faith on how many natures after the union would a person confess: one or two? If one, then Chalcedon was necessarily rejected.

[39] This was his local nickname: Timothy "the weasel." Friends said it was because he was ascetically thin; enemies said it was he was politically slippery.

support the Chalcedonian settlement. Zeno had, however, seen for himself the furor this encyclical roused on the part of the Chalcedonians, especially from the Romans, who were now advancing the policy, comparable to their attitude to Nicaea 325, that this council of 451 should never be touched, never revised, but must remain the single and standard confession of christological orthodoxy for all and for all time. So when Zeno took power he instructed Acacius to prepare a more sophisticated draft along similar lines of desiring the reconciliation of the Miaphysites, but being less weighted toward the anti-Chalcedonian positions.

Acacius, as we saw in chapter six, drew up a memorandum of union that came to be widely called the *Henotikon*. Zeno wanted him to issue it out of the patriarchate, so the emperor would not be seen to be interfering, but Acacius "took out insurance" by declaring it had the imperial approval. As a subtle rebuke to Roman intransigence (Chalcedon or nothing), Acacius repeated the conciliar doctrine that the creeds of Nicaea 325 and Constantinople 381 were the fundamental doctrine of the Christian church. In the *Henotikon* he then described two unbalanced poles of thought: Nestorius, who separated the natures so radically he conceived of two persons in the incarnation, and Eutyches, who confused them so muddily that he ended up with a new kind of single, mixed, hybrid nature. These two positions were to be execrated, he said, as heresies that were troubling the church of his day.

In setting out the argument this way, he knew that Chalcedonians would not see themselves as Nestorian (as some Miaphysites had complained) and that the Miaphysites would not see themselves as Eutychian (as some Chalcedonians had accused them of being), and that the implied Aristotelian "golden mean" might thus be acceptable to both parties: namely that the Christology of Cyril of Alexandria as expressed in its radical form, in the *Twelve Anathemata* attached to his *Third Letter to Nestorius*, could be proposed as the positive doctrine that ought to be accepted by everyone. It was a clever attempt, because in the Byzantine world both Chalcedonians and anti-Chalcedonians had agreed that Cyril's theology was the proper expression of christological orthodoxy. But in the West it was immediately apparent to all how Acacius had arrived at to his platform of unity: by deliberately omitting all mention of Chalcedon, not offering any resolution to the issue of "one or two natures," and certainly forgetting to refer in any way to Leo's *Tome*. And the Romans were not going to have any part of it, as a result.

In 482 Zeno promulgated the *Henotikon* as a doctrine that had force of imperial law behind it and initiated a widespread deposition of higher clergy, both Chalcedonian and anti-Chalcedonian, who would not support its use as an instrument to restore the communion of the churches. The provinces of Syria and Egypt were then under great pressure from the Sassanid armies, and he wanted the people there to feel the emperor had care for them. The patriarchs of Constantinople, Antioch, and Alexandria acceded to the policy.[40] Hope for any broader unity with the West, however, started to fade in 484, when the pope called a synod at Rome and excommunicated Acacius as a heretic. Acacius responded by removing the pope's name from the list of orthodox bishops prayed for in the great cathedral. This was the first great schism that had divided Rome and Constantinople and was to be a sign of more tensions to come related to the issue of the practical unity of global Christianity.

Life at Constantinople carried on regardless of the Roman excommunications. Acacius died in 489, and Emperor Zeno followed him in 491. The new emperor, Anastasius, continued the policy of the *Henotikon*, along with the incumbent patriarch Euphemios (489–495), but one of his generals, Vitalian, eventually mounted a rebellion on the platform of "saving Chalcedon" and protesting the emperor's poor treatment of the border troops. In 515 he had secured a string of victories and marched on the capital itself, forcing Anastasius to offer him terms, which included his cessation of the pro-Miaphysite policy. Anastasius therefore opened negotiations with Pope Hormisdas in Rome to seek reunion, but the latter's terms were harsh and demanded that the emperor must condemn the memory of Acacius and Zeno, and this Anastasius refused to do. As a result Vitalian led back his troops to overthrow the emperor but was decisively defeated and went into hiding.

At Anastasius's death in 518, he sought and received pardon from his successor, Justin (518–527). The new emperor announced in 519 that the pope's terms would be accepted and reunion accomplished. Zeno and Acacius were anathematized. Unity with the West came at a cost. Antioch and Alexandria still refused to accept the preeminence of Chalcedon. The emperor had an adopted son he greatly favored. To him he would leave the throne. His occupancy of it (527–565) would leave him renowned as "Justinian the Great." He was not only a superlative strategist and politician; he was also a great reformer, as his work on the codification of Roman law shows.[41] He was also a seriously interested lay theologian, and his interest in resolving the great post-Chalcedonian schism adds a last act to this saga.

## THE COUNCIL OF CONSTANTINOPLE II 553

This important synod has entered history retrospectively as the fifth ecumenical council, held in the Eastern capital. There were 165 Eastern bishops in attendance, along with

---

[40] Peter of Alexandria thereby alienated many of his Miaphysite followers. They were subsequently called the "headless ones" (*akephaloi*), since they had detached from their leader/head.

[41] See further J. A. McGuckin, *The Ascent of Christian Law* (New York: St. Vladimir's Seminary Press, 2012).

Pope Vigilius (who did not come to the sessions) and Patriarch Eutychius of Constantinople. The council was convoked at Hagia Sophia by Justinian to try to make a lasting christological settlement among the pro- and anti-Chalcedonians. The example of the posthumous condemnation by the pope of a patriarch of Constantinople and an emperor who had previously tried this process gave grounds for thought. It also gave a new perspective on the possibility of turning away from the theology of a previous hierarch. Like it or not, Leo and his controversial *Tome* were not the essence of Chalcedon. For all the *Tome*'s close and detailed precision, avoiding "confusion" and concepts of "merging" in the two natures of Christ, and for all its orthodoxy in asserting one single person uniting two natures, the *Tome* remained a source of great contention in the East for its binary style of talking about two natures "operated by" a person (it was seen, as it is, heavily mechanistic in its sense of personhood). Moreover, by Justinian's day many were realizing that Chalcedon had failed in its attempt to be a synod of reconciliation. Instead of bringing unity, it was now itself a cause of continuing division. The conciliar proceedings of 451 were increasingly seen as a "forced synod" (one conducted under heavy military supervision and directed by imperial pressures) one that would not otherwise have accepted the Roman two-nature Christology in that form.

The anti-Chalcedonian Easterners were willing to accept the statement that the one Christ came "out of two natures" (insofar as they were not Eutychian and acknowledged the perfect authenticity of the divinity and humanity in Christ), but not that he subsisted "in two natures." The Roman and Chalcedonian position was that "union" was indeed compatible with the continued claim that there still subsisted two natures in Christ after the union. A fairly skilled theologian himself, Justinian was convinced that the reconciliation of the eastern pro- and anti-Chalcedonians was possible on the basis of a return to a strong emphasis on the Cyrilline theology they shared. He took elements out of the *Henotikon*, especially its suggestion that a basis of union could be found in the twelve anathemas of Cyril.

Between 543 and 551 Justinian gathered together the writings of three earlier Syrians most opposed to the thought of Cyril of Alexandria (Theodore Mopsuestia, Theodoret of Cyr, and Ibas of Edessa) and issued no less than three separate decrees condemning the Syrian christological school most decisively. This was a popular policy, appealing to every faction (except the minority continuing Assyrian church that remained loyal to the memory of Nestorius, though many of the Syrian hierarchs had, since the days of Nestorius, come over to a radical Cyrilline position themselves). Justinian classed this dossier of documents as the "Three Chapters."

Having thus put out his bona fides, all that was necessary for stage two was to keep the Romans in the dialogue. Here lay the problem, for nothing had changed their policy that Chalcedon and Leo's *Tome* should remain untouched. The West acknowledged but remained suspicious about the condemnations of the Three Chapters, because it feared it was just an opening of the door to sideline Chalcedon. Justinian decided that the best way to secure Roman agreement was to involve the papacy in it, willing or not. This was why he forced Pope Vigilius to be present in Constantinople. The pope vacillated continuously while the synod was in session, fearing to go too far in asserting his rights in case he incurred a synodical sentence of censure from the assembled bishops, which he knew Justinian would certainly enforce, but also fearful in case his people at home thought he had let the side down. He was eventually compelled to sign the acts and agree to the condemnation of the Three Chapters. His distaste for the whole process was the reason the West took a very long time in retrospect to accept this council as one of the core ecumenical synods. It eventually did so but has always acted as if Chalcedon were the last word, paying no attention to the radical way that the acts of 553 reinterpret the teaching of Leo's *Tome*.

The council affirmed the previous great synods as ecumenical (namely Nicaea, Constantinople I, Ephesus, and Chalcedon). It strongly signaled its radical rejection of all forms of "Nestorianism" by condemning the Three Chapters once again. Its eleven *capitula*, or statements, decisively rejected the Syrian "Christology of duality" (which was also where the unspoken critique of Leo's *Tome* lay). In fifteen *anathemata* appended to its acts, the synod also addressed the divisive issue of Origenism, as it was upsetting the peace of the monasteries of Egypt and Palestine. In the eleventh anathema the name of Origen himself appears listed as a heretic. Recent scholarship has since argued that the name was inserted as a later interpolation into the conciliar acts legally to justify the burning of his books (though many propositions from Evagrius and the Origenist monks of the desert were certainly condemned synodically in 553).

The archbishops of Milan and Aquileia broke communion with Pope Vigilius because of his acceptance of this council, and its acts would not be accepted as "ecumenical" throughout the West until the end of the sixth century (and at Aquileia not until the end of the seventh century). The christological statement made by the synod observes the clarity and precision of the Chalcedonian settlement but deliberately makes no mention at all of Leo and returns to affirm the strongest form of Cyril's christological statement (the *Twelve Anathemas* of the *Third Letter to Nestorius*), which had been passed over at Chalcedon in favor of adding in the Roman texts rejected at Ephesus 449. So it was that the vivid language of theopaschism (God suffered in his own flesh), so important to the Miaphysites, was admitted into the conciliar tradition.

The council of 553 was a bold attempt to reconcile the Syrian and Egyptian parties, on the basis of Cyrilline theology, retaining Chalcedon, but glossing it so as to reduce the impact of Leo's *Tome*. It failed, in the end, to achieve what was hoped for, largely because Egypt and Syria were soon lost to the Byzantine world through the Islamic invasion of the seventh century and because the Western churches were distracted by the increasing chaos affecting the Roman governance of their provinces. The council has, in modern times, been the subject of renewed interest for the possibility of a renewed ecumenical rapprochement between the Byzantine, Latin, Coptic, and Armenian traditions, which were divided after Chalcedon. The Byzantine tradition has always preferred the tenor of christological theory represented in the intellectual trajectory of Ephesus 431, culminating in Constantinople 553. In the West, Christology has always been predominantly interpreted through Chalcedon 451 as read through the resolving lens of the *Tome of Leo*, and very little notice has, accordingly, been given to Constantinople II. Even so, for its ability to have entered into the ecumenical synodical tradition, Constantinople II remains one of the high marks of christological rapprochement and one of the genuine achievements of Justinian's reign, even though it did not bring him his hoped-for results of ecclesial peace.

## BYZANTINE PLATONISM AT ATHENS AND PALESTINE

With Justinian (who merits a book on himself but will have to be content with a short synopsis in the following chapter) we come to a climactic point of church politics and culture in the complicated sixth century. His reign has often been elevated as one of those arbitrary (but nonetheless significant) markers of "great moments in history." In his case it has been as a watershed figure between the world of late antiquity and that of the Middle Ages. If he was to fall any side of that, it would surely be to the side of late antiquity. Another example of that: the last moment, in some senses, of the church's capacious resting in the premises of the ancient Greco-Roman thought world is given to us in this period. It begins with Justinian's alleged "closing" of the philosophical academy of Athens, which, as we have noted earlier in chapter six, is rather to be interpreted as the Christian refusal to have compulsory acts of paganism attached to school studies in the sixth century and a concomitant imperial program of favoring Christian teachers there. And it ends with a Christian response to how the Platonic academy might look if it were rebuilt with Christian stones; and this was the work of a very intriguing philosopher-theologian who called himself (but did it for motive of retaining anonymity) Dionysius the Areopagite.[42]

---

[42]The "real" or historical Dionysius the Areopagite was a disciple of St. Paul in his mission to Athens in the first century. Our writer (often called Pseudo-Dionysius) was a theologian-philosopher of the sixth century.

***Damascius of Athens and the neo-Platonic school.*** Justinian's Edict of 529, noted earlier, which stopped funding of pagan professors in state educational establishments, caused the seven leading pagan philosophers of the neo-Platonic school at Athens to move to the Persian Sassanid court to seek patronage there.[43] They liked it so little, however, that they returned to the empire two years later and were welcomed back by Justinian, though he still refused to endow their chairs. The Byzantine historian Agathias gives us their names.[44] Damascius was the head of the school among their company.

It might be illuminating to compare Damascius's thought with that of a near-contemporary Christian thinker, whose real name is not known to us but who goes under the pseudonym of Dionysius the Areopagite, and whose works mark a high point, in one sense, of how the gospel might look when read through the lens of the academy. Some have interpreted his writing as a lamentable "Hellenization of the gospel," though others have seen it, with deeper appreciation, as a dynamic missionary strategy, nothing short of the "evangelization of Hellenism."

Damascius was a Syrian in origin. So too was Dionysius. The real character behind that latter pseudonym seems to have been a monastic *higumen* in Beth Shan, Byzantine Palestine. As both men represent, Hellenism had clearly moved eastward long before this date. The Christianizing of Plato is, therefore, not an unexpected form of that penetration of Greek culture of which the New Testament is but the bridgehead, not the end. The move by Justinian to defund the pagan school at Athens was most likely initiated because the professors there had provocatively demanded their Christian students ought to take part in the pagan rites of ceremonial instituted to mark their graduation. This had caused great offense and was reacted against strongly. Justinian, as we have seen, did not make any generic move against pagan schools: he left the Hellenistic academy at Alexandria completely unaffected, for example. The whole era was a ferment of exchange between different schools of philosophy, and Christians were increasingly claiming (certainly after the time of Origen) that their gospel was the fulfillment of all the dreams of philosophers for establishing religious truth.

---

[43]"We wish to widen the law once made by us and by our father of blessed memory against all remaining heresies (we call heresies those faiths that hold and believe things otherwise than the catholic and apostolic orthodox church), so that it ought to apply not only to them but also to Samaritans [Jews] and pagans. Thus, since they have had such an ill effect, they should have no influence, nor enjoy any dignity, nor acting as teachers of any subjects, should they drag the minds of the simple to their errors and, in this way, turn the more ignorant of them against the pure and true orthodox faith; so we permit only those who are of the orthodox faith to teach and accept a public stipend." *Codex Theodosianus.*

[44]Agathias, *Histories* 2.30-31: Damascius the Syrian, Simplicius of Cyrene, Eulamius of Phrygia, Priscian of Lydia, Hermes and Diogenes of Phoenicia, and Isidore of Gaza.

Neo-Platonism was a highly religious interpretation of Plato.[45] It is a later school of Platonic commentary most associated with Plotinus (c. 204–270). He was a student, as probably was the Christian Origen of Alexandria, his near contemporary, of the Alexandrian teacher Ammonius Saccas.[46] His greatest work of commentary is the *Enneads*, written after 253 and prepared for publication from notes by his disciple, the second of the neo-Platonists, Porphyry. Plotinus picks up on certain religious-metaphysical themes already present in Plato, notably in the *Symposium*, *Thaetetus*, and *Timaeus* tractates, and develops them further than his teacher, but with equal philosophical elegance and force. He describes how three originating principles mediate reality to the sublunar cosmos (our world). They are the One, the Nous or Logos, and the Soul. The latter two begin a series of extensive emanations caused by the One, which link all being. The Nous is comparable to the Demiurge of Plato's *Timaeus*. The Soul, or World Soul, is divided into an upper and lower aspect. In it higher aspect it is the agency that emanates all souls, animated life, seeking union with the One. The lower element is more or less what we mean by nature, the grounding of life.

When Plotinus was forty (around the same time Origen was teaching in Palestine), he came to Rome to set up school. Plotinus teaches the One is sublime and transcendent. No attribution can be made in reference to it, for such would be to induce binary categories, reducing it from the state of One to that of the many. It cannot be any existing thing, nor is it the sum of all things that exist, for it is prior to, and transcendent before, all that is. It is beyond all attribution and attributes, even those of being and nonbeing. If we insist on thinking about it, though no thought or word can approach it, we might approach it by intimating that it is pure energy, potentiality (*dynamis*). The One is synonymous with the Idea of Good and the principle of Beauty.

But Plotinus is firm in his insistence that the One cannot be understood as a particular being, self-aware, or a creator deity.[47] In this his system clashed with the Christian conception of God as supreme personhood. At *Enneads* 5.6.4 Plotinus describes the One as "Light," the divine Nous (the first movement of will toward Good) as "the Sun," and the Soul as "the Moon" whose light is a derivative accumulation of light from the Sun. The One is therefore the source of all that is: even if not in a direct,

---

[45]The term is an invention of the nineteenth-century classicists to describe how Plato's academy takes this religious turn in the era of late antiquity.

[46]Plotinus was also influenced by the works of Alexander of Aphrodisias, Numenius, and the Stoic school. Neo-Platonism gained its character from the outset and therefore was an eclectic movement. It is legitimate to see Christianity in the hands of some of its interpreters, not least Dionysius, as a rival branch of that school: using not the Greek myths as illustrative and authoritative textual support for its metaphysics but rather the scriptural writings, symbolically interpreted.

[47]*Enneads* 5.6.3, 6.

creator-ly, willing sense, since activity cannot be attributed to the transcendent, unchanging One; but in the sense that the imperfect has to emanate from the perfect. All stages of creation therefore issue out from the One, in descending degrees of perfection. The highest of all perfections is the creative force of the Logos. In advanced contemplation, the philosopher (almost akin to a mystical experience) can ascend to an intuition of the One, when the mind goes beyond all multiplicity, speech, and ratiocination and achieves unitive contemplation (*henosis*). Porphyry claimed in his biography of his master that Plotinus achieved this unitive ecstatic vision four times in his lifetime.[48] It is by virtue of dedication to the Good and the Beautiful that the individual philosopher/contemplative can first recognize the One in material things, and thence in the Ideal Forms.

The next great successor to this potent fusion of philosophy and mysticism (and he was actually entitled "the successor"—*diadochus*) in the Platonic schools was Proclus (412–485). He and Damascius form the apex of the development of Plato's and Plotinus's ideas. He too (more so than Damascius) was very influential, along with Plotinus, on the later development of Christian (and Islamic) metaphysical and mystical thought. He was born in Constantinople to a renowned family of lawyers, and he studied philosophy and mathematics in Alexandria. He abandoned law in 431, when he went to Athens to study the neo-Platonic tradition with Plutarch of Athens, the head of the academy there. He took a house near the theater of Dionysius, which has been recently excavated.

After Plutarch and Syrianus, Proclus himself became the leader of the academy. Proclus admitted more an element of theurgy into neo-Platonism, the rituals of the old gods, and the desire to combine the life of the mind with the ritual acts designed to summon divine energy into the sublunar world, as Iamblichus had earlier taught. He was especially adept in the Orphic and Chaldaean oracles. His two major works are, first, the *Elements of Theology* (*Stoicheiosis theologike*), a manual of more than two hundred fundamental propositions, demonstrating a method that begins with a proof outlining how all things start with the existence of the divine unity and descend by means of souls to the material world. Second is *The Platonic Theology*, which systematizes arguments from Plato's dialogues in the cause of demonstrating the inherent divine orders within the cosmos, and which parts of the universe are closest to the One. For Proclus the role of the philosopher was to assist the soul in the struggle for liberation and the return to primal unity, by mastering the distracting passions in making it able to focus on the Good and the Beautiful. Many

---

[48]"Porphyry: On the Life of Plotinus and the Arrangement of His Works," in *Neoplatonic Saints: The Lives of Plotinus and Proclus by Their Students*, ed. M. Edwards (Liverpool: Liverpool University Press, 2000).

Byzantine-era Christian monastics found his agenda comparable to theirs and thus understood their lifestyle to be as much philosophical as "religious." Dionysius the Areopagite was a close and careful reader of Proclus and brought his ideas to many generations of Christian mystics thereafter. Boethius was another Christian thinker who used his system.[49]

In Justinian's time Damascius and Simplicius were the two most renowned of the Athenian sages, and Damascius stood as the most famed interpreter of Plato, continuing and completing the neo-Platonic tradition of Plotinus and Proclus, while Simplicius was renowned for his work on Aristotle, Epictetus, and Eulamius. We know this not despite Justinian, but rather only because their works were valued, reproduced, and transmitted down the ages by Byzantine Christian monastics who published successive editions of them in Greek and Latin. Damascius and Simplicius revived the declining fortunes of the Athenian schools. Wallis thinks it is this significant revival that brought down on their head Justinian's reaction.[50] But it is more likely the manner in which they reintroduced ritual and theurgic elements back into the school's curriculum, but now in the context of an increasingly Christianized town that found such ritual elements scandalous.

Damascius (c. 458–538), so named from his native town of Syrian Damascus, is often called the last of the neo-Platonists. He wrote three commentaries on the opus of Plato that were widely read by pagan and Christian intellectuals alike. He also composed a metaphysical work titled *Difficulties and Solutions of First Principles*. In his early years he studied rhetoric in Alexandria for twelve years, and then, moving to Athens, he majored in philosophy, science, and mathematics. His mentor then was Isidore of Athens, whom he succeeded as head of the Academy circa 515. After his self-imposed exile in Persia, protesting Justinian's cutting off of state funds, he probably returned to work in Alexandria after 531.

The writings of Plotinus, Proclus, and Damascius heavily influenced the thought world of the Christian theologian Dionysius the Areopagite, who, however, significantly biblicizes their thought world and renders the divine Henad, the Logos and World Soul, in ultrapersonalist (hypostatic) terms in harmony with the trinitarianism of the fourth-century Fathers (who have also read Plotinus). One author has recently claimed that Damascius was himself the author of the Dionysian corpus and has called it "the last counter-offensive of paganism," though it is a thesis that has gained

---

[49] Boethius's poem in book 3 of the *Consolation of Philosophy* is a digest of ideas taken from Proclus's *Commentary on the Timaeus*, and book 5 of the *Consolation* echoes Proclus's principle that all things are known not according to their own nature but according to the character of the subject that knows.

[50] R. T. Wallis, *Neoplatonism* (Indianapolis: Scribner, 1972), 138.

no following but rather is demonstrative of a mindset among some classicists that finds it hard to believe there are independent intelligentsia among the monastics of the Byzantine world.[51] It is far more likely that the anonymous Dionysius, like Damascius's colleague John Philoponus (who later converted to Christianity), were both members of the Athenian school in the course of their youth.[52]

Damascius's main work is the *Difficulties and Solutions of First Principles*, which examines the nature and attributes of the One (the first principle) and the Soul. The One is ineffable and unimaginable, an infinite depth, complete, one and undivided, and thus incomprehensible. All divine attributes are credited to God (such as goodness, knowledge, power) only by inference from their effects in the material world. Damascius and the other Neo-Platonists see themselves as commentators on and rescuers of the Platonic tradition. The originality of their project lay in their attempt to provide a coherent (systematic) structure to both Plato's and Aristotle's teachings (seeing them as harmonious aspects of a common tradition, not as conflicting schools). The lack of ancient systematic was felt acutely among these thinkers: Aristotle was notorious for his obscure style (though it was deliberately adopted so as to conceal the deeper truth from the uninitiated—as Proclus had optimistically suggested), and his treatises were little more than elaborated lecture notes; Plato, on the other hand, indiscriminately mixed poetry, rhetoric, and propositional argument. Both of them, therefore, really lacked a formalized system. The commentators saw their role as giving shape to the tradition of Plato and Aristotle and synthesizing it with the best insights derived from other leading schools (Stoics) and venerable religious traditions (theurgy, Chaldaean oracles, Orphism). Many of them adopted Galen's scientific method as a model for their own methodology. This was especially true of Proclus.

This overriding purpose of neo-Platonism, especially its metaphysic of orders and ascents and descents, came about as a result of their focus on a few key philosophical treatises, especially Plato's *Parmenides* and *Timaeus* and Aristotle's logical and metaphysical treatises. The neo-Platonic school tradition was very much geared toward the *Parmenides* as far as metaphysics was concerned, and toward the *Timaeus* and Aristotle's *Physics* as far as the theory of nature was concerned (physics of the planetary spheres and of our sublunar cosmos), and they heavily leaned on Aristotle's *Organon* as far as logic and propositional method were concerned.

---

[51] C. M. Mazzucchi, "Damascio, Autore del Corpus Dionysiacum, e il dialogo Περι Πολιτικης Επιστημης," *Aevum: Rassegna di scienze storiche linguistiche e filologiche* 80, no. 2 (2006): 299-334.

[52] John Philoponus (c. 490–570) was also known as John the Grammarian or John of Alexandria. He was a noted Byzantine Christian philosopher and was posthumously condemned as heretical (for his trinitarian views) in 681.

In their theology as such, metaphysics was identified with theological inquiry, as the science of first principles. This view of metaphysics as a declining series of emanations from the sublime Henad was grounded in the *Parmenides*. Plotinus was the first to exegete the second part of that dialogue (particularly the first three hypotheses of part two of the treatise) as delineating the three fundamental hypostases of being; namely the One, the Nous/Logos, and the Soul. After that primal statement, neo-Platonic theology becomes the devolved study of the structures of reality, including their preferred triad: those layers putatively located beyond being, those that partake of being, and those that descend in ranks all the way to nonbeing. The notion of absolute simplicity as stated in his *Parmenides* originally led Plato to the conclusion that the One does not participate in being, and there can be no knowledge or opinion of it.

The neo-Platonists modify that presupposition and are deeply interested in mystical apprehension of divine unity. Plotinus's notion of the Intelligible Triad is a marked advance on the apophatic simplicity of Plato. In Porphyry's hands even the First Supreme Being was spoken of as self-differentiated and self-reflective, which made a very broad bridge in the direction Christian intellectuals were moving. Damascius stresses the principle that Ineffable Unity only has meaning in contradistinction to the many (or plurality) and therefore belongs, in some sense, to the sphere of relative reality.[53] In his work *On the Ineffable*, Damascius strongly advocates an apophatic method:

> But the most venerable thing of all cannot be apprehended by any conception or by any speculation, since even among things here, whatever escapes toward that which is higher with respect to our thoughts is more lofty than whatever is ready to hand, and so that which escapes our conceptions most completely is the most valuable of all. If this is nothing, then that "nothing" must be of two kinds, one greater than the One, the other inferior to it. If, then, we are stepping into the void when we speak this way, then even "stepping into the void" must also have two meanings, where the one falls out of speech into the Ineffable, and where the other falls into what has no kind of existence at all. The latter is also ineffable, as Plato says, but in an inferior way, while the former is so in a superior way.[54]

This is most particularly the point where Damascius's project overlaps metaphysically with that of Dionysius the Areopagite: where religion and philosophy become fused in late antiquity.

---

[53]Damaskios, *On First Principles* 1.5-6. Cf. Wallis, *Neoplatonism*, 118.
[54]S. Ahbel-Rappe, trans., *Damascius' Problems and Solutions Concerning First Principles* (Oxford: Oxford University Press, 2010), 71.

***Dionysius the Areopagite.*** This name was the pseudonym of an unknown Syrian bishop or priest-ascetic who was a leading theologian of the early sixth century. His aim, clearly enough, was to make a dynamic synthesis between the religious insights of the late neo-Platonist school and emerging Byzantine mystical theory. Four relatively short treatises of Dionysius (and ten *Letters*) are among the most important of early church literature dealing with mystical prayer. They all represent a serious and profound attempt to express the evangelical spirit of divine communion and ascentive enlightenment in language that would be recognizable to the Hellenistic philosophical tradition. Plotinus, Proclus, and Damascius are the chief philosophical influences on this writer, and among his major Christian influences are Origen of Alexandria, Gregory the Theologian, and Gregory of Nyssa—all the patristic-tradition giants who also wished to make a synthesis of scriptural revelation and philosophical wisdom.

It is no coincidence that these works of Dionysius were offered to Byzantine intelligentsia society (and also, of course, for pagan readership in a missionary spirit) at the time when the pagan chairs of philosophy were defunded by the state, and philosophy at Athens and Constantinople was only going to be subsidised henceforth if taught by Christian *magistroi*. His desire to reach out to pagan intelligentsia and demonstrate Gregory of Nazianzus's thesis that within Christian philosophy was the true encounter with divine Logos might explain why the author chose to describe his opus as the reflections of Dionysius the Areopagite, the philosophical companion and disciple of St. Paul preaching the gospel in Athens.

Although the authorial subterfuge was not taken seriously when the texts first surfaced in Byzantine theological dialogues (Severus of Antioch first mentions them in 533), the great attractiveness they had as soon as they appeared made it perhaps inevitable that within a generation or so the tradition of their "apostolic origin" was eventually believed, and with this dramatic label the works went on to have a profound influence for centuries to come, especially on Maximus the Confessor and Andrew of Crete in the East, and Pope Gregory the Great, John Scotus Eriugena, Bonaventure, and Albert the Great in the West. Even into the eighteenth century they were widely believed to belong to the first century, and J. P. Migne reprints them in the very early sequence of his nineteenth-century collection of patristic texts in the Patrologia Graeca. They were the main inspiration behind the later medieval mystical revival of the West, as evidenced in the great English treatise *The Cloud of Unknowing* and in such mystics as Meister Eckhart and Tauler.

Dionysius's work *The Divine Names* discusses the essential attributes of God, teaching that deity is beyond any direct knowing and relates to creation through the saving dynamic of divine emanation in the agency of the Logos. The book introduces the influential concepts of kataphatic (affirmative) and apophatic (ineffable or speech-transcending) theology. The treatise *Celestial Hierarchy* describes how nine ranks of angelic beings mediate between God and his creation. The book teaches the subsequently influential view that evil is unreal in itself: the absence of the good, devoid of essential being. The treatise *Ecclesiastical Hierarchy* shows how the principle of emanations continues to provide the substructure of the mystical church of Christ on earth (as well as in heaven). Here, three orders of priests (bishops, priests, and deacons) mediate three mystical orders (baptism, Eucharist, and chrismation) to the three orders of Christians (monks, laity, and catechumens), a ninefold (*ennead*) order or *taxis* that mirrors the angelic mediating ranks. The system of mediation and emanation is dynamically conceived as a process (as in Origen of Alexandria, Gregory the Theologian, and Gregory of Nyssa) whereby the soul ascends to the divine presence (*anabasis*), which in turn stoops down (*katabasis*) to the creation as its savior and healer. The treatise *Mystical Theology* describes the soul's ascent to deification (*theiopoiesis*), in a transcendence of all sense and utterance (encountering the divine darkness of unknowing). In Dionysius the system of the soul's rising up to God is marked by a triadic character of purification, illumination, and perfection of union. This scheme had overwhelming authority with the subsequent Christian mystical tradition.

Its importance is contained in numerous points, of which a brief synopsis is probably all we have time for here. One hopes it will be instructive, though the fear is it might be too dense to be other than deeply obscure. Nevertheless, the converging lines of connection between the Dionysian, late patristic project and the religious metaphysics of the neo-Platonists did something profound for the Christians of the early Byzantine age. First, it gave immense encouragement (in an era when Origen's school was heavily under attack, and, so it seemed, along with it a Christian intellectual tradition) to Origen's ancient principle that the believer must go *opou Logos agei* ("wherever the mind leads"—the pun here being, of course, that where reason leads, so too is God the Logos beckoning). Too often religion has served as a force of obscurantism and oppression in human history, rather than enlightenment and liberation. The Christian intelligentsia who seized on the possibilities of transmitting their evangelical insights using contemporary philosophical language were celebrating their spiritual freedom in an age when many conservative voices were pressing for closure of the open mind. Such a premise remains perennially important, in my opinion.

Second, they found in the neo-Platonists a dialogue partner, not a series of texts to be plagiarized. Far too much careless thought has led, in the past, to accusations that Dionysius and other patristic writers are "Platonists" or simply aping the neo-Platonic agenda. Such critiques can only be raised by people who have never read the primary texts but rely on clichés of superficial secondary literature. The likes of Dionysius are actively critiquing neo-Platonism and heavily adapting its fundamental insights in accordance with evangelical and patristic principles. They are thus quintessentially and authentically Christian, but demonstrate refined intellect and a generous missionary spirit that wishes to translate the Semitic gospel to a Hellenized world. In short, they are creating a new school of thought, which they pose to the Hellenistic world as the fulfillment (*teleiosis*) of all the aspirations of the cultured past, just as the gospel was the *teleiosis* of all the prophets.

Third, the dynamism of the mutual schools lies in its manner of seeing metaphysics as a related system of descent from the First Principle: the Sublime Ineffable. All being holds it coherence from the One. In Christian hands, in Dionysius, this amounts to a massively ordered understanding (a sacred hierarchy) of the cosmos where God is all in all, and all are bonded to God in a caring, intersocial communion of initiation (the heavenly and earthly church). The marks of the Logos are within all things. Dionysius and Maximus Confessor (whom we shall look at shortly) are masters of this approach. Not only are the fingerprints of God in all matter and in all thought and moral choices, but life itself becomes quintessentially marked as either an ascent to God or a decline from him (and thus a decline from Beauty, Truth, and Order). To connote this great scheme of metaphysical cosmology they adopted the soteriological principle of "deification by grace." Salvation is to be near God, to merge with God by virtue of God's desire to lift up his created order into union with himself as life-giving source of all being. This is deification by grace (*theiopoiesis kata charin*), and it would become the meeting ground of high patristic theology and mystical reflection of a very deep order in the hands of the Byzantine theologians to follow.

Fourth, the aspects of the Dionysian project concerned with how to speak about God—*apophatically*, using negation of words and ideas, or *kataphatically*, using ideas taken from the material world—pressed to their limits analogically, became the greatest of all Christian systems dealing with the correlation of mysterious revelation and spiritual experience, and deducted Christian theology. In other words, it became one of the great originators of deep theological systematics still in use to this day, still marking the Christian attempt to hold together its twin commitments to sacramental mystery and revealed truth. The school took seriously the church's duty to proclaim its message and insight to an external world using the tools of the secular academy if necessary.

Last, the stress on order and dependent relationships in the ascent to God, which Dionysius emphasizes so much in his view of angels and clerical ranks in his treatises on the *Hierarchies*, provided immense intellectual stimulation to the Christian Western world in its Dark Ages, and to the Byzantine East it offered a view of the processes of the ascent of consciousness (from inductive *Logismos* to transcendent *Noesis*) that gave coherence and inspiration to innumerable early medieval mystics and eventually brought into the light of day the great Byzantine school of Hesychastic spirituality.

## A SHORT READER

**Second Letter of Cyril to Nestorius.** From Cyril: greetings in the Lord to the most righteous and reverend fellow minister Nestorius. I hear that there are some who are talking wildly of the esteem I afford to your reverence, a thing that frequently happens when meetings of those who hold authority afford them an opportunity. Perhaps they hope in this way to please your ears, and so they spread abroad unlicensed defamation. But these are men who have suffered no wrongdoing, but, on the contrary, whom I have exposed for their own benefit; one because he oppressed the blind and the poor, the other because he drew a sword on his mother, a third because he stole someone else's money in collusion with a maidservant and since then has lived with such a reputation as one would hardly wish on one's worst enemy. In any case, I do not intend to waste more words on this subject in order, for I ought not to elevate my own mediocrity above my teacher and master's or above the fathers, because however one may try to live, it is impossible to escape the malice of the evil, men whose mouths are full of cursing and bitterness and who will have to give an account of themselves before the judge of all. And so I turn to a subject more appropriate to myself and remind you, as a brother in Christ, always to be very careful about what you say to the people in matters of doctrine and concerning your thoughts about the faith. Keep in mind that to scandalize even one of these little ones who believe in Christ lays you open to unsupportable wrath. If the number of those who are distressed is very large, then surely we should use all our skill and attention to remove scandals and to expound the healing word of faith to those who seek the truth. The most effective way to achieve this end will be to occupy ourselves zealously with the words of the holy Fathers, to esteem their words, to examine our own words to see whether we are holding to their faith as they have written it, and to conform our thoughts to their correct and irreproachable teaching. The holy and great synod, therefore, stated that: The only begotten Son, begotten of God the Father according to nature, true God from true God, the light from the light, the one through whom the Father made all things, came down, became incarnate, became man, suffered, rose on the third day and ascended to heaven. We too ought to follow these words and these teachings and consider what is meant by saying that the Word of God took flesh and became man. For we do not say that the nature of the Word was changed and became flesh, nor that he was turned into a whole man, made of body and soul. Rather, we assert that the Word, in an manner that is ineffable and inconceivable, hypostatically united to himself flesh animated by a rational soul, and in this way became man and was called Son of Man, not by God's will alone or by good pleasure, nor simply by the assumption of a person. No, for two different natures came together to form a unity, and from both arose one Christ and one Son. The distinctness of the natures was assuredly not destroyed by the union, but rather divinity and humanity together perfected one Lord and one Christ for our sake, combining together wondrously and mysteriously to form a unity. And so, he who existed and was begotten of the Father before all ages is also said to have been begotten of a woman according to the flesh, without the divine nature either beginning to exist in the holy Virgin or needing any second begetting of itself after that he received from his Father (for it is absurd and stupid to speak of the one who existed before every age and who is coeternal with the Father needing a second beginning so as to exist). The Word is said to have been begotten according to the flesh, because he hypostatically united to himself what was human, for us and for our salvation, and came forth from a woman. For he was not first begotten of the holy Virgin, as a man like us, and then the Word descended on him; but rather, from the very womb of his mother he was thus united and then he underwent generation according to the flesh, appropriating this begetting of his own flesh as his very own.

Likewise, we say that he suffered and rose again, not meaning that the Word of God suffered blows or piercing with nails or any other wounds in his own nature (for the divine, which is devoid of a body, is incapable of suffering), but rather because the body that became his own suffered these things, and so he is said to have suffered these things for us. For he was without suffering, while his body suffered. Something similar is true in relation to his dying. For by nature the Word of God is, of itself, immortal and incorruptible, and is life, and life giving, but since on the other hand, by God's grace, as the apostle says, his own body tasted death for the sake of all, then this is why the Word is said to have suffered death for us, and not as if he himself had experienced death as far as his own nature was concerned (for it would be sheer lunacy to say or to think that), but because, as I have just said, his own flesh tasted death. So too, when his flesh was raised to life, we refer to this again as his resurrection, not as though he had fallen into corruption (God forbid) but because it was his own body that had been raised again.

This is why we confess one Christ and one Lord. We do not adore the man along with the Word, in order to avoid any appearance of division by using the word *with*. But we adore him as one and the same, because the body is not apart from the Word but takes its seat with him beside the Father, again, not as though there were two sons seated alongside one another, but only one son, made one with his own flesh. If, however, we reject the hypostatic union as being either impossible or too unfitting for the Word, then we fall into the fallacy of speaking of two Sons. Then we shall have to make a distinction so as to speak of the man who was honored with the title of *Son*, and again of the Word of God, who naturally possesses the name and the reality of Sonship, each in their own way. But we must not split the one Lord Jesus Christ into two Sons this way. Such a way of presenting an orthodox exposition of the faith would be most unhelpful, even though some do go on to speak of a union of persons. You see, Scripture does not say that the Word united the person of a man to himself, but rather that he became flesh. The Word's becoming flesh means nothing other than that he shared in flesh and blood just like us. He made our body his own and came forth as man from woman without ever casting aside his divinity or his generation from God the Father, but rather when he assumed the flesh he remained what he was.

This is the account of the true faith that is professed everywhere. This, we shall find, is what the holy Fathers believed. This was why they dared to call the holy Virgin "mother of God" (Theotokos), not as though the nature of the Word or his godhead received their origin of being from the holy Virgin, but rather because from her was born his holy body with a rational soul, with which the Word was hypostatically united and is thus said to have been begotten in the flesh. I write these things to you out of love in Christ, exhorting you as a brother and calling on you, before Christ and the elect angels, to hold and teach these same things with us, in order to preserve the peace of the churches and so that the priests of God may remain in an unbroken bond of concord and love.

**The Second Letter of Nestorius to Cyril.** Nestorius sends greeting in the Lord to the most religious and reverend fellow minister Cyril. I pass over the insults against us contained in your extraordinary letter. They will, I think, be cured by my patience and by the answer that events will offer in due course. On one matter, however, I cannot be silent, for silence would in such a case be very dangerous. On that point, therefore, avoiding long-windedness as far as I can, I shall attempt a brief discussion and try to be as free as possible from revolting obscurity and indigestible wordiness. I shall take my start from your Reverence's own wise statements, setting them down word for word. What, then, are the words in which your extraordinary doctrine finds expression? "The holy and great synod states that the only begotten Son, begotten of God the Father according to nature, true God from true God, light from the light, the one through whom the Father made all things, came down, became incarnate, became man, suffered, and rose." These are the words of your Reverence. Perhaps you recognize them? Now listen to what we say, which takes the form of a brotherly exhortation to piety of the type of which the great apostle Paul gave an example in addressing his beloved Timothy: "Attend to the public reading of Scripture, to preaching and teaching, for by so doing you will save both yourself and your hearers." Tell me, what does "attend" mean here? By reading in a superficial way the tradition of those holy Fathers (being guilty of a pardonable ignorance), you concluded that they affirmed that the Word who is coeternal with the Father was passible. Please look more closely at their language, and you will find out that that divine choir of fathers never said that the consubstantial Godhead was capable of suffering, or that the whole being that was coeternal with the Father was recently born, or that it rose again, seeing that it had itself been the cause of the resurrection of the destroyed temple. If you apply my words as a fraternal medicine, I shall set the words of the holy Fathers before you and shall free them from the slander you raised against them, and through them against the Holy Scriptures.

"I believe," they say, "also in our Lord Jesus Christ, his only begotten Son." See how they first lay as foundations "Lord" and "Jesus" and "Christ" and "only begotten" and "Son," for these are the names that belong jointly to the divinity and humanity. Then they develop on that foundation the tradition of the incarnation and resurrection and the passion. In this way, by prefixing the names that are common to each nature, they intend to avoid dividing out expressions applicable to sonship and lordship, but at the same time avoid the danger of destroying the distinctive character of the natures by absorbing them into the one single title of "Son." Doing this they were following their teacher St. Paul. When he remembers the divine becoming man and then wishes to introduce the notion of suffering, he first speaks of "Christ," which, as I have just said, is the common name of both natures, and then he adds an expression that is appropriate to both of the natures. For what does he say? "Have this mind among yourselves, which is yours in Christ Jesus who, though he was in the form of God, did not count equality with God a thing to be grasped," and so on until: "he became obedient to death, even death on a cross." For when he was about to mention this death, in order to prevent anyone imagining that God the Word suffered, he says "Christ," which is a title that expresses in one person both the impassible and the passible natures, in order that Christ might be appropriately called both impassible and passible: impassible in Godhead, while passible in the nature of his body.

I could say much more on this subject, primarily that those holy Fathers, when they discuss the economy, are not speaking of the (divine) generation but rather of the Son becoming man. But I recall the earlier promise I made to be brief, and this restrains my discourse and thus moves me on to the second topic your Reverence brought up. In that I applaud your division of natures into humanity and Godhead and their conjunction in one person. I also applaud your statement that God the Word needed no second generation from a woman, and your confession that the Godhead is incapable of suffering. Such statements are truly orthodox and equally opposed to the evil opinions of all heretics about the natures of the Lord. However, if what followed was an attempt to introduce some hidden and incomprehensible wisdom to the ears of the readers, it is only for your wit to decide. In my opinion, your subsequent views seemed to subvert all that came first. They suggested that he who had at the beginning been proclaimed as impassible and incapable of a second generation had now somehow become capable of suffering and newly created—as though what belonged to God the Word by nature had been destroyed by his conjunction with his temple, or as though people considered it not enough that the sinless temple, which is inseparable from the divine nature, should have endured birth and death for sinners; or finally as though the Lord's voice was not deserving of credence when it cried out to the Jews: "Destroy this temple and in three days I will raise it up." He did not say, "Destroy my Godhead and in three days it will be raised up."

Once again I should like to develop on this matter but am restrained by the memory of my promise. I must speak, therefore, but only briefly. Holy Scripture, whenever it recalls the Lord's economy, speaks of the birth and suffering as belonging not to the Godhead but to the humanity of Christ. And this means that the holy Virgin is more accurately designated "mother of Christ" than "mother of God." Listen to the words that the Gospels proclaim: "The book of the generation of Jesus Christ, son of David, son of Abraham." It is clear that God the Word was not the son of David. Listen to another witness if you please: "Jacob begot Joseph, the husband of Mary, of whom was born Jesus, who is called the Christ." Consider this further piece of evidence: "Now the birth of Jesus Christ took place in this way. When his mother Mary had been betrothed to Joseph, she was found to be with child of the Holy Spirit." But who would ever consider that the Godhead of the only begotten was a creature of the Spirit? Why do we need to mention "the mother of Jesus was there"? And again what of: "with Mary the mother of Jesus," or "that which is conceived in her is of the Holy Spirit," and "Take the child and his mother and flee to Egypt," and "concerning his Son, who was born of the seed of David according to the flesh"? Again, Scripture says when speaking of his passion: "God sending his own Son in the likeness of sinful flesh and for sin, he condemned sin in the flesh"; and again "Christ died for our sins," and "Christ having suffered in the flesh"; and "This is my body, broken for you": not my Godhead.

Ten thousand other expressions witness to humanity that we should not think that it was the Godhead of the Son that was recently put to death but rather the flesh that was joined to the nature of the Godhead. This is why Christ also calls himself the lord and son of David: "'What do you think of the Christ? Whose son is he?' And they said to him, 'The son of David.' Jesus answered and said to them, 'How is it then that David inspired by the Spirit, calls him Lord, saying, "The Lord said to my Lord, sit at my right hand"?'" He said this as being truly son of David according to the flesh, but David's Lord according to his Godhead. The body, therefore, is the temple of the deity of the Son, a temple that is united to it in a high and divine conjunction, so that the divine nature accepts what belongs to the body as its own. Such a confession is noble and worthy of the Gospel traditions. But to use the expression "accepts as its own" as a way of diminishing the properties of the conjoined flesh, such as its birth, suffering, and entombment, is a mark of those whose minds are led astray, my brother, by Greek thinking, or are sick with the lunacy of Apollinarius and Arius or the other heresies, or rather something more serious than these. For if we value propriety we ought to make God the Word share, as is fitting, the experience of being fed on milk, of gradual growth, of terror at the time of his passion, and of standing in need of angelical assistance. I pass over circumcision and sacrifice and sweat and hunger, all of which belong to the flesh and are adorable as having taken place for our sake. Even so, it would be entirely wrong to apply such ideas to the Godhead and would involve us in just accusations because of our calumny.

These are the traditions of the holy Fathers. These are the precepts of the Holy Scriptures. This is how someone should write in a godly way about the divine mercy and power, "Practice these duties, devote yourself to them, so that all may see your progress." This is what Paul says to us all. The care you take in laboring for those who have been scandalized is well taken, and we are grateful to you both for the thought you devote to divine things and for the concern you have even for those who live here. But you should realize that you have been misled either by some here who have been deposed by the holy synod for Manichaeism or by clergy of your own persuasion. In fact, the church daily progresses here, and through the grace of Christ there is such an increase among the people that those who behold it cry out with the words of the prophet, "The earth will be filled with the knowledge of the Lord as the water covers the sea." As for our sovereigns, they are in great joy as the light of doctrine is spread abroad and, to be brief, because of the state of all the heresies that fight against God and of the orthodoxy of the church, one might find that verse fulfilled: "The house of Saul grew weaker and weaker, and the house of David grew stronger and stronger."

This is our advice from a brother to a brother. "If anyone is disposed to be contentious," Paul will cry out through us to such a one, "we recognize no other practice, neither do the churches of God." I and those with me greet all the brotherhood with you in Christ. May you remain strong and continue praying for us, most honored and reverend lord.

**The Third Letter of Cyril to Nestorius.** We follow the confessions of the holy Fathers in every instance, for they made them with the Holy Spirit speaking in them, and we follow the direction their opinions move to, and so, as if setting out on the Imperial Road, we say that the only begotten Word of God, he who was begotten from the very essence of the Father, true God from true God, light from the light, and the one through whom all things in heaven and earth were made, came down for our salvation and emptied himself out and became incarnate and was made man. This means that he took flesh from the holy Virgin and made it his own, undergoing a birth from her womb, like ours, and came forth a man from a woman. He did not cast aside what he was, but although he assumed flesh and blood, he remained what he was, namely God in nature and truth. We do not say that his flesh was turned into the nature of the Godhead or that the unspeakable Word of God was changed into the nature of the flesh. For [the Word] is unaltering and absolutely unchangeable and ever remains the same, as the Scriptures say. For although visible as a child and wrapped in swaddling cloths, even while he was in the bosom of the virgin who bore him, yet as God he filled the whole of creation and was fellow ruler with the One who begot him. For the divine is without quantity and dimension and cannot be subject to circumscription.

And we confess the Word to have been hypostatically made one with the flesh, and so we adore one Son and Lord, Jesus Christ. We do not divide him into parts and separate man and God in him, as though the two natures were mutually united only through a unity of dignity and authority; that would be an empty expression and nothing more. Nor do we give the name *Christ* in one sense to the Word of God and in another to him who was born of woman, but we know only one Christ, who is the Word from God the Father along with his own flesh. As man he was anointed along with us, even though he himself gives the Spirit to those who are worthy to receive it, and beyond measure, as the blessed Evangelist John says.

However, we do not say that the Word of God dwelt as in an ordinary man born of the holy Virgin, so that Christ may not be thought of as a God-bearing man. For even though "the Word dwelt among us," and it is also said that in Christ dwelt "all the fullness of the Godhead bodily," we understand that once he had become flesh, the manner of his indwelling is not defined in the same way as he himself is said to dwell among the saints. Rather, he was united by nature and not turned into flesh, and he made his indwelling in such a way as we might say that the soul of a man does within his own body. There is, therefore, one Christ and Son and Lord; but not with the sort of conjunction that a man might have with God, such as a unity in terms of dignity or authority. Equality of honor by itself is unable to unite natures. For Peter and John were equal in honor to each other, being both apostles and holy disciples, but they were two realities, not one. Neither do we understand the manner of conjunction to be one of juxtaposition, for this is not enough for a natural union. Nor yet is it a question of relative participation, as we ourselves, being united to the Lord, are (as it is written in the words of Scripture) "one spirit with him." Rather, we altogether deplore the term *conjunction* as being inadequate to express the idea of union.

We do not call the Word, who comes from God the Father, the God or Lord of Christ. To speak in that way would apparently split the one Christ, Son and Lord, into two, and so we could fall under the charge of blasphemy, making him the God and Lord of himself. For, as we have already said, the Word of God was hypostatically united with the flesh and is God of all and Lord of the universe, but is neither his own slave or master. It is foolish, or rather irreverent, to think and speak in this way. It is true that he called the Father "God" even though he was himself God by nature and in his being. We recognize that at the same time as he was God he also became man, and so was subject to God according to the law that is appropriate to the nature of humankind. But how could he ever be God or Lord of himself? Accordingly, as man and as far as it was fitting for him within the limits of his self-emptying, it is said that he was subject to God like ourselves. This is how he came to be under the law while at the same time himself speaking the law and being a lawgiver, as God.

When speaking of Christ we avoid the expression "I worship him who is borne because of the one who bears him; and because of him who is unseen, I worship the one who is seen." It is scandalous to say in this context: "The assumed shares the name of God with the one who assumes." To speak in this way once again divides him into two Christs and sets the man apart by himself and sets God likewise by himself. Such a saying blatantly denies the union, according to which one is not worshiped alongside the other, nor do both share in the title "God," but rather Jesus Christ is considered as one, namely the only begotten Son together with his own flesh, honored with one single worship.

We also confess that although the only begotten Son who was born of God the Father was not subject to suffering in terms of his own nature, nevertheless he suffered in the flesh for us, according to the Scriptures, and was in his crucified body, and though he was himself without suffering he made the sufferings of his own flesh his own, because "by the grace of God he tasted death for all." For that purpose he gave his own body to death, though he himself was by nature life and resurrection, and this was so that, having trodden down death by his own ineffable power, he might first in his own flesh become the firstborn from the dead and "the firstfruits of those who sleep." And so that he might prepare a way for human nature to return to incorruption by the grace of God, as we have just said, "he tasted death for all," and on the third day he returned to life, having despoiled Hades. And so, even though it is said that "through man came the resurrection of the dead," yet we understand that man to have been the Word that came from God, through whom the power of death was overcome. At the right time he will come again as one Son and Lord in the glory of the Father, to judge the world in justice, as it is written.

We need to add this also. Proclaiming the death according to the flesh of the only begotten Son of God, that is Jesus Christ, and professing his return to life from the dead and his ascension into heaven, we offer the liturgy of the sacrifice in the churches and so proceed to the mystical thanksgivings and are sanctified having partaken of the holy body and precious blood of Christ, the Savior of us all. We receive his body not as ordinary flesh, heaven forbid, nor as that of a man who has been made holy and joined to the Word by some union of honor, or as that of someone who had a divine indwelling, but rather as truly the life-giving and real flesh of the Word. For being life by nature, as God, when he became one with his own flesh, so he made that also to be life giving, as he also told us: "Amen, I say to you, unless you eat the flesh of the Son of Man and drink his blood . . ." For we must not think that it is the flesh of a man like us (for how can the flesh of man be life giving of its own nature?), but as being made the true flesh of the one who, for our sake, became the Son of Man and was so designated.

We do not divide up the words of our Savior in the Gospels as if to two hypostases or persons. For the one and only Christ is not binary, even though he can be thought of as from two distinct realities, brought together into an unbreakable union. In the same sort of way a human being, though he is composed of soul and body, is not thought of as a binary, but rather is one out of two. Therefore, in thinking rightly, we refer both the human and divine expressions to the selfsame person. For when he speaks about himself in a divine manner, such as "he that sees me sees the Father," and "I and the Father are one," we think of his divine and unspeakable nature, according to which he is one with his own Father through identity of nature and is the "image and imprint and brightness of his glory." But when, honorably aware of the limits of his humanity, he says to the Jews: "But now you seek to kill me, a man who has spoken the truth to you," again no less than before, we recognize that he who is God the Word, because of his equality and likeness to God the Father, stands also within the limits of his humanity. For if it is necessary to believe that though he was God by nature he became flesh, that is, man ensouled with a rational soul, why on earth should anyone be ashamed of the expressions uttered by him, insofar as they happen to be appropriate to his stature as a man? For if he does not want to accept terms suitable to him as a man, who was it who forced him to become a man like us in the first place? Why should he who submitted himself to voluntary self-emptying for our sake reject expressions that are precisely suitable for such a self-emptying? All the expressions that occur in the Gospels, therefore, are to be referred to one and the same person, the one enfleshed physis of the Word (*mia physis tou theou logou sesarkomene*). For there is one Lord Jesus Christ, according to the Scriptures. Even though he is called "the apostle and high priest of our confession," since he offers to God the Father the confession of faith that we make to him, and through him to God the Father and also to the Holy Spirit. Again, we say that he is the natural and only begotten Son of God, and we shall not assign to another man apart from him the name and reality of priesthood. For he became the "mediator between God and humanity" and the establisher of peace between them, offering himself as an odor of sweetness to God the Father. This too is why he said: "Sacrifice and offering you would not have, but you prepared a body for me.... Then I said, 'Behold I come to do your will, O God,' as it is written of me in the scroll of the book." For our sake and not for his own he offered his own body as an offering of incense. Indeed, what offering or sacrifice for his own sake would he ever have needed, since he was superior to all manner of sin, being God? For though "all have sinned and fall short of the glory of God," and for this reason are prone to disorder, and human nature has fallen into the weakness of sin, this is not the case with him. Consequently, we are behind him in glory. How, then, can there be any further doubt that the true Lamb was sacrificed for us and on our behalf? The suggestion that he offered himself for himself as well as for us is inseparable from the charge of impiety, for he never committed a fault at all, nor did he sin in any way. What sort of offering would he then need, since there was no sin for which offering might rightly be made?

When he says of the Spirit, "he will glorify me," the correct understanding of this is not to say that the one Christ and Son was in need of glory from another and that he received glory from the Holy Spirit; for his Spirit is not better than he, nor is it above him. But because he used his own Spirit to display his divinity through his mighty works, he says that he has been glorified by him, just as if any one of us should perhaps say of his inherent strength, for example, or his knowledge of any subject, that they "glorify" him. For even though *the* Spirit exists in his own hypostasis and is thought of on his own, as being Spirit and not Son, even so he is not alien to the Son. He has been called "the Spirit of truth," and Christ is the truth, and the Spirit was poured forth by the Son, as indeed the Son was poured forth from God the Father. Accordingly, the Spirit worked many strange things through the hand of the holy apostles and so glorified him after the ascension of our Lord Jesus Christ into heaven. For it was believed that he is God by nature and works through his own Spirit. This is why he also said: "He (the Spirit) will take what is mine and declare it to you." But we do not say that the Spirit is wise and powerful through some sharing with another, for he is all perfect and in need of no good thing. Since he is the Spirit of the power and wisdom of the Father, that is the Son, he is himself, evidently, wisdom and power.

And so, because the holy Virgin bore in the flesh God who was hypostatically united with the flesh, for that reason we call her Theotokos, not as though the nature of the Word had the beginning of its existence from the flesh (for "the Word was in the beginning and the Word was God and the Word was with God," and he made the ages and is coeternal with the Father and shaper of all things), but because, as we have said, he hypostatically united things human to himself and underwent a birth according to the flesh from her womb. This was not as though he needed a birth in time and in the last times of this age out of any necessity or for the sake of his own nature, but in order that he might bless the beginning of our existence, in order that seeing that it was a woman who had given birth to him united to the flesh, the curse against the whole race should thereafter cease that was consigning all our earthy bodies to death, and in order that the removal through him of that curse—"In sorrow you shall bring forth children"—should demonstrate the truth of the words of the prophet: "Strong death swallowed them up," and again, "God has wiped every tear away from each face." This is why we say that in his economy he blessed marriage and, when invited, went down to Cana in Galilee with his holy apostles.

We have been taught to hold these things by the holy apostles and Evangelists and by all the divinely inspired Scriptures and by the true confession of the blessed Fathers. To all these things your Reverence ought to agree and subscribe without any deceit. What is required for your Reverence to anathematize we now subjoin to this epistle:

**The Twelve Anathemas *Appended to Cyril's Third Letter to Nestorius.*** [55] 1. If anyone does not confess that Emmanuel is truly God, and therefore that the holy Virgin is the mother of God (for she bore in a fleshly way the Word of God become flesh), then let him be anathema.

2. If anyone does not confess that the Word from God the Father has been hypostatically united with the flesh and is one Christ with his own flesh, and is therefore God and man together, let him be anathema.

3. If anyone divides the hypostases after the union, in the one Christ, joining them only by a conjunction of dignity or authority or power, and not rather by a coming together in a union by nature, let him be anathema.

4. If anyone distributes between the two persons or hypostases the expressions used either in the Gospels or in the apostolic writings, whether they are used by the holy writers of Christ or by him about himself, and ascribes some of them to him as to a man, thought of separately from the Word from God, and ascribes others to him (the ones appropriate to God) as to the Word from God the Father, let him be anathema.

5. If anyone dares to say that Christ was a God-bearing man and not rather God in truth, being by nature one Son, even as "the Word became flesh," and is made partaker of flesh and blood precisely like us, let him be anathema.

---

[55] Not endorsed at the Council of Ephesus in 431, where they were first read out, but accepted into the conciliar record at Constantinople II in 553 and thereafter known as the *Twelve Chapters*.

6. If anyone says that the Word from God the Father was the God or master of Christ, and does not rather confess the same both God and man, the Word having become flesh, according to the Scriptures, let him be anathema.

7. If anyone says that as man Jesus was activated by the Word of God and was clothed with the glory of the only begotten, as a being separate from him, let him be anathema.

8. If anyone dares to say that the man who was assumed ought to be worshiped and glorified alongside the divine Word and be called God along with him, while yet being separate from him, (for the addition of "with" must always compel us to think in this way), and will not rather worship Emmanuel with a single veneration and send up to him a single doxology, even as "the Word became flesh," let him be anathema.

9. If anyone says that the one Lord Jesus Christ was glorified by the Spirit, as if making use of an alien power that worked through him and as having received from him the power to master unclean spirits and to work divine wonders among people, and does not rather say that it was his own proper Spirit through whom he worked the divine wonders, let him be anathema.

10. The divine Scripture says Christ became "the high priest and apostle of our confession"; he offered himself to God the Father in an odor of sweetness for our sake. If anyone, therefore, says that it was not the very Word from God who became our high priest and apostle, when he became flesh and a man like us, but, as it were, another who was separate from him, in particular a man from a woman, or if anyone says that he offered the sacrifice also for himself and not rather for us alone (for he who knew no sin needed no offering), let him be anathema.

11. If anyone does not confess that the flesh of the Lord is life-giving and belongs to the Word from God the Father, but maintains that it belongs to another besides him, united with him in dignity or as enjoying a mere divine indwelling, and is not rather life giving, as we said, since it became the flesh belonging to the Word, who has power to bring all things to life, let him be anathema.

12. If anyone does not confess that the Word of God suffered in the flesh and was crucified in the flesh and tasted death in the flesh and became the firstborn of the dead, even though as God he is life and life giving, let him be anathema.

**The Synodical Condemnation Against Nestorius at Ephesus 431.** The holy synod said: Since, in addition to everything else, his Excellency Nestorius has declined to obey our summons and has not received the holy and God-fearing bishops whom we sent to him, we have of necessity started on an investigation of his impieties. On the basis of his letters, his writings that have been read out, and from the things that he has recently said in this metropolis that have been witnessed by others, we have found him to be thinking and speaking in an impious fashion; and as a result we have been necessarily compelled, both by the canons and by the letter of our most holy father and fellow servant Celestine, bishop of the church of the Romans, to issue this sad condemnation against him, though we do so with many tears. Our Lord Jesus Christ, who has been blasphemed by him, has determined through this most holy synod that the same Nestorius should be stripped of his episcopal dignity and removed from the college of priests.

**The Dogmatic Definition (Ekthesis) of the Council of Chalcedon, 451.** The sacred and great and ecumenical synod, assembled in Chalcedon, the metropolis of the province of Bithynia, by God's grace and by decree of your most religious and Christ-loving emperors, Valentinian Augustus and Marcian Augustus, meeting in the shrine of the holy and victorious martyr Euphemia, issues the following decrees:

In establishing his disciples in the knowledge of the faith, our Lord and Savior Christ said: "My peace I give you, my peace I leave to you," so that no one should disagree with his neighbor regarding religious doctrines but rather that the proclamation of the truth would be uniformly presented. But the evil one never stops trying to smother the seeds of religion with his own weeds and is forever inventing some novelty or other opposed to the truth; so the Master, exercising his usual care for the human race, stirred this religious and most faithful emperor to zealous action, who summoned to himself the leaders of the priesthood from all places, so that by the working of the grace of Christ, the master of all of us, every injurious falsehood might be fended off from the sheep of Christ and they might be fattened on fresh growths of the truth. This is in fact what we have done. We have driven off erroneous doctrines by our collective resolution, and we have renewed the unerring creed of the Fathers. We have proclaimed to all the creed of the 318 (Nicaea); and we have made our own those fathers who accepted this agreed statement of religion—the 150 who later met in great Constantinople and themselves set their seal to the same creed.

Therefore, while we also stand by the decisions and all the formulas relating to the creed from the sacred synod that took place formerly at Ephesus, whose leaders of most holy memory were Celestine of Rome and Cyril of Alexandria, we decree that preeminence belongs to the exposition of the right and spotless creed of the 318 saintly and blessed fathers who were assembled at Nicaea when Constantine of pious memory was emperor: and that those decrees also remain in force that were issued in Constantinople by the 150 holy fathers in order to destroy the heresies then rife and to confirm this same catholic and apostolic creed: the creed of the 318 fathers at Nicaea, and the same of the 150 saintly fathers assembled in Constantinople. This wise and saving creed, the gift of divine grace, was sufficient for a perfect understanding and establishment of religion. For its teaching about the Father and the Son and the Holy Spirit is complete, and it sets out the Lord's becoming human to those who faithfully accept it. But there are those who are trying to ruin the proclamation of the truth, and through their private heresies they have spawned novel formulas: some by daring to corrupt the mystery of the Lord's economy on our behalf, and refusing to apply the word *Theotokos* to the Virgin; and others by introducing a confusion and mixture, and mindlessly imagining that there is a single nature of the flesh and the divinity, and fantastically supposing that in the confusion the divine nature of the Only-begotten is passible.

Therefore this sacred and great and universal synod, now in session, in its desire to exclude all their tricks against the truth, and teaching what has been unshakable in the proclamation from the beginning, decrees that the creed of the 318 fathers is, above all else, to remain inviolate. And because of those who oppose the Holy Spirit, it ratifies the teaching about the being of the holy Spirit handed down by the 150 saintly fathers who met some time later in the imperial city—the teaching they made known to all, not introducing anything left out by their predecessors, but rather clarifying their ideas about the Holy Spirit by the use of scriptural testimonies against those who were trying to do away with his sovereignty. And because of those who are attempting to corrupt the mystery of the economy and are shamelessly and foolishly claiming that he who was born of the holy virgin Mary was a mere man, it has accepted the synodical letters of the blessed Cyril, bishop of the church of Alexandria, as written to Nestorius and to the Orientals, as being well-suited to refuting Nestorius's mad folly and for providing an interpretation for those who, in their religious zeal, desire an understanding of the saving creed.

To these it has suitably added, against false believers and for the establishment of orthodox doctrines, the letter of the primate of greatest and older Rome, the most blessed and most saintly Archbishop Leo, written to the sainted Archbishop Flavian to put down Eutyches's evil-mindedness, because it is in agreement with great Peter's confession and represents a foundation we have in common.

It is opposed to those who attempt to tear apart the mystery of the economy into a duality of sons; and it expels from the assembly of the priests those who dare to say that the divinity of the Only begotten is passible; and it stands opposed to those who imagine a mixture or confusion between the two natures of Christ; and it expels those who have the foolish idea that the form of a servant which he took from us is of a heavenly, or some other, kind of being; and it anathematizes those who profess two natures of the Lord before the union but imagine a single one after the union.

And so, following the holy Fathers, we all teach unanimously the confession of one and the same Son, our Lord Jesus Christ: the same perfect in divinity and perfect in humanity, the same truly God and truly man, of a rational soul and a body; consubstantial with the Father as regards his divinity, and the same consubstantial with us as regards his humanity; like us in all respects except for sin; begotten before the ages from the Father as regards his divinity, and in the last days the same for us and for our salvation from Mary, the Virgin Theotokos, as regards his humanity; one and the same Christ, Son, Lord, only begotten, acknowledged in two natures that undergo no confusion, no change, no division, no separation; at no point was the difference between the natures abolished because of the union, but rather the property of both natures is preserved and comes together into a single person and a single hypostasis. He is not parted or divided into two persons, but is one and the same only begotten Son, God, Word, Lord Jesus Christ, just as the prophets taught from the beginning about him, and as the Lord Jesus Christ himself instructed us, and as the creed of the Fathers handed it down to us.

Since we have formulated these things with all possible accuracy and attention, the sacred and universal synod has decreed that no one is permitted to produce, to write down or even compose, any other creed or to think or teach differently. As for those who dare either to compose another creed or even to promulgate or teach or hand down another creed for those who wish to convert to the recognition of the truth from Hellenism or from Judaism, or from any kind of heresy at all: if they be bishops or clerics, the bishops are to be deposed from the episcopacy and the clerics from the clergy; if they be monks or laity, they are to be anathematized.

**The Synodical Anathemata Against the Three Chapters: Council of Constantinople II (553).** 1. Whoever refuses to confess that the Father, Son, and Holy Spirit have one nature or substance, and that they have one power and authority, and that there is a consubstantial Trinity, one Deity to be adored in three hypostases or persons: let him be anathema; for there is only one God and Father, from whom all things come, and one Lord Jesus Christ, through whom all things are, and one Holy Spirit, in whom all things are: so let such a man be anathema.

2. If anyone will not confess that the Word of God has two nativities, one which is before all ages from the Father, outside time and without a body, and a second nativity of these latter days when the Word of God came down from the heavens and was made flesh of the holy and glorious Mary, Mother of God and ever-Virgin, and was born from her: let him be anathema.

3. If anyone declares that the [Word] of God who works miracles is not identical with the Christ who suffered, or alleges that God the Word was with the Christ who was born of woman, or was in him in the way that one might be in another, but that our Lord Jesus Christ was not one and the same, the Word of God incarnate and made man, and that the miracles and the sufferings that he voluntarily underwent in the flesh were not of the same person: let him be anathema.

4. If anyone declares that it was only in respect of grace, or as a principle of action, or of dignity or in respect of equality of honor, or in respect of authority, or of some relation, or of some affection or power, that there was a unity made between the Word of God and the man; or if anyone should argue that it was in respect of good will, as if God the Word were pleased with the man, because he was well and properly disposed to God, as Theodore claims in his madness; or if anyone says that this union is only a sort of synonymity, as the Nestorians allege, who call the Word of God Jesus and Christ, and even designate the human separately by the names "Christ" and "Son," quite obviously speaking about two different persons, and only pretending to speak of one person and one Christ when the reference is to his title, honor, dignity or adoration; and finally, if anyone does not accept the teaching of the holy Fathers that the union occurred of God the Word with human flesh possessed by a rational and intellectual soul, and that this union is in terms of synthesis or person, and accordingly that there is only one person, namely the Lord Jesus Christ, one member of the holy Trinity: let him be anathema.

5. This notion of "union" can be understood in many different ways. The supporters of the wickedness of Apollinarius and Eutyches have asserted that the union is produced by a confusing of the uniting elements, because they advocate the disappearance of the elements that so unite. Those who follow Theodore and Nestorius, rejoicing in the separateness, have brought in a union that is only in terms of "good will." The holy church of God, rejecting the wickedness of both sorts

of heresy, professes her belief in a union between the Word of God and human flesh that is by synthesis, that is, by a hypostatic union. In the mystery of Christ the union of synthesis not only conserves the elements that come together, without confusing them, but also allows no division.

6. If anyone understands by the single hypostasis of our Lord Jesus Christ that it covers the meaning of many hypostases, and by this argument tries to introduce into the mystery of Christ two hypostases or two persons, and having thus introduced the notion of two persons then talks of one person only in respect of dignity, honor, or adoration, as both Theodore and Nestorius have written about in their foolishness; and if anyone falsely represents the holy synod of Chalcedon, making out that it accepted this heretical view by its terminology of "one hypostasis," and if such a person does not acknowledge that the Word of God is hypostatically united with human flesh, and that on account of this there is only one hypostasis or one person, and that the holy synod of Chalcedon thus made a formal statement of belief in the single hypostasis of our lord Jesus Christ: let him be anathema, for there has been no addition of person or hypostasis to the holy Trinity even after one of its members, God the Word, became human flesh.

7. If anyone maintains that when one describes the holy and glorious ever-Virgin Mary as the Mother of God, it is only an inexact way of speaking, not a true title, or if they say that she is this only in some relative way, since she bore only a man and since God the Word was not made into human flesh within her, but rather the nativity of a man was notionally referred to God the Word since he was with the man who came into being; or if anyone misrepresents the holy synod of Chalcedon, alleging that it claimed that the Virgin was the Mother of God only according to that heretical understanding that the blasphemous Theodore put forward; or if anyone says that she is the mother of a man or simply the Christ-Bearer, that is, the Mother of Christ, intending to suggest that Christ is not God; and if such a person will not formally confess that she is properly and truly the Mother of God, because he who before all ages was born of the Father, namely God the Word, has been made into human flesh in these latter days and has been born to her, and that it was in this reverent understanding that the holy synod of Chalcedon formally stated its belief that she was the Mother of God: then let him be anathema.

8. If anyone does not confess a belief in our one Lord Jesus Christ, when speaking about the two natures, as understood both in his divinity and his humanity, so as by this means to signify a difference of natures from which an

ineffable and unconfused union has been made, in which neither the nature of the Word was changed into the nature of human flesh, nor was the nature of human flesh changed into that of the Word (for each remained what it was by nature, even after the union, since this had been made hypostatically); and if anyone understands the two natures in the mystery of Christ in the sense of a division into parts, or if he expresses his belief in the plural natures in the same Lord Jesus Christ, God the Word made flesh, but does not consider that the difference of those natures, out of which he is composed, is only in the onlooker's mind, that is a difference which is not compromised by the union (for he is one from both and the two exist through the one) but rather uses the plurality to suggest that each nature is possessed separately and has a hypostasis of its own: then let him be anathema.

If anyone confesses a belief that a union has been made out of the two natures, divinity and humanity, or speaks about the one nature of God the Word made flesh but does not understand these things according to what the Fathers have taught, namely that from the divine and human natures a hypostatic union was made, and that one Christ was formed, but from these expressions tries to introduce one nature or substance made out of the deity and human flesh of Christ: let him be anathema. For, in saying that it was in respect of hypostasis that the only begotten God the Word was united, we are not alleging that there was a confusion made of each of the natures, one into another, but rather that each of the two remained what it was, and this is the way we understand that the Word was united to human flesh. Accordingly, there is only one Christ, God and man; the same one being consubstantial with the Father in respect to his divinity, and also consubstantial with us in respect to our humanity. Both those who divide or split up the mystery of the divine dispensation of Christ and those who introduce into that mystery an element of confusion are equally rejected and anathematized by the church of God.

9. If anyone says that Christ is to be worshiped in his two natures, and by that wishes to introduce two adorations, a separate one for God the Word and another for the man; or if anyone (either in order to remove the human flesh or to mix up the divinity and the humanity) horribly invents one nature or substance brought together from the two, and thus worships Christ, but not by a single adoration as God the Word enfleshed along with his human flesh, as has been the tradition of the church from the very beginning: then let him be anathema.

10. If anyone does not profess belief that our Lord Jesus Christ, who was crucified in his human flesh, is truly God and the Lord of glory, and is one of the members of the holy Trinity: let him be anathema.

11. If anyone will not anathematize Arius, Eunomius, Macedonius, Apollinarius, Nestorius, Eutyches, and Origen, as well as their heretical books, and also all other heretics who have already been condemned and anathematized by the holy, catholic, and apostolic church and by the four holy synods that have already been mentioned, and also all those who have thought or now think in the same way as the aforesaid heretics and who persist in their error even to death: let him be anathema.

12. If anyone should defend the heretical Theodore of Mopsuestia, who said that God the Word is one, while the Christ was quite another, who was troubled by the passions of the soul and the desires of human flesh and was gradually separated from that which is inferior, and became better by his progress in good works, so that he could not be faulted in his way of life, and as a mere man were baptized in the name of the Father and the Son and the Holy Spirit, and through this baptism received the grace of the Holy Spirit and came to deserve Sonship and to be adored "as if" he were God the Word, in the way that one might adore a statue of the emperor, and that after his resurrection he became immutable in his thoughts and entirely without sin; this heretical Theodore who also claimed that the union of God the Word with Christ was rather like that which, according to the apostle's teaching, is between a man and his wife, where "the two shall become one"; who along with innumerable other blasphemies dared to allege that, when the Lord breathed on his disciples after his resurrection and said, "Receive the Holy Spirit," he was not truly giving them the Holy Spirit, but breathed on them only as a sign who similarly claimed that Thomas's profession of faith made after the resurrection, when he touched the hands and side of the Lord, namely "My Lord and my God," was not said about Christ, but that Thomas was in this way rather extolling God for raising up the Christ and expressing his astonishment at the miracle of the resurrection (and Theodore makes a comparison that is even worse than this when, writing about the Acts of the Apostles, he says that Christ was like Plato, Mani, Epicurus, and Marcion, alleging that just as each of these men arrived at his own doctrine and then had his disciples called after him Platonists, Manichaeans, Epicureans, and Marcionites, so Christ found his teaching and then had disciples who were called Christians); well then, if anyone offers a defense for this most heretical Theodore, and his heretical books, in which he throws up the aforesaid blasphemies and many other additional blasphemies

against our great God and Savior Jesus Christ, and if anyone fails to anathematize him and his heretical books as well as all those who offer an acceptance or defense of him, or who allege that his interpretation is correct, or who write on his behalf or on behalf of his heretical teachings, or who are or have been of the same way of thinking and persist until death in this error: let them be anathema.

13. If anyone defends the heretical writings of Theodoret that were composed against the true faith, against the first holy synod of Ephesus and against holy Cyril and his *Twelve Chapters*, and also defends what Theodoret wrote to support the heretical Theodore and Nestorius and others who think in the same way as the previously mentioned Theodore and Nestorius and accept them or their heresy; and if anyone, because of their influence, shall accuse the doctors of the church who have stated their belief in the hypostatic union of God the Word of being heretical; and if anyone does not anathematize these heretical books and those who have thought or now think in this way, and all those who have written against the true faith or against holy Cyril and his *Twelve Chapters*, and who persist in such heresy until they die: let them be anathema.

14. If anyone defends the letter that Ibas is said to have written to Mari the Persian, which denies that God the Word, who became incarnate of Mary the holy Mother of God and ever Virgin, became man, but alleges that he was only a man born to her, whom it describes as a temple, as if God the Word were one and the man someone quite different; which condemns Saint Cyril as if he were a heretic, when he gives the true teaching of Christians, and accuses Saint Cyril of writing opinions comparable to those of the heretical Apollinarius; which censures the first holy synod of Ephesus, alleging that it condemned Nestorius without going into the matter properly by a formal examination; which claims that the *Twelve Chapters* of Saint Cyril are heretical and opposed to the orthodox faith; and which defends Theodore and Nestorius and their heretical teachings and books so if anyone defends the said letter and does not anathematize it and all those who offer a defense for it and allege that it, or a part of it, is correct, or if anyone defends those who have written or shall write in support of it, or the heresies contained in it, or supports those who are bold enough to defend it or its heresies in the name of the holy Fathers of the holy synod of Chalcedon, and persists in these errors until his death: let him be anathema.

15. These, then, are the propositions we confess. We have received them from Holy Scripture, from the teaching of the holy Fathers, and from the

definitions about the one and the same faith made by the previously mentioned four holy synods. Moreover, condemnation has been passed by us against the heretics and their impiety, and also against those who have justified or shall justify the so-called *Three Chapters*, and against those who have persisted or will persist in their own error. If anyone should attempt to hand on, or to teach by word or writing, anything contrary to what we have regulated here, then if he is a bishop or somebody appointed to the clergy, insofar as he is acting contrary to what is appropriate for priests and his ecclesiastical status, let him be stripped of the rank of priest or cleric, and if he is a monk or layperson, let him be anathema.

## FURTHER READING

### Patriarchates

Congar, Y. M. J. *I Patriarcati orientali nel primo millennio.* Rome: Pontificium Institutum studiorum orientalium, 1968.

Sardes, M. de. *Le patriarcat Oecuménique dans l'Église orthodoxe.* Paris: Beauchesne, 1975.

Wries, W. de. *Orient et Occident. Les structures écclesiales vues dans l'histoire des sept premiers conciles oecuméniques.* Paris: Editions du Cerf, 1974.

———. "Rom und die Patriarchate des Ostens und ihr Verhaltnis zur papstlichen Vollgewat." *Scholastik* 37 (1962): 341-66.

### Chrysostom

Baur, C. *John Chrysostom and His Times.* 2 vols. London: Sands, 1960.

Kelly, J. N. D. *Golden Mouth: The Story of John Chrysostom: Ascetic, Preacher, Bishop.* Ithaca, NY: Cornell University Press, 1995.

Lawrenz, M. *The Christology of John Chrysostom.* Lewiston, NY: Edwin Mellen, 1996.

Liebeschuetz, J. H. W. G. *Barbarians and Bishops: Army, Church, and State in the Reign of Arcadius and Chrysostom.* Oxford: Oxford University Press, 1990.

Wilken, R. L. *John Chrysostom and the Jews: Rhetoric and Reality in the Late 4th Century.* Berkeley: University of California Press, 1983.

### The Origenistic Crisis

Clark, E. *The Origenist Controversy: The Cultural Construction of an Early Christian Debate.* Princeton, NJ: Princeton University Press, 1992.

Crouzel, H. "Les condamnations subies par Origène et sa doctrine." In *Origeniana Septima,* ed. W. A. Bienert, 311-15. Louvain: Peeters, 1999.

———. "Origenism." In *Encyclopedia of the Early Church,* ed. A. Di Berardino, 2:623-24. Cambridge: Clarke, 1992.

Daley, B. "What Did 'Origenism' Mean in the Sixth Century?" In *Origeniana Sexta,* ed. G. Dorival et al., 627-38. Louvain: Peeters, 1995.

Diekamp, F. *Die origenistischen Streitigkeiten im sechsten Jahrundert und das funfte allgemeine Concil*. Münster: Aschendorff, 1899.

Harding, E. M. "The Origenist Crisis." In *The Westminster Handbook to Origen of Alexandria*, ed. J. A, McGuckin, 162-67. St. Louis: Westminster John Knox, 2004.

Hombergen, D. *The Second Origenist Controversy: A New Perspective on Cyril of Scythopolis' Monastic Biographies as Historical Sources for Sixth Century Origenism*. Rome: Pontificio Ateneo S. Anselmo, 2001.

Ledegang, F. "Anthropomorphites and Origenists in Egypt at the End of the Fourth Century." In *Origeniana Septima*, ed. W. Bienert et al., 375-79. Louvain: Peeters, 1999.

Prinzivalli, L. "The Controversy About Origen Before Epiphanius." In *Origeniana Septima*, ed. W. Bienert et al., 195-213. Louvain: Peeters, 1999.

### The Fifth-Sixth Century Conciliar Debates

Davis, L. D. *The First Seven Ecumenical Councils: Their History and Theology*. Wilmington, DE: M. Glazier, 1987.

Frend, W. H. C. *The Rise of the Monophysite Movement*. Cambridge: Cambridge University Press, 1979.

Gray, P. T. R. *The Defence of Chalcedon in the East. 451–553*. Leiden: Brill, 1979.

Grillmeier, A. *Christ in Christian Tradition*. Vol. 2, part 2. London: Mowbray, 1995.

Hardy, E. R. *Christology of the Later Fathers*. Philadelphia: Westminster, 1964. Pages 378-81.

Kalamaras, M. *He Pempte Oikoumenike Synodos*. Athens: Athenai, 1985.

McGuckin, J. A. "Il Lungo Cammino Verso Calcedonia." ("The Long Road to Chalcedon: The Unfolding Nexus of Christological Definition from Origen to Dioscorus.") In *Il Concilio di Calcedonia 1550 Anni Dopo*, ed. A. Ducay, 13-41. Rome: Libreria Editrice Vaticana, 2002.

———. "Mystery or Conundrum? The Apprehension of Christ in the Chalcedonian Definition." In *In The Shadow of the Incarnation: Essays on Jesus Christ in the Early Church in Honor of B. E. Daley*, ed. P. W. Martens, 249-59. Notre Dame, IN: University of Notre Dame Press, 2008.

———. *St. Cyril of Alexandria and the Christological Crisis: Its History, Theology, and Texts*. Leiden: Brill, 1994; Crestwood, NY: St. Vladimir's Seminary Press, 2004.

Trostyanskiy, S., ed. *Seven Icons of Christ: The Teaching of the Seven Oecumenical Councils*. Piscataway, NJ: Gorgias Press, 2016.

### Neo-Platonism

Cleary, J., ed. *The Perennial Tradition of Neoplatonism*. Ancient and Medieval Philosophy 1.24. Leuven: Leuven University Press, 1997.

Corrigan, K. *Reading Plotinus: A Practical Introduction to Neoplatonism*. West Lafayette, IN: Purdue University Press, 2005.

Dillon, J. M., and L. P. Gerson. *Neoplatonic Philosophy: Introductory Readings*. Indianapolis: Hackett, 2004.

Gerson, L. P., ed. *The Cambridge Companion to Plotinus.* Cambridge: Cambridge University Press, 1996.

———. *Plotinus.* New York: Routledge, 1994.

O'Meara, D. J. *Plotinus: An Introduction to the Enneads.* Oxford: Clarendon, 1993.

Rist, J. M. *Plotinus: The Road to Reality.* Cambridge: Cambridge University Press, 1967.

Segonds, A. P., and C. Steel, eds. *Proclus et la Théologie platonicienne: Actes du colloque international de Louvain (13–16 Mai 1998) en l'honneur de H. D. Saffrey et L. G. Westerink.* Ancient and Medieval Philosophy 1.26. Leuven: Leuven University Press, 2000.

Wallis, R.T. *Neoplatonism.* Indianapolis: Hackett, 1972.

**Dionysius the Areopagite**

Gersh, S. *From Iamblichus to Eriugena: An Investigation of the Prehistory and Evolution of the Pseudo-Dionysian Tradition.* Leiden: Brill, 1978.

Koch, H. "Proklus als Quelle des Pseudo-Dionysius Areopagita in der Lehre von Bösen." *Philologus* 54 (1895): 438-54.

———. *Pseudo-Dionysius Areopagita in seinen Beziehungen zum Neuplatonismu und Mysterienweses.* Mainz, 1900.

Louth, A. *Denys the Areopagite.* Wilton, CT: Morehouse-Barlow, 1989.

Luibheid, C. *Pseudo-Dionysius: The Complete Works.* Classics of Western Spirituality Series 54. New York: Paulist, 1987.

Rorem, P. *Biblical and Liturgical Symbols Within the Pseudo-Dionysian Synthesis.* Toronto: Pontifical Institute of Mediaeval Studies, 1984.

———. *Pseudo Dionysius: A Commentary on the Texts and an Introduction to Their Significance.* Oxford: Oxford University Press, 1993.

Rorem, P., and J. C. Lamoreaux. *John of Scythopolis and the Dionysian Corpus.* Oxford: Oxford University Press, 1998.

# THE EMERGENCE OF CHRISTIAN BYZANTIUM IN THE SIXTH TO NINTH CENTURIES

**JUSTINIAN THE GREAT**

Flavius Petrus Sabbatius Justinianus (482–565) was one of the most powerful of the Byzantine Christian emperors, and his reign marked a revival of the Roman imperium after long years of decline. He is known, for this reason, as well as for his cultural contributions, as Justinian the Great. He studied law and theology before his elevation to power, and this specialist knowledge of church affairs is evident in all his subsequent policies. He was patronized by his uncle Justin, a (relatively uneducated) military commander who assumed the throne on behalf of the army after the death of Emperor Anastasius in 518. From the outset Justinian directed policy in his uncle's administration, already conscious of the need to bring internal unity to the eastern provinces, especially Egypt and Syria, which had been racked by christological dissensions rising up in the aftermath of the Council of Chalcedon (the Monophysite movement).

In 525, having petitioned his uncle to change the law that forbade senators from espousing lower-class artistes, he married Theodora (497–548), a noted actress, who became a skilled partner in his rule (they are depicted together in the resplendent robes of state in a famous mosaic in Ravenna). Although she was subject to scurrilous tales, not least by the court rhetorician and historian Procopius, who worked for them both but also cherished secret resentments against them, she was far more than a circus entertainer who had risen high because of her looks. Her sharp mind and sophisticated political acumen matched that of Justinian, and they made a strong regnant team. Justinian often used her, not least in his policy toward the Monophysites, as a "gentle advocate" contrasting with his "stern hand." It is inconceivable that she would have sheltered leading Monophysite clergy in the imperial palace, for example, and offered gold subsidies to them, without the explicit knowledge and approval of her imperial husband. Previous commentators have often failed to appreciate the delicately nuanced nature of their policy of reconciliation, seeing it in too black-and-white terms that presumed it was "self-contradictory," and that she was somehow working against her husband's religious policy rather than being an integral part of it.

In 527, on the death of Justin, Justinian succeeded peacefully to the throne himself. But there were rumbling resentments among the old aristocracy, who despised the ascendancy of the military classes. Ten years later the Nika revolt, fomented by a party of aristocrats in the capital, almost brought Justinian's life to an end.[1] The Hippodrome factions of the Blues and Greens, which were also basic political caucuses at the capital, broke out in deadly fights inside the arena that soon turned into a major statement of dissatisfaction against Justinian himself. He and Theodora were in the imperial box at the Hippodrome when the riots began, and the mob threatened to overwhelm the royal balcony. The old cathedral of Hagia Sophia was set on fire, and many other buildings of the center of the city. Justinian was ready to make his escape from the capital, into exile, but his wife's cool-headedness set a different policy. The dictum afterward associated with Theodora, preventing the flight, was "Imperial purple makes the finest of shrouds." Instead of running, Justinian gave orders to the troops he had stationed within the Hippodrome to band together in military formation and systematically start hacking their way through the mob with their swords. It did not take long for the aggression of the crowds to turn to panic, and many hundreds were slaughtered on the day, quelling all resistance to Justinian's rule.

The widespread damage to the capital's key buildings near the Hippodrome, in the aftermath of the Nika revolt, inaugurated Justinian's major building campaign at Constantinople. He had already constructed the magnificent church of the soldier saints Sergius and Bacchus, but now he amplified his ambitions to produce the greatest church in the world, the magnificent replacement for the old basilica of St. Sophia, which had been burned down.[2] Even today, in its threadbare and denuded condition, Hagia Sophia still evokes wonder.[3] In its heyday it was the most splendid building in the world, and it retains some claim to be in the short list of places that can still claim that title. The dramatic and daring architecture of the new cathedral, along with its awe-inspiring size, had the effect of making the eyes of the whole

---

[1] So called from the rioters' shouts of "Nika!" ("Victory!").
[2] The church of the soldier saints Sergius and Bacchus is in the aristocratic quarter, below the Hippodrome, and is now a mosque called Little Hagia Sophia. It is a jewel box of Byzantine ecclesiastical architecture.
[3] In Istanbul, the twentieth-century renamed city of Constantinople.

Christian world turn toward Constantinople and take note of its art, its liturgy, and theology for many centuries to come. Justinian's magnificent center symbolized, in many ways, the role that Constantinople was to have for almost a millennium to come as the undisputed focal point of Eastern Christian affairs. It is reported that when he went into the completed building for its dedication and looked around him, Justinian said, "Solomon, I have surpassed you!"

Having concluded a peace settlement with Persia, the traditional enemy of the Romans, Justinian was at last able to turn his attention to the western territories, which for a century past had been lost to the empire because of occupying Arian German tribes. His western wars were to last over twenty years: North Africa was reclaimed from the Vandals in 534; Italy from the Ostrogoths in 555; Spain from the Visigoths in 555. The ancient boundaries of the Roman imperium were almost restored, but the cost of overextension was too great, and Justinian's restoration did not last. Perhaps it can even have served to diminish the idea, which had at one stage been elevated as a distinctive theological hope in the patristic era, of a single Romano-Christian polity for the world: one Lord, one faith, one baptism, one earthly kingdom of the Christians on earth. Certainly the cost of the war to regain the West fell heavily on the West itself, and the fiscal hardship the recovery imposed led many Latin-speaking Christians to resent the imperial yoke (increasingly seen as Greek and foreign) and wish it gone, rather than feeling anything like a "return" to a Roman imperial homeland. From this time onward, the papacy is increasingly seen to be attracting to itself a lot of the former claims of the imperium: a kind of priestly dominion.

Turning his attention to the larger issues of Roman cultural and social coherence, a refreshment of Roman values that were being sensed as increasingly antique in the sixth century (a policy he described as *renovatio*, or renewal), Justinian inaugurated a major review of Roman law, which, in 529 (and again in 534), was issued as the famed *Codex Justinianus*. A collection of *Digests* were issued in 533 along with the *Institutes*. All three of these collections became the *Corpus of Civil Law* (*Corpus Iuris Civilis*), which was to have determinative effect on later European (and Islamic) civil law as well as on the church's canon law in both the Eastern and Western parts of the empire.

In this project Justinian used the lawyer and historian Tribonian, a notable political leader at Constantinople, who was a close friend, and to whom he had already given many of the highest state offices.[4] Tribonian began his career with Justinian as *magister officiorum* (secretary of state in the imperial administration). He was the minister of justice in 530 (*quaestor sacri palatii*), but on account of the continuing

---

[4]For a contemporary account, see Procopius, *Anecdota* 13.12, 20.16-17. For a wider consideration, see T. Honoré, *Tribonian* (London: Duckworth, 1978).

strict measures taken by his agents against the populace after the Nika revolt, he lost the favor of the people, and so was moved sideways by the emperor so as to become *magister officiorum* once again. After the publication of the first parts of the *Codex* he again resumed the post of *quaestor sacri palatii*. After his death in 546, Justinian's legal project lost much of its forward impetus. Another major contributor was Theophilus, who was professor of law (*antecessor*) in the school of Constantinople. The skills of Dorotheus and Anatolius were soon co-opted as chief members of the inner circle for planning the work. They were the chief professors of law in the prestigious Roman legal school at Beirut.

On February 13, 528, Justinian issued the edict entitled *Constitutio Haec*, which set up a ten-member commission, including Tribonian, but chaired by the *quaestor sacri palatii*. The task set to them was to bring the antiquated legal collations of the emperors Diocletian and Theodosius to a systematic completion and to codify all the still-valid imperial constitutions into a single, manageable collection. This basically meant that they were to collate together the Gregorian, Hermogenian, and Theodosian codices and add in all the imperial constitutions issued between 438 and 539. They were empowered by the emperor to delete all perceived obsolete elements and eliminate contradictions or superfluities, adding whatever they thought necessary to bring the prescripts up to date, and reestablish their authority for the whole of the empire.

Fourteen months later, on April 7, 529, the completed work was published under the title of *Codex Constitutionum* (often simply known as the *Codex Justinianus*) by the decree of the imperial *Constitutio Summa* and was set to come into force on April 16. Thereafter no Roman law that was not found within the codex was permitted to be cited in any court of the empire. The chronological arrangement of earlier codex models was again followed here, along with the listing under subject titles, making the codex both comprehensive and easily negotiated by the legal researcher. The success of the project and its rapid completion gave encouragement to the chancery of Justinian to press on with amplifications of the reform. So it was that in 534 a revised version was issued that has come to be called the new code.[5]

Even at the time of the publication of the code of 529, it was already clear to Justinian's commission that a new and revised edition was badly needed, if only because of the significant extent of Justinian's own legal decrees of recent years. More than this, the extensive scholarly sifting through the old source materials for the code had clearly demonstrated to Justinian's commissioners the pressing need to address the problem that the earlier generations of reforms had been systematically

---

[5]The first edition being thus designated as *Codex Vetus* by scholars. A fragment of its index was discovered in Egypt by Grenfell and Hunt in the nineteenth century (Papyrus Oxyrhyncus XV.1814). This is all that survives of the manuscripts.

avoiding, namely the forceful bringing into some kind of order and coherence the teeming mass of legal opinion from the historical (and still revered) classical Roman jurists, which served as the contextual background for the interpretation of all Roman legal enactments. The earlier systematization introduced by the Roman *Law of Citations* had not managed to bring much order into this practical process of citing juristic opinion. Now having the basic texts in order, in the *Codex*, made it all the more imperative to prioritize (and weed out) the body of juristic commentary that actually formed the main basis of practical legal pleading in the Byzantine-era courts. Justinian himself saw the problem posed by the commentaries of the jurists (the dead weight of tradition in the handling of law) and resolved to attack it just as forcefully as he had the collation of the ancient enactments.

As a preliminary measure he issued an imperial decree on November 17, 530, titled *Quinquaginta Decisiones*, or "The Fifty Decisions." In this he formally noted the inconsistencies in the major authoritative source of the interpretation of Roman law and decreed resolutions to the major controversies that they had listed as open points of interpretation, simultaneously issuing definitive solutions. Having thus established his imperial credentials as the *Renovator Traditionum Romanorum*, that which was the quintessential role of the emperor as he saw it, namely to renew the springs of Roman culture, he set out on his own authority that this work of revision would be definitive: after it no alternative sets of sources would be admitted, no further scholiastic commentaries on his *Codex* would be allowed.[6]

The implication was also given here that a similar all-inclusiveness (for example, the forbidding of independent editions of his code, or the publication of new independent books of legal philosophy) would mark his attack on the body of juristic opinions, though that work would take more time and effort on the part of his legal experts. *The Fifty Decisions*, nevertheless, is an early signal to the entire legal profession that he intended to take the minor revisions of the code much further, a project that would eventually see the day as the Justinianic *Digests*.

The work of the first revision of the code began in early 534. Tribonian and Dorotheus of Beirut, then resident in Constantinople, and three of the lawyers who prepared the *Codex Vetus* set to work to complete this. Their task was simply stated: to adapt the first code by introducing the Justinianic decrees postdating 529, and especially the terms of the *Fifty Decisions*. But they also took the opportunity to repair perceived gaps in the historical coverage of the *Vetus Codex* and eliminate duplications. On November 16, 534, the new code was published by the decree

---

[6] A few editions with Byzantine scholia (notes) did appear as time went on, however, mainly explaining the technical language of the codex and simplifying it for popular Greek usage.

*Constitutio Cordi* under the title of *Codex Repetitae Praelectionis*, and it came into force on December 29, 534.

The Code of Justinian is an impressive architectural work, like many of his state and church buildings in stone. It was meant to show even the casual observer the glory and power of Roman culture, and in expressing it anew, perhaps to reiterate for the world of his own age the precise vision of what the Christian imperium would offer as an enduring sequence of imperial dynasties stretching out from Constantine to himself. If so, the preponderant message was one of continuity with classical culture. The whole is structured as twelve books (a deliberate allusion to the archaic and classical "Twelve Tables of Rome"), each one being subdivided into several titles relating to different legal topics. The titles present the constitutions of the emperors in chronological sequence under the imperial name of the issuer and that of the original addressee of the decree. The constitutions are further divided into paragraphs (propositional divisions that allow for easier citation). The first of these in each major heading is always designated the *principium*. Book one concerns jurisdictional and ecclesiastical matters. Books two through eight treat private law. Book nine sets out terms of criminal law. Books ten through twelve relate to administrative law. The whole code contains approximately forty-five hundred acts of law dating from the time of Hadrian in the early second century. The majority of the decrees emanate from Diocletian's reorganization in the late third and early fourth centuries.[7] Justinian's own decrees account for four hundred of the enactments, accounting for 10 percent of the total.

**The Digest *(or* Pandects*) of Justinian.*** The rapid and efficient production of this first experiment encouraged the emperor to attempt the more difficult enterprise of simplifying and digesting the writings of the jurists. Thus, on December 15, 530, Justinian issued the Constitution *Deo Auctore*, which instructed Tribonian, who had by then moved to become the *quaestor sacri palatii*, or justice minister himself, to form a new commission of sixteen eminent experts with the charge of bringing order and system into the juristic texts and publishing a single, supremely authoritative compendium within the space of ten years. It would in fact take them only three years to bring the work to completion.[8] The groundwork for this major

---

[7]Twenty-seven percent of the total derives from Diocletian.
[8]The speed of the work was aided, doubtless, by the fact that the idea had already had a long gestation—in the air from the time of Theodosius. Also, some of the later Roman jurists had already started to try to systematize the chaos. This can be seen, for example, in the work of Masurius Sabinus (*Libri tres iuris civilis*). Scholars surmise that the sixteen members undoubtedly split up into specializing subcommittees. F. Bluhme argued a method of composition that has commanded widespread agreement: "Die Ordnung der fragmente in den Pandektentiteln," *Zeitschrift fur geschichtliche Rechtswissenschaft* 4 (1820): 257-472.

compendium, which became known as the *Digest* or the *Pandects*, had already been laid by the numerous annotations the compilers of the code had made as to the inconsistencies that had to be dealt with in the mass of juristic opinions that comprised the traditional *Ius Romanorum*.[9]

Tribonian appointed as leading members Dorotheus and Anatolius, professors of the law school in Beirut, as well as Theophilus and Cratinus, chief teachers in the law school of Constantinople. He appointed also the palace official Constantinus and eleven notable lawyers. The scope of their collating work was to be restricted to those Roman jurists who in times past had been afforded the highest rank and weight by preceding emperors, or in other words given the status of the *ius respondendi*. Their juridical opinions had for a long time enjoyed the force of custom at law. But there were others also whose names customarily carried weight. The commissioners were instructed not to allow custom to stand as a blind guide. The traditional fame of a jurist of the past was not to outweigh the practical value of his opinions; and all the collection was to be ordered in a coherent way according to the judgment of the panel, whose decisions were to have absolute and binding force.[10]

Jurists who were not mentioned in the law of citations were able to be consulted, but those that the commissioners finally omitted from the *Pandects* were never to be cited again in Roman legal cases, nor were opinions of famous jurors to carry any more weight except as authorized in the *Digest*, ad locum. Nor would there be any appeal against the commission's decisions on what had become obsolete in the law. The limit was set of not covering material that had already been sufficiently covered in the *Codex*. The *Digest* was thus the accompanying interpretative material for the *Codex*, which because of the support given to it by the *Digest* was meant to be the final and definitive version of Roman law henceforth. Once it was published it was intended that any reference to the original treatises of the ancient jurors would be forbidden in the courts.

The seriousness of this centralizing work of reference was underlined by the emperor's forbidding any further creation of legal treatises commenting on the *Digest* itself. Only cross-translation (from the original Latin to the vernacular Greek) and short annotations (*scholia*) and brief quotations were to be allowed. An obvious reason for this was to avoid the problem of "accumulations" that had clogged up the reform attempts of Diocletian and Theodosius. It might also be the case that this very close encounter with the classical (pagan) Roman law sources revealed to Justinian's

---

[9] *Digest* (derived from the Latin *digerere*) means "the systematization"; *pandects* (derived from the Greek *pan dexesthe*) means "encyclopedia."

[10] As to the conflicted material emerging in the review of old law, to which the commissioners intruded decisions and made specific alterations, these instances have been known since the sixteenth century as the *Interpolationes Triboniani*.

court just how much the early medieval Byzantines now moved within a different thought world. The old sources, interpreted in the light of the cult of the ancient gods of Rome, were primary guides to societal life, fundamentally social but far from secular. The Byzantine commissioners lived in a society where the religious parameters were significantly different; the very conceptions of justice and equity had moved in fundamental new ways.

Modern commentators sometimes express surprise that although Justinian himself was a profoundly religious Christian, a dedicated theologian whose vision of what Rome's glory involved clearly depended on extending Christian orthodoxy to the limits of his jurisdiction, even so the *Code* and *Digest* that bear his name seem incredibly "secular" in tone, almost devoid of any overtly Christian message.[11] Two things can be borne in mind in relation to this. The first is that when one deals with a code of law rooted in ancient precedents, one is not dealing with a direct mirror-reality of society in any case. Most reviewers now agree that the Justinianic code is an accurate reflection neither of how law operated in the pagan imperial past nor in his own day. It is not, to that extent, a clear reflecting mirror on either set of societies. It is more in the fashion of an attempt to secure a bridgehead between the world of Roman antiquity and the emerging world of the Christian early Middle Ages. It can be seen as a Christian Roman attempt to keep faith with the past while moving energetically onward.

To this extent Justinian's reordering of the classical Roman sources, which he instinctively felt were the bedrock of Byzantine security precisely because they "were" Roman, is as much a determination to draw a line under the influence of ancient Roman values as it is a concern to reaffirm their authority. In more ways than geographical we have certainly moved from old Rome to new Rome. The Byzantines, therefore, are trying to keep faith with a classical imperial past, but not entirely committing to it, which is why Justinian fully asserts his own stamp and affords his commissioners such total mastery of power over the "quality" of the classical record. The inevitable loss of historical resources it signified (the varied historical contexts of individual antique jurors that it would cut loose from the legal history of Rome were de facto not liable to survive a further passage through time regardless of how venerable they were) was a fair price to pay for the way the Romans of Justinian's day reasserted themselves as masters of their own tradition, not slaves to it. And perhaps this might have been another reason why Justinian ordered a ban on further commentary on this work of review.

The second thing that has to be kept in mind if one muses over the apparent "secularity" of the Justinianic code is that the emperor had a very refined awareness of the massive legal codes that had already accumulated in relation to the religious

---

[11] See for example A. Watson, *The Spirit of Roman Law* (Athens: University of Georgia Press, 1995), 45.

law codes of the empire. These are the canon laws, and from the outset they were fundamentally Christian in tone and spirit, and by the sixth century had become extensive, rising into a formal level of legal significance not merely at the local level (where the episcopal judgments bore force in Byzantine society) but even at international imperial level, when the canons of the great councils (councils that could only be declared by imperial constitution) were given active force in Roman law by the emperor's decree subsequently acknowledging and accepting the work of these major synods of bishops. If one wonders at the relative absence of specific Christian legislation in the Justinianic Code, one needs to bring alongside it what every Byzantine would have regarded as the "parallel" religious dimension to the law of Christian Rome, namely the collections of canons that were under the immediate concern of the hierarchy, who were basically the functioning *quaestores ecclesiasticae*, that is, the lawmakers of the *ekklesia*. The two sets of law, civil and ecclesiastical, were both given civic (imperial) force in Byzantium and regarded in theory as having a *symphonia*, a harmonious single voice.

The *Digest*'s authoritative status was announced and established by the imperial decree *Constitutio Tanta* (given in Latin) and duplicated in the Greek as *Dedoken*, which was issued on December 16 and set to become law as from December 30, 533. Justinian notes in the preamble that the commission surveyed approximately two thousand books containing three million lines, reducing them to 150,000 lines of text and altering "many things of the highest importance" in the process. The work of thirty-nine classical Roman jurists was abstracted in the *Digest*, ranging in time from 100 BC to AD 300. The earliest commentators were Quintus Mucius Scaevola and Aelius Gellus; the last was Arcadias Charisius, who lived in the mid-fourth century. Eighty percent of the cited opinions were taken from the five leading Roman authorities of the late principate (Ulpianus, Paulus, Papinianus, Gaius, and Modestinus); Ulpianus himself commanded 40 percent of all the citations, and Paulus came a close second after him. The other thirty-four jurists mentioned in the work contributed collectively the remaining 20 percent. The leading five classical jurists, of course, had by that time already established an overwhelming level of authority and had the most complete editions of their work extant in the libraries of the law schools.

The *Digest* was composed of fifty books. Each was divided into titles (*tituli*) and then subdivided into *fragmenta* (also called *leges*) and in some cases then into sections, and also paragraphs (the first of the series of the latter being the *principium*).[12] As Justinian had commanded, the titles were drawn up to reflect the titles used in the codex. Cross-referencing was the heart of the matter. The beginning of each

---

[12] The exception is books 30-32.

*fragmentum* in the *Digest* lists the name of the jurist in question, together with the legal title under discussion and the section of the original book from which the citation was taken.[13]

The first four books, called the *Prota*, deal with generic matters, such as how to conduct affairs in court, who the various public official were and what were the proprieties of their rank, and what the limits of jurisdiction were. Books five through eleven were entitled *De Iudiciis* and concerned judicial proceedings and cases. Books twelve through nineteen set out contract law and personal actionable cases (*De Rebus*), while books twenty through twenty-seven dealt with various domestic issues such as marriages, guardianship, rights of mortgage holders, and so on (*Umbilicus Pandectarum*). Books twenty-eight through thirty-six (*De Testamentis*) specifically legislated for wills and testamentary trusts. Books thirty-seven through forty-four concerned legal exceptions, ownership and property rights, and problems associated with intestacy. Books forty-five through fifty dealt with obligations, civil injuries, and the process of appeals, as well as local government processes and public works administration. At the heart of this section, in books forty-seven and forty-eight, could be found the Byzantine criminal code, bearing the specific title of the "Awesome Volumes" (*Libri Terribili*). Eighty copies of the whole work were ordered to be made for use in the palace departments, the law schools, and throughout other sections of the capital's administration. Of these original eighty manuscripts one has survived, though most of the numerous copies of the work that we now possess date to the eleventh century.[14]

**The Institutes *of Justinian*.** While the *Digest* project was clearly also meant to serve as the future primary source of reference for trainees in the law schools of Beirut and Constantinople, the very size of the text made it necessary for the commissioners to think about a shorter, classroom-friendly project that could be expected to be part of the library of every provincial town as well as of every successful lawyer. For centuries past the classical textbook the *Institutes of Gaius* had served this purpose. This was now determined to be overhauled and reissued in a form that corresponded to the arrangement of the *Codex* and *Digest*.

In 533 Justinian commanded the textbook should be revised so as to form a new book of instruction for the schools. A commission of three was appointed for the

---

[13] This layout leads to the common way of citing material from the Justinianic *Digest* in a fourfold numerical system: by book, by title, by fragment, by section. If there is no section because of the shortness of the fragment, it reduces to a threefold reference. It is similarly reduced if only the *principium* of the fragment is being cited.

[14] The lone surviving manuscript came to Italy in the tenth century and from the twelfth century lodged at Pisa. It was captured by the Florentines in 1406. It is now known as the *Littera Florentina* or *Codex Florentinus*. The Latin versions that circulated were predominantly partial copies, usually omitting all the Greek material as a matter of course.

task. Tribonian led the panel and was accompanied by his long-standing colleagues, the law professors Theophilus from Constantinople and Dorotheus of Beirut. The remit was once more the same: to abbreviate, delete the duplications, and cut what was obsolete from the record. The majority of the editorial work had already been completed as part of the process of dealing with the jurists in the *Digest*, and so the finished work, subsequently known as the *Institutes of Justinian*, was ratified by the imperial Constitution *Imperatoriam maiestatem* on November 21, 533, and published as law together with the *Digest* by the *Constitutio Tanta* (Greek title: *Dedoken*) on December 30, 533.

Two-thirds of the *Institutes* directly reproduces the older text, the *Institutes of Gaius*. The editors also introduced material from Gaius's other famous volume *Res Quottidiane* (*Book of Daily Affairs*), and various elementary materials were brought in from the other leading classical jurists, Ulpianus, Paulus, Marcianus, and Florentinus. Some of the simpler materials from the *Digest* were also set out as test cases for students. The edited work retained the structure plan of Gaius's original in the main, making a threefold division in four books, related to law of persons, property, and actions, but now subdivided more consistently to reflect the contents of the sections in the titles and paragraphs of the *Codex* for ready reference. Where the *Digest* was composed basically of synopsized extracts, the *Institutes* was made up more from narrative essays on the topics in hand, making it much more relevant for educational use.

**The Novels *of Justinian*.** Between 534 and his death in 565, Justinian continued to issue a great number of ordinances that dealt with many subjects and that significantly altered the classical statement of the law on many points. These ordinances, falling as they did out of the scope of the *Codex*, came to be called the "New Constitutions" (*Novellae Constitutiones Post Codicem*). In recent English studies they have been customarily referred to as the *Novels*. By the time of his death they amounted to more than 150.[15] Most of them concern administrative or ecclesiastical law. He had intended (as announced in his *Constitutio Cordi* of 534) to bring these *Novels* into a systematic new volume when they had sufficiently accumulated, but it is probable that the intervening death of Tribonian in 546 took the energy out of this project.

---

[15] The *Collectio Graeca* manuscript contains 168 but extends into the reigns of Justin II (565–578) and Tiberius II (578–582). The manuscript tradition of the *Novels* now dates back to the eleventh century at the earliest, but collections were first made in Justinian's time by Julianus, professor of law at Constantinople (*Epitome Juliani*), for export to the newly recaptured territories of Italy. There is also a separate version by an anonymous collator (the *Authenticum*, containing 134 constitutions). The *Collectio Graeca* was the standard version known throughout all the history of Byzantium, but it was largely unknown to the West until fifteenth-century refugees introduced it there after the collapse of 1453. It became a major source of inspiration for Renaissance scholars of the law thereafter.

***Justinian's* Corpus Iuris Civilis.** All four parts of the entire Justinianic law program, namely the *Codex*, the *Digest*, the *Institutes*, and *Novels* are today collectively called the *Corpus Iuris Civilis*. It is a term invented by renaissance scholar Dionysius Gothofredus (1549–1622), who produced one of the first early modern critical editions of Justinian's code, which remained a standard text until the nineteenth century. This *Corpus Juris* of Justinian, with a few additions from the ordinances of succeeding emperors, continued to be the center and focus of all legal ordinance and philosophy in what survived of the Roman world. The codification of the classical heritage and its emended adoption by the Byzantines allowed Roman law to be passed on as the common heritage of most later European cultures, both Eastern and Western.[16] By bringing the ancient Roman tradition into manageable order, and by showing in the civic sphere what the church fathers had already done in the fourth century, that the secular heritage of classical Rome could be adopted and adapted confidently by Christians, Justinian achieved an enduring legacy. Most significantly, he was able to ensure that the ancient achievement of the concept of the rule of law, arguably the highest social philosophy of the ancients (however partially it had been applied in history), was able to pass alive into the ferment of the medieval world, in the process guaranteeing Roman law a foundational place in the ongoing history of Greco-Latin civilization.

Justinian was one of the most proactive of all the Christian emperors in terms of regulating church life. He was not just a guardian but a prosecutor of orthodoxy, summoning synods as well as deposing bishops and arresting popes where necessary. He was deeply opposed to the Origenist monks, though not very successful in suppressing Origen's influence among the ascetical intelligentsia despite his orchestration of a posthumous synodical condemnation of the ancient theologian in 543. His chief ecclesiastical policy was aimed at the reconciliation of the Monophysite schism, and accordingly he tried to follow a difficult path: moderating the authority of Chalcedon, without alienating Rome, by making Cyril of Alexandria's authority preeminent once more.

The Council of Constantinople II in 553 was his design and issued severe condemnations of the Syrian theologians whom Cyril had fought against a century before (the *Three Chapters Controversy*). In the long term his efforts did not so much reconcile as serve to mark and underscore the significant differences in tone and character between the Syrian church (soon to leave the Byzantine political orbit), the Alexandrian and Ethiopian churches (which denounced Chalcedon and did not find

---

[16]Roman law had less impact on Saxon and Celtic cultures. The common law codes of England, Wales, and Ireland are much less indebted to it.

Constantinople II to be sufficiently radical for them), and the Byzantine and Roman churches (which held to Chalcedon's centrality but in notably different styles).

Justinian actively suppressed the signs of pagan culture enduring in his day with legal penalties. As mentioned previously, in 529, in response to neo-Platonist professors at the Athenian academy instituting theurgic pagan rituals that they expected their pupils to take part in, he reacted by ordering the cessation of state-subsidised salaries for non-Christian teachers at Athens. He also suppressed Samaritan and Jewish worship in Palestine, definitively ending the attempts by some to rebuild the Jewish temple in Jerusalem. He commissioned the missionary (Monophysite) bishop John of Ephesus to organize mass conversion expeditions among the pagans of Asia Minor, and reports of seventy thousand baptisms were recorded in this period. His empire, especially, Constantinople, was set back severely on two occasions by the appearance of the Black Death, bubonic plague. Estimates of upwards of 20 percent population loss have been advanced at this time, factors that set in process the resumption of the slow decline of the Eastern empire after Justinian's death in 565.

## THE EMERGENCE OF THE MONOPHYSITE CHURCH

The disaffection with Chalcedon that continued to brew in the Byzantine Egypt throughout the latter part of the fifth century, becoming a hardened set of divisions and formal schisms by the sixth century, stemmed originally from the feeling that the political honor and ecclesial heritage of all Egypt had been deeply insulted in 451 when Dioscorus, the archbishop of Alexandria, had been tried and deposed from office. After his condemnation the entire Egyptian hierarchy left the proceedings, declaring that they could no longer take part "without their head." The refusal to accept Dioscorus's condemnation as valid, the deep suspicion of Chalcedon's "two-nature language," and an abiding hostility toward Leo's *Tome* (considering it tantamount to Nestorianism) all began to be increasingly summed up in catchwords. To the majority of the Egyptians, the Chalcedonians were "two-naturists" (Dyophysites), implying that they had a separatist, nonunitive thought system about Christ; and the Chalcedonians in turn began to call them "one-naturists" (Monophysites), implying that their stress on the unitive dynamic of the incarnation had turned into a confused "mixture" (*krasis*) of Godhead and humanity (also known as Eutychianism).

Some of the opponents of Chalcedon undoubtedly did follow a line of thought that paid less than sufficient attention to Christ's human actuality. Reverently wishing to stress Christ's overwhelming dominance of Godhead in his incarnate life, some of them did tend to follow in varying degrees in the steps of Apollinaris of Laodicea and sometimes believed that to affirm human limitation was a disservice to the confession of the divine Christ. Thinkers such as Julian of Halicarnassus and Eutyches of Constantinople represented this kind of confused piety. There were others, however, such as Philoxenus of Mabbug, Timothy Aelurus (nicknamed "the weasel" or "the cat"), and Severus of Antioch, whose sophisticated theology cannot be reduced to this level.

The major argument, if hostile apologetics (both ancient and modern) can be cleared away, turns around two closely related issues: first, that Cyril of Alexandria (who from the middle of the fifth century had become a towering authority on Christology in the East) had used certain terms simultaneously in two senses. Chalcedon, for the sake of clarity, wished to move toward one agreed technical christological vocabulary and had vetoed some of Cyril's early expressions. His followers (especially those in the Egyptian church) refused to accept such a veto, placing Cyril's authority higher than that of the Council of 451. Cyril had spoken of the seamless union of divine and human activity in a single Christ under the party slogan of his own day: "one *physis* of the Word of God incarnate" (*mia physis tou theou Logou sesarkomene*). Here he applied *physis* in the antique semantic sense of "one concrete reality," which was more or less a synonym for the central idea of his (and Chalcedon's) Christology that there was only "one single hypostasis" in Christ.

Unfortunately, even in Cyril's own time, the word *physis* was coming to be taken as a common synonym for *ousia*, or nature understood not as a concrete reality (a subjective presence, which hypostasis connoted), but more as a set of (natural) properties, or attributes (such as "human nature" and "divine nature"). Thus, to describe Christ as one single *physis*-nature, in this sense, was generally taken by those who did not have a vested veneration of Cyril as a theologian (non-Cyrillians, who included Romans as well as many Syrians) to be advocating for a new form of hybrid nature (a divino-human synthesis) in Christ. This was widely heard, outside Egypt, at least, to be a revival of Apollinaris of Laodicea's christological solution by fusion, and in the fifth century it was felt no longer to be tolerable since it degraded the sense of the authentic humanity of Jesus.

In his own day Cyril felt such graphic language of *physis* unity (the *mia physis* or "single concrete reality" of the Christ) was necessary, for he was worried that those parties who ostensibly wished to defend the authenticity of human experience in Christ, and the differentiated spheres of human and divine actions in his life (notably, intellectuals of the Syrian church), had actually strayed into such a polarization that the incarnation had become artificial, a disunion rather than a union of God and man. We have to be circumspect in our use of modern English in all this debate, because to woodenly translate *mia physis* as "one nature" and *dyo physeis* as "two natures" seems to suggest that the two sides were speaking of completely different things: How could a person confessing one nature be the same as one professing two natures? Well, the Cyrilline sense of single *physis*, if accepted as the same as the single hypostasis of Chalcedon, can explain the logical possibility. So too the Chalcedonian profession of two natures (*ousiai*) unconfusedly united (*henosis*) can explain why they were not binary divisionists but also (alongside the Monophysites) wished to confess the singularity of the union of natures Christ effected in his own divine person. The modern preference to speak of the Monophysite secession as Miaphysites tries in modern discourse to indicate the possibilities of ecumenical rapprochement.

Cyril's followers, alienated after the Council of Chalcedon, were more and more labeled in the Byzantine and Latin churches as Monophysites and accused of teaching the doctrine of a confused hybrid of natures (Eutychianism). They themselves saw their defense of the "strong union of natures" as a last stand for the belief in the deification of the human race that came from the dynamic of the incarnation of God. In their turn they regarded the Chalcedonians as no better than defenders of Nestorianism. In this they were quite wrong (just as their opponents were often wrong to see them as Eutychians), but the semantic confusions made the controversy run for centuries, and after the Islamic seizure of Syria and Egypt in the seventh century, the possibilities of reconciliation with the Byzantine and Roman traditions became increasingly slight.[17]

The best of the so-called Monophysites actually represent the *mia physis* formula of Cyril's early theology (before his reconciliation with John of Antioch after the Council of Ephesus 431). The anti-Chalcedonians consistently rejected any two-nature language as both a betrayal of Cyril (hence of Ephesus 431) and of the belief that the incarnation was a dynamic of unity. For refusing to join in the reconciliation dialogue that Chalcedon represented (a dialogue meant to keep Roman, Byzantine, and Egypto-Syrian thinkers still talking to one another) the anti-Chalcedonians were increasingly prosecuted by the imperial government. It is one of the great tragedies of the patristic era that so many attempts to reconcile the dissidents failed, when clearly the central issues (integrity of humanity and divinity in the Christ, who is but a single divine person) were fundamentally agreed on both sides. Political and ethnic factors played a considerable part in this.

---

[17] It is now one of the longest enduring of the many fractures the Christian *ekklesia* has endured in history, and the dialogue between pro- and anti-Chalcedonians is still immured in deep misunderstandings. See further J. A. McGuckin, "The Mia-Physis Doctrine of St. Cyril of Alexandria and Chalcedonian Dyophytism," in *The Dialogue Between the Eastern Orthodox and Oriental Orthodox Churches*, ed. C. Chaillot (Volos Academy Publications, 2016).

## HERACLIUS AND THE EXALTATION OF THE CROSS

Heraclius (575–641) was the regnant emperor of Byzantium between 610 and 641. He was the son of the exarch, or senior imperial governor, of Carthage in North Africa. Having been trained well as a high military commander, and with his father's connivance, he mounted a coup against the much-hated Emperor Phocas in Constantinople, who was holding on to power there by means of a reign of terror, and successfully ascended to the throne at age thirty-five. With his wife, Eudoxia, he thought for a time of transferring the Byzantine capital to Carthage, a more defensible site given the significant influx of the Slav and Avar tribes into the Balkans at this period as well as the advance of the Persian forces into Syria, Palestine, and Egypt.[18] Fortunately, he thought better of the idea, and Constantinople remained the capital from which he started a great revival of Byzantine affairs. His new dynasty would last for the next century.

It seemed to him at the beginning of his reign that the expanse of the Christian empire had come to an end. All around him were loss of territories, loss of prestige, immense flux from migrating barbarian tribes setting up their own systems of settlement, stagnation in the arts, dissonance and schism in the church, increasing separation of Latin and Greek mentalities. The loss of the Syrian territories and the holy places in Palestine was a bitter blow, symbolizing the impotence of a Christian emperor who could not even defend Bethlehem or Jerusalem. Heraclius (named Heraklios after the hero Hercules/Herakles) was determined to make good his claim to be the authentic God-protected emperor, a concept that was not so much vested in dynastic succession lines for the Byzantines, but rather (like the rights of David compared to Saul in the Old Testament) rooted in the notion that the man whom God had chosen to lead his people would be signified as such by his righteousness and above all by his victories.[19]

Heraclius's immediate impact on Byzantium was his energy. His civil and military reforms brought stability to a fragmenting Roman society. Heraclius began by consolidating the army. He reduced reliance on foreign mercenaries and co-opted more peasants into the frontier forces, local men who had a vested interest in defending their own lands and crops. Reorganizing the fiscal system of the empire, Heraclius was able to ensure the troops were paid more regularly, which more than anything else had a high effect of remoralization. He personally resumed the position of supreme commander of the troops (the old meaning of the word *imperator* or emperor)

---

[18] Heraclius encouraged the settlement of the Slavs and arranged for missions to convert them to Christianity, thus cementing their long-term allegiance to the empire.

[19] For use of the Davidic imagery in the imperial art of the era, customary since the time of Justinian, see S. S. Alexander, "Heraclius, Byzantine Imperial Ideology, and the David Plates," *Medieval Academy of America* 52, no. 2 (April 1977): 217-37.

and instituted a ring of defensive forts around the borders, also introducing new training techniques for his soldiers.

In 622 he moved against the greatest threat of all: the Persian armies, which were bent on taking and settling Syria and Palestine.[20] For six years a war of attrition raged on without significant result. The tide began to turn in 626, however, when Heraclius was able to celebrate the definitive liberation of the capital at Constantinople from all threats of barbarians, following a great naval victory against the insurgent Avars. After this he could turn all his attention to Palestine, and in 627/8 he celebrated a very striking victory over the Persian armies at Nineveh. In its aftermath Sassanid King Khosrau II (titled the "ever victorious") was abandoned by his aristocracy. In February 628 they freed the heir, Khavadh II, from his imprisonment and assassinated Khosrau. Once liberated, however, Khavad was so ill that he thought he was dying and sent urgent envoys to Heraclius, asking him to deliver peace immediately and protect the rule of his infant son, Ardeshir. He promised complete withdrawal from all Roman territories and favorable terms of tribute. This collapse of Persian arms proved to be a fatal blow to the old empire that had always been the great superpower rival to Rome in the ancient world. As a goodwill gesture the Sassanid ruler ordered the relic of the true cross, which had been captured in Jerusalem and laid prone in the Zoroastrian temple at their capital as a war trophy, to be returned with all honor to the emperor in the field.

Heraclius's acceptance of the cross became one of the great symbols of the success of his reign (despite the fact that soon he would preside over several significant reversals in war), and for many centuries after it endured as a symbol of the hopes of the Christian world that it would never be abandoned by providence. The story of the true cross is this: After Constantine had risen to supreme power and established his capital at Constantinople, he had sent his mother, Helena, on a tour of the Christian holy places, to endow them with imperial donations and establish churches that would elevate the Christians more in the public eye. His building of the churches at Bethlehem and Jerusalem, one over the place of Christ's birth and the other over the places of his death and resurrection, were cardinal events in the international establishment of the new church. The liturgical rituals of Jerusalem from the fourth century onward spread across the Christian world in a very influential way. Although the holy places always remained, in a real sense, Christian backwaters after the fourth century, they had a very high symbolic and liturgical visibility. Some of the Jerusalem exports, for example, were the Feast of Theophany (Epiphany), which involved the

---

[20]See further M. H. Dodgeon, G. Greatrex, and S. N. C. Lieu, eds., *The Roman Eastern Frontier and the Persian Wars (Part I, 226–363 AD)* (London: Routledge, 2002).

blessing of the waters of Jordan, a local event that soon became observed as a great festival in every Christian church of the ancient world. Another was the Feast of the Discovery of the True Cross. Later accounts after Helena's time recorded how she had ordered the foundations to be built for the Church of the Resurrection, and as they were excavating the builders discovered three wooden crosses.[21]

Excitement ran high, and wishing to know which one of these was Jesus' true cross, they laid the sick upon all three, and one of them effected an immediate cure: the wood was then lifted up in great honor and became one of the great pilgrim foci of the new church, set up for the veneration of multitudes of Christian pilgrims who came to kiss it on the way to pray at the tomb.[22] Between the fourth century and the time of Heraclius, possession of even a small part of this greatest of all Christian relics was a thing every church longed for but few possessed. Constantine ordered parts to be brought to Constantinople, along with other relics of the passion. We can gain a small sense of the powerful hold of relics on the ancient mind when we also learn that Constantine took personal possession of the metal nails that were reputed to have been found near the cross of Jesus and had them reforged and hammered into a bit for his horse's mouth. The immediate puzzlement of this becomes clear, of course, when it is realized that he had not the slightest doubt that this was the most powerful talisman he could ever have to protect himself in battle. The Feast of the Discovery of the True Cross, spreading across the Christian world liturgically, was one of the central symbols of the ascent of the Christian faith. When one reflects on the loss of the cross to the Persians, therefore, and the manner in which the cross was laid flat on the floor before their own gods, it was comparable to the loss of the ark of the covenant. The recovery of it in the field seemed miraculously significant to the Byzantines.

Two years later, in 630, Heraclius triumphantly liberated Jerusalem and led the procession on horseback into the holy city, bearing the true cross on his own shoulders.[23] The Feast of the Rediscovery of the Cross was soon instituted, and it too quickly went around the international community to become an established "great feast," held each year on September 14. Soon it became known as the Feast of the

---

[21] The Jerusalem archaeological service, under Dan Bahat's leadership, has since confirmed that the Anastasis Church was indeed built over the ancient quarry at Jerusalem that was outside the city walls and had been used as a place of burial from earlier times than Jesus. The Christians of the city had long kept note of where Jesus' tomb originally was, and Constantine's architects labored to level the site so as to be able to build the church. The results of this are still visible in the multitudes of floor levels present today. It was an immensely costly thing to do, so much cheaper to build elsewhere, and they were undoubtedly compelled to build there because of the local ecclesial tradition that demanded that place and none other.

[22] Variants of the tradition speak of the resurrection of a dead man.

[23] See further N. H. Baynes, "The Restoration of the Cross at Jerusalem," *English Historical Review 27,* no. 106 (1912): 287-99.

Exaltation of the Cross. Legends tell how the patriarch of Jerusalem had asked Heraclius not to bring back the cross into the Holy City in such a militaristic way, and when the emperor insisted, he and his horse found the burden so heavy that he could hardly move. Removing his crown in an act of humility, it is said that he suddenly could move easily once more. The telling and retelling of the tale was obviously charged with many subtle messages; but there can be no doubt that the "exaltation of the cross" was widely seen as a kind of "renewal of the Christian covenant."

Heraclius, therefore, knew the immense propaganda value this festival would encapsulate when he returned the treasured relic to its place in the Church of the *Anastasis* (Resurrection), known more commonly in the West as the Church of the Holy Sepulchre. However, he also knew well enough that the Palestinian province still remained dangerously unstable, and so he also quietly removed many large sections of the wood of the cross and had them sent on to more defensible Christian centers such as Constantinople, and Rome, where they were set with precious stones in resplendent reliquaries. Some of them can still be seen, as for example, in the Treasury of St. Peter's in the Vatican, or the repository of relics taken from Constantinople in the thirteenth century at Sainte Chapelle, or even (most peculiarly) the foyer of the Morgan Library in New York.[24]

Emperor when the cross was once more "exalted," Heraclius was ever after associated with the restoration of the affairs of the Christian empire.[25] This great positive propaganda value, however, masked two things: first, that very soon after the Persian victory, the net gains unraveled very quickly, and all the territories that had been won in Syria, Palestine, and Egypt were eventually lost once more to the Arabs; and second, that the emperor's attempt to consolidate unity within the churches in the aftermath of this great news largely fell on unyielding ground. Indeed, the refusal of the churches to cooperate has often been linked to the manner in which Syria and Egypt would pass forever out of Christian control in this period. The radical collapse of Persia as a world superpower following on Heraclius's victory caused the vacuum that allowed the Arabs to move out of the Arabian peninsula and bring their conquests along with their new religion, Islam, the one fueling the other onward. In 634 the Arab Muslims invaded Roman Syria and in 636 defeated Heraclius's brother, the Byzantine general Theodore, at a great battle at Yarmuk. In

---

[24] How the most sacred relic of Christendom could end up exposed to all in this highly secular manner would surely have struck the ancients as worse than its location in the fire temple of Zoroaster, where at least it was recognized as a charged and sacral thing.

[25] The double meaning of this "exaltation" (*hypsosis*) was "venerated," that is, held up for veneration once more after being lost, and then also picked up from the floor (of the Zoroastrians' temple—like the ark being recaptured after the Philistines took it).

638 Jerusalem once more fell, this time to Arab forces. In 639/40 they occupied Armenia, and from there began the campaign to take Egypt, which would soon be lost forever to Byzantine control. The Arab spread into Mesopotamia and Egypt was the beginning of the establishment of a permanent caliphate in the East and the long erosion of Christian culture that would follow on it.

## MONOENERGISM AND MONOTHELITISM

Several scholars have suggested that this loss of territory, especially in Syria and Egypt, was not without the cooperation of the local Christians, who (at least in the early stages) preferred the rule of overlords with a different religion to the oppressions of Christian emperors at Byzantium who were bent on foisting on them the decrees of what they regarded as the heretical Dyophysitism of the Council of Chalcedon. Heraclius consulted his patriarch at Constantinople, Sergius (610–638), and asked for a new policy that might relaunch the several failed attempts that had been made (one remembers the Acacian schism) to heal the post-Chalcedonian divisions. He accepted Sergius's suggestion that a theological thesis of Monoenergism might be acceptable to all parties.

According to this approach, it would be beneficial if all involved in christological discussion avoided the fraught term of *natures* (either one or two) and instead tred to reconsider the whole question of Christ's personhood on the basis of a new platform of how the Christ manifested energy and action. His dominant idea was that the energy and action of Christ derived directly from his singularity of personhood. Thus his deeds were at one and the same time divine and human, neither one nor the other, so there were no "merely human acts" such as sleeping or eating, and other "divine acts" such as miracles, but rather each and every act was a divino-human energy. On this basis one could leave unstated the details, avoid altogether such categories as natures, and attribute all Christ's activities to his single divino-human energy (*energeia*) instead of to two distinct natures (Chalcedonian Dyophysites) or a single nature as the anti-Chalcedonian (Monophysites) wished to. Heraclius approved the plan, and Sergius began slowly to gather episcopal theologians into his party who would propagate the teaching in the East. Bishop Cyrus of Phasis in Colchis agreed to the utility of the plan and was rewarded by Heraclius with the office of patriarch of Alexandria in 631. His early years there showed some success in reconciling parties of the Egyptian anti-Chalcedonians to the imperial (*Melkite*) church.

Sergius was more cautious in his approach to Pope Honorius in Rome. Well aware that the success of the whole enterprise depended not only on finding a strongly unitive christological model for the East but also in finding a way that did not explicitly reject Leo's tradition of distinction of natures and acts as set out in the *Tome* (hardly a Monoenergistic model of theology!), Sergius trimmed his sail to the wind in his westward conversations. He wrote to Honorius a flattering letter acclaiming him for all the benefits he had brought to the unity of the churches and now asked for his assistance. Could theologians now be told to lay aside the terms of "one energy" and "two energies" (we note he avoids the issues of natures, since this would clearly involve an explicit revision of Chalcedon) and instead speak only in terms of how the only begotten Son had "worked" (*energein*) in divine and human ways, and that each and every energy, both divine and human, derived inseparably (the term was derived from the Chalcedonian decree) from the one and the selfsame incarnated Logos (the terms were derived from the Miaphysitism of the early Cyrilline school)?

Honorius affirmed Sergius's solution and told him to proceed with papal approval. As far as the pope was concerned the formula preserved everything that Chalcedon wanted to defend: the single divine subjectivity of the incarnate Christ and the sense that his humanity and divinity ought not to be dissolved. The actions, which could be seen as visible aspects of the *energeia*, proceeded from the will of the Lord, which he understood to have evidently a divine character. So the singular personhood of Chalcedon was being buttressed, in his opinion, with a new moralistic, or voluntarist, approach, based on the sacred and unfalteringly obedient will of Christ, which manifested the singularity of his divine personhood now incarnated.

Encouraged by this success at Rome, Heraclius initiated efforts in Armenia and Syria, too, aimed at a reconciliation of the churches. The policy was quickly labeled by the Byzantines as Monoenergism. Its purpose, however much one said one would avoid the issue of "one or two," was clearly to insist that as there was one divine person in the incarnate Lord, and so too the acts he accomplished were issued from one singular power: his divine will now acting in an incarnate body and thus issuing as a single divino-human center of activity. Unlike Leo's notion in the *Tome* that the Lord did some things in his human nature and some things in his divine nature, the Monoenergism of Sergius came back more closely to Cyril's insistence that the one Lord did all things in his singularity as God-made-man, and that the through-flow of divine power in the incarnate flesh irradiated with divine power all that it touched, basically effecting the salvation and sanctification of the human material element because of its proximity to the divine. This sense of "transference of energy" was how the Monoenergistic school conceived of the Chalcedonian *communicatio idiomatum*.

It was a very subtle and richly ecumenical scheme, but it had two flaws in it that were soon hit on by its opponents. The first was its continuing implicit criticism of Chalcedon. It was hardly likely that by simply not speaking about one or two natures, the old problem would go away. This was especially the issue of to what extent the full reality of the humanity of Jesus was preserved in the act of incarnation. If Jesus showed only divino-human energy in all he did, was there never a time he was "just like an ordinary man," or was subject to the common limitations of what an ordinary human nature means?

The second was the manner in which the theory elevated voluntaristic ideas to the fore: that is, the stress it placed on the singularity of the incarnate Christ as a willing subject. As there would be a single divino-human *energeia*, so it was presumed logically self-evident that there was a single willing subject with a single will. And that, obviously, had to be a divine will, if Jesus was to be acclaimed as the incarnate Lord who saved the world by his incarnation. What God did in the body was precisely to will to save the world by reference to his own adoption of humanity in himself, so as to present the adoption of all the human race, in himself, to the Father.

Both flaws were seen at an early stage by opponents on the Chalcedonian side. Many Chalcedonians wanted no ecumenical rapprochement with the Monophysites at all, just a complete victory over them. Others suspected that anything the emperor did as an appeasement to the Monophysite party had to be a denial of Chalcedon because of the vehement opposition that council had caused in Egypt and Syria, and so they were carefully on the look out for any "new" policy. Two notable opponents rose up in the person of Sophronius, the patriarch of Jerusalem, and the monk Maximus, who would later be called Maximus the Confessor. He was one of the greatest of the Byzantine theologians, whose works are a dazzling confluence of high theology and philosophy.

Sophronius was the first to move publicly against the imperial policy. In an *Encyclical Letter* he sent out widely after his election to the Jerusalem patriarchate, making sure copies got to Rome and Constantinople and to all the monasteries of Palestine, he argued that it was impossible to locate the notion of the energy of any living being in the person, or the voluntarist capacities of the individual person (hypostasis). The will of God, or that of a man, or that of an animal for that matter, were all different things, manifesting very different capacities, which all derived from the radical differences of their natures. Will, therefore, was simply an aspect or attribute of a nature (*ousia*), not of a hypostasis. The divine will was a manner of conceiving the unlimited power of creation that ever flowed out of the divine being: to will a thing was to effect it on the part of God. To simply will a thing, however, is definitely not to effect it on the part of a human being; or else all "beggars would ride," as they say.

So the will, the theologians concluded, was a fundamental aspect of the "nature" of a thing, not the hypostasis. As such, if Christ was to be considered a real, authentic, and complete human being, (as Chalcedon had affirmed—*homoousion* with us humans in all things related to his human nature), it was absolutely essential that he be confessed to be in possession of a truly human will, deriving from that complete human nature and manifesting its most elevated spiritual capacities (as Gregory the Theologian had already argued in his refutation of Apollinarism in his *Letters to Cledonius* in the late fourth century). Since the incarnate Lord, clearly as God the Word, possessed a divine will, it followed, therefore, that Christ had to be affirmed as possessing two wills, just as he possessed two natures.

This uncompromising reaffirmation of the validity of Chalcedon, refined so as to allow it to speak to the psychological and moral aspects raised by Monoenergism, was clearly a major threat to Sergius and Heraclius's scheme of reconciliation. Most of Sophronius's extensive writings in opposition to Monothelitism are now lost, but it is known he traveled widely, for example to Alexandria in 633, in the cause of persuading the leading Melkite clergy not to be co-opted into the imperial policy for the churches.[26]

In 638, alarmed in case this very cogent philosophical argument might cause his policy to falter, the emperor asked Sergius to compose a more precise document in response, and this he published with the force of imperial law as the imperial *ekthesis* in 638. In this iteration Sergius advocated a refinement of the doctrine and urged a moving off the concept of energy and adopting instead the insistence that it was the will of Christ that really mattered and that was the real locus of his *energeia*. The whole matter and ground of agreement now had to be the affirmation that the Christ had only one will, and that a divine one. Within a very short time this was called the position of Monothelitism: the concept that the single will in Christ was a divine one. Sergius died in the December of the same year, 638, as saw the issuing of the *ekthesis*. It was also the year Pope Honorius died at Rome. Three years later Heraclius himself would be dead. Though this policy was at first largely accepted in the Eastern church as a more refined form of Monoenergism, the death of the three leading minds behind it certainly weakened its ability to withstand criticism.

At Rome, they woke up to the issues Honorius had not seen as problematic, now alerted by Sophronius and Maximus, and they were gravely disturbed by the central implication of Monothelitism, namely that Jesus did not possess a truly human will and thus could not properly be seen to have chosen or decided on anything in his human or moral life, as an ordinary man would. This seemed to the Romans to be the denial of the very heart of all it means to be a human being, and thus an admission

---

[26] The name *Melkite* comes from the Syriac term for "king's men," meaning pro-Chalcedonian clerics following imperial church policy.

of the worst excesses of Monophysitism as the West conceived it, a denial of the full and complete humanity of the incarnate Lord. The Byzantine court would become so tired of the disputes that rose up after every attempt to resolve this crisis that ten years after the *ekthesis* was issued, Heraclius's grandson, Emperor Constans II, retracted it in 648 and simply forbade under pain of legal penalty any further public disputation or publication that even mentioned one or two energies or wills in Christ. This decree was known as the *Typos*. The whole set of approaches were once more to be buried under the sands. Even so, the issue of the disunity of the Eastern churches still grumbled on, and the theological division was a philosophical issue that tormented the empire's Christian intellectuals. However much the court wished to bury it, it simply would not just go away.

Maximus the Confessor (c. 580–662) was a learned monk from Palestine who also knew and supported Sophronius. He had deeply immersed himself in the writings of Origen of Alexandria, Gregory the Theologian, and Dionysius the Areopagite. As a master synthesizer he blended this high theological philosophy very dynamically in his writings to show, especially to the monks, how this related to the themes of mystical ascent and purification that they sought after in their ascetical lives. In 614 Maximus had entered the monastic life at Chrysopolis, near to the imperial capital. The disruptions of the Persian war in 626 caused him to move to Crete, Cyprus, and finally North Africa.

In 654 the Greek monastery at Carthage became the site of a public staged debate between Maximus and Pyrrhus. The latter was the successor of Sergius at Constantinople, but he had lost his position in the riots of 641, when he was accused of plotting with Empress Marina against Constantine III. The exiled patriarch of Constantinople was advocating at Carthage that the West should not abandon the Monothelite Christology of the *ekthesis*, which the court was still officially advocating. Maximus regarded the Monothelite position not only as a betrayal of Chalcedon in the (forlorn) hope of reconciling the Monophysites, but also as a dangerous heresy that depicted a less than fully human Savior, a Christ who was not possessed of a true human will. For him Monothelitism was a vision of the Savior's humanity that verged on the mechanical.

The Western bishops strongly encouraged Maximus, aware that his knowledge of the undercurrents of Greek theology and philosophy were much greater than could be found in the West, and they adopted him as a chief spokesman for the defense of Chalcedon and their decision to defy the emperor's policy, which Honorius had tacitly agreed to. In the course of the debate at Carthage, Pyrrhus declared himself convinced that Maximus was correct (he would later change his mind, consummate politician that he was). Several African synods soon condemned Monothelitism as a heresy, and Rome followed suit, with Pope Martin specifically anathematizing the doctrine in the Lateran Council of 649. Pope Martin also criticized there the *Typos* of Constantine.

In 653, the emperor was determined to seize these two leading Western critics who were on the point of sinking the imperial policy of reconciliation, and so, taking a leaf from the book of Justinian, who had arrested Pope Vigilius, he issued warrants for the arrest of Pope Martin and the monk Maximus. He brought both dissidents to Constantinople. Martin died en route and was immediately regarded as a martyr to the faith in the West. At Constantinople Maximus adamantly refused to sign his agreement to the terms of the *Typos* and was exiled. He was recalled in 658 and 661, and on his third and final refusal to stop agitating against Monothelitism he was tortured. Tradition has it that his tongue and right hand (which had continued to defy the emperor by preaching and writing) were cut off (hence his title *Confessor*). He died soon after in exile in Georgia.

His many works attack the Monothelite Christology, advancing in its place a powerful doctrine of the freedom of the human person, which is assured by the incarnation of Christ. The incarnation, seen as the high point of all human history, is what Maximus sees as the dynamic method and means of the deification of the human race. He teaches that the adoption of humanity into the life of the Godhead in the person of the incarnate Logos is no less than a spiritual re-creation of human nature that now allows individuals the freedom needed to practice virtue, since all humans were formerly enslaved by passions and had lost pure moral freedom to choose the good. By Christ's healing of the human defective will (after Adam's fall damaged it in all human beings) in the archetype of his own pure human will, which the Lord seamlessly united (by obedience) to the divine will, the incarnation turned on the very issue of two natures, two wills, made perfectly one in the spiritual harmony of salvation.

For Maximus the "losing" of the human will in Christ did not make any sense as an ecumenical rapprochement, since it fundamentally destroyed the coherence of the incarnation seen as a salvific force, the healing of the deranged wills of human beings and the refashioning of the human race into saving obedience. Maximus seamlessly combines his theological philosophy of the freedom of personhood with a mystical vision of the Christian life as an ever-deepening communion with God. His ascetical writings (chiefly *The Ascetic Life* and the *Chapters on Charity*) and his theological commentaries on difficult subjects (*The Ambigua* and *Questions to Thalassius*) are profound works that have increasingly attracted attention after the latter decades of the twentieth century. His liturgical studies (*Mystagogia* and *Commentary on the Our Father*) show a powerful intellectual who is also capable of writing lyrically on prayer.

If it was Sophronius's warning that set the main tone of the opposition to the imperial policy, it was rather Maximus's theology that caught the imagination of the Byzantine world and led christological thinking forward out of the pedantic morass it had entered into, with debates about "one or two" natures and rather static posturing as to whether one had to defend Leo to the death or could only stand by the reputation of the early Cyril, against all other insights. Ossification of thought was certainly not present in Maximian theology. But, remembering the disgrace posthumously heaped on the court and patriarchate in the time of the Acacian schism, the Eastern emperors were unanimously determined about one thing: never would the reputation of an emperor be cast down because of the demands of a pope or patriarch. The dragging of Pope Martin to the East, where he died on the forced march, was not an intended sentence, though a harsh one to make sure clergy of all ranks knew where to place their loyalties.

The condemnation of Maximus, however, was enforced as someone whom the Byzantines regarded as little better than a traitor. In less than twenty years after his death, it was Maximus's ideas that were largely adopted at the great council that was summoned to address the enduring christological controversy. His theology matches that of Cyril of Alexandria, therefore, as the work of an gifted individual that represents the best insights of a generation. Unlike Cyril, it is remarkable how his name and memory continued to be damned at Constantinople. For all the influence of his teachings present there, Maximus is never once referred to at the Third Council of Constantinople. His theology was accepted; his person was not. It was the monks, not the court or hierarchs, who nevertheless acclaimed him as a great theologian and monastic martyr. In recent times he has come to be appreciated as one of the deepest intellects of the age.

### THE COUNCIL OF CONSTANTINOPLE III 680-681

What is now reckoned as the sixth of the seven ecumenical councils was the last of the imperially sponsored attempts to resolve the christological crisis—now not so much by virtue of imperial decrees sidestepping the principle of calling a general council of the world's leading bishops, but rather meeting the issue head-on and summoning the last of the great councils to be specifically bound up with the christological question. It was summoned by Emperor Constantine IV and opened with the agreement of Pope Agatho, who sent a three-person Roman delegation. The council was organized under the presidency of Patriarchs George of Constantinople and Macarius of Antioch (the latter who was then resident at the capital). It convened in the Domed Hall (*Troullos*) of the imperial palace and is, accordingly, sometimes known as the "Council in Trullo" (a name also, rather confusingly, given to the so-called Fifth-Sixth Council, otherwise known as the "Quinisext," which was a synod called in 692 to supply a list of reformatory canons, retrospectively, to the fifth and sixth ecumenical councils of 553 and 681). More than 164 bishops were in attendance at Constantinople III.

The gathering together of yet another great synod representing all the world's great sees was hoped to bring an end to several controversies that resulted from the Monophysite rejection of Chalcedon and the failed attempts of the various imperial policies to resolve the matter extrasynodically. By 680 it was abundantly clear to the Byzantine emperors that their attempts to suppress christological arguments in the East, or to control them either by imperial dictat or a policy of stick and carrot, had utterly failed. The council was a serious attempt to think through and resolve some of the problematics still remaining. In this sense it was the last gloss, or rationale, offered to the earlier conciliar christological tradition, which it read and studied carefully before it started its own work.

This council has attracted very little study in later times, which is unfortunate, for the issues raised here extend very deeply and were one of the few times Christian theologians of antiquity explicitly considered the dimensions of personal freedom and psychological identity. The synodical meetings extended over eighteen sessions, the first eleven of which were presided over by the emperor in person. Macarius of Antioch opened debate by insisting that the admission of two wills in Christ (Dyothelitism) was tantamount to a revival of Nestorianism. For him two wills meant two persons. The majority of bishops, however, followed the teachings of Sophronius that will was a "natural" attribute deriving its quality from nature, not hypostasis, and agreed with Maximus the Confessor, who had argued strongly that to deny a human will to Christ was to render his humanity specious in the most important aspect of humanity—its moral freedom.

In terms of Monoenergism the council concluded that to see Christ merely as a single divine "force" betrayed the previous conciliar tradition relating to Christology, which clearly taught that the single Christ performed acts both divine and human, working as one and the same person both according to the humanity and according to the divinity, and thus exercised two energies of life, both of which were perfectly harmonized in his single divine person. In other words, whereas Monoenergism posited that the term of christological union should be located in the concept of dynamic force or act, Maximus, and the conciliar fathers following after him, argued it had to be posited in the concept of a free and gracious personal choice. Christology was thus a mystery of personal engagement (God's salvation of his created people through love), not a simple manifestation of an abstract power.

As a result of the opening debate Macarius of Antioch was deposed from office both as conciliar copresident and as archbishop. In the final session the names of previous supporters of the Monothelite and Monoenergist positions were also anathematized: Patriarch Sergius and Pope Honorius being named chief in that list. It is one of the rare times a pope has been posthumously condemned as a heretic. The council professed a doctrine of Christ having two wills (divine and human), which were both perfectly harmonized in his single divine person: harmonized in one unconfused and inseparable reality, just as the divine person perfectly harmonized all the other operation of his two natures, in a perfect unanimity and unity.

This dyothelite (two-will) Christology, as it came to be known, was really the last nail in the coffin as far as the Monophysites were concerned. They read the insistence on two wills in the way Macarius of Antioch had heard it: that here was the real inner sense of Chalcedonianism, a refusal to affirm the spiritual singular subjectivity of the Word of God made flesh. After more than two centuries of argument it seemed that both sides, with only slightly different senses of the same desire to affirm the spiritual unity of Christ, were no closer than ever in hearing or understanding each other. So it has remained for the following fifteen and a half centuries.

## ISLAM AND ITS IMPACT ON EASTERN CHRISTIANITY

Islamic tradition records that Muhammad was lifted up by God as a prophet and received the revelation from the archangel Gabriel (resulting in the Qur'an) over a twenty-three-year period beginning when he was forty years of age, on December 22, 609, and ending in the year of his death, in 632. The rise of Islam among the Arabs of the Arabian peninsula brought the two religions in contact first of all in the person of the Ethiopians. On hearing a report of the principles of early Islam, the Ethiopian court encouraged it as a move to teach monotheism among the idolatrous nomadic tribes. At first there were reasonably good political relations with the two powers so close to one another across the waters. From the perspective of the Byzantine court, which was so much farther away by a difficult land journey, Islam was not so much seen as a separatist religion (and would not be deemed a "new religion" for many centuries to come), rather than the "heretical" or ill-founded religious impetus of the Arab tribes who were rebelling against the long-held dominions of the Christians. Like the Ethiopians, the Byzantines positively acknowledged the move to monotheism from idolatry that Islam brought to the tribes. It took them longer to see the political implications of this new faith.

Several of the greatest provinces that the Arab Muslims were now contesting had been the cradles of earliest Christianity, the holy places, Jordan and Egypt chief among them. Most of the early emperors, after Heraclius, regarded the loss of these provinces as a temporary matter. Few could believe that the nomadic Arabs posed any significant long-term threat, and it was this lack of closer intelligence about the political religiosity of the new faith that led the Byzantines to ignore them for so long. It would take many centuries, probably up to the time of the First Crusade at the end of the first millennium, before the Byzantine world really grasped the sense that these areas of the former empire really had been permanently lost and a new religious *politeia* informed a new "people" now joined together by a sense of religious belonging, comparable but opposed to the religious covenant that held Christian Byzantium in being.

Islam from the beginning had to fight for its existence. In repulsing the pagan Arab forces that tried to extinguish it in the first generation, it soon canonized the concept of holy war, lifting many of the ideas behind this notion of the winning of a "holy land" from the Old Testament texts on the conquest of Canaan, which influenced it. Even in the lifetime of Muhammad, Islam had come across Byzantine (probably Nestorian) monks in the Arabian desert, as well as several dissident Christian sects. Several strands of Christian influence gleaned from antique apocrypha, as well as oral traditions, appear in the Qur'an also, such as the Gnostic traditions that Jesus did not die on the cross, and the high veneration of Mary the mother of Jesus. Many other aspects of the evangelical tradition were appropriated, and in that appropriation recast significantly. Jesus' prophecy of the coming Paraclete, for example, was referred to Muhammad himself, and the Christian doctrine of the divine Trinity was refracted into a doctrine of Jesus' human prophetic status, and the subsistence of the Holy Spirit was taken as a manifestation of the archangel Gabriel, who delivered the revelation to Muhammad.

The overall sense of the Christian impact on earliest Islam is one that is partial and largely based on hearsay: much like the way Islam was received by the Byzantines in the first millennium. The absorption of both the Old Testament and the New as preambles to the Islamic revelation that were separately seen as incomplete, or defective, allowed the new religion to treat Jews and Christians (the latter of which completely meant Byzantine Christians for the first millennium) as significantly different from the pagans around them, whom they were commanded to convert even by force if necessary. Jews and Christians, in contrast, were afforded the status of "people of the book," or communities of divine revelation, by the developing Islamic law, and if they refused to be converted to what the Muslims saw as their own higher light, they were allowed by the authorities to keep the practice of their religion, subject to taxation and significant restrictions on lifestyle and preaching.

Early military campaigns against the Byzantines, targeting Constantinople, were easily dismissed. Heraclius, who had engaged in battle with the first wave of Arab insurgency, entered Arab history with a good reputation for being a "noble warrior." But the Arabs, as such, especially as motivated by a new religion, did not as yet make an impact on the Byzantine mind. It was not until the eighth century that they are registered, and then we see the immediate birth of a strong polemic. By the end of the eighth century Baghdad had emerged as a significant cultural center of the new faith and polity. Its wealth and art were beginning to be noticed as fresh rivals to the capital at Constantinople. Just before this period, there is a critical letter of Emperor Leo III to Islamic Caliph Omar II (717–720). In it the emperor complains that the Muslims are torn apart by religious schisms more severe than any that have been known in Christian history. This internal lack of harmony and unanimity speaks ill, the emperor argues, of Islam's religious claims to have a polity destined for the whole world. The Islamic retort was to mock the Christians as a people who had retained their divisions into no less than seventy-two races.

Arabic Christian intellectual Theodore Abu-Qurra (750–823) set out one of the first defenses of Christian teaching designed for Muslim readers at a common level. He was the bishop of Harran in Mesopotamia, a Syriac writer who was also one of the first Christians to use Arabic.[27] Some of his works were translated also into Greek.[28] His work strongly defends Christianity against anti-Chalcedonian attacks on the one side, and Islamic criticisms on the other, for the use of images in Christian worship.[29] Islamic theologian Isa ibn Sabih al-Murdar (d. 840) is reported to have written a refutation aimed against him.

Theodore, in his work *On the Existence of God and True Religion*, imagines himself as a having lived all his life in seclusion on a mountain and then descending to the people on the plains and asking them the basics of how religion was faring today. He presents to his readers the sense of scandal that so many divisions and arguments should raise in the heart of any true God-lover. Starting from the basics, he sets out what he considers to the true course of development of religion, culminating in a strong defense of the superiority of the Christian faith in metaphysics, morals, and sacramental structure that can meet human beings on material levels and lead them up to spiritual wisdom.

---

[27] C. Bacha, *Les oeuvres arabes de Théodore Aboucara* (Beirut, 1904); R. Glei and A. Khoury, *Johannes Damaskenos und Theodor Abu Qurra. Schriften zum Islam* (Wurzburg: Echter, 1995).
[28] See PG 97.
[29] S. H. Griffith, "Theodore Abū Qurrah's Arabic Tract on the Christian Practice of Venerating Images," *Journal of the American Oriental Society* 105, no. 1 (1985): 53-73.

John of Damascus (Yanan ibn Mansur) (655–750), had firsthand encounters with Islamic government in his time as an aristocrat in Damascus, then moved in old age to become a monk in the Palestinian desert and composed a monumental compendium of Christian doctrine called the *Fount of Knowledge*. In the course of the second section of this work he has a long section on the many varieties of Christian heresies. Here he catalogues Islam as the one hunded and first heresy to afflict the Christian church. One notices how he still refuses to admit it as a separate, new religion. But he saw it mainly as a defective corruption of Judaism that, like antique Arianism, had rejected the revelation of the divine incarnation and the holy Trinity. His tone is dismissive and hostile, as can be seen from the chapter "On the Heresy of the Ishmaelites," which is reproduced in the reader following. John's canonization as one of the great Byzantine saints in the aftermath of the iconoclastic crisis ,which won him a reputation as great poet and defender of the faith, meant that this view of Islam became a majority Byzantine position, insofar as the chapter in question was a highly republished text of one of the great Fathers.

In the early part of the ninth century Theophanes the Confessor (d. 822) is one of the earliest Byzantine historians who takes account of the spread of Islam. He explains for his readers in his *Chronicles* various stories about the origins of Muhammad, which are all highly critical. He blames Jewish critics of Christianity for having given to early Muslims false views about the Christian faith, but also reports stories about how Muhammad himself was a disappointment to the Jews and how he used a religious excuse to mask the malady of epilepsy:

> At the beginning of his advent the misguided Jews thought he was the Messiah . . . but when they saw him eating camel meat, they realized that he was not the one they thought him to be. It was these wretched ones who taught him wicked things hostile to us Christians, and still supported him. . . . He himself consorted with Jews and Christians when he came to Palestine and inquired of them about scriptural matters. He was afflicted with epilepsy. When his wife became aware of this, she was greatly distressed, insofar as she who was a noblewoman realized she had married a man like himself, not only indigent but epileptic. He tried to calm her by deceit, saying: "I regularly see a vision of a certain angel named Gabriel, and being unable to bear the sight of him, I faint and fall down."

Theophanes's tone of Muhammad being a deceitful, false prophet becomes the standard version of the Greek writers. Those writing in Syriac, and from within predominantly Islamic territories, were more circumspect about what they said in relation to the founder. However, the renunciation of false views and the "false prophet" himself entered into the ritual for accepting coverts to the Christian faith from this period on, and when Emperor Manuel I (regnant 1143–1180) settled many Turks in Byzantine territory and tried to have the harsh anathemas removed from the conversion ritual, the clergy strenuously objected to his interference. For most of the time between the ninth century and the early modern period, the Byzantine church demanded of converts from Islamic backgrounds that they explicitly anathematize the theology of Muhammad, his person, and all the caliphs after him, before proceeding to baptism. If a Christian was converted to Islam, either by choice or forcibly, to return to the practice of the faith the clergy required a repetition of the baptismal chrismation rite, as signifying the repentance someone who had radically apostatized from the faith rather than simply lapsed.

Another theologian of the latter half of the ninth century, Niketas Byzantios, known as "the Philosopher," was one of the first Byzantine writers who actually studied the Qur'an firsthand, most likely from a Greek translation he had. He composed a systematic apologia against Islam organized around theological, moral, and political conceptions. Theologically, the refusal to acknowledge monotheism as possible in any other form than monadism was taken by Niketas as a failure of sophistication. Casting out the divine Logos, for him, meant that the Muslims had "deprived God of his mind" (he takes the witticism from the writings of Gregory the Theologian attacking the fourth-century Arians) and had broken the logic of the link between the sublime transcendent and the world of material forms. Niketas accuses Islamic metaphysics of being philosophically naive, and resulting in a deity that was *holosphairos* (all spherical) and *holosphyros* (profoundly materialistic or mythologically fixed in the cosmos).

In terms of morality, he accuses the religion of favoring polygamy and tolerating sodomy, and of encouraging its believers to regard paradise as a hedonistic reflection of the best of "paradisial" lives here below. Niketas finds Islamic fatalism, and some aspects of its predestinationism, to be a depressing tendency and contrasts it strongly with a Christian sense of free will as a sharing in the divine charism of dominion. He had an interesting encounter with a Muslim theologian who defended the rightness of holy war.[30] Niketas refutes the argument that killing can be seen as divinely permitted and thus jihad validated as a godly thing. Killing, even in time of war, is always murder, he replies, and it is blasphemous to assign such an evil to the will of God.[31]

Polemical relations were the norm between the two faith systems. The apologias from the Islamic side slow down and dwindle away after the eleventh century. It

---

[30] See further D. Krausmuller, "Killing at God's Command: Niketas Byzantios' Polemic Against Islam and the Christian Tradition of Divinely Sanctioned Murder," *Al-Masāq: Journal of the Medieval Mediterranean* 16, no. 1 (2004): 163-76.
[31] See also J. A. McGuckin, "A Conflicted Heritage: The Byzantine Religious Establishment of a War Ethic," *Dumbarton Oaks Studies* 65-66 (2011–2012): 29-44.

coincides with the greater political assurance of the Islamic regimes. Those from the Byzantine side, however, continue to the end of the empire. Increasingly they rely on patristic writings from an earlier period far more than any effort to engage directly. Neither side was ever willing "to live and let live," theologically speaking: that is, in the sense that they could admit the validity of differing ways to God's truth. Both sides were convinced that they were the highest revelation and the other was a corruption. Islam had a more venerating approach to Nabi Jesus, the prophet Jesus, whom Muhammad greatly respected. For its part Byzantium regarded Muhammad as a false visionary whose hedonism increasingly emerged as his life progressed, demonstrating, in his lack of ascetical discipline, the dark origins of his religious teaching, which was another "diabolical heresy" meant to attack the kingdom of God on earth, which it did in political form, not merely doctrinal. Two later emperors composed treatises attacking Islam on such grounds, namely John VI Katakouzenos's (1292–1383) *Treatise Against Islam* and Manuel II Palaiologos's (1350–1425) *Dialogue with a Persian*. In down-to-earth politics, and surely in the local scenarios where the two systems actually rubbed against each other, there was undoubtedly more give and take between the two powers, and regularly a realpolitik manifested itself once Islam was recognized by the Byzantines as a serious world power.

The advent of Latin Crusaders in Constantinople and Palestine, with a much more naive political attitude, would shatter the tenuous basis of even that relationship at the end of the first millennium. After the disastrous loss to Islamic Seljuk armies at the battle of Manzikert in 1071, the Turkish gains were relentless, and Byzantium was in constant mode of shrinking territories and influence. The depredations of the Fourth Crusade in the early thirteenth century further weakened the imperial control of the eastern territories, and the sense that God had handed over the Christian Eastern world to Islamic suzerainty chillingly became widely felt. The imperial capital itself would fall in May 1453 to the Ottoman armies of Mehmet II the Conqueror, and his commandeering of the Great Church of Holy Wisdom as his mosque symbolized all that the Byzantines had increasingly feared for the last two hundred years.

The collapse did not substantially change the stubborn resistance to the Islamic faith. While the Ottomans saw the conquest of Rome as a great sign of God's favor on their religion, one that gave them hopes of soon conquering the Latin West as well, the Byzantines remained convinced that the religious system that sponsored such powerful force against them was a destructive force from a very different source than God, and one that God permitted, as he permitted all evils, to fall on the race of Christians on account of their infidelity and their sins. The lot of the "people of the book" in an era when there was no great Christian power left to speak for or defend them became more harsh than the theory of the Qur'an would lead one to think. After the fall of the last emperor, Mehmet appointed the patriarch of Constantinople to be the single representative leader (*ethnarchos*) of all Christian factions (Chalcedonian, Monophysite, Armenian, Balkan, Arab, or Latin) in his increasingly vast Ottoman empire. This would give to the Greek Byzantine Christian faith a more monolithic priority than it had hitherto enjoyed in the East, a situation that would last (though challenged by the Russians after the sixteenth century) until the increasing collapse of Ottoman power in the nineteenth century.

## THE BYZANTINE ICONOCLASTIC CRISIS

In the eighth century, however, these were visions of a bleak future for Eastern Christianity that had not come to pass. Closer to hand was a crisis of more immediate concern concerning the internal rationale of the Christian faith. It was one that took place predominantly in the Byzantine world, and yet again caused immense strain in the relations of Eastern and Western Christianity. To this day it remains one of the causes of the parting of the ways of the two church traditions. It concerns iconoclasm. The word means "the smashing of the icons." The Western church found religious art, at times, useful. It never really (either in Protestant or Catholic versions of its traditions) placed such an important stress on relic and icon as did the East. It tended to see an icon (a holy and venerable image of Christ or the Virgin or one of the saints) as a didactic device—like stained-glass windows, a way of teaching biblical stories to the illiterate. The Eastern tradition tended to see the icons as far more than didactic devices, more as sacramental vehicles of divine grace. The controversy has been called by some the only thing comparable to a "Reformation" that the Eastern church ever experienced. Scholars are still puzzling the reasons, whether political or theological, it all happened.

Iconoclasm massively disrupted the life of Byzantine Christianity in two periods. The first iconoclastic era was instituted by the Syrian imperial dynasty (Leo III, and his successor and son Constantine V, Copronymos) and lasted from 726 to the accession of his younger son, Leo IV (775–780), when it began to abate, probably because it had been so largely prosecuted as a centrally mandated imperial policy and interest was waning. After Leo's death his wife, Irene, had become regent for their son (Constantine VI), and in the face of much palace opposition from her husband's ministers she began to reverse the iconoclastic policy, culminating in her arrangement of the Council of Nicaea II (the seventh ecumenical council) in the time of Patriarch Tarasius. She summoned this universal synod at Constantinople in 786, but because of troop riots in the capital she transferred its sessions to Nicaea in the following year.

The council set out a dogmatic statement explaining not only the legitimacy of the veneration of icons of Christ, the Virgin, and the saints, but also the central necessity of such veneration, in order to safeguard the belief in Christ's divine status. The images were seen to serve as channels to transmit the veneration of the church to the "prototypes" represented by those icons. Adoration and worship of God (now technically defined as *latreia*) was strongly distinguished from all veneration of saints and holy things (now defined more closely as *proskynesis* or *douleia*). *Latreia* could only be offered to God, including Christ and the Spirit. Only Christ could be depicted imaginstically, however, since he alone of the Godhead was incarnated in history and made visible. If *latreia* were offered to any human or material thing, it would be idolatry.

The saints, however, were also decreed as fitting recipients of Christian respect and veneration (*proskynesis*), which included bowing down and the offering of respectful rituals such as incensing or kissing the images. The theological principle that was elevated was one that related directly to Christian liturgy: that all respect offered before an icon transmitted directly to the person (hypostasis) of the one who was represented in the icon. It was never transmitted to the icon itself, which served only as a sacramental medium. Thus if a believer bowed down and kissed an icon of Christ, he or she was offering an act of adoration (*latreia*) to God, given that Christ was the incarnation of God himself (this was why the icon was seen to be a proof case of authentic christological doctrine). If they bowed before an icon of the Virgin or a saint, however, they were offering veneration (*proskynesis*), not adoration, on the grounds that the great power of the Godhead in the incarnate Lord passed to his saints in the form of the charism of abundant grace (*charis*), and this grace, which lived in their glorified persons in heaven, was given as a blessing (*eulogia*) to those who reverenced them on earth.

At Nicaea II the works of John of Damascus (c. 655–750) (*In Defense of the Holy Images*) and Patriarch Germanos of Constantinople (c. 634–733), the chief anti-iconoclastic theologians, were afforded "patristic" status. John outlined the chief arguments against the iconoclastic claim that icon veneration was idolatrous and unbiblical by clarifying the distinction between idol worship and the Christian honor given to the Savior through the medium of his icon in churches. He also demonstrated from the Scriptures the amount of times God explicitly commanded images to be made for the process of worship (the imagery on the ark of the covenant, or temple curtains, for example), and made the point that it was idolatry that was forbidden, not image making per se, despite what Jewish and Islamic propagandists might say. In an unenlightened age, he argued, the two might have been seen as synonymous, but in the time of enlightenment after the advent of God in the flesh, the icon is now a suitable theological medium for expressing belief in the profound sacramentality of matter. Just as Christ's own body was deified, and deifying, so the icon too becomes a material sacrament of a divine presence and thus a source of healing grace for those who use icons in their forms of worship. For John, hostility to the principle of icons serving as sacramental forms manifested an aversion to the fundamental principles involved in the authentic revelation of God enfleshed. Thus icon veneration was not really an "indifferent" matter but actually central to the orthodox faith. Iconoclasm was, therefore, not merely a rigorist puritanism but more precisely a christological heresy.

The second period of iconoclasm was revived by Emperor Leo V of the Byzantine Armenian dynasty and lasted from 814 to 842. The second phase of the attack against icons and their supporters (the "iconodules") was once again centered in the court and the army, and once again resisted by the monks. It was probably more violently prosecuted than the first. It ended with the death of Emperor Theophilus in 842. After that point the empress-widow Theodora elevated the iconodule theologian Methodius to the patriarchal throne, and together they instituted a great festival to coincide with the first Sunday of Lent. This great "triumph of the icons," involving the street procession of the sacred images of Byzantium, was immensely popular and marked a definitive end to the iconoclastic tendencies of the army, whose most active dissident forces were dissolved.

In the second period of iconoclasm the leading theologians representing the legitimacy of icon veneration were Theodore the Studite (795–826) and Patriarch Nikephorus of Constantinople (758–828).[32] The celebration of the "restoration of Orthodoxy" was afterwards institutionalized in the Byzantine liturgy for the first Sunday of Lent and is now known as the "Feast (or Triumph) of Orthodoxy," when all ancient heresies are liturgically anathematized, culminating in the iconoclasts. It was this, perhaps, that led to the radical "slowing down" of the notion of holding ecumenical councils, a belief that Nicaea II had capped the whole series. It was a tendency that was exacerbated by the imminent rupture between the Latin and Greek churches in 1054, initiating a series of increasing alienations of the Eastern and Western churches that were fixed at the fall of Constantinople to invading Latin armies in 1204.

---

[32]Theodore's anti-iconoclastic works (*Antirrhetici adversus Iconomachos*) can be found in PG 99, pp. 327-436. A selection from them has been issued in translation by C. P. Roth, *On the Holy Icons* (Crestwood, NY: St. Vladimir's Seminary Press, 1981). Nikephoros issued three major writings against the iconoclasts: an *Apologeticus minor*, prior to 814, meant as a simple account for nonspecialists of the first phase of the iconoclastic policy; an *Apologeticus major* comprising three *Antirrhetici* (*Refutations*) directed against iconoclast Emperor Constantine V Copronymos and giving a heavily sourced patristic account of why icon veneration was a true expression of Orthodox faith; and last a large *Refutation of the (Iconoclast) Synod* of 815.

## PHOTIUS THE GREAT (C. 810–897)

The ninth century in Constantinople was also the "age of Photius." It was a time when learning was held in high esteem and men of letters flourished. Chief among them was one of the most learned men of his day, Photius. He was an aristocrat and a scholar who rose to great prominence in the church and brought into the light of day, to the puzzlement of those who then clearly observed it, as if for the first time, the long-existing tendency in world Christianity of the Latin and Greek forms of the faith to have significantly moved apart from each other in ethos and tendency. This manifested itself most acutely in two respects in Photius's lifetime: first, the Latin doctrine of the double procession of the Spirit (that the Spirit of God proceeds in the Trinity "from the Father and the Son"). In Latin this is known as the *filioque*. Second was the open claim of the papacy in Rome to have jurisdictional rights over every other episcopal see in Christendom, most particularly over the patriarchal see at Constantinople. It was a charge Photius robustly denied, learning in the course of his arguments against "papal ambition" that it was not merely a whim of an overzealous bishop of Rome (Nicholas I) but rather an idea that had taken root in the West and now emerged as a distinct aspect of Latin dogmatic ecclesiology (the doctrine of the church).

Photius was born in Constantinople to a wealthy family that had distinguished itself in the earlier iconoclastic crisis. He was known to the court and trusted with high office. In 858 the regnant emperor Michael III deposed the current patriarch Ignatius, on the advice of his regent Bardas, and asked for the diplomat Photius to succeed him, even though he was still a layman. Pope Nicholas I, however, through his legates present at a council in Constantinople in 861, supported Photius's legitimacy as patriarch, despite Ignatius's appeal, possibly on the understanding that Photius would be more amenable to his claims. He began to use the opportunity of the conflict between Ignatius with the monastic party against Photius and the court to assert a strong claim for papal supremacy even in Constantinopolitan affairs.

By 862, when it became clear Photius was his own man, the pope disavowed his legates' signatures at the synod of 861 and instead issued a statement to the Eastern bishops that he regarded Ignatius as the rightful patriarch and held Photius's episcopal ordination to be null and void. When this failed to elicit any reaction, the pope held a synod at Rome in April 863, which threatened to excommunicate Photius if he did not submit. Photius replied to Pope Nicholas to remind him that he was the subject of the emperor and as such should seek to be loyal. The communication implied that the papacy's closeness to the Carolingian dynasty (a pope had even crowned Charlemagne on Christmas Day of 800 as Holy Roman Emperor in defiance of the imperial dynasty at Constantinople) was a treasonable matter.

The schism that eventually resulted was exacerbated by the dispute that also arose in 865 over the newly established Bulgarian church—whether it should look to Roman or Constantinopolitan ecclesiastical jurisdiction. Photius vehemently opposed Roman missionaries in Bulgaria and began to assemble reasons why the Orthodox East had the right claim. It was to be the foundations of an argument that historically resulted in the wider culture of the Orthodox Slav world. Throughout his patriarchal ministry he fostered missionary expeditions to the Bulgarians and Russians. The Russian mission would develop spectacularly after his death. His chief argument for this presidency was that the canons of the Council of Chalcedon had assigned all new missionary territories to the governance of the patriarchate of Constantinople. Rome's desire to intervene in Bulgaria (the Bulgarian ruler was playing the fault line of allegiance between East and West for all it was worth) was taken to be a flouting of an ecumenical conciliar decree by papal ambition. Nicholas's response was to send eight separate letters to the emperor and the senate at the capital to demand obedience to his decree that Bulgaria should be regarded as Latin ecclesiastical territory and should adopt the Latin rite. His intention was made known in advance to the emperor, who sent troops to turn back the three papal legates by force. None of their letters were delivered. The pope's peremptory tone cost him any support he had at Constantinople. For Nicholas the matter was becoming a matter of the East's refusal to acknowledge the jurisdictional primacy he was claiming in the name of Peter.

In the course of a Council at Constantinople in 867, Photius marshaled a series of arguments against papal supremacy along with complaints about the pope's behavior in relation to Bulgaria. To the charge of an excessive development of papal theory (hinting that it was unorthodox or at least nontraditional) he added a very specific charge that the pope was responsible for propagating heresy in the form of tolerating the spread of the Latin *filioque* theology. This taught that the Spirit of God proceeded from the Father (as the creed of 381 stated) but also "and from the Son" (Latin *filioque*), which the creed did not state. The charge of canonical irregularity that Rome had leveled against Photius was now repaid much more seriously in the attack on the whole Latin tradition of trinitarian theology.

Photius, who knew his patristic theology very well, was aware that the *filioque* contradicted the insistence of Gregory the Theologian, architect of the theology of the Creed of Constantinople 381, that the Father himself was the source of all trinitarian unity by virtue of being the sole cause (*arche*) of both the Son's generation and the Spirit's procession. To make the Son a co-cause of the Spirit was seen in the East as a serious deviation from patristic precedent: enough, at the very least, to label Pope Nicholas as unorthodox. The synod of 867, accordingly, solemnly anathematized him.

The ultimate alienation of the Byzantine and Roman churches has often been posited in 1054, but the work of Photius marked the first real occasion (there had been many prior divisions and would be several others after) that the Eastern and Western churches officially and instinctively drew apart on significant theological issues, particularly related to the manner in which papal authority was felt by the Easterners to have changed the ancient pattern of the Christian ecumene.

Photius, as the emperor's representative, sought after better relations with the Saracens then governing the Holy Land, seeking to establish better conditions for Christians there and also safe passage for pilgrims. His own personal security, however, started to be rocked in 866 when Bardas, his friend and the imperial regent, was murdered, and Basil the Macedonian declared himself coruler with Michael III. A year later Basil murdered Michael and seized the throne for himself, deposing Photius and restoring Ignatius as patriarch once more, ten days after the death of Pope Nicholas at Rome. Emperor Basil was anxious to secure his legitimacy by healing the schism and reconciling with the new pope, Adrian, and so Ignatius took the opportunity, at a Council in Constantinople in 869–870, with papal legates present, to anathematize Photius. This synod was regarded in the West as the "Eighth Ecumenical Council," though not so in the East. Photius was held in house arrest at Stenos, on the European side of the Bosphorus, deprived of his books as a punishment.

Relations with Rome, however, were not improved one jot when Ignatius immediately appointed new senior bishops to administer the Bulgarian church. Photius kept in correspondence with many influential friends and bishops and in 876 was recalled to the capital in the role of tutor to the royal household. In 877, three days after Ignatius's death, Photius was reappointed as patriarch, and in 879 a reconciliation with Rome, in the person of Pope John VIII, was brought about. It was once more strained in 882 when Pope Marinus was elected and Photius protested irregularities in the canonical process at Rome! In 886, on the accession of Emperor Leo VI, Photius was dismissed from his see, as the new emperor (his former pupil) appointed his nineteen-year-old brother to the position. He was retired to the Armenian monastery of Bordi, where he died around 897.

Throughout his life Photius had been a lover of reading, and in Constantinople he presided over a circle of intellectual friends who read and reviewed literature from antiquity to their own day. He was a fluent and interesting writer on his own terms.[33] His access to the great libraries of the capital was unequaled. The results of his reading circle were published by Photius in his most famous work, titled *A Thousand Books* (*Myrobiblion*—also known as *The Library*, or *Bibliotheca*). This work is a digest and

---

[33] His works are collated in PG 101-4.

annotated bibliographical review (often with rare and precious extracts from the originals) of 280 works, many of which are now known to history only through Photius's comments. The work, therefore, is of inestimable historical importance.

His volume *Amphilokia*, dedicated to his friend Amphilochius of Cyzicus, is a series of three hundred questions and answers chiefly on matters of biblical interpretation and concerned especially with self-contradictory passages in the Bible (the so-called *enantiophanies*). He draws heavily from earlier patristic commentary and values Theodoret considerably. His treatise *Mystagogy of the Holy Spirit* became a foundational study for later Eastern Orthodox theology, and one that for centuries to come focused the mind of the Byzantine world on why it held Latin Catholicism in suspicion, both in terms of ecclesiastical organization and in relation to its doctrine of God's trinitarian life because of the *filioque* addendum it made to the creed. Photius's core argument is that the *filioque* introduces two principles of origination in God and thus destroys the internal unity of the Trinity and flies in the face of all patristic teaching (even the Latins, such as Ambrose and Augustine, whom Photius assembles and quotes, and the popes from Damasus to Adrian III). *His Dissertation on the New Appearance of Manichees* is one of the first times a theologian of the East takes notice of the Paulician movement and connects its dualism (probably brought to Constantinople by tribal movements) with the ancient school of Manichaeism. Photius gives an account of their teachings and uses the earlier work of Petrus Siculus.[34]

## THE BYZANTINE SLAVIC MISSIONS

The mission to the church of Bulgaria in the ninth century prefigured the larger mission to the Slavs, which would open up a vast "new world" for the Eastern Orthodox Church under Constantinople's patronage and cultural influence. At this period, when Byzantine affairs were at their zenith, the empire expanded its sphere of influence by a vast system of federation and alliances with outlying states and peoples.[35] To be adopted by the emperor, or to be married into the imperial family, was a way that a political web of treaty and interdependence was extended far and wide as a form of kinship relation of princes all looking to the Byzantine emperor as the center. This spreading nexus of political liaison inevitably came with the Byzantine expectation that the new territories and tribes must adopt Christianity as proof of their sincerity to be allied in a common view of civilized values. And so with the diplomats traveled the priests and monastic missionaries, and thus the gospel spread into the new regions with which Byzantium came into contact.

---

[34]Petrus Siculus, *Historia Manicheorum*, PG 104, p. 1240.
[35]See further D. Obolensky, *The Byzantine Commonwealth* (New York: Praeger, 1971).

With the Christianization of the Eastern European tribes came also books and literacy. The mission that would have, perhaps, the furthest-reaching effect was the evangelization of the pagan Slavs, who lay to the north and northwest of the Byzantine borders: the tribes of the Moravians, the Bulgars, the Serbs, and the Rus, all precursors of great Christian nations to come. Patriarch Photius of Constantinople had especially encouraged the Slavic mission and blessed two Greeks from Thessalonica to organize it: Constantine (826–869) and his brother Methodius (c. 815–885). They are more commonly known as Saints Cyril and Methodius.[36] As children they had already encountered Slavic tribes migrating near their city and had gained familiarity with their language. Inventing a script (now called "Cyrillic"), based on Greek letters but with extra sound-signs added, Cyril and Methodius prepared extensive translations of church service books and Gospel translations into this dialect. It would have a phenomenally wide transmission as "Church Slavonic" and is still the common ecclesiastical language of Russia, Bulgaria, and Serbia. Photius's encyclical letter to the Eastern patriarchs already speaks of the mission to the Bulgars and Rus as having had great and immediate fruit. But the endurance of paganism among the Russians would actually endure far longer than the optimistic accounts of the missionaries would lead one to believe.

When the two brothers left Constantinople they disseminated the literature, the language, and the spiritual culture of Orthodoxy wherever they went. Their mission was hampered by a conflict with German missionaries who were also at work trying to Latinize Moravia and Bulgaria. Issues of divergence between the two Christian traditions soon led to acrimony, and the brothers appealed to the papacy to limit the range of the hostile German preachers and to allow them to use their vernacular method of spreading the gospel. Pope Adrian II gave them his support, siding with them against the Germans, but Cyril died in Rome, and when Methodius returned he found the papal blessing actually counted for very little on the missionary field. His work was hindered at every turn by German ecclesiastics in Moravia, and after his death his followers were expelled.

However, the dramatic failure of the Byzantine-Slav mission in Moravia was not the case elsewhere. The work took root in Bulgaria and Serbia, and among the Rus, the ancestors of Russia. At the very end of the reign of Tsar Simeon (893–927) Bulgaria was recognized as an autonomous patriarchal church, the first national Christian church of the Slavs. Serbia became progressively Christianized in the later ninth century. The traditional date of the Christianization of Russia is set in Kiev (now the capital of Ukraine, but then the princely capital of the Rus) when Prince

---

[36] Constantine adopted the new name on his tonsuring as a monk.

Vladimir received baptism at Chersonesus in 988 prior to his marriage to the Byzantine princess Anna Porphyrogenita, and soon after called all his people to be baptized in solidarity with him (or risk his disfavor) in the River Dnieper. The account of the events is given in a colourful manner in the *Russian Primary Chronicle*, otherwise known as *The Tale of Bygone Years* or the *Chronicle of Nestor*. It is a history of Kievan Rus from around 850 to 1110, written at Kiev about 1113.

This dramatic turning point in Vladimir's reign was preceded by Princess Olga of Kiev's baptism on her visit to Constantinople in 945 (or perhaps 957) with her attendant priest, Gregorius. She requested a mission of priests to attend her back to Kiev. Her son Sviatoslav (regnant 963–972) remained a pagan, worshiping the god Perun and arguing that his troops would never respect him if he converted to the religion of Christ. Members of the Kievan royal house afterward oscillated in their relations with Byzantine Christianity and local pagan tradition. It might have been the case that Prince Yaropolk was Christianized (in the Latin rite), but the chroniclers pass over this in the cause of focusing attention on Vladimir's seminal conversion in the Byzantine rite. The great celebration of the millennium of the Christianization of Russia in 1989 was one of the factors responsible for hastening the end of communist oppression of church life, and a significant factor in the rapid collapse of the communist leadership a few years later.

## A SHORT READER

***Justinian*, The Institutes, *book 1, "On Persons," prelude.1-4, "On Justice and Law" (sixth century).*** Justice is the constant and perpetual wish to render everyone his due. Jurisprudence is the knowledge of things divine and human, the science of the just and the unjust. Having explained these general terms, we think we shall commence our exposition of the law of the Roman people most advantageously if we pursue at first a plain and easy path, and then proceed to explain particular details with the utmost care and exactness. For if at the outset we overload the mind of the student, while yet new to the subject and unable to bear much, with a multitude and variety of topics, one of two things will happen: we shall either cause him wholly to abandon his studies, or, after great toil, and often after great distrust to himself (the most frequent stumbling block in the way of youth), we shall at last conduct him to the point, to which, if he had been led by an easier road, he might, without great labor, and without any distrust of his own powers, have been sooner conducted. The maxims of law are these: to live honesty, to hurt no one, to give everyone his due. The study of law is divided into two branches; that of public and that of private law. Public law regards the government of the Roman empire; private law, the interest of the individuals. We are now to treat of the latter, which is composed of three elements, and consists of precepts belonging to the natural law, to the law of nations, and to the civil law.

**Severus of Antioch, Letter 1, To Count Oecumenius, On the Properties and Operations of Christ** *(c. 508).*[37] I am not worthy to speak of the righteousness of God, or to take his covenant in my mouth. However, since this time of present conflicts does not admit of silence, I accept an honorable defeat from you, and turn to the question in hand.... Know then, great lord, that for us to anathematize those who speak of properties of natures is not permissible (I mean the Godhead and the humanity of which the one Christ consists). Flesh does not depart from its existence as flesh, even if it has become God's own flesh, nor has the Word seceded from his nature, even if he has been hypostatically united to flesh that is possessed of a rational and intelligent soul. Rather, the difference also is preserved, and that propriety in the form of natural characteristics of the respective natures of which Emmanuel consists. For the flesh was not converted into the nature of the Word, nor was the Word changed into flesh. I speak of course in regard to the matter of natural characteristics; I do not mean that those that were naturally united are singly and individually separate and divided from one another: this is the position of those who split our one Lord Jesus Christ into two natures. For, since the union in hypostasis is acknowledged, it follows that those things that were united are not separated from each other. There is one Son, and one nature of God the Word himself incarnate, as the holy Cyril also says in the work he wrote against Diodore: "Let him know therefore that the body that was born at Bethlehem, even if it is not the same as the Word from God and the Father (I mean in terms of natural characteristics), nevertheless became his own, not anyone else's separate from the Son: and thus we recognize one Son and Christ and Lord and Word who took flesh." Accordingly, those who confess one incarnate nature of God the Word and do not confuse the elements of which he consists recognize also the propriety of those things that were joined in union. I mean here property as that which exists in the form of a manifestation of natural differences. They do not ascribe the acts of the humanity only to the human nature, and impute again those of the Godhead

---

[37]Severus was one of the greatest of the anti-Chalcedonian "Monophysite" theologians. See E. W. Brooks, ed., *Severus of Antioch: A Collection of Letters from Numerous Syriac Manuscripts* (Paris: Firmin-Didot, 1915).

separately to God the Word, but they recognize the difference only, never admitting a division: for the principle of union does not admit of any division. ... This why we do not anathematize those who confess the properties of the natures of which the one Christ consists, but we do anathematize those who separate the properties and attribute them to each nature considered separately. When the one Christ has thus been divided (and he is divided by the fact that they speak of two natures after the union), it follows that along with the natures that have been so cut apart into a duality and separated into a distinct diversity, so will go the operations and properties that are the offspring of this division. And this is how the text of Leo's wicked *Tome* holds it, in his words: "For each of the forms effects in partnership with the other that which belongs to itself, the Word doing that which belongs to the Word, and the body performing the things which belong to the body." Against these things it is good to set up the much-honored words of the holy Cyril, which refute impiety. In the *Scholion* that speaks of the coal he speaks as follows:

> Nevertheless, we may see in the burning coal (Is 6:1) a figure of how God the Word was united to the humanity but has not cast off being that which he is, but rather changed what had been assumed or united into his glory and operation. For, just as fire when it takes hold of wood and is introduced into it prevails over it and does not make it cease being wood, but rather changes it into the appearance and energy of fire, so as to perform all its own acts in it, and is already reckoned as one with it, thus is just how we should understand the case of Christ also. For, since God was ineffably united with humanity, he has preserved it as what we say it is, and he himself has also remained what he was. But, after he has once been united, he is reckoned as one with the humanity, appropriating its qualities to himself, while he himself also carried on the operation of his proper (divine) nature in it.

If, then, the Word changed the humanity that he had hypostatically united to him, not into his nature, for he remained that which he was, but rather into his glory and operation, and things that manifestly belong to the flesh have come to belong to the Word himself, how shall we allow that each of the forms performs its own separate acts? Thus, we must anathematize those who confine the one Christ in two natures and say that each of the natures performs its own acts. ... I have written these things though I am poor in intellect and praise the greatness of your God-loving understanding; and because, as you are wise, I give you an opportunity to attain wiser results. Forgive me that on account of the lack of leisure caused by the present struggles I have been late in writing. Greet your honored consort, who is a partner and a helper in the affairs of God.

**The Statement of Faith (Ekthesis) of the Council of Constantinople III (681).**
The holy and universal synod stated the following: This reverent and orthodox creed favored by God was surely enough for a complete knowledge of the orthodox faith and complete establishment in it.[38] But since from the first, that worker of evil things could never rest, first finding an accomplice in the serpent and through this means bringing on human nature the poisonous sting of death, so even in our day he has found instruments suited to his own purpose, namely Theodore, who was bishop of Pharan, and Sergius, Pyrrhus, Paul, and Peter, who were all bishops of this imperial city, and furthermore Honorius, who was pope of Old Rome, and Cyrus, who held the see of Alexandria, and Macarius, who was so recently bishop of Antioch, and the latter's disciple Stephen. He [Satan] has been hard at work using them to rouse up false stumbling blocks for the universal church, using new forms of argument to sow the heresy of a single will and a single principle of action in the two natures of the one member of the holy Trinity, Christ our true God, among the orthodox people. This is a heresy in harmony with the evil belief of the wicked Apollinaris, Severus, and Themistius, and it is ruinous to the mind.[39] Its aim and goal is to remove the perfection of the incarnation of the same one lord Jesus Christ our God, through certain tricky arguments, which all lead on to the blasphemous conclusion that his rationally animated flesh is devoid of a will and a principle of action. And so, for this reason, Christ our God has stirred up the faithful emperor, that new David, finding in him a man after his own heart, who, as the Scripture says, did not allow his eyes sleep or his eyelids to find rest until through this holy assembly of ours, which has been assembled by God, he found the perfect proclamation of right belief.[40] For according to that God-uttered saying, "Where two or three are gathered together in my name, there am I in their midst" (Mt 18:20).

This same holy and universal synod, here present, dutifully accepts and welcomes with open arms the memorandum of Agatho, most holy and most blessed pope of Old Rome, which was sent to our most reverend and most faithful emperor Constantine, which rejected by name those who proclaimed and taught (as has already been explained) one will and one principle of action in the incarnate

---
[38] The creed of Nicaea, which they recited at the outset of their teaching.
[39] Severus of Antioch, author of the preceding letter, who is here denounced as a Monophysite.
[40] Like David, who would not rest until he had brought back the ark from captivity.

dispensation of Christ our true God. Similarly, it also approves that other synodal report sent to his God-Taught Serenity,[41] from the synod of 125 bishops, all dear to God, which met under the same most holy pope, as being in accord with the holy synod at Chalcedon and with the *Tome* of the all-holy and most blessed Leo, pope of the same Old Rome, which was sent to Flavian,[42] who is now among the saints, and which that synod called a "pillar of orthodox belief," and also in accord with the synodal letters written by the blessed Cyril against the wicked Nestorius and to the bishops of the East.

Following the five holy and ecumenical synods and the holy and accepted Fathers, and making its definition in harmony, the synod professes our Lord Jesus Christ our true God, one of the holy Trinity (which is of one and the same being and is the source of all life), to be perfect in divinity and perfect in humanity, the same truly God and truly man, of a rational soul and a body; consubstantial with the Father as regards his divinity, and the same consubstantial with us as regards his humanity, like us in all respects except for sin; begotten before the ages from the Father as regards his divinity, and in the last days the same for us and for our salvation born of the Holy Spirit and the Virgin Mary (who is properly and truly called Mother of God) as regards his humanity; one and the same Christ, Son, Lord, Only begotten, acknowledged in two natures, which undergo no confusion, no change, no separation, no division; for at no point was the difference between the natures taken away through the union, but rather the property of both natures is preserved and runs together into a single subsistent being; he is not parted or divided into two persons, but is one and the same Only begotten Son, Word of God, Lord Jesus Christ, just as the prophets taught about him from the beginning, and as Jesus the Christ has himself instructed us, and as the creed of the holy Fathers has handed down to us.

And equally we proclaim two natural volitions or wills in him and two natural principles of action, which undergo no division, no change, no partition, no confusion, in accordance with the teaching of the holy Fathers. And the two natural wills are not in opposition, as the impious heretics have said, far from it, but his human will follows, never resisting or struggling, rather, in fact, is subject to his divine and all-powerful will. For the will of the flesh had to be moved, and yet to be subjected to the divine will, according to the most wise Athanasius.[43] For just as his flesh is said to be, and is, flesh of the Word of

---

[41] Emperor Constantine Pogonatos.
[42] Patriarch of Constantinople in the fifth century.
[43] Athanasius of Alexandria.

God, so too the natural will of his flesh is said to belong, and does belong, to the Word of God. This is what he himself says: "I have come down from heaven, not to do my own will, but the will of the Father who sent me." Here he calls his own will that of his flesh, since his flesh too became his own. For in the same way that his all-holy and blameless flesh endowed with a soul was not destroyed in being made divine but remained in its own limit and category, just so his human will also was not destroyed by being made divine, but rather was preserved, according to Gregory the Theologian,[44] who says: "For his act of willing, when he is considered as Savior, is not in opposition to God, being made divine in its entirety." And so we hold there to be two natural principles of action in the same Jesus Christ our Lord and true God, which undergo no division, no change, no partition, no confusion; that is, a divine principle of action and a human principle of action, according to the godly words of Leo, who says most clearly: "For each form performs, in a communion with the other, that activity which it possesses as its own: the Word working that which is the Word's and the body accomplishing the things that are the body's."[45] For of course we will not grant the existence of only a single natural principle of action of both God and creature, lest we elevate what is created to the level of divine being or indeed reduce what is most specifically proper to the divine nature to a level befitting creatures; for we acknowledge that the miracles and the sufferings are of one and the same according to one or the other of the two natures out of which he is, and in which he has his being, as the admirable Cyril has said. Therefore, protecting on all sides the principle of "no confusion" and "no division," we announce the whole matter in these few words:

Believing our Lord Jesus Christ, even after his incarnation, to be one of the holy Trinity and our true God, we profess that he has two natures shining forth in his single subsistence,[46] in which he demonstrated the miracles and the sufferings throughout his entire providential dwelling here on earth, not in appearance but in truth; the difference of the natures being made known in the same single subsistence in so far as each nature wills and performs the things that are proper to it in communion with the other. Moreover, in accordance with this reasoning, we hold that two natural wills and two principles of action[47] meet together in correspondence for the salvation of the human race. So now that these points have been formulated by us with all

---

[44]Gregory of Nazianzus.
[45]From the *Tome of Leo*.
[46]Two *ousiai* (divine and human), one (divine) hypostasis.
[47]Contradicting Monothelitism and Monoenergism at the same time.

precision in every respect and with all care, we definitively state that it is not permissible for anyone to produce any other faith; that is, to write or compose or consider or teach others. Those who dare to compose another faith, or to support or teach or hand on another creed to anyone who wishes to turn to knowledge of the truth,[48] either from Hellenism or Judaism or indeed from any heresy whatsoever, or those who dare to introduce new formulations, inventing new terms so as to overturn what has now been defined by us; such persons, if they are bishops or clerics, are to be deprived of their episcopacy or clerical rank, and if they are monks or laity they are to be excommunicated.

**John of Damascus, Fount of Knowledge, book 2, chapter 101, "On the Heresy of the Ishmaelites" (Islam) (eighth century).** There is also the superstition of the Ishmaelites to consider, which to this day still prevails and keeps people in error and is a forerunner of the antichrist. These people are descended from Ishmael, son of Abraham by Agar, and for this reason they are called both Agarenes and Ishmaelites. They are also called Saracens, which is derived from *Sarras kenoi*, which means "destitute of Sara," because of what Agar said to the angel: "Sara hath sent me away destitute." (Gen 16:8). These people used to be idolaters and worshiped the morning star and Aphrodite, whom in their own language they called Khabár, which means the great one. And so down to the time of Emperor Heraclius they were very great idolaters. From that time to the present, a false prophet called Muhammad has appeared in their midst. This man, after having accidentally found the Old and New Testaments and, so it would seem, having conversed with an Arian monk, devised his own heresy.[49] After having insinuated himself into the good graces of the people by a show of apparent piety, he made out that a certain book had been sent down to him from heaven. He had put down some ridiculous compositions into this book of his and he gave it to them as an object of veneration. He says that there is one God, creator of all things, who has neither been begotten nor has begotten (Qu'ran, sura 112). He says that the Christ is the Word of God and his Spirit, but a creature and a servant, and that he was begotten virginally, of Mary the sister of Moses and Aaron (Qu'ran, sura 19; 4.169). He maintains that Word and God and Spirit entered into Mary and she brought forth Jesus, who was a prophet and

---

[48]Namely, catechumens being instructed in the faith.
[49]There is a tradition that Muhammad as a child met a Nestorian monk (Bahira or George/Sergius of Bostra), who laid his hands on him and said that he could recognize in the youth the signs of a prophet.

servant of God. And he says that the Jews wanted to crucify him in violation of the law, but that they seized only his shadow and crucified this, but that the Christ himself was never crucified and never died, because God had such love for him that he lifted him up into heaven beside him (Qu'ran, sura 4.156). And he also says that when the Christ had ascended into heaven God asked him: "O Jesus, did you ever say: 'I am the Son of God and God'?" And according to him, Jesus answers: "Be merciful to me, Lord. You know that I did not say this and that I did not scorn to be thy servant. But sinful men have written that I made this statement, and they have lied about me and so have fallen into error." And he says then God answered and said to Jesus: "I know that you never said such a word" (Qu'ran, sura 5.116). There are many other extraordinary and quite ridiculous things in this book, which he boasts was sent down to him from God. But when we ask: "And who is there to testify that God gave him the book? And which one of the prophets foretold that such a prophet would rise up?"—they are at a loss to answer. Yet we observe that Moses received the law on Mount Sinai, with God appearing in the sight of all the people in cloud, and fire, and darkness, and storm. And we say that all the prophets from Moses on down foretold the coming of Christ and how Christ our God, the incarnate Son of God, was to come and be crucified and die and rise again, and how he was to be the judge of the living and dead. Then, when we say: "How is it that this prophet of yours did not come in the same way as these others bearing witness to him? And how is it that God did not present this man with the book to which you refer in your presence, even as he gave the law to Moses, with the people looking on and the mountain smoking, so that by this means you too may have certainty?" Then they answer that God does as he pleases. To which I say: "This I well know, but we were asking how the book came down to your prophet." Then they reply that the book came down to him while he was asleep. Then we wryly say to them that, as long as he received the book in his sleep and did not actually sense the operation, then the popular adage must apply to him [which runs: "You are spinning me dreams"].[50] And when we ask again: "How is it that when he himself commanded us in this book of yours not to do anything or receive anything whatsoever without testimony of witnesses, you did not ask him: 'First, can you show us by witnesses that you are indeed a prophet and that you have come from God, and show us just what Scriptures there are that testify concerning you?'" then they are ashamed and remain silent. So, although you may

---

[50]The manuscripts do not quote the adage in question. The editor of the Damascene, LeQuien, suggests he meant this one from Plato.

not marry a wife without witnesses, or buy anything, or acquire property; although you cannot purchase a donkey or take possession of a beast of burden without witnesses; although you can possess wives and property and donkeys, and so on, only through witnesses, is it the case that only in reference to your faith and your scriptures you hold matters completely unsubstantiated by witnesses? Because the one who handed all this down to you has no warranty from any source, nor is there anyone known who testified about him before he came. On the contrary, he received it all while he was asleep!

What is more, these people call us *hetaeriasts*, or associators, because, they say, we introduce an associate with God by declaring that Christ is the divine Son of God. We say to them in reply: "The prophets and the Scriptures have delivered this to us, and you, as you persistently maintain, accept the prophets. So, if we wrongly declare Christ to be the Son of God, it is they who taught this and handed it on to us." But some of them say that it is by misinterpretation that we have represented the prophets as saying such things, while others say that the Hebrews hated us and deliberately deceived us by writing in the name of the prophets so that we might be lost. So again we say to them: "As long as you say that Christ is the Word of God and Spirit, why do you accuse us of being *hetaeriasts*? For the word, and the spirit, is inseparable from that in which it naturally has existence. And so, if the Word of God is in God, then it is obvious that he is God. If, however, he is outside God, then, according to you, God is devoid of word and devoid of spirit. Consequently, seeking to avoid introducing an associate with God you have ended up mutilating him. It would be far better for you to say that he has an associate than to mutilate him, as if you were dealing with a stone or a piece of wood or some other inanimate object. And so, you speak falsely when you call us *hetaeriasts*; we will reply by calling you the 'mutilators of God.'" Moreover, they also accuse us of being idolaters, because we venerate the cross, which they abominate. To this we make reply: "How is it, then, that you rub yourselves against a stone in your Ka'ba and kiss and embrace it?" Some of them say that Abraham had relations with Agar upon this stone, while others say that he tied his camel to it when he was going to sacrifice Isaac. But we make the reply: "Since Scripture says that the mountain was wooded and had trees from which Abraham cut wood for the holocaust and laid it on Isaac (Gen 22:6) and left his asses behind with two young men, why are you talking nonsense? For in that place there are no thick woods, nor is there passage for asses." Well may they be embarrassed, but they still assert that the stone is Abraham's. So we say: "Let it be Abraham's, as you so foolishly maintain. But just because Abraham had relations with a woman on it or tied a camel to it, are you not ashamed to kiss it? And even then you find fault with us for venerating the cross of Christ, by which the power of the demons and the deceit of the devil was destroyed." This stone that they talk about is really a head of that Aphrodite, whom they once used to worship and whom they called Khabár. Even to the present day, traces of the carving are visible on it if you look carefully. Now, as I have stated, this Muhammad wrote many ridiculous books, to each one of which he set a title. For example, there is the book titled *On Woman* (Qu'ran, sura 4), in which he plainly makes legal provision for taking four wives and, if possible, even a thousand concubines, that is, as many as one can maintain over and above the four wives. He also made it legal to put away any wife one wishes to, and, if anyone desires, to take another wife in the same way. Muhammad had a friend named Zeid. This man had a beautiful wife, with whom Muhammad fell in love. Once, when they were sitting together, Muhammad said: "Oh, by the way, God has commanded me to take your wife." The other answered: "You are an apostle. Do as God has told you and take my wife." In fact, to tell the story over from the beginning, he said to him: "God has given me the command that you should put away your wife." And so he put her away. Then several days later he said: "Now God has commanded me to take her." Then, after he had taken her and committed adultery with her, he drew up this law: "Let whoever wills it put away his wife. And if, after having put her away, he should return to her, let another marry her. For it is not lawful to take her unless she has been married by another. Furthermore, if a brother puts away his wife, let his brother marry her, if he so wishes" (Qu'ran, sura 2.225). In the same book he gives such precepts as this: "Work the land which God has given you and beautify it. And do this, in such a manner" (Qu'ran, sura 2.223), for I do not wish to repeat all the obscene things that he did.

**John of Damascus, In Defense of the Holy Images *(eighth century).*** Now, since we are talking about icons and worship, let us analyse the exact meaning of each term. An icon is a likeness of the original with a certain difference, for it is not an exact reproduction of the original. Thus, the Son is the living, substantial, unchangeable Image of the invisible God, bearing in Himself the whole Father, being in all things equal to Him, differing only in being begotten by the Father, who is the Begetter; whereas the Son is begotten. The Father does not proceed from the Son, but the Son from the Father. It is through the Son, though not after Him, that He is what He is, the Father who generates. In God, too, there are representations and icons of His future acts, that is to say, His counsel from all eternity, which is ever unchangeable. That which is divine is immutable; there is no change in Him, nor shadow of change. Blessed Dionysios (the Areopagite) who has made his focus the divine things that are in God's presence, says that these representations and images are marked out beforehand. In His counsels, God has noted and settled all that He would do, the unchanging future events before they came to pass. In the same way, a man who wished to build a house would first make and think out a plan. Again, visible things are images of invisible and intangible things, on which they throw a faint light. Holy Scripture clothes in figure God and the angels, and the same holy man (Dionysios) explains why. When sensible things sufficiently render what is beyond sense, and give a form to what is intangible, a medium would be reckoned imperfect according to our standard, if it did not fully represent material vision, or if it required effort of mind. If, therefore, Holy Scripture, providing for our need and ever putting before us what is intangible, clothes it in flesh, does it not make an image of what is thus invested with our nature, and brought to the level of our desires, yet invisible? A certain conception through the senses thus takes place in the brain, which was not there before, and is transmitted to our faculty of discernment, and added to the mental store. Gregory (of Nazianzus), who is so eloquent about God, says that the mind, which is focused upon transcending corporeal things, is incapable of doing so. For the invisible things of God, since the creation of the world, are made visible through images. We see images in creation which remind us faintly of God, as when, for instance, we speak of the holy and adorable Trinity, imaged by the sun, or light, or burning rays, or by a running fountain, or a full river, or by the mind, speech, or the spirit within us, or by a rose tree, or a sprouting flower, or a sweet fragrance.[51]

***Photius*, Mystagogy of the Holy Spirit *1.3-5* (ninth century).** For if the Son and the Spirit came forth from the same cause, namely, the Father (even though the Spirit is by procession while the Son is by begetting); and if, as this blasphemy cries out, the Spirit also proceeds from the Son, then why not simply tear up the Word (Logos) and propagate the fable that the Spirit also produces the Son, thereby according the same equality of rank to each hypostasis by allowing each hypostasis to produce the other hypostasis? For if each hypostasis is in the other, then of necessity each is the cause and completion of the other. For reason demands equality for each hypostasis so that each one exchanges the grace of causality indistinguishably. Some others recognize that the Son's generation does not impair the indescribable simplicity of the Father.

---
[51]Translation by M. H. Allies, *St. John Damascene on Holy Images* (London: T. Baker, 1898), 10.

But since it is claimed that he proceeds from two hypostases, the Spirit is brought to a double cause, thereby obscuring the simplicity of the Most High. Does it not follow from this that the Spirit is therefore composite? How then is the Trinity simple? But, on the other hand, how shall the Spirit not be blasphemed if, proceeding from the Son, he in turn has no equality by causing the Son? O impiously bold tongue, corrupting the Spirit's own proper dignity! Who among our sacred and renowned Fathers ever said the Spirit proceeds from the Son? Did any synod, acknowledged as ecumenical, ever proclaim it? Which assembly of priests and bishops, inspired of God, affirmed this understanding of the Holy Spirit? For these men, having been initiated into the Father's Spirit, according to the Master's teaching, loudly proclaimed the splendor of the Master's teaching. These prophetic writings and books, predetermined from ancient times, are sources of light, and in accordance with righteousness anticipate the composite divisions and apostasies of this new ungodliness. Indeed, they subjected all who believed otherwise to anathema for being scorners of the catholic and apostolic church; for the second of the seven holy and ecumenical synods (Constantinople 381) directly taught the doctrine that the Holy Spirit proceeds from the Father. The third council (Ephesus 431) received it by tradition; the fourth (Chalcedon 451) confirmed it; the fifth (Constantinople II 553) supported the same doctrine; the sixth (Constantinople III 681) sealed it; the seventh (Nicaea II 787) sealed it in splendor with contests. Accordingly, in each of their luminous proclamations the godly doctrine that the Spirit proceeds from the Father and not also from the Son is boldly asserted. Would you, then, O godless herd, draw away toward unlawful teaching and dispute this teaching of the Master himself?

***The Russian Primary Chronicle*, The Baptism of the Rus, 116-19.** Vladimir took the princess and Anastasius and the priests of Chersonesus, together with the relics of St. Clement and of Phoebus his disciple, and selected also sacred vessels and images for the liturgy. In Chersonesus he thus founded a church on the mound that had been heaped up in the midst of the city with the earth removed from his embankment; this church is standing even to the present day. Vladimir also found and appropriated two bronze statues and four bronze horses, which now stand behind the Church of the Holy Virgin, and which the ignorant think are made of marble. As a wedding present for the princess, he gave Chersonesus over to the Greeks once more, and then departed for Kiev. When the prince arrived at his capital, he directed that the idols should be overthrown and that some should be cut to pieces and others burned with fire.

He thus ordered that the idol of Perun should be bound to a horse's tail and dragged down Borichev to the stream. He appointed twelve men to beat the idol with sticks, not because he thought the wood was sensitive, but to affront the demon who had deceived men in this guise, so that he might receive chastisement at the hands of men. Great art thou, O Lord, and marvelous are thy works! Yesterday this thing was honored of men, but today it is held in derision. While the idol was being dragged along the stream to the Dnieper, the unbelievers wept over it, for they had not yet received holy baptism. After they had thus dragged the idol along, they cast it into the Dnieper. But Vladimir had given this injunction: "If it halts anywhere, push it out from the bank, until it goes over the falls. Then let it alone." His command was duly obeyed. When the men let the idol go, and it passed through the rapids, the wind cast it out on the bank, which since that time has been called Perun's sandbank, a name that it bears to this very day. Thereafter Vladimir sent heralds throughout the whole city to proclaim that if any inhabitants, rich or poor, did not betake himself to the river [for baptism], he would risk the prince's displeasure. When the people heard these words, they wept for joy and exclaimed in their enthusiasm, "If this were not a good thing, the prince and his boyars would not have accepted it." On the next day, the prince went forth to the River Dnieper with the priests of the princess [Anna] and those from Chersonesus, and a countless multitude assembled. They all went into the water: some stood up to their necks, others to their breasts, and the younger near the bank, some of them holding children in their arms, while the adults waded farther out. The priests stood by and offered prayers. There was joy in heaven and on earth to behold so many souls saved. But the devil groaned, lamenting: "Woe is me! How am I driven out from this place? For I thought to have my dwelling place here, since the apostolic teachings did not dwell in this land. Nor did this people know God, so I rejoiced in the service this people rendered to me. But now I am vanquished by the simple, not even by apostles and martyrs, and my reign in these regions is at an end." When the people were baptized, they returned to their own dwellings. Vladimir, rejoicing that he and his subjects now knew God himself, looked up to heaven and said: "O God, who has created heaven and earth, look down, I beseech thee, on this your new people, and grant them, O Lord, to know you as the true God, even as the other Christian nations have known you. Confirm in them the true and unalterable faith, and help me, O Lord, against the hostile foe, so that, hoping in you and in your might, I may overcome his malice." Having spoken in this way, he commanded that wooden churches should be built and established where pagan idols had previously stood. He thus founded the Church of St. Basil on the hill where the idol of Perun and the other images had been set up, and where the Prince and the people had customarily offered their sacrifices. He began to found churches and to assign priests throughout the cities, and to invite the people to accept baptism in all the cities and towns. He took the children of the best families and sent them for instruction in book learning. The mothers of these children wept bitterly over them, for they were not yet strong in faith, but mourned as though for the dead. When these children were assigned for study, there was fulfilled in the land of Rus that prophecy that says, "In those days, the deaf shall hear words of Scripture, and the voice of the stammerers shall be made plain" (Is 29:18). For these persons had not formerly heard any words of Scripture, and now heard them only by the act of God, for in his mercy, the Lord took pity upon them, even as the prophet had said: "I will be gracious to whom I will be gracious" (Ex 33:19).

## FURTHER READING

### *The Age of Justinian*
Baker, G. P. *Justinian*. London: Nash and Grayson, 1931.

Browning, R. *Justinian and Theodora*. London: Weidenfeld and Nicolson, 1971.

Downey, G. *Constantinople in the Age of Justinian*. Norman: University of Oklahoma Press, 1964.

Meyendorff, J. Chapter 7 of *Imperial Unity and Christian Divisions*. Crestwood, NY: St. Vladimir's Seminary Press, 1989.

Wesche, K. P. *On the Person of Christ: The Christology of the Emperor Justinian*. Crestwood, NY: St. Vladimir's Seminary Press, 1991.

### *Monothelitism and Monoenergism*
Baynes, N. H. "The Restoration of the Cross at Jerusalem." *English Historical Review* 27, no. 106 (1912): 287-99.

Berthold, G., trans. *St. Maximus the Confessor*. Classics of Western Spirituality. New York: Paulist, 1985.

Davis, L. D. *The First Seven Ecumenical Councils: Their History and Theology*. Wilmington, DE: M. Glazier, 1987.

Dodgeon, M. H., et al., eds. *The Roman Eastern Frontier and the Persian Wars (Part I, 226–363 AD)*. London: Routledge, 2002.

Frend, W. H. C. *The Rise of the Monophysite Movement*. Cambridge: Cambridge University Press, 1972.

Grillmeier, A., with T. Hainthaler. *Christ in Christian Tradition*. Vol. 2, part 4, *The Church of Alexandria with Nubia & Ethiopia After 451*. London: Mowbray, 1996.

Kaegi, W. A. *Heraclius, Emperor of Byzantium.* Cambridge: Cambridge University Press, 2003.

Louth, A. *Maximus the Confessor.* London: Routledge, 1996.

Luce, A. A. *Monophysitism Past and Present: A Study in Christology.* London: SPCK, 1920.

Meyendorff, J. *Christ in Eastern Christian Thought.* Crestwood, NY: St. Vladimir's Seminary Press, 1975.

———. *Imperial Unity and Christian Divisions: The Church AD 450–680.* Crestwood, NY: St. Vladimir's Seminary Press, 1989.

Rheinink, G. I., and B. H. Stolte, eds. *The Reign of Heraclius (610–641): Crisis and Confrontation.* Louvain: Peeters, 2002.

Thunberg, L. *Microcosm and Mediator.* Lund: Gleerup, 1965.

### The Council of Constantinople III (681)

Davis, L. D. *The First Seven Ecumenical Councils: Their History and Theology.* Wilmington, DE: M. Glazier, 1987.

Trostyanskiy, S., ed. *Seven Icons of Christ: An Introduction to the Christology of the Ecumenical Councils.* Piscataway, NJ: Gorgias Press, 2016.

### Christianity and Islam

Bertaina, D. "An Arabic Account of Theodore Abu Qurra in Debate at the Court of Caliph al-Ma'mun: A Study in Early Christian and Muslim Literary Dialogues." PhD diss., Catholic University of America, 2007.

Kazhdan, A. "Polemic Against Islam." In *The Oxford Dictionary of Byzantium*, 2:1017-18. Oxford: Oxford University Press, 1991.

Khoury, A. T. *Polémique byzantine contre l'Islam.* Leiden: Brill, 1972.

Meyendorff, J. "Byzantine Views of Islam." *Dumbarton Oaks Papers* 18 (1964): 113-32.

Vryonis, S. "Byzantine Attitudes Toward Islam During the Late Middle Ages." *Greek, Roman, and Byzantine Studies* 12 (1971): 263-86.

### Iconoclasm

Anderson, D., trans. *St. John of Damascus: On the Divine Images.* Crestwood, NY: St. Vladimir's Seminary Press, 1980.

Barasche, M. *Icon: Studies in the History of an Idea.* Crestwood, NY: St. Vladimir's Seminary Press, 1995.

Bryer, A. M., and J. Herrin. *Iconoclasm. (Papers Given at the Ninth Spring Symposium of Byzantine Studies. Birmingham University 1975.)* Birmingham, UK: Centre for Byzantine Studies, University of Birmingham, 1977.

Chase, F. H., trans. *St. John of Damascus: The Fount of Knowledge.* Fathers of the Church 37. Washington, DC: Fathers of the Church, 1958.

Hussey, J. M. Pages 30-68 in *The Orthodox Church in the Byzantine Empire.* Oxford: Oxford University Press, 1986.

Louth, A., trans. *Three Treatises on the Divine Images (St. John of Damascus).* Crestwood, NY: St. Vladimir's Seminary Press, 2003.

McGuckin, J. A. "The Theology of Images and the Legitimation of Power in Eighth Century Byzantium." *St. Vladimir's Theological Quarterly* 37, no. 1 (1993): 39-58.

O'Rourke-Boyle, M. "Christ the Eikon in the Apologies for Holy Images of John of Damascus." *Greek Orthodox Theological Review* 15 (1970): 175-86.

Nasrallah, J. *St. Jean de Damas: Son Époque, sa vie, son oeuvre.* Harisah, Lebanon: Imprimerie St. Paul, 1950.

Roth, C. P., trans. *On the Holy Icons (St. Theodore the Studite).* Crestwood, NY: St. Vladimir's Seminary Press, 1981.

Sahas, D. J. *John of Damascus on Islam: The "Heresy of the Ishmaelites."* Leiden: Brill, 1972.

Salmond, S., trans. *St. John of Damascus. On the Orthodox Faith. NPNF* second series 9. Grand Rapids: Eerdmans,1899.

**Photius the Great**

Dvornik, F. *The Photian Schism: History and Legend.* Cambridge: Cambridge University Press, 1948.

Freese, J. H., trans. *The Library of Photius.* Vol. 1. London: SPCK, 1920.

Treadgold, W. T. *The Nature of the Bibliotheca of Photius.* Dumbarton Oaks Studies 18. Washington, DC: Dumbarton Oaks Center for Byzantine Studies, Trustees for Harvard University, 1980.

White, D. S. *Patriarch Photius of Constantinople.* Brookline, MA: Holy Cross Orthodox Press, 1981.

# THE FLOURISHING OF MEDIEVAL ROME IN THE SEVENTH TO TENTH CENTURIES

## BENEDICT AND BENEDICTINISM

St. Benedict of Nursia (c. 480–547) came to be popularly regarded in Latin Christian history as the veritable "founder" of Western monasticism, comparable to the way Antony the Great, or Basil of Caesarea, had assumed the title of "father of monks" in the East. Antony, of course, was not the first monk or sole inventor of the monastic way of life any more than Benedict was; and the notion of any single founder is inapplicable in terms of the real and much more complex history of the origins of monasticism. Even so, such titles represent the manner in which their subsequent reputations elevated them hagiographically among their monastic successors, and it gives testimony to the very real influence on the early formation of monastic practice that these significant founders genuinely had.

Benedict did not actually add all that much to the monastic formulae that had already evolved in the West over the previous century, but what he did contribute in terms of a clear rule of life, set down as a daily observance, was significant and had a long-lasting effect, and this was more along the lines of what we might call an ethos rather than a single distinctive invention. His great contribution was his character: a melding together of a Roman genius for organization and regularity, with a compassionate sense of pastoral welfare. These two things, organized communal life and the overarching context of a "family" atmosphere for monastics, still make up the distinctive *charisma* of his Benedictine disciples around the world today.

In his own lifetime, and even for close on a century after it, it would have been a matter of some surprise for contemporaries to have learned of his great posthumous glory, for while he was active as a monastic teacher Benedict had only a very small following and little more than local fame. It was his rule, or plan for organizing an imagined monastic community, that made him posthumously famous, propagated along with Pope Gregory the Great's praises of him a generation later in the latter's second book of his widely influential *Dialogues*. It is this book (also full of legendary elements) that gives us more or less all the historical information we actually possess about Benedict.

Born to a wealthy Italian family, Benedict came from the Apennine village of Nursia and as a young man traveled to Rome for the final stages of his education in rhetoric. Rome at this period was in a serious economic and political decline. Here he experienced some form of life crisis. We are told by Pope Gregory that the quality and morality of city existence disgusted him, and so he decided to retire to a secluded life first at Enfide (now Affile in Italy) and shortly after at Subiaco, a country region near the capital. At Subiaco he headed his own monastic household near Vicovaro. His organizational genius drew attention, and soon he established twelve monasteries in the Aniene valley, each with twelve monks under the authority of an abbot: modeling the pattern of Christ with his twelve apostles. His organization of these common-life (cenobitic) houses met with the resistance and lively opposition from established ascetics in the area, who felt their eremitical independence was being attacked. Around 529 Benedict left Subiaco after discovering plots being made against him (Pope Gregory speaks of the legend of an attempted assassination by means of a poisoned chalice), and then he established a community at Monte Cassino inside the ruins of a pagan temple.[1] Monte Cassino was a secure hilltop settlement halfway between Rome and Naples, which served him and his monks well in those troubled times of war-torn Italy.

It was here that he composed his rule, probably by adapting earlier monastic regulations (especially the prototype called the *Rule of the Master*), setting out the detailed regimen of his house: its spiritual goals as well as the minutiae of its organization and daily *horarium* or schedule.[2] In adapting the *Regula Magistri* Benedict added a particular stress of his own on the critically essential ethos of gentle paternal care that should characterize the monastic abbot or leader. His monks were to find their salvation in obedience, and accordingly the abbot was to be a true pastor, a veritable Christ figure to his charges. The stress in all his work was on monasticism

---

[1] The saint's iconography shows him blessing the cup at a meal, and the poisoned chalice thereupon breaks. If the story is based on historical memory, it is interesting to note how deep passions ran among some of these ancient hermits: though a constant theme of the Benedictine literature is that communal monasticism is beneficial and familial, and solitary lifestyle leads to eccentric madness—so this trope that hermits wanted to murder him might well be an exaggeration of a group of anchorites trying to drive him and his builders off "their" mountain.

[2] Some scholars think the *Rule of the Master* is later than Benedict's rule.

understood as a matter of the common, or cenobitic, life. For Benedict the chief function of the monastery was the *opus Dei*—"God's work" of sustaining a constant rhythm of prayer and liturgy each day in a nexus of monastic buildings gathered around the church. The prologue and seventy-three chapters of the rule stress the monk's duty to fulfill the return to God (repentance) on a pilgrimage of obedience. Obedience is elevated as one of the fundamental monastic attributes.

Having had a jaundiced experience of hermits in his early years as a monk, and also having looked to the Eastern monastic notions of wandering (Byzantine monastics were much freer and often traveled from house to house seeking the guidance of different elders), Benedict dismisses the concept of free moveability as too open to abuse, and directed his monks to take an oath or vow of *stabilitas loci*, "stability of place," meaning the commitment to the monastic lifestyle would be made quite discretely to obedience to a specific abbot, in a single residence, for life. Benedict himself looks to Pachomius, Basil the Great (of Caesarea), and John Cassian as the best of spiritual masters for monks. His own rule, however, was looked to in turn as a marvelous example of humane moderation by his successors.

The essence of the "Benedictine" spirit was to balance labor and work. The motto "work and pray" (*ora et labora*) was to become the guiding axiom for the constructive life of the monk, and prayer was above all to be understood in a communal liturgical context. The office of hours (matins, or morning prayers, and then short offices of psalm singing at the turn of every three hours—terce, sext, none—ending with evening vespers, and compline) as well as the daily eucharistic liturgy, served by a priest-monk, were the chief foci of the house.[3] Benedict's renown as a holy man grew with the extent of his monastic foundations, and the Ostrogothic king Totila (r. 541–552), then engaged in a campaign with Justinian's general Belisarius for command of Rome, made a special journey to see him on Monte Cassino before the saint's death, probably some time near 547.

Benedict's monks were forced from Monte Cassino by Lombard incursions around 575, and they took refuge in Rome, from which center their new rule really became popularized. At Rome Pope Pelagius II gave them a new monastic center adjacent to his cathedral of the Lateran basilica. Gregory the Great adopted the rule from his intimate knowledge of these monks when he turned his own villa on the Caelian Hill into St. Andrew's monastery. It was from here that the prior Augustine set out at Pope Gregory's command, with forty companions in 595, to evangelize the English, in the course of which demonstrating how suitable Benedictinism was as a missionary force.[4]

---

[3] The Roman "first hour" was 6 a.m., the third (*Terce*) was 9 a.m., and so forth.
[4] C. Butler, "Was St. Augustine a Benedictine?," *Downside Review* 3 (1884).

Some members of Augustine's mission, seeking to be dispensed from their task, brought their rule to Lerins and so introduced Benedictine practices to the monasteries of Gaul.

The Holy Roman Emperor Charlemagne in the ninth century, taking cognizance of Gregory the Great's high praises of St. Benedict, insisted on elevating Benedict's rule alone as the standard of all the monasteries in his domains. His son, Louis the Pious, sustained this policy, and so the Carolingian support gave the Benedictine rule a kind of archetypal status as "norm" for monks in the West. St. Benedict of Aniane was the religious charismatic who presided over this development. His influence over Emperor Louis was intense, and he persuaded the ruler to establish a monastery adjacent to his Royal Palace at Aix La Chapelle. Benedict introduced the Benedictine monastic ethos to a much more positive attitude toward Eastern monastic praxis and writing, a deeper spirit of ascetical practice, as he had known it from his early life. The only exception to the rapid spread of Benedictinism in Western Europe was in Scotland, Wales, and Ireland, where the old Celtic monastic rules and practices retained their grip strongly for several more centuries to come.

After the tenth century, Benedict's rule achieved an increasingly dominant status throughout Western Europe, characterizing most monastic organization there and thereby giving to the entire Latin church a cohesion of core systems that would mark it deeply. Nothing comparable to this centralization was ever found in the ascetical life of the Eastern church, where all monastic founders of houses retained the right to draw up their own regulations if they so wished.[5] Even though all monastic literature emphasises the right of the abbot to rule "as if he were Christ himself," the reality was very different. Of all monastic charters it is perhaps the Benedictine in the West and the Pachomian in Egypt that take most seriously the concept of complete and explicit obedience to the abbot of the house. Allied to this the Benedictine insistence that a monk should not leave the monastery he first joins gave the Western monks a spirit of obedience that was almost militaristic in character. It was to prove of great value in the missionary expanse of the church westward into pagan tribal territories, where married clergy would not venture, but small monastic families under tight discipline were more fitted for survival. Germany in the seventh and eighth centuries was remissionized by English Benedictine monks Willibrord and Boniface, who established several renowned monasteries at the heart of the church structures. From there mission and Benedictine monasticism were exported together to Scandinavia.

---

[5] Byzantine monastic rules did eventually tend to cluster around Basil of Caesarea's writings (very vague in style) and Theodore the Studite's ninth-century rule for the Stoudium monastery at Constantinople, but even so there is no comparison to the centralizing force Benedictinism brought to the Western monastic families.

The familial aspect of Benedictinism is sustained even to this day by the nature of the sense of authority among Benedictine monastic houses. Unlike many religious orders that have a tightly hierarchical order of precedence, leading from superiors of houses to provincial directors and an abbot or prior general in Rome, the Benedictines are organized as highly independent families in individual houses and in terms of larger (national) congregations. The cohesion is not so much provided, however, by personal allegiances and obediences of superiors within a rising hierarchy (although the pope retains a jurisdiction over all) but rather by virtue of a sense of common allegiance to the rule, which shapes all to the same end.

At first the Benedictine individual house was autonomous under its abbot, who governed from the rule. Soon, however, a system of acknowledging the authority of the local bishop had to be worked out; and this was done by admitting his "governance" on fixed times, which were a kind of limited external "visitation." After the eleventh century the custom of larger houses founding smaller offshoots led to the concept of mother and daughter houses, where the mother house retained precise and circumscribed legal rights over the later foundation. It was this that finally grew into the concept of federated congregations that lasted into the second millennium of Benedictinism.

The move toward making Benedictinism a system, like the sense of a "religious order" we would recognize today, was symbolically made at the abbey of Cluny in Burgundy, France, in 910. The abbot, St. Berno, had made a highly impressive federation of dependent houses adhering to Benedictine inspirations. By the twelfth century this comprised no less than 314 houses. Its routines, liturgical practices, and spiritual ethos exercised an immense influence over worldwide Benedictine imagination. In turn the principles of Cluny brought a system of reform, as it were, by modeling a charism within the structure. Some of the later "reform" movements of this type produced monastic developments that, while still retaining allegiance to the rule of Benedict, created orders with a distinctive new spirit (often one that sought more contemplative independence or greater ascetic simplicity than the main Benedictine family). The best known was that which grew from the Abbey of Citeaux in 1098, and which issued in the Cistercians. There are also the Camaldoli hermits from 1009, Vallombrosa from 1039, Grammont from 1076, Fontevrault (a double monastery of both sexes ruled by an abbess) from 1099, Savigny from 1112, Monte Vergine from 1119, the Sylvestrine monks from 1231, the Celestines from 1254, and the Olivetans from 1319; all developed out of the spirit of the Benedictine rule.

## GREGORY THE GREAT AND HIS SUCCESSORS

Pope Gregory (c. 540–604), who is now known as the "Great" to distinguish him from many other papal namesakes after him, was one of the most important of the early bishops of Rome: an outstanding political administrator in a time of great social unrest in Italy, no less than the beginning of the Dark Ages, and a highly practical theologian, whose work actually marks the birth of "pastoral theology" in the Western church.

Gregory belonged to an aristocratic Christian family in Rome at a time when the fortunes of both Italy and the ancient city were in decline because of Justinian's wars of reconquest and later (from 586) raids from Lombardian insurgents. The Lombard tribes had flowed into Italy in the vacuum left behind by the exhausting wars between the Byzantine armies sent by Justinian to remove the Ostrogothic rulers. Very quickly they absorbed the remaining Ostrogothic leaders and set a permanent wedge between Italy and any hope of Byzantine reconquest. Gregory was politically astute enough to know that the future of Europe lay more in its own hands than in any protection it could hope for from Constantinople. The emperor's exarch was still stationed at Ravenna, in the north, but now with only a small body of troops that were reluctant to engage with the Lombards. As time went on Gregory increasingly came to realize they would not offer much in the line of political protection.

Gregory was a skilled politician from his early youth. His father had been a senator at Rome, loyal to Justinian's court, and in 573 Gregory himself became the prefect of Rome (the highest imperial civic office possible). Soon afterward he announced his retirement from public life and dedicated his extensive properties in Rome and Sicily to the cause of Christian asceticism. His large villa on the Caelian Hill, near the Colosseum, became his monastery of St. Andrew (still functioning), where he lived a life of scholarship and prayer with companions. This was the classic life of *otium*, or secluded leisure, that was traditional for retiring Roman nobility and was often couched in that era in terms of philosophic reflection and as such "askesis." Gregory was different, however, from such earlier retired noblemen as Paulinus of Nola, insofar as he actually did engage himself with ascetical community life. He greatly admired the Benedictine spirit.

Having declared himself in a public way as a "man of the church," however, his plans for self-determination were rudely interrupted, because Pope Pelagius II, now his ecclesiastical "superior," quickly determined to reemploy his talents for the service of the church. The pope ordered Gregory to resume public ecclesiastical service, not monastic retirement, and so he was ordained deacon and sent as the senior papal representative (*apocrisarius*) to the court of Constantinople, where he lived from 579–586. In this time at the Eastern capital he learned many things about liturgical practice, chant systems and so on, which became the seed of several innovations he brought back to the Western church. Later ecclesiastic practices were also attributed to him and became collectively known as the "Gregorian reforms." He crossed swords at this time with the Greek patriarch Eutyches and, learning from this experience, set himself to become a champion of the primacy of the popes, increasingly freed from political control of the emperors. He had firsthand experience of the manner in which first Ostrogoth kings, usurping Byzantine rule, then Lombard barbarians, had all disrupted Italian government. The greatest cause of the impoverishment of his country had perhaps been Justinian's determination to win it back once more for Byzantium, but all the political turmoil had certainly conspired to make his view of any external control over church affairs a lamentable and sacrilegious thing. This, of course, was itself a blasphemous (not merely treasonable) idea to the Byzantine world, which saw the emperor's role, including a high degree of governance of the church and its bishops (though not in dogma), as part of the basic canonical charter of the Christian world. In Gregory's time this parting of the ways between Western and Eastern ecclesiologies, especially in terms of the independent authority of the Roman popes, became sharpened.

During this time in Constantinople, Gregory began one of his greatest literary works, the *Magna Moralia in Job*, which was designed as an ascetical commentary on the biblical text of Job for the use of his monastic companions in the East. After resuming his duties as papal secretary back in Rome, Gregory administered the church as its effective executive officer during the time of the great plague in 590 because the pope himself was ill. When Pope Pelagius died later in that same year, Gregory was rapidly elected pope (much against his own inclination) and named Gregory I. He rallied the city with extensive penitential processions through the streets to ask for God's mercy and an abatement of the plague. Later tales spoke of a vision that occurred at this time, of an angel putting away his sword over Hadrian's mausoleum (now Castel San Angelo), where today the statue of the same is a familiar Roman landmark.

With the cessation of troubles of invasion and plague, Gregory began a highly efficient administration in Rome. It stood out all the more brightly as a symbolic end to a long decline of the Roman church. When he assumed the papacy he actually spoke of himself as being possibly the last of all the popes and describes the church as an old, beaten ship whose timbers are now rotten. Rather than despair, he set about the task of rebuilding with great energy; and like his reaction to the plague, his instinct was that if one returned to penitence and fervent discipline, God's favor would be granted abundantly. This, and also because he could rely on his own chosen men, is why he profoundly monasticized the Roman church administration, despite protests of the nonmonastic clergy. In this he began a long tradition along these lines that would mark Western catholicism ever afterwards.

His successful leadership over Rome and its province led to his papacy becoming almost a paradigm of how the papal office could develop in the future. Increasingly frustrated with the unwillingness and incompetence of the Byzantine exarch at Ravenna, Gregory independently negotiated a military peace with the Lombard invaders, offering them terms of tribute. This was reported to Constantinople as tantamount to a treasonable act. Symbolically, it marks the moment when the popes became one of the religio-political rulers of the West, even though they lacked a significant army.

Gregory's considerable writings on theological matters were chiefly pastoral, biblical, and hagiographical. His extensive biblical exegesis and theological comments were a moderated and simplified form of Augustine. He was an intellectual in a time of great educational cutback, and his simplified "synopses" of the earlier writers were welcomed at a time when there were increasingly fewer intellectuals and innovative thinkers. Gregory did more than any other (except perhaps Prosper of Aquitaine) to elevate Augustine's influence over the whole Western church, giving a theological preeminence to the doctrine of grace, and adding to Augustine's speculations on the possibility of afterlife spiritual progress his own more developed views on purgatorial purification. *Purgatorium* meant "place of purification," and this notion of a state neither heaven nor hell where final preparation was made for souls to be fitted for the sight of God and cleansed of all minor sins became a view that eventually grew into the distinctive Roman doctrine of purgatory.

His *Pastoral Rule* (written largely for himself soon after he assumed the papacy) was designed as a guidance manual for a Western bishop on matters such as administration and preaching. It became a standard text in Western church schools afterwards. He sees the bishop above all else as a pastor of souls, a leader and expositor of the divine word of Scripture. The minister's chief task is to try to live the gospel purely, but especially to preach it effectively and allow the Word itself to reform the Lord's own church. Gregory's exegetical works also standardized the Western view of biblical exegesis as comparable to the three stages of house building: the foundations were the exposition of the literal and historical sense of the text; followed by the roof and walls of the allegorical sense, which interprets higher Christian mysteries present symbolically within the old narratives; and finally the beautiful decorations and fittings that perfect a building in the form of moral counsels designed to elevate the lives of the hearers. His insistence that a preacher should pay attention to all three aspects of a text proved determinative for the later Middle Ages. Indeed many parts of Western preaching to this day, across Catholic and Protestant churches, owe an often unconscious debt to Gregory.

His *Dialogues* were also immensely popular. In these four books Gregory recounts the lives of Italian ascetic saints. The miraculous element abounds, marking an important stage in the development of the cult of the saint at a time when, in both Byzantium and the West, the fundamental idea about how to access the divine presence and favor was undergoing radical reconstruction and experiencing local democratization. Local saints were seen as the agents of God who actually cared most for their own local people. This movement is reflected in a great increase of saints' lives (hagiographies) produced in this era. In the second book of *Dialogues* Gregory popularized Benedict, the ascetic of Nursia, but really his own favored "local saint" insofar as he had discovered Benedictinism at Rome. This high profiling of Benedict as a saintly protector of Italy in one of its most dangerous times provided an enormous impetus to the spread of Benedictine monasticism.

Gregory's spiritual writings had a similarly determinative effect on the Latin Middle Ages insofar as he strongly elevated the monastic life as the "perfect" way of contemplation, far excelling the lay married state. Well into the twentieth century it was common for Western catholicism to adopt this doctrine that monasticism was the "superior" Christian lifestyle, and marital vocations were relatively inferior. He similarly interpreted the story of Mary and Martha at Bethany (Lk 10:40-42) to mean that the contemplative life, one of reflective prayer withdrawn from the world, was innately superior to the "active" life of a Christian, even if engaged in works of mercy, since access to God in prayer for the sake of the world was the greater philanthropy. This view, propagated widely on his papal authority, gave a very strong boost to the monastic life in its formative era.

## THE CAROLINGIANS AND THE HOLY ROMAN EMPIRE

After Justinian's general, Belisarius, returned to Constantinople, the Byzantine gains of his campaign in Italy against the Visigothic kings started rapidly to unravel. He had, however, fatally wounded the Gothic ability to keep hold of the governance of Italy. Into that political vacuum had entered the Lombards, whose early and aggressive campaigns did not spare the church from any bloodshed or plunder. In 751, senior Lombard warlord Aistulf, who had declared himself king in 749, captured Ravenna, the seat of the Byzantine exarch and the alleged garrison of defensive imperial troops.[6] Having neutralized and threatened that city, he declared his intent

---

[6] He had been duke of Friuli since 744. He claimed the kingship of Lombards when his brother Ratchis abdicated and retired to a monastery. Aistulf died in a hunting accident in 756.

to march on Rome, a threat that frightened the inhabitants there enough to give him a tax tribute instead. In the same year he captured the region of Istria, driving out the last remnants of Byzantine forces. It was his immensely successful campaign that led the Roman popes to more or less give up on the idea of Italy being part of the Byzantine empire and being able to call on useful Byzantine military protection.

They looked anxiously to see where else could they call for protection. They would put their hopes in a stable and rising kingdom in the West that had shown itself to be a loyal admirer of Latin Christianity: the court of Charles Martel. From his Christian name derives the concept of the dynasty he represents, Carolingians. The most famous of their kings would be Charlemagne, or Charles the Great, Martel's grandson. The Carolingian dynasty began as overlords within the kingdom of the Franks. Pope Gregory III was the first to explicitly invite Charles Martel to intervene in Italy and take command of the chaos. This, if it had been heard in Constantinople, would have been treated as high treason. Charles, occupied with his own struggles elsewhere, refused the invitation. In 753 Pope Stephen II made a visit to Charles's son, Pepin III the Short, who had been crowned, with his papal predecessor's blessing, as king of the Franks in 751.[7] The Pope anointed Pepin as king at the abbey of Saint Denis, near Paris, and blessed his two sons, Charles and Carloman.

As an offering of thanks for the papal support of his dynasty, Pepin crossed the Alps southward in 754 (with a second campaign in 756) and defeated the Lombard king Aistulf, taking from his control the lands of Aemilia-Romagna and the Pentapolis, which the latter had seized as his center of operations, wresting them out of the control of Ravenna and the Ducatus Romanus. In 756, Pepin then restored the territory, including large parts of central Italy, not to the Byzantine emperor but to the pope. The move signaled a new era in which the rights of the emperor at Constantinople were increasingly disregarded, the Byzantine dynasty was regarded as "foreign" to Roman affairs, and the antique idea of one church, one God-appointed emperor in one coherent sacred politeia of the holy empire, was being sidelined.

And yet, even as it was being set aside (and in place of the ancient idea of one church and one dominion came the concept of separate nation-states), it was carefully being emulated and copied. Except this time, it was to be installed back in the Latin-speaking West. Kings would model themselves on the emperor in the East. He in turn would pretend (as he had done in Italy for a long time) that they were not really kings, simply his exarchs or junior caesars. The popes would be regarded, especially by

---

[7]The papal intrusion ended the Merovingian dynasty, which had been founded by Childeric (457–481). His son Clovis (481–511) extended their rule to cover all of antique Gaul. In March 752 Pope Zachary deposed the Merovingian King Childeric III. The Carolingian dynasty would replace it when Zachary's successor anointed Pepin.

themselves, as sacred princes, and the kings would mutually vie for dominance. Soon the popes themselves were in the thick of it alongside them, vying for political authority as high priest-kings superior to the ranks of lesser, "secular" monarchs, whom they believed they could install, consecrate, or even depose, by virtue of the supreme authority vested in them by their appointment from Christ via St. Peter.[8]

This break with Byzantium was of monumental import. It can rightly be called the true moment of the "Great Schism" (though that would not manifest itself until the early eleventh century), but it largely passed unnoticed at the time except as an annoyance to the rulers in Byzantium. They could not foresee the long-term separation of the halves of the church that would result from it. It also set the papacy on a course from which it would not swerve for many centuries to come: the arrogation to itself of the right to political rule as well as spiritual governance.

At this period the forgeries known as the *Donation of Constantine* gained prominence.[9] They were letters allegedly written by the fourth-century emperor Constantine purporting to give to his contemporary, Pope Sylvester, independent rights of political governance. The parallelism is obvious: the papal approval elevates priestly authority as higher and more sacred than earthly dominion. From the heavenly gift earthly authority takes its origin. Once elevated, earthly kings should support the church's mission as faithful sons in loyal obedience to the popes. In return the popes' authority validates their rightful succession and inheritance as heirs of Constantine. It is the birth of the concept of the Holy Roman Empire, but now a Christian Romanity rebuilt in the West without any sense of owing allegiance to Constantinople.

The way the popes looked at it, of course, with themselves as the undisputed top of the triangle, was not necessarily the way the earthly rulers would take up this notion of independent national sovereignty. The tension of this relationship between the nation-kings of the second millennium and the power of the papacy would be a perennially recurring problem in church history. The *Donation of Pepin* would become the basis for the papal states, over which the popes would rule as princes until these lands were taken by force into the kingdom of Italy in 1870. In 772 Pope Adrian I in turn called on Charlemagne, Pepin's son, to assist him in ridding Italy of the disruptions caused by the Lombards. Charlemagne's campaign definitively ended the dominion of the Lombards in Italy.

---

[8]See further U. R. Blumenthal, *The Investiture Controversy: Church and Monarchy from the Ninth to the Twelfth Century* (Philadelphia: University of Pennsylvania Press, 1988).

[9]One of the first times they appear cited as an authority is when Pope Hadrian wrote to Charlemagne (the son of Pepin who had made the donation of Italian lands to the papacy) in 778 to follow the example of the Emperor Constantine and make generous grants to the Roman church.

The popes were still not secure. After being attacked in the streets of Rome, Pope Leo III once more traveled over the Alps to meet Charlemagne at his court in Paderborn. The content of their discussions has not survived in any account, but a definite result was Charlemagne's state visit to Rome in 800 to secure the city for the pope. In a (now-famous) ceremony in Constantine's basilica of Saint Peter's on Christmas Day 800, Charlemagne brought his son to church to be chrismated as his legal heir.[10] As Charlemagne himself kneeled in prayer, the pope instead placed a crown on his head and declared him to be emperor of the Romans. Leo had reversed the political order. Instead of being nominated and legally validated by the emperor's decree from Constantinople, he had now claimed the right to be sacred kingmaker, even to the level of appointing a new Roman Emperor in the West. No one in the Constantinopolitan court recognized the events, but they spelled the end of the antique order. A ruler of a federated kingdom made up out of alliances of Germanic tribes, acclaimed by the popes, had become the new world order in the West. They increasingly saw Byzantium, both in its ecclesiastical order (where no single super-bishop was allowed to be above the king or the collective order of other bishops) and in its political claims (one single ruler of all the Christians, who was also the temporal administrator of church affairs outside the dogmatic realm) as "dissident."

The West's embarking on the new path meant that Byzantium came to be seen as "Greek," not Roman, and its archaic religious-political theories were reclassified (in an age where archives were very sketchily kept) as degenerated innovations. The rights of the papacy were cast back into the church's very origins, long before Constantine gave any "donation" of rights to Sylvester, and all the Byzantine emperor's claims, on the contrary, were more and regarded as doctrinally defective. The political rift of Christmas Day 800 is, in a real sense, the parting of the ways of the Eastern and Western churches. It happened as a result of the collapse of effective Byzantine rule in the West and also because of the ascending claims of the medieval papacy, but also, truth to be told, because the literate and theological classes were now no longer able to be bilingual. For centuries past they had not been able to read and communicate with each other, their traditions had moved apart in several dimensions, and they increasingly resented the number of differences they now saw to be prevalent in one another's Christian practices.

The formal establishment of a Holy Roman Empire in the West would come about in the next century. It would be the political organizing principle of the medieval European Christian world. But it is all there in the nutshell of the title Charlemagne

---

[10] Now only the columns of the old church and parts of the confession of Peter's shrine remain from Constantine's building.

adopted that Christmas Day, when, with suitable modesty, he pretended he was annoyed with the pope, who had "surprised" him by offering the imperial crown out of the blue. Having accepted it nonetheless, he would be known henceforth as "Charles, most serene augustus, God-crowned, great and pacific emperor, governing the Roman empire." Among Charlemagne's immediate policies for the church in his domains were his strong support of the papacy in Rome, the spreading of the Benedictine system in monasticism, and the encouragement of a more learned priesthood than was present in the contemporary Frankish clergy.

Charlemagne's literary adviser, Alcuin (735–804), had been trained in the archepiscopal see at York under Egbert. Between the 780s and 790s he had a high standing in the Carolingian court. He became abbot of the monastery of Tours in 796. His literary remains include many fine poems as well as doctrinal works. Alcuin's poem on the Viking attacks on Lindisfarne, *De clade Lindisfarnensis monasterii*, is the only surviving version of the events. He writes, "Never before has such terror appeared in Britain. We see the church of the holy Cuthbert, smeared with the blood of God's priests, and robbed of its ornaments." Alcuin's argument to Charlemagne that faith was an act of a free will, and religion could not be compelled, persuaded the king to remove the death penalty in 797 from those Franks who insisted on continuing pagan rites. Alcuin is described in the scholar Einhard's *Life of Charlemagne* as "the most learned man to be found in any place."[11] Alcuin is reputed to have been the source of the phrase *vox populi vox dei*, meaning that when the people make very clear their deepest feelings in ecclesiastical matters, their religious leaders need to take note of it as bearing an inspired weight.[12]

Charlemagne's palace school at Aachen was a renowned center of learning that was based on the seven liberal arts of the classical tradition and brought together the children of the nobility, but also highly intelligent youths from the lower classes. It has been seen as the first example of a large-scale interest in the education of the laity who were destined to govern. Charlemagne instituted several other schools and in so doing laid the foundations for the medieval system of education across Europe. In 787, his issuing of the "Capitulary of Baugulf" (who was abbot of the important monastery of Fulda) commanded that in each monastery there should be a concern for studying (not always a factor in earlier monastic houses). In 789 he issued another capitulary ordering that each monastery and bishop's palace should contain a school for boys, who should learn reading, chanting, grammar, and mathematics.

---

[11] Einhard or Eginhard (775–840), *Vita Caroli Magni*, chap. 25.
[12] *Vox populi vox dei* means "the voice of the people is the voice of God."

As well as Alcuin, Theodulf of Orleans was a renowned ecclesiastical scholar at the Carolingian court. Either he or Alcuin was probably responsible for the *Libri Carolini* (the *Caroline Books*), which came out under Charlemagne's name and attacked the Byzantine church both for the recent iconoclast council of 754 and for the contrary teachings of the seventh ecumenical council of 787 (then obviously not having been afforded ecumenical status in the West) for what it complained had commanded "excessive" veneration to be afforded to images. The Latin translation of the acts of Nicaea II that was used to make the refutation was highly defective, making it appear the council of 787 advocated the "adoration of icons," which was, of course, exactly what it did not teach.

Theodulf (c. 750–821) was of Visigothic descent and came from Spain at the time of the Islamic invasion to Charlemagne's court, eventually ending as bishop of Orleans. A visit to Rome convinced him of the importance of monastic schools, and he was a strong advocate throughout his life of episcopal and monastic centers of learning. Two capitularies that he issued as bishop summarize his reform charter. The first was addressed to all his priests and advocates the importance of clerical chastity, manual labor, study, and prayer.[13] The second was a charter for penitential reform.[14] It lists a variety of sins—murder, incest, false witness, fornication—and discusses how they can be dealt with in the confessional. It raises a warning against clergy who commit adultery in secret or who live openly in a sexual relationship. He has seventy-nine poems surviving in his *opera*.[15] The Latin hymn "Gloria laus et honor," which is commonly sung even today—"All glory, laud, and honour, To Thee, Redeemer, King; To whom the lips of children, Made sweet hosannas ring"—is perhaps Theodulf's most famous writing.[16]

His treatise *De Spiritu sancto* is one of the first Latin defenses of the *filioque*, the double procession of the Spirit from Father and Son. As was the case with the *Libri Carolini*, the underlying agenda of these attacks on Eastern Christian theology was to enhance Charlemagne's right to the title he had assumed as the sole Roman emperor (he denied the legitimacy of Empress Irene, who had assumed rule at Constantinople) who had the defense of the Orthodoxy of the church in his remit.

Theodulf built a palace complex of his own in France, which was inspired by the Carolingian court at Aachen. Today there survives from his Gallo-Roman villa the splendid private chapel, or Oratory, which is at Germigny-des-Prés, which he built in 806. It has a fine ninth-century apsidal mosaic of the making of the covenant. Other

---

[13]*Capitula ad presbyteros parochiae.*
[14]*Capitula altera Theodulpho episcopo Aurelianensi adscripta.*
[15]Works in PL 77, 1309-1432.
[16]J. M. Neale's translation.

renowned Carolingian church scholars in this bright period of intellectual renaissance included Rabanus Maurus (c. 780–856), Einhard the historian (c. 775–840), Paulinus of Aquileia (726–802) the "apostle of the Slovenes," Adalhard of Corbie (c. 751–827), Benedict of Aniane (747–821), and the poet and eucharistic theologian Abbot Paschasius Radbertus (785–865).[17]

Rabanus (or Hrabanus) was perhaps the most prolific of the group of Carolingian theologians. He was given his nickname of Maurus by his teacher Alcuin, in honor of Saint Benedict's most beloved disciple, St. Maur.[18] His own numerous works later won him the title *praeceptor Germaniae* or "teacher of all Germany." He spent much of his life in the Frankish monastery of Fulda by the Rhine. Like Alcuin, Rabanus had a deep knowledge of the earlier church fathers and worked out of them as sources. He was a monk at the Benedictine Fulda monastery until elected abbot there in 822. There he stayed for the next twenty-five years also, until he was elected archbishop of Mainz, where he died nine years later.

One of his most famed poetic pieces is the "Praises of the Holy Cross" (*de laudibus sanctae crucis*), written probably at the Fulda monastery around 800. It is oen of the finest of all examples of the ancient genres of figured poem (*carmina figurata*), made up of twenty-eight separate poetic parts set out like a grid on which scribes pictured relevant images or geometric figures in a very complex and sophisticated manuscript style. Rabanus is also known for his manual of clerical formation (*de institutione clericorum*), which lays out a basic seminary program and describes the various orders, offices, types of sacraments, and vestments to be worn. His other works included a *Commentary on Matthew's Gospel* and a table of how to compute the date of Easter (*De computo*), as well as a treatise on the soul (*Tractatus de anima*), one on the nature of the priesthood (*De sacerdote*), and a collection of specimen sermons (*Homiliae*). The most famous work of all, however, was his treatise *On the Nature of Things* (*De rerum naturis*), which is an encyclopedia designed to aid Bible commentators in regard to natural phenomena that they might discover when reading the Scriptures. In the 820s he entered a period of controversy with the monk Gottschalk, who had advanced a strong defense of predestinationism, and wrote a refutation of the latter's condemnation of the practice of admitting young children

---

[17]Benedict of Aniane was the first Latin theologian to clarify what would soon become the Latin eucharistic doctrine of transubstantiation, or the method of the "real presence" of Christ in the sacrament. In his treatise *On the Body and Blood of the Lord*, written for his disciple Placidus of the monastery of New Corbie in 831, later reedited for Charles the Bald as a Christmas gift in 844, he argues that "the substance of bread and wine is effectually changed (*efficaciter interius commutatur*) into the flesh and blood of Christ." See further R. McKitterick, *The Frankish Church and the Carolingian Reforms 789–895* (London: Royal Historical Society, 1977).

[18]Rabanus studied with Alcuin at Tours between circa 796 and 803.

to the Benedictine monasteries as oblates (*de oblatione puerorum*), who would be educated for a future life as monks.[19]

## THE MEDIEVAL PAPACY

It is remarkable to see in the larger context of the social collapses that marked the aftermath of the Justinianic war against the Gothic kings of Italy how the papacy emerged as one of the few governance institutions in the Roman West that retained any credibility. At the very time that the papacy was in its lowest point, politically speaking, it rose up to a phenomenally important new prominence in seizing the political and religious initiative out of the hands of Constantinople. From earliest Christian times, as demonstrated perhaps even as early as Pope Victor in the second century, who wrote to exercise some governing control over the observance of Pascha in the Asia Minor Quartodecimans churches, Rome had long expected to exercise an office of ecclesial jurisdiction "of some sort" over all Christian churches. What that sort of jurisdiction was, how extensive it might be considered to be, was, of course, an issue for both the Western churches and those of the East, and after the expansion of papal claims in the aftermath of Pope Damasus's rule, in the later fourth century, the development of the office and role of papacy became a much more important thing than it had been in the primitive church (which is not to say it was negligible then). With its importance came an expansion of its claims, and with that there followed, hand in glove, increasing controversy over the nature of the centralizing office it exercised with such remarkable but not unresisted success.

To begin with, to put it simply, Rome's ecclesial prominence in the first three Christian centuries was related to two primary issues. The first was that it was the capital of the Roman world. Like global cities such as New York and London today, it had served as a magnet to attract to itself all the exceptional talent of the far-flung empire. The courts of Rome were world renowned, and much of the papacy's earliest prestige and significance among Christians was provided by the manner in which it served as a court of appeal: What was best in international practice? What was acceptable polity in terms of local governance conflicts? Rome was the undisputed center of ecclesial life in the West, even though in the earliest centuries other great Christian cities, such as Milan, Trier, or Poitiers, had their zones of influence, too. But it was largely, as a bishop among bishops, who was a bishop of the more important city, that the popes had standing on the wider platforms.

---

[19]Hincmar of Rheims would commission John Scotus Eriugena to refute Gottschalk concerning predestination, but the latter's own work drew criticism from the German bishops.

The second factor, which grew in stature as time went on, was that the pope presided over a church that had a very large number of martyr shrines. The heavy toll of deaths in times of persecution at Rome was remarked on worldwide. These were martyrs who were often famous figures, not simply local farmers or laborers. Towering over them all were the shrines of Peter and Paul, which attracted pilgrims at an early date. Christ's promise to Peter, "I will give you the keys of the kingdom of heaven," and that he would be the rock (*petros*) on which the church would be built (Mt 16:18-19), although, (ironically) textually fashioned in the Gospel of Matthew to be a claim for the church of Antioch to have precedence (where Peter was first claimed as bishop), was soon claimed by Rome to be transmissible to the incumbent bishops of the Italian capital. Here was where Peter died, in the Neronian circus on the Vatican Hill, here was where he was buried, and here was where Constantine built over the graveyard his basilical church of St. Peter's "confession," or martyr shrine.

Roman bishops after Damasus began to call themselves the "vicars of St. Peter" in a particular way. They developed the *theologoumenon* peculiar to Rome, but thereafter exported to the larger West as Rome developed its governance of missions to the further Western horizons, that the bishops of Rome were not really inhabiting the throne of episcopal governance in their city, simply "holding it" as locum tenentes on behalf of the real bishop of the church, who was Peter, still mystically alive in their midst and indwelling his martyr's shrine as a living spiritual presence. The present pope of any period, on the basis of this theory, was really Peter, and enjoyed that authority that Christ had personally given to Peter as an extension of his own unique level of authority over the church. This theology of the Petrine Vicariate thus departed, after the fourth century, from the earlier idea of the Roman bishops being the adjudicators in the last court of appeal into becoming an implicit claim that Christ's personal authority as Lord over the church was inheritable, by a bishop who stood out from all others as uniquely privileged in jurisdictional terms.

Damasus, in the latter part of the fourth century, laid down an architecture of the developed papal theory that his successors built on in a strong local tradition that increasingly extended out into the increasing number of "daughter" Western mission churches. The unique position of Rome as the solitary "great and ancient see" in all the Western territories gave to the papacy an increasingly magnetic force as the Byzantine imperial structures faltered in the time of the great migrations. Damasus's immediate successor, Siricius, was the first to define the papacy's essential claim (distinct, that is, from the mystical idea of the "Petrine presence"), which was "an office of oversight over all the churches" (*solicitudo omnium ecclesiarum*). But it was Popes Leo (r. 440–461) and Gregory the Great (r. 590–604) who were subsequently the chief continuators and developers of the theory of papacy and passed it on to the later medieval popes, who made significant final changes to the claim for jurisdictional oversight it now contained—altering the claim to be the vicars of Saint Peter into a title that has lasted into the present, elevating their office to be no less than the earthly "vicars of Christ."

As the papal claims advanced, from the seventh century onward, so too did the Eastern church's answer to them. From the early fourth century, as evidenced in the collective decision of the Council of Nicaea to regard state divisions of governance (*imperial dioceses*) to be the systems that ought to be paralleled in the administration of churches, the opinion grew in the East that cities should have ecclesial dominance, according to their size and political weight, but not necessarily jurisdictional rights over another church. The idea can be seen in the canons of Chalcedon relating to the primatial role of Constantinople in the East, which it means to parallel that of Rome for the West, defining both roles as regional-primatial. This dominance for ease of governance was generally thought to be best expressed by having the bishop of the large imperial city as the head of the local synod of regional hierarchs. Such an incumbent would be the president of the synodical assembly and would have administrative rights. But always the collective decision of the synod would remain the ultimately higher authority.

This was why, in the East, nothing like the papal Petrine theory ever developed, even in regard to great sees such as Antioch, Alexandria, or Constantinople. The synodal and patriarchal system would not permit it. Claims such as Rome advanced, that it derived its refined apostolicity from Peter in person, were matched by the Eastern church's argument that apostolicity was attributed to any see of a bishop who manifested authentic fidelity to apostolic doctrine, as determined by the church's tradition and secured by its synodical episcopal collegiality. In this way apostolicity was ensured and supervised by the entire college of bishops, not by any single one. The Eastern churches, therefore, came to regard the papal claims as either purely honorific, a matter of local tradition (a *theologoumenon* that might have some force in the local area of its origins but not elsewhere) or as simply irrelevant. In later centuries, after long ages of effective separation of the Greek and Latin churches, the papacy, which had energetically developed its sense of particular jurisdictional charism in the meantime, emerged no longer as a symbol of unity for the churches but as a special point of contention and division over varying ways to interpret apostolicity.

In its later iterations, papal theory argued that since apostolicity was ensured by communion with Peter's see, then if communion with that see was broken, the apostolicity of all those who were not in communion with Rome was lost. By this stage the Eastern churches regarded the theory (as Rome had long been explicitly arguing) as no longer a harmless *theologoumenon* but rather a serious doctrinal claim: one, however, that they regarded as warping the concept of how apostolicity is secured in the church—communally, not monarchically. Because of this the Eastern church began to list the papal claims as one more instance of the West's departure from classical patristic tradition. By the late Middle Ages several Byzantine theologians were coming to regard the Latin *filioque* doctrine and claims of papal primacy as instances of heresy, and retrospectively attributing to them the causes of the separation of the churches.

With the loss of Christian Alexandria, Antioch, and Jerusalem to the forces of Islam, Constantinople began to emerge as the Eastern equivalent of a magnetic center of church life: the center from which all liturgical developments and organizational innovations would flow. After 1453, when the Ottoman armies captured the imperial city itself, this ecclesiastical centralism around Constantinople actually increased, as the sultans made the patriarchs the surviving agents (*ethnarchs*) of dealing with subjected Christian peoples of all kinds within their dominions. But always the older models of synodical government and communion of the college of bishops prevented the rise of a parallel "papal" theory in the Orthodox East.

Although the papacy received immense support from the Carolingian dynasty, the closeness of such a powerful set of kings, which had given to the papacy lands, gold, and political protections, also caused deep unrest. The sacral claims of the Carolingians were bent on matching those of the Byzantine emperors they emulated at the same time as despising them. But a new form of Byzantine sacral emperor was not at all to the liking of the Roman pontiffs, who saw in this development a challenge to their own central authority as lawmakers of the church and even kingmakers. It is in this context of tension that the *Pseudo-Isidorean Decretals* first appeared, sometime between 833 and 857. The documents were fathered onto Isidore of Seville (c. 560–636), who then had a high reputation as an authoritative Latin father of the church but also the utility of someone whose works were not all that closely read. Around his alleged authorship a dossier of texts was gathered, some of them specially written for the occasion, others recording the lives of earlier Roman bishops, all collated to demonstrate the thesis that the papal authority was of antique foundation and could not be challenged by laymen, even if they were kings. No lay voice could interfere in the priestly regulation of the churches, which had been handed over to Peter's successor.

Pope Nicholas I (858–867) is the first known to use the *Decretals* to bolster his case against John the archbishop of Ravenna. He had summoned the latter to Rome to stand trial for corruption, but John had denied his authority to act. After holding a synod in Rome to depose John, much controversy was stirred up against Nicholas's actions. Famed scholar-bishop Hincmar of Rheims (806–882) had himself deposed a bishop in his own provincial synodic area of governance. The deposed cleric appealed to Rome, and once more Nicholas appealed to the *Decretals* to make out a case for superior jurisdiction in all ecclesiastical courts. He reversed Hincmar's decision and instituted the process for the first time that provincial synodical decisions could be sidestepped. Hincmar himself expressed doubts as to the historical legitimacy of this dossier but was a good enough canon lawyer to make use of it to bolster some of his own arguments about clerical authority. On the basis of the *Decretals* all bishops in the Latin church were now encouraged to appeal directly to Rome. In thus weakening the power of provincial archbishops, the authority of the papacy was greatly enhanced. Nicholas's extension of papal rights brought the Roman see into intense conflict with Constantinople, especially in the time of the patriarchate of Photius.

If Nicholas extended the reputation of the papacy in the ninth century, however, then several incumbents of the tenth century brought it into disrepute. When Sergius III became pope in 904, it was with the collusion of Count Theophylact of Tusculum, who was the military commander of the Roman region. Popes now were looked on as great political lords as well as church leaders. Theophylact's young daughter, Marozia, became the pope's mistress and bore him a son. After Sergius's death in 911, she remained a power to contend with and, in 927, she arrested Pope John IX (914–928) and put out his eyes in prison, where he died soon after. Marozia governed the elections of the next three popes, one of which was her own son by Pope Sergius, who reigned as John XI (931–935). After she arranged the assassination of her husband in 932, her son Alberic overthrew her and assumed the dominion of Italy between 932 and 954. The Roman senate was persuaded to appoint Alberic's son as Pope John XII in 955. His reputation as a debauchee included accusations of the selective rape of female pilgrims to the shrine of Peter. The holding of the papal office for several generations at this period passed from one Italian noble family to another, reducing the status of the office in their wrangling. The Tusculum and the Crescenti clans in the eleventh century held the papacy between them from 1003 to 1045. To have laid such a weight of jurisdictionally centralized theory on one ecclesiastical office, and then to have reduced it to an early medieval Italian princely court, commenced a sad era of decline, which in some ways prefigured the corruptions of the Renaissance papal courts preceding the Reformation.

At the same period the fortunes of the Eastern empire were suffering. A long and slow decline of military stability came to a climactic head on August 26, 1071, at the battle of Manzikert, when Seljuk Islamic forces, led by Alp Arslan, crushed a fully mounted imperial Roman army in the field and captured Emperor Romanus IV Diogenes. It was a humiliating and degrading defeat that broke a major gateway of the Byzantine borders and allowed the Turkish people to settle in eastern imperial territories. By 1080 the Turkish tribes occupied thirty thousand square miles in Anatolia, the old heartland of the empire. From there they could never be dislodged, and it was from that moment on a story of the gradual erosion of territory to Byzantium, until the ancient borders shrank back and back to the point of nonsustainability in a few centuries to come. The whole period, in both East and West, was one of tension, new beginnings, and premonitions of antique endings.

## A SHORT READER

**Rule of St. Benedict 5, On Obedience.** The first step of humility is quick and ready obedience. This is the special virtue of those who hold nothing more dear than Christ; who, because of the holy ministry they have professed, and the fear of hell, and the glory of life everlasting, as soon as anything has been ordered by the abbot take it as a command of God himself and cannot bear any delay in executing it. It is of these the Lord speaks: "As soon as he heard, he obeyed me" (Ps 17:45). And again, he says to those who instruct: "Whoever hears you, hears me" (Lk 10:16). These are the ones who immediately leave off their own affairs and abandon their own will, and stop the work they were engaged on, even leaving it unfinished, with the alacrity of obedience, to follow up with action the voice of the one who commands. And so, it is as if at the same moment the master's command is given the disciple's work is completed, both things being speedily accomplished at the same time in the readiness of the fear of God by those who are motivated from the desire of attaining life everlasting. That desire is their spur for choosing the narrow way, of which the Lord speaks, "Narrow is the way that leads to life" (Mt 7:14). Thus they do not live according to their own choice, nor do they obey their own desires and pleasures, but rather they walk by the judgment and command of another, and they dwell in monasteries and desire to have an abbot over them. In truth, the likes of these fulfill that saying of the Lord in which he says, "I have come not to do my own will, but the will of him who sent me" (Jn 6:38). Even so, this very obedience will be acceptable to God, and pleasing to all, only if that which is commanded is obeyed without hesitation, or delay, or vacillation, grumbling, or protests. For the obedience given to superiors is given to God, since he himself has said, "He who hears you, hears me" (Lk 10:16). And disciples should offer their obedience with a good will, because "God loves a cheerful giver" (2 Cor 9:7). For if a disciple obeys ungraciously and grumbles, not even with his lips but simply in his heart, then even though he may fulfill the command, even so his work will not be acceptable to God, who can sees that his heart is grumbling. And far from gaining a reward for such work, the disciple will incur the punishment due to grumblers, unless he should make satisfactory amends.

**Rule of St. Benedict *33, Should Monks Own Anything of Their Own?*** We must cut out this vice from the monastery above all others and by the roots. Let no one presume to give or receive anything without the abbot's permission, and let no one possess anything as his own, nothing whatsoever; whether book or tablets or pen or whatever else it might be, because monks are not allowed to have even their own bodies or their wills at their disposal. So, for all things that are needful, let them look to the father of the monastery. And let it be unlawful to have anything that the abbot has not given or permitted. Let all things be common to all, as it is written (Acts 4:32), and let no one ever assume or call anything as his own. So, if anyone is caught indulging in this most wicked vice, let him be admonished once and even a second time, but if he fails to improve let him undergo punishment.

**Rule of St. Benedict *73, That the Full Observance of Justice Is Not Established in This Rule.*** We have composed this rule so that by its observance in monasteries we may show that we have attained some degree of virtue and the rudiments of the religious life. But for those who would hasten to the perfection of that life, there exist the teachings of the holy Fathers, for by observing these we are led to the heights of perfection. What page or what saying is there of the God-inspired books of the Old and New Testaments that is not an infallible rule for human life? Or what book of the holy catholic Fathers does not loudly proclaim the way we can come by the royal road to our Creator? Then there are also the *Conferences* and the *Institutes* [of John Cassian], and [Pope Gregory the Great's] *Lives of the Fathers*, as also the rule of our holy Father Basil [of Caesarea]. And what else are they all but tools of virtue for observant and obedient monks? Nevertheless, for us who are lazy and disreputable and negligent, such things are a source of shame and confusion. And so, whoever you may be who wish to hurry on your way to the heavenly homeland, observe this little rule, with the help of Christ, which I have written for beginners. Because then, with God's protection, you will attain to the greater heights of teaching and virtue that we have mentioned above.

**St. Gregory the Great,** The Pastoral Rule 1, *That the Unqualified Ought Not to Seek an Office of Authority.* No one would ever presume to teach an art, if he had not first set out to learn it with careful attentiveness. Accordingly, how rash it is for those who are not skilled to assume a pastoral authority, because the government of souls is the art of all arts. We know that the wounds of people's souls are more complex than the wounds of their bodies, and yet how often do those who have no knowledge at all of spiritual precepts recklessly profess themselves to be physicians of the heart, while those who had no knowledge of the various effects of drugs would blush to set themselves up as worldly doctors. But now, because by God's providence the great nobles of this present age are inclined to hold religion in reverence, there are some who look for the glory of distinction by means of the trappings of dominion in the holy church. Such people long to appear as teachers, they long to be in positions of power over others, and, as the Truth himself attests, they look for the first greetings in the marketplace, the first places at feasts, the first seats in the assemblies (Mt 23:6-7), while all the time they cannot properly administer the office of pastoral care they have abrogated to themselves, because they have attained the position of teachers of humility from a motive of self-aggrandizement only. In a teaching position, language itself is confounded when one thing is learned while another is being taught. Against these the Lord complains by means of the prophet, when he says: "They have reigned, but not by me; they have been set up as princes, though I knew it not" (Hos 8:4). For such people assume rule of their own will and not by the will of our supreme Lord. Without the benefit of virtues and never having been called, but rather inflamed by their own cupidity, they seize rather than attain supreme rule.

**St. Gregory the Great,** The Dialogues *32, On the Death of a Courtier Whose Grave Burned with Fire.* Maximianus, Bishop of Syracuse, a man who led a holy life, and who for a long time in this very city [Rome] had the government of my own monastery, several times told me this dreadful story. It happened in the province of Valeria. A certain courtier, at the vigil of Pascha, stood as godfather to a young woman, who, after the fast was ended, returned home to his house. There, having drunk more wine than he should, he desired that his goddaughter would stay with him. And that night, horrible though it is to speak of, he caused her utter ruin. In the morning, he got up and went to the bath with a guilty conscience, as if the waters of that place could have washed away the filthiness of his sin. Even so, he went and washed himself. Then he began to worry in himself, whether he should go to church or not. He was afraid on one side what men would think of him if he did not attend so great a festival; but on the other hand he trembled to think of God's just judgment. In the end his shame before the world overcame him, and so he took himself off to church. There he stayed with great awe and dread, fearing all the time in case he might be handed over to the devil and tormented in the sight of all the people. All through that solemn mass, he shook greatly in his fear, but even so he escaped all punishment and so came home joyfully from church. The next day he came to church without any fear whatsoever; and so for the rest of the octave's observances he went on quite happily thinking to himself that either God had not seen his abominable sin or else that he had mercifully pardoned the same. Yet, on the seventh day, by sudden death he was taken out of this world, and he was buried. And for a long time afterward, in the sight of the whole town, a flame of fire issued forth from his grave, which burnt his bones for a long time, until it consumed the very grave itself, so that the earth, which was raised up in a little mound, appeared sunken lower than the rest of the ground. By this fact almighty God declared what fate this man's soul suffered in the other world, when even a flaming fire consumed his dead body in this world. And so he leaves to us a fearful example, and we can learn from it what the living and sensible soul will suffer for sins committed, when even the material bones were burnt to nothing by such a punishment of fire.

**St. Gregory the Great, Moralia on Job, epistolary preface.3.** It should be known that there are some parts [in the Job commentary] that we will go through in a historical exposition, some we will trace out allegorically in an investigation of the typological meaning, and some where we open up lessons of moral teaching alone, allegorically conveyed. But there are some passages where we need more particular care to search out how, using all these different ways together, we can explore them in a threefold method. First of all, we will lay historical foundations; then, by pursuing the typological sense, we will erect a structure of the mind that will be a stronghold of faith; and then, as our last step, by the grace of moral instruction, as it were, we shall drape the entire building with a final coat of color. For how else are the dogmas of truth to be reckoned, except as food that refreshes the mind? If we treat them all, using alternate applications of different methods, we shall serve up a menu of instruction that will prevent any satiety in the reader, whom we have invited in as our guest. And he will be invited to consider all the things laid before him, and take for himself whatever he takes to be the most appetizing. And yet, we ought not to neglect to make clear the plain sense of the historical message, so as not to take too long in coming to the hidden senses, for often these cannot be understood according to the letter for, when taken superficially, they offer no manner of teaching to the reader but only engender error. In one place, for example, it is said: "Under whom they are bent who bear the world?" [Job 9:13]. Now, in the case of this great writer we must realize that he certainly does not follow the empty fictions of the poets, so as to imagine that the weight of the world is supported by the labor of the giant [Atlas]. In another place, again, under the pressure of great woes Job exclaims: "My soul prefers strangulation and death rather than life" [Job 7:15]. But what man in his right senses would believe that such a praiseworthy individual, whom we know received from that great Judge of all the reward of his patience, had decided in the midst of his sufferings to end his life by hanging himself? So evidently, sometimes even the very literal words forbid us to think they ought to be interpreted according to their literal sense.

***Einhard,*** **Life of Charlemagne 28.** When Charlemagne made his final journey to Rome, he also had other ends in view. The Romans had inflicted many injuries on the Pontiff Leo, tearing out his eyes and cutting out his tongue, so that he had been compelled to call on the King for help. Accordingly, Charles went to Rome, to set the affairs of the church in order, which were then in great confusion, and he passed the whole winter there. It was then that he received the titles of emperor and augustus, to which at first he had so great an aversion that he declared that he would never have set foot in the church on the day that they were conferred, even though it was a great feast day, if he knew in advance what the pope intended to do. He bore very patiently with the jealousy that the Roman emperors showed on his assumption of these titles, for on their part they took this step very badly; and in the course of frequent embassies and letters, in which he addressed them as brothers, he made their haughtiness yield to his magnanimity, a quality in which he was unquestionably much their superior.

***Alcuin,*** **Letter to Bishop Higbald of Lindisfarne.** To Bishop Higbald and the whole community of the church of Lindisfarne, good sons in Christ of a most blessed father, the holy Bishop Cuthbert, Alcuin, a deacon, sends you greeting and blessing in Christ. When I was with you, your loving friendship gave me great joy. Now that I am away, your tragic sufferings daily bring me sorrow, for the pagan [Vikings] have desecrated God's sanctuary, shed the blood of saints around the altar, laid waste the house of our hope, and trampled the bodies of the saints like filth in the streets. I can only cry from my heart before the altar of Christ: "O Lord, spare your people and do not give your inheritance over to the Gentiles, lest the heathen say, Where is the God of the Christians? What assurance can the churches of Britain have, if Saint Cuthbert and so great a company of saints do not defend their own? Is this the beginning of the great suffering, or the result of the sins of those who live there? It has not happened by chance but is the sign of some great guilt." But you who survive, stand like men, fight bravely, and defend the camp of God. Remember how Judas Maccabaeus cleansed the temple and freed the people from a foreign yoke. If anything needs correction in your way of gentleness, correct it quickly. Call back your saintly patrons who left you for a season. It was not that they lacked influence with God, but they were surely silent. We cannot tell why. Do not glory in the vanity of dress, for that is cause for shame rather than pride in priests and servants of God. Do not blur the words of your prayers in drunkenness. Do not seek after the indulgences of the flesh or the cupidity of the world, but rather stand firm in the service of God and the discipline of the monastic life, so that the holy Fathers, whose sons you are, may not cease to protect you. May you remain safe through their prayers, as you surely walk in their footsteps. Do not be degenerate sons, having such fathers as these. They will not cease protecting you, if they see that you are following their example. So do not be dismayed by this disaster. God chastises every son whom he finds acceptable, and perhaps he has chastised you more because he loves you more. Jerusalem, a city that was loved by God, was destroyed, along with the temple of God, in Babylonian flames. Rome, too, surrounded by its company of holy apostles and countless martyrs, was devastated by the heathen, but it quickly recovered through the goodness of God. Almost the whole of Europe has been laid bare with fire and sword by Goths and Huns, but now by God's mercy it is again as bright as ever with churches as the sky is with stars, and in them the offices of the Christian religion grow and flourish. So encourage each other, saying, "Let us return to the Lord our God, for he is very forgiving and never deserts those who hope in him." And you, holy father Higbald, leader of God's people, shepherd of a holy flock, physician of souls, flame set on a lampstand, be a model of all goodness to all who can see you, and a herald of salvation to all who hear you. May your community be of exemplary character, so as to bring others to life, not to damnation. Let your meals be sober, not drunken. Let your clothes befit your station. Do not copy the men of the world in vanity, for vain dress and useless adornment are a reproach to you before men and a sin before God. It is better to dress your immortal soul in good ways than to deck out with fine clothes that body that soon rots into dust. Clothe and feed Christ in the poor, that by so doing you may reign along with Christ. Redemption is a man's true wealth. If we loved gold we should send it to heaven to be kept safe there for us. We have what we love: let us love the eternal, which will not perish. Let us love true riches, not the transitory type. Let us win the praise of God, not of man. Let us imitate those saints whom we praise. Let us follow in their footsteps on earth, so as to be found worthy to share their glory in heaven. May divine goodness keep you from all adversity and bring you, dear brothers, to the glory of the heavenly kingdom with your fathers. When our lord the King Charles returns from defeating his enemies, by God's mercy, I plan to go to him, and then if I can do anything for you about the boys who have been carried off by the pagans as prisoners, or about any other of your needs, I shall make every effort to see that it is done. Fare well, beloved in Christ, and be ever strengthened in doing good.

**Alcuin's poem on the Nightingale ("De Luscinia").**

> Whoever stole you from me, from that bush of yellow broom,
> My little nightingale, was envious of my happiness,
> For oft you lifted my sad heart up from its sorrow
> And drowned my soul in streams of melody.
> And I wanted all the other birds to come,
> And join with me in singing out your melancholy tune.
> How dull you were in coloring,
> But never dull in song.
> In your tiny throat, what depths of harmony,
> All through the gathering night, never ceasing your music,
> Ever singing to your Creator;
> Worshiping him through your little voice,
> So beautiful and gracious.
> No wonder that the Cherubim and Seraphim
> With resounding chorus
> Continually offer praise to Him,
> When to such a tiny bird
> So great a grace was given?
> *Carmina Alcuini.*[20]

---

[20]H. Waddell, *Medieval Latin Lyrics* (London: Constable, 1929), 88 (slightly altered).

***Paschasius Radbertus,*** **On the Body and Blood of Our Lord *1.2; 4.1-2.*** It is plain, therefore, that nothing is beyond the will of God or contrary to it; rather, that all things are subject to him. So no one ought to be disturbed about the body and blood of Christ, in that in this mystery there is real flesh and real blood if God the Creator has so willed there to be. And because it is his will, although the figure of bread and wine remain, nevertheless these are only a figure. After the consecration we must believe that there is nothing else there than the flesh and blood of Christ . . . and if I may speak more in tune with the wonder of it, this is indeed no other body than that which was born of Mary, which suffered on the cross, and rose from the tomb. . . . Since it is not fitting that Christ should be torn by our teeth, he has willed that in this mystery the bread and wine are potentially created his true flesh and blood by the consecration of the Holy Spirit. And in so being created they are mystically sacrificed each day for the life of the world so that, just as his real flesh was created from the Virgin without any paternal generation but from the operation of the Holy Spirit, so too by the operation of the same Spirit, the same body and blood of Christ are mystically consecrated from the substance of bread and wine. So what is it that men eat? Well, we can see that all men, without qualification, receive the sacraments of the altar regularly. Clearly they so receive: but one spiritually eats the flesh of Christ and drinks his blood, while another certainly does not, even though he can be seen to receive the morsel from the priest . . . even so, he does not eat and drink the flesh and blood to any benefit to himself, for rather he takes it to his judgment, even if he appears to take the sacrament of the altar alongside all the others. The virtue of the sacrament is withdrawn in his case, and what is more the judgment on his guilt is made all the more heavy on account of his presumption.[21]

***Paschasius Radbertus,*** **Letter to Frudegard.** When [Christ] broke the bread and gave it to them, he did not say: "This is," or "There is in this mystery a kind of figure or virtue of my body." No, he said plainly enough: "This is my body." And so it is a matter of what he himself said, not what someone else pretends to be the case. . . . This is why I am amazed that there are now some[22] who wish to argue that there is not the reality of the flesh and blood of Christ in the sacrament, but rather a kind of virtue of the flesh, not the flesh itself, a virtue of the blood, not the blood itself; that is, a figure rather than a reality; a shadow more than a body.[23]

---

[21] PL 120.1267.
[22] His contemporary, Ratramnus of Corbie. See O. M. Phelan, "Horizontal and Vertical Theologies: 'Sacraments' in the Works of Paschasius Radbertus and Ratramnus of Corbie," *Harvard Theological Review* 103, no. 3 (2010): 271-89.
[23] PL 120.1357.

## FURTHER READING

### Benedict and Benedictinism
Chapman, J. *St. Benedict and the Sixth Century*. London: Greenwood, 1929. Reprint, 1971.

Elder, R., ed. *Benedictus: Studies in Honor of St. Benedict of Nurcia*. Kalamazoo, MI: Cistercian Publications, 1981.

Fry, T., et al. *The Rule of St. Benedict in Latin and English with Notes*. Collegeville, MN: Liturgical Press, 1981.

Kardong, T. G. *Benedict's Rule: A Translation and Commentary*. Collegeville, MN: Liturgical Press, 1996.

———. *The Life of Saint Benedict by Gregory the Great: Translation and Commentary*. Collegeville, MN: Liturgical Press, 2009.

Lindsay, T. F. *St. Benedict: His Life and Work*. London: Burns and Oates, 1949.

Matt, L. von., and S. Hilpisch. *Saint Benedict*. Chicago: H. Regnery, 1961.

McCann, J. *The Rule of St. Benedict*. London: Burns, Oates, and Washbourne, 1952.

Vogüé, A. de. *Reading Saint Benedict: Reflections on the Rule*. Translated by Colette Friedlander. Kalamazoo, MI: Cistercian Publications, 1994.

### Gregory the Great and His Successors
Dudden, F. H. *Gregory the Great*. 2 vols. London: Longmans, Green, 1905.

Evans, G. *The Thought of Gregory the Great*. Cambridge: Cambridge University Press, 1986.

Kelly, J. N. D. *The Oxford Dictionary of the Popes*. Oxford: Oxford University Press, 1986.

Markus, R. A. *From Augustine to Gregory the Great*. London: Variorum Reprints, 1983.

Richards, J. *Consul of God: The Life and Times of Gregory the Great*. London: Routledge and Kegan Paul, 1980.

Straw, C. *Gregory the Great: Perfection in Imperfection*. Berkeley: University of California Press, 1988.

Tillard, J. M. R. *The Bishop of Rome*. London: SPCK, 1983.

Ullmann, W. "Leo 1 and the Theme of Papal Primacy." *JTS* 11 (1960): 25-51.

### The Carolingian Scholars
Appleby, D. "Beautiful on the Cross, Beautiful in His Torments: The Place of the Body in the Thought of Paschasius Radbertus." *Traditio: Studies in Ancient and Medieval History, Thought, and Religion* 60 (2005): 1-46.

Archibald, L. "Latin Writing in the Frankish World: 700–1100." In *German Literature of the Early Middle Ages*, ed. B. Murdoch, 73-85. Rochester, NY: Camden House, 2004.

Blumenthal, U. R. *The Investiture Controversy: Church and Monarchy from the Ninth to the Twelfth Century*. Philadelphia: University of Pennsylvania Press, 1988.

Chazelle, C. "Figure, Character, and the Glorified Body in the Carolingian Eucharistic Controversy." *Traditio: Studies in Ancient and Medieval History, Thought, and Religion* 47 (1992): 1-36.

Contreni, J. G. "The Carolingian Renaissance." In *Renaissances Before the Renaissance: Cultural Revivals of Late Antiquity and the Middle Ages*, ed. W. T. Treadgold, 59-68. Stanford, CA: Stanford University Press, 1984.

Kottje, R., and H. Zimmermann. *Hrabanus Maurus: Lehrer, Abt, und Bischof.* Mainz: Steiner, 1982.

Matter, A. E. "The *Lamentations Commentaries* of Hrabanus Maurus and Paschasius Radbertus." *Traditio: Studies in Ancient and Medieval History, Thought, and Religion* 38 (1982): 137-63.

Phelan, O. M. "Horizontal and Vertical Theologies: 'Sacraments' in the Works of Paschasius Radbertus and Ratramnus of Corbie." *Harvard Theological Review* 103, no. 3 (2010): 271-89.

Waddell, H. *Medieval Latin Lyrics*. London: Constable, 1929.

# THE FORMATION OF CHRISTIAN LITURGY

## EARLIEST ORIGINS OF LITURGY

The word *liturgy* derives from the pre-Christian Greek term *leitourgia*, meaning "public works," which could connote civic good deeds, political service, or the formal recognition of a patronal divinity's benefactions to a town. The word had already been adopted into biblical usage by the Septuagint translators of the Bible, to designate the (civic) worship of God in the Hebraic state cult, the sacrificial and prayer rituals of the temple in particular. Thus from here it made its appearance in the New Testament writings, where it is somewhat "spiritualized," no longer referring to animal sacrifices but more especially being used to connote the sense of the service of Christ (Heb 8:6) or of Christians one for another (Phil 3:20), or the ministry of church leaders (Acts 3:12; cf. Didache 15.1), or the heavenly and spiritual worship of praise conducted by the angels (Heb 1:14).

Pope Clement of Rome, at the end of the first century, was the first patristic writer to use the term as a marked contrast to the cultic practices of the Old Testament, arguing that now with the worship services that characterize the church only spiritual praise is offered.[1] Third-century Roman theologian Hippolytus defined a Christian minister as one who has been ordained for the service of the church's *leitourgia*, and it was this meaning, liturgy as public Christian worship, that soon gained the predominance. The Latin equivalents of the word were *ministry* (that is, "service"), or *divine office* (*ministerium, officium, munus*). Only in much later times did the Latin church adopt the Greek form of the word once more.

To this day Latin church usage tends to include the Divine Office (the services of psalms appointed for the various hours of the day) in its broad conception of liturgy, whereas the Eastern church restricts the meaning of the word to the sacramental rites of the church and most particularly the "Divine Liturgy," that is, the eucharistic

---

[1] 1 Clement 40-41, 44.

service. Liturgies proper begin here with the priestly invocation: "Blessed is the kingdom of the Father, and of the Son, and of the Holy Spirit." If the kingdom blessing is not given, the ritual is a service of several different kinds, rather than liturgy proper. Similarly, in the Eastern liturgical traditions, only a bishop or priest can celebrate a liturgical service, for which he must be formally vested, though other ministers, monks, or laity can preside over other prayer services. In the Eastern traditions the monastic offices of psalms are simply designated as services or "hours."

Christian liturgy in this sense of the development of specific worship services has a complex and very profound history. It was hardly ever controversial, very different from the history of doctrinal matters, and because of that liturgical history progressed in quiet, incremental style over the centuries. The great rites of the Christians developed in stages: first, the rituals of Eucharist and baptism, and then other sacramental rites, and finally the services of monastic prayer that turned into the "Divine Office," services of psalmody and intercessory prayers that marked off the hours of the day. All these factors would coalesce by the fourth century to make a rich synthesis.

The earliest roots of Christian prayer are undoubtedly to be found in the Jewish traditions of prayer, using the Psalms, and reading the sacred Scriptures. Christians added to this the definite specificity of reading the sacred text (what they later called the "Old Testament") in the light of the events and signs of Jesus' life. This was indeed the root of the making of what came to be the New Testament, which is a set of ancient writings that fundamentally seeks to interpret the covenant in the light of Jesus' person and deeds, especially rotating around the signs of the cross and resurrection. This is why so much of Christian liturgical prayer is focused on the death and resurrection of the Savior, considered as the covenant of salvation: for which thanks of the new people of God ought to be rendered collectively.

By the ninth century the generic shape of all the liturgies of the ancient Christian churches were more or less formed and had an immense staying power, as liturgical change was significantly slowed after that point, and what changes there were presented themselves as traditionalist, or seeking the forms of the (sometimes imagined) past rather than any designer-maneuvered future. Specific attempts to reformulate Christian liturgy wholesale would not be seen until the Reformation era. There were times of lively development in the patristic era, and this is particularly true of the fourth to fifth centuries: so much so that most of the ancient Roman rite and the current liturgies of the Byzantine and Oriental churches are still profoundly steeped in patristic thought forms, theological imagery, and language.

Christian liturgy probably began with the adoption of the Jewish practice of morning and evening prayer (Mk 1:35; 6:46; Lk 10:17). The rites of baptism and

Eucharist were also quickly adopted internationally (though their precise proto-history is still shrouded with obscurity because of paucity of textual information). In both cases the intellectual foundations for the ritual acts were provided in the New Testament apostolic writings. Other sacramental rites (such as marriage or ordination) also found their inspiration in Jesus' acts (such as the wedding at Cana or the selection of the apostles), but in such cases the symbolic "start" provided in the New Testament archetypes really had to be filled out quite extensively by later patristic reflection on the nature of the mysteries. So, for example, the early Christian ordination rituals took some time to take a definitive shape, although they were universally based around the New Testament pattern of the "laying on of hands." A fuller form of ordination rite can be found in the *Apostolic Tradition*, and the version as practiced east of the Jordan in the second century can be seen in the Clementine epistles.[2] It was not until the early fourth century that marriages were considered something that should be brought before the bishop to bless in the name of the church; and even after that point the ritual still continued in the form of a blessing set within a larger service (often the eucharistic rite) but attended with legal forms to "witness it" publicly. The rituals of crowning with leaves and blossoms (in the East) or veiling and unveiling (in the West) were civil practices the church simply adopted and adapted to its own use.

The book of Revelation and the letter to the Hebrews were two early and important texts that demonstrate how extensively a cultic, or liturgical, spirituality had already permeated the Christian imagination. The fundamental theological principle enunciated in both these texts, that the events of the liturgy in heaven are mirrored by the heavenly liturgy of the church on earth, was formative on Christian liturgical theology. By the end of the second century, the church's eye was set on the liturgical books of the Old Testament, and it increasingly took the temple rituals as a form of archetypal instruction, even to the ordering of Christian buildings after the fourth century (which were modeled on the temple's division of space into the threefold pattern of uninitiated [narthex or porch], baptized faithful [nave], and ordained clergy [sanctuary]). There was, however, always a lively awareness of the differences between Christian "spiritual" worship on the one hand (by which they meant moral awareness and the "offering" of prayer and intercession services) and the notion of physical sacrifice on the other hand (a common enough experience not only in Judaism but throughout antiquity). Christian aversion to physical sacrifices marked off the church distinctively from the earliest times, but incense and prayer offerings were given notable stress, particularly in the early Syrian church.

---

[2]*Apostolic Tradition* 2-3, 7-8; *Clementine Homilies* 60-72.

The basic origins of Christian liturgy seem to derive from the custom of meeting for Eucharist on Sunday as the first day of each week (Acts 20:7-11; Didache 14.1). Justin Martyr is the first patristic witness to give an account of such a Sunday eucharistic service, which he does in very broad lineaments, a factor that exists in most liturgical accounts of the early centuries, which seem to wish to explain things without actually giving noninitiates much detailed information.[3] Other accounts of the pre-Nicene liturgy can be found in several other places in early Christian writing.[4] The pattern of the Eucharist from the fourth century onward is more widely attested, with much more specifically "liturgical treatises" then being composed, partly to attract a large wave of new converts in the post-Constantinian church. There are from this time important instructional treatises written by bishops addressing themselves to their annual Paschal catechumens, who are approaching the mysteries of baptism and Eucharist.

One of the most famous of these is Cyril of Jerusalem's *Catechetical Lectures*, which sets out to explain to neophytes in the Easter triduum the rites of their new faith, which they will celebrate in a few days' time. There is also an early fourth-century bishop's altar book that survives in the form of Serapion of Thmuis's *Euchologion* (or prayer book for the altar). It seems to be the case that early eucharistic prayers, and other formularies probably, were composed spontaneously at first by the presiding bishop, only becoming more fixed as they were written down in later times. The third and fourth centuries witness more and more legislation restricting the principle of spontaneous composition of liturgical prayers. Several of the liturgical manuals from this time are published as "models" of how to pray at a liturgy, and they served their purpose by directing what must have been more diverse forms of prayers before them into a standardized set of commonalities across a wide range of the churches.

The eucharistic rites as they were celebrated in Syria had a special impact on Eastern forms of liturgy and can be seen (in developed form) in the liturgies still commonly used in the Eastern Christian world: of Basil the Great, and the liturgy of Saint John Chrysostom, which we shall observe shortly. There were numerous "families of liturgies," and much modern scholarship has been concerned with drawing out the relationships between them all, both Eastern and Western. The main divisions can be listed as the liturgical traditions of Alexandria (Coptic and Ethiopic), Jerusalem and Antioch (known as Eastern and Western Syrian, respectively), Cappadocia (Armenian), and Constantinople (Byzantine), the last one predominating in the long period when the city was a world capital and synthesizing

---

[3] Justin, *First Apology* 65, 67.
[4] *Apostolic Tradition* 4; Didache 9-10; *Anaphora of Addai and Mari*; *Anaphora of St. Mark*.

many of the other Eastern forms. In the West, the main liturgical path of development was more coherent, less varied, but local traditions are certainly noticeable in the churches of Rome, Milan, Spain, Gaul, North Africa, and the Celtic western islands. Rome's ever-expanding influence tended to absorb and subordinate alternative liturgical traditions in a powerful fashion.

## THE CLASSICAL PATRISTIC-ERA FORMULATIONS OF LITURGIES

***Eucharistic.*** One of the earliest Christian terms for the rite of Communion seems to have been *fractio panis*, the breaking of bread, probably a reminiscence of Luke's account of the Emmaus disciples who recognized the risen Lord "in the breaking of the bread" (Lk 24:35; Acts 2:42). The term *Eucharist* eventually came to supplant this, derived from the Greek word for "giving thanks" (*eucharistia*), which was the central theme of the main prayer (anaphora) of the president of the Communion rite, who recounted all the deeds of the Lord, from creation to redemption, culminating in the covenant made in Jesus' death and resurrection, as synopsized in his own commandment to repeat the Last Supper (called the *Mystical Supper* in the Eastern churches) "in memory of him" (Lk 22:19). The word is seen in Ignatius of Antioch at the end of the first century and already has this technical ritual sense.[5] The word *anamnesis* is also used by Ignatius. It denotes that special "memory" of the Christ's salvific events, which is not mere recollection of things past but a sense of entering into the saving events in the here and now. *Anamnesis*, when used by Christian thinkers in a liturgical sense, is charged with eschatological significance. The sacred covenant is made new when the eternally fresh event of Christ's death (the fracturing of the bread and the pouring of the wine) is made one with his resurrection (the distribution of the mysteries as communion with the glorified Lord) at each celebration of the Lord's Supper in his church, which is ever constituted and renewed by its celebration. In this sense Christian eschatology (the ultimate nonsignificance of linear time-distance in God's plan for the life of the world) as a vital genre of thinking remains vividly alive in the liturgy, often when it has dwindled and dimmed in many other areas of later Christian life.

The Eastern churches preferred the term *mysteries* (*mysteria*) to designate the eucharistic gifts, while the Latin (following Tertullian) used the notion of *sacrament*, derived from *sacramentum*, the sacred oath of allegiance a soldier would give, in Christian terms signifying the closeness of the earliest eucharists to the first baptismal profession. The two sacraments were seen as extensions, therefore, of initiation rites; one once for all, the other continuously renewed. After the fourth

---

[5]Ignatius, *To the Ephesians* 13.1; *To the Philippians* 4; *To the Smyrnaeans* 8.1.

century the colloquialism "dismissal" (or *Ite Missa est*, from the final words of the Latin liturgy) became widespread in the West, giving the popular term *Mass*.[6] The East retained the concept of Divine Liturgy instead.

In the first century the eucharistic origins probably grew from a combination of meal fellowships with synagogue service of readings, which the Christians redrew to their own ends by showing how the story of the passion and resurrection of Jesus "threw light on" the covenant histories of the old law.[7] A reading from the Old Testament, a psalm or several of them, and then a reading from the Gospel were a basic structure into which eventually a parallel reading from the Pauline epistles was intruded. In eastern ritual eventually the Old Testament readings were dislocated from the eucharistic liturgy and read, instead, on the vigil vespers of the evening before, leaving only Psalm antiphons, a Pauline reading ("the apostle"), and the Gospel in the Eucharist itself. The bishop's sermon was given after the Gospel reading, although this was later dislocated and often given after Communion.

Many examples of episcopal preaching from the ancient church survive, and many of them were later written up by some of the more renowned fathers of the church in the form of biblical commentaries. As time passed, many medieval bishops made heavy use of the patristic homilies that most monasteries and episcopal palaces held in their libraries. Origen's work was extensively used, even though his name was often removed from the exemplar. Some of the most fluent biblical interpreters of the ancient period who must also be reckoned as among the church's greatest early preachers were Origen, Chrysostom, Theodore of Mopsuestia, and Theodoret of Cyr for the Greeks; and Jerome, Ambrose, Augustine, and Gregory the Great for the Latins.

From as early as the end of the first century the role of the bishop in the liturgical assembly was heavily stressed. As the eucharistic bread was broken from one piece into many for distribution and so became a symbol of the church's unity in diversity, so too the single presiding bishop served to represent a focal point of unity in and around the Eucharist. The Eucharist at one altar, with one bread, one bishop, one single community, became a symbolic bulwark against the many secessions that threatened to fragment Christian cohesion in the early days. This corporate sense was physically rooted around the sacrament. Early theologians developed the idea

---

[6] Ambrose of Milan, *Epistle* 76; Egeria, *Itinerary* 25.10.
[7] Many antique religious and business societies or special interest groups used the form of a meal to bind members together. It was a kind of specialist supper club. Christian meals were taken with both sexes present, which was unusual. Christian scriptural theology is thus born liturgically, reading the Old Testament in the light of the New and reading the New as a fulfillment of the "types" and adumbrations of the Old.

of ecclesiology (a doctrine of the church) on the basis of eucharistic unity: the church was where the bishop and presbyters and people joined together in eucharistic worship. For many years the inevitable splitting up of the bishop from his council of presbyters at eucharistic concelebrations was resisted because of the fear of losing this visible symbol of one church (building), one altar, and thus only one single church community for each locality.

Pressure of numbers after Constantine's conversion forced the presbyterate out into the suburban and rural regions in order to found new parish communities; but even so rituals were observed (such as the breaking of a portion of the eucharistic bread and dropping it into the chalice) to remind the congregation that the "other" churches having communion were also "in communion" with them, making up the larger communion of the *ekklesia*.[8] Episcopal letters of peace (*eirenika*) were given to traveling laity and clerics to introduce them to neighboring bishops, who would thus welcome the strangers to the new community and admit them to communion. The exchange of eucharistic communion eventually became the litmus test for doctrinal and disciplinary commonality. It was thus the manner of showing who was, or was not, in catholic communion.

The New Testament accounts of the Last Supper were, of course, dominant influences on the shape of the eucharistic liturgy. And from as early as Justin's first account of a post–New Testament Eucharist, the consecratory prayer over the bread and wine took the form of a greatly extended prayer of thanksgiving (*eucharistia*): for all the benefits of God the Father's creation, his constant renewal of the springs of salvation and enlightenment on earth, the goodness of the world, and especially how all of this "loving providence" culminated in the sending of the Son to act as the incarnate Savior, when all those salvific deeds were completed (in the sense of reaching their telos, their goal, or their *teleiosis*, their perfection) in the self-offering of the Son in his passion.[9] Irenaeus is one of the first classical-era bishops to show this central way the eucharistic prayer "sums up" salvation history and serves as a centrally cohesive force in organizing the church's identity around a Christology of the passion-resurrection as God's victory (*nike*) over the forces of evil in the world.[10] This death (the broken body, symbolized in the breaking of the bread, and outpoured blood in the chalice) and the resurrection that lifted it to triumph were juxtaposed in the liturgy as the symbiosis

---

[8]The Roman bishops eventually commanded deacons to bring to the papal altar different fragments from all the other suburban liturgies being celebrated on the same Sunday so that they could be added to the pope's chalice and show that there was still only "one altar" in Rome. The Latin Mass still commemorates this today.

[9]Justin, *First Apology* 65, 67.

[10]See Irenaeus, *Adversus Haereses* 4.17-18. Christ is the fulfillment of all earthly offerings and all the harvests of God.

of consecration and communion, the first looking to the Last Supper, the cross and tomb; the second to the resurrection and the regathering of the church. One of the first of these nonlinear, eschatological reflections on the closeness of the two sides of the one salvation mystery was penned by Luke in his extended account of the disciples at Emmaus, who could not understand the sufferings of Jesus nor recognize his risen glory until the mystical moment of the *fractio panis* (Lk 24:13-35).

At first the words of the central prayer of the anaphora, or eucharistic consecratory prayer, would have been made up extempore by the presiding celebrant.[11] This is why the earliest officers of the communities, such as bishops or presbyters, were elected on account of their charismatic ability to pray and intercede with God. Soon, however, it became clear that holiness and rhetorical ability do not always go hand in hand, and by the end of the third century there was a widespread desire to have "good models" of what a fine eucharistic prayer should be like. The Apostolic Constitutions is one of the earliest examples of a text written to show a good exemplar. It reflects the still deeply Jewish nature of worship at Rome in the late third century. The elements of the eucharistic prayer here go back over the same constitutive elements (Trinity, creation, fall, salvation history, the incarnate redemption) as are known to have formed the pattern of the earliest baptismal catechesis, and the link cannot be accidental.

Many of the patristic-era writers, from the earliest anti-Gnostic apologists who were protesting at the attempt to excessively spiritualize Jesus to the anti-Origen theologians of the sixth century, laid a great stress on the reality of the presence of the risen Christ in his mystical body, that is, the consecrated bread and wine made into the "life-giving blessing" of his risen flesh (as Cyril of Alexandria calls it). The concept of the "real presence" did not emerge explicitly until after the Carolingian debates of the ninth century prepared a vocabulary for it; after this point the idea dominates Latin thought. But the notion is certainly present in all the patristic writings on Eucharist. The later medieval thought excessively polarizes approaches to Eucharist that see it as either spiritual or physical. In fact, the earliest thinking does not operate on this dichotomy at all. It sees the risen presence of the Lord in his mysteries as an eschatological event (the death and resurrection entering again into the sacrament of the present moment by the consecratory power of the Holy Spirit), which is at one and the same time spiritual and physical, just as his incarnate body was deified in the incarnate transaction.[12]

---

[11] *Anaphora* literally means "offering up."

[12] Thus the once-for-all event is never repeated; only the church is ever brought back into the dynamism of the same salvific event, despite time and distance, which are eschatologically foreshortened across the ages of the church.

The Eastern liturgies lay especial transfigurative force on the consecratory prayer that follows the words of institution.[13] The consecration of the "gifts" into becoming the "mysteries" was attributed to the Spirit, just as he made the body for Christ in the Virgin to begin with. It is known as the *epiclesis*, or "prayer of calling down."[14] In Latin liturgical tradition a greater stress was laid on the priest's recitation of Jesus' words of institution as consecratory in effect. Following Cyprian's third-century reflections on the priest as *alter Christus*, that is, another Christ, the mystical change was regarded as happening rather at this moment.

**Baptismal rites.** How baptism first came into the Christian church as a major initiation rite is not clear. It is possible that it was elected in memory of the many links the first apostles (and Jesus) had with the movement of John the Baptist. His ritual washing to symbolize the forgiveness of sins was comparable to the *mikveh* rites of the Jews. When a majority of Gentiles formed the basis of the Christian communities, and with Paul's insistence that circumcision was no longer necessary, it was an understandable development to seek for another dramatic sign of marking entrance to the community of the "new covenant." *Mikveh* washing had long been used as the ritual that sufficed for a Gentile female who wished to become an Israelite after a period of probation as a proselyte in late antiquity. The extension of the rite of washing to male as well as female Christian converts is possibly how it spread to be a dominant solution, even though no one could remember any authority of Jesus during his ministry to command baptism (Jn 4:2), a deficiency that was more than made up for in one of the very last "editions" of the multilayered Matthean Gospel (Mt 28:19), adding to the penultimate verse of the Gospel the explicit posthumous command of Jesus to observe trinitarian baptismal rites. This evidently shows the context of a church at the end of the first century looking back to formalize the liturgical practice then prevalent by means of a prophetic word from the risen Lord.

The forms of very early post–New Testament baptismal ritual are witnessed in Didache 7.1-2; Justin Martyr's *First Apology* 61; and Hippolytus's *Apostolic Tradition* 15-21. So by the second century it had clearly become established universally as a common Christian ritual of repentance, exorcism, and washing from sins, so as to enter into the "mysteries" of the church; and by the third century it was widely recognizable. Since many of the earliest converts were previously active members of other religions, and since the early Christians largely tended to regard these "gods"

---

[13]"This is my body, which is broken for you.... This is my blood of the new covenant," etc.
[14]The Byzantine *epiclesis* reads as follows: "Again, we offer you this spiritual and bloodless worship, and we ask and pray and supplicate you: send down your Holy Spirit upon us and upon these gifts here set forth, and make this bread the precious body of your Christ, and what is in this chalice, the precious blood of your Christ, changing them by your Holy Spirit."

they served as nothing more than daimons, terrestrial and hostile spirits of evil, as they considered them, that is "demons," then it was understandable that preliminary rituals of baptism began with exorcisms.

The company of exorcists had been a powerful aspect of primitive Christianity. To serve their needs as missionary preachers, much of the New Testament account of the ministry of Jesus, a kind of proto-Gospel, had already been assembled. It looked, in many ways, like a manual for an exorcist: how to deal with this or that different type of demon possession in the course of the kerygmatic preaching. These earliest of all missionary travels in the first expansion of Christianity would probably begin with the exorcists and healers (the two things were seen as one) collecting a crowd in the agoras of the towns to which they had come and practicing exorcism "in the name of Jesus." Having assembled a body of listeners, the preachers would then deliver a fuller form of the Jesus *kerygma*.

Rudolf Bultmann and other form critics have successfully laid bare once again the "format" of the exorcism as it was originally performed among the Christians of the first century: a *diakrisis* or diagnosis to see what "kind" of demon it was that dominated the person, a command to the demon to name itself, a rebuke of the demon, then a demand of the demon to depart from the person using the formula "in the name of Jesus."[15] In cases of "difficult" spirits, examples of good practice were laid down in these most ancient of Christian texts, using Jesus himself as the model in each case. It was highly inadvisable to engage in a dialogue with the demonic force, for example, so a basic question-and-answer regime was established. The exorcist was encouraged to use the Lord's own authority to deal with the spirit. But if it was recalcitrant, such as, being commanded to give its name, it then "played deaf," for example, then the exorcist was shown how to put his finger in the person's ear; if it was playing dumb, to touch the tongue, and so on (Mk 7:33-35). In the baptismal rituals as they have come down today, especially the Greek, but the Latin, too, the remains of the exorcisms are still visible.

After this initial rite, the candidates were enrolled in the church's register as *catechumenoi*, by means of a cross signed on the brow. They were catechumens, or candidates being instructed (receiving *catechesis*) in the basics of Christian faith, morals, and church praxis. When they were deemed ready for baptism (the professions of soldiering,[16] wizardry, and prostitution were prohibited from being considered) the presbyters assembled them together regularly during the Lent preceding Pascha (or Pentecost), at which great feast they would be baptized by the bishop, and used the

---

[15] See further G. Twelftree, *In the Name of Jesus: Exorcism Among Early Christians* (Grand Rapids: Eerdmans, 2007).

[16] At least until the fourth century.

meetings to scrutinize the past behavior of their charges. From this the ritual came to be known as *scrutinies*. In some churches it was a rigorous cross-questioning about one's moral life, past and present: preparing the person to be ready to confess all things and be prepared to embark on a new fashion of moral lifestyle, which would now be more closely demanded of the initiate rather than the catechumen. Augustine was relieved, when he came to Milan, to find that this church was less intrusive in its questions than his native churches of North Africa. But he faced so many criticisms when he returned to Africa and became a cleric, when it was known he had escaped that ritual of penance, that he eventually composed his own public admission of his spiritual life, on his own terms, now famous as the *Confessions*.

Toward the end of Lent the presbyters would start teaching the catechumens the fundamental prayers they would need, especially the "Our Father," which they had to learn by heart, and some form of a creedal profession of faith. After the fourth century the Nicene Creed became dominant at baptisms. Immediately before Pascha, the local bishop would take over and present a series of lectures to the candidates about secret matters (known as the *arcana*, or hidden things). We have a few of these catechetical lectures surviving, from renowned bishops such as Cyril of Jerusalem and Theodore Mopsuestia. But these texts were the discourses later prepared for publication, and do not contain, for anyone to read, the heart of the *arcana*, which seems to have been the nature of the inspiration of the Holy Spirit and his work in the believer at baptism, and also aspects of Christian praxis that the candidate had to keep strictly private from all others who were not initiated, matters concerning the eucharistic ritual in the main. This was similar, in many respects, to the *disciplina arcana* of the pagan Greek mystery religions, where devotees swore not to reveal the inner secrets of the sect to any outsider. For Christians in time of persecution, this matter of secrecy was a life-and-death matter of trust as well as a way of stressing what were the most important parts of Christian sacramental faith. But it presents a problem for us today, as the early liturgical sources are, deliberately, never telling the whole story.

Finally, as the Paschal vigil began (a night on which many of the early churches thought they would witness the second coming of the Messiah), the bishop took the candidates away separately (while the rest of the believers began the eucharistic service with a long prelude of psalms and antiphons), and with the aid of male and female deacons, anointed the naked bodies of those who were to be baptized (oiling the skin was a common ritual of the bathhouses of the time, as it served the function of modern soap), explaining the anointing as a sign of spiritual strengthening. After the oil, the candidates were led into the water and there immersed under the surface three times as the threefold name of Trinity was invoked on them (*The servant of*

*God \_\_\_\_\_ is baptized in the Name of the Father, and of the Son, and of the Holy Spirit*). Affusion (or sprinkling the head with water) was allowed only for life-and-death emergencies, though it later became the standard practice in the West. At first it was called *clinicus* baptism, and if a recipient recovered from the illness that caused this emergency economy, he or she was expected to come to the church to receive the fuller completion of the mysteries.

The baptismal full immersion was explained to candidates (following Paul's letter to the Romans) as a symbolic entrance into the death of Christ, like an entombment, and the death of the old, sinful, Adam, so as to be born again (*palingennesia*) in a forgiven newness of life. After rising from the waters, the newly cleansed Christians were dressed in a shining white robe. It is from this that the term *candidate* derives ("dressed in white"). For eight days they wore white garments to celebrate their initiation. Many who were admitted to mystery religions in ancient times wore specially radiant clothes for the octave following. For Christians in times of troubles, this was often the time when it became clear to their neighbors, from their costume, what they had done; and for some it was a real test of faith, a veritable risking of their lives.

The main part of the baptism, however, was not yet completed. The ancient ritual always consisted of three things. The third element has fallen out in some later Christian rituals, particularly among some of the Reformed churches, but in antiquity baptism was made up of three interrelated and deepening aspects of rebirth. The first was the catechumenal anointing, symbol of gaining strength; the second was the washing for the forgiveness of sins; the third was the chrismation.[17] *Chrisma* was specially consecrated oil mixed with perfumes and myrrh by the bishop's hand. It was seen as the sacramental matter for conveying the "gift or seal of the Spirit" (*sphragis tou pneumatos*). The doors to the senses (the eyes, ears, nose, mouth, heart, hands, and feet) were anointed with perfumed chrism so that the newly baptized would be "sealed in the Spirit of God." This highly perfumed oil would remain on the new Christian for the octave also, until it was wiped off carefully when the white garment was laid aside in church. In the baptismal ritual the sealing with the Spirit is accompanied by prayers that convey to the believer that they have thus been consecrated with charisms of priesthood, prophecy, and kingship. It was to emphasize that the chrismation was the core culmination of the whole initiation rite that *baptism* was not the preferred term for the sacrament in the Eastern churches, where it was known more generally as *photismos:* illumination or the sacrament of enlightenment.

It was the fourth century that really saw a development and formalization of these ritual elements, so as to make of baptism the awe-inspiring ritual of initiation

---

[17] Only in Syria did the chrismation seem to precede the baptism itself.

it must have been in the ancient church. In many places today, where infant baptism is the norm and a tiny trickle of water is spread gently over the infant's brow, it is a far cry from the ancient events, which must have been emotionally and psychically shattering for their participants. Certainly, when Augustine thinks back to his own baptism, in his *Confessions*, it is striking how he chooses to end the entire narrative of his Christian life (senior bishop though he then was when he was writing) at the moment he realized he had completed the initiation, and how the waves of emotion took him. All that remained was for the now–luminously robed initiates, with lighted candles in their hands, to be led by the deacons to rejoin the main assembly of the believers in the church, where the Eucharist was still proceeding but had been halted so that the newcomers could come in pride of place to the altar and receive the eucharistic gifts for the first time. Many liturgical sermons attendant on baptism, distinct from catechetical lectures, have been preserved, including some fine examples from Gregory of Nazianzus, John Chrysostom, and Augustine.

***Penitential rites.*** The Christian theologians who first speak of baptismal initiation regard it as a once-for-all forgiveness of sin. The question "What happens if one sins after baptism?" would have been regarded as impertinent, a sign that the radical commitment for a new life was not properly there. But soon, the era of bitter persecutions, when ordinary men and women were dragged from their homes and subjected to torture and even execution, not only made a harvest of martyrs but also produced a very large amount of recidivists: people who fell away simply from fear at the final stages and were cowed into submission and the denial of their faith: ready in the end to honor the gods of Rome if this was what the authorities wanted, but at the same time, perhaps, also making mental reservations that these were not gods at all.

Serious lapses from Christian commitment (the traditional three great sins were listed as murder, adultery, and apostasy) were regarded as effectively not having any remedy in the earliest generations. Those who committed them after baptism were no longer members of the church. As the third and fourth century persecutions showed, however, this was not a realistic pastoral policy to sustain in the longer term. Many of those who lapsed were seriously distressed that they had not the courage to endure torture and petitioned for some form of readmission to the community. This was the spur to develop an early form of the theology and praxis of penitence. It seemed it was especially developed by three classes of ministers: the prophets (there is a very early instance of appeals for greater leniency in the first-century Shepherd of Hermas), the confessors (who had suffered nobly in the persecutions and survived, claiming the right to offer spiritual consolation to their brothers and sisters, as we can see at Rome and Carthage in the middle of the third century), and the bishops (who ultimately emerged as the constructers of the formal rites of penance, which began to function as control gateways to the sacramental rituals, especially admission to the Eucharist).

The concept of penance derives from the Latin word *paenitentia*, "repentance." In patristic theology it predominantly refers to the system of postbaptismal forgiveness of sins that was developed especially through the third to eighth centuries, when it reached a specific form with some variations in the Eastern and Western churches. The concept of penance covers the related Greek concepts of *metanoia* and *exomologesis* (repentance and confession). The earliest iterations of the gospel message understood that forgiveness was central to the *kerygma* and that it was fundamentally a grace of God invoked by the salvific work of Jesus (the gift to the church of the *dynamis*, or potency, of the passion and resurrection) and appropriated through the repentance of the believer.

The parable of the tax collector and the Pharisee (Lk 18:9-14) demonstrates the high profile Jesus gave to repentance in humility. The developing organization of the churches, and the deepening sense of the holiness of the sacramental altars, led to problems with the concept of repentance, however, as it conflicted in several instances with the equally developing sense of the church as the eschatological new community of the elect, who had been bought by the blood of Christ and made into his spotless bride, or into the sacred temple of God, whose defilement was a sin calling for divine vengeance (1 Cor 3:16-17; 6:18-20). Even in the Gospel of Matthew there are signs that the "problem" of believers who remain "sinners" needs to be addressed.

In a text that is generally believed to represent late first-century reflections, the church (probably of Antioch) adopted a position of forgiving repeated offenders, up to a certain point, but then disciplining them by "treating them as a tax collector" (Mt 18:15-18), which presumably (at that stage) meant imposing some form of excommunication on them. In this text the community for the first time claimed the power of "binding and loosing" to be inherited from Jesus as an active disciplinary measure (see also Jn 20:22-23). Incipient forms of penitential discipline based around exclusion from the community and its common prayers (especially the eucharistic ritual) are already visible in the Pauline churches (cf. 1 Cor 5:1-5, 11-13; 10:21; 11:26-29; 2 Cor 2:5-11; 6:14-18; 1 Tim 1:20), and in the slightly later catholic epistles the sense is clearly growing that the church, as the community of the last age, has no room within it for habitual offenders (1 Pet 4:7; 2 Pet 2:20-22; 1 Jn 3:4-6.).

This theology of the "pure elect lady," whose company could tolerate no defilement, grew strongly as the sacrament of baptism was more and more elaborated as the archetypal and supreme mystery of forgiveness and initiation. This seems to have displaced the more primitive sense of the Eucharist itself as the preeminent sacrament of reconciliation. In the course of this displacement, anxieties started to grow about potentially defiling the Eucharist by admitting sinful people to the altar, instead of the concept of sinners needing to have recourse to the Eucharist to wash away their sins in the fire of the body and blood "shed for the forgiveness of sins."

But having so stressed the unrepeatable nature of baptismal regeneration, the pastoral problem soon became critical: how to cope with the reality of postbaptismal sin among their members (cf. 1 Jn 1:8-10). While this remained on the level of "interior attitudes" (rather than public scandals) it was not seen as overtly troubling, often being addressed by proto-ascetical solutions, such as forgiveness sought and gained by prayer, fasting, and almsgiving. Many who came from Christian families but were not willing to undertake the rigorous moral code of the church in all its fullness would often defer baptism until later in life (sometimes to the end of life), thus, somewhat artificially and formalistically, preserving the church's self-understanding as the initiated community of the saints.

Where the sin became a matter of public knowledge (especially the three "unforgivable sins" of murder, adultery and apostasy), it was sometimes regarded as a sign that the individual had never "properly" been a Christian at all. Perhaps his baptism had never "taken," as it were. Even into the late fourth century many Christians deferred baptism until the onset of old age or the imminent threat of death. The Shepherd of Hermas is a text much concerned with the issue of preserving purity among the church members and shows an anxiety about the process of seeking forgiveness for regular sins. Such is also a concern of the Johannine letters (perhaps written at the same period of the late first century and early second century), which introduce the notion of sin in general, which all Christians had to confess, and "sin that was to the death" (1 Jn 5:15-17), which seems to be a sin so serious that it demonstrated that the sinner was no longer part of the church. The writer of the Johannine letters probably had schism in mind when he introduced the idea, but the concept of "ordinary-level" (venial) sins and "mortal sins" soon became a commonly held distinction, especially in the West, where monastic theologians, particularly in the Celtic lands, worked toward codifying a list of sins in order of significance.

Texts such as the Didache demonstrate how the earliest penitential system seemed to work, with the idea of "regular sins" being confessed in prayer with private fasting and philanthropic acts of repentance, seeking God's forgiveness. The old disorder gave way before the third-century persecutions, however, and the weight of those who had lapsed and were thus regarded as having committed apostasy but were then seeking readmission. The church of Carthage in the time of

Cyprian was particularly exercised with this problem. Cyprian, the Carthaginian bishop, composed his treatise *De Lapsis* to resolve the problem and so brought the whole matter of public reconciliation rites out into the open in a controversial way. Several of the Carthaginian confessors (potential martyrs who had survived) regarded it as their prophetic prerogative (surviving a martyrdom blamelessly was regarded as having raised a Christian to at least presbyteral status in many places) to indicate the Lord's forgiveness to repentant sinners, in contradiction of the commonly established belief that such sinners ought never to be readmitted to eucharistic communion. The Novatianist sect is a testimony to this, but many other churches also held to the rigorist view that for postbaptismal serious sin there could be no forgiveness at all.

As a result of the chaos of discipline that was threatening, an international system agreed between Alexandria, Rome, and Carthage was put into effect and soon spread widely. A system of "graded" penance was established in most churches that allowed those who had fallen during times of duress to return to the Christian assembly in the role of a penitent. Tertullian is one of the first to agonize on paper whether the grave sinner could ever be reestablished. In his treatise *De Paenitentia*, which he would renounce after he became an admirer of the Montanists and came to regard it as too lax, he reluctantly acknowledged that one "second" repentance is possible if demonstrated by the adoption of a life of severe penance involving long prayers, fasting, prostration in the churches and before the presbyters, and a special prayer of intercession before God from the church community, when the presbyters would lay hands over the sinner's head.[18]

After Constantine established an international peace for the churches in the fourth century, the system of canons governing this process began to be generally agreed through a series of conciliar assemblies. The Western churches had the system more openly arranged, and here it amounted to the stages of (1) petitioning the bishop to be received as a penitent, (2) belonging to the order of penitents for a longer or shorter time (sometimes for the whole of one's life), and (3) final readmission (*reconciliatio*) to eucharistic communion through a ceremony of the laying on of hands (usually in the West at Maundy Thursday). The entrance into the order of penitents disbarred a person from marital relations or holding any form of public ministry, and was, accordingly, usually postponed until late in life. Clergy could not participate in this process in any sense, the two states being regarded as incompatible, and serious public wrongdoing among clerics was dealt with instead by deposition from orders.

---

[18]*De Paenitentia* 7, 9-10.

The system had so many defects within it that a more popular practice arose after the seventh century, first witnessed among the monastic communities, of confessing one's inner life to a spiritual father or confessor. The confessor (the Irish called him *anam cara*, or soul friend) took on a role of high authority over the disciple and imposed "penances" for different offenses, such as periods of fasting, or numerous prostrations, or other acts of self-abnegation. Soon a "tariff" system (certain penances fitted to various sins) became common in the Western churches, where the Irish monks introduced the process more generally.

Carolingian clergy on the continent in the ninth century tried to resist this Celtic system, which they thought was crude, in favor of retaining a remembrance of the ancient disciplinary canons; and so the two clashing penitential approaches marked the Western church throughout the patristic era. In the Byzantine world the system of monastic counseling also spread to become the common ecclesiastical process of confession. In the late fourth century Patriarch Nectarius at Constantinople abolished from his roll of official ministers the archaic office of grand penitentiary, the cleric who once supervised all of this process. It is a demonstration that the entire system had run its course in the East and was going to be replaced with an entirely "personal" approach to clergy by laity seeking a private blessing of reconciliation, which would deal with "run of the mill" sins, while public scandals were left to the discretion of the bishop and his spiritual court. In both the Greek and Latin churches sometime after the ninth century, this private confession to the soul guide was absorbed into the formal sacramental process and became established as "sacramental confession" (*confessio, exomologesis*), finally administered solely by the priest or bishop.

The Western medieval church adopted a more ready approach to "penitential commutations," a system of dispensing with the full rigor of the penalties attached to sins in the tariffs, thus allowing the confessor considerable discretion in imposing retributive penances on the individual. In the Byzantine world the penitential canons (as established in several ascetical writings, notably the *Canonical Letters* of Basil the Great) were regarded as "fixed" penalties for various sins, and so (because of the severity of these ancient rules) the system of private penance was never as popular there as it would become in the West. In several of the different churches of the East today, there remains a great disparity in the practice of the sacramental rites of penance. The Slavic-influenced churches, for example, insisted on confession before anyone approached communion. The Greek post-Byzantine churches, on the other hand, tended to regard confession as something one approached more in times of life-changing events, great sickness, spiritual trouble, or great scandal.

## THE LITURGICAL CYCLE OF FEASTS

The annual cycle of Christian feasts took some time to establish. It began with the observance of Pascha (Easter). It is first noticed in Asia Minor (Melito's *Peri Pascha* gives much information) and from there spread internationally very quickly, so that by the middle of the second century it was a universal aspect of Christian observance. The Epistle of the Apostles (written c. 135–140) gives a very early account of Paschal liturgy and attributes the feast to a divine commandment. Early Paschal festivals were based around an all-night vigil service of prayer, during which extensive scriptural readings demonstrated the link between the exodus experience and the Christian Passover of Jesus' death and glory. A Eucharist celebrated at daylight on the Sunday of Pascha itself inaugurated fifty days of rejoicing afterward.

Some communities, especially those in Asia Minor in the first three centuries, wished to celebrate not on the Saturday-Sunday, but on the fourteenth of the month of Nisan (April), in memory of the Lord's day of execution. This caused a crisis in many places, as the churches first realized because of this liturgical deviation that a common system of praxis was more a thing to be aspired to than presumed. Seeing it as a worrisome scandal (because there was also the widespread belief that Christ would come back to earth to judge during the Paschal vigil and would expect his church to be awake and ready to "greet the Bridegroom at midnight"), the Roman church, under Pope Victor, exercised its influence to argue for the suppression of the Asian practice in the interest of common observance (the so-called Quartodecimans controversy). He had mixed results, but eventually the Roman practice prevailed over that of Asia Minor and became the common norm, until it was so fixed by the Paschal canons of the Council of Nicaea in 325, which set a standard for all churches how to compute the recurrence of Pascha on a lunar cycle.

By the late fourth century the basic shape of a "liturgical year" was in evidence. It was very basic: namely, a Great Pascha, preceded by forty days of Lenten observances and followed by feasts celebrating the Lord's ascension and the spiritual Pentecost. In the fourth century the East, for the sake of uniformity of observance, followed the lead of Rome in observing the nativity (Christmas) on December 25. Rome had initiated this in order to set up a Christian festal alternative to the continuing pagan winter solstice celebrations there. From this developed the logic of the Feast of the Annunciation, or conception of Jesus, on March 25. The West in its turn took on the Feast of Epiphany from the Eastern church and marked it on January 6, adapting it a little from its Eastern stresses (the blessing of holy waters in memory of Jordan) and leaning it toward the revelation of Christ to the Gentiles in the persons of the three Magi (who soon became "kings"). Christmas was soon preceded by another, smaller Lent, called Advent, and the last element to be added was the cycle of great feasts of the Lord and the Virgin and the multitude of martyr's festivals and other saints.

The practices of the Jerusalem church were widely copied from the fourth century onward in both East and West. When a feast is celebrated today by both Greek and Latin churches, it is a sign that it was established before the fifth century. After that date the calendars of both churches begin to fill out extensively, especially with local martyrs, bishops, or ascetics, and wonderworking healers; but their very "localism" meant that international commonality was increasingly lost. The calendars of both the Latin-Roman and Byzantine churches today are packed, with a feast of a martyr, bishop, or other saint in the spaces that the great cycles of festivals have left vacant. There are often five or more saints packed into one day.

In the tenth century the Byzantine calendar of festivals was already so sprawling that Simeon Metaphrastes (his surname means "translator" or "editor") took pruning shears to it all. He moved around all the relatively "modern" saints to share a name day no longer on the day of their death (the original commemoration of a saint's festival— remembering the martyrdom event that originally began the calendar of local saints) but on the day of the most famous saint of that name. In some cases this led to conflation and confusion. The story of Santa Claus (St. Nicholas of Myra) is one such example.[19] Little is known of Nicolas of Myra, the fourth century bishop from Anatolia who attended the Council of Nicaea, other than that he was a fervent opponent of Arius and had a reputation for miracles. The later medieval Byzantine saint, Nicholas of Sion, was a bishop who had a particular care for the poor, and in his life it is recorded that he gave gold to a father who was considering selling his daughters into serfdom so that they would have a freewoman's dowry. After the editorial work of Metaphrastes, putting all the various "Nicholases" together in the calendar on December 6, the first Saint Nicholas's day, the stories merged into the making of one new "supersaint." This maximalized Nicholas became one of the great patrons of the later Middle Ages. His life and legend(s) dominate Russian Christian iconography.

## LATIN STYLES OF LITURGY

The Western churches had several different rites present concurrently in the ancient period. The various Western rites are normally catalogued as the Roman, the African, the Ambrosian, the Hispano-Visigothic (or Mozarabic), the Gallican-Gothic, the

---

[19]The original story, that is, not the nineteenth-century American reworking of it that goes back via Coca Cola to Nordic Thor the thunder god (with his flying reindeer sleigh)! For an explanation see my op-ed article in the *New York Times* on Christmas Day 2007: "St. Nick in the Big City," page A27, www.nytimes.com/2007/12/25/opinion/25mcguckin.html?r=0.

Italic (comprising the churches of Campania, Benevento, Aquileia, and Ravenna), and the Celtic rite. These energetic churches outside Rome developed particular rites and ceremonies in an early period that rivaled those of the great Latin center of all church life, which was Rome. Eventually the great magnetic force of Rome, and its ecclesial stability in the long years of Italy, Gaul, and Spain's immense political instability, meant that the Roman rite would dominate and overshadow all the adjacent churches and would, by virtue of Rome's presidency over the great missionary expansion of the church to the German tribes, bring the Roman ritual as standard across a vast swath of western territories. By the time of Gregory the Great in the seventh century, the Roman triumph was assured, and Gregory himself did much to formalize and refine the Roman liturgical traditions, not being averse to adding ceremonial elements derived from his experience of life at Constantinople, where he served as papal representative (*apocrisarius*) to the imperial court.

*The African rite.* Elements of the African rite can be witnessed in the writings of Cyprian of Carthage in the third century, and also in the work of St. Augustine in the fifth, especially in his *Letters 55-56*, *To Januarius*. Other North African Latin theologians who give details are Optatus of Milevis (d. c. 390), Victor of Vita (d. after 484), Ferrandus of Carthage (c. 523), and an otherwise unknown bishop, Voconius of Castellanum, who is mentioned by the writer Gennadius (who wrote a continuation of Jerome's *Lives of Famous Men*) as having composed an African *Sacramentary* book. Psalms, and prayers derived from them, were given a place of high honor in the African rituals. The antique and rough-and-ready Latin version of the Bible, known as the *Vetus Latina*, was clung to in preference to other editions as a hallowed sacred text. Eucharist was celebrated very early in the morning, as the sun rose, having been preceded by a vigil service of psalmody and prayer.

With the fall of Roman North Africa, first to the Arian Vandals in the fifth century and then to the Muslim Arabs in the seventh, the African ritual was pruned at an early stage and did not have much chance to pass internationally, though aspects of its ideological basis did pass through the growing influence of Augustine. One of those exports was the belief that children had to be baptized at an early stage, for if they died unbaptized their souls could not enter heaven but remained in a state of metaphysical limbo. The African rites partly passed into the Hispano-Visigothic and the Gallican rites and so did not disappear entirely.

*The Ambrosian rite.* The Ambrosian rite was attributed (often these attributions are more symbolic than historical) to its namesake, Ambrose the fourth-century bishop of Milan. He, in all probability, did revise the liturgy of his church, for he followed after an Airan predecessor, Auxentius, and as a stalwart Nicene believer he most certainly reordered all christological references and introduced trinitarian doxologies. However, the records of the Milanese calendar of saints (*Liber notitiae sanctorum Mediolani*), written in the early fourteenth century and containing ancient historical records, name bishop Simplicianus of Milan (d. 401) as having a large hand in finalizing the shape of the liturgy and describe the Milanese bishop Eusebius (c. 449–452) as having added numerous liturgical hymns, after the example of Ambrose himself (who actually wrote few of them, though these produced numerous later imitations).

The Milanese ritual of the prayers of the Divine Office were renowned for antiphonal hymn signing and developed chant traditions. Auxentius, who was from Cappadocia, and then Ambrose, both brought "oriental" elements into the Western liturgy at Milan, especially vigils and hymn singing. The Ambrosian rite in an ancient form also had the *epiclesis* prayer after the words of institution, as did the Byzantine rite. After the fourth century the history of the rite enters obscurity until Carolingian age, where it reappears, fighting against Frankish royal and later papal attempts to suppress it. This fight for the right to exist clarified the ritual and gave it the character of a very fixed and local, tradition. It did not travel far. Much of the distinctiveness of the rite consists in the different order in which prayers come.[20] Some Byzantine elements remain: the thuribles, for example, have no top cover (as in early Byzantine style), and the deacons wear their stoles on top of the outer Dalmatic vestment, not underneath it, as in the wider Latin tradition. Funeral, baptismal, and Holy Week ceremonies have significant differences from those of the Roman rite.

***The Mozarabic rite.*** The Mozarabic (or Hispano-Visigothic) rite still survives in the Latin church in a few places in Spain to this day.[21] It gained its name from the post-Reconquista period when, the rite having been terminated in Spain in favor of the Roman ritual, it still continued in the Christian churches in those dominions in Al Andalus that had not yet been conquered and were still under Arab control. The ritual shares so much with the Gallican that it clearly has a common set of origins. After the sixth century it appears in literature, at the same time that the Visigothic kingdoms were passing out of Arianism into catholicism, and the liturgy (as was the case with the Ambrosian rite in the fourth century) was evidently being christologically revised. The overall structure of the liturgy is taken from the sacramentary of Rome, but Spanish bishops (the seventh-century

---

[20] The Gospel is followed by a short antiphon; the prayers of the faithful follow the homily; the kiss of peace comes before the offertory; the creed is recited before the prayer over the gifts; there is no *Agnus Dei*; many of the secret prayers of the priest are particular; the final blessing is preceded by a threefold *Kyrie Eleison*; and the rite has its own form of lectionary of readings.

[21] Also called Gothic, Toledan, or Isidorian rite. It survives in the Capilla Muzarabe in Toledo Cathedral, and (more rarely) the chapel of San Salvador in Salamanca Old Cathedral.

bishop St. Isidore of Seville [d. 636] is customarily associated with the rite) added particular elements in the form of added prayers, differences of lectionary and psalm use, and distinctive Spanish hymns.

In 924 the differences of the ritual were enough to call it into suspicion, and Pope John X sent a papal legate to Santiago to examine its orthodoxy. The report was favorable, and papal approval was given, though the differences in the words of consecration in the eucharistic liturgy were not allowed and were ordered to be changed to match those of the Roman ritual. In 1064 Pope Alexander II sent Cardinal Hubertus Candidus as his legate to attempt the suppression of the rite across Spain, but the resistance of Spanish clergy and the support of Spanish kings kept it alive against the face of the irresistible spread of Roman ritual in the Western churches. One of its distinctive ceremonial ideas spread widely: the use of ashes to signify penitential devotion, and was popularized as Ash Wednesday to begin the Western Lenten period.

*The Gallican rite.* The Gallican-Gothic ritual developed in southern Gaul, now France, from the fifth century onward and was the specific liturgical tradition of those lands until it was submerged in the time of the Carolingian kings of the ninth century onward. It merged elements of the Eastern liturgy with the Roman rite, which some scholars think can be dated back to the time of Pothinus (d. 177) and Irenaeus (d. c. 202), who were bishops originating from Asia Minor who settled in Gaul. Gaul attracted, from earliest imperial times, merchant settlers from the East, among whom Christianity first took root. The Gallican rite also showed some traces of the African, Roman, and Spanish rites. It is another indication that in this early period of the formation of the great liturgical families, much international flow was visible, much interchange and adaptation. But as time went on the liturgical traditions became more and more conservative and fixed in form. The shape of the early Gallican rite can be seen in the writings of Hilary of Poitiers (his *Tractatus Mysteriorum*). Gennadius of Marseilles (d. 505) recounts that Bishop Venerius of Marseilles instructed his presbyter Musaeus sometime around 459 to draw up an ordered form of the liturgy, and that his successor bishop Eustathius prepared a specific lectionary, a psalm responsorial book, and a sacramentary.[22] Sidonius Apollinaris also writes that the presbyter Claudianus of Vienne had composed an anthology of readings for festival throughout the year.[23] A later form of the ritual can be seen also in Gregory of Tours's (d. 594) sacramentary, the *libellus missarum*.[24] By the end of the eighth century the specific Gallican elements of the ritual had faded away, more or less wholly absorbed under the Roman rite's predominance.

---

[22]Gennadius, *De Viris Illustribus* 79, PL 56.1103.
[23]*Monumenta Germaniae Historia. Auctorum antiquorum* 8.63.
[24]*Monumenta Germaniae Historia. Script. rerum Merovingiarorum* 1.1.67-68.

***The Celtic rite.*** In the sixth and seventh centuries the establishment of Christianity in Ireland, and its monastic focus with also a strong emphasis on missions to Britain and the Continent (under Columbanus), led to the formation of specific characteristics in the Irish Latin liturgy. The surviving *Bangor Antiphonary* is one of the major literary sources indicating what these were. The liturgical specific differences show the influence of the liturgies of Rome, Milan (the Ambrosian rite), and the Gallican ritual: countries the Irish passed through, clearly adopting local practices as they traveled. The specifically Irish elements are really only to be found in the hymns, where the local bardic traditions retain their strong flavor.

All these original, local specifics testify to the early flexibility of liturgical life in the patristic-era churches, where a standard basic form was illustrated with many local differentiations of detail. The overarching story in the Western churches, however, is one where the Roman ritual, strong from the outset because of the ancient prestige of the church that first formulated it, begins to dominate all other forms and magnetically attracts itself into them, finally overlaying them, either wholly or to a very large degree, by force of practice or by papal decree at the end of the first millennium. The process goes hand in hand with the developing scope of papal jurisdiction, until the West has an increasingly monolithic liturgical appearance.

## THE EASTERN RITES

The story of liturgical development in the East is similar in many ways: a pattern of several different local forms of worship, increasingly giving way to the unifying force of the liturgy attached to the one "super-church" of the latter part of the first millennium. In the case of the eastern Christian world, that was Byzantium, the church of Constantinople. But Constantinople was a latecomer on the Christian scene. It was a tiny, insignificant ecclesial center until it was elevated by Constantine in the mid-fourth century, but only began to have ecclesiastical weight after the early fifth century. So by the time the Byzantine rite started to gain ground and overshadow other traditions, it had already itself been formed in the crucible of other, more ancient forces that fed into it as its own sources. In this way the Byzantine rite shows the survival of a larger scatter of liturgical traditions that go back to early Christian times. In its present form, however, the Byzantine liturgy often demonstrates a mature shape, such as it had attained by the ninth century, when Patriarch Photius made amendments to its order. It is formally attributed to the work of St. John Chrysostom in the early fifth century, who may also have made some amendments, possibly abbreviating some of the eucharistic prayers (for the longer forms are found in the eucharistic liturgy of Saint Basil). But the roots of the Byzantine rite go back beyond Chrysostom.

Eastern liturgy has been categorized by scholars into various families that first accumulated around the practices of the greater sees. Rome, Milan, Ravenna, and Aquileia comprised the group that mixed in the West, eventually giving way to the predominance of Rome. In the East the great sees were Jerusalem, Antioch, Alexandria, and last Constantinople, which served as the synthesizer. The Eastern families fall into two major forms, representing the liturgical traditions of Antioch and Alexandria.

*The Antiochene liturgical family.* Antioch was the dominant superepiscopal see when Constantinople was founded, and for many years was its mother church until the emperors, and successive ecumenical councils, gave increasing privileges to Constantinople, allowing it to take to itself a large ecclesiastical territory cut from the former domains of Antioch, Nicomedia, and Ephesus. As the political fortunes of Antioch started to fall, so too did those of Byzantium rite, and so it was that the Antiochene rite assumed its greatest geographical extent by being taken over by the imperial capital. The anaphora, or great prayer of eucharistic intercession, in this family, is an unvarying form of words (it has no festal variable parts in the priest's recitation), but there are several different possibilities of anaphora in different regions. The *epiclesis* prayer, the petition that the Holy Spirit will descend on the gifts of bread and wine, typically comes after the words of Christ's institution that have been spoken over them, but the gifts are recognized as blessed and sanctified only after the prayer to the Spirit.

In the eastern parts of the ancient Antiochene patriarchate, the churches ran into Persia and often used Syriac. Liturgies in this East-Syriac division of the rite place the *epiclesis* prayer after a series of intercessory prayers. They were further divided by ecclesiastical division concerning whether the churches supported or denied the Ephesine and Chalcedonian councils. The so-called Nestorian rite is represented by the anaphoras of Addai and Mari, Mar Theodoros (of Mopsuestia), and Nestorius. The Anaphora of Addai and Mari is distinctively peculiar in that it completely lacks an institution narrative. Dependent variations of the East-Syriac rite are found in the Chaldaean and the Syro-Malabar rites. The East-Syriac ritual reached its most developed form in the sixth to seventh centuries, when it was carried far afield by Nestorian missionaries moving eastward as far as China and Java.

The Western Antiochene family, or West-Syriac family of rites, is composed of four strains: the Antiochene proper, which derives from the liturgical ritual of the great patriarchal see of Antioch when it was independently active (especially in the fourth to fifth centuries), and then the Maronite (Lebanese), Armenian, and Byzantine rites, which are variations on it. The earliest literary indications of the Antiochene source can be seen in the classic early texts of the Didascalia Apostolorum and the Apostolic Constitutions. The liturgical remarks in the writings of John

Chrysostom also represent his knowledge of the ritual, for he was a priest of the Antioch cathedral before assuming the see of Constantinople. It can be readily identified by the prayers of intercession being placed close after the *epiclesis*, not before it. The liturgy of Jerusalem was also very close to it. In the second millennium the Antiochene rite underwent many adaptations, involving Arabic influences and Latinization after the era of the Crusades.

After the Council of Chalcedon, Constantinople was granted extensive subordinate ecclesiastical territories (canon 28) in Asia, Pontus, and Thrace. The eventual great extent of the cultural influence of Byzantium led to slightly variant forms of the liturgy in Greek, Slavonic, Georgian, Albanian, and Italic. The two main eucharistic liturgies in use were those of John Chrysostom (for most of the year) and that of St. Basil the Great (for Lent and certain great feasts). In Lent, when a eucharistic liturgy was not celebrated, a solemn ritual of vesperal communion was offered instead, called the Liturgy of Pre-sanctified Gifts, attributed to Pope Gregory the Dialogist.[25] The Liturgy of St. Chrysostom is fundamentally an abbreviated form of the priestly prayers of the Liturgy of Saint Basil. The anaphoras are formed of rich amalga of Nicene patristic prayers celebrating the incarnational economy of God the Word made flesh.

As this liturgy was that of the imperial capital, it was surrounded with ever increasing and dramatic ceremonials of great solemnity. It also encountered, at several periods, the liturgical traditions of Jerusalem, as preserved and developed by the great monastic houses of Palestine, especially Mar Saab, near Bethlehem. This mixed into the ceremonial pomp an extensive use of psalmody and highly ornate hymns, greatly extended from scriptural narratives. This Sabbaite usage and the so-called cathedral rite of Byzantium being combined led to an elaborately complex liturgy that gave a common spiritual, and very elevated, character to the whole Eastern communion under the presidency of Constantinople. Nothing like the "low Mass" of the Western rite ever developed in the Byzantine world. To this day the liturgy takes many hours to celebrate and is always sung, never simply recited.

***The Alexandrian liturgical family.*** The Alexandrian rite symbolically claims the authorship of St. Mark the Evangelist, which indicates its ecclesial origin in Africa. The family is characteristically marked by having the great series of intercessory prayers in the Eucharist come before the Sanctus, and by having two prayers of *epiclesis* (invocation of the Spirit over the eucharistic elements), one before and one after the words of institution. Before the split of the Miaphysites and Chalcedonians that took place after the middle of the fifth century, the language of the Alexandrian church had been Greek. Patristic writers who give evidence as to the Alexandrian liturgy comprise

---

[25] The Byzantine manner of referring to Gregory the Great, author of the *Dialogues*.

a roll call of the great theologians of Alexandria: Athanasius, Didymus, Timothy Theophilus, and Cyril; as well as theologians from adjacent towns in the archdiocese: Synesius of Cyrene and Isidore of Pelusium.

Coptic, which had also been a language more in evidence outside the great Romano-Egyptian capital, is evidenced in the altar book (*euchologion*) of Bishop Serapion of Thmuis (d. 362) and many ancient papyri and pottery fragments. There are later Coptic sources with three distinct anaphoras: those attributed to St. Cyril of Alexandria, St. Gregory the Theologian, and St. Basil of Caesarea (the latter not the Byzantine rite of the same name). The Alexandrian family includes not only the Coptic rite but also the Ethiopic, but the latter is differentiated by having within it a series of influences from the missionaries (the "nine saints") who came to Ethiopia (then known as India) from the Antiochene patriarchate in its missionary expansion in the sixth century. There then followed a mixing of the Coptic and East-Syriac rites in Ethiopia. Ethiopian liturgy is now known only from relatively late manuscripts, but the tradition is richly poetic, with many Marian hymns. It uses Ge'ez as its sacred language. Bohairic Coptic was the main language of influence in Alexandria after the ninth century, and Coptic monasticism had a strong effect on the liturgical forms. A major concern was to defend the christological unitive tradition of St. Cyril of Alexandria and resist Chalcedon's apparent dualism.

Christian liturgy, and the many variations it demonstrates, is a profoundly rich environment that has sustained Christian identity, almost (if not entirely) devoid of controversial battles, but rather focused on an ecstatic and eschatologically elevated sense of God's redemptive presence in and to his church. Most of the classical liturgical forms were forged in the fires when Christian intellectual life was at its height, and the majestic prayers that make up the eucharistic rites are not only deep and insightful but trained generation after generation of Christians in the fundamental traditions of the faith. Far more than a doctrinal creed (though these too were often incorporated into the liturgies), the liturgy presented the Christian faith as a set of saving deeds by God, whose life ran into this world in a trinitarian outreach and whose mercy was cause for celebratory thanksgiving.

Hearing these great prayers repeated week after week in great communal celebrations (the liturgy was never a personal prayer, but an occasion for the whole clan, parish or city, to gather) formed an international consciousness of the faith that embedded itself in a wholesale cultural memory that is deeply comparable from the highlands of Ethiopia to the forests of Russia, from the borders of China to the Byzantino-Greek territories of southern Italy. At times of persecution, conquest by foreign foes, and general cultural loss, it was the liturgy that sustained continuity and hope across Christian centuries. It did not need an educated clergy, a cadre of theologians, or even supportive institutions for it to live. It lived out of collective memory and long familiarity with ancestral prayers. Its vivid eschatological character (often evoked in the Eastern rites by lengthy repetitions) and its deeply poetic forms provided the lifeblood to Christianity in ages past. Classical liturgy worked through a very slow rhythm and provided a genetic imprint for the church in antiquity. In many places this remains true to this day, and it is a considerable loss when liturgical rites are (generally) excluded from the formal study of significant moments in historical theology: for in relegating liturgical studies to the sidelines, as if they were merely about rubrics for ceremonial, scholars of Christian history might sometimes overlook the most characteristic evidence of Christian theology: its spiritual application in communal prayer.

## A SHORT READER

***Justin Martyr,* First Apology 65.** But after we have washed him in this manner,[26] when he has been convinced and has given assent to our teaching, we then bring him to the place where those who are called the brethren are assembled, so that we may offer heartfelt prayers in common both for ourselves and for the newly illuminated person, and for all people in all places, so that we may be counted worthy, now that we have learned the truth, and also by our works to be proven good citizens and keepers of the commandments, so that we may be saved with an everlasting salvation. Having ended the prayers, we greet one another with a kiss. There is then brought to the president of the brethren bread and a cup of wine mixed with water; and taking them, he gives praise and glory to the Father of the universe, through the name of the Son and of the Holy Spirit, and offers thanks at considerable length for our being counted worthy to receive these things at his hands. And when he has concluded the prayers and the thanksgivings, all the people present express their agreement by saying "Amen." This word *Amen* answers in the Hebrew language to "let it be so." And when the president has thus given thanks, and all the people have expressed their agreement, those whom we call the deacons give to each of those present a portion of the bread and wine mixed with water, over which the thanksgiving was pronounced, and they carry away a small amount to those who are absent.

***Justin Martyr,* First Apology 66.** And among ourselves we call this food the Eucharist. And no one is allowed to share in it except those who believe that

---
[26] Baptism rituals.

the things that we teach are true, and who have been washed with the washing that is for the remission of sins, for regeneration, and who are so living as Christ has commanded us. For we do not receive these things as if they were common bread and common drink; but just as Jesus Christ our Savior, having been made flesh by the Word of God, bore both flesh and blood for our salvation, just so have we been taught that this food, which is blessed by the prayer of his word and from which our blood and flesh by transmutation are nourished, is the flesh and blood of that same Jesus who was made flesh.

**Cyprian of Carthage,** **Epistle *63.14*.** If our Lord and God, Christ Jesus, is himself the high priest of God the Father, and first offered himself as a sacrifice to the Father, and then commanded this to be done in remembrance of himself, then it is most certain that the priest truly acts in Christ's place when he reproduces what Christ himself did; and he then offers a true and complete sacrifice to God the Father if he begins to make the offering as he sees Christ himself has offered it.

**Cyril of Jerusalem,** **Catechetical Lectures *20.1-6*.** These daily introductions into the mysteries, and new instructions, which are the announcements of new truths, are profitable to us, and especially to you, who have been renewed from an old condition to one that is new. And so it is necessary for me to lay before you the sequel of yesterday's lecture, that you may learn the symbolism behind those things that were administered to you in the inner chamber. As soon as you entered, then, you took off your tunic; and this was an image of putting off the old man with all his deeds (Col 3:9). Having stripped yourselves, you were naked; and in this you also imitated Christ, who was stripped naked on the cross, and by his nakedness he cast off from himself the principalities and powers and openly triumphed over them on the tree. And because the hostile powers made their lair within your members, this is why you may no longer wear that old garment. Her I do not speak of the visible tunic, rather the old man, which grows corrupt in the lusts of deceit (Eph 4:22). May the soul, which has once put this old man away, never again put him back on, but rather confess with the spouse of Christ in the Song of Songs: "I have put off my garment, how shall I put it on again?" (Song 5:3). This is a marvel. You were naked in the sight of all and were not ashamed; for truly you then bore the likeness of the first-formed Adam, who was naked in the garden and was not ashamed. Then, when you were stripped, you were anointed with sanctified oil, from the very hairs of your head to your feet, and were made partakers of that good olive tree, who is Jesus Christ. For you were cut off from the wild olive tree, and grafted into the good one, and were made to share the richness of the true olive tree. The holy oil, therefore, was a symbol of the participation of the richness of Christ, being a blessing to drive away every trace of demonic influence. As it was with the breathing of the saints over you, and the invocation of the name of God, which like a fierce flame, scorched and drove out evil spirits, so also this sanctified oil receives such virtue by the invocation of God through prayer, so as not only to burn and cleanse away the traces of sins but also to chase away all the invisible powers of the evil one. After these things, you were led to the holy pool of divine baptism, just as Christ was carried from the cross to the tomb, which is here before our eyes.[27] And each of you was asked whether he believed in the name of the Father, and of the Son, and of the Holy Spirit, and you made that saving confession of faith, and descended three times into the water and ascended again; here also hinting by means of a symbol at the three-day burial of Christ. For just as our Savior passed three days and three nights in the depths of the earth, so you also in your first ascent out of the water represented the first day Christ spent in the earth, and by your descent, the night; for just as he who is in the night no longer sees, but he who is in the daylight remains in the light, just so in your descent, as in the night, you saw nothing, but in ascending again you were as in the day. And at one and the same moment you were both dying and being born again; and that water of salvation was at once your grave and your mother. What Solomon spoke, concerning others, will suit you also; for he said: "There is a time to give birth, and a time to die" (Eccles 3:2); but for you, it was in the reverse order, for there was a time to die and a time to be born, and one and the same time brought about both of these things, and so your birth went hand in hand with your death. What a strange and inconceivable thing! We did not really die, we were not really buried, we were not really crucified and raised again; but our imitation of these things was in a type, yet our salvation was in reality. Christ was actually crucified, and actually buried, and truly rose again; and all these things he has freely bestowed on us, that by sharing his sufferings by our imitation of them, we might gain salvation in reality. What surpassing loving-kindness! Christ received nails in his undefiled hands and feet, and suffered anguish; while he freely bestows salvation on me without pain or toil, merely by fellowship in his suffering. Let no one ever think that baptism is merely the grace of the remission of sins, or what is more, only the grace of adoption, such as was that of John, whose baptism conferred only the remission of sins. No. We know full well, that just as it purges our sins and ministers to us the gift of the Holy Ghost,

---

[27] Cyril was speaking in the Church of the Resurrection in Jerusalem.

so also it is the counterpart of the sufferings of Christ. This is why Paul cried aloud so recently and said: "Or are you ignorant that all we who were baptized into Christ Jesus were baptized into his death? We were buried therefore with him by baptism into his death." He said these words to some who were disposed to think that baptism ministers to us only the remission of sins and adoption, but has not beyond this given us also the fellowship, in type, of Christ's true sufferings.

**Cyril of Jerusalem, Catechetical Lectures 23.1-11.** By the loving-kindness of God you have heard sufficiently at our former meetings concerning baptism, and chrism, and partaking of the body and blood of Christ; and now it is necessary to pass on to what is next in order, meaning today I will set the crown on the spiritual building of your edification. You have seen the deacon giving water to the bishop and presbyters who stand around God's altar, to wash with. He did not offer this because of any bodily defilement; it is not for that. For we did not enter the church at the beginning with defiled bodies. No, the washing of hands is a symbol that you yourselves ought to be pure from all sinful and unlawful deeds; for since the hands are a symbol of action, it is clear enough that by washing them we represent the purity and blamelessness of our conduct. Did you not hear the blessed David explaining this very mystery, and saying, "I will wash my hands in innocence, and so will walk around your Altar, O Lord?" The washing of hands, therefore, is a symbol of immunity from sin. Then the deacon cries aloud, "Receive one another; and let us give one another the kiss." Do not suppose that this kiss is of the same type as those we offer publicly among friends. It is not like this. This kiss blends souls one with another and brings about complete forgiveness for them. The kiss, therefore, is the sign that our souls are mingled together and banish all remembrance of wrongs. This is why Christ said, "If you are offering your gift at the altar, and there you remember that your brother has anything against you, leave your gift there upon the altar, and make your way first to be reconciled to your brother, and then come and offer your gift." The kiss, therefore, is reconciliation, and for this reason it is holy: as the blessed Paul somewhere cried out, saying, "Greet one another with a holy kiss" (1 Cor 16:20); and Peter said, "with a kiss of charity" (1 Pet 3:15). After this the priest cries aloud, "Lift up your hearts." For truly in that most awesome moment we ought to have our heart on high with God, and not below, thinking of earth and earthly things. This is why the priest bids us all in that moment to dismiss all the cares of this life, our domestic anxieties, and to have our hearts in heaven with the merciful God. Then you all answer: "We lift them up to the Lord," giving your assent to this by your avowal. But no one can do this properly if he only says "We lift up our hearts to the Lord," with his mouth, but in his mind all his thoughts are fastened on the cares of this life. But at all times God should be in our mind, but if this is impossible by reason of human infirmity, at least at that moment it should be our heartfelt effort to make it so. Then the priest says, "Let us give thanks to the Lord." And indeed it is our duty to give thanks, because he called us, even though we were unworthy, to so great a grace; and he reconciled us even when we were his enemies, in order to grant to us the Spirit of adoption. Then you all respond: "It is right and fitting." In giving thanks we certainly do a fitting thing and a right thing. He, however, did not do right: he did more than right, in doing us this benefit and counting us worthy of such great benefits. After this, we make mention of heaven, and earth, and sea; of sun and moon; of stars and all the creation, rational and irrational, visible and invisible; of angels, archangels, virtues, dominions, principalities, powers, thrones; of the cherubim with many faces; in effect we repeat that call of David when he said: "Magnify the Lord with me." We make mention also of the seraphim, whom Isaiah in the Holy Spirit saw standing around the throne of God, with two of their wings veiling their face, and with two their feet, while with two they flew and cried out "Holy, Holy, Holy, is the Lord of Sabaoth" (Is 6:2-3). The reason we recite this confession of our God, as delivered to us from the seraphim, is that we too may share with the hosts of the world above in their hymn of praise. Then, having sanctified ourselves by these spiritual hymns, we pray to the merciful God to send forth his Holy Spirit on the gifts lying before him, that he may make the bread into the body of Christ, and the wine into the blood of Christ; for whatever the Holy Ghost has touched is most certainly sanctified and changed. Then, after the bloodless ministry of the spiritual sacrifice is completed, we beseech God, over that sacrifice of propitiation, for the common peace of the churches, for the welfare of the world; for kings; for soldiers and allies; for the sick; for the afflicted; and, in a word, for all who stand in need of help, we pray together and offer up this sacrifice. Then we commemorate also those who have fallen asleep before us, first patriarchs, prophets, apostles, martyrs, so that through their prayers and intercessions God will receive our petitions. Then we pray also on behalf of the holy fathers and bishops who have fallen asleep before us and, in short, all for who in past years have fallen asleep among us, believing that it will be a very great benefit to their souls, if the supplication is sent on high while that holy and most awful sacrifice is still set forth. And I wish to show you this by means of an illustration. For I know that many say that once a soul has departed from this world, either in sin or without sin, then what use is it if it is then commemorated in prayer. Well, if a king were to banish certain people who had offended him, and then their kin should weave a crown and offer it to him on behalf of those undergoing punishment, would he not grant a remission of their penalties? In the same way we, when we offer to him our supplications for those who have fallen asleep, though they be sinners, weave no crown, but instead we offer up Christ, who is sacrificed for our sins, propitiating our merciful God for them as well as for ourselves. Next, after these things, we say that prayer that the Savior delivered to his own disciples, with a pure conscience calling God our Father, and saying, "Our Father, who are in heaven." O what excellent and surpassing loving-kindness of God! He has bestowed such a complete forgiveness of evil deeds on those who rebelled against him, and so came to the utmost extremes of misery, and so great a share of grace that they can even call him their Father. "Our Father, who are in heaven"; and indeed they indeed are a heaven themselves who bear the image of the heavenly (1 Cor 15:49), in whom is God, dwelling and walking in them (2 Cor 6:16).

**Byzantine Liturgy of St. John Chrysostom, Priestly Prayer of the Cherubic Hymn.** None of those who are entangled in carnal desires and pleasures is worthy to approach or draw near or minister to you, King of glory; for to serve you is great and awesome even for the heavenly powers. Yet on account of your inexpressible and boundless love for humankind you became man without change or alteration and were named our high priest; and as master of all you have committed to us the sacred ministry of this liturgical sacrifice without shedding of blood. For you alone, Lord our God, are ruler over all things in heaven and on earth, mounted on the throne of the cherubim, Lord of the seraphim and King of Israel, the only holy one, resting in the holy place. Therefore I entreat you, who alone are good and ready to hear: Look on me, your sinful and unprofitable servant, and purify my soul and heart from an evil conscience. By the power of your Holy Spirit enable me, who am clothed with the grace of your priesthood, to stand at this your holy table and celebrate the mystery of your holy and most pure body and your precious blood. For to you I come, bending my neck and praying: Do not turn away your face from me, nor reject me from among your children, but count me, your sinful and unworthy servant, worthy to offer these gifts to you. For you are the one who offers and is offered, who receives and is distributed, Christ our God, and to you we give glory, together with your Father, who is without beginning, and your all-holy, good and life-giving Spirit, now and ever, and to the ages of ages. Amen. Let us who mystically represent the cherubim and sing the thrice-holy hymn to the life-giving Trinity now lay aside all earthly cares, that we may receive the King of all, invisibly escorted by the angelic hosts. Alleluia, alleluia, alleluia.

**Byzantine Liturgy of St. John Chrysostom, the Holy Anaphora.** It is fitting and right to hymn you, to bless you, to praise you, to give you thanks, to worship you in every place of your dominion; for you are God, ineffable, incomprehensible, invisible, inconceivable, ever existing, eternally the same; you and your only begotten Son and your Holy Spirit. You brought us from nonexistence into being, and when we had fallen, you raised us up again, and left nothing undone until you had brought us up to heaven and had granted us your kingdom that is to come. For all these things we give thanks to you, and to your only begotten Son and your Holy Spirit; for all the benefits that we have received, known and unknown, manifest and hidden. We thank you also for this liturgy, which you have been pleased to accept from our hands, though there stand around you thousands of archangels and tens of thousands of angels, the cherubim and the seraphim, six-winged and many-eyed, soaring aloft upon their wings—singing the triumphal hymn, shouting, proclaiming, and saying: "Holy, holy, holy, Lord of hosts; heaven and earth are full of your glory. Hosanna in the highest. Blessed is he who comes in the name of the Lord. Hosanna in the highest." With these blessed powers, Master, lover of mankind, we also cry aloud and say: "Holy are you and all-holy, you and your only begotten Son and your Holy Spirit; holy are you and all holy, and magnificent is your glory." You so loved your world that you gave your only begotten Son, so that whoever believes in him might not perish but have eternal life. And when he had come and had fulfilled the whole dispensation for us, in the night in which he was given up, or rather gave himself up for the life of the world, he took bread in his holy, most pure, and blameless hands and, when he had given thanks, and had blessed it, sanctified and broken it, he gave it to his holy disciples and apostles, saying: "Take, eat, this is my body, which is broken for you, for the remission of sins." Likewise, after supper he also took the cup, saying: "Drink from this, all of you; this is my blood of the new covenant, which is shed for you and for many for the remission of sins." Remembering therefore this command of our Savior and all that has been done for us: the cross, the tomb, the resurrection on the third day, the ascension into heaven, the sitting at the right hand, the second and glorious coming; offering you your own of your own, because of all things, and for all things—[**People:** "We praise you, we bless you, we give thanks to you, O Lord, and we pray to you, our God"]—Again we offer you this spiritual and bloodless worship, and we ask and pray and supplicate you: send down your Holy Spirit on us and on these gifts here set forth, and make this bread the precious body of your Christ, and what is in this chalice, the precious blood of your Christ, changing them by your Holy Spirit [**People:** "Amen, Amen, Amen"] so that those who partake of them may obtain vigilance of soul, remission of sins, the communion of your Holy Spirit, the fullness of the kingdom of heaven, boldness to speak in your presence, and not judgment or condemnation. Also we offer you this spiritual worship for those who have gone to their rest in the faith, ancestors, fathers, mothers, patriarchs, prophets, apostles, preachers, evangelists, martyrs, confessors, ascetics, and every righteous spirit made perfect in faith; especially for our most holy, most pure, most blessed, and glorious Lady, the Theotokos and Ever-Virgin Mary; for the holy prophet, forerunner, and Baptist John, the holy, glorious, and all-praised apostles, for our holy patron saint, and for the saints whose memory we keep this day, and for all your saints, at whose prayers visit us, O God. Remember too all those who have fallen asleep in hope of resurrection to eternal life, and give them rest where the light of your countenance watches. Also we beseech you: Remember, Lord, all Orthodox bishops, who rightly proclaim the word of your truth, the whole order of priests, the diaconate in Christ, and every order of clergy. Also we offer you this spiritual worship for the whole world, for the holy, catholic, and apostolic church, for those who live in chastity and holiness of life; for the leaders of this land. Grant them, Lord, a peaceful administration, so that in their tranquility we too may live calm and peaceful lives in godliness and holiness. Among the first, remember, Lord, his Grace our bishop, and grant that he may serve your holy churches in peace, safety, honor, health, and length of days, rightly proclaiming the word of your truth. Remember, Lord, the city in which we dwell, and every city, town, and village, and the faithful who dwell in them. Remember, Lord, those who travel by land, air, water, [or space,] the sick, the suffering, those in captivity, and their safety and salvation. Remember, Lord, those who bring offerings, those who care for the beauty of your holy churches, and those who remember the poor, and send down on us all your rich mercies: and grant that with one voice and one heart, we may glorify your all-honored and majestic name, of the Father, the Son, and the Holy Spirit, now and ever, and to the ages of ages. Amen.

**The Ethiopic Anaphora of St. Gregory the Theologian, priests' preface.** We give thanks to our Great Benefactor, the merciful God and Father of our Lord God and Savior Jesus Christ. We give thanks to you, our holy God, compassionate God, merciful God, who are slow to anger, full of mercy, and righteous. You are our God who has no beginning, and our Savior who has no end. His right hand is fire, and the authority of his word is indestructible; the length of his years is uncountable, and there are no bounds to the extent of his dominion. He is no respecter of persons, and neither does he turn his face away from giving an answer. He does not bow down to a rich man because of his riches, nor dismiss the poor because of their poverty. For you see what is hidden from the outset and gaze on everything even to the last breath. [The deacon says: "Let us look on the beauty of the glory of our God."] This is he who made heaven. This is he who built the earth. His divinity is unfathomable. It has neither height nor depth, nor length nor width. It has no right or left or center, but rather fills all the ends of the world. He is hidden from the minds of all angels, for none can know his nature and none can count the things he formed with his own hand. He came from above, the heavens, which are his own firmament, and taking our nature he was incarnated and was made man, taking the body of his first creature, he descended without being emptied of the joy of his divinity, and through his death he brought us to life. And so, we lift up the eyes of our hearts to you, and we bow down our stubborn hearts before you. We give you our submission. We glorify your kingdom. And with your archangels we offer to you this incense.... [The people say: "Remember us, O Lord, in your kingdom"].

## FURTHER READING

### Early Liturgy

Bradshaw, P. *The Search for the Origins of Christian Worship.* Oxford: Oxford University Press, 2002.

Carroll, T., and T. Halton. *Liturgical Practice in the Fathers.* Wilmington, DE: M. Glazier, 1988.

Deiss, L. *Early Sources of the Liturgy.* London: Geoffrey Chapman, 1967.

Dix, G. *The Shape of the Liturgy.* London: Dacres, 1978.

Jones, C., G. Wainwright, and E. Yarnold, eds. *The Study of Liturgy.* Oxford: Oxford University Press, 1978.

Jungmann, J. A. *The Early Liturgy to the Time of Gregory the Great.* Notre Dame, IN: Notre Dame University Press, 1959.

Schulz, H. J. *The Byzantine Liturgy.* New York: Pueblo, 1986.

Srawley, J. S. *The Early History of the Liturgy.* Cambridge: Cambridge University Press, 1947.

Taft, R. *The Byzantine Rite: A Short History.* Collegeville, MN: Liturgical Press, 1992.

### Eucharistic Liturgy

Botte, B., ed. *Eucharisties d'Orient et d'Occident.* Paris: Editions du Cerf, 1970.

Goguel, M. *L'Eucharistie des Origines à Justin Martyr.* Paris: Fischbacher, 1910.

Hamman, A. *L'Eucharistie dans l'antiquité chrétienne.* Paris: Desclée de Brouwer, 1981.

———. *Prières eucharistiques des premiers siècles.* Paris: Desclée de Brouwer, 1957.

Hanson, R. P. C. "Eucharistic Offering in the Pre-Nicene Fathers." *Proceedings of the Royal Irish Academy* 76 (1976): 75-96.

LaVerdiere, E. *The Eucharist in the New Testament and in the Early Church.* Collegeville, MN: Liturgical Press, 1996.

McGowan, A. *Ascetic Eucharists: Food and Drink in Early Christian Ritual Meals.* Oxford: Clarendon, 1999.

Sheerin, D. J. *The Eucharist.* Message of the Fathers of the Church 7. Wilmington, DE: M. Glazier, 1986.

Triaccca, A. M. "Liturgy and Tradition." In *Encyclopedia of Ancient Christianity*, ed. A. Di Berardino, 587-95. Downers Grove, IL: InterVarsity Press, 2014.

Wainwright, G. *Eucharist and Eschatology.* London: Epworth, 1978.

### Rites of Penance

Langstadt, E. "Tertullian's Doctrine of Sin and the Power of Absolution in the *De Pudicitia*." *StPatr* 2 (1957): 251-57.

Turner, H. E. W. *The Patristic Doctrine of Redemption.* London: Mowbray, 1952.

Vogel, C. *Le pécheur et la pénitence dans l'Église ancienne.* Paris: Editions du Cerf, 1966.

Ward, B. *Harlots of the Desert: A Study of Repentance in Early Monastic Sources.* Kalamazoo, MI: Cistercian Publications, 1987.

White, L. M. "Transactionalism in the Penitential Thought of Gregory the Great." *Romische Quartalischrift fur christliche Altertumskunde und Kirkengeschichte* 21 (1978): 33-51.

# THE GREAT PARTING OF THE WAYS

## Greek East and Latin West in the Tenth to Eleventh Centuries

### BYZANTINE MONASTIC RENEWAL: SYMEON THE NEW THEOLOGIAN AND HESYCHASM

In the formative years of Constantinople in the late fourth century, monasticism had already taken an early foothold. It especially took advantage of the military protection offered by the great walls of Constantine, and several monasteries were built, half hermitages, half cenobitic or common-life communities, in the semicultivated land outside the walls. Soon, however, the space contained within Constantine's first city walls proved far too constricting, and the great defensive land walls of Theodosius were constructed considerably farther out, now enclosing some of the earliest religious houses within the city. Thus was born at the imperial city the phenomenon of city monachism: traditions of desert spirituality, but now lived out in the teeming heart of a great metropolis.

One of the immediate results of this was that at the capital monastics were deeply involved in many aspects of state and civic life. As literate and trustworthy stewards, they were in high demand as civil servants. Many monasteries flourished in Constantinople throughout its long history, and as most houses in the Byzantine world followed their own charter (which the founder had the right to draw up and specify the particular focus of the house), they represented different specialisms. Some were houses devoted to study, the collection of libraries, and the copying and preservation of texts. The great Stoudium monastery became world famous for its invention of small-case writing, called minuscule, which allowed it to copy texts with greater rapidity. Others were renowned for the quality of their liturgical life. The Evergetinos monastery was once large and prestigious. Today no trace of it can be found in

Constantinople's archaeological remains, but it certainly exists "virtually," for its extensive liturgical manuscripts turn up in many of the world's great libraries and testify to the high quality of its ritual and prayer life.[1] Other monasteries were famed for their political abbots (*higumens*), leaders, and poets. The sixth-century Romanos the Singer (*Melodus*) composed hymns in the great cathedral of Hagia Sophia that traveled all over the Greek-speaking world.

At the end of the first millennium, monasticism at the great city underwent something of a renaissance. It can be particularly seen in the life and works of one of the most extraordinary mystics of the Byzantine world: Symeon the New Theologian (949–1022). Symeon was a controversial figure in his time. His works are among the most vivid of the Eastern Christian church's tradition, with their appeal to direct personal experience. His title "New Theologian" began, in all probability, as a denigration from his enemies. As an "innovator," his work and person would be held in low esteem in the highly traditional theological circles of medieval Byzantium. Soon, however, his disciples turned the sarcasm to their advantage, elevating him and his work (even though he is hardly a theologian in the traditional sense of a leading patristic dogmatician) to the rarefied heights of only two others who were given that designation of *theologos* in Eastern Christian thought: the apostle John and St. Gregory of Nazianzus. Symeon's life was spent in a highly volatile political period of the empire, when powerful aristocratic clans were in high tension with the central imperial administrations. It gives us much interesting information about conditions in the Byzantine Empire during a relatively unknown period.

His spiritual teaching coincides with a period in Byzantine religious life in which a new pneumatological interest can be discerned. He was afterward to be regarded as a forefather of the Hesychast movement, although the influential treatise assigned to his name, concerning the physical method of hesychastic prayer, so highly prized among the Athonites and preserved in the *Philokalia* under his name, is not by him.[2] Nor can certain noted characteristics of later Hesychastic method be found in his work, such as devotion to the practice of the Jesus prayer or emphasis on monologistic invocations.[3] Nevertheless, his ecstatic, light-centered mystical enthusiasm

---

[1]The Byzantine department of Queen's University Belfast has made a special study focused around it in recent years.
[2]Hesychastic prayer is the "Jesus prayer." Hesychastic spirituality (so named from the Greek word *hesychia*, or "spiritual quietness"), was particularly expansive in the eary years of the second millennium. It reinterpreted classical monastic mysticism in a more personalist and ecstatic style. See further J. A. McGuckin, *Standing in God's Holy Fire* (London: Darton, Longman, and Todd, 2001). The *Philokalia* is the great collection of the church's mystical writings from the early to medieval periods, collated in the eighteenth century and published in the nineteenth. It has been translated in several volumes by P. Sherrard, G. Palmer, and K. Ware (London: Faber, 1979–1999).
[3]Long repetitions of a short phrase from the Scriptures.

laid a path that later writers would develop. In a real but heavily qualified sense he can be regarded as a founder of what later (and independent of him) came to be Byzantine Hesychastic mysticism.

Symeon was born in 949 (named George before his monastic profession) to a wealthy Byzantine family, provincial aristocrats from Galata in Asia Minor. The family had several highly placed court connections in the capital, and they intended the young George to follow in a courtly profession and so had him eunuchized as an infant—a common practice in that period for younger sons, as many high court positions were restricted to eunuchs. His father brought him to Constantinople for his education in 960, and his uncle served as patron of the boy, advancing him toward a glittering political career. In the bloody street fighting of 963, Symeon's uncle was one of the casualties as Nicephorus Phocas seized the imperial throne. Symeon's hagiographer, Nicetas Stethatos, tells us only that the uncle was "ushered out of life in no ordinary manner," for he is ever bent on removing any sign of controversy from the *Vita* of his subject, whom he knows to have been very controversial in his lifetime, and he suggests that the child abandoned his education at this point from motives of piety. In fact, after a short time Symeon reappears in an elevated social setting. An unknown senator had taken him onto his household staff. He attended the palace daily and soon assumed senatorial rank himself.

In 969, when George was twenty, he describes himself as a somewhat rakish youth, traveling to and from court on business (probably family business). He first encountered the Studite monk Symeon Eulabes at this time, and like other aristocrats gathered round this odd but generously charismatic figure who served as a confessor-father to the group. Symeon visited him whenever he was in the city, and the monk gave him spiritual books to read, but clearly there was little more to the connection until the occasion, around this time, that he had an experience that he described, much later as a monk himself, as having been highly significant for him. He tells us, then, in an autobiographical retrospective, that he had been in a state of anxiety (there was another palace coup in the same year that John Tzimisces seized the throne), overwhelmed by the thought of his sins and searching for a figure who could truly reconcile him to Christ. At this time he was praying in his room when he saw a shining light and behind it an even more radiant light. He later interprets this as his spiritual father, Symeon, spiritually present and interceding for him with Christ. Nothing much seems to have changed in the outward circumstances of George's life subsequent to that, but it was a decisive moment nonetheless, a hook on which he would later build the structure of his whole spiritual autobiography, where conversion and repentance form central motifs.

Years later, when he emerged as a leading spiritual master himself, he locates his whole experience of the spiritual father's critical mediatory role for a disciple on the basis of his own experience of Symeon Eulabes's intercession for him with Christ. His own conception of the transmission of the Christian faith is based on this prophetic model (he calls it a golden chain of "saints of the present generation"). Seven years later, in 976, when he was twenty-seven years old, another palace coup initiated a sequence of events that changed his life permanently. The *paracoemomenos* (palace administrator) Basil seized the throne, allegedly on behalf of the young prince (Basil II), and Symeon's family seems to have been clearly marked by the new regime as hostile elements. His political career was definitively terminated at this point, and he seems to have taken temporary refuge with his spiritual father at the Studite monastery. Here he tells us that he once again he experienced an overwhelming vision of light. He saw the radiance of Christ, directly this time, he tells his readers, and this became for him a definitive conversion point. It marks his definitive entrance into the monastic state.

In a short time Symeon was moved from the Stoudium to the nearby St. Mamas monastery at the Xylokerkos Gate in the capital. His hagiographer of the next generation, Nicetas, and those who follow him too trustingly, have seen this as an "expulsion." It ought to be read as his promotion and his permanent protection by sympathetic patrons outside the court, for only three years later, in 979–980, Symeon was confirmed as abbot of the same household. It is a fact that indicates the significant patronage he could bring as a powerfully connected leader, for he continued his leadership, now out of politics, but still protected by many powerful friends in the influential circles of the Byzantine church, where monastic and aristocratic lifestyles were closely allied. His elevation to the office, recently vacated by the previous *higumen* of St. Mamas, who was in advanced age, came under the patronage of the patriarch Antony the Studite (rather than the sequence of patriarchs Nicetas suggests in the *Vita*—which is often confused on dates and personages or wishes to hide many serious elements of conflict in the life of his subject).

Symeon was able to command a very significant outlay of money at this time. He substantially refurbished the site of St. Mamas, and at this period he also began to deliver the traditional morning *catecheses*, or spiritual instructions, to the monks of the community, teachings that have survived as the central body of his work. There were more than thirty monks, making it a significant household. Much of his approach in the monastic *Catecheses* is traditional Studite observance, but much of the original verve that also characterizes his writing and discourse emanates from what he learned from Symeon the Studite (*Eulabes*). So, for example, he places extreme stress on the personal, dedicated obedience he expects the spiritual father should be given by his monks. He stresses the necessity for direct personal experience; he lays great emphasis on the need for regular shedding of tears from a deeply moved spirit, even insisting that without tears a monk should never approach the Eucharist. This dramatic underlining of the traditional allegiance that the antique monastic discipline had expected that neophytes should give their spiritual fathers, and its reclaiming and refurbishing now in the hands of the abbot of St. Mamas, applied to the entire community, however experienced they were, led to serious disruptions within his community.

In 986–989 the wider Byzantine society was disrupted by another aristocratic attempt to topple the throne, under Bardas Phocas (drawing support from aristocrats in Asia Minor, Symeon's homeland). In 986 Basil II dismissed his regent and assumed total power. After Phocas's defeat in 989 he moved against his enemies, among whom he seemed to outnumber Symeon. In the same period (986–987) Symeon Eulabes died at the Stoudium monastery, leaving Symeon as the new head and leader of his school of disciples, a circle that included both monastics and lay aristocrats.

Some time between 995 and 998 the growing opposition to Symeon's discipline and teaching broke out in the form of a revolt by a large number of his community at St. Mamas. They threatened him at morning service and lodged an official complaint about his behavior at the patriarchal court. The hagiographical *Vita Symeonis* attempts to minimize the significance of the revolt and has a confused version of how the protesters were exiled yet brought back at Symeon's own insistence so that they could live with him under his charity. A more careful reading might interpret this as clear evidence that while the initial complaint was not sustained, there remained a determined focus of opposition to Symeon's rule, right up to the time of his deposition and exile a few years afterward.

The rising of the monks possibly coincides with the death of Patriarch Nicholas Chrysoberges and the installation of the first appointment of Emperor Basil II in his own right, namely Patriarch Sisinnius II (995–998). Sisinnius was succeeded by Sergius II Manuelites (999–1019), and his court also instituted legal proceedings against Symeon. These processes were more vigorously pursued and resulted eventually in Symeon's exile. The first formal arraignment turned around the issue of the unofficial cult of the master, which Symeon had instituted in memory of Symeon Eulabes. The elder's reputation was attacked in an attempt to discredit the younger Symeon, and after 995 his cult (veneration of his icon) was forbidden at St. Mamas. The hagiographer tries to make out that the opposition to Symeon was neither patriarch nor emperor but Stephen of Alexina, the metropolitan of Nicomedia. The attempt to distance Symeon from official censure is unconvincing. Stephen was not only the patriarchal chancellor but also a trusted confidant of Basil II and had been used before by him in the delicate imperial mission to negotiate with Bardas Sclerus.

The emperor, therefore, chose to move against Symeon by means of the ecclesiastical court process. In 1003 an attempt was made to entangle Symeon in a more formal theological debate concerning his trinitarian orthodoxy (it produced as his response the *Theological Chapters*).[4] He returned an officially satisfactory answer to the charges but also took the opportunity to lambaste Stephen of Alexina for attempting to theologize without first having experienced spiritual impassibility and the direct experience of the divine light. Such a polarized way of seeing and professing the theological task was tantamount to a declaration of war with the official hierarchy. The attrition carried on for six years, culminating in a patriarchal synodical sentence of deposition in 1005, followed by house arrest and then exile in 1009.

The hagiographer tries to depict the cause of the conflict as Symeon's defense of the holy icons, as if it were a revisitation of the ninth-century iconoclastic crisis, but the real causes were more personal and immediate. Symeon himself certainly regarded the issue as "doctrinally" based and localized in his insistent right to claim that a saint can live in the present generation and must judge in accordance with his own God-given lights, above any external, or formalistic, authority. We might extend the definition of *doctrinal* at this point in order to note that in this argument, which is almost synonymous with Symeon's central theological thrust to argue that only the initiated mystic has the right to theologize, the central matter is one of authority. This struggle to assert the proper locus of authority—be it in the imperially controlled circuit of palace and patriarchal throne or in the more diffused and independent networks of aristocratic relations, governed by charismatic, spiritual holy men—was critically important, not merely on the "theological" front proper but also in the wider context of Basil II's determined efforts to assert his predominance over against aristocratic clan groups of all kinds.

On January 3, 1009, Symeon was exiled to Paloukiton, on the Asian shore near Chrysopolis, opposite but definitively closed out from Byzantium. The hagiographer says (though it is highly doubtful) that the patriarch later repented and offered him an episcopal throne, which he refused. Symeon soon found himself able to begin again, for his inner circle of disciples accompanied him into exile, and one of the wealthy aristocrats among them supplied the money to buy the oratory of St. Marina and lands attached to the neighbouring *metochion* of the Eugenios convent. Here, in exile, Symeon wrote some of his most famous works, including the exquisite *Hymns*

---

[4] Which I translated as a student in 1982 (repr., 1992) for Cistercian Press (Kalamazoo, MI).

*of Divine Eros*, which are a rhapsodic classic of Byzantine religious writing.[5] They mark him out as one of the Christian tradition's leading mystics.

In his final years we are told of his journeys to family estates in Asia Minor. On one of his journeys, he suffered an attack of dysentery and died at the age of seventy-three. His relics were preserved at the oratory and could not be brought back into the capital; such was the enduring controversy over his legacy, until the fateful year of 1054. Nicetas's *Vita Symeonis* was partly designed to prepare for their reception in the city.

Symeon was received as a great master of the inner life by the Athonite monks, and his reputation was championed there as a forefather of Hesychasm. In recent decades he has attracted increasing scholarly attention. His teaching is important and significant for the historical light it throws on a difficult and dark period of Byzantine affairs, but more so for the spiritual and mystical themes it treats with such freshness and authority. In a more restricted sense Symeon is also important for the doctrine of spiritual fatherhood, which he represents to such a strong degree and which has had a marked impact on Orthodox spiritual praxis.[6] His *Hymns of Divine Eros* are classics of spiritual writing, depicting the relationship with God in rhapsodic poetry as a matter of fiery passion, which washes the true believer in the cleansing light of the divine presence itself.

## BYZANTINE INTELLECTUAL LIFE

**John Mauropous.** John Mauropous was a brilliant Byzantine intellectual and teacher at the center of a remarkable school of disciples and colleagues at the dawn of the eleventh century.[7] He was born in Paphlagonia, Asia Minor, circa 1000, and came to Constantinople to make his name in the schools there. One of his most devoted pupils was Constantine (Michael) Psellus, who was a favorite of the emperor Constantine IX Monomachos, and through him John was introduced to the court, and elevated as court orator. Along with Psellus, he seems to have fallen from favor around 1054, and just as Psellus was forced to become a monk, so too, probably at this time, John was ordained to church service as Metropolitan bishop of Euchaita (c. 1050–1075+), a "promotion" that at one and the same time rendered him unable to continue in active politics and also required him to leave the capital for a life in the far-off provinces.[8]

He knew it was an exile, and in several letters asks his friend Psellus, once the latter had been restored to favor following the death of Constantine IX, to see whether he

---

[5]Translated by George Maloney (Denville, NJ: Dimension Books, 1975).
[6]See further H. J. M. Turner's monograph on this theme, *St. Symeon the New Theologian and Spiritual Fatherhood* (Leiden: Brill, 1990).
[7]*Mauropous* is a nickname meaning "black foot."
[8]See A. Karpozilos, "The Biography of Ioannes Mauropous Again," *Hellenika* 44 (1994): 51-60.

could manage to get him recalled to life in the capital, where there were libraries and discussions with intelligentsia.[9] In 1047 he had petitioned the emperor to forgive and rehabilitate the conspirators in the rebellion of Leo Tornikios, and this might well have served as a bad mark against him. In his time of exile he composed many fine late Byzantine poems. They have only had an Italian translation into a modern language to date.[10] Toward the end of his life, Mauropous retired as an active bishop and came back to Constantinople and took up residence in the monastery of St. John Prodromos in the Petra district. He died sometime between 1075 and 1081.

His work celebrates the power of oratory as it was used in classical Greek times and in the great patristic past, both to rouse great leaders and to chart a course for them to follow. To this extent he presided as intellectual leader over a circle of very brilliant students, whose works were often more accomplished than his own specific exercises. But it was he who conceived the program for a new renaissance of intellectual leadership of the state. His own body of work, especially after his exile, is composed of a large amount of poetry. Much of it is dedicated to the new genres of ecclesiastical canons, spacious religious poetic forms that were used in the liturgies of the hours. As well as these liturgical poems, he wrote many other poetic works (a cycle of ninety-nine in all), a collection of epigrams, a hagiographical text, and seventy-four extant letters.

Much of his work concerns the fragility of life and the uncertainty of human hopes.[11] He reflects the great uncertainty of political life in his time. When Psellus wrote a panegyric on him at the end of John's life, he focused on his elevation as a bishop as the acme of his career, but his real impact on history was his occupation of the highest point of Byzantine culture (before Psellus tried to supplant him in that role), for he formed a circle in which Greek literary life was resurrected and studied with great care and elegance, and a religious vision was sketched out in which culture and the pursuit of beauty were seen as the handmaidens of true religion, not its seducers. His *Chronographia*, or history of his time, was regarded with disfavor at court, because it tended to be antimilitaristic in a time of great pressure from the advancing Turks.

John Mauropous strongly defended the great philosophers of the past, especially Plato and Plutarch, against the charges raised by many of the monastic faction that

---

[9]These have been collated by A. Karpozilos, *The Letters of Ioannes Mauropous Metropolitan of Euchaita* (Thessaloniki: Association for Byzantine Research, 1990); see also J. M. Hussey, "The Writings of John Mauropus," *Byzantinische Zeitschrift* 44 (1951): 278-82.

[10]R. Anastasi, *Giovanni Mauropode, metropolita di Euchaita, Canzoniere* (Catania: Facoltà di lettere e filosofia, Università di Catania, 1984).

[11]A touching reflection on his exile from home (possibly meaning his forced departure from Constantinople, his "true home") can be found in C. Livanos, "Exile and Return in John Mauropous: Poem 47," *Byzantine and Modern Greek Studies* 32, no. 1 (2008): 38-49.

they were atheists and thus undeserving of study. One of his long-lasting liturgical innovations was the composition of the office for the thirtieth of January, a new feast to celebrate the Three Holy Hierarchs. The three great patristic fathers Basil of Caesarea, Gregory the Theologian, and John Chrysostom each had their own feast day, and their own devotees in the ranks of the students of Constantinople. Monastics lauded Basil the Great, father of monks; theologians and seminarians preferred Gregory; and rhetoricians and preachers held Chrysostom to be the greatest of the three. On the respective feast days the mutual vying for the honor of their patron saint, like university factions in many other times and places, often led to recurring bouts of street violence. Mauropous thought that by combining the three together in one elaborate feast for Greek Orthodox culture, as well as for these men who exemplified the best of Christianity combined with classical learning, that mutual rivalry among the Constantinopolitan students could be avoided and a common vision could be projected that Byzantine Christianity celebrated a great and happy synthesis between Hellenistic culture and Christian faith. In many ways this vision is the synopsis of all his intellectual work.

**Constantine (Michael) Psellus.** Constantine Psellus was one of the leading intellectuals in Constantinople at a time of high cultural renaissance.[12] He was born to a modest, middle-class family in 1018 and rose by his wits as a philosopher and author, dying some time after 1081.[13] Psellus was a brilliant young student in the capital, but at the age of ten he was sent out of the city to serve for several years as a legal assistant to a judge (from whose service he learned a great deal about case law). He returned to the city and once more resumed higher studies under John Mauropous, with whom he formed the center of a caucus of closely related fellow students, numbering two future patriarchs, Constantine Leichoudes and John Xiphilinus, as well as the future emperor Constantine X Doukas (1059–1067). Having served as a provincial judge, he returned to Constantinople some time before the accession of Constantine IX Monomachus.

In the reign of that emperor (1042–1055) he was promoted to the position of secretary to the chancery and from there rose to increasingly higher court positions. At the height of his career he was named the court philosopher, *hypatos ton philosophon*, making him not only a personal adviser to the emperor but also head of the University of Constantinople. Possibly because of his controversial theological views, he soon after fell into disfavor and was forced to resign his state positions in 1054, being ordered also to take the monastic habit, then a civilized alternative to undergoing a

---
[12] Psellus was possibly a joke nickname in Constantinople; it means "stammerer"—attached to one of the most eloquent men of his age.
[13] He makes out that he had patrician roots, but he is known for much exaggeration.

more severe punishment, for it was a legal way of definitively ending a person's political activity, as no one in clerical orders could hold state executive rank of any kind. The monastic name he assumed at that time was Michael, by which he is now more commonly known. He went to Bithynia and entered the Olympus monastery but was soon recalled under Empress Theodora (1055–1056). He regained the trust of the imperial family and served for a long time as a respected political adviser, being involved in two sensitive transitions of imperial power.[14] Under Emperor Michael VII (Doukas) he left the capital city definitively, and little is known of him afterward. His reputation suffered an occlusion for a long time after.

Even so, when he was at the height of his powers he was one of the most prolific of Byzantine intellectuals. His work ranges over philosophy, history, rhetorics, poetry, law, and theology.[15] There is also a collection of *Letters* extant. He stirred up much controversy in church circles of the time by arguing, from an Aristotelian reading of Plato, that the cosmos, though created by God's energy, was set up to work on the basis of its own inherent laws. The miraculous, so much a feature of the Byzantine worldview, he found to be unnecessary as an explanation for phenomena. There might indeed be miracles, but those that are genuine are extremely rare, and they were more generally invoked as explanations by those who did not understand the cosmic laws. Philosophy, he argued, had a right to expound matters under the terms of its own laws and logics. This was a controversial stance to take.

By the time he took such a position, theological and philosophical studies had long been divorced in the Byzantine schools. The growing concern with purity of Orthodox faith had led the patriarchs to remove the entire study of theology from the university curriculum and restrict it to those seeking ordination, and only as conducted by clerical professors in the patriarchal academy. The university environment where liberal and mathematical arts were fostered thus became, in increasing ways, in heightened tension with the ecclesial tradition, which stressed mysterious providence and now majored in miraculous hagiography rather than any further forays into doctrinal metaphysics such as those conducted by the earlier classical Greek fathers (who nevertheless remained greatly studied and admired).

---

[14]From Michael VI Bringas Stratioticus (1056–1057) to Isaac I Komnenus (1057–1059); and again from Romanos IV Diogenes (1068–1071) to his former student Michael VII Doukas (1071–1078).

[15]In rhetoric, he left three funeral orations on notable patriarchs—Michael Caerularius, Constantine Leichoudes, and John Xiphilinus—as well as a manual of rhetorical training exercises for the schoolroom; lessons on grammar and rhetorical forms in poetic meter; and specimen apologetic speeches against various heresies such as the Bogomils and Euchites, as well as examples of his court speeches before the emperors. On poetry, see L. G. Westerink, ed., *Michaelis Pselli Poemata* (Stuttgart: Teubner, 1992). On theology, see Paul Gautier, ed., *Theologica I* (Leipzig: Teubner, 1989); L. G. Westerink and J. M. Duffy, eds., *Theologica II* (Leipzig: Teubner, 2002). A taxonomy of demons (*De Daemonibus*) is no longer thought to be by his hand.

Psellus prided himself on having restored the light of Greek philosophical inquiry in the schools of Constantinople.[16] He reintroduced the serious study of the late Platonic (neo-Platonist) tradition. His school friend John Xiphilinus, now the Byzantine patriarch, felt he had "forsaken Christ to study Plato" and became a strong critic. The same criticism attached itself even more to his successor as head of the school of philosophy, John Italos, who was actually brought to ecclesiastical trial and made to recant his errors publicly after having been charged with resurrecting Plato's doctrines of the eternity of the world and the transmigration of souls.

Psellus's *Chronography* is a history of the empire between the years 976 and 1078, from Basil II of the Macedonian dynasty (the time of Symeon the New Theologian) to Michael VII, in the middle of the Doukid dynasty, who was one of his own pupils.[17] He was a living witness to many of the events he describes. Seeing cosmic events from the "center of the world," at Constantinople, he tells the story aware of the traditions of Greek historiography stretching back to Herodotus and Thucydides. But his personal strength as a writer is the fresh style he gives to the Byzantine manner of telling history through biographical cameos of rulers. His version of events takes a particularly strong psychological approach. Humans are moved to do certain things, wise or foolish, with good or disastrous results, as an expression of strong passions, conflicts or intrigues.[18] These forces, issuing from human social interactions, explain larger events that follow as effects from causes.

As an historian he seeks to put his philosophy into literary form and show how humans cause historical eventualities, deliberately departing from many Byzantine writers before him, who had laid much greater stress on the plans of divine providence unfolding through the sacred empire as a form of continuing "sacred salvation history" embodied in the Christian empire. The manner in which he presents himself as a leading factor involved in many of these events is generally reckoned to be an exaggerated case of wishful thinking more than strict reality. As a historian he

---

[16] Several of his philosophical writings have received modern editions: J. M. Duffy, ed., *Philosophica minora I* (Stuttgart: Teubner, 1992); D. J. O'Meara, ed., *Philosophica minora II* (Leipzig: Teubner, 1989); A. R. Dyck, ed., *Essays on Euripides George of Pisidia, Heliodorus and Achilles Tatius* (Vienna: Verlag der Österreichischen Akademie der Wissenschaften, 1989).

[17] Only one twelfth-century manuscript of the work survived. See K. N. Sathas, ed., *Michael Psellus. Chronographia. Bibliotheca graeca medii aevi*, vol. 4 (Paris: 1874). There is an English translation of it by E. R. A. Sewter (New Haven, CT: Yale University Press, 1953), which is also accessible online at http://sourcebooks.fordham.edu/basis/psellus-chronographia.asp (accessed May 29, 2016). See also S. Papaioannou, *Michael Psellos: Rhetoric and Authorship in Byzantium* (Cambridge: Cambridge University Press, 2013).

[18] See C. Chamberlain, "The Theory and Practice of Imperial Panegyric in Michael Psellus," *Byzantion* 56 (1986): 16-27.

introduces a more realistic style than previous writers, who sought to offer more rigid and formalist models of good and bad behavior. He prefers to draw a picture in grays rather than black and white. His character study of Constantine IX Monomachus is just such a "flawed picture" he presents, inviting the reader to appreciate the strong points of the man despite his personal weaknesses. In the latter part of his work there emerges an increasingly evident motive to defend the reputation of the Doukid dynasty, with whose fortunes he felt especially associated. He seems to be the most psychologically aware of the Byzantine writers and is one of the very few to speak of the theme of sexual desire openly in his work.

**John Xiphilinus.** John Xiphilinus was another of the close circle of Mauropous and Psellus. Born circa 1010 in Trebizond of a wealthy family that boasted many intellectuals and political figures, he came to study at Constantinople in the circle of Mauropous and would eventually rise to become John VIII, patriarch of Constantinople. He too was embroiled in the controversy with Emperor Constantine IX that saw the fall from grace of Mauropous and Psellus, and around 1054 he retired from his appointment as imperial *nomophylax*, which constituted him head of the law school at the University of Constantinople, and entered the monastic life at Mount Olympus, with Psellus, his friend and colleague. It was ten years later, in 1064, that he was elevated to become the patriarch of Constantinople under Emperor Constantine X Doukas, to fill the place of his classmate Constantine Leichoudes. When Psellus wrote a letter congratulating him on his ascent, Xiphilinus replied with a more acerbic letter back accusing Psellus of not having sacrificed philosophy in favor of Christ. He remained friends with Psellus, nevertheless, and owed his appointment and preferment to him; but his decision to become a monk allied him more fully with the narrower theological faction of the city, and he distanced himself from the liberal faction Psellus now headed. He left behind treatises on Roman law and several ecclesiastical homilies in high rhetorical style.

**Constantine Leichoudes.** Constantine Leichoudes was another member of that remarkable circle of Mauropous's students, a fellow classmate of Psellus and Xiphilinus; he eventually preceded the latter in the office of patriarch, holding the see after the dismissal of Michael Cerularius from 1059–1063. Unlike his fellow students, Constantine was a native of Constantinople. He was given honor in the reigns of Michael V and Constantine IX. First appointed imperial *protovestiarios*; he then became the *proedros*, or president of the senate. He was chief adviser to Constantine IX with the office of *mesazon*. After the dismissal of the circle of Psellus from Constantine's court, Constantine probably continued to live on the revenues from the imperial mangana, whose titles (*pronoia*) Constantine had given to him as an income stream.[19] Under Isaac I Komnenus he was elevated to the patriarchate, undoubtedly on Psellus's recommendation. Psellus describes Constantine as a man of most practical mind, who married philosophy and religion: again the watchword of their circle. His broad-mindedness was a welcome relief to all at Constantinople after the rigid zealotry of Caerularius. In the Eastern Orthodox Church he is considered a saint, with a feast day on July 29.

Like Michael Psellus's most renowned student, John Italus, a philosopher and neo-Platonist (who would cause great controversy with his continuation of the theme of marrying Christianity and Greek culture and nearly bring it all into ruin after his own trial for heresy), this circle of brilliant academicians focused a strong light on the role of learning and letters in refining Christian faith. The school lifted Eastern Christian culture out of the hands of monastic ascetics, who had little time for scholarly pursuits and none at all for the wisdom of the pagans. The scholars of the circle of Mauropous were university men before they were monastics, and even after they entered the church (largely for their own personal safety in parlous times) they kept faith with the tradition of the great fourth- and fifth-century Fathers, who believed in the harmonization of truth from whatever source: marrying the best of human culture with the insights of the gospel. Great fourth-century writer Gregory the Theologian had described his vision of that task as "plucking the roses of Hellenism but then removing the thorns." Their legacy remained cherished in the Eastern church as a kind of renaissance of the patristic spirit, but now with a more serious concern to save and pass on an antique culture that was no longer a common syntax of understanding in a medieval and more uncertain world.

## APOLOGIA AND CONFLICT:
## MICHAEL CERULARIUS AND THE GREAT SCHISM

Michael Cerularius appears here for his role in history as the patriarch of Constantinople on whose watch the Great Schism of the churches of East and West took place in a way that would not be healed for a millennium, with no end in sight. He was born between 1005 and 1010 and died in exile, subject to a trial for heresy, which was being prepared under Emperor Isaac Comnenus I's insistence, in the hands of Michael Psellus. His death precluded his judgment. The Comnenan emperor had turned against him, as Michael resisted imperial attempts to sequestrate church property, although it was Michael who had advised the previous emperor to abdicate quietly once the army had shown its support for Isaac.

---

[19]For a long time *mangana* was thought to be the monastery of the same name; now it is considered more likely to have been the imperial mangana bureau that administered extensive imperial landholdings in Constantinople and its environs.

Suspecting him of intriguing against his throne, Isaac exiled Michael to the Hellespont in 1058, where he died in the winter of the same year. He had long been a high political player and was related to Constantine Doukas, who eventually took the throne between 1059 and 1067. His family numbered many senators in their history. In 1040 Michael, then a layman, was caught in a plot to overthrow Emperor Michael IV Paphlagonian (1034–1041), and in order to avoid a more severe penalty for treason, he was induced to adopt the habit of a monk. In the reign of Constantine IX, however, he was restored to favor, and the latter appointed him as patriarch of Constantinople in 1043, after the death of Alexius the Studite. His tenor of mind was that of a conservative, and he increasingly came to dislike the liberal intellectual circle gathered around Constantine, including John Mauropous, Psellus, and his colleagues. With great popular support in the capital, and using the resources of a close confidant, the theologian Nicetas Stethatos, Cerularius eventually seems to have turned the imperial favor away from the circle around Psellus and negotiated their (temporary) dismissal.

It was Michael who first popularized the designation *ecumenical patriarch* for his office. This was no large matter in itself; the word simply meant the "Roman world," and in all probability carried with it no other connotation than the rights of his see to administer affairs for all "new territories" across the world, which had been given to it in the Council of Chalcedon. But it appeared in letters he exchanged with the papacy in a time of conflict, and then, in that context, it was the fire that set the explosion between the two sees at the height of their aspirations to dominate the Christian world. The papacy had long been expanding its own self-definition, using the Petrine *theologoumenon* to argue to all who would listen that it had jurisdictional rights in all churches. The Byzantine world had never interfered with this or doubted it application in the Western territories but had afforded Roman ecclesiastical claims no more than a right to preside honorifically at international synods and a right to make its voice heard as "first among equals."

This, in the era of the high claims for universal jurisdiction, now struck the Roman popes as a major attack on their understanding of church order. The issue had flared briefly in the time of Photius, then, as now, had also been a secondary matter attached to a theological dispute. In Photius's time it was a question of divergences between Eastern and Western theology of the procession of the Holy Spirit. The East held to the antique tradition that the Spirit of God proceeded only from the Father. The West adopted the later Spanish *theologoumenon* that the Spirit proceeded both from the Father and from the Son (*filioque*). In the course of fighting that one out, the issue of the papal primacy had risen, and Photius had resisted this also. But the matter had been set aside, seemingly because no one wished to drag it out into the open. For the Romans the papal primacy had continued to develop since then until it was almost universally accepted in the Western churches. As the Roman ritual had spread everywhere after the Carolingian age, so too had the Petrine theory of jurisdiction by right of law. The popes had started to circulate the texts containing the alleged "Donation of Constantine," arguing that the emperor had long ago given the papacy the right to temporal as well as spiritual dominion in the West. When these texts were shown to Cerularius, in an attempt to cow him, he was less than impressed.

The Byzantine world increasingly came to regard the papal claim to a quasi-monarchial right to rule over the churches as something hostile to the traditional ecclesiology of the church that placed no single bishop, of any see whatsoever, in a higher position than a general council. There began to be a sense that Rome's claims were no longer ceremonial matters of precedence and protocol but were actually advancing a different model of church order from what had been traditionally adopted in classical patristic times. The Eastern Christian world, now dominated by the patriarchate of Constantinople, instinctively recoiled from this position, which it saw as an innovation verging on a heresy. For the West, it was almost the opposite: to refute the Roman claims was now almost seen as a heretical matter, or at best cause to censure the dissident by declaring them to be in "schism," a state of loss of communion slightly less serious than heresy as such but involving a church in a loss of potency in the administration of sacraments and such like until it returned to obedience to the Roman popes. Rome had used this threat to good effect with several dissident sees in the West in prior times. It had not, for some time, threatened the East with withdrawal of communion.

The threat here, however, did not carry as much weight with it as it did in the West. There the common agreement was that catholic ecclesial communion was ensured by communion with the Roman see. Rome, that is, embodied catholic communion, and if someone was not in communion with Rome, they could not claim to be a catholic Christian at all. Schism between any see and Rome in the West, therefore, was a very serious matter. For Byzantium, on the other hand, catholic communion meant primarily the sustaining of orthodoxy of belief (according to the creeds and conciliar decisions), supported by a common ecclesial relationship with all the other "catholic" sees that shared the same orthodoxy. This commonality was held in place by intercollegiality and synodical agreements among the greater sees: Constantinople, Alexandria, Antioch, Jerusalem, and Rome. So the concept that one of those sees only could hold the rest to ransom, by claiming to be the sole locus of catholicity, was seen as untraditional and disturbing.

This was the point where another factor precipitated matters. The southernmost tip of Italy had long been Byzantine ecclesiastical territory, and that tradition, of course, had a very different liturgical style and set of customs from the Roman liturgy. As the papal claims had extended geographically, so had the overwhelming dominance of the Roman rite spread outward, absorbing all that stood before it. It was only a matter of time before the great diversity between Latin and Greek ritual came to a clashing head in southern Italy. Rome was reaching out increasingly to incorporate these areas into the Latin practices. Within two hundred years the process was largely completed; and one remembers how Francis of Assisi could now only find a church of Byzantine rite (San Damiano, where the crucifix spoke to him) in ruination. Rather than speaking to the whole issue, on the question of antique tradition where some areas had followed different ritual forms for centuries, the medieval contemporaries at this time attached more easily to small symbolic "differences," which they seized on to stand for a greater argument that they might not have been able to address more directly. One immediate difference between the two rituals, of course, is that the Latins used unleavened bread for Communion, in the form of flat wafers, while the Greeks used leavened bread and distributed Communion in the double forms of bread and wine.

The Latin theologians started to advance a claim that unleavened bread was used in Christian Eucharists from the very beginning, and the Greeks had broken with tradition and must stop using leavened bread. There is no evidence that they are correct in terms of historical tradition, but the argument was launched that Jews only used unleavened bread at Passover and so the Last Supper must have been celebrated with unleavened bread. Latin theologians after the Carolingian age had also been stressing the adorable nature of the Eucharist, turning it more away from the concept of a shared meal (with a substantial piece of bread dipped in wine) to the notion of a great and pure mystery that ought to be looked at in adoration and awe more often, perhaps, than it ought to be approached by sinners for consumption. The Latin Eucharist at this period, out of motives of extreme respect, was being heavily clericalized.

The crisis started with a sharp exchange of letters between the renowned theologian Leo Metropolitan of Ohrid (in Bulgaria) to his episcopal colleague John of Trani, a bishop in Apulia. His complaint was a list of divergences that the West had allowed to creep in to Christian tradition, with little respect for ancient practice. In particular the use of unleavened bread in the Eucharist and the habit of fasting on Saturdays were held up for censure. The issue of unleavened bread was the most emotionally freighted one and soon gathered the name of the *azymes* controversy.[20]

---

[20] *Azymes* being the Byzantine term for "unleavened."

The letter outraged John of Trani, who forwarded it on quickly to Pope Leo IX, who took it up with the patriarch Michael as well as with Leo.

This already acerbic exchange was sharpened by two things. The first was in 1053, when Michael responded in kind to the events happening in southern Italy and closed the Latin churches in Constantinople, refusing them permission to celebrate any longer in the Roman rite in his diocese. The second was when the pope noticed Michael was claiming the title of ecumenical patriarch in his less-than-submissive replies to papal complaints. Michael had called Pope Leo his brother, not his father, and Leo censured him for this as well as for his apparent claim for an international jurisdiction. Leo was an aristocratic German holder of the papacy, a reformist pope who was holding a series of synods in the West to root out abuses and enforce celibacy across the ranks of the Latin clergy. He announced that only he, as pope and successor of Peter, had the right to claim any ecumenical jurisdiction. In this initial exchange of letters the East first came to know of the theory of the so-called Donation of Constantine. By now it is clear enough that the papacy put full confidence in the historical authenticity of this dossier of forged texts. Byzantium did not. Pope Leo wrote also to Patriarch Peter III of Antioch, asking his support in the matter, but was put out when Peter independently agreed with Michael's position.

Pope Leo then sent a senior legate, Cardinal Humbertus de Silva Candida, to assert his rights in person and gain from the patriarch an agreement, if not an apology. Michael was in charge of all official church delegations coming to his city, however, and treated Humbertus to a long waiting game, giving him very little access to the patriarchal palace and none to the emperor, and systematically reducing the quality of his food and lodgings, all of which raised the irascible cardinal's temper and blood pressure to alarming levels. He knew he was being humiliated, and his behavior mounted up toward increasing arrogance, accordingly, for he felt his shame would be that of his papal master. The legation never opened up any serious discussion of the *azymes* issue, but Cerularius commissioned Nicetas Stethatos, a disciple of the famed Symeon the New Theologian, to prepare a refutation of the Latin practices. It was given the title *Panoplia*.

Realizing that he was going nowhere and that his legation was increasingly being mocked in the city streets, Humbertus arranged a grand procession of all the Latin clergy in Constantinople and Pera from his lodgings, on July 16, 1054, through the streets to the great Cathedral of Hagia Sophia. He had drawn up a papal bulla, a formal document with the papal seal on it, which announced the excommunication of Patriarch Michael by Pope Leo IX. Humbertus was probably unaware that his papal master had actually died in Rome several months beforehand, so his actions sealing the document in Leo's name were actually invalid—but nevertheless it was taken by all parties concerned as valid and fervently intended. Humbertus, in his cardinal's robes, accompanied by candles and incense, marched into the cathedral and straight up to the iconostasis, where he entered through the sanctuary doors, laid the bulla on the high altar, and departed. The Greek subdeacons who were in attendance that day were completely puzzled by the appearance of the procession, unannounced to them, and by the whole procedure.

When it became clear to them that it was not a friendly act, they took the scroll from the altar, and discovering it was a bulla of excommunication, they ran down the aisle after the departing procession, pulling at Humbertus's robes and begging him to take it back. He refused to speak to them and swept out of the cathedral; at which point the subdeacons threw his bulla out into the street after him (though it was surely collected up once more when the Latins were out of sight to show to the patriarch). When the contents of the bulla were translated for him, Michael immediately ordered that the pope's name be struck off the list of those great church leaders commemorated in the Constantinopolitan liturgy. This removal from the liturgical diptychs was tantamount to an act of cutting off communion with the see of Rome.

So it was that this date, July 16, 1054, has come to mark the Great Schism of the Latin and Eastern churches. Cerularius did not take it all that seriously. But he did continue to pressure the remaining Latin communities of his immediate jurisdiction to stop holding services in the Roman rite, to match the pressure being applied in southern Italy. And he also defiantly ordered that a new patriarchal seal should be cut that had inscribed on it his title of "ecumenical patriarch." It would take many more years before this rupture took on the ever-increasing dead weight of a long-lasting schism. In the twelfth century Theodore Balsamon, the patriarch of Antioch, then resident in Constantinople, concluded that of old the Latins had been regarded as one in faith, but in his day if they sought communion in any of the Byzantine churches a statement of faith ought to be required of them first and hands ought to be laid on them. This is the real mark that the schism had become deeply established. Despite attempts to repair it in the twentieth century by the popes and patriarchs of Constantinople, very little progress has been made toward any state where intercommunion might be expected to be reestablished.

Emperor Constantine IX Monomachus was very agitated that a rupture should be made with the pope, because he was hoping that the papacy would side with him and censure Norman military expansion into southern Italy, which was the political factor behind the ecclesiastical clash in the first place. When Pope Leo led out his own armies to stop the Norman invasion of Apulia, however, he suffered a resounding defeat in the field in 1053, and after that point Constantine IX had little more to expect from him. The pope was held as a hostage at Benevento from June 1053 until March 1054, and released only after he had acknowledged the right of the Normans to occupy Apulia.

Michael Cerularius's antipapal position was massively endorsed by the populace from the outset, however, and by summer of 1053 the emperor himself had to concur with his patriarch's stand against the pope. This in itself raised Cerularius's profile even higher, and after Constantine's death in 1055, he was one of the most powerful men in the empire: a kingmaker, who brought his influence to bear against Empress Theodora, who had decided to rule in her own person (1055–1056). She tried unsuccessfully to depose him, but he in turn successfully brought Emperor Michael VI to the throne (1056–1057) and just as easily negotiated with him to abdicate when the army showed its preference for Isaac Comnenus (1057–1059). Cerularius arranged the consecration of Isaac and at the same time himself adopted the wearing of purple slippers, formerly a right of ceremonial dress reserved to the royal family. In an increasingly bitter relationship Cerularius resisted all Isaac's religious policies, especially when he attempted to rein in church revenues. In one angry exchange Michael is said to have threatened to "break Isaac like a clay oven I have built myself," and the breach became definitive.

The intellectual party rallied together with the military around Isaac, and so the emperor demanded Cerularius's resignation and departure from the capital (where he had much popular support). He refused, and so the emperor deposed him and exiled him anyway, announcing that he would be put on trial for unorthodox opinions. He asked Michael Psellus to draw up the accusation, but Cerularius's death on a march into the Thracian countryside made the issue irrelevant, and Psellus was rewarded by being allowed to nominate his former colleague Constantine Leichoudes as the patriarchal successor.

Pope Leo's successor in 1054 was another German, Pope Victor II. He was much occupied with keeping peace in the Holy Roman Empire after being entrusted with the protection of the young heir on the death of Henry IV. Matters between Constantinople and Rome slipped into a state of forgetfulness, but in the East the pope's names were not replaced in the liturgical commemorations, and so it was that the state of schism grew into a hardened condition over several generations to come. Whenever the churches became aware of each other again, the concept of the special privileges of the papacy was soon to become a stumbling block in rapprochement. A twelfth-century Byzantine bishop, Nicetas of Nicomedia, expressed the common sentiment, writing to a Western correspondent,

> My dearest brother, we do not deny to the Roman church the primacy amongst the five sister Patriarchates; and we recognize her right to the most honorable seat at an Ecumenical Council. But she has separated herself from us by her own deeds when, through pride, she assumed a monarchy which does not belong to her office. . . . How shall we accept decrees from her that have been issued without consulting us and even without our knowledge? If the Roman Pontiff, seated on the lofty throne of his glory, wishes to thunder at us and, so to speak, hurl his mandates at us from on high, and if he wishes to judge us and even to rule over us and our churches, not by taking counsel with us but at his own arbitrary pleasure, what kind of brotherhood, or even what kind of parenthood can this be? We should be the slaves, not the sons, of such a church, and the Roman See would not be the pious mother of sons but rather a hard and imperious mistress of slaves.[21]

Further disturbances such as the Crusades, culminating in the infamous Fourth Crusade in 1204, when Latin armies sailed into Constantinople itself to capture and pillage it, and the establishment then of a separate and parallel hierarchy of leaders (even a new Latin patriarchate) to the incumbent Orthodox bishops, signaled to the Eastern church that the Latin West was no longer any ally they could count on, and even less a family member in communion with them in the deepest matters of the faith. All further attempts to reconcile the churches at high level (and several were undertaken in the later Middle Ages) would come to grief on the rocks of popular Byzantine resentment of the highhanded way they felt they had been treated in the thirteenth century when their political fortunes were at a very low ebb.

## THE RISE OF THE UNIVERSITY SCHOOLS IN THE WEST

That remarkable renaissance of letters in Constantinople in the eleventh century we have already noted was matched by a similar renewal of academic life that came to a peak in the West in the early thirteenth century. The seeds of it were also noticeable at this period, and whereas Constantinople's fortunes were set to a slow but inevitable descent, worn away by the attritions of war and financial collapse, those of the West were set only to rise. By the thirteenth century the phenomenon of the birth of universities was a notable feature of many of the greater cities around Europe.

At first education had been strictly the preserve of the clergy and the upper classes. The schools of the Carolingian court in the ninth century demonstrate the pattern: rulers educated for leadership by clergy drawn to the great courts, where libraries and schools clustered around them. The antique idea of a few notable orator-philosophers heading private schools had given way in the later Middle Ages to the cathedral or monastery school, staffed by clergy and focused mainly on the

---

[21]Cited in S. Runciman, *The Eastern Schism* (Oxford: Clarendon, 1955), 116.

copying of patristic and liturgical texts, and the education of clerics for the literary and numerate tasks required for administration of lesser estates. From Charlemagne's time the concept spread that evidently intelligent children, even from humble families, ought to be taken into the church and given an education suitable to their abilities and commitments.

In 1079 Pope Gregory VII (Hildebrand of Sovana) issued a papal decree mandating the creation of schools attached to cathedrals that would oversee the education of candidates for holy orders. It was this that fostered the expanse of higher-level university centers in the following century. The university in this time took its concept from a center of learning that would range in its scope beyond that which was necessary for practical administration. Such a school would thus be a *studium generale*, defined as such by drawing students from a wide geographical area, not simply the local candidates for orders; by having a broad curriculum; by having a teaching staff mainly consisting of *magistri* (with a higher degree); by allowing its *magistri* to enjoy their clerical benefices without having to fulfill local residency requirements usually required by canon law; by the university enjoying a degree of autonomy from local civil and episcopal authorities; and by affording the teaching staff the *ius ubique docendi*, that is, the right to teach in any other higher-level school without undergoing further examination. These conditions allowed a nexus of schools to create, over the next few generations, a veritable new concept of academic culture that was to have great force.[22]

In Italy the University of Bologna took its foundation in 1088. The University of Paris rose out of an amalgamation of various monastery schools at the cathedral of Notre Dame around 1119, and in 1231 under the sponsorship of one Robert Sorbon, a theological school was established that would eventually become renowned as the Sorbonne. Salerno was perhaps the third most prestigious and ancient school, particularly renowned for its medical school, which had functioned there at least from the tenth century before it associated with Naples and extended to a *studium generale* in 1253. At Oxford various superior colleges were established by the church between 1096 and 1167 (when Henry II banned English students from attending the University of Paris), which entered into loose association as the University of Oxford (still formed on a strongly independent collegiate basis). A protest among scholars there led to the foundation of a rival establishment in the Fens at Cambridge in 1209.

By the early to mid-thirteenth century there were growing universities also at Vicenza, Palencia, Salamanca, Padua, Toulouse, Orleans, Siena, and Valladolid. More

---

[22]See further D. Hay, *Europe in the Fourteenth and Fifteenth Centuries* (New York: Holt, Rinehart, and Winston, 1989).

would follow in the fourteenth century. The academicians were aware of the strength of the artisanal guilds that formed such a part of medieval social life and were probably emulating their structure, seeking strength in association. Many popes founded such institutions and conferred high privileges on them in their charters. Before 1300, Europe could boast twenty-three *studia generalia*, and soon the right to confer degrees was associated with the power of the king or the pope. Older schools (such as Oxford, which had private collegiate founders in the main) were universally reckoned to have that right *ex consuetudine*, by long-standing custom. By the later medieval period *studium generale* passed out of common use, and *universitas* (our *university*) became the general term to signify the collective body of scholars in town (many of them aliens or foreigners) who were under the necessary protection of the academic establishment.

It is in this ferment of the close juxtaposition of political and military instability in both Eastern and Western Christian cultures, along with a rapidly growing rift between the cultures and traditions of Latin and Greek ecclesiality, that we leave the Christian world of the first millennium. The papacy was now a secular power of great significance in its own right, as well as its incumbent holding a spiritual influence of immense force all over the Western churches.

The outreach of this papal centralism did not carry to Byzantium, but the powers of the Eastern Empire were clearly being eroded in every passing generation by the expanse of Islam and the arrival of powerful Eastern tribes who have amassed armies. The battle of Manzikert on August 26, 1071, saw the bitter defeat of the armies of Byzantium by the forces of the Seljuk Turks. It was the first time that a Christian Roman emperor had been defeated by an Islamic ruler, in this case Alp Arslan. When Romanus IV Diogenes was brought before the sultan, covered in dirt and blood, he was a sorry spectacle. The sultan forced him to kneel, and putting his foot on his neck, made him kiss the ground before him. After that, however, he held him only for a short while, making punitive treaties before sending him back to Constantinople unharmed. It was Romanus's own people who shortly afterwards blinded and deposed him. As a result of the collapse of Roman power in Anatolia, the ancient heartland of the empire, by 1080 the Seljuks had occupied no less than thirty thousand square miles of land, which they never relinquished.

The imperial historian Princess Anna Komnene some time later wrote of this aftermath:

> The fortunes of the Roman Empire had sunk to their lowest ebb. For the armies of the East were dispersed in all directions, for now the Turks had over-spread, and gained command

of, all the lands between the Euxine [Black] Sea and the Hellespont, as well as the Aegean and Syrian Seas [Mediterranean], with the various bays, especially those which wash Pamphylia, Cilicia, emptying themselves into the Egyptian [Mediterranean] Sea.[23]

The Eastern Christian empire after this point is a dwindling reality. It had lost its landholdings, which ensured its wealth, and from then onward its military defensive capacities were fatally weakened. Byzantium had other brief moments of renaissance, especially in the Paleologan period of the mid-fourteenth century, which saw a splendid revival of art and cultural achievements; but the writing was on the wall for the independent existence of the Christian East, and the Ottoman Turks would eventually capture the capital in May 1453, leaving its Christian populations now under the oversight of the patriarch of Constantinople under Ottoman suzerainty. The patriarch was compelled to serve as an official of the court of the sultan, as ethnarch of all Christian people in the East, responsible to him for their good behavior and above all for collecting in their taxes. The twilight of the Christian East, however, witnessed the great and splendid rise of the civilization of Western Christianity, which was about to enter into its most luminous phase in the dawn of the second millennium.

## A SHORT READER

### *Symeon the New Theologian, a mystical prayer.*

Come, true light.
Come, eternal life.
Come, hidden mystery.
Come, nameless treasure.
Come, Ineffable One.
Come, Inconceivable One.
Come, endless rejoicing.
Come, Sun that never sets.
Come, true hope of all who wish to be saved.
Come, awakening of all who sleep.
Come, resurrection of the dead.
Come, Powerful One who ever creates and recreates
    and transfigures by your simple will.
Come, Invisible One beyond all touch or grasping.
Come, eternally Motionless One, ever active
    to come to us and save us who lie in hell.

---

[23] Anna Komnene, *Alexiad*, book 1.

Come, beloved name repeated everywhere
>   whose existence and nature we cannot express or know.
> Come, eternal joy.
> Come, untarnished crown.
> Come, royal purple of our great King and God.
> Come, jeweled belt of shining crystal.
> Come, unapproachable sandal.
> Come, imperial vestment.
> Come, sovereign right hand.
> Come, Lord, whom my miserable soul has longed for, and longs for still.
> Come, Solitary One, to this solitary, for as you see I am all alone.
> Come, for you have alienated me from all things,
>   and made me be alone in this world.
> Come, you who have become my desire,
>   and have made me desire you, the Inaccessible One.
> Come, my breath, my life.
> Come, consolation of my poor soul.
> Come, my joy, my glory, my endless delight.
> For I must give you all my thanks for making yourself one with me in spirit.[24]

**Nicetas Stethatos, The Gnostic Chapters 21, 27.** Souls that are purified and illuminated by the rays of primordial light, in a radiance of mystical knowledge, are not only filled with every goodness and luminosity, but are carried up to the intellective heavens through the contemplation of natural essences. The action of the divine energy does not stop here, however, but continues until it has finally made them one with the One, through wisdom and mystical knowledge of ineffable things; making them abandon their former multiplicity and become one in themselves. In the first ranks of the highest angelic powers some circle with eternal motion around the divine presence, burning with fire and gazing clear-sightedly on the Godhead; while others contemplate God in mystical wisdom, since this is that divine condition that sets them in endless revolution around the deity. It is the same with souls who have become like the angels. They too burn with fire for God and are clairvoyant, advanced in wisdom, in spiritual knowledge, and mystical perception. As God affords them, in their limited way, these souls also wheel endlessly around the divine presence. . . . Having been

---

[24]*Prelude to the Hymns of Divine Love*, ed. J. Koder, SC 156, pp. 150-52.

firmly established in the enlightenment, they have received and, sharing in the very life of the One Who Is, they share generously with others, teaching them by word about his enlightenment and graces.[25]

**Leo Metropolitan of Ohrid, Letter to Bishop John of Trani in Apulia.** God's great love and the depth of his compassion have persuaded me to write to your holiness, and through you to all the archbishops of the Franks, and to the most venerable pope himself,[26] in order to bring up the question of the *azyma* (use of unleavened bread) and the (fasting on the) Sabbath: for in these matters you have an inappropriate communion with the Jews in the manner of the Mosaic law. The Jews indeed were instructed by Moses to observe the sabbath and keep unleavened bread, but Christ is now our Paschal Lamb, who agreed to be circumcised so he would not be regarded as pagan, and at first celebrated the lawful Passover, but then after ceasing this observance inaugurated a new rite for us. The holy Evangelist in the Gospel according to Matthew speaks in this way about the mystical supper and says: "On the first day of the Passover festival, Jesus' disciples came to him and said: Lord, where do you wish that we should prepare the Passover festival for you?" . . . But now since the Jewish law has ceased to have hold over us, as the apostle tells us, so too, of necessity, has the unleavened bread (*azyma*). The same thing took place in regard to the paralyzed man whom Jesus made whole on the sabbath day. And because of this [that Jesus did not observe the sabbath] those who still keep the sabbath and the *azyma* and claim that they are Christians prove themselves neither to be good Jews nor good Christians. They are instead like the coat of a leopard, as Basil the Great says, whose hair was neither black nor white. . . . You already know these things, O man of God, and have taught them yourself to your people many time over and have written about them. Now give instruction that these practices ought to be altered among those who observe them, and do this for your soul's salvation. And send also to the archbishops and bishops of the thrones of Italy, and have them all take an oath that they will alter these practices in order that you will have the greatest of rewards in such matters as in other good things in your life. And if you do this, then I shall write to you, in a second letter, about greater and more extensive

---

[25]In *Philokalia*, ed. G. Palmer, P. Sherrard, and K. Ware (London: Faber and Faber, 1984), 3:331-32.
[26]He wrote with the knowledge and approval of Patriarch Michael Cerularius. John was one of the bishops in the formerly Byzantine-rite territory of Apulia in southern Italy, which was then under military occupation by the Normans (to papal annoyance) and undergoing forced conversion to the Roman ritual (with papal approval).

matters,[27] as further evidence of the true and divine faith and glory of God, and the salvation of those who choose to believe correctly in the orthodox manner, for whom Christ gave up his own life.[28]

**Cardinal Humbertus, Anathema of Michael Cerularius (1054).** Humbertus, by the grace of God cardinal-bishop of the holy Roman Church; Peter of Amalfi; Frederick Deacon and Chancellor: to all sons of the catholic Church. The holy Roman, the first and Apostolic See, towards which, as towards the head, belongs the special solicitude of all churches, for the sake of the peace and benefit of the church, has seen fit to appoint us as legates to this city in order that, in accordance with our instructions, we might come over and see whether it is the case or not that the clamor still continues which comes to the ears of Rome; or, if this is no longer the case, that the Holy See may learn about the present condition. And so, above all else, let the glorious emperors, the clergy, the Senate and the people of this city of Constantinople, and the entire catholic church, know that we have taken note here of very great and good things, on account of which we deeply rejoice in the Lord. But we have also perceived a very great evil here, and because of this we are deeply saddened. For with respect to the pillars of the empire and its wise and honoured citizens, the city is most Christian and Orthodox. However, with regard to that Michael who is falsely called patriarch, and his followers in folly, too many weeds of heresies are daily sown in its midst.... Although admonished by our Lord Pope Leo regarding many errors and many other deeds, this Michael has disregarded all warnings contemptuously. And towards us, the pope's legates, who seek only to root out zealously the cause of such evils, he has refused to admit us into his presence, and has closed the churches against us in which we might celebrate Mass: just as earlier he had closed the Latin churches in Constantinople. He has called the Latins *azymites* and has hounded them everywhere in word and deed. In truth, in the person of its sons, he has thus cursed the Apostolic See, in opposition to which he has signed himself "Oecumenical Patriarch." And so, refusing to endure this unheard of slander and insult to that first and holy Apostolic See and seeing that the catholic faith has been attacked in so many ways, by the authority of the Undivided and Holy Trinity, and of the Apostolic See whose embassy we constitute, and by the authority of all the orthodox fathers of the seven councils, and that of the entire catholic church, whatever our most reverence lord the Pope has denounced in Michael and his followers, unless they repent, we declare now to

---

[27]Probably meaning to address the *filioque* dispute.
[28]PG 120.836-44.

be anathematised. May this Michael, false neophyte patriarch, who only assumed the monastic habit out of human fear, and is now known to many in all notoriety because of his most wicked crimes; and long with him the Archdeacon Leo, who is called bishop of Ohrid, and his treasurer Michael, and Constantine, who have all trampled with their profane feet upon the Latin sacrifice,[29] and all their followers in their aforesaid errors and presumptions, now be anathematised along with the Simoniacs, Valesians, Arians, Donatists, Nicolaites, Severians, Pneumatomachians, Manichaeans, and Nazarenes, and along with all heretics and even indeed the Devil and his angels—unless, by some chance they might repent. Maranatha. Amen. Amen. Amen.[30]

***Michael Cerularius,*** **Decree of the Standing Synod of Constantinople** *(July 1054).* A decree in response to the bulla of excommunication cast before the holy altar by the legates of Rome, attacking the most holy patriarch Michael in the month of July in the seventh indiction. When Michael, our most holy lord and ecumenical patriarch was presiding, certain impious and disrespectful men (how else could we call them) who rose out of the darkness (they were begotten in the West) came to this reverent and God-protected city, from which the springs of orthodoxy flow as if from on high and thus disseminate righteous teachings to the ends of the world. To this city they came like a thunderbolt or an earthquake, or a hailstorm; or to phrase it more accurately, like wolves trying to defile orthodox belief by their difference in dogmas. Setting aside the Scriptures,[31] they deposited an accusation on the holy altar, according to which we, and especially the Orthodox Church of God, and all those who do not agree with their impiety (since we who are Orthodox wish only to preserve what is orthodox and reverent) are charged with, among other things, the fact that unlike them we do not accept the shaving of our beards [as priests]. Nor did we want to transform what is natural for men into what is unnatural.[32] Moreover, we do not forbid anyone

---

[29] The Eucharist—by closing Latin churches in the city in retaliation to the closure of Byzantine-rite churches in southern Italy.

[30] Cited in D. J. Geanokoplos, *Byzantium: Church, Society and Civilisation Seen Through Contemporary Eyes* (Chicago: University of Chicago Press, 1984), 208-9.

[31] Humbert moved aside the Gospel book on the high altar to leave there his decree of excommunication in Hagia Sophia. But he is also using the idea symbolically—that their act was not in accordance with scriptural principles of communion.

[32] He is making innuendos about Humbertus's sexual proclivities, but he chiefly means by this that he refused to endorse the current papal policy of insisting on celibacy for all deacons, priests, and bishops. It had been the custom from ancient times that Eastern clergy should be married, if they wished, except those in episcopal orders.

from receiving Communion from a married priest. In addition to all of this we will not tamper with the sacred and holy creed, which holds its authority inviolate from synodical and ecumenical decrees, by the use of wrongheaded arguments, unlawful reasoning, and excessive temerity.[33] And unlike them we do not wish to say that the Holy Spirit proceeds from the Father and the Son, for this is an artifice of the devil. We say instead that the Holy Spirit proceeds from the Father. For our part we state that they do not follow the Scripture that tells us not to shave our beards. Nor do they seem to want to understand that God the Creator appropriately created woman and decreed that it was not right for men to be alone. They have also dishonored the fourth canon of the Synod of Gangra, which says to those who despise marriage: "If anyone hesitates about receiving Communion from a married presbyter, let him be anathematized." . . . And we continue to observe inviolate the ancient canons of apostolic perfection and due order, and so we wish to restate that the marriages of ordained men should never be dissolved, and they should not be deprived of having sexual relations with their wives, which is fitting from time to time. . . . So if anyone[34] dares to act against the apostolic canons and removes any of the clergy, either priest or deacon or subdeacon, depriving him of his lawful bond with his wife, then let him be excommunicate. . . . Moreover, they do not wish to understand, and this is why they affirm that the Holy Spirit proceeds from the Father and the Son, even though they have no evidence for this blasphemy against holy doctrine from the Gospels or the ecumenical councils. For the Lord our God spoke of "the Spirit of truth, which proceeds from the Father," but the fathers of this new impiety speak of the Spirit "which proceeds from the Father and the Son." . . . A document written against us in Italian letters was deposited by this impious man in the presence of the subdeacons who were officiating in the second week on the holy altar of the Great Church of God. Later it was removed from the holy altar by the subdeacons, and the subdeacons suggested it ought to be taken back, but since the legates refused to accept it, it was thrown to the ground and then fell into the hands of many. But so that the blasphemies it contained should not become common knowledge, it was taken up by Our Mediocrity,[35] who then shortly after asked certain men

---

[33] He is referring to the Latin addition of the *filioque* clause. Humbert had mistakenly accused him of deleting it from the Nicene Creed. He now complains the Latins have added it without legal authority.

[34] Pope Leo had recently commanded this in the West.

[35] Cerularius himself.

(Protospatharios, Kosmas, Romanus, Pyrrhus, and the monk John the Spaniard) to translate it from Latin to Greek. . . . Unable to tolerate such audacity and impudence against our piety, by remaining silent, or to permit it to stand unpunished, we communicated all this to our powerful and sacred emperor.[36] . . . [The emperor replied] "Let the document with the anathema be burned in the presence of all, including those who have advised, composed and published it,[37] and even of those who have any knowledge of it."

***Michael Psellus,*** **Chronographia 6.22-28.** Several persons, on more than one occasion, have urged me to write this history. Among them were not only men in authority and leaders in the senate, but also students of theology, who interpret the mysteries of Holy Writ, and men of great sanctity and holiness. Through the passing of time the historical evidence has already proved inadequate for the writing of a proper record. There is a danger that events may be hidden in the remote past, so forgotten that our knowledge of bygone days rests on no sure foundation. These gentlemen, therefore, asked me to do what I could to remedy those deficiencies: it was not right, they argued, that our own contemporary history should be concealed and utterly obscured, while events that took place before our time were thought worthy of record by succeeding generations. Such was the pressure and such the arguments with which they urged me to take up this task, but for myself I was not particularly enthusiastic for the undertaking. It was not that I was lazy, but I was afraid of two alternatives, either of which could not be disregarded: I might pass over, for reasons that I will explain later, things done by certain individuals, or distort my account of them, and so be convicted not of writing a history, but of mere fabrication, as if I were composing a play. That was one alternative. The other was that I might go to extreme lengths in hunting down the truth and so become a laughing-stock to the critics. They would think me not a lover of history, but a scandal-monger. For these reasons I was not very eager to tackle the history of our times, especially as I knew that in many things I would clash with the emperor Constantine, and I would be ashamed of myself if I did not seize every opportunity of commending him. I should be ungrateful and altogether unreasonable if I did not make some return, however small, for his generosity to me, a generosity that showed itself not only in positive acts but in the indirect ways in which he

---

[36] The text then recounts how the emperor summoned the legates back into the city, but they refused to attend on Michael and also refused to answer any charges before his synod. The emperor allowed them immunity because of their ambassadorial status but sympathized with his patriarch because of the inappropriate behavior of Humbertus.

[37] So, in the end, Humbertus was compelled to be present at the public incineration of his bulla.

helped me to better my condition. It would be shameful if I did not prove my gratitude in my writings. It was therefore because of this man that I consistently refused to compose the history. I was most anxious to avoid imputing any blame to him. I did not want to reveal by my words any actions not to his credit and things it is better to keep dark. I was loath to put before the public a dishonest story, yet at the same time I was unwilling to shame the hero of my former eulogy. In my opinion, it was wrong to exercise literary talents, which I had perfected because of his encouragements, to do him harm. Philosophers will tell you that the vain and superfluous are of all things on earth the most despicable. For them the object of life is to understand those things that are necessary to their nature. All else is regarded as merely so many external attributes. However that may be, I cannot use such an argument as an excuse for ingratitude, especially to one who honored me above my deserts and raised me above my fellows. What I would like, therefore, is either to commemorate him in a panegyric or to pass over in silence those actions in his life that did not spring from worthy motives. If, having set out to eulogize his career, I then rejected those deeds that were the fit object of praise and gave the impression that I had lumped together all that was reprehensible, I would be the worst scoundrel on earth, like the son of Lyxes, who selected the worst deeds of the Greeks for his history. On the other hand, suppose I set aside this project for the moment and propose to write a history of the lives of the emperors, how, when I leave unsaid things that belong to the province of history, am I to deal with those which are the proper object of eulogy? It would look as if I had forgotten my purpose or was caricaturing the art of history by failing to distinguish its subject matter and by confusing the role of two forms of literature whose aims are incompatible. Actually I had composed many panegyrics in honor of Constantine before I undertook this work, not without commendation from the public. The high praises I lavished on him were not undeserved, but other writers have failed to understand my methods of composition. The truth is, the actions of emperors are a conglomerate patchwork of bad and good, and these other writers find themselves able neither to condemn without reservation nor to commend with sincerity, because they are overmuch impressed by the close conjunction of opposite qualities. In my own case, I do offer criticism, but only for form's sake or in dramatic passages where the prose is affected. In the composition of a eulogy, in fact, my subject matter is not chosen usually with complete indifference to good or bad: the latter I reject, the former I set on one side, afterward putting it in proper order. So a homogenous pattern is worked out, a tapestry of the finest cloth. Such is the method I have adopted in composing eulogies of Constantine, but now that I have undertaken to write a history, this plan becomes impossible, for I cannot bring myself to distort the facts of history, where truth is of more importance than anything else, in order to escape the reproaches of my contemporaries. They may accuse me of blaming, where in their opinion I should praise, but I prefer to ignore such criticisms. What I am writing now is not an indictment, not a speeds for the prosecution, but a true history. Then again, had I seen other emperors pursuing an uninterrupted, invariable course of noble action, on all occasions displaying an admirable character, whereas the reign of Constantine alone was marked by deeds of the opposite kind, then I would have said nothing about him at all. Yet no one on earth is faultless, and we judge a man by the trait that chiefly distinguishes him from everyone else. So why should I feel ashamed to declare openly whatever injustice or indiscretion this emperor, in common with the rest, may have committed? Most men who have set themselves to record the history of the emperors have found it surprising that none of them kept his reputation untarnished in every particular. Some won greater praise for their conduct in early life, others impressed more in their latter years, and while some preferred a life of pleasure, others dabbled in philosophy, only to confound the principles they had elected to follow and end in muddle. For my own part, I find such inconsistency nothing to marvel at; on the contrary, it would be extraordinary if someone were always unalterable. Of course, it is possible that you may discover some ordinary citizen who pursued the same undeviating path throughout life, from the very beginning to the very end (although there cannot be many examples of such consistency), but an emperor, one who inherited from God supreme power, especially if he lived longer than most, would never be able to maintain the highest standards all through his reign. In the case of the ordinary man, his own nature, plus a good start in life, may be sufficient to ensure virtuous conduct, for the simple reason that he is not overmuch troubled by outside affairs, nor do external events have any effect on his private disposition. How different it is with an emperor, whose private life is never, even in its most intimate detail, allowed respite from trouble! Consider how brief are the moments when the sea is calm and peaceful, and how at other times it is swollen, or lashed by waves, as Boreas, or Aparktias, or some other storm wind disturbs its rest—a sight I have seen myself many a time. An emperor's life is like that. If he seeks recreation, at once he incurs the displeasure of the critics. If he gives rein to kindly sentiments, he is accused of ignorance, and when he rouses himself to show interest, they blame him for being meddlesome. If he defends himself or takes blunt reprisals, everyone levels abuse at his "wrath" or his "quick temper." And as for trying to do anything in secret: Mount Athos would be more likely to hide itself from human gaze than an emperor's deeds to escape the notice of his subjects! No wonder then that no sovereign's life has been blameless. Naturally, I would have wished that my favorite emperor had been perfect, even if such a compliment was impossible for all the others, but the events of history do not accommodate themselves to our desires. And so, divine soul, forgive me, and if sometimes in describing your reign I speak immoderately, concealing nothing and telling the truth, pardon me for it. Not one of your nobler deeds shall be passed over in silence. They shall all be revealed. Likewise, whatever derives not from the same nobility, that too shall be made manifest in my history. And there we must leave the matter and return to our narrative.

## FURTHER READING

### Symeon the New Theologian

Alfeyev, H. *St. Symeon the New Theologian and Orthodox Tradition.* Oxford: Oxford University Press, 2000.

de Catanzaro, C. J., trans. *Symeon the New Theologian: The Discourses.* Classics of Western Spirituality. New York: Paulist, 1980.

Golitzin, A. *St. Symeon the New Theologian.* 3 vols. Crestwood, NY: St. Vladimir's Seminary Press, 1995–1997.

Hausherr, I. *Un grand mystique byzantin: Vie de S. Syméon le Nouveau Théologien par Nicétas Stéthatos.* Orientalia Christiana XII 45. Rome: Pontificium Institutum Orientalium Studiorum, 1928.

Krivocheine, B. *In the Light of Christ.* Crestwood, NY: St. Vladimir's Seminary Press, 1987.

Maloney, G. *The Hymns of Divine Love.* Denville, NJ: Dimension Books, 1975.

———. *The Mystic of Fire and Light.* Denville, NJ: Dimension Books, 1975.

McGuckin, J. A. "The Notion of Luminous Vision in 11th C Byzantium: Interpreting the Biblical and Theological Paradigms of St. Symeon the New Theologian." In *Acts of the Belfast Byzantine Colloquium—Portaferry 1995*, 90-123. Belfast: Queens University Press, 1996.

———. "St. Symeon the New Theologian and Byzantine Monasticism." In *Mount Athos and Byzantine Monasticism*, ed. A. Bryer, 17-35. London: Variorum, 1996.

———. "St. Symeon the New Theologian (d. 1022): Byzantine Theological Renewal in Search of a Precedent." In *Studies in Church History* 33, *The Church Retrospective*, 75-90. Oxford: Boydell, 1996.

McGuckin, P. (J. A.). *Symeon the New Theologian: Chapters and Discourses.* Kalamazoo, MI: Cistercian Publications, 1982. Reprint, 1994.

Pelikan, J. "The Last Flowering of Byzantium: The Mystic as New Theologian." In *The Spirit of Eastern Christendom*, chap. 6. London: University of Chicago Press, 1977.

Turner, H. J. M. *St. Symeon the New Theologian and Spiritual Fatherhood.* Leiden: Brill, 1990.

**The Great Schism**

Chadwick, H. *East and West: The Making of a Rift in the Church; From Apostolic Times Until the Council of Florence.* Oxford: Oxford University Press, 2003.

Dvornik, F. *Byzantium and the Roman Primacy.* New York: Fordham University Press, 1966.

Runciman, S. *The Eastern Schism: A Study of the Papacy and the Eastern Churches During the XIth and XIIth Centuries.* Oxford: Oxford University Press, 1955.

**Medieval Academic Life**

Courtenay, W. J. *Teaching Careers at the University of Paris in the 13th and 14th Centuries.* Notre Dame, IN: University of Notre Dame Press, 1988.

Ginther, J. R. *The Westminster Handbook to Medieval Theology.* Louisville: Westminster John Knox, 2009.

Holopainen, T. J. *Dialectic and Theology in the 11th Century.* Leiden: Brill, 1996.

Pedersen, O. *The First Universities: Studium Generale and the Origins of University Education in Europe.* Cambridge: Cambridge University Press, 1997.

Sewter, E. R. A., trans. *Fourteen Byzantine Rulers: The Chronographia of Michael Psellus.* London: Penguin Books, 1966.

# PART TWO

# A WINDING ROAD: SELECT THEMES AND IDEAS

# THE BIBLE AND ITS INTERPRETATION IN THE EARLY CHURCH

### OLD AND NEW BIBLICAL INTERPRETATION

The twentieth century witnessed a veritable explosion in scholarly interest in biblical-hermeneutical issues—that is, interpretive concerns related to the meaning and status of Holy Scripture in Christian life and thought, especially including issues of methodological approach to biblical interpretation. This explosive expansion of the field of biblical criticism happened in the twentieth century predominantly, though it was being built up on the patient labors of eighteenth-and nineteenth-century (predominantly Protestant) literary critics. As in the aftermath of other kinds of intellectual explosions, the resulting field of new biblical analysis is not a tidy one but presents to the interested eye many possibilities of "new build." If commentators look back from a century ahead and try to synopsize the chief concerns of the intellectual life of twentieth-century Christianity, I suspect that it is this literary ferment over the status and deeper meaning of scriptural interpretation that will probably present to them one of the most distinctive aspects of the church in this age, and one of the primary (though largely unrecognized) causes behind much of the current flux, in its moral, doctrinal, and social aspects, of church life in America and Western Europe.

Before the eighteenth century, Christian preaching out of the Bible had been done in a more or less unbroken tradition stretching back to the patristic age. Two approaches were dominant and unchallenged and really characterized every single differentiation of Christian experience (ancient or modern, Catholic, Protestant, or Orthodox—despite the much-vaunted denominational claims that different churches "read" differently), and these were first of all a common-sense reading of what the text said and an attempt to derive a moral inspiration from it for the reader's life, and then a symbolic reading of the (large amount) of material that did not immediately fit that simpler pattern (such as historical materials, stories where the literal meaning was somewhat dubious—rapes, murders, wars, and the like), which was usually in the form of allegorical readings of the text in hand, abstracted now for Christian usage as symbols of higher truths. An example of the simple moral approach would be the application of the Ten Commandments as a code of moral values across societies (even though interpretation was at work heavily here, of course, transforming the Bronze Age Jewish legal code into an enduring moral "goal" for later era societies) or the taking of Jesus' instructions (such as the Beatitudes [Mt 5:2-12]) as primary personal moral directives. An example of the allegorical approach would be the taking of the psalm reference advocating taking the babies of one's enemies in wartime and dashing their brains out on a rock (Ps 137:9) as a symbol of the necessity of eradicating the evil tendencies of a human heart.[1] These were hermeneutical procedures employed and systematized by the early Christian fathers. They were not invented by them but rose out of their own immersion in Greco-Roman rhetorical techniques as commonly taught in the schools of the day.

Origen of Alexandria marks a watershed in Christian biblical interpretation.[2] Before him the biblical interpretation of the earliest communities tends to be isolated proof-texting (a verse or narrative incident lifted out of the larger fabric of the biblical materials and used as a type [a prefigured symbolic reference] to the Jesus story). In this way the earliest approaches to exegesis, for example, turn around such passages as Second Isaiah's Suffering Servant (an approach already intimated, of course, in Matthew's Gospel), or the exodus story of the Paschal Lamb, as a sermon parallel for considering the sacrificial death of Jesus. Or, as in Melito of Sardis's *Peri Pascha*, one of the earliest full liturgical homilies we have extant from the Asia Minor church, the passing through the waters of the Red Sea is lifted as an extended metaphor for baptism.[3]

This latter type, already suggested in the writings of Paul, was given shape and focus by the demands of episcopal preaching at the Christian liturgies in the first two centuries. This tendency toward proof-texting, lifting up of randomly chosen citations (fulfilled by Christ) or parallel narratives that are recognized by the Christian preachers as prophetically symbolic, was an atomistic kind of approach that relied on

---

[1] The patristic allegorical reading of this text was that the secret tendencies of the heart toward vice were the "children of Amalek" (the king opposed to Joshua/Jesus, and thus the prefigured symbol—or type—of Satan), and the war for the promised land was to be fought constantly within each individual—now spiritually. So by means of allegorical reading, what was once an abhorrent ancient war practice (kill the babies so that a next generation of warriors cannot come back and wreak their vengeance on you in your old age) is rendered into a useful moral message for evangelical purposes.

[2] See further J. A. McGuckin, *The Westminster Handbook to Origen* (Louisville: Westminster John Knox, 2004).

[3] An excerpt is given in the short reader following.

the inspired character and gift of the preacher (normally the eucharistic president, one imagines) to put together. Patterns of this kind of approach had already been witnessed as subtextual patterns still visible behind the literary form of the later Gospel, Acts, and epistolary accounts of earliest Christianity. A classical exposition of these patterns can be found in English theologian C. H. Dodd's *The Apostolic Preaching and Its Developments*.[4]

Through the course of the twentieth century many literary and historical studies of the Scriptures seemed to detach themselves from any concern to represent ecclesial interests in the Scripture considered as "sacred literature." New genres of criticism developed that approached the canon of Old Testament and New on simple historical and literary-analytical terms. These generally privileged the so-called higher criticism of the Bible and regularly dispensed altogether with any reference to patterns of biblical interpretation (patristic, medieval, or early modern) that had been offered by Christian ages before the nineteenth century. Detaching themselves from an ecclesial tradition, they usually scorned allegorical traditions of readings (the predominant ancient approaches), and it became very rare indeed to find any "critical commentary" that made any reference to the rich history of interpretation. It was almost as if the question of biblical interpretation began again at year zero in the twentieth century, and many commentators began to wonder whether dispensing with the ecclesial concept of biblical theology meant the necessary rejection also of concepts such as the unity of the Testaments, the notion of inspired canon, inerrancy, and the host of other attitudes and approaches to Scripture the church had elevated in its exegetical philosophy when it predominantly approached the texts as inherently holy revelations and fundamentally authoritative sources of Christian identity.

And so there was some sense of reassessment taking place at the beginning of the twenty-first century into what was a viable ecclesial concept of Holy Scripture and how contemporary critical work could be related to generations of Christians past, who had lived out of the Bible without much dependence on the style of critical approach that had emerged in the new academic study. There was movement in many parts of the church to distance itself from the higher criticism and cling to a simple, literal reading. But the general sentiment was expressed by the Scottish biblical theologian James Barr who, though noting the challenge this form of study had given to an "ecclesial reading," went on to point out what seemed to be obvious to most who worked in the academy, that the achievements of historical criticism were manifold and would be long-lasting, even if many

---

[4] C. H. Dodd, *The Apostolic Preaching and Its Developments* (London: Harper, 1964). Available online at www.religion-online.org/showbook.asp?title=539.

smaller details, and the concept of an ecclesial mentality in regard to Scripture, came to be reconsidered over time:

> Some of the main positions achieved [by biblical criticism] have remained as essential reference points for the discussion, and no alternatives have been proposed that have gained anything like the same degree of assent. Still more important, the general intellectual atmosphere of criticism, with its base in language and literary form, its reference grid in history, and its lifeblood in freedom to follow what the text actually says, has established itself as without serious challenge. Serious work on scripture can only be done in continuity with the tradition of biblical criticism.[5]

## RELATIVISM AND THE ECCLESIAL MIND

Today, the task of reconciling contemporary critical study of the Bible (still heavily historically based) with earlier forms of more theological reading of the text considered as sacred literature for church (an approach heavily favored in more popular, devotional forms of church literature on Bible) still remains to be done coherently and systematically. One step forward in this process might be the efforts of scholars to realize that the historical record of prior biblical analysis is not something antagonistic to critical method, nor something that ought to be cast aside as useless (completely neglected, as it has been in most twentieth-century works of analysis). The ancient biblical commentators were not doing the same things as modern literary analysts; but they were experts in the task of close and reverent reading of a sacred text, and accordingly they elevated the first architecture of what the church came to mean by inspiration, canonicity, and authoritativeness of the biblical corpus. Even for this their work would remain important and worthy of study.

More than this, however, in many cases the biblical exegesis of the ancients is dominated by a mystical and attentive spirit, which although it strikes modern readers as being in an oddly different key signature, is eye opening and profound in many challenging ways. One result of the restoration of a sense of patristic biblical hermeneutic, alongside modern analytical techniques, I might suggest, is a healthy underlining that there is rarely (if ever) "one single meaning" to a text: and certainly not a single meaning that our latest techniques have revealed for the first time ever.

The "critical" presupposition that each previous age has obscured the truth that now at last is to be laid bare by "objective" historical research in our time, or newly sharpened philosophical acumen, is both arrogant and uninformed, misunderstanding the nature of history and textuality, as well as deliberately cutting itself off

---

[5]James Barr, "History of Interpretation," in *The Oxford Companion to the Bible*, ed. B. Metzger and M. D. Coogan (New York: Oxford University Press, 1993), 324.

from any communion or solidarity with the originating communities of discourse. No historical context, or text, exists in some disembodied space that can be objectively scrutinized by an infallible academic voice. Neither do text, context, and interpretations merge into one another in an intertextual world where it is no longer proper to speak of meanings.

This does not mean either that the church is required to elevate fundamentalistic devotional readings simply because they claim to be "reverent," or to be enslaved to the latest critical speculations that are divorced from the common sense of the church (meaning here chiefly the common spiritual instinct of the Christian ages). The recognition and perception of meaning is undoubtedly driven by human epistemological systems that have only recently come to be more fully understood, but the philosophical step forward from this, namely that humans have created meaning rather than recognizing it (so central to the relativism that postmodernism wishes to inculcate), is a secular "act of faith" (not fact). It is an act of faith that stands in contradiction to much that is held valuable in human culture at large, and certainly to most of what the (worshiping) church would recognize, generally, as the patterns of revelation within the created order and, particularly, as the location of the sacred charism of divine revelation within the expansive sacramentality of the scriptural text.

Far from text being detached in a disembodied space, text (at least ancient text such as the Scripture) is rather is the collective "song of the community." The interpreter who understands this is one who is sensitive to the community of meanings that constitute the "community's meaning." In theological terms this means that the text of the Bible "belongs to" the church as much as the church belongs to the Bible; and the ecclesial reading of the *ekklesia*'s song, therefore, is very much a matter of harmony with, or conformity to, the appropriate modalities of interpretation. Much contemporary criticism, of course, finds this highly objectionable on methodological grounds. The ancients, especially the Christian fathers, never failed to argue that true interpretation demands a *symphonia* of understanding between the discourses brought into association: that "like can only be known by like" (a principle first insisted on by Plato but refined by Origen to insist that only a mind illumined by Christ's values can properly appreciate the texts that first described Christ). But, in the wider and unbroken consensus of the church's perspectives, the very concept of Scripture is, after all, a theological notion, not a simple literary one. Holy Scripture is a sacramental mystery of the church, not simply an artifact of history.

Even so, a key result of much modern "hermeneutic of suspicion" has been has been the systematic rejection of other perspectives that conflict with the axiomatic ideologies of the new hermeneutic that is being applied, and an unwillingness to subordinate the critical commentator to canons of judgment other than his or her own selected "principles." From the first, this visibly resulted in an exile of patristic analysis from modern biblical study. The vast collection of patristic sermons on Scripture was banished from all serious academic discussion of biblical hermeneutics as hopelessly irrelevant. At a stroke, that community that strenuously elevated the canon of the Bible and faithfully preserved it in kerygmatic preached discourse was eliminated from our considerations of how to interpret it.

Today, very few biblical commentaries seriously consider how a pericope has been interpreted in the past. The rich and nuanced body of patristic material has been caricatured as all of a piece "allegorical" or "typological" analysis and set aside. Such crudity of categorization, one that is rarely based on serious study of the data, is often the fruit of a narrow ideology. The same is suggested by the observation that only at the very end of the twentieth century were any serious scholarly analyses of patristic biblical hermeneutics making their appearance.[6]

In the church's inner life, its intimate attitudes, the fundamental ideology behind this prevalent "hermeneutic of suspicion" preferred by the secular academy's approach to biblical texts will rarely find a ready acceptance. The church has a sense of continuity of faithfulness from Jesus and the apostles, to whom he entrusted the message, through the successive generations who shaped the forms and canon of the scriptural corpus, to the long generations who have since accepted these texts as gifts from God. Behind it all is the "ecclesial mind," or the consciousness that the church of every age claims not only continuity with the church of the originating ages but even an awareness of being authoritatively the same spiritually enlightened community as the churches of the apostolic period (though of course in a different environment).[7]

It is not so much a hermeneutic of suspicion that is active here in the ecclesial approach to Bible but a hermeneutic of familial trust. This is what contemporary criticism would call "grand narrative imposition" of a high order, but what I would suggest is actually the primary drive and instinct of the church's self-recognition across the ages. Denominationalism has not been able to destroy this, though it has certainly detracted from it in the dogma wars of the last six hundred years, and ultimately when

---

[6]Such as M. Simonetti, *Biblical Interpretation in the Early Church* (Edinburgh: T&T Clark, 1994); T. Stylianopoulos, *The New Testament: An Orthodox Perspective* (Brookline, MA: Holy Cross Orthodox Press, 1997); Archbishop D. Trakatellis, *Hoi Pateres Hermenevoun: Apopseis Paterikes Biblikes Hermeneias* (Athens: Apostolike Diakonia, 1996); J. Panagopoulos, *He Hermeneia Tes Agias Graphes Sten Ekklesia Ton Pateron*, vol. 1 (Athens: Akritas Press, 1994); A. Hauser and D. F. Watson, eds., *A History of Biblical Interpretation*, vol. 1, *The Ancient Period* (Grand Rapids: Eerdmans, 2003); and the monumental *Handbook of Patristic Exegesis*, by Charles Kannengiesser (Leiden: Brill, 2006).

[7]This is a doctrinally prevalent belief in all the major Christian communities across history, that they have equal access to the presence and mind of the risen Christ in their midst—fundamentally, that is, that Christianity is not a sect honoring a dead and past master for his historical teachings.

the latest and most speculative forms of postmodern hermeneutic have grown gray with age and seem less than "trendy and challenging," it will be the church's spiritual instinct that will continue to cherish its "Holy Scriptures" and approach them reverently (as if standing before holy things) for enlightenment, not merely knowledge.

If we can call this attitude to hermeneutics the principle of the ecclesial reading, we will see how basically it matters that a Christian interpreter shares a "consonant" motivation for interpreting the sacred text—consonant, that is, with the kerygmatic motive of the earlier saints, preachers, and biblical commentators whose works have been "received" by the church at large.[8] This commits "ecclesial" interpreters, of course, to a large body of biblical interpretation that may not be particularly "accurate" but that remains good insofar as it proved its utility in building up the faith of the community and entering into the heart of the community.[9]

If previous meanings have fallen out of the heart (and memory) of the community, so be it. It would be ridiculous in the name of authenticity to patristic tradition, for example, to resurrect some of the patristic biblical homilies that were warmly welcomed in earlier centuries but that to modern congregations of worship would simply sound fanciful and prove a barrier to the comprehension of the core biblical message of salvation. Some element of falling out of memory, and falling out of favor, in the life of the church is an important aspect of the self-renewal of the tradition of the saints and ought not to be interrupted by the work of "archaizers" any more than the work of new historical speculators who wish to draw up fresh canons of what they want to regard as Scripture.[10]

## THE PRINCIPLE OF CONSONANCE

In some sense this ecclesial reading to which I wish to draw attention here as a core element of the early church's exegetical macrotheory can be summed up as a "principle of consonance" with a broader tradition, or spiritual mindset. It is not so much

---

[8]The prevenient notions of divine inspiration and apostolic authority are not, strictly speaking, hermeneutical, though of course they too affect mainstream Christian understandings of appropriate interpretative process.

[9]Some of it, frankly, is historically inept and based on symbolic rhetorical elaborations of the texts, not serious contextual analysis. But not to discard it signifies that the ecclesial mind is not enslaved to a historical-critical methodology, since symbolic forms of truth telling can be equally revelatory of deeper mysteries, especially if they speak to deep-seated patterns of Christian thinking across the ages. Not to discard historical method equally demonstrates that the church will not abdicate critical methods of qualitative insight in relation to its apprehension of spiritual meaning and thus will stand open to antique senses it might have forgotten and need to relearn, as well as maintaining a defense against immature and inappropriate readings of Scripture applied without discretion.

[10]The Jesus Seminar, for example, would have left the church with a much smaller set of Gospel materials and a massively shrunken Christology.

demanding that everyone, all over the world, should adopt and demonstrate the selfsame things,[11] which would not take into account a wide range and degree of richness and maturity in the church's approach to biblical meanings, as much as stating that the Christian sense of Scripture is transhistorical (enduringly communitarian across ages) and metahistorical (eschatological and time explaining, not merely timebound), as well as historical.[12] This sense of ecclesial consonance asks of the modern biblical interpreter to stand within the mind of the saints, who themselves shared the mind of Christ (the *phronema Christou*; 1 Cor 2:16; Phil 1:27; 2:5; 3:14-16).

This concept is best expressed in the ancient literature by Origen, who insists in almost all he writes that since the biblical text is a matter of sacramental revelations from the divine Logos, the primary qualification of the interpreter has to be mystical maturity (through a deep life of prayer) allied with moral purity, and then sharpened by literary and rhetorical skills.[13] Origen's two close readers, Gregory of Nazianzus and Athanasius of Alexandria, both epitomize this.[14] Athanasius's instructions to his church on how to read the Scriptures, written in a time of great conflict over the Arian controversy, have been elevated by later generations as a classical exposition of the early Christian method of the totalist and spiritual reading of Holy Scripture.[15] For him clarity of soul is necessary to apprehend the sacred text insofar as it bears the mysteries of the Spirit.

Basil the Great also says much the same thing in his *Treatise on the Holy Spirit* when he describes how the interpreter of the oracles of the divine Spirit needs to be rendered clear by the working of the same Holy Spirit (using the image that only when glass is clear can it mediate the sun).[16] This kind of interpretation requires "consonance." Using the words of St. Paul, the communion with the Holy Spirit who inspires the text is a fundamental precondition for the authentic "opening up" of the

---

[11]In formulating this theory of tradition Vincent of Lerins made, it has to be said, one of the most woodenly simplistic iterations of it—that Christian tradition was "that which is believed everywhere, at all times, by everyone." Not only is it impossible to demonstrate such a theory, but it is fundamentally a useless one.

[12]In its formal exegesis, as well as its more general preaching through the ages, Christianity has evidently been capable of inspired heights as well as bathotic stupidities and meanness. The ecclesial reaction to Christ in each generation is qualitatively different, according to individual achievement, maturity, and inspiration.

[13]Athanasius, in his *De Incarnatione* account, refers to moral purity as "that virtue which is of Christ." Here, virtue (*arete*) is not simply moral probity but connotes the energy of direction and instinct for knowing when one has arrived at truth, elements of the divine power of the Logos communicated to the church, which Athanasius is deliberately adding in to his account in 57.1-3.

[14]In Gregory's *First Theological Oration* (*Oration* 27). Excerpted in the short reader at the end of this chapter.

[15]*De Incarnatione* 57.1-3. Excerpted in the short reader below.

[16]*De Spiritu Sancto* 9.23.

sacred book (Rom 8:9; 1 Cor 2:12-13; Eph 1:17-18). Without that, there might be many levels of historical and morphological comment possible on the biblical text, but no *exegesis* as the church properly understands it.

This leads us to the conclusion that, for the early Christian fathers, biblical exegesis belongs properly to the internal community of the church, which is defined by the possession of the charism of the Spirit. Individual biblical interpreters supplement their own possession of the charism of the Spirit's illumination, with the gift of illumination that over the centuries has been granted to preceding generations of the church. It strongly suggests that no interpreter can presume to disregard, or ridicule, the serious interpretative efforts of previous generations, least of all those of the saints who have been preserved in the tradition as particularly worthwhile and authoritative. Consonance in this case is certainly not the same as monotonous repetition of past utterance, which would amount to strict conformity and would signal the end to intelligent development of biblical analysis; on the contrary, I think that what is signaled here is that new applications of biblical interpretative methods proceed reflectively "within the communion," just as variations on a theme are self-evidently linked to the master theme, which they in turn set out to elaborate, illuminate, or extend.

This principle, of course, allows biblical interpreters from within the communion to make use of a large range of biblical readings, methods, and styles that have not been produced by those within the same communion and perhaps not written with much regard for what one might call the "inspired" character of the sacred text, but it commits the ecclesial interpreter to view and process all of that extrinsic material in the light of the church's inner principles of receptivity. In all things the method is an interpretative tool, merely a tool. The guiding metaphysic (the process toward authentic reception of the sacred exegesis of the Bible) has to be the reception of the sacrament of revelation in the present moment: what the early Fathers called the *mysterion Christou*, the mystery of Christ's abiding presence in the church.

The principle of consonance (which we could also, then, call the principle of communion) is extensively set out, and most elegantly so, in the first of the *Five Theological Orations* by St. Gregory the Theologian, who elsewhere throughout his work describes the biblical commentator as a priest who is allowed entry into a temple, but the deeper the progression into the sacred areas (beyond the veil no human can go in this earthly life), the more pressing is the need for purity of heart and acumen of mind.[17] Both things, moral and intellectual power, are seen by

---

[17] *Oration* 27.

Gregory to be significant charisms that cannot be neglected, and if they are not present in the manifested works of the interpreter, the priestly act of biblical exegesis will be rendered into sacrilege.[18]

The several patristic writers who speak of consonance with the mind and spirit of the biblical author are largely echoing Origen, who, in turn, is developing his principles of biblical interpretation from the Pauline starting point of "seeking the mind of Christ." For Origen, that mind (which also in the Greek means "mindset") is a matrix that the *energeia* of divine inspiration lays down in the mind of the apostolic author. His starting point for this is, of course, the apostolic dictum in 1 Corinthians 2:16, which is itself the summation of one of the first ever considered essays on the Christian theology of inspiration from the hand of the apostle himself:

> And I came to you in weakness and in fear and in much trembling. My speech and my proclamation were not with plausible words of wisdom, but with a demonstration of the Spirit and of power, so that your faith might rest not on human wisdom but on the power of God. Yet among the mature we do speak wisdom, though it is not a wisdom of this age or of the rulers of this age, who are doomed to perish. But we speak God's wisdom, secret and hidden, which God decreed before the ages for our glory. . . . These things God has revealed to us through the Spirit; for the Spirit searches everything, even the depths of God. For what human being knows what is truly human except the human spirit that is within? So also no one comprehends what is truly God's except the Spirit of God. . . . Now we have received not the spirit of the world, but the Spirit that is from God, so that we may understand the gifts bestowed on us by God. And we speak of these things in words not taught by human wisdom but taught by the Spirit, interpreting spiritual things to those who are spiritual. Those who are unspiritual do not receive the gifts of God's Spirit, for they are foolishness to them, and they are unable to understand them because they are spiritually discerned. Those who are spiritual discern all things, and they are themselves subject to no one else's scrutiny. "For who has known the mind of the Lord so as to instruct him?" But we have the mind of Christ [1 Cor 2:3-16].

This is not to imagine that sophisticated biblical theologians such as Origen, Athanasius, and Cyril, or the Cappadocian fathers, ever envisaged a direct or literal transference of information from God to the human author (something the later icon painters somewhat naively depicted as a ray of light leaving God's hand and entering the Evangelist's ear), but rather that they imagined inspiration as being a divine *energeia* that inspired the charism of "comprehension" of the things of God in a human heart. Such comprehension was seen to be partial (inevitably so, since no human mind

---

[18]See J. A. McGuckin, "The Vision of God in St. Gregory Nazianzen," *StPatr* 32 (1996): 145-52.

could fully comprehend the purposes of God) but substantively accurate insofar as it represented the will of God concerning the issues of human salvation.

Accordingly, the Fathers understood the differences in the biblical accounts of Jesus, for example, as fundamentally related to the quality of the inspiration of each of the various evangelists. John and Paul were always recognized, in almost all patristic literature, as being clearly more in possession of the "mind of Christ" than most of the others. Origen explicitly lifted up a list of those parts of the Scripture that had pre-eminence of authority over all others and to which all other biblical texts had to be subordinated. Chief in the list were John, then Paul, then the Psalms and the remaining Gospels, then the greater prophets and the apostolic letters, then the remaining parts of Scripture. Although he regarded all Scripture as inspired, in no way did he regard each and every verse being equally freighted with enduring authority.

Origen expressed this sense of degrees of inspiration among the biblical writers in a regularly repeated image: that some of the apostles were called to the mountain with Christ to see things that the others could not witness directly but had to hear of only through later report (he has in mind the episode of the transfiguration in Mk 9).[19] He also depicts John as that apostle who had "reclined on the bosom of the Logos" (Jn 13:23-26; 21:20) and heard secrets, as contrasted to other witnesses who did not receive such great initiations. The patristic idea of consonance, however, was fundamentally one that resisted the atomization of biblical texts into disparate trends, or parts. It is this essentially "totalist" vision that accounts for the church's refusal to allow Marcion and the Gnostics to divide the Testaments. It derived from Origen's insistence that it was core to the church's faith that the divine Logos was the single author of all Scripture and thus gave the whole (sprawling) corpus a consistency that historical and literary approaches alone could not comprehend.

The same idea is also at the heart of the early church's building and defending the biblical canon: that whatever is recognized as canonical literature is endorsed as sharing in that communion of spirit that is authentically the Jesus tradition. Not all parts of the Jesus tradition share the same level of inspiration, this implies, but they all share the same communion of authority. It follows that the contemporary principle of affording the highest level of authority to chronologically earlier materials (such as the so-called Jesus Seminar endlessly arguing over what is or is not an authentic utterance of the historical Jesus) is deeply inimical to these principles of biblical interpretation. There is no hidden canon within a canon, a pure core of historically verifiable materials (as

---

[19] Origen's central insights into the process of biblical criticism were collected by the Cappadocians Gregory and Basil and assembled in the *Philocalia of Origen*. English trans. by G. Lewis (Edinburgh: T&T Clark, 1911). See further J. A. McGuckin, *The Transfiguration of Christ in Scripture and Tradition* (New York: Mellen, 1987).

distinct from what later disciples added to the Ur-tradition) to be established by the sagacious modern historian, but rather a collegiality of *kerygma* beginning with the preaching of Jesus and from there extending back over the whole comprehension (or reception) of the Old Testament itself, and extending forward over the whole unrolling of Christian civilization (the culture of the church) even to the time of the eschaton.

## THE PRINCIPLE OF AUTHORITY

For the early church commentators the Scriptures commanded authority, therefore, as a primary witness of the apostolic preaching, and thus the lens through which the church, and its biblical interpreters in a later age, could share in a commonality of experience of the Christ mystery. Dominical and apostolic utterances become, as it were, the set key signatures, within which the present music of the reexpression of the evangelical *kerygma* can be extrapolated: that music which is the essential expression of the church from age to age.[20] The Scriptures thus stand as an authority over Christian tradition and a guarantee of the latter's authenticity, in the manner that fugal form necessarily guides a composer in the creation of a fugue, or in the way a sonnet is required to rhyme.

Irenaeus, in the second century, had much to say about the creativity of tradition, which was not open to endless "redefinitions" (in his case he was attacking the speculations of the Gnostics). In another place I have more extensively considered the "open-endedness" of ecclesial tradition as indeed being a closure system.[21] This is not a contradictory notion, as some might presume; no more than is the notion of bounded infinity with which modern cosmologists understand the strange reality of the ever-expanding universe as it appears to scientific observation. Irenaeus amplified the biblical sense of apostolic tradition (first seen in the New Testament epistolary literature) with the concept of apostolic succession of bishops in the mainline "apostolic" churches. His point was that if one first discerned, then scrutinized, the apostolic tradition of Christian doctrine, one would find that there was perfect unanimity as to the *regula fidei* and his own current interpretation of Scripture. This was proven by appeal to the record of the main apostolic centers—those ancient and leading churches that already commanded international Christian emulation. This notion of universality gave rise to the idea being designated as the principle of catholicity.[22] Irenaeus was here suggesting a universal "test of authentic tradition," as well as invoking a

---

[20]Including its spiritual and liturgical life but also its intellectual and social culture.

[21]J. A. McGuckin, "Eschaton and Kerygma: The Future of the Past in the Present Kairos [The Concept of Living Tradition in Orthodox Theology]," *St. Vladimir's Theological Quarterly* 42, nos. 3-4 (Winter 1998): 225-71.

[22]*Kath 'olon* being the Greek term for widespread validity, universal adoption.

particular claim for the authenticity of his own charism as a Christian teacher: namely, that he stood within the church's consensus, not without it.

Irenaeus further developed his thought by suggesting that the apostolic churches had the *charisma veritatis* ("charism of truth"), which could not be presumed to be at work elsewhere.[23] For him, this essential *charisma* was manifested above all in the manner in which the leaders of the great churches interpreted the Scriptures soberly and with catholic consensus. It was in this context that he developed his famous image of the interpretative "key" (*hypothesis*) to the Scriptures, which the church has but which others do not possess. It was to grow into the later patristic concept of the *mens ecclesiae*, the "mind of the church," what Athanasius was to call the church's *dianoia* and its sense of the *skopos* of Scripture and tradition—meaning that comprehensive overview given to the Spirit-illumined faithful, which was radically partialized and distorted by Arian and other dissidents, who hereticized themselves precisely by refusing the consensus of illumination.[24]

For Irenaeus, the chief thing that was wrong about Gnostic exegesis was its lack of a harmonious sense of direction. He regarded this as proof that they did not possess the "key" to the Scriptures. They were like people, he said, who broke up and then reassembled the pieces of a mosaic. He uses the image of an original mosaic of a king that then turns up as an image of a dog after the careless workers have "reconstituted" the tesserae in their workshop. He mocks them for claiming that the new image is authentic because it was made up out of nothing other than the original parts.[25] Irenaeus added further to the fundamental vocabulary of the theology of tradition when he developed the argument that the key to biblical interpretation was the "canon of truth," which in the Latin version of his works gave to the West, decisively so in the hands of Tertullian, the principle of the *regula fidei*, or *regula veritatis*.[26] This *regula*, Irenaeus argued, was the strongest refutation of Gnostic variability, for it is maintained in all the churches and goes

---

[23] *Adversus Haereses* 4.26.2. This does not mean to suggest it is always absent elsewhere—but that it cannot be presumed to be consistently operating elsewhere.

[24] *Dianoia: ten ekklesiastiken dianoian* (Athanasius, *Contra Arianos* 1.44). *Skopos*: ibid., 3.35. Heresy after the fourth century comes to mean a dissident sect; but before this, when it is still being used precisely in this larger argument, it meant an intellectual position that was minority and eccentric instead of being majority consensual, a "division" within a school of thought.

[25] *Adversus Haereses* 1.8.1.

[26] On the canon of truth, see ibid., 3.2.1 (*kanon tes aletheias*). Irenaeus speaks of the church having the "body of truth": 2.27.1. Tertullian pressed the legal context much more than Irenaeus. For him tradition was transmitted within the churches that were linked by "familial" apostolic relationship. Tradition is thus the legal patrimony of the apostolic churches: a patrimony that is the legacy left by the legal founder of a corporation. It belongs only to the legitimate heirs. False pretenders to the legacy, such as the heretics, must be excluded by a legal *praescriptio*: that is, their claims are voided by default (*De Praescriptione Haereticorum* 19-21).

back to the apostles. Apostolic succession, then, is not primarily a matter of succession of individual bishops one after another (as it has often been presented in later ages), but chiefly the succession of apostolic teaching from the time of apostles to the present.[27]

## THE PRINCIPLE OF UTILITY

Beyond the principle of consonance, many other early Christian commentators on Scripture point regularly to a most important aspect of the church's authentic biblical interpretation, which is its "edificatory" character. The biblical commentary, in this understanding, is not, essentially, a historical essay or a semantic analysis but an expression of the charism of preaching within the church. We might call this the principle of utility: how the proclamation of the faith is rendered "appropriate" from age to age; how in one era (the first generation, say) the discourse is suitably Semitic and poetical, while in another (the patristic age, for example) the framework of Greek rhetoric and hymnody works most effectively, and in another age does not work so well and might require simpler forms of reexpression.

Origen (who certainly saw the act of biblical commentary as an extension of the prophetic charism of preaching the word) expressed this principle in his own time by describing the commentator as a "spiritual herbalist," whose duty was to know the values of all the contents of the herbarium and be able to make a potent mix for the benefit, not the bane, of the recipients: "The saint is a sort of spiritual herbalist who culls from the sacred Scriptures every jot and every common letter, discovers the value of what is written, and its use, and finds then that there is nothing in the Scripture that is superfluous."[28] This, in short, is a caution to the church's biblical commentators of the future, that commentary cannot be separated from the task of kerygmatic proclamation; and, since the latter includes dogmatics at its heart, it is a serious caution against divorcing systematic theology, biblical interpretation, and pastoral theology, a series of divorces that have, in fact, been much in evidence in the latter centuries of Christian intellectual life.[29]

After Origen had taken back the art of writing biblical commentaries from the Gnostics, he made sure that the genre in the church would always be faithful to the letter,

---

[27] *Adversus Haereses* 3.3.3; cf. 4.26.2; 4.33.8.
[28] *Philocalia of Origen* 10.2.
[29] It might well be that the life of the academy in the last century, especially as it related to theology and literary interpretation, was unable to cope in any other way with the burgeoning complexities and increasing literature of its subfields; but the progressive atomization of domains of expertise has been a bane of twentieth-century humanities and cannot be presumed to be a desirable path for the future (although there seems to be at least a century of "lag time" before educational establishments repair large-scale defects in curricula).

using careful grammatical and historical observations.[30] But he also set the bar for all who came after him and insisted that a commentary that only looked to the letter, not to the deeper spirit, was a poor thing. The vast amount of biblical commentary that he produced in his relatively short lifetime was a spur to generations of other early church writers, who produced extensive and often movingly deep commentaries on sacred Scripture.

Origen laid down theories of interpretation that were abstracted by the Cappadocian fathers, Gregory of Nazianzus and Basil, in the form of the *Philocalia Origenis*. This is one of the earliest of all handbooks for a Christian preacher—how to handle the biblical data. It was later reconceived by Pope Gregory the Great in the sixth century, as part of his labors in making Augustine's thought more transmittable in simplified form. The pope's exegetical theories are basically a "common man's" Augustine. Gregory's influential work, produced in 591, is entitled *Liber regulae pastoralis*, or *The Pastoral Rule*, and it gives very practical advice to clergy how to preach scripturally.[31] It moderates the highly symbolistic and mystical-philosophical approaches of Origen and affirms a more common-sense moralistic reading of the narratives, mediated by the preacher and fitted to the pastoral needs of his listeners at liturgy. The book had an immense readership because of the increased prestige of the early medieval Latin papacy and so became the standard exegetical handbook of the Christians in the West for more than a millennium, forming the substrate of a common tradition of mildly symbolic style of preaching biblical texts that culminated in the search for a moral point, and which has endured to the present in most churches.

The Syrian churches of antiquity had also developed a similar approach to that of Gregory in the West. Both schools deliberately diverged from some of Origen's more extended symbolisms. The earlier Syrian exegetes had insisted on close literal readings of the Scripture, avoiding allegorical readings that moved too far away from the sense. The doyen of this school, a direct critic of Origen, was fourth-century exegete Mar Theodore of Mopsuestia.[32] Theodore and his disciple, Diodore of Tarsus, were noted for their robust attacks on the "excesses" of Alexandrian allegorism. Theodore preferred what he regarded as a "straightforward" reading of the text's historical-moral meaning. Most of his exegetical work has been lost. The catalogue

---

[30]Heracleon, a disciple of Valentinus, is the first Christian known to have composed a commentary on a scriptural book: the Gospel of John. Origen systematically critiques it in his own magisterial *Commentary on John*.

[31]The text is in PL 77; English trans., Henry Davis, *Gregory the Great: Pastoral Care*, Ancient Christian Writers 1 (New York: Newman Press, 1950); see also R. A. Markus, *Gregory the Great and His World* (Cambridge: Cambridge University Press, 1977).

[32]See further R. A. Norris, *Manhood and Christ* (Oxford: Clarendon, 1963); D. Z. Zaharopoulos, *Theodore Mopsuestia on the Bible* (New York: Paulist, 1989).

originally included commentaries on Genesis and the other books of the Pentateuch, on Psalms, the Major and Minor Prophets, Job, Ecclesiastes, and a letter on the Song of Songs; as well as commentaries on Matthew, Luke, John, Acts, and the major and minor Pauline epistles. All that survives from this large body of biblical work are Greek fragments from the *Genesis Commentary* from the first three chapters; the *Commentary on the Minor Prophets* (in the original Greek text); *Commentary on John* (in a Syriac version); *Commentary on Paul's Minor Epistles* (in a Latin version); fragments from the *Commentary on Paul's Major Epistles*; and a modern reconstruction by Devreesse (relating to the first eighty psalms only) gathered from various quotation fragments (*catenae*) in various places.[33]

Theodore's custom was to preface his detailed comments on a biblical text with a generic preface, where he outlined the book's overall character (its ethos) and discussed its author and the context in which it was composed. This is very similar to the standard Aristotelian canons for literary comment, which had been established in the Great Library at Alexandria. His comments on the Psalms show that he had already noted that many of the episodes narrated in the Psalms (such as the invasion of Jerusalem) were later than David's lifetime, but they were still composed by David, he argues, since he is traditionally known as the author of the Psalms and so was acting proleptically in visionary terms as a prophet when he spoke of these things. There is rarely any explicit doctrinal application in Theodore's exegeses. Most of his writings become, as a result, an extended paraphrase of the biblical story. He especially wishes to root out the (Origenian) habit of cross-relating texts from different scriptural books, and he regularly fights against number symbolism, denying it has any mystical associations whatsoever.

Theodore retains the Alexandrian sense of typology as underlying some passages of the Bible but massively reduces the scope and extent of the types as compared to the Alexandrians.[34] His chief legitimate types are Jonah as a symbolic foretelling of the death and resurrection of Jesus, the exodus as a type of the

---

[33]His works were scattered and widely disapproved of in Byzantium (and the West) because of his posthumous condemnation by the Second Council of Constantinople in 553, which tarred him by association with Nestorius.

[34]A "type" being a prefiguration of a New Testament reality in the narrative structure or the prosopography of the Old Testament text. The concept derives from the idea of *typos*, or seal, which left an impression in wax. The seal was a reverse image that became clear only when seen in its later "stamping." Like a key of an old typewriter, the metal was difficult to read because of its reversal but became clear when used later. So, it was argued, the Old Testament narratives "adumbrate" and become clearer in the light of the New Testament revelation. An example would be the story of Jonah in the whale being a type of Christ in the tomb; or Abraham setting off to sacrifice his son Isaac (who bears the wood of the sacrificial fire on his back), which adumbrates the "true Son" Jesus carrying his cross to Calvary.

Passover of Christ, and the bronze serpent as a symbol of the passion. In short, he either follows a New Testament precedent or a liturgically established tradition. Whereas Athanasius had taken the whole book of Psalms to have christological reference, Theodore says there are only four psalms that can be so interpreted (Pss 2; 8; 44/45; 109/110).

Numerous Old Testament texts that had, until his time, commonly been taken christocentrically or ecclesiologically, he says can be entirely explicated as having reference to events that were accomplished in the time of the prophets themselves.[35] Theodore is the only patristic commentator who denies that the bride and groom of the Song of Songs is a mystical reference to Christ and the church. He tries to give a systematic rule to explain when typology should be followed and when avoided. To be useful as a type, he argues that the Old Testament episode must have (1) obvious correlations with its New Testament antitype, (2) be inferior in its import and contextual weight to the New Testament episode it adumbrates, and (3) have a good moral impact that can be applied sensibly in preaching.

Theodore's very heavy restriction on the use of the Old Testament for typological interconnections demonstrates his generic preference for reading the Hebrew Bible as a closed system that maintained a pre-Christian religious dispensation that was superior to Hellenism but was destined to give way before the coming of the new covenant. The latter, he argues, was ushered in by the newly revealed doctrine of the Trinity. Christ's incarnation, Theodore elevates as a key theme, reveals the new economy (*oikonomia*) between God and humanity; and this is synopsized in the doctrine and belief of the Trinity, into which a new race would be baptized. The economy of the incarnation makes a new holy text, for Theodore, that brings its own meaning, illuminating the old, not being illuminated by it.

He lays over all his exegeses a macrocontext of his particular doctrine of the "two ages." Christ's incarnation ushers in the future age. The New Testament is, therefore, the initiation of the next age and looks to the future, never to the past. It is in its core genre an eschatological literature. Typology, for Theodore, is a theological trend that seems to want to make the New Testament tied to the Old. But he sees the latter as a series of books that cannot do other than look to the past. As they are rooted in history, they have to be historically unraveled. As this is their core ethos, the method of their analysis has to be entirely historical, too. But since the New Testament is focused in another direction, looking to an apocalyptic future, proleptically charged, then it cannot be explicated by history, since it explicates history itself, and thus can only be interpreted in the light of eschatology.

---

[35]Such as Mal 4:2 (that is Mal 3:20 in the LXX), concerning the "sun of righteousness."

Theodore's established custom of reading the text literally and sequentially makes his *Commentary on John* one of the least inspiring versions of that Gospel in patristic literature. Some see his polarized sense of the strong difference between the two Testaments as helping his analysis of Pauline thought. Previous Pauline exegesis in the Fathers had tried to harmonize all aspects of Paul with the Old Testament because of a widespread anti-Marcionite anxiety prevalent in the church after the second century. John Chrysostom and Theodore are probably the best of the ancient commentators on Paul. Modern commentators, not always seeing the point of Theodore's distinction between historical and transhistorical hermeneutics, have often (quite wrongly) hailed him as a precursor of modern historico-critical biblical interpretation.

The moderated Syrian style, surviving after Theodore and Diodore, is best exemplified in the very large corpus of exegetical works left by St. John Chrysostom. His name is a title derived from the term for "golden-mouthed," and he became one of the most loved writers of the early Byzantine period, and in this form dominated Byzantine Greek exegetical styles (though the Greek intellectuals never lost sight of the works of Origen either). Chrysostom exemplifies the Antiochene style of close reading of the common sense of the narrative, but he also applies the widely accepted symbolic readings that Theodore had disputed. In this sense he serves as a reconciliation of Alexandrian and Antiochene traditions. He does this effortlessly, as he was also the leading Greek rhetorician of his age, in that period of the late fourth century when Antioch of Syria was the world capital of Hellenistic rhetoric. When Chrysostom was invited to be the archbishop of the capital at Constantinople, he was placed in a position (as exegete and renowned martyr) where his works permeated the whole Byzantine world. He impressed even leaders of the Alexandrian church, such as Cyril (who quietly incorporates much of his exegesis) and moderated the more severe strictures of earlier Syrian exegesis. This reconciliation became the standard "Byzantine" way of reading Scripture for many centuries to come. Indeed, even in the present day, Chrysostom is the writer who sets the tone for most Eastern Orthodox preaching.

It would be no exaggeration to say that the vast majority of early Christian writing, if not focused on the right interpretation of Scripture, is concerned with initiating deeper forms of prayer and worship. These are its primary areas of interest. It is only in the early modern age that European commentators have given precedence to the "dogmatic controversies" of the early Christian writers and confected for the modern world the idea that they were early examples of systematicians. They are, above all else, meditators on the Word: and this for the simple reason that the Word of God was extensively commented on in the course of the weekly eucharistic liturgies of the early communities.

Today the once neglected (and massive) domain of early Christian exegesis is taking its place in theological curricula (slowly). It is being helped to return not as a replacement of historical-critical method but as a parallel resource to it. Reformed church theologians such as Tom Oden, who have regarded ancient exegesis as a neglected treasure, have made monumental efforts to get this rich material out and available in English versions that would be useful for modern Christian preachers. His series Ancient Christian Commentary on Scripture has digested patristic analysis and arranged it around each book of the canon, verse by verse.[36] In the medieval church St. Thomas Aquinas had anticipated him by a similar exercise in Latin called the *Catena Aurea*, or *Golden Chain*.

## A SHORT READER

### *Melito of Sardis,* On the Pascha *6-10 (second century).*

> In this way the slaughter of the sheep,
> The Passover ritual and the writing of the law
> Have come to Christ,
> For whose sake everything that is in the law took place,
> Which is even more so in the New Word.
> And indeed the Law has become Word,
> The Old has become New,
> Emerging out of Zion and Jerusalem.
> The commandment has become grace;
> The Type, Truth;
> The Sheep, Man;
> The Man, God.
> For the Son has been given birth
> As the Lamb has been led forth.
> And the Sheep has been slaughtered
> As the Man has been buried,
> And God has risen from the dead:
> By nature God and Man.
> He who is all things:
> As the one who judges, Law;
> As the one who teaches, Word;
> As the one who saves, Grace;

---

[36] A magnificent series published by InterVarsity Press.

As the one who gives birth, Father;
As the one who is given birth, Son;
As the one who suffers, Sheep;
As the one who is buried, Man;
As the one who rises, God.
This is Jesus the Christ,
To whom be glory for ever. Amen.
Now this is the mystery of the Passover,
Just as it is written in the Law,
And as it has just now been read out.

***Origen of Alexandria,*** **De Principiis** ***preface.3, 8*** **(third century).** Now it ought to be known that the holy apostles, in preaching the faith of Christ, delivered themselves with the utmost clearness on certain points that they believed to be necessary to everyone, even to those who seemed somewhat dull in the investigation of divine knowledge; leaving, however, the grounds of their statements to be examined into by those who should deserve the excellent gifts of the Spirit, and who, especially by means of the Holy Spirit himself, should obtain the gift of language, of wisdom, and of knowledge.... Then, finally, [they taught] that the Scriptures were written by the Spirit of God, and have a meaning, not such only as is apparent at first sight, but also another, which escapes the notice of most. For those [words] that are written are rather the forms of certain mysteries and the images of divine things. Concerning this there is one opinion prevailing throughout the whole church, that the whole law is indeed spiritual; but that the spiritual meaning that the law conveys is not known to all, but only to those on whom the grace of the Holy Spirit is given in the word of wisdom and knowledge.

***Origen of Alexandria,*** **De Principiis** ***4.7-10*** **(third century).** "For we have the treasure in earthen vessels," so that the excellence of the power of God may shine out, and not be thought to have originated from us mere humans (2 Cor 4:7). For if the old methods of rhetorical demonstration that we commonly use had been successful in convincing people reading the Bible, then our faith might well have been supposed to rest on the wisdom of humans, rather than on the power of God (1 Cor 1:20-25). But as it is it is clear to everyone who has eyes, that the Word and preaching have not prevailed among the masses because of persuasive words of wisdom, but by demonstration of the Spirit and of power (1 Cor 2:1-5). Since a celestial (even a supercelestial) power compels us to worship the only Creator, let us accordingly leave behind the doctrine of the beginning of Christ, that is, the elements of it, and make it our task instead to progress toward perfection, so that the wisdom spoken to the perfect may be spoken to us also. For he who possesses it promises to speak wisdom among the perfect, and it is a wisdom that is other than that of this world, and that of the princes of this world, which is has been brought to nothing. This wisdom will be distinctly stamped on us and produce a revelation of that mystery that was kept silent in the eternal ages, but that has now been manifested through the prophetic Scriptures and the appearance of our Lord and Savior Jesus Christ, to whom be glory for ever and ever: Amen. Having spoken thus briefly on the subject of the divine inspiration of the Holy Scriptures, it is necessary to proceed to consider the manner in which they are to be read and understood, because numerous errors abound as a result of many never having found the appropriate method for the scrutiny of the holy texts. And both those who have a hard heart, and the agnostics belonging to the circumcision, evidently have not believed on our Savior.... Now the cause, in all the points previously enumerated, of the false opinions, and of the wicked statements or ignorant assertions about God, appears to be nothing other than the inability to grasp the spiritual meaning of the Scripture, and only reiterating it according to its merely literal sense. But to those who believe that the sacred books are not the compositions of men but were rather composed by the inspiration of the Holy Spirit, conformably to the will of the Father of all through Jesus Christ, and that so have they come down to us, we must point out the correct methods of interpretation as they understand it who cling to the standards of the heavenly church of Jesus Christ in accordance with the succession of the apostles. For there are certain mystical economies made known by the Holy Scriptures, and surely even the most simple believers in the Word understand this? But as to what they are, most honest and humble believers will admit to being unsure: even perplexed about such things as Lot's incest with his daughters, or the two wives of Abraham, or the two sisters married to Jacob, and the slaves who bore him children.... And what need is there to speak of the prophecies, which we all know to be filled with enigmas and obscure sayings? And if we come to the Gospels, even here an exact understanding of them depends on having the mind of Christ, which requires the grace that was given to the one who said, "But we have the mind of Christ," that we might know the things freely given to us by God, which things also we speak, not in the words that human wisdom teaches, but rather that the Spirit teaches (1 Cor 2:16; Phil 2:5).

***Athanasius of Alexandria,*** **De Incarnatione 57.1-3** ***(fourth century).*** What are the requirements for the searching of the Scriptures, and for true knowledge of them? An honorable life is needed, and a pure soul, and that virtue that is of Christ. For the intellect must apply this to guide its path, and then it shall be able to attain to what it desires, and to comprehend it, insofar as it is possible for a human nature to learn of things concerning the Word of God. But, without a pure mind and the modeling of one's life after the saints, a person could not possibly comprehend the words of the saints. If we wanted to see the light of the sun, for example, we would certainly wipe our eyes to brighten them and would purify ourselves in some appropriate way related to what we desire. So, for example, the eye, by becoming light, would then be able to see the light of the sun. Or take the case of a person who wanted to see a certain city or country. Such a person would surely journey to the place in order to be able to see it. It is exactly the same for someone who desires to comprehend the mind of those who speak of God. Such a person must begin by washing and cleansing their own soul, and by addressing their manner of living. They should approach the saints by imitating their own works. By such consonance with the saints in the conduct of a shared life, a person may understand also what has been revealed to them by God. From that time onward, because they are so closely in communion with the saints, they too may escape the perils of sinners and the fires of the day of judgment, and they will receive what is laid up for the saints in the kingdom of heaven, those things that "no eye has seen and no ear heard, things that have never entered into the heart of humankind," the very things that have been prepared for those who live a virtuous life and love our God and Father, in Christ Jesus our Lord: through whom and with whom be to the Father himself, with the Son himself, in the Holy Spirit, honor and might and glory for ever and ever. Amen.

***Athanasius of Alexandria,*** **Contra Arianos 13.[53]** ***(fourth century).*** But [the Arians] argue that it is written in Proverbs, "The Lord created me the beginning of his ways, for his works" (Prov 8:22). And in the epistle to the Hebrews the apostle says: "Being made so much better than the angels, just as he has by inheritance obtained a more excellent name than them" (Heb 1:4). And soon after: "And so, holy brethren, partakers of the heavenly calling, consider the apostle and high priest of our profession, Christ Jesus, who was faithful to him who made him" (Heb 3:1). And in the Acts: "Therefore let all the house of Israel know most truly, that God hath made that same Jesus whom you have crucified, both

Lord and Christ" (Acts 2:36). They have offered such passages as these at every turn, mistaking their sense, with the thesis that they proved that the Word of God was a creature, a work, and one of the things that have been originated. This is how they deceive the thoughtless, by making the language of Scripture their pretense. And yet instead of the true sense, they have scattered over it the poison of their own heresy. For if they had only known, they would not have blasphemed against "the Lord of Glory" (Acts 2:36) and would not have twisted the good words of Scripture. But if they have set themselves on adopting the path of Caiaphas and have determined on Judaizing and acting as if ignorant of the text that "Truly God shall dwell upon the earth" (Zech 2:10; cf. 1 Kings 8:27; Baruch 3:37), then let them stop investigating the apostolic sayings. For this is not the custom of the Jews. But if they want to side with the godless Manichaeans and deny that "the Word was made flesh" (Jn 1:14) and deny his incarnate presence, then in that case they ought not to adduce the book of Proverbs, for this is inappropriate for Manichaeans. But if, out of a desire for personal advancement and the longing for money that accompanies this, or the desire to have a good standing in the world, they did not want to be seen to deny that text "the Word was made flesh," since it is written as such, then it follows that they should either interpret the words of Scripture correctly, about the embodied presence of the Savior, or, if they still deny their sense, let them deny also that the Lord became man at all. For it is most inappropriate to confess that "the Word became flesh" and yet be ashamed about what is then written of him and on that account set out to corrupt the sense.

**Gregory of Nazianzus (the Theologian), Oration 27.3 (First Theological Oration) (fourth century).** It is by no means appropriate for every person to discourse about God.[37] Indeed, it is not for everyone. The subject is not as cheap or vulgar as that! What is more, it is not proper to do so before any audience, at any time, or on every point; only on certain occasions, in the presence of select people, and within certain limits. It is not for everyone, because it is lawful only to those who have been duly tested and are past masters in meditation, who have been purified beforehand in both soul and body; or at least are in the process of being purified. It is never safe, we might safely say, for the impure to handle what is pure, no more than it is safe for weak eyes to be fixed on the Sun's rays. So what is the permissible occasion? It is when we are free from all external defilement or agitation, and when our guiding

---

[37] Literally "to theologize," which included biblical interpretation for Gregory, one of the most learned rhetoricians of the fourth century.

spirit is not confused with troubling or wandering images, which would be like persons who mix up good writing with bad, or sweetly perfumed ointments with stinking filth. One needs true peace to know God and, when we can find the appropriate time, to discern the high road of the divine matters in hand. So who are the people for whom such things are permissible? They to whom the subject is of real moment, and not those who make it a subject of pleasant domestic chatter, or gossip after the races or the theatre, after concerts, or dinner parties: not to mention still lower employments.

**Basil the Great, On the Hexameron 1.2 (fourth century).** "In the beginning God created the heaven and the earth" (Gen 1:1). I stop here, struck with admiration at this thought. What shall I myself say first about it? Where shall I begin my story? Shall I demonstrate the vacuity of the pagans? Shall I exalt the truth of our faith? The philosophers of Greece have made a great fuss over explaining "nature," but not one of their systems has remained firm and unassailed, each one being overturned by its successor. It is a waste of time to refute them; they are sufficient in themselves to destroy one another. Those who were too ignorant to rise to a knowledge of God could not allow that an intelligent cause presided at the birth of the universe. It was the primary error that involved them in lamentable consequences. Some had recourse to material principles and attributed the origin of the universe to the elements of the world. Others imagined that atoms, and indivisible bodies, molecules, and channels, combined in union so as to form the nature of the visible world. Atoms reuniting or separating produced births and deaths, and the most durable bodies only owe their consistency to the strength of their mutual adhesion. It was a veritable spider's web woven by these writers who give to heaven, to earth and sea, so weak an origin and so minimal a consistency! And this was all because they did not know how to say "In the beginning God created the heaven and the earth." Led astray by their inherent atheism, it appeared to them that nothing governed or ruled the universe, and instead all was random chance. But, to guard us against this error the writer on the creation, from the very first words, enlightens our understanding with the name of God: "In the beginning God created." What a glorious order! He first establishes a beginning, so that it might not be supposed that the world never had a beginning. Then be adds *created* to show that which was made was a very small part of the power of the Creator.

**John Chrysostom, Homily 9, On Colossians (*late fourth century*).** Listen carefully to me, I beg you.... Get for yourself books that will be medicinal for the soul.

... At least get a copy of the New Testament: the letters of the apostle [Paul], the Acts, and the Gospels, so as to be your constant teachers. If you fall into any sorrow, dive into them as if into a chest of medicines and take from them comfort for your trouble; whether that is loss, or death, or grieving the departure of relatives. And don't just dive into them: swim around in them. Keep them constantly in your mind. The cause of all evils is the failure to know the Scriptures well.

***Augustine of Hippo,*** **De Doctrina Christiana *1.35-36 [39-40]* (fifth century).** We ought to understand most clearly that the fulfillment and end of the law, and of all the Holy Scripture, is the love of an object that is to be enjoyed, and the love of an object that can enjoy that other in fellowship with ourselves. For there is no need of a command that each man should love himself. The whole temporal dispensation for our salvation, therefore, was framed by the providence of God that we might know this truth and be able to act on it; and we ought to use that dispensation, not with such love and delight, as if it were a good to rest in, but rather with some feeling of transience, such as we have toward the road, or carriages, or other such things that are merely means to an end. Perhaps some other comparison can be found that will more suitably express this idea: namely, that we are to love the things by which we are carried up only for the sake of that toward which we are carried up. And so, whoever thinks that he understands the Holy Scriptures, or any part of them, but puts such an interpretation on them as does not tend to build up this twofold love of God and our neighbor, clearly does not yet understand them as he should. If, on the other hand, a man draws a meaning from the Scriptures that can be used for the building up of love, even though he does not strike on the exact meaning which the author whom he reads had intended to express in that particular place, then even so his error is not a serious one, and he is wholly excused from the charge of deception.

***Augustine of Hippo,*** **De Doctrina Christiana *2.8.[12]* (fifth century).** Now, in regard to the canonical Scriptures, one must follow the judgment of the greater number of the catholic churches; and among these, of course, a high place must be given to such churches as have been thought worthy to be the seat of an apostle and to receive epistles. Accordingly, as to what are the canonical Scriptures a man will judge according to the following criteria: to prefer those books that are received by all the catholic churches to those that some do not receive. Among those, again, that are not received by all, he will prefer such books as have the sanction of the greater number and those churches of greater authority, to such as are held by the smaller number and those of less authority. If, however, a man shall find that some books are held by the greater number of churches, and others by the churches of greater authority (though this is not a very likely thing to happen), I think that in such a case the authority on the two sides is to be looked on as equal.

**Augustine of Hippo, De Doctrina Christiana 2.9.[14] (fifth century).** In all these [canonical] books, those who fear God and are of a meek and reverent disposition seek the will of God. And in pursuing this search the first rule to be observed is, as I have said, to know these books, if not yet with the understanding, still to read them so as to commit them to memory, or at least so as not to remain wholly ignorant of them. Next, those matters that are plainly laid down in them, whether concerning rules of life or rules of faith, are to be searched into more carefully and more diligently; and the more of these a reader discovers, the more capacious will his understanding become. For among those things that are plainly laid down in Scripture can be found all matters that concern faith and lifestyle, namely, hope and love, of which I have spoken previously. After this, when we have made ourselves to a certain extent familiar with the language of Scripture, we may proceed to open up and investigate the more obscure passages, and in doing so we should draw examples from the plainer expressions to throw light on the more obscure ones, and use the evidence of passages about which there is no doubt to remove all hesitation in regard to the doubtful passages. And in this matter memory counts for a great deal; but if the memory should be defective, no rules can supply the deficiency.

**FURTHER READING**

Blowers, P. M., ed. *The Bible in Greek Christian Antiquity.* Notre Dame, IN: University of Notre Dame Press, 1997.

Dawson, D. *Allegorical Readers and Cultural Revision in Ancient Alexandria.* Berkeley: University of California Press, 1992.

de Margerie, B. *Introduction à l'histoire d'Exégèse.* Vol. 1, *Les Pères grecs et orientaux.* Paris: Editions du Cerf, 1980.

Froehlich, K., ed. *Biblical Interpretation in the Early Church.* Sources of Early Christian Thought. Philadelphia: Fortress, 1984.

Hall, C. A. *Reading Scripture with the Church Fathers.* Downers Grove, IL: InterVarsity Press, 1998.

Hauser, A. J., and D. Watson, eds. *A History of Biblical Interpretation.* Vol. 1, *The Ancient Period.* Grand Rapids: Eerdmans, 2003.

Kugel, J., and R. Greer. *Early Biblical Interpretation.* Philadelphia: Fortress, 1986.

McGuckin, J. A. "Structural Design and Apologetic Intent in Origen's Commentary on John." In *Origeniana Sexta,* ed. G. Dorival and A. Le Boulluec, 441-57. Bibliotheca Ephemeridum Theologicarum Lovaniensium CXVIII. Leuven: Peeters, 1995.

———. *The Transfiguration of Christ in Scripture and Tradition.* Lewiston, NY: Mellen Press, 1987.

———, ed. *The Westminster Handbook to Origen.* Louisville: Westminster John Knox, 2004.

Simonetti, M. *The Interpretation of the Bible in the Early Church: An Introduction to Patristic Exegesis.* Edinburgh: T&T Clark, 1994.

Torjesen, K. J. *Hermeneutical Procedure and Theological Method in Origen's Exegesis.* New York: de Gruyter, 1986.

Trigg, J., ed. *Biblical Interpretation.* Message of the Fathers of the Church 9. Wilmington, DE: M. Glazier, 1988.

Young, F. *Virtuoso Theology: The Bible and Its Interpretation.* Cleveland: Pilgrim Press, 1993.

# THE CHURCH AND WAR

## CONFLICT AS BLESSING OR BANE?

How do we look on war? As a blight on human history? A scourge on civilization? Even as the greatest of all moral defects of the human race? Or do we load it with "honors," celebrate it with intellectual trophies, like many of the ancient societies whose storytelling cycles elevated fighting as the supreme arena for the manifestation of human courage and that greatest of ancient values: *andreia*, "manliness"? The Christian ethicists of the earliest age took the very word for virtue (*virtus*) as a loanword from the earlier Greek tradition that had used the warrior-athlete's effortless grace and strength as the chief "icon" for what human perfection was. Aristotle, we might remember, was the tutor to Alexander the Great. What would be the difference between such a "heroic age" ethic of war (one that still lives on into contemporary life in a variety of guises) and that of the core Christian tradition? Have not many Christians through the centuries, at different times and conditions, not looked on war as an example of righteous intervention? Have they not celebrated the "virtue of war" as a way of maintaining and sustaining civilizations?

Both attitudes to war, the appalled and the laudatory, have not only been regularly manifested across human history, but they have also been regularly reflected within Christian experience and canonized in its history. The study of the Christian approach to war has itself been a curiously conflicted one. The issue seems to have been problematic since earliest times, and is still a matter where opinions can run very differently and raise the temperature.[1] Today studies on the problem are extensive, and a synopsis of the primary sources has

---

[1] The key academic studies of the early church's peace tradition had to wait until the twentieth century. They appeared in two clusters, both of them the immediate aftermath of the great conflicts of 1914–1918 and 1939–1945, followed by a longer "tail" that was overshadowed by the Cold War's generic fears of nuclear holocaust and that produced a more thoroughgoing tenor of the "suspicion of war" in academic circles. Studies in the aftermath of the wars tended to elevate the macro view that Christianity was pacifistic before Constantine, and militaristic after him, which has been a cliché all too often reproduced since.

not long ago been collated in a useful ready-reference volume, with a good contextualizing discussion.[2]

One initial distinction that might help us navigate the area is to be ready to discern when writers, ancient or modern, are speaking about war as a global factor or a local, personal, one. In regard to the first, there is a profound sense in pre-Christian Greek and Roman culture, for example, or in Israelite culture as manifested in the Old Testament (and thus on to the Christians by both classical and biblical channels) that the "elect nation" has a "manifest destiny," and this is afforded a God-given mandate for it to be protected at all costs. In order to retain the preeminence necessary to the elect people, violence that would otherwise be seen as wicked is blessed. This global view is a subset of a theology of providence. The ancient Romans had it in abundance. Might was literally right for them, since their conquests demonstrated sufficiently, in their eyes, that the gods were on their side. Ancient Israel had it also, but their lack of military success (faced with the overwhelming superiority of their neighbors Egypt, Assyria, Babylon, Greece, and Rome) also made this theology of providence-on-our-side a severely stressed one after the reverses of exile they endured.

In regard to the second, the approach to war on personal and local terms: the stress is usually on the force of the violence suffered as an inevitable corollary of war, in terms of moral evil. If a village or town is burned to the ground and all the inhabitants robbed or raped or killed, the damage is not merely done to the victims. The

---

[2] The chief sources in English are R. H. Bainton, *Christian Attitudes Towards War and Peace: An Historical Survey and Critical Re-evaluation* (Nashville: Abingdon, 1960); C. J. Cadoux, *The Early Christian Attitude to War* (London: Headley Bros., 1919; repr., New York: Seabury, 1982); H. A. Deane, *The Political and Social Ideas of St. Augustine* (New York: Columbia University Press, 1963), chaps. 5-6; A. von Harnack, *Militia Christi: The Christian Religion and the Military in the First Three Centuries*, English trans. (Philadelphia: Fortress, 1985); J. Helgeland, "Christians and Military Service: AD 173–337," PhD diss., University of Chicago, 1973; A. M. Hornus, *It Is Not Lawful for Me to Fight: Early Christian Attitudes to War, Violence and the State*, English trans. (Scottdale, PA: Herald Press, 1980); H. T. McElwain, *Augustine's Doctrine of War in Relation to Earlier Ecclesiastical Writers* (Rome: Istitutum Marianum, 1972); J. A. McGuckin, "A Conflicted Heritage: The Byzantine Religious Establishment of a War Ethic," *Dumbarton Oaks Papers* (2011–2012): 65-66; T. S. Miller and J. Nesbitt, eds., *Peace and War in Byzantium: Essays in Honor of G. T. Dennis* (Washington, DC: Catholic University of America Press, 1995); E. Ryan, "The Rejection of Military Service by the Early Church," *Theological Studies* 13 (1952): 1-32; W. R. Stevenson, *Christian Love and Just War: Moral Paradox and Political Life in St. Augustine and His Modern Interpreters* (Macon, GA: Mercer University Press, 1987). A synopsis is in L. J. Swift, *The Early Fathers on War and Military Service*, Message of the Fathers of the Church 19 (Wilmington, DE: M. Glazier, 1983). Extensive evidence for early Christian views on military service and war is given by Cadoux, *Early Christian Attitude to War*, 51-57, 116-22, 183-90, 269-81, 402-42, 564-96. For another detailed consideration, see J. F. Ubina, *Cristianos y Militares: La iglesia antigua ante el ejército y la guerra* (Granada: Universidad de Granada, 2000); brief discussion in M. Whitby, "Emperors and Armies, 235–395," in S. Swain and M. Edwards, eds., *Approaching Late Antiquity: The Transformation from Early to Late Empire* (Oxford: Oxford University Press, 2004), 156-86, esp. 175-79.

perpetrators themselves have been diminished in their humanity. In classical religious terms, "sin has abounded." In the study of war as a personal reality, humanity itself suffers on every ground: physical, moral, and cultural. There is always an immense strain in postexilic Jewish, and Christian, attempts to combine the moral lamentation of war as an evil with the elevation of the "just" or "holy" war that is "in this instance" validated by God for the sake of his righteous nation.

## IS CHRISTIANITY A PEACEFUL RELIGION?

In reference to a moral compass point for a Christian ethic of war, one could, on good grounds, think of the pacific figure of Jesus, who advocated nonviolent resistance to evil (Mt 5:38-41; 6:14-15) at such great personal cost (and was a figure of such inspiration for Gandhi, Tolstoy, and other significant pacifist leaders of the modern age). Jesus himself defined Lordship by rejecting earthly dominion.[3] And yet that same Lord often envisaged the coming judgment of God in metaphorical terms of righteous war meant to eradicate the forces of evil.[4] If one thinks of the long Christian record over the ages, the church has many serene and courageous witnesses of antiviolence to offer and inspire. It equally is weighed down in its history with numerous examples of bloody intolerance, such as the Inquisition's burning of dissidents, and all too often it has sought the justification of religion for torture, imprisonment, and execution, extremely bizarrely in the name of the very Jesus who readily forgave his murderers (Lk 23:24). Is Christianity a peaceful religion? Or is it inherently militaristic? Or can it never make up its mind: inclined to be propeace in quiet times and all too ready to justify violence in the name of true religion when politics become hot? In the large sources of its written and unwritten tradition there are conflicting authorities on this most deadly and important topic.

In ancient civilizations, such as the heroic age of Greece, or pre-Christian Roman imperialism, for example (and in this they are typical of most ancient societies before them), war was religiously and politically legitimated by the protective deities of the various peoples. The winners of the wars in question were those whom the gods favored. War was thus a "judgment of the gods" (an attitude that many later Christian commentators continued from pagan sources). It was on such socio-theological bases that we see the accounts of the favors of the gods woven into the central fabric of the Homeric poems of the Trojan War, and on such a term that Rome defended and

---

[3]Jn 18:36: "My kingship is not of this world"; Mk 10:42-45: "The Son of Man came not to be served but to serve."
[4]E.g., Mt 24:30-31; 26:34. Mt 26:52-53 tells the disciples that Jesus *does* command heavenly legions, though his *politik* is not determined by earthly armies but by God's all-encompassing power and judgments.

indeed gloried in its militaristic imperialism. Ancient Near Eastern societies, when they went to war and conquered other peoples, asserted their right to existence over against these other nations.

One of the most defining moments of the end of ancient war was to take the defeated gods (the temple imagery and cultic materials from the holy shrines) and lay them at the feet, in the temple, of the conquering gods ("our gods," the winners, as opposed to "their gods," the losers). The shock to ancient Israel of the ark of the covenant being carried off to Babylon in 597 BC (2 Kings 24:13-14) is demonstrative of this ancient attitude that the gods cannot be separated from the military affairs of their client peoples, and so too are the Psalms. At the exile the Lord of Israel was popularly seen to have been carried off in captivity along with Judah's royal court when Jerusalem fell to Nebuchadnezzar; and it was this theological shock to the system that forced Israel to reconsider its rather mono-linear theology of providence, namely that God would always protect his nation from the depredations of its enemies.

Postexilic Hebrew theology is much more sophisticated in its reexpressions of theodicy. The preexilic triumphalism, however, remained in the canonical Old Testament texts and was read afresh by hundreds of later generations, including, eventually, the Christian and Islamic peoples. It is largely because this surviving textual voice spoke more loudly and to a wider audience than the actual bitterly learned experience of Israel that such positivistic and triumphal ideologies carried on into Christianity and Islam. The Qur'an lauds war as a medium of religious propagation and conversion, as well as an unquestionable good and holy deed in the cause of the spread and defense of Islam.[5] Historically, Islam has, as a result, never much fretted over the justifiability of war with the "outsider." It does not have within its range of foundational holy texts (doubtless because they all came about within so narrow a psychological and historical range and from such a highly militarized environment) oppositional traditions to suggest that violence represents stunted morality.

Christianity, however eschatological in framework it might be, is much more ambivalent than Judaism or Islam in adopting to itself the role of "Lord of history," even if some in its past have adopted wholeheartedly (and widely reapplied) the scriptural ideology of the war for Canaan. Most of the early Christian exegesis of the violent imagery of this and other verses about war in the Psalms and the kingly books, for example, was read in deliberately nongraphic ways as a symbol of spiritual combat—the need to conquer the forces of evil within the heart. Amalek, the king whom Joshua destroys in the war for Canaan, is read, for example, as a "type" for

---

[5] Qur'an 2:191-93, 216; 8:15; 61:9.

Satan.[6] So when God commands the Israelites to strike down Amalek and every one of his army (Ex 17:13-16), in one of the bloodiest of all jihadist passages in Scripture, what this "really meant" for Christian exegetes in the early period was a specific "withdrawal" of the biblical right to conquer (a morally imperfect shadow) and a shifting of the attention to a new morality (the call to a purer and more devoted life).

Christianity, generally speaking, was well aware in its more sober moments of the message of the later prophets (since Jesus referred to them significantly in addressing his own theology of his passion) that straightforward military triumphalism was not the core witness of the Scriptures; but his church often turned directly to the preexilic texts celebrating the God of war (the Lord *Sabaoth*) or to the books of Maccabees (which it read fervently in the time of the fourth-century persecutions as a prophecy of its destiny to struggle). Furthermore, it sometimes forgot its more generic and subtle conclusion that Israel (whether old Israel or new Israel) had to learn from progressive experience, developmental revelation, that the wisdom of the later prophets might exceed and be deeper than that of the earlier kingly texts, or that the shadow of the cross and the evangelical message of peace and reconciliation might actually have radically reformatted the war theology of the ancients.[7]

The latter position (that God's providence might at one time be triumph in conquest, and another time the cup of suffering and defeat) was a subtlety of theology that did not always commend itself to the soldier, however. And thus a modern (especially, perhaps, one who has never personally witnessed the powerful currents that swirl round within a society at war) tends to be left in wonder at the sight of one Christian army (take the English at Agincourt, for example) singing the *Te Deum*, using words from the Psalms to praise God for the great slaughter inflicted on the French by the use of the longbow. The forest of Agincourt was then cut down and shipped to reroof the basilica of the Lord's Nativity at Bethlehem as an act of pious homage. Clearly, here there was no pause in the theological process that carried on believing that God would take sides in a war, even if this might now be conducted against coreligionists.

---

[6]A type is a biblical cipher, something in the original text that "stands in" for a deeper message when read allegorically in Christian exegesis. Allegorical interpretation is extensive in the Christian appropriation of the Hebrew Scriptures: the conquest of the Promised Land is "really" signifying the entrance into heaven; the victory over the Egyptians and Canaanites is "really" signifying the victory over the forces of evil in our lives.

[7]Not necessarily new things being revealed, in the manner of the nineteenth- and twentieth-century theory of development of revelational facts, but more in the way of developing profundity in the reading of the relative priorities of biblical revelations: why the church renders many things in its inherited codes obsolete while honoring them as once having force (sabbath observance, Judaic food regulations) and why it retains other biblical prescripts: a matter of spiritual and moral acuity of discernment.

The records of the Christian church, therefore, show the coexistence, however uneasy that juxtaposition might be, of both pacifistic and militaristic strands. Both parties claim the high ground—that their approach is the "authentic" one and the other side has manipulated the evidence or betrayed the original simplicity by a partial radicalism. That view is especially recognizable in many modern studies of the "church and war" that frequently impose a form of argument that does violence to the actual history of the church: claiming, for example, in many popular books (those that take a rather cavalier approach to the actual evidences) that before Constantine the Great the church was pacifistic in attitude, and after him militaristic and imperialist. This approach is far too simplistic to command much serious attention: but it still clutters the literature on the theme, with many books having predecided the issue morally before ever examining it historically.

## STRUGGLING WITH CONFLICTING SOURCES ON RELIGIOUS VIOLENCE

It is doubtless because of its inheritance of the Old Testament as its scriptural book of prayer that so many warlike images passed on into early Christianity. They were regularly used metaphorically to describe the "battle" for gospel fidelity (though mainly transmuted into personal symbols of inner struggle). The constant presuppositions of the Old Testament that the land mattered and was an actual physical land that had to be fought over, or that God would rout the forces of evil violently and with justice to establish the apocalyptic kingdom (casting down the "empires," as in the book of Daniel), or that God ought to be prayed to extend his strong right hand and crush his foes, permeated into the church's consciousness.

Jesus himself has many sayings that seem to suggest he had a nonviolent attitude. He describes wars and revolts as parts of the inescapable order of the world but also as matters that cannot frustrate the divine plan for the cosmos (Mk 13:7-8). Earthly unrest and violence is not an expression of the irrefragable might of the powerful, but rather an incitement to the intervention of God in justice within history. In this Jesus follows the classical doctrine of the prophets, albeit with a definite eschatological sharpening. He is very skeptical as to the utility of political military might, and among his recorded sayings is one that appears to be a mockery of Alexander the Great (Mk 8:36) (the supreme "hero" of the Hellenistic world) as well as a cold view of the profession of soldiering, with his dictum that "whoever lives by the sword shall die by the sword" (Mt 26:52). And yet some of the parables fundamentally lean on the metaphor of a king who expresses his will by force of arms, and this as a symbol of how God will vindicate his justice over Israel (Mt 22:2, 7).

The political program of God's overthrowing earthly power (understood, of course, as Rome) to vindicate the righteous was, however, a vision that was best kept quiet in the actual context of the early Christians within the Roman Empire. Apart from the book of Revelation, which produces its call for violent vengeance from God in the light of a recent and savage persecution, most Christian writings of the earliest period are remarkably pacific and advocate communities conform to the political authorities peaceably. Such is the message of Paul, who encourages his Christians to be good citizens and taxpayers and to pray for the welfare of the rulers. Similarly in the Pastoral Epistles and the Letters of Clement, the churches and their members are urged to be models of good citizenship. Military images, which abound in Paul more than most New Testament writers (1 Thess 5:8; Rom 13:12; Eph 6:10-17; 2 Tim 2:3) are generally rendered into allegories of spiritual readiness (2 Cor 10:3-4). Clement of Rome, in his letter to the Corinthians, composed just after Domitian's persecution (c. 96–98), still expresses admiration for the military profession.[8]

The Roman military, a profession that was known for particular brutality and oppression in a world generally inured to it, retained (for many Christians) something of an aura about it, and not only because (one supposes) those enjoying the political stability brought by Roman force of arms did not want to bite the hand that fed it, but also perhaps partly because the stories of Jesus' admiration for the centurion's faith (Lk 7:1-10) or Peter's baptism of the centurion Cornelius (Acts 10), or the testimony of the captain of guards at the crucifixion (Mk 15:39). All were core stories of the faith embedded into the holy texts and meant to show how the message of faith could transform even the military.

Of course, if the gospel message ever became popular with the middle ranks of Roman soldiery, it could only be a matter of time before Christianity permeated into the very substructure of the empire. This it did, of course, by the late third century; and by the fourth century Christian soldiers were a third column that could not be disregarded. In regard to early church attitudes to war it is instructive to see the earliest levels of cautious noninvolvement give way in that era to a first position that is generally hostile to any potential Christian recruit continuing in the profession of soldiering, then turning to an attitude that is much more ready to accept a role in the shaping of the destiny of Rome.[9]

---

[8] 1 Clement 37.
[9] Hostility toward soldiering was not simply because the profession was a brutal one, it would seem, but also because the entire structure of the soldier's day was built around acts of devotions to the gods of Rome and the divine genius of the emperor, seen by the early bishops as inherently idolatrous. The sexual mores of the soldiers were also highly suspect, as barracks life encouraged the use of surrogates for many decades while on active service.

The third-century soldier-emperor Philip the Arab was quite possibly a Christian. A Christian bishop censured him and barred him from communion because of the blood he had spilled. This makes sense only if he were known to be a baptized believer. It also shows a clerical attitude still hostile to the very notion of the shedding of blood and insisting on the incompatibility of eucharistic worship and blood defilement (a liturgical context that continued to color the church's attitude to war for centuries).[10] But if Philip was a Christian who had already assumed imperial power through the medium of a military career, it cannot be doubted that there were many other Christians in the Roman army. Commentators have insisted that Christians in the army were always a minority until well into the Byzantine period. And that might be so, though the evidence is obscure and it is difficult to judge. But even if it is the case, one must not underestimate the presence of Christians in the military; and given the "local" nature of ancient army recruitment, a clustering together of Christians in garrisons from the same regions cannot be discounted.

### CONSTANTINE AND THE "CHRIST-LOVING ARMED FORCES"

It is surely the case, though again the precise data is hard to come by, that Constantine recognized that the Christians in the armies of both East and West were critically important to his hopes to rise to supreme power in the civil war of the fourth century. He composed prayers for the army that were bland and all-inclusive but nonetheless definitely leaning toward Christian public religious demands: acclaiming monotheism, morally interpreted, and rejecting all forms of sacrificial cult (to the annoyance of many of Constantine's soldiers). Christians were a real presence politically by the third century, and that means, by default, a presence militarily. Constantine's monotheistic leanings were something they could energetically get in line with, and Constantine himself increasingly comes in line with their thinking as his reign progresses.[11]

The final stage is nothing less than the deep penetration of all the empire's structures by Christianity after the age of Constantine. Although there is enduring evidence that the army remained the most secular area of the Christian civilization, even on into tenth-century Byzantium, it was governed by Christian leaders and subject to a new Christian consciousness that was, in many respects, very different from the old Roman ideologies. Even so, after the time of Theodosius, in the late

---

[10]In the fourth century the Christian Lactantius (*Divine Institutes* 6.20.10), though a counselor of Constantine, still thinks Christians must be barred from the office of magistrate because of the inevitability of having to spill blood in that office's judicial aspects.

[11]While always remaining his "own man" in terms of his sense of his own high-priestly (pontifical) status, which later Christian apologists constantly soften and manipulate in the cause of showing him to be "Christian" long before his baptism.

fourth century, patristic writers generally speak only about moderating the moral evils of war, no longer about abolishing it or fleeing from it as an absolute evil.

## MAJOR CHRISTIAN THEORISTS

***Pre-third-century writers.*** Although second-century writer Tatian was always deeply hostile to the military profession, it is really Tertullian who was the first patristic writer to engage the problem of war as an ethical notion.[12] At first he was open-minded about the profession of arms, but in his later work his view changed to the position that soldiering was inherently incompatible with belief in Christ.[13] Part of this can be explained from the constant requirements of a soldier to engage in pagan cultic acts, but the fundamental aspect of a life dedicated to sustaining power, whether morally so or not, cannot be excised from his thinking.[14] Clement of Alexandria was equally forthright: soldiering was nothing other than a machination of the devil, for war is fundamentally contrary to the Christian spirit.[15] And he is echoed by Cyprian of Carthage.[16] Both writers had the benefit of seeing how easily the machinery of the state could be turned against the church. But, writing privately to high-ranking soldier acquaintances, he speaks like any conservative and philosophically inclined Roman gentleman, praising generals for "maintaining the standards entrusted to them."[17]

***Origen.*** Third-century philosopher-theologian Origen was one of the first truly international minds the church had yet produced. He clearly thinks things through, often in the company of a circle of advanced students, whom he used like a sounding board in a seminar. He considers that it was God's plan that the church arose at the very time in human history that had brought about the possibility for international dissemination of ideas along a brilliant transport network. In other words, the rise of Rome as a global empire was used by God to evangelize the world. However evil might have been the empire's "roads of ascent," they were used by the providence of God for the expansion of Christianity to all the world. When he turned his mind to the question of the army, however (and he lived through at least two state-sponsored persecutions of the church), he thought that it was no place for Christians. He took

---

[12]Tatian, *Oration to the Greeks* 11.1; 19.2; 23.12. He caustically criticized Roman "pagan" colonialism throughout his work and saw its military conquests, in biblical terms, as an evil outreach. Tertullian (c. 160–225) was the son of a pagan centurion serving in North Africa and was educated in rhetoric, assuming the legal profession and converting to Christianity as an adult.
[13]*Apologeticus* 30.4.
[14]*On Idolatry* 19; *On the Crowns.*
[15]*Miscellanies (Stromateis)* 5.126.5; 4.8.61.
[16]*To Donatus* 6.
[17]*Epistle* 73.10.

what was to become the "clerical" Christian view, that those engaged in the life of holiness could not be engaged with the traffic of war. He was most sternly against the notion of the church advocating its transmission and spread by force of arms.[18]

To offset the church's distaste for military service (we note he never completely forbids Christians from being in the profession of soldier—simply suggests this is not a good lifestyle), he maintained to his critics that the church had the duty of praying for the emperor and his forces, which it would observe diligently.[19] In this he was trying to line up Christianity with the privileges afforded to Judaism as a *religio licita*, not simply calling for a cessation of state persecutions but also attempting to deflect the criticisms that a sharp critic such as Celsus had already thrown against the church a hundred years before him when he argued that the new religion's tendency to pacifism in its core Scriptures unarguably made Christianity a religion that sapped the vigor of the empire at best and made it a reed that could not be relied on in times of trouble.[20]

It was certainly Origen who put into his disciple Eusebius of Caesarea's mind, in the next century, the idea that the *Pax Romana* established by Constantine was the providential fulfillment of the promise that Rome's imperial infrastructure could rapidly internationalize the gospel. In his wider exegesis Eusebius shows himself consistently to be a follower of his teacher's lead, and the Old Testament paradigms of the "downfall of the wicked" are what are generally at play in both Origen and Eusebius when they highlight biblical examples of vindication or military collapse. Several scholars misinterpret Eusebius radically, however, when they read his laudation of Constantine as some kind of proleptic justification of the church as an asserter of rightful violence. His rather sycophantic *Panegyric on Constantine* should not be given such theoretical weight, just as a collection of wedding congratulatory speeches today would hardly be perused for a cutting-edge analysis of the times. In applying biblical tropes and looking for their fulfillments in his own day, Eusebius (certainly in the wider panoply if all his work is taken together, not simply his court laudations) is looking to the past, not to the future, and is intent only on celebrating what for most in his generation must have truly seemed miraculous—that their oppressors had fallen, and that they themselves were now free from the fear of torture and death.

---

[18] See N. McLynn, "Roman Empire," in *The Westminster Handbook to Origen of Alexandria*, ed. J. A. McGuckin (Louisville: Westminster John Knox, 2004), 185-87.
[19] *Against Celsus* 8.73.
[20] Celsus was a second-century pagan philosopher who closely studied copies of the Gospels that had been seized in the persecutions. In a treatise called *The True Word* he heavily criticized the church on doctrinal and ethical grounds.

Origen and Eusebius might have set a tone of later interpretation that could readily grow into a vision of the church as the inheritor of the biblical promises about the Davidic kingdom (that the boundaries of Christian power were concomitant with the kingdom of God on earth, and thus that all those who lay outside those boundaries were the enemies of God), but there were still innumerable dissidents even in the long-lasting Byzantine Christian *politeia* (especially the monks) who consistently refused to relax the apocalyptic dimension of their theology and who resisted the notion that the church and the imperial Byzantine borders were one and the same thing.[21]

**Lactantius.** Fourth century Latin apologist Lactantius is an unusual voice, however, because his objections to the military are not concerned, as are most of the others, with individual matters of right and wrong but with a more global view. He denounces war as evil because it is the machinery of murder attempting to masquerade as patriotism or a special category of "invasion."[22] He wryly notes that if an individual were to pillage and kill a neighbor, he would be denounced as heartless, but if a nation wades in blood as it subdues other lands and peoples (he is criticizing the great Roman heroes, especially Scipio Africanus) it is generally praised as a great "peacemaker."

Yet Lactantius, in his *Deaths of the Persecutors*, equally advocates and supports Constantine as God's chosen ruler. For him God has elevated this emperor above all others because he alone protected and nurtured the church. Even so, if truth were told, Constantine rose to power by a bloody ascent through civil war and familial murders. In an age of brutal warlords, he stands out as particularly violent in his deeds, while simultaneously being reverent in his claims to be an establisher of the peace. Bishop Eusebius of Caesarea, another of Constantine's panegyricists, and a younger contemporary of Lactantius, cannot deny that war is an unmitigated calamity, but he seamlessly slides over issues as he depicts Constantine as Roman *imperator*, now receiving blessing from a new god of war, no longer Mars but Christ, as he instructs his soldiers to write the new divine cipher of the cross on their shields.[23]

**The fourth-century Fathers.** The Constantinian age changed attitudes. Christians were now a dominant force within the army and the imperial court, a fact that alarmed the emperors Diocletian and Galerius considerably and led to the outbreak of the Great Persecution. They were such a force that even years of purges could not shift them, and after Constantine they would not be ready to relinquish power again. After the fourth century, however, they had to face a new context of ethical reflection.

---

[21]For a further elaboration of the argument see J. A. McGuckin, "The Legacy of the Thirteenth Apostle: Origins of the East Christian Conceptions of Church-State Relation," *St. Vladimir's Theological Quarterly* 47, nos. 3-4 (2003): 251-88.
[22]*Divine Institutes* 6.20.15-17.
[23]Eusebius, *Church History* 1.2; *Life of Constantine* 2.4; 4.56.

It was easy enough for theorists to argue a radical pacifist position before the church had responsibility for being the moral guidance of the state, but how could Christianity now claim to guide a new political order without a readiness to bless war? Would it not be the case, as Celsus had once mockingly claimed in the second century, that if there ever were a Christian emperor, he would have to be hopelessly pacifist and thus leave Rome to be ravaged by its enemies?[24]

The patristic writers of the fourth century show their awareness of the new problem only gradually and partially. Some, such as Eusebius of Caesarea, were perhaps content to allow the God of the armies to change, from pagan to Christian, and then continue with military politics much as before. But the change was nevertheless marked. A much more pacific philosophy had entered into the heart of Roman moral thinking in the Christian empire. It is instructive to see how later Byzantine ages always preferred negotiated settlement to force of arms, and it is one of the fundamental reasons historians, beginning with Ammianus Marcellinus in the fifth century and continued by Gibbon in the eighteenth, have denounced Christianity as the force that destabilized the empire, because of its condemnation of the idea of aggressive war and its advancement of the justification for military action being lodged solely in the concept of self-defense.

The latter idea is epitomized by Basil of Caesarea, who agonized over the whole idea of war as something that is inherently incompatible with the gospel of love. It was a concept that he already found in the earliest collection of episcopal canons, rules of early synods where we find the Eastern bishops trying to regulate the morals of their lay followers.[25] Basil, however, was bishop of a military town at an important crossroads on the road to an unstable Eastern frontier, and in his time his people were suffering from raids of local warlords. His solution to the problem was to urge his local Christian soldiers to form war parties and punish the perpetrators of the attacks. If these righteous warriors spilled blood, however, they would "perhaps" be debarred from Communion for several years. But, if they refused to fight, they would be equally guilty in the eyes of God, for they would be responsible for not protecting the innocent, and they would be debarred from Communion as being guilty. Clergy, who represented the church as a "pure type" of Christian, were under no circumstances ever allowed to take up arms or engage in violence or killing. If they spilled blood, they should not function any longer as ministers of the altar. Basil's canonical letters set the tone for this approach to war in most of late Eastern

---

[24]Origen, *Contra Celsum* 8.68-71.
[25]The Western bishops, however, such as those at the Council of Arles in 314, were ready to censure Christians who tried to escape the ranks of the military during peacetime. Canon 3 threatens Christian deserters with excommunication. *Apostolic Tradition* 16; *Canons of Hippolytus* 14.74.

Christianity: strictly avoiding any suggestion of a "just war" theory in favor of a view that regarded it as the least of evils that needed to be adopted to safeguard the good of protecting the innocent.

Some have called this position a "confusion of thought," but it is in fact a carefully balanced statement of the limitation of what is seen as a "necessary evil" when defensive (or punitive) military action is unavoidable. Basil's ideas once again arise from the ancient context of Christian ethical thought meant to protect the purity of the eucharistic altar, but here in his canonical edict (and this became widely prescriptive for later Eastern Christianity, which was thereby closed off from adopting the "just war" theory of the Western church) he has extended his thinking into the wider civic domain to argue that sometimes morality requires us to do a right thing that involves acts of violence (against the violent).

Though Basil has been accused of being inconsistent (ordering his young men to go to fight on the borders and then barring them from communion for several years if they spilled blood), what I have argued elsewhere is that he is really setting a limit on the legitimacy of war: the returning "Christian heroes" are honored (and when victorious the church has never needed to strike up the band, as so many seem ready to do so anyway); when they return to church they are welcomed (Basil commands that they are brought into the eucharistic experience in the nave, not relegated to the porch with the public sinners) but designated as in some real sense "defiled" by the shedding of blood.[26] Standing for up to three years in the condition of core members of the church, but members temporarily barred from full communion, a subtle message is preached by the church to fence the legitimacy of war. If this is fudge—it is better fudge than the adoption of Cicero's just war theory to exegete Jesus' doctrines. But the West, generally, had little time for such subtleties, whereas the Byzantines were often aware of the need for a certain "ambivalence" in difficult areas.

Some of the later Latin writers were more overtly "patriotic." Ambrose of Milan praised the very idea of military faithfulness and set it as an example of virtue to his congregation. The old Latin philosophy rears its head again here, for *virtus* was, of course, the pre-Christian Roman term for *virtue*: "manly strength." Ambrose actually lists the strength of a warrior among the chief virtues he can think of.[27] Gregory of Tours was even more explicitly warlike. He is, indeed, one of the first examples of a "bellicose bishop," a type that would make its appearance more extensively in the early Middle Ages.

---

[26]Cf. McGuckin, "Conflicted Heritage."
[27]Ambrose, *De Officiis* 1.129.

*Augustine.* The old criticisms of Celsus (that the church's diffident attitude to the profession of arms was rooted so deeply that Christianity could never defend the imperial glory of Rome) were once more raised against the Christians by pagan senators in the time of the sack of Rome in the early fifth century. This suspicion among the surviving pagan aristocracy of the West that the newly ascendant Christians would be hopeless in governing the empire they had subverted was so keenly felt by lay Christian politicians at Rome, who heard it regularly leveled against them in the senate house, that one of their leaders, Marcellinus, commissioned from Augustine his monumental treatise *On the City of God*.[28]

Here the saint wrestles with the whole notion, so deeply and at such length and grimness that an unsympathetic pagan reader might well conclude the future of Rome was indeed bleak in Christian hands, since all the delight in self-aggrandizement and self-assurance that had given rise to Roman civilization (including its militarism and conquests) is dismissed by Augustine as the spoiled fruit of sin and pride. There is no real substrate soil in the whole of this great, foundational work of social polity for what one could call a "theology of civilization," let alone a theologically considered theory of culture. Skirting, without reference, the great irony that Attila the warlord who had sacked the eternal city was himself a Christian, Augustine tried to give Marcellinus a large-scale answer to his difficult questions. He first decided to make up a large book blasting pagan critics for claiming their corrupt imperial history was anything to boast about in the first place. But after many chapters of this (several of which survive as the first part of his *City of God*) he passed on that apologetic demolition job to one of his disciples and set his mind to considering the real issue: what was Christianity's proper attitude to social culture?

In terms of military force (which is an integral part of that discussion), Augustine was the first Christian theorist to attempt a moral justification of the profession of arms. Not finding any predecessors he could rely on here, he took the basic ideas of a just behavior in time of war from Cicero and set out what would be the terms and conditions of a Christian "just war."[29] Amazing though it might be to think that the leading Latin Christian intelligence of his day imported a pre-Christian pagan theorist into his work to account for the church's ethics of war, nevertheless this is what happened. Cicero approaches war from a Stoic viewpoint and seeks a theory that

---

[28] The literary and intellectual exchange between Augustine, Evodius, Marcellinus, and Volusianus the pagan was a significant learning experience for Augustine. Volusianus was proconsul of Carthage and uncle of the Christian ascetic Melania the Younger. He was a significant though open-minded pagan critic of the Christian philosophy, and his objections led Augustine to formulate several responses to the critique that an eschatological religion dealt badly with *realpolitik*. See Augustine, *Letters* 132, 135-38. *The City of God* is the major work that deals with the problem.
[29] Augustine, *Epistle* 138.15; *Against Faustus* 22.69-76.

will limit its impact. His is a moral realism that seeks to apply restrictive rules of engagement. Augustine seems to prefer this to the eschatological demands of the gospel, conveyed in Jesus' enigmatic references to the morality of bloodshed. He himself was not too sure how to resolve the problem otherwise. He is personally convinced that war is a moral evil. He simply cannot see how else to reconcile the eschatological terms of the New Testament with the demand in his own day for a realist ethic for the Christians living in an enduring society.

In his sermon 302 *On the Feast of Lawrence*, he writes, "Brothers, I tell you explicitly, and so far as the Lord allows, freely: only bad men use violence, and do so against other bad men. The actions of the authorities are a different matter. A judge only unsheathes the sword usually when forced to it. When he strikes, he does so unwillingly."[30] He seems here, rather hopefully, to try to posit the view that personal violence is always evil, but sociopolitical violence will always tend to be in the cause of justice. A few minutes' thought would tell us that he must have known this was a ridiculous idea. His motivation for advancing it, of course, is an overriding theory that the public lapses of social order are always less than the social chaos that would result if individual morality were to lapse. He too has adopted a limited form of moral social realism when it comes to assessing the moral status of violence. One finds it interesting, nonetheless, that this great Latin theologian needs to look for solutions to the problem of war so far removed from Christian sources. Most writers of the Latin church followed Augustine after that point.

Another of the early warlike church leaders, Gregory the Great, urges Christian princes not to hesitate to make war when necessary for the defense or extension of the faith. He propagated Augustine's views, often ironing them flat to remove all ambivalence from them. Pope Gregory was determinative in setting the Latin church after the seventh century on a course of adopting war as a religiously permitted reality, under qualifying conditions. Overall, Augustine's influence over Western Christian moral thought has been monumental, continuing on into the present day. Reinhold Niebuhr in the twentieth century was still using a moderated form of Augustine's moral realism to negotiate ethics in a society worried about world wars and nuclear armament.

**Byzantine attitudes.** The Eastern, Greek-speaking world never gave Augustine much credence (rarely read him). It continued its largely liturgical and canonical approach to violence as a cultic problem of the shedding of blood, a more individually focused ethic, but always resisting the idea that war, as such, could ever be legitimated in the abstract. It refused in the course of this approach to bless the

---

[30]See also Augustine, *Letters* 189 and 220 to Boniface on military violence, and *Letter* 229 to Darius.

concept of a just war, though this came at the cost of never having a strongly coherent theory of the social morality of war. The Byzantine theologians laid stress on the justification for applying violence (which always remained a moral evil) only in terms of defensive wars. The borders of Byzantium were seen as coterminous with the people of God (the Christians), hedged around on all sides by enemies of the faith, not merely foes to the crown. Wars were therefore a defense of the kingdom of God as it existed on earth: a defense of Christian women, churches, monasteries, institutions; and therefore in accordance with a Christian's duty. Canonically those who refused to fight in a defensive war were to be sanctioned by the church, not merely by public opinion, since they had neglected a moral duty.

Even so, the Eastern church applied the canons of St. Basil to those who returned successfully from war: the victor was to be celebrated, but the evil of bloodshed was to be remembered by making those who had actually spilled blood refrain from the taking of the Eucharist at the altar for a number of "penitential" years. Clergy were never permitted to shed blood (an old liturgical approach that in many other contexts too had tried to make clerical standards of behavior "pure" and absolute, even if wider social Christian morality was more "compromised"). This elevated the clergy around the altar as the "pure standard" of pacifist morality, and it implicitly added that to sustain this purity one needed a protective army around them, to prevent the unacceptable evil of the burning down of churches.

Byzantine approaches to war, as a result of this deeply ingrained approach, tended to favor negotiation (including political bribery, treaty making, and the old technique of setting one's enemies against themselves). All their wars were not defensive, of course. The Byzantine armies were, for most of their existence, a locus of Eastern Christian thinking and praxis that held "jaundiced" views about monastic and pacific attitudes; though the chaplain's rituals of blessing, forgiveness, and commendation show that for them, like many others, the number of atheists in the foxholes often dwindled.[31] It is not a clear or wholly admirable record on the part of the Byzantines, and not by any means a witness to the evangelical spirit that turns away from violence, but it does show some real sense among a long-rooted Christian society that it is not logical on the basis of the Christian foundational texts to canonize war as justifiable or good: it is rather always a moral evil, which in some cases has to be entered into, but with a view to getting out as quickly as possible and a consequent seeking of purification. On this point, however, it stands in marked contrast to the records of the West.

When the two worlds came into one another's view after many centuries of separation at the shocking instance of the Fourth Crusade in 1204, the Eastern church was

---

[31] The iconoclastic crisis shows what hostility simmered between the army and the monks.

not merely appalled by the sight of Christian Crusader knights attacking its holy city and churches of Constantinople; more than one commentator expresses profound shock at the sight of Latin bishops and priests dressed in war gear and taking an active part in battle. It was this encounter with the very different mentality of the Latins about legitimating reasons for violence that served as the real cause for the deep alienation of the two churches, East and West, that has endured down to the present day.[32]

## A SHORT READER

***Clement, pope of Rome,* 1 Clement *1.37.1-4 (circa 96).*** Brethren, let us zealously serve as good soldiers under [Christ's] irreproachable command.[33] Let us remember the discipline, obedience, and submissiveness that our governmental troops demonstrate when they fulfill their orders. It is not everyone's place to lead a thousand men, or a hundred, or fifty, or some such number. No, each one carries out the emperor's orders according to his own rank. Those with greater responsibility cannot dispense with those who have less, and vice versa. All together they make up a whole, and that is where the benefit lies.

***Justin Martyr,* First Apology *39.2-3 (circa 150).*** When the Spirit of prophecy speaks and foretells the future he says this: "The law shall come out of Zion, and the words of the Lord from Jerusalem. And he will judge the Gentiles and reproach many, and they will beat their swords into ploughshares, and their spears into pruning hooks. And nation will not raise its sword against nation, and they will longer learn the arts of war." You can believe that this even this prophecy was fulfilled;[34] for twelve ignorant and unskilled men went out from Jerusalem to the wide world and with God's help proclaimed to every race of people that they had been sent by Christ to teach God's word to all. And we, who formerly killed one another, now not only refuse to make war on our enemies, but even go willingly to our deaths, confessing Christ, so as to avoid even lying to our interrogators or deceiving them.[35]

---

[32]The Crusaders attacking Constantinople were told that the punishment of the "schismatic Greeks" justified the violence taken against them.

[33]Writing to the Christian community at Corinth at a very early stage to chide them for overthrowing their leader (*episkopos*), this leader of the early Roman church mentions the (pre-Christian) Roman army incidentally, but in terms that make it clear he has some admiration for them. The issue of Christians serving in the ranks does not seem for him, as it will soon enough for Tertullian, to be a scandal. His point however, is to offer the Corinthian church the army as a model of good discipline and orderliness—where authority is obeyed, not cast over.

[34]His pupil Tatian claimed that all wars were inspired by demons (*Address to the Greeks* 19.2-4), dousing with cold water any attempt in this era to mount a "just war" theory.

[35]PG 6.388.

### *Celsus,* True Word, *cited in Origen,* Against Celsus *8.68 (circa 180).*

Pagan philosopher Celsus (*Celsus*), writing a scathing attack on the Christians titled *The True Word*, around AD 180, finds this pacifism and advocacy of nonviolence civically distasteful. Nonviolence, he argues, is both socially illogical and religiously contradictory, for it hands over the governance of the body politic to the worst class of human beings. His charges would be left unanswered for a whole generation until Origen finally took up the pen to argue with him posthumously:

If everyone followed your [Christian] example, there would be nothing to prevent [the emperor's] being left alone and deserted, while earthly affairs fell under the sway of the most lawless and uncivilized barbarians; and no one on earth would hear anything about your religion or the true wisdom.[36]

### *Origen,* Against Celsus *3.8; 7.26.*

Origen's answer to this charge is very generic but twofold: (1) if the pagan Romans and the barbarians accepted Christ's teaching, as they will eventually do, since more and more were coming over to Christ every day, then there would soon be no more war; and (2) that the service the Christian can supply to the empire in lieu of military action is that of spiritual warfare: praying for the emperor and vindication of the just cause.[37] His overall thinking about armies and war is that the Christian dispensation is fundamentally a witness to a peaceful and nonviolent lifestyle.[38]

If war and military actions were once permitted to the Jewish nation by God, they are no longer permitted under the covenant of peace, which supersedes the older, less perfect covenant; and thus Old Testament instances cannot be called on to offer direct evidence for Christian moral positions.[39]

### *The* Apology *of Tertullian 42.2-3.*

Tertullian, who is a great critic of the pagan army and finds it an incompatible lifestyle for a Christian because he sees no distinction between murder and wartime killing (*On the Resurrection* 16.7-8), nevertheless in other parts of his work, when he is not being specifically antimilitarist, shows that the earlier picture of a totally nonviolent early church is a rather idealized abstraction from reality. In this passage he remarks how Christians have expanded in the first century and now inhabit all walks of life, the military included:

So it is that we live in the world, sharing with you the forum, the market, the bathhouse, the shops and factories, market days and all other commercial

---

[36]SC 150, p. 330.
[37]Origen, *Against Celsus* 8.68, 73 (SC 150.332, 344).
[38]Origen, *Against Celsus* 5.33 (SC 147.98).
[39]SC 136.26; 150.72.

life. No less than you do, we sail the sea, serve in the armed forces, farm the land, and do all manner of buying and selling.[40]

**Tertullian, On Idolatry 17.2.3 (early third century).**

> One of Tertullian's major problems about Christians belonging to the army was the way in which pagan sacrificial cult was an unavoidable element of daily life. Even to collect his pay the soldier would be called on to offer incense to the genius of the emperor. Tertullian wonders whether a Christian solider can retain his cultic faithfulness in such circumstances, and for a long time the early bishops agreed with him, making the occupation of soldiering (along with that of prostitutes and magicians!) one of the professions that debarred a candidate from baptism. Here Tertullian recounts that parts of his congregation have argued that civic and military office ought not to be closed off to Christians. His reply is highly sardonic. He says "maybe," but he clearly means "no!":

An argument has arisen lately as to whether a servant of God can hold any position of honor or authority, given that he can manage to avoid any appearance of idolatry . . . after the manner of Joseph and Daniel. These functioned as governors of all Egypt or Babylonia, enjoying the honor, power, and privileges of office, but remained free from idolatry. Well, let us grant that a person could hold such a position in a purely honorary capacity—that is, if you can believe that it is possible then to avoid sacrificing, or authorizing sacrifices, paying for sacrificial victims, managing the maintenance of (pagan) temples, putting on the arena games at his own or public expense, or presiding over the staging of spectacles, issuing solemn edicts or statements, or even taking an oath.[41] Provided a man can do this and moreover avoid the functions of the office, that is, administering judicial decisions that affect the life or character of a person, . . . putting someone in chains or in prison, or setting him to torture, then I would say you could hold office in an honorary fashion.[42]

**Tertullian, On the Crown 19.1-3 (211).**

> In 211 Tertullian wrote again on the matter in a treatise titled *On the Crown* (the military chaplet worn by soldiers at time of [pagan] worship). In this treatise, as in the work *On Idolatry*, he marshals the two chief reasons he thinks the soldiering profession is a betrayal of baptism: first, that it involves a believer in bloodshed,

---

[40]CCL 1, p. 157.
[41]Each of the things Tertullian mentions was an integral part of public office in the second century, and all of them involved the protagonist in the pagan cults—legal aspects of the office demanded oaths by the gods of Rome.
[42]CCL 2.1118.

and second, that it catches the participant in pagan cult at every turn. To those of his own flock who seem to have disagreed with him and called on the symbols of the Old Testament warriors, he had this answer:

> Can a one of the faithful become a soldier? Or can a soldier be admitted to the faith, if they were a simple member of the lower ranks who was not required to offer sacrifice or decide on capital charges? I can't see how there can be any relation between the oath given to God and that made to man;[43] or between the flag of Christ and that of Satan; or between the camp of Christ and the camp of darkness. The soul cannot serve two masters: God and Caesar. I know Moses carried a rod and Aaron wore a military belt . . . and if one wants to be clever, that Jesus [Joshua] the Son of Nun led an army and the Jewish people went to war. But how can a Christian do this? How can a Christian serve in the army even during peacetime, without carrying that sword that Jesus Christ has abolished? . . . Even if the centurion became a believer, the Lord, by taking away Peter's sword (Jn 18:11; Mt 26:52), disarmed every soldier after that point. It is not lawful for us to wear any uniform that symbolizes so sinful an act.[44]

### *Hippolytus,* Apostolic Tradition *16 (third century).*

At roughly the same time, in the early third century in Rome, a surviving church "order" book called the *Apostolic Tradition*, attributed to the theologian Hippolytus, shows the same hostile attitude to military service. It speaks this way in relation to catechumens thinking of an army career:

> A soldier in the lower ranks is not allowed to kill anyone. If ordered to do so he shall refuse.[45] And he must not take the oath.[46] If he does not care to comply with this ruling, let him be dismissed [from communion]. If anyone exercises the power of the sword or is a civil magistrate who wears the purple, let him either give up that office or be dismissed. A catechumen or member of the faithful who desires to join the army ought to be dismissed, since they have shown contempt toward God.[47]

### *Clement of Alexandria,* To the Greeks *10.100.2.*

The contemporary writer Clement of Alexandria, however, while following much the same line in his general writings about Christ ushering in a new era of peace and

---

[43] The baptismal profession and the oath taken to enter the Roman military.
[44] CCL 2.1120.
[45] A capital charge of mutiny in itself.
[46] Meaning, of course, that he could not enter the ranks in the first place.
[47] SC 11.72.

the church's commitment to nonviolence, does not show the same anxiety about keeping soldiers out of the church. He does not appear to think a soldier is required to renounce his profession:

> It is in the very nature of a man to be on intimate terms with God. Just as we do not force the horse to the plough, or the bull to part of the chase, so we take care to appoint each animal to that kind of work that is most natural to it. In the same way we call out to humanity, truly a heavenly creature made for the vision of God, to come to a knowledge of God. I advise you to take charge of what most intimately and particularly belongs to us (as distinct from other living beings) and fit yourselves for holiness as the preparation for your eternal journey. If you are a farmer, I would say, till the earth: but recognize the God of farmers. If you love the life of the sea, sail on, but do not forget to call on the heavenly Pilot. If you were in the army when you were seized by the knowledge of God, obey that commander who gives just commands.[48]

### *Lactantius,* The Divine Institutes *6.20.15-17 (fourth century).*

Fourth-century Christian philosopher Lactantius, who taught rhetoric (and possibly Christian ethics) to the young prince Constantine at Nicomedia before his "conversion," is one of those who sustained the strong Christian aversion to all forms of bloodshed. For him all killing is ethically wrong, whether that done in war or judicially. His opinions did not command much following after him: but his strong and elegant rhetoric ensured him a regular reading among Latin theologians afterward (until he was superseded by Augustine).

> It is not right for a righteous man to serve in the army: justice itself ought to be his special form of service. Nor is it right for a just man to indict a person under a capital charge. It is no different if you kill a man with a sword or with a word, since it is killing itself that is prohibited. And so there must be no exception to command form God. Killing a human being, whom God willed to be sacrosanct, is always wrong.[49]

Lactantius has some of the most severe indictments of war that can be found in any of the early Christian fathers and is a particular sharp critic of Roman military imperialism, which uses the idea of righteous war as a mask for bloody venality.[50] Even so, however, in his extensive late work *On the Death of the Persecutors*, he draws a strong implicit parallel between the "wicked kings" of the Old Testament (who always came

---

[48]SC 2.168.
[49]CSEL 19.558.
[50]*Divine Institutes* 1.18.8 (CSEL 19.68).

to a bad end because of God's providence) and the righteous kings, whom God upheld in their battles. He applies this matrix onto Constantine, lauding the emperor who gave to the world the new era of peace by protecting the innocent Christians. He is somewhat silent, however, about Constantine's road to that effective protection—that is, by instigating a very bloody civil war and by executing all of his military rivals, not to mention members of his own family. Even in this case of a rare Christian thinker who truly was a pacifist, the logical link between the rhetoric and the actuality of war theory was not always maintained. His turn toward the possibility that there just "might be" a case for a just war if it is for a just cause can be noted in another late work.[51] The overwhelming sense, for him, that God had raised up Constantine like a new David seems to make his wars a special case.[52] Greek theologian bishop Eusebius of Caesarea, who also knew Constantine personally, established much the same idea for the Eastern church, describing Constantine's ascent to power as a divine providence, ushering in a strong government as a guarantor of social peace.[53]

**Acts of the Christian Martyrs, "Acts of Maximilian the Martyr" 1-2 (fourth century).**

Just before the Diocletianic persecution started, at roughly the same time Lactantius was writing, we see the old conflict about Christian service in the army, whether it was permissible or not, was still current. A dramatic record of the trial of a young man, Maximilian, in North Africa in 295, recounts how he was executed for his refusal to perform military service. The text shows what we also learn from the "purges" Diocletian soon ordered against Christians in the imperial palace: that many members of the church by the beginning of the fourth century held positions in the army and state bureaucracy:

Dion the Proconsul said: Join up and accept the military seal.

Maximilian said: I will not accept it. I already have taken the seal of my God, Christ.

Dion answered: I will soon send you to your Christ!

He answered: If only you would! That would be glory for me. . . .

Dion said: Join up and receive the seal, or you will die a miserable death.

Maximilian said: I will not die. My name is already in the presence of my Lord. I cannot serve in the army.

Dion said: Have a thought for your youth and join up. It is appropriate for a young man to do so.

Maximilian answered: I am committed to serving my Lord. I cannot serve

---

[51] *Epitome of the Institutes* 56.3-4 (CSEL 19.739).
[52] Something that can be observed in his laudation of Constantine, victor in the civil war and protector of the church, in *Divine Institutes* 1.1.13-16 (CSEL 19.4).
[53] Eusebius of Caesarea, *Demonstration of the Gospel* 3.7.140; *In Praise of Constantine* 16.3-7.

in an army of this world. As I have told you already, I am a Christian.

Dion the Proconsul said: The sacred bodyguard of our sovereign lords Diocletian and Maximian, Constantius and Maximus, has Christian soldiers who serve within it.

Maximilian answered: They know their own interests best. But I am a Christian and I cannot do what is wrong.[54]

> A similarly vivid account is given of the trial of the Veteran Christian soldier Julius, shortly after this, who fell foul of the decree of Diocletian for members of the army to offer sacrifice to the old gods of Rome (an attempt to purge the army of Christians). The imperial anxiety, as well as the dialogue, typical of the martyr accounts that often keep close legal records of events, suggests how many Christians there must have been in the army at this period.[55]

### *Basil of Caesarea, Canonical Epistle (fourth century).*

> St. Basil of Caesarea, writing in the later fourth century, in a pastoral ruling that had a long and lasting influence, represents something of the "compromise of economy" (a thing might not be very good but might be tolerated as a "lesser evil" in straitened circumstances) that the Greek church took in regard to violence and cultic purity. It was this (what many commentators have found to be slightly paradoxical) that allowed the Eastern church never to subscribe to any theory of a "just war" such as can be found among the Latins:

Our predecessors[56] did not consider killing in war as murder but, as I understand it, made allowances for those who fought on the side of moderation and piety. Nevertheless, it is a good thing to insist that those whose hands are unclean[57] should abstain only from communion[58] for a period of three years.

### *Augustine of Hippo,* **Epistle *189.9, 4* (fifth century).**

> Augustine is the thinker who, more than any other, affected the Latin Church's thinking on war. He did not address the subject directly in any specific treatise but was rather led to his positions piecemeal. He is, for example, the thinker who retrieved Cicero's theory of a just war and dusted it off for Christian application.[59] But his mindset was formed first of all by his views on anthropology. Humanity was so corrupted by sin that entropy marks

---

[54]H. Musurillo, *The Acts of the Christian Martyrs*, Oxford Early Christian Texts (Oxford: Oxford University Press, 1972), 244.
[55]See "Martyrdom of Julius the Veteran," in ibid., 260.
[56]Bishops in Cappadocia making moral rulings about who could or could not access the Eucharist.
[57]For having spilled blood even in the defense of the innocent.
[58]That is, they would be allowed all other liturgical privileges, such as standing in the church with the believers—not being considered as excommunicates.
[59]Augustine, *Against Faustus* 22.75; *City of God* 1.26; *Questions on the Heptateuch* 6.10.

society fundamentally: all goes astray, almost inevitably, because of human sin and unrestrained desire (concupiscence).[60] This being the case, there can be no true peace on earth. The "city of God" is always going to be contrasted starkly with the city of Babylon: any "theology of culture" is suspect. In this light the main thing to be concerned about is the restraint on evil tendencies that Christian social theory demands. Augustine approaches the idea that as wars will happen, as a natural outflow of human wickedness, so they need to be limited: the chief ethical aspect is to realistically limit the scope of human wickedness. God is seen by Augustine to will social order (and thus the hardships contained within that restraint) as a necessary means of reining in the otherwise irrepressible "lust for dominance" that is at the heart of all human wickedness. He sums up his theory of "economy" in a letter of advice he sent to the Roman Christian general Bonifatius in 418:

Peace should be your goal. War should be a thing of necessity, so that God might free you from necessity and keep you in peace. One does not pursue peace in order to wage war: one wages war to attain peace. Even while engaged in waging war, therefore, have a care to maintain a peaceful disposition; for then, when you defeat your enemies, you can bring them the benefits of peace.... And so let it be out of necessity, rather than your own desire, that you kill the enemy who fights against you.[61]

He comes full circle to Tertullian, now telling Bonifatius:

Do not believe that it is impossible for a person to serve God while on active duty in the army. The holy David, with whom God was most pleased, was a military man; and so too were many other of the righteous in his time. The same is true of the centurion who said to the Lord: "I am not worthy that you should come under my roof."... And John answered [those who came to him]: "Do not strike anyone or make false accusations. Be content with your pay." If he told them to be content with their pay, he was certainly not intimating to them that they could not be soldiers.[62]

## FURTHER READING

Bachrach, D. S. *Religion and the Conduct of War c. 300–1215*. Woodbridge, NY: Boydell Press, 2003.

Bainton, R. H. *Christian Attitudes Towards War and Peace. An Historical Survey and Critical Re-evaluation*. Nashville: Abingdon, 1960.

———. "The Early Church and War." *Harvard Theological Review* 39 (1946): 189-212.

---

[60] Humanity after the fall became a "mass of sin." Augustine, *To Simplicianus on Diverse Questions* 1.2.16.
[61] CSEL 57.135; see also *Epistle* 138.2.
[62] CSEL 57.133; see also *Epistle* 138.15.

Brundage, J. A. *Crusades, Holy War and Canon Law*. Aldershot, UK: Variorum, 1991.

Cadoux, C. J. *The Early Christian Attitude to War*. London: Headley Bros, 1919. Reprint, New York: Seabury, 1982.

Deane, H. A. Chapters 5-6 in *The Political and Social Ideas of St. Augustine*. New York: Columbia University Press, 1963.

Elster, W. L. "The New Law of Christ and Early Pacifism." In *Essays on War and Peace: The Bible and Early Church*, ed. W. M. Swartley, 108-29. Elkhart, IN: Elkhart Institute of Mennonite Studies, 1986.

Fontaine, J. "Christians and Military Service in the Early Church." *Concilium* 7 (1965): 107-19.

Friesen, J. "War and Peace in the Patristic Age." In *Essays on War and Peace: The Bible and Early Church*, ed. W. M. Swartley, 130-54. Elkhart, IN: Elkhart Institute of Mennonite Studies, 1986.

Harnack, A. von. *Militia Christi: The Christian Religion and the Military in the First Three Centuries*. English trans., Philadelphia: Fortress, 1985.

Helgeland, J. "Christians and Military Service: AD 173–337." PhD diss., University of Chicago, 1973. Summarized in Helgeland, J. "Christians and the Roman Army. AD 173–337." *Church History* 43 (June 1974): 149-61.

Helgeland, J., R. J. Daly, and J. P. Burns, eds. *Christians and the Military: The Early Christian Experience*. Philadelphia: Fortress, 1985.

Hornus, A. M. *It Is Not Lawful for Me to Fight: Early Christian Attitudes to War, Violence and the State*. English trans., Scottdale, PA: Herald Press, 1980.

Klassen, W. *Love of Enemies*. Philadelphia: Fortress, 1984.

Long, M. G., ed. *Christian Peace and Nonviolence: A Documentary History*. Maryknoll, NY: Orbis, 2011.

McElwain, H. T. *Augustine's Doctrine of War in Relation to Earlier Ecclesiastical Writers*. Rome: Istitutum Marianum, 1972.

McGuckin, J. A. "A Conflicted Heritage: The Byzantine Religious Establishment of a War Ethic." *Dumbarton Oaks Papers* (2011-2012): 65-66.

Miller, T. S., and J. Nesbitt, eds. *Peace and War in Byzantium: Essays in Honor of G. T. Dennis*. Washington, DC: Catholic University of America Press, 1995.

Reimer, A. James. *Christians and War: A Brief History of the Church's Teachings and Practices*. Minneapolis: Fortress, 2010.

Ryan, E. "The Rejection of Military Service by the Early Church." *Theological Studies* 13 (1952): 1-32.

Slack, C. K. *Historical Dictionary of the Crusades*. Lanham, MD: Scarecrow Press, 2003.

Stevenson, W. R. *Christian Love and Just War: Moral Paradox and Political Life in St. Augustine and His Modern Interpreters*. Macon, GA: Mercer University Press, 1987.

Swift, L. J. *The Early Fathers on War and Military Service*. Message of the Fathers of the Church. Wilmington, DE: M. Glazier, 1983.

Wengst, K. *Pax Romana and the Peace of Jesus Christ*. Philadelphia: Fortress, 1987.

# THE DEVELOPMENT OF CHRISTIAN HYMNOGRAPHY

When one considers the literary record of the early church, the first thing that comes to mind is the considerable amount of doctrinal controversy or philosophy or exegesis that, in translation, takes up the major share of the archival library shelves. The extent of this literature is a partly true reflection of the church's interests across the centuries. We say "partly," because these highly intellectualist and controversial writings might not necessarily reflect the church's deepest interests; and this on the principle that controversy generates a lot of paper (then as now), while more settled matters often passed with little comment. That they so passed, often unnoticed and unmentioned, is no indication that they were not extensive, popular, and even more important (than the controversial matters) in their own time. It is the same today: the more substantial matters of family life, for example, often pass unrecorded, taken for granted in their normalcy, as it were; while peak events (marriages, births, divorce, or death) clamor to get into text or photographic record. But in antiquity the literary record must not be taken for the whole story. It is only the record of the top 3 percent of the literary leaders. So, for example, we have numerous canons or regulations from clerical leaders about how to deal with problematic moral cases in early Christianity, and a massive volume of papers detailing the ins and outs of such doctrinal controversies as Arianism from the pens of Christian litterateurs.

But in relation to liturgy, prayer, and worship, where there was rarely a large enough controversy to generate the mountains of paper, we have a relative paucity of sources and are left with a large set of silences as to earliest origins. One thing we can surely conclude is that the Christian community was embryonically formed within the womb of worship: it is just that they did not explicitly talk "too much" about how they conducted themselves in it. What we know from the earliest levels of Christian worship is either incidental or controversial. Paul, or James, for example, tell us their solutions to problems of eucharistic behaviour in the ancient churches (1 Cor 11:18-34; Jas 2:1-7); and we have glimpses of quotations of hymn and creedal fragments, quite probably from the first generation (Phil 2:5-11; 1 Tim 3:16; Lk 1:46-55; 2:29-32; Rev 19:1-3).[1]

Now this is not to say that these liturgical matters did not generate enough literature of their own: but it tends to be in that great deposit of texts in the ancient languages that later European scholars did not much concern themselves with and thus did not put themselves to the bother of translating into modern language bases. Even so, Greek, Latin, and Syriac Christian hymns are a massive part of the surviving literary record of the ancient church. They have rarely attracted the level of scholarly attention that they deserve. One of the reasons for this is surely the manner in which the genre of hymn had been, by the early modern era, firmly established in the life of the various churches as one of the most popular levels of common devotion and liturgical "involvement"; and familiarity, in this case, perhaps bred contempt.

In Europe after the eighteenth century, there was a veritable explosion of interest in hymnody, one that was given further impetus by the Oxford high church movement under such scholars as J. Keble, J. H. Newman, and J. M. Neale (1818–1866), who did much to bring the lyrics of ancient Greek Christian hymns back to a higher level of popular awareness.[2] In more recent times translation works of noted Syriac scholars have shown to a wider and more interested Christian audience the great riches of the Syriac tradition in relation to hymnody and poetry. Up to the mid-nineteenth century, however, many scholars of Christian antiquity regarded the hymn, with some disdain, as a "leveling down" of high theology into popular ditties, and looked on the genre as a form of low-level catechesis. This was a mistaken attitude; how mistaken became clearer only after the late nineteenth century, when scholars W. Christ and M. Paranikas brought out what is still one of the most important collections of ancient Greek hymnography.[3] Cardinal Pitra issued a large collection titled *Hymnographie grecque* at Paris in 1867. In 1876, classical scholar and Anglican priest Allen Chatfield combined his theological and linguistic skills in the first serious publication of Greek hymns in English.

After 1890 the Anglican church's "Lincoln Judgement" officially allowed the practice of hymn singing in English church parish services.[4] This in turn prompted

---

[1]See further J. A. McGuckin, *At the Lighting of the Lamps: Hymns from the Ancient Church* (Oxford: SLG Press, 1995); J. T. Sanders, *The New Testament Christological Hymns* (Cambridge: Cambridge University Press, 1971); D. Liderbach, *Christ in the Early Christian Hymns* (New York: Paulist Press, 1998).
[2]In the *English Hymnal* of 1906, there were no less than sixty-three hymns from the early church translated by Neale, along with six of his own composition—including the famed "Good King Wenceslaus."
[3]W. Christ and M. Paranikas, *Anthologia Graeca Carminum Christianorum* (Leipzig: Teubner, 1871).
[4]Issued by E. W. Benson, then archbishop of Canterbury.

a large flurry of contemporary hymn writing in the nineteenth century by Anglicans, a practice that in turn stimulated Catholics and more radical reform circles to follow suit. Among the Catholics and Anglicans there was a lively interest in refurbishing the hymns of the ancient church for modern congregational usage. In reviewing these early efforts, Neale once commented that they hardly merited the epithet of "translation." Neale was great admirer of the Eastern churches, and his introduction of Greek patristic-era hymns into standard Anglican use was widely influential.[5]

In more recent times C. Trypanis brought out a very useful (and massively select) bilingual collection of all Greek poetry from Homer to Seferis in a popular Penguin edition.[6] In this edition the collection of Christian Greek hymns from the early church as well as from Byzantium received generous space; the book, however, soon went out of print. More recently, F. F. Church and T. J. Mulry composed an anthology of the ancient Christian hymns that also gives a good flavor of the corpus, having the added benefit of representing the mainstream church literature in Greek and Latin, as well as the New Testament hymns gathered together with the Gnostic and Syriac hymnal literature.[7] But there are still no scholarly editions, and no complete English versions, of the hymnography of some of the major Christian writers, such as John of Damascus (eighth century), Andrew of Crete, or Joseph the Hymnographer. Some of these neglected hymns, however, are masterpieces of early Christian literature and do not deserve the dust of neglect that has fallen on them. The giving of close attention to hymnographic elements (instead of purely apologetic and controversial literature) from Christian antiquity would revolutionize the way we approach the forms of Christian theology: restoring, as is right and proper, the overarching matrix of worship to all that the Christians did, and said and thought, in the early centuries.

## ORIGINS OF THE GREEK CHRISTIAN HYMNS

It used to be a standard axiom of the textbooks that Christian worship grew directly and immediately out of Jewish cultic practices; and so the earliest Christian hymns were biblically derived. But there is little hard evidence to support this. The earliest New Testament hymnal remains show dependence on both biblical and Hellenistic forms of religious poetry, and neither are left unchanged. Certainly Old Testament

---

[5] As was his *Introduction to the History of the Holy Eastern Church*, published in two volumes in 1850. His scholarly interests were reflected in his deep ecumenical concerns: in 1864 he founded the Eastern Church Association, aiming at the eventual reconciliation of Eastern Christianity and the Anglican Communion. It survives today as the Anglican and Eastern Churches Association.
[6] C. Trypanis, ed. and trans., *The Penguin Book of Greek Verse* (Harmondsworth, UK: Penguin, 1971).
[7] F. F. Church, and T. J. Mulry, trans., *The Macmillan Book of Earliest Christian Hymns* (New York: Macmillan, 1988).

symbolic "archetypes" of worship had an influence on post-fourth-century Christian reflection on liturgy, and then specific parallels were drawn between the temple cult and the Christian *ekklesia*, with post-Constantinian church building reflecting the threefold division of the Jerusalem temple and its plaza: with its areas for the priests alone, reserved sections for the laity, and an outer place for the wider public, including Gentiles. As mentioned earlier, later Christian churches reflected this in the narthex (outer porch for the use of noninitiated catechumens), the nave (for the baptized), and the altar (or sanctuary), where the clergy congregated. At the same time, however, it was remembered that Jesus himself had adopted a very ambivalent attitude toward the temple and to the sacrificial cult it primarily represented; and after AD 70 it was razed to the ground, its institutions and practices scattered to the winds.[8] Jewish synagogue practice did not bear any continuing relation to the cultic sacrificial rites in anything other than a "notional" way.

One can presume that Psalms and biblical readings and prayers remained important in both the early synagogue and the early Christian assemblies. Apart from the Psalms (the *hallel* psalms were sung at the Last Supper itself, according to Mk 14:26), there were many other hymnic forms within the Old Testament, some of which the Christians designated as "the odes" (Ex 15:1-18; Judg 5:3-5; Job 5:9-16; 12:13-25; Is 42:10-12; 52:9-10; Sirach 39:14-35; 42:15–43:33). Psalms was the very first material to be used by the Christian ascetics of the fourth century to build up a structure of long prayer services that spread through the night (vigils). The book of 150 psalms was divided into sections (*kathismata*, or "sittings") so that it could be entirely recited by ascetics in church over the course of one week.

From the later Pauline literature of the middle to end of the first century it is already clear that hymnody had an established place in Christian prayer (e.g., Eph 5:19-20). The writer of Colossians is already beginning to standardize the hymnal forms as psalms, hymns, and odes (Col 3:16). The author of Acts 16:25 represents Paul himself as a great "singer." Important fragments and quotations from this very earliest level of Christian hymnody can be found as surviving fragments in several places within the New Testament (Jn 1:1-18; Col 1:15-20; Rev 15:3-4; 19:1-3). Perhaps the most famous example of a New Testament hymn is that found in the authentic writings of Paul, and therefore no later than mid–first century, but which itself appears to be a preexisting Christian hymn the apostle is quoting back to the local church to demonstrate their core belief to them (Phil 2:5-11). If it predates Paul's own ministry, this must be very early indeed after the crucifixion of Jesus, and so one of

---

[8]See J. A. McGuckin, "Sacrifice and Atonement: An Investigation into the Attitude of Jesus of Nazareth Towards Cultic Sacrifice," in *Remembering for the Future* (Oxford: Pergamon Press, 1988), 1:648-61.

the most ancient liturgical ways of theologizing the suffering, death, and glorification of Jesus as a pattern of behavior for his disciples.

Many of the others among these earliest fragments are deeply christological in character, and some of them (e.g., 1 Tim 3:16) are clearly "creedal" in form, trying to "sum up" the basic structures of the faith in memorable imagery. In this way the church began a very long tradition, for what we today recognize as the great baptismal creeds of Christianity, which as time went on began to assume greater length and even greater status as core dogmatic texts, generally began life as catechumenal hymns of faith.[9] Several of St. Luke's New Testament hymns are rightly famous. They sit on the borderline between hymn (song) and poetic prose. They are clearly indebted to Old Testament archetypes but also consciously aware of the wider Hellenistic tradition, and rising out of both they become significant songs of praise in their own right. In this regard one can think of the Magnificat, the Benedictus, and the Nunc Dimittis (Lk 1:46-55, 68-79; 2:29-32). That one can so readily identify them by titles shows how extensively these sections have been used in Christian worship throughout history. It was not a far step to make from the poetic Aramaisms of Jesus to the rolling, rhythmic phrases of the Greek Testament. Even in translation, the Beatitudes cannot be mistaken for mere prose (Mt 5:2-10; Lk 6:20-26).

## RELIGIOUS HYMNS AMONG THE PRE-CHRISTIAN GREEKS

The use of hymns in Christian worship after the third century was also likely to have been influenced by common temple practice in the wider Hellenistic world. Hymn singing was, of course, the ancient bedrock of ancient Greek religion. Most of the early Christians in Asia Minor, if not having spent time as pagan temple worshipers themselves, lived close among the culture and had friends whose religious practices they knew very well. Nothing could be more false than to picture the early Christians as a sect cut off from society, even though their own moral and cultic practices were distinct. The earliest surviving collection of Greek hymnody to the Greek gods is the magnificent poetry from the seventh century BC known as *The Homeric Hymns*, which are dedicated to a number of the Olympian pantheon.[10] The classical poets Pindar and Bacchylides later established two major genres of Greek hymnography: paeans and prosodies. The first were acclamations to the gods sung on religious occasions, while *prosodia* were processional songs, meant for recitation during the sacrifices.

---

[9]The Nicene Creed is a prime example. See further J. N. D. Kelly, *Early Christian Creeds* (London: Continuum, 2006).

[10]Trans. A. Athanassakis (Baltimore: Johns Hopkins University Press, 2004).

The *Orphic Hymns*, which come from around the second century AD, are the largest extant collection of pre-Christian Greek hymnography.[11] They consist of eighty-seven temple songs from Asia Minor.[12] They are attributed to Orpheus, the famed theologian and musician, and were part of the mystery cult (Orphism) that bore his name. The long list of titles covers most of the Olympian gods and mythic spiritual forces (such as the winds, sleep, or death). This early establishment of forms for hymnal composition by highly skilled Greek litterateurs (the hymns are exercises in fine rhetorical style) had an important impact on Christian writers from the high intelligentsia, such as Clement of Alexandria, Gregory of Nazianzus, and Synesius of Cyrene, who each had been educated in Greek letters, including reference to the corpus of Greek religious hymnography.

As Christian rhetoricians most of them (especially Gregory of Nazianzus, who was the author of a massive amount of Christian poetry) wished to claim Greek letters for the service of the gospel: *logoi* in the service of the *Logos*, as Gregory wittily put it. This was not simply a matter of reapplying older forms of worship for a new application: in several cases among the Christian fathers it was a specific reference to the unsettled dispute between Aristotle and Plato in late antique intellectual life, as to the place religious poetry held in any serious attempt to speak about reality. Plato, for example, had dismissed the Greek religious poets as fundamentally dealing in lies and materialist falsifications. He wanted none of them to be included in his new republic.

Gregory the Theologian wished to reclaim for the church an earlier view prevalent among Greek pagan poets that the inspiration of *poesis* was a divine *afflatus*.[13] Religious poetry did not need to be thrown away as a wholly lying (mythic) matter; rather, it needed to be purified of its gross material reductions and used to express the spiritual insights of the gospel in a fittingly spiritually refined manner. He believed that in the élan of inspiration, the Holy Spirit of God worked in a very special and developed way within the purified soul (here he meant purified by baptism, monotheism, and an ascetically observant life of prayer).[14] It was a special wish of his to reclaim the Greek hymn back from the hands of the pagans: a counterstrategy,

---

[11] Trans. A. Athanassakis and B. Wolkow (Baltimore: Johns Hopkins University Press, 2013).

[12] See "The Orphic Hymns 1-40," *Theoi E-Texts Library*, www.theoi.com/Text/OrphicHymns1.html (accessed May 30, 2016).

[13] See further J. A. McGuckin, "Gregory of Nazianzus: The Rhetorician as Poet," in *Gregory of Nazianzus: Images and Reflections*, ed. T. Hagg and J. Bortnes (Copenhagen: Museum Tusculanum Press, 2005), 193-212. *Afflatus* is an inspired breath of the Spirit.

[14] In his *Theological Orations* 27, Gregory sets out an important principle for most Greek Christian theology that followed him: that refinement of mind was necessary for the perception of the truth and that this was produced by careful study as much as careful living. Gregory was the most quoted of all Christian writers in Byzantium. His poetry stimulated countless others to emulate it, and his theology of aesthetics was never to be challenged in Byzantium.

as it were, to the contemporary emperor Julian the Apostate, who had recently tried to ban Christian intelligentsia from teaching the Greek classics in any public forum on the grounds that those who did not believe in the gods ought not to be allowed to teach classical literature.[15] The efforts of these early Christian intellectuals in turn influenced later patristic and Byzantine-era hymnographers.

The "high literary" writing of the Christian hymn simplifies the pagan hymns in the sense that the long litanies of titles and divine invocations are reined in, perhaps remembering Jesus' instructions not to "go on" in prayer, like the pagans did.[16] So almost all Christian hymnography represents this "chastened" style of invocation of God. The Christian hymns are thus more a revision of pagan hymnography than a continuation of it, for they intended from the outset to be missionary strategies. Like the Salvation Army in Victorian England, the Christians "refused to let the devil have all the good tunes." But the style of Christian worship then prevalent, one that put a premium on whole congregational response, demanded a simplification of hymnal texts, along the lines of psalm verses and antiphonal refrains for communal singing. This set to a lower level of utility those forms of ancient Greek hymns that were a long declamation of the deeds of the god performed by a solo orator or cantor. The polytheistic context was also cut out, of course, but just as the pagan hymns often retold the *mythos* of the god in question, so too the Christian versions still focused on recounting the Christian story in ways that showed its application, or relevance, to the life of the worshiper.

The refrain was used in the Christian congregations to "draw the moral inference," or how the mercy of God called out for a response of graciousness on the part of the faithful. This response, one of thankfulness, led to the hymns being fundamentally "eucharistic" (thanksgiving) in character. Quite a lot of these high literary compositions of the Christians, those that were made up of many lines of skillful verse composed with an eye to the subtleties of meter and syntax, without intervening refrains, were most probably written more for private publication and less likely ever to have been intended for use in real-time congregational worship. The Greek poems of the later (Byzantine) Christian hymn-writers are simpler in form and language, and those of the Latin church too (beginning with its great Latin hymnographer Ambrose of Milan in the fourth century) are clearly written with a strong, short, and memorable line in mind, designed for congregational memorizing and common chanting. The early Christian fathers preferred whole

---

[15] Julian's *Edict on the Professors*, June 17, 362.
[16] Mt 6:7-8: "And in praying do not heap up empty phrases as the Gentiles do, for they think that they will be heard for their many words. Do not be like them, for your Father knows what you need before you ask him."

congregational chant to that led by solo cantors, which could have been more musically developed. Accordingly, their reflections on church music are surprisingly few and far between.[17]

There are several patristic treatises *De Musica*, including one from Augustine. But they are not so much about music in the sense we would understand as about mathematical ratios, part of the philosophical cabinet of ancient thought. The works of Augustine (*De Musica*) and Niceta of Remesiana (*De Utilitate Hymnorum*) had a particularly wide influence in the West and tied in hymn singing with the theory and practice of psalmody.

## PRE-NICENE CHRISTIAN HYMNODY

The Christian hymn appears very early in what looks to be a domestic context with the late second- or early third-century hymn *Phos Hilaron*.[18] The idea of the "cheerful light" that the householder lit to mark the onset of dusk (all ancient lighting being then tallow candles or oil lamps) is applied to Christ, who is also the cheering light of the world who drives off darkness. What simplicity of metaphor this is, yet memorable too as an act of worship bound tightly in to the simplest of nightly domestic rituals: for soon this hymn was spread across a wide territory of the Christians and became a custom to sing as the first lamps of evening were lit in the homes. It has survived to this day as one of the chief points of the ancient ritual of vespers (evening prayer) in the Eastern churches. Like several other short hymns from the third and fourth centuries, the *Phos Hilaron* is more akin to rhythmical rather than to metrical text, in other words, poetry; and in this it is clear enough that the hymns of the early Christians are predominantly popularist literature. This

---

[17]Generally they were filled with distaste at the instrumental music used in pagan temple worship (*pompa diaboli*) and wished to distance themselves from it. Music, to the ascetically minded Fathers, was a thinly veiled form of licentious behavior—and indeed flute girls and singers at *symposia* were often a synonym for courtesans. See, for example, Clement of Alexandria, *Paedagogus* 2.4: "Leave the panpipes to shepherds, and keep the flute for superstitious devotees in a rush to serve their idols. We completely forbid the use of these instruments at our temperate banquet." For Clement the *symphonia* of the common chant demonstrated spiritual communion and wholeness among the Christians, whereas pagan polyphony and individualist performance signified spiritual dissonance (*Protrepikos* 9). St. Gregory of Nazianzus (*Oration* 5.25) contrasts the pagan use of lights, flute playing, and hand clapping with the simpler spiritual joy and purity of those who participated in the service of the true God. Later Fathers recommended that the only instrument that should be used in church is that which God himself had created: namely, the human voice. Chrysostom laments the passing of common psalmic chant in the services (*Homily* 36 in *Homiliae in epistulam i ad Corinthios* [PG 61, 313]). See O. Casel, "Die *logike thusia* der antiken Mystik in christlich-liturgischer Umdeutung," *Jahrbuch für Liturgiewissenschaft* 4 (1924): 37-42.

[18]Greek text in Christ and Paranikas, *Anthologia Graeca Carminum Christianorum*, 40; trans. McGuckin in *At the Lighting of the Lamps*, 19. It is reproduced in full in the short reader at the end of this chapter.

freedom that they have from the formal canons of Greek and Latin poetic writings (which had long been an intellectual affair) gave them a robust vividness. Ambrose, who is careful to use properly quantified metrical lines, is thus a Latin poet who cleverly expresses his craft in writing Christian songs for the masses.

There are only a few very early fragments surviving of other hymns from this time that have adopted a definite Greek poetic (*anapaestic*) format—metrical "feet" composed of two short stresses and one long.[19] Truly formal poets among the Christians start to appear after the fourth century. Sedulius, Merobaudes, Prudentius, and Paulinus of Nola all composed works that have stood the test of time, and among the Greeks, the poetic writings of Gregory of Nazianzus, who was a litterateur of exceptional brilliance, wrote in every genre and meter known to classical Greek literature—just to show he can do it, partly. Many of his poetic works are very beautiful and for almost a thousand years they made up the literary curriculum of the schools of Byzantium (alongside Homer and the other classics), showing that Christians were no less civilized than their pagan forebears. But these high literary compositions did not tend to enter the daily liturgy of the Christians to the same extent that the shorter, simpler congregational hymns did. Of course, the same is true today: what works well in a liturgical assembly as a common hymn often will not stand much scrutiny outside the act of worship as a piece of literature.

In the early years of the second century, Pliny the Younger, a Roman aristocrat serving as a provincial governor in Bithynia, reported back to his emperor, Trajan, on the manner in which he was interrogating and punishing local Christians. A rare glimpse of the early forms of Christian liturgy escaped from two Christian slave women, whom Pliny tells us were called "deaconesses." Both these liturgical ministers had been subject to torture, as was then common practice in initial interrogations of the lower classes, and under duress they revealed that

> they were accustomed to meet on a fixed day before dawn and *sing an antiphonal hymn to Christ as if to a god*, and they bound themselves to a solemn oath, not to commit any wicked deeds, never to commit any fraud, theft, adultery, never to falsify their word, and not to deny a trust when they should be called on to deliver it up. When this was over, it was their custom to depart and to assemble again to partake of a meal, but one composed of ordinary and innocent food.[20]

So here again the christological hymn "sung with responses" stands out as an element of matins and the Eucharist. Next to nothing is known about Latin hymnody

---

[19] The Oxyrhyncus and Amherst papyri: *Oxyrhynchus Papyri* 15.1786; *Amherst Papyri* 1.2.
[20] Gaius Plinius Secundus, *Letter* 10.96-97, *To Trajan*.

of the first three centuries, although Tertullian (160–225) does refer to it as an aspect of church life.[21]

## HYMNS OF THE HETERODOX-ORTHODOX STRUGGLES

The hymns sung in Greek religious circles were influenced, toward the Christian era, by the chants of the mystery religions. It is possible that this was an influence on the "sophianic" (wisdom initiation) character of the hymns that appear in Christian Gnostic circles in the second to third centuries. Marcion was known as a hymn writer. Several of the Christian Gnostics, such as Valentinus at Rome, and Bardesanes and his son Harmonius (note the musical name) in Syria, were very interested in hymnic theology. Because of the larger church's disapproval of the Gnostics after the mid-third century, only a few fragments of these Gnostic-type hymns have actually survived.

One important collection is the Odes of Solomon, a Syriac set of pseudepigraphical compositions of the second century "pretending" to be biblical.[22] The Odes are probably the very first collated Christian hymn book. The exact date is uncertain, but the earliest manuscripts are third century, indicating an earlier origin. They had been known (and even then reckoned as obscure texts) since the time fourth-century African Latin theologian Lactantius quoted a fragment of one of the Odes, thinking it was a prophecy by Solomon of the coming of Christ. But they were not generally recognized (as they were, again, in fragments) among the Gnostic texts that were starting to reemerge in scholarly consciousness after the eighteenth century. They really became largely known only in 1909 and 1912, when Assyriologists James Rendel Harris and F. C. Burkitt separately issued manuscript discoveries with larger parts of the originals, eventually finding no less than forty-one hymns.[23]

The Odes are a Christian composition, though their romantic-fictional self-depiction as Solomonic (the great "prophet of love") actually led certain literally minded ancient Christian editors to include them in some manuscripts of the Septuagintal Old Testament. They are deeply modeled on the Psalms and biblical writings, but with a christological flavor of their own, and as an exemplar of an early theological dossier they are certainly among the very earliest records of Syrian

---

[21] *Adversus Marcionem* 3.22; *De spectaculis* 19, 39; *Ad uxorem* 2.8.8. The Latin church adopted a mid-third-century hymn to the Virgin, the *Sub tuum praesidium* ("Under your care we take refuge, Theotokos. Do not despise our prayers but save us in our distress from all dangers, only pure only blessed one"). It is found first in a Greek Alexandrian papyrus (see *Catalogue of the Greek and Latin Papyri in the John Rylands Library, III, Theological and Literacy Texts* [Manchester: Manchester University Press, 1938], 46-47), dating from perhaps the persecutions of Valerian or Decius. It is the earliest of all Marian prayers.

[22] They have an eye very closely on the Song of Songs, attributed to Solomon, and on several psalms.

[23] The second ode is still to be discovered, which would make up forty-two.

Christianity, possibly Palestinian. My reading of them suggests to me we have the work here of one of the cadre of early Christian "prophets," who are a feature of Christian congregational worship in the first two centuries (someone also immensely gifted literarily and theologically significant).[24]

When they were first unearthed there was much debate as to whether these were "Gnostic" pieces or orthodox. But the terms applied were often anachronistic, for the pre-Nicene Semitic traditions were highly sophianic in nature, radically ascetical, unlike much of the familiar forms that were dominant in other Greek-speaking Christian churches, and profoundly scriptural in tone. Scholarship today is increasingly of the opinion that they are not what the word *Gnostic* would connote, but from the mainstream of the very early Syrian church.[25]

Christ, who was with God before the incarnation (Odes 22, 41) is presented as a "crown" of each individual (Ode 1). He is the beloved (Ode 3), the brother, the Savior and Son (Ode 10) who lifts up the soul's understanding (Ode 17) to realize its restored union with God. Christ is the deliverer of souls from the shadows of Hades, and the joy of the saints in the delights of paradise (Ode 11).[26] There are signs in the corpus of poems that the prophet-author was concerned with giving consolation and encouragement to his church in time of political crisis, perhaps persecution (Odes 8, 9, 29).

Slightly later than the Odes of Solomon we find a similarly sophianic hymn addressed to Christ the Shepherd (Christ-Wisdom) by Clement, a second-century presbyter of Alexandria who was also a professor teaching Christian rhetoric to private students in the Egyptian capital.[27] This, presented in full below, is a hymn of initiates chanting to their heavenly pedagogue, as if in a mystery cult, using mystical and cryptic symbols of faith, hailing the divine *psychopompos*, and celebrating Christ's redemptive guidance.

Some of the wisdom elements and personal mysticism of the early hymns led some earlier interpreters to posit a theory that hymnody belonged to the heterodox groups at first (writers such as Bardesanes, Valentinus, Marcion, Arius were all held up), and the orthodox only adopted the genre after the Nicene crisis (stimulated to it by Arian use of chants to propagate their doctrine) had come to a head, just as in Syria Ephrem set himself the agenda of matching the female cantors of Harmonius's circle with his own pro-Nicene tradition of hymns for virginal choir.[28] But this argument was

---

[24] We can think of someone like Philip the evangelist (see Acts 21:8-11) or his school.
[25] J. Charlesworth, "The Odes of Solomon—Not Gnostic," *Catholic Biblical Quarterly* 31, no. 3 (1969): 357-69.
[26] Fourth-century Syrian poet Ephrem reuses much of this imagery in his own *Hymns of Paradise*.
[27] This is a slightly better term than the ill-fitting concept of "orthodox-Gnostic."
[28] Harmonius was the son of Bardesanes. He was renowned for creating choirs of women to sing his compositions, which became immensely popular in Syriac Christianity.

overelaborated. The hymn itself was used in most of the religious communities of the day: pagan, orthodox, or heterodox. If Arius had recourse to poetic forms in his *Thalia*, and Athanasius largely steered away from hymnic forms, not too much can be deduced from this, given that in the second generation of Arianism, in the late fourth century, Gregory of Nazianzus, one of the greatest of the Nicenes, was a prolific poet and hymn writer, whereas his leading neo-Arian opponents Aetius and Eunomius showed no interest in verse whatsoever. Ephrem's *Hymns of Virginity* likewise used a model of secular *erotikai* (love songs), just as Scripture and the Odes of Solomon did before him and the Byzantine poets (such as Symeon the New Theologian) would do much later.[29] Hilary of Poitiers (315–367) and Ambrose of Milan (c. 339–397), among the Latins, certainly used the form of theological song to combat Arianism, which was renowned for having good tunes and witty chants that synopsized its doctrines. Unfortunately, none of Hilary's authentic hymns seem to have survived.[30]

In the Eastern church, at the Synod of Laodicea called in late 363 or 364, after the ending of the Persian war and the reestablishment of a Christian emperor (Jovian), the Asia Minor bishops issued a large set of liturgical reform instructions. Among them were two laws relating to ecclesial singing. Canon 15: "No others shall sing in the church except the formally appointed cantors, who shall go up into the ambo and sing from a book." And canon 59: "No psalms that have been composed by private individuals and no non-canonical books may be read in the church, but only the canonized books of the Old and New Testaments." Although this seems to censure the practice of communal singing, which had been extending widely as a liturgical practice up to this time, I think its meaning ought rather to be exegeted in the larger sense of the decrees of this council, which seem to be bent on clearing out noncanonical literature from the assemblies. It would spell the end of using such things as the Odes of Solomon but especially (and this was perhaps the whole point) the end of anyone using Gnostic materials (apocryphal Gospels, Acts, and hymns), even if they seemed harmless enough in sentiment.

The post-Nicene hymns that survive are now more and more marked by their dogmatic, that is, theologically didactic, character. They were all led to conclude with a trinitarian doxology and mainly teach aspects of high trinitarian thought, or the royal glory of God, or the soteriological aspects of the incarnation, rather than the earlier tendencies of personal mystical union evoked in the second-century materials. This more intimate psychic aspect of hymnic writing passed on into the ascetical

---

[29] With his magnificent *Hymns of Divine Eros* from eleventh-century Constantinople.
[30] Although several are traditionally attributed to him, such as *Lucis largitor splendide, Deus Pater ingenite, Beata nobis gaudia, Iam meta noctis*, and *Ad coeli clara. De Viris illustribus* 100 notes that he was the author of a *liber hymnorum*.

literature of the Eastern church. To an extent, the Latin poets who are not writing metaphysical exercises in dogmatics tend to stick to a generic form of personal bucolic poetry: such as can be seen in Paulinus, Prudentius, and Sedulius Scotus.

## HYMNOGRAPHY AFTER THE ARIAN CRISIS

**Latin hymns.** The Latin hymn reaches its golden age in the post-Nicene era. The challenge to teach Nicene thought in a popular way stimulated much hymnal writing. Several of the literary leaders of Latin Christianity took up Lactantius's challenge in the early fourth century to demonstrate that the church was not wholly devoid of literary and intellectual culture.[31] When Jerome's pagan literary correspondents laughed at him for the "ignorant" quality of Christian discourse, he replied, "David is our Simonides, our Pindar and Alcaeus."[32] Jerome's labors to make the Bible version more elegant than the (rather crude) *Vetus Latina* that was common in the church before him resulted in the splendid Vulgate text, which had a very long lifespan after him. In the East notable theologians such as Apollinaris Elder and Junior, along with Gregory of Nazianzus, turned their hand to making very elegant metrical paraphrases of the Scriptures for use in schools: partly to teach the Bible, but to do so in a way that also gave advanced instruction in literacy using Christian materials instead of pagan myths.

In Latin, Juvencus's *Evangelia* similarly offered a Gospel harmony written in hexameter poetic form.[33] He was a high-ranking Spanish priest writing about the year 330. As the preface to this work, Juvencus wrote a programmatic for Christian poetry, which was very influential in the later church. He contrasts his literary philosophy with that of Vergil and Homer. The church, he argues, must turn away from the streams of pagan religious sentiment and bellicose morals, and present its own themes from the Scriptures. Where they called on the lying muses, Christians must invoke the inspiration of the Holy Spirit. The pagan poets had aspired for immortality through their verses, he says, but the Christian poet alone will actually attain immortality, by the virtuous submission of his work to Christ, who will welcome him at the day of judgment.[34]

Fourth-century Roman noblewoman Valeria Faltonia Bettitia Proba, whose family was of the ancient Anicii clan and held several offices of consuls and urban prefects, took a slightly different line. She composed a very skilful and renowned *cento*. This was a literary device of lifting lines from the earlier poets and reassembling them for other ends: a pastiche, as it were. Homer and Vergil were the traditional

---

[31] *Divine Institutes* 1.1.10; 6.21.9. His own style of theological Latin won him the epithet of the "Christian Cicero."
[32] *Epistle* 53, 8 (PL 22.547).
[33] Works of Gaius Vettius Aquilinus Juvencus in PL 19.53-346.
[34] Juvencus, *Praefatio* 15-24. For Juvencus's details see Jerome, *De Viris Illustribus* 84.

quarries for such efforts. Some time after her conversion to Christianity, around 362, she worked up a *cento* from Vergil's work, celebrating Christ's gifts to the world. It is known as the *De Laudibus Christi*.[35] Its literary skill annoyed Jerome, who called her "an old chatterbox who wants to teach Scripture before she has understood it" (he seemed to be jealous of her literary skill), but it grew to be one of the most heavily used scriptural teaching devices in the western Middle Ages, leading Boccaccio to list her on his roster of most famous women.[36] The publication of her *De Laudibus* in an edition of 1472 gives her claim to be the first ever woman to appear in print.

The first truly great, original poet of the Christian Latin world was Aurelius Prudentius Clemens (c. 348–410). He was a lawyer in the Western imperial administration and after achieving high rank (urban prefect, proximus, and count of the first order) retired to an active second career as litterateur sometime after the death of Theodosius in 395. A visit to Rome and the numerous martyr shrines there impressed him deeply with the sense of how the gospel had taken over the soul of the empire and was destined to build a "new civilization." Returning to his estates in Spain, he set about sketching out this programmatic in poetry. In a *Preface* of forty-five verses Prudentius set out his own poetic philosophy:

> Now at the end of my life, my sinful soul shall rid itself of folly. At least by its voice, since it is no longer able with its works, it will send up praise to God. Day and night without ceasing I shall sing to the Lord with hymns; I will combat heresies and explain the catholic faith. I will destroy the temples of the pagans and will put your idols to death, O Rome. I will dedicate my poems to the martyrs and exalt the apostles.[37]

Prudentius knew all the poets and major Latin authors intimately and was a master of meter. Constantine's baptism is described in his work as the "coming of age" of Rome itself. He published his main work, the long poem *Cathemerinon* (*Book of Daily Affairs*), in 405 at the age of fifty-seven. It stands as a classic Christian example of "conversion" narrative in which he tells of his turning to a life of retirement as a religious rite of cleansing of his soul in ascetical simplicity. Some of its twelve poems celebrate the life of Christ, while the first six are concerned with shaping the hours of the day in prayer. Theologically he defends the Nicene Christology and trinitarian faith against Arianism. His other main work is the *Peristephanon* (*Crown of Martyrs*), in which in fourteen hymns he praises the martyrs of Spain. His *Hamartigenia* is a poem of 966 hexameters dedicated to the problem of the origin of evil. It is a sustained attack on Marcionite dualism and a defense of the providence and dominion of the one God.

---

[35] PL 19.802-18.
[36] *Epistle* 53.7 to Paulinus of Nola.
[37] *Praefatio* vv. 34–35.

His *Psychomachia* is an epic and sustained allegory of the spiritual warfare that is necessary for the possession of the soul. It kept the energy of eschatological thought alive for the Western church: the struggle against primal evil that was shown in the martyr's fight is the same as the warfare that ever rages in the heart that strives to be true each day to God, for it is the same struggle to achieve the glorious kingdom on earth. Prudentius's *Apotheosis* is an elegant hexameter poem on the incarnation.

Several of his poems have been abstracted into the services of the Western Catholic church, but many of them were of such epic length and dense quality that they were not exactly suitable for congregational use unless heavily edited and abbreviated. His achievements, however, set the bar for all Latin Christian poetry to follow. His contemporary Paulinus of Nola is as elegant and elevated as he but does not match the theological range of Prudentius. Coelius Sedulius, a mid-fifth-century Italian priest, is also a notable poet in the style of Vergil. His long poem *Carmen Paschale* follows Juvencus's lead with greater skill and range.[38] His poem celebrating the life of Christ, *A Solis Ortus Cardine*, is typical of the Ambrosian style of vigorous meter that was used in common congregational chant, and excerpts from it have entered the Latin church's liturgy.[39] Merovingian bishop Venantius Fortunatus, writing at the end of the fifth century, is the last of the line of Latin Christian poets writing in the old style of classical meters. He was an important bridge to medieval Christian poetry.[40]

***Pre-sixth-century Syro-Byzantine hymns.*** In the Greek world, the learned bishops Gregory of Nazianzus (329–390) and Synesius of Cyrene (370–413) are two examples of a general sign of the times in the late fourth-century church: the increasing presence of highly educated rhetoricians and literary stylists in the episcopate. The lists could be expanded significantly, including men such as John Chrysostom (c. 347–407), whose fluid prose rhythms were outstanding and who was known to have encouraged hymn singing in the cathedrals where he served (Antioch and Constantinople); or Proclus of Constantinople, an equally gifted rhetor (d. 447), who wrote the first memorable Marian hymns describing her as the new Penelope, who "wove the flesh of Christ" on the loom of her humanity. The life and miracles of Christ and the figure of the Virgin Mary were twin poles around which much Greek hymn writing revolved.[41]

---

[38] PL 19.533-752.

[39] The first stanza is typical of the beat: *A solis ortus cardine / Adusque terre limitem / Christum canamus principem / Natum Maria virgine* ("From the rising of the sun, to the farthest bounds of earth, The Lord Christ is our song, born of the Virgin Mary"; PL 19.763-70).

[40] There are excellent recent studies of his life and work by M. Roberts, *The Humblest Sparrow: The Poetry of Venantius Fortunatus* (Ann Arbor: University of Michigan Press, 2009); and J. W. George, *Venantius Fortunatus: A Poet in Merovingian Gaul* (Oxford: Clarendon, 1992).

[41] See G. E. Woodward, *The Most Holy Mother of God in the Songs of the Eastern Church* (London: Faith Press, 1919).

Synesios's corpus of nine hymns is a fusion of Christian and neo-Platonist themes concerned with the ascent of the soul to divine perception and communion.[42] He allegorizes pagan themes in the new Christian direction. Christ appears in the guise of a divine hero, rising through the spheres, to show the way to immortality to his initiates. The harrowing of hell is told as an account of Christ as the new Hercules who sends Cerberus (Hades) cringing back into his lair. The result is a strikingly beautiful conceit, but better suited, perhaps, to a symposium in the bishop's apartments, with his pagan literati friends, rather than a typical Christian small-town liturgical synaxis.

Gregory of Nazianzus, on the other hand, not only had a greater following and entered the Greek liturgy at many points but also came to be the single most-read author in the later Byzantine culture. The extent of his manuscripts is only exceeded by copies of the Greek Bible. The Eastern church found in him a centrally important Nicene theologian (he is the articulator for the Eastern church of the classical doctrine of the Trinity as well as the conception of redeeming grace as the deification of the soul).[43] Gregory of Nazianzus and Synesius, the elite of Christian rhetoricians in the patristic era, had both attempted to write in quantitative Greek meter. They gained few later disciples in this respect. Most of the subsequent Greek hymnody stayed with accentual meter as its preferred form: an easier genre in which to compose. Much of Byzantine hymnography also preferred to adopt a popular style of language, rather than the self-conscious classicism of the earlier late antique rhetors who loved to use rare forms and archaisms.

The Syrian roots of the Byzantine tradition always remained as a shaping force in its hymnographic and liturgical traditions.[44] The styles and forms of Ephrem's Syriac poetry can be witnessed centuries later in midrashic liturgical composition, now in elegant Byzantine Greek, that retells the scriptural narratives in extended and dramatic form. The Byzantine liturgy, being the worship of the imperial capital, began to have a very large remit of influence. It was the liturgy that dominated Greek Christian poetic composition and gave occasion for most of further hymnic development. Liturgical songs, known as *troparia*, such as the "Only Begotten Son" (*Monogenes Huios*), traditionally ascribed to Justinian, or the "Cherubic Hymn" (*Cherubikon*), exemplify this.[45] But the Syrian style of retelling the narrative in an expanded form is seen most

---

[42]The poems of Synesius can be found in PG 66.1587-1616. The tenth in the collection is the well-known hymn "Lord Jesus, Think on Me and Purge Away My Sins." It is the work of tenth-century Byzantine monk George Hamartolos.
[43]See further J. A. McGuckin, *St. Gregory of Nazianzus: An Intellectual Biography* (Crestwood, NY: St. Vladimir's Seminary Press, 2001).
[44]Constantinople had been a satellite of the church of Antioch before it rose to prominence after the fourth century as an imperial capital.
[45]In the reader below.

clearly in one of the greatest of all Byzantine poets, sixth-century deacon of Constantinople's cathedral Romanos the Singer (or Melodist).

Romanos the Melodist (fl. 540) was one of the greatest composers of the *kontakion* style of hymn. He introduces his compositions with a theme-setting *proimion* and then binds together a long series of strophes in the same metre (called *oikoi*) with initial letters of the line that make up an acrostic when read vertically. The favored device of Romanos was "Of the Humble Romanos" (*tou tapeinou Romanou*). It was a clever habit that prefigured copyright laws: for the watermark of attribution was impossible to hide. It was also a good technique to assist in the correct memorization of the *kontakion*, for any forgotten lines would glaringly emerge in text when the acrostic no longer worked. There were traditions that Romanos himself was a Jewish convert. He most likely was a Syrian by birth. Eighty *kontakia* have come down under his name, though not all are genuine. Some of them are literary masterpieces. His *kontakia On the Birth of Christ, On the Lamentation of the Virgin for her Dead Son*, and *On the Resurrection* are in this inner circle.[46]

In the *Kontakion on the Nativity* Romanos sets the whole hymn around the worried musings of the Virgin Mary, who has just given birth and wishes to protect her baby from all the disruption that seems to be coming in from outside: magi, shepherds, and the like. She is the central character "pondering these things in her heart" (Lk 2:19) and so serving in the role of a guide (*psychopompos*) for the less initiated as to the essential meanings of these various mysteries. In his *Kontakion on the Resurrection*, the cross is set up on Golgotha, and its foot pierces the rocky ceiling of Hades. Hearing the noise of the intrusion, Satan and Death (personified) have an alarmed dialogue with each other. Death complains that he feels (mortally) sick, and Satan is bewildered as to why his age-old rights have been trampled in such a way that escapes his comprehension.

In the *Kontakion on the Death of Christ*, which is still part of the Great Friday passion services in Orthodoxy (just as the *Nativity Kontakion* forms a large part of Christmas services), the Virgin is depicted as a bleating ewe. The mother sheep runs around the field crying out inconsolably for her lost lamb. The image is more difficult for moderns to empathize with but was widely taken in antiquity as a moment filled with pathos, and one that must have been very familiar even to city dwellers in Paschal springtime, when the lambs were culled from the flock. The dramatic imagery of Christ speaking from the cross, which occurs in both Latin and Greek Good Friday services,

---

[46] For a fine English translation see E. Lash, trans., *St. Romanos The Melodist: Kontakia on the Life of Christ* (San Francisco: HarperCollins, 1995).

My people, what have I done to you,
how have I offended you?
I hung the stars upon the frame of heaven,
but you hung me upon a cross. . . .

derives from Romanos's hymns. Another of his significant devices is to juxtapose strong contrasts and christological paradoxes. The refrain in the nativity *kontakion* is typical of this: "A tiny child, who is God before the ages."

Romanos began a period of Greek hymnological flowering that lasted to the eleventh century. This is a considerable body of literature that for centuries has remained largely unknown outside the domain of the Orthodox Church, which still uses these hymns in the fabric of its offices of prayer (especially matins and vespers). Even today much remains untranslated or is available only in poor versions. Some of the great masters, such as Romanos, are now available in English, but for others, equally significant, such as Joseph the Hymnographer, Kosmas of Maiouma, or John Damascene, there is still no collected edition to allow popular access. One outstanding piece, using the person of the Virgin Mary to tell the tale of the gospel, is the *akathist* hymn.[47] It has (wrongly) been attributed to Romanos but probably dates to the time of Proclus of Constantinople in the fifth century, with an added seventh-century *proemium* by Patriarch Sergius (d. 638).

After the seventh century many liturgical changes were in process in the Eastern church. The shock of the loss of the Holy Land to the Persians, and then to the Muslim Arabs after 614, led to a renewed interest in hymn writing for liturgical use. *Canons*, a term now meaning new forms of liturgical poetry divided up into nine *odes*, came into vogue in the Greek offices of prayer (especially matins). Mar Saba monastery near Bethlehem (which remained a center of free Christian culture while Jerusalem was ceded to the caliph) initiated a set of reforms of liturgical practice that gave greater precedence to psalmody and hymn chanting, used as a device to teach the faithful basics of the faith. In the ranks of these later monastic Byzantine poets we should note Andrew of Jerusalem (or Andrew of Crete, c. 660–740); John of Damascus (c. 655–750); his kinsman, Cosmas of Maiouma (c. 675–751); and Joseph the Hymnographer (c. 810–886). Theodore the Studite (759–826) and Theophanes (800–850) are also noted hymn writers who have left a mark in the Greek service books.

Christian women were leading sponsors of the writing of hymns. The large collection of *Hymns of Virginity* by Ephrem was sponsored by the community of Syrian

---

[47] *Akathist* means "not sitting down"—in other words, it was a processional hymn. See V. Limberis, *Divine Heiress: The Virgin Mary and the Creation of Christian Constantinople* (London: Routledge, 1994); L. M. Peltomaa, *The Image of the Virgin Mary in the Akathist* (Leiden: Brill, 2001). The first stanza is rendered below.

virgins for whom he wrote, and who (presumably) sang these compositions in their prayer services. Christian women, however, did not have such ready access to the processes of manuscript copying throughout history, the chief force in the process of manuscript transmission; and so their compositional efforts were always more vulnerable than those of the male and clerical monastics. This is why it is predominantly the compositions of men that feature in the liturgy.

Nevertheless, there are some notable exceptions and survivals of female hymnographers. Chief among them is ninth-century Byzantine aristocrat lady (and monastic) Kassia (also known in the manuscripts as Eikasia and Kassiane).[48] Her works passed through the manuscript tradition with great vitality and were highly treasured. Of the forty-nine attributed hymns, probably half are genuine. The manuscript tradition in regard to poetry and hymns was not generally careful in recording authorships, and famous writers generally attracted the works of lesser-known artists. Twenty-three of Kassia's poems have entered the Eastern Orthodox liturgical tradition as festival hymns. In the twelfth century critic Theodore Prodromos noted that Kassia had originally authored the four-ode *Canon for Holy Saturday*, but that it had been reattributed to Cosmas of Maiouma on the grounds that it was thought to be unseemly to sing on such a holy day a song a woman had written! One of her most powerful compositions, a *sticheron* turning around the figure of the lamentation of the sinful woman in the Gospel (Lk 7:36-50), features in the matins of Wednesday of Holy Week.

Whereas Romanos (who deals with the same episode in his own poetry) makes much of this woman's "shame" as a prostitute, Kassia sees more deeply into the point of the Gospel symbolism and identifies rather with the deep and sacred passion of the woman's repentance and the love for Christ, which it exemplifies and which the Lord himself exalts as a model of discipleship. Another *canon* of Kassia's composition, 252 verses on the theme of the burial of the dead, is the only piece of hers that did not make its way into the service books in some form or other. In the fourteenth century, when Nicephorus Callistus Xanthopoulos drew up a list of Byzantine hymn writers, Kassia was entered as the only female poetess of note. Modern scholarship has since then drawn attention to several others, though most of them are now only known by name, such as Theodosia, Thecla, and Palaiologina.[49]

Already by the late ninth century the golden age of Byzantine hymn writing was passing away, with notable exceptions such as Symeon the New Theologian from eleventh-century Constantinople, whose *Hymns of Divine Eros* surely count among

---

[48] See A. Tripolitis, *Kassia: The Legend, the Woman, and Her Work* (New York: Garland Press, 1999); E. Catafygiotou Topping, *Sacred Songs: Studies in Byzantine Hymnography* (Minneapolis: Light and Life Publications, 1997).

[49] See E. Catafygiotou Topping, "Theodosia, Melodos and Monastria," *Diptycha* (1987): 384-405.

the world classics of mystical literature, yet are still more or less entirely unknown, deserving a far greater readership.[50] The Christian hymn has been too long overshadowed by its noisy neighbors, apologetics and philosophy. But when appreciated for what deep glories it has to offer—a fusion of religious sensibility and culture—it can still shine out like a bright star in the firmament of the house of theology. Unfortunately, it remains highly vulnerable to the skills of the interpreter: for its beauties depend greatly on the nuances of the original languages, and too many efforts to date to bring this material back to life in artistic English forms have been shipwrecked on the rocks of bad translation.

## A SHORT READER

*Pauline community, 1 Timothy 3:16, a song of Christ (first century).*

How truly great
Is the mystery of our religion:
He was revealed in the flesh,
Vindicated in the spirit,
Seen by the angels,
Proclaimed among the nations,
Believed on in the world,
Lifted up in glory.

The opening subject of the hymn (line 3, "He was . . .") is stated in the original scribal hand of the main New Testament manuscript witness (Codex Sinaiticus) as *hos*: namely, "He who . . ." Origen in the third century followed this reading, but a later scribe corrected Sinaiticus to read *theos* as the subject (God), which is followed by Gregory of Nyssa and the Byzantine lectionary. Probably in the course of the citing of this hymnal element within other texts the original grammatical subject of the hymnal unit has been damaged and is now impossible to recall, although it was obviously referring back to the incarnate Lord and not (as some have rendered it) looking back to the last neuter subject of the text, that is, the "mystery of faith." In short, this was probably one of the most ancient of all Christian Logos hymns, and many of its concerns mirror those of the Johannine prologue, which it predates.[51] Here in Timothy it has an undoubtedly "creedal" character that wishes to synopsize the main elements of the Christian faith. The "mystery of faith" hymn is thus one of the earliest of all creeds.

---

[50]See J. A. McGuckin, "A Neglected Masterpiece of the Christian Mystical Tradition: The Hymns of Divine Eros by the Byzantine Poet Symeon the New Theologian (949–1022)," *Spiritus* 5 (Summer 2005): 182-202.
[51]The Johannine prologue is itself a midrashic rewrite of Sirach 24.

The "truly great" of the first line is literally "confessedly" great. The philological nuance of *exomologesis* is certainly present in this protocreedal statement. *Omologesis* was the "confession" of faith required of baptismal candidates (still required in the ancient liturgical rites of the Catholic and Orthodox churches, where the Nicene "creed" is now generally used for the purpose). The first two stanzas, then, serve to introduce the "confession of faith" itself, which is presented as a *mysterion*, another liturgical word that was used in the early church as a synonym for "sacrament," with all the associations that term had for baptismal initiation.

Lines three and four, with their antitheses of "revealed ... vindicated," "in flesh ... in spirit," are reminiscent of the balanced juxtaposition of polarities that is found elsewhere in the surviving Pauline creedal fragments (see Phil 3:6-11). "Flesh" is the domain of the visible element of world history: what Jesus seemed to be (crushed and conquered, mortal and fallible), while "spirit" is the domain of what he truly was in the eyes of God: exalted Lord, triumphant conqueror.

Line five, "seen by the angels," evokes the core notion of Christ's *anastasis* (resurrectional) glory. In antiquity, the concept of triumph (*nike,* or "victory") was closely related to "epiphany." The triumph had to be publicly demonstrated, massively celebrated, and thus the witness to it (its confession) was integral. Epiphany is thereby also a godlike quality. The epiphany is part and parcel of the divine vindication. For Jesus to have been "seen by angels" is thus an essential part of his exaltation as angelic Lord. In this epiphany to the angels Jesus is demonstrated as far more than a mere mortal.

In the final line, "Lifted up in glory" or "Taken up in glory," evokes the Lukan scene of the ascension (*analepsis*) of Christ. The cluster of New Testament words relating to the "glorification" of the Lord is much more extensive than "resurrection" (which has subsequently tended to overshadow the others). It includes resurrection, ascension, exaltation, glorification, reception of the name, and experience of the Spirit. Here the key concepts in this hymnic unit are ascension and acclamation, when Christ has an epiphany before the angels. Part of the church's faith confession in this hymn is to echo what angels have already been brought to confess: the Lordship of Jesus in the heavenly, earthly, and cthonic domains (see the echo of this in Phil 2:10). The six lines of the confession are a *chiasmus* of two triplets: the revelation, vindication, and manifestation of Jesus in the heavenly dimension (the exaltation) precedes and is reflected in his earthly *kerygma*, belief, and acclamation within the church.

### Clement of Alexandria, Christ the Shepherd (c. 150–215).

Bridle for wild horses,
Wing of birds unerring,
Dead-set helm for ships,
Shepherd of royal lambs,
Gather your simple children

To praise in holiness,
To sing in guilelessness,
With innocent mouths,
Christ, the Guide of children.
King of saints,
All-Mastering Word
Of the Most High Father,
Lord of Wisdom,
Strong support in sorrows,
Rejoicing in eternity,
Jesus Saviour of the Mortal Race,
Shepherd, Ploughman,
Helm and Bridle,
Heavenly Wing
Over the all-holy flock,
Fisher of men
Who have been saved.[52]

Clement's christological Wisdom hymn takes its title from the reference to Christ as the pedagogue in line nine. The pedagogue in ancient times was commonly a slave in the house. Thus his composition "hides in plain sight" Christ's title as *servus* (Son and servant). Here Clement presents Christ to his rhetoric students as the apex of the world's quest for wisdom. The imagery throughout is redolent of the mystery cults, and the language of neophyte initiation (heavenly milk and other esoteric symbols of "Gnostic" wisdom). Using terms already familiar to mystery initiates, Christ is described as the *psychopompos* (mystical soul-guide) of the elite, and Christian (baptismal?) initiation is suggested as their ultimate goal in their educational progress.

The description of "royal lambs" in line four is the first of several "royal" titles ascribed to Christ in this poem. The context of political persecution of only "educated" Christians in Alexandria at this time makes this interesting. The phrase "rejoicing in eternity" in line fifteen evokes an epithet of the ancient Hellenistic gods: "those who were blissful in their immortality." Clement here presses pagan theology to Christian ends: one of his missionary strategies in composing hymns of this kind.

The following line, sixteen, where Jesus is called Savior, again brings out a common enough christological title for the Church, but one in the context of ancient Alexandria, which had a sharp resonance: for here in this city Ptolemaic dynasty had notoriously claimed the divine title *soter* (savior) for themselves, which the

---

[52]Text in Christ and Paranikas, *Anthologia Graeca Carminum Christianorum*, 37-38 (line 3 emended). Also see the critical edition of the *Paedagogus* in SC 70, 108.

Christians were ready to resist to the death. The ploughman in line seventeen is at first an unusual christological image, but then we might recall the extent of bucolic images of God's dominion over the afterlife, which are so frequent in early Christian art and relate to mystery themes. That "Heavenly Wing" in line nineteen is possibly reminiscent of Mt 23:37, a "half-hidden" New Testament reference that only a Christian initiate would "get," while it would pass over a pagan as a meaningless concept.

In the final two lines ("Fisher of men / Who have been saved") Clement begins with an allusion to Mk 1:18 (coming to know the Lord, beginning one's Christian vocation) as the path to salvation. But the term *salvation* here carries two senses: metaphysical redemption and also physical safety in time of persecution. The list of "strange" christological titles here (which would not be familiar to anyone overhearing this hymn) is part of Clement's strategy elsewhere (as when he advises his students what finger rings and other ciphers would be appropriate for Christians), which is to use common devices (ship, anchor, etc.) to "stand in for" the mystical centrality of Christ—but things that could not be used by hostile pagan authorities to entrap them.

**Odes of Solomon (extracts) (second-century Syria).**

*Ode 1.*

The Lord is on my head like a crown,
And I shall never be without Him.
This crown of truth has been woven for me
And it has caused your branches to blossom within me.
This is no withered crown that does not bloom
For you live upon my head, and have blossomed upon me.
Your fruits swell and are brought to fullness,
They are replete with your salvation.

*Ode 6.*

Like the wind gliding through a harp to make the chords sing
So the Spirit of the Lord speaks through my members
Just as I speak through his Love.
He purges all that is alien, so that all is of the Lord,
For so it was from the beginning, and so it shall be until the end,
So that nothing shall be opposed to Him, nothing hold out against Him.
The Lord has spread his knowledge abroad
How filled with zeal He was
That the works of his grace in us should be made manifest.
It was his praises that he gave us for his Name's sake.
And so our spirits praise His Holy Spirit. . . .

*Ode 19.*

I was offered a cup of milk, and I drank it in the sweetness of the Lord's mercy.
The cup is the Son.
The Father is the one who was milked.
The Holy Spirit is the Milkmaid.
For his breasts were full and it was not right his milk should be wasted.
So the Holy Spirit opened her bosom
And there mixed the milk of the two breasts of the Father
And gave the mixture to an unknowing generation.
But those who have received it
Are now in the perfection of the right hand.
The womb of the Virgin received it
And she conceived and gave birth.
So it was that she became a mother in great mercy
And painlessly, according to the purpose, did she labor and bear a son.
She needed no midwife since it was he who caused her to give life.
Like a mighty man did she bring forth gladly.
She gave birth according to the revelation
And in accordance with the Great Power did she receive.
With Redemption she loved.
With kindness she watched over.
with glory she cried out: Hallelujah.[53]

These short excerpts give a flavor of the whole. Highly artistic, mystical, and prophetic in character, they speak of the soul's bridal relation to Christ. The reference to the crown in Ode 1 to us suggests immediately a royal connotation, but to the ancient, of course, the primary resonance was the marriage rite, in which the couple was crowned with flowering orange blossom. The passion (the crown of withered thorns offered to Christ by his enemies) gives way to a living, blooming, life-filled crown of grace when the believer has soul union with the Spirit of the Lord. The gifts of the Spirit (including here prophecy and prayer) flow out in the heart of the believer like "living water," bringing all things to fruit.

In the excerpt from Ode 6 the image of the theologian-singer as the harp of the Spirit (also a reference to the book of Scriptures) is applied in ways the explicitly

---

[53] A larger collection of the Odes of Solomon in English can be found in Church and Mulry, *Macmillan Book of Earliest Christian Hymns*, 33-55; and the full complement in translation by James Charlesworth can be found on the web: "Odes of Solomon, Translation by James Charlesworth," http://users.misericordia.edu//davies/thomas/odes.htm (accessed March 2014).

mimic the book of Psalms. The *Hymn of Nativity* in Ode 19 gives the sense accurately enough of just how striking these poems are, yet also how "strange" their mystical-erotic symbolism would appear to the later Christian mainstream, which soon would neglect them.

### "The Hymn of the Pearl," in Acts of Thomas (by Bardesanes?), an abbreviated digest (third-century Syria).

> When I was a little child dwelling in the kingdom of my father's house
> I lived at ease amidst all the luxury and riches of my teachers.
> But then from the East my parents sent me forth,
> > they gave me a load easy to bear . . . of gold, and silver, chalcedony, and agate . . .
> But I had to strip off my glorious garment which their love had made for me,
> > my purple toga woven and measured to fit me exactly.
> They made an agreement, and inscribed it on my heart
> > so that it would not be forgotten:
> Go down into Egypt and bring back the single pearl,
> > which is in the middle of the sea, entwined by the hissing serpent.
> Then you can put back on the glorious garment, and your toga,
> > and will become with your brother, our deputy, the heir in our kingdom.
> So I left the East and came down with two guardians
> > since the road was so dangerous and hard. . . .
> Finally I came down into the middle of Egypt where my companions left me.
> I went straight to the serpent, waiting there until it fell asleep before I snatched the pearl.
> Thus I became single, and alone, to my fellow-lodgers a stranger.
> But the Egyptians recognized I was not one of them . . . and made me eat their food.
> So I forgot I was the son of kings, and I forgot the pearl. I fell asleep.
> When my parents perceived my oppression they were grieved for me.
> Hence a proclamation was made in our kingdom
> > and all the nobles of Parthia hurried to make a plan
> So that I might not be left, bereft, in Egypt.
> And so they wrote me a letter, and all signed.
> It read: "From your father the King of Kings,
> > and your mother Governor of the East,
> > and from your brother our deputy, to our son in Egypt:
> Peace. Awake and rise from your sleep.

> Remember you are a son of Kings. Think on your current enslavement.
> Remember the Pearl. Think of your glorious garment."
> I awoke and kissed the letter, and because of what was inscribed in my heart
> I remembered I was the son of Kings.
> Then my free soul longed for its natural state, and I remembered the Pearl.
> So I charmed the serpent by invoking my Father's name over it,
> > and that of the deputy (our Twin) and that of my mother the Queen of the East.
> I snatched the Pearl and turned back to my father's house.
> Stripping off their filthy garments I left them in their country.
> I turned back to the light of our native land. . . .
> My parents sent on the glorious garment which I had divested.
> I could not remember its fashion, since it was in childhood I had left it behind.
> But suddenly as I received it again, the garment seemed like a mirror of my self.
> I saw all of it in myself, and received all things within it :
> > two in distinction, but one as in form—
> My glorious garment, covered in precious stones.
> I clothed myself in it and ascended to the palace of peace and worship.
> With all the teachers I worshipped the brightness of the father who sent it,
> And I was received into the Kingdom where all the servants were rendering praise.
> I hastened with my offering, with the Pearl, so to appear before the King.
> This is the hymn of Judas Thomas, the Apostle
> > which he spoke in prison. It is ended.[54]

Some would classify this as a "Gnostic" piece, but it more accurately represents the Encratite (strictly ascetic) tradition of Syria, such as seen, for example, in the apocryphal Acts of Thomas. Here virginity (or at least celibacy) was required as a prerequisite of all those going forward for Christian baptism and eucharistic initiation. This tradition lasted widely in the Syrian Church until late into the third century. The hymn is preserved in a few manuscripts of the Acts of Thomas (who is known as the Lord-Twin, or Mar-Addai—Didymus of the Fourth Gospel tradition).[55] The *Hymn of the Pearl* has

---
[54] The full text of the hymn can be found in J. Ferreira, *The Hymn of the Pearl*, Early Christian Studies 3 (Sydney: St. Pauls Publications, 2002).
[55] The Acts of Thomas can be read complete in a free version online in volume 8 of the *ANF* series (www.newadvent.org/fathers/0823.htm), and the book has also been rendered by M. R. James, trans., *The Apocryphal New Testament* (Oxford: Clarendon, 1924).

been attributed by some scholars to Bardesanes, the early Syrian Christian Gnostic poet-theologian.

The hymn is designed to report the spiritual biography of Mar-Addai the apostle as a paradigm of salvation. It represents his coming to earth (trailing heavenly glory and then forgetting his true origins). It is his speech to his brothers and sisters in prison (the flesh). Thomas's fall from glory to earth is a parallel of sorts to the incarnation of the Logos, who delivers all souls from ignorance to enlightenment. In the hymn the Father presides over all grace, the mother stands for the Holy Spirit, the deputy or twin is Christ, to whom Thomas-Addai is bound in union and thus saved by liberating grace.

Some have seen the hymn as a purely Manichaean document, but though the Manichaeans took and preserved this as holy text (whereas the mainstream church increasingly sidelined it on account of its potential heterodoxies), it is now generally thought that it did not originate with the Manichaeans. The use of Thomas-twin motifs and the parables of the prodigal son and the pearl of great price are implicit throughout here, pointing to a Christian origin. As can be readily seen, the genre is one of rhythmical prose rather than poetic meter.

### "Wedding Song of the Maiden," *in Acts of Thomas 1.6-7 (third-century Syria).*

The Maiden is a daughter of the light.
The proud radiance of kings lives and abides in her.
She is luminous with beauty and gladness. [Ps 45:3, 10-18]

Her garments are like the flowers of spring
Giving off the odor of perfume.
In the crown of her head is the King established
Who nourishes all those who are founded on him
With the food of immortality.
Truth is established in her mind [Jn 17:17, 19]

And her feet are accompanied by gladness. [Is 52:7]

She opens her mouth, most fittingly. [Prov 10:31; 31:10, 26]
Thirty-two singers chant her praises.
Her tongue is like a curtained doorway
Swaying to allow entrance within.
Her neck is a flight of steps as fashioned by the First Maker. [Song 4:4; 7:4]

Her two hands manifest symbols,
Announcing the dance of the Beatific Ages,

And her fingers point out the gates of the City.
Her secret chamber is radiant with lights
And redolent of the sweet perfumes of Myrrh and Indian Leaf.
Within there are myrtle leaves and scented flowers scattered on the floor.
Garlands are entwined around the doorposts.
Seven groomsmen attend her, whom she herself has chosen,
And seven are her bridesmaids who dance before her.
Twelve handmaidens serve and obey her,
And they look to the Bridegroom,
For sight of him is their enlightenment,
And they shall be with her forever in that unending joy,
At that marriage feast where princes are gathered,
Who attend the banquet where the everlasting are found worthy.
And they shall put on royal raiment, clad in bright robes.
In their great joy and exultation they shall give glory
To the Father of All, whose noble light they have received.
By the vision of their Lord they are enlightened,
Whose immortal food, wholly pure, they have taken,
And who have drunk of that wine that gives no thirst or desire.
And thus they have given glory and praise
With the Living Spirit, the Father of Truth, and the Mother of Wisdom.

In the course of the Acts of Thomas story (the apostle is telling of the glories of the state of the chastely, celibate disciple of the Lord), this extraordinarily lovely hymn is sung by the apostle at a royal feast, and by it his spiritual nature is made known. The text is clearly a mimesis of an *epithalamium*, a wedding night song or an *erotikon*, such as were commonly sung at wedding feasts. Ironically, then, as is the case with lots of other Syrian Christian poetry (such as Ephrem's *Hymns of Virginity*), the case for celibacy is made by reference to the gorgeous and erotic images of divine marriage (union in the bridal chamber of Christ). This is a theme that is also found in eucharistic imagery, and throughout the hymn there is regular and recurring reference to the taking of the eucharistic "food of immortality." But like the biblical Song of Songs, whose text it often alludes to, it applies the motifs of the beautiful bride, the joy of the wedding attendants, and the delights of the wedding chamber to a symbolic end: it is a song of wisdom. Like Sophia, the beautiful bride is a symbol here of the soul that has been enlightened by Christ and has found in that enlightenment a radiant union with the Trinity. The final stanza describes the Trinity in the specific and unusual Syrian terms of Father of truth, the living Spirit, and the mother of Wisdom (the latter figure standing for Christ as divine Sophia: see Sirach 24; Jn 1:1-16).

**"Phos Hilaron" ("Jesus Christ the Cheerful Light") (*third century*).**

Jesus Christ, The Gladdening Light
Of the deathless Father's holy glory;
The heavenly, holy, blessed one.
As the sun reclines
We see the light of evening
And sing our hymn to God,
The Father, Son, and Holy Spirit.
Worthy are you, O Son of God,
Through each and every moment,
That joyful songs should hymn you.
You are the giver of our life,
And so the world gives glory.[56]

The short, beautifully simple, and elegant hymn is one of the earliest liturgical elements still surviving in daily worship of the Christian church. This is the version used to this day in the Greek liturgy of the hours (hymn of vespers—the bringing in of the light). Its author is anonymous (c. third century). By the mid-fourth century the custom to sing this hymn when the twilight came and the Christians first used to light the olive lamps inside their houses was already established. In Byzantine culture the fading of the light of the day began the new day (a Jewish custom also; it was marked by the ending of labor and a pleasant time of rest, eating, and sharing). So it was that, liturgically speaking, the new day began to be celebrated at sunset. The evening prayers (vespers) of the church carried the censer with smoking incense (a symbol of the grace of the Holy Spirit) and a candle (a symbol of the light of Christ entering the world) in procession into the church, and the priest blessed the people with the censer and candle while saying, "The light of Christ illumines all."

### *St. Gregory of Nazianzus,* **Hymn 1.1.34,** *A hymn of thanksgiving (eucharistic hymn) (fourth century).*

In Gregory's retirement this renowned theologian composed a massive dossier of Christian poetry, parts of it very fine indeed.[57] Most of his works emulated the classical meters of the great Greek poets before him. Sometimes he makes a specific rendering of Christian themes in the (then archaic) Homeric language. Many of Gregory's poems, therefore, and this one seems a case in point, probably were meant to be declaimed by a single cantor. In the present-day Orthodox Church, several of his

---

[56] For the Greek text and translation see McGuckin, *At the Lighting of the Lamps*, 18-19.
[57] Further historical context can be found in McGuckin, *St. Gregory of Nazianzus*; "The Vision of God in St. Gregory Nazianzen," *StPatr* 32 (1996): 145-52.

verses (edited down in scale) have survived to be elements of the Byzantine liturgy. This song is an extended prayer of repentance that envisages how the repentant prayer of a sinner can ascend to join the immortal chorus of the prayers of the angels. In a manner typical of the early church, the eucharistic rite is envisaged as joining together the angelic orders and human beings in a time moment that elides time and space and unites heaven and earth as one. Gregory uses this image to advance his generic theology that God calls humanity through Christ to transcend the limitations of its small nature (*physis*) eventually to find in Christ a transfiguration into glory, such as the angels presently have in heaven. In other writings he calls this the core and energy of redemption: deification by indwelling grace (*theiopoiesis kata charin*).[58]

All thanks to you, the King of All, and Maker of all things.
All thanks to you who by your Word,
   commanded spiritual and material forms
And summoned into being what was not there before,
   from nothingness to bring them forth.
Those perfect singers of your praise stand gathered round your throne,
The myriad of angelic ranks, untold myriads yet again,
That fiery chorus all unmarred, since time has first begun,
The first-born nation, with a choir of radiant stars,
Those spirits of your righteous saints, the souls of all the just,
All are gathered in as one, to stand around your throne,
To make their hymn with ceaseless joy and awe.
They chant a song both endless and sublime:
"All thanks to you Most Mighty King and Maker of all things."
A hymn indeed sublime, that issues from that heavenly choir.
And yet, I too shall make my prayer: Immortal Father,
Before you I shall bend the knee, to signify my heart; Immortal Father,
In your presence, I lay down my inmost mind prostrate.
I rest my brow upon the ground, to make my prayer to you.
And so I lie, a suppliant. My libation is my tears.
For how could I be worthy, to raise my eyes above?
Merciful Father, take pity on me.
Have mercy on your servant who thus implores your grace.

---

[58] See further J. M. McGuckin, "Deification in Greek Patristic Thought: The Cappadocian Fathers' Strategic Adaptation of a Tradition," in *Partakers of the Divine Nature: The History and Development of Deification in the Christian Tradition*, ed. M. Christensen and J. Wittung (Teaneck, NJ: Fairleigh Dickinson University Press, 2006), 95-114; "Gregory of Nazianzus," in *The Cambridge History of Philosophy in Late Antiquity*, ed. L. Gerson (Cambridge: Cambridge University Press, 2011), 1:482-97.

Stretch forth your hand, and cleanse my inmost thoughts,
And snatch me then from out the claws of death.
Of your Spirit never let me be bereft,
So pour your courage and your strength into this soul of mine,
That I may hymn you with my heart and voice.
I am your servant, but be a Father unto me,
And grant to me a blameless life, and grant a blameless end;
Grant me the hope to do the good, your mercy, and your grace,
That overlooks so many sins committed since my youth.
For you are my Good King indeed. To you all thanks are due.
All thanks are due to you. And unto every Age.[59]

**Ambrose of Milan, "Eternal Maker of All Things" (fourth century).**

Eternal Maker of all things
Who rules both night and day,
Setting timely limits on the times
To lighten our weary load,
The herald of the day now sounds
Ever-watchful through the deepest night,
Like a watchman's lantern for the traveler,
That marks off night from night.
This Lucifer, once roused,
Dissolves the skies from darkness.
At this, all the choir of error,
Leaves off its harmful ways.
At this the sailor gains new strength,
And the billows of the sea subside.
At this singing, that very rock
Of the Church, washed away his guilt.
So let us get up eagerly.
The cockerel rouses those abed,
And nags at all the somnolent,
Shouting down who would protest.
At the cockerel's cry, hope comes back,
Health invigorates the sick once more,
The robber sheathes his sword.

---

[59] PG 37.515-17. English trans. in McGuckin, *At the Lighting of the Lamps*, 28-31, 94.

The lapsed find faith returns.
O Jesus, look upon us who have fallen,
And by your gaze correct us.
If you look on, our faults shall fall away,
And guilt dissolve in tears.
You who are Light, shine in our senses
Scatter the phantoms of our mind.
Our voice shall greet you first this day,
Offering our vows to you.

Ambrose of Milan is called the "father of the Latin hymn." He was a powerful advocate for the application of hymns in the Latin churches, noting how this hymnic revival had already had great effect in the Greek-speaking churches of his day. Ambrose wrote in his *Commentary on Psalm* 1,

> The apostle commands women to be silent in church, but they may surely sing the psalms, for this is fitting for every age and for both sexes. In such chanting old men lay aside the rigor of age; despondent middle-aged men respond in the cheerfulness of their heart; younger men sing without the danger of lewdness; children sing without danger to their yet-impressionable age . . . tender maidens suffer no harm to the adornment of chastity, and young widows can let their rich voices sound forth with endangering their modesty. For it is a powerful bond of unity . . . when all sing in community, the Holy Spirit, as the artist, permits no dissonance.

In the above, one his most famous hymns and one of the four definitely genuine ones that Augustine enumerates as poems of Ambrose, the author jumbles together a lot of images about daybreak and associates them with the cheerful Lucifer (light-bringing angel), which is Christ in his resurrection. The cockerel (here called the herald of the day) was an ancient (hidden-in-plain-sight) cipher for the risen Christ. At daybreak the church would sing the hymns of matins (morning prayer) and focus on the rising sun as a chief symbol of the *anastasis* glory. This is the end moral of the hymn—and probably indicates that this was how it was used as an opening hymn for matins in the Milanese cathedral.

Ambrose spent by custom a large part of the night in writing and prayer. He often returns to this theme of daybreak in his poems. Christ the light of the world scatters darkness (the choir of error, or the demons prowling, and all manner of earthly villainy) and gives hope to human hearts—such as the sailors who after a stormy night are cheered when they see the dawn and find new hope of being saved at sea; or in the final stanzas like Peter, who wept when he heard the cock crow in the passion of Christ, and in his weeping found absolution from his sins.

***Ambrose of Milan, "Splendor of the Father's Glory" (fourth century).***

Splendor of the Father's glory
Light coming forth from light,
Day illumining the day
With firstfruits of new light.
True Sun come down
Glinting with eternal gleams,
And pour into our inner sense
The radiance of the Holy Spirit.
And let us call in prayer on the Father,
Father of eternal glory,
Father of commanding grace,
That he may forgive our guilt.
May he bring us to committed action,
And bridle the teeth of those who envy.
May he help us through all bitter times,
Giving us grace to endure.
May he guide and rule our mind.
May our faith spring into flame,
As we keep ourselves faithful and chaste,
Innocent of the poison of deceit.
May Christ himself be our food,
And may our drink be faith itself,
That, ever joyful, we can drink
That sober drunkenness of the Spirit.
Joyful may this day pass by.
Let shame be only a glimmering dawn,
Though faith like noonday sun,
Our mind not recognizing dusk.
For dawn sets forth its chariot:
Now dawn complete appears.
Just so is the Son entirely in the Father,
And the Father entirely in the Son.

This poem is attributed to Ambrose by scholars in the second division of those that are "probably genuine." (He was so famous as a hymn writer that a lot of Latin songs were "fathered back" on to him.) The second line, "Light coming forth from light," is an allusion to the Nicene Creed (Light from Light), which the whole hymn sets out to paraphrase: a typical modality of the post-Nicene Orthodox hymn writers. It thus describes the Son's relation to the Father as light from light, taking the notion of the sunrise (a hymn for dawn) as its central image of the relation of the Logos coming forth from the Father as radiance. It was a theological theme already set out in Tertullian, who used the ideas of light and beam, spring and river, root and plant as acceptable images of the Father's relation to the Son. If the line is taken very exactly (which perhaps it ought not to be), it suggests that Christ (the Light of the Father) himself "brings forth" (*proferens*) a light from the light. In other words, this could be an early allusion to the concept of the double procession of the Spirit of God: from the Father and the Son. I think this is probably overtranslating Ambrose, whose point here is chiefly that the Son issues from the Father's light in the manner that dawn pours new light on the world at dawn.

In line four Ambrose uses the liturgical concept of the sacrificial firstfruits. The glimmerings of new day at dawn are themselves resonant with sacrificial imagery. Christ is the firstfruits of the father's glory (his eternal or "primordial" radiance), as given to the world as a new dawn, just as the prayer of the church (Ambrose's dawn hymn) is the firstfruits of the church's response to God—its "glorification." In line six the reference to "eternal gleams" has a christological association meant for pagans. Here as in the later line "radiance of the Holy Spirit" (*jubar*) Ambrose alludes to the common Greco-Roman notion that the gods are clothed in light. The term *jubar* is actually the concept that evokes the radiance of the gods and is a cultural vehicle for his present teaching on the divine status of the Son, in Nicene perspective. The hymn then goes on to center on trinitarian images. What the Father possesses (glory, radiance) is equally the possession of the son. The church approaches the Father through the Son's mediation in the Holy Spirit. So here is clearly set out the Nicene theological agenda. In this context his reference to those who gnash their teeth in envy is probably a reference to his Arian opponents in Milan. In line twenty-four the interesting reference to "sober drunkenness" is a theme that is found extensively in early Syrian Christianity—as, for example, in Pseudo-Macarius's *Spiritual Homilies* from this same period—and is an ascetical notion that refers to the sense of elation that the inner workings of the divine Spirit produce within the believer's heart in prayer.

The whole Nicene faith is neatly summarized in the final two distichs of the hymn: the Father is entirely in the Son and the Son entirely in the Father: two persons, each divine, but one Godhead indivisible. Ambrose also illustrates here, incidentally, how the trinitarian faith that he defends so carefully in this hymn did not find it necessary, as yet, to explicate the part that he Spirit played in that bilateral relation. It would fall to Augustine in the younger generation to develop that theological theme.

### *St. Ephrem the Syrian*, **Hymns of Paradise 6.1-2 (*fourth century*).**

The keys of dogma,
Which unlock all the books of Scripture,

Opened up before my eyes the book of Creation itself,
The Treasury of the Ark, the Crown of the Law.
This is a book that more than all others
Has made the Creator manifest in its narrative
    and passed on his works
Taking cognizance of all his craftsmanship and
Revealing all his artistic creations.
*Responsorial:*
*Blessed is He who opened up Paradise by means of his Cross.*

So Scripture led me to the gate of Paradise
And my spiritual intellect stood amazed
And in wonderment as it entered in.
My conscious mind grew dizzy and weak,
For the senses found all its treasures,
Too magnificent to comprehend for long.
It could not deal with all its flavors;
It could not find analogies for all its colors;
It could not take in all its beauties;
Or find words that could depict them.

Ephrem was much concerned to bring his Syrian ecclesial tradition into greater harmony with the international Nicene synthesis of the wider church of his day, so although he is very representative of the special poetic and literary particularities of Syriac Christian thought (its highly symbolistic and poetic style of discourse), he is specially interested in representing Nicene doctrinal themes in the medium of his poetry. Here he sets the correct interpretation of Scripture on the fundamental basis of true doctrine (*ortho-doxia*): if the interpreter is a member of the church and starts from the basis of correct belief, then all things in the Scriptures will be revealed and clarified (stanza 1, lines 1-3). The interpretation of the sacred text is a door into paradise, which is itself the revelation of the proper order of creation: and the key to this is the study of the Law (*Torah*), which, beginning from the Genesis account of the creation, shows the hand of God in all time and space and history. From this close study an attentive mind can find God by looking at the beautiful works the craftsman has left in the created order as revelation of his presence (stanza 1, lines 4-8).

    In the second stanza the poet moves on from the approach to the Scriptures as the book of created revelation to the notion of how Scripture is the book of uncreated mysteries: from a sense of God's presence in history, the mind is elevated into greater wisdom, a wisdom of incomprehension as the divine mystery comes closer to the human mind and in its great immensity demonstrates to human consciousness (by transcending its capacity) something of the infinite grandeur of the divine presence, "known in unknowing." Ephrem, an important ascetical writer, gives a dense and rich statement that the exegete and theologian must also be the selfsame as the mystic: for only in union with God will the truth of God be revealed, a truth that cannot be captured in mere syllogisms.

**The Cherubic Hymn, Liturgy of St. John Chrysostom (fifth century).**

We, the mystic symbols
Of the Cherubim,
Also offer the thrice-holy hymn
To the Trinity that gives all life.
So let us lay aside all earth-bound care,
To receive the King of All,
Who comes escorted by the ranks of unseen angels.

The Cherubic Hymn was (and still is) sung on the occasion of the "great entrance" (offertory procession) of the Byzantine eucharistic liturgy. It was first composed circa fifth century at Constantinople for use in the great Cathedral of the Divine Wisdom (Hagia Sophia). In ancient times it was chanted by the corps of imperial eunuchs in a high pitched, eerie castrato. As Jesus had referred to the angels in heaven as "neither marrying nor being given in marriage," it became a Byzantine custom to regard the eunuchs as being symbols of the angels in their liturgical roles, and icons of the angels and archangels always depicted the heavenly beings as imperial eunuchs of high rank. The eunuchs made this liturgical processional hymn "their own."

In line one the "mystic symbols" are literally we who are "mystically iconizing." The eunuchs become living symbols of the angels during the mysteries—that is, during their liturgical chant, they mimic the angels, who sing to God in heaven the chant of "Holy, Holy, Holy."

The cherubim (line 2) are the angelic order on which God himself was enthroned ("He who sits upon the cherubim"), and which serve as the accompanying bodyguard of the Lord (see last stanza) as Christ is invoked to make a royal descent among his believers in the course of the liturgical rite.

In line three the Trisagion, "Holy, Holy, Holy," is the song of the angels recorded in Isaiah 6, when the prophet saw the angelic liturgy taking place in the temple (an iconic "type" of the Byzantine liturgy). Here it is actually the threefold alleluia that is sung. The Trisagion hymn actually takes place at another part of the Byzantine rite, just before the scriptural readings.

In the last line of the hymn the term *escorted* is actually the more precise word: "Borne up, by the spear-guard." When children were selected for imperial service in the palace in Byzantine times and eunuchized shortly after birth, their physiological growth was accelerated in adolescence. This made young eunuchs immensely powerfully built, with much upper-torso growth and its accompanying strength. When they surrounded the emperor at court and church functions, they were like a "scrum" protecting him from any assassination attempt. The emperor was thus literally "borne up" by his attendants. The hymn finally refers to the "ranks" of angels: in Byzantine theology they were enumerated as nine in all, the different orders (*taxeis*) of angels who attended on Christ in glory. The cherubim and seraphim were the highest of them and most closely accompanied Christ in the heavenly court, and on earth when the heavenly mysteries were reenacted during the liturgy.

While short in length on the page, this hymn, when chanted in Byzantine modalities, can often last for ten minutes or so while the long processions are being made in the church. It is one of the more solemn moments of the eucharistic rite of St. John Chrysostom and is sung with solemn repetitions and long, flowing melodies that linger over the words.

### St. Paulinus of Nola, On St. Felix's feast day (fifth century).

Spring has given back a voice to the birds.
My own tongue has also found its Spring
On the birthday of Felix,
Whose radiance has made the very winter
Burst into bloom for the rejoicing people.
Though the season is still dark and cold,
And winter still casts hoarfrosts in our midst,
That festal light wakes up a frozen year with singing lands,
And godly joys turn it for us to happy Spring.
Sadness, that winter of the soul,
Drops from hearts laden with care,
And clouds of sorrow scatter from our heart's serenity.
How well the gentle swallow knows its days of welcome,
Along with Magpie, and the holy Turtle Dove.
How silent are the thickets of thorn
Until the moment new Spring arrives
How each bird wanders silent through the shaggy hedge,
But the moment Spring comes back the birds burst with rejoicing
With so many different tunes, and what resplendent wings.
Just so, I too recognize that day
Which holy festivals renew each year
in fitting honor for the great Felix.

Now the Spring I love is reborn for me, and the year rejoices.
Now is the right time to offer up songs and hymns.
I celebrate the Spring with a fresh offering of rhetoric.

The text comes from a much longer poem celebrating the feast day of the martyr St. Felix. Paulinus had first retired from a senatorial career to his wife's estates in Spain but then moved to the Bay of Naples, where he had served as the governor and where he also had estates. There he headed an ascetical Christian community near the shrine of the martyr Felix. His conversion to a clerical and ascetical life was a cause célèbre among the literati of his day. Along with his priestly rural duties he continued to write elegant verses, especially *natalicia*, or festal remembrances of the martyr's birthday (his date of execution, January 14).[60]

This present one was clearly intended as an exercise in classical bucolic poetry (along the lines of Horace) to show he had not lost his literary gift, rather than anything meant to be sung in church; but even so it makes reference to the fact that songs and (processional) hymns very much made up part of the daily routine of a shrine church in this period, and doubtless Paulinus penned quite a few of these liturgical efforts too, which he probably thought were not worthy to be put among his literary remains. His intended audience is his own circle of literate friends. Indeed, the poem is part intended to celebrate *amicitia*, that spiritual friendship that forms a central part of Latin ecclesiastical scholarly writing, a beautiful example of which can also be seen in the excerpt from Sedulius below.

### *Prudentius,* **Cathemerinon 10 (excerpt) (fifth century).**

*Hymn at the Funeral of A Christian*

Matrons, now leave off your weeping
Cease lamenting your dearest kin
For such a death is simply life renewed;
Like a dried-up seed, when laid in earth,
Will sprout again, even though long dead,
And renew the harvests of past years.
Now Earth, receive him to your care
And clasp him to your gentle breast.
A man's body I commit to you,
Noble remains I entrust to you.
For this was once the dwelling of a soul
Made by the word of God Himself;

---

[60]Paulinus's poems can be found in English: P. G. Walsh, *Paulinus of Nola: Poems*, Ancient Christian Writers 40 (New York: Newman Press, 1975).

This was the shelter of that fire
Of Wisdom, under Christ's own rule.
Cover this body I leave with you now.
Its Maker and Author will not forget it
But will turn to seek once more his gift,
That icon of his very countenance. . . .
We rely on your words, Redeemer,
Conquering the darkness of death,
When you called the brigand
Your companion on the Cross,
To walk in your own footsteps,
Thus opening for the faithful
A shining path to spacious Paradise,
Within the grove a Serpent once closed off to all.
And so, best of Guides, order it so
The Spirit of this your servant
May be consecrated in its native home,
From which it came out wandering in exile.
Meanwhile, we shall care for these buried bones
With gifts of violets and green fronds
Sprinkling sweet perfume on this cold headstone.

The *Cathemerinon* 10 of Prudentius is a long discourse on a funeral ritual for a Christian friend. It is the first known example of such a thing. The line he takes, between tenderness, pity, consolation, and eschatological hope built out of the Gospel sayings (to the thief, Lk 23:43: "This day you shall be with me in paradise") and the concept that paradise was the ancestral home for the soul as image of God. As well as being most elegant verse, it is a highly artistic theology.[61]

### The Akathist, first stanza (sixth century).[62]

An Angel of the highest rank was sent from Heaven
To acclaim the Mother of God: All Hail![63]
But seeing you, O Lord, assuming bodily form, he stood in awe,
And with bodiless voice he cried aloud to her such things as these:
Rejoice, you through whom joy shines forth once more.

---

[61] Prudentius's corpus of poetry can be found in English translation by H. J. Thomson, *Prudentius*, 2 vols. (Cambridge, MA: Harvard University Press, 1949, 1953).
[62] Attributed by some to Romanos the Melodist.
[63] Also meaning "Rejoice!" (*chaire*).

Rejoice, you through whom the curse shall be blotted out.
Rejoice, restoration of lapsed Adam.
Rejoice, ransom of Eve's tears.
Rejoice, height too difficult for human thought to climb.
Rejoice, depth beyond the eyes of angels.
Rejoice, you who are the royal throne.
Rejoice, for you sustain him who sustains all things.
Rejoice, star that made the sun appear.
Rejoice, womb of divine Incarnation.
Rejoice, through whom Creation is renewed.
Rejoice, through whom the Creator becomes a child.
Rejoice, bride unwed.

This is the first stanza of a very long hymn celebrating the Virgin Mary's role in the incarnate plan of redemption. It takes the biblical themes and reflects on them meditatively—a style of Syro-Byzantine hymn writing that develops from its Syriac past (though now expressed in most elegant Byzantine Greek) and its roots in midrashic exegetical narrative. The poem begins with a witty meditation on the annunciation. Gabriel, an archangel described as if he were a grand courtier of the emperor, is sent by the Logos to the home of the Virgin of Nazareth. He is rehearsed in what he "should" say (namely, what the reader knows is in the New Testament, and what he or she thus expects to hear: "Hail, Mary, who is full of grace. The Lord is with you" (Lk 1:28). But as the angel descends with great speed to Earth, the Logos himself is imagined as getting there even faster. So when the angel arrives, the first thing he sees (with his "bodiless" eyes) as he begins to deliver his instructed message is the Logos himself, the supreme bodiless one, taking shape as flesh within the Virgin's womb.

This causes him so much wonderment that he forgets the message, as it were, and stutters with ecstatic mumblings, "Rejoice, you who are . . ."—the first word of his message endlessly repeated, as if he cannot get past the shock of his vision. The poem's extensive accumulation of the word *Rejoice!* communicates to the congregation the wonderful joy of the "good news," which is the incarnation of God to save humanity, through Mary. This became one of the most popular of all Christian hymns in the Orthodox East and is still used throughout Lent in church services.

**Romanos the Melodist, "Hymn on the Nativity," vv. 4, 6 (sixth century).**

When she heard the magi seeking the infant,
The maiden cried to them, "Who are you?"
And they in turn replied:
"And who are you, who have borne such a child as this?

Who is your father, or she who bore you,
That you should become mother and nurse of a fatherless son?
On seeing his star we understood that there had appeared to us:
*(Refrain): A tiny child, who is God before the ages."*

When Mary heard these wondrous words,
She bowed low and worshiped the child of her womb.
In tears she said, "How great, my child, how great
Is all that, in my poverty, you have done for me.
For behold. Magi are outside who seek you.
The kings of the East seek your face,
The richest among your people beg to see you,
For truly your people are those to whom you have been revealed as:
*(Refrain): A tiny child, who is God before the ages.*

So, since they are your people, my child, bid them come under your roof,
That there they may see riches in poverty, precious beggary.
As I have you as my glory and pride, I am not ashamed.
You are the grace and beauty of my dwelling, and myself.
Nod and let them enter. My poverty does not distress me.
You whom I hold are the treasure kings have come to see;
For kings and magi know that you have appeared,
*(Refrain): A tiny child, who is God before the ages."*

The midrashic style of Byzantine hymnology is shown at its most developed here in this sixth-century masterpiece of Romanos's writings. The biblical story of nativity is taken out and developed in an extended dialogue of characters. The reader becomes privy to the thoughts and dialogues of inner meanings, and in this way the exegesis of the simpler biblical text is sketched out in sound and radiant imagery of a charming domestic nature. These long hymns were led in the Great Cathedra of Constantinople and would have had, in their own day, something of the power and pathos of a Bach St. Matthew Passion.

Romanos loved juxtaposing paradoxes (the word in Greek also means "strange," which features throughout his works). The strange paradox of the incarnation becomes a high christological theme (the poverty of the human child, recently born, who is simultaneously the divine and everlasting Lord). The refrain (as here) was a catchphrase meant to be sung by the congregation to sum up the quintessence of the theological paradox, or mystery, the feast was concerned with celebrating. In this case on the Feast of Christmas, the poet acclaims the great paradox of the tiny child . . . who is God before the ages.

**Sedulius Scotus, Carmen *70* (ninth century).**

> The seasons take flight and leave on whirling wings;
> The cupped sphere of the starry heaven knows it all too well.
> September hurries off. October, with puffing breath, runs in;
> Autumn ever swelling to its own completion and demise.
> Hoar-haired Winter with crackling ice hurries on the shivering;
> Brings with it cloud-piled skies and all their sadness of rain.
> My famous teacher, once you would be my comfort, my springing hope
> Against these awful blasts of gusting wind.
> Pity me. Here I lie sluggish, like some cricket in a hole,
> Not even strong enough to stir, to see my dear one.
> I find this awful thorny time more bitter than ever,
> For my charming shepherd, my sophist, has gone away.
> Light has become as shadow for me. Lamplight is as night.
> Ah, pity me. I can no longer look upon my own bright lamp.
> But soon he shall come back again, ever more delightful in our sight,
> And all the thorns will then give way; noxious gloom shall leave,
> Then will clouds of sorrow clear from the hearts of the just;
> For we shall have peace again, and good repose: an Easter in our breast.
> May the grace of the Lord be with you many years to come.
> May the Lord's grace exalt you greatly.
> See I have not forgotten you. This little poem bears witness.
> My prayer is that you have not forgotten me.
> For indeed I have not forgotten you.

Sedulius Scotus ("the Irishman," not Sedulius the fifth-century Christian poet) left his native Erin as a wandering scholar and traveled to Liège, where he settled down under the patronage of Archbishop Hartgar. Carolingian Emperor Lothair I, Charlemagne's grandson, appointed him as tutor to his sons, and during this time Sedulius composed a treatise on the art of statesmanship for the princes Lothair and Charles. In his lifetime he was a veritable center of Irish culture on the continent and had a large circle of friends, among whom he celebrated (as he does here) the art of spiritual kinship (*anam cara*—the soul-friend relationship). This poem represents Sedulius calling to mind a clerical scholar friend whose absence through a long winter Sedulius has grieved over.

The spring promises to bring him, and his intelligent conversation, back again. *Amicitia*, "friendship," a theme much celebrated in late antique Roman literary circles, is taken up by the later Christian scribes and elevated to a spiritual status: the soul-friendship of soul to soul, mind to mind, heart to heart, among the Christians, consecrated in the grace of Christ as a sign of that communion that is the mystical body of the church. A similar, and perhaps even more beautiful, poem of his on the joys of Easter Eve and its promise of friends returning from afar (*Carmen* 3.2, lines 17-26), I translated some time back.[64] The unavailability of any significant collection of his works in English translation is a sorry thing.[65]

**FURTHER READING**

Adey, L. *Hymns and the Christian "Myth."* Vancouver: University of British Columbia Press, 1986.

Bingham, J. *Origines Ecclesiasticae: The Antiquities of the Christian Church.* Reprint, London: Bohn, 1845.

Brière, E. *Scripture in Hymnography: A Study in Some Feasts of the Orthodox Church.* DPhil diss., Oxford University, 1982.

Carpenter, M. *Romanos the Melodist.* Translation and commentary. 2 vols. Columbia: University of Missouri Press, 1970, 1973.

Catafygiotou Topping, E. *Sacred Songs: Studies in Byzantine Hymnography.* Minneapolis: Light and Life Publications, 1997.

———. "Theodosia, Melodos and Monastria." *Diptycha* (1987): 384-405.

Christ, W., and M. Paranikas, eds. *Anthologia Graeca Carminum Christianorum.* Leipzig: B. G. Teubner, 1871.

Church, F. F., and T. J. Mulry, trans. *The Macmillan Book of Earliest Christian Hymns.* New York: Macmillan, 1988.

Conomos, D. E. *Byzantine Hymnography and Byzantine Chant.* Brookline, MA: Holy Cross Press, 1984.

Di Berardino, A. "Christian Poetry." In *Patrology* IV, ed. J. Quasten, 255-341. Westminster: Christian Classics, 1986.

Edden, V. "Prudentius." In *Latin Literature of the Fourth Century*, ed. J. W. Binns, 160-82. London: Routledge and Kegan Paul, 1974.

Gilbert, P. *On God and Man: The Theological Poetry of St. Gregory of Nazianzus.* Crestwood, NY: St. Vladimir's Seminary Press, 2001.

Grosdidier de Matons, J. *Romanos le Mélode et les origines de la poésie religieuse à Byzance.* Paris: Beauchesne, 1977.

Hughes, H. V. *Latin Hymnody.* London: Faith Press, 1922.

---

[64]See McGuckin, *At the Lighting of the Lamps*, 83, 100.
[65]The works of Sedulius Scotus can be found in PL 103.9-352. The poetry is in L. Traube, ed., *Monumenta Germaniae Historia*, vol. 3, *Poetae* (1896), 151-240. The present hymn is *Carmen* 70, in I. Meyers, ed., *Sedulii Scotti: Tom. CXVII*, Carmina Corpus Christianorum, Continuatio Mediaevalis (Turnhout: Brepols, 1991), 113. For further commentary on this piece, see my translation and notes on Sedulius in J. Leemans, ed., *Corpus Christianorum 1953–2003: Xenium Natalicum* (Turnhout: Brepols, 2003).

Jeffrey, P. "The Earliest Christian Chant Repertory Recovered: The Georgian Witness to Jerusalem Chant." *Journal of the American Musicological Society* 47 (1994): 1-39.

Julian, J. *A Dictionary of Hymnology*. London: J. Murray, 1892. Reprint, Grand Rapids: Kregel, 1985.

Klijn, A. E. J. *The Acts of Thomas* Leiden: Brill, 1962.

Krueger, D. *Writing and Holiness*. Philadelphia: University of Pennsylvania Press, 2004. See esp. chap. 8, "Textuality and Redemption, the Hymns of Romanos the Melodist."

Lacombrade, C., ed. *Synesios de Cyrene: Hymnes*. Paris: Les Belles Lettres, 1978.

Lash, E. trans. *St. Romanos The Melodist: Kontakia on the Life of Christ*. San Francisco: HarperCollins, 1995.

Liderbach, D. *Christ in the Early Christian Hymns*. New York: Paulist Press, 1998.

Limberis, V. *Divine Heiress: The Virgin Mary and the Creation of Christian Constantinople*. London: Routledge, 1994.

Lingas, A. "Hymnography." In *The Encyclopedia of Greece and the Hellenic Tradition*, ed. G. Speake, 1:786-87. Chicago and London: Fitzroy-Dearborn, 2000.

McGuckin, J. A. *At the Lighting of the Lamps: Hymns of the Ancient Church*. Harrisburg, PA: Morehouse Press, 1997.

———. "Gregory of Nazianzus: The Rhetorician as Poet." In *Gregory of Nazianzus: The Hellenist, The Christian*, ed. T. Hagg and J. Bortnes, 193-212. Copenhagen: Museon Press, 2005.

———. "A Neglected Masterpiece of the Christian Mystical Tradition: The Hymns of Divine Eros by the Byzantine Poet Symeon the New Theologian (949–1022)." *Spiritus* 5 (Summer 2005): 182-202.

———. "Poetry and Hymnography: The Greek Christian World." In *The Oxford Handbook of Early Christian Studies*, ed. S. Ashbrook Harvey and D. Hunter, 641-56. Oxford: Oxford University Press, 2008.

———. trans. *St. Gregory of Nazianzus: Selected Poems*. Oxford: SLG Press, 1986.

———. *Standing in God's Holy Fire*. Maryknoll, NY: Orbis Books. 2001.

McKinnon, J. *Music in Early Christian Literature*. Cambridge and New York: Cambridge University Press, 1987.

McVey, K. *Ephrem the Syrian: Hymns*. New York: Paulist Press, 1989.

Maloney, G. *Symeon the New Theologian: Hymns of Divine Love*. Denville, NJ: Dimension Books, 1976.

Neale, J. M. *Hymns of the Ancient Eastern Church*. Reprint, New York: AMS Press, 1971.

Peltomaa, L. M. *The Image of the Virgin Mary in the Akathist*. Leiden: Brill, 2001.

Quasten, J. *Music and Worship in Pagan and Christian Antiquity*. Washington, DC: National Association of Pastoral Musicians, 1983.

Roberts, M. J. "Poetry and Hymnography: Christian Latin Poetry." In *The Oxford Handbook of Early Christian Studies*, ed. S. Ashbrook Harvey and D. Hunter, 628-40. Oxford: Oxford University Press, 2008.

Rovière, P. La. *Veteres Graeci Poetae.* Geneva, 1614.

Sanders, J. T. *The New Testament Christological Hymns.* Cambridge: Cambridge University Press, 1971.

Skeris, R. A. *Chroma Theou: On the Origins and Theological Interpretation of the Musical Imagery Used by the Ecclesiastical Writers of the First Three Centuries, with Special Reference to the Image of Orpheus.* Altotting: A. Coppenrath, 1976.

Strunk, O. *Essays on Music in the Byzantine World.* New York: Norton, 1977.

Taft, R. *The Byzantine Rite: A Short History.* Collegeville, MN: Liturgical Press, 1992.

Thompson, J. J. *Poems of Prudentius.* Loeb Classical Library. 2 vols. London: Harvard University Press, 1949, 1963.

Touliatos, D. "Women Composers of Byzantine Medieval Chant." *College Music Symposium* 24 (1984): 62-80.

Tripolitis, A. *Kassia: The Legend, the Woman, and Her Work.* New York: Garland Press, 1999.

Trypanis, C., ed. and trans. *The Penguin Book of Greek Verse.* Harmondsworth, UK: Penguin, 1971.

Wainwright, G. "Christian Worship: Scriptural Basis and Theological Frame." In *The Oxford History of Christian Worship*, ed. G. Wainwright and K. B. Westerfield Tucker, 1-31. Oxford: Oxford University Press, 2006.

Ware, K., and Mother Maria, trans. *The Akathistos Hymn to the Most Holy Mother of God, and Office of Small Compline.* Wallington, UK: Ecumenical Society of the BVM, 1987.

Ware, K., and Mother Maria, trans. *The Festal Menaion.* London: Faber, 1969.

Wellesz, E. *A History of Byzantine Music and Hymnography.* 2nd ed. Oxford: Clarendon Press, 1961.

White, C. *Early Christian Latin Poets.* New York: Routledge, 2000.

———. *Gregory of Nazianzus: Autobiographical Poems.* Cambridge Medieval Classics. Cambridge: Cambridge University Press, 1996.

Woodward, G. E. *The Most Holy Mother of God in the Songs of the Eastern Church.* London: Faith Press, 1919.

# WAYS OF PRAYER IN THE EARLY CHURCH

## GATHERING FOR PRAYER

The Christians have always prayed publicly, together, as well as privately, apart. From the beginning Jesus instructed them to perform the common ritual of the Eucharist: breaking bread and sharing a common cup (Mt 26:26-28). The communal experience was critical to the notion of "communion" (joining together in harmonious union) that the ritual symbolized and created in the moment of symbolizing it. But he also advocated that prayer should be conducted in secret, in the quiet of one's own inner rooms (Mt 6:6-8). Throughout the centuries, therefore, Christian prayer has had both a public and a more deeply personal aspect. This chapter will concern itself mainly with the more domestic rituals of private prayer.

The church's public ceremonials were soon called the Divine Liturgy, borrowing the word *leitourgia* from the Septuagint Greek translation of the Old Testament, which in turn had borrowed it from classical Greek use (meaning public works of civic import), now to connote the Jewish temple rituals. Noting this use of *liturgy* in the Septuagint Bible, Christians reapplied the word after the fourth century to mean public worship in the churches, especially the sacramental rites of Eucharist and baptism. Soon, and more so in the Western churches, the concept of liturgy broadened to include the monastic "offices" of prayer throughout the day, namely evening prayer (vespers), night prayer (compline), morning prayer (matins or orthros), and daytime prayers at the various marking off of the "hours" (such as first, third, sixth, ninth, and so on).[1] These more formal prayer ceremonies are discussed in the chapter dedicated to the development of Christian liturgy and are only lightly touched on here.

---

[1] The ancient way of reckoning the clock worked from first hour (dawn or 6 a.m.) in increments of three hours, up to prayers of sunset (vespers), nightfall (compline), and middle of the night (*mesonyktion*).

There was not a strong division between private prayer and prayers in the churches, as many of the same forms of vocalized prayers in use would obviously overlap (such as the Our Father or litanies of petition), and heavy use of the Psalter as a prayer book can be presumed at all times in Christian history; but clearly there were different emphases. Prayer in the private or domestic context was more interior and personal; that in the public forum always had a more didactic and ceremonial role. Domestic prayer might use vocal forms (set forms of prayers) or be silent. Obviously in the latter case it soon became a matter of more secret initiation. One cannot write about silent prayer very fluently. And yet after the fifth century the monastic movement, whose devotees evidently had a great and vested interest in the ways of prayer, developed an extensive set of doctrines about "prayer in the secret of the heart." We can still access many of those written materials. It is, however, also largely a matter of person-to-person initiation, and that is harder to reconstitute, though one can have a lively sense of it, as the initiations into the ways of private prayer are still practiced in the surviving monasteries of the Christian world, and those of the Eastern traditions have changed little since the patristic era.

The ancient writers on prayer developed terms to describe the issue: *kataphatic*, a word meaning "to say expressly," covered that which in prayer or theology could be well enough described, categorized, or defined within terms of human language. *Apophatic*, the term for "turning away from speech," described that aspect of prayer and the divine experience that exceeded the capacity of human discourse or written words to capture. Most modern approaches to Christianity, especially its contemporary historians, theologians, and apologists, seem to presume for much of the time that words can capture and express all. Is it an academic's fallacy? If there is a problem in theology, therefore, it seems only that we need a new form of words to discover in order to put it all across more efficiently and relevantly. The ancients who spoke, paradoxically, about apophatic realities (to discuss that which cannot be spoken of) had an approach to the mystery of religion that tended to understand Christianity, perhaps more fully than we do today, as first and foremost a mystery religion, a mystical experience.

Since the Reformation church developments of the last five centuries set this trend in motion, European Christians have much preferred to dwell in the domains of rationalization and activism than mystery and meditation. This is undoubtedly why the ancient literatures on prayer and mystical perception were so heavily neglected by the modern church, to the extent that most Christians, even highly literate ones, would probably never even have heard of the great spiritual masters of the past or the works they produced that formed the foundational constructs of Christian mysticism, making it one of the world's greatest religious traditions of mystical prayer. This is why, when American Protestant, or formerly Protestant, men and women in the middle part of the twentieth century started to look around for more satisfyingly "mystical" traditions, it was San Francisco and New York that became the laboratories for a Western encounter with Buddhism or Vedanta. The Christian mystical tradition was unknown and unsuspected to them.[2]

In the beginning the Christians found themselves in an old world that prayed often and at length. Prayers (to the gods of state and hearth) were so normative that they reached from domestic existence to civic and imperial governmental life. A refusal to worship the old gods of Rome was listed to the early church as the capital legal crime of high treason. Involvement with the gods, and sometimes the very specific ones the state mandated as the epitome of its political fortune (who was also a goddess called Fortuna), was not optional in the ancient world. Philosophical and skeptical attitudes to the gods were known and tolerated, but even as skeptical a man as Cicero was careful not to publicly mock the system and would occupy priesthoods of old cults, which were also seen as the defining mark of the upper class rulers. The pre-Christian emperors were themselves the *pontifices maximi*, the high priests, as it were, of Roman religion.[3]

In late antiquity the Christians found that the common Greek word for prayer was *euche* (pronounced *ef-keh*). From the outset they decided to change their preferred term for prayer to *proseuche*. The only clear motivation for this, a striking change that can be noticed in all the literature, is that from the very beginning they must have wished to dissociate themselves from all other (pagan) ways of making prayer. In particular the Christians had a deep distaste for that part of Hellenistic worship that can best be called "aversion rituals": the darker side (both theologically and psychologically) of the Greek cults that dealt with keeping the hostile gods placated and their attention turned away from humans so that they might not cause mischief or hurt.

Such gods were for the Christians subsumed under the category of the demons: and it was widely believed among the early Christians, and many of the Jews, that the demons were fallen angels who had snared human beings into worshiping them (in

---

[2]Kerouac's *Dharma Bums* is an example. The writings of Japanese Zen master D. T. Suzuki exemplify this movement. Those trying to reclaim the Christian mystical tradition as a more public form of knowledge were also apparent at that time, such as Thomas Merton (*The Seven Storey Mountain*), but it would take Merton many more years, living as a Cistercian monk, to discover the riches of even the patristic tradition on prayer.
[3]*Pontifex maximus* was the title of priesthood of the Roman cult appropriated by the emperor. It means "greatest bridge builder" (between the affairs of earth and the gods). It was later appropriated as one of the honorific titles of the popes of Rome.

the pagan cults) by performing miracles so as to lead them into building temples in their honor and establishing rites and festivities.[4] For most Christians of the early centuries, Greek worship was a demonic delusion. There was little pluralistic give and take. The church leaders regarded any form of involvement with cultic pagan worship (even down to the smallest offering of a pinch of incense, which most ordinary pagans would have seen as a social nicety as much as an act of religion) as an apostasy. Those preparing for baptism were strictly instructed how to remove themselves from any lingering attachments to the ubiquitous cults around them. This marked them out socially in quite dramatic ways and earned them the reputation of being "atheists."

Among Hellenistic cults, it was a common ancient presupposition that the gods had to be persuaded to listen to human petitions (so routinely predictable in the sense that yet another need was being presented). Ancient non-Christian theologies, therefore, advocated that sacrifices were a fundamental part of successful prayer. It was transactional in its fundamental character: namely, give the god something like an *eulogia* (the word meant a goodwill offering but could also connote "bribe") and then present your petition. The best offerings were animal sacrifices or incense offerings to be burned on their altars. The key element was something precious offered up and something expected in return.

This transactional basis of ancient prayer was also critically important to the Jewish temple rituals (e.g., Ps 66:13-15). Animal sacrifice formed the heart of the "covenant" between God and Israel (Ps 50:5). The very term to enter into covenant in Hebraic theology was derived from the sacrificial ritual of dismembering and termed *karat berith* ("to cut up a contract"). Israel offered up sacrifices, incense, and prayers; and God sent down in return his divine favor and protection (Ps 20:3). If the relationship was disrupted, the terms of the transactional engagement would be suspended. This is why the Hebrew prophets so recurrently see Israel's lapse from purity of cult or worship as the chief reason political disasters befall them (e.g., Ps 106:28-29, 37-42). Just as Israel falls away from its duty of regular and pure sacrifice, so God in turn neglects his part of the bargain to keep Israel safe.

This aspect of transactional covenant thought carried on in several places into Christianity, with this modification: that from the very outset Christians seemed to have turned away radically from the notion of offering animal sacrifices. This was undoubtedly because Jesus himself was such a critic of the theological transactional principle. Many times in his references to prayer and divine relationship, he criticized

---

[4]The ancient Greek notion of the lesser gods, *daimones*, was not usually negative. These were more likely to be interested in the affairs of humans approaching them. For Christians, like the Jews before them, *daimones* were quickly translated into satanic demons, and the pagan cult was regarded as the most depraved of human sins, much to the puzzlement of their pagan neighbors in antiquity.

the concept of sacrificial negotiation—as if God had to be persuaded to be beneficent. His stories frequently insist that God's mercy is not poured out dependent on the quality of the offering made but, on the contrary, is free and startlingly generous, even to those who might least expect it.[5]

This, an aspect of his theology of the kingdom, had a direct bearing on the doctrine of prayer he taught his disciples: a connection that is nowhere more obvious than in the content of his most personal doctrine of prayer as recorded by the apostles, namely the Lord's Prayer, which is in essence an invocation of the kingdom in the form of the rabbinic practice of the "hallowing of the name" (Mt 6:9-13).[6] What is very noticeable in Jesus' teachings, nevertheless, is his turning away from the concept of sacrifice as transactional dealing with this God who is habitually so unexpectedly merciful (Lk 11:9-13). He lifts up this prophetic axiom to his opponents who seem to have found his informality about cultic attitudes distasteful: "Go and learn what this text means—'I desire mercy, not sacrifice.' For I came not to call the righteous, but sinners" (Mt 9:13). And time after time he advocates that the interior attitude of the heart and conscience carry more weight with God than the externals of cultic probity (Mt 5:23-24; 12:6; Mk 12:32-34), a theme that is also found in the Psalms and later prophets (Ps 51:7; Is 1:11-17).

Overall it is remarkable how opposed Jesus seems to sacrificial cult.[7] And, therefore, probably it is no surprise how those who brought about his judicial murder were the priests of the Jerusalem temple, who did so in the immediate aftermath of his deliberately provocative sign of overturning the tables in the temple precincts. All of these things related symbolically to the sidelining of sacrificial cult. Even Jesus' reference to the temple as his Father's "house of prayer," rather than what the old ritual defined it as (a place of sacrifice), reveals his substantial change of direction (Mt 21:12-13). Even though the first generation of apostolic teachers, following him, tended to use sacrificial motifs to describe Jesus' own death, it is clear enough that Jesus' passion was seen as an "ending of sacrifice" among the Christians as much as any continuation of it. Sacrificial worship was seen to have been consummated, reached perfecting fulfillment (*teleiosis*) and in a sense exhausted by Jesus' death on the cross. It might well have been his Christian advisers who persuade Constantine,

---

[5]Jesus' stories of the prodigal son (Lk 15:11-32) or the Pharisee and publican (Lk 18:10-14) illustrate this, as do many other *logia*, such as how prayer ought to be short and heartfelt (Mt 6:5-8; 21:22).
[6]See further J. A. McGuckin, "Authority, Obedience and the Holiness of God: The New Testament Sense of the Kingdom," in *Power & Authority in Eastern Christian Experience*, ed. F. Soumakis, Sophia Studies in Orthodox Theology 3 (New York: Theotokos Press, 2011), 17-32.
[7]For a more carefully evidenced argument see J. A. McGuckin, "Sacrifice and Atonement: An Investigation into the Attitude of Jesus of Nazareth Towards Cultic Sacrifice," in *Remembering for the Future* (Oxford: Pergamon Press, 1988), 1:648-61.

in the fourth century, to be the emperor who so decisively ended animal sacrifices, that universal staple of antique religion, by legally proscribing them.

The place of sacrifice was, as already adumbrated in Psalm 51:16-17, becoming the "interior altar" of the heart for the Christians, and so it is that conscience starts to become the master theme of the Christian literature on prayer. The "heart" thus becomes a dominant motif of the spiritual literature. This had been present in the Greek philosophical literature of antiquity to some extent already. Most of the time the terms for interior sensibility among the philosophers had been *logismos* (rational thinking) or *nous* (intellectual perception); the concept of heart (*kardia*) being mainly reserved by the Greeks to describe the generic passionate or emotional life of a person, or sometimes the moral choices a person might commit to.[8]

And yet already in those key Platonic dialogues that the Christians would read most attentively, that is, the *Symposium* and the *Timaeus*, Plato demonstrates the small beginnings of a semantic that did identify heart (*kardia*) with soul (*psyche*), demonstrating at least the "potential" for compatibility between Platonic and Christian anthropologies on this point.[9] It was, of course, going to be a synthesis that could only be worked out much later, in the works of the fourth-century Greek fathers and onward. Apart from this Platonic witness, we can also see among the Stoics, the school that influenced Christian moral thought most profoundly, that the concept of heart had also begun to be used as the central locus of intellectual reason, the source from which feeling and moral choice proceeded.[10] This was similar to the way that the Platonic tradition employed *nous*, as well as being comparable to several biblical texts where the authors discourse on moral choice rising from the inner heart.

## THE HEART AS SANCTUARY IN THE OLD TESTAMENT

What both these major Greek traditions notably lacked, however, was that central biblical sense of the heart of a human being as a fundamentally *sacred locus*: the inner place where the creature stood under the eye of God.[11] The Septuagint, or Greek translation of the Hebrew Bible, however, had already made the connection, and this proved decisive for the Christians who immersed themselves in it to the extent of rarely ever looking at the Hebrew text. In the Septuagint translation the term *heart* is elevated as a synonym of the soul or the spiritual intelligence of a

---

[8] Cf. J. Behm, "Kardia Among the Greeks," in *Theological Dictionary of the New Testament*, ed. G. Kittel (Grand Rapids: Eerdmans, 1965), 3:608-9.
[9] *Symposium* 218a; *Republic* 6.492c; *Timaeus* 100a. Texts in Behm, "Kardia Among the Greeks," 608.
[10] Such a concept is attributed to Chrysippus and found explicitly in Diogenes of Babylon (his immediate disciple), and also in Diogenes Laertes. Cf. Behm, "Kardia Among the Greeks," 609.
[11] Behm (ibid., 609n7) notes that the correlation of *kardia* with religious sentiment is traceable only in a few magical papyri in the later Hellenistic period.

person (*dianoia, psyche*).[12] In this aspect biblical anthropology is similar in several respects to Pharaonic Egyptian religion, which also understood the heart as a cipher for the moral conscience, and perhaps this is why the spiritual doctrine of prayer of the heart made its first postscriptural appearance in the desert monasteries of fourth- and fifth-century Egypt.[13]

In this semantical shift the Septuagint translators summed up an entire spiritual doctrine of the Old Testament—an anthropology of the spirit, as it were, which gives the heart of a human being a high spiritual significance. The heart here becomes a biblical cipher for the whole spiritual personality, especially considered as the true and deep reality of a person. It is the center of the human creature's spiritual intelligence, that spiritual consciousness that is partly intellective but more fundamentally expressed by the word *wisdom* (*sophia*; Prov 19:8; 18:15; Job 34:10; 1 Kings 3:12). In the Old Testament, thought rises naturally from the heart as the seat of spiritual intelligence. The heart is the place where thoughts reside in a creature (Dan 2:30; Judg 5:16) and is therefore a deeply moral quantity that directs a human being's life according to the "thoughts of the heart" (Jer 11:20; 23:20; Is 10:7; 1 Kings 8:17; Ezra 7:10). The heart is the arena of all moral obedience—one serves the Lord "with all one's heart" (1 Sam 12:20, 24). And the scripture sums this up by saying that the "fear of God" (reverence) thus dwells within the heart (Jer 32:40). The movement of the heart also describes the chosen purposes, or the life commitments, that have been adopted as a fixed allegiance and are stabilized as the firm establishment of a human being within the "way of the Lord" (Pss 27:14; 119:36; Job 11:13; Prov 3:5), meaning at

---

[12]Rarely does it connote *nous*, reflecting the general principle that the biblical anthropology is more holistically concerned to represent the sense of a spiritual intelligence under the eye of God: the creature scrutinized by the divine reality and learning to recognize its own deep reality in its own spiritual scrutiny of the self, from which arises wisdom and stability of personhood in relation to the divine—in essence what the patristic and Byzantine tradition exemplifies through its elaboration of early monastic ascetical theology.

[13]The *Hymn to Amen Ra* speaks of the heart as the place of encounter between the high god and those he has made—both lesser gods and humans: "Hail to Thee, O Ra, Lord of Truth / whose shrine is hidden, the Lord of the gods . . . / Who gave commands and the gods came into being . . . / Who hears the prayer of the captive / Gracious of heart to those who appeal to him. . . . / In whose beauty the gods rejoice / Their hearts live when they see him" (in A. M. di Nola, ed., *The Prayers of Man* [London: Obolensky, 1962], 226-27). Pre-Christian Egyptian religion, as can be seen graphically from the hieroglyphic depictions of the judgment of the dead, also had a vivid conception of the heart as the moral conscience. The person to be judged stood before the scales while Thoth carried the dead person's heart in his hand, balancing himself, and it, against truth on the other side of the scale. The ancient Egyptian liturgy of burial wrapped the scroll of absolution with the mummy to ensure Osiris's favorable judgment. It also testifies to the synonymity of the heart with the soul in Egyptian theology: "Behold the deceased in this hall of double truth. / His heart has been weighed in the balance / in the presence of the great spirits / the very lords of Hades / and it has been found true" (Egyptian burial liturgy, in di Nola, *Prayers of Man*, 235).

first obedience to the terms of the Torah and something the Christians will come to look on as the life of faith.[14]

The Psalms and Wisdom traditions of the Scriptures presented a tighter form of this same doctrine, directly relevant for the doctrine of prayer, and one that the early monks were to assimilate from their constant recitation of phrases taken from the book of Psalms in their daily prayer offices. Here the heart is the arena not only of conscience and fidelity but the place in consciousness where the soul stands nakedly before its God. The Psalms teach that the Lord knows the secrets of the heart (Ps 44:21). He sees that humans find their deepest selves in the heart (Prov 23:7), which has depths that can cause wonderment (Ps 73:7). But he sees also that humans work wickedness in their hearts (Ps 41:6; 58.2). In the heart a creature can resist God blatantly, the root of all subsequent evil (Ps 103:6), and such rebels God rejects because of their pride and arrogance of heart (Ps 101:4-5). God is close to those whose hearts are broken (repentant; Ps 34:18) and is the friend of those whose hearts are established in him (Ps 112:8), for such establishment sets the creature firmly within the number of the servants of the living God. Equally, however, the heart might wither and become fixed in opposition to God, and the human who has hardened his or her heart shall fall away (Prov 28:14).

## THE NEW TESTAMENT DOCTRINE OF THE HEART

In the New Testament the idea of the human heart takes these Old Testament interiorizing trends to a further pitch. More so than the Septuagint, the New Testament employs the heart as the supreme symbol of the inner spiritual condition and center of energy in a human being. The anthropology remains monistic and dynamically concrete. This is true even of Paul, who lays the basis for the Christian adoption of the more common Hellenistic forms of dichotomous or trichotomous anthropology.[15] Paul, even when he imagines human beings as tri- or bipartite in composition, still speaks of the heart as the synonym for the "inmost self," that is, the whole inner person longing for salvation (Rom 7:22).

---

[14]This is found extensively in the LXX Old Testament: Hannah's prayer, rising from deepest sorrow and need, was uttered "in her heart" (1 Sam 1:13), and God heard her. Solomon prayed for understanding of heart to perceive the moral demands of God (1 Kings 3:9), and his wisdom and favor with God derived from the "largeness of heart" that God had given him (1 Kings 4:29). A human might look on the outer appearance of another person, but God always looks on the heart (1 Sam 16:7). Humans devise evil in their hearts (Zech 7:10; Prov 6:18), but it is also the source of their repentance, when God makes the heart of the nation to melt (Josh 14:8), or when David's heart struck him (1 Sam 24:5).

[15]*Pneuma*, *psyche*, *sarx/soma*. The anthropology witnessed in the Qumran texts, especially in the hymns, reflects more of a spirit-body dualism, and both patterns (trichotomous and dualist) occur in the New Testament letters, which have not settled on a firm anthropological model as yet.

The anthropological doctrine of the Gospels is not specifically or carefully elaborated (really just presupposed in a utilitarian way), but it takes its point of departure from spiritual soteriology[16] and consistently reaffirms that the heart is the seat of spiritual understanding, the source of reflection and contemplation (Mk 7:21; Mt 12:34; Jn 12:40; Lk 1:51; 2:35; 9:47; 24:25, 38; Acts 7:23; 8:22; Heb 4:12). As in accordance with the scriptural doctrine, it is thus the source of volition and moral decision (Jn 13:2; Acts 5:3; 11:23; 1 Cor 4:5; 7:37; 2 Cor 9:7; Col 4:8; Eph 6:22; Rev 17:17). It is, for these reasons, the center of creaturely consciousness, to which God turns when he reveals his presence in the world, making the heart the center of the divine encounter and revelation. Like a personal Sinai, the heart is the arena in which the human being knows and relates to God in the deepest seat of religious awareness (Mt 13:15, 19; 18:35; Mk 7:21; 12:30; Lk 8:15; 16:15; Acts 15:9; 16:14; Rom 2:15; 5:5; 8:27; 10:9-10; 2 Cor 1:22; Gal 4:6; 1 Thess 2:4; Heb 8:10; 10:16, 22; 2 Pet 1:19; Rev 2:23).

Following Paul, the later Christian tradition habitually thinks of the inner spiritual heart as a personal sanctum, a shrine or holy place within, which is the holy of holies in a human being where the Holy Spirit comes to dwell in the person of the saints. Paul phrases it succinctly: "May your hidden self grow strong so that Christ may dwell in your heart by faith" (Eph 3:17). Jesus himself is surely thinking more of the Sinai image when he utters his most memorable saying: "How blessed are the pure in heart, for they shall see God" (Mt 5:8).

We might sum up, then, by understanding that for the early Christian teachers on the spiritual life, it was not necessary to seek the heart, as if it were a complex idea, for the Scripture is taking it for granted that it is the heart itself in a human being that is restless for God and wishes to do the seeking. But a highly important part of this ascetical and anthropological doctrine is that the heart is not alone in seeking, for God has elected the heart as the holy ground of revelation and encounter. It is the place of his indwelling and is thus to be seen as a potential sanctuary or holy place. What they mean by the prayer of the heart, then, is not merely the turning of the whole self to God. More than this, it is the seeking after the heart by God himself, who is restless to save and bring life to his creature. The heart in the Christian spiritual masters is not a mere part of the human creature but, in a deeply rooted biblical understanding, the whole creature understood as having a capacity for a higher life, and ultimately a capacity for God, who has given that creature the instinct for the divine presence by means of the heart's sacred character.

The heart, therefore, is the person understood as a creature under the eye of God, a mysterious and holy reality even though fallible, mortal, and limited. The heart

---

[16]The concept of the salvation of the soul.

signifies the whole person who can enter in, or might draw back from, the sacred space, which is that geography of the divine encounter that later spiritual writers will wish to discourse over in terms of the syntax of spirituality. The particular geography of this terrain of the heart is stark and apocalyptical, like the desert. It is either the holy ground of fiery revelation or the desolate wasteland of the creature's rebellious and isolated sterility. Prayer, itself a reflection of the condition of this inner heart, retains this character of *krisis*, or judgment, that we find especially in the Gospel sayings about the human heart. It is not, in the first instance, an emotional or comfort-laden cipher. The character of their prayer is, like it or not, a profound indicator of the quality of a Christian's true discipleship. This graphic, monistic, and dynamic understanding of the human being in the face of God remains at the core of all the subsequent East Christian understandings of prayer and the spiritual life.

## PRAYER IN THE EARLY CHRISTIAN MONASTIC MOVEMENT

The early monastics in Egypt were most concerned with directions to their disciples about how to live a dedicated life of prayer in the practical limitations of the severe desert conditions they chose in order to have sufficient peace and simplicity to focus their lives on this task above all others. Poverty and chastity (the simple lifestyle of a subsistence desert dweller, allied to celibate lifestyle) were the attendant contexts of this complete dedication to prayer. But even with the best will in the world, the monks found that they could not live on prayer alone: they had to organize their days also with work, food, and rest in mind. Many of them probably prayed for around ten hours each day, not considering the formal "offices of prayer" they completed using the psalms and canticles of the Scriptures to vocalize their prayers. Most monks in the early deserts of Syria and Egypt began to pray at dusk and used the coolness of the night to complete their meditations until the sun rose, when they would take something to eat and rest for a while before beginning their physical labors with intermittent use of psalms. During the day they engaged in various times of vocal and silent prayer.

The significant teachers among them soon began to attract disciples, who pressed them for advanced teaching about prayer. Some of the greatest have left magisterial collections: theologians and ascetics such as Evagrius of Pontus, Macarius the Great, Diadochus of Photike, Isaac of Niniveh, Sadhona the Syrian, and many others.[17] This literary tradition soon accumulated into a vast library of texts concerning prayer written

---

[17]Generously scaled discussions of their life and doctrine can be found in A. Di Berardino, ed., *The Encyclopedia of Ancient Christianity* (Downers Grove, IL: InterVarsity Press, 2014); or the classic multivolume reference work, *Dictionnaire de Spiritualité ascétique et mystique* (Paris: Beauchesne, 1933–). A smaller introduction can be found in J. A. McGuckin, *Standing in God's Holy Fire* (London: Darton, Longman, and Todd, 2001).

by these early monastics. It is today called ascetical literature, and the great interest in its rediscovery over recent generations past has led to the issuing of many of these seminal texts in English for the first time in more than a millennium and a half.

One notable thing about the Egyptian desert teachings on prayer is their immediacy and simplicity. They often do not state their own obvious contexts, which is why it is useful to remind ourselves of them and not simply lift the words out of place, as collections of spiritual writings (*florilegia*) in popularly available spiritual books often do. To begin with, these instructions are those of ancient schools. In other words, they are issued to small groups of immediate and intimate disciples who are constantly under the eye of a master who has considerable authority over his charges. They are not issued as if they were Sunday homilies, take it or leave it. They belong, therefore, to the genre of practical instruction, rather than theoretical discussion. In addition to this, they belong to a closed circle of the family of those for whom they were designed—that is, small communities of celibates living hard, subsistence lives in desert conditions. Abstinence from sexual relations, hard physical labor, grueling external environments, and many hours each day spent in mental focus on transcendental concerns were all staples of such communities of monastics.

Even when monasticism moved away from deserts into more suburban conditions, and these teachings were still preserved as the monastic manuals of prayer, many of these conditions survived as the backdrop of all that was found to be relevant. This kind of prayer, therefore, is a desert dweller's prayer. In speaking of these matters to modern groups, I was struck one day by a respondent who said, "We still live in a desert, except the topography has changed a little." He meant that the relevance of the instructions endured; and doubtless that is why the literature was so faithfully copied and recopied across the centuries, a legacy that gave testimony to the utility of the corpus for hundred of generations of practitioners. Even so, most moderns, living busy lives in a city, going to work, raising children, negotiating intimate relationships, have to stretch their imagination to consider the direct (as opposed to symbolic) application of these norms of prayer that are being talked about in daily life. The desert monks would be expected to use prayer techniques to radically reorient processes of mental consciousness in ways we rarely encounter today outside contexts of radical therapy.

One common technique was known as *monologistos* prayer. It means taking a short phrase and extending it before the individual consciousness. A phrase from the Scripture or from a spiritual teacher would be selected (or given) to the monk, such things as "The Lord is my light and my salvation" (Ps 27:1), or "Love the Lord your God with all your heart" (Mt 22:37); but endless possibilities were possible, and the text chosen by the teacher was often one he or she thought was fitting to the present condition of the disciple. It became a custom in the desert to greet a spiritual master, as if expecting such instruction, with the words "Father, give me a word."[18] The monk was meant to take the "word" (*logion*) in its form, as either scriptural aphorism or short story of instruction (parable) from the master, and use it as mental reflection for the rest of the day. In other words, as they went on their daily tasks they kept turning this over and over in their minds. If it was a short phrase they repeated it many thousands of times, like a prayer or incantation.

Since the works that were encouraged in the Egyptian desert were predominantly of a simple physical nature (the weaving of baskets, gardening, cleaning, building), this repetition of a phrase for hours at a time, when the body was occupied with simple tasks, became a powerful tool for simultaneously charging and reorienting the human consciousness, focusing it, as it were, like a lens on the singleness of the idea of the presence of God.[19] Ancients, like us today, were well aware that our consciousness, especially at times of prayer, has the tendency to wander around aimlessly. One might begin prayer with an intention to be focused (recollected) but after very few minutes, the mind is making images for itself, and the attention is everywhere else except where it should be. *Monologistos* prayer was designed, therefore, to be the first stage in training for beginners.

The practice reflected the anthropology we have noticed earlier. The Christians regarded the body (with its physical impulses and needs), the soul (with its range of feelings and desires), and the *nous* (the spiritual intellect with its aspirations for God) as three intimately related realities. If the body was too hot, or sick, or agitated, none of the other two "ranges" or zones of human consciousness could operate independently. They would all be pulled down into the zone of dominance of the body. Usually the body was accustomed to be in charge of the human trifold reality, like the elder sister who had the driving license and took charge of the whole car and where it was going. The monks wanted the body to be put into the back seat. Physical drives toward sexuality, increase of wealth, and comfort had to be managed carefully in such a life, if they were not to completely derail the spiritual consciousness of the practitioners. The monks were nothing if not realists.

But how could bodily needs be controlled? Their answer was toward redirection. Fasting and hard labor were the primary manners they had to sustain chastity as singles, but it was harder to manage thoughts and physical desires. And in the

---

[18] See further D. Burton-Christie, *The Word in the Desert: Scripture and the Quest for Holiness in Early Christian Monasticism* (Oxford: Oxford University Press, 1993).

[19] Some monastic groups favored intellectual pursuits, seminar-like discussions and later text copying, but these were never the preponderance in Egypt, except in the circle around Evagrius.

hours of prayer when awareness was being raised, the monastics found that such things as physical attention and mind wandering had a tendency to raise a storm. This was one initial reason why the phrase had to be repeated so many hundreds of times. It stilled thought. There was no possibility to reason one's way out of the body's complaints that it was not getting enough attention from such a desert lifestyle. So the body was given the tasks of weaving with the hands, plowing the earth, while all the time the mind repeated a simple phrase sotto voce. If conflicting thoughts and distractions became unmanageable, the phrase was repeated aloud for some minutes until the order of things had been reestablished. So this was like a dethronement of the body as the chief of the "three sisters" that made up the ancients' tripartite psychology.

But the soul, too, was not a fully stable reality. The soul in antiquity was the zone of empathy, feelings, and intentions, and involved much of what we today would call thinking processes. Higher levels of reflection (ideals, metaphysics, theology) they located in the *nous*, which was the upper and most refined level of spiritual consciousness. It was in this second level of soul (*psyche*) consciousness (psychic, we could even say) that most thinking people lived habitually. Their prayer lives also were rooted here, and rarely, if ever, left the psychic domain to travel in the higher levels of noetic consciousness. And this was the intent of the *monologistos* prayer also: to quieten down the psyche by using the mental faculties to so focus on the words of the prayer phrase that it stopped its habitual processes of generating ideas and images associated with its words and thoughts. In other words, thoughts habitually generate thoughts. Words make more words. Using a single *monologistos* prayer was meant to kill words and thoughts by means of a single word and a single thought constantly returned to.

When the monk became aware that he or she had intellectually wandered away into daydreams or their own world of thoughts, they returned back, via the vocalized focus on the phrase and its meaning, to a state where thought and thought generation were stilled once more. The two noisier sisters in the house, as it were, had been given something to do (as if to shut them up) so that the quieter sister, the *nous*, might be coaxed out of retirement so as to come into the leadership role in prayer. The *nous* in this Christian anthropology was understood as the higher functions of human thought, namely terms of awareness of metaphysical order and, for the monks especially, the sense of transcendent presence: the monk's presence before God, and God's presence to the monk.

It was this sense of "being in the presence" that all monastic theory of prayer looked to. The *monologistos* phrase was a means to this end: so to still the agitations of the body and the soul that the human *nous* could sustain moments of being aware of the presence in a pure and unmediated way. It was not that the monks despised vocal prayer or meditation on the scriptural texts; they knew these had their place and often rotated forms of prayer with many times of scriptural reading and recitation of the Psalms. It was just that they knew that prayer consisted chiefly of standing in the presence of their God: an active, living presence, as real to them now as he was to prophets and apostles of old. But to stand for more than an instant in this noetic awareness was immensely difficult for a human being. Bodily awareness and soul awareness are like unruly children, demanding so much attention because for the great majority of their lives and histories the monks had lived in these domains most of the time, as had most other people. They had to learn first of all how to access noetic awareness, and then once attaining to it, how to abide in it. This was the "prayer of the heart" in real, sustained, practice.

One of the most favored forms of *monologistos* prayer evolved from the New Testament came also to be known as the Jesus prayer. It has endured as a major form of Christian mysticism in the Eastern monasteries to this day. The *Philokalia* tradition (a compendium of the eighteenth century dedicated to reproducing these patristic teachings on prayer) is dedicated to it.[20] The Jesus prayer adopted as the basis of its monologistic recitation a conflation of two Jesus events: the episode of the blind man on the road from Jericho to Jerusalem who "cried out" (a type of successful prayer), and the parable of the Pharisee and the tax collector in the temple (where Jesus gave a "word" about the character of true prayer; Lk 18:10-14; Mk 10:46-52). The stories offer up the first and second parts of the Jesus prayer, which digests and summates them: "Lord Jesus Christ, Son of God, have mercy on me, a sinner." The monks regarded this as a summation of the gospel itself: a way of praying the whole gospel in one sentence. They advocated the repetition of this many hundreds of times a day to retrain the consciousness toward noetic capacity of the divine presence.

The arrival at the awareness was a state where the prayer would lapse into silence, even though it would mentally continue in order to keep the body and soul in stasis, as it were, but if attention lapsed the prayer would be resumed vocally until spiritual order was reestablished. In saying the prayer at first aloud, then after many times making it sotto voce, the first half of the phrase was instructed to be recited in the

---

[20]See G. Palmer, et al., eds., *The Philokalia*, vol. 1 (London: Faber, 1983). See further J. A. McGuckin, "The Making of the Philokalia: A Tale of Monks and Manuscripts," in *The Philokalia*, ed. B. Bingaman and B. Nassif (Oxford: Oxford University Press, 2012), 36-49; McGuckin, "Rasskaz Strannika: The Candid Tale of a Pilgrim to His Spiritual Father," in *Contemplative Literature: A Comparative Sourcebook on Meditation and Contemplative Prayer*, ed. L. J. Komjathy (Albany: SUNY Press, 2014); McGuckin, "St. Paisius Velichovsky: 1722–1794. An Early Modern Master of the Orthodox Spiritual Life," *Spiritus* 9, no. 2 (2009): 157-73.

in breath (breathing in the holy name, as it were) and the second part on the out breath, exhaling the symbol of evil along with the prayer for mercy. The breathing itself was regulated and slowed a little, so as to aid quietness (*hesychia*). This focus on mental quietness gave many monastics attached to this spiritual movement, in later times, the name *Hesychasts*.[21]

The Egyptian teachers themselves were able to describe all of this (complex as it might seem to us who are not practicing it too much of the time) in lapidary and simple manners. Antony the Great, one of the first major monastic teachers, put it this way: "The Abba Antony said this: Whoever sits in solitude and is quiet has escaped from three wars, those of hearing, speaking and seeing. Yet against one thing shall the monk never cease to wage war: his own heart."[22] John Climacus, the abbot of Sinai monastery in the seventh century, was a strong advocate of monologistic prayer.[23] He drew the connection between it and how the process would bring attentiveness (*prosoche*) to the soul of the monastic in training. Again, with simple, graphic images he makes this into very approachable didactic material: "Be concentrated without self-display, withdrawn into your heart. For the demons fear concentration as much as thieves fear dogs."[24]

Another early masters of the spiritual life was Diadochus, who became bishop of Photike in Greece in the fifth century. He demonstrates the close interconnection between the doctrine of the heart and the practice of monologistic prayer. He argues that since the Christian's interior heart is the image of God, then the observation of the heart is like looking into a divinely placed mirror. This is the first step toward a living, divine encounter. But the fall has darkened the mirror, corrupted its facility for clear reflection: "And after the fall," he says,

> it became hard for the human *nous* to remember God or his commandments. We should, therefore, always be looking into the depths of our heart, with continual remembrance of God, and should pass through this deceitful life like people who have lost their (outward) sight . . . because the person who dwells continually within the heart is detached from the attractions of this world, and such a person lives in the Spirit and becomes ignorant of the desires of the flesh.[25]

---

[21] See further J. A. McGuckin, *The Orthodox Church: An Introduction to Its History, Doctrine and Spiritual Culture* (Oxford: Wiley-Blackwell, 2011), 346-52.

[22] *The Sayings of the Fathers* (*Vitae Patrum*) 5.2.2, trans. H. Waddell, *The Desert Fathers* (Oxford: Sheed and Ward, 1936), 81.

[23] See further D. Chitty, *The Desert a City* (Oxford: Blackwell, 1966), 170-75. Climacus's chief text is available in C. Luibheid and N. Russell, trans., *John Climacus: The Ladder of Divine Ascent*, Classics of Western Spirituality (New York: Paulist, 1982).

[24] John Climacus, *The Ladder of Divine Ascent* 7.15.

[25] Diadochus, *On Spiritual Knowledge* 56-57, in *Philokalia*, ed. G. Palmer, P. Sherrard, and K. Ware (London: Faber and Faber, 1979), 1:269-70.

For Diadochus, the heart is a source of the knowledge of God, which needs attentive introspection (*prosoche*) to cause the spring of divine love to flow out despite the passions that tend to distract it: "Whenever we fervently remember God we feel the divine longing well up within us, from the very depths of the heart."[26] And this work of spiritual regeneration is the Spirit's salvific grace, a work of the Lord from start to end: "The communion of the Holy Spirit brings this about within us, for unless his divinity actively illuminates the inner shrine of our heart, we shall not be able to taste God's goodness with the perceptive faculty undivided."[27] He constantly returns to the core doctrine that the ascetic must seek to dwell within this sacred shrine, or temple, of the heart, focusing its attentive awareness like a worshiper waiting for the epiphany of the Lord, and using the invocation of the holy name of Jesus (the Jesus prayer) to achieve this until the light of God's revelation breaks forth.

Diadochus was a careful reader of the great fourth-century philosopher-monk Evagrius and popularized some of his more esoteric doctrines of prayer. One of those influences Diadochus demonstrates when he talks of how the soul of the person advanced in prayer becomes luminous. When he speaks this way about the light that is sometimes revealed to the attentive heart having its own luminosity, he does not seem to be speaking merely symbolically. He argues that this is a luminosity it possesses exactly insofar as it becomes the renewed and cleansed icon of the "true image of God," who is the Logos, the archetypal Creator of the soul:

> it is written that none can say Jesus is Lord except in the Holy Spirit (1 Cor 12:3). Let the spiritual intellect, then, continually concentrate on these words within its inner shrine, with such intensity that it is not turned aside to any mental images. Those who meditate unceasingly upon this glorious and holy name in the depths of their heart, can sometimes see the luminosity of their own intellect. For when the mind is closely concentrated upon this name, then we grow fully conscious that the Name is burning off all the filth that covers the surface of the soul.[28]

Prayer, for the ascetics, was regarded as one of the most important moral cleansers of the soul, one of the key aspects of keeping the entire ascetical philosophy and lifestyle on the rails. One of the tales of the desert masters recounts how a disciple once complained to his teacher that his prayer life was getting nowhere: just pointless repetitions day after day and no results to speak of. The master told the disciple to leave the cave and walk a mile or so to the spring and get water. But he gave him a worn-out and filthy wicker basket in which to do it. After walking all the way and

---

[26]Diadochus, *On Spiritual Knowledge* 78; *Philokalia* 1:280.
[27]Diadochus, *On Spiritual Knowledge* 29; *Philokalia* 1:261.
[28]Diadochus, *On Spiritual Knowledge* 59; *Philokalia* 1:270.

back, the water had leaked out entirely. The old man sent him back for water several times without comment, and always the same result.[29] Eventually the young monk lost his patience and complained that the whole thing was ridiculous. His obedience of the water trip was foolish, his work was pointless. This, of course, was a parabolic trope of his previously vocalized spiritual attitudes toward his new vocation in the desert. The old man then quizzed him. "Do you see anything you have accomplished? Do you see any difference at all?" The young monk puzzled about it and then said: "No, the only thing that is different is that the basket is now shining and clean." And the master replied to him, "That is the point with prayer. Keep at it." Prayer was itself the greatest askesis in the desert. It was the battleground where the heart was brought into true obedience to God, rendered clean and bright.

## SYRIAC CHRISTIAN TRADITION ON THE PRAYER OF THE HEART

While monastic asceticism was developing in Egypt in its characteristic ways, the ecclesial life of Syria continued its own stress on asceticism, not least through the ancient tradition celebrated there of the communities of *ihidaya*, the single-minded (and celibate ones) who had dedicated their life in virginity to the Lord. These ascetics often lived in smaller communities near the local church and were from the beginning more closely integrated into the urban life of the churches in Syria. The Semitic syntax of their language gave the Syrian Christians, from the outset, a profound awareness of biblical idiom, and there the doctrine of the heart standing in prayer before God was carried on from pure biblical sources in a very dynamic manner. The Syriac writers, by the time of the late fourth century onward, had fused within their literary and theological traditions a deeply biblical spirituality with advanced Greek rhetorical forms.

Some of the Syrian spiritual writers after the time of Mar Ephrem would be critically important in forming the later Greek Byzantine spiritual synthesis. The rediscovery of the writings of the Syrian masters in the late twentieth century has given a major impetus to spiritual theological enquiry in our time. Translation was the key to this. Syriac scholars such as Robert Murray, Sebastian Brock, Susan Ashbrook-Harvey, Kathleen McVey, and David Miller undertook the patient labor needed to make the Syrian spiritual writings available in English, giving them, undoubtedly, their largest ever exposure in the history of the church and at the same time demonstrating their profound importance for a more balanced understanding of Christian origins.[30]

---

[29]The teacher monks were called "old man" (*geron*) or Father (Abba), titles that have survived to this day in the church for its clergy and monastics.
[30]So Sebastian Brock begins his study "The Prayer of the Heart in Syriac Tradition," *Sobornost* 4, no. 2 (1982): 131-42, to which I am indebted here.

Early fourth-century Syriac writer Aphrahat the Persian Sage is (after Origen) the first person to have written specifically about prayer in Christian tradition.[31] He interprets the words of Christ about praying with the door of one's chamber closed shut (Mt 6:6) to refer to wordless prayer in the sacred chamber of the heart. The first of the mysteries to take place in the divine encounter is the purification of the creature to be fit for theophanic encounter with the Lord.[32] The passage synthesizes in a wonderfully rich liturgical manner the most profound of the biblical themes:

> Our Lord's words tell us to pray in secret, that is in your heart, and to shut the door. What is this door he says we must shut, if not the mouth? For here is the temple in which Christ dwells, just as the Apostle said: "You are the temple of the Lord." And Christ comes to enter into your inner self, into this house, to cleanse it from everything that is unclean, while the door (that is your mouth) is closed shut.[33]

For Aphrahat the heart is the new temple of the Lord's presence, and as such it is the place where the true spiritual sacrifice spoken of by the Scripture is to be offered.[34] The liturgical and sacral concept is why Aphrahat stresses so much the need for purity of heart. The sacrifices offered from a cultically impure site, as the Scripture taught, will not be acceptable in the eyes of God, so now that prayer is the new Christian sacrifice, the heart itself must be rendered pure so that the sacrifice will be acceptable.[35] If the sacrificial offering and the priest who offers it are pure, only then, Aphrahat says, will fire descend from heaven to consume the offerings.[36] For Aphrahat the beginning of pure prayer is the raising of the heart like a liturgical-eucharistic anaphora:

> As I urged you above, the moment you start praying, raise your heart upwards and turn your eyes downward. Enter inside your inner self and pray in secret to your heavenly Father. All this I have written to you on the subject of prayer: how it is heard when it is pure, and not heard when it is not pure.... You who pray should remember that you

---

[31] Origen, *De Oratione*. English trans., J. J. O'Meara, *Origen of Alexandria: On Prayer and The Exhortation to Martyrdom*, Ancient Christian Writers 19 (Westminster, MD: Newman Press, 1954). Aphrahat takes the general lines of the allegorical reading of heart standing for the "secret (bridal) chamber" from Origen.

[32] "Purity of heart constitutes prayer more than do all the prayers that are uttered aloud. And silence united to the mind that is sincere is better than the loud voice of someone crying aloud." Aphrahat, *Demonstration* 4.1.

[33] Ibid., 4.10. *Patrologia Syriaca* 1.157-60. English trans. in S. Brock, *The Syriac Fathers on Prayer and the Spiritual Life* (Kalamazoo, MI: Cistercian Publications, 1987).

[34] Cf. Mal 1:10-11; Ps 140:2; Ben Sira 32 (35).8.

[35] The same idea is taught in Isaac of Nineveh, *Discourse* 22. Text in Brock, *Syriac Fathers on Prayer and the Spiritual Life*, 256-57. Sahdona in his *Book of Perfection* also develops much on the idea of spiritual sacrifice from the altar of the heart.

[36] He is thinking about 1 Kings 18:38; 1 Chron 21:26; cf. also Lk 12:49. Cf. Aphrahat, *Demonstration* 4.2-3 (Brock, *Syriac Fathers on Prayer and the Spiritual Life*, 6-8).

are making an offering before God. Let not Gabriel who presents the prayers be ashamed by an offering that has a blemish.[37]

The prayer of the heart, for him, is quintessentially the inner condition of a spirit attuned to God: "Realise that the person who is bound up in Our Lord and ponders on Him continuously, possesses hidden prayer of the heart. Let us pray with our body as well as with our heart, just as Jesus prayed and blessed in the body and in the spirit."[38] The idea will be further developed in later Syriac writers such as the seventh-century Sahdona. By this time the concept of watchfulness (*prosoche*) and penitent sorrow (*penthos*) are more evidently to the fore in the spiritual literature.[39] The monk is expected to be the "gladsome mourner." Sadhona teaches that the heart is the place of true sacrifice, an altar area that must be kept pure so that God will accept the sacrifice that rises from it. Only if prayer rises like incense (Ps 141:2) from a pure heart, deeply conscious of the Presence, will it be true prayer. Some of his texts are in the reader following.

In the late fourth century, another great Syrian teacher of the spiritual life was operative. He composed in Greek and was connected in some way with the Cappadocian circle of monastics. Gregory Nyssa knew and used his writing. His real name is unknown, but the works (certainly adapted and emended in later times) were later attributed to the Egyptian Abba Macarius and so came down in the tradition under that pseudonym.[40] He is now commonly called Pseudo-Macarius.[41] For this Macarius, the landscape of the heart is an apocalyptic arena:

> The heart itself is but a small vessel, yet dragons are there, and there are also lions; there are poisonous beasts and all the treasures of evil. There are rough and uneven roads;

---

[37] Aphrahat, *Demonstration* 4.13 (Brock, *Syriac Fathers on Prayer and the Spiritual Life*, 17-18).

[38] *Book of Steps* (*Liber Graduum*). English trans. in Brock, *Syriac Fathers on Prayer and the Spiritual Life*, 45.

[39] See further I. Hausherr, *Penthos: The Doctrine of Compunction in the Christian East*, Cistercian Studies 53 (Kalamazoo: Cistercian Publications, 1982).

[40] Some scholars have recognized him as Symeon of Mesopotamia, but the identification is speculative. It was thought that he had originally been part of the "Messalian" movement, which was condemned at various times, including finally at Ephesus 431, for objectionable doctrines relating to spiritual "enthusiasm" (wishing only to pray and not to work; believing that demons inhabited souls even after baptism and had to be exorcised by constant prayer; resisting the governance of local bishops by their nomadic monastic communities; teaching the necessity of radical *encrateia* for all Christians). Recent scholarship has tended to show that Pseudo-Macarius is, in fact, from the outset a restraining influence on these Syrian-Greek religious tendencies. He does prioritize the need for spiritual experience but moderates many of the recognizable "Messalian" characteristics in the warp and woof of his doctrine (not just in an editorially "corrected" text by way of excisions). Cf. C. Stewart, *Working the Earth of the Heart* (Oxford, Oxford University Press, 1991); S. Burns, "Charisma and Spirituality in the Early Church: A Study of Messalianism and Ps. Macarius," PhD diss., Leeds University, 1999.

[41] We shall dispense with the "pseudo" in what follows.

there are precipices; but there too is God, the angels, life and the Kingdom, light and the apostles, the heavenly cities and treasures of grace. All things are within it.[42]

In this same *Spiritual Homily* 43 Macarius gives a taxonomy of the heart in regard to a human's interior spiritual condition. His theology, despite the constant stress that the heart is prey to demonic influences (temptations), remains optimistic and in accord with the main patristic tradition of the enduring force of the image of God within humanity. Christ, he says, has illuminated the human heart like a torch, and in the communion of his light the nature of the church as a sacrament of Christ is revealed:

> As many torches and burning lamps are lit from a fire, though the lamps and torches are lit and shine from one nature, so too is it that Christians are enkindled and shine from one nature; namely the divine fire, the Son of God, and they have their lamps burning in their hearts, and they shine before Him while they live on earth, just as He did. This is what it means when it says: So God has anointed you with the oil of gladness (Ps. 45.7).[43]

As the Spirit of God illumined Christ's humanity, and set his heart on fire, so too Macarius says, it is the case with the true disciple, otherwise the spiritual life counts for nothing:

> If the lamp of a Christian is not enkindled from the light of the Godhead within them, then they are nothing. The Lord was that "burning lamp" (Jn. 5.35) by means of the Spirit of the Godhead which dwelt substantially in Him, and set his heart on fire, according to the humanity. Consider this image: a dirty old pouch filled with pearls inside. So too Christians in the exterior person ought to be humble and of lowly esteem while, interiorly, in the inner self, they possess the "pearl of great price" (Mt. 13.46).[44]

Macarius constantly urges spiritual vigilance as the foundation of the life of prayer. This is what he calls "working the earth of the heart" like a farmer.[45] Vigilance (*prosoche*) is required for the heart, just like a gardener in an orchard that is bordered by a river whose waters can wash away the foundations if care is not taken. This is why he advocates the practice of "constant prayer." The demonic forces that can corrupt the inner self will have no force over a disciple whose heart is founded in

---

[42]Macarius, *Homily* 43.7 (trans. in G. A. Maloney, trans., *Pseudo Macarius: The Fifty Spiritual Homilies and the Great Letter*, Classics of Western Spirituality [Mahwah, NJ: Paulist, 1992], 222).
[43]Macarius, *Homily* 43.1 (Maloney, *Pseudo Macarius*, 219).
[44]Macarius, *Homily* 43.2 (Maloney, *Pseudo Macarius*, 219).
[45]A phrase Columba Stewart has taken in his fine study of the spiritual themes of this school, *Working the Earth of the Heart*.

the grace of the indwelling Spirit, for constant prayer burns them up like wax in a fire, but should carelessness leave the heart unguarded, spiritual disasters occur:[46]

> Take the example of a garden having fruit-bearing trees and other sweet-scented plants in which all is beautifully laid out. It also has a small wall before a ditch to protect it. . . . But should a fast-flowing river pass that way, even if only a little of the water dashes against the wall, it tears away the foundation. . . . It enters and . . . destroys the entire cultivation. So it is with the heart of a person. It has the good thoughts but the rivers of evil are always flowing near the heart, seeking to bring it down.[47]

Macarius seems to envisage the constant warfare giving way to progressive stages of stability: at first the heart is constantly hostage to evil thoughts and influences within it, but then its turning to the Lord and advances in the spiritual life make the presence of the divine Spirit more and more perceptible to the Christian. This growing purity of the heart invites Christ to take up his dwelling within, like a king establishing his kingdom.[48] It was in this aspect of his doctrine, the sense of God's movement to take command of the heart, that Macarius was to have his greatest influence over the later Byzantine teachers of the early medieval period. When combined with Evagrius's and Diadochus's suggestion that the purified heart can sometimes see its own spiritual luminosity, and added to the Syrian fathers' stress on the purity of heart that leads to divine theophany, all the materials for the later Byzantine Hesychast doctrine of prayer (and its distinctive theology of revelation)[49] are in place, waiting for their resolution.[50] It is a process that begins with renewed vigor in late tenth-century Byzantium with its monastic reform movements and a newly invigorated pneumatology, such as can be perfectly seen in the writings of Symeon the New Theologian.[51]

The Syrian writers' recurring stress on spiritual attentiveness is closely comparable to the celebrated image of fourth-century Syrian poet-theologian Ephrem the Syrian in regard to the learning of prayer, when he likened God's patience in teaching creatures

---

[46] Macarius, *Homily* 43.3 (Maloney, *Pseudo Macarius*, 220).
[47] Macarius, *Homily* 43.6 (Maloney, *Pseudo Macarius*, 221).
[48] Macarius, *Homily* 43.6 (Maloney, *Pseudo Macarius*, 221).
[49] See further J. A. McGuckin, *The Book of Mystical Chapters: Meditations on the Soul's Ascent from the Desert Fathers and Other Early Christian Contemplatives* (Boston: Shambhala Press, 2002); *Standing in God's Holy Fire: The Spiritual Tradition of Byzantium* (London: Darton, Longman, & Todd, 2001).
[50] "When the *Nous* has divested itself of its fallen state and clothed itself with the state of grace, then in the time of prayer it can even see its own inner condition, which is something like sapphire, or the azure blue of the sky. It is what scripture calls the dwelling place of God which the elders saw on Mount Sinai." Evagrius, *On Discrimination*, in Palmer, *Philokalia*, 1:54.
[51] See J. A. McGuckin, "St. Symeon the New Theologian and Byzantine Monasticism," in *Mount Athos & Byzantine Monasticism*, ed. A. Bryer (Aldershot, UK: Variorum Press, 1996), 17-35; "A Neglected Masterpiece of the Christian Mystical Tradition: The Hymns of Divine Eros by the Byzantine Poet Symeon the New Theologian (949–1022)," *Spiritus* 5 (2005): 182-202.

to be aware of him to a man trying to teach a parrot to speak and using a mirror to fool it into thinking it was chatting with another bird.[52] Even so, this language was something that did not come naturally. Only the squawk arose spontaneously, but the gracious discourse with God was, even at its heights of achievement, something laughable, and yet touchingly wonderful too: awesome in what it revealed of the patient, attentive care bestowed on the dumb animal by an ineffably transcendent power who had compassion on the creature's weakness. The parrot's primary problem in learning this strange syntax was its lack of attentiveness, like the soul's lack of awareness of the divine milieu to which it was being summoned by the Presence. In wandering away from the sense of that presence time after time, its failed in its task. On the occasions when it learned by heart, or rather from the heart, it was capable of addressing its master: for in that moment it saw its Lord face-to-face, just as a human does when the heart dares to lift itself up in the presence of the Holy One, and, at that moment, is in the full conscience of his presence. Ephrem, however, normally uses the concepts of the illumination of the mind by God, or the seeing of the soul (*nephesh*) of the human being under the gaze of God.[53] The heart under the eye of God is not a primary symbol of his theology, and he does not develop on it in any relation to prayer.

It is certainly otherwise with Mar Isaac of Nineveh, the seventh-century Syrian teacher.[54] Isaac lays high stress on the essential requirement of purity of heart in the person desiring true prayer. Isaac was a highly influential figure in the history of spirituality. In his own reading and exquisitely written teachings he followed further the lead of Macarius toward combining many of the Evagrian ideas about the ascent of the *nous* into imageless prayer, with the more biblically rooted Syrian doctrine of the pure heart.[55] Evagrius laid great stress on the doctrine that if a soul

---

[52] Mar Ephrem of Nisibis (c. 306–373), *Hymns on Faith* 31.
[53] On the illumination of the mind, see, for example, *Hymn on the Nativity* 13.8. "The mind wanders among your attributes, O rich one. Copious inner chambers." In Ephrem the Syrian, *Hymns*, trans. K. McVey (New York: Paulist, 1989), 138. On the soul of the human under the gaze of God, see *Hymn on the Nativity* 14.6. "You are a son of the poor; know what is in the spirit of each of the poor." In McVey, *Hymns*, 142.
[54] Mar Isaac (d. circa 700) came from Qatar and was a monk at the monastery of Beth Abe in Kurdistan. He was consecrated bishop of Nineveh by the catholicos of the church of the East, but (whether from opposition he encountered or a desire for a life of solitude) he retired to live the solitary life in Khuzistan (Iran) shortly afterward. Becoming blind in his old age, he moved to the monastery of Rabban Shabur. Here at the end of his life he edited his spiritual teachings in the form of the *Ascetical Homilies*. These have been given a splendid modern translation and edition by Fr. Mamas (D. Miller) of the Holy Transfiguration Monastery in Brookline (Boston: Transfiguration Monastery Press, 1984). This edition has been used here, with some adaptations of the translation.
[55] The vivid personality of this spiritual master emerges on every page: "Often when I was writing these things my fingers failed me in setting down all onto paper; they were unable to endure the sweetness that descended into my heart and silenced my senses." *Ascetical Homilies* 62 (Miller, 297-98).

wished to approach to the formless God in prayer, it must banish all reliance on material imagery from its imagination. Such prayer would be formless, wordless, imageless: apophatic in character, befitting the God who surpassed all human reckoning. This synthesis of imageless prayer and heart-centered prayer, where the noetic language was fused with affective spiritual language in a way that subsumed the one into the other, had a profound effect by the fifth century on harmonizing the diverse spiritual traditions of the East.

Isaac was aided in this work by the fact that the Syrian translation that had been made of Evagrius's works in the late fifth century had already suppressed many of the objectionable metaphysical elements about the fall of preexistent noetic realities into materiality. It is quite revealing to read the Evagrius that Syrian theologians would have known. Apart from the "corrected" *Kephalaia on Prayer* (for which the original Greek still survives), the *Admonition on Prayer* attributed to Evagrius circulated widely. This latter text is only extant now in Syriac. It is a world away from Evagrius the speculative thinker and presents to us a clear and practical discourse on the need for purity of heart, repentance, and patient perseverance. The *Admonition* has remarkably "Syrian" attitudes to the purity of heart that produces the vision of God: "Allow the Spirit of God to dwell within you; then in His love He will come and make a habitation with you. He will reside in you and live in you. If your heart is pure, you will see Him, and He will sow in you the good seed of reflection upon His actions, and wonder at His majesty."[56]

Isaac had a great impact not only in his own era and region, but also in the ninth century, when he was translated into Greek at the monastery of Mar Saba and thence introduced to Byzantium, a cultural and religious center now destined (after the fall of the Syrian and Egyptian cradles of Christianity to Islamic domination) to become the disseminator of all monastic ascetical teachings through the Eastern Christian world.

Isaac too insists that the single-mindedness required for true prayer is profoundly simple, but apocalyptic in its extent and correspondingly awesome for those who grasp the implications:

> Purity of mind is one thing and purity of heart is another, just as a limb differs from the whole body. Now the mind is one of the senses of the soul, but the heart is what contains and holds the inner senses. It is the sense of senses, that is their root. But if the root is holy, then the branches are holy. But this is not the case if it is just one of the branches which is sanctified.[57] Now if the mind, on the one hand, is a little diligent in reading the divine scriptures, and toils a little in fasting, vigil, and stillness, it will

---

[56] Text in Brock, *Syriac Fathers on Prayer and the Spiritual Life*, 66-73.
[57] Greek: "If the heart is purified then all the senses are evidently purified."

forget its former activity and become pure, as long as it abstains from alien concerns. Even so its purity is not permanent, for just as it is quickly cleansed, so too it is quickly soiled. But the heart, on the other hand, is only made pure by many afflictions, deprivations, separation from all fellowship with the world, and deadness to all things. Once it is purified, however, its purity is not soiled by little things, nor is it dismayed by great and open conflicts.[58]

Closely allied to this notion of purification is the term that recurs often in Syriac writers—illumination of the heart that produces pure prayer or "limpid" or "lucid" prayer, as it is designated in the Syriac texts. Brock notes how the origin of this tradition is probably the Jewish Targum of Genesis, discussing the sacrifice of Isaac (Gen 22). The spiritual perfection of the two patriarchs is described by the term "lucidity of heart."[59] The ideas of purity are, for the first time, associated with the concept of transfigured radiance: luminosity. Isaac connects the purity of heart with radiant capacity for the vision of God, which we could, in this instance, best understand in terms of the awareness of the Presence.

The connection is not propounded as an abnormal or extraordinary condition of ecstatic envisioning.[60] It is taught, by Isaac, as the gift of God to those who are pure in heart, for in them the kingdom of heaven dwells: "Behold, heaven is within you (if you are indeed pure) and within it you will see the angels in their light and their Master with them, and in them."[61] This, like most of the other Syrian teachings on the vision of light is in form a midrashic exegesis of the promise to the pure of heart that Jesus made in the Beatitudes.[62] The luminous vision rises from the guarding of the heart. They are arguing that once the heart is cleansed of the turmoils of the passions, it assumes the limpid condition God destined for it both in its original making and in its remaking through Christ.

Like Macarius, Isaac teaches that the revelation of the presence of God within the heart produces an inevitable sensation (*aisthesis*).[63] The heart and the vision of the mind are inextricably linked in Isaac. The heart sees the presence intellectively and feels it empathetically:

---

[58] *Ascetical Homily* 3 (Miller, 21).
[59] *Shafyut lebba*: Brock, *Syriac Fathers on Prayer and the Spiritual Life*, 135-36.
[60] The nature of a human creature is, in its deepest essence, a sacramental mystery of divine communion. The mystery has been renewed in the incarnation of the Word and is destined to be fully revealed in the next age, but even while on earth the human heart and intellect, if it sees God in a purified state, has a "hypostatic theoria" that results "from its primordial condition" Cf. Isaac, *Homily* 43 (Miller, 214).
[61] *Ascetical Homilies* 15 (Miller, 84).
[62] Connected here with Lk 17:21. *Midrash* is an extended form of literary commentary on Scripture.
[63] In *Ascetical Homilies* 68, Isaac gives a taxonomy of spiritual sensation (*aesthesis pneumatike*) prefiguring the later Byzantine hesychast teachers. Miller, 332-33.

> The love of God is fiery by nature and when it descends in an extraordinary degree on to a person it throws that soul into ecstasy. And so, the heart of the person who has experienced this love cannot contain it or endure it without unusual changes being seen . . . the face becomes lit up, full of joy; the body becomes heated; fear and shame depart from such a person who thus becomes like an ecstatic. . . . The gaze of this person's intellect is fixed inseparably and deliriously upon Him. Though he is distant he speaks with Him as one who is near at hand. . . . This vision is natural, but inaccessible to sense-perception. In his actions as well as in his appearance, such a one is enflamed. . . . This is the spiritual passion which inebriated[64] the apostles and martyrs.[65]

These affective movements of the heart, however, are not the goal of pure prayer. If the heart is taken away by fervor and moves too freely (that is, moves without a certain character of stillness, or spiritual affliction) then it is a sign of fervor, certainly, but also an indication for Isaac that the spiritual intellect has not yet understood the light that is surrounding it: "If the heart flows out smoothly and abundantly, with long, drawn out prayer, combined with intensity of diverse stirrings, then this is a sign of fervour; it is also an indication that the mind has not yet become aware of the light contained in the words, nor yet received experience of the knowledge which illumines the inner eye during the time of prayer."[66]

For Isaac, compassion is the preeminent sign of lucidity and purity of heart:

> Let this be for you a luminous sign that your soul has reached limpid purity: when after thoroughly testing yourself, you find that you are full of mercy for all humankind, and that your heart is afflicted by the intensity of your pity for people, and burns like a fire, without making distinctions between people. By this, when it constantly occurs, the image of the heavenly Father will be seen in you.[67]

This connection of the purified heart and the lucidity in which God confers the divine communion is a theme that occupies much of the subsequent Syrian tradition. It marks the essential and intimate connection that all the Christian writers see between prayer and the inner, moral state of the soul. As God is holy, and essentially so, so too prayer requires advancing purity of heart in all those who approach to the divine presence in prayer. This aspect makes early Christian teaching on prayer as much an ethical construct as a theological one. The great stress that Christian teachers on prayer also laid on the use of Scripture (entering into the treasury of Scripture formed, as it were, the syntax of prayer) made the literature on prayer very

---

[64] The Syrian spiritual masters often call the ecstasy that arises in prayer "drunken sobriety."
[65] *Ascetical homilies* 35 (Miller, 158).
[66] Isaac of Nineveh, *Centuries on Knowledge* 4.67. Brock, *Syriac Fathers on Prayer and the Spiritual Life*, 269.
[67] *Ascetical Homilies* (Miller, 392).

close to scriptural exegesis and kept the practice of exegesis always close to the center of most ancient Christian writing: certainly a deep commitment of the monastic movement at all times, whose writings are predominantly and extensively given over the mystical themes. Ascetics would formally recite the Psalter in its entirely once a week, and in Lent twice a week. No ascetic in the early church could be ordained bishop without being able to recite the Psalter by heart. Such immersion in the mind and the world of Scripture tied in the life of prayer to the foundational biblical record, not only in the formal liturgical ceremonies of the church but also in the private lives of the praying believers.

Prayer in this sense, therefore, is the secret tradition of Christianity. Some call it its hidden interior soul. The Greek word for that which is secret and not spoken of publicly is *mystikos*, and eventually the concept of mysticism rose from this. What it meant in antiquity was not so much the raptures and revelations that this term came to signify after the high Middle Ages, but, as we have seen, in the early level of the literature, a deep sense of interior, private dedication to reform one's life and seek after the face of God in a serious manner. This close attention to the inner workings of the *psyche* and the *nous* made this desert literature the real foundations of Western psychology: centuries before the twentieth-century theorists returned to the notion so fruitfully in our own time. Indeed, many of the desert masters, such as Evagrius with his analysis of the various states of despondency that can afflict the human mind, clearly understood the affinity between introspection for reasons of devotion and for the requirements of therapy. This ancient doctrine of prayer is, in many respects, a treasure of the Christian tradition still waiting to be discovered. I have compiled a beginner's compendium of texts for those interested, and the short reader following will demonstrate not only the profundity of this (extensive) material, but also how elegant, useful, and approachable these ancient materials can still be.[68]

## A SHORT READER

***Gospel of Matthew 6:5-15 (first century).*** And when you pray, you must not be like the hypocrites, for they love to stand and pray in the synagogues and at the street corners, that they may be seen by men. Truly, I say to you, they have received their reward. Rather, when you pray, go into your room and shut the door and pray to your Father who is in secret; and your Father who sees in secret will reward you. And when you pray, do not pile up empty phrases like the Gentiles do, for they think that they will be heard on account of their many words. Do not be like them, for your Father knows what you need before you ask him. Pray then

---

[68]McGuckin, *Book of Mystical Chapters*.

in this way: Our Father in heaven, hallowed be your name. Your kingdom come. Your will be done, on earth as it is in heaven. Give us this day our daily bread; and forgive us our debts, as we also have forgiven our debtors; and lead us not into temptation,[69] but deliver us from the evil one. For if you forgive people their trespasses, your heavenly Father also will forgive you; but if you do not forgive people their trespasses, neither will your Father forgive your trespasses.

***Abba Ammonas of Skete,*** **Third Letter of Ammonas *(fourth century).***[70]
I write to you as to those who love God and seek Him with all your heart. For God will listen to such when they pray, and will bless them in all things, and will grant all the requests of their soul when they entreat Him. But those who do not come to Him with all their heart, and are rather in two minds, who perform their works so as to be glorified by men—then such as these will not be listened to by God in anything that they ask Him. God gives them none of the requests that they ask of Him, but rather resists them. For they do not their works in faith, but superficially. Therefore, the divine power does not dwell in them, but they are diseased in all their works, in whatever they set their hand to. For this reason they have not known the power of grace, nor its freedom from care, nor its joy, but their soul is weighed down with a load in all their works. The greater part of our generation are such. They have not received the divine power that fattens the soul, prepares it to rejoice, and brings it day by day that gladness which makes the heart fervent in God.[71]

***John of Apamea (or John the Solitary),*** **Letter to Hesychius *65 (fifth century).***
When you stand in prayer before God, take care that your mind is recollected. Push aside any distracting thoughts so as to feel in your soul the true weight of the glory.[72] Purify the movements of your thoughts. If you have to struggle with them, be persistent in your struggle, and do not give up. When God sees your persistence then all of a sudden grace will dawn in you and your mind will find strength as your heart begins to burn with fervour, and your soul's thoughts become radiant. It may even be the case that that wonderful intuitions of God's majesty will burst forth in you: this comes as a result of much supplication and luminous understanding; for just as we do not put choice perfumes into a foul-smelling container, neither does God stir up intuitions

---

[69]That is, "do not put us to the test" (in case we fail).
[70]Ammonas was the disciple of Antony the Great and his successor as spiritual master in the Egyptian desert. He was the abbot of the monastery of Pispir.
[71]S. P. Brock, trans., *Letters of Ammonas* (Oxford: SLG Press, 1979), 3-4.
[72]*Kabod*—the heavy weight bearing down, the glory of the presence of God.

of his true majesty in minds that are still ugly.[73]

***Dionysius the Areopagite,* The Mystical Theology *1.1 (sixth century).*** O Trinity. Higher than any being, any divinity, any goodness! Guide of Christians in the wisdom of heaven! Lead us up beyond unknowing and light, up to the farthest, highest peak of mystic scripture, where the mysteries of God's Word lie simple, absolute and unchangeable in the brilliant darkness of a hidden silence. Amid the deepest shadow they pour overwhelming light on what is most manifest. Amid the wholly unsensed and unseen they completely fill our sightless minds with treasures beyond all beauty.[74]

***Maximus the Confessor,* The Ambigua *(seventh century).*** For they say that God and man are paradigms one of another, that as much as God is humanized to man through love for mankind, so much is man able to be deified to God through love, and that as much as man is caught up by God to what is known in his mind, so much does man manifest God, who is invisible by nature, through the virtues.[75]

**The Life of Abba Philemon *(sixth century).*** A certain monk called John came to the Abba, and clasping his feet said to him: "What must I do to be saved Abba? I see that my mind is distracted and it wanders here and there where it ought not to go." After a short silence Abba Philemon said to him: "This is a sickness suffered by those who are externalists. It remains in you because your love of God is not yet perfected. Up to this moment the fire of the love and knowledge of God has not yet risen up within you." So, the brother asked him: "Then what shall I do?" The Abba said to him: "Go now and practice secret meditation in your heart. This will cleanse your mind of its sickness." The brother did not understand what he was told and so said to Abba Philemon: "But what is this secret meditation Abba?" "Go," he told him again, "preserve sobriety in your heart and soberly, with fear and trembling, repeat constantly in your mind: Lord Jesus Christ have mercy upon me. For this is what the blessed Diadochus prescribed for beginners."[76]

---

[73] Brock, *Syriac Fathers on Prayer and the Spiritual Life*, 96 (slightly adapted).
[74] In C. Luibheid, trans., *Pseudo-Dionysius: The Complete Works* (New York: Paulist, 1987), 135.
[75] Maximus Confessor, *The Ambigua* 10.3, in A. Louth, ed., *Maximus the Confessor* (London: Routledge, 1996), 101.
[76] Diadochus of Photike in Epirus. *The Chapters on Spiritual Knowledge* he composed can be found in G. Palmer, et al., eds., *The Philokalia* (London: Faber, 1983), 1:251-96. The present excerpt is from the *Apophthegmata Patrum* in K. Ware, ed., *The Art of Prayer*, compiled by Igumen Chariton, trans. E. Kadloubovsky and E. M. Palmer (London: Faber, 1966, 1981), 76-77.

***Sadhona the Syrian,*** **The Book of Perfection 2.8.20 *(seventh century).***[77] So, provided the beginning of our prayer is watchful and eager, and with true feeling of heart we wet our face with tears, and our whole time of prayer is performed with God's will, then our prayer will be accepted in His presence, and the Lord will be pleased with us and find delight in our offering, catching the sweet savour that wafts from the purity of our heart. And then He will send down[78] the fire of His Spirit, which consumes our sacrifices, and raises up our mind along with them in the flames heavenward, where we shall behold the Lord—to our delight and not to our destruction, as the stillness of His revelation falls upon us and the hidden things of the knowledge of Him are portrayed within us, while spiritual joy is granted in our heart, along with hidden mysteries which I am unable to disclose in words to the simple. In this way we establish our body as a living, holy, and acceptable sacrifice which, in this rational service, is pleasing to God.[79]

***Sadhona the Syrian,*** **The Book of Perfection 2.4.9, 8 *(seventh century).*** Blessed are you, O heart that is lucid, the abode of the deity. Blessed are you, O heart that is pure, and which beholds the hidden essence. Blessed are you flesh and blood, the dwelling place of the Consuming Fire. Blessed are you mortal body made from dust, wherein dwells the Fire that sets the worlds alight. It is truly a matter for wonderment and astonishment that He, before whom even the heavens are not pure, who puts awe into his angels, should think to take delight and pleasure in a heart of flesh that is filled with love for Him, a heart that is opened wide to Him; a heart that is purified so as to act as His holy dwelling place, joyfully ministering to Him in whose presence thousands upon thousands, ten thousands on ten thousands, fiery angels stand in awe, ministering to His glory. Blessed is that loving person, who has caused God Love Himself, to dwell within the heart. Blessed are you O heart; so small and confined, yet you have caused Him whom heaven and earth cannot contain, to dwell spiritually in your womb, as in a restful home. Blessed that luminous eye of the heart which, in its purity, beholds Him lucidly: the One before whose sight even the Seraphim must veil their faces.... How blessed are the pure in heart![80]

---

[77]In the Greek spiritual tradition he is known as Abba Martyrios.
[78]Brock, "Prayer of the Heart in the Syriac Tradition," 137. The verbal root is *aggen*, as found in the overshadowing of the Virgin in the conception of Jesus (Lk 1:35). Cf. S. Brock, "Passover, Annunciation, and Epiclesis," *Novum Testamentum* 24 (1982): 222-33; "Mary and the Eucharist," *Sobornost* 1, no. 2 (1979): 58.
[79]Text in A. de Halleux, ed., *Corpus Scriptorum. Christianorum Orientalium*, 252-53. Translation given in Brock, "Prayer of the Heart in the Syriac Tradition," 136-37.
[80]Translated in Brock, "Prayer of the Heart in the Syriac Tradition," 141-42.

***Abba Hesychios of Sinai*, On Watchfulness and Holiness 5, 89, 104, 132 (eighth century).** Attentiveness (*prosoche*) is the stillness (*hesychia*) of the heart, unbroken by any thought. In this stillness the heart breathes and invokes, endlessly and without ceasing, only Jesus Christ, who is the Son and God himself. Through this invocation enfolded continually in Christ, who secretly divines all hearts, the soul does everything it can to keep its sweetness and its inner struggle hidden from men, so that the devil does not lead it into evil.... Because every thought enters the heart in the form of a mental image of some sensible object, the blessed light of the divinity will illumine the heart only when the heart is completely empty of everything and so free from every form. Indeed, this light reveals itself to the pure intellect in the measure to which the intellect is purged of all concepts.... The heart that is constantly guarded, and is not allowed to receive the forms, images, and fantasies of the dark and evil spirits, is conditioned by nature to give birth from within itself to thoughts that are filled with light. For just as a coal engenders a flame, or a flame lights a candle, so will God, who from our baptism dwells within our heart, kindle our mind to contemplation when he finds it free from the winds of evil and protected by the guarding of the intellect.... For when the heart has acquired stillness (*hesychia*), it will perceive the heights and depths of knowledge; and the ear of the now stilled intellect will be made to hear marvelous things from God.[81]

## FURTHER READING

Allen, P., ed. *Prayer & Spirituality in the Early Church*. Vol. 1. Queensland: Australian Catholic University, Centre for Early Christian Studies, 1998.

Bradshaw, P. *Daily Prayer in the Early Church*. London: SPCK, 1981.

Brock, S. "The Prayer of the Heart in Syriac Tradition." *Sobornost* 4, no. 2 (1982): 131-42.

———, trans. *The Syriac Fathers on Prayer*. Kalamazoo, MI: Cistercian, 1987.

Bunge, G. *Earthen Vessels: The Practice of Personal Prayer According to the Patristic Tradition*. San Francisco: Ignatius Press, 1996.

Cabrol, F. *Liturgical Prayer: Its History and Spirit*. Westminster, MD: Newman Press, 1950.

Guillaumont, A. "Le coeur chez les spirituels grecs à l'époque ancienne." In *Dictionnaire de Spiritualité*, 2:2281-88. Paris: Beauchesne, 1936.

Hamann, A. *Le Pater expliqué par les pères*. Paris: Editions franciscaines, 1952.

———. *La prière: tom. 1. Les origines chrétiennes*. Paris: Editions franciscaines, 1959.

Hammerling, R., ed. *A History of Prayer: The First to Fifteenth Century*. Leiden: Brill, 2008.

Hausherr, I. *La méthode d'oraison hésychaste*. Rome: Pontificium Istitutum Orientalium Studiorum, 1927.

---

[81] In *Philokalia*, 1:163, 89, 177, 104, 180, 132, 185.

Hvalvik, R., ed. *Early Christian Prayer and Identity Formation.* Wissenschaftliche Untersuchungen zum Neuen Testament 336. Tübingen: Mohr Siebeck, 2014.

Jones, C., et al., eds. *The Study of Spirituality.* Oxford: Oxford University Press, 1986. Pages 159-60, 175-83, 235-58.

Maloney, G. *The Prayer of the Heart.* Notre Dame, IN: Ave Maria Press, 1981.

McGuckin, J. A. *The Book of Mystical Chapters: Meditations on the Soul's Ascent from the Desert Fathers and Other Early Christian Contemplatives.* Boston: Shambhala Press, 2002.

———. "Christian Spirituality in Byzantium and the East (600–1700)." In *The Blackwell Companion to Christian Spirituality*, ed. A. Holder, 90-105. Oxford: Blackwell, 2006.

———. "The Prayer of the Heart in Patristic and Early Byzantine Tradition." In *Prayer & Spirituality in the Early Church*, ed. P. Allen, W. Mayer, and L. Cross, 2:69-108. Queensland: Australian Catholic University, Centre for Early Christian Studies, 1999.

———. "The Shaping of the Soul's Perceptions in the Byzantine Ascetic Elias Ekdikos." *St. Vladimir's Theological Quarterly* 55, no. 3 (2011): 343-63.

———. *Standing in God's Holy Fire: The Spiritual Tradition of Byzantium.* London: Darton, Longman, and Todd, 2001.

Neyt, F. "The Prayer of Jesus." *Sobornost* 6, no. 9 (1974): 641-54.

Palmer, G., et al., eds. *The Philokalia.* Vol. 1. London: Faber, 1983.

Regnault, L. "La prière continuelle 'monologistos' dans la literature apophtégmatique." *Irenikon* 47 (1947): 467-93.

Simpson, R. L. *The Interpretation of Prayer in the Early Church.* Philadelphia: Westminster, 1965.

Spidlik, T. "The Heart in Russian Spirituality." In *The Heritage of the Early Church: Studies in Honour of G.V. Florovsky*, 361-74. Orientalia Christiana Analecta 195. Rome: Pontificium Institutum Studiorum Orientalium, 1973.

———. *The Spirituality of the Christian East.* Kalamazoo, MI: Cistercian Publications, 1986.

Sponheim, P. R. *A Primer on Prayer.* Philadelphia: Fortress, 1988.

Ware, K., ed. *The Art of Prayer.* Compiled by Igumen Chariton. Translated by E. Kadloubovsky and E. M. Palmer. London: Faber and Faber, 1966, 1981.

———. "Ways of Prayer and Contemplation (Eastern)." In *Christian Spirituality: Origins to the Twelfth Century*, ed. B. McGinn, J. Meyendorff, and J. Leclercq, 395-414. New York: Crossroad, 1993.

# WOMEN IN ANCIENT CHRISTIANITY

## GREEK SILENCE

Early Christian writing followed many of the social customs and intellectual presuppositions of the ancient Greek world. In that intellectual universe women were of the "private" domain, while men were of the "public" domain. This axiomatic polarity drove much of the Greek social theory related to gender issues in antiquity and has remained in place to the present day as a shadow reflection in the glass behind much of contemporary attitudes too. In many places of the world today, of course, other than the developed countries, the ancient attitudes toward gender differences are still very much in place in a similar archaic modality—places that ostensibly cling to more antique cultural mindsets, even, perhaps, when hurriedly adopting the modern resources such as biological self-determination, advanced education, and wealth-generating capacities that were the ultimate chief liberators of women in the post–Industrial Revolution era in the West.

For the ancient Greeks, the home and domestic interiority were seen as an intellectually "female" reality, and the open space of the agora, together with association in public and (most important for our present purposes) "intellectual discourse" (*logos*), was imagined as a male phenomenon. Textuality (the Greeks always understood the "word" as a proclaimed discourse before ever it was a written one) was thus part of the male domain. And textuality, one remembers, became the primary means of transmitting the historical record. Women, so the philosophers and medics theorized, were not suited much to intellectual discourse (including text), as they were biologically unstable. The "wandering" of their womb (*hystera*) made them tend to the "hysterical" rather than the rational.[1]

---

[1] This endured partially even into Victorian times, when women who were feeling faint attributed their unease to "a touch of the vapors." Aretaeus had surmised that the womb wandered because it had a dislike for fetid smells and a preference for pleasant ones and so moved up from the vagina to the throat when it could and was induced to move down again by smelling things, or

First-century medical theorist Aretaeus, writing in Greek and working in Rome in Nero's time, puts it succinctly:

> In women, in the hollow of their body beneath the ribs, lies the womb. This is very much like an independent animal within the animal, for it moves around of its own accord . . . and is quite erratic. If the womb moves upwards it can quickly cause the woman to suffocate and choke by cutting off her breath. She becomes incapable even of struggling in pain or shouting out to call for assistance. In many cases the inability to breathe takes immediate effect. In others it is an inability to speak.[2]

It is clear enough that wealthy women in antiquity were educated, often to a very high level. A female philosopher such as Hypatia, in Alexandria in the fifth century of the Christian era, commanded an international reputation. It is obvious too that ancient women were also textual. One of the most rhapsodic poets of the Greek literary tradition is Sappho of Lesbos. Later, when the Christian philosopher Origen of Alexandria was composing the opening books of his monumental commentary on John, his sponsor's advance of money allowed him to have more than twenty female stenographers in the lecture room, busily taking down the words as he declaimed them to his class. And among that class we know that there were several prominent female Christian philosopher-disciples. We learn this from the records of their subsequent martyrdom as recounted by Eusebius of Caesarea in his *Ecclesiastical History*.[3] Herais, Marcella, and "the celebrated Potamiaena" were each burned to death, for impiety and capital offenses against the state, under the governor Aquila.[4] They had been condemned to execution in the pogrom initiated in third-century Alexandria against Christians who were of the upper classes, an aggression that paradoxically excluded Origen himself from legal penalty because the authorities did not think he was of sufficiently elevated social stature to merit punishment.[5]

---

by regular pregnancies, which anchored the womb most effectively. H. King, *Hysteria Beyond Freud* (Berkeley: University of California Press, 1993).

[2]*On Diseases* 2.11.1-3; 6.10.1-4.

[3]He devoted book 6 of the same to the life and times of Origen and names the martyred disciples of his hero there. See *Ecclesiastical History* 6.4 for the names of those who died in the Severan persecution and after.

[4]It was a form of execution meant to make a point: the condemned person was stripped, then dressed in the *tunica molesta*—a whole-body covering made of stiff papyrus steeped in flammable oils that made it impossible to move the head—and set in a bonfire as flammable oil; pitch was poured on them from above. In Roman law, crimes against religion were all given a capital status, which is why so many early martyrs are depicted as having been executed in this way.

[5]In the legal terms of the persecution, addressing itself to converts of the upper classes, Origen, as a mixed-race noncitizen, was not liable for arrest. We are told that he endured the jeers of the crowds as he attended the execution of some of his disciples. See J. A. McGuckin, ed., *The Westminster Handbook to Origen of Alexandria* (Louisville: Westminster John Knox, 2004).

Even so, it was never a common thing for women to be educated, at least not in the higher levels of an ancient rhetorical school in one of the great cities. Such an education was a feature of life for the daughters of the wealthy elite. Things must have been even more limited, educationally speaking, in the poorer towns and villages. This leads inevitably to the great problem of the drastic "textual invisibility" of women in the records of Greco-Roman society, and especially in the annals of Christianity in the early period, when its educated wealthy elites must have been very small indeed. Women are spoken of in ancient texts, extensively so, but always from the male perspective.

The stage dramas of ancient Greek literature summarize this problem exactly: the characters who present the views of women are using words entirely supplied to them by male authors, for the (almost) exclusive benefit of male viewers, and are themselves (as the law required) male actors impersonating females. Drew Kadel, when compiling a list of female Christian writers in 1982, found that he could identify no more than 250 between the earliest centuries of Christianity and the fifteenth. And of that number many of the texts had been lost while only the names survived. Lisa Bellan-Boyer actually titled a 2003 study "Conspicuous in Their Absence: Women in Early Christianity."[6]

In the early church, this cultural matrix dominated. Women were disadvantaged by this ubiquitous Greek invisibility. The intellectual traditions of Christianity, that is, almost all of that which would come into printed form and thus be transmitted across history, was deeply rooted in that Greek tradition. Social patterns were deeply established in ancient society, and the rhetorical traditions of *paideia* were part of the forces that made that conformity extensive and enduring. Women in antiquity were married young, in their mid-teens, often to considerably older men, who enjoyed extensive authority over them, physically, socially, and financially. The families of women wealthy enough to count usually made the decision of marriage for them, and with a life ahead of childbirth and (except for the few elite rich) domestic labor, without sophisticated medicines, the death rate was very high. It would not be unusual for a woman then to be regarded as being in advanced old age by her late forties. As women played no great part in the formation of the great patristic textual tradition (being closed out of the major leadership offices of bishop and priest in the early church), they have largely been passed over in Christian history, up to the present century, except for a few notable cases of aristocratic women who were educated and entered the textual tradition themselves. We shall come to those names shortly.

---

[6]Article in *Cross Current* 53, no. 1 (2003): 48-63.

Although the story of the church in the patristic era has generally been a one-sided and heavily patriarchal one, the mid- to late twentieth century has witnessed a remarkable flowering of women's studies, not least in the domain of early church life.[7] The significant presence of female apostles in the earliest Jesus movement has been reclaimed for the record by many notable feminist biblical scholars, and decades of scholarship by skilled female patristic theologians and historians of late antiquity has only recently begun to make a mark, excavating the dust of the "Greek silence," to reveal a fuller picture of the impact women had on early Christianity from the postbiblical age to the early Middle Ages.

As a result of that pioneering work, it has become clear that asceticism was taken and used by many early Christian women as a channel for self-development that allowed them new vistas of opportunity. Today the path of virginity might look to us as a narrowing of prospects, but the liberation from marriage and the capacity to determine one's own financial and social identity were nurtured imaginatively by important female ascetics, several of whom were obviously respected teachers in their lifetimes, such as Macrina, Syncletica, Melania, and Olympias.[8] The church's acclamation of virginal life thus offered new options above and beyond domestic drudgery.[9] The autonomy and partial independence offered in the ascetical circles made the fourth century an important era for the development of Christian women, though successive centuries saw the gradual erosion of those rights as episcopal authorities brought all forms of ascetical communities under their canonical control.

The scholarly attempt to break the silence about early Christian women meets increasing difficulties, however, as it begins to move away from the fruitful ground of the place of Christian women in asceticism, or in the occupancy of ministerial offices such as deacon, prophet, or widow, and now begins to move out into the issues of women in general social standing, familial life, and Christian social networks. The problems are the perennial ones: not enough archaeological data and not enough textual record. But much of what is being produced by recent critical narrative that

---

[7] E. Schüssler Fiorenza, *In Memory of Her: A Feminist Theological Reconstruction* (New York: Crossroad, 1994); L. Schottroff, *Lydia's Impatient Sisters: A Feminist Social History of Early Christianity*, trans. B. Rumscheidt and M. Rumscheidt (Louisville: Westminster John Knox, 1995); R. S. Kramer and M. D'Angelo, *Women and Christian Origins* (New York: Oxford University Press, 1999); J. Lieu, "The Attraction of Women into Early Judaism and Christianity: Gender and the Politics of Conversion," *Journal for the Study of the New Testament* 72 (1998): 5-22; R. Stark, "Reconstructing the Rise of Christianity: The Role of Women," *Sociology of Religion* 56, no. 3 (1995): 229-44; C. Trevett, *Christian Women and the Time of the Apostolic Fathers* (Cardiff, UK: University of Wales Press, 2006).
[8] Syncletica's name is lost; her rank is simply recorded by this title.
[9] See E. Castelli, "Virginity and Its Meaning for Women's Sexuality in Early Christianity," *Journal of Feminist Studies in Religion* 2 (1986): 61-88; V. Burrus, *Chastity as Autonomy*, Studies in Women and Religion 23 (Lewiston, NY: Mellen, 1987).

is more attentive to "ordinary" life in ancient times (as distinct from the old preferences of historians for kings, queens, and authors) is enlivening the whole field of patristics, dragging it into the wider world of late antique social, religious, and philosophical research.[10] The present enthusiasm of a new generation of female scholars of Christian antiquity promises still to bear a fruitful harvest in decades to come.

## WOMEN IN THE FIRST CENTURIES OF THE CHURCH

It is not difficult to find several notable female disciples named in the New Testament texts. However, some of the most significant of these early female leaders (one would imagine they were powerful in the early communities since they feature at all) appear in such a way that we know almost nothing about them historically. For example, what is known about Mary the mother of Jesus, speaking for the historical record, would not fill a page. Mary Magdalene gets a few lines. Like the male apostles, these New Testament women exist in a literary form (the genres of the Gospels) that is so focused on Jesus himself that all other characters are minimally sketched so as to serve as mere highlights for the portrait of Jesus and his acts.

Later disciples such as Priscilla (Acts 18:2, 18, 26), Tabitha-Dorcas (Acts 9:36-39), and the "apostle" Junia (Rom 16:7) are mentioned, in their turn, chiefly as backstage props for the literary exploits of a few leading (male) apostolic figures (Peter or Paul).[11] Later legend, in the hands of Christian hagiographers, will supply the imaginative (and highly speculative) details for some of these. The legend of Mary Magdalene is one of those going strong even in our own time, and the less historicity the corpus has to it the better it serves the purpose:[12] a factor that is already apparent in second-century Christianity among the (largely fictionalized) apocryphal Gospels that sprang up, filling in the gaps.[13]

In the New Testament literature, as Antonova points out, the accounts are not necessarily the more accurate for being the less embroidered, for even then the role of the female disciples of Jesus are only recorded in the narrative to serve the purposes of highlighting the missionary endeavors or charismatic graces of the male

---

[10]See, for example, *A People's History of Christianity*, vol. 2, *Late Antique Christianity*, ed. V. Burrus (Minneapolis: Fortress, 2005); vol. 3, ed. D. Krueger, *Byzantine Christianity* (Minneapolis: Fortress, 1989).

[11]Junia's name is even masculinized in the later New Testament textual tradition to Junias, with scribes not being able to believe the apostle Paul had afforded the title apostle to a female. See V. Fabrega, "War Junia(s), der Herrvorragende Apostel (Rom. 16.7) eine Frau?," *Jahrbuche fur Antike und Christentum* 27-28 (1984–1985): 47-64.

[12]Though see M. R. D'Angelo, "Reconstructing the 'Real' Women in the Gospel Literature: The Case of Mary Magdalene," in Kramer and D'Angelo, *Women and Christian Origins*, 105-29.

[13]See B. Ehrman and Z. Plese, *The Apocryphal Gospels* (Oxford: Oxford University Press, 2011).

disciples who feature as heroic figures in the tales.[14] The occlusion of their role as the first witnesses of the resurrection appearances is evidently done, across the range of Synoptic Gospels, because the reliance on women's narratives for such a striking *kerygma* seemed scandalous to the first disciples in trying to put together a strong apologia before those (many) of the time who were more than skeptical about the apostolic proclamation and would have ridiculed the idea of relying on female testimony in any judicial context.[15]

The letters of Paul have recently been the subject of close scrutiny by scholars interested in seeing what picture can be drawn of the position and roles of women in the earliest Christian communities.[16] It is clear enough that there were several women of high standing in the earliest churches, several of whom Paul singles out for praise. Some of these were undoubtedly his patrons. It is difficult to deduce a general picture, other than that a wealthy woman in antique times would always break the mold by virtue of the manifold social freedoms and roles of patronage that her possession of wealth would allow. Moreover, it is difficult to deduce general patterns from Paul's writings, considering they are so highly "occasional" in character. Chloe in 1 Corinthians 1:11, however, is surely a woman of high standing, and she is mentioned along with "her people," suggesting she has leadership of a considerable household or faction in the church. When Paul mentions Prisca (Priscilla) and her husband, Aquila (1 Cor 16:19; Rom 16:3-5; see also Acts 18), she is listed, unusually for the time, first in order. This couple were missionaries and preachers of some standing. They owned a household where the church met, clearly presidents of one of the first level of house churches that formed the archaic structure of the Christian movement.

At this period where Christianity was formed out of clusters of worshipers gathered around house churches, of which the largest were surely the biggest villas (of the wealthy) that could accommodate the largest numbers safely on one occasion, it is clear enough that being a wealthy house owner afforded significant leadership roles to the *matrona* who so sponsored the Christian assembly. Nicola Denzey's study of how upper-class Christian women were notably associated with gathering the remains of executed martyrs in Rome (they were not as liable as men to attract

---

[14] S. Antonova, ed., *Women in the Eastern Christian Tradition* (New York: Theotokos Press, 2013).
[15] The women at the tomb are the heroes of what seems to be the preevangelical version of the stories: the only ones with the courage to attend the death and burial rites of the master. But in the accounts as they appear in the Gospels their "womanly" foolishness and fearfulness is brought to the fore, so as to cast doubt on the reliability of their testimony. They remain the "apostles of the apostles" nevertheless. See ibid., 20-22.
[16] M. McDonald, "Reading Paul: Early Interpreters of Paul on Women and Gender," in Kramer and D'Angelo, *Women and Christian Origins*, 236-53; W. Cotter, "Women's Authority Roles in Paul's Churches: Countercultural or Conventional?," *Novum Testamentum* 36 (1994): 350-72.

unwanted legal attention and had the resources to rebury the victims) goes on to point out that having thus reburied the martyrs near their own properties, they had thus, de facto, founded pilgrimage sites and house churches.[17] The map that the frontispiece of the book offers, showing the *martyria* shrines and *tituli* churches of Rome that were associated with female Christian founders, is strikingly full.

The Shepherd of Hermas, a late first-century text that once almost made it into the New Testament canon, gives us a glimpse of such a situation.[18] Its author was, quite possibly, a captured Jewish priest brought to Rome after the war of AD 70. He tells us in the opening parts of the book that he was sold to a wealthy Roman lady named Rhoda, who after some years also became a Christian herself. It is likely through Rhoda's patronage that Hermas himself rose to become a significant leader of the Christian house church to which he belonged (Rhoda's?). His visionary and prophetic discourses, eventually written down in the text and circulated to great renown in the second and third centuries, show Hermas to have been one of the early Christian prophets who are mentioned in several places of the New Testament. What is relevant, for the moment, however, is the status of Rhoda, who, as it were, is the power behind this high-status leader, whom she elevates to be the spiritual guide of her local community. This is the social situation of Roman Christianity that we meet in the time of Paul. At the end of his letter to the Romans, the apostle appends to his text a list of names of notable Christians that he knows personally. It is an attempt, as it were, to offer some form of references for himself to a church already established, where he does not already have established disciples and which he knows he is about to visit. In this list of his notables, it is significant that ten women's names appear. Among them Phoebe is described as "sister and deacon" (*adelphe, diakonos*) of the church at Cenchreae and a benefactor (*prostatis*) of many, including Paul.

If he relied on the patronage of these powerful Christian leaders, however, it is also notable that in his own churches, those he feels he can legislate for since his preaching founded them, Paul forbids women to speak in the prayer assembly, stressing their subordination and making the extraordinary conclusion, "For it is shameful for a woman to speak in church."[19] His ambivalent evidence about Christian women's evangelical status (accepting patronage to fulfill his own mission

---

[17] N. Denzey, *The Bone Gatherers: The Lost Worlds of Early Christian Women* (Boston: Beacon, 2007).
[18] It is still bound in with the New Testament in the fourth-century great Codex Sinaiticus, held in London's British Library. Origen (in his *Romans Commentary*) thought the author was the Hermas mentioned in Rom 16:4.
[19] 1 Cor 14:33-36. He offers an argument in 1 Cor 11:2-14 as to why women should not be regarded as a normative part of the Christian prophetic ministry. Again it is one that operates out of the Roman household code: leaders must not be chosen from among the "subordinate" class (females or slaves).

but refusing them a local role in his own foundations) tells us something about the diversity of practice we might expect to have found in the earliest communities in terms of leadership roles and gender roles. It also reveals something about Paul's own conservative values and his overwhelming anxiety about keeping the Roman household code intact.[20]

At times, however, his conservatism was set aside: as in Galatians, where he makes his famous (and very radical) statement: "There is no longer Jew or Greek; there is no longer slave or freeman; there is no longer male and female: for all of you are one in Christ Jesus" (Gal 3:28). Perhaps outside his own communities (which he felt to be under constant hostile scrutiny from Jerusalem) he was more relaxed. But it would be his negative and narrower views about gender that would have a long-lasting impact, establishing the praxis of later Christian communities in relation to leadership roles of Christian women. This was in the aftermath of his own posthumous canonization as "apostle of the Gentiles," and in the aftershock, as it were, of the Montanist movement, with its dissident women prophets, which had been so heavily criticized by the episcopal leaders of Asia Minor in the early second century.

The trend to limit women's leadership roles can already be seen in the deutero-Pauline literature. The theme of preserving the expected values of the Roman household and subordinating women is especially notable in the Pastoral Letters (1 and 2 Timothy and Titus). The state of the ordinary (Roman) family is taken here as a model of how to construct a church community. All is respectable and calm. The picture is, perhaps, too good to be true; and underneath the surface many have suspected that the Christians had already gained a notoriety for disrupting families with their excusive religious claims, their peculiar views on chastity, and pagan ritual nonobservance. The Pastoral Letters, therefore, are "trying hard" to appear normal and respectable, in a wider world that knew they were anything but respectably bourgeois. This is exactly the time when the first social reactions against the church start to occur (spontaneously before they are taken up at imperial level) and come to be known as "the persecutions." Schüssler Fiorenza has concluded from this historical trend that Christianity veered away from a radical path at the end of the first century and instead adopted a social program of "love patriarchy"; that is, adopting the hierarchical values of antique Roman society as a good "order"

---

[20]The "code" was the common bourgeois Roman attitudes of the first century regarding male superiority and female subordinationism. Paul's agenda here is not to allow any social controversy to threaten his spreading of the good news in antique society. For the same reason he refuses to critique, in any substantial way, the practice of ancient slavery, commanding rather that slaves should obey their masters (Col 3:22) so as to offer them a good report of Christianity, rather than alarming them, presumably, with more radical moral lessons.

for communities but adapting their harsher features by an ethic of loving-kindness.[21] This theme also dominated in the writings of the early apostolic fathers, who have probably taken all their cues on the subject from the Pauline literature anyway.

The Gnostic literature does not offer us any greater light on the subject of female leadership, although there were communities of Christian Gnostics (attacked for this by Tertullian) who had revolving liturgical offices (even presidency of the Eucharist, it would seem) that circulated within the community and were open to women as much as to men. The Gnostic texts in general are very antithetical in character. They delight in making pairs of observations: light/darkness; truth/error; enlightenment/blindness. High among these pairings is that of male/female. In every case where this is applied as a spiritual trope, the idea and concept of female is presented as a symbol of foolishness, ignorance and error. The (Valentinian) cosmic myth of Sophia presents her in female type as "going astray" into sexual creation and producing a world out of her womb that is more or less "an abortion" in its chaotic and disgusting nature. According to Clement of Alexandria in his *Stromata*, Gnostics tended to regard sexual or gender differentiation as negative because it stood for the "works of the female," which Jesus had come on earth to destroy.[22] As Antonova explains,

> The enigmatic phrase the "works of the female" designates human reproduction, birth and corruption, that are overcome by abstinence and by the attempted transcendence of one's gendered state. More often than not, the transcendence of human sexuality and gender are represented as the transcendence of femaleness, both in an abstract and in a concrete sense.[23]

Much of early Christian asceticism approaches the idea of holiness in this desexualized way.[24] Female ascetical figures are typically described as "this female holy man of God."[25] In the highly ascetical Thomas traditions from Syria, we find in the Gospel of Thomas Jesus promising to Mary Magdalene that he will "make her male" so that she can be perfected.[26] This notion of the woman becoming male by her virtue lasts a long time. It can be seen especially in the ascetical literature of the

---

[21] E. Schüssler Fiorenza, *But She Said: Feminist Practices of Biblical Interpretation* (Boston: Beacon, 1992).
[22] Or *Book of Miscellanies*, chap. 3.
[23] Antonova, *Women in the Eastern Christian Tradition*, 31.
[24] See R. R. Ruether, "Misogynism and Virginal Feminism in the Fathers of the Church," in *Religion and Sexism: Images of Woman in the Jewish and Christian Traditions*, ed. R. Ruether (New York: Simon and Schuester, 1974), 150-83.
[25] G. Cloke, *This Female Man of God: Women and Spiritual Power in the Patristic Age. 350–450* (London: Routledge, 1995); J. M. Petersen, *Handmaids of the Lord. Contemporary Descriptions of Feminine Asceticism in the First Six Christian Centuries* (Kalamazoo, MI: Cistercian Publications, 1996).
[26] Gospel of Thomas, logion 114: "Behold, I will guide her so as to make her male, so that she too may become a living spirit resembling you males. For every female who makes herself male will enter the domain of heaven."

fourth century. Jerome and Ambrose echo Thomas when they both speak of woman finally becoming male when she leaves behind the things appropriate to her gender and lives the spiritual life in Christ.[27] None of it is particularly cheery in terms of positive roles for women, it would seem.

## WOMEN IN ANCIENT CHRISTIAN EPIGRAPHY

There exist several funerary stone inscriptions from the very early period that mention significant early Christian women by name (significant even by virtue of merely having such a stone, a very expensive artifact then, which lifted them out of the ordinary and the forgotten). But in general they are few and far between, and though they have been the subject of intense debate as to their significance (as to how much of a leadership role these women occupied), the interpretation of what these cryptic monuments might mean is still very much up in the air.[28] The later literary evidences continue the conspiracy not to allow antique religious women to speak for themselves. This is partly because of the transmission process for texts across such a long period. It was an expensive and laborious business, and the church's scriptoria after the fourth century were largely filled with monks producing literature that was relevant to them.

So, for example, while we know that several of the major church fathers conducted extensive literary exchanges with leading Christian female intellectuals and philanthropists of their day (such as Basil's correspondence with his ascetic sister Macrina, or John Chrysostom with the millionaire deaconess Olympias, or Jerome's correspondences with the widows Paula and Marcella), only the church father's side of the correspondence was reproduced by the monastic copyists. The opinions and queries of the women were not thought worth the effort of being copied and so are completely lost unless the patristic writer either cites them (usually to correct them) or alludes to them sufficiently so as to give us the sense of what had been said. In the *Alphabetical Collection* of the sayings of the desert fathers, only three out of 120 chapters are devoted to women. Other ancient monastic overviews, such as the *History of the Monks of Egypt*, have nothing whatsoever about female ascetics, as if

---

[27]Jerome, *On the Letter to the Ephesians* 3.5 (PL 26.567). "As long as woman is for birth and children, she is as different from man as body is from soul. But when she wishes to serve Christ more than the world, then she will cease to be a woman, and will be called a man." See also Ambrose, *Exposition on the Gospel of Luke* 10.101 (PL 15.1844).

[28]See Margot Houts, "Visual Evidence of Women in Early Christian Leadership," *Perspectives* 14, no. 3 (1999): 14-18. Is a mention of a *presbytera* (female elder or priestess) in this time an indication that women were ordained to the presbyterate, contrary to the weight of the textual evidence, for example? Or is it simply the indication of an honorific title for a deceased presbyter's wife (the practice in the Eastern church to this day), where the priest's wife is the *presbytera*, the deacon's wife the *diakonissa*, and so on?

they did not exist. Palladius's *Lausiac History* has more mention of ascetic females and their circle of influence, probably because he knew his work would be read by circles of higher-class female ascetics back in the imperial city or Jerusalem, where educated women had gathered already in ascetical communities such as those led by the aristocratic women Olympia and Melania.

### WOMEN IN THE AGE OF PERSECUTIONS

There is one case, however, where the Christian women suddenly did burst onto the scene in a societally shocking way—and that was in the age of persecutions. One remarkable thing about the early church was that it kept records very well. As a result the code of silence about women was well and truly shattered, by the church itself, and partly by accident, for it recorded its female martyrs with pride and held them up for emulation as eschatological heroes of the faith, while at the same time (by doing this) giving unconscious testimony that it was precisely the fact that Christian women would so defy social and legal prescriptions that made the pagan society around them filled with anxiety about how "ungovernable" Christian women were becoming.[29]

In its public face the (male) Christian writers and bishops wanted to portray women in the communities as being obedient, docile, and self-effacing—just like the cliché of good behavior that emerges from the pastoral literature's elevation of the Roman household code. But the second- to fourth-century martyrdom stories, which included so many Christian women, clearly tell another story. The quite extraordinary ratio of women who were put to death in these martyrial accounts clearly shows that Christian women were not docile and shy housewives: on the contrary. In this way the ecclesial records open a window onto the reality behind the code of silence, almost despite themselves. These martyr accounts (soon to be replete with legends) are filled with very detailed versions of how nobly, yet how terribly, the Christians suffered.

Literary tropes could not help abounding here: ideas of the endurance of the sage (drawn from Stoic archetypes) tended to elevate the ordinary Joe and Mary Christian martyr into noble philosophers who despised pain and cannot be deflected from the confession of their faith, no matter what awful legal tortures were applied to make them recant. The reality must have been both more banal and more terrifying. It is clear enough from the great jungle of church legislation that sprang up after the persecutions, dealing with how to reconcile Christian deserters and apostates who had caved in and offered sacrifice and renounced their faith, that the persecutions did not only elicit heroic nobility across the board but caused what happens after

---

[29]See F. Cardman, "Acts of the Women Martyrs," *Anglican Theological Review* 70 (1988): 144-50.

every period of persecution and tyrannical oppression—a great amount of divisions and disparate behaviors.[30]

In its martyrial literature the church lifted up the extraordinary cases for emulation and edification, ascribing to those who either suffered (confessors) or died (martyrs) great spiritual powers of intercession in heaven.[31] The extent of women in these martyrdom records (for their deaths inscribed them into the church's lists of its liturgically commemorated saints, and their names have been remembered even to the present) is a very loud testimony indeed to the way in which Christian women stood out from ancient society in terms of their defiance of social mores in defense of the faith.[32] This was not how ancient women were supposed to behave, according to the household code.

One of these early women martyrs actually breaks the conspiracy of textual silence, too. She was a wealthy educated woman and thus literate. Her name was Vibia Perpetua, a young mother with child at the breast who was a catechumen in the North African church. During the games held at Carthage in celebration of the birth of Caesar Geta in the year 203, local criminals were used in the arena. The games were moments of important social statement of loyalty to the augustus as divine *Kyrios*-Lord and were a pagan cultic celebration, in essence. Christians who refused obedience to both the cult and the imperial title stood out on these occasions, and several of the early martyrdoms occur in the context of games.[33] Those executed that day included a group of new Christian converts who had refused to recant.[34] Among them were Perpetua and her slave Felicitas. They were eventually thrown before wild cattle, gored, and then trampled to death. In her time of incarceration after her trial it is clear enough from the account that survives that the magistrate had ordered

---

[30]The canons of the early councils after Nicaea are full of legislation on how to punish yet reconcile those who renounced their faith under threat of torture, death, or confiscation of goods. See further J. A. McGuckin, *The Ascent of Christian Law: Patristic and Byzantine Reformulations of Antique Civilization* (Crestwood, NY: St. Vladimir's Seminary Press, 2012).

[31]See J. A. McGuckin, "Martyr Devotion in the Alexandrian School (Origen to Athanasius)," in *Martyrs & Martyrologies*, ed. D. Wood, Studies in Church History 30 (Oxford: Blackwell, 1993), 35-45.

[32]The Roman *martyrology* or the Litany of the Saints still commemorates them. In the Eastern church the female martyrs are remembered at every eucharistic liturgy, and almost every day of the year lists a female martyr to be commemorated. In the liturgical commemorations, the memory that innumerable women were among the company of early martyrs endures. The *proskomedia* ritual commemorates them this way: "In honor and memory of the holy apostle, protomartyr, and Archdeacon Stephen; of the holy Great-martyrs Demetrios, George, Theodore the Recruit and Theodore the Commander, of Thekla, Barbara, Parascheva, Katherine, and all the holy martyrs . . ."

[33]One recalls the deaths of Polycarp at Smyrna, Ignatius at Rome, and the martyrs of Lyons. Translations of select texts in B. Chenu et al., *The Book of Christian Martyrs* (London: SCM Press, 1990).

[34]Conversion was specifically forbidden by the legislation of Emperor Septimius Severus so as to limit the spread of Christianity among the elite.

Perpetua's pagan father to "bring her to her senses" and make her conform. All she needed to do was renounce her conversion, and she would be liberated and could return to her domestic life as dutiful daughter and wife. The husband never features at all in the account. It seems he had well and truly distanced himself from his wife, perhaps because of her conversion, which was, therefore, a massive act of independent rebellion against his domestic authority.

Perpetua left behind a diary memoir of her time in prison, which is not only dramatic and very moving but also an incredibly rare firsthand account of an early Christian female martyr. Perpetua is very concerned that her mother and newly converted Christian brother bring up her new baby (another indication that her husband has renounced her). The father is described as being in a great rage because Perpetua will not obey him and renounce her faith so as to come home. She takes comfort from prophetic (dream) visions she is encouraged to have while in prison, because of her status as a God-beloved confessor, but also realizes from them that she cannot avoid death. Her mounting anxiety about being exposed to public view in the arena, thinking she might be stripped or violated, is demonstrated in part of her dream when she encounters a fearsome Egyptian warrior (a symbol of Satan) and "Some handsome young men came forward to help prepare and encourage me.[35] I was stripped of my clothes, and behold![36] Suddenly I was a man."[37] A brief excerpt from this extraordinary document is given in the reader below.

After Perpetua's death an editor from the Carthaginian church completed the narrative with the account of her martyrdom. Some have thought it was Tertullian himself, though there is no compelling external evidence to believe so. If it had been, it would be an ironic counterbalance to the more general picture of Tertullian (that emerges from other writings) as a strident voice trying to keep Christian women "in their place" and that place silent and conformist and repentant (as can be seen in the excerpt provided from his writings also in the reader below). But perhaps this is not so surprisingly a contradictory thing if one thinks about it more deeply: for Tertullian would not have spent so much literary passion insisting that Christian women should

---

[35] However psychologically revealing this might be (she was only twenty-two when she died), it was meant as a theological symbol of the handsome young men of New Testament narratives, namely angels.

[36] For contest now as a fighter in the arena, just as in the men's gymnasium. She is a man among men by virtue of the courage she feels. Her fears, as a respectable Roman *matrona*, about this shameful exposure were fulfilled; in details added posthumously, the account tells how she was stripped naked along with her slave while the games' organizers gave them gladiatorial nets. But seeing their fragility (and probably knowing her honorable family name), the local crowd reacted against their treatment, and so they were taken back inside, clothed, and set before a charge of long-horned cows, which fatally injured them, as was necessary to complete the criminal sentence.

[37] *Passion of Perpetua and Felicity* 10.

be "seen and not heard" if this was already widely established as the case.[38] Other writers than Tertullian are equally inconsistent in their views of Christian women.[39] Rather, he might write about it with such vehemence in order to try to make it a reality. In his later life Tertullian came under the influence of the Montanist movement, which gave to women visionaries a high spiritual status (interpreters of divine dreams and communications of the Spirit). Whoever composed the final edition of Perpetua's *Dream Narratives* was most likely a sympathizer of this tradition.

## CHRISTIAN WOMEN IN THE PATRISTIC AND BYZANTINE ERA

The later church writings feature women predominantly in ascetical terms. Asceticism might seem to us a narrow perimeter in which to expect women to expand their horizons, but Christian women of the fourth century and after made a startlingly creative use of ascetical practices to afford themselves a degree of social liberation hitherto rare.[40] Christian canon law from the very outset had been strict about regulating marriages. Believers were allowed one marriage. If a partner died, for the survivor to take another partner was regarded as inadmissible. It was a failure to profess faith in the reality of the eschaton. Such persons were called digamists and were canonically censured by exclusion from communion. Of course, as time passed, the church legislation (canons) on this matter relaxed, allowing second marriages to be contracted after a spouse's death without penalty. But always a single, unrepeated marriage, or virginity, was held in highest honor in ecclesial mentality.

In the Eastern church divorce was allowed, and church-sanctioned remarriage up to three times, a position that St. Gregory the Theologian argues for as a philanthropic dispensation from Christ in his *Oration* 37. The oration was occasioned by the queries of the new Western general Theodosius, who had been appointed augustus of the East and who asked him in 380, as bishop of the imperial city, why the different parts of the Christian world had different legislation on this matter of remarriage. Gregory noted how marriage law was a major way that women were treated unfairly in Roman society, and his explanation of why the lawgiver (Christ) would always tend toward mercy

---

[38] Texts from antiquity have so often, in the past, been taken woodenly, at face value, as describing accurately the reality they allude to, and not enough account has been taken of the fact that they are rhetorical attempts to establish an ideal the writer wishes to establish. Historical analysis demands more subtlety of the modern interpreter and a greater awareness of the rhetorical devices that so abound in ancient (as well as modern!) literature.

[39] M. H. Keane, "Woman in the Theological Anthropology of the Early Fathers," *Journal of Theology for Southern Africa* 62 (1988): 3-13; D. Kinder, "Clement of Alexandria: Conflicting Views on Women," *Second Century: A Journal of Early Christian Studies* 7 (1989–1990): 213-20; S. Davies, "Women, Tertullian, and the Acts of Paul," *Semeia* 38 (1986): 139-43.

[40] See E. A. Clark, "Ascetic Renunciation and Feminine Advancement: A Paradox of Late Ancient Christianity," *Anglican Theological Review* 63 (1981): 240-57.

rather than severity "for men and women swimming in a sea of misery" is also a major early statement on why all Christian canonical legislation must define and treat the genders as completely equal. A selection from his text is offered in the reader below.

In modern times four factors above all others have led to the ascent of women to social status and liberation: greater degree of control of their reproductive biology, equality under terms of law, educational advancement, and the application of the three preceding factors to allow the secure accumulation of wealth in their own name. In antiquity women achieved standing and relative freedom from oppression by a combination of the same factors, but in different ways. The Christian ascetical movement offered them an important vehicle to bring all four into play. According to Roman custom, men of social rank married late and women early. After the marriage had produced an heir, it was common for the different wings of the villa to live separate lives: the men entertaining in their own quarters and the women in theirs. Children were brought up in the *gynecaeum* until they were about eleven, and then passed over into the care of the father, who would arrange the child's tutorial governance and train them for a profession. Women were so generally uneducated that the men's activities never considered them as likely partners for social discourse (the *symposia* and gatherings of the powerful and influential that made up the round of upper-class Roman conviviality and patronage circles). As Plato had argued, a man's soul companion was more than likely going to be another man, and this even apart from any sexual aspect. It was just that those who had been educated together would naturally relate together and continue to pursue the same sets of values with one another, in business as well as leisure and culture. It was literally the boys' club. But if men married late in life, to produce heirs, it followed that they also tended to die first, in the natural order of events. So if a man was married by his early forties (what we today would probably equate with a sixty-year-old) and his wife might be in her teens at the time of marriage, it was likely that a lot of widows would be around.

The poor standards of health care, of course, also meant that the rate of deaths by childbirth was also high. This, incidentally, meant that those choosing virginity had a distinct life advantage and also a premium opportunity to enjoy the years of independence (from child care) necessary to accumulate an advanced education as well as the social contacts necessary for a political life in ancient society. In the case of widows of wealthy men, Roman law was very careful to make sure the estate patrimony would not remain with the bereaved wife but revert back to the male line of family descent.[41] The widow, if she wanted to retain any social place at all, needed to remarry as quickly as she could. Christian women of the upper classes put this

---

[41] The word *patrimony* itself shows how the wealth of the estate belongs to the "pater," the father.

system to the test, using the canons to their advantage: those very canons that had forbidden a second marriage.

One of the first that we see making this move was the renowned Macrina (c. 327–380), sister of St. Basil the Great and his younger brothers Naucratios, Peter, and Gregory, later the bishop of Nyssa. Macrina never features in the writings of St. Basil himself. In all likelihood she was closely attached to the circle of Eustathius of Sebaste, a renowned and radical ascetic who taught that Christian monastic communities should abolish within themselves all distinctions among their members of class and gender.[42] He believed that female Christian ascetics should be "manly virgins," cut their hair short, travel where they liked in the service of the church, and wear the same simple tunic-style dress as male ascetics. Basil himself had once looked to Eustathius as his mentor, and the latter had first ordained Basil and employed him as an anti-Arian speaker at several synods he attended. But soon the two had parted company. Basil disliked his style of monastic communality and would legislate differently. But he also had serious doctrinal difference with Eustathius, that later came to a head when Basil and Gregory of Nazianzus argued strenuously for the hypostatic nature of the Spirit of God, *homoousion* with the Father and Son, and Eustathius (though Nicene in his Christology) preferred not to follow the same high pneumatology. Because his sister stayed loyal to Eustathius, this was probably the reason he never referred to her, it not being considered proper to denounce one's own family members in any text for whatever reason.

His younger brother, however, Gregory of Nyssa, had been more or less entirely brought up and educated by Macrina, and he felt no reserve in lauding her as one of the wonders of the church in her generation. His *Life of Macrina* presents her rhetorically as a kind of dying Socrates.[43] He tells how he came to her monastery while she was on her deathbed in 379, and she spoke to him about the immortality of the soul in an edifying conversation.

For Gregory, Macrina's ability to discourse without fear on the concept of spiritual immortality proclaimed her to be a leading female philosopher-ascetic. It is, in fact, a canonization hagiographical text. And here the usual problem of women in texts applies: first of all, it is entirely written from Gregory's own perspectives, as a male bishop, addressing the memory of a beloved sister he had difficulty persuading his elder brother should be mentioned in any way at all, though when Basil died, Gregory was

---

[42]Cf. Sozomen, *Church History* 3.14; Socrates, *Church History* 2.43; Basil, *Epistle* 223. It is probably Eustathius and his nomadic ascetics who raised the ire the bishops against them and led to the legislation produced by the Synod of Gangra in 340.

[43]V. C. Woods, trans., *St. Gregory of Nyssa: Ascetical Works*, Fathers of the Church 58 (Washington, DC: Catholic University of America Press, 1967), 159-91.

able as a bishop himself to restore the honor. Gregory was one of the leading intellectuals of the day, and though he had been trained in rhetoric by some of the leading scholars of the time, including St. Gregory the Theologian, his *Life of Macrina* is a statement that he regarded her as one of his supreme teachers.[44] And here is the usual problem: the conventions of ancient rhetoric mean that Macrina emerges as a symbol. Nothing of her own teachings is recorded at all. Between the *topos* of Socrates's dying words to his disciples, from the Platonic writings, and Gregory's own concerns as a writer to shape her memorial hagiographically, hardly anything of the real woman, Macrina, emerges. And yet, some deduction can allow us to look behind the screen.

Macrina's monastery was at Annesos, the country estate of his family. When she was still young her father (a millionaire landowner) had betrothed her to a neighboring landowner in a political match. She had not yet gone to live with the man when he died. Since she was now of practical marriageable age, her father immediately started to find another match for her. But she played the ecclesial card. According to the canons, she argued, the first betrothal was regarded as a full marriage, albeit not consummated. And the church's legislation frowned on second marriage. Intending to be a dutiful daughter of the church, she refused to engage in an illicit second union. She had the weight of church law behind her now, to counterbalance her father's demands, and was able to continue living at home as a dedicated virgin.

Soon after her father himself died. The mother Emmelia had no head for business, so although Basil was the heir, Macrina took Emmelia and the younger brothers off to their country estate of Annesos, where she set up an extended household, designating it, for herself and Basil (who came after her there and learned the skills he later put to effect in legislating for monastic communities), as an ascetic complex. Eventually Basil's clerical career placed him more in the urban flow of Cappadocian Caesarea, where he eventually became the archbishop, and so he left the Annesos complex more or less to Macrina, where it seems she applied Eustathius's ideas of classless living. It is recorded that the nuns there did various works together regardless of rank. At the time of her death, when Gregory Nyssa visited, she has appointed another abbess as successor, who clearly has legal control over the whole land and buildings and offers Gregory only a small "memento" of his sister.[45] Macrina's election of virginity, therefore, effectively had placed her at the head of the

---

[44]See further J. A. McGuckin, *St. Gregory of Nazianzus: An Intellectual Biography* (Crestwood, NY: St. Vladimir's Seminary Press, 2001).

[45]He tells the story triumphantly in that what was on offer was either a rich-looking object or a plain metal cross. He chooses the latter, knowing well enough that it contained a relic of the true cross. What is interesting, though, is that it seems to emerge from this that he has no legal power of command over the community, even as bishop and surviving family member, nor did he inherit the land and buildings.

household. Her brother Basil was legally the head, immediately after his father's death, but Macrina persuaded him to adopt the ascetic life, too. By means of virginity she achieved independence, control of the family estate (at least the country estate), and an advanced education. It all mounted up to making her one of the leading Christian women of Cappadocia in the fourth century. Yet even so, we know her by reputation alone, as if by the shock waves her life left as ripples in the sand.[46]

Other female millionaires had more of an impact. They did not suffer from the immediate theological disapproval of such as the Cappadocian fathers, for example, and so appear in the literature as great patronesses. Melania the Elder (c. 342–410) and her granddaughter Melania the Younger (c. 385–439) used their immense monetary resources along with an ascetic identity to forge identities for themselves as leading Christian intellectuals.[47] Melania the Elder's monastery on the Mount of Olives sheltered both Rufinus of Aquileia and Evagrius of Pontus, along with many other Christian intellectuals of the day, and became known as one of the Christian world's great centers for the study and dissemination of the works of Origen of Alexandria.

Melania's son, left behind in Rome, as she did not want to be encumbered by the infant, having done her duty and provided the heir to the family millions, must have been dismayed when his own daughter told him that she too did not wish to marry but spend her life and her dowry in the pursuit of a Christian career. He forced her to marry Pinianus, an equally rich nobleman. Melania the Younger tried to persuade her new husband that they should live together as virgins. He was not impressed. When she was pregnant, she prayed earnestly, so her hagiographer tells us, that she would not be hindered in her vocation by the birth of children: and later that night she gave birth to a stillborn infant. The writer of her life advances this as a sign that she and Pinianus would no longer be concerned with earthly things. They both traveled widely away from Rome (subject to Gothic invasion in 410) and settled together with other wealthy Roman refugees on their estates in North Africa, founding two monasteries at Thagaste, where they made the acquaintance of St. Augustine. In 417 they moved to Palestine and stayed with St. Jerome at Bethlehem. After Pinianus's death in 431, Melania founded a monastery of her own on the Mount of Olives, near the one her grandmother had built.[48] She visited Constantinople

---

[46] See further S. Elm, *Virgins of God: The Making of Asceticism in Late Antiquity* (Oxford: Clarendon, 1994); P. Wilson-Kastner, "Macrina: Virgin and Teacher," *Andrews University Seminary Studies* 17 (1979): 105-17.

[47] F. X. Murphy, "Melania the Elder: A Biographical Note," *Traditio* 5 (1947): 59-77.

[48] Its ruins are probably those visible on the grounds of the Dominus Flevit Church on the Mount of Olives.

before her death at Jerusalem in 439. The priest Gerontius, who took over charge of her monastery, wrote an account of her life soon afterward.[49]

Like Macrina, Melania is thereby rendered largely into a silent type of holiness and benefaction by her biographer, and this despite her evident prominence as an intellectual and director of a theological school and monastery in her own lifetime. She leaves no written teaching of her own firsthand. If this happens to the millionaires, what can we imagine was the lot of their innumerable more impoverished sisters? Wealth distribution in antiquity was comparable to the Majority World today: a few immensely wealthy families controlling all the land and fluid cash resources, and the 99 percent living subsistence lives. There was no middle class to speak of, but rather a small tranche of skilled professionals (rhetoricians, musicians, and so on) who depended utterly on the patronage of the rich households for their (equally subsistent) livelihoods.

So the vast majority of Christian women in this era were most likely uneducated and illiterate. This is a far cry, however, from being synonymous with "stupid." Then, as through long centuries and into the present, in terms of church life, it was the silent generations of mothers and grandmothers who chiefly passed on the faith to new generations. In times of stress and persecution (as in recent decades in Russia or Eastern Europe), it was innumerable unnamed Christian women who kept the flame of Christian life alive when the more obvious structures of the church were left devastated: buildings destroyed, clergy assassinated. Of all the many "offices" and governance structures of Christianity, the most unsung and yet the most important of all is surely that of grandmother telling the old stories and passing on a love of things Christian from one generation to the next two. So the ubiquitous invisibility of women in times past has not always been a disadvantage. It often allowed survival and succession of the deeper truths, as it still does today.

This hagiographizing abstraction of important women Christians is also visible in the way that St. Gregory of Nazianzus gives us information about the women of his own family: his mother, Nonna (d. 374), wife of the bishop Gregory, who was his father; and his sister Gorgonia (d. 370), married to a military commander in Cappadocia. Gregory's mother, he tells us, belonged to a long-standing Christian family. Gregory, a consummately skilled rhetorician himself and one of the most learned bishops of his age, was the first Christian to adapt the ancient Hellenistic genres of the funeral *encomium*, to make it serve as one of the earliest strands of Christian hagiography (apart from martyr narratives). He domesticated the genre in the process. His

---

[49]E. A. Clark, *The Life of Melania the Younger: Introduction, Translation and Commentary* (Lewiston, NY: Mellen, 1984).

*Funeral Oration for Gorgonia* sets up many tropes that will characterize later female hagiography (the "diamond of her sex," the dutiful wife, zealous person of prayer, notable benefactor, and so on) but is also important for offering the first detailed text focusing specifically and precisely on a Christian woman notable. Gregory clearly tries in every way he can to canonize his sister as akin to being a martyr, yet the text equally reveals she never had anything remotely like an experience of martyrdom. Her sufferings were mainly, he tells us, to have "fallen out of her carriage."

Even so, it was an experience that probably hastened her death. Gregory tells us also that in a state of desperation about not finding relief in the healing remedies she was offered, Gorgonia broke into the local church one night and smeared her body with the eucharistic elements that were kept in the altar area. Gregory explains to his (probably shocked) listeners that this was an act of "bold" piety, for she expected a cure from her Lord. But as the text ends it becomes clear that at the time she had not even been baptized: for she received that sacrament *in extremis*. And so her odd behavior with regard to the Eucharist might well have been that she never had actually witnessed how the faithful received the mysteries in church. The "pious boldness" Gregory attributes to her is also probably explicable on the basis that she and her husband had probably built the church and furnished it in the first place, and the local priest must surely have been one of her estate workers: liable to a duty to her as much as to his bishop.

Gregory's funeral sermon, one senses, is partly intended to smooth down any controversy arising from her unusual end. Once more, we get a glimpse of something between the curtains that is not the text's immediate intent to provide. Gregory's text speaks in place of Gorgonia, only partly for her. And the Gorgonia that results is the hagiographic symbol. In this case it is unlikely that Gorgonia had much personal involvement in the life of Christian letters. She exercised her patronage out of her wealth. Even so, the building of churches was part of the very fabric of the expanse of Christianity in the post-Constantinian generation, as significant as literature. But not having produced any text of her own that merited copying, Gorgonia's icon lies in the hands of her male relatives. Much the same could be said of most of the other notable Christian women of this period. They are noted as companions of the great male teachers: the rich widow Anthusa, who educates and forms her son John Chrysostom to become the leading Christian rhetorician of the fifth century; the millionaire deaconess Olympias, who owned extensive properties in Constantinople and founded an order of ascetic educated women in the imperial capital; and the learned women around Jerome, particularly the intellectual theologian Marcella (325–410). The latter was widowed at seventeen years of age and joined the core circle of Jerome at Bethlehem. We are told that priests and learned men journeyed to consult with her to find answers to questions that troubled them. It is also reported that she gave her answers in the name of Jerome, rather than herself, so as not to cause scandal at the aspect of a woman teaching in the churches.

## WOMEN IN THE LATER BYZANTINE HAGIOGRAPHIES

The hagiographical texts, early medieval lives of the saints that had a popular consumption, especially the Greek Byzantine ones written for the educated classes of the imperial cities, continue to feature women in them occasionally. Some of them adapt the old Egyptian desert literature with its focus on heroic fasters of the deserts and bring in the central character as a woman. Two in particular are worthy of notice, both offering the reader strange complexities of interpretation. The first is the *Life of Mary of Egypt*. The second is the *Life of St Marinos/Marina*.

The *Life of Mary of Egypt* is a seventh-century reworking, probably by Sophronius the literary patriarch of Jerusalem, of earlier traditions of the Palestinian desert communities.[50] The eponymous hero, in Sophronius's account, is Mary, a prostitute from Alexandria who began her trade at twelve and followed it until she was twenty-nine. And then, one September when the boats left the docks in Alexandria to take pilgrims on their journey to the holy shrines at Jerusalem for the Feast of the Exaltation of the Cross, she decided to go along with them, paying for her passage by offering sexual services to the crew. The sex workers were not allowed by the church authorities to enter the holy places themselves if they were identified. There in itself a window is opened for us onto ancient practices. Not only was Mary only twelve when she was given (sold?) into prostitution, but the trade clearly, as ever, followed the crowds, whether it was at the pagan circus or at the Christian shrines.[51]

The tale tells us that Mary not only decided to go to Jerusalem when she disembarked but also took the opportunity to visit the Anastasis church.[52] There, at the door, we are told, invisible hands held her back, refusing her entry. In day-to-day life, deacons (symbolically vested in services as the angels) would actually serve as security police for the church buildings and would have been well used to refusing entry to men and women whom they considered to be inappropriate visitors. In the story, however, it is real angels who invisibly hold Mary back. She is so distressed at this

---

[50] It has been translated recently by Maria Kouli, in A. M. Talbot, ed., *Holy Women of Byzantium: Ten Saints' Lives in English Translation* (New Haven, CT: Harvard University Press, 1996), 65-93. Sophronius (560–638) was patriarch of Jerusalem, 634–638.

[51] A common fate for orphans in late antiquity.

[52] In the West it has long been called the Church of the Holy Sepulchre. Its two central loci were the relic of the cross of Christ and the place of the tomb.

rejection that she vows to reform her life if she can enter to venerate the place of the cross, and immediately the invisible power releases her, and inside the church she experiences God's mercy and repents from the heart. True to her word, Mary then renounces her former life and, taking only three loaves into the wilderness, lives unseen for forty-seven years, pursuing a life of radical prayer and fasting. In the stark desert conditions her clothes rot from her back until she is clothed only by the long hair that reaches down to her knees. Her skin withers, and she lives on next to nothing.

It was the custom of the monasteries of the Judean desert at this period to set their monks wandering and living off the land, together with a few dried loaves they could take with them, as the manner of accomplishing the Lenten fast. It was a way of seeing which monks could live up to the ancient traditions most successfully before having to come back to the shelter of the monastery. The story tells us that one of these monks, the priest Zosimas, during his time of Lenten wandering, came across her. At first sight he thinks she is a demon in the desert and is afraid. He soon realizes that she is a great saint, possessed of clairvoyance and powerful prayer. She makes him promise to come back next year and bring her the Eucharist. When he does so, she walks across the waters of the River Jordan to approach him, and this time he is afraid of her because of her holiness. The following year, again obeying the instructions she gives for her burial, he comes to find her body lying unattended in the desert. He is unable to bury her himself, but then a lion mysteriously comes by and patiently digs the grave for him.[53]

This story became an international bestseller for centuries afterward.[54] It was probably read in the refectories of the great pilgrimage centers, as a warning to pilgrims not to misbehave when away from home; but also as a very dramatic story of sin and repentance, basic theological elements summarizing the chief aspects of Christian spirituality in a cartoon-like manner. The literary genre is a masterpiece of storytelling: women walking on the waters, levitating, lions appearing out of nowhere.

Sophronius developed his story out of a real account of a typical desert-dwelling monastic. The narrative first appears in the *Life of St. Kyriakos*, written by Cyril of Scythopolis in the sixth century.[55] Cyril tells how he heard from the Palestinian monk John how he had encountered in his wanderings a solitary female ascetic living in a cave in the Judean desert. She told him she had once been a cantor in the Jerusalem

---

[53]A detail lifted, probably, from Jerome's *Life of Paul the First Hermit*.
[54]Numerous manuscripts in Greek and Latin can be found (the earliest now dates to the ninth century), and there are ancient translations extant in Syriac, Armenian, Ethiopic, and Slavonic. The legend of St. Mary also entered the liturgical tradition. The *Vita* itself is still read in the Eastern churches during the Thursday of the fifth week in Lent.
[55]Greek text: E. Schwartz, *Kyrillos von Skythopolis* (Leipzig: Hinrichs, 1939), 233-34; translation, R. M. Price, *Lives of the Monks of Palestine* (Kalamazoo, MI: Cistercian Publications, 1991), 256-58.

church but had become a hermit, living in the cave for eighteen years in complete isolation, living off her jar of water and a basket of dried vegetables that she had first brought with her. When he came to visit her again some time later, he found her dead body in her cave and so buried her there. This tale is more or less paralleled in John Moschos's seventh-century collection of monastic tales, *The Spiritual Meadow*, which adds the detail that the woman in question had formerly served as a nun in one of the churches of Jerusalem before becoming a solitary ascetic in the desert.[56]

So far then, the tale is a standard introduction of an ascetic woman into the tales of the desert fathers. It is remarkable because the woman is advanced as an example to the male readers of the Palestinian monastic literature, that a woman could do far better than any of them. She is not a reformed prostitute but a holy nun who lives an unbelievably strict life (miraculous in character), putting them all to shame. It strikes the monastics as a wondrous story because of the courage needed, first of all for someone to live so radically a cave existence in that dangerous wilderness, and second because that ascetic was female.[57]

In this light Sophronius's literary alterations become more noticeable. The rationale for Mary's life of askesis is now the shame attendant on her previous life as an Egyptian prostitute. Although she has clairvoyance to know the future, can levitate, and command the wild beasts, this Mary still insists to the priest Zosimas that the grace that clergy have is superior and demanding of all reverence even from the most ascetic of laypeople. Once can easily recognize Sophronius's added literary interests. As the clerical leader of the Jerusalem church, one that contained within it so many renowned ascetics and "holy men," he must have had great difficulties controlling the charismatic conflicts of his varied flock. In the aftermath of the Council of Chalcedon, as Cyril of Scythopolis tells us often in his narratives of the Palestinian monks that the divisions between Monophysites and Dyophisites were acute and bitter.[58] Several of the leading holy ascetics of each side attempted to demonstrate their theological correctness, and the folly of their opponents, by miraculous signs attendant on their respective Eucharists. In his text Sophronius is trying to put charismatic holiness into its proper and respectful place. He is also turning the narrative around toward more of a lay audience. In the course of this, however, the actual woman, the mystic and nun Mary, is repainted as a harlot. It is

---

[56]PG 87:3049. Translated by J. Wortley, *The Spiritual Meadow of John Moschos* (Kalamazoo, MI: Cistercian Publications, 1992), 148-49.
[57]Dangerous because of the climate, the wild beasts, and the numerous brigands wandering through there.
[58]Those rejecting the "two nature" Christology of Chalcedon were called Monophysites, those accepting it Dyophisites.

a travesty of the actuality. So, Sophronius thought, the demands of his literary masterpiece demanded.

Perhaps he was right: but clearly he thought that since it was a woman at the core of the narrative, he was under no obligation whatsoever to keep any link to historical reality. It would have been, indeed was, different if the hero in question had been a man. Between the fourth to sixth centuries his work started a number of other "repentant harlot" stories. They have been gathered together in the study by Dame Benedicta Ward.[59] The popularity of this genre might well represent an important impact Christian monasticism had on the ranks of female sex workers, which were very large in these times, leaving a large body of women without much in the way of social or financial security. Perhaps their appearance as female ascetic penitents in the latter stages of their careers does indeed mark one road out of the "oldest profession" that was adapted by enough women at this period to have made a mark on the literature in this way. Perhaps, however, the duplication of the tales merely represents a literary trope establishing itself because of its titillation value in male monastic refectories. It is difficult to tell. Certainly the way the female penitents behave is usually a trope of one excess of debauchery, followed by an excessively severe life of virtue, to demonstrate a message for emulation by present-day ascetics. One suspects the readership is predominantly male.

The last example of Byzantine hagiography I would like to lift up briefly in this regard is the *Life of Marina/Marinos*.[60] The ending of the original Greek is gender-ambivalent for a reason. This is one of that genre of hagiographic lives that has recently been called "transvestite saints," and this in the sense that the plot turns around the identity of an ascetic everyone has taken for years to be a man but who at death turns out to have been a woman. It includes the life of Pelagia, a saint who is often confused with Marina because of the similar maritime derivations of the names. The *Life of Pelagia*, however, is one of the corpus of repentant harlot stories, though like Marina, when she dies after a life of strenuous asceticism, having excelled as one of the leading monks of the Jerusalem church, she is found, at her laying out, to be female; and the whole church is "full of wonder" and celebrates her achievement.[61] Marina too poses as a man in order to avail herself, paradoxically, of the freedoms of the ascetic life, which would have been closed to her as a woman.

---

[59]B. Ward, *Harlots of the Desert* (Kalamazoo, MI: Cistercian Publications, 1987). She includes here translations of the *vitae* of other renowned Christian "harlots": Pelagia, Thais, and Mary the niece of Abraham.

[60]Text edited by L. Clugnet, *Vie et Office de Sainte Marine*, in *Bibliothèque hagiographique orientale*, vol. 8 (Paris: Picard et Fils, 1905).

[61]The English text can be found in Ward, *Harlots of the Desert*, 66-75.

The story tells how her father, Eugenius, wished to enter the monastic life after his wife's death and arranged to marry his daughter Marina off before he left. She, however, insists on entering monastic life beside him, and so accompanies him, cutting her hair and adopting the guise of a young boy. Her father dies, and she remains as a young servant monk in the community. One day she is sent out on an errand of monastery business that requires her and three other monks to stay in a wayside tavern overnight. The innkeeper's daughter at the tavern that same night sleeps with a traveling soldier, and nine months later gives birth to a child. Her outraged father forces her to confess who the father of the baby was, and having no idea where the soldier might be, she decides to blame the handsome, beardless young monk who had passed by on monastery business.

The family brings the baby to the monastery and demands that the monks take charge of it and accept the public shame. All the community are convinced of the young monk's guilt, and the abbot commands Marinos to work outside the monastery and bring up the child, doing the most menial works at the beck and call of all. Marinos will not say a word in his/her own defense and accepts the baby to raise. In iconographic representations of her she is usually shown in monastic garb with a child clinging to her leg. After many years Marinos becomes ill and dies, and as the monks gather around to wash the body and put it in its shroud, they discover her hidden truth—that all the while she was a woman and had suffered all the calumnies in patience over so many years. The story went through many translations, editions, and variations of detail.[62] But the central symbol remains the same: an ascetic who refuses to justify herself when even a word would have revealed her vindication.

The point of it is not so much an "erotic" tale, though the sexual interest factor doubtless made for the popularity of such tales in a communal, chiefly male celibate, audience of monks. The issue of disguise and revelation here is mainly about status and gender.[63] These tales represent a twofold trope: that monasticism is a life of forgetfulness of self where reputation no longer matters, and that God sees the truth of the inner life. The motif of the woman masquerading as a man in order to finally be revealed as excelling the men (who judge their betters with a harsh judgment), in both the Pelagia story and the Marinos narrative, reveals yet again the issue of the "disguised female" of our ancient sources.

Many regard the Marinos story as wholly legendary; but it can throw some light, perhaps, on the manner in which life in a Byzantine men's monastery, however forbidding that might seem to us moderns, was for an early medieval Christian woman

---

[62]Greek, Latin, Syriac, Armenian, Coptic, Arabic, and Ethiopic.
[63]As modern transvestism, psychologically approached, can also be. See V. L. Bullough, "Transvestites in the Middle Ages," *American Journal of Sociology* 79, no. 6 (May 1974): 1381-94.

a more liberative prospect than many available alternatives—a life that offered security, access to literature, chant, domesticated labor, and prayer in a supportive and nonpredatory extended family. For many ancient women, such terms of existence would have seemed blessing indeed. This hagiographic genre of the female in monk's clothing plays with the radical notion of celibate community life rendering gender obsolete. It thus refers to a monastic trope that the ascetical virgins on earth fulfill Christ's prophecy that "they shall be as the angels are" in heaven (Mt 22:30), where "there is neither male nor female" (Gal 3:28) but only communion in Christ.

As with many other things in the Christian tradition, the role of women in the foundations of the church and their innumerable contributions to the development of the evangelical preaching have tended to be overlooked and forgotten, blurred, or even falsified. It has often and usually been difficult for the church to escape from enthrallment with Aristotle and his views of the deficiency of womankind. The church has often, unthinkingly, allowed Aristotle's pagan ideas about gender to thrive long past their natural lifespan. This remains an overwhelming challenge. Our own time, when women have, in so many places in the developed world, accessed self-determination, wealth, education, power, and safety, is now understandably marked also by a desire to return to sources and find far more positive exemplars for the Christian future than those who worked in the dominantly patriarchal structures of the past. Christian male theorists of late antiquity all too often lifted up Aristotle's (toxic) views of the fixity of natures and ranks and wrapped them in the Genesis narrative of the fallibility of Eve, to make a heavy burden for its own (and womankind's) back.

## A SHORT READER

***Aristotle,*** **Politics *1.260a.*** There are, established by nature, the different classes of rulers and ruled. For the free man rules the slave; the male the female; the man the child, all in different manners; just as all humans possess the various parts of the soul, but hold them in different ways. For a slave does not have the deliberative part of the soul at all; and while the female does possess it, it is devoid of complete authority, while the child possesses it only in an undeveloped form.

***St. Paul, 1 Timothy 2:8-15 (first century).*** It is my desire, therefore, that in every place the men should pray, lifting up holy hands without anger or quarreling; also that women should adorn themselves modestly and sensibly in appropriate dress, not with braided hair or gold or pearls or costly clothes, but by good deeds, as befits women who profess religion. Let a woman learn in silence with all submissiveness. I permit no woman to teach or to have authority over men; she is to keep silent. For Adam was formed first, then Eve; and Adam was not deceived, but the woman was deceived and became a transgressor. Yet woman will be saved through bearing children, if she continues in faith and love and holiness, with modesty.

**Tertullian, On the Dress of Women *1.1-10 (second century).*** If there dwelt on this earth a faith that is as great as shall be that reward of faith that we look for in the heavens, then, dearest sisters, not one of you, from the time that you first came to know the Lord and know the truth of [woman's] condition, would ever cherish a desire for a cheerful or ostentatious style of dress. You would prefer rather to go about in humble clothing and demonstrate a simple appearance, walking around like a repentant and mourning Eve, so that by the clothing of repentance you might more fully expiate that which you derived from Eve, namely the shame of the first sin and the disgrace of human perdition. "Woman, in shame and anxiety shall you bear children. And you shall incline to your husband, who shall be master over you." So do you not know that you are Eve? God's sentence on your sex endures to this age, and so it follows that the guilt must also survive. You are the devil's gateway, the pillager of the forbidden tree. You are the first deserter of the divine law. You are the one who persuaded him whom the devil was to strong enough to attack. You destroyed with great ease man who is the image of God. On account of your penalty, which was death, even the Son of God had to die. So how do you have a thought to adorn yourself more elaborately than your tunics of skins? If from the very origins of the world the Milesians had learned to shear sheep, the Serians how to weave fibers, the Tyrians how to dye, the Phrygians how to embroider with the needle, the Babylonians how to work the loom; if pearls had already gleamed, and onyx stones glittered; if gold had already emerged from the ground (with all the obsessive longing that accompanies it); if the mirror too had already learned to lie so magnificently, I suppose that Eve herself, even when expelled from paradise to death, would also have coveted these things. But now, if Eve wishes to live again, she should neither crave or use those things that, when Eve was alive, she had neither possessed or owned. All of these things, therefore, are the fripperies of a woman in her condemned, her dead state, and are appointed only to make up appearances for her funeral.

**The Passion of Perpetua and Felicity *2-4 (second century).*** At this time the young catechumens, Revocatus and Felicity (who was a slave like him) and Saturninus and Secundulus, were arrested. With them also was Vibia Perpetua, a nobly born woman who had been educated in a liberal manner and wedded honorably, having a father and mother and two brothers, one of them who was also a catechumen, as well as a son, who was a baby at the breast. [Perpetua] herself was about twenty-two years of age. What follows hereafter, she shall tell herself; for the whole order of her martyrdom is as she left it written with her own hand and in her own words. When we were still under legal surveillance (she tells) and my father was pleased to harangue me with his words and constantly tried to break my faith (because he loved me), I said to him: Father, can you see this pot lying here, a pitcher or whatever it is? And he said, I do see it. So I said to him: Can it be called by any other name than that which it has? And he answered me: No. And I said to him: And that is why I can be called no other name other than that which I am: a Christian. And my father was made very angry by these words and came at me as if to tear out my eyes; but he only shouted at me, and then went away a beaten man: him and the devil's own arguments. Then because I was without my father for a few days I gave thanks to the Lord, and I was comforted because of his absence. In this same space of a few days we were baptized, and the Spirit declared to me, after the water, that I ought to pray for nothing else except for the endurance of the flesh. After a few days we were taken into the prison, and I was greatly afraid then, because I had never known such darkness. It was a bitter day! There was a great heat because of the crowd inside, and the soldiers handled us savagely. I was also greatly anguished because of my nursing of the child. Then Tertius and Pomponius, the blessed deacons who ministered to us, spent money so that for a few hours we could be taken to a better part of the prison for some refreshment. The others went out of the prison for some relief, so then I suckled my child, who was already faint with hunger. And being very anxious about him, I spoke to my mother and encouraged my brother and commended my son to their care. I grieved because I saw they were grieving for my sake. I suffered such cares for many days, but I managed it that the child should stay with me in prison, and then I immediately became well and my labor and care for the child were all lightened for me. Suddenly the prison became a palace for me, so that I would rather be there than anywhere else. Then my brother said to me: Lady, my sister, you are now in high honor, even to the point that you could ask for a vision, and it would be shown you whether this trouble will result in your suffering or your deliverance. And I, because I knew that I spoke to the Lord, for whose sake I suffered all these things, made him no promise him, because I was not sure. But I said to him: I will let you know tomorrow. But I did ask. And this was what was shown to me. I saw a ladder of bronze, incredibly high, reaching up even to heaven; but it was very narrow, such that no more than one person could ascend at any time. And in the sides of the ladder all kinds of iron things were embedded: swords, spears, hooks, and knives; so that if any person climbed up in a careless way, or did not keep his eyes fixed straight up, they would be cut, and their flesh would stick in the iron. And right by the foot of the ladder there was a serpent lying, incredibly large, and lying in wait for any who would try to ascend, to frighten them so that they would not go up. And then Saturus went up first (who afterwards had of his own free will given himself up for our sakes, because it was he who had inspired us; and when we were arrested he had not been present). And he came up to the top of the ladder, and he turned around and said to me: Perpetua, I am waiting for you; but take care that the serpent does not bite you. And I said: In the name of Jesus Christ it shall not hurt me. And then as if it was afraid of me it put out its head gently under the ladder, and I stepped upon it as if treading on the first rung. And I climbed up, and I saw a very great and spacious garden, and in the middle there was a tall, white-haired man sitting, in shepherd's clothing, milking his sheep; and standing around all dressed in white were many thousands. And he raised his head and looked at me and said to me: Welcome, child. And he called to me, and from the curd he had from the milk he gave me a little piece; and I took it with joined hands and ate it; and all those who were the bystanders said: Amen. And at the sound of that word I woke up, but still eating something sweet; I did not know what. And then immediately I told my brother of this. And we both knew it meant my suffering. And from that time we no longer had any hope in this world.

**St. Gregory of Nazianzus, Oration 37.6-7 (fourth century).** Why did [the Roman law] penalize women but act indulgently to men? Why was it that a woman who sinned against her husband's bed is named an adulteress, and the penalties of the law applied for this are very severe, and yet if a husband commits fornication against his wife, he has no legal case to answer? Such legislation as this, I do not accept. Such customs as these I cannot approve. Clearly those who made this law were men, and this is why their legislation is hard on women. They likewise placed children under the authority of their fathers, while leaving the weaker sex without protections. God does not act like this. He says, "Honor your father and your mother," which is the first commandment with a promise attached to it, "so that it may be well with you.

And whoever curses father or mother, let him die the death." This is how God assigned honor to what was good and punishment to the evil. Again it is said: "The blessing of a father strengthens the children's households; but a mother's curse uproots the foundations" (Sirach 3:11). Note the equability of the legislation here. There is but one Maker of man and woman; one debt is owed by children to both their parents. So why do you demand chastity [of the married woman] but do not observe it yourself? How can you demand what you will not give? Though you yourself are the same body, how can you legislate in this imbalanced way? Suppose you take the worst scenario as answer. "The woman sinned!" Well, so did Adam. The serpent deceived them both; and one was not found to be the stronger while the other was weaker. Suppose you take a better scenario. Then Christ saves both by his passion. Was he made flesh only for the man? No, he was incarnated also for the woman. Did he die only for the man? No, woman also is saved by his death. Do you think that it is the man who is honored when Christ is called "of the seed of David"? (Rom 1:3). Well, remember, he is born of a virgin, and this is surely on the woman"s side. He himself tells us: "These two shall be one flesh"; accordingly, let this single flesh enjoy equal honor. Paul also legislates for chastity by the example of Christ. How, you ask; in what way? He tells us: "This is a great mystery. I speak concerning Christ and the church" (Eph 5:32). It is a good thing for the wife to reverence Christ through her husband: and it is equally good for the husband not to dishonor the church through his wife. Paul tells us: "Let the wife see that she reverence her husband, for in this way she reverences Christ." But he also commands the husband to cherish his wife, as Christ cherishes the church.

**St. John Chrysostom, On the Kind of Women Who Ought to Be Taken as Wives 4 (fifth century).** By custom, our life is organized into two spheres: public affairs and private concerns. And God determines both of them. The presidency of the household is assigned to woman; to man falls all the business of state, the markets, and all the administration of justice, governance, or military matters, and things like this. . . . Truly all this is a work of God's love and wisdom, that he who is skilled in greater things can be completely useless and incompetent in seeing to the less important ones. And in this way, the work of the woman is rendered necessary. For if a man was able to undertake both sorts of activities, the female sex might easily be despised. And on the other hand, if all the important and more beneficial enterprises were turned over to the woman, she would go quite mad.

## FURTHER READING

Antonova, S. "Chosen to Follow and to Lead: Women in the Ancient Christian Church." In *Women in the Eastern Christian Tradition*, ed. S. Antonova, 15-37. New York: Theotokos Press, 2013.

———, ed. *Women in the Eastern Christian Tradition.* New York: Theotokos Press, 2013.

Burrus, V. *Chastity as Autonomy.* Studies in Women and Religion 23. Lewiston, NY: Mellen, 1987.

Cameron, A., and A. Kuhrt. *Images of Women in Antiquity.* Detroit: Wayne State University Press, 1983. Esp. chaps. 11, 17, 18.

Castelli, E. "Virginity and Its Meaning for Women's Sexuality in Early Christianity." *Journal of Feminist Studies in Religion* 2 (1986): 61-88.

Clark, E. A. *Ascetic Piety and Women's Faith.* Lewiston, NY: Mellen, 1986.

———. *Women in the Early Church.* Message of the Fathers of the Church 13. Wilmington, DE: M. Glazier, 1983.

Clark, G. *Women in Late Antiquity: Pagan and Christian Lifestyles.* Oxford: Oxford University Press, 1993.

Cloke, G. *This Female Man of God: Women and Spiritual Power in the Patristic Age. 350–450.* London: Routledge, 1995.

Eisen, U. E. *Women Office-Holders in Early Christianity: Epigraphical and Literary Studies.* Translated by L. Maloney. Collegeville, MN: Liturgical Press, 2000.

Elm, S. *Virgins of God: The Making of Asceticism in Late Antiquity.* Oxford: Oxford University Press, 1994.

Harrison, V. "The Feminine Man in Late Antique Ascetic Piety." *Union Seminary Quarterly Review* 48, nos. 3-4 (1994): 49-71.

Heine, S. *Women and Early Christianity: A Reappraisal.* Translated by J. Bowden. Minneapolis: Augsburg, 1987.

Kadel, A. *Matrology. A Bibliography of Writings by Christian Women from the 1st to 15th Centuries.* New York: Continuum, 1982.

———. "Writings of the Mothers: Women Authors of the Eastern Church Before the Fifteenth C." In *Women in the Eastern Christian Tradition*, ed. S. Antonova, 45-54. New York: Theotokos Press, 2013.

Karras, V. "Patristic Views on the Ontology of Gender." In *Personhood: Deepening the Connections Between Body, Mind, and Soul*, ed. J. Chirban, 113-15. Westport, CT: Bergin and Garvey, 1996.

Kramer, R. S. *Maenads, Martyrs, Matrons, Monastics: A Source-Book on Women's Religions in the Greco-Roman World.* Philadelphia: Fortress, 1988.

Kramer, R. S., and M. D'Angelo. *Women and Christian Origins.* New York: Oxford University Press, 1999.

Lang, J. *Ministers of Grace: Women in the Early Church.* London: St. Paul's Publications, 1989.

Laporte, J. *The Role of Women in Early Christianity.* Lewiston, NY: Mellen, 1982.

Lieu, J. "The Attraction of Women into Early Judaism and Christianity: Gender and the Politics of Conversion." *Journal for the Study of the New Testament* 72 (1998): 5-22.

Limberis, V. *Divine Heiress: The Virgin Mary and the Creation of Christian Constantinople.* New York: Routledge, 1994.

McNamara, J. "Muffled Voices: The Lives of Consecrated Women in the 4th Century." In *Medieval Religious Women: Distant Echoes*, ed. J. A. Nichols and L. T. Shank, 11-29. Kalamazoo, MI: Cistercian Publications, 1984.

Pantel, P. S. *From Ancient Goddesses to Christian Saints.* Translated by A. Goldhammer. Vol 1. of *A History of Women*, ed. G. Duby and M. Perrot. Cambridge, MA: Belknap, 1992.

Petersen, J. M. *Handmaids of the Lord: Contemporary Descriptions of Feminine Asceticism in the First Six Christian Centuries.* Kalamazoo, MI: Cistercian Publications, 1996.

Rowlandson, J. *Women and Society in Greek and Roman Egypt: A Sourcebook.* Cambridge: Cambridge University Press, 1998.

Ruether, R. R. "Misogynism and Virginal Feminism in the Fathers of the Church." In *Religion and Sexism: Images of Woman in the Jewish and Christian Traditions*, ed. R. Ruether, 150-83. New York: Simon and Schuster, 1974.

Sawyer, D. *Women and Religion in the First Christian Centuries.* New York: Routledge, 1996.

Scholer, D. M. *Women in Early Christianity.* New York: Garland, 1993.

Schottroff, L. *Lydia's Impatient Sisters: A Feminist Social History of Early Christianity.* Translated by B. Rumscheidt and M. Rumscheidt. Louisville: Westminster John Knox, 1995.

Schüssler Fiorenza, E. *In Memory of Her: A Feminist Theological Reconstruction.* New York: Crossroad, 1994.

Simpson, J. "Women and Asceticism in the 4th Century." *Journal of Religious History* 15 (1988): 38-60.

Stanton, G. N. *Women in the Earliest Churches.* Cambridge: Cambridge University Press, 1988.

Stark, R. "Reconstructing the Rise of Christianity: The Role of Women." *Sociology of Religion* 56, no. 3 (1995): 229-44.

Trevett, C. *Christian Women and the Time of the Apostolic Fathers.* Cardiff, UK: University of Wales Press, 2006.

Yarborough, A. "Christianization in the 4th Century. The Example of Roman Women." *Church History* 45 (1976): 149-65.

# HEALING AND PHILANTHROPY IN EARLY CHRISTIANITY

## HEALING IN ANCIENT HELLENISM

Each of the Gospels demonstrates an intense and lively interest in the healing ministry of Jesus.[1] Even before Mark put together the literary form of the Gospel genre, it is clear enough that a preevangelical narrative structure had explicitly compared Jesus' miracles of healing with those of Elijah and Elisha before him.[2] This concern with miracles of healing, understood chiefly as signs of the godly authenticity of the healer, was something inherited from the Scriptures that carried on into the early church and has been present in varying degrees for the rest of Christianity's history.[3]

In the generic context of first-century Hellenistic religions, healings were often seen as epiphanies of the power of the gods. The cults of several deities were particularly associated with healings, notably Isis (especially at the great temple at Menouthi near Alexandria), or the several shrines of the god Aesculapius, whose cult celebrated his nocturnal visitations of worshipers who came for incubational rest in his temples and there received healing ministrations from the priests as well as epiphanic visitations in dreams. The accounts of these healings can still be found inscribed on the

---

[1] Mark alone demonstrates how much the healing stories provide the core of his Gospel narrative. See Mk 1:29-34; 1:40–2:12; 3:1-6; 5:21-43; 6:30-44, 53-56; 7:24-37; 8:22-26; 10:46-52.

[2] The Elijah cycle determines the shape and order of the miracles of Jesus in the New Testament. It does not seem to be part of Mark's invention, but rather an inheritance of the Aramaic proto-Gospel. The great Elijah and Elisha multiply bread in a crisis, heal a leper, raise the dead son of a widow, have an epiphany on a mountain, cross dry-shod over water, and suffer from wicked princes. All of these miraculous events accumulate to an "Elijah cycle," as it were, that has clearly influenced the manner in which the miraculous ministry of Jesus is recounted, even though all the Evangelists are uneasy about drawing too close an association with the ancient prophet(s), wishing to set Jesus' miracles (and person) on a new basis.

[3] In the sense that they were the validation of the prophet's authority to speak for God, or in the New Testament were signs of Jesus' *exousia*. John uses the structure of the seven "great signs" to show how Jesus' works of power are manifestations of his inner reality as divine Logos.

walls of the ruined sites.[4] At Menouthi the exiled Jerusalem patriarch Sophronius later mistook them for the records of the Christian shrine that had supplanted the Isiac cult in the fifth century.[5] At one of the ancient world's greatest healing shrines, on Cos, the inscriptional narratives show that the healings offered there were based on practical therapeutic techniques in the tradition of Hippocrates.

The early Christians, who did not deny the veracity of these acts, usually attributed them to demonic power intent on confusing the witness of Jesus' uniquely divine healings. What the devotees of the old cults saw as helpful *daimones* behind their cures, the Christians denounced as demons, intent on snaring the devotees more deeply into false cult by offering the appearances of philanthropy. The symbol of Aesculapius as the serpent entwined around the staff (today still a symbol of doctors and hospitals) and the close association of this with Jesus in John 3:14 is more than coincidental. So too, perhaps, is the shrine of Aesculapius the healer discovered within Jerusalem at the excavations of the pool of Bethzatha, the site of Jesus' cure of the paralyzed man in John 5:1-18. Early Christian missionary strategy seems to have used both healing and exorcism, "in the name of Jesus," to serve as a platform for its kerygmatic preaching of the good news.[6] The interface between Jewish, pagan, and Christian understandings of divine philanthropy represented by the medium of healing and deliverance was well suited to its communication needs.

The ancient world, therefore, certainly regarded the healing arts as immensely important, and the profession of doctor was well established in pre-Christian antiquity. As Greek philosophy rose up from the close observation of mental and physical phenomena and, especially after Aristotle, as the empirical method flourished in Greece, so too medical observations of what actually worked for healing and what did not work (not ever an exact science then or now) grew apace to become the foundation of the civilized world's body of medical knowledge. The key moment, as it were, is attributed to Hippocrates of Cos in the age of Pericles, whose systematizations of therapeutic observation first distinguished medicine as a distinct

---

[4] A fifth-century BC inscription from the Asclepion at Epidaurus reads, "Ambrosia from Athens, blind in one eye. She came as a suppliant to the god. Walking about the sanctuary, she ridiculed some of the cures as being unlikely and impossible, the lame and the blind becoming well from only seeing a dream. Sleeping here, she saw a vision. It seemed to her the god came to her and said he would make her well, but she would have to pay a fee by dedicating a silver pig in the sanctuary as a memorial of her ignorance. When he had said these things, he cut her sick eye and poured a medicine over it. When day came she left well." Inscription A4. L. R. LiDonnici, *The Epidaurian Miracle Inscriptions* (Atlanta: Scholars Press, 1995), 89.
[5] See further J. A. McGuckin, "The Influence of the Isis Cult on St. Cyril of Alexandria's Christology," *StPatr* 24 (1992): 191-99.
[6] G. Twelftree, *In the Name of Jesus: Exorcism Among Early Christians* (Grand Rapids: Eerdmans, 2007).

field from the areas of philosophical anthropology or magical theurgy, under which it had formerly been theorized.[7]

The theory behind ancient Greek medicine, however, was predominantly praxis oriented. The profession of doctor was largely a service for the wealthy. The care of the sick poor, who were not likely to provide any suitable fee to the physician or the surgeon, was left to local, less educated help. Toward the lower end of the medical market, as today, scientific and textual knowledge increasingly gave way to magical incantation and folk remedies of very dubious worth. If any theory of illness existed at all in pre-Christian Hellenism it was that the gods often sought out hidden sins, or, less moralistically, simply that bodies often went wrong. In the theological version of the Greek theory, sickness was logically deserved. To put it into more recognizable form today—if illness was a divine punishment, then the medical interference to apply healing was at best ill-judged, or at worst a rather irreverent interference with karma. But more often than not, the only theory that was actually applied by practitioners in terms of ancient medical healing was utility: did the intervention work or not? If the latter, how could it be best repeated in future cases? And this is why one of the first and most important contributions to ancient medical theory was the aspect of the Hippocratic oath that a doctor should "do no harm."[8] Among the ordinary people most illness was terrifying—a real reminder of their close proximity to death, and an instance where they looked anxiously to their god to exercise their role as *soter*, savior.

## HEALING IN EARLY CHRISTIAN PERSPECTIVES

Within the Gospels, the healings of Jesus, like the exorcisms he performs, are presented as manifestations of the advent of the kingdom. He is not presented as a healer per se but rather presents healings as a "sign" of his authority (*exousia*) and a manifestation that is meant to elicit wonder and faith (Mk 2:11). For much of late antiquity, but certainly among Jews and early Christians, sickness was a manifestation, if not of demonical possession, at least of demonical assault. This is why the exorcisms and healings are placed in such proximity in the Gospel accounts, and why later church writers always tended to associate healing with a necessary attitude of repentance on the part of the sick person. The earliest continuations of

---

[7] Hippocrates of Cos, c. 460–370 BC.
[8] The common phrase referring to the Hippocratic oath "first do no harm" is actually a paraphrase popularized by Liverpool surgeon Thomas Inman (1820–1876). The oath itself, however, does prioritize "do no harm" in this form: "With regard to healing the sick, I will devise and order for them the best diet, according to my judgment and means; and I will take care that they suffer no hurt or damage. Nor shall any man's entreaty prevail upon me to administer poison to anyone; neither will I counsel any man to do so. Moreover, I will get no sort of medicine to any pregnant woman, with a view to destroy the child."

the healings of Christ, as can be seen in the accounts of the apostolic healing miracles, run on in the same manner of presenting healings as signs to validate and empower the earliest *kerygma* of the kingdom of God (Acts 3:1-10; 9:36-42; 14:8-18). They are recorded as signs meant to elicit faith in their agent and his message (Acts 2:43; 3:6-10; 5:12-16; 9:32-35; 14:3; 1 Cor 2:4; 2 Cor 12:12; Acts of Paul 50-55; Acts of John 38-45).

The apostle Paul lists healings as one of those charisms expected in the church as the community of the new age, possessed of the *energeia* of the Lord's resurrection.[9] But, more and more, as generations passed, the healing ministry was restricted to the elders of the community, a tendency that is first witnessed in James 5:14-16, where healing is sacramentally conceived through the form of anointing by the presbyters. By the second century, the attitude to healings has moved away from being seen as a sign of the advent of the new age (except in cases related to the cult of martyrs) and reverted more to the generic attitude found in the Psalms and other parts of the Old Testament, where frequently the psalmist prays for deliverance from affliction (Pss 6:1-10; 31–32; 38) or asks the intercession of the prophet or holy man of God (Is 38:1-20; 1 Kings 17:22-24; 2 Kings 5:1-14).

Healings were expected by the Christian faithful from those who were about to receive martyrdom, a sign of their proximity to the kingdom, and soon the charism of healing was widely transferred to the ascetic saint, whose intercessory powers worked wonders, like the prophets of old.[10] Second-century pagan apologist Celsus dismissed Christianity's claim to offer healings as another example of its reliance on tricks to support its bogus religious claims, and it was a charge that Origen was careful to refute.[11] The latter does not deny that the church frequently witnessed healings as part of its regular life cycle, but he is most anxious to distance the practice from what he characterizes as the "magical" invocation of healing that was widely used in the polytheistic religions around him.[12]

In the third-century church there were still those who had the charism of healing who were not ordained elders, and the Roman presbyter-bishop Hippolytus says that they ought to be acknowledged for their gift but not enrolled among the clergy simply because of it.[13] But more and more the gift of healing was appropriated by the Christian presbyters in a liturgical setting, and it is indicative of this that a clear

---

[9] 1 Cor 12:9; see also Justin, *Second Apology* 13; *Dialogue with Trypho* 17, 30; Irenaeus, *Adversus Haereses* 3.18.4; 4.20.2; 5.3.1-2; Origen, *Against Celsus* 7.32; Cyprian, *Epistle* 74.2; 76.2.
[10] Eusebius, *Martyrs of Palestine* 1.1; *Passion of Perpetua and Felicity* 9.1; 16.4; Athanasius, *Life of Antony* 80; Gregory of Nyssa, *Life of Gregory the Wonderworker* (PG 46.916); Jerome, *Life of Hilarion* 8.8.
[11] Origen, *Against Celsus* 3.52.
[12] Ibid., 1.46; 3.71-72.
[13] Hippolytus, *Apostolic Tradition* 1.5.

reference to the charism of healing is found in the church's most ancient ordination prayers.[14] From the late fourth century onward this double pattern of healings became normative. In the first place, healing was accepted as a continuing part of God's manifested mercy in the church, understood as the harbinger of a new creation, and it was thus regarded as something that should be readily available as a ministration of prayer or through the sacraments (anointing and Eucharist were the normal channels) by means of presbyteral invocation and laying on of hands.[15] Accordingly, there were many rituals of healing available in the church's service books from ancient times.

In the second place, however, the act of healing was still regarded as a wondrous phenomenon, eschatologically charged, a particular in-breaking of the kingdom of God for the special end of manifesting an epiphany or of eliciting faith. This aspect is especially emphasized in the early Byzantine hagiographies, and the act of power manifested in the healing is now taken as a mark of great sanctity on the part of the (saintly) agent of healing. The healings of the saints were soon attributed to their relics, and as the latter increasingly came to be associated with the church buildings of the post-persecution-era relics of healing saints and thus were at the center of the experience of Christian pilgrimage from its very inception: not just holy places, then, but also holy people and loci of sought-after cures.[16]

If ancient Greek anthropology had set out the theoretical terms that illness was a curse of the gods, and several of the Old Testament texts had implied that it was a punishment for disobedience or a sign of God's abandonment of the individual, it was Christians of the patristic age who first made a radical development of these anthropological theories, and it was one that allowed medicine to make a dramatic advance in the fourth century. It was the Christian fathers of that era who were driven to make a synthesized dialogue between Hellenistic philosophy and scriptural heritage in order to supply the reason why a human being should be valued enough to extend healing care even to the ranks of the poor: namely, that each human being, poor or rich, was equally graced by God with the divine image (*eikon*) and thus stood equally valued as a child of the kingdom. This insight, elevated now as an axiom, revolutionized the antique concept of a rigidly hierarchical set of valuations attributed to human beings according to wealth, power, social status and education.

---

[14] Apostolic Constitutions 8.16, 26.
[15] So the most ancient eschatological perspectives on healing had been preserved and reinterpreted—occluded, perhaps, but never wholly forgotten.
[16] Altars were built over the relics of the martyr saints, and later other great saints, monastics, and bishops were entombed within the church buildings themselves, their tombs becoming foci of their veneration and the pilgrimage of those seeking to ask their healing intercessions.

This notion of equality as it existed in the canons of the church went far ahead of Roman civil law, where the concept of equality of status for persons was not afforded to the lower classes until much later (if ever); for the earlier set of ancient Greek values and presuppositions about the relative worth of men and women of course did not disappear overnight from Hellenism, nor even Christian Hellenism, nor have they faded away even in our own time, as the perennial inequities in most nation's health care systems will readily demonstrate. Ancient Greek attitudes are perhaps still the predominant way that societies tend to organize themselves: assessing worth of persons, and rights of access to medical care, depending on wealth and social status. Even so, the doctrine of the kingdom of God deeply challenged that archaic system and continues to challenge it; and the notion of philanthropy, after the fourth-century theologians, entered into human social thought no longer on the basis of the accidental "kindness of strangers" (that is, the ancient social duty of hospitality) but now on the basis that philanthropic charity became the substrate of justice in a new society where the poor had been honored with no less than the image and likeness of God.

Among the very first intellectuals to press this new anthropology in an explicitly medical way was the fourth-century St. Gregory the Theologian (of Nazianzus). In his *Oration* 14, *On the Love of the Poor*, Gregory directly addresses the Greek philosophers who had regarded sickness as a divine curse, in order to contradict them. It is the first time in Christian writing that we find a systematically elaborated argument of this type, and we shall return to it shortly in greater detail.[17] Sickness, Gregory argues (and he decides to take it at its most extreme example in the form of the ongoing mutilation of leprosy), is a sign offered to the church so that it might be stirred to react against the disfigurement of the icon of God. The suffering of the poor is not a sign of their abandonment by God but should rather be read as an emergency call to the (God-imitating) philanthropy of the Christ community. This, he argues, must mirror the mercy of God to the poor in the praxis of support for the sick if it is to remain faithful to that God who wishes his icon to be preserved in all creatures and repaired where necessary through the media of Christian mercy. Nothing like this can be found in pre-Christian classical literature.

At this juncture the church's works of mercy, medicinal among them, Gregory argues, become part and parcel of its maintenance of the sacred cult: that is, a liturgical

---

[17]See further J. A. McGuckin, *St. Gregory of Nazianzus: An Intellectual Biography* (Crestwood, NY: St. Vladimir's Seminary Press, 2001), 145-55; "Embodying the New Society: The Byzantine Christian Instinct of Philanthropy," in *Philanthropy and Social Compassion in Eastern Orthodox Tradition*, ed. M. Pereira, Papers of the Sophia Institute Academic Conference December 2009 (New York: Theotokos Press, 2010), 50-71.

duty and action. Basil's own *Address to the Rich* and the Basilian *Homily on Justice and Mercy* give us an equally robust insistence that while Gregory laid out the theoretical argument, and sent his *Oration* to Constantinople in the cause of gathering money for it, Basil was occupied with the practicalities of building.[18] Here Basil also makes a dramatic and controversial alteration to the protocols of Christian monasticism, as it had developed up to his time, and appoints his own diocesan monastics to staff the leprosarium in a larger social-philanthropic complex that eventually became known as the Basiliad.[19] Monastics who had hitherto been characterized by a flight from society were here first used to staff diocesan philanthropic institutions. It was to be the first in a long sequence of such moves in the church.

Gregory himself, his brother Caesarius, his cousin Amphilochius of Iconium, his friend Basil of Caesarea, and Basil's brother Gregory of Nyssa, all Christian leaders of the fourth century, each personally exemplified the lengthy education expected of wealthy landowners at this period. As a core curricular part of their rhetorical and philosophical training they all underwent medical studies. Caesarius decided to specialize in medicine at Alexandria, then one of the world's leading medical centers. He went on to become the imperial physician at Julian the Apostate's court at Constantinople. The others (as was the custom among many of the ascendant social class of fourth-century bishops) learned enough medical lore to treat their estate workers and family. It is why writers such as the Cappadocian fathers, and others such as Nemesius of Emesa, John Chrysostom, or Theodoret of Cyr, have fairly extensive medical reflections in the course of their theological works.

Gregory of Nyssa referred to medicine as "an example of what God allows humans to do when they work in harmony with him, and with one another." Writing to his friend the physician Eustathius, he expresses the opinion that the exercise of the medicinal arts is one of the greatest acts of philanthropy any Christian can perform, making the profession one of the most noble imaginable.[20] Basil of Caesarea maintained that "God's grace is just as visible in the healing power of medicine and its medical practitioners as it is in miraculous cures."[21] And John Chrysostom, the fifth-century archbishop of the imperial city, highlighted

---

[18] *Homily on Justice and Mercy* has recently been supposed not to be by Basil, though it is listed in his complete opera, but from a century or so later. Texts in English translation in C. P. Schroeder, trans., *St. Basil the Great: On Social Justice* (Crestwood, NY: St. Vladimir's Seminary Press, 2009).

[19] The complex became so large and renowned, on the outskirts of Cappadocian Caesarea, the provincial capital, that today the present-day city of Kayseri in Cappadocia is actually built over the site of the Basiliad, not the ancient town, which is some miles away.

[20] St. Gregory of Nyssa, *De pauperibus* (PG 46.454-90).

[21] St. Basil, *Regulae fusius tractatae interrogatio* 55 (PG 31.1048).

the responsibility and special role that medical workers have to make their gifts available to the community.[22]

This is the beginning of a distinctive trend in the early Byzantine church toward the aspect of elevated sanctity as an extraordinary *philanthropia*, in the form of being an unmercenary healer: namely, a doctor who provides the astonishingly innovative concept of free services to the poor. The tradition of the unmercenary saints derives from this. The most renowned among this particular Byzantine category of hagiography were Panteleimon and Hermolaos or Cosmas and Damian, for example, or the martyric *myrobletes* saints, such as Demetrius the Great Martyr at Thessaloniki, and many others throughout history, whose relics and healing shrines were seen as a continuance of a healing ministry after their deaths.[23] The sermon of St. Cyril of Alexandria on Saints Cyrus and John describes the manner in which fifth-century Egyptian Christianity used the healing shrines of such saints, again staffed by monastic guardians, to counteract and eventually displace the pagan ancient healing cults such as the Aesculapia or (in the case of Cyril) the temple of Isis at Alexandrian Menouthi, along the Great Canopic Way.[24] The success of that latter strategy could be measured already in the seventh century, when the accounts of the miracle cures carved into the ruined walls of the Isis temple were being commonly read as an archive of the cures effected by Saints Cyrus and John. Today the place name Menouthi (the greatest temple of Isis in the world) is wholly forgotten, yet the locality still bears the Arabic name Aboukir, a corruption of Abba Cyrus.[25]

Several later Byzantine hagiographies associated with healing saints show that incubational practices, including dream visitations and diagnoses, carried on in Byzantine healing shrines similar in superficial respects to pre-Christian temple practice. In the churches, however, the healings were attributed to Christ's power of resurrection, working through the medium of the saint, and were closely attached to the liturgical life of the shrine: the tombal relics of the saint, and especially the eucharistic mysteries, which then, as indeed now, were seen as primary vehicles of healing and forgiveness.

In the New Testament, following on from a dominant trend in early Hebraic thought, illness was generally seen as a manifestation, if not of demonical possession, at least of demonical assault. This is why the exorcisms and healings are placed in

---

[22]St. John Chrysostom: "Because God gave [physicians] a special talent to save others from pain and sometimes even death, they have a pressing responsibility to share their talents." *De perfecta caritate* (PG 56.279-80).

[23]*Myrobletes* refers to saints whose relics emitted healing myrrh.

[24]Cf. McGuckin, "Influence of the Isis Cult on St. Cyril of Alexandria's Christology."

[25]St. Cyrus.

such proximity in the Gospel accounts, and why the early church always associated healing with a necessary attitude of repentance on the part of the sick person. The same juxtaposition of ideas can still be traced in all the healing rituals of the later Byzantine altar books and is especially prevalent in the service of the seven anointings, where confession of sins is placed at the core of the prayers of healing. The church's ritual is not implying here that all sickness is explicable on the basis of personal sin, but it insists that the first step in all healing must be the confession of the sickness of the soul, which is intimately related to the body. Healing begins with the return of the soul to harmony in Christ. In other words, the restoration of the body cannot be considered independently. This aspect is crucial to Eastern Christian thought. Though some of the patristic theologians continue the archaic theme that sickness is proof of divine disfavor, most of the greater Christian fathers are insistent that sickness and death are not from the hand of God at all. His hand, on the contrary, is health-giving and salvific. Death and sickness derive from sin. They are the consequences of it in the way that certain lifestyle choices inevitably result in foreseen, ignored, and unhappy results.

This approach to theodicy can be seen, for example, in St. Basil's *Homily That God Is Not the Cause of Evil*.[26] To believe that sickness comes from God's hand would be, as Basil says, to destroy our faith in his innate goodness: "God made the body," he goes on, "but he did not make illness, just as he made the soul, but by no means did he make sin."[27] Even so, existence in the body is entirely and universally qualified by sickness. No human being escapes it, if we take senescence as an extrapolation of sickness even for the most healthy among us. All life, in fact, rolls toward death, which is equally a noteworthy factor in the patristic teaching in anthropology. Considering the rootedness that death has in our systems as mortal creatures demands a qualification be made to the global patristic statement, but not such a qualification perhaps as to countermand it. To opponents who even in his own day argued against Basil's optimism and said that human mortality proved we could not truly be in the image of the lifegiving God, St. Gregory of Nyssa, Basil's brother, made the reply:

> The abnormal nature of our present conditions of human existence are not enough to prove that humanity has never been in possession of the full benefits [of the divine image]. Truly, since we are the work of God whose own goodness inspired him to give us life, then it would be unreasonable to conclude that a creature that owes its very existence to divine goodness could have been plunged into suffering by the Creator.

---

[26] "God is not the cause of suffering. It is madness to believe that God is the cause of our sufferings. Such a blasphemy . . . destroys the concept of God's goodness." St. Basil, *Homily: That God Is Not the Cause of Evil* 2 (PG 31.332B).
[27] St. Basil, *Homily: That God Is Not the Cause of Evil* (6.344B).

> There is another cause for our present condition and for the factors that have deprived us of a more enviable state of existence.[28]

In this he is underscoring the Wisdom doctrine of the late Old Testament books, especially the passage in the book of Wisdom that states "God did not make death, nor does he delight in the death of the living. For he created all things that they might exist" (Wisdom 1:13-14). Many other of the later Fathers continue this central patristic stress that human nature was not designed to suffer either illness or death, and that God, accordingly, cannot rightly be seen as the source (thus, implicitly, the willing sender) of present sickness and death in humans.[29] St. Gregory Palamas continues this stress on into the late Byzantine period, when he says, "God did not create death, or illnesses or infirmities."[30]

This doctrine is more of a realistic and nuanced one than the head-in-the-clouds affirmation of divine providence it might first appear to be. For just as the Fathers affirm the centrality of life at the core of creation, they equally know that human nature, as we now experience it, is bound in subjugation to death and corruption. They insist it is the original icon that is radiant and immortal, what humanity was in God's design and is still in his design. But that icon of redeemed humanity lies outside our power to attain to it again, except through and in Christ, whose immortal humanity was gifted to humans in the remaking of the corrupted human nature in the divine incarnation. Several of the Fathers, especially those following the school of Origen, argue that humanity returns to the immortal condition in and through Christ.[31] St. Gregory of Nyssa opines that the bodily condition that Adam first enjoyed was incomparably lighter and more ethereal than that which we now drag around and was devoid of the material heaviness that presently describes (but does not define) the mortal condition.[32] This is why physical death is the ending not of our human nature but of that corrupted state of the second Adamic nature (not the original archetype), which the second Adam reversed by his resurrection. In this perspective, the resurrection body will thus be the condition of our return to our true self in the kingdom of God.

---

[28] St. Gregory of Nyssa, *Catechetical Oration* 5.8-9; see also 5.11; 7.4; *Treatise on Virginity* 12.2.
[29] St. Maximus Confessor, "When God created human nature he did not introduce . . . suffering into it." *To Thalassios* 61 (PG 90.628A); 41 (PG 90.408C).
[30] St. Gregory Palamas, *Homily* 31 (PG 151.396B). He says, "God did not create either the death of the soul or the death of the body." *Theological & Ethical Chapters* 51.
[31] Athanasius, *Against the Pagans* 2-3; St. Basil, *Homily 7, That God Is Not the Cause of Evil* (PG 31.344C); Gregory Nyssa, *Catechetical Oration* 5.6; 5.8; St. John Damascene, *On the Orthodox Faith* 2.12.
[32] See J. Daniélou, *Platonisme et théologie mystique. Doctrine spirituelle de saint Grégoire de Nysse* (Paris: Editions Montaigne, 1944), 56-59. Maximus the Confessor follows him in this: *Ambigua* 45 (PG 91.1353A); St. John Chrysostom suggest it was like the angelic condition, *Homilies on Genesis* 16.1.

So, allowing for the fact that humans were originally designed neither to die or suffer, where does human nature stand in the present economy, where suffering is an inescapable part of human experience? As we have seen, the Fathers imply that suffering is the direct result of sin and the companion of sin. Again, this is the logic why all appeals to God for healing of physical illness first begin with the appeal for sacramental healing of moral transgressions. In the patristic vision, departure from the presence of God is death in and of itself: a decay of both spirit and flesh. Closeness to God is life; severance from him is decline, corruption, and mortality. The collapsed state of the human system in our present *stasis*, outside the fulfillment of the kingdom, is thus seen as an elongation of a state of illness that will be remedied only in the entrance into the kingdom of God.

In short, this is a sophisticated doctrine of illness and sickness, not the hamfisted optimism of Pangloss that it might first appear to be at a careless reading.[33] It is not denying the reality of suffering in our world, simply stating two very dramatic, and perhaps counterintuitive, things: first of all, that God is not the source of sickness and can never be cited as the cause of the collapse of the beauty of the icon (it is always to be seen as an evil thing fallen on a person) but rather shall always be regarded as the comforter and healer of our ills; and second that the perfect healing of human sickness and sorrows will be in and through death.

Death is thus the ultimate gift of God's mercy, perfecting the transfiguration in Christ that has been the disciple's lifelong pilgrimage in the church. Through death in Christ, the disciple thus makes the same pilgrimage that he made, from suffering and death to immortal glory. So this is not the cheery doctrine that since death and sickness are not part of God's plan it ought to be the reasoned response in each instance of sickness to ask God to remove our sorrows. But it does imply that God will be responsive to prayers for his mercy, since such sorrow is not in accordance with the beauty of the divine icon rooted in the human being; and that God's will is constantly set on bringing his disciples closer into the perfection of that icon in Christ. Nevertheless, maybe that will involve the church in suffering alongside the beloved Son, "who thus entered into his glory" (2 Cor 1:3-6; Phil 3:10-12; Col 1:24; Heb 2:9-10). As the apostle points out, it was the sufferings of Jesus that perfected his sanctifying grace and constituted the community of the saved:

> We see Jesus, who for a little while was made lower than the angels, crowned with glory and honor because of the suffering of death, so that by the grace of God he might taste

---

[33] Pangloss, the satirical caricature of Leibniz the philosopher as he appears in Voltaire's *Candide*, with his reiterated mantra, in the face of all catastrophe that "all is for the best in the best of all possible worlds."

death for everyone. For it was fitting that he, for whom and by whom all things exist, in bringing many children to glory, should make perfect the captain of their salvation through suffering. For he who sanctifies and those who are sanctified have all one origin. That is why he is not ashamed to call them brethren. (Heb 2:9-11)

The patristic approach to sickness and healing, then, is not ultimately about defending a coherent theodicy (somehow that all is always for the best) but is rather a biblically rooted theology of the cross and resurrection of Christ. If we had to sum it up philosophically, it would be an extended and very refined doctrine of philanthropy.

## *PHILANTHROPIA* IN CLASSICAL GREEK THOUGHT

The early church fathers, and the Byzantine writers after them, predominantly use the term *philanthropy* to discuss what acts of mercy within society are expected in terms of the evangelical spirit. The word is the Greek term for the love of one's fellow human being. It connotes neither what the term Christian *charity* means today, nor the revolutionary spirit of what contemporary liberation theology has been speaking about in the past generation, with its more structural approaches to the concept of social justice. Nevertheless, it is an interesting idea and a more radical one than the concept of alleviation of suffering by charitable assistance offered sporadically or individually, which has often been operative in parts of the Christian historical tradition in earlier times.

The early church applied the notion of philanthropy first of all to God, who was described as the "lover of humanity" (*theos philanthropos*), and then imposed the character of philanthropy as a duty on all human beings, and particularly Christians, so that they should understand their primal role as icons of God on earth and so act in society that indigent men and women would be reminded by their compassion of the ultimate mercy of God. The Christians did not apply the word only from their reading of the Scriptures but were well aware that in this use of the very plastic concept of *philanthropia* they stood on the shoulders of a long and venerable tradition of the word's ethical significance in classical antiquity, one that they synthesized with biblical imperatives to make something new of it. New Testament notions of divine kindness from the New Testament were fused with christological ideas about the *kenosis* of the suffering Lord, often with the crucible of the Divine Liturgy serving as both text and context for the interchange and fusion.[34] In the use and renovation of the concept of philanthropy as a primary way of negotiating ideas about what we moderns would

---

[34] With one exception, the LXX use of *philanthropia* shows no significant difference from the classical Greek concept of beneficent kindness of patron to client. See 2 Maccabees 6:22; 9:27; 14:9; 3 Maccabees 3:15; 4 Maccabees 5:12. That exception is a significant one—for the Wisdom tradition applies *philanthropia* as a quintessential mark of Wisdom, a tradition that underlined the Byzantine use of *philanthropia* in the christological tradition. See LXX Wisdom 1:6; 7:23; 12:19.

tend now (rather flatly, perhaps) to call social ethics, Byzantine Christian society shows its creative élan in refashioning two older societal visions, that of the Hellenes and that of the Hebrew prophets, in a way that gives a newly universalized priority to the underlying rationale of *why* mercy ought to be shown to others.

In the first instance, the Hellenic vision of a civilized order in which loyalty and respect ought to be shown to kin and beneficent *agape* to strangers (*agape* being something we can translate in this context as "kindly regard") is upgraded by its elevation to *philia*: the active kindness of a friend.[35] This very simple question of why we ought to show *philanthropia* to another, and especially to one in need, is one that might seem self-evident in a social context formed by Christian values over so many centuries. It was not at all self-evident to classical society. As can be still discerned in some Eastern civilizations today, ancient thought was dominated by the ubiquity and irreversibility of fate. If there were indigent, underprivileged, and sick people around in society: this was not the fault of society. It was the will of the gods. Karma mattered, to put it in more recognizable terms. If one intervened by giving extraordinary charity to someone who was in the depth of misery and wretchedness (we can think of blind Oedipus, for example), one risked the strong possibility that a mere mortal intervened in the established punishments of the gods. This was the widespread way in antiquity that suffering, sickness, and poverty were cosmologically explained. It was the fate that had fallen on this or that individual.

The very first example in the history of Greek rhetoric where a philosopher (consciously modeling himself on Demosthenes) argued the case that the wretched and sick were not God-despised but rather icons of God that called out to all men and women, but especially to Christians, to assist them as a moral imperative (an aspect of true worship, since the icon of God could not be allowed to corrupt) was Gregory the Theologian in his *Oration* 14, when he made the extraordinary claim (for ancient ears) that the lepers of his time, far from being abandoned by God, were objects of divine compassion. Gregory argued that the wretched on earth were lifted up by the divine command (of mercy) so as to stand dramatically before the eyes of society and function in the church as positive moral examples, so that the healthy could in them learn the character of divine compassion by acting graciously in God's stead. In such an instance, altruistic outreach to the poor and suffering made the believers rise up to their true status as authentic icons of God, recognizing the poor as equally authentic, though suffering, icons of the Savior. Nowhere else in ancient literature can we find such an extraordinary claim. After Gregory, the Byzantine philosophy

---

[35]G. Downey, "Who Is My Neighbor? The Greek and Roman Answer," *Anglican Theological Review* (January 1965): 1-15.

of philanthropy developed so as to bring the concept of compassion as an act of worship to central stage.[36]

If Hellenistic cultural philosophy is here transfigured by synthesis, we can also note, in the second place, how the Hebraic concept of duty to the poor and stranger that ought to characterize the elect community of the covenant is also upgraded in the way Gregory now roots this notion for the New Testament community in the basis of a universalized anthropology. In his hands it is now *phil-anthropia*, the love of humanity itself, that is the reason that undergirds social compassion for the Greek fathers. Kinship, on the one hand, and race or tribe on the other, as ways of organizing societal obligations, have passed away as foundational reasons in a new synthesis of the Byzantine gospel that saw, in the *kenosis* of Christ, a model of alterity of an utterly new and universalized kind. There is no longer Greek or Hebrew; things are being made new in Christ, to paraphrase the apostle (Col 3:10-13).

It was this fundamental change of vision at the level of deepest *theoria* that can be traced in the new semantic of the Byzantine use of the term *philanthropia*. This was an intellectual reordering of major proportions that would, inevitably, produce an effect in the domain of praxis sooner or later. The actual record of early medieval Byzantine philanthropic foundations will be the concrete evidence for this. But it is the mental shift of perspective that precedes that reordering of society, and this is something that happens extensively almost from the moment that the Greek Christians commanded the imperial system sufficiently to ensure stable political associations. That context was in place by the mid-fourth century. By the fifth, bishops had entered philanthropic work so fundamentally into the ecclesial substructure that they had earned the common-parlance title of *philoptochos* (friend of the poor). By the sixth century the great philanthropic foundations of leprosaria, hospitals, orphanages, geriatric homes, and food-relief centers had become common in the greater cities of the Byzantine world.[37]

From the fifth century onward, such philanthropic institutions became a constitutive mark of the church's presence throughout all its later history and more or less across all its geographical extension. The work of philanthropy can even be said to have emerged as a distinctive mark (if not a formal creedal one) of the church's integral mission. We might not be amiss in adding (as a necessary ecclesiological descriptor), to the creedal definition of one, holy, catholic, and apostolic, this extra

---

[36] See McGuckin, *St. Gregory of Nazianzus*, 147-55 (*Oration* 14, *On the Love of the Poor*); see also S. Holman, *The Hungry Are Dying: Beggars and Bishops in Roman Cappadocia* (Oxford: Oxford University Press, 2001).

[37] The "food liturgy," known even at ancient Athens and Rhodes, and organized for poor relief in exceptional circumstances.

dimension of "philanthropic": the fifth authentic mark of the church of Christ on earth. The church can never forget that heritage. Even now, with diminished resources in the shattered social structures of Eastern Europe, and in the developed West, where governmental agencies undertake so much of the philanthropic labor, it remains the duty of the church to work out in *theoria* and praxis how society can understand and implement principles of philanthropy nurtured in the freedom and dignity of the person, understood as icon of the divine.

For the Byzantines, this fundamental commitment to the principles of *philanthropia* marked the very essence of what a civilized society meant. They had learned much from the ancient Greek philosophical tradition, although they were to take the ideas further. In the poets as well as in Plato, philanthropy signified the generic love that the deity had for humankind.[38] It was a pacific, detached regard of beneficence that undergirded the mission of various *daimones*, spiritual entities, that took charge of the governance of races and societies in order to allow justice to flourish among mortals and to cause a cessation of wars and hostilities. The spirit of philanthropy that thus arose when hostility was laid aside directly allowed civilization to flourish.

Philanthropy was, therefore, a prime characteristic of the divine ethos for the pre-Christian Hellenes. It was the defining mark, and thus the separator, of the superior over and against the needy inferior. The deities offer to humankind, as patrons to their clients, all the benefits of a happy life, the fruits of the earth, and so on.[39] Deriving from this divine character of beatitude, philanthropy also meant, in many Greek sources, the affective attitude of a human that marked them as beneficent and civilized in their manners. Philanthropy as shown by human to human, for the Hellenes, was the attitude of politeness, kindness, generosity, and the manifesting of deeds that supported one's city or state.[40] It derived from the divine *philanthropia*, and its expression raised the human out of the ranks of the merely animal. Among animals savagery was understood as a constant backdrop of all interrelation. Accordingly, savagery could not be accounted to them as a fault, but neither could that complex level of social interaction be expected of them that would ever merit the name civilization. Civilization demanded a divine ethos, a divine spur.

The Hellenes, before the gospel, generally doubted strongly whether the *barbaroi* would ever rise to that status either. Yet, when humans rose to the level of philanthropy, in Greek thought, they became the fulfillment of their own higher destiny

---

[38] Aristophanes, *Peace* 392f; Plato, *Laws* 713d. "God, insofar as he is *Philanthropos* toward us, has set the daimones to have governing charge over our race . . ."

[39] Xenophon, *Memorabilia* 4.3-7.

[40] S. Lorenz, "De Progressu Notionis Philanthropias," diss., Leipzig, 1914; H. Martin, "The Concept of Philanthropia in Plutarch's Lives," *American Journal of Philology* 82 (April 1961): 164-75.

and acted beneficently to one another just as the gods acted. Thus philanthropy is the very root and core of all that is meant by civilized values. For this reason, throughout much of Greek literature it is presumed that the most godlike among human society, namely the kings, are characterized as royal precisely because of the philanthropy they show (far more than the power that they can command).[41] The Spartan king Aegesilaos (398–360 BC) is described by Xenophon as *philanthropos* because of three distinguishing characteristics of his dominion: his merciful policy toward prisoners of war, his care for destitute orphans, and his compassion for the aged who were without protectors.[42]

The rhetor-philosopher Isocrates laid out for Philip of Macedon his ideal of what a true Greek king would be: an iconic representation of the divine Heracles who spent his life on the defense and establishment of justice on earth, working tirelessly for the benefit of humankind and advocating high moral standards.[43] The care of the orphan and the aged were particularly elevated as marks of true philanthropy among the ancient Greeks.[44] Works of philanthropy thus defined the civilized city-state and were used by the Hellenes to demonstrate their great distance from barbarian societies that lacked both the *theoria* of that term and its praxis. Many ancient city-states had established works of public assistance for orphans and the aged, and the redemption of captives was always held to be one of the highest demonstrations of true philanthropy.[45] In like manner hospitality was often taken in Greek writing to be a quintessential mark of philanthropy. The kindly regard for the stranger (*xenos*), and assistance to the indigent, are among the notable marks of the morally good person as Homer describes him in the *Iliad* and *Odyssey*. It is his equivalent of the concept of *philanthropia*, without him actually employing that term as yet. The epitome of evil and shame, conversely, is manifested by the abusers of hospitality. The symbols of Circe and the suitors at the house of Penelope spring to mind readily. For Demosthenes it was the exercise of *philanthropia* among citizens that defined the state, guaranteed its character as civilized, whereas toward enemies the state had to adopt a protective attitude of enmity and hostility.[46]

Most of these efforts, however, were a reflection of the city organization: generally the work of the elite leaders of the Greek city state. After the age of the city-state had passed into the age of the strings of imperial cities, each with their vast hinterland

---

[41] Isocrates, *Oration* 9.43.
[42] Xenophon, *Agesilaos* 1.21-23.
[43] Isocrates, *To Philip* 48-49.
[44] C. B. Gulick, "Notions of Humanity Among the Greeks," in *Harvard Essays on Classical Subjects* ed. H. W. Smyth (New York: Harvard University Press, 1912), 38, 41.
[45] L. Lallemand, *Histoire de la Charité* (Paris: Picard et Fils, 1902), 1:55-100.
[46] Demosthenes, *On the Chersonese* 2.70-71.

of rural support systems feeding into the urban environments of the late antique age, this responsibility for the works of *philanthropia* was continued chiefly by town *curias* and by vastly wealthy plutocrats, who often used philanthropy as a replacement of the old system of the *leitourgia*, or civic work program, and thereby advanced themselves politically as well as emerging as a new model of philanthropy from on high.[47] The notion of claiming back the philanthropic process as a common enterprise, a more democratically balanced affair, is not seen again among the Hellenes until the early Christian era, when it is then presided over by the bishops who stood in as "friends of the poor."

Even so, the rootedness of the Hellenic conception of philanthropy as a mimesis of the gods makes the concept of patronage a fundamental aspect of all ancient philanthropic thought. We have to add to this theoretical judgment, of course, the economic observation that in this form of society more than 90 percent of all disposable wealth was held by less than 5 percent of the ancient landowning aristocracy. There is a chasm existing here between the wealthy and the poor, with no middle class in between (the kind of environment assumed in Jesus' parable of Dives and Lazarus, where he explicitly applies the word *chasm*; Lk 16:19-31). We might think that this has shifted today, and perhaps it has, relatively speaking, though much of the world still labors under economic conditions reminiscent of antiquity, and even in the highly developed West striking imbalance is taken as normal. The *New York Times* has recently reported, for our edification, the statistic that in the beginning of the third millennium, the collective wealth of the richest 1 percent in modern America is greater than the collected wealth of the bottom 90 percent combined.[48]

After an extensive review of the evidence, however, J. Ferguson characterized the essence of this pre-Christian Greek theory of *philanthropia* as fundamentally related to immediate kinship structures.[49] In short, charity begins (and ends) at home. And D. J. Constantelos, following A. Monnier, also sums up the whole of the Hellenic effort as having high spots of symbolic value but very limited range of applicability:[50] "As a rule," he notes, "no underlying and widespread spirit of *philanthropia* prevailed. . . . The limitations of ancient Greek *philanthropia* were defined by their ideas of responsibility for one's fellow man. Their philanthropy was practiced in a limited

---

[47]*Curia* is a local administrative council.
[48]Bob Herbert, "Stacking the Deck Against Kids," *New York Times*, Nov. 28, 2009, A19.
[49]"The 'Love of man for man' [*philanthropia*] found its actual outlet in application to relatives, friends, fellow citizens, or allies." J. Ferguson, *Moral Values in the Ancient World* (London: Methuen, 1958), 107-8.
[50]A. Monnier, *Histoire de l'assistance publique dans les temps anciens et modernes* (Paris: Guillaumin, 1866).

field and was directed mostly toward the civilized Hellenes."[51] Constantelos, in an engaging and innovative study, went on to excavate Byzantine philanthropic establishments, developing the thesis that here at last was a genuinely outreaching altruistic philosophy that built institutions to exemplify its *theoria* and can be legitimately contrasted with Hellenic values and social welfare institutions.

I do not wish to contradict that overall thesis, but its needs more qualification than he tended to offer, for some of the evidence he presents tends to be somewhat decontextualized, and it is an area of research that could be fruitfully reengaged. It is significant to note, for example, that the Byzantine orphanages cannot simply be elevated as signs of how the Byzantine legal system had kindly regard for orphans as such. Orphans in the legal literature are specifically wealthy minors devoid of fiscal protectors, since their mothers were nonpersons for long stretches of time under Roman law and could not, as widows, straightforwardly assume the running of the household (*oikos*) after the death of their husband. Thus there were often people lining up in the streets to become the guardians of these and assume the administration of their estates, which is why the state intervened. What is not said in this regard is just as significant as what is said: for children abandoned on the country roads or in the marketplaces of Byzantium, ordinary poor children whose parents had died or just did not want them, were not regarded as "orphaned," simply as abandoned. Their lot, and it must have been the lot of the large majority of invisible ordinary cases, was to be picked up eventually for service as country serfs, prostitutes, or household workers. Similarly, the available beds in the Byzantine hospitals at Constantinople could have been able to hold, I would estimate, no more than one in a thousand per capita. It is not a negligible thing by any means (given that standard medical care in Byzantium was presumed to be home based, not institution based); but neither is it the ideal panacea we might wish it to be.

The Greek notion of *philanthropia* was so infused with the concept of the earthly magnate mimicking divine benefactions among society as *philanthropos soter* that the early church held it at first in deep suspicion, as part and parcel of the pagan cult of the divine ruler.[52] It was therefore with some audacity that the idea was subverted when applied to Christ and claimed as the title of the Lord Jesus, who in his humble *kenosis*, his incarnation, brought it to a culmination in laying down his life for his friends. The Johannine passage that describes the kenotic self-sacrifice of Christ is the basis for the theological connection in the church of *philanthropia*, with

---

[51] D. J. Constantelos, *Byzantine Philanthropy and Social Welfare* (New Brunswick, NJ: Rutgers University Press, 1968), 11.

[52] *Philanthropos soter* is a title that mimics the deities—"saviors and benefactors of humankind." It was such a title, assumed by Antiochus Epiphanes, that sparked the Maccabean rebellion.

that mutuality of love that must henceforth describe the nature of church (Jn 10:15; 15:13-17). We note that the Hellenic spirit of patronal superiority over another in need is set aside, in John, in the manner in which the Lord-as-servant elevates his disciples to the status of "friends" (*philoi*), who are able to put into effect what the Father has revealed to the Son and that in turn has been passed on and understood so that the disciples can go out and "bear fruit that will endure." It is thus a different kind of mimesis that is set in place here: a radical turning aside of the spirit of Hellenic *philanthropia* acting from privilege toward a mutuality of communion. Stripped of its aristocratic ideology, therefore, the notion of *philanthropia* soon assumed a powerful status in early Christian thought to indicate the act of supreme compassion of God for the world: the stooping down of the Logos to the world in the incarnation. A key description of this can be found in Titus 3:4-8, which can be found in the short reader at the end of this chapter.

The connection here between the recognition of the kenotic and liberative philanthropy of God in Christ and the response of the church's own philanthropy is a very strong one. Christian philanthropic work is described as a mimesis of God's action on earth, just as it was throughout most of Hellenic thought; but now the motive is different, profoundly related to the ethical imperative in a way that no writer in the Hellenic philosophical tradition ever connected it. For nowhere in the long vocabulary of pre-Christian Greek *philanthropia* did the philosophers attach it strongly to ethics or develop it as a major branch of ethical theory. It was left in the Greek tradition simply as part of the popular folk tradition of good behavior and did not enter the vocabulary of the philosophers as such until well into the Middle Platonic period, slightly after the New Testament itself.[53]

Justin Martyr and the Syriac Thomas traditions are influenced by the combination found in the New Testament letter to Titus of philanthropy and merciful kindness (*chrestotes*).[54] And both reflect on the abundant mercy of the Lord, who showed compassion so richly toward humanity in the selfless love of the Christ. Philanthropy, thus, for Christians became exemplary of the perfection of love as manifested in the cosmos, something more public and social than *agape* (which reflected chiefly the mutuality of charity among members of the church) and something closely allied to the church's duty to reflect in the world the impact of the

---

[53]G. Luck describes this popular folk tradition as one in which only the rhetoricians (not the philosophers) were "following polite popular ethics when they lauded the virtue of *philanthropia*: e.g. Demosthenes *Orat.* 20.165." In G. Kittel and G. Friedrich, eds., *Theological Dictionary of the New Testament* (Grand Rapids: Eerdmans, 1974), 9:108-9.

[54]*Dialogue with Trypho* 47.5; Acts of Thomas 123, 156, 170, the latter designating Jesus as the Messiah *philanthropos*.

philanthropy of God experienced within it that released it from bondage toward a new sense of compassion and love.

The second- and third-century Alexandrian theologians Clement and Origen are the ones who pass these insights on to the Byzantine church and set the terms for the way in which philanthropy is consistently referred to thereafter.[55] It regularly now comes with its paired cognates *agape* and *chrestotes*, love and loving-kindness, but always connoting a stronger sense of action: love as made manifest to the other in the form of help. The christocentric context is fixed as basic in the Alexandrian tradition. Christ is the perfect summation of the love and mercy of God to humanity, and his philanthropy encompasses the entire cosmos in its scope. The philanthropic love that God stirs up in the hearts of believers is a spiritual force that manifests the gift of salvation that has been accomplished in the Logos's illumination of his chosen elect. For this reason the works of love within the church are an essential part of its manifest charism of closeness to its indwelling Lord. Once again we can conclude that, for all intents and purposes, the sense is urged that philanthropy is the fifth mark, or note, of the church's identity: one, holy, catholic, apostolic, and philanthropic. In the church's philanthropy within the cosmos, the world can recognize the authentic features of the Christ made present to it again in mercy.

The work of the Fathers, is, from the outset (as can be seen in the Cappadocians establishing monastic establishments at Caesarea that serve a medical function, or Chrysostom's relief work at Constantinople, or the deep traditions of hospitality and medical care for travelers in the Egyptian and Palestinian monasteries) a theory that is grounded in the practicalities of applying the church's "treasure chest" for socially merciful ends. Each one of the varied Byzantine establishments, often imperially endowed and supported, in the form of *gerocomeia* (old-age homes), *ptochia* (houses for the indigent), *xenones* (hospices for travelers and sick foreigners), *orphanotropheia* and *brephotropheia* (homes for orphaned children and abandoned infants), and *typhlocomia* (homes for the blind), merits further and deeper study. Constantelos's pioneering work has been partly continued, but there remains more work to

---

[55]In *Stromateis* 2.9, Clement defines *philanthropia* as God's creative action toward humankind (*Protreptikos* 10; *Quod Dives Salvetur* 3), as the church's charism of a "spiritual love of the brotherhood," and as a fellow feeling toward those of the same communion who have been brought together by the Spirit of God. It is for him principally an ecclesial virtue. Its root is in the prior outreach of God to humanity in and through the kenotic incarnation of the Logos (*Pedagogus* 1.8; *Stromateis* 7.2). St. Athanasius classicized this approach in his *De Incarnatione* 1.3; 4.2. For Origen, see *Commentary on John* 2.26 (on Jn 1:5); 1.20 (on Jn 1:1). In *Contra Celsum* 1.67, Origen describes how the very name of Jesus creates philanthropy and kindliness (*chrestotes*) in those to whom it is manifested. In *Commentary on Matthew* 10.1, he describes the supreme philanthropy of the divine Logos making his way, by incarnation into time and space, to bereft creatures who had utterly lost the capacity to make their way to him.

be done in cataloguing and describing the regularity with which monastic establishments, the patriarchal administration, and the imperial and aristocratic families collaborated to constitute a nexus of philanthropic welfare systems in the Eastern empire. Here, I wish only to make symbolic reference to a few incidences of how the Byzantines elevated philanthropy as a major term of theological reference, two in particular: how they referred to it in the liturgy and also how they tried to exemplify it in some of the medical establishments they created.

## PHILANTHROPY IN THE BYZANTINE DIVINE LITURGY

Let us begin with the Divine Liturgy, as I would certainly posit this as the most extensive spiritual formative force for the ordinary Byzantine, intellectual or nonintellectual, rich or poor, male or female: a theological force of *paideia* repeated throughout centuries of Byzantine Christian civilization. Over innumerable times in the course of each person's civic and ecclesial life the words and phrases of the eucharistic liturgy were spoken and sung over them, so that they entered into the fabric of the heart and consciousness of each individual in a way that is hardly imaginable for a modern.

John Chrysostom shows the classic Byzantine approach to the theology of compassion when he begins with the divine initiative and contrasts the compassion and generosity of God with the immeasurably smaller compass of the human heart's openness to others. The divine mercy, he says, always challenges the paucity of its earthly reflection: the philanthropy of God is like the fathomless waves of the sea, a profundity of loving outreach in the divine nature that cannot be encompassed by human speech.[56] The liturgy that bears his name represents the divine philanthropy quintessentially in the prayer of the Trisagion, which recounts God's prevenient and abundant gifts to humankind.[57] The same sentiment is expressed in the preface to the anaphora.[58]

---

[56] Chrysostom, *Homily on Matthew* 18.23.

[57] "O Holy God at rest in the holy place, hymned by the Seraphim with the thrice-holy hymn, glorified by the cherubim and worshiped by every heavenly power; out of nonexistence you brought the universe into being and created humankind according to your image and likeness, adorning us with every gift of your grace. You give wisdom and understanding to those who ask, and you do not reject the sinner, but for our salvation you have established repentance. Although we are your humble and unworthy servants, you have counted us worthy to stand at this time before the glory of your holy altar and to offer you due worship and praise. Master, accept the Thrice-Holy Hymn even from the mouth of us sinners and visit us in your philanthropy. Pardon us every offense, voluntary or involuntary; sanctify our souls and bodies, and grant that we may worship you all the days of our life; through the prayers of the holy Theotokos and of all the saints who have been well-pleasing to you in every age." *Liturgy of St. John Chrysostom*.

[58] "It is fitting and right to hymn you, for you brought us from nonexistence into being, and when we had fallen raised us up again and left nothing undone until you had brought us up to heaven . . ."

The priestly prayer concluding the litany of the Lord's Prayer entrusts the entire life of the faithful to the Christ *philanthropos*:[59] "To you, O Master and lover of humankind, we commend our entire life and our hope, and we pray, entreat and implore you to count us worthy to share in your heavenly and awesome mysteries." The prayer immediately after this continues the same sentiment:

> We thank you, invisible King, who through your boundless power created all things, and in the abundance of your compassion brought them into being from out of nothing. Master, look down on those who have bowed their heads before you . . . and make smooth the path for our good in what lies before us, according to our several needs: sail with those who sail, journey with those who journey, heal the sick, since you are the physician of our souls and bodies. Grant this through the grace and compassion and philanthropy of your only begotten Son, with whom you are blessed together with your all-Holy Spirit, now and ever and to the ages of ages.

The thanksgiving prayer after the reception of the mysteries continues the selfsame theme: "We thank you, Lord *philanthropos*, benefactor of our souls, that you have counted us worthy this day of your heavenly and immortal mysteries. Make straight our way, make firm our steps, watch over our life, and establish us all." The prayer of thanksgiving immediately after the liturgy concludes describes philanthropy in these terms:

> Master and *philanthropos* who died for our sake and rose again, and gave us these awe-inspiring mysteries for the well-being and sanctification of our souls and bodies: grant that these gifts may also bring me healing of soul and body, the repelling of all adversaries, enlightenment in the eyes of my heart, peace in my spiritual powers, faith unashamed, love without pretense, fullness in wisdom, the guarding of your commandments, the increase of your divine grace, and the gaining of your kingdom . . . that I may no longer live as for myself, but instead for you, our Master and benefactor.

There could be many other examples brought forward. The common titles of Christ in the liturgical texts are: *Philanthropos Theos, Philoptochos, Philanthropos Evergetis, Kyrios Philanthropos, Eleimon Theos, and Philopsychos*.[60] But let it suffice for the present to sum up this vastly extended liturgical *paideia* about God's philanthropy by noting that it is used as a dense synoptic motif in the ever-recurring Byzantine doxology: "For you are a merciful God, and *philanthropos*, and to you we ascribe glory: to the Father, and to the Son, and to the Holy Spirit, now and ever and to the ages of ages."[61]

---

[59] "Lover of humankind."
[60] Respectively: "human-loving God"; "lover of the poor"; "human-loving benefactor"; "merciful God"; "lover of the soul."
[61] As taken, for example, from the liturgical rite of anointing and so many other places.

The Divine Liturgy and the prayers of the hours repeated so extensively, so civically, in the life of Byzantium, spread, as it were, a tapestry of a spirituality of *philanthropia* over the members of the church, a woven garment that constantly reiterated fundamental truths about this biblical and patristic doctrine: namely, that God's abundant philanthropy was endlessly renewed over creation, that it restored the weak and the failing, and that it called out to the one who was lifted up to lift up others in mimesis of the selfless love of God. Such was the quintessential synopsis of the Christian religion that the liturgy celebrated as the "awesome mysteries of Christ." The healing it envisaged was not a spiritually disembodied one, but a one of body and soul; not an isolated individual phenomenon, but a matter of compassion for all who sail, or journey, or labor, or are sick. The liturgy teaches that it is in the communion of the philanthropic mercy of Christ, first and foremost experienced in powerlessness, that the believer truly experiences the authentic presence of the God who wishes beneficence on all and who sets this example of philanthropy as the gold standard of discipleship. It was no wonder that the Byzantine Christian immersed in such a *paideia* was suffused with this notion and grew up with it inculcated as the primary aspect of God, so much so that by the Paleologan period it was standard to inscribe the Christ icons with the title *Christos Philanthropos*, and crosses with the superscription *Philanthropos Theos* ("the God who loves humankind").

## THE HOSPITAL AS SYMBOL OF THE CHURCH

How far did this mystical doctrine of Christ's proximity to his church in philanthropy carry over into a program of actual philanthropic work in Byzantine daily life? I want to ground that question here with a very short review of some of the principles evoked in the establishment of houses of philanthropy in the Byzantine Christian capital. These few symbolic remarks simply point up the need for a further, full-scale, ethical study that can combine the Byzantine social evidence with the religious premises that underlay it. In one sense we can take for granted the operation of charity from the basis of the monastic houses, which regularly offered forms of support for the indigent of the various localities. The offering of hospitality and poor relief is so fundamentally structured into the monastic *typika*, or rules, that it can often be taken for granted. But the large extent of monastic establishments in the capital at Constantinople made it a unique center of urban asceticism and thus provided within this queen of cities at least a considerable ring of institutions where the indigent were looked after with some stability. The hospital attached to the Stoudios monastery was renowned in the city for the quality of its care.

946 | PART TWO: A WINDING ROAD: SELECT THEMES AND IDEAS

In Justinian's time the Xenodochion, or hostel-cum-hospital, of Sampson, located between the Hagia Sophia cathedral and the Church of Saint Irene and which had been functioning for some time, was burned down in the Nika revolt.[62] Justinian rebuilt it on a grander scale and endowed it with an annual income so that it could extend its range of services to the sick of the capital. From this time onward Byzantine hospitals began to function proactively as centers where doctors assembled together professionally to practice healing arts on sick people who were brought to the hospital. It proved to be a major stimulus to the medical capacity and skill of the profession. In Byzantine hospitals, unlike many of their medieval Western counterparts, the treatment of the inmate was undertaken with concerted team-based action.

As his own foundation, and that of Theodora, Justinian also established the two *xenones*, "hospices," of the House of Isidore and the House of Arcadios. It is recorded that he also constructed large hospitals at Antioch and at Jerusalem.[63] In the latter case he responded favorably to the petition of the ascetic St. Saba that the pilgrimages to Jerusalem left many arriving visitors sick, exhausted, and in need of special care. In this instance we know that Justinian supervised the building of a center that contained two hundred beds and was endowed with an imperial gift of annual income of 1850 gold solidi for its maintenance: a very large sum of money. Justinian's successor, Justin II (565–578), established the Zotikon hospital for lepers (*leprocomion*) in the peripheral suburb of Irion across the Bosphorus, probably on the hill where Pera began in the Galata region. It was headed by the imperial protovestiarios Zoticus, who had served Justinian and then retired, and from him it took its name ultimately. The first foundation was burned by Slav raiders in the early seventh century, rebuilt in wood by Heraclius soon after in 624, restored and expanded in the tenth century by Constantine Porphyrogenitus (913–959) and rebuilt and expanded again by John Tzimisces (969–976), who left half his personal property to it in his will.[64] We hear of it again in the eleventh century, when an earthquake destroyed the buildings and caused emperor Romanus Argyrus to rebuild it in 1032.

Other hospitals are known to have been established by Constantine Monomachus IX, next to the "Church of St. George."[65] In each case we are doubtless dealing with what we today would regard as the partial redistribution of imperial largesse gained from an economy of a massively repressive type. In this respect it is important not

---

[62]Procopios, *Buildings* 1.2.15.
[63]Ibid., 1.2.17; 2.10.80.
[64]George Cedrenos, *Historiarum Compendium* 1.698-99; Theophanes Continuatus, *Chronographia* 449.4; Leo the Deacon, *History* 6.5.
[65]R. Janin, *La Géographie ecclésiastique de l'Empire byzantin. 1: Le Siège de Constantinople et le Patriarcat Oecuménique*, vol. 3, *Les Églises et les Monastères* (Paris: Institut français d'études byzantines, 1953), 78.

to allow the rhetorical excesses of the sources to carry us away with their praises of the beneficence of the rulers. One such example of fulsome rhetoric along these lines is the panegyric of Anna Comnena for her father, Emperor Alexios, in the eleventh century, who built and endowed hospitals in the by-now-classical imperial manner. What is interesting, however, above and beyond the state propaganda is the rhetoric that constantly associates the emperor's philanthropy as an earthly mimesis of that of Christ himself. The Basileus, therefore, becomes the God-beloved, *Theophilestatos*, precisely to the extent that he iconizes the mercy of Christ to the people.

In this sense the Byzantine religious system reined in its reliance on the archaic Hellenic sense of the superior patron dispensing largesse and retained its New Testament heritage concerning the duty of all humanity to serve the other in mercy. In other words, the church allowed the emperor to iconize Christ's philanthropy, but only on a more spectacularly larger scale than all other Christians were expected to iconize that mercy. He was not elevated above others in his capacity for philanthropy, merely expected to demonstrate that philanthropy was a fundamental religious duty to his people. It might seem a small difference in the massively unbalanced economic systems of the ancient world, but I think it is a significant one, and it points to the way Eastern Christianity, although availing itself regularly of imperial and aristocratic donations, never reduced philanthropy to the status of merely charitable patronage but held to the archetype of philanthropic exercises as an icon of kenosis, expected as a response in duty to suffering humanity, whom God elevated as particular occasions of his concern.

The twelfth-century hospital of the Pantocrator was one of the most prestigious of the hospitals of the capital.[66] It was founded in 1136 by Emperor John Comnenus II.[67] Its *typikon* survives, as do extensive buildings, recently restored from dilapidation and closed as a mosque to reopen as a museum. There were five clinics operating at the Pantocrator: three of them for special treatments (a ward of ten beds for surgery; a ward of eight beds for ophthalmic and intestinal illness; a ward of twelve beds for gynecological problems, staffed by women medics), and two larger clinics for general illnesses, with twenty-seven beds in each. It is clear from the extensive and detailed instructions in the Pantocrator *typikon* that treatment of the diseases was actively pursued, and cures expected. The staff are constantly urged by the terms of the establishment to treat the sick as if they were entertaining Christ himself. Physicians were required by terms of their contract of employment to attend in person at the institution and examine the inhabitants. It is an extraordinary

---

[66]See Constantelos, *Byzantine Philanthropy and Social Welfare*, 171n105.
[67]See ibid., 171.

testimony to a civic sense of philanthropy developed beyond anything else comparable in medieval society, even into modernity in some respects—a philanthropy incarnated and concretized in particular instantiations.

Of course, a phenomenon like the imperial relief houses at Constantinople relied on an economic system that could hardly be sustained over the long term and that fell back more and more as the loss of territories in the hinterland reduced the realities of Byzantine taxation to a small circle around Constantinople itself. The legacy it left, however, was a perennial challenge and stimulus for the church. The Byzantine legacy offers paradigms but not blueprints, as circumstances have changed so profoundly. No longer will charitable patronage be enough. The church will never again, perhaps, be entrusted by the wider society with the sole care of its philanthropic missions. But the church did propose to society in times past, and can do so again, that the starting point of all philanthropic action is an anthropology of love, a divine anthropology, an iconic philosophy that values all men and women as symbolic and transcendent images of God incarnated out of motives of love. To place healing and the medical care facilities in a theoretically grounded ethos of dignity and loving care, understood as a sacred action of mercy, is one of the church's great and enduring contributions to civilized life. Without it, the world of medicine will simply burgeon off into another corporate scheme where money matters most, and the rich shall always have great precedence and dominant privilege.

The church was able, with its newly articulated vision of the dignity of humankind, to steer away from charity as merely a patronizing emergency relief to token cases of an underclass that no one really wanted to liberate. So much of philanthropy in our modern world has returned to the pre-Christian Hellenic model and is motivated by concomitant patterns of guilt, accompanied by loathing and neglect for the marginalized (a state of affairs so brilliantly satirized by Kafka's image of Gregor the cockroach in his tale *The Metamorphosis*). In such a context of growing techno-impersonalism even in the advanced medical establishments, the Christian anthropology first witnessed in its systems of philanthropia has never been more needed.

## A SHORT READER

***Book of Wisdom 1.12–2.1 (second century BC).*** Do not invite death in because of the error of your life, and do not bring on destruction because of the works of your hands. For God is not the maker of death, and he does not delight in the death of the living. For he created all things so that they might exist, and the generative forces of the world are indeed wholesome, and there is no destructive poison in them; and the dominion of Hades does not stand on earth, for righteousness is immortal. But ungodly men have indeed summoned death by means of their words and deeds. They have considered him a friend and pined away, and they have made a covenant with death, because they are fit to belong to his party. For they have reasoned falsely, saying to themselves, "Our life is short and sorrowful, and there is no remedy when a man comes to his end, since no one has been known to return from Hades."

***Sirach (Ecclesiasticus) 38.9-15 LXX (second century BC).*** My son, when you are sick, do not become negligent, but rather pray to the Lord and he will make you whole. Desist from sin and order yourself correctly. Cleanse your heart form all wickedness. Offer a sweet-smelling [sacrifice] and a memorial offering of fine flour, and make an animal offering, to the extent you can afford. And then, give the physician his place. For the Lord created the physician, and do not distance yourself from him, for you have need of him. There are times when they have good success in their hands, since they also shall pray to the Lord so that he might prosper what they offer for your alleviation and as remedies to prolong life. If someone has sinned before his maker, let him fall into the hands of the physician.

***Gospel of Luke 13:1-5 (first century).*** There were some present at that very time who told [Jesus] about those Galileans whose blood Pilate had mingled with their sacrifices. And he answered them, "Do you think that these Galileans were worse sinners than all other Galileans, because they suffered in this way? I tell you, it is not the case. But unless you repent, you will all perish in similar fashion. Or what of those eighteen on whom the tower in Siloam fell and killed them? Do you think that they were worse offenders than all the others who lived in Jerusalem? I tell you it is not the case. But unless you repent, you too will perish in similar fashion."

***The Letter of St. James 2:14-18 (first century).*** What use is it, my brethren, if a man says he has faith but does not have works? Can his faith save him? If a brother or sister is badly clothed and in lack of daily food, and one of you says to them, "Go in peace, be warm and no longer hungry," but does not give them any of the bodily things they need, what use would that be? So faith by itself, if it has no works, is dead. But some one might reply: "You have faith and I have works." Show me your faith apart from your works, and I, by my works, will show you my faith.

***The Letter of St. James 5:13-16 (first century).*** Is there any one among you who is suffering? Let him pray. Is anyone among you cheerful? Let him sing praises. Is any among you sick? Let him call for the presbyters of the church, and let them pray over him, anointing him with oil in the name of the Lord; and the prayer of faith will save the sick man, and the Lord will raise him up; and if he has committed any sins, he will be forgiven. And so, confess your sins to one another, and pray for one another, so that you may find healing. The prayer of a righteous man has great power in its effects.

**Letter of Paul to Titus 3:4-8 (first century).** But when the goodness (*chrestotes*) and philanthropy of God our Savior appeared, he saved us, not because of deeds done by us in righteousness, but in virtue of his own mercy, by the washing of regeneration and renewal in the Holy Spirit, which he poured out on us richly through Jesus Christ our Savior, so that we might be justified by his grace and become heirs in hope of eternal life. The saying is sure. I desire you to insist on these things, so that those who have believed in God may be careful to apply themselves to good deeds; these are excellent and profitable things for all.

**St. Gregory of Nazianzus, Oration 14.5, 10-13, 18, 22-23, On Love of the Poor (fourth century).** If we place any reliance on Paul, or on Christ himself, then we shall take love as the first and greatest of the commandments, no less than the summation of the law and prophets, and, accordingly, we shall take love for the poor as the highest pinnacle of charity . . . for "mercy and truth walk before our God" (Ps 88:15 LXX), and nothing more than this befits a God who "prefers mercy to justice," and in no other way whatsoever can God be served religiously except through the medium of mercy. . . . But who is there even among the most gracious and humane of men who does not habitually show himself hostile and inhumane to the leper? This is the only case where we forget this is someone who is flesh like us and must bear the same fragile body we have. But imagine, if you will, what the mother of one of these must feel. What lamentation will she not raise when she sees her son before her very eyes like a living corpse? "O wretched son of a tragic mother," she will say, "Stolen away from me by this disease. O pitiful child; son I can no longer recognize. You who must now live among wild animals in deserts and craggy mountains, with only rocks as your shelter, nevermore to see humankind except for the most holy among them." . . . With cries such as this she will pour out fountains of tears. . . . The lepers themselves define as a charitable man, not him who gives them donations, but rather the ones who do not drive them away with fierce blows. . . . I have given this speech to help you change your minds. What has all this vast, unending sea of the misery of humankind got to do with today's festival, you may ask? I suppose I had better stop developing the theme of tragedy, for otherwise I shall spoil your fun by moving all of you to tears, though I suspect some grieving may be better for you than what you'll soon go to see on stage, and a few teardrops may be more worthy for you than the bawdy jokes you'll soon be sharing.... We must renounce our inhumanity to the wretched. Why do we spend so much on superfluous luxuries instead of helping them? Why do we do these things, my friends and brothers? Why are we so sick in soul like this? For it is indeed a sickness, far worse than any bodily illness to act like this. Why do we not rush to help while we still have time? Why do we sit and glut ourselves while our brothers are in such distress? God forbid I should enjoy such superabundance, when the likes of these have nothing at all. So dedicate a little to God, from whom you received so much. Even give him everything, for he gave you all that you have. You will never be able to surpass God's generosity to you, not if you gave away every single thing you owned, even selling yourself into the bargain.... And therefore, "Know thyself!" Know from what source comes all that you possess, all your breathing, your knowing and your wisdom. And this is the greatest of all—to know God, to hope for the kingdom of heaven, the same honor as the angels, and the vision of glory. For now we see that we are the children of God, and coheirs of Christ, only as if in a mirror, in dark reflections, but then we shall see more clearly and more purely (1 Cor 13:12). And, if I may put it a little more daringly, we shall see that we have even been deified.[68]

**Pseudo-Basil, Homily on Mercy and Justice *(fifth century)*.** You must blend together mercy and justice; holding your possessions with justice, but dispensing them with mercy, according to what is written: "Preserve mercy and justice, and ever draw close to God" (Hos 12:6 LXX). God loves mercy and justice, and so whoever practices mercy and justice is indeed one who draws close to God. Accordingly, every person should examine themselves well. The rich should carefully weigh up their means, out of which they intend to make offerings [to the church], in order to make certain they have not lorded it over the poor, or employed force against the weak, or committed extortion against those beneath them. We are commanded to maintain justice and equity, even toward slaves. Do not use force because you have dominion. Do not commit extortion just because you are able to do so. Rather, demonstrate the qualities of justice even while you enjoy the trappings of authority.... If, after taking what belongs to the poor, you give back to the poor, you ought to

---
[68]PG 35.864, 869, 872-73, 880, 885, 888.

know this, that it would have been better if you had neither extorted from them in the first place nor offered them charity.[69]

**FURTHER READING**

Agourides, S. "The Social Character of Orthodoxy." *Greek Orthodox Theological Review* 8, nos. 1-2 (Summer–Winter 1962–1963): 7-20.

Amantos, C. *He Ellenike Philanthropia Kata Tous Mesaionikous Chronous*. Athens: P.D. Sakellarion, 1923.

Avalos, H. *Health Care and the Rise of Christianity*. Peabody, MA: Hendrickson, 1999.

Batson, D. *The Treasure Chest of the Early Christians*. Grand Rapids: Eerdmans, 2001.

Bell, H. I. "Philanthropia in the Papyri of the Roman Period." In *Hommages à J Bidez et F Cumont: Collection Latomus II*, 31-37. Brussels, 1949.

Constantelos, D. J. *Byzantine Philanthropy and Social Welfare*. New Brunswick, NJ: Rutgers University Press, 1968.

———. "*Philanthropia* as an Imperial Virtue in the Byzantine Empire of the tenth Century." *Anglican Theological Review* 44, no. 4 (October 1962): 351-65.

———. "Philanthropy in the Age of Justinian." *Greek Orthodox Theological Review* 6, no. 2 (Winter 1960–1961): 206-22.

Deaut, R. Le. "*Philanthropia* dans la littérature grecque jusqu'au Nouveau Testament." *Mélanges Eugène Tissserant* 1 (1964): 255-94.

Downey, G. "*Philanthropia* in Religion and Statecraft in the Fourth Century After Christ." *Historia* 4 (1955): 199-208.

———. "Who Is My Neighbor? The Greek and Roman Answer." *Anglican Theological Review* (January 1965): 1-15.

Ferguson, J. *Moral Values in the Ancient World*. London: Methuen, 1958.

Frost, E. *Christian Healing: A Consideration of the Place of Spiritual Healing in the Church of Today in the Light of the Doctrine and Practice of the Ante-Nicene Church*. London: Mowbray, 1940.

Giordani, I. *The Social Message of the Early Church Fathers*. Paterson, NJ: St. Anthony Guild Press, 1944.

Grant, R. M. *Miracle and Natural Law in Graeco-Roman and Early Christian Thought*. Amsterdam: North Holland, 1952.

Gulick, C. B. "Notions of Humanity Among the Greeks." In *Harvard Essays on Classical Subjects*, ed. H. W. Smyth, 38-41. New York: Harvard University Press, 1912.

Holman, S. R. *The Hungry Are Dying: Beggars and Bishops in Roman Cappadocia*. Oxford: Oxford University Press, 2001.

Hunger, H. "Philanthropia. Eine griechische Wortpragung auf ihrem wege v. Aischylos bis Theodorus Metochites." *Anzeiger der Osterreichischen Akademie der Wissenshaft. Philosophisch-Historische Klasse* 100 (1963): 1-20.

---

[69]PG 31.1708-9.

Imbert, J. *Les Hopitaux en droit canonique*. Paris: Vrin, 1947.
Janin, R. "Les monastères du Christ Philanthrope à Constantinople." *Revue des études byzantines* 4 (1946): 135-62.
———. "Un ministre byzantin; Jean L'Orphanotrophe. 11-ième siècle." *Echos D'Orient* 34 (1931): 431-43.
Kee, H. C. *Medicine Miracle and Magic in Early Christian Times*. Cambridge: Cambridge University Press, 1986.
Koukoules, P. "L'assistance aux indigents dans l'empire byzantin." In *Mémorial Louis Petit*, 254-71. Mélanges d'histoire et d'archéologie byzantines. Bucharest: Institut Français d'études byzantines, 1948.
Lallemand, L. *Histoire de la Charité*. 2 vols. Paris: Picard et Fils, 1902–1903.
Leclercq, H. "Charité." In *Dictionnaire d'archéologie chrétienne et de liturgie*, vol. 2, cols 599-656. Paris: Letouzey et Ané, 1903.
Lorenz, S. "De Progressu Notionis Philanthropias." Diss., Leipzig, 1914.
Luck, U. "Philanthropia." In *Theological Dictionary of the New Testament*, ed. G. Kittel and G. Friedrich, 9:107-22. Grand Rapids: Eerdmans, 1974.
Magoulias, H. J. "The Lives of the Saints as Sources of Data for the History of Byzantine Medicine in the 6th and 7th Centuries." *Byzantinische Zeitschrift* 57, no. 1 (June 1964): 127-50.
Martin, H. "The Concept of Philanthropia in Plutarch's Lives." *American Journal of Philology* 82 (April 1961): 164-75.
McCasland, S. V. *By the Finger of God*. New York: Macmillan, 1951.
McGuckin, J. A. "The Influence of the Īsis Cult on St. Cyril of Alexandria's Christology." *StPatr* 24 (1992): 191-99.
———. "The Vine and the Elm Tree: The Patristic Interpretation of Jesus' Teaching on Wealth." In *The Church and Wealth*, ed. W. J. Sheils and D. Wood, 1-14. Studies in Church History 24. Oxford: Blackwell, 1987.
Miller, T. S. *The Birth of the Hospital in the Byzantine Empire*. Baltimore: Johns Hopkins University Press, 1985. Reprint, 1987.
Monnier, A. *Histoire de l'assistance publique dans les temps anciens et modernes*. Paris: Guillaumin, 1866.
Niederev, F. "Early Medieval Charity." *Church History* 21 (1952): 285-95.
Nissiotis, N. A. "Church and Society in Greek Orthodox Theology." In *Christian Social Ethics in a Changing World*, ed. J. C. Bennett, 78-104. New York: Association Press, 1966.
Phan, P. *Social Thought*. The Message of the Fathers of the Church 20. Wilmington, DE: Michael Glazier, 1984.
Santa Ana, J. de. *Good News to the Poor: The Challenge of the Poor in the History of the Church*. Maryknoll, NY: Orbis Books, 1979.
Schroeder, C. P., trans. *St. Basil the Great: On Social Justice*. Crestwood, NY: St. Vladimir's Seminary Press, 2009.

Sheather, M. "Pronouncements of the Cappadocians on Issues of Poverty and Wealth." In *Prayer and Spirituality in the Early Church*, ed. P. Allen et al., 375-92. Queensland: Australian Catholic University, Centre for Early Christian Studies, 1998.

Shewring, W. *Rich and Poor in Christian Tradition*. London: Burns, Oates, and Washbourne, 1966.

Temkin, O. "Byzantine Medicine: Tradition and Empiricism." In O. Temkin, *The Double Face of Janus and Other Essays in the History of Medicine*, 202-22. Baltimore: Johns Hopkins University Press, 1977.

Troeltsch, E. *The Social Teaching of the Christian Churches*. Vol. 1. New York: Harper, 1960.

Uhlhorn, G. *Christian Charity in the Ancient Church*. New York: Scribner's Sons, 1883.

Winslow, D. F. "Gregory of Nazianzen and Love for the Poor." *Anglican Theological Review* 47 (1965): 348-59.

# THE EXERCISE OF AUTHORITY IN THE CHURCH

## Orders and Offices

The history of Christianity represents a complex set of variations in the church's relations with those who held power over the course of its long progress through human society: whether those in authority tried to suppress its very existence, like the early Roman emperors, or used their power and wealth to endow and privilege Christian institutions, such as Constantine I and the Christian rulers who came after him. When the church was being threatened by the Roman law that had first ruled it an illicit religion and then determined that it therefore had no rights to assembly, further representation, or appeal (since a crime of religion under the early emperors was equated with high treason and carried a capital penalty), some of the church's rhetoricians who had themselves been educated in legal process turned their minds explicitly to questions of law and justice.[1] It was a matter of life and death that had so focused their attention. These works of the early apologists grew especially out of the systematic persecutions of the third and early fourth centuries. Some of them take a wider view and consider issues such as the use and abuse of authority in human society, what would constitute the "just ruler." But many were only concerned with trying to represent the church in a better light than the hostile prejudices of the day allowed. For most of the time in its early generations the church was content enough simply to be left alone.

After the fourth century, when it became an object of support by Christian emperors, it was forced to turn its attention once more to issues of governance on national and

---

[1] Apologists such as Tertullian chief among them. See further J. A. McGuckin, *The Ascent of Christian Law: Patristic and Byzantine Reformulations of Antique Civilization* (Crestwood, NY: St. Vladimir's Seminary Press, 2012).

international scales that it could never have imagined scarcely half a generation before. After the fourth century there developed a large range of Christian attitudes to society, culture, and power. It is not surprising, then, that there remains a large disparity of attitudes to the same things in the current international Christian movement: with some concepts of the church envisaging it as a force meant to be within the heart of human society and cultures, and others seeing it as a world apart from "the world," which it inhabits temporarily but is never meant to belong to. All manner of variation on these poles can also be found in all times and places. If we look, then, at the concepts of authority, governance, and order within the Christian movement, perhaps a good place to begin is with how these things were given articulation in the foundational sources.

## NEW TESTAMENT POLITY

Jesus clearly had some radical views about authority that can be classed as both theological and societal. In the first instance, the idea of God's authority palpably manifested on the earth is the core meaning of that chief theological idea he preaches: the kingdom (or rule) of God (*basileia tou theou*). The term *authority* (*exousia*) is thus a critically important one in New Testament thought and relates to the notion of divine power and how it is shared with the representatives of God on earth (a priesthood, kingly dynasty, or prophetic order).

In the second place, how Jesus imagined his community to be ordered (its governance and institutional polity) is an interesting concept that might illustrate for us some of the implications of that theology of authority conveyed by the idea of the kingdom of God—for the patterning of the earliest and later Christian communities surely stands as an elaboration of how divine order and governance "ought to be" expressed among the elect. To this extent the ancient ecclesiology (concept of the church) can manifest for us the earliest patterns of the use and application of power within the Christian community. So we have a two-way scrutiny: first, how the church looked at external powers acting against or for it; and second, how it thought it should organize itself internally as the ideal community. Let us begin with the biblical evidences.

## AUTHORITY IN HELLENISTIC AND CHRISTIAN USAGE

*Exousia*, which is the Greek scriptural word for *authority*, illustrates a remarkable range of paradoxes for us, because it was also the customary word in Hellenistic texts for legal permission and thus freedom from constraint.[2] The ancient Greeks used

---

[2] In the LXX version of the Old Testament, which was that used by the early Christians, and throughout the New Testament. In the Septuagint, the Hebraic term for authority, *memshalah*, is rendered consistently as *exousia*, especially signifying the rightful dominion of God: the kingdom where his authority holds sway. Passing on into the New Testament, the concept of the *exousia* cannot be

the word *exousia* to connote the freedom to do a thing, as distinct from the issue of the ability or capacity (*dynamis*) to do it. *Exousia* is thus the authority needful to do a thing. *Dynamis* is the power or skill to be able to do it. In classical literature referring to the acts of kings or gods the two things were often presumed to be one and the same, but not so in ordinary civic life. In late antiquity the Roman law codes deduced from this axiomatic observation an important cultural distinction that still massively impinges on the Christian legal and civic construct: the distinction between *potestas* and *auctoritas*, which we today might translate as the difference between executive power (such as that exercised by the emperor, who really was in that era the "commander in chief" of the armies) and moral authority (such as that claimed by the senate, as theoretical representatives of the traditions of the people).

In the late empire of the early Christian era, there was definitely a sense growing, helped along by the widespread dissemination of Stoic ethical reflections on human culture, that "might is not always right." This might seem to us today a banal observation, but it brought into human society of the time a revolutionary change from more antique notions that the will of the gods on earth was primarily manifested by, and in, the might of kings, since kings were the images of the divine power, the source of law and order, and had been raised to their powerful role by the favor of attendant gods. Revolutionary dissidence, then, was fundamentally an irreligious act in antique imagination. Subversive behavior, such that threatened the established order, was quite liable to be labeled an attack on the divine plan for human society. It was exactly under such political and religious premises that the persecutions against the Christians were conceived and justified. There was some built-in critique to this theory of godly kings: for example, if the ruler showed signs of tyranny, ancient political thought would theorize that *hybris* and irrationality had perverted the true exercise of power, and ancient political theology expected the will of gods to be manifested in a way that brought down the tyrant through war or the rebellion of a just warrior to reset the balance.

Apart from freedom or permissibility under term of law, the word *exousia* also connoted in common Greek discourse in antiquity what we today would call "the government," understood as a system of ordering and commanding, power that is expressed in the realpolitik.[3] This sense is largely absent from the Hebrew Scriptures,

---

separated from that of the kingdom (*basileia*). At its heart is the notion of the true Israel, on whose praises the Almighty is enthroned (Ps 21:2-4). In Hellenistic texts, see Plato, *Symposium* 182e; *Crito* 51D; *Gorgias* 526A, 461E; *Oxyrhynchus Papyri* II 237 col. 6.17. See G. Kittel and G. Friedrich, eds., *Theological Dictionary of the New Testament* (Grand Rapids: Eerdmans, 1978), 2:562-74; H. Cremer, *Biblico-Theological Lexicon of New Testament Greek* (Edinburgh: T&T Clark, 1883), 236-38.
[3] See, for example, Plato, *Alcibiades* 1.135B.

though it reappears in the later epistolary literature of the New Testament to describe the "powers that be" in the political realm, who, even if they might be hostile to the church, are still deserving of believers' obedience and respect. In this sense of "government" Plato defined *exousia* as the *epitrope nomou*, or the "guardian of law."[4] Aristotle in the *Nicomachean Ethics* described the ruling body of his day in the very modern sense of "those in authority" (*oi en tais exousiais*), a term we find exactly paralleled in a very important New Testament passage at Matthew 20:25, though here used with very heavy irony indeed, to correct this notion's presumptive equating of governmental powers with true and rightful authority. The term of *exousia* in this instance of Matthew's Gospel appears so much in the manner of a severe brake, and caustic comment, on the Hellenistic political thought of the day that we can suspect from the outset that the Christians had a more complicated view on the "powers of the day" than appears from the rather bland counsel to be obedient in all things that we find in the later apostolic letters. Of course, in the time of Jesus, a biblical sense of *politeia* (the order intended by God for his elect people) clashed prophetically with the realpolitik of Roman-occupied Palestine; and on that fracture line we see flashes of a revelation of what it was that Jesus evoked by his prophetic preaching of the advent of the kingdom of God, as well as his personal evocation of what that would look like, performatively displayed, in his own life as the holy agent of God (the import of most of the christological titles we see in the Gospel texts).

In the Septuagintal version of the Old Testament, *exousia* is a word that has a profoundly legal usage, heavily coloured by the identification of law as Torah and chiefly connoting the sense of having the right from God to do something, or having the legal right under the terms of the Jewish law for certain conducts that thereby prescribe what are the boundaries of the true Israel—moral, not merely geographic.[5] It is chiefly in this sense too that we find the word associated with Jesus' ministry of preaching and exorcism in the Gospels (his ability to exorcise being itself a manifestation of how he holds his authority from God). In its precise reference to the Torah, *exousia* in the Septuagint signifies God's rights over the chosen people who signal their allegiance by the observance of his law and by their veneration of the holy name in right worship.

On other occasions, however, especially in the Psalms, the word refers to God's supreme rights as Lord (*basileus*), not simply over Israel but over the entire universe, even though many a lesser power (*dynamis, ischys, kratos*) might contest or stand against the *pantokrator* (all-powerful God) in the short term. These lesser powers,

---

[4]Cremer, *Biblico-Theological Lexicon of New Testament Greek*, 236.
[5]See Tobit 2:13; see also this typical usage applied in halakhic disputation by Jesus in Mk 2:24-26; 3:4; 6:18; 10:2.

envisaged in the Scriptures, can be rebellious angels, earthbound demons, or earthly princes hostile to God's Israel (and thus hostile to God's glory—*doxa*). When the entire cosmos is in "right order," it naturally sings out the glory of the holy name. This is a theme that underlies much of the beautiful nature poetry of the Psalms and Wisdom literature.

Late prophetic literature expresses this idea classically in the following terms taken from Daniel 4:27: "The Lord lives in heaven, and his authority (*exousia*) holds sway over all the earth." It is in Daniel too that we first see clearly how the term *basileia* (or "kingdom" of God), can effectively stand in for the notion of *exousia*: God's moral right to have the obedience and glorification of the whole world, but above all that of Israel. We should note, however, that *exousia* is the broader term that carries *basileia tou theou*; it is not the other way around, as has been suggested in many recent approaches to the theme. We cannot understand the moral implications of this ancient biblical idea of divine authority if we have not understood the theological premise behind it; in other words, Israel can only initiate the *politeia* of the kingdom because it has first glimpsed the *doxa* of the divine holiness; and this is why the halakhic, or moral, aspects of the theme are intimately related to the political and apocalyptic elements—they not the disparate themes that have seemed to puzzle many later commentators concerning their relationship.

Healings and exorcisms have the same intellectual signification in the New Testament world, though we moderns have often separated them, because healing remains a living concept to us while exorcism has been marginalized. For the world of the New Testament, human sickness is simply a manifestation of the force of demonic hostility against humanity.[6] A healing in the text is, therefore, in the same category as an exorcism. The Gospel accounts of the ministry present Jesus most commonly in the role of an exorcist. Both sickness and demonic oppression are understood to belong to the *krateia* (power) of the "prince of this world." Liberation from this oppression by evil forces belongs to the kingdom where God's holy name is present, uniting men with angels and driving out the forces and traces of the *krateia* of the present age.[7] This is why, for example, so many of the evangelical instances of the use of the word *exousia* belong to the instructions Jesus gave about exorcisms to his disciples (Mt 10:1; Mk 3:15; 6:7; Lk 4:36; 9:1). Such a determinative authority from God (by which I mean that the authority is not

---

[6] Sickness being one form of demonic oppression over mortality, since death was brought into this world as part of the "envy" of the evil one. Cf. Heb 2:14.

[7] Which is why one sees the inescapable political associations of Jesus' theological message, and why Rome was so willing to execute him, since the *krateia* of Rome was not seen by any rabbi of the time as God-given; and if not from God, then from where?

simply that Jesus is empowered to perform liberative healings but rather than the healings and exorcisms are proffered as signs that he possesses the divine *exousia*) is claimed in fullness by Jesus (Mt 9:6; Mt 28:18), recognized in him by insightful characters of the Gospel narratives (Mt 7:29; 8:9), and passed on by him to his subordinate agents of mission (Mt 10:1).

In a very significant discourse Jesus also considered the practical implications of the exercise of this high authority within the ongoing life of the community (see also Mk 10:42; Lk 22). Here he makes a strong contrast between the way *exousia* is manifested among the elect and the way that power (dominion, or *kyriotes*) is used as the basis for a pagan organization of society: "But Jesus called [the disciples] to him and said, 'You know that the rulers of the Gentiles (*archontes*) lord it over them (*katakyrieuousin*), and their great men (*megaloi*) exercise authority over them (*katexousiazousin*). It shall not be like this among you.'" In stark contrast to the force that holds together pagan society, the church is to be held together by a spirit of service, humble *kenosis*, and love. Never has such a radical change of social polity been sketched in so few words.

It is clear enough from this that the charter for the church's sense of *exousia* has been set up on a collision course with "secular" society. The same sense of radical separateness, even opposition, between the ecclesial understanding of how God's authority is manifested in the elect community and how that is reflected (from a demonic source) in secular understandings of power and glory is given in the extraordinarily deep hymn of Christ's victory given in the late first-century text of Ephesians 1:18-23. Here the *exousia* of the universal kingdom is given to Christ as a trophy of his passion, beginning with the conquest of the evil powers (listed in the text) but running out to the church as the vindicated place on earth where the two ages collide in a permanent capacity for offering glory:

> May he enlighten the eyes of your mind, that you may know the richness of the glory (*doxa*) of your inheritance . . . and the immeasurable greatness of his power (*dynamis*) in us who believe, according to the force (*kratos*) of his great might (*ischyos*), which he accomplished in Christ when he raised him from the dead and made him sit at his right hand in the heavenly places, far above all rule (*arche*) and authority (*exousia*) and power (*dynamis*) and dominion (*kyriotes*), and above every name that is named, not only in this age (*aion*) but also in that which is to come; and he has put all things under his feet and has made him the head over all things for the church, his body.

Here we see the emergence of *exousiai* (authorities) along with rulers, powers, thrones, and dominions, as actual titles for categories of (originally evil) spirits in the nascent

New Testament demonology.[8] All the titles denote *krateia*, oppressive domination. The name of God alone has the force of true *basileia* and it is manifested cosmically in the risen Christ among his church in the world, which now occupies an interstitial condition held in both sites, through the act of *doxa* that constitutes its being "in Christ."

From a similar first-century school and context the hymn in Colossians 1:11-20 expresses the same dynamic sense of the kingdom when it effectively renders the poem above in creedal form, turning it more specifically as a doxology of the name and saying,

> May you be strengthened with all power (*dynamis*), according to the power (*kratos*) of his glory (*doxa*), for all endurance and patience with joy, giving thanks to the Father, who has qualified us to share in the inheritance of the saints in light. He has delivered us from the governance (*exousia*) of darkness and transferred us to the kingdom (*basileia*) of his beloved Son, in whom we have redemption, the forgiveness of sins. He is the image of the invisible God, the firstborn of all creation; for in him all things were created, in heaven and on earth, visible and invisible, whether thrones or dominions or principalities or authorities (*exousiai*)—all things were created through him and for him. He is before all things, and in him all things hold together. He is the head of the body, the church; he is the beginning, the firstborn from the dead, that in everything he might be preeminent. For in him all the fullness of God was pleased to dwell, and through him to reconcile to himself all things, whether on earth or in heaven, making peace by the blood of his cross.

This remarkable proto-creed of Christendom demonstrates to us how the kingdom has been given to the Son. It is his name that now commands, and in commanding reveals the light of the glory of the revelation of the new age (Mt 28:18). His name is caught up in the praise of God the Father or, in other words, is in the *Shekinah* light itself, becomes the holy place of the *Shekinah*, and thus serves as the mediator of all other cosmic praise of God for the elect of Israel. This is how, for the early church, Christ's name (his titles) thus shares the attributes of the unutterable name of the Father: Creator (*Ktitor*), beginner before all things (*arche*; cf. Jn 1:1), icon of the invisible, firstborn (*prototokos*), head of the body (*kephale*). It is this selfsame doctrine that the Evangelist John never tires of repeating: for every instance of the appearance of the word *authority* in his Gospel returns to the same doctrine that there is but one *exousia* of Father and Son, inseparable (see Jn 5:27; 5:30; 7:17-18; 8:28; 12:49; 14:10; 16:13). In a very short space, therefore, considered both chronologically and

---

[8]*Exousia* (an "authority") actually seems to have been a term invented at this time by Christian exorcists developing the theology of the kingdom through exercising the power of the name in their ministry of *didache*. See 1 Cor 15:24; Eph 1:21; 3:10; 6:12; Col 1:16; 2:10, 15; 1 Pet 3:22. These spirit titles are later transferred in the writings of the Christian theologians into titles of the various orders of the (good) angels.

intellectually, this doctrine of the authority of the name that was first expressed as an aspect of early Christian demonology (that itself served to illustrate the manner in which the kingdom's *exousia* was manifested among mortals) has risen up to the full heights of a cosmic Christology of glory.

The scriptural sense of *exousia*-authority emerges, therefore, not as a simple doctrine of ecclesial authorizations (or how authority should be exercised in the church through history) as much as a deeply theological, eschatological, and mystical doctrine of the fundamental shape of the kingdom of God among human beings who gather themselves to give glory to the unutterable name (thus a working biblical definition of Christ's *ekklesia* or church). This deeply mystical doctrine of authority suggests that the root of all legitimate authority in Christ's church is dependent on conformity to the glory of God, by assuming "the mindset that was in Christ" (*phronema*), as Paul phrases it (Phil 2:5). This is a remarkable doctrine: subverting brute force (*krateia*), or the principle that "might is right" (or at best the concept of leadership "by the great") by advocating instead a polity of obedience and *kenosis*.

Now, to ask how much the later history of the church put this into effect is another matter altogether. The temptation to thrust aside the *kenosis* of Christ and seize a *krateia* that used Christ's name to justify it has always been a temptation throughout Christian history. But here, at the foundational charter point, is a very clear statement: to elevate in Christ's church models of authoritative governance that assume *krateia* is the standard norm for godly governance is to deny the eschatological imperative of Christ's victory on the cross, the only source of divine blessing to the new people, and to forget the Lord's own warning: this is how things are done among the pagans, with their "great men"—"But it must never be like this among you" (Mt 20:25).

A text that we might do well to look at, before we leave the New Testament evidence, is the extraordinarily sophisticated theology witnessed in the letter to the Hebrews. This text, one of the most developed theological and literary pieces that is extant in the New Testament, derives from a disciple of Paul, in the half-generation after him, but someone who was clearly still writing in the first century and possessed of an immense authority and charism. It is curious that the name of the author has dropped from the tradition. By the fourth century, writers such as Jerome and Augustine reassigned it to the apostle Paul, mainly to confirm its "apostolic" status. More attentive critics like Origen mention the ascription to Paul but indicate that the literary style is clearly not his.

In this text the concept of the Old Testament priesthood is assigned to Christ. He is a high priest (*archi-iereus*—the sacrificing priesthood of the temple, as referenced in the LXX version of the Scripture). To distance the sense in which Christ is a high priest, both from that of the Jewish temple *kohanim* and the pagan cults of sacrificial priesthood (who also applied the same word *hiereus*) the author ascribes Christ's priesthood to "the order of Melchizidek," a mystical figure of a kingly priest who offers bread and wine to God when Abraham visits him (Gen 14:18-20; Heb 7). Christ's high priesthood thus radically reinterprets and assigns new values to the concept of priesthood found in the Old Testament (Heb 7:12). This becomes a founding principle for all later Christian reflection on priesthood and ministerial office.

It is out of this letter to the Hbrews that most patristic theologians after the late second century start their reflection and assign the concept of priesthood (*hiereus*, *hierateuma*, *sacerdos*) to the various Christian offices (especially apostle, bishop, and presbyter). Christ is at once the offering priest and the sacrificial victim. His priestly offering ends the old system, by fulfilling it perfectly and eternally (Heb 7:27). His triumphant offering is part of his glorification and enthronement with God: "Every priest stands daily at his service, offering repeatedly the same sacrifices, which can never take away sins. But when Christ had offered for all time a single sacrifice for sins, he sat down at the right hand of God" (Heb 10:11-12). This passage is very formative for Christian thought about the priestly office of bishops and presbyters, later.

Major Christian theologians of a wide representation follow the lead:[9] that priesthood as it is experienced in the church will be (1) of a new type (namely, Christ's mystical Melchizidekian priesthood),[10] (2) that it will concern the offering of special gifts (bread and wine, symbolic of the Eucharist), and (3) that it does not simply bear the character of the generic priestly character of the people of God (Ex 19:5-6; Is 61:6; 1 Pet 2:9-10), which is taken as a preeminent symbol of the holiness to which disciples are called and their obligation to "make the offering" of prayer, but rather is distinctly characterized by the charism of *hierateuma*, the elect priestly offering (eucharistic), which requires a special consecration to effect, a priesthood derived distinctively from the high priesthood of Christ.

So much for some important scriptural foundations. But all societies, even those attempting to be eschatologically pure in a hostile world, nevertheless need systems of governance to organize themselves. How did the early church put its theory of

---

[9]From the third century: Tertullian, Hippolytus, Origen; from the fourth century: Eusebius of Caesarea, Basil of Caesarea, the Council of Constantinople, Cyril of Jerusalem, Gregory of Nazianzus, Macarius of Egypt, Gregory of Nyssa, Didymus of Alexandria, Apostolic Constitutions; from the fifth century: John Chrysostom and Augustine. Common to all the writers is the application of the concept of *hierateuma*, the priestly character of Christ the *archiereus* as witnessed in the charism of the "priestly" ministers (*episkopoi* and *presbyteroi*) who "make the offering" of the Eucharist. See J. Blenkinsopp, "Presbyter to Priest: Ministry in the Early Church," *Worship* 41 (August–September 1967): 428-38.

[10]Insofar as Melchizidek serves as a "type" of what it to occur in Christ, the fulfillment (*teleiosis*).

divine authority into effect in terms of the "offices of authority" it established? From the outset one suspects we shall witness in the historical record of how Christianity approaches offices and orders within its polity, a definite tension between the eschatological imperative and the demands of common order within the day-to-day affairs of the church. There are various poles of possibility: from attributing quasi-divine authority to earthly ministers (a source of immeasurable harm to religious societies and a fund of potential abuse, as can be rehearsed in innumerable examples from Christian history) to attributing all authority to the community and next to none to a particular leadership (an equally unreliable system of governance—as communal insight has often proved inferior at times to that of an inspired set of individuals).

Christianity has, in times past and present, appealed to both models for its ideas of correct governance: a collegial model built on the principle of apostolic balance (putting the Johannine theology alongside that of the Synoptic, not instead of it) or episcopal colleges, where the wisdom of the majority can serve to balance and moderate any possible excesses of an individual or particular group (thus allowing monarchical episcopate in the early church, but heavily moderating its effect by subordinating the local bishop's decisions to the synod of the provinces other bishops). An example of this approach to authority is the important use of "compromise" in Christian history and development. The apostles James and Paul are hardly in close theological harmony in their own time: the church subsequently "harmonizes" them itself in its later praxis. In Byzantine times the emperor and the high patriarchs (bishops of the major capitals, such as Rome or Constantinople) certainly exercise a high executive authority over church affairs and are able to back this up with enforceable laws. And yet, the decisions of both emperors and high bishops are often opposed in Christian history, even in ancient times, by the will of the people exercised in numerous avenues of protest or acclamation, correction or endorsement.

The formal concept of an ecumenical council, seen as the very highest source of earthly authority in the church and the surest exemplification of the will of God for the present moment, was once (as it still remains in the Eastern church) only a retrospective concept.[11] In other words, an ecumenical council could not be called "in advance": it had to be seen from the reaction of the whole people of God, over time, whether it was recognized as such. If it could not command assent (as being in harmony with the foundations of Christian faith), it could not claim the status of

---

[11] The term *ecumenical* derives from the Greek word for "universal"—signifying that an international synod of bishops was gathered, representing all the great sees of Christendom, to adjudicate matters of the greatest import. The gathering of the leaders of the worldwide community of Christians was seen to be endowed with the status of a collation of prophetic charism. So decisions were sought from unanimity, not by majority.

ecumenicity. Here is at once an example of very high authority imposed from above (for the council was an international example of episcopal synod) yet also requiring assent from below. The Christian emperor was also afforded some real status as governor of the church in secular matters. He exercised a symbolically monarchical rule (one that was of course highly qualified by all manner of checks and balances to it that usually went unstated—but were nonetheless real, given the amount of emperors whose rules were cut short by their violent overthrow); and his monarchy was seen as iconic of God's single dominion over the world.

But even this was symbolically, and carefully, qualified in turn. The emperor in pre-Christian times was the "font and origin of all law." In Christian times, he was seen as the supreme adjudicator and enforcer of the law. There is a great difference. The Christian emperor derived his power from Christ. His allegiance was to the gospel. If he did not uphold the gospel, God's favor would be withdrawn from him, and thus his authority would have no basis. To represent this, the Byzantine emperor always occupied a double throne. The two seats on it were not, however, for him and the empress. It was for him to occupy a seat alongside the book of the Gospels that was always enthroned there and left there when the emperor himself was not physically present.

These complex symbols represent a whole set of theoretical checks and balances within the Christian theory of governance that are not merely restricted to rhetorical texts. Too often theorists have looked simply at the texts of those concerned with formulating theories of governance. It should not take us long to realize that these were penned by those who had most to gain from them: figures trying to articulate or extend their powers. But these are not necessarily the best sources to illuminate for us what is going on within the church's polity. To gain the fuller picture, we always need to keep in mind this aspect of "receptionism": how those arguments actually worked in their respective historical contexts. Let us take the matter into a more precise instantiation by reviewing the practice surrounding church orders and offices.

## ORDINATION AND OFFICES IN EARLY CHRISTIANITY

*Apostles.* The New Testament–era churches clearly established apostles, deacons, and prophets as primary titles of the officers of the generation following Jesus. Later institutional thought, after it had established a threefold system of ministerial office of bishops, presbyters, and deacons, thereafter misread the deacons that had been mentioned in the New Testament source materials as if they were the "lesser" ordained clergy of later times: third in rank of the office of priesthood. But the threefold ministerial system of the later, post–New Testamental, generation is a developed theology and praxis of priesthood, and one that is not yet entirely to the fore of the materials in the earlier New Testament foundations. There, the system of offices and titles of orders is still embryonically fluid: being sorted and sifted by the way the communities experience "best practice."

The writer of Acts, however, is already bent on reducing the importance of the system of governance by deacons or prophets and elevating the apostolic order as the highest rank of office. He follows out this agenda with a formative (but heavily "shaped") tale that suggests the apostles in Jerusalem cannot be distracted from their sacred duties of preaching the word by the more trivial matters of attending to good order at the table feasts (that is, ministering to the dole of bread the church gave out to the widows it supported; Acts 6:1-6). This manner of classifying deacons as servants of the table, or administrators of the goods of the church under supervision, became a classical formative influence on the later history of the diaconate.

But the strategy of Luke–Acts has too often been superficially exegeted. It is not just about "serving at table" (this is a code reference to precedence in the eucharistic assembly) but more likely that the Hellenist Christians (present with some degree of friction in first-century Jerusalem alongside the Hebraic party, as Acts itself manifests; Acts 6:1) are here recorded as having had a different system of ordering their internal church "authorities" from that of the Hebraists, who were in the majority at Jerusalem. Some studies of the Johannine church community have located the latter's base in Samaria also with a center of operations outlasting the original Jerusalem church in the region of the Decapolis in modern-day Jordan.[12]

This (now only dimly imagined) leadership system of seven deacons (*diakonoi*), if taken out of the imaginative horizon of the later threefold orders of ministry, presents the ideal role model of the successive leadership after Jesus as, literally, "the servants." This notion of the leader being the servant, of course, directly reflects Jesus' own concept of kenotic discipleship, being preferred to the *krateia* sought after by

---

[12] Studies of the Johannine church community include that by doyen of Johannine scholars Raymond Brown: *The Community of the Beloved Disciple* (New York: Paulist Press, 1979); *The Churches the Apostles Left Behind* (New York: Paulist Press, 1984). Richard Bauckham, *Jesus and the Eyewitnesses* (Grand Rapids: Eerdmans, 2008), has since made an argument for a closer relationship between the Gospels and their eyewitness (first-generation) "sources" and has abbreviated many of Brown's putative "stages of community development" in terms of the authorship process of the Fourth Gospel. The Samaria hypothesis comes from the symbolic importance of the woman at the well narrative in John 4, concerned with foundations, establishments, of faith communities. The Jerusalem church was devastated in AD 70 by the Roman war, and its "international" authority over the Christian movement set back forever. Even when Jerusalem was functioning again as an important international center of Christian affairs and a renowned pilgrimage center, it was subordinated to the bishop of Caesarea Maritima (as a small church of primarily symbolic importance). It gained importance as disseminator of liturgical praxes between the fourth to sixth centuries, but its lack of any real international status in the postapostolic era was a reality that did not change even after it assumed patriarchal honorific status after the Council of Chalcedon in 451.

the powers and great men of this world. The title was applied to the Lord himself as above all else the "Suffering Servant." The complete and total silence throughout the Fourth Gospel of any reference to the word *apostle* is a highly eloquent silence: the term is clearly set aside there. If we follow the lead of Luke–Acts, we have an indication of how this system of the deacons developed in the Palestinian-Hellenist community with initial leaders such as Stephen, Philip, Prochorus, Nicanor, Timon, Parmenas, and Nicolaus of Antioch.

Now these names might not be particularly resonant to us, but two of them (the first names) were evidently highly significant theologians and leaders of the primitive Hellenist Christian community, and both of them were described in terms that suggest they were also charismatic prophetic visionaries.[13] So perhaps the Hellenist deacons and the prophets were not mutually exclusive categories. Stephen's extensive speech (Acts 7:2-4) is presented in Acts, echoing this theology of the new temple and the concept that God's covenant has always been based in the renewal of the charismatic gift of the Spirit among his people, (themes that we see throughout the Fourth Gospel). Stephen himself is presented as a prophetic visionary of the end age.

The Philip of Acts 8:5 is listed immediately after the Stephen narrative and so gives a demonstration of the life and times of this second of the seven "deacons" mentioned earlier. This is why he has generally been identified (in later times) as other than the "Philip the apostle" who appears in the Fourth Gospel (but not in the apostolic lists of Matthew), as a Hellenist from Bethsaida, which was the town of Peter and Andrew. Philip the deacon of Acts, however, seems to be the same as Philip the evangelist (which might simply mean preacher of the gospel, not simply writer of a Gospel text).[14] Eusebius identified the apostle and the evangelist Philip as one and the same, but whether from historical memory or from simple conflation of biblical references is not clear.[15] His conflation was not followed by many church writers after him, but this largely because of equally "symbolic" reasons (not historical), based on the strong

---

[13] Stephen the first martyr claims the vision of the end days, an eschatological "rending of the heavens," as he dies (Acts 7:55-57), one that echoes the baptismal narratives of the Gospels and the passion story of Christ (Mt 26:64-65), with which it is clearly linked (Lk 22:68-70). Philip is equally given text that elevates his status as a major figure of the earliest communities. He is associated with Luke–Acts's narratives of the expansion of the church to the Gentiles (the Ethiopian eunuch and Simon Magus's conversion). In the Fourth Gospel Philip is the theological symbol of how Jesus' death will open the gate to the inclusion of the Gentile world in Israel (Jn 12:20-28). For me this argues a very close symbiosis between these two figures.

[14] Who was also a highly charismatic leader and theologian of the Palestinian church who had converted the Ethiopian eunuch (an important episode in Acts symbolizing the missionary expansion of the Christians), converted Simon Magus in Samaria, and settled at Caesarea Maritima with four daughters who were also prophets.

[15] *Ecclesiastical History* 3.31.5.

doctrinal distinction that had then been established on the basis of a theology of orders that "succeeded" the lost age of the apostles.

What is clear enough is that memories of the apostolic generation, with the exception of a very few great leaders from the early times (whose memories are soon incorporated into canonical texts for the second generation), most of the first generation leaders fade into legend. Next to nothing is known of them, and to fill the gap later Christian writers indulge in many historical romances. As was the case with the original seven deacons, the apostolic band also had faded away in memory except for a few leading protagonists among them, whose preaching careers were formative for the (Greek) literary Christian traditions of the second generation.

A historian might well deduce from this fact that the leadership pattern of the apostles of Jesus' time faded even in the first-century communities and was superseded by alternative charismatic polity, such as represented by the Hellenist *diakonoi* and other charismatic preachers. Paul is a prime example of the latter (claiming status as apostle, prophet, visionary, evangelist, and lawgiver all in one), and he makes a lot of effort against prevailing winds to harmonize his separate charismatic claims to status with an epitomizing insistence that he too was a thirteenth of the twelve apostles.[16] So the seven deacons that might have provided the highest level of leadership of the Hellenists itself became a pattern of earliest church order that was soon subordinated in the historicizing texts (Luke–Acts already makes this argument) to the concept of the twelve apostles, whom Jesus had himself established as a structure of "officers."[17]

Here is perhaps the clue as to why there was a confusion, or at least disagreement in the earliest sources, that has been resolved by Luke–Acts, but not entirely cleanly. If Jesus had established a pattern of discipleship, as he seemed to do when he appointed twelve men to serve as *shaliakhim*, missionaries sent out in his name to deliver his message to the towns of Galilee, then maybe this ought to

---

[16] How much throughout his ministry Paul felt he had to insist that he was "really" an apostle, not a wandering prophet, can be seen by a simple word search of the word *apostle* in his writings. The prophet (the wandering charismatic and evangelical revivalist) was already being seen as an inferior ministry to that of the apostle, who see seems, in this mid-first-century era, to have oversight of the fundamental nature of the constitution, or establishment, of churches. Paul's radical sense of the inclusion of Gentiles as coequal partners in the Jesus movement made several of the original apostolic corpus wary of him.

[17] In the sense that it is patently nonsensical to read Stephen and Philip in Acts 6–8 as mere servants of the bread dole, in contrast to the real theological preachers, the apostolic twelve, as Luke would have us do, for sake of simplifying the (evidently confused) origins of the leadership succession after Jesus' execution. Luke's historicizing account in his Gospel and in Acts at many times turns around this form of simplification by providing one (conflational) narrative line out of the several overlapping possibilities that made the original story more confusing and conflicted than his final version allows it to be.

be the pattern of leadership the churches ought to adopt in the aftermath of his death? It was a reasonable "first" supposition; but one that clearly fitted the ethos of a moving missionary set of communities, rather than an established urban church of later times. If we take it to be the case that the passion and death fell on the proto-Jesus community as a massive shock (the Gospels speak eloquently of the disarray of the survivors and only their slow charismatic rebuilding), then the issue of Jesus' succession might well never have been thought about; and so precedences from Jesus were naturally sought. The establishment of this act of Jesus, who had personally appointed twelve missionaries, was thus understandably elevated as the first pattern of continuing "offices" among the disciples. But it was not without problems, for the appointment of *shaliakhim* was a particular symbolic movement to represent the princes of the twelve tribes, meant to call Israel back to repentance through the signs of preaching and mighty works of healing and exorcism (see, e.g., Mt 10:1-16).

The Hebrew concept of *shaliakh*, the "one sent," is the source from which the Greek term *apostolos* is first derived.[18] Theologically, in Jesus' own ministry it claimed that the one sent came with all the *exousia* of the Lord, who had sent his agent (his Son or servant) to proclaim his message. So the term fused together the notion of the herald and the plenipotentiary agent. In other words, it is a term that derives its first set of meanings from the concept of the classical Old Testament prophet who has been validated by God to deliver a message and to demonstrate the power of the word by the signs that accompanied it. Jesus' adoption of the number twelve is an eschatological twist on this, meant to connote the role the preachers would have as presiding over the twelve tribes of a renewed and restored Israel (Mt 19:28).

When this term and notion was first used, in the great precedent established by Jesus, of sending out twelve of the disciples to evangelize the lake towns of Galilee as a temporary extension of his own preaching mission, they were given precise instructions as to how to comport themselves. Their mission was portrayed as a charismatic extension of that of their leader, their authority an extension of the *exousia* that God had given to him (Mt 10:5-8). But already in this first-century account of the historical mission to the lakeside towns, the incident has been elevated into a generic account by the Evangelist of how the church's international preaching ministry would attract opposition that would inaugurate persecution; and it is couched, moreover, in terms reminiscent of Paul's already-famed career and meant to endorse, theologically, Paul's (historically anachronistic) claim to

---

[18] See further H. von Campenhausen, "Le concept d'Apôtre dans le Christianisme primitive," *Studia Theologica* 1 (1947–1948): 96-130; J. N. Bakhuizen, "Tradition and Authority in the Early Church," *StPatr* 7 (1966): 3-22.

have been one of these *apostoloi* (Mt 10:18, alluding to Paul before Felix and King Agrippa; see Acts 24–26).[19]

The lost apostle Judas was soon replaced to keep the symbolic number of princes of the twelve tribes intact (see Acts 1:16-26). This apocalyptic symbol of new Israel was evidently important. Beyond the recorded work of Peter in Jerusalem, Antioch, and Rome, and that of James in Jerusalem, the actual postresurrectional careers of the Twelve are immensely obscure. There are no grounds for doubting that their mission might well have disseminated geographically, as later traditions suggest; but equally there are next to no grounds for thinking that their *kerygma* would have transmitted in Greek. And not being in that universal language meant that its passage into the second generation's corpus of literary retrieval was strictly curtailed.

In most respects, therefore, the apostolic generation served, for the second generation, to be a source of "memoirs" and testimonies about Jesus' own words and teachings. The hermeneutical researches of twentieth-century New Testament scholars have demonstrated that the interconnective materials of the various Evangelists (the redactive narrative joints that are not part of the *logia* tradition of Jesus) are predominantly made up by the Evangelists themselves, rather than based on sensible geographical or historical data. Also, the (large) extent of the manner in which Paul corrects James, or the Evangelist Mark corrects Peter, has left us with a vivid sense of the manner in which "honor was saved" in the making of lines of tradition transmission (the honor due to original companions of Christ) but also how the early communities did not afford the apostles any monarchical role in claiming a supremacy of inspiration as to the interpretation of the meaning of the gospel tradition.[20]

In some respects, then, visionary and charismatic traditions were equally weighted, and the succession to Jesus ensured as much by a democratized sense of access to the Spirit, as it was by reliance on the princely authority of eyewitness accounts (which were always given high status in the preaching tradition). The actual title and office of early Christian prophet thus seems to have been extremely important for the transitional generation. By the time of the second-generation church, as can be seen already in its marked turn to textuality (the embryonic canon of the New Testament), the reliance on charismatic gifts to lead the communities has been

---

[19]Paul, of course, interprets the required qualification (Acts 1:21-22) to have seen and been with Jesus from the beginning and to have heard Jesus' teachings, as fulfilled by his Damascus road experience (Acts 9:3-7; 2 Cor 12:2-4), for he renders the supreme "apostolic" qualification to be the election by Christ as witness to the resurrection.
[20]For further analysis on a case study related to transfiguration story see J. A. McGuckin, *The Transfiguration of Christ in Scripture and Tradition* (New York: Mellen Press, 1987).

tempered, and soon the very concept of prophet as significant officeholder fades away. The sociological reasons for this reordering of priorities are obvious. Let us briefly discuss the concept of *prophetes* before we go on to outline the authoritative offices that emerge in the second century and endure for the rest of the millennium.

**Christian prophets.** St. Paul is already trying to make an ordered sense out of the competing claims for charismatic gifts as early as the mid-first century, as can be seen in 1 Corinthians: "And God has appointed in the church first apostles, second prophets . . ." (1 Cor 12:28). He is evidently struggling here to show how his own charism as apostle trumped his local critics, who had claim prophetic status to criticize him. Overall, he extends that claim to more than just "ministerial" arguments, for Paul appeals to his abilities as a prophet and visionary as being just as good as anyone else's, if not better (1 Cor 9:1-2; 2 Cor 12:1-6). The texts of the Didache and Shepherd of Hermas show us how this role of prophet continued significantly into the church of the late first and early second centuries before being occluded in the very manner in which Paul had already sketched out: that is, it was subordinated to the roles of social governance within the community.[21] Prophets standing up in a community and "speaking for God" (that is, with theoretically absolute authority and brooking no dissent) once subordinated to another authority (such as Paul's, or an early council of presbyters) were effectively downgraded from Christ's living prophetic mouthpieces to being mystical visionaries, whose words might or might not be worthwhile, depending on the adjudication of them by other (perhaps less charismatic) authority figures in the community.

In other words, their downgrading is a major theological redrafting of how the Christian communities would accept, admit, and understand the nature of the prophetic charism (whose archetype is laid down in the Old Testament literature). It accepts "prophecy," as can be seen in almost all the theological narratives that it produces, in the sense of a foretelling of the future mysteries: a biblical anticipation of the coming of Christ.[22] This is why the age of prophets is also felt to be fading away: shadows disappearing before the advent of light. Such an approach makes it obsolete even as it endorses it. This is also why professors of Old Testament theology have to constantly remind Christian students that prophecy in the actual Old Testament text and pre-Christian experience is not really restricted in this style of "foreseeing." Another way of saying this is that the early second-century Christian church radically redefines the concept and function of prophecy among its communities.

---

[21]See further J. Reiling, *Hermas and Christian Prophecy: A Study of the Eleventh Mandate* (Leiden: Brill, 1973); H. K. Stander, "Prophets in the Early Christian Church," *Ekklesiastikos Pharos* 66-67 (1984–1985): 113-22.

[22]See, for example, Mt 1:22; 2:17; 4:14; and numerous other instances.

One can see the tensions that would always exist in this relationship of spiritual charismatic authority on the one side (especially if this was dramatically apocalyptic in character) and "common-sense" officers of a Christian community, who might be concerned both with the manner in which such words impacted on the safety and stability of the community, and with the way these "new prophecies" related to the growing body of prophetic teachings already established (the forming canon of tradition and Scripture). Indeed, this ever-felt tension between the charismatic, spirit-filled sense that the risen Christ still speaks in his community and the concerns of God-appointed leaders to govern the church safely and wisely has marked Christian history from the origins to the present day; and has on several occasion been the cause of notable crises, from the Montanist movement to the Reformation, as well as being the root of deep Christian tensions that might not have ripped the fabric of the church (caused a schism, that is) but twisted it decisively into new shapes, such as the rise of the Christian monastic movement.

The early Christian doctrine of the resurrection (*anastasis*) should be seen, more precisely, as the larger concept of the glorification (*doxa*) of Jesus. The latter contains the former, of which the resurrection accounts are merely one stream. Another stream of the same thing is the sense, very vivid among the still eschatologically charged churches of the first and second centuries, that the glory of Jesus was manifested on earth by the outpouring of the Holy Spirit on the community of believers. The prophets, therefore, were seen as primarily a testament to the glory of the risen Lord, still active in the church, and made present (as was the eucharistic and baptismal grace) by the ever-present stirrings of the Holy Spirit.[23] Paul speaks often about the gift of the Spirit in the community (Rom 8:9-11; 1 Cor 6:19; 1 Thess 4:8). The Spirit gift possessed by the prophets was a sharp instantiation of it (Acts 4:8; 1 Cor 12:4-11).

It has been deduced from the Pauline evidences (especially 1 Corinthians and 1 Thessalonians) that there were quite a few who prophesied in the early churches, but that it was not so much an office as a function. And yet there were signs that some were seen to be especially elevated as prophets. Agabus, who dramatically foretold Paul's imprisonment, seems to have been one (Acts 11:28; 21:10-12). He moved between Jerusalem and Antioch. The author of the book of Revelation clearly sees himself as a prophet in the old style, and his book as a work of prophecy (Rev 1:3; 10:11; 22:7, 10, 18). He personally stands opposed to the female Christian prophet of the Thyatira community (whom he caustically calls Jezebel), who seems to have

---

[23] See further D. E. Aune, *Prophecy in Early Christianity and the Ancient Mediterranean World* (Grand Rapids: Eerdmans, 1983); D. Hill, *New Testament Prophecy* (Atlanta: John Knox, 1970).

followed the Pauline teaching that meat offered in sacrifice to idols was not de facto defiled (Acts 15:29; 1 Cor 8:4-9; Rev 2:20).

This John of the book of Revelation knew the situations of a large circle of churches in Asia Minor, suggesting that he too was an itinerant preacher, who often (as his text reveals) spoke *in persona Dei*, that is, not as if he were some authority speaking out of his own sense of what the tradition was but rather speaking out in the name and character of the risen Lord himself. There are traces of how such itinerant prophets continued up to the second century. The Didache identifies prophets and apostles and counsels that if they appear, they ought to be given the presidency of the eucharistic celebration (which means being allowed to utter the great prayer of prophetic thanksgiving over the gifts, which at this stage had not yet become fixed in any way).[24] Their word is not to be tested, since this is the unforgiveable sin. And yet this part of the Didache is full of signs of reining in, or testing, the authority of the prophet (1 Jn 4:1-3). If they stay more than three days, they are not a real prophet. If they ask for money or parties, they are proven false. If they do not conform to established teaching or demonstrate "the ways of the Lord," they are not to be trusted; and so on.

So it seems that such direct and overwhelming authority, with no way to question the spirit, was more than a community could regularly live with, and the Didache establishes that speaking in the spirit of God is not the same as being an apostolic prophet (meaning one who claimed authority in his person by virtue of his function). If the prophet does conform to the Christian spiritual tradition, however, they are to be greatly welcomed, regarded as the "high priests," and receive firstfruits from the community.[25] The church's clash with the Gnostic and Montanist movements, who established community polities that gave high value to prophecy, led to the mainstream communities moving away from this office as an ecstatic one. Doubtless the number of charlatans that had been experienced, claiming to be prophets, had already set in some disillusionment.[26]

Already in the early second century *episkopoi* such as Ignatius have started to fold the prophetic charism in to their episcopal role—and not surprisingly, since the offering

---

[24]Didache 11-13.
[25]Ibid., 13.4.
[26]Shepherd of Hermas, Mandate 11.12; Didache 11.6, 9. Lucian's caustic satire on Peregrinus Proteus, the Cynic philosopher who had once been a Christian and assumed an authoritative role in the church before being expelled, gives a sense of the wanderings of such charismatic leaders. Lucian clearly sees him as a fake. Lucan, *De Morte Peregrini* 11, 16. See G. Bagnani, "Peregrinus Proteus and the Christians," *Historia: Zeitschrift für Alte Geschichte* 4, no. 1 (1955): 107-12. Lucian mocks the church at this period (c. 120–140) in these terms: "any charlatan or trickster" who comes to them "quickly becomes rich by imposing on such simple people."

of the eucharistic anaphora, a prime function of the early bishops, was first and foremost a matter of exercising prophetic voice to give thanks viva voce and extemporaneously to God in the assembly.[27] Ignatius speaks of exercising the prophetic gift in the assembly of the people: probably now meaning the office of interpreting the Scriptures and offering the prayer. His absorption of the prophetic office exemplifies the teaching of the Didache, which regards bishops and deacons as the normal replacement for the prophets by this time.[28] Ignatius sees his role as *episkopos* in no less charismatic terms than that of prophet. But it is a stationary order and office, suited to the longer-term teaching and development of a stationary community. So, while the role of Christian prophet faded away before the rise of the bishop-presbyters, even so a few particularly outstanding prophets of the second century remained in the "annals of the heroes."

Eusebius the bishop-historian of the fourth century, so alive in his work to the presence of charlatans and heretics in the history of the church, still recalls, as great figures, the lady Ammia of Philadelphia as well as Quadratus of Athens, who was just as active, he says, as the virgin prophetess daughters of Philip the evangelist (Acts 21:9) and who also wrote an apologia in defense of the faith in the time of Hadrian.[29] The Shepherd of Hermas, written at the very end of the first and first few decades of the second century, shows us a Christian prophet functioning in a large church, that of Rome. The author seems to have been a Palestinian (some have thought him a temple priest brought to the capital as spoils of the Jewish war of AD 70). He has visions and works in an apocalyptically charged environment but also seems to rise up as a significant administrative figure in the church. His special concern is with moral discipline: all the characteristics we see overlapped, in fact, with the office of presbyters and bishops. Hermas gives us a test case of the merging of the more disparate office patterns of the first two generations, with a simplification of titles and roles settling down around the administration of the eucharistic assembly.

The strength of commitment among Christians to the prophetic movement can be seen in the Montanist movement, a name given by the episcopal heresiologists to the self-styled "new prophecy," which seems from its own title to have been a revivalist movement: an attempt, perhaps, to bring back prophetic structures at a time when the episcopal order had supplanted them? In doing so it was firmly opposed by the bishops. We have considered the movement already in our discussion of the history of the second century. It is enough here to remind ourselves how prophecy at this period was represented especially by the two female companions of the prophet Montanus, Prisca and Maximilla, around the latter half of the second

---

[27]Didache 14-15.
[28]Ibid., 15.2.
[29]Eusebius, *Historia Ecclesiastica* 5.17.3-4; 3.37.1; 4.3.1-2.

century.[30] We see here a strong and rigorous ethical sense, a highly sharpened sense of apocalyptic end times (not least a welcoming of martyrdom opportunities), a habit of speaking *in persona dei* (which was then heavily criticized as presumptuous by the surrounding church leaders), and an itinerant practice that was seen increasingly at odds with the more sedentary nature of the church communities. The movement faded away in Asia Minor where it first began and was there branded from the outset as secessionist. It moved westward, however, and was taken up popularly by many congregations in a more moderated form that was attractive, especially to many Christian communities in North Africa. Tertullian in Carthage was a convert in his later years to the Montanist movement and became a positive advocate for it. In his hands it seems to have adapted to become a slightly more charismatic and puritanical form of Christian observance, which he (rigorist that he is) found to be refreshing.

**Presbyters.** *Priest* is the English rendition of the Greek term *presbyteros*. Initially it meant primarily "old man" or "elder." Before it grows into an institutional order, therefore, it represents in the Christian communities the basic fact that age and age's wisdom were a precious commodity in antiquity. Most people simply did not live long enough to be elderly: or at least not elderly and in possession of active faculties. The wisdom of the aged was thus a very important factor in ancient community systems for transmission of memory and maintenance of custom. These things were highly prized among the Christians, who, because of their eschatological philosophy, looked back to the age of the founder as a charter time. Clearly one system of governance of the early communities was to allow the old men a primacy of honor in the worship. There is some indication that female elders were given honor in some of the earliest communities (*presbytidae*), and indeed in the New Testament era some women were the founders of the community.[31] These important (one presumes also

---

[30] Eusebius, *Historia Ecclesiastica* 5.16.6-9; 6.20.3; Hippolytus, *On Heresies* 7.19.1.
[31] About ten tombal inscriptions survive from across the ancient Christian world mentioning *presbytidae* (see K. Madigan and C. Osiek, *Ordained Women in the Early Church: A Documentary History* [Baltimore: Johns Hopkins University Press, 2005]). They have been much discussed in modern arguments concerning the ordination of women in the catholic tradition of the churches. Their evidence value is not always clear (are these from mainstream communities or secessionist ones? Are they referring to female presbyters or male presbyters' spouses?), which is why they have been the source of heated controversy. See Ute Eisen, *Women Office-Holders in Early Christianity: Epigraphical and Literary Studies* (Collegeville, MN: Liturgical Press, 2000); M. A. Rossi, "Priesthood, Precedent and Prejudice: On Recovering the Women Priests of Early Christianity," *Journal of Feminist Studies in Religion* 7, no. 1 (1991): 73-94; Madigan and Osiek, *Ordained Women in the Early Church*, 163-98. Some Gnostic Christian churches (Hippolytus, *Refutation of Heresies* 6.35; Irenaeus, *Adversus Haereses* 1.13.1-2; Epiphanius, *Against All Heresies* 42.4; Tertullian, *On the Prescription of Heretics* 41) and several Montanist communities (cf. Cyprian, 75.10; Epiphanius, *Against All Heresies* 49.2) seem to have had female presbyters who both baptized and celebrated

wealthy) foundresses are analogous to the *archisynagogai* or leading women of the Jewish communities we also hear of in sources. Some of them, such as Junia, attract the designation of apostle.[32]

The issue of women's leadership has been a much discussed topic in mid-twentieth-century scholarship as an ordained female "priesthood" (as distinct from ministry) has been reintroduced in many parts of the church and has become a source of controversy between different church traditions. Some of the scholarly studies have not successfully distanced themselves from the apologia. One thing to keep in mind is that the same title (as we have seen with *diakonos* and *apostolos*) is not necessarily referring to the same thing in these very different and embryonic centuries, until after the third, when these "orders" become more or less established.[33] There is much ambivalence in the earliest sources about the various orders of governance (and doubtless a considerable stretch of different praxis in local communities), and it has been pressed by both sides (for and against women's ordination to presbyterate in the modern era) in apologetic ways.

The Roman senate started out with a similar designation of officers, the word *senator* deriving from the Latin *senex*, or "old man." Synagogue practice also recognized the *zaken*, or "elder," who was a member of a council that had the duty of determining issues of the interpretation of the Torah, regulating good behavior in the synagogue worship, and settling larger matters of dispute in the local communities. The judicial nature of a council of elders is already indicated in the Old Testament texts (Deut 21:18-21; 1 Kings 21:8-12). One notes immediately about the Christian use of the title that pre-third-century communities tend to represent the presbyter always in a council or fellowship. It is very rare that we find the term used in a singular reference.[34] It could be argued that in adopting the governance system of a council of elders the Christian communities simply continued synagogue

---

the Eucharist. Epiphanius in the fourth century argues (in an apologetic context about women's orders in general, which he complains is a secessionist practice) that *presbytidae* was simply a title given to the senior widows: "Deaconesses serve bishops and priests on grounds of propriety, for example in connection with the care of sick women, or perhaps in the baptismal rites . . . but the Word of God does not permit a woman to teach in the church (1 Cor 14:34), or to lord it over men. . . . This also you should note carefully, that only the office of female deacon was established in the ecclesiastical order. Widows are mentioned by name, and the most senior among them are called elders (*presbytidas*), but these have never been made women presbyters (*presbyteridas*) or women priests (*sacerdotissas*)." *Panarion* 79.4.

[32]Rom 16:7; Junia's gender often disappears in this text's rendering.

[33]A good review, with sources, can be found in Madigan and Osiek, *Ordained Women in the Early Church*, 163-98.

[34]The author of the second and third letters of John describes himself as "the elder." This is a rare singular usage. When Peter the apostle is described also by this title, he is classed as a "fellow elder" and "eyewitness": a conflation of the apostolic title with that of the council of presbyters. These documents represent late first- or early second-century contexts.

practice. The development of the theology of presbyters, however. was something else, and from early times the concept of priesthood (*iereus, sacerdos*) was stirred into the mix, using archetypes derived from the priestly offices of the temple *cohanin* and Levites. This latter development is a liturgical "theology of orders," as distinct from their social impact, which we will look at shortly.

Presbyters appear in the New Testament literature as having many of the same functions as the Jewish council of elders: overseeing community discipline and maintaining the traditions of teaching (Acts 14:23; Jas 5:14). Yet they also emerge as having charismatic functions such as healing and blessing. These contexts surely made the common liturgy of the group a place where the presbyteral council was most visible on a regular basis. Through the table fellowship discipline was exercised (by inclusion or exclusion), and core tradition was not only maintained but created. It is in a liturgical context, to be sure, that the very archetypal texts were fashioned. The core and heart of the Markan Gospel is a passion narrative composed for recitation of the Christian Pascha, and from out of the recitation of the "saving deeds" (*haggadah*), Christian doctrine is first "put together" in the context of communal liturgy. Soon enough, therefore, presbyterate among the Christians would be more and more determined by liturgical functions. The sacred blessing of healing that is spoken of in James 5:14, as a particular function of the presbyters (a medium of charismatic holiness and grace from God), is, of course, the selfsame way that presbyters were themselves constituted after selection. The ordination ritual among the Christians has always been, more or less, a solemn ritual of collective blessing on the head of the chosen person.[35]

Some of the literature of the second century, from several places stretching from Asia Minor to Rome, reflects the situation that local churches were then governed by councils of presbyters alone.[36] Several New Testament texts show that not a great distinction was always being made in the first century between officers called *episkopoi* and those designated *presbyteroi* (Acts 20:17, 28; 1 Pet 5:1-4; Tit 1:5-7). Another important collection of letters from Antioch, those of the bishop (*episkopos*) Ignatius, show a different pattern: there the council of presbyters was gathered around a strong leadership of a single "overseer" (which is the literal meaning of *episkopos*). We can return to that notion of *episkopos* shortly, but once again we note that even when the presbyteral office is subordinated (no longer the chief

---

[35]The "laying on of hands" is synonymous with blessing (Mt 19:15) and the conveyance of divine charism (Mk 5:23; 6:5; 8:23-25). It becomes the standard form of consecration to ministry in the New Testament (Acts 8:17; 9:17; 19:6; 1 Tim 4:14; 5:22; 2 Tim 1:6; Heb 6:2).

[36]*Epistle of Polycarp* 5-6, 11; *Second Epistle of Clement* 17.3; *Ascension of Isaiah* 3.23; Sibylline Oracles 2.264-65.

leadership of a community) it serves to function "around" the bishop, surely as an advisory council.[37]

By the fourth century, bishops would start to gather around each other, and then the council of bishops definitely overshadows the presbyteral council in terms of significance and precedence. In Ignatius's letters from the second decade of the second century, however, it is clear enough that the presbyteral council represented the "college of apostles" (Ignatius argues that the bishop was the ecclesial symbol of Christ, around whom the apostles gathered).[38] They seemed to have served especially as maintainers of the church discipline. Tertullian in the second century and other writers through to the fourth, across a wide geographical range, all speak of the presbyters as having the arbitration of moral cases and the administration of penance in the churches.[39] Well into the fourth century the presbyters retain the roles of preparing catechumens (including their exorcism rites), even when the bishops begin to claim more and more the role of teaching (homiletic and doctrinal instruction as the president of the Eucharist) to themselves.

By the end of the fourth century, however, that movement to develop the episcopate, by restricting certain functions to it alone, was checked to a certain extent by the fact that the number of churches needed in a newly expanded Christian environment meant that presbyters started to leave the council of the cathedral church and go off to serve singly in outlying village churches. There, functioning effectively as the single president of the Eucharist, they reclaimed the role of doctrinal teaching and preaching. They did not reclaim any role of independent laying on of hands for ordination. This remained the prerogative of the *episkopos*, but all the other, "special" episcopal ministries were claimed back by the presbyterate: baptism, chrismation, presidency and offering of the Eucharist, reconciliation, and marriage. Even the ordination ritual of presbyters demanded the presence of the council of presbyters (or at least representative presbyters) who also laid hands on the candidate, along with the bishop, though in silence. The ordinational laying on of hands for the diaconate was restricted to the bishop, as was the consecration of a new bishop, requiring a quorum of three bishops to perform it, in the presence of the presbyters and deacons, but not using their laying on of hands.

An attempt to hinder this development of the presbyteral status was the institution of the role and function of the *chorepiskopos*: a small village bishop who basically was an archpriest in a town not large enough to merit a proper episcopal

---

[37]See B. Botte, "The Collegiate Character of the Presbyterate and Episcopate," in *The Sacrament of Holy Orders* (Collegeville, MN: Liturgical Press, 1962), 75-97.
[38]Ignatius, *Letter to Polycarp* 6; *To the Trallians* 3; *To the Smyrnaeans* 8.
[39]Tertullian, *Apology* 39; *Paenitentia* 9; Hippolytus, *Contra Noetum* 1; Epiphanius, *Haereses* 42.

presence. If the episcopate had managed to establish this system of "suffragan" bishops wholly subject to their authority (and not allowed to ordain independently of the city bishop who had authority over them), then the presbyteral order would probably have stayed in the cathedral, as an honorary council, and might never have developed in the way that it did. The system of *chorepiskopoi*, however, was already an anachronism by the early fifth century, and the presbyterate did not allow the episcopate to claim to itself alone the office and title of priesthood. By the fifth century, we see St. Augustine applying the idea of *sacerdotium* (priestliness) to all the people of God, but in the specific sense (meaning those who make the eucharistic offering in the churches) to bishops and presbyters only.[40] A tensile theology of ministerial priesthood exists in the Orthodox and Catholic churches to this day: that presbyters, as members of the council of elders, derive their representative authority from the bishop in whose diocese they serve; but they derive their priestly charism of making the offering not from people, but from God alone, and at the altar they represent not the bishop but Christ himself, the high priest of the church's eucharistic offering.

The church in Egypt had a distinctive pattern and retained many aspects of governance that were at odds with the emerging standard patterns of the churches of Asia Minor. In the fourth century Jerome looks back and recalls that the great Alexandrian church had customarily been led by a council of twelve presbyters, who elected, from out of their own midst, a single president as bishop.[41] This was so unusual by the fourth century as to draw notice. After the fourth century the episcopate wished to draw a more and more radical line of distinction between itself and the presbyterate, conceived as a lesser form of orders. Jerome used the ancient example of Alexandria apologetically, to maintain that a bishop was simply a presbyter with extra powers (chiefly rights to initiate ordinations and presidency of governance). Jerome's argument to make the bishop out to have been a presbyter writ large was part of an apologetic argument he was then having with the local bishop, John of Jerusalem, who was trying to rein in this recalcitrant theologian. But even apart from Jerome's tendentious arguments, many other writers of the fourth century remembered and noted that the New Testament evidence suggested the identity of elders and bishops before they were later distinguished more markedly.[42]

---

[40]*De Civitatis Dei* 10.20.
[41]Jerome, *Epistle* 146; also Eutychius, *Annals* (PG 111.982).
[42]Jerome, *Epistle* 146; *Ad Titum* 1.5; Ambrosiaster, *Commentary on Ephesians* 4.11; *Commentary on 1 Timothy* 3.10; Theodore of Mopsuestia, *Commentary on 1 Timothy* 3; John Chrysostom, *Homily 2 on Philippians* 1.1.

The *Didascalia Apostolorum* is an early third-century Syrian example of a set of books that began to appear at this period called "Apostolic Orders."[43] They are works that try to regularize and standardize the process of things such as liturgical practice. Their treatment of orders gives us a window into the manner in which the broader disparity of earlier practice is coming into a more common shape by the end of the second century, and being standardized across a large geographical area throughout the third. Many scholars have seen this as largely an ideological conflictual matter, citing disparities of praxis between orthodox and heterodox communities, those with demonstrable female leadership (such as the Montanists or some Gnostic groups) or those without such evidences. But I suspect this is not how the patterning of religious leadership fanned out to an ever-increasing commonality in the ancient church, but rather the means by which such systems generally spread and are adopted in a given era before there is any form of common compulsion to order them to be adopted: and that is by the principle of emulation of good working practice from a recognized center.

Local Christian communities saw what was emerging in the larger city-center churches (Rome, Antioch, and Alexandria have a dominant role to play in this making of the international order of things) by virtue of their higher visibility, and the standards adopted there increasingly came to be communal forms across a wider range of churches who "held communion" with each other, not least by recognizing one another's systems, governance plans, doctrines, and sacred books. Just as the orthodox communities of the second century more and more definitively refused to recognize the holy books of the Gnostic communities, so it probably followed that they also refused to admit their polity. So it was that female leadership among ordained offices was possibly put into the shadow because of a perceived need to "separate" from the secessionists. The function of significant writer-theologians in establishing polity is also not to be discounted. These do not so much create a pattern as articulate it from reflection on existing forms, in my opinion. Tertullian and Irenaeus are two of the most important early writers in this regard. In relation to the doctrine of episcopate, shortly, we can exegete some of Irenaeus's thinking about orders.

One deliberately retrospective book of polity, the *Didascalia Apostolorum*, is aware of and incorporates elements from important second-century literature such as the Didache, Shepherd of Hermas, and letters of Ignatius.[44] In the fourth century it was

---

[43] J. V. Bartlet, *Church Life and Church-Order During the First Four Centuries with Special Reference to the Early Eastern Church-Orders* (Oxford: Blackwell, 1943); R. H. Connolly, *Didascalia Apostolorum: The Syriac Version Translated and Accompanied by the Verona Latin Fragments* (Oxford: Clarendon, 1929).

[44] *Didascalia Apostolorum* is a third-century Syrian text (originally composed in Greek but now with only the Syriac version surviving, and some Latin parts). See Connolly, *Didascalia Apostolorum*.

itself incorporated into the first six books of the Apostolic Constitutions, and its canonical rules for church order were given a large international authority.[45] Here the presbyters have devolved into a council of advisers and associates of the bishop.[46] When they joined in the celebration of the Eucharist in a cathedral setting they were ranged in the apsidal seats, fanned out alongside the presiding bishop, a pattern that is still observed in the Catholic and Orthodox churches to this day. Fourth-century documents begin to set down a minimum rule of age before ordination: thirty years of age as a minimum for presbyters and fifty for bishops.[47] By the time the presbyters are regularly functioning on their own, not in concelebration with the bishops in the cathedral but serving as the normal minister of the village or town churches, then obviously they assumed the presidency of the Eucharist and preaching as their most notable functions, with issues of larger governance and the duty of maintaining the public doctrine of the church falling to the episcopate. There would always remain in the churches presbyters whose theological skills served to advise the bishops (Origen, a presbyter-theologian, was called in by the bishops of Palestine to serve as a *peritus* in a third-century Arabian synod dealing with the doctrinal aberrations of Bishop Heraclides), but their theological role was seen as subordinate to that of the episcopate, especially as gathered together in synodical assembly.

The increasing number of episcopal synods witnessed after the fourth century produced a large body of canons, or regulations concerning the clergy. In the main they were all directed at keeping the standards for clergy (both moral and intellectual) higher than the norms expected of the rest of the people of God. This increasing aspect of separateness (cultic purity) as well as the fact that ordination was increasingly regularized by being noted in the church archives was responsible for a growing distinction between *laos* (the people of God) and the ordained priesthood (of bishops, presbyters, and deacons).[48] This division of clergy and laity grew after the fourth century, along

---

[45]See: J. Donaldson, trans., *The Apostolic Constitutions*, Ante-Nicene Christian Library 17, part 2 (1870); also in *ANF* 7 (1886), 385-505; D. A. Fiensy, *Prayers Alleged to be Jewish: An Examination of the Constitutiones Apostolicae* (Chico, CA: Scholars Press, 1985); C. H. Turner, "Notes on the Apostolic Constitutions," *JTS* 16 (1915): 54-61, 523-38.
[46]*Didascalia* 26.
[47]Council of Neo-Caesarea (AD 315), canon 11; Apostolic Constitutions 2.1.
[48]The Latin word *ordinatio* means ranked and "entered in lists" for public office. It had the benefit, as far as Christians were concerned, of being a word wholly divorced from any of the connotations associated with pagan priesthood. The Greek equivalent would be *kathistatai*, but the more commonly used term *cheirotonia* carries the same sense as well, along with the concept of "laying on hands." For more on the origins of the technical term *ordinatio* see G. Dix, "Ministry in the Early Church," in *The Apostolic Ministry: Essays on the History and Doctrine of the Episcopate*, ed. K. E. Kirk (London: Hodder and Stoughton, 1946), 193-96; and P. van Beneden, *Aux origins d'une terminologie sacramentelle: Ordo, ordinare, ordinatio, dans la literature chrétienne avant 313*, Spicilegium Sacrum Lovaniense 38 (Louvain: Université catholique de Louvain, 1974).

with the extension of the theology of ordained priesthood.[49] Even so, all the ancient theologians accepted that the root of all priesthood in the Christian community was the single high priesthood of Christ, given as a charism to all at baptism.

Writers of the patristic period, however (unlike theologians of the age of the Reformation), also argued that this did not preclude a specific and unique form of priesthood allotted to those who were formally ordained. Patristic treatises on the priesthood, especially those of Gregory the Theologian, John Chrysostom, and Gregory the Great, were much valued in Christian antiquity and had a wide circulation, establishing norms of preparation for priestly (episcopal and presbyteral) ordination for centuries to come.[50] Chief commonalities of these treatises are approaches to the concept of Christian priesthood that redefine it away from the sacrificial cults of the pagan religions and ground it now in terms of governance of souls, exegesis of the Scriptures, and the offering (anaphora) of the eucharistic prayer.

**Bishops.** The word *bishop* is the old English variant of the New Testament Greek term *episkopos*, which originally meant "overseer" or "superintendent." Episcopacy is an office first mentioned in the Pastoral Epistles, in reference to one who has oversight of the Christian community (Phil 1:1; 1 Tim 3:1-7; Tit 1:7; 1 Pet 2:25). In Paul's letter to the Philippians the office is closely connected with that of the deacons of the church. In other texts it is closely associated with the presbyteral council. The association of episcopate and diaconate was strengthened after the third century, when the members of the presbyteral (concelebrating) council tended to leave the cathedral churches in order to staff an increasing amount of village churches, and the deacons then remained to become special episcopal attendants, serving liturgical functions and putting into effect the bishop's administration of church goods. At the end of the first century, 1 Timothy 3:1-7 established the basic qualifications of an *episkopos*:

> This dictum is true: If any one aspires to the office of bishop, he desires a noble task. But a bishop must be beyond reproach, married only once, temperate, sensible, dignified, hospitable, an able teacher, not a drunkard or violent, but gentle; not quarrelsome, or money-grabbing. It is imperative he has managed his own household well, securing the obedience and respectability of his children in all things, for if someone does not know how to manage his own household, how can he care for God's church? He must not be a recent convert, or he may be puffed up with pride and fall into the condemnation of the devil. He should be well regarded by outsiders, or he may fall into reproach and the snare of the devil.

---

[49]The fourth-century imperial law first recognizes the existence of the *ordo ecclesiasticus* as a separate social status in *Codex Theodosianus* 16.26.
[50]See St. Gregory the Theologian, *Oration 2, On the Priesthood*, trans. C. G. Browne, *NPNF* second series, vol. 7 (1894); John Chrysostom, *On the Priesthood*, trans. G. Neville, Popular Patristics (Crestwood, NY: St. Vladimir's Seminary Press, 1996); St. Gregory the Great, *Pastoral Rule*, trans. H Davis, Ancient Christian Writers 11 (New York: Paulist, 1950).

Management of the *oikos* is at the center of this vision of early ministry. This pattern is demonstrable throughout the Pastoral Letters of the New Testament and it is also seen emerging in the writings of Ignatius of Antioch and the Clementine literature, both of which come from the hand of early *episkopoi* who are conscious of a high degree of spiritual authority, but whose zealous arguments to project and sustain this, rhetorically, also suggest that this was not universally accepted by all the communities. The writer of 1 Clement actually put pen to paper to berate a community in Corinth who had forcibly retired their *episkopos* (apparently) for incompetency.

Third-century Latin bishop Cyprian of Carthage affected the theory of episcopate considerably by associating the office with the symbolism of the Old Testament high priesthood.[51] For Cyprian, the bishop is the *sacerdos*: the high priest of the Christian community (but the word had until then been used in non-Christian contexts to indicate the sacrificial priesthoods of the cults). So he is fashioning a new set of resonances but using symbolic associations primarily drawn from his new reading of the Bible.[52] One key thing he wishes to stress is the superiority of the episcopal range of authority compared to that of the presbyters.

In the third-century East, particularly the large cities such as Alexandria, other changes were also in progress, tending to make the bishop stand out more and more clearly from the larger ranks of the presbyters. Although Jerome still protested in the fourth century that bishop and presbyter are really the same thing, his argument was already falling on deaf ears by this period.[53] The bishops of great cities, and Rome is a prime example, were able to develop the role and function of their office considerably because of the prestige of their respective sees. Such large cities attracted all manner of traffic; not least among that was Christians making

---

[51] *Epistle* 63.14; *Epistle* 3; *On the Unity of the Church* 17. The connection of Christian ministers with the typology of the priests of the Old Testament was first made by Clement of Rome (1 Clement 43-44), but Cyprian developed it apace. Cyprian also underlined the notion of the priest as the "other Christ" (*alter Christus*), which became important for the West and also contributed to the growing sense of priesthood as something that was primarily claimed by ordained ministers, who sacramentally iconized Christ in the liturgical ritual of the churches. In the Greek Christian world the word corresponding to the Latin *sacerdos*, that is, *hiereus* (sacrificing priest), never became quite so favored, although in both churches the developing theory of the Eucharist as sacrifice contributed greatly to the evolution of priesthood (both that of the presbyter and that of the *episkopos*) as a matter fundamentally different from the "priesthood of believers" spoken of in 1 Pet 2:5.

[52] He was himself a recent convert elevated directly to episcopal rank in time of persecution. His knowledge of Scripture is that of a rapidly self-taught thinker. Cyprian had a lifelong difficulty with his council of presbyters, who did not trust his decisions or his judgment on many points. His underlining of the episcopal authority, over against them, is understandable in the light of his situation.

[53] As we have noticed, *presbyteros* and *episkopos* are terms that are interchangeable in the New Testament (Acts 20:17, 28; 1 Pet 5:1-4; Tit 1:5-7), and Clement of Rome uses the term *bishops* in the 90s to refer to all the clergy of Rome: 1 Clement 42, 44.

an appeal for adjudication (redress, vindication, support) to an influential bishop who might help them on many levels.

In the East, Demetrius of Alexandria, in the first quarter of the third century, was one of the first of this new breed of monarchical leaders to insist on the clear demarcation of the bishop from the presbyters. A rhetorical appeal to the concept of monarchical authority (the bishop as the icon of Christ in the church and subject to no other authority) had been witnessed as early as Ignatius of Antioch, but the actualities of the latter's governance of the Antiochenes undoubtedly needs to be more richly contextualized in a nexus of other church "authorities" that included teachers and confessors.[54] Ignatius shows signs in his letters to other *episkopoi* he talks to that the order of virgins at Antioch gave him trouble. His authority might not have been all that ideally unchallenged as he describes in his letters.

Clement of Rome's first letter to the Corinthians present us with a picture of a late first-century Roman bishop who was well conscious of his position as the most important spokesman and president of the council of presbyters. He presents the case to the Corinthians (he has surely received a prior appeal from the deposed bishop of Corinth) that even though the community elects its bishop, that does not give it the right to overthrow him subsequently. From the second century onward, election seems to have been an important element in the choice of all new bishops. The right of election features in the Didache 15. Such communal power had dwindled in later Byzantine times to a mere consultation of the people (often they were expected simply to "acclaim" the new leader sent to them by the emperor or the local synod of bishops), but even so there were many instances of a bishop being unable to assume duties because of the implacable hostility of a local church who felt their wishes had been overlooked (such as the case of Proclus of Constantinople in the fifth century).

By the end of the second century one finds lists of bishops being drawn up (one of the first known is that of the Palestinian writer Hegesippus [110–180]).[55] He traveled over a range of different churches and, seeing the extent to which various Gnostic movements had divided the second-century Jerusalem church, came to the conclusion that an internationally agreed-on doctrine for basic Christianity would only be assured by the collaboration of the most gifted bishops of the world acting in concert. His travels from Jerusalem through Rome to Corinth had impressed him with many examples of excellent organization of the church life in those places that had strong episcopal guidance. His list of the bishops of the various churches was offered as a way to ensure a form of "pedigree" for a church's purity of faith.

---

[54]*Epistle to the Magnesians* 6.1. Dated to the end of the first century.
[55]See N. Hyldahl, "Hegesippus Hypomnemata," *Studia Theologica* 14 (1960): 70-113; M. J. Routh, *Reliquiae Sacrae* (Oxford, 1846), 1:207-84.

The Exercise of Authority in the Church | 985

The list of the earliest bishops of Rome preserved in Epiphanius is thought to have derived from Hegesippus's *Memoirs Written Against the Gnostics*, which Eusebius also used as a source for his later *Ecclesiastical History*.[56] The idea of composing (and then archiving) such episcopal lists devolved from Irenaeus's argument that the way the bishop succeeded the apostles (his doctrine of the "apostolic succession" of bishops) was a guarantor of authenticity of teaching.[57] Irenaeus and other *episkopoi* of the second century seemed to have been alarmed by the way Gnostic Christian community leaders identified them, and their flocks, as "low-level" believers, the common mass of more crass fideists who had not seen the light, been enlightened in the particular *gnosis* on offer. As a reaction to this form of constructing Christianity as wisdom initiations, Irenaeus constructs a system of how to recognize "authentic" Christian tradition. This is the birth of the concept of orthodoxy in Christian transmission and, of course, it depends on the opposite term to make sense of it: namely, heterodoxy. From the second century onward (though the idea has made a sharp early appearance in the Johannine and Catholic Epistles of the late New Testament literature) there is a definite movement taking place in many churches to try to draw up a schema of recognizing the commonality of Christianity.

It seems to me, though the point has been hotly disputed in the last thirty years as the Gnostic movement has been heavily made over as a viable form of identifying legitimate Christianity rather than secessionist movements within Christianity, that a bishop such as Irenaeus, for all he poses as an intellectual setting out a new book of systematic advice (the *Adversus Haereses*), is actually just putting together the customary and basic elements of Christian community lifestyle. He makes a "systematic" out of what is already happening in the wider horizon of churches that he knows in different parts of the world, keeping an eye out especially for what the larger and older churches are doing. So, for example, as there is a tendency to publish new Gospels and apocrypha to broadcast a new Gnosticizing doctrine, Irenaeus calls for a policy to admit none others than the traditional four Gospels that have already been established in church, as matter for reading in the liturgical assembly, and leans toward the closing of the canon.

Moreover, when new creeds are set forth, he calls for an acknowledgment only of that creed in which the community majority were baptized: the simple, straightforward narrative of salvation effected in the descent, life, death, and resurrection of Jesus, born of a virgin. He designated this the "rule of faith" (*regula fidei*). Against wide-ranging and much varied speculative metaphysical theories of redemptive regeneration being offered to the communities, he posits the figure and the teachings

---

[56]Epiphanius, *Refutation of Heresies* 27.6.
[57]Irenaeus, *Adversus Haereses* 3.3.1-3.

of the "real Jesus" as a constant point of departure and return for all Christians. These things make up three corners of a fourfold systematic of "orthodox tradition" for Irenaeus. They are highly practical, already in existence (rather than needing to be invented). What he does is bring them forward from the core of liturgy to be a canonical rule against which he can measure alternative approaches to Christian faith. These first three of his corners of his structure can be rephrased as a fixed canon of Scripture, maintaining the simple rule of faith as expressed in traditional prayer and liturgy, and a christocentric focus tied into the historical narratives of the Gospels.

His last element in this four-footed approach was the development of the episcopal role, as guardian of the faith. This too had already been established in the churches before his day. He is not inventing it, but as an *episkopos* himself he saw that the leadership of the local president of the Eucharist had to be clear and decisive: should new books be admitted as authorities in his communities of worship, if their provenance raised doubts? Should new creeds be constructed to reflect the concerns of the latest school of theologians? Irenaeus, as eucharistic president, falls back on conservative tradition as being extremely important in one aspect (maintaining a historical core of what constitutes the Jesus tradition as handed down from the Christian witnesses), but in another aspect he elevates the judgment, or spiritual discernment, of the *episkopos* as being of critical importance in being flexible and adaptable enough to make decisions in the immediate context of a controversially divided church. This is where the development of the concept of the office of *episkopos* became significant.

Irenaeus defined the bishop as quintessentially the inheritor of the now-defunct office of apostle. The ministry was not the same as that of an apostle, but it was the heir of the apostolic charism. His notion for this was that the bishop stands in the line of "apostolic succession." This became the fourth corner of the quadrant of ideas he elevated against the Gnostics and the one that organized the others, just as the *episkopos* in daily praxis organized the ritual life of the communities (supervising what sacraments they celebrated, what creeds they recited, and what scriptural texts they read). By apostolic succession, what Irenaeus especially has in mind is the way the bishop makes sure that the apostolic teachings are preserved in the daily life of the communities. This means, quite precisely, evangelical teaching. The concept of apostle is thus redefined, just as is that of the bishop.

Christian doctrine, to be authentic (or orthodox), Irenaeus is arguing, has to be traditionally canonical (ruling out the apocrypha) and has to be liturgical (rooted in the traditional acts of prayer and worship that have been familiar for past generations) and has to be validated by a leadership of the communities that can show its "lineage" in terms of its relation, if not to the apostles themselves, then to their deposit of doctrine as represented in the canon. That is, the church has to be governed and led forward by conservative-leaning *episkopoi*, not the speculative, intellectualist *didaskaloi*-theologians who tended to front the Gnostic communities.[58] This set up a tension between episcopal congregation leaders and theologian intelligentsia in the Christian movement that, perhaps, has not disappeared to this day.

Two things, then, stand out in this last aspect of Irenaeus's argument for apostolic succession: the authority of the single leader of the liturgical community is underlined (he carries the weight of an apostle and can expect obedience, as Paul once did); and he justifies his authority by preserving the evangelical tradition in the churches under his remit. The large number of "issues" raised about the nature of Christian tradition by the Gnostic movements brought about this increased focus on the principle of episcopal governance. Despite Irenaeus's primary focus on the single, local *episkopos* in his *Adversus Haereses*, what emerges at this same time in the mid-second century is the very practical effect of checks and balances that is usually seen in Christian churches when it comes to the exercise of power—for the scope of the individual bishop was hemmed in by demanding that they coordinate their opinions, customs, and approaches with common practice and common mindset among the other bishops of a province's community.

So it is, for example, that in Irenaeus's own lifetime we see him commuting to Rome to consult with Bishop (Pope) Victor over attitudes how to relate to the Quartodecimans movement in Asia Minor. Tertullian, writing from Carthage at the same time, also speaks of how such meetings of many of the bishops of a single place (it was also apparent in the reaction to the Montanists) regularly gathered to resolve matters of dispute among themselves. Such meetings came to be known in the churches as synods. By the early fourth century this system of episcopal monarchy, subject to the guidance of a council of presbyters on the local scene, and subject to a council, or synod, of fellow bishops on the provincial scene, was common practice, soon to become mandated, for all the churches in the Constantinian empire.[59] A final level of

---

[58]Such as Valentinus (or his disciple, the exegete Heracleon), who was prominent as an intellectualist Gnostic leader at Rome. Several Gnostic teachers claimed that their doctrines were only apparently innovative, since they had actually been committed in secret by Jesus to his apostles and were now being revealed by the *didaskaloi* who had inherited them (Irenaeus, *Adversus Haereses* 3.2.1; Epiphanius, *Against All Heresies* 33.7.9).

[59]Canon 4 of the Council of Nicaea (325) mandates the principle that bishops' ordinations need to be done on a province-wide basis and shows how the earlier system of maintaining this idea of provincial correlation was most likely done by letter. Canon 38 of the mid-fourth-century *Apostolical Canons* (book 8 of Apostolic Constitutions) reflects the pattern then probably common: "Let a synod of bishops be held twice in the year, and let them ask one another the doctrines of piety; and let them determine the ecclesiastical disputes that happen—once in the fourth week of Pentecost, and again on the twelfth of the month Hyperberetaeus."

sophistication was to be added to this in the aftermath of the Christianizing of the empire in the mid-fourth century: namely, the elevation of the province-wide synod of bishops, in cases of large-scale controversy among the churches, to the concept of an ecumenical synod.

The word derives from the Greek *oikoumenikos*, pertaining to the whole world. The synods were presumed, as a gathering of the higher priesthood of the church, to be specially directed by the inspirations of the Holy Spirit. This was argued as even more applicably the case in a worldwide council of international bishops gathered for the most serious reasons. Such meetings, therefore, did not proceed by basis of common debate and searching for a consensus, but rather by demanding a unanimity of vote, as fitting for a prophetic and hierarchical assembly declaring (not searching for) the ancient faith of the church in times of confusion and uncertainty.[60] Those who refused to go along with the consensus at such meetings, therefore, were soon afterward deposed from their office and order. The so-called ecumenical council remains, to this day, the highest of all Christian authorities in the polity structure of the Eastern churches. In Roman Catholicism of the second millennium the developing office of the monarchical papacy outstripped it.

In combating what he saw as the excessively innovationist speculations of Gnostic *didaskaloi*, Irenaeus had laid great stress on the "common-sense" principle that Christ had demonstrably taught a single, coherent, and simple truth, to simple fishermen. The Gnostics had complicated and corrupted this doctrine, he argued, and had made it fantastically, and mythically, elaborated. Nevertheless, the truth Christ had taught was passed on as a heritage to the fishermen-apostles, who in their own turn taught it to their disciples. This simple and open "apostolic heritage" was to the present day represented by the bishops within the public communities of worship, for their own doctrine was simple and apostolic in contrast to the clever complexity of the intellectualist *didaskaloi*. The idea that this (the core of Christian doctrine) was a set of teachings that were coherent, uniformly witnessed in the major communities of the Christian world, and demonstrable in the bond of intercommunion that existed in the relations of bishops of various cities seems to have grown apace between the first and end of the second century.

Since, as Irenaeus and others had argued, the apostolic doctrine was quintessentially that represented in the New Testament writings, just so all the faithful of every generation could hear the authentic teaching of Christ as preserved by the apostolic tradition, because of the bishop's fidelity to the Scriptures. The true bishop

---

[60]Though this is not to say that common debate was absent from the structures of such meetings. Nicaea in 325 began with several days of public debate, with rhetoricians and philosophers presenting cases, before the bishops convened their episcopal synod.

would thus be recognized by his simple, open, and accurate biblical teaching: and would accordingly be recognized as the legitimate church leader, not only by the local community, but by the larger *concilium* of churches in the area, led by their own, equally legitimate bishops. Against the Gnostic vagaries, then, the episcopal ranks had clearly and conservatively closed: and in this process was established the lineaments of a theology of orthodox doctrine that defined apostolic succession as historically rooted, commonly comprehensible, and unanimously adopted.

The latter aspect (that the authentic Christian doctrine would be widely recognized by some form of broad consensus) came to be known as the principle of catholicism (from the Greek word *katholikos*, meaning "large-scale commonality"). From this time onward the ideas of catholicity and orthodoxy became very closely connected. Along these same lines, *didaskalos*-philosopher Justin Martyr (d. 165) argued that the chief characteristic of apostolic doctrine was its international uniformity.[61] The same idea was advanced by Tertullian (160–225) in his treatise *On the Prescription of Heretics*, which followed the line established by Irenaeus.[62] The argument eventually matured into the necessary inclusion of apostolicity as one of the four cardinal identifiers of the Christian church as set out in the confession of the creed: "one, holy, catholic, and apostolic."[63]

If the doctrinal friction with the Gnostics had accelerated the episcopacy toward an increased qualified-monarchical status in the course of the second to third centuries, the equally fraught doctrinal controversies of the fourth century served to elevate it even more. At that period, the relative failure of the synodical process in establishing a common consensus of agreed doctrine (manifested in the number of contradictory synods held in the fourth century meant to resolve the Arian crisis) threw emphasis back yet again on the notion of the single theologian-bishop who could stand for the truth even against a majority of teachers who were advocating a different compromise. This idea of the "father of the church," or patristic theologian, took hold in the early fourth century as great rhetor-bishops such as Athanasius of Alexandria, Paul of Samosata, Eustathius of Antioch, Basil of Caesarea, and Gregory of Nazianzus emerged as figures who were increasingly looked to (especially by the fifth century, when the dust of the Arian crisis had begun to settle) as bishops who had personally incarnated the gospel values and teachings in their own lives and doctrines.

In the second and third centuries, however, this concept of the outstanding philosopher-bishop was not a common reality. Many, if not the majority, of pre-fourth-century

---

[61] *First Apology* 42.
[62] *De Praescriptione Haereticorum* 20-21, 32.
[63] Later to be known as the four defining marks of the church: *notae ecclesiae*, the essence of what constitutes apostolic catholicity.

bishops were rural and not well educated men. After Constantine's fourth-century legislation elevated bishops to local magistrate status, the quality of episcopal education began to improve, and by the later fourth century many bishops of the larger cities were indeed figures to be reckoned with on both the academic and political scenes. All of this made for the ever-increasing status of the episcopal office. Presbyters and bishops after that point became like magnets, attracting in to themselves a whole range of other offices and functions that had, in more ancient times, perhaps been more diffuse in the worship communities. One of the areas to suffer from this expansion was the range of offices Christian women had once occupied.

By the fourth century onward we find Christian bishops advising emperors, even belonging to the imperial family or to immensely wealthy and aristocratic families. Bishops such as Athanasius or Ambrose of Milan, who headed large churches as skilled rhetoricians, showed how they could influence imperial policy by applying political pressure in the manner redolent of the governors of imperial provinces. Ambrose even made Emperor Theodosius publicly repent for executing dissident citizens: a thing that would have seemed unthinkable to the emperors of a previous generation.

After the fourth century the Christian emperors increasingly honored the episcopate and gave it legal status and rank as a high office of state. A tension can, of course, be noticed now between episcopacy's original conception as an office of liturgical president and teacher and its new functions as magistrate and administrator for a (very) large diocesan area. The bishops of powerful cities in the empire inevitably came to have a greater influence than their colleagues from small towns, although the primitive principle of the equality of all bishops as icons of Christ was maintained. Even so, the bishops of the large cities came to rank as "metropolitans" and commanded the governance of larger matters such as episcopal ordinations and the care of synods. The older idea of unanimity among the high priests of the Lord inspired by the selfsame Spirit was balanced out judicially by the quaintly vague idea of the metropolitan archbishop as being the "first among equals." The four really great cities of the empire, after the time of Justinian, in the sixth century, claimed the title patriarch.[64] Jerusalem was added to the main four, merely for honor's sake, and a pentarchy of patriarchates was thus evolved, whose bishops enjoyed particular prestige and legal precedence in international affairs.[65] That Rome was the only patriarchate in the West contributed significantly to the evolution of the

---

[64]Rome, Alexandria, Antioch, and Constantinople. The jockeying of these four for relative status and position in the ranks of the "first among equals" was a factor that determined a great deal of the formation of international Christian establishment from the fourth century through to the end of the first millennium.

[65]See further chapter eight, "The Rise of the Ecumenical Conciliar System in the Fifth to Sixth Centuries."

monarchical papacy after the fifth century. Augustine's definition of the bishop as "the servant of the servants of God" (*servus servorum dei*) remained a constant reminder of the pastoral nature of the office, even after the phrase was taken up in the seventh century by Gregory the Great to become a particular designation of the Roman popes, who have kept it as a specific title to this day.[66]

**Deacons.** The title originally signified "servants" or "ministers" and, as such, could stand for almost any Christian ministry, though by the dawn of the second century it would emerge as a precise title for the third order of ministerial office alongside bishops and presbyters. As we noted earlier, the word first appears as a first-generational title of officeholder among the Hellenist communities in Palestine. The seven deacons of Acts 6:6 was a symbolic number and order of highly important theologian-leaders, many of whom seem to have been charismatic prophet-theologians. But already (as can be seen in the the book of Acts's narrative about the Hellenists) it is being subjugated to the concept of the more important primacy of apostles (missionary preachers). After the third century the term is more or less wholly subsumed in the way it has evolved as part of the threefold office structure of bishops, presbyters, and deacons. Luke's rationalizing account in Acts 6, of the way the deacons were really more "practical" and sedentary agents in the Christian assembly, led to the developing office being chiefly focused, ever afterward, on the administration of practical affairs and philanthropic works in the communities.

With the inclusion of female candidates in the ordained office of diaconate, women clearly exercised priesthood in the Eastern church, in the diaconal degree, at least until the high medieval period (when political insecurity and antagonistic monastic pressures led to the disappearance of the order as an active cathedral ministry). Unlike Greek theological thought, the Latin theology of priesthood tended to exclude diaconate from its purview of the "three degrees" of *sacerdotium*, and the female diaconate was also more quickly suppressed in the West than it was in the East.

Paul mentions that there were women deacons in the very earliest communities (Rom 16:1), and Pliny the Younger in the early second century tells us that in the course of investigating the Christian communities in Bithynia, in the time of the emperor Trajan (98–117), he put to torture two female deacons, who gave him information about the early eucharistic rite.[67] The origins of a specific order of female deacons in the main church communities (though they were already prominent in the more fluid clerical structures of Montanist and Gnostic communities) only separates clearly from the female orders of widows and virgins later in the fourth century,

---

[66] *Epistle* 217; *Epistle* 1.1, 36; 6.51; 13.1.
[67] Pliny, *Letter* 10.96.8.

mainly by the ever-increasing conflation of all three orders into the diaconate as time goes on.[68] Female deacons were especially prominent in Constantinople, serving at the Great Cathedral, and were clearly an ordained order, who ministered at the altar not merely an ancillary role simply honorifically called deacons (as some later writers have argued). The ordination rite for them, surviving from Byzantine times, places the character of their office in the category of the three major orders of the priesthood.

From earliest times the office of deacon was attached to the episcopate as an administrative helper (Phil 1:1; 1 Tim 3:8). In the letters of Ignatius of Antioch the deacons appear for the first time, at the end of the first century, as the third-ranked office in the triad of Christian ministries. At Rome the deacons were powerful clergy who often rose to become the popes. So close was the association of bishop and deacon (the same administration) that deacons often moved from the third order to the first, sidestepping the presbyterate. Of the thirty-seven men elected pope at Rome between 432 and 684, only three had been presbyters before their election. This prominence of the deacons of large cities can be seen not only at Rome but also at Alexandria and Constantinople. The early medieval Western church developed such a dominant order of archdeacons that, at times, especially between the eighth and thirteenth centuries, they rivaled their own bishops in power and prestige and were (paradoxically) often ordained presbyters.

At the Council of Nicaea (325), the liturgical powers of the deacons were defined and limited. They were then explicitly forbidden to "offer" the gifts.[69] The same concern to separate diaconate from the priestly task (proper to bishops and presbyters) of "offering the gifts" is noticeable in the fourth-century *Apostolic Tradition*. Here, a careful distinction is made concerning how the diaconal order was excluded from the priestly office and thus set apart from episcopate and presbyterate.[70] In later Greek theology, however, the deacon is more closely bound in with the "threefold order" of the priesthood in various degrees than he was in the West, where this stronger sense of exclusion from "priestly" charism per se was sustained. In the seventh century at the Council of Toledo in Spain (633) and the Synod in Troullo (692) at Constantinople, the bishops made other synodical legislation to restrict their (still) growing influence. Deacons were again prohibited from celebrating the Eucharist except as assistants to bishops and presbyters.

---

[68]Canon 15 of the Council of Chalcedon 451; Apostolic Constitutions 8.20.

[69]Council of Nicaea, canon 18: "It has come to the attention of this holy and great synod that in some places and cities, deacons give communion to presbyters, even though neither canon nor custom allows this to be done: that those who do not have the power to make the offering should give the body of Christ to those who actually do make the offering."

[70]*Apostolic Tradition* 9.2: "[The deacon] is not ordained to the priesthood but to serve the bishop and to carry out the bishop's commands. He does not take part in the council of the clergy."

After the seventh century, the order of deacons faded back somewhat. In the Eastern churches the office of a lifelong deacon remained common enough: they served in the church as the representative of the people at prayer, leading litanies and petitions and generally dealing with the people of God assembled, while the presbyters took more and more of a role at the altar. In the Western churches, the office increasingly became more of a temporary one, a transitional step on the way to priesthood. The (male) diaconate continued with much vitality in the Eastern churches, where it still often remains a lifelong ministry.

The deacons accumulated specific liturgical functions, such as the singing of the Gospel, the proclamation of the prayers of the people (the litanies), the reading of the diptychs (the lists of names to be prayed for publicly), the care of the eucharistic vessels, the administration of the Eucharist (with the other officiants), and the general regulation of conduct in the church buildings. Male deacons oversaw the conduct of the men, and female deacons that of the women, in church. Their stole of office was worn long and diagonally over one shoulder and distinguished them from bishops and presbyters, who wore the stole of office around the neck hanging straight down. At times the male deacons wrapped the stole tightly around them in a cross-shaped band. It came to represent the manner in which they liturgically symbolized the angels (who in icons are shown dressed in this manner), and the custom is still followed in Eastern Christian liturgies. It probably grew originally from the practical need to tie up loose clothing before distributing the gifts in the churches.

Female deacons developed strongly as an ordained order in the third and fourth centuries. It is difficult to make more precise determinations about matters between the first and fourth centuries, partly because (one suspects) the female deacons thrived more in the greater town churches than the smaller village communities (certainly this was the case at Constantinople, where aristocratic women occupied the office), and partly because the word for *deacon* in the male semantic form (*diakonos*) is used in the pre-sixth-century literature indiscriminately to cover both males and females.[71] So one is never quite sure whether a female is being referred to in the sources.[72] The functions of the female deacons are outlined in the Apostolic Constitutions and the Didascalia. The latter demands that they be at least fifty, a requirement reduced to forty at the Council of Chalcedon. The motive was to put them past

---

[71] See Rom 16:1, where Phoebe is called a *diakonos*.
[72] The short text from St. John Chrysostom in the reader at the end of this chapter shows that he found it necessary in the fifth century to insist on the existence of female deacons in the church. He was a strong advocate of the order of female deacons and worked closely with the wealthy aristocrat Olympias, who was a leader among the order there, which engaged in many charitable and liturgical works, not least organizing special vesperal services for women in the cathedral.

childbearing age, and generally after the third century they were ordained out of the celibate ranks of the ascetics, the widows, and virgins, though several married female deacons were known, including possibly the wife of St. Gregory of Nyssa.

Female deacons did much the same as their male counterparts, especially taking charge of dole to the poor women, baptismal anointing and catechesis of women, and the supervision of the women's galleries in the great churches. Many female deacons, including aristocrats, were on the staff of Hagia Sophia at Constantinople in the sixth century. John Chrysostom had made it a concern to bring their ministry more to the fore in his time in the cathedral there a century earlier, possibly reflecting a more public appearance of female deacons in the Syrian church at Antioch. They also attended the local bishop, as chaperones, whenever he had to have personal dealings with women of the diocese. The male and female deacons were ordained within the course of the liturgy, invested with the stole, and celebrated at the altar.

In later times many abbesses and heads of convents were given this title, and it signified in many cases a lesser range of official duties than the earlier female deacons: probably hearing the nuns' confessions, presiding over the service of the offices, and distributing Communion to the community in the absence of a chaplain priest. There is little clear evidence about it. One of the first of these so mentioned, in the fourth century *Life of Macrina*, is Lampadion, the female deacon who served in the convent of Gregory's sister, the abbess Macrina. The office of female deacons went into decline first in the West in the sixth century. Here, the councils of Epaon (517) and Orléans (533) ruled to abolish the female diaconate, though it survived elsewhere in the West until the eleventh century, and later than that in the Eastern churches (to the late nineteenth century among the Armenians). In both cases pressure from an increasingly monasticized male clergy was probably the root cause of hostility to the female order. The ordination rite for female deacons, however, still survives in the service books of the East.

**Widows.** It is notable that almost all the women mentioned in Luke–Acts as being significant leaders in the affairs of earliest Christianity were either single or widows. The freedom from spousal (legal) control and expectation must have been a very determinative issue for any ancient woman who wished to exercise a vocational ministry in the church. Moreover, the significant extent of what appears to be a ministerial office of widows in the Christian communities of late antiquity was a natural result of the custom of Roman marriage, in which older men often espoused very young girls. On the death of the husband, the legal wealth-holder, the familial property (when it existed in the first place) sidestepped the widow and was recirculated along the line of the nearest male inheritors. The widows, then, had no patrimony, and even those who had formerly been wealthy were often rendered destitute by the deaths of their husbands. With little prospect of earning anything themselves, they were a particularly vulnerable class.[73]

Some of the earliest reference to widows in the New Testament refer to them as a class of recipients of Christian communal dole.[74] But clearly by the early second century, as evidenced in the earliest form of instructions we possess for recognition as a "Christian widow," namely 1 Timothy 5:9-10, the social plight of being a widow had transmuted into something else within the communities: the concept of the widow as the elder woman who had special time and availability for prayer and charitable action on behalf of the local church. It was a development that is first witnessed in the Pseudo-Clementine *Recognitions*, where the idea of instituting such a ministerial office is attributed to the apostle Peter.[75] This might be an indication that the initiative originated in the church of Antioch. The writings of Ignatius, bishop there at the end of the first century, show several references to the widows as an order. He identified widows with virgins in his text.[76]

Later Syriac ascetical writing through to the third century gives several references to the widows as having specially powerful prayer. Their hearts are compared to an altar of coals, from which the incense of prayer arises before God's sight.[77] This perhaps indicates that they were assembling in church for what was the kernel of offices of prayer and later grew into the monastic offices of the hours. Other writings of the late third century, from Egypt and Syria, suggest that the offices of nursing the sick, evangelizing and catechizing pagan women who were interested in joining the church, and the task of administering public alms among the women of the town, on behalf of the church, were frequently exercised by the widows.[78] By the later third century we see them clearly acknowledged as an order of Christian minister by

---

[73]They had been regarded as such from Old Testament times, as can be seen in Ex 22:22; Deut 10:18.
[74]Jas 1:27; Shepherd of Hermas, Mandate 8.10; Similitudes 1.8; 5.3; Ignatius of Antioch, *Letter to Polycarp* 4; *First Letter of Clement* 8; Apostolic Constitutions 4.2.
[75]Ps.-Clement, *Recognitions* 6.15.
[76]"I salute the families of my brethren, along with their wives and children, and also the virgins who are called widows. I pray in the power of the Holy Spirit that you will all be strong. Philo, who is with me, also greets you." Ignatius of Antioch, *To the Smyrnaeans* 12. In his letter to the Philippians, however, he distinguishes them: *To the Philippians* 15: "Philo and Agathopus the deacons salute you. I myself salute the company of virgins and the order of widows. May I have joy of them. I salute all the people of the Lord, from the least to the greatest."
[77]See C. Osiek, "The Widow as Altar: The Rise and Fall of a Symbol," *The Second Century* (1983): 159-69. The *Epistle of Polycarp* 4 says this: "The widows ought to be discreet, pledged to the Lord in their faith, praying unceasingly for all, refraining from gossip, slander, and false testimony, and love of money. In fact, they should abstain from all evil in the knowledge that they are the altar of God, where everything is examined for blemishes, and nothing escapes him, either in terms of thoughts or feelings, or the secrets of the heart." The image is repeated also in *Didascalia Apostolorum* 14.
[78]Clement of Alexandria, *Stromateis* 3; Apostolic Constitutions 3.5.

Origen, then a presbyter at the church of Caesarea in Palestine.[79] By this stage, then, it was something more than the list of widows registered for official church support.

In the fourth century John Chrysostom wrote a special encomium entitled *The Widow Is Chosen* (*Vidua eligatur*), in which he notes how the status of a once-despised and impoverished social class of persons had been reversed and elevated by the high honor the Christian church had given to it. But even as he wrote, the office itself seemed to have been fading away: taken over by the (perhaps) more energetic order of virgins that had been developing alongside it, and that, of course, could admit younger, unmarried women into its ranks, unlike that of the widows. The office of widow, and that of virgin, were basically subsumed into the larger wave of interest in the burgeoning ascetical movement of the fourth century. Soon the remains of both early offices of widows and virgins would disappear, subsumed into the female diaconate. It is not stated anywhere in the sources that the widow was appointed by any laying on of hands. It was not, therefore, an "ordained" office of the church, more a charismatic ministry. This is a point that the Apostolic Constitutions insists on in a marked way: they are not ordained but appointed to serve in the exercise of prayer.[80]

**Virgins.** Virgins too, were not ordained but dedicated for a special way of life. While they did not have any office at the altar of the church, they seem to have exercised presiding functions in communities of religious women: something that grew eventually into the ritual of the monastic offices. Virgins are not mentioned as a specific "order" in the *Didascalia Apostolorum* of the third century. But by the following century they do appear as such in the Apostolic Constitutions. From very early times Jesus' sayings about subordinating sexual desire to the demands of the kingdom (Mt 19:12), and Paul's recommendation that celibacy was a suitable response to the proximity of the end times (1 Cor 7:25-31), can be seen to be reflected in the polity of such very ancient Asian churches as those reflected in the book of Revelation, where the (heavenly) virgins are presented as the true pure of heart, the core elect of the church, who closely attend the heavenly Christ, and who are the "firstfruits" of all the redeemed (Rev 14:4). This exaltation seems to correspond in some way with the existence of virgins as an ascetical and zealous group in the churches.

In other New Testament evidences there is a correlation of the state of virginity and the exercise of the prophetic function. A passing mention in Acts 21:9 tells us that the "evangelist Philip" had four daughters who were virgin prophets. According

---

[79]Origen, *Commentary on John* 32.7.
[80]"[A widow] shall not be ordained, because she does not offer the oblation and does not have a liturgical ministry. Ordination is for the clergy on account of their ministry. But the widow is appointed for prayer, which is a task for all Christians." Apostolic Constitutions 11.

to Eusebius's *Church History* two of them remained active as such all their lives.[81] For Eusebius, this aspect of Christian virgins using their ascetical lifestyle to advance a highly apocalyptic office as "witnesses" of the gospel marks a very early and very strong tie in Christian thought between the idea of evangelical detachment from the cares of the passing world and the renunciatory sign of sexual abstinence. In other words, earliest Christianity elevates sexual abstinence not as a social factor (Paul had advanced that idea in his general recommendation of the single life as a "useful state" in 1 Cor 7:28) but rather as a distinct eschatological "sign of contradiction." The virginal lifestyle is still described as such by Athanasius of Alexandria at the end of his *De Incarnatione* (48).

An early pattern of Christian virgins, such as represented by Syrian practices in the second to third centuries, suggests they lived in the heart of the urban communities; if they were female, they were sheltered within the house of parents or other family. The two Pseudo-Clementine letters show that virginal communities remained a fairly common part of church life in Syria in the third century. They still appear in this way in the church manual *Apostolic Tradition* (of Hippolytus), where they are designated as an "order" of virgins who live at home, under the spiritual guidance of the bishop. But by the fourth century they were found more commonly living together in buildings adjacent to the church, under the supervision of the bishop.

We see a tension between the *episkopoi* and the virgins first manifested in the writings of Ignatius of Antioch, who cautions his younger episcopal colleague Polycarp about the "pride of virgins."[82] His words suggest that he had occasion to rue their social influence at Antioch, all of which reminds us that the standard episcopal expectation of obedience might not always have been fulfilled. Several female ascetics later came from the ranks of wealthy aristocrats and often ensured that their institutions had physical distance from, and financial independence of, the local bishop.[83] When this was the case, the issues of episcopal governance of female communities can be presumed to be more difficult. In Gregory of Nyssa's account

---

[81] Eusebius, *Church History* 5.24.2.
[82] Ignatius of Antioch, *Letter to Polycarp* 5.2.
[83] Gregory of Nyssa's *Life of Macrina* tells us of his famous ascetical sister, who had been formed by the controversial ascetic Eustathius of Sebaste. She is one renowned example in Cappadocia of this phenomenon of wealthy women adopting the ascetical lifestyle. Other wealthy women we know of include Syncletica in Alexandria, Melania the Younger at Jerusalem, Olympias of Constantinople, and even the fifth-century empress Pulcheria, sister of Theodosius II, all of whom who used the dedicated virginal life as a means of retaining personal control of familial properties and extending the limited range of self-determination then available for women in ancient society. It might seem surprising to us today, but is nevertheless true that the adoption of an ascetical virginal lifestyle by ancient Christian women in all-female communities was a very liberating social move for most of them.

of the death of his sister Macrina, something of this tension can be traced in Gregory's relations with Macrina's community of nuns, on the property of what (had once) been his own familial lands. The relations are all very respectful but notably not warm. Independent women challenged the deep roots of late antique patriarchalism inside and outside the church.

In the third century Origen of Alexandria composed, at Caesarea, his *Commentary on the Song of Songs* to encourage the community of virgin ascetics. And at the end of that same century the theologian-bishop Methodius of Olympus composed a Christianized version of Plato's *Symposium*, titled *The Banquet of the Ten Virgins*, in which he gives an extended encomium of the virginal life. Hymnographer and deacon Ephrem the Syrian was, in the fourth century, commissioned by such a group of female ascetics to compose his *Hymns of Virginity*, for them, celebrating their state of espousal to Christ their bridegroom and meant to be used in their offices of prayer. In some parts of Christian Syria between the second and third centuries, dedicated celibacy was propagated as a necessary condition for a serious dedication to the evangelical way of life, even to the extent that baptism was preached as especially fitting and proper to those who had so dedicated themselves to celibacy.[84] This led, of course, to a large number of Christian catechumens who deferred baptism until late in life and a significant minority leadership of younger leaders of the communities who were ascetics.[85] These male and female virgins (for the word designates celibates more than anything else) were known in Syrian Christianity as the *ihidaya*, the solitary "sons and daughters of the covenant." They existed here long before the fourth-century monastic movement popularized this lifestyle more widely in Christianity and then made it more institutionally central (especially after the fifth century, when most bishops were expected to be celibate).

In accordance with late antique norms about the appropriateness for females to live enclosed (domestic) lives, while males should occupy the public forum as their "proper" domain, it tended to happen, one suspects, that once male Christians adopted the celibate lifestyle and symbolically occupied the office of "spiritual virgins," they dramatically brought this office out from the domestic zone into the ecclesial public domain and set the stage for what would be more common after the fourth century, that is, the increasingly wholesale co-option of ecclesiastical offices by male celibate ascetics. Monastic, ascetical, celibate communities of men are found in many places in the fourth century actively seeking a public voice in church affairs.

---

[84]This practice was abandoned in the late third century and was retrospectively denounced as Encratism.
[85]Because only the baptized (celibates) could be advanced to orders.

Some evidence exists to show that celibate Christian communities of male and female ascetics coexisted. These were probably originated as a defense of a household of Christian virgins by their celibate male counterparts. But they attracted a lot of formal episcopal censure. A few "moral lapses" might have occurred by so juxtaposing the sexes in this way, but the real reason they were institutionally frowned on seems to have been the eyebrow raising that the practice (of celibacy generally) appears to have caused among non-Christians.[86] Always sensitive to criticism, the church authorities disliked leaving themselves open to ribald critique. A Syrian text called *Letter to the Virgins* is one of the first to protest against this practice of common domestic living for male and female ascetics.[87] Canon 3 of the Council of Nicaea extends the prohibition to all clergy for all time.[88]

After the explosion of the ascetical life in the fourth century, many Christian women increasingly looked to a life lived in an organized monastic community as an attractive and powerful Christian vocation. From the late third century onward, and especially in the fourth, patristic rhetoricians, who were themselves increasingly representative of the ascetic class, drew up several elaborate treatises recommending the virginal life as something even superior to marriage. Cyprian of Carthage was the first to write one of these in third-century Africa, in which he develops the themes that a Christian virgin is espoused to Christ and to this end she lives an ascetical life.[89] He chastises some of the virgins of his church who still go to the public baths and appear naked, or to wedding parties, or who wear makeup and jewelry. These virgins, he says, are like "diseased sheep" that need to be cut off from the pure flock. Tertullian also gives much information from the previous generation of the same church in his treatise *On the Veiling of Virgins*. After his and Cyprian's writings on virginity, it seems that the custom of "taking the veil" and the wearing of very simple tunics became the distinguishing outward habit of the Christian virgins.

In fourth-century Egypt Pachomius offered rules for women monastics on the Nile and gave the direction of his first women's monastery (strictly segregated from the male community by the River Nile itself) to his sister. In Upper Egypt Shenoude supervised a very strict rule for what appears to have been large communities of rural virgins. Augustine of Hippo, in fifth-century Africa, himself wrote a rule for the

---

[86] The episcopal rhetors describe the situation as irregular "living together," but one suspects that for the most part it was a matter of communities, and separate houses, placed defensively close to one another.
[87] Later given the morally murky designation of *subintroductae* ("sneaked-in ladies").
[88] Nicaea Canon 3: "The great synod severely forbids any bishop, presbyter, deacon, or any one of the clergy at all, to have a *subintroducta* dwelling with them: except only a mother, or sister, or aunt, or only such persons as are beyond all suspicion."
[89] Cyprian, *On the Dress of Virgins*.

convent governed by his own sister within his diocese. Jerome also gave a rule of life to his female disciple, the ascetic lady Paula. One of the classic accounts of the integral "superiority" of the ascetical virginal life (taken in most of the patristic writings as a high philosophical state) is given in Gregory of Nazianzen's poem *In Praise of Virginity*.[90] After Pope Gregory the Great reiterated this belief in the intrinsic "superiority" of virginity over the married state in his *Dialogues*, it became an established attitude in Latin Christianity up to and beyond the high Middle Ages. Other noted theologians of the fourth and fifth centuries, such as Gregory of Nyssa, Ambrose, Basil of Ancyra, John Chrysostom, and Augustine, all wrote extensive treatises *On Virginity*.

The power of the virgin saint as intercessor became a notable factor in early Christian hagiography and iconography (the north wall of San Apollinare Nuovo at Ravenna illustrates this abundantly). This was even more true when that virgin-saint was also a martyr, as several of the earliest female ascetics were, doubtless because they attracted the attentions of the persecutors precisely because of their high local notoriety as Christians. The extent of female virgins in the lists of the early martyrs is remarkable. Most of the patristic writings, all of them by men, laud virginity as a "spiritual betrothal" to Christ. Thus even in celebrating the ascetic renunciation of marriage, the male theologians seem to have been able to conceive of it only in marital terms. There is little alternative suggested from the extremely rare female voices that managed to be textualized in the early Christian period. The distinct office of Christian (female) virgin did not so much ever disappear from the church but was certainly absorbed (and to that extent disappeared) into the larger ascetical movement and into the female diaconate.

## A SHORT READER

***Ignatius of Antioch*, To the Philadelphians 4.** Masters, be gentle toward your slaves, as holy Job has taught you; for there is one nature and one family of humankind. For "in Christ there is neither slave nor free." Let governors be obedient to Caesar; soldiers to those who command them; deacons to the presbyters, as to high priests; the presbyters and deacons and other clergy, together with all the people, the soldiers, the governors, and even Caesar, to the bishop; the bishop to Christ, even as Christ is to the Father. For in this way shall unity be preserved in all. Do not permit the widows to be socializing wanderers, or take delight in luxuries, or to flit from house to house; but let them be like Judith, who was noted for her seriousness, or like Anna, who was renowned for her sobriety.

---

[90]Gregory of Nazianzus, *Carmen* 1.2.1.

***Ignatius of Antioch,* To the Antiochenes 8.** You who are presbyters should "feed the flock that is among you," until such time as God will make clear to you who it is who will hold the governance over you. For I am now ready to be offered up, so that I may win Christ. Let the deacons understand what dignity they have, and let them study to be blameless, so that they may be disciples of Christ. Let the people be subject to the presbyters and the deacons. Let the virgins know to whom they have consecrated themselves.

***Ignatius of Antioch,* To the Antiochenes 12.** I salute the holy presbyters. I salute the sacred deacons, and that person most dear to me, whom God grant I may behold in the Holy Spirit, occupying my place when I shall attain to Christ.[91] I offer my soul for his. I salute the subdeacons, the readers, the singers, the doorkeepers, the workers, the exorcists, the confessors. I salute the keepers of the holy gates, the deaconesses in Christ. I salute the virgins betrothed to Christ, of whom may I have joy in the Lord Jesus. I salute all the people of the Lord, from the smallest to the greatest, and all my sisters in the Lord.

***Clement of Alexandria,* Miscellanies 3.6.53.** Peter and Philip had children, and Philip married some of his daughters off to men.[92] And Paul is not afraid in one of his letters to call a woman his "wife" whom he did not take with him on his journeys, because she was not of use to his great ministry. Does he not say in the same letter: "Do we not have the power to take with us a sister wife, as the other apostles do?" For these apostles, giving themselves without respite to the work of evangelism as befitted their ministry, took women along with them, not as wives but as sisters, to share in their ministry toward women who lived at home: and so by their agency the Lord's teaching reached the women's quarters without causing scandal.

***Tertullian,* On the Prescription of Heretics 41.1-8.** I will not fail to give an account also of the conduct of the heretics—how frivolous it is, how secular, how merely human, devoid of seriousness, without authority or discipline, as befits their creed. To begin with, it is hard to see who there is a catechumen and who is a believer; for they all alike have access, they all indiscriminately

---

[91] Ignatius was on his way to trial and probably execution in Rome when he wrote this letter back to his church. He is not naming the cleric whom he has (probably) already indicated ought to succeed him as bishop of Antioch on the news of his expected death.

[92] While three remained virgins. Clement point here to the extent of the (eschatological) charism of virginity among the earliest ministers of the gospel. This practice of celibates of different sexes living together chastely as mutual support for the evangelical life was heavily disapproved of in later times and eventually condemned by the Council of Nicaea, canon 3; Council of Ancyra, canon 19.

hear and pray, even pagans, if any of these come among them by chance. So "that which is holy they have cast to the dogs," and they "have flung their pearls before swine," though doubtless they were fake ones! They think that simplicity consists in the overthrow of discipline and consider that we pay too much attention to it. When it comes to the offering of peace, they huddle up with all who come any way at all. Right order is of no matter to them, provided they can band together to storm the citadel of their "one and only truth." All are puffed up, all offer you their knowledge. Their catechumens are perfect even before they are fully taught. And how bold are the women of their party! They have the audacity to teach, to dispute, to perform exorcisms, to undertake cures, and, perhaps, even to baptize. As to their ordinations, these are carelessly administered, capricious, and changeable. At one time they put neophytes in office; then at another time, men who are bound to some secular employment; and yet another time they appoint persons who have apostatized from our community, so as to bind them there by vanity, since they cannot do so by force of truth. Nowhere is promotion easier than in the camp of these rebels, where the mere fact of being there is a high service. And so it comes to pass that today one man is their bishop, but tomorrow someone else; today someone is a deacon who tomorrow turns out to be a reader; today one person is a presbyter who tomorrow becomes a layman. Yes, for even on laymen they impose the functions of priesthood.

**The Apostolic Constitutions 2.1.** As to what concerns bishops, we have heard from our Lord that in each congregation a pastor who is to be ordained a bishop for the churches must be blameless and beyond reproach, free of any kind of wickedness common among other men; never less than fifty years of age; for such a one will be in the main past the disorders of youth and beyond the slanders of the heathen, as well as the reproaches that are sometimes cast on many by certain false brethren who do not consider the word of God in the Gospel: "Whoever speaks an idle word shall give an account of it to the Lord on the Day of Judgment" (Mt 12:36). And again: "By your words you shall be justified, and by your words you shall be condemned" (Mt 12:37). If it is possible, let the candidate be well educated, but if he is illiterate, let him at least be a skillful preacher and of a competent age. But if it is a small community and no one of advanced age can be found, then let a younger person, who stands in good repute among his neighbors and has been counted by them as worthy of the office of bishop, be ordained in peace; someone, that is, who after due examination and after receiving a good general report can be shown to have comported himself from his youth with meekness and regularity, like a much elder person. For Solomon was king of Israel when he was twelve years of age, and Josiah reigned righteously when he was eight (2 Kings 22:1), and similarly Joash governed the people when he was seven (2 Chronicles 24:1; 2 Kings 11:3-4). So, even though the person may be young, let him be meek, gentle, and quiet. For the Lord God says through the prophet Isaiah: "On whom shall I look, except the man who is humble and quiet, and always trembles at my words?" (Is 66:2). The Gospel says likewise: "Blessed are the meek, for they shall inherit the earth" (Mt 5:5). Let him also be merciful; for again it is said: "Blessed are the merciful, for they shall obtain mercy" (Mt 5:7). Let him also be a peacemaker; for again it is said: "Blessed are the peacemakers, for they shall be called the sons of God." Let him also be a man of good conscience, purified from all wickedness, evil, and unrighteousness; for as it is said again: "Blessed are the pure in heart, for they shall see God" (Mt 5:8).

***The Apostolic Constitutions 2.2.*** Let the bishop, therefore, be sober, prudent, decent, firm, stable, not given to wine; not someone who uses beatings, but a gentle person, not a brawler or a covetous man. Let him not be a recent convert in case he becomes puffed up with pride and falls into condemnation and the devil's snare, "for every one that exalts himself shall be cast down" (1 Tim 3:6; Lk 14:11). A bishop must have been the "husband of one wife" (1 Tim 3:2), and she herself must have had no other husband. He should have "ruled well over his own household" (1 Tim 3:4). So, in this manner when he is to receive ordination and be placed in his bishopric, let an examination be conducted to determine whether he is serious, faithful, and decent; whether he has a serious and faithful wife, or has formerly had such a one; whether he has educated his children reverently, and has "brought them up in the fear and service of the Lord" (Eph 6:4); whether his servants fear and respect and obey him; for if those who immediately surround him in relation to worldly concerns are seditious and disobedient, how will others who are not of his family learn to be obedient to him when they come under his management?

***Ritual Prayer of the Laying on of Hands, in* Euchologion: The Ordination of Presbyters in the Byzantine Church.** The divine grace, which always heals that which is infirm, and completes that which is lacking, ordains the most reverend deacon (*name*) to the office of priest. Let us, therefore, pray for him, that the grace of the all-Holy Spirit may come on him.

O God who have no beginning or end, who are before every created thing, and who honor with the title of presbyter those whom you have considered worthy, to serve the word of your truth in the divine ministry of this order: you, the same sovereign Master, preserve in purity of life and in unswerving faith this man whom you have been pleased to ordain through me by the laying on of hands, graciously imparting to him the great grace of your Holy Spirit, making him wholly your servant, well-pleasing to you in all things, and worthily exercising this great honor of the priesthood, which you conferred upon him by the power of your wisdom. For yours is the kingdom, and the power, and the glory, of the Father, the Son, and of the Holy Spirit, now and ever, and to the ages of ages.

**Gregory of Nazianzus, Oration 2.95, In Defense of His Flight.** Since these things impressed themselves on me—how no one is worthy before the greatness of God, and the sacrifice, and the priesthood, who has not first presented himself to God as a living and holy sacrifice and offered that reasonable and God-pleasing service (Rom 12:1) and sacrificed to God that sacrifice of praise in a contrite spirit, which is the only sacrifice required of us by the giver of all—then how could I dare to offer to him the public sacrifice, the antitype of the great mysteries? How could I clothe myself with the name an vestment of a priest, before such time as my hands had been consecrated by holy works, and before my eyes had become accustomed to gaze safely on created things; amazed in the face of the Creator but without risking creaturely disaster (Ex 33:20)? How could I [assume the priesthood], before my ear had been sufficiently opened to the instruction of the Lord, and he himself had opened up my ears to hear him readily, and he had set a golden earring (Ezek 16:12) with precious stones (that is, the words of wisdom) in an obedient ear? How could I, before my mouth had been opened (Ps 40:6) to draw in the Spirit; opened wide so as to be filled with the spirit of speaking mysteries and doctrines (1 Cor 14:2), and before my lips had been bound, so as only to use the words of wisdom, filled with divine knowledge (and, I might add, set loose in due season [Ps 119:171])? How could I, before my tongue had been filled with exultation, so as to become an instrument of divine melody, awaking with glory, waking in the early dawn, and laboring till it "cleave to my jaws" (Ps 22:15; 137:6): before my feet had been set on the rock, made to become like a hind's feet, and my footsteps directed in a godly fashion so that they should not make a slip (Ps 94:18); or before all my members had become instruments of righteousness (Rom 6:13) and all mortality had been put off, and swallowed up in life (2 Cor 5:4) so as to yield to the Spirit?

**John Chrysostom, Homily 11.1.** When Paul says: "The women likewise," he meant the women deacons (τας διακονους). There are those who think that here he was only talking about women in general. But that is not the case. It would have made no sense to have inserted here something about women in general. He was referring to those who held the dignity of the diaconate (της διακονιας) . . . when the text goes on: "Let deacons be the husband of one wife." This is also appropriately said of women deacons (γυναικων διακονων), for such monogamy is necessary, useful, and proper to the highest ranks of the church.[93]

**The Testament of the Lord** *40-41, Prayer for the Appointment of Widows.* Let the appointment be made in this way. As the widow prays before the entrance to the altar, looking down, let the bishop say quietly, but so that the presbyters can hear, this prayer: O God, Holy One, Most High, who looks down on the humble, who has chosen the weak and the mighty; you the honored one who has created even things that are despised, now, Lord, give also to this your handmaid, your spirit of power, and strengthen her in your truth, so that in fulfilling your commandments and serving in the house of your sanctuary, she may be an honored vessel in your sight and may glorify you on that day when you shall glorify your poor, O Lord. Grant to her that she may cheerfully fulfill your teachings, which you have set as a rule for your handmaid. Give her, O Lord, the spirit of meekness, and power, of patience and kindness, so that hearing of your yoke, she may endure hardships with ineffable joy. Lord, you who know our weakness, make perfect your handmaid for the praise of your house. Strengthen her to edify and give good example. Make her wise and comfort her, O God. For blessed and glorious is your kingdom, O God our Father, and to you is due praise, with your only begotten Son our Lord Jesus Christ, and the holy, good, adorable, and life-giving Spirit, who are consubstantial with you, now and ever and to the ages of ages. Amen.[94]

## FURTHER READING

Aune, D. E. *Prophecy in Early Christianity and the Ancient Mediterranean World.* Grand Rapids: Eerdmans, 1983.

Bakhuizen, J. N. "Tradition and Authority in the Early Church." *StPatr* 7 (1966): 3-22.

---

[93] PG 62.553.
[94] A fifth-century church order book from Syria or Egypt. See J. Cooper and A. McLean, trans., *The Testament of the Lord* (Edinburgh: T&T Clark, 1902).

Beneden, P. van. *Aux origins d'une terminologie sacramentelle: Ordo, ordinare, ordinatio, dans la literature chrétienne avant 313.* Spicilegium Sacrum Lovaniense 38. Louvain: Université catholique de Louvain, 1974.

Blenkinsopp, J. "Presbyter to Priest: Ministry in the Early Church." *Worship* 41 (August–September 1967): 428-38.

Botte, B. "The Collegiate Character of the Presbyterate and Episcopate." In *The Sacrament of Holy Orders*, 75-97. Collegeville, MN: Liturgical Press, 1962.

Campenhausen, H. von. "Le concept d'Apotre dans le Christianisme primitif." *Studia Theologica* 1 (1947–1948): 96-130.

Clark, E. A. *Women in the Early Church.* Message of the Fathers of the Church 13. Wilmington, DE: Michael Glazier, 1983.

Collins, J. N. *Diakonia: Re-interpreting the Ancient Sources.* New York: Oxford University Press, 1990.

Colson, J. *La fonction diaconale aux origines de l'Église.* Paris: Desclée de Brouwer, 1960.

Cunningham, A. *The Bishop in the Church: Patristic Texts on the Role of the Episkopos.* Wilmington, DE: M. Glazier, 1985.

Daniélou, J. *Le ministère des femmes dans l'Église ancienne. La Maison Dieu* 61 (1960): 70-96.

Dix, G. "Ministry in the Early Church." In *The Apostolic Ministry: Essays on the History and Doctrine of the Episcopate*, ed. K. E. Kirk, 185-303. London: Hodder and Stoughton, 1946.

Dubois, J. "Les listes épiscopales, témoins de l'organisation ecclésiastique et de transmission des traditions." *Revue d'histoire de l'Eglise de France* 62 (1976): 7-256.

Eisen, Ute. *Women Office-Holders in Early Christianity: Epigraphical and Literary Studies.* Collegeville, MN: Liturgical Press, 2000.

Elm, S. *Virgins of God: The Making of Asceticism in Late Antiquity.* Oxford and New York: Oxford University Press, 1996.

Ferguson, E. "Church Order in the Sub-Apostolic Period. A Survey of Interpretations." *Restoration Quarterly* 11 (1968): 225-48.

Gryson, R. *The Ministry of Women in the Early Church.* Collegeville, MN: Liturgical Press, 1976.

Hill, D. *New Testament Prophecy.* Atlanta: John Knox, 1970.

Jay, E. G. "From Presbyter-Bishops to Bishops and Presbyters." *TSS* 1 (1981): 125-62.

Madigan, K., and C. Osiek. *Ordained Women in the Early Church: A Documentary History.* Baltimore: Johns Hopkins University Press, 2005.

Martimort, A. G. *Deaconesses: An Historical Study.* San Francisco: Ignatius Press, 1986.

McGuckin, J. A. "Eschaton and Kerygma: The Future of the Past in the Present Kairos. The Concept of Living Tradition in Orthodox Theology." *St. Vladimir's Theological Quarterly* 42, nos. 3-4 (1998): 225-71.

Methuen, C. "Widows, Bishops, and the Struggle for Authority in the *Didascalia Apostolorum*." *JEH* 46, no. 2 (1995): 197-213.

Osiek, C. "The Widow as Altar: The Rise and Fall of a Symbol." *The Second Century* (1983): 159-69.

Reiling, J. *Hermas and Christian Prophecy: A Study of the Eleventh Mandate.* Leiden: Brill, 1973.

Rossi, M. A. "Priesthood, Precedent and Prejudice: On Recovering the Women Priests of Early Christianity." *Journal of Feminist Studies in Religion* 7, no. 1 (1991): 73-94.

Stander, H. K. "Prophets in the Early Christian Church." *Ekklesiastikos Pharos* 66-67 (1984–1985): 113-22.

Thurston, B. B. *The Widows: A Women's Ministry in the Early Church.* Minneapolis: Fortress, 1989.

Tillard, J. M. R. "Sacerdoce." In *Dictionnaire de Spiritualite Ascetique et Mystique, Doctrine et Histoire*, 14:2-11. Paris: Beauchesne, 1990.

Trevett, C. *Christian Women and the Time of the Apostolic Fathers. (AD 80–160).* Cardiff, UK: University of Wales Press, 2006.

Turner, C. H. "Ministries of Women in the Primitive Church: Widow, Deaconess, and Virgin, in the First Four Christian Centuries." In *Catholic and Apostolic,* ed. H. N. Bate, 316-51. London: Mowbray, 1931.

Wijngaards, J. *Women Deacons in the Early Church: Historical Texts and Contemporary Debates.* New York: Crossroad, 2006.

# CHRISTIANS AND MAGIC

CHRISTIAN THOUGHT FROM THE EARLIEST TIMES has been very careful to distance itself (what it does in its sacraments and worship ceremonies, and how it sees the world working) from the world of magic. This carefulness has usually manifested as anxiety. One might cite the popular manner of evoking "the three kings" at school nativity plays instead of the "three wizards" (*magoi*) of St. Matthew's text (Mt 2:1). Even commentators who are more scrupulously careful to use the actual New Testament terms usually render it as "three wise men," even though an ancient reader knew well enough that professional (Zoroastrian) astrologers were meant here. From the time of the first Christian missions, this line in the sand between Christian (ritual) acts of power and Hellenistic magic has been drawn firmly, even though many outside observers in antiquity would have regarded the zones of operation between Christians and those commonly labeled *magoi* as overlapping in significant dimensions (such as investment in exorcisms, dream interpretation, healing rites, prophetic foretelling of the future and so on). One can think, for example, of St. Paul working as an exorcist in Ephesus and by this means convincing some of the other (presumably professional) exorcists in the city to give up their trade and burn their "magical texts," even though these could have been sold for a very high price (Acts 19:11-20). It was Paul, here in Acts, who set the tone for defining every magician (in the person of his foe Elymas) as potentially a "son of the devil, an enemy of all righteousness, full of all deceit and villainy" (Acts 13:8-12). But in this extraordinary account of the earliest missions, it is again Paul who "corrects" Elymas by making him go blind: an action that someone not so keenly aware that Christians "never did magic" would have interpreted as being "better magic" than his opponent's.

This kind of established Christian "thought" that marks so clear a line between religion and magic in this context has largely come down through Christian history in the form of text; and text has almost exclusively been the product of the educated classes, usually where these have coincided in Christian times with the leading clerical elites. If we were to consider the question from the broader viewpoint of popular religion across the Christian ages, however, it would be more difficult to extricate the world of ancient religion from the "magical" milieu that is so pervasive in antiquity, for the clear distinction theologians might like to impose between magic and superstition on the one side, and true religion and effective prayer on the other side, is often more occluded in popular culture than such a categorization might allow.

This is true even today in ways in which official church rituals and consciousness might radically exclude "superstition," while at a more popular level strange inconsistencies can be found among Christian peoples of widely different cultures: astrology, spells, amulets, aversion rituals, multiple-cult attachments, and much more. It is not enough to presume that magic was what pagans did, and religion was what Jews and Christians did in antiquity (though this was once a common presumption). It still runs on in those definitions of magic that see it as all "acts committed by a disapproved-of religious system." But this does not help much. In ancient times magic was not so much clearly defined as broadly agreed on as a very bad and dangerous thing, in other words, largely "presumed" to be something collectively, when a modern sociologist might not classify it as such.[1] What comes across in all the ancient references to it is that it is seen first of all as a low-class concern, ostensibly a peasant interest of the uneducated (though this belied the fact that at times many highly educated protagonists were involved with it, especially in late Platonist circles); and, second, a movement that is largely malevolent in character (*maleficia*), much concerned with curses (*defixiones*) (though again this is belied by the fact that it also seems much concerned with cures and liberative exorcisms, according to the vast amount of spells that have survived).[2]

## ANTIQUE FEARS OF BLACK MAGIC

The Romans, who first give us that marvelous term *superstitio*, reveal much in what it originally meant: superstition was a level of excessive fear of the gods, a religious dread that sought to void itself in aversion rituals. So "magic" for them was a darker and corrupt side of mystical rite, where there was central focus on bargaining with the gods, or appeals to the darker (*chthonic* and elemental spirits—lesser *daimones*), and especially where great stress was laid on the details of the ritual itself (the exact words to be used, the specific "powers" of the individual sorcerer or *magus*, for example).[3] This is what distinguishes magic from religion. Today a skeptically minded

---

[1] R. MacMullen, *Enemies of the Roman Order* (Cambridge, MA: Harvard University Press, 1966).
[2] But contra see R. S. O. Tomlin, "The Curse Tablets," in *The Temple of Sulis Minerva at Bath*, vol. 2, *The Finds from the Sacred Spring*, ed. B. Cunliffe (Oxford: Oxford University Committee for Archaeology, 1988), 59-278; J. Gager, *Curse Tablets and Binding Spells from the Ancient World* (Oxford: Oxford University Committee for Archaeology, 1992).
[3] *Chthonic* means "dark earthbound forces."

secularist might regard all religious belief, and especially all presumption that God works in history through sacred rituals (eucharistic presence, healing sacraments, and so on), as "magical thinking." This can serve to remind us that much in the allegedly "solid" wall between religion and magic rests on theological premises.

What we might conclude from the ancient approach to magic (we shall not attempt to dignify it with the status of a definition) is that it was something the literary and governing classes despised as a dangerous and violent aspect of the underclass's superstition. That there was a lot of it around in ancient society is borne out by the number of references to it in the ancient writers, but even more so by the extraordinary amount of spells and ritual incantation remains that have survived in the papyrus finds. The magical texts were first collected in the mid-nineteenth century, but in 1974 a critical edition in two volumes was made by Karl Preisendanz and issued as the *Papyri Graecae Magicae* (*PGM*). Hans Betz made a substantial English version of these surviving remains in 1986, and their extent has proven surprising even to those who might have suspected it.

Late antique Roman writers of the old religion themselves were very worried about magic and saw a clear divide between it and what was being pursued in the state rites. Christian apologists attacked them, of course, lumping in official Roman religious procedures (such as oracular divination) with a broad attack on all forms of non-Christian (and non-Jewish) worship as demonically based and thus maleficent in substance if not always in intent. But in doing so they were simply turning back on Roman heads an argument that had first been leveled at them; for it was Roman authorities who first began to proscribe Christian communities as practitioners of magic.

We see this instanced in Suetonius's accusation that the Christian religion was *malefica*. In that charge the Roman authorities had their first legal basis for taking legal action against Christianity, and it is probably that factor that accounts for two noticeable things in the later Christian attitude to magic: (1) that the church "officially" refuses to be associated with the term in any way at all, and (2) that it saw a powerful apologetic being put to work against it under the heading of the term *magic* and decided to throw back the same brick at its persecutors, this time classifying all Greco-Roman rites as demonic (evil) when they themselves claimed, of course, that they were effective, religiously speaking, exactly to the extent that they were authentically *daimonic* (able to ensure human contact with the invisible world of the spirits).

Much confusion remains in this area of assessing early Christianity and magic, partly because the Christian apologetic about a *noncommunicatio* between the church and pagan senses of ritual and divination has been uncritically presupposed in so much reflection up to the twentieth century, and also because such attitudes ran over unconsciously (for the most part) into much classical-studies criticism up to the end of the nineteenth century, when scholars so often imported a deep Protestant distaste for image veneration and sacramental ritual into the great post-Reformation debates with continental Catholicism and (with the consequent masking of apologetic arguments at play) actually read the cases of classical Greco-Roman religion through the spectacles of (a peculiarly narrow) reading of Christian apologetics. As we have noticed, even today it is difficult, in speaking about such a complex subject, to arrive at a definition of key terms that actually works. What is magic? What is religion? How differentiate them?

Early Christians who wrote about the matter followed the line established by Roman apologists before them: namely, magic was a low-class affair, and in turning to the darker *daimones*, was a manifestly wicked business. The Christian theorists also followed much first-century Jewish thought in being clear that religion was the worship of the true God, and prayer was a medium of effecting the communication of effective divine power to the believer, while magic was an offshoot of the cult of the (false) gods (whom Jews and Christians widely defined as demonic) that characteristically tried to "force" these demonic powers to the ends of the *magus*, the witch, or the *theurge* (the philosopher-magician of late Platonism). There is, therefore, a lively continuance in the Christian era of that apologetic against magic that was first laid down in the Old Testament texts combating nonmonotheist worship.[4]

Even when the early Christians sustained this tight definition that relegated all magic to the realm of defective cult and irreverent arrogation of divine power, it is still clear enough that at some times and places what would have been widely accepted as "magic" by most people in the ancient world was a strong part of folk

---

[4] Several of the oldest level of Old Testament references to magical praxis are neutral—that is, they presume the power of the works of Egyptian priest-magicians (for example) but allude to them only to show the superiority of the Jewish agent (Aaron or Moses or another prophet). The prophetic power (from God) is shown off in the light of the (lesser) cultic power of the servants of the Egyptian gods. This uses the category of "magic" as a kind of common factor in a broader context of henotheism (the God of Israel is the best in a pantheon of other spiritual powers): see Gen 41:8, 24; Ex 7:11-12; 8:18-19. In later Israelite theology there is a growing background of hostility toward magical rites (especially those related to necromancy) insofar as they represent departures from obedience to the law (and thus covenant impurity). Two things have changed in this later period: henotheism is no longer operative under a stricter context of monotheism, and (following from this) alternative spiritual powers are seen as de facto hostile to God, thus evil. So, for example, we see the "woe" to those who practice magical rites in Ezekiel (Ezek 13:18-20); the classification of all magic rites as "delusion" in Wisdom 17:7; and the remarks in Leviticus that magical involvement cuts a person off from Israel (Lev 19:26, 31; 20:6). It is this Levitical model that is closely followed in Acts of the Apostles, where the story of Peter and Simon Magus is set out to "warn off" Christians from being involved in magical ritual. Here to be a magician is to be "in the bonds of iniquity" (Acts 8:20).

practice among the Christians, as well as their pagan neighbors.[5] Marvin Meyer's recent focus on Coptic incantational papyri that look for all the world like materials that a classicist in other circumstances would classify as "magical," has in recent times reinforced the caution that Christianity's "theory" about religion expelling magic might have been stronger on the page than it was in the ancient village—more forceful coming from the pen of clerical authorities than from the oral tradition of the suburbs. And so, although Christians have generally and always been somewhat anxious in relation to this category of magic, one might suspect that it has possibly been a much more common part of folk Christian practice than previously thought, albeit highly disapproved of by Christian clerical leaders and dismissed by them as superstition among the church.[6] For such reasons, in the ancient world it was not specifically looked at in great detail, and a picture of what was happening in terms of common Christian superstition needs to be retrieved almost from the margins of the early Christian visual field.

## MAGICAL AMULETS

A lot of sacramental practice (blessing and healing ritual, the use of holy objects, crosses, icons, saints' images, and relics, for example) might also be fruitfully understood in apologetic terms as Christian missionary attempts to dislocate the use among the people of magic amulets, or body or domestic images of the old gods, by a new *cultus* that reoriented older ideas using familiar praxis to new ends.[7] By the fourth century Christians were widely found wearing neck crosses, engraving Christian symbols on household objects such as lamps (used in prayer rituals), and avoiding any even nominal iconic representations of the old gods (such as mosaic floor or wall decorations) by adapting them to Christian forms. The reapplication of a ceiling mosaic of Apollo the sun god as a tomb mosaic of Christ the heavenly light giver, found in the third-century cemetery under St. Peter's, adjacent to the "Red Wall" of the apostle's tomb, is a clear example of religious fusion tipped decisively in

---

[5] Not least the early Coptic Christians, who seem to have left behind a mountain of incantational papyri. See J. Mercier, *Ethiopian Magic Scrolls*, trans. Richard Pevear (New York: G. Braziller, 1979); M. Meyer and R. Smith, eds., *Ancient Christian Magic: Coptic Texts of Ritual Power* (Princeton, NJ: Princeton University Press, 1999); P. Mirecki, "The Coptic Wizard's Hoard," *Harvard Theological Review* 87 (1994): 435-60.

[6] In the fifth century St. Augustine sarcastically recounts what one of his wealthy Christian congregation had told him in an outraged way when the bishop complained about his dabbling in magic: "Certainly, I visit the [temples of the] idols, and I consult magicians and soothsayers, but I do not forsake the church of God. I mean to say! I am a catholic Christian." Augustine, *Psalmos* 88, *Sermo* 3.4 (PL 37.1140).

[7] See A. A. Barb, "The Survival of Magic Arts," in *The Conflict Between Paganism and Christianity in the Fourth Century*, ed. A. Momigliano (Oxford: Clarendon, 1964), 100-125; C. Bonner, "Magical Amulets," *Harvard Theological Review* 39 (1946): 25-55.

favor of a new Christian iconography. Often little needed to be done. The Vatican Roman cemetery shows Phoebus made into Christ by the simple addition of a cruciform nimbus around the head. Hermes Criophoros, carrying a lamb on his shoulders, could be rendered even more easily into the Good Shepherd.

Sts. John Chrysostom and Augustine regarded even the use of Christian amulets as no more than remnants of pagan religiosity, and in their works, as well as in several synods of the West, Christian clergy regularly complained about such things.[8] The use of Christian magic, however, ran on into medieval times and beyond, but is not the same as the developing use of Christian iconography in paraliturgical use.[9] In the Byzantine era and in the early medieval Latin West, fusion of magical and orthodox attitudes was widespread: magical rings, incantations, amulets against the evil eye, and so on. The ubiquitous blue *oculus* to ward off *baskania* (the "evil eye") is still found today all over Christian Greece. But not all instances of icon and relic can be placed in the category of "magic," despite a strong Protestant apologetic that since the sixteenth century has applied such a stringent view of icon and relic to the Christian past. The widespread fear of demonic influence (spirits of place, hostile *chthonic* powers prevalent everywhere) was a force to reckon with in antiquity. That Christianity offered such a strong *theologia victoriae*—the sign of the cross as the putting of all demons to flight—was a powerful incentive for attracting ancient people to the ranks of the church: indeed, surely one of the earliest forms of the "theology of liberation."[10]

A symbol of this kind of religious fusion that is not merely Christian-pagan "slippage" is perhaps the manner in which in the fifth century in Egypt the queen of magic herself, the goddess Isis, whose cultic power was widely seen as very potent in regard to fertility and home life, had her title of the "mother of the god" (Horus) stolen from her by highly sophisticated Alexandrian theologians, beginning with Origen and culminating with Cyril the patriarch. All the popular devotion to the

---

[8] Council of Orleans, canon 30 (511); Council of Auxerre, canon 41 (573); and Council of Clichy, canon 16 (626).

[9] The use of rituals involving holy water, relics of the saints, dust from the Holy Land as *eulogia* or "blessings"; icons of saints and Christ himself, viewed as possessed of sanctifying power (the formula was that the reverence given to the icon passed directly to the Lord or saint depicted, and the blessing of the holy figure fell in return on the one who venerated the image).

[10] St. Athanasius of Alexandria, who was himself accused before the emperor (falsely, one should add, but the charge was seriously considered) of cutting off a rival cleric's hand for use in occult magic, elevated the fearlessness of Christians in the face of pagan magic as one of the public signs of the authenticity of the gospel message: "At the sign of the cross all magic ceases, all witchcraft is rendered void, all idols are abandoned and denied, all superstitious longings cease, and everyone raises their eyes to heaven. . . . Only say aloud the name of Christ and you will see how at that the spirits flee, augury stands dumb, and all magic and sorcery are brought to no account." *De Incarnatione* 31.

great magician goddess, who could especially bless her female devotees with fertility and happy home lives, was rechanneled to the Virgin of Nazareth, proclaimed by the bishops in synod at Ephesus in 431 as Theotokos, Mother of God. When the synodal bishops emerged from the church at Ephesus on that June night in 431, they were met by crowds of women carrying lighted torches, anxious to hear whether they had affirmed the Theotokos title for Mary, anxious to defend the honor of the heavenly patroness of their city.

Artemis of the Ephesians (Acts 19:23-28) had been ousted by Mary of Nazareth. Now this cultural "borrowing" has often been dismissed by careless readers as a "corruption" of the church in a supposed "Hellenization of the gospel," as Adolf von Harnack once called it disapprovingly. It might be more accurate to regard it as an often-repeated strategy of the evangelization of Hellenism: for the end result, here the elevation of the figure of Mary as axiomatic as a Christian symbol of love, takes us not sideways in a parallel displacement but rather in a radically new set of directions. In both the terms of the Isis iconography (which Marian iconic traditions seizes) and in terms of the theological applications of the title Theotokos for Mary, we see not evidence of religious "fusing," but rather a dynamic reappropriation for new ends: in short, religious displacement.[11] Simply put, Mary is by no means Isis in disguise: she is the radical evangelical reclaiming of ideas of how God presides over the sexual fertility, home life, and dealing with difficulties.

However, in order to properly clarify the issues involved, it is best to begin by looking briefly at what magic meant in terms of Greco-Roman religion in the ancient world, and then move on to how Christians might have been pulled into these truly ancient religious attitudes by mimesis, or repelled by them—moved, as it were, by abundantly present magical practices around them to make a contrary statement about how they saw the energy of God active in the world and the proper way for the devotee to access divine powers. In former eras Roman religion was often held up, because of its numerous and hostile references to "magical" practices, as being a paradigm of the rationalist purification of religious ritual from lower forms of magical practice.

Much of this approach is now being seen as heavily, often unconsciously, and certainly anachronistically influenced in itself by late antique Christian apologetics

---

[11] The figure of Isis the queen is shown seated on a royal throne, either holding the divine child (Horus) on her lap and presenting him to the viewer as regal lord, or suckling him, symbolizing the gift of immortal life. In Marian iconography Mary is shown, after the fourth century, seated on the throne, holding the Christ child on her lap. She becomes his throne, as it were, and is designated *Platytera*—wider than the heavens—since "she contains within her womb, him whom the heavens could not contain," as one church hymn puts it. Also borrowing from Isis iconography, Mary is sometimes shown seated suckling the Christ child—what Christians in Egypt elevated (on the back of Isis memories) as a symbol of the Eucharist.

that demonized the world of the *daimones*. Religion was alleged to deal only with the high and refined aspects of cultic worship (elevating moral aspirations and monotheistically inclined cosmic reverence), while magic was classed as a shoddy and opaque set of goings-on concerned in the main with love potions, curses, attempts to force the gods to petty, day-to-day concerns. Recent classical scholarship, however, is more and more suggesting the interpenetration of magical rites with ancient religious rites: the effect being that our categories of approaching such issues have largely been radically called into question in the last several decades, and the issue has to be thought out again as the range of what is seen as relevant evidence alters substantively.

Magic (anyone's magic) worried ancient Roman legal writers and apologists mainly in the sense of malevolent interest in curses and "black arts" used against living people. The Romans genuinely feared the power of witches and necromancers, not merely for the ancillary social damage such a practice could incite (acquisition of corpses and illicit body parts, possible abduction and mutilation of minors) but also for the dread of the invocation of dark spirit forces that could defile the state-sponsored cult of the gods and thus damage the special standing Rome was thought to enjoy from its divine patrons because of its *pietas*.[12] The trial of Apuleius as a *magus* demonstrates that fear in practice. The generally sensible historian Suetonius gives an early external definition of the Christian religion as *nova et malefica*: to do with revolution and malicious magic.[13] Pliny in his investigation (under torture) of two Christian deaconesses in 112 in eastern Bithynia also called the religion "an extravagant superstition," and acquiesced in Trajan's decree that it merited punishment if discovered but was not necessary to be sought after and exterminated.[14] Similarly, Emperor Marcus Aurelius mentioned Christians with the distaste reserved for secretive and maleficent magic sects, calling them *lucifuga et latebrosa natio*: "a secessionist people that flees the light to lurk in shadow."[15]

## EXORCISTS AND MAGI

In the late Roman Empire Jewish *magi* (exorcists, healers, soothsayers, and so on) were widely known in the Roman world as magical "specialists."[16] Tiberius employed a per-

---

[12] In Apuleius's *Golden Ass* the witches of Thessaly sought to secure body parts from corpses laid out for their wake.
[13] *Lives of the Caesars: Nero* 16.2.
[14] Pliny, *Letters* 10.97.
[15] Recounted in Minucius Felix, *Octavius* 8.4.
[16] Jewish magic seems to have been very conservative and long-lasting. Elements of Jewish magical practice from late antiquity, such as found in the Qumran scrolls and other temple-era literature (not merely the Jewish elements of the *Papyri Graecae Magicae*), still turn up in the medieval

sonal Jewish exorcist in his household. Juvenal satirizes them collectively, and Lucian speaks of them also.[17] Accordingly, the earliest Christian insistence on Jesus' works of power as demonstrative of his authority (prevalent in Mark's Gospel) to initiate the kingdom would have had a different, more magical, resonance to Romano-Hellenistic ears, than the "eschatological" theological message intended by the Evangelists.[18]

So there is clearly a lively religious apologetic turning around the concept of magic from earliest Christian times. Third-century neo-Platonic philosopher Porphyry finds Christ himself to have been an exemplary moral character but depicts the religion that grew after him as a lamentable case of corrupt magic led by Peter, whom he describes as a dabbler in the black arts.[19] Jewish apologetic in the early Christian times also attempted to discredit Jesus by classifying him as a *magus*. The original text of that *Testimonium Flavianum* in the *Antiquities* 18.3 (before it was heavily reworked by Christians to remove the offensive elements) seems to have described Jesus more or less as a *magus* who worked such signs as would impress those who fell for such things.[20] Justin Martyr in the second century was still working hard to discredit such

---

period—magical names and incantations in the "antique" mold even then gaining extra force by their very antiquity.

[17] Juvenal, *Satire* 3.13; 6.542-47; Lucian, *Tragedy* 174. His (hostile) satire on Cynic philosopher Peregrinus Proteus (born AD 95; *On the Death of Peregrinus*) is also a caustic view on the fusion of magic, philosophy, and spiritual guru-ism that was widespread at this time. In the latter work he accuses Peregrinus of having easily passed for a Christian wonderworker at one point of his career.

[18] G. H. Twelftree sets the scene for the interplay between wider Hellenistic and New Testament exorcism: "Jesus and Magic in Luke-Acts," in *Jesus and Paul: Global Perspectives in Honor of James D. G. Dunn. A Festschrift for his 70th Birthday*, ed. B. J. Oropeza, C. K. Robertson, and Douglas C. Mohrmann, Library of New Testament Studies 414 (London: T&T Clark, 2009), 46-58; *In the Name of Jesus: Exorcism Among Early Christians* (Grand Rapids: Baker Academic, 2007). My own study ("Authority, Obedience and the Holiness of God: The New Testament Sense of the Kingdom," in *Power and Authority in Eastern Christian Experience*, ed. F. Soumakis, Sophia Studies in Orthodox Theology 3 [New York: Theotokos Press, 2011], 17-32) sets out what I think was Jesus' own and the core early Christian theological intentionality behind accounts of his "works of power."

[19] As cited in Augustine, *De consensu evangelistarum* 1.32.49 (PL 34.1066); *De Civitate Dei* 18.53: *Petrum autem maleficia fecisse subjugunt*.

[20] J. P. Meier has reconstructed the possible "original" form of Josephus's words about Jesus as fairly disapproving but in a sophist mode: "Now there was about this time Jesus, a wise man. For he was a doer of startling deeds, a teacher of such men as receive the truth with pleasure. And he gained a following both among many Jews and many of Greek origin." Meier's reconstruction has removed such obviously Christian interpolations such as "if it is lawful to call him a man" qualifying the phrase "wise man." But the text originally, in my estimate, was even more hostile than this. Josephus was not calling Jesus a "wise man" who taught those who "receive truth with pleasure" (*hedone*)—that is, depicting him as a populist philosopher who had a following for a time and then was crucified. Rather, he was complaining that Jesus was a *magus* who did "wondrous deeds" (i.e., magic) for those who received "such phenomena" with pleasure. Pleasure here is not a positive concept at all, and in the first version was not related to "truth." The substitution was probably another of the extensive edits of the Christian interpolator, who was concerned to launder out the caustic dismissal of Jesus here as a false messiah using magical works to confuse the lower (nonphilosophical) classes. The Josephan text comes in a series of other such "false messiahs" that he lists. It still is, incidentally,

a charge.[21] It was picked up and continued up by many Roman writers who were themselves hostile to Christianity, and the concern that this charge caused the church is mentioned by several Christian writers up to the fourth century.[22] Julian the Apostate, even though he himself was invested in *theurgy* (a philosopher's use of magical rite), returned to it as a weapon against the Christians.[23]

The usual Christian "reply" to that charge (one that carried an implicit legal threat against the church) was that the pagans had badly misread their alleged ecclesial "magic," when it was in essence "countermagical." In other words, Christian ritual was all about subverting the power of the demons on earth, and the church thus marked a radical break with the power of evil and demonic influence and stood diametrically opposed to magic, which emanated from those demons.[24] Gregory of Nazianzus, in his *Diatribe Against Julian*, accuses the emperor of panicking when he was shown the invocation of the demons theurgically and disgracing himself in his Athenian initiation by making the sign of the cross over himself instinctively and thus spoiling the theurgic rites.[25] This formal argument (magic is demonic, Christian ritual is angelic and divine, and thus they are two opposite poles of spiritual *dynamis*) soon becomes standard in the church and is found in the intellectuals Justin, Tertullian, Cyprian, and Chrysostom, eventually to be given a classical expression in the fifth century by Augustine.[26]

The Byzantine church continued that position strongly, through the medium of "highly wondrous" miracle tales in the numerous hagiographies (saints' lives) it produced. In these popular, lively accounts (often contextualized in the evangelization of the country regions) the struggle of the church, in the figure of the saint (bishop or monk) against magic, is a dominant theme.[27] This too shows that the popular conflation of "magic and miracle: pagan and Christian" was an enduring problem, needing to be addressed by clerical catechesis through the early medieval era. The

---

a remarkable nonevangelical source, confirming Jesus was renowned in his lifetime for "works of power"—whether one classed those as magic or miracle. The Christian "fixer's" heavy hand still allows us to see the magical charge underlying the original.

[21] Justin, *Dialogue with Trypho* 69.7; 108.2; *First Apology* 30.

[22] *Clementine Recognitions* 1.58; Tertullian, *Ad Uxorem* 2.4, 5; Origen, *Contra Celsum* 7.69; Lactantius, *Divine Institutes* 5.3.19.

[23] See Socrates, *Ecclesiastical History* 3.13.11, 12.

[24] A charge of the use of magic against an opponent could carry the death penalty with it and was greatly feared even among the intelligentsia: cf. Ammianus Marcellinus, 15.7.7-8; 30.5.11.

[25] It is a wonderful story—whether it actually happened or not—and is brilliantly recaptured in C. Cavafy's masterly poem "Julian at the Mysteries."

[26] Augustine, *De doctrina christiana* 2.35-36.

[27] See D. Abrahamse, "Magic and Sorcery in Hagiography of the Middle Byzantine Period," *Byzantinische Forschungen* 8 (1982): 3-17; see also H. J. Magoulias, "The Lives of Byzantine Saints as Sources of Data for the History of Magic in the Sixth and Seventh Centuries AD: Sorcery, Relics and Icons," *Revue des etudes Byzantines* 37 (1967–1968): 228-69.

Byzantine theologians continue the patristic approach: that the power of the saint is that which relied on God, and at the sign of the cross or a holy thing all the power of magic will dissolve, since the latter all emanates from demonic evil, and is shown to be a malevolent force but ultimately specious. The circus factions of Christian Constantinople between the fifth to ninth centuries were notorious for hiring magicians to curse their opponents' teams, and Christian high officials who fell sick often attributed their illness to the "evil eye" cast on them by rivals resorting the magic arts. The shrine church of St. Hypatios at Rouphinianai in Bithynia was renowned as a place of healing for those suffering from the curses of sorcerers (*goetai*).

So for many centuries (even into the present, of course) the unease of appropriate "discernment" as to what was magical superstition and what was an experience of true religious wonder (or miracle) continued. In early times, both the church and the synagogue set up a major distinction that works chiefly on theological terms and has continued down through the Christian ages. Magic is chthonic, powered by demonic forces, and malevolent, and intends to seduce souls from the path to God and life. Religion, by contrast, has a force that works to the beneficent healing of human souls and bodies, is energized by Christ, the Virgin, or the saints, through the medium of blessed things or rites, and is philanthropically transfigurative. The former is superstition. The latter is a work of faith and meant to confirm faith. The former is "pagan"; the latter is Christian. The church, therefore, does not know magic: it only celebrates God's power handed to it in Christ's gift of the continuance of his presence and grace in history. The pagan world still resorts to magic of different forms, because it still resists the church and the call to God's grace, preferring the seductions of the offering of independent powers over the world.

An important element of this apologetic construct is the large classification it makes between the elect and the reprobate. But more than this, it places the magicians and the followers of the non-Christian pantheon alike into the category of "pagans." This was a clever apologetic term of offense: the word derives from "country simplicity." In other words, practitioners of magic (and devotees of the old religion alike) were little better than village hicks. The force of the argument rose, of course, after the greatest gains to the Christian movement were found in the cities, and the old religion lingered on for many centuries more in the conservative rural areas.

Idolatry, the ultimate abomination of evil, which Jews and Christians alike thought merited an everlasting alienation from God, and loose morals, which demonstrated adherence to demonic overlords, were attributed to the wider society outside the synagogue and the church. This too was a remarkable apologetic. I do not mean to say that ancient Greco-Roman societies were not decadent, but rather that two things ought to be discerned in the Christian apologetic process against magic: first, the exclusion of the corrupt society served to tighten the lines defining the very society that excluded it. In other words, such an apologetic was part and parcel of Christianity's own emerging self-definition, and social organization. Second, that the wholesale lumping together of all Greco-Roman society under a collective heading of pagan idolaters and loose livers served to bring down several birds with one apologetic shot. It was relatively easy pickings for an aggressive church apologetic aimed at ancient cults, which had slightly ridiculous *mythoi* and little ethical coherence. These could be derided for their failure to lead their devotees to a higher standard. Christian apologia delighted in the tales of the immoralities of the Olympian gods and the theological explanation of the "wonders" of the pagan cults in terms of demonic operations.

But the collective denunciation overlooked the fact that "paganism" as such was entirely a Christian invention: it did not exist in these real terms. On the contrary, Greco-Roman religion was a vastly complex affair—perhaps a little like Hinduism today. It ranged from crass superstition, to bizarrely symbolic ritual systems, to rigid social and class rules, to the higher levels of metaphysical, mystical, and ethical thought. In relation to magic, superstition, or theurgy, even its ritual incantations, its "mysteries" and popular spells, carry within them a wide range of practice and theological significance. The same can be said, of course, with regard to ritual, incantation, relic icon, and hagiographic wonders in the Christian world. It is thus probably enough, therefore, to leave the consideration of this sprawling and intriguing area with the simple notice that the church's apologetic construct of pagan magic is a lot more sharply delineated than the historical contexts might have been "on the ground" in ancient times.

## A SHORT READER

> In this first example, taken from a papyrus fragment, we have five examples (the fifth is largely lost) of ancient magical incantation from a recipe book of a *magus*. They are written with short separations, indicated by short dashes, the *paragraphos* in Greek. I have added numbers to them for ease of reference. They come from a papyrus in the collection of the University of Michigan (p. Mich. 3.154; published in K. Preisendanz, et al., *Papyri Graecae Magicae. Die Griechischen Zauberpapyri*, 2 vols., 2nd ed. [Stuttgart: Teubner, 1974]) and (written in Greek) derive from Egypt in the third or fourth centuries of the Christian era. It would have been the custom of the *magus* to sell the charms, teach them viva voce to the devotee, and perhaps pass on each one individually inscribed on an amulet.

### *Hekate Charms.*

(1) ... name ... a favor charm, a charm to dissolve a spell, an amulet, and a victory charm: *aa emptôkom basum*, protect me.

(2) Charm of Hekate Ereschigal against fear of punishment: If she comes forth, let her say: "I am Ereschigal, holding her thumbs, and not even one evil can befall her." But if she comes close to you, hold your right heel and say: "Ereschigal, virgin, dog, serpent, wreath, key, herald's wand, golden is the sandal of the Lady of Tartaros," and you will prevail on her.

(3) *Askei kataski erôn oreôn iôr mega semnuêr bauï* (three times), Phobantia, remember, I have been initiated, and I went down into the chamber of the Dactyls, and I saw the other things down below, virgin, dog, and so on. Say it at the crossroads, and turn around and flee, because it is at those places that she appears. Say it late at night, about what you wish, and it will reveal it in your sleep; and if you are led away to death, say these things while scattering seeds of sesame, and it will save you.

(4) *Phorba phorba breimô azziebua*. Take bran of first quality and sandalwood and vinegar of the sharpest sort, and shape cakes from it. And write his name on them, and so hide them, saying into the light the name of Hekate, and: "Take away his sleep from so-and-so," and he will be sleepless and worried.

(5) Against fear and to dissolve spells: Say, . . .

> The first charm fragment, above (1), ends with a series of (apparently meaningless) sounds: *aa emptôkom basum*. These are the so-called *voces magicae*. Such sound-resonant phrases appear in multitudes of ancient spells and carried a significance of magical power, mysteriousness innate in the very sounds (special "recipes" sold to the client by the magician, who was "in the know" about such things—Gnostic initiation). They are the grandfather of *voces magicae* that have endured in a pale form even to this day: *abracadabra*; *hocus pocus*, and the like. Some of the extant charms consist only in such *voces*, pages of them and nothing else. The magical concerns of domination of others, protection from seen or unseen foes, and exorcismic liberation, all come together at once in this short incantation, clearly an "all-purpose" insurance.
>
> The second through fourth spells turn around the figure of the goddess Hekate— here equated with the Babylonian goddess Ereschigal, so as to give the "true and ancient" name of the goddess as a key element of the charm's power. Hekate is an ancient Greek deity, later depicted as triple-formed (one head of a dog, one of a horse, one of a serpent), who in her iconography carried a lighted torch or a key and cultically was seen to preside over magical rites, household cults to do with entrances, fires, herbs, and lamp lighting. She was the goddess who inhabited crossroads (making them a suitable place to bury the condemned); a fearsome chthonic figure reverenced by rituals of aversion (nighttime sacrifices); adept in poison and necromancy (summoning the dead). One popular devotion to her was to leave offerings of meat at crossroads (presumably to be consumed by her familiar animal, the dog).

The second of our charms here offers protection against her, an aversion of any punishment that might befall the practitioner of magic for bending the goddess to do one's will. The third charm also contains an emergency saving clause: say it while scattering sesame seeds at a crossroads (ready to run, in any case!), and these will save the adept from the goddess trying to murder the initiate in their sleep, revenge for being summoned. The spirit of place (the crossroad) is significant here, but this charm sells itself as working *oneiromantically*, to induce visions in sleep: presumably those foretelling the future.[28]

The fourth incantation also begins with *voces magicae* at its heart and a supportive ritual of making shapes with the name of the person you wish to attack written on them. This is a psychic attack spell. In several cases such hex charms have turned up with human figures adjacent to them with pins stuck in them. The last fragment was obviously a recipe against such a psychic attack being waged back.

### *A Love Binding Spell.*

Only half of this second- to fourth-century spell from Egypt (p. Mich. 757) is reproduced here—it is one of the longest surviving *defixiones*. Apart from its size, and the fact that it was inscribed on a lead amulet (so it would have a long and active life), it is very typical in its style. It begins with columns of *voces magicae* and then continues:

*ablanathanalba, aeêiouô, iaeôbaphrenemoun, ôuoiêea, akrammachamarei . . . aberamenthô oulerthexa n axethreluo ôthnemareba*, I deposit this binding spell with you, chthonian gods Pluto and Kore *uesemmeigadôn* and Koure Persephone Ereschigal, and Adonis, also called barbaritha, and chthonian Hermes-Thoth *phôkensepseu earektathou misonktaich*, and mighty Anubis *psêriphtha*, who holds the keys to those who dwell in Hades, and chthonic spirit gods, and those who suffered an untimely death, boys and young girls, year by year, month by month, day by day, night by night, hour by hour. I adjure you, all spirits in this place, to assist the ghost. Rouse yourself for me, ghost, whoever you are, whether male or female, and go into every place, into every quarter, into every house, and find Kopria (whom her mother, Taesis, bore), the hair of whose head you have, to bind her for Ailourion (whom his mother, named Kopria, bore), that she may not submit to vaginal or anal intercourse, or gratify any other youth or man except Ailourion alone

---

[28] The main forms of popular divination (*manteia*) in antiquity were *geomancy* (lines appearing in dust thrown on the earth), *pyromancy* (reading the shapes in a fire), *libanomancy* (watching the swirls of rising incense), *ooscopy* (reading the shapes made by an egg broken over fire), *hydromancy* (scrying into a bowl or body of water), *lithomancy* (crystal gazing), and *oneiromancy* (exegeting the oracular significance of dreams). *Necromancy* (the use of magic rituals aided by body parts from corpses, or the summoning of spirits of the dead) carried severe penalties under Roman law.

(whom his mother, named Kopria, bore), so that she may not even be able to eat or drink or get any sleep or enjoy good health or have peace in her soul or mind, because of her desire for Ailourion (whom his mother, Kopria, bore), until Kopria (whom her mother, Taesis, bore), whose hair you have, will spring up from every place and every house, erotically burning, and come to Ailourion (whom his mother, named Kopria, bore), loving, adoring with all her soul, with all her spirit, with unceasing and unremitting and constant erotic binding, Ailourion (whom his mother, named Kopria, bore), with a divine love, from this very day, from the present hour, for the rest of Kopria's life. For I adjure you, ghost, by the fearful and dreadful name of him at the hearing of whose name the earth will open, at the hearing of whose name the spirits tremble with fear, at the hearing of whose name the rivers and seas are agitated, at the hearing of whose name the rocks are cleft, by *barbaritham barbarithaam chelmobra barouch ambra Adônaiou* and by *ambrath Abrasax sesengenbarpharangês* and by *Iaô Sabaôth Iaeô pakenpsôth pakenbraôth sabarbatiaôth sabarbatianê sabarbaphai mari glorious marmaraôth* and by *Ouserbentêth* and by *Ouserpatê* and by *marmarauôth marmarachtha marmarachthaa amarda maribeôth*. Do not disobey my commands, ghost, whoever you are, whether male or female, but rouse yourself for me and go into every place, into every quarter, into every house, and bind Kopria . . .

> This long and repetitive spell is clearly as much a psychic assault as it is a "love spell." The recipe adds on a ritual of making two human figures, one male and armed, the other female, kneeling with hands tied behind her back, penetrated by thirteen copper needles. The amulet (and figurines) were meant to be placed in the tomb of someone who had died violently or prematurely so as to become a restless ghost. The command would force the ghost to do the will of Ailourion and deliver to him an erotically charged Kopria, in love only with him. One notes the obsessive desire to specify the correct person by matrilinear line. The reference to hair already given refers perhaps to the use of real hair taken from Kopria's house and attached to the figurine left in the grave.
> 
> The titles of the *daimones* and gods here have the usual suspects: Pluto, Kore, Hermes-Toth—all gods of the underworld from whose hands the ghost is wrested by Ailourion so as to become his servant; but toward the end we see mentioned *Iao Sabaoth*, a reference to the Lord *Sabaoth* (God of Hosts) of the biblical tradition. *Abrasax* also makes an appearance—a very common *daimon* in the magical traditions, sometimes used by Sethian Gnostic Christians as an invoked spirit. The phrase "I adjure you, ghost, by the fearful and dreadful name of him at the hearing of whose name the earth will open, at the hearing of whose name the spirits tremble with fear, at the

hearing of whose name the rivers and seas are agitated, at the hearing of whose name the rocks are cleft" is highly reminiscent of the prayers of exorcism at the Christian baptismal ritual (reception of catechumens),[29] and is indicative of the "religious fusion" that such magic represents at popular level. Archaeologists have found several instances of magical amulets in early Christian tombs, especially in North Africa; and in Egypt there is broader evidence of a Christian desire to "lightly evangelize" the practice of amulets, by making "magical crosses"—incantational inscriptions written in the form of a cross, or the engraving of the name of Christ on scarabs.[30]

**Canon 36 of the Council of Laodicea 363.** They who are of the priesthood, or of the clergy, shall not be magicians, enchanters, mathematicians, or astrologers; nor shall they make what are called amulets, which are chains for their own souls. And those who wear such, we command to be cast out of the church.

## FURTHER READING

Aune, D. E. "Magic in Early Christianity." *ANRW* 2.23.2 (1980). 1507-57.

Barb, A. A. "The Survival of Magic Arts." In *The Conflict Between Paganism and Christianity in the Fourth Century*, ed. A. Momigliano, 100-125. Oxford: Clarendon, 1964.

Betz, H. D., ed. *The Greek Magical Papyri in Translation, Including the Demotic Spells.* Chicago: University of Chicago Press, 1986.

Bonner, C. "Magical Amulets." *Harvard Theological Review* 39 (1946): 25-55.

Brown, P. "Sorcery, Demons, and the Rise of Christianity: From Late Antiquity to the Middle Ages." In *Religion and Society in the Age of St. Augustine*, 119-46. London: Faber and Faber, 1972.

---

[29]The exorcism prayer surviving today in the Byzantine baptismal rite goes, in part, as follows: "I charge you by God, who revealed the tree of life and arrayed in ranks the cherubim and the flaming sword that turns all ways to guard it: be banned [Satan]. For I charge you by him who walked on the surface of the sea as if it were dry land and banned the tempests of the winds; whose glance dries up the deep and whose command makes the mountains melt away. Now, through us, he bans you. Fear, be gone and depart from this creature, and do not return, nor hide yourself in him, nor seek to meet him, nor to influence him, either by night or by day, either in the morning or at noonday; but depart to your own infernal abyss until the great day of judgment that is ordained. Fear God who sits on the cherubim and looks on the deeps; before whom angels and archangels, thrones, dominions, principalities, authorities, powers, the many-eyed cherubim and the six-winged seraphim all tremble; before whom, likewise, heaven and earth do shake, the seas and all that they contain. Leave, and depart from this sealed, newly enlisted warrior of Christ our God. For I charge you by him who rides on the wings of the wind, and makes his angels spirits and his ministers a flaming fire: leave, and depart from this creature, with all your powers and your angels." The Christian baptismal rituals all began with exorcisms. But still, the *Traditio Apostolica* 16 shows that wizards, astrologers, and diviners were not to be admitted to baptism at all, doubtless because of suspicions that they would relapse and thus bring the practices into the heart of the church.

[30]F. Dolger, "Amulets," in *Antike und Christentum* (Münster: Aschendorffsche Verlagsbuchhandlung, 1929–1950), 2:230-40. See Barb, "Survival of Magic Arts"; Bonner, "Magical Amulets."

Ciraolo, L. J. "Supernatural Assistants in the Greek Magical Papyri." In *Ancient Magic and Ritual Power*, ed. M. Meyer and P. Mirecki, 279-96. Leiden: Brill, 1995.
Cramer, F. H. *Astrology in Roman Life and Politics*. Philadelphia: Memoirs of the American Philosophical Society, 1954.
Dickie, M. W. *Magic and Magicians in the Greco-Roman World*. London: Routledge, 2001.
Eliade, M., ed. "Magic." In *The Encyclopedia of Religion*, 9:81-115. London: Macmillan, 1987.
Faraone, C. A., and D. Obbink, eds. *Magika Hiera: Ancient Greek Magic and Religion*. Oxford: Oxford University Press, 1991.
Fowler, R. "Greek Magic, Greek Religion," *Illinois Classical Studies* 20 (1995): 1-22.
Gager, J. *Curse Tablets and Binding Spells from the Ancient World*. Oxford: Oxford University Press, 1992.
Gallagher, E. V. *Divine Man or Magician? Celsus and Origen on Jesus*. Chico, CA: Scholars Press, 1982.
Graf, F. *Magic in the Ancient World*. Cambridge, MA: Harvard University Press, 1997.
Hamann, A. "Magic." Page 517 in *Encyclopedia of the Early Church*. Institutum Patristicum Augustinianum. Edited by A. di Berardino. English trans. by A. Walford. Cambridge: James Clarke, 1992.
Hull, J. M. *Hellenistic Magic and the Synoptic Tradition*. Studies in Biblical Theology. London: SCM Press, 1974.
Janowitz, N. *Magic in the Roman World: Pagans, Jews and Christians*. Religion in the First Christian Centuries. London: Routledge, 2001.
Luck, G. *Arcana Mundi: Magic and the Occult in the Greek and Roman Worlds*. Baltimore: Johns Hopkins University Press, 1985.
MacMullen, R. *Enemies of the Roman Order*. Cambridge, MA: Harvard University Press, 1966.
Martin, M. *Magie et magiciens dans le monde gréco-romain*. Paris: Editions Errance, 2005.
Mercier, J. *Ethiopian Magic Scrolls*. Translated by Richard Pevear. New York: G. Braziller, 1979.
Meyer, M., and R. Smith, eds. *Ancient Christian Magic: Coptic Texts of Ritual Power*. Princeton, NJ: Princeton University Press, 1999.
Mirecki, P. "The Coptic Wizard's Hoard." *Harvard Theological Review* 87 (1994): 435-60.
Preisendanz, K., et al. *Papyri Graecae Magicae. Die Griechischen Zauberpapyri*. 2 vols. 2nd ed. Stuttgart: Teubner, 1974.
Tomlin, R. S. O. "The Curse Tablets." In *The Temple of Sulis Minerva at Bath*, vol. 2, *The Finds from the Sacred Spring*, ed. B. Cunliffe, 59-278. Oxford: Oxford University Committee for Archaeology, 1988.

# THE CHURCH AND WEALTH

## CLASSICAL GREEK INHERITANCES

In antiquity (and the archaic idea has survived into our time in so many respects) the source and character of a group's wealth determined its perceived social value. The same was applied to individual estimations of a person's worth—even of their identity. In the Greco-Roman context of the early church, this was an idea built on the archaic concept that social position was determined by control of land (primarily) and movable wealth (a close second). The landowning wealthy man (which invariably meant "slave owning") thus possessed the rank and status of *kalokagathon*: the gentleman.[1] This social rank carried with it legal and political privileges, so extensive that the wealthy were not, in any sense, to be considered as ordinary mortals under the law. The upper echelon of magistrates, and the lawyers who serviced the courts, were all drawn from this same narrow band of landowners and their retinues. The notion of *kalokagathon* carried with it an implicit sense that this was also the "virtuous man" whose nobility had been rewarded by the favor of the gods (lifting him out of the mire of the poor and uneducated, by a privileged "bloodline").[2]

For most of antiquity it was the divinely appointed destiny of the rich to be so, that of the poor to be wretched. This pre-Christian Greek fatalism ran deep. Though it did resist it, with a vision of a common nobility for the redeemed family of God and a stress on the equality of all under the eyes of God, even so the church never quite escaped from the pull of its ideological current in most of its social teaching, and certainly in its praxis. Arguably it still hasn't.

If it was ultimately the gods who allotted men and women their conditions and expectations (through bloodline and birth heritage and all the mysterious sublunar events that determined the sorting of human rank and privilege for ancient society),

---

[1] Ancient society took slave owning so much for granted that it would not think it necessary to make a note of a "gentleman" possessing slaves. Accordingly, the writers (including wealthy Christian rhetoricians, one presumes) who held household slaves rarely mention their existence in the pages of their rhetoric. They are seen largely "in the tangent" of historical literary evidence.

[2] The very Greek term literally means "the beautiful and good person."

then it followed, as a corollary to the wealthy being intrinsically blessed and hallowed, that the wretched on the face of the earth were that way because either the gods had cursed them, or because they had not been gifted by "eminent character," those intrinsic virtues of blood and heritage that marked them out socially as people of stature. This presumption that the wealthy were thus virtuous was certainly a closed circle of thought, but among their expected capacities was the virtue of philanthropy. This was not an insignificant factor, for example, in a world where social welfare programs were almost nonexistent and charitable giving was the base currency of poverty alleviation.[3] This generic attitude also implied, however, that to worry about the lot of the poor was as futile as seeking to alter their karma by positive social actions. It was widespread belief in Hellenistic society that this (often wretched) disparity of lot was simply how things were in the greater cosmic order. Imbalances were not injustices. The attitude (still prevalent today, of course, as an often-unvoiced supposition in many venues) was at the core of pagan Roman ideas on wealth and status.

The gospel's very different approach to entitlement (based on what was a ridiculous idea to wider Greco-Roman society—that all men and women were equals as the consecrated images of God on earth) was a veritable clash of civilizations. Stoicism, in the century or so before the arrival of the church, had begun to introduce the idea of "humanity as a family," especially through the legal writings of its Roman disciples (it can be seen in the works of Cicero and Seneca, for example), but it had not made much headway in any systemic social sense.[4] The clash of values that resulted from Christianity's ascent, and the religion of the gospel bearing that idea of equality under the eye of God into the core of its ethical values, meant a potential grinding of tectonic plates between the conflicting presuppositions about this theory after the third century, when the church really started to make headway among the richer classes of Greco-Roman society.

The theological theory of human coequal value, of course, did not agitate anyone until it became a matter of asking precise fiscal questions: why are the rich living so well, in the face of so much common misery? The question only started to burn with a lively flame once actual redistributions of wealth were touched on. The church is quite willing to idealize poverty—be it as the Lady Bride of St. Francis, or the "poor in spirit" of the Beatitudes—indeed, too willing to make this concrete source of bitter

---

[3] See further J. A. McGuckin, "Embodying the New Society: The Byzantine Christian Instinct of Philanthropy," in *Philanthropy and Social Compassion in Eastern Orthodox Tradition*, ed. M. Pereira, Papers of the Sophia Institute Academic Conference December 2009 (New York: Theotokos Press, 2010).

[4] The idea of humanity as a family is still alluded to (though weakly today—as widespread scorn for human rights across the twentieth century damaged the idea) as the "brotherhood of man."

suffering into a dreamy aspiration of "holy simplicity." But once the discussion should turn toward the actualities of equitable wealth distribution, all sides of the question become agitated. Poverty, in Christian reflection (very like attitudes to chastity and obedience, a triad in which it has often been theorized), has always been regarded as a core evangelical issue, an important thing for the church to represent, but perhaps one that was best left to someone else to sort and attend to, lest there be too heavy a price to pay on the home front.

In one of the earliest of all Christian reflections on the character of wealth (the Gospel parable of the sower and the seed; Mk 4:18-19) the possession of riches by a Christian is compared to a bramble bush that strangles every other plant in its vicinity.[5] The Evangelist clearly applies the trope to signify (probably in the context of an early persecution of the church) how some wealthy Christians have preferred to keep hold of their wealth rather than their faith. The exact nature of that strangulation by brambles has usually been that widespread human problem, no less prevalent in the church than outside of it, of self-protective inaction, a flexible facility to keep one's eyes closed and one's ears shut to the cries of the needy in case they impact too heavily on us. Between the readiness of the Greco-Roman world, on the one side, to justify its immense wealth inequities and their concomitant social oppressions (such as slavery, which was the basis of so much of power of the few) and, on the other side, the Christian ideal, which depicted a common mercy binding together a coequal family of God, there was a profound chasm indeed. To change the deep-rooted Greco-Roman ideology in the human hearts of men and women was a monumental labor facing the church, requiring no less than an axiomatic revolution.

In Hellenistic society, what we today would see as the inhuman and tragic disparities between rich and suffering poor were regularly a cause of laughter. This, of course, was a satiric tradition the church felt uncomfortable with and generally set aside (thus contributing, paradoxically, and unintentionally, to the progressive "silencing" of the voice and presence of the ancient poor). The Greco-Roman comic poets found the poor, even those occupied in trades, and especially those who made piles of money from their labor, as stock characters for ridicule. The idea of the nouveau riche was the funniest thing on the stage of the Hellenistic theatre (other than the star-crossed lover). This attitude to labor and social class also indicates how much that period of classical antiquity had witnessed the decline of so many landed families and the rise of others to prominence. Such a social upheaval, financially motivated, would again be the case in the third century of the Christian era. This

---

[5]The analogy of wealth as a strangling bramble bush comes in the exegetical remarks of the Evangelist attached immediately after the original story of Jesus, as its commentary, and thus is probably dateable to Rome in the era of Nero.

too was a time of massive inflation and crisis for the old landed families, as well as being the moment when a small number of Christians first made an appearance in the ranks of the ultrawealthy and thus occasioned the first really sustained Christian reflections on the ethics involved in possessing wealth.

This idea in the Hellenistic literature that the *nouveau arrivé* was someone utterly risible, however, shows close dependence on the archaic Greek idea that a person is innately what he or she was born to—not merely inclusive of gender and class but in particular the social reality given by possession of wealth. To gain large cashflows was funny to an ancient Greek because it was a short-term phenomenon of one thing illegitimately trying to become another thing. In the case of axiomatic thinking about social strata in Hellenistic society, it was tantamount to a less-than-human subject (a poor person) trying to become a real person (a landowning citizen of antique standing). Thus, to be fully human in the classical era Athenian understanding, one had to be leisured. The "virtuous life" (*arete*) was one in which a man lived in leisure: or at least lived equably, overseeing his estates.[6]

Aristotle, one of the most acute political empiricists of his epoch, simply cannot see how slaves, peasants, or shopkeepers could possibly live out happy (that is, "virtuous") lives: for his definition of such was "lives that were at once prosperous and noble." For the Greek world (and it carries on with some force into early Christianity) *arete* (virtue) is synonymous with excellence (*aristeia*) and is thus a quintessentially "aristocratic" commodity. As Paul Veyne put it succinctly, "No one who leads the life of a worker or laborer can practice virtue," and this is also why Aristotle went on to conclude that only the rich and leisured can legitimately be citizens.[7] Now, the implicit anthropology in this runs even deeper and darker still: only the rich and leisured citizen class can be properly human. It was such an ideology, of course, that legitimated the violence necessary on the poor to inaugurate and sustain systemic slavery. Slavery was an antique mode of living that was vast in its extension, at least once imperial Rome's military expansion gave a ready supply of

---

[6]It was always understood as a man only who could do this—women were ruled out by other factors, not least their gender understood in an essentialist way.

[7]P. Veyne, *A History of Private Life*, vol. 1, *From Pagan Rome to Byzantium* (Cambridge, MA: Belknap Press, 1992), 119. Greek philosopher Xenophon said that manual crafts and labor "feminized" those men who engaged in them because, like domesticated women, "these too had to sit all day in the shade, or even spend whole days by the fireside" (cf. Veyne, *From Pagan Rome to Byzantium*, 123). Note here the close coupling of the issues of poverty, the social status of women, and the right to claim "humanity" in this powerful Greek pre-Christian cocktail of prejudices. Echoing this, Seneca, the Stoic Roman tutor to the emperor Nero, once wrote, "The sordid arts are those the philosopher Posidonius says which are practiced by manual labourers, who spend all their time earning a living. There is no beauty in such occupations, which bear little resemblance to the Good" (cited in Veyne, *From Pagan Rome to Byzantium*, 120-21).

cheap labor from prisoners of war. This sustained an economy based on such wildly uneven terms that only the ever-present threat of violence could sustain antique's society's continuation.

Real humankind, then, began for the pre-Christian Greeks at the rank of landowner.[8] The wealthy did not so much consider themselves superior to the poor: rather, they saw themselves as qualitatively different from the poor. The poor were unformed human beings. Slaves (and even more so "barbarian" foreigners) were seen under these Greek preconception as simply less than human. The issue of patrimony was central to this way of thinking. The moral discussions of wealth that were produced by the Greek philosophers (one can think of Plato's *Euthydaemon* and Aristotle's [now lost] *On Riches*) turned around the distinctions of good as opposed to bad *acquisition* and good as opposed to bad *application* of wealth. The two central terms were *patrimony* (the substantive body of wealth that defined a family, a kin group, and the individual within it) and *usufruct* (the manner in which that wealth was set to work societally).[9] In the main it was understood among the Greeks that a civic goal (such as a rise to power—*dynamis*) or recognized political influence (*doxa*—glory) was the main "point" of family wealth, and the ultimate goal (*telos*) of using what status wealth conferred.

For the Greek world, and the Romans following them, patrimony itself was god-given—not simply a graceful gift of the gods but a specific divine endorsement of the worth of those who held it (and by antithesis the worthlessness of those who did not, who were not god-favored, not meritorious). The social distinctions that followed from all of this (the relative differences between real human beings, lesser humanity, and subhumanity) were also seen as "given by the gods."[10] Poverty was, therefore, a curse from the gods, or at best a sign of the indifference of the gods to the plebs. The idea that the poor, by virtue of their plight, were a worthy object of attention, solace, and compassion by wider society was, therefore, a thoroughly un-Hellenistic notion.

---

[8] In Rome, citizens were divided on the basis of wealth into civic orders: simple citizens, decurions, equestrians, senators. But when the census was taken (i.e., listing those who "really" existed) the only basis recognized for "wealth" was the extent of landholding, not portable wealth or industrial assets.

[9] We must remember that in classical philosophy of this era, Greek thought did not regard "personhood" as a substantive category, but rather saw it as a peripheral (accidental) one. We today have laid such emphasis on the "rights of the person" that perhaps we cannot imagine how issues such as personal value could be articulated in a philosophical environment where personhood did not yet have a strong semantic to lift it as a significant argument in ethics. It was to be one of Christianity's philosophical achievements that it elevated the concept of personhood (through its christological and trinitarian arguments) into a substantive category, affording it ontological status and thus enabling it to be used as a powerful ethical tool.

[10] Wealthy, poor freedmen, and slaves.

These distinctions about patrimony and usufruct went on to determine almost all the moral discussion on wealth through Christian centuries up to the late Middle Ages. Christianity had a hard time introducing the idea that the very concept of the human person was not (either philosophically or morally) subordinate to the concept of societal standing and wealth. It is debatable, of course, whether it ever got that philosophical message across to society at large. Those in the classical world who passed on this ideology were often the rhetoricians, and among them were many who approached the matter with sardonic unease, caught as they were between two worlds. As poor intellectuals they were simultaneously "real people" insofar as they were philosophers, and "unreal people" in so far as they were impoverished. More than one rhetor had to earn his place by educating the young. They were oddly situated in the households of the rich who were their *patroni*, like the dependent governess in Victorian society.

## CHRISTIAN ATTITUDES TO WEALTH

The biblical record of Israel is marked by a deep opposition to much of this core Hellenistic tradition. If it is not too much of a generalization, one might describe the ancient Greek approach to wealth as urban, elitist, personal; while that of Israel tended to be rural, familial, rooted in concepts of clan covenanting (ecclesial). It is this biblical root that grows on and over the Christian tradition in most of its respects, though the Hellenistic urban contexts of the first Christian churches certainly impacted its thinking, too.

The Scriptures of Israel show a God who has a marked concern for justice for the poor: the poor of Israel, they largely mean. We do not see, necessarily, a generic reflection on human worth as yet. With the "poor whom God defends" we are dealing less with a universal philosophical anthropology and more with a distinct subset of covenant theology, or how to preserve the cultic purity of the nation (the people of God). If we ask what ideas were prevalent in ancient Israel about the rights of non-Israelites, there is some movement in this direction, in the later prophets, in terms of the concept of the "stranger in your midst," who needs to be protected and helped as a moral imperative, but even this is rarely rises to any universal notion of philanthropy. Even so, the biblical tradition that God was the defender of the poor, the orphan, and the widow made from the very start a massive dent in the Hellenistic tradition. The God of Israel was the Lord of the poor, not because being poor was a good or virtuous thing in itself, of course, but because he was the God who protected the covenantally sanctified Israelites, especially those who were least able to protect themselves. The oppression of these by other members of Israel was an infraction of the covenant virtues, thus an offense to the honor of God, which he would avenge. Being the "poor of the Lord" thus had some value conceptually and morally: a revolutionary development that Israelite religion brought to social affairs in germinal form.

From the outset, the generic Christian attitudes to wealth and philanthropy were a complex mix of Hellenistic and biblical traditions. Some times the biblical tradition won out (and one might even say generally did so in creating an overall moral ethos in the church), but frequently the structural presuppositions of Hellenism's intellectual argumentation carried on into ecclesial thinking, as an unconscious cultural inheritance. Is it a cause for wonderment that it took Christianity so long (so many weary centuries of injustice) before it came out with a complete denunciation of the evil of slavery—when attitudes to human worth were so intimately allied with Hellenistic notions of personhood as derived from possessed substance?

One of the earliest Christian theorists even began the church's approach to defining "person" as "that which possesses a nature."[11] Ownership was so basic a category of thought in Greco-Roman culture that it was taken as the basis even for thought on personalism. Can it even be said today that the church is a society that recognizes merit regardless of social standing? One might like to think so, but sociology often convicts the moral and theological aspirations of the church. This problem was already manifested in Paul's Corinth as well as James's Jerusalem. The apostles castigate both communities for the behavior of the wealthy classes, who had introduced distinctions and privileges for themselves at the local Eucharists to the disadvantage of the poor members of the churches (1 Cor 6:5-8; 11:26-34; Jas 1:9-11; 1:27–2:9; 5:1-6).

The scriptural texts, by the end of the second century, had become increasingly authoritative for the church and constitutive for its creation of a theology of wealth and poverty. Its own apostolic writings distill and systematize the evidence accumulated in the Old Testament literature. But that evidence, unfortunately, was not all that clear to interpret; and throughout Christian history since, there have been many Christians who have elevated Jesus himself, and the apostles following him, as advocating the abandonment of all possessions, just as there have been those voices arguing that this is not a pattern of behavior that Jesus intended his wider church to follow as an example. Likewise, the Old Testament texts often approach wealth possession (from an ancient agrarian context) as a sign of manifest blessing from God on the righteous and concomitantly imply that poverty is a sign of God's disfavor. Importing this view on the basis of biblical authority into the early Christian Hellenistic matrix, of course, tended to validate the pagan Greek construct we have been

---

[11] Tertullian, in his reflections on the christological debate; note the adoption of the word *persona* to connote subject reference in Christ.

looking at, rather than challenging it; even though, as I see it, the overall pattern of the Hebraic theology actually does give status to the poor as "God's elect *anawim*."[12]

The issue remains an axis of disagreement within the core biblical sources. Those who elevate the Old Testament texts as having "equal authority" to the New Testament (a peculiarly modern approach in terms of Christian history) tip the balance of the texts' evidences toward the archaic views: wealth possession is good and desired by God for his church. Such is the intellectual trajectory of those who support the theory of the "gospel of prosperity." Those who give priority to the New Testamental texts see that there is a certain conflict in the core biblical evidences about wealth and its application. Let us review that evidence briefly, for it is a general rule that if the foundational documents are not entirely of one mind about a core issue, then the subsequent Christian tradition across the first millennium also tends to be ambivalent about it, something that is evidently the case in terms of Christian attitudes to wealth, where we have, simultaneously, great cathedral builders, filling the churches with silver and gold decorations (even when those outside are in rags), and yet also impoverished ascetics calling for all the devout to be wary of all possessions, even to renounce them in the selfless service of the poor.

**Scriptural evidences.** Some of the early Old Testament texts clearly seem to advocate wealth as a positive blessing from God. There is no moral question mark over the holding of great resources, even though in terms of the ancient economy the possession of a great concentration of wealth inevitably had to be seen in terms of the 2 percent wealthy and 98 percent on subsistence level or less. It is a one-dimensional theology. The wealthy Israelite is the righteous person, insofar as he is the living sign on the community of God's majesty and favor. The book of Chronicles puts this in terms of a doxology to God in this way: "Yours is the sovereignty, Lord, wealth and riches come from you. It is you who bestow greatness and might on whomsoever you please" (1 Chron 29:12).[13] The Psalms express this same idea as follows: "Blessed is the man who fears the Lord, who greatly delights in his commandments. His descendants will be mighty in the land; the generation of the upright will be blessed. Wealth and riches are in his house; and his righteousness endures forever" (Ps 112:1-3).

---

[12]The "poor of the Lord" considered as a theological category, implying both covenantal blessing and divine protection over them even in their sufferings. This started out as a "theology of the nation," of course, but could also be applied to the state of the individual (righteous) Jew who suffered (and thus became a source of great consolation to Israel in its later vicissitudes). It is also the basis for much contemporary Christian liberation theology.

[13]In similar vein, in 2 Chron 1:12, Solomon asks from God wisdom to rule the people. God is pleased that he did not ask first for riches and power, but promises, along with the wisdom, to give him riches and power also, such as no king has ever had before. The gift of wealth and power is here an integral part of the ethical universe.

The divine gift of riches are a reward, part of the ancient text's imagination of how God as king of Israel would spread out beneficent rewards on his faithful retinue: "When the Lord gives someone riches and property and the ability to enjoy them, it is truly a great gift from God" (Eccles 5:19). The wealth that is given to the individual here is for his or her enjoyment; there is no sense of moral "application," we would say today, no social grounding of that wealth considered as societal production. Under the terms of ancient society's political imagination, the land belonged to the king. If Israel theologizes this, it affords to the Lord the same privileges as an earthly monarch dispensing favors. Such an approach deeply validates the rights of the wealthy over the poor.

And yet—there remained in biblical wisdom a deep sense that wealth was also a dangerous thing: since it led people to trust in their possessions and power rather than in the God who gives wealth. This somewhat socially subversive notion is witnessed from as early as the premonarchical days of Israel (for the affirmation of a royal messianic tradition was not uncontested in the biblical record, and even when it was elevated as a high messianic theology, the actual experience of Israel under the rule of kings was historically limited), and it approached the idea of Israelite society more collectively as a covenant community of all. We see, in the Psalms, warnings about the wealthy relying on themselves rather than on God. The wealthy here are first described as oppressors and predators (Ps 49:5-6). The righteous Israelite is counseled not to fear them, since death will destroy their presumption.[14] The psalmist concludes by setting the "wisdom tradition" over against the old doctrine that wealth was always a divine blessing: "Man cannot endure in his pomp; he is like the beasts that perish" (Ps 49:20).

Throughout the later prophets, also there are an increasing amount of denunciations of the rich, who are castigated for abandoning the ideals of Israel by their pitiless self-referentialism and oppression of the poor. The prophets also denounce the way in which riches can lead to moral blindness and carelessness as to the plight of the poor. Zechariah imagines the restoration of Israel as not least witnessed in the divine rejection of the wealthy leaders (priests and shepherds) who have brought the nation to ruin. "Those who buy [the flock of Israel] slaughter them, and go unpunished; and those who sell them say: 'The Lord be blessed! I have become rich.' Their own shepherds have no pity on the flock" (Zech 11:5). Similarly, the prophets tend to look back on Israel's simple, rural past as an idyllic time and thus denounce "present-day" (urban) affluence as one of the causes of Israel's sinfulness. This explains their castigation of a desire to acquire more than was necessary for a simple and happy life.

---

[14] Ps 49:1-17: "Do not be afraid when a man becomes rich, or when the glory of his house increases. For when he dies he will carry nothing away; his glory will not go down after him."

The idea of necessity and superfluity here comes into play morally and becomes a major part of the ethical character of prophetic literature. This idea becomes a trope for the later Christian fathers, who merge it with the Hellenistic philosophical trope that a wise man seeks to live simply. The concept of charging interest on loans strikes at the essence both of the notion as Israel as a covenant family and of this idea that the simple life has to give way to depersonalized "high finance." For this reason, this practice of "usury" is universally regarded in early Hebrew and early (to medieval) Christian tradition as fundamentally evil. It was, of course, progressively abandoned as a moral outrage by both traditions, as part of the rise of capital-based systems of complex banking. But for both traditions, in a major part of their inspired foundations, the making of money from the plight of the indigent was widely regarded as a fundamental lapse from covenant values. As an antithesis to this, the free distribution of wealth to the needy (both those belonging to the Christian community and often those outside, though it began within the community to the widows, sick, and orphans) was seen as a renewal of baptismal commitment and as such a source of the forgiveness of sins.[15] Until the institution of a system of penance in the late third century, prayer, fasting, and almsgiving was the only source of institutionalized "forgiveness of sin ritual" among the Christians. In both the Gospels and the Hebrew Scriptures, therefore, the use of wealth, through almsgiving and free lending to the needy, is taken as a primary sign of covenant fidelity.

Overall, then, the general impetus of the pre-Christian biblical tradition is not entirely clear on the subject of wealth: whether it was a danger, a curse, or a blessing. This ambivalence (wealth was a sign of God's blessing, but it was equally a source of potential moral corruption) is carried on directly into the New Testament. It is not the case, then, that the New Testament advocates the insignificance of wealth or riches—it might utter dire warnings about wealth, but it also sees the merciful application of wealth as a fundamental "living out" of the gospel. To this extent the New Testament has an implicit theology of the needfulness of some (albeit simple and basic) property and wealth holdings.

It is difficult to make generic application of a New Testament doctrine of wealth for contemporary times primarily because in making a straight transference we neglect the predominantly eschatological context in which the message of Jesus was first delivered. *Eschatology* means the "doctrine of the last things." It is a larger context of thought that conditions late Judaistic theology and the early Christian era. Most of what Jesus teaches presumes this intellectual and moral context.

---

[15]The first recorded instance of this free distribution of wealth is the support dole given to the widows of the church of Jerusalem, Acts 6:1-3. Jesus is recorded to have kept a purse for support of the poor in the course of his ministry, Jn 13:29.

*A tradition rooted in eschatology.* There are two major issues concerning the interpretation of the New Testament data about wealth. The first is, to what extent are Jesus' attitudes to wealth occasional or systematic? In other words, was he teaching a standard to be adopted throughout his movement and by all (that is, giving a core kingdom doctrine), or was he dispensing temporary advice for an itinerant community that he had brought together solely for the purposes of preaching a program of repentance in the local towns during the spring and summer seasons? In one case, the command "follow me" commits the latest as well as the first apostles to abandoning their fishing boats (families, children, homes, and possessions).[16] But a closer reading of the evangelical tradition shows that those boats and nets were still there, somehow, available to the same apostles when the preaching ministry was concluded (Jn 21:1-7). So it looks as if the "leaving all possessions" to follow Jesus is being used more symbolically in the texts than realistically. When the juxtaposition of "follow me" and "leave all" is actually placed together in the text, we find either enigmatic response (Mt 8:21-22) or inability to agree on it (Mt 19:21-23). Did Jesus expect his traveling companions to be poor (leave your nets and boats) and celibate (leave your wives, families, and children) precisely because they had to be itinerant, not static, during the (presumably limited) period that he gathered them for preaching to the hill towns of Galilee?

If this is the correct scenario, then poverty, chastity, and obedience are virtues of the traveling evangelist, not necessarily permanent states of virtue set out as absolutes for all followers at all times. Jesus is then not making a statement about wealth at all, except that it ought not to stand in the way of readiness to move when God's call is perceived and mediated to his disciples by his authoritative voice. This would be similar to the manner in which the passing of military emergency regulations supersedes civic law in temporary specific circumstances: such as a general calling up of citizens in times of war, when they have to leave possessions and family bases for other duties that demand their attention. In this way we can imagine that Jesus' teachings about wealth are occasional and eschatological (the extraordinary circumstances of the "last age" put other, more traditional and static attitudes into a new light for some who are called), but not necessarily systematic or universal.

The second interpretative issue is to what extent this eschatological context itself is fundamental or accidental to the doctrine of wealth. In this sense we can compare

---

[16]Mk 1:16-20: "And passing along by the Sea of Galilee, he saw Simon and Andrew the brother of Simon casting a net in the sea, for they were fishermen. And Jesus said to them, 'Follow me, and I will make you become fishers of men.' And immediately they left their nets and followed him. And going on a little farther, he saw James the son of Zebedee and John his brother, who were in their boat mending the nets. And immediately he called them; and they left their father Zebedee in the boat with the hired servants and followed him."

Jesus' doctrine about possessions to Paul's doctrine, in 1 Corinthians 7:7-9, about whether a Christian should marry or remain single. In the latter case the apostle is clearly teaching a "common sense" doctrine about preferring celibacy as a general rule of church governance. But it is only common sense, of course, given his generic presupposition that the end time is coming in a radically foreshortened history.

If it was not the case that the last days would come in a few years, would Paul have continued to regard his advice, about preferring celibacy for all, any longer as common sense? Similarly, if Jesus' doctrine about possessions calls for the prioritization of an itinerant community (the apostolic preachers of repentance) because of the impending nearness of the kingdom of God as the ending of world history, does it matter whether the imminent end of social affairs is not in the shortened time scale first foreseen? Or does it not matter? In other words, does necessary celibacy, abandonment of possessions, and self-submission to the commands of the charismatic leader (poverty, chastity, and obedience) not still remain as the supreme witnesses of the first Christian community (the apostles) to their eschatological belief? Would not these three cardinal virtues still stand as fundamentally eschatological acts of faith? If so, would they not retain an enduring, not merely temporary, significance in the larger Christian community that progresses in an increasingly deeschatologized view of history and society?

The parables of Jesus are a key element in helping us understand the import of Jesus' mind in this regard. They appear only superficially like homey tales. They refer to land, farms, flocks, weeding, threshing, barn building, and so on, but always take these things as symbols for a deeply eschatological message. In other words, it is a major mistake to read the parables as intending to offer any sedentary farming wisdom. The eschatological context appears deeply apocalyptic (by which I mean concerned with the significance of a radical sense of approaching nearness of divine judgment). The attitude to land (which we can take as a cipher for "possession") shows actually no vested interest in land per se. Jesus himself refuses to be an adjudicator of who was right or wrong in terms of possessions, and at the same time the poor subsistence farmers depicted in Jesus' parables can hardly live off their labors while the wealthy are consistently shown as villains.[17] This was much more critical than anything found in contemporary Hellenistic literature about the oppression the rich often foisted onto the poor in the cause of advancing their own interests.

Jesus, in this classic body of parables, is an agrarian "friend of the poor." Of that there can be no question. But it does not follow from this that he intends the poor to have a

---

[17] See, for example, the parable of the prodigal and elder sons (Lk 15:11-32) with its crazy attitude (to the ancient world) of the father toward rights and possessions; or the refusal to serve as a judge over legitimacy of possessions, which he defines as mere snares: Lk 12:13-15.

better and more just hold over social wealth. He continues the prophetic strand of God's judgment on the rich oppressor and the theme of God's deliverance of the downtrodden throughout his teachings, and the overall context of argument seems to be the call for the purification of the people of God, collectively, by repentant return to a familial sense. This is why the figure of the tax collector matters so much to Jesus: the lost son of Israel who has bought from the Roman oppressor the right to collect taxes and add to the unjust imposition even greater exactions of his own making (so that he can make a profit on the deal). In this light the use of the land and the impositions of the tax collectors stand as a primary symbol of the refusal to acknowledge God's dominion over Israel. And Jesus' calls for repentance over "this form of wealth distribution" are subservient to his cultic claims: socially subversive though they obviously are.

Even so, Jesus' repeated statements, on his itinerant preaching tours, that wealth is at best a dangerous snare (Mk 4:19), certainly weakens and undermines that older biblical theology that having many goods is a sign of blessing that ought to be sought after. Jesus' message places it low in priorities: "Therefore, do not be anxious, saying, 'What shall we eat?' or 'What shall we drink?' or 'What shall we wear?' For the Gentiles seek all these things, and your heavenly Father knows that you need them all. But seek first his kingdom and his righteousness, and then all these things shall be yours as well" (Mt 6:31-33). This is not the text that any "business leader" would advance as an inspirational model. It saps the very energy of seeking to accumulate a career, wealth, success. But at the same time that it places reliance on the God of Israel to care for the needs of those who submit to his overarching dominion, the phrase "and then all these things" seems to suggest the loss will not be felt if the surrender to God's dominion is accepted.

What are "all these things" that "shall be added" to the obedient disciple, however? They do not seem to be the goods of this world, as an easy reading might initially suggest. It seems to be the basic necessities (food and drink and clothes sufficient to the day), which Jesus suggests God's providence supplies in any case, as he is the originator of all good things. So is this not another radical call for detachment to wealth? God the Father, for Jesus, is the giver of the "bread for this day" (Mt 6:7-13). What is at issue here is the "abandonment to divine providence" that for Jesus is the mark of faith considered as implicit trust (*pistis*) in the God of providence:

> Therefore I tell you, do not be anxious about your life, what you shall eat or what you shall drink, nor about your body, what you shall put on. Is not life more than food, and the body more than clothing? Look at the birds of the air: they neither sow nor reap nor gather into barns, and yet your heavenly Father feeds them. Are you not of more value than they? And which of you by being anxious can add one cubit to his span of

life? And why are you anxious about clothing? Consider the lilies of the field, how they grow; they neither toil nor spin; yet I tell you, even Solomon in all his glory was not arrayed like one of these. But if God so clothes the grass of the field, which today is alive and tomorrow is thrown into the oven, will he not much more clothe you, O men of little faith? (Mt 6:25-30)

The rather romanticized notion that Jesus was a wandering poet without any possessions at all is a very dubious image to project on the Gospels. It takes the conditions of what were probably Jesus' two missionary campaigns and extrapolates them as absolute conditions for all time and place.[18] But as we all know, one lives quite differently on a camping trip than one does normally. We know too from almost incidental references that the ministry of Jesus around Israel was financed by some very powerful rich people.[19] Accordingly, several of the "poverty" sayings in the Gospels, such as "the Son of Man has nowhere to lay his head" (Mt 8:20), are not poverty sayings as such (statements about a philosophy of wealth) but rather instructions for the first missionaries.[20] They belong to a category of missionary instructions and were probably preserved as aphorisms to guide missionaries among the Christian prophets during the late first and early second centuries. To absolutize them (as has often been done—though usually only in highly symbolic ways) leads to major misunderstandings of the original impact of the teaching.

Indeed, many of these poverty/missionary sayings are even softened when they appear in secondary Synoptic Gospel versions. A classic example of this gradual movement from the literal to the symbolic, is how the injunction "Blessed are the poor" of Luke's version of the Beatitudes (Lk 6:20) is rendered "Blessed are the poor in spirit" in Matthew (Mt 5:3). The figure of the poor in the parable of the rich man's feast (Lk 14:13, 31), however, does see these poor as the real-world indigent. But here the invitation to the feast is not so much as a sign of the poor being given some share in social wealth distribution, but rather the elevation of the socially defiled outcast to a seat at the festal table—a sign of the cultic restoration of a pure Israel.

As happened with so many other sayings of Jesus, the Hellenistic trend to allegorically interpret literature made for an increasingly "spiritualizing" approach to Jesus' difficult commandments, not least those referring to wealth and possessions. No better example of that can I think of than the very difficult saying "It is easier for a camel to go through the eye of a needle than for a rich man to enter the kingdom of God" (Mt 19:24; Mk 10:25; Lk 18:25). How elastically has Christian preaching

---

[18]First around the towns of Galilee, and then, next year, on the road to Jerusalem.
[19]Not least Joanna, the wife of King Herod's steward, Chuza (Lk 8:3).
[20]And Luke especially seems to accumulate such references to bring them together as a collective admonition for the disciple to adopt "spiritual poverty."

through the ages interpreted that as "not meaning exactly what it says"? But however one softens this saying by means of symbolic, allegorical, exegesis, it still remains as an indigestible aside meaning clearly what it precisely intends to say: attachments are deadly dangers for anyone who wishes to make the godliness of the kingdom a priority. Does this mean it is impossible, then, for anyone who is rich to enter the kingdom? Because it is surely impossible for a camel to go through a needle's eye? Well, even here no, the *logion* goes on; it is not impossible for a rich person to be saved, after all, and despite what the saying has implied, because (as the text adds), "With God nothing is impossible."

Historical exegetes are left wondering whether the "get-out clause" that comes after the hard saying is part of the original Jesus *logion* that denounces the rich, or whether it is a case of the hard saying being "spiritually" softened somewhat by the end of the first generation of (urbanized) disciples, because the original appeal for apocalyptic impoverishment had by then become a liability for the gathering in of disciples to the Jesus movement in the growing communities of the second generation. When Jesus did turn his mind toward the subject of money explicitly, the comparison that sprang to his mind first, apparently, was the double-mindedness of "paganism." When he says "You cannot serve God and money," he made money synonymous with *mammon*, that is, the cult or worship of a false idol (Mt 6:24).

Yet, on the one occasion we know of that Jesus encountered a systematically arranged banking service (the case of the moneychangers in the Jerusalem temple; Mt 21:12) the results were far from happy. It was undoubtedly this single attack on the vested financial interests of the temple and its priesthood that immediately initiated Jesus' arrest and execution—despite later disciples' concerns to widen the reasons for his arrest into a much broader theological prospectus. And yet, the throwing over of the moneychangers' stalls, despite attempts by some modern scholars to suggest it was because the rates of exchange were unfavorable to the poor or because the priesthood had systematically oppressed the laity, seems rather to have been theologically motivated: to sustain Jesus' vision that God's mercy over all, and generous providence to all, precluded a view of the cult that demanded "organization" to this extent. Jesus is decidedly antipathetic to the concept of sacrifice as a way of accessing God's mercy, but in this instance the fiscal "sign" that he gives is more in relation to the concept of the pure temple as a "house of prayer for the nations" (Mk 11:15-18, alluding to Is 56:7; Jer 7:11) than as a serious attack on the validity of sacrifice as such, which was a seriously expensive affair, commanded by the Torah.[21]

---

[21] See further J. A. McGuckin, "Sacrifice and Atonement: An Investigation into the Attitude of Jesus of Nazareth Towards Cultic Sacrifice," in *Remembering for the Future* (Oxford: Pergamon Press, 1988), 1:648-61.

In what is perhaps his only other reference to organized banking (this time on a Roman model) Jesus uses the idea in a commendatory way. The man who was given the talents by his master and buried the money and made no return on the investment is criticized for not having had the sense to at least invest it (Mt 25:27). It is comparable to us wondering how a person could not have made any money on a capital investment, when they could at least have deposited it in the bond market. But once again, extrapolating this image from the core of a larger parable that is concerned with using talents on a wide front and also discerning the signs of God's demands on a believer does not allow us to deduce that this was an endorsement on the part of Jesus of the ancient banking system. His prioritization of the message of the kingdom, in the face of the fear that response to the call of righteousness might unsettle one's social substance, is summed up in the lapidary phrase, "Do not lay up for yourselves treasures on earth, where moth and rust consume and where thieves break in and steal, but lay up for yourselves treasures in heaven" (Mt 6:19-21). There remains, then, no systemic doctrine of wealth and poverty as such: only an insistence from Jesus that submission to the demands of God's righteousness is all important, and issues of wealth and property (like any other thing) must never be allowed to get in the way. This is a doctrine of detachment, certainly, but not a systematically followed-through doctrine of possessions.

On a smaller scale than his attack on temple trading, we might also observe Jesus' institution of a charitable burse at the heart of his missionary movement. This shows his interest in organizing, even as a traveling missionary, the funds of the community over which he presided. It is symbolic of much of what was to come later as the idea that the church ought to preside over a treasury, whose core concern ought to be the relief of the poor. Jesus delegated one apostle (Judas Iscariot, according to the Gospels) to serve as dispenser of alms to the needy. Was this more than the common Jewish practice of almsgiving as a work of righteousness? The Evangelist John uses the connection with Judas as holder of the purse to offer us a startling observation on the relative importance of alms. He depicts Judas grumbling over the woman who poured out costly ointment on the feet of Jesus. As he does so he makes Judas guilty of avarice, as does Mark in a parallel version of the story (Jn 12:3-8; Mk 14:3-11). Jesus defended the woman who poured the ointment over him, rather than adding the donation to the charitable purse, with the words, "The poor you have with you always; you will not always have me." Jesus, of course, is not pleading here for a personal allowance as leader of the movement that includes expensive perfumes; rather, the whole episode is meant as a poignant evocation of how the Messiah will be chrismated (i.e., Christ-ed, anointed or manifested by God as the Messiah)—that is, not with the regal ointments that were used in the days past, but in his case with burial spices. This episode, in short, cannot be taken as any indication of "attitude of Jesus to wealth" at all, although it has often been used as such and elevated misguidedly as an absolute indicator that the poor are not the top priority of the church's mission but come somewhere lower down the list. This text, for example, has often been misused to justify the building of luxurious churches in areas of urban poverty.

The evocation of the last judgment in Matthew, however, says something to the contrary of this and presents love and care for the poor as actually the core and basis of Christian worship: "What you did to the least of these . . . you did to me" (Mt 25:36-40). Some scholars think that the form of these sayings about the last judgment here are later than the first level of Jesus' materials in the New Testament. But whatever the case, it is clear enough that Jesus' own attitudes to riches as a "bramble patch," a dangerous distraction from the demands of God's kingdom, and his regular sardonic references to the blind paralysis that so often accompanies the condition of being wealthy and self-sufficient (Lk 1:23, 53; 6:24; 12:18-20; 16:19-26; 18:18-24; 21:1-3), remained as an enduring legacy and deep memory among the Christian community: enough so as to make his subsequent Christian disciples who were rich never completely easy before the challenges of the evangelical tradition.[22]

**Wealth in the earliest Christian centuries of the church.** A general approach among the post-Testamental church to the issue of the warnings and woes against the rich in the Jesus tradition has been to classify the call to poverty as a "counsel of perfection," something Jesus wants the best of his disciples to do, not necessarily all to adopt. Spiritualized into a gentle symbol of renunciation, poverty has often been treated like this in Christian spirituality. The locus classicus of this is the exegesis of the rich young man story in Luke 18:23, with the moral pointed up to the aspirant disciple: "If you would be perfect . . ." Such an approach has long been at the heart of the monastic movement: the elevation of a class of ascetic disciples within the larger body of disciples.

This spiritualizing tradition in and around the word *poverty* would go on to have a long history in Christianity. Along with the idea that true zealots would live out the renunciation sayings literally (though even then it is important to note that monasteries were significant social centers of wealth acquisition, and even individual monastic ascetics were always seen as suitable recipients of external philanthropy, thus fiscal support) there grew up also the idea that most Christians would be content with modest amounts of possessions that allowed them to live simply and

---

[22]And probably that condition did not apply until the second generation of the church.

to disburse a suitable level of external philanthropy to others. Wealth in this exegesis is justified as a benefactory charity. Those who moved out of this category of relative modest wealth sanctified by philanthropy, that is, the phenomenally wealthy, were regarded as having to do more to justify their holdings; but even here their philanthropy would render their wealth acceptable to God.[23]

This overall position became very widespread in the Christian consciousness. But even so, is it not dangerous to transmute poverty into a "spiritual" symbol? Poverty is actually profoundly noxious to health and human life. It is not "spiritual detachment" we mean when we normally speak of poverty, but bad health, bad education, bad housing, social oppressions, injustice, and often violent lives. And the endemic "spiritualizing approach" to poverty (glossing it in a bourgeois manner as long as the bitter effects of impoverishment have passed the commentator by) has often masked what is nothing other than the wealthy's tolerance of inequity under a cloak of pious romance.

In the late parts of the New Testament literature and the early patristic period, the problem of wealth acquisition is, more often than not, simply metamorphosed into a moral-spiritual symbol, a metaphor of beneficence. One thinks of Paul's attitude to the concept of money: seeking funds, for example, to continue his own mission or relieve the fiscal problems of the Jerusalem church. In Romans, his mind turns naturally to the "philanthropic" notion that God is "rich" to all (cf. Rom 10:12; Eph 2:4), or the trope that as an apostle he is personally poor but has made others "rich" with his message (2 Cor 6:10). Some very early Christian prophetic texts sidestep this "spiritualizing" approach and continue the tradition of giving the rich a hard time. At the end of the first century, Laodicea (a city that had only recently recovered its prosperity after a devastating earthquake) is denounced for saying "I am rich again" (Rev 3:17). The heavenly judgment raised against it is that "you are neither hot nor cold. I will spew you from my mouth."[24] On the other hand the city of Smyrna, which at the time was poor and whose Christian community was in some hardship, is described as really the Christian community that is "spiritually the rich one before God" (Rev 2:9).

By the mid-second century rhetorician-philosopher Clement of Alexandria shows how much the Christian community of that city contained wealthy members among it. For the affluent Christian circles in Alexandria, he wrote a "table manners

---

[23] The ancient economy made the phenomenally poor and the phenomenally wealthy the two largest contingents. The "modestly comfortable" might have actually been a small class of those very littérateurs who are reflecting in the issues in texts that have come down to us: men such as Clement of Alexandria, whom we shall look at shortly.

[24] A sardonic reference to the fact that the wealth of the city was based on the role it played as a hot springs and therapeutic center, where the "waters" were oddly flavored.

guide" called the *Paidagogos*, or *Christ the Tutor*. This text has several passages clearly meant to give his class members a guide to social manner for the upwardly mobile. His other treatise *Quis dives Salvetur* (*Who Is That Rich Man That Can Be Saved?*) is the first attempt of a Christian thinker systematically to portray an attitude to wealth that is nonapocalyptic yet renunciatory. Clement continues Jesus' message about detachment and obedience, but in a relatively deeschatological frame of reference. He argues axiomatically that Jesus was an intelligent philosopher, and so when he advocated the suspicion and avoidance of wealth he knew that this would be socially ruinous both for the individual and the community, and thus improper. So, obviously, what he *really meant* by such a deliberate aporia was a challenge to his hearers to interpret him less hyperbolically (to learn not to be stupid and literalist), namely, that a righteous disciple should be "relatively detached" from possessions. Clement argues (honestly and well, it has to be said) that total impoverishment is an unalleviated human evil in all circumstances. Moderate wealth (an honest income honestly earned) is, he argues, a salutary blessing for society. Christians, according to Clement, therefore, ought to work hard, earn honest wages, and bring up their own households in moderation, while providing philanthropic support to outside society from their labors. This makes the disciple into that "rich man who finds salvation," as adumbrated in Jesus' enigmatic teaching.

**The patristic-era teachings.** Gregory of Nazianzus, late in the fourth century, simultaneously opens up new vistas of Christian reflection on social justice while penning poems praising his family slaves, who were still working on his estates (though he did free them in his will). Gregory was vastly rich, as was his friend and contemporary Basil the archbishop of Caesarea. Both men's careers witness the rise of a new kind of Christian aristocrat who used episcopal rank to advance their political status. They both appeared as bishop-rhetors in the presence of the emperors themselves. Their social program is a mix of Greek and Christian notions. Gregory of Nazianzus's *Oration* 14, *On Love for the Poor*, is a major new landmark in Christian reflection on the social duty to provide philanthropy in a wide remit in society.[25] Gregory argues the case that the poor person is de facto the image of God, and even if all the rest of human society cannot see the connection, Christians must begin to see it. He lifts up the figure of the leper as the iconic example of the "poorest of the poor" and challenges the Christian community to be judged on the basis of how well it cares for these most wretched of all human beings. The Christian philanthropist who supports those poor who cannot make a repayment, he argues, is at that instant

---

[25]See S. R. Holman, *The Hungry Are Dying* (Oxford: Oxford University Press, 2002); J. A. McGuckin, *St. Gregory of Nazianzus*: An *Intellectual Biography* (Crestwood, NY: St. Vladimir's Seminary Press, 2001), esp. references to *Oration* 14 in situ.

acting like God (merciful and philanthropically) and demonstrating the perfect example of true discipleship.[26]

Even so, according to Gregory, patrimony is given to individuals by God. It is the mark of a perfect man to despise wealth (an old sophistic theme), but God also commands love as the primary virtue, and the rich have a duty to share their beneficence with those who suffer from not having enough money: especially the lepers, widows, and orphans. The expenditure of wealth for the poor (who cannot repay) is a mark, for Gregory, of greatest eminence and earns the Christian benefactor a *skene* (tabernacle) in heaven (Jn 14:2). The immediate context of his fourteenth oration was as a fundraiser for his and Basil's new project of a leprosarium at Caesarea (the Basiliad). The oration was so successful that the emperor Valens himself was moved to send funds to pay for the hospital. This was a major first in the long subsequent history of the church being associated with the establishment of philanthropic institutions aimed at education, healing, old-age support, and child care. Here we have the first glimmerings of Christian philanthropy moving to a deeper and more systemic social level. But here again the building of a new Christian polity of justice on earth sits uneasily with the eschatological imperative "Here we have no abiding city."

Gregory's younger friend and student, Basil's brother Gregory of Nyssa, is the most significant thinker in the patristic church who denounced the condition of slavery as "always wrong" and needing to be disowned in the church (probably because of his sister Macrina, and Eustathius, the radical monk-bishop who represented this stance). Eustathius was attacked for his radicalism by the Synod of Gangra, who condemned his disruption of the local nature of the church. Eustathius had subjected communities to roving subversion through impoverished monk-disciples, and he advocated monasticism as a way for slaves to leave their masters and enter a new society of impoverished equals who refused to recognize distinctions of rank before admission. The bishops of the third and early fourth century (more so afterward) are increasingly acclaimed by the local Christians on the basis of their philanthropic capacity to be *philoptochoi*: "friends of the poor" (founders and funders of the church and its support programs). This, of course, meant that they had to be rich and powerful.

The conflict between all these disparate elements in Christian practice and theory in regard to the possession or use of wealth has never really been resolved. It was not satisfactorily resolved in the transition from the first missionaries of Jesus, who were happy enough to follow the prescripts of their master in the exigencies of following him on the preaching tour from Galilee to Jerusalem. It was not resolved in

---

[26] As in the logion of Jesus at Lk 14:13.

the second-century church, which saw, for the first time, the expansion of rich and affluent Christians in the midst of the congregations. It was not resolved when the church hierarchy were given the task of organizing Hellenistic towns under a new series of Christian emperors (though their partial response—which was to invent the association of Christian churches and institutes of philanthropy—was undoubtedly a brilliant one). It was not resolved during the Middle Ages, when the church acquired great land wealth. And it was not resolved even during the radical protests of the reform age (despite some radical experiments in wealth equalization in some circles such as Calvin's early Geneva or the Shakers).

What is more, it has not been resolved to this day in the Christian world. The tension has been a source of many historical difficulties in the course of the Christian centuries, as well as many absurdities, but the tension has also served as a motivator of superb spiritual force in multitudinous varieties of Christian societies.[27] One thing is certain: wealth—its use, its renunciation, its acquisition and protection—is a fundamental force in defining the character and setting the goals of the energy of a whole human life and entire societal values. In analyzing how wealth is valued, one sees the essential "treasure" of a person and a whole social system. This arena of human life and passion is, accordingly, one of the clearest manifestations of how seriously a church or an individual takes seriously the values established by the charter of the gospel. To reduce the whole matter, as some contemporary Christian circles do, to an issue of "tithing" does not begin to do justice to the centrality of the question. The challenge is perennially what Jesus originally said, to his (generally poor) disciples: "Where your treasure is, there will your heart be also" (Mt 6:21).

## A SHORT READER

### *Letter of James 2:1-7.*

> In his first-century letter to the churches, James draws attention in his second chapter to the problem of the governance of early Christian assemblies, which seems to have been an issue also for the church of Corinth in the mid-first century, when Paul was writing (cf. 1 Cor 11:18-34). The common (eucharistic) meal was beginning to be so ordered in some places that social "distinctions" were beginning to be observed: one imagines special seats reserved for the wealthy and so on. The author of this very early text protests that to abandon impartiality is to abandon the very affirmation that all men and women have found equality in Christ. In the following excerpt, however, the author makes a revealing ad hominem argument after stating his general

---

[27] One recalls the poor little church of Francis of Assisi—the Porziuncula—wrapped later (and today) in a monstrous basilica.

point: and why should you give any special consideration to the rich? He describes them in caustic terms: it is from their ranks that hostility to the gospel can be expected, not from the poor. This is one of the earliest examples of what moderns have called the "preferential option for the poor":

My brethren, show no partiality as you hold the faith of our Lord Jesus Christ, the Lord of glory. For if a man with gold rings and in fine clothing comes into your assembly, and a poor man in shabby clothing also comes in, and you pay attention to the one who wears the fine clothing and say, "Have a seat here, please," while you say to the poor man, "Stand there," or "Sit at my feet," have you not made distinctions among yourselves, and become judges with evil thoughts? Listen, my beloved brethren. Has not God chosen those who are poor in the world to be rich in faith and heirs of the kingdom that he has promised to those who love him? But you have dishonored the poor man. But is it not the rich who oppress you? Are they not the ones who drag you into court? Are they not the ones who blaspheme that honorable name that was invoked over you?

### *Clement of Alexandria (150–215),* **Paidagogos 3.7.**

Clement was a philosopher-theologian, possibly a Christian presbyter, working in the great African city at the delta of the Nile. He is called the first great representative of the "school of Alexandria," a tradition that would run on after him in the figure of the great philosopher Origen and countless other great hierarchs of that church up to the Islamic invasion of the seventh century. Alexandrian Christianity is always characterized by an intellectualist approach. Jesus is understood as fundamentally a wise philosopher. Clement is intrigued how Jesus would advocate radical poverty for all men and women when, if everyone followed this literally, social chaos would follow, and misery would afflict so many families. He concludes that a literal understanding of Jesus' words about total abandonment of goods is a misguided fundamentalism. The text or words of the philosopher, whether Jesus or any other great teacher, have to be interpreted wisely, since they are enigmatic examples of deep wisdom that challenge the hearer to obey, but to obey with wisdom and understanding.

Accordingly, he interprets the dispossessive statements of Jesus in a more symbolic manner (allegorically), as advocating the need (1) for simplicity of life in the case of a genuine disciple of the poor Lord, and (2) as an advocacy for detachment of heart from riches, so that those who possess the goods of this world will be prepared to share them with the indigent. Note in the passage below how the staff Jesus commands his pilgrim followers to have (in Mt 10:9-10) is allegorically rendered as "philanthropy" by Clement. His overall approach, that what Jesus meant was spiritual detachment and practical philanthropy, went on to have a profound influence on the later Christian interpretation of the poverty sayings. In his book

> *Christ the Teacher* (*Paidagogos*) he puts together a lot of aphorisms and practical advice for young, upwardly mobile Christians (those who were capable of following his courses). Among other things, he teaches his hearers how to behave at banquets and what kinds of jewelry are appropriate. And here he touches on the issue of usufruct, how to apply the wealth of the shared household:

We ought to possess only what we can carry with us on our journey (Mt 10:9-10): a light burden, that is. Husband and wife should share the same attitude to this. Thrift is a good traveling companion for those who are on the road to heaven. The limit for our possessions is our body, just as the limit for a shoe is a foot. What remains as surplus, that is, all the fripperies that the rich like to collect, is only a nuisance, and no proper adornment for the body. Anyone who wants to climb the hard path (Mt 7:13-14) should have a good staff, namely, the practical assistance of the poor. Any who want to share the true rest[28] should show themselves generous to the afflicted. Note that Scripture says "Anyone who is rich has to pay a ransom" (Prov 13:8). What this means is that the rich can be saved by giving away their money to anyone in need whom they encounter. Consider the case of a well of spring water. We draw some off, but the water returns to its previous level. It is just the same with true generosity, in which case the spring is love of one's neighbor. When generosity offers a drink to the thirsty, it wells up once more and straightway is full again, just as a mother's milk flows back into her breasts the moment the babe has sucked.[29]

### Basil the Great, Commentary on the Psalms 33.

> Basil, archbishop of Caesarea in Cappadocia (330–379), is known to history as "St. Basil the Great." His works has a wide influence on the formation of classical Christian doctrine. He was especially renowned for his ascetical writings and is a major figure in the Eastern church who inspired and spread the monastic movement. Here Basil interprets the poverty sayings of the Gospels in the mode of a "counsel of perfection." It is a message explicitly aimed at encouraging ascetical withdrawal, organized monasticism, in other words, whose daily practice involved the recitation of the Psalter as the backbone of church services. And we can note that here he is talking about the issue of poverty in the context of a *Commentary on the Psalms* that monks would use. But his

---

[28]That is, of heaven. The image of rest, or leisure (*otium*), is regularly attached in early Christian literature to the concept of what the heavenly life would be like. This leisure corresponds with the ancient Hellenistic idea of how the truly "wise man" (*sophos*) ought to live, the latter idea being dependent on having enough wealth not to work, but rather to devote oneself to philosophy and politics like a "true" human being. The early Christians projected such a "true humanity" democratically into the next age and thus implicitly refuted the Hellenistic anthropology that drew a very sharp line between the rich and the poor in this life.
[29]PG 8.609.

words also have a deliberate scope aimed at the wider laity of his church, for, ascetic though he was, he was also a very practical and political bishop of a major Roman city.

What Basil elevates most of all here is the element of free choice: if a disciple follows Christ fully, then poverty is inevitably an important element of discipleship. But he lays down no commands, no laws, letting the individual freedom determine the manner in which this element of the gospel will be adopted or not. This might seem, on the face of it, to underline a rather solipsistic and hyperpersonal approach to issues of wealth and not to take into account the social elements involved in wealth distribution. On other occasions, however, Basil showed himself to be more than aware of the need for social action. His initiative started one of the most famous and early examples of Christian social welfare when he gathered the money to build a major leper hospital and welfare colony on the outskirts of his city. The complex, known as the Basiliad, was staffed by monastics and grew so successfully that it eventually rivaled the town in size. In his commentary on Psalm 33 he says,

Not all forms of poverty are praiseworthy. This is only the case when poverty represents a free choice according to the gospel commandment. There are many who are poor in terms of what they possess but are very miserly in spirit. And those people will not be saved through their poverty but rather may be damned because of their attitude of mind. So clearly, not every poor person is worthy of praise (Lk 6:20), but only those who by free choice put the Lord's commandments ahead of all the treasures of this world. These are the people the Lord speaks about when he says "Blessed are the poor in spirit" (Mt 5:3). He does not say "poor in possessions," but refers to those who have freely chosen poverty in spirit. What is involuntary cannot merit blessedness. Every virtue has to be a free choice, and this applies to poverty in spirit most particularly. The same argument applies in Christ's case also. In his own nature he is rich (Jn 1:16), and everything that the Father has is his (Jn 16:15). Even so, "For your sake he became poor so that by his poverty you might become rich" (2 Cor 8:9). The Lord himself has first experienced everything that can lead us to blessedness. So he offers himself as an example to his disciples. Consider the Beatitudes (Mt 5:2-12), analyze them stanza by stanza, and then you will realize that the theoretical teaching they contain is drawn directly from practical experience.[30]

### *Basil the Great,* Commentary on Psalms 14.

St. Basil, in this following excerpt, gives us a window on the sharp practices of the bankers of his day when he gives his Christian congregation a warning never to fall into the clutches of moneylenders who charge interest on loans:

---

[30]PG 31.561.

The miser sees a man kneeling in front of him, begging him for money, resigning himself to any humiliating act, prepared to make any argument at all. The miser is without pity for the wretched supplicant. He is unbending in his refusal to help. . . . He is not moved at all by the man's tears. He simply repeats that he does not have any money at all and that even he needs to look to someone else to lend him money. He even will swear to this by an oath. But once the petitioner mentions interest and collateral pledges: ah, then at once the miser's eyebrows go up and he smiles. He then remembers the friendship that once linked their parents. He starts looking on the man as one of his own family, someone who ought to be treated as a friend. He says: "Let us see if I by chance have a little money here. Yes, I do have some money that belongs to another friend. He loaned it to me for a little affair. Sadly, he is asking a very high rate of interest on it. But for you I will make a discount. I will make you a loan at a lesser rate." These are the lies with which he will trap the unfortunate beggar, who then is immediately chained into a contract and will never stop being pestered from that point on. This is how the beggar was freed from distress only to be enslaved. Anyone who agrees to pay interest becomes a slave for the rest of his life. . . . Dogs will be satisfied if you throw them a bone, but a moneylender will become even more fierce when you pay him back his money. He will keep on growling and demanding ever higher rates of interest. He will search out all that you have at home and poke into all your business affairs. If you try to leave your house, he will drag you by force to his office. If you try to hide at home, he will stand at your door, banging on the knocker. . . . Do you think you should try for a deferment? Do you think this will help you? Poverty is like a galloping horse. It catches up with you soon enough and begins to chase you once again, and soon enough you will find yourself in trouble once more, except this time you are even more in debt than before. A loan does not remove poverty; it only postpones it. Since this is the case, put up with the hardships of poverty today and do not defer them until tomorrow. If you do not ask for the moneylender's help today when you are poor, tomorrow you will be equally poor, but certainly no more poor. But if you ask for the moneylender's help tomorrow, then you most certainly will be worse off than today, because the interest charges will deepen your poverty. Today no one will blame you for being poor. It is a misfortune and not your fault. But tomorrow, if you become a slave of the moneylender, everyone will accuse you of being stupid to subject yourself to interest payments.[31]

---

[31] PG 31.265, 269.

### St. Basil the Great, Commentary on Psalms 14.

> Bishop Basil had some caustic things to say to the moneylenders whose usury had brought misery to many of his congregation. But he starts off by "talking their language" and advocating a reform in banking practice in the town:

If you help a poor person in the name of the Lord, you are making a gift and at the same time granting loan. You make a gift because you have no expectation of being reimbursed by that poor person. You grant a loan because the Lord himself will settle that account.... "Those who are kind to the poor lend to the Lord" (Prov 19:17). Would you not like to have the Lord of all on your side? ... So make a present of what money you have to spare without asking for interest. It will benefit you and others. It will benefit you because you will have made your money safe. It will benefit others insofar as they are able to put it to work. If you are still looking for some profit, be content with that which the Lord will give to you.... The profit that you will gain from the poor surpasses all bounds of cruelty. You make your profit out of wretchedness. You squeeze your money out of tears. You persecute a defenseless being. You hound a starving man. You may think the profit you make out of the poor is just, but Scripture says: "Woe to those who put bitter for sweet and sweet for bitter" (Is 5:20). Are grapes gathered from thorns, or figs from thistles? (Mt 7:16) Can kind relations be gathered from usury?[32]

### St. Basil the Great, Epistle 236.7, To Amphilochius.

> In this passage from a letter of advice he wrote to the younger bishop Amphilochius, he sets a standard course of patristic Christian theology: riches are neutral in themselves. Their moral significance derives from the use to which they are applied. The attitude to wealth reveals a person's moral standing. The truly good person approaches wealth as a matter of distributive justice. Such an attitude can tame the possessiveness by which wealth often ensnares the unwary:

Last, we come to your inquiry as to what manner things that are neutral and indifferent are ordained for us, whether by some random chance at play, or by the righteous providence of God. And my answer is this: health and sickness, riches and poverty, honor and shame, insofar as they do not render their possessors good, are not in the category of things that can be described as naturally good, but, insofar as they make life's current flow more easily, in each case the former quality is to be preferred to its contrary and has a

---
[32]PG 31.277.

certain kind of value. To some men these things are given by God for stewardship's sake, as for instance to Abraham, to Job, and such like. To lesser souls they are a challenge to improvement. For a man who persists in unrighteousness, even after so many kind tokens of love from God, they subject him to inexcusable condemnation. But a really good man will not turn his heart to wealth when he has it, nor will he seek after it if he does not possess it. He will treat what is given him as given not for his selfish enjoyment but rather for wise administration. No one in his right senses runs after the trouble of distributing other people's property, at least, not unless he is trying to court the praises of the world, which admires and envies anyone in authority.

### St. John Chrysostom, On the First Letter to the Corinthians 21.5.

> St. John Chrysostom (c. 345–407), a renowned archbishop of Constantinople, reflects the social needs of the poorer classes of Christians in his cathedral sermons with numerous exhortations to them to be more liberal with their philanthropy. His reiterated calls for greater social justice in a capital clearly marked by great social divisions and disparity of income eventually alienated the upper classes and imperial family, who sent him into exile. In this sermon he preempts the objections of the wealthy person to giving "street charity" to unreliable beggars and does it in this robust way:

Is it not folly, sheer madness, to fill our wardrobes full of clothes, but to regard with indifference a human being, made in the image and likeness of God, who stands naked, trembling with cold, hardly able to stay upright? You may reply: "But that fellow there is only pretending to shake, and be feeble." But even so, what does that matter? If that poor man is putting on an act, it is only because he is trapped between his own wretchedness and your cruelty. Yes! For you are cruel and guilty of inhumanity. If he hadn't indulged in this playacting, you would not have opened your heart to his destitution, would you? If he was not driven by necessity, why would he behave in this humiliating manner, simply to get a piece of bread? His made-up tales are evidence of your hardness of heart. His begging prayers, his laments, his tears, his wandering around the city all day long: all of it hardly secured for him the barest pittance to live on. The shame and blame for his masquerade falls less on him than on you. He has a right to be pitied for falling into such an abyss of destitution. You, however, deserve a thousand punishments for having reduced him to such humiliation.[33]

---

[33] PG 61.177.

### *Augustine of Hippo,* Sermon 14.7-8.

> The great Latin theologian St. Augustine of Hippo (354–430) also approaches poverty as a moral choice of the individual believer, but he also stresses the evangelical warnings about the soporific nature of possessions, how they can smother the zeal for God and love for the neighbor in a believer's spirit. He holds up the example of Christ's personal life in this lyrical sermon he offered to his congregation of workers in a Roman port town in North Africa:

Lord, when I came into this world I did not bring anything with me, and when I leave it I shall not take anything out. So as long as I have something to eat and some clothes to wear, I am happy. You see, if you long to become rich, you fall into temptation, into foolish desires that will carry you away and lead toward death. The root of all evil is covetousness (1 Tim 6:10). How many who have coveted wealth have turned aside from the faith, and found only affliction. As for me, I will find you [my Christ], you, the truly poor one. Because although you were rich, for my sake you became poor. Who could possibly have an accurate conception of how rich you are? Likewise, who could ever comprehend your poverty? What poverty was the poverty of my Lord! Conceived in a Virgin's womb, you were locked in the body of your mother. What poverty! You were born in a tiny room, where they wrapped you in swaddling clothes and laid you in a manger. And then the king of heaven and earth, the creator and maker of all things visible and invisible, drinks, eats, cries, grows up, reveals his age, and hides his majesty. Eventually he is arrested, flogged, mocked, spat on, slapped in the face, crowned with thorns, nailed to a cross, pierced by a lance. What poverty! Lord, whenever I meditate on your poverty, all the things I look at afterwards lose their attraction for me. Give me instead something eternal. Grant me a taste of eternity.[34]

### *Sicilianus Anonymous,* On Riches.

> Augustine, however, was seen by some Christians in the surrounding African countryside (who have come to be known as Donatists) as too cozy with the colonial Roman establishment. His thought has often been used in later times to justify social divisions as "necessary accommodations" for the sake of social stability. Christian country dwellers in ancient times were often in a different and much poorer position than urban Christians. Many lived and worked on large farms or plantations (*latifundia*), where numerous slaves were still used to do the heavy labor for the benefit of wealthy (and regularly absentee) landowners. From fifth-century

---

[34]PL 38.115.

Sicily, a province where such agricultural practices impoverished the locals for the benefit of elite landlords, we find a (relatively rare) sharply caustic voice of a dissident Christian writer railing against the predations of the rich:

> Get rid of the rich, and you will find no poor. Let no-one have more than is necessary, and everyone will have as much as is needful. For the few rich are the cause of the many poor.[35]

### *Philoxenus of Mabbug,* Homily 9.338-40.

The fifth-century writer Bishop Philoxenus (440–523) of the Syrian town of Mabbug was an important author whose works, both because they were composed in Syriac and because he belonged to the anti-Chalcedonian movement, were sidelined in the later church. His life and writings are now coming under reconsideration, and his importance as a theologian and spiritual writers is being more widely acknowledged. In this homily he is tackling one of the hard sayings of Jesus: to what extent did the Lord's command to sell all and give it to the poor actually impact the day-to-day lives of a fifth-century church congregation?

The following text is part of a sermon he is giving to a wide range of townspeople (not just monastics). In his argument he plays on the notions of natural and normal, compared to unnatural and abnormal, and calls back the tradition of Christian poverty out of the rut it had already fallen into (namely, that monastics ought to be the "new martyrs" and offer the witness of poverty and chastity as representatives of his the church can fulfill the commands of Jesus). He insists that such a martyrdom (the word originally means "witness") is a major part of the core human tradition, and is a testimony that all Christians ought to emulate. He does not specify how; only that a Christian of any condition ought not to conclude that such radical seeming commandments "do not apply" to them. In Philoxenus's view the possession of anything more than our own bodies is a temporary and accidental condition. It is a philosophy that echoes Jesus' own detachment and undercuts any view that sees possessions and wealth as an absolute "right."

It might strike you as an extraordinary thing to do: to sell all you have and give the proceeds to the poor (Lk 18:22), but actually it is a natural action. It is like going back to the creation, back to our own birth. When Job lost all his possessions, he did not think that what had happened to him was anything abnormal. He calmed his sorrows by saying to himself: "Naked I came from my mother's womb; and naked shall I return" (Job 1:21). This was as if he had concluded: "All that has happened to me is that I find myself once more as I was when I was born." You see, it is a natural thing for human beings to be deprived

---

[35]Cited in A. Caspari, ed., *Anonymi Scriptores Pelagiani* (Brussels: Brepols, 1964), 48.

of everything, and end up with nothing other than their own bodies. But if a person does this by free choice, out of love for God, then it becomes far greater than a merely natural thing. It becomes like death: and to die for God is martyrdom. When Adam and Eve were created they did not possess anything. Not only had they no wealth, they did not even have any clothes. They were like an infant that comes naked from its mother's womb. They were in that same position Job describes. They were as Paul describes: "We brought nothing into the world, and we cannot take anything out of the world" (1 Tim 6:7). So let us look at our beginning and our end, and strive to be like that also during the time we have between.[36]

## FURTHER READING

Avila, C. *Ownership: Early Christian Teaching.* Maryknoll, NY: Orbis, 1983.

Batson, D. *The Treasure Chest of the Early Christians.* Grand Rapids: Eerdmans, 2001.

Christophe, P. *L'Usage chrétien du droit de propriété dans l'écriture et la tradition patristique.* Théologie, Pastorale et Spiritualité 14. Paris: P. Lethielleux, imprimerie, 1964.

Constantelos, D. *Byzantine Philanthropy and Social Welfare.* New Brunswick, NJ: Rutgers University Press, 1968.

De Ste Croix, G. E. M. *The Class Struggle in the Ancient Greek World.* London: Duckworth, 1976.

Giordani, I. *The Social Message of the Early Church Fathers.* Paterson, NJ: St. Anthony Guild Press, 1944.

Hamman, A., and M. Rostovtzeff, eds. *The Social and Economic History of the Roman Empire.* 2nd ed. Oxford: Oxford University Press, 1957.

Hengel, M. *Earliest Christianity.* London: SCM Press, 1986.

Holman, S. R. *The Hungry Are Dying: Beggars and Bishops in Roman Cappadocia.* Oxford: Oxford University Press, 2001.

———, ed. *Wealth and Poverty in Early Church and Society.* Grand Rapids: Baker Academic, 2008.

Lallemand, L. *Histoire de la charité.* Librairie de la Société Bibliographique. Paris: Picard et Fils, 1876.

Mara, M. G. "Poor—Poverty." In *Encyclopedia of the Early Church*, ed. A. Di Berardino, 2:703. Cambridge: Clarke, 1992.

McGuckin, J. A. "Embodying the New Society: The Byzantine Christian Instinct of Philanthropy." In *Philanthropy and Social Compassion in Eastern Orthodox Tradition*, ed. M. Pereira, 50-71. Papers of the Sophia Institute Academic Conference, December 2009. New York: Theotokos Press, 2010.

———. *St. Gregory of Nazianzus: An Intellectual Biography.* Crestwood, NY: St. Vladimir's Seminary Press, 2001, esp. 145-55, 205-11.

---

[36]SC 44.301-2.

———. "The Vine and the Elm Tree: The Patristic Interpretation of Jesus' Teaching on Wealth." In *The Church and Wealth*, ed. W. J. Sheils and D. Wood, 1-14. Studies in Church History 24. Oxford: Blackwell, 1987.

Miller, T. S. *The Birth of the Hospital in the Byzantine Empire*. Baltimore: Johns Hopkins University Press, 1985.

Mullin, R. *The Wealth of Christians*. Exeter, UK: Paternoster, 1983.

Pereira, M., ed. *Philanthropy and Social Compassion in Eastern Orthodox Tradition*. Sophia Institute Papers. New York: Theotokos Press, 2010.

Phan, P. *Social Thought*. The Message of the Fathers of the Church 20. Wilmington, DE: Michael Glazier, 1984.

Queré-Jaulmes, F. *Riches et pauvres dans l'Église ancienne*. Paris: Grasset, 1962.

Ramsay, B. "Christian Attitudes to Poverty and Wealth." In *Early Christianity: Origins and Evolution to 600*, ed. I. Hazlett, London: SPCK, 1991.

Santa Ana, J. de. *Good News to the Poor: The Challenge of the Poor in the History of the Church*. Maryknoll, NY: Orbis, 1979.

Schroeder, C. P., trans. *St. Basil the Great: On Social Justice*. Crestwood, NY: St. Vladimir's Seminary Press, 2009.

Sheather, M. "Pronouncements of the Cappadocians on Issues of Poverty and Wealth." In *Prayer and Spirituality in the Early Church*, ed. P. Allen, 375-92. Queensland: Australian Catholic University Press, 1998.

Shewring, W. *Rich and Poor in Christian Tradition*. London: Burns, Oates & Washbourne, 1948.

Uhlhorn, G. *Christian Charity in the Ancient Church*. New York: Scribner, 1883.

Veyne, P. *A History of Private Life*. Vol. 1, *From Pagan Rome to Byzantium*. Cambridge, MA: Belknap Press, 1992.

Vinne, M. J. de. "The Advocacy of Empty Bellies: Episcopal Representations of the Poor in the Late Empire." PhD diss., Stanford University, 1995.

Wilkins, J., D. Harvey, and M. Dobson, eds. *Food in Antiquity*. Exeter, UK: University of Exeter Press, 1995.

Winter, B. W. *Seek the Welfare of the City: Christians as Benefactors and Citizens*. Grand Rapids: Eerdmans, 1994.

# CHURCH AND SLAVERY IN AN AGE OF OPPRESSION

## SLAVERY IN ANCIENT SOCIAL STRUCTURES

The attitude of the early church to slavery in the late imperial era is an interesting test case in ancient Christian ethics, as well as being a large window onto the way ancient daily life was affected by Christian philosophy. Did Christianity, for example, so often presented as a liberative religion in its internal mindset, actually do much to ameliorate the often-wretched condition of the poorest classes in the world in which it emerged? Today we are perhaps more attuned to such a "live" question as this because of the impact in the twentieth century of liberation theology, which has questioned the (prevalent) rhetoric of Christian liberationism by testing it against its impact in social actuality. Black theology has also shown a large gap between the rhetoric of Christian equality and brotherhood, and the ongoing reality of racism in the lives of the modern-era churches. Such a live question is one that can often penetrate the generic rhetoric of theologians, moderns as well as ancients, who might be "looking the other way" too much.

Many of the leading bishops of the early church were themselves slave owners, a fact they would not be likely to celebrate in their church homilies, a fact they might not have spent too much time reflecting on as being all that morally significant, as in their worldview it might have been accepted as a commonplace that radical social divisions such as those between wealthy and poor, or between free and servile, were part of the "human order" established by God. Rhetoric (and that means largely all texts that we have to consider from the early church) celebrated the worldview of the elite, educated, wealthy upper classes. But what was it like down at the bottom? Where can we find accounts, evidences, of the life of the poorest of the Christians? Did Christianity actually help the poor, the enslaved, the wretched, or not?

Before we develop on this theme, it might also give us pause to realize that more than ever before, our own generation needs to be alive to such questions. Our own much-vaunted age of personal freedoms that has certainly led us to be more aware than scholars perhaps were before of iniquitous social conditions prevailing in the early ages that were often masked by rhetorical constructs—this age is itself an age that (after a relatively short hiatus) has reinvented slavery in radically new ways. It has been recently estimated that in this globally wired and justice-seeking new world, there are currently between 10 and 13 million people on the planet living in conditions that can only be described as slavery: a slavery real, not metaphorical, and deliberately fostered (as it was in the past) precisely because it makes money quickly. There are possibly (given the vast population expansion compared to ancient times) more slaves alive today than ever before in human history. Child brothels and tied-labor brick kilns, farms and carpet factories in rural outposts, put a prize on the bodies of the young; and the slavers, who are richer than Croesus, are more than careful to ensure the work remains always in the shadows, where the sexually and economically entrapped will not upset the consciences of the far-off rich buyers by being brought out into the light of day. Even today, as it was in antiquity, the slave (generally speaking) is either invisible in the sheds of the country plantation, or quiet and silent, occupying the side alleys where the fortunate would never dream of walking. House slaves always had a better deal and were often more educated, but the image of ancient slaves as theoretically being able to earn their own *peculium* (private income) and work their way up the social ladder to freedom and wealth was and is mainly fantasy.

Slavery existed in ancient times as a vast institutional and economic underpinning of the late Roman Empire. Both as a personal reality and as an economic and political way of organizing whole societies, slavery was common in most ancient societies. It is not simply a "pagan" reality, Earlier church historians have often attempted to regard it as a "pagan" phenomenon, which Christianity first softened and then abolished as soon as it could: pagan in the sense of it being rooted in reductionist views of the value of human beings and antagonistic to the Christian anthropological sense of the eternal and coequal status of the human family under the eyes of God. Slavery is thus laid to the door of a venal Greco-Roman reality in contrast to the "more just" biblical and early Christian conception of how society "ought to be." The evidence, unfortunately, does not really support such a self-congratulatory account. Christianity's record in regard to slavery seems to have been a confused half-rejection of Greco-Roman principles behind the institution of slavery, and a sense of compromise with economic and social "realities" seems to have overcome their earlier, more eschatological instincts.

If the early church looked to the Old Testament for authoritative guidance, of course, it found there too that the institution of slavery was legislated for, and thus, to an extent, vindicated as part of a divinely appointed Israel. This was to be a lamentable theological argument that was to be used in early modern societies onward to relaunch the practice of slavery and bring it with an exceptionally new form of bitterness into the New World. In the Old Testament, as was the case with the later Roman Empire, slavery grew out of war conquest, part of the ancient unwritten and also legal codes that presumed a people conquered in hostilities and spared should belong to their captors as lifelong servants and chattels. Israelite law was more attuned, it is true to say, to the scandal of enslaving Israelites and introduced limitations to the notion of lifelong servitude (the so-called system of jubilee, or amnesty in the seventh year; Ex 21:2; Lev 25:39-40), and Deuteronomy's legislation allows the early Israelite cities to become more or less zones of safety for slaves who have run away from their enslavement in the surrounding nations (Deut 23:15-16); but it cannot be said that slavery, as such, was not part of the biblical mindset and just as commodifying of human labor as anything we find in Greco-Roman antiquity (Ex 21:20-21).[1]

Roman imperial society was such a vast war machine that there never was a chance of slave stock being exhausted. Slaves in the Roman system bred slaves. If ever numbers threatened to drop, there were more than enough wars to supply new populations. From a root in limited regional tribal wars, however (as are imagined in all the relevant Old Testament literature and that applied to most ancient societies), slavery in the time of the late Roman Empire had become something entirely different. It had been reinvented on a hitherto unimaginably massive scale. The Roman Empire, and the extensive civilizations that grew in and out of it, could not have existed on any other economic basis. Accordingly, any political, philosophical, or religious system that advocated a wholesale abolition of slavery would be regarded as anarchistic.

Even if early Christianity could have imagined the abolition of slavery on the basis of its new philosophy of inestimable individual worth, it could not explain how it could bring this mysterious reality about. For such reasons it rarely did imagine such a thing and took centuries before it could advocate it as a "good idea"; and meanwhile, even in its foundational scriptural sources (the New Testament Pastoral Letters), it generally commended patience and long-suffering to the enslaved, and lauded their obedience as a virtue that aided in stabilizing society. When the slavers of the early modern New World took as their basic library the writings of the Greek and Roman philosophers, the Old Testament now considered as of equal authority to the New, and the New Testament texts advocating slave passivity—a heady and

---

[1]The worth of a slave was thirty shekels of silver (Ex 21:32).

somewhat poisonous cocktail was ready for the brew, resulting in some of the worst realizations of slavery ever known.[2]

Slavery, therefore, was a base "presumption" of almost all ancient developed societies. Even so, Christianity in its early period was forced to deal afresh with the moral questions raised by the issue of enslavement. Many aspects of the proto-Christian preaching of the kingdom of God, envisaged as a time of equality and justice when God had no favoritism other than on the basis of the quality of a person's righteousness and depth of faith, simply flew in the face of the acceptance of such a system of radical inequality and violent oppression that was fundamental to the continuance of slavery. What is more, many of the first adherents of the Christian movement in the larger cities and towns of its first diaspora were themselves slaves or freed slaves and had little romantic attachment to the status quo in that sense, whatever their leaders had commended to them as the virtuous life of silent suffering. Any Christians who had directly experienced the condition of slavery knew that the life of the slave in a rural factory farm was little more than a bestial condition of unimaginable harshness.

What small evidence we have concerning Christian bishops denouncing slavery wholesale tends to come from the rural regions, where bishops themselves were of more modest backgrounds and probably knew their laity's conditions at close and uncomfortable quarters—in the role of chaplains on the later plantations (*latifundia*), though with this difference to later clergy (say of the eighteenth-century New World) that the ancient rural bishops also served as ecclesiastical and civil-law magistrates whose courts were open to the appeals of slaves against such things as often went unnoticed in the real civil courts administered by wealthy secular magistrates in the cities—things that mattered in an episcopal court, such as sexual exploitation. The rural bishops, therefore, had more of the ear of the suffering slaves and were more vested in ensuring that all Christians, rich or poor, held to similar moral standards.

---

[2]Leaving aside the issue that such people of this age and state of developed civilization "ought to have known better," they practiced the breaking up of families of slaves in ways that even the ancient world would have considered cruel and that the canons of the early church had long since banned as immoral. In the early modern era, when Charles V ordered a great debate at Valladolid in 1550 to settle the moral question of whether Spain could attack the Indians and enslave them in advance of preaching the gospel, leading disputants Juan Gines de Sepulveda and Fra. Bartolomé de las Casas both took as their starting point the Aristotelian doctrine of the "natural condition of slavery" of some people. Cf. L. Hanke, *Aristotle and the American Indians* (London: Hollis & Carter, 1959). Plato and Aristotle set the tone for the Greeks in arguing that *barbaroi* (crude foreigners) were generally speaking "slavish by nature." On the other hand, a person superior in intellect and character could never be a slave, even if in a condition of enslavement (Aristotle, *Politica* I.6, 1255$^a$25-26. St. Paul uses the latter argument (as did the Stoics before him) to suggest words of encouragement to the slaves in his Christian audience; but like the Stoics before him, this was often done to pacify their discontent rather than seek any social amelioration.

All this was well enough if the bishop himself was not a slave-owning landowner: but several of them were. So although this recourse to the bishop as "friend of the poor" (*philoptochos*) was theoretically possible and was a noted factor in the fourth-century rise to prominence of episcopal courts of appeal and the concomitant rise to civil authoritativeness of ecclesiastical canons, even so it remained in later times as always an appeal of the unrepresented, the voiceless, and the poor for the justice and mercy of the represented, the powerful and the rich.

Though little was said about it openly (something true for antiquity as well as later times), slavery in the ancient domestic setting also customarily masked a massive amount of sexual exploitation on the part of the masters, which the church feebly (but nevertheless still) opposed in its liturgical rules. The New Testament literature shows considerable tension in regard to the issue of slavery: never quite feeling confident enough to come out and denounce it explicitly, since to do so would have been tantamount to a declaration of social revolution and would have involved a death penalty for those fomenting such a change as well as for those attempting to put it into effect, presumably by fleeing from their masters with little real hope of escape. The concept of flight was not a real incentive. Those who fled the harsh condition of the plantations would face flogging and even worse treatment than before when recaptured (as they usually were, since there were no free zones of hiding in the empire), and those who rebelled in a domestic, urban situation faced the ever-present threat of demotion to the rural slave farms or even punishment in the salt mines and quarries, where workers were sent to be worked to death. There were thus numerous invisible fetters on both bodies and minds. Real chains were rarely necessary.

If slavery is not simply a Greco-Roman phenomenon, however, it also has to be said that no people in previous history had ever extended the system of slavery as much as the Romans did in their extensive empire. As we have noted, it all began out of the vastly expanded slave market following increasingly global Roman military conquests. The vanquished were given choice of surrender with enslavement or death. The ritual of enslavement was the much-feared "passing under the yoke": prisoners were lined up and made to walk under an ox yoke (*sub iugum*) as a symbol that their lives were henceforward spared only for the (agricultural) service of their victor-masters, like beasts of the field, without honor or rights. Slaves produced children, thereafter, who were themselves "legally" born into slavery.

The law enshrined this system of commodification of conquered people, and in due course the peculiarities of postwar exactions entered into the mainstream of Roman society. The sight of the mark of the common household slave (the broad leather belt) was a most common one in all Roman cities. One notes, for example, in Pompeii, that so many of the "body casts" of the dead were men and women wearing the broad belt. Contrary to supposition in the past, the people of Pompeii were not caught unawares by the eruption of Vesuvius; the ones who died there were chiefly those who had been ordered to stay behind to protect their master's property, namely, the slaves of the rich villa owners.

The Roman comic writer Plautus gives the modern reader a bird's-eye view into ancient city society in Roman times. In the course of his plays, we find listed in his cast of characters the following categories of slaves: grooms, stewards, fowlers, jewelry attendants, plowmen, footmen, singers, dancers, storekeepers, wardrobe masters, cooks, messengers and secretaries, poultry keepers, chain-gang laborers, market gardeners, doorkeepers, reapers, baby nurses and child minders, obstetricians, shepherds, children's guardians and tutors, attendant bodyguards, pageboys and pagegirls, fieldworkers, hairdressers, and masseurs. Hardly any aspect of life was not represented by slaves. Most kitchen and tavern staff in the ancient world also doubled as sexual surrogates.

Politician, elite ruler, and army warrior were (obviously) not part of the slave class's tasks or potential professions, though these did provide ways out of slavery for a very few educated and talented elite, whom we often meet in their later life as freedmen of powerful families. The slaves of the rich families were expected to reflect the wealth of the *familia* (clan) they served and were often much better educated and considerably richer in terms of personal finances than the free poor of Rome, who always eked out a tenuous existence. The latter, of course, might still have one or more domestic slaves themselves. Slaves of the working class, and especially those who labored in the fields, were regarded as "the worst of all social types" in general estimation. Their life must have been, as Hobbes later phrased it, "Nasty, brutish, and short." As the slave population of Rome increased, the free poor were unable to compete with them in securing jobs, and the later empire saw increasingly large numbers of the free poor reduced to a dire quality of life subsisting on the state dole of bread for citizens, whereas slaves of moderately rich city families could enjoy more stability and affluence, even to the point of saving disposable income and buying their own freedoms.

A freedman is a regular aspect of the Roman literature of the early Christian age; and here the figure of the newly socially ascendant exslave was treated as a stock figure of fun in the satiric literature, often contrasted with the poor free scholar who has to depend on the comparatively crass family of the nouveau riche. But again, this is how the view appears from the perspective of the literary class, who must have felt uncomfortably close (by virtue of their genteel shabbiness) to the much-feared fate of the poorer classes, from whom they so desperately wanted to distance themselves. Then as now, riches soon enough leveled out issues of rank.[3]

Slaves in Rome could retain personal property in some cases, especially the educated slaves who ran the business of their masters and mistresses. Rich slaves might eventually buy back their freedom or could be freed (manumitted) in the wills of their late owners. There is some indication in the episcopal city literature that Christian families were encouraged to manumit slaves, and the church certainly offered its services (after Constantine allowed bishops to exercise some magisterial functions) to make the manumission process simple enough to be attractive. In 321 and again in 325, Constantine legislated that slave manumissions performed by clergy in a church were as legally binding as those performed in the secular magistrates' courts.[4] Writers such as John Chrysostom, the bishop of the Eastern capital at Constantinople in the fifth century, were strong rhetorical advocates for the poor and for better treatment among Christians of slaves.

But in all the extant works of the early Christian bishops it is only fourth century bishop-theologian Gregory of Nyssa whom comes out explicitly to say that slavery is a moral offense in the church. His *Homily on Ecclesiastes*, where he makes this arguent, is excerpted in the reader following. Gregory's mentors, Bishop Eustathius of Sebaste and his own sister Macrina, might have been factors in leading him to this position. They were, in their own turn, significant innovators of an ascetic lifestyle in Cappadocia (later to be folded into the church's history of monasticism), which put a premium on communities of simple living that renounced degrees of rank and privilege. Eustathius's teaching on this subject alarmed the local bishops of the region where he preached the new way of life so much that they issued a set of synodical instructions (the Synod of Gangra) deploring the social unrest such radical views would cause.[5] In particular the synodical letter condemned the manner in which slaves were welcomed into this movement and given "new clothing," and the legislative third canon of the synod precisely condemns the practice of those Christian ascetics with Eustathius of encouraging slaves to consider themselves free (which means they must have offered a means of liberative escape).[6]

---

[3] As Ovid gnomically expressed it, *dat census honores*, "It is property that confers rank." *Amores* 3.8.55.
[4] *Codex Theodosianus* 1.27.1 (episcopal tribunals), and 4.7.1 (*Address to Bishop Hosius*).
[5] Held in Asia Minor in 340.
[6] "These people were found to be stirring up separations from the houses of God and the church, treating the church and its members with disdain, and establishing separate meetings and assemblies, with different doctrines and other things contrary to the churches and the customs of the church; such as wearing strange clothing, abolishing common customs of dress; making distributions, among themselves and their adherents as saints, of the firstfruits of the church, which have from earliest times been given to the church; and slaves leaving their masters, who, because of their own strange apparel, began acting insolently toward their masters." *Letter of the*

In many cases slave families were held together as part of the Roman extended family system (unlike the very harsh practice of early modern American slavery, where slave families were often deliberately split apart to prevent bonds of association forming). Slaves were so extensive and pervasive a part of Roman society that very few thinkers, Christian or otherwise, ever questioned the institution. It is an estimate, but possibly up to 50 percent of the Roman imperial population in early Christian times might have been in the slave category. For society to have survived and run on a regular course must have involved a very large amount of "taking slavery for granted" among all classes, not least the slaves themselves.

Some notable exceptions to this "nonquestioning" of the institution of slavery, of course, can be provided by the very dramatic slave revolts (such as that of the gladiator Spartacus, who eventually led an army against Rome). A revolt might not be a considered philosophical treatise, but it gets its point across clearly enough.[7] The (generally misleading) supposition that life could be fairly comfortable as a Roman villa slave (though in some cases it could) primarily reflects the conditions of an urban family of moderate to great wealth who kept slaves. These villa slaves could number in the hundreds. At the top end of the social scale, the Emperor Nero had four hundred personal slaves in his imperial household, for example.

The general reality of slave life, however, namely that many, if not most, Roman slaves were used in factory labor and in heavy labor-intensive farming rather than in "domestic service," must have been unquestionably harsher and more cruel a reality than if we were to take our snapshot on slavery solely against the backdrop of urban city life. It is the latter scenario that is most commonly reflected in the Latin literature of the stage, where slaves appear in the texts of the leisured classes. They are the stage paraphernalia, often the buffoon or the butt of the action: a prefiguration, perhaps, of the manner in which African Americans appeared on Hollywood's celluloid "stage" through most of the first half of the twentieth century.

---

*Synod of Gangra*. The "strange apparel" was an early form of monastic habit worn by both males and female followers. It was meant to signify that in the ascetical Christian life there was no longer any place for distinction between male and female, slave or free (cf. 1 Cor 12:12-13; Gal 3:28). The bishops clearly wish to protect "customary" practice of secure ecclesiastical incomes (protected from the likes of these wandering ascetics, who must have attracted popular support from local Christians supporting their mission), and they are genuinely alarmed at the disruption the ascetics have had on marital stability and slave owners. The extent to which the movement actually affected society on these matters remains obscure. In terms of the ancient rhetorical and legal complaints' process, it would only require a single case of a woman divorcing her husband to follow the ascetical life, or a single slave breaking free, to justify a complaint that the urban bishops of this area seem glad enough to have supported. Canon 3 reads, "If any one shall teach a slave, under pretext of piety, to despise his master and to run away from his service, and not to serve his own master with good will and all honor, let him be anathema."

[7]See K. R. Bradley, *Slavery and Society at Rome* (Cambridge: Cambridge University Press, 1994).

As we observed in the context of our earlier discussion on wealth, Greek and Roman philosophy conspired together to say that only free men could be "true men" (we note that slaves and women are on these terms by definition "defective in humanity"). The free man (an idea that emanated from ancient Greece in the first instance) had to prove his humanity by the capacity for reflection and philosophy. For this reason workers (children, slaves, women, and the free working poor) were regarded as defectively human because they did not have the leisure (*otium*) necessary to devote to thought. Slaves are primarily (philosophically speaking, that is) units of production, whereas philosophical types (littérateurs, the wealthy, the leisured thinking class) were elevated as the only true humanity. This was why there was next to no moral reflection on the plight of the poor in what was an extensive late imperial moral literature (for example, see the text cited in the reader below from Seneca) and why there was no real incentive throughout ancient society for leaders to better the lot of slaves.

When Christianity introduced to Greco-Roman society the notion of the equality of men and women under the eye of God, it was widely received as a ridiculous idea, contrary to common sense. This explains why the idea took so long (even among Christians) to take root in socioeconomic reality. We can lift up *Oration* 14 by St. Gregory of Nazianzus, *On the Love for the Poor*, written in the last quarter of the fourth century (by a millionaire landowning bishop) for a significant and historical moment, being the introduction of this agenda by Christian rhetoricians into the thought world of ancient Greek opinion. St. Gregory's sermon is the first time in recorded Greek thought that an argument was raised for valuing human beings solely on the infinite value they had in the eyes of God, and not on the relative value they had in the estimation of society.[8] In his oration he allied this notion with the (more generally accepted philosophical and Christian-endorsed) theory that no person could expect wealth and possessions as an absolute right. All possession was tentative, conditional, and related to the good use one made of it as temporary "steward." The two ideas juxtaposed effectively demolished the possibility of making a moral defense of the practice of slavery, but noticeably Gregory did not explicitly say this in as many words. Even so, such thought was indeed revolutionary.[9] In this instance, however, Gregory proposed it not in the cause of instigating a revolution in social mores, more

---

[8] The text of *Oration* 14 is discussed in J. A. McGuckin, *St. Gregory of Nazianzus: An Intellectual Biography* (Crestwood, NY: St. Vladimir's Seminary Press, 2001), 145-55; and also in S. Holman, *The Hungry Are Dying: Beggars and Bishops in Roman Cappadocia* (Oxford: Oxford University Press, 2001).

[9] Cicero asks, rhetorically, in his *De Officiis* (2.73, and see also 2.78, 83-85; 1.21), what greater malevolence could there be than to advocate an equal distribution of property (*aequatio bonorum . . . qua peste quae potest esse maior?*). His argument is, broadly, that states were primarily established, politically speaking, to defend individual property rights.

in the cause of soliciting funds from rich colleagues in order to aid his colleague Basil of Caesarea in building a leprosarium to alleviate the throngs of lepers who crushed in to the Cappadocian market towns on the festivals of the martyrs (also market days) seeking some very basic form of social assistance and growing restless at their more or less total dismissal by organized society of the time.

This instance of building a leprosarium is, of course, a continuance of the late Roman philanthropic tradition (the very rich demonstrating their preeminence by social works) Before (in the fourth century) Christian orator-theologians made the highly sacramental case that even the poor, the sick, and the slaves had to be recognized as "icons of God," it was widely presumed as a given that the sick, the wretched, and the poor were in this condition as part of their lot appointed by the gods—their karma, as it were. Interfering with that by misplaced philanthropy or social revolution would not be a moral act, therefore, but an act contrary to common sense, hostile to the will of the gods, who had appointed differing human destinies, and massively injurious to societal stability (the latter also seen as fixed by the will of the gods).

There were others among the Christians, however, who could see how the implications of a new anthropology—that all humans were of equal importance in the eyes of the divine—could revolutionize social ideas above and beyond the concept of philanthropic charity considered as a trickle-down welfare system. Gregory of Nazianzus's rhetoric student (and Basil's brother) the bishop Gregory of Nyssa was certainly one of those who reflected deeply on the concept, as we have already noted, and his empathy allied with a very sharp philosophical mind produced the first Christian sermon denouncing slavery as an unacceptable evil within the Christian church. Even so, the fourth century continued its way with a lot of wealthy Christian bishops still holding personal slaves and not thinking much about it.

Because of slavery's pervasive and extensive role as a "given" substructure of Roman society, it took Christians a long time to notice it properly and reflect on it in anything like serious moral and theological manner. At first a large proportion of the ranks of Christians were from the social classes of the slaves and the free poor. It is only in the second century onward that we start to notice the advent of rich people into the church—namely slave owners, since all rich people in the first three centuries (including early Christian bishops, though that fact will often not be stated) can be presumed to be slave owners.

## SCRIPTURAL APPROACHES TO SLAVERY

The first New Testament literature on the subject advocates a cautious line, found in Paul's letter to Philemon and 1 Peter 2:18-25, in which these church leaders are clearly worried that Christian slave converts might get the idea that, because they are equal in the eyes of God, that should be reason enough for them to be free in the eyes of the state. This earliest level of literature advocates "patience" and an obedience in society's eyes that will "commend" Christianity to the powers at large. It has to be remembered, of course, that this attitude is observed in the face of an overwhelming hostile social structure, which could easily (and did) crush Christian communities violently and mercilessly when it wished to do so. Any hint coming from the church in the first centuries that it was out to subvert the slave system would have been enough to earn it the relentless suppression of the state police system. Paul, who reads as dramatically libertarian in many respects and who uses the image of freedom from slavery regularly as a core metaphor for Christian life (Rom 6:22; 1 Cor 9:19), basically commands his converts who are slaves to "remain in that condition" in which they were first called, although he advises them to seek the opportunity to become free if it arises.[10] There is no overwhelming sense here that the church ought to resist this institution as an unbridled evil. But it is a curious addendum: to seek freedom, should the opportunity arise. Was it really a matter that servitude did not bear so heavily on members of Paul's urban congregations that they needed encouragement to seek freedom?

Writing to an audience of Christians, Paul, in Ephesians 6, actually commands slaves to obey their masters as if they would obey Christ, thus giving the state of servitude a religious value; albeit this is a position he takes, probably, as a consolation for those laboring under inescapable terms of bondage.[11] In this case it can be read as an encomium trying to help Christian slaves see how they might sanctify the conditions they could not otherwise avoid, rather than any endorsement of the present state of affairs. But even so: imagine the ramifications of being placed in a situation of systemic daily abuse in the context of belonging to a society of worship that demanded purity of conduct. When Paul commands the Christian slave to obedience, he also adds a warning to the masters to behave with humanity, as they are under the eye of God, who judges between them with impartiality, since both master and slave are servants of the same Lord.[12] The owners he addresses are, presumably, Christian ones. In his

---

[10] "Everyone should remain in the state in which he was called. Were you a slave when called? Never mind. But if you can gain your freedom, avail yourself of the opportunity. For he who was called in the Lord as a slave is a freedman of the Lord. Likewise, he who was free when called is a slave of Christ. You were bought with a price; do not become slaves of men. So, brethren, in whatever state each was called, there let him remain with God" (1 Cor 7:20-23).

[11] Jerome and Theodoret are two Christian writers who press this argument of the value of servitude literally, now (in the fifth century) devoid of its eschatological origin to justify the "religious duty" of a slave in the Christian imperium.

[12] "Slaves, be obedient to those who are your earthly masters, with fear and trembling, in singleness of heart, as to Christ; not in the way of eye-service, as men pleasers, but as servants of Christ, doing the will of God from the heart, rendering service with a good will as to the Lord and not to men,

letter to Philemon he strongly suggests to this Christian slave owner to manumit Onesimus, who has served as the intermediary messenger and has brought help to Paul. It might not be the stronger kind of message we would hope for, but it was a text that was canonized in the Scriptures precisely because of this witness to philanthropy (for the letter contains little else memorable), and the image of an apostle leaning toward the ending of the slave condition set a tone, if nothing else.

But there is a great caution throughout Paul's writings (occasional though they are) in being anything that appeared too radical. The apostle is dominated by two contexts that determine his attitude to the condition of slavery: the first that he was terrified of suggesting to the outside authorities that Christianity was courting revolutionary positions on the liberation of slaves. This comes out quite clearly in his advice to his younger colleague the missionary Timothy: "Let all who are under the yoke of slavery regard their masters as worthy of all honor, so that the name of God and the teaching may not be defamed" (1 Tim 6:1). And the second is that his laissez-faire attitude to more radical social change was undoubtedly conditioned by his belief that the eschaton was coming imminently. The sad condition of a slave would not endure long, in his telescoped vision of history. This is why in 1 Corinthians he places together the issues of single people getting married and the condition of being a slave: neither class is advised to undergo the trouble of changing status, given what he thinks is the short time remaining for secular society to run its course.

This first publicly expressed "policy" on Christian slaves needing to be "docile" and obedient (as in the Pauline letters, or the second-generation Christian authors Clement of Rome or Ignatius of Antioch) takes its cue from what is known as the late Roman household code. After the first great slave revolts, the secular, still pagan, Roman leaders knew that their system rested on a city-majority of slave power. The very thought of slave revolt terrified the Roman authorities at every age of the empire. Laws to punish slave disloyalty were immensely harsh (held over people's heads rather than being uniformly prosecuted); but if a slave assassinated a master in a house, the entire household of slaves was routinely put to death as complicit in the crime—and crucifixion was the slave's punishment: one of the most dreadful and widely feared forms of execution, still enforced up to the early fourth century.[13]

---

knowing that whatever good any one does, he will receive the same again from the Lord, whether he is a slave or free. Masters, do the same to them, and forbear threatening, knowing that he who is both their Master and yours is in heaven, and that there is no partiality with him" (Eph 6:5-9).

[13] In AD 61, Pedianus Secundus, the prefect of Rome, was murdered by one of his slaves. The senate held a debate as to whether in this case, according to tradition, all the household slaves of an assassinated master should be executed. The problem was acute since Pedianus held four hundred of them, the vast majority of whom were clearly innocent of all crime. The lawyer Gaius Cassius went on record then to say, "You cannot restrain this scum except by terror." Despite widespread

The literature of the apostolic fathers, coming immediately after the late New Testament texts, continues the same cautious support of the Roman household code. Basically it amounted to the admonition, "Slaves and wives, do not cause trouble, for heaven's sake!" together with encouragement that the Lord sympathized with them and called them to obedience just as he himself had been pressed into obedience. There is, however, also the injunction emanating from early Christian literature that masters must treat slaves well, with kindness and justice. It is presumed that abuses (as were well known to occur in pagan households), such as sexual domination and pimping, would (or at least should) not happen among Christians. The elements of mutual respect are slowly brought out in the Christian literature. Ignatius of Antioch's *Letter to Polycarp* 4.3 suggests there ought to be always a deep mutual respect between slave and master, but he also openly opines that the common treasury (of the local churches, I think he means) should never be used for manumitting slaves (only for more generic poor relief). Slaves, Ignatius thinks, "ought to endure slavery for the glory of God," here showing a deep reliance on Paul's arguments.[14]

It would not be for another three hundred years that we have an important church document advocating the opposite practice should be the case and suggesting that church funds in the larger cities, at least, could and should be used for the purposes of manumission.[15] This is a testimony in itself that slaveholding had drastically reduced in its social scope. It is, of course, difficult to judge from the occasional references in legislative documents just how widespread the practice of slave redemption was on the part of the church. It seems from episcopal synodical legislation in the West that church ownership of slaves continued there for much longer than it did in the East. Similar (conformist) ideas about the respect that has to be nurtured between owners and slaves in a Christian environment are found in the second-century writings of the Didache and in the Shepherd of Hermas, the latter written by a former slave who rose to hold high office in the Roman church, sponsored in that rise to prominence by his aristocratic (Christian) female owner.[16]

By the third century Clement of Alexandria writes that rich Christians ought to strive to reduce their holdings of slaves and to work to better the existence of

---

rioting from the common citizens of Rome, the execution of all the slaves was ordered and carried out. De Ste. Croix comments critically (G. De Ste. Croix, M. Whitby, and J. Streeter, *Christian Persecution, Martyrdom, and Orthodoxy* [Oxford: Oxford University Press, 2006], 346) that the statute remained on the books even in the time of the Christian emperor Justinian. He does not note that it could, and would, never have been implemented in his day.

[14] Ignatius of Antioch, *Letter to Polycarp* 4.3.
[15] Apostolic Constitutions, which emanates from fourth-century Constantinople.
[16] Didache 4.10; Shepherd of Hermas, Precepts 8.10 and Similitudes 1.8; 9.28.

those slaves they insist on retaining.[17] Cyprian of Carthage, a newly converted pagan aristocrat, writes as a newly elected bishop to Demetrian, a rich slave owner, at the end of the third century, giving substantially the same advice (*Ad Demetrianum* 8). Augustine, in a more provincial African town but with an eye to a broader philosophical horizon, recognized the slave master's property ownership rights but advocated kind treatment for slaves (*Exposition on the Letter to Galatians* 64). He was shocked, however, when dissident Donatist Christians of the North African country regions ("Circumcellion" gangs, whom he regarded as terrorist thugs, but who regarded him as a colonialist collaborator) started a policy of torching slave-owner plantations and forcibly liberating slaves. The Donatist country bishops, where the scandal of slave farm factories loomed as a major aspect of daily life, led the way for a call to finally end the practice of slavery in the Christian empire.

In his day, regarding the social disruption of these "dissidents" as schismatics, Augustine eventually advocated bringing in the state police to put down the Donatist movement by force of arms.[18] He is the first Christian theologian to advocate the "justification" of state control of Christian affairs. Keeping the peace was for him a higher goal than the liberation of slaves—even though in his office as magistrate bishop in the port city of Hippo Regius, he did, on more than one occasion, surreptitiously arrange for members of his church community to raid slave ships in the harbor and free their prisoners. What Augustine could not quite see his way to was the way to banning of the concept of slavery by law. His understanding was that slavery was a reflection of the depraved nature of the human race—always seeking to advance its own desires at the expense of others. Society was a compromise—not an ideal aspiration for the good, but a practical restraint of even greater evils.

When the Donatists tried to burn slave plantations to the ground, Augustine preferred to suppress them in the cause of preserving a "peaceful" state order. Augustine argued that slavery was a blot on society that was caused by man's depravity and tendency to sin and hardness of heart. He did not think it part of the natural or intended order of humanity (in other words, not part of the pure order of things), but he goes on, "Though not natural, [slavery] is nonetheless penal and is appointed by that law that enjoins the preservation of the natural order and forbids its

---

[17]Clement of Alexandria, *Miscellanies* 4.19.
[18]He famously applies the penultimate phrase of the parable of the rich man's feast (Lk 14:16-24), "Compel them to come in," as his theological justification for what he said was a reluctant conclusion in the face of violent recalcitrance.

disturbance."[19] In other words, it could be seen as a deserving punishment for sin and potentially instructive for the sinner caught in its web, and overall the desires of the slave for freedom did not outweigh the "superior law" of good order in society.

This was an attitude that was largely to be followed for many Christian centuries, and it certainly took the impetus out of any far-reaching social change spearheaded by the church. As one modern scholar observes,

> Relations between master and slave were as divinely ordained as those between husband and wife. [Slaves] were part of a natural order whose disturbance was forbidden. The Western Fathers were thus impervious to ideas of social change.[20] Radicalism henceforth would be linked to schism and heresy, and liable to religious as well as secular penalties. Even the epic martyrdoms now circulating in the West tended to emphasize the high birth and noble antecedents of the hero. Slaves such as Blandina, the heroine of Lyons, were no longer the subject of praise.[21]

Overall, by the fourth century there was clearly a growing awareness that slave trafficking and slaveholding was regarded with Christian disfavor. Yet even into the end of that century we find clergy and church institutions among those who are holding slaves. Gregory of Nazianzus, who writes (in *Oration* 14) a stirring defense for the rights of the poor and dispossessed, also mentions (almost in passing) in his will that he frees (manumits) several household slaves, of which otherwise we hear nothing in his voluminous works. He mentions, in passing, in a poem, that he specially loves his two household slaves: twins who are both called "Eupraxios" (the name means "good worker" or "handyman"). By this period church legislation insists that slaves and free ought to communicate together at worship as equals (a practice we presume was an ancient liturgical one). The papacy in the second century had (under Pope Callixtus, who was himself a freed slave) set out legislation (to the scandal of some other parts of the Christian world, notably the theologian Tertullian in Africa) that slaves could marry the freeborn in a legitimate church marriage (it was not at that stage a legally recognized marriage, but church law led the way to the changing of Roman law under the Christian emperors). Slave marriages were thus afforded the full status of church recognition, while in secular law they were regarded as *contubernium*, not *connubium* (a higher form of concubinage rather than a real marriage).

---

[19] Augustine, *City of God* 19.15.
[20] W. H. C. Frend (*The Rise of Christianity* [Philadelphia: Fortress, 1985], 570) notes here how with the exception of John Chrysostom, the Greek fathers were generally less impressed by the argument that sin was the cause of slavery and that thus to some extent the state of servitude was a deserved punishment. The more notable theme of the Greek fathers was that humanity, as image of the divine on earth, was created free and equal, the sovereign inhabitants of a world that God had created as "their royal dwelling place." Gregory of Nyssa, *On the Making of Man* (PG 44.132-33).
[21] Frend, *Rise of Christianity*, 570-71.

Elsewhere conciliar legislation by the bishops shows the peculiar weight social status still had over their views of what should, or should not, cause moral outrage. Canon 5 of the Council of Elvira (Granada in Spain) mooted (obviously from a real-world case that had come before it) that a slave mistress who had beaten a slave to death in a fit of uncontrolled rage ought to undergo seven years of excommunication from the Eucharist if the death had been premeditated, and that this should be reduced to a five-year sentence of excommunication if the death had been "accidental." No civil penalty is envisaged. This places beating a slave to death on the same moral scale, for these Spanish bishops, as first-offense adultery. It obviously mattered that the Christian woman was of a high class, and the slave was of "no class," according to their moral register (a legal factor of that day), though it has to be said that some of the rules that emanate from some of the early Spanish synods generally are odd in character: harsh beyond what one normally finds in synodical records of the same era elsewhere.

By admiring and admitting a system of spiritual hierarchies and values, as taking precedence over secular rank and status, the offices of the church were theoretically open to men of all classes. Pope Callixtus (a former slave and gravedigger who had risen to prominence in the church) and the author of the Shepherd of Hermas (probably a former Jewish temple priest and Christian brought to Rome as a slave captive after the Jewish war of AD 70) were among the highest leaders of the Christian communities of Rome who had risen in the church from the ranks of the poorest. There were many others who came from the lowest classes (though equally after the fourth century it was expected that the rich and politically connected would more normally provide the leadership candidates).

In the fourth century, the Council of Elvira, a local synod of Spanish bishops, brought the issue of slavery for the first time into the light of legislation among the Christians, making it an excommunicable offence for a slave master who was a Christian to inflict his (secular) legal right of the death penalty on any one of his slaves. The same tendency to move toward legal protection for slaves influenced the Christian revision of Roman law that occurred in the fourth-century *Codex Theodosianus*, which introduced several measures to alleviate the practical social conditions of slaves and to protect their independent moral rights.[22] Ownership of Christian slaves by non-Christians was first forbidden by law, and the right of the church to make legal manumissions and arrange this process much more easily than secular courts would was widely established.[23]

---

[22] Cf. *Codex Theodosianus* 9.12.1.
[23] Augustine, *Sermon* 21.6; *Canons of Hippolytus* 6.36.

In the early fifth century John Chrysostom, a highly popular preacher, encouraged a growing campaign for widespread manumission of slaves among Christians. In his church at Antioch and later, when he became archbishop at Constantinople he was a strong advocate of the church extending its legal right to manumit the slaves of others. For this he was widely respected among the poorer classes but fell foul of court intrigue and ended his career with exile and state-ordered death (he was starved to death, more or less, on an enforced march into exile). Chrysostom advocated that masters ought to train their slaves in a profession before manumitting them into society as free men and women.[24] The Council of Chalcedon in 451 in its fourth canon authorized slaves to be admitted publicly into the ranks of the monks, if they had the consent of their owners. But the church also secured the agreement of the state authorities that if a runaway slave escaped and became a monk, without detection, for more than a year, it was held as a full legal enfranchisement, whatever his origin. It was clearly a pattern of several monastic colonies to hide and shelter runaways among them.

Theologically there is hardly a voice that says among the early Christians, "Slavery is an out-and-out abomination in a civilized society." The historian De Ste. Croix opines that the Christian writers were even more supine than the late antique (pagan) philosophers when it came to denouncing the evils of slavery. The former, at least, he says, could call it an "unnatural" condition, but the later Fathers, mimeographing Paul, tended to regard it as a state to be endured in "spiritual freedom" (perhaps an advice that only a free man could have the temerity to give to a slave?), and even recommend obedience to masters as a duty to be performed under God. This shocked De Ste. Croix. His view is worth quoting in full:

> The exhortation to the Christian slave to regard himself as "Christ's freedman" (in the same sense that the Christian who is a free man is "Christ's slave," (1 Cor. 7: 22) may well have afforded him greater spiritual comfort than the pagan slave could obtain from the familiar philosophic view that if he was a good man he was "really" free already; but it was basically the same view. And if, as by philosophic pagans, Christian masters are briefly enjoined to treat their slaves fairly (Coloss. 4: 1; Ephes. 6: 9; Philem. 10-18) the yoke of slavery is fastened even more firmly upon Christian slaves as the emphasis on obedience to their masters becomes even more absolute. Certain phrases in the Pauline epistles, (Ephes. 6: 5–8; Coloss. 3: 22–4; 1 Tim. 6: 1–2; Titus 2: 9–10; 1 Pet. 2: 18–20; 1 Cor. 7: 20–4) such as that in Ephesians (6: 5), exhorting slaves to obey their masters "with fear and trembling, in singleness of heart, *as unto Christ*," had sinister implications which were made explicit in two post-apostolic works, the *Epistle of Barnabas* (19.7) and the *Didache* (4.11): they expressly tell the

---

[24]*Homily* 45, *On 1 Corinthians*; see also Augustine, *Letter* 31.6.

slave that he must serve his master "as a counterpart of God" (*hōs typōi theou*), "in reverence and fear." I know of nothing that goes as far as that in pagan literature. Whatever the theologian may think of Christianity's claim to set free the soul of the slave, therefore, the historian cannot deny that it helped to rivet the shackles rather more firmly on his feet.[25]

In my opinion, De Ste. Croix's unalleviatedly bleak view of Christianity's record in this regard needs some leavening.[26] My reading of the Fathers is that, while they are certainly writing from the bourgeois perspective of an upper class, or at least a class of littérateurs that did not wish to rock the social boat, there is nevertheless a pervasive sense, among those who reflected on it, that slavery was undoubtedly an evil that came into society as a result of humankind's fall from grace. There is nothing comparable in the pagan philosophers that slavery is part of sin, rises out of sin's domain and sin's effects in human society. Moreover, the literary bishops are not the whole church, merely its upper-class voices. The theological position even among them, however, was collectively that slavery and other forms of human misery rose out of the sinful alienation of humanity from God. In this environment cruelty grew, and harsh social conditions such as servitude. Since they clearly put slavery into the category of a morally dubious lapse from the good, to this extent (at least) they took away from the socioeconomic machinery of that empire (that fostered and relied on slavery to uphold the ancient economy) any form of moral high ground, any form of religious "recommendation" of the system. If the church endorsed (as many of its powerful leaders clearly did) that slavery could not be overthrown because of the legally defensible rights of possession that owners held, it did not support the view that those rights extended into the high moral domain. Christianity's doctrine of the spiritual equality of all souls in Christ's church, and its core doctrine of the moral imperative to "love others as oneself," weakened the fundamental ethos that allowed slavery to continue to be regarded—certainly as a moral good, and even, I would say, as a morally neutral thing. To this extent, Christianity fatally weakened the ancient institution of slavery.

---

[25] "Early Christian Attitudes to Property and Slavery," in De Ste. Croix, Whitby, and Streeter, *Christian Persecution, Martyrdom, and Orthodoxy*, 349-50.

[26] "It is often said that Christianity introduced an entirely new and better attitude towards slavery. Nothing could be more false: Jesus accepted slavery as a fact of his environment" (ibid., 349). He lists the New Testament texts that mention slavery but does so significantly out of context. His chief point is that Jesus was a rural figure who more or less took the Old Testament worldview on most matters for granted. There is next to no awareness in his work of an eschatological dimension to Jesus' doctrine of the kingdom of God, nor the extent to which this was conceived as a politico-social as well as a "spiritual" program. The same is true of his exegesis of Paul. His wholesale disparagement of the later Christian theorists similarly lacks nuance and passes over close attention of those who deferred from the Aristotelian premises, in favor of those whom he demonstrates to have been social conformists.

Latin theorists such as Augustine and Ambrose, who write at times almost as if they were elite defenders of a colonial status quo (which they partly were), can attempt to justify the ongoing condition of slavery in terms that suggest the old pagan arguments (that some men could not be free by nature and so do better when they are mastered by others) or that the continuance of slavery is better for society than the revolutionary unrest that would ensue if all were treated equally and afforded freedom (a truly revolutionary concept for ancient men and women); but in associating it with sinfulness and cruelty, the moral energy had unarguably been taken out of the idea of slavery. It had lost its rationale (that it was a proper thing to do to enslave subhuman classes so as to protect the wider social good) and thus any moral (as distinct from economic) reason why it should continue out of a pagan notion of society into a Christian one.

And this is why, I think, slavery evolves into feudalism by the seventh century; a slow change, to be sure, and one that we might be disappointed with, but nevertheless one that the church wished to encourage, wished to be part of in encouraging the emancipation of slaves "voluntarily." Feudalism is not simply an accidental parallel development to this, but an inevitable corollary of the ending of the dominance of the great imperial cities (*poleis*), their tendency to suck dry the resources of the rural hinterlands, and the inevitable decline of heavy agro-business depending on slaves to meet the demand. In other words, as the social decline of the empire after the seventh century finally brought about the conditions where widespread abandonment of a slaving economy was now practical, it is no accident that the moral climate itself had changed enough (because of Christianity's intellectual impact) to allow the transition to be effected.

De Ste. Croix is right, I would say, in his overall conclusion that the problem with Christian theory in this matter of not being able to see the "high ground" of moral outrage in regard to enslavement of others and their commodification, on the one side, while simultaneously lauding them as the images of God, on the other, is that the Christians adopted as their authorities viewpoints that were dominated by a deeply "personalist" point of view. However, I would recast that perspective (which he expresses in the end of his study in terms of the class struggle better illuminated from a Marxian perspective) and would prefer to argue that the Christians see such personalism (the value of the soul, rather than the social condition of, the man) from a significantly "eschatological" view. As we have noted, when Paul tells his slaves not to worry too much about their condition, he does so not from callousness but from a firm belief that they will not have to endure that sorrow for much longer anyway. This context probably lasted as a significant coloration of thought until the fourth century, by which time the habituation had damaged the church's ability to think afresh; and at the same time it started to adopt and adapt pagan philosophical rationales for many of its longer-term social stances, in which context the preexisting philosophical understandings of the "innate condition of servitude" proved to be a very damaging inheritance from Aristotle.

Gregory the Theologian and John Chrysostom argued more pointedly than their Latin counterparts that slavery rose out of this groundswell of sinfulness in society but evolved especially because of the ingrained sin of greed among humans.[27] St. Gregory of Nyssa theologized that masters did not have any rights over slaves at all, since the whole institution was morally reprobate and wholly corrupt, and he asserted that slavery was a contravention of the created order. It had not been appointed by God in the Edenic condition and was thus a creation of humankind acting out of rebellious pride.[28] This is not merely the old philosophic argument that slavery was "unnatural" taken to a higher pitch, but more: that it was sinful, that is, inherently immoral. Fourth-century early monasticism, in its rural forms, also probably served as a leveling force: the "new society" created by more eschatologically radical Christians who had detached themselves from the iron shackles of Roman imperial market philosophy, which probably made them more ready than city-dwelling Christian rhetoricians to see that slavery and Christian brotherhood were fundamentally incompatible partners: one of them had to go.

And so, although the church's record on slavery in ancient times left much to be desired, it cannot entirely be dismissed as supine conformity to the mores of secular Roman society. Christianity's philosophical affirmation of the divine dignity of the human being considered as spiritual creature made deep legal and moral inroads into the pre-Christian Greek and Roman supposition that the intelligent and rich alone were truly human, and it advocated constantly the alternative concept (new and very radical in its day, and still radical if it were to be applied in politics) that the poor and the humble were even more favored in the eyes of God than the rich and cultured. Such an idea might have burned on a slow fuse in the early church, but it had an inevitable force in changing the structure of the pagan late empire. By the seventh century, slavery among Christian societies had by and large been rendered as a relic of the past—and society was on its way toward a (slightly less onerous) feudal system of organization.

"Freedom" might never have been a prime philosophical factor in all of this (economic harsh necessity governing the bare-subsistence life conditions of more than 90 percent of the ancient empire's inhabitants), but the concept of the rights

---

[27] Gregory of Nazianzus, *Theological Poems* 2.36; John Chrysostom, *Homily* 22, *On the Epistle to the Ephesians*.
[28] *Homily* 4, *On Ecclesiastes*.

of Christian men and women as equal moral agents under the eye of God had certainly been introduced and established as a core issue of what was commonly understood as a "Christian civilization," and however wide the gap between moral aspiration and ethical reality (a problem affecting society today as much as any before it), an ideal of equal dignity under the eyes of God, once stated, can never be forgotten: precisely because of its luminous idealism that casts into even darker shadow the many failures to realize it in social reality as an ethic of love running to serve justice. De Ste. Croix's castigation of the church comes in the barely masked apologetic context of suggesting a Marxian philosophy would have liberated the poor much more quickly, honestly, and efficiently. But it is a historical hypothesis that can only be regarded as laughable in the light of all known instances where Marxism has imposed itself as a dominant social structure in our own time.

## A SHORT READER

### *Gospel of Matthew 20:25-28.*

> The following passage from the Gospel, attributed to Jesus, makes a very significant point about the core of Jesus' ministry being based on self-emptying service, manifested in the Lord's suffering. The distinction is here made between service (*diakonia*) and slavery (*douleia*). The last two lines of the text might be a first-century commentary on the duplicate logion that precedes, or even if not stand as a clarification of the twofold logion, where the higher the status in the church, the deeper the service must be. Jesus calls himself here the *doulos*, "slave," insofar as he is Lord. Thus in himself he exemplifies the overturning of the tables of social expectation where lords ought to expect service and slaves ought to provide it. The theology of Jesus here goes back to the Suffering Servant concept found earlier in Isaiah; but it is none the less instructive that Jesus' apparently tangential allusion to the ancient (social) practice of slavery provides a premise that dissolves it:

Jesus called them to him and said, "You know that the rulers of the Gentiles lord it over them, and their great men exercise authority over them. It shall not be so among you; but whoever would be great among you must be your servant (*diakonos*), and whoever would be first among you must be your slave (*doulos*); even as the Son of Man came not to be served but to serve (*diakonethenai*), and to give his life as a ransom for many."

### *The apostle Paul.*

> St. Paul's writings, in the middle of the first century, are full of references to real-world slaves. They must have formed a significant number of the earliest Christian

congregations. I am listing no less than eight excerpt here, for this corpus of writings indubitably had the greatest effect on forming the Christian mentality in regard to the ethical attitude to slavery. Paul's original eschatological constraints and his wariness of what he might be able to suggest before calling down the wrath of the empire against him and his congregations colored his remarks deeply. His eventual rise to immense status as canonical authority in the second century onward gave his words a power and weight they neither had nor perhaps intended. Some of his advice is clearly for the comfort and alleviation of slaves (see the second, third, fifth, and eighth passages). Other things, once taken out of an eschatological context, provided fodder for those who wished to sustain the pagan status quo in regard to enslavement (see the first, fourth, sixth, and seventh passages).

*1 Corinthians 7:17-24.* Only, let everyone lead the life that the Lord has assigned to him, and in which God has called him. This is my rule in all the churches. Was anyone at the time of his call already circumcised? Let him not seek to remove the marks of circumcision. Was anyone at the time of his call uncircumcised? Let him not seek circumcision. For neither circumcision counts for anything, nor uncircumcision, but keeping the commandments of God. Everyone should remain in the state in which he was called. Were you a slave when called? Never mind. But if you can gain your freedom, avail yourself of the opportunity. For he who was called in the Lord as a slave is a freedman of the Lord. Likewise, he who was free when called is a slave of Christ. You were bought with a price; do not become slaves of men. So, brethren, in whatever state each was called, there let him remain with God.

*1 Corinthians 12:13-17.* For by one Spirit we were all baptized into one body, Jews or Greeks, slaves or free, and all were made to drink of one Spirit. For the body does not consist of one member but of many. If the foot should say, "Because I am not a hand, I do not belong to the body," that would not make it any less a part of the body. And if the ear should say, "Because I am not an eye, I do not belong to the body," that would not make it any less a part of the body.

*Galatians 3:27-29; 4:6-7.* For as many of you as were baptized into Christ have put on Christ. There is neither Jew nor Greek, there is neither slave nor free, there is neither male nor female; for you are all one in Christ Jesus. And if you are Christ's, then you are Abraham's offspring, heirs according to promise.... And because you are sons, God has sent the Spirit of his Son into our hearts, crying, "Abba! Father!" So through God you are no longer a slave but a son, and if a son then an heir.

*Ephesians 6:4-12.* Fathers, do not provoke your children to anger, but bring them up in the discipline and instruction of the Lord. Slaves, be obedient to those who are your earthly masters, with fear and trembling, in singleness of heart, as to Christ; not in the way of eye-service, as people pleasers, but as servants of Christ, doing the will of God from the heart, rendering service with a good will as to the Lord and not to people, knowing that whatever good any one does, he will receive the same again from the Lord, whether he is a slave or free. Masters, do the same to them, and forbear threatening, knowing that he who is both their Master and yours is in heaven, and that there is no partiality with him.[29] Finally, be strong in the Lord and in the strength of his might. Put on the whole armor of God, that you may be able to stand against the wiles of the devil. For we are not contending against flesh and blood, but against the principalities, against the powers, against the world rulers of this present darkness, against the spiritual hosts of wickedness in the heavenly places.

*Colossians 3:5-15.* Put to death, therefore, what is earthly in you: fornication, impurity, passion, evil desire, and covetousness, which is idolatry. On account of these the wrath of God is coming. In these you once walked, when you lived in them. But now put them all away: anger, wrath, malice, slander, and foul talk from your mouth. Do not lie to one another, seeing that you have put off the old nature with its practices and have put on the new nature, which is being renewed in knowledge after the image of its creator. Here there cannot be Greek and Jew, circumcised and uncircumcised, barbarian, Scythian, slave, free man, but Christ is all, and in all. Put on, then, as God's chosen ones, holy and beloved, compassion, kindness, lowliness, meekness, and patience, forbearing one another, and if one has a complaint against another, forgiving each other; as the Lord has forgiven you, so you also must forgive. And above all these put on love, which binds everything together in perfect harmony. And let the peace of Christ rule in your hearts, to which indeed you were called in the one body. And be thankful.

*1 Timothy 6:1-8.* Let all who are under the yoke of slavery regard their masters as worthy of all honor, so that the name of God and the teaching may not be defamed. Those who have believing masters must not be disrespectful on the ground that they are brethren; rather, they must serve all the better since those who benefit by their service are believers and beloved. Teach and urge these duties. If anyone teaches otherwise and does not agree with the sound words of our Lord Jesus Christ and the teaching that accords with godliness, he is puffed up with conceit, he knows nothing; he has a morbid craving for controversy and for disputes about words, which produce envy,

---

[29]Paralleled in Col 3:22–4:1.

dissension, slander, base suspicions, and wrangling among men who are depraved in mind and bereft of the truth, imagining that godliness is a means of gain. There is great gain in godliness with contentment, for we brought nothing into the world, and we cannot take anything out of the world; but if we have food and clothing, with these we shall be content.

*Titus 2:9.* Bid slaves to be submissive to their masters and to give satisfaction in every respect; they are not to be refractory, nor to pilfer, but to show entire and true fidelity, so that in everything they may adorn the doctrine of God our Savior.

*Philemon 10-20.* I appeal to you on behalf of my child, Onesimus, whose father I have become in my imprisonment.[30] Formerly he was useless to you, but now he is indeed useful to you and to me. I am sending him back to you, sending my very heart. I would have been glad to keep him with me, in order that he might serve me on your behalf during my imprisonment for the gospel, but I preferred to do nothing without your consent in order that your goodness might not be by compulsion but of your own free will. Perhaps this is why he was parted from you for a while, that you might have him back forever, no longer as a slave but more than a slave, as a beloved brother, especially to me but how much more to you, both in the flesh and in the Lord. So if you consider me your partner, receive him as you would receive me. If he has wronged you at all, or owes you anything, charge that to my account. I, Paul, write this with my own hand, I will repay it—to say nothing of your owing me even your own self. Yes, brother, I want some benefit from you in the Lord. Refresh my heart in Christ.

### *The book of Revelation 18:10-14.*

> The desire to be "quiet and good" in the face of the might of imperial Rome is not so prevalent in the writings of the prophet from Asia Minor who penned the book of Revelation at the end of the first century. For him, Rome was the great persecutor, covered in the blood of saints, in which habitual attitude it proved its demonic origin and end. The reference to the end of the slave trade comes in a list of all the things he rejoices in imagining as he pulls down the pillars of the house in God's judgment over Rome's venality and cruelty:

Woe! Woe! you great city, you mighty city, Babylon! In one hour your judgment has come. And the merchants of the earth weep and mourn for her, since no

---

[30]Onesimus was the slave of Philemon, to whom Paul was writing, and had been loaned to him as a secretary-companion on his journey.

one buys their cargo any more; cargo of gold, silver, jewels and pearls, fine linen, purple, silk and scarlet, all kinds of scented wood, all articles of ivory, all articles of costly wood, bronze, iron and marble, cinnamon, spice, incense, myrrh, frankincense, wine, oil, fine flour and wheat, cattle and sheep, horses and chariots, and slaves, that is, human souls. The fruit for which your soul longed has departed from you, and all thy dainties and thy splendor are lost to you, never to be found again!

**Apostolic Constitutions.**

> This book is a fourth-century (archaizing) collation of earlier church "order" books (notably the Didache and *Apostolic Tradition* of Hippolytus) whose canons entered the church's international tradition and had an impact, even if the book as a whole cannot always be relied on as a real-world guide to liturgical practice in the fourth-century church. This passage following probably represents the growing practice of the time it was composed, rather than an earlier age. In the fourth century the church's status and the growing extent of the episcopal courts (chanceries) made manumission easier in practice than it had been. To manumit a slave was regarded as a "forgiveness of many sins" for the liberating owner. Here the unknown author advocates to church leaders that the church's common funds should be used for liberating slaves, and that the congregations ought to be encouraged to this philanthropy:

Say to the people under you what the wise Solomon says: "Honor the Lord out of your just labors, and pay your firstfruits to him out of your fruits of righteousness, so that your barns may be filled with abundance of wheat, and your presses may overflow with wine." In this light, then, maintain and clothe those who are in want from the proceeds of the righteous labor of the faithful. And order such sums of money as have been collected from them, in the manner we have mentioned, to be expended in the redemption of the saints, in the deliverance of slaves, and captives, and prisoners, and also of those that have been abused, and those who have been condemned by tyrants to single combat and death on account of the name of Christ. For the Scripture says: "Deliver those who are led to death, and do not neglect to redeem those who are ready to be slain."[31]

---

[31]The text, like the book at large, sets itself in an earlier age of persecutions. But if, as seems most likely, it is a mid-fourth-century Constantinopolitan document, most of the list it offers as good examples of church spending will no longer apply (Christians were no longer forced to be gladiators in the capital, where this had been abolished), leaving the manumission of slaves and the rescue of the abused (slaves living with predatory masters) standing out as the two works that are to be inculcated.

### Gregory of Nyssa.

St. Gregory of Nyssa is an important voice articulating the later Christian sentiment that slavery was a moral evil. In an early work called *On the Making of Man* (*De Opificio Hominis*) he set out to complete his famous brother Basil's treatise *On the Hexaemeron*, the making of the world in the six days Genesis suggests. Basil had died before he could finish it fully. His younger brother Gregory designs this treatise as a memorial tribute and the "anthropological" part of what Basil omitted. In setting out his ideas on Christian anthropology Gregory comes at the issue of dominion and the use of power in society from a deeply considered aspect. His voice is one of the first of the Christian fathers to locate freedom of mind and soul as a core defining anthropological factor.

He is influenced in this work by the Stoic theorists, but his chief argument is drawn from the concept of humanity as made in the divine image and thus reflective of the glory of God. If God's freedom and dignity of dominion is not honored in humanity, then it is an offense against God. This is a new argument in the ancient world, following on from Gregory of Nazianzus's *Oration 14* (Gregory was his rhetorical and theological teacher). The implications it brings concerning the quintessentially immoral state of enslaving other human beings flows from it. These early sentiments in the *De Opificio Hominis* are taken to a pitch in his later work commenting on Ecclesiastes, which will shall notice later. In this first passage Gregory takes freedom (the root of a moral sentient being) out of the domain of compulsion. The logic of the position is that enslavement has to be antihuman, antiethical, and anti-God:

**De Opificio Hominis 16.10-11.** I hope no one will be impatient with me if I bring what might seem a remote argument to bear on the present subject. God, in his own nature, is all that which our mind can conceive of good. More accurately, he transcends all good that we can conceive or comprehend. God creates humanity for no other reason than his innate goodness; and being such, and having this as his reason for embarking on the creation of human nature, it follows that God would not exhibit the power of that goodness in any imperfect form, as if he were to give our nature some of the things at his disposal but begrudge it a share in other. The perfection of the form of goodness is witnessed by the fact that God both brings humanity into being out of nothing and completely supplies it with all good gifts. It would be out of the question to enumerate all those gifts one by one, since there are so many of them. This is why Scripture talks about them all gnomically in a comprehensive phrase, when it says that humanity was made "in the image of God." This is the same as to say that God made human nature participant in all good. Since, if the Godhead is the fullness of good, and this is his image, then the image must find its resemblance to the archetype insofar as it is filled with all good. This is why there is in humanity the principle of all excellence, all virtue and wisdom, and every higher reality that we can conceive. Nevertheless, preeminent among all of this is the fact that we are free from necessity and do not stand in bondage to any natural power but have free choice of decision within our own power. For virtue is altogether a voluntary thing, subject to no dominion. That which is the result of compulsion and force cannot be virtue.

> In another passage from this study, which he wrote early in his career, Gregory makes the important and fundamental Christian point that the divine image is located in all human beings, not in any single part of the race (such as philosophers before him had argued that some were natural slaves and others were naturally free). In applying the divine image to all humanity and giving this honor the sanction of the divine will and the divine plan for the order of creation, Gregory effectively sinks the Aristotelian doctrine of the two types of humankind that slavers used so often (then and later) to justify inhuman treatment to the "lower orders." This anthropology Gregory defends became the basis of all subsequent Christian reflection on human nature.

**De Opificio Hominis *16.17-18.*** Now, just as any particular human being is limited by his bodily dimensions, and just as the specific size of his physical manifestation is the measure of his distinct existence, just so, I think, all the complete fullness of humanity was included in one conceptual body by the God of all, by virtue of his own power of foreknowledge. This is what that text teaches us when it says, "God created man; in the image of God he created him." But the image is not in any part of our nature, nor is its grace in any one of those things found in that nature. On the contrary, this power extends equally to all of the human race. The sign of this is that rationality is implanted in all humans, since all have the power of understanding and deliberation and all those other things in which the Godhead finds its image in that which was made according to it, namely, man who was manifested at the first creation of the world, and he that shall exist after the consummation of all, are alike. They equally bear in themselves the divine image. For this reason the whole race was spoken of as one man, since as far as God's power is concerned nothing is either past or future, but even that which we look to is comprehended by the all-sustaining energy at the same time as that which presently exists. Accordingly, our whole nature, as it extends from the first to the last, is, so to say, one single image of Him Who Is.

Gregory of Nyssa's important fourth homily on the Old Testament book of Ecclesiastes is a work of his late maturity. It is one of the most direct statements from early Christianity arguing the out-and-out evil of slavery as an institution. It was written around 380, a time when he was soon to be raised to high honors by the imperial household and appointed as an international "arbiter of affairs" for the Christian church:

**Homily 4 on Ecclesiastes.** Speaking about himself, the author [of Ecclesiastes] lists all those qualities that allow us to recognize the vanity of this life. He now seems to place an even stronger censure on men's deeds and accuse them of passion rising out of arrogance. Among the vanities he lists are: an expensive home, many vineyards, lovely gardens, pools and orchards. Here we also find the man who regards himself as lord over his fellow man, for he writes: "I obtained servants, maidens, slaves born to me in my house" (Eccles 2:7). Can you see here that pride that originates false pretensions? Such words as these rise up against the face God, for, as prophecy has told us, all things serve God, whose power is over them (Ps 118:91). This kind of person abrogates to himself what belongs to God and attributes to himself power over the human race as if he were its lord. What arrogant claim, transgressing human nature, makes this person look upon himself as different from those he rules over? "I obtained servants and maidens." What are you saying? You are condemning to slavery humankind, who is both free and self-determinative. You are contradicting God by perverting the natural law in this way. Like a sinner and a rebel against the divine commandment, you have put man himself under the yoke of servitude, when he was created as lord over the earth. You have forgotten the limits of your authority, which consists in dominion only over the brutish animals. Scripture tells us that humankind shall rule over birds, beasts, fish, four-footed animals, and reptiles [Gen 1:26]. So, how can you rebel against that state of subjection that has been laid on you and raise yourself against humanity's very freedom? . . . Even then, when you have freed yourself from servitude and bondage, you desire to have others serve you: "I have obtained servants and maidens." What value is this, I ask? What merit do you see in their humanity? How cheaply have you estimated them? What price would you set on that nature that God himself has crafted? It was God who said, "Let us make man according to our image and likeness" (Gen 1:26), and since we are created according to the divine likeness and are appointed to rule over the whole earth, then tell me: who is that person who can buy and sell others? Only God can do this. But such a thing is not appropriate even for him, for "the gifts of God are irrevocable" (Rom 11:29). You see,

God called human nature into freedom though it had become addicted to sin, so he would never subject it to slavery again. God's dominion is incontestable, and he refuses to subject freedom to slavery. How could man, who is the lord of the whole world, obtain dominion, since everything related to possession requires corollary payment? How could we estimate the cost of the whole earth and all its contents in any accurate way? But if these things are inestimable, then how much greater is the value of man himself, who is lord over them? In all of the world you would not find anything comparable to the honor of man. That one who indeed knows human nature himself says that the whole world is no adequate exchange for a man's soul (Mt 16:26). When the Lord of the earth himself bought humanity, he acquired nothing more precious.[32] He will defend his possession of humanity, along with the earth, the islands, the sea and all the things they contain. What was the deposit God put down? What will he receive from the contract by which he has received possession?[33] Do you delude yourselves that a bill of sale, a written contract, a paltry amount of money, can gain for you possession of the image of God? Oh, what self-deception! The contract can perish; moths can corrode the bills of sale, and dripping water can destroy them entirely; so then, where are your contracts of domination? I can see nothing more than legal title underwrites your case. What authority so enhances your nature? Believe me, it is neither time nor beauty, not honor or virtue.[34] All these qualities have brought you to lead a life equally dominated by passions of both soul and body: suffering and cheerfulness, joy and sadness, grief and pleasure, anger and fearfulness, pain and death. Do not all these things belong to both slave and master? Do they not both breathe the same air and look upon the same sun? Does not food serve to nourish them both? Do not they have the same insides? Do not they both become dust when they die? Is there not one standard for all? Is there not a common rule and a common hell? So, how can

---

[32]Gregory here envisages how Christ purchased the human race, redeeming it from bondage though his death and resurrection and thus abiding as its true owner and master.

[33]His argument is that contractual law of possessions cannot come near to explaining the infinite philanthropy by which God took the human race to himself as his own: a liberative "possession" of humanity. By contrast, those who think they can commodify humanity in a possessive legal transaction (such as slavery) delude themselves: the human race is not for sale; God's liberative ownership of humanity defends it against the predations of others who have wished to enslave it. Gregory elsewhere lists Satan as the chief enslaver. Human slavers are thus, like him, rebels against God's creation order.

[34]Here Gregory considers the legal arguments then in force to justify the rights of slave owners (ancient family rights, superior status, superior natural or moral endowments) and rejects them all.

you who are equal in all things claim such a superiority that though being a man, you consider yourself as man's ruler and say: "I have servants and maidens" as if they were goats or cattle?[35]

**Ephrem the Syrian, Hymns on the Nativity 17.5-10.**

> The Syriac poet-theologian Ephrem, writing in the late fourth century, graphically depicts the events surrounding the incarnation of the Lord for his clients, who had asked him to compose hymns for their monastery: probably a community of Syrian female ascetics who would sing these hymns of nativity in their vigil prayer services. In one of his hymns he describes the Virgin Mary's meditations on how this event of her son's birth will "transform all of creation." There is a significant reference to slavery, in the context of how it shall be abolished in the Christian dispensation. Some scholars have interpreted the phrasing of this as suggesting only that slaves could be released if they entered a monastery. But at this period, baptism of the laity in Syria was restricted to those who promised celibate observance, so the invitation seems to be couched in larger terms: admission to the church is a promise of liberation. Whether, or how, this was acted out in practice in Syria is a matter of uncertainty. Evidence from Theodoret, himself a Syrian bishop, who suggests slaves owed a "duty of obedience" to masters as the apostle had advocated, would suggest that it was not widely enacted. Even so, the fact of Ephrem's putting into the mouth of the Virgin Mary at least an aspiration for widespread emancipation carried moral weight, for Mary's iconic status in the early church was immense:

Blessed is that woman whose heart and mind you indwell [my Son]. She is a castle of the king for you, the king's son, and holy of holies; for you the high priest. Such a woman does not have the anxiety or labor of a household and husband . . . for you are our bread, our bridal chamber, the robe of our glory. . . . Whoever has a body let him come to be a brother to my beloved. Whoever has a daughter or kinswoman let her come to be the bride of my noble one whoever owns a slave, let him release him so as to come and serve his Lord. My Son, one is the wage of the freeborn man who has taken up your yoke. But the slave, who has suffered the double yoke of two masters, the one above and one below, shall receive two blessings and two wages for his double burden. My son, the freedwoman is also your servant, if she serves you. And the slave woman becomes a freedwoman in you. She is consoled by you that she really is a freed woman. If she loves you, she will find invisible emancipation placed within her heart.

---

[35]PG 45.665-68.

### John Chrysostom, Homily 40, On 1 Corinthians.

John Chrysostom, the chief preacher in the cathedral of Antioch before he rose to become archbishop of Constantinople, was renowned for his regular complaints against the rich of the city and their oppressions of the poorer classes. This is his view of servants and the institution of slavery:

Why do you keep so many slaves? In the case of dress, we ought to follow our need alone, so too the case with our eating habits: and so too should it be in respect to the slaves we keep. And there what is our need? We have no need at all. One master should only employ one servant; rather, two or three masters only need one servant. If you think this is outrageously hard, consider those people who have no servant at all but then enjoy more ready service of their needs. For God made everyone well capable of attending to themselves and to their neighbor as well. If you do not believe me listen to Paul, who says: "These very hands ministered to my own necessities, and those of my companions" (Acts 20:34). And this is why God gave us hands and feet in the first place, so that we might not stand in need of servants. You see, the class of slave was not introduced out of any perceived need, otherwise when Adam was made, slaves too would have been formed. No: it is the penalty of sin and disobedieince that accounts for the introduction of slaves. But when Christ came, he put an end to all this.... So that it is now no longer necessary to hold a slave. But if you insist it is necessary, then keep one only, at most two. What is the point of holding swarms of slaves? Our rich men now pad around in the forum and baths as if they were sheep dealers or slave auctioneers. Even so, I will not be too exacting. I allow you to keep a second servant. If you collect more than this you are not doing it out of humanity but rather for self-indulgence. If you have any care for them, do not emply them in serving your own needs; rather, when you have purchased them and taught them trades wherein they can support themselves, then let them go free. But if you scourge them or put them in chains, know this: this is not a work of humanity. I know I am disgusting some of my hearers, but what can I do? I am set on this course, and I shall never cease saying these things, whether anything comes of it or not.

### Augustine of Hippo, City of God 19.14-15.

In the Latin world patristic thought was often less philosophically speculative or daring, more rooted in legal constructs. Statements from Cyprian, Jerome, or Ambrose do not show much concern to change the status quo about slaves. In his great work the *City of God,* Augustine set himself the task in the fifth-century context of imperial decline of seriously considering what effect Christianity had on human society and how society could be explained in theological terms. Here one might expect an ideal opportunity to advocate new principles. But one of Augustine's dominant ideas was the extent to which sinfulness, pride, and hardness of heart had seeped out from humankind's first sin of rebellion against God's order, so as to corrupt everything, without exception, in the human order. He thus drew a radical distinction between the affairs of the city of God, the heavenly Jerusalem (where all might be free as the image of God), and the earthly city, Babylon, where nothing existed that was pure or true.

In regard to slavery, Augustine himself was a kindly man, and on occasion was known to encourage his congregants to liberate the slaves from a transport ship that had ill-advisedly docked in the local harbor. The slave owner, despite Augustine's protests that he had "nothing to do with it himself," knew well enough to take him to court (the secular magistrate's court) to seek compensation for his loss. But in his theoretical work Augustine, having stated that slavery is one of the results of pride and sinful hardness of heart, went on to temper any conclusion that it was thereby a thing to resist, with the (to him) equally important principle that the extent of sin in human society called for a "realist politic" that did not seek to establish perfect conditions as much as defensible and attainable standards. For such reasons he advocated the state had a right to assert violence: not that this was good, but that it was better in real terms than the alternative of allowing social disorder. He applied the same argument to slavery. To abolish it, though it resulted from sinful alienation from the standards of love, would cause too much social unrest. In the present state of a deficient world, it ought to be endured. His ruminations went on to carry much weight, well into the Middle Ages and beyond:

And this is the system of [social] concord: that a man should, first, injure no one, and second, should do good to all within reach. So first and foremost a man's own household is his care; for the law of nature and society gives him readier access to them and greater opportunity of serving them. This is why the apostle says: "Now, if any does not provide for his own, and especially for those of his own house, he has denied the faith, and is worse than an infidel" (1 Tim 5:8). This is the origin of domestic peace, and the well-arranged concord between those in the family who rule and those who obey. For it is the ones who care for the rest who rule: the husband over the wife, the parents over the children, the masters over the servants. And those who are cared for should obey: women their husbands, children their parents, servants their masters. Even so, in the family of a just man who lives by faith, who is still a pilgrim journeying on to the heavenly city, even those who rule are servant of those whom they seem to command. For in such a case they do not rule from any love of power but out of a sense of the duty they owe to others. They do not rule because they are proud of their authority but because they love mercy. This is prescribed by the very order of nature: for this is how God has created humanity. He it was who said: "Let them have dominion over the fish of the sea, and over the fowl of the air, and over every creeping thing that creeps on the earth" (Gen 1:26). God did not intend that his rational creature, who was made in his own image, should have dominion over anything but the irrational creation, certainly not man over man, but rather man over the beasts. And this is why the righteous men of primitive times were made shepherds of cattle rather than kings over men; for so God intended to teach us what the relative position of the creatures was, as distinct from the outcomes of sin. For it is indeed the case, I think, that the condition of slavery is the result of sin. And this is why we do not find the word *slave* in any part of Scripture until the time that righteous Noah branded the sin of his son with this name. Slavery, therefore, is a name introduced to the world by sin and not by nature. The origin of the Latin word for "slave" is supposed to derive from the fact that those who were about to be executed according to the laws of warfare were sometimes preserved by their victors and were thereafter called servants.[36] But these circumstances could never have arisen except as a result of sin.

**FURTHER READING**

Bergada, M. M. "La condemnation de l'esclavage dans l'Homélie IV." In *Gregory of Nyssa: Homilies on Ecclesiastes*, ed. S. G. Hall, 185-96. Berlin: De Gruyter, 1993.

Bradley, K. R. *Slavery and Society at Rome*. Cambridge: Cambridge University Press, 1994.

Brown, P. *Poverty and Leadership in the Later Roman Empire*. Lebanon, NH: University Press of New England, 2002.

De Ste Croix, G. E. M. "Early Christian Attitudes to Property and Slavery." *Studies in Church History* (1975): 1-38. Reprinted in G. E. M. De Ste Croix, M. Whitby, and J. Streeter, *Christian Persecution, Martyrdom, and Orthodoxy*. Oxford: Oxford University Press, 2006.

Flint-Hamilton, K. "Images of Slavery in the Early Church: Hatred Disguised as Love?" *Journal of Hate Studies* 1, no. 2 (August 2003): 27-45.

Garnsey, P. *Ideas of Slavery from Aristotle to Augustine*. Cambridge: Cambridge University Press, 1995.

Garnsey, P., and C. Humfress. *The Evolution of the Late Antique World*. Cambridge: Cambridge University Press, 2001, esp. chap. 9.

Glancy, J. A. *Slavery in Early Christianity*. Oxford: Oxford University Press, 2003.

---

[36]*Servus*, related to the concept "save."

Goldenberg, D. *The Curse of Ham: Race and Slavery in Early Judaism, Christianity, and Islam.* Princeton, NJ: Princeton University Press, 2003.

Gulzow, H. *Christentum und Sklaverei in den drei ersten Jahrhunderten.* Bonn: R. Halbelt, 1969.

Harrill, J. A. *The Manumission of Slaves in Early Christianity.* Tübingen: Mohr (Siebeck), 1995.

Holman, S. *The Hungry Are Dying: Beggars and Bishops in Roman Cappadocia.* Oxford: Oxford University Press, 2001.

Malherbe, A. J. *Social Aspects of Early Christianity.* Philadelphia: Fortress, 1983.

Nardo, D. *The Life of a Roman Slave.* San Diego, CA: Lucent Books, 1998.

Pomeroy, S. *Goddesses, Whores, Wives, and Slaves.* New York: Schocken, 1975.

Ramelli, H. *Social Justice and the Legitimacy of Slavery.* Oxford: Oxford University Press, 2016.

Steinmann, A. *Sklavenlos und Alte Kirche.* Monchen-Gladbach, Germany: Volksvereinsverlag, 1922.

Talamo, S. *La schiavitu secondo padri della Chiesa.* Rome: Unione cooperativa editrice, 1927.

Wiedemann, T. *Greek and Roman Slavery: A Sourcebook.* London and New York: Routledge, 1989.

# ATTITUDES TO SEXUALITY IN THE EARLY CHURCH

## PHILOSOPHICAL RENEWALS OF INTEREST

Recent historical research has been much interested in the issue of sexuality and sexual identity in the ancient world. It has been an area of much critical writing from a variety of disciplinary standpoints: especially postmodernist philosophy, feminist studies, and studies of human cultural identity. That the axial turning point of a distinct "change of attitude" to human sexuality among the Christians can be located fair and square in the fourth-century ecclesiastical era (and is most particularly manifested in the writings of the early church) makes this historical moment of special interest to a range of contemporary theorists—and it has proved most interesting to see such "old" subject areas of Christian asceticism (monastic renunciation) being given a complete makeover by such an array of scholarly disciplines.

It is perhaps not surprising that our own age (the age following after Freud and Jung), especially the mid-twentieth century onward, has itself been an axial point in terms of cultural attitudes to sexuality. The immense desire to articulate the sexual dimension to human experience has been a defining one for our contemporary civilization. Michel Foucault's third volume in his *History of Sexuality* turned its attention very closely to antique Greek, Roman, and early Christian approaches to sexual theory, in an attempt to discover the origins of concepts of selfhood and meaning invested in this fundamental human potency.[1] His philosophical inquiry has proved highly influential for many scholars of the early church, after the '80s of the twentieth century, although his own historical judgments in his work (especially his remarks about antiquity) are often facile and controvertible. He is more a philosopher than a historian.[2]

---

[1] M. Foucault, *The Care of the Self* (New York: Vintage Books, 1986).
[2] A famous "sin of omission" was Foucault's complete disregard of women and ancient Judaism in his account of Western sexual history. Foucault had in a sense been seduced himself by the ancient Greek presuppositions on identity, namely that a person became a person by *his* relations (it had to be a man, as the Greek view of women, comparable to their view of slaves and workers, was that they were manifestations of a lesser form of humanity that could not reach the norm of

In classical approaches to Christian sexual ethics, it was often presumed (largely on the basis of the writings of the church fathers, who heavily emphasized this view) that human bodies were manifests of fixed "natures." The body was a delimited factor that was a constant. It could not be changed, as neither (so it was believed) could one's gender be changed, nor one's patterns of "normal" human behavior, that is, those described by fixed "norms" that were constituted by the nature itself. For the ancient Greek world, then, sexual behavior followed "norms" (or disobeyed norms, as the case may be) that were themselves manifestations of the fixed terms of a given human nature.

This view had a large uptake among early Christian theorists. One might recall how common a view this was when one thinks of how homosexual practice (for example) was defined by several of the church fathers writing on sexual ethics as a "contradiction of a law of nature." This is an idea that still finds ethical proponents to the present day, not least central parts of Orthodox and Roman Catholic ethics. The presumption that bodies were manifests of fixed natures was particularly a "Stoic" notion. It was a common idea (or axiom) in that ancient pre-Christian school of thought. Ethical behavior among the Stoics, and the several early Christian fathers who based themselves on such premises, was generally understood as a matter of human beings conforming themselves to such laws of nature as they could see (by the light of reason) revealed in the world about them.

The impact of this style of thinking has not only been prevalent in Christianity in the domain of sexual ethics but is especially visible today also in the field of modern bioethics. This classical "Stoic-Christian" approach has been subject to constant revision over the centuries, most notably in the recent assaults on it in late twentieth-century critical theory. Bordo, in the following citation, comes at the issue from a postmodern feminist viewpoint: "Over the past 150 years under the influence of a variety of cultural forces, the body has been forced to vacate its long term residence on the 'Nature' side of the Nature-Culture duality, and encouraged to take up residence, along with everything else that is human, within culture."[3]

---

the free, landholding citizen) to money, power, his own body, his wife's body, young boys' bodies, and the body of the truth (philosophy) mediated to him by a sage pedagogue. Foucault elevated especially the last of that list of six as the cardinal axis of identity making among the Greeks. For this, some recent feminist thinkers have accused him of not merely reproducing the Greek myopia but even deepening its pejorative effect.

[3] S. Bordo, *Unbearable Weight: Feminism, Western Culture, and the Body* (Berkeley: University of California Press, 1993), 33. The citation is typical of a lot of rather loose philosophical-ethical thinking insofar as it removes the overstrict categorization of body = nature toward an equally unsupportable axiom of body = human culture. But while bodies (and natures) might not be as fixed as antiquity thought, neither are they simply cultural constructs. They still occupy time and space and are subject, like it or not, to determinative laws of physics.

As we have briefly noted, one of the key theoreticians who opened up this recent research interest in the theme of human sexuality as a key to interpreting past and present power plays (disparities of power and relations in societies) was Michel Foucault, with his influential three-volume study of the *History of Sexuality*. Foucault started research in this area almost accidentally, but soon realized that what he was turning up forced him to reassess the importance of the whole theme of human sexuality in history. He was immensely puzzled by the fundamental question of "How, why, and in what forms, was sexuality constituted as a moral domain?"[4] It was clear to Foucault that a veritable sea change had happened between the happy-go-lucky Greeks, with their love of nakedness, the body as a locus of pleasure, and the intrigues of love affairs, on the one side; and on the other side the sober, inward-looking, and morally judgmental Christians, who had taken their master's words in the Gospel about the sinfulness of lustful thoughts (Mt 5:28) to such a pitch that they equated sexual fantasy with adultery and made the issue of purity of internal moral consciousness one of the primary goals of philosophical (ethical, we would say) behavior. Take a tour of any collection of ancient Greek vases and see the large range of sexual behaviors so graphically depicted, and then take a tour of Christian pottery of the early Byzantine period, with its restrained symbols and geometric designs, and ask, what has happened? For Foucault this interior moralization of the body, the forced relocation of sexuality from the exterior to the interior, was one of Christianity's major contributions to world culture.

His overall thesis in his *History of Sexuality* is that while in the first two centuries of the Christian era several Greek non-Christian sources can be noticed already as bringing a new and puritanical strain to bear on the issues of sexuality and embodiment, it was entirely the result of the fourth-century ascetical Christian impact on philosophy[5] that radically changed long-standing Greek attitudes to the body, merging them in a new synthesis with Old Testament ideas and philosophical "ethics of reason and order."[6] For Foucault this resulted in several marked social themes that in turn went on to dominate medieval and modern consciousness, enduring in many respects until the modern era. He lists these as a profound negativization of sex; a focus shift in philosophy, and its remit, away from cosmological

---

[4] M. Foucault, *The History of Sexuality*, vol. 2, *The Use of Pleasures* (New York: Vintage Books, 1985), 5, 10.
[5] Especially seen as manifested by those writers who were both intelligentsia and ascetics: the Fathers of the fourth and fifth centuries. Athanasius of Alexandria, a major dogmatician, who also composed the *Life of Antony*, is a prime example of this symbiosis.
[6] The New Testament Pastoral Letters and writings such as the Clementine epistles show the effect of what has often been called the Roman household code, a set of presumptive guides for good behavior: modesty, humility, chastity, obedience to authority, and so on.

speculation and toward the interior dimensions of the scrutiny of the self (asceticism) as being the higher goal of the philosophical quest; an emphasis on obedience and discipline as the primary ethical modalities; and a critical emphasis on the overarching goal (*telos*) of purity, through the preferred means of self-renunciation.[7]

## GREEK LOVE

At the end of his work Foucault claims that "sexuality" is a thoroughly modern thing. He did not mean by this that we had invented sex, of course, but rather that the notion of sexuality that is so central to modern life and thought is fundamentally and peculiarly a modern creation. Foucault placed its origins in the eighteenth to nineteenth centuries. Then, he argued, the notion of "the separate, knowable, sexual identity" came into human discourse. This, his final thesis, has proved to be highly controversial. His generic point, however, continues to raise interesting questions. Other scholars have raised parallel questions, asking whether the ancient Greeks had any concept of homosexuality in the way a modern might apply the idea.[8] Male-to-male sexual relations were certainly known in ancient Greece, of course, and socially favored there in a way that cannot be said was true about Semitic societies (such as the world of the Hebrew Scriptures), but the sexual theory that emerges from the Greek writings is almost entirely concerned with "inequities of social status" inherent in such relations.[9]

The ethical reflections of typical ancient Greek thought concerning homosexuality are more or less entirely circumscribed by questions of honor and shame. The dominant partner would be honorable, the passive partner shameful (as occupying the inferior status of a woman). The homoerotic context of two males (an elder and a junior) would be ideally and nobly exercised in the elder educating and refining the younger (through gifts, patronage, and *paideia*).[10] Plato gives space to this idea of the perfect form of love. The male-to-male relation is presumed by several Greek rhetorician-philosophers to be the perfect manifestation of the purest ideal of human love, one that is godlike in its character. Plato, we might recall, had a very peculiar approach to embodiment anyway, seeing it as a paradigm of metaphysical illusion. He

---

[7] Foucault called this emphasis on obedience and discipline the "mode of subjection" in Christianity. See Foucault, *Care of the Self*, 235-40.

[8] Such as D. Halperin, ed., *Before Sexuality: The Construction of Erotic Experience in the Ancient Greek World* (Princeton, NJ: Princeton University Press, 1990).

[9] In the Hebrew Scriptures homoerotic love is either castigated or obscured.

[10] An ideal distanced from modern culture—but when one considers how women were married in antiquity to much older men when they were little more than adolescents who had often never received any education worth speaking of, it is more understandable that an ancient educated man would look to his own class of peers for emotional cameraderie and would have found the idea of searching for this in a marriage laughable.

regarded the male-to-male lover relation, once it was purged of its obsessive desire to possess the other sexually, as the paradigm of divine love itself (*to kalon*).[11]

This manifests in a nutshell the great difference that exists between the classical Greek approach to sexual relations and the ancient Judeo-Christian tradition, which from the outset was hostile to male-male relations.[12] Behind the Greek favoring of the male-male relation (and this is the point Foucault wished partly to draw out) is not a favoring of homosexuality over heterosexuality (as we moderns would classify those concepts), but rather an emphasizing of the nature of power positions in society. The reaction of a thinker like the apostle Paul (who systematically applies Stoic philosophical notions to homosexuality in his letters and speaks of the "contrariety of natures") brings in a tonality to the discourse on sex that cannot be found in classical Greek ethics. This aspect brings well to the fore the quite evident aspect that matters of sexuality in the late classical Greek world, and on into the early Christian world, were fundamentally matters of power imbalance. Women were subordinate, men were dominant. Sexual relation was fundamentally about the interplay of honor/shame, that is, (to them) dominance/subjection, master/subservient relation. There is only the sense of sexual expression as "mastering" here; no hint of it in a sense of equalizing, bonding, affection, or love.

Into this maelstrom of ancient cultural axioms and expectations—how did Christianity enter? What impact did it make? We know it changed the scene drastically. (In relation to homosexuality, for example, the Christian emperor Theodosius at the end of the fourth century passed an imperial law that would have made the ancient world shudder [and did make the late antique world gasp]: the forced burning alive of men who regularly took the passive position in homosexual relationships.) This law, of course, was not extensively enforced (and the "of course" is not unworthy of remark, since it balances a showcasing law with the common reactions of a morally sensitive society that shied away from its savagery.) Justinian is also on record for having two homosexually practicing bishops publicly mutilated to send a message out somewhere for some end. Contexts being generally missing in the law codes, we are now not quite sure of what that was. His administration also extensively overhauled marital regulation, abortion, and prostitution laws—so there is evidence in the societal record of the sixth century that the sea change of attitude to sexuality was having a new and "toothy" embodiment in social legislation.

---

[11] An unstated implication of the relation being that of an "older" man to a younger. It is technically not so much pedophilia as *ephebism*. The word *kalon* not only means the good but more precisely the beautiful and desirable.

[12] From Lev 18:22 or Lev 20:13, attaching to it a death penalty in Bronze Age times, to Paul's inclusion of it (1 Cor 6:9) as among those things that exclude from the kingdom.

But the generic question that remains, still seeking an answer, is, as Foucault sensed, how (and how deeply) did Christianity actually change the scene in late antiquity? For what reasons? And with what results? We should note, in passing, that the "burning" Justinian ordered for male-male sexual relations was mandatory only for one partner in the sexual transaction: namely, that passive partner who has offended the new Greek-Christian society's sense of its "honor" by virtue of a male adopting a female posture. For all the "difference" it seems to bear with it, this law simply absolutizes the archaic Greek moral attitude to sexuality, rather than striking out in a new direction. This decree (like all other Roman laws on the statute books) also has to be contextualized rather than being elevated into an overweening symbol of Christian intolerance of homosexuality. For example, we have little evidence that it was ever used. It was certainly soon dropped into obscurity by the rise of a more pervasive sense of larger Christian tolerance. It might, in any case, only have been aimed at suppressing the rise in the capital (for which read the Hippodrome area under his palace windows) of a larger class of male prostitutes than was usual. To correct a perceived imbalance in the capital was often a reason for sweeping Roman laws to be issued.

Nevertheless, just taking this one litmus case, we might still sense that the larger Christian tradition remained hostile to "Greek love," as homosexuality came to be called. Even if this can be concluded, however, the historical question has to be further nuanced by the weighing of nonlegal, nontextual evidences as against the literary and legal sources. For example, we need to remember just how very much the human sexual tradition was nontextual before the nineteenth century. And this being the case for antiquity, we need to ask parallel questions, alongside the literarily explicit intolerance of Justinian, about how many homosexuals during his reign found refuge within the church, and likewise over the centuries—not simply those who lived a secretive life, hiding homosexual relations from public perception and committed to Christian ascetic celibacy, for example, but whose "lapses" (repented and forgiven with regularity) were always of the male-to-male type. How would it be possible to enumerate this?

The older Christian pattern of rhetoric (and it is still sometimes the case today within parts of the churches) meant that much strident homophobia in Christian texts could often arise from undisclosed homosexual theologians wishing to protect themselves by deflection, or to denounce in print tendencies that they feared in themselves as well as in others. Many of the medieval treatises on male-to-male idealized love (see, for example, St. Aelred of Rievaulx's medieval *Treatise on Friendship*) resume the ancient Greek pattern of Platonic erotics as a paradigm for divine love, almost exactly as it had been left in pre-Christian late antiquity: but they set it, this time, in a monastic (ascetical) context.

Ancient Greek philosophical and literary society found it hard to focus on the fact that there could be any pattern of woman-to-woman erotic love. This is worth noting. It knew that there was such a thing, of course. It was famously celebrated in the love of the elder woman for the young girl in Sappho's poetry, which we shall note shortly, and was there a rite of passage in upper-class Greek circles in antiquity. But it was a very closed affair: private to the household. It was not a socially, publicly recognized reality. Accordingly, we have next to no text that shines any light on it. Bernadette Brooten in recent studies has labored in trying to uncover the few texts that have survived that suggest what might have been going on. Greek philosophical and medical sources constantly imply that the nature of woman is promiscuous and unstable without the discipline of the male household head. An abiding issue in antiquity regarding female sexuality was the immense anxiety that the male householder harbored that his domestic females (wife, daughters, or female slaves) might be impregnated by someone else not under his control. This would be fatal to his honor and often prove fatal (literally so) to the woman in question when, or if, found out.

Because female homosexuality in ancient Greece did not matter to this basic aspect of "warding off dishonor" to the male authority structure, as a result interfemale eroticism barely enters the intellectual or textual record and so is difficult to access by the historian. Sappho's love poetry (one of the most beautiful collections of lyric poetry among the ancient Greeks) has often been cited as a paradigm of lesbian literature (Sappho hailed from the island of Lesbos and so has given her name and her island's to the whole sexual movement). Her poetry celebrates the last stage of a free Greek girl's life, that stage of blossoming sexuality, which would then have been about twelve or thirteen years of age—just a few life moments before the girl would be commandeered to be part of some new (male-dominated) household.

It is necessary to read these texts in a correct historical context to see that they celebrate a philosophical, idealized eroticism (comparable to the male-male sense of "the beautiful [male] athlete" that we can so readily see on the Greek sporting vase trophies). For Sappho's circle, which possibly consisted of her young educational charges, wealthy Greek girls, it was a poetry of farewell, of regretful separation, of the love bonding that was being forged between female intellectuals to serve as a parallel form of kinship. The latter is present as a powerfully subversive notion that often escapes modern attention because it is looking elsewhere for evidence of the more overtly sexual; but overall, if the context of Sappho is one of *paideia*, the depth of relationship invoked surely celebrates much that is similar to what Plato had idealized about the relation of the older man to the younger and thus more malleable (educable) "beautiful youth" (*kale nymphe*).

## SOME NONPHILOSOPHICAL GREEK ATTITUDES TO SEXUALITY

The philosophers or pedagogues, of course, and to that extent the poets and littérateurs too, might not be the best people to give us a snapshot of common societal attitudes to sexuality in the ancient world. As with the Hebrew Bible's approach to sex (very cultic, very concerned with procreation and purity issues), we might expect that we are being given only a "partial view." The Bible, for example, is commonly "corrective" literature. It is the literature of the preacher of reform: the tonality often fulminates and seeks redress of a common pattern of behavior that it wishes to redirect. One presumes that it was common by virtue of the repeated injunctions to control it. Similarly, the ancient Greek philosophical tradition can be suspected of drawing an idealized picture, a concept of loving relation purified of the "grosser physical dimension" of male-male relations, or male-female dominance sex relations, that must have formed the common majority of experience in antiquity.

This should remind us, if we have not already become very conscious of it, that the element of sexual romance is conspicuously missing here. It is a particularly "modern" phenomenon. There is hardly anything at all from antiquity that we could call "romantic sexual literature." It is near enough a nonexistent category of thought or writing for ancient times. The ancients (men) bury wives of many years' standing with the same kind of sentiment that one finds on the "Amiable Child Monument" near where I presently live, adjacent to Grant's Tomb in New York. The "Master of the estate's" infant son fell off a bluff over the River Hudson one day, and the tombstone reads, "Erected to the Memory of an Amiable Child, St. Claire Pollock, Died 15 July 1797 in the Fifth Year of His Age." It is chilling in its Stoic abstraction. Ancient dead wives, similarly, were celebrated as faithful matrons, modest, dutiful and faithful. Any grief is hidden by the text's formality: rank is what matters, and the restraint is the badge of it on the tombstone. The formal cliché all but renders the empassioned reality invisible.

It does not take too long to think of modern parallels, of course. We might receive lectures on sex from philosophically minded teachers at the podium of the Academy, though it is hardly a common event, but we would hardly say any one of us has "learned" about sex from such a source. And so, as ever when dealing with such archaic literary and epigraphic sources, one needs perhaps to allow the texts evidential primacy, yet never to trust them entirely.

## GREEK MEDICAL NOTES ON SEXUALITY AND GENDER

If we were to turn our attention away from philosophical theorists, we find some interesting and equally "strange" material in the pre-Christian Greek medical writers. It is worthy of note that Christian theorists produced next to no medical literature of their own, and only a very few reproduced the classical medical learning, chiefly interested in it for anthropological doctrines.[13] For such reasons ancient Greek medical knowledge was "frozen" in the Christian tradition for centuries to come, being passed on even when it was patently anachronistic and redundant.

Of the classical non-Christian writers Galen (AD 129–200) wrote one of the most influential of all medical handbooks.[14] His remarks on women (written by a man for a male readership) manifest the philosophical underpinning to the Greek sexual theory we have already noted. For Galen, male bodies are hot, dry, dynamic, and intellectual. Female bodies are wet, cold, passive, and sensual by inclination. This "scientific theory" of the humors would have an immensely long run in Western civilization (still present in some medical curricula of the nineteenth century) and would determine much gender-based philosophy even to the present day.[15]

He thought that female bodies could try to engage in intellectual endeavor (which is also hot and dynamic and thus quintessentially male) but can overstrain themselves in this attempt to strive against their proper nature and thus run the constant risk of "hysteria." This derives from *hystera*, the Greek term for "womb." So, women, in this approach, were "womby" and always dominated by their womb instabilities. As a cold and passive element of nature, Galen argued that womankind needs to live out its life in the private domain, in the seclusion of the sheltered and protected household. The man, on the other hand (the writers always mean the free, landowning man), ought to live out his existence in the public domain, typically the agora, where all intellectual and political discourse and all exercises of *arete* (virtue, strength, and honor displays) take place.

In sexual terms, the female body, as Galen outlines it, was primarily designed to supply blood, like a liquid "feed," to the human seed, which is given to its care temporarily by the man, and after birth it is meant to supply milk. All the generative power was believed to be contained in the male seed and life force alone, which the womb simply "fed" as it developed. Women were to be entrusted with the education

---

[13]Such as fourth-century Syrian father Nemesius of Emesa. His treatise is called *On the Nature of Man*. His was the first Christian work to focus on medical matters, and it endured to have a long influence in Byzantium and the medieval West. Its medical knowledge is all classically derived. He assigns Stoic categories but argues for a greater sense of moral freedom constituting humanity as against antique determinism.

[14]See further R. J. Hankinson, ed., *The Cambridge Companion to Galen* (Cambridge: Cambridge University Press, 2008); V. Nutton, *Ancient Medicine* (London: Routledge, 2004).

[15]Even Renaissance surgeons, dissecting bodies and seeing with their own eyes that Galen was wrong (he had conducted his own epoch-making experiments in dissection on macaque monkeys), nevertheless republished his treatises and sought to make their new discoveries conform to his matrix of thought on the humors. His influence was still explicitly present in some nineteenth-century medical curricula.

of the young, for a short time only, but a male child in a wealthy house in antiquity would be formally "taken away" from the *gyneceum* (the woman's quarters of a house) at about five years of age and given over the male part of the household, as part of the ritual of finally becoming a "man" (and by this they certainly implied "fully human"). Women were dominated by passions and affections, as Galen believed, and this was the source of all unbalance in human life. *Paideia* thus was most centrally about the control of passions. One sees how this theory leads up to a view of sexuality as that area of life most in need of control. Ideas of control, direction, suppression, are at the core and heart of it all. Galen clearly depended significantly on Stoic ethical presuppositions, and he was a significant influence, in his theory of passions, that transferred this ethical approach to sexuality into the heart of ancient Christian theory.

This picture of how men and women are, this sexual anthropology, so odd to us now, was axiomatic not only for the ancient Greeks but for all Christian culture to up to very late medieval times. The Christian fathers largely adopted the then-"scientific" view of the passions (*ta pathemata*) needing the control of reason (*logos*) to supply to them direction (*telos*). In the case of sexuality the philosophers come up with only one rationale—procreation. Where today we might suggest affectivity and psychic balance as significant "ends" of human sexuality, the ancient thinkers categorized such things as simply further examples of *pathemata*. This dogged theoretical underpinning can also be seen to go back to the ancient Greek social theory of honor/shame, dominance/passivity, that we have noted earlier.

Classical Greek and Roman vase evidence contains a lot of sexual imagery. It is difficult to interpret, however. There remains a large unresolved tension between the classical view of the sexual honor of the matron (in a private familial context) and the unrestrained sexual license of the "public" sexually explicit vases. The Greek *krater* vases, however, were generally presents given by older men to younger men whom they admired, having watched them exercising naked in the town public gymnasium. Many vases have male-male erotic themes, but many others have male-female sexual postures graphically depicted. The genre of the vase, therefore, is akin to the continuing paradox of the publicization of a sexuality that is predominantly private. As such it is similar to a form of ancient pornography, in the sense that its context was for the male part of the household: never meant for female eyes at all, but something like the "Maja" de Goya painting: the clothed version meant for daytime exposition (in the Spanish prime minister's apartment), and the unclothed version of the same figure, hung above it on pulleys, for substitution in the men's after dinner get-together.[16]

---

[16] Exco, Manuel de Godoy. The two versions of the Goya painting are now hung next to each other in the Prado Museum, Madrid.

These ancient Greek *kraters* circulated among men, for purposes of male bonding and the bestowing of "honor." Men's sexual relations are here idealized; the male-female sexual "coupling" is shown with women in submissive postures. Was this meant as an erotic joke against women or a depiction of sex as a nonprudish part of life?[17] It is difficult to read all the nuances today, but the social context of the all male society among which these vases circulated was close to the symposium, the male drinking club, where courtesans were usually on the menu as well as philosophical discussions, at least before everyone usually succumbed to the abundance of wine. The word *symposium*, after all, means a drinking session. The vases might thus depict the last stages of a drunken night out celebrating an athletic victory when the *hetairae* (paid call-girls/musicians/dancers) were offered sexually to the handsome victors. On the day after, the (now sober) young men could reflect on the nobility of the (older) man who gave them such a finely crafted trophy, and on the purity of his philanthropic loving regard, in contrast to the violent animalism of the drunken sex they had enjoyed with the lowest class of Athenian society, the female sex worker whose presence on the elegant and noble *krater* serves to mark a contrast in types of love available to the young and beautiful athletes. If this is a correct context of interpretation, perhaps the heterosexual *krater* depictions are simply meant to enhance the male-male philosophico-sexual ideal and do not offer an alternative "robust heterosexual paradigm" at all, as some commentators have argued.

The notion of depicting sexual relations with one's wife for others to see or read about would be deeply sacrilegious to an ancient Greek, a profound defamation of the honor of the household, and it never occurs. This kind of sex is never to enter the public domain. The ancient wife is depicted (as on the Greek funeral *stelai*) as the honorable matron, the wealthy woman who reflects the husband's social glory, and (generally) as the tender mother. She was meant to bring tears to the viewer's eyes when depicted as distraught by grief, draped in sorrow over the tomb of her dead husband, or sitting demurely with children gathered around her, if she predeceased him. Apart from these surviving (epigraphic) evidences of the wealthier classes, it is worthy of note that "sexual availability" in the late antique empire was widespread. Almost every tavern or wine shop would have staff on offer to clients every day in the upstairs rooms. *Waitress* was a synonym for "sex worker" in the ancient world. In addition, the sexual use and abuse of vast numbers of household slaves was endemic and rarely thought worthy of remark.

---

[17]Several commentators have taken it at face value, arguing that the pre-Christian Greeks were devoid of hangups about sex until Christians came along. But this is a large part of a twentieth-century propaganda and adopts many unsupported presuppositions, not least that the *krater* evidence is self-explanatory—which it certainly is not.

## HELLENISTIC JEWISH APPROACHES TO SEXUALITY

So what would we take as our iconic summation of Hellenistic sexual attitudes? The *Hetairae*? The poet of Lesbos? The strict and demure Greek matron? The male-on-male bonding going on in the gymnasia where naked youths wrested, oiled and dusted with bronze powder? The (joking) statues of the satyrs chasing after semiclad nymphs that still crowd our museums and the galleries holding our nineteenth- to twentieth-century classicizing artists?

But if a Greek male youth would think nothing of going naked in the public space of the gymnasium, the very thought of it would have horrified the typical rural Jew of the intertestamental period. Such "Hellenism" and Greek attitudes (which were being imported into Israel of the second century BC by the ruling families of the era) were regarded as morally distasteful and covenantally suspect. The one culture was seen to be superseding the other, and since the temple priesthoods were held by just that class of wealthy elite that valued Greek *paideia*, serious religious repercussions were set off in this "Hasmonean" era.[18] Sexual "excess" was taken as a prime sign of the disregard for the old covenant values (just as in ancient times the sexual aspects of the hilltop rituals of Baal were contrasted in a hostile way with covenant fidelity).[19]

The older Israelite biblical tradition had its own, lively erotic tradition, of course (consider that remarkable *epithalamium* or marriage song—the Song of Songs, which celebrates erotic love in the context of a royal wedding), but the clash between Hellenistic and old biblical (rural) values such as transpired in the century and a half preceding the birth of Christ turned Jewish theological writing away from the genres of love poetry and toward theologies set in contexts of war and conflict.[20] This era sees the flourishing of the genre of apocalyptic literature, one of the important matrices for New Testament thought. Here the imagery preferred for God's action in Israel is no longer the charming domesticity of God's tender leading strings (as for a wayward child), or the love of God for a beloved if errant wife (as in Hosea's image of the Lord and Israel), but rather visions of war, destruction, loss, and renewal. The old order is about to be swept away (probably violently), and a new order, a new heaven and earth (Rev 21:1) established. The New Testament classically calls this new order the dominion, or kingdom, of God (*basileia thou theou*).

---

[18]The Hasmoneans were the kings of Judea between 140 and 116 BC. They were conquered by Rome and incorporated as a client state in 63 BC and yielded to the Herodian dynasty in 37 BC.
[19]Deut 23:17-18. The sacred prostitute was called *qadesha*, derived from "sanctified woman"; the male was *qadesh*, a word that was also used to connote homosexual.
[20]See further the excellent study by David Carr, *The Erotic Word: Sexuality, Spirituality and the Bible* (Oxford: Oxford University Press, 2003).

In the Hellenistic period, Judaism's larger culture had been caught up in a growing negativity toward sexuality. The Greek attitude had itself partly been responsible (mainly as a reaction in Roman Palestine to much of what was perceived to be objectionable about the Greco-Roman way of life), but there was also an internal movement to negativity and a growing effort among scholars to idealize celibacy. Philo and Paul definitely represent this negative phase, and though several have characterized it in the past as a "reaction" toward Hellenistic cultural values (a more sober and puritanical spirit at work), it is actually a sign of indebtedness to that part of the Greek tradition that has a heavy reliance on Stoic values.

The rabbis of the second century of the Common Era tried long and hard (with some success) to reestablish as a norm within Judaism the celebration of marriage and family and sexual productivity. This was not merely a spiritual reformation but a necessary emphasis to rebuild the scattered nation (and a similar movement is currently under way in contemporary American Judaism in reaction to the crisis of population decline). Christianity, however, took the negativity of its foundational era onward with it for a much longer time than Judaism did. It has to be noted, for example, that after Rabbi Akiba in the second century, Judaism more or less turned its face away from the apocalyptic idiom. Christianity remained (intellectually) rooted in the apocalyptic mindset for a longer period, and then it was displaced by the radical ascetical movement, which similarly had small place within it for a celebration of erotic love or familial intimacy. The latter also had a prevailing idiom of "war" against the world and the flesh. These two contexts of apocalypticism followed by radical asceticism are determinative for early Christianity's philosophy of embodiment. The apocalyptic mentality always turns toward the collapse of the present order, always subverts domesticity.

Philo, the Jewish philosopher from Alexandria, writing just after the time of Jesus, elaborated a view of "ascetic" behavior as purely "philosophic," that ideal life to which God was calling his people. In his writings he is, therefore, very enthusiastic about groups of Jewish zealots he enumerates such as the Therapeutae and the Nazirites.[21] At the same time the Stoic Greek tradition was encouraging the Judeo-Christian ascetical view of human life, thus "problematizing sex" for society. Hellenistic Stoic moralist Musonius (AD 30–101) put in words a sentiment that Philo and many of the Christian moralists around his time would endorse enthusiastically: pleasure is bad, detachment is the (apocalyptic/wise) moral idea. He argues as follows:

---

[21] Some have thought that the Therapeutae were the Qumran community. Nazirites were those who had taken the vow described in Num 6:1-21. It became a way later Jewish writers had of elevating Jewish "ascetical" traditions as being akin to but older than the philosophical asceticism of the Greek tradition.

A large element of promiscuity attaches to the sexual pleasures. The degenerate require their little "pets," and not only legitimate pets, but unlawful pets too, both female and male. They chase one love after another. They are never satisfied with the standard available offerings but seek after the more exotic type of pet as well, those who require the more shameful kind of embraces. All of this is a great indictment against humanity. If you are not degenerate, if you are not an evil person, then you should consider that sexual pleasure is justified in one setting only—namely, within marriage, and even here justified only when it accomplishes the task of the procreation of children. The begetting of children is lawful. Pleasure hunting is wicked and unlawful, even if it is within marriage.[22]

Paul does not go as far as this in castigating the pleasure principle per se, nor is there anything substantive in the New Testament tradition that would do this, but his Stoic influences in ethics have led him to take the radicalism of apocalyptically charged celibacy as a norm, since "the world is passing away."[23] To this extent the Christian writers from the first through the fourth centuries are being pulled into an ambit of "making sense" of sexuality through the twin lenses of apocalypticism and Stoic "reasons of nature" thinking. What about the Jesus tradition itself?

## THE NEW TESTAMENT EVIDENCE ON SEXUAL MORALITY

Jesus does not show any particular dependence on the Greek Stoic tradition. This is not unexpected. His approach to human sexuality is occasional (he did not devote a systematic set of reflections to it), and it is undoubtedly dependent on his overall views of the apocalyptic in-breaking of the kingdom of God, considered in the light of the prior prophetic tradition of the Scriptures. If we were to synopsize that, it would mean that Jesus' ethic of sexuality is a biblical-covenantal one, using his eschatological doctrine (his experience of the implications of the kingdom of God) as mediated through his own ministry and vocation to offer a halakhic commentary on the prophetic heritage.[24] We might distinguish three stages in this ongoing development, this "new tradition" rooted in an older one. First, the earliest Jesus traditions; second, the writings of Paul and the early church legislators, such as the later parts of Matthew; and third, the literature of the very end of the New Testament

---

[22] Musonius, *Discourse* 12.
[23] "What I mean, brothers, is that the appointed time has grown very short. From now on, let those who have wives live as though they had none . . . for the form of this world is passing away" (1 Cor 7:29-31).
[24] The word *halakhic* derives from "walking the covenant" (how to put its demands into praxis, ethically, in accord with the Torah). It can be understood in Jesus' case as rabbis authoritatively using present events (the imperatives of Jesus' own preaching ministry, for example) to offer a precise and incisive commentary on how the ancient scriptural prescripts about "belonging to the covenant community" are realized, adapted, or clarified by pressing immediacies.

period (the Pastoral Letters together with such works as the Clementine writings and the Shepherd of Hermas). We will end our review of this development by looking at how the patristic tradition took it up and once more melded it into the Greek Stoic traditions of ethics, providing a patristic synthesis that would have a large and enduring effect on Christian attitudes to sexuality.

*The Jesus tradition.* One of the strongest impressions gained from the earliest Jesus tradition is an even deeper problematization of family and erotic bonding than can be seen in contemporary Hellenism. The context here is all important. Considering Jesus as an itinerant apocalyptic preacher, we should not expect extensive materials on domesticity. The issue of applying a suitable (historically authentic) context of interpretation of what Jesus originally meant by his aphoristic references to sex and sexual morality remains highly problematic to this day. In the wider Christian tradition of the second century onward, however, the issue of "problematized context" did not register at all—the words of the Lord were simply applied as absolute dicta—universal, general laws to be maintained under all occasions. If we attempt to contextualize them in situ in the context of his missionary travels, we might see another picture emerging.

In either case the Jesus evidence is ambivalent and highly problematic in regard to sexuality. Was the advice to renounce wife and children and family meant as a temporary encouragement for his (married) apostles to leave home for purposes of the seasonal "preaching season" of late spring and early summer: taking the first apostles off from home in the good weather and back to the village before harvest time? Or was it a striking at the root and branch of domestic kin bonds in the cause of creating an alternative society (challenging them to be celibate "as the eunuchs, and angels, are") in which all the bonds are created around the concept of extreme obedience to the kingdom pressing in apocalyptically?[25] Was his dictum that the heart's very thought of lust was tantamount to committing adultery (Mt 5:27-28) meant as a serious stricture on all male-female socializing, or meant as a levity, a small witticism on the need to watch over the heart's fallibility? Were these occasional references to "guarding sexual thought and desire" meant for all disciples at all times, or precisely (and designedly) for those disciples he had taken away from home (from wives and children) for a temporary preaching ministry, where he was specifically warning them about wandering eyes and thoughts during their (presumably temporary) period of religious celibacy undertaken for the preaching ministry?

The "context of intent" matters desperately, one would think, and yet the actual historical context is always what the Gospel genre of logia discards. Jesus' doctrine

---

[25]Mt 19:12; 22:30 (where for "resurrection" implicitly read "in the eighth age of the eschaton").

on sexual relations has been seized by disparate parts of the church equally to justify marriage as a supreme sacramental sign of the kingdom and to justify the wholesale renunciation of marriage as the perfect seeking out of the kingdom. We have familial interpretations of it and renunciatory interpretations of it equally present in the later reception of the tradition. Jesus through history has thus been posited at one and the same time as the heart of the "holy family" and the first patron of monks (virgin son of a virgin mother). What might we make of the teachings on sexual ethics if we were to presume that they had a coherence and precise point in them? This would presume, of course, that we had fixed on the correct "interpretive context" from the outset.

The tangential references to sexuality occur in only a very few circumstances. The first thing to note is the extent to which Jesus' teachings on the kingdom revolve around the notion or image of the (wedding) banquet. This must have been one of the few occasions in an ancient base-subsistence economy, such as first-century Roman Palestine, where ordinary villagers (not the type to be invited to aristocratic banquets) could look forward to a meal of surfeit, with wine and dancing and merriment. The festal meal is elevated by Jesus to a primary symbol of how God's advent to Israel in the eschaton might be conceived.[26] We can think of several parables of the kingdom where this wedding feast, or festal celebration, is at the center (Mt 9:15; 22:2-14). Of course, integral to this notion of the wedding feast is that which stands at the core of the image, namely the concept of the bridegroom and the bride. In biblical theology, both prophetic and sophianic, this is a cipher image for the relationship of God to Israel. So the intimacy (sexual intimacy evoked by the concept of the bridal chamber) of the wedding is a high theological symbol at the heart of the idea of the joyous return of God to Israel in the eschaton. To have used this concept in such an elevated way implies that the concept of sexual (marital) intimacy is a highly positive one for Jesus.

The same highly positive regard for marital intimacy as a factor underlying spiritual and theological communion (so high, in fact, the apostles complain it is unrealistic) is witnessed in another important logion of Jesus, where he complains that divorce was not part of the created order emanating from God but part of an unnatural "economy" instituted by Moses to cater to the "hardness of heart" of Israel (Mt 19:3-11). In this text where he argues with the Pharisees that divorce is a countersign of God's covenant, Jesus describes marriage as a becoming one flesh, a higher value than the law's command to venerate parents, something instituted and guaranteed by God himself, and a mystery that emanates out of the heart of the creation

---

[26]See further J. A. McGuckin, "The Sign of the Prophet: The Significance of Meals in the Doctrine of Jesus," *Scripture Bulletin* 16, no. 2 (Summer 1986): 35-40.

ordinance (not as a legal construct applied over society). These four cascading and ascending arguments give the icon of marital intimacy a massively "high order" in the teaching of Jesus. Once again, it is not marriage as such that is being theologized about (rather the elevation of marriage as an icon of the covenant relation of God to Israel), but there can be no doubt that Jesus attaches immense value to the reality of sexual marital love. If it is important to him as a symbol of the kingdom, it can only be such because it has a deep integral value per se as well.

But in Matthew 22:23-30, Jesus theologizes about the end, the supersession, of marriage in the eschaton of the eighth age (the kingdom). The Sadducees (who denied the resurrection from the dead) put to Jesus a case meant to be a "ridiculous conclusion" type of argument. Weighed against the Torah's definite and precise command (of Levirate marriage so that the line of one's kin would not die out), the doctrine of resurrection was for them to be considered suppositious and vague. Their case study imagines a widow who goes through seven brothers, one after another, before dying herself. "So, in the resurrection, to which of these seven will she be a wife?" they ask Jesus. The theological argument Jesus returns is quite robust: "How wrong you are. For you do not understand either the power of the scriptures or the power of God. For in the resurrection they neither marry nor are they given in marriage, for they are like the angels in heaven." Angels, who are symbols of the eighth age of the kingdom, are devoid of the need to reproduce sexually: hence there is no need of marriage. Later Christian tradition would make the angels devoid of gender as well, iconographically depicting them as Byzantine eunuchs.

What can we deduce from this ad hominem argument with the Sadducee party about Jesus' attitude to sexual ethics? Not much, really. Once again, it is a revelation more precisely about Jesus' conception of the eschatological eighth age, that is, his doctrine of the kingdom, where transformation (*metamorphosis*) into angelic glory is the foreseen destiny of the elect. The angelic metamorphosis will make sexual differentiation irrelevant, but this along with a lot of other radical transformations too: for there will be neither death, nor sorrow, nor injustice, when God's will shall be all in all.

What we might deduce from this, therefore, is that sexuality (like many other things that are important to us in the here and now) will be rendered passé in the kingdom to come. Saying this same thing in a slightly different way is probably also the reason why Jesus commands his disciples who are serious about the eschaton to be ready to make such things as sexuality, family, money, and prestige all subordinate to the demands of the kingdom and its preaching, such that they might even be called on to end up as "eunuchs for the sake of the kingdom" (Mt 19:12). After the generation of Jesus, this eschatological matrix to his thought faded somewhat, and his logia, or sayings, began to be collected rather as apodictic laws: "If the Lord had said this, then this is what must be done in the church."

It is an entirely understandable move, but the loss of an originally eschatological context significantly changes the import of the meanings. For example, once the saying about adultery being a matter committed in the heart and mind is taken out of the eschatological domain of symbolism and located in the ethical instructions for the day to day, it radically internalizes and personalizes a sexual ethic in an ascetically zealous way: "You have heard that it was said, 'You shall not commit adultery.' But I say to you that everyone who looks at a woman lustfully has already committed adultery with her in his heart." The question remains: Was this a general ethical teaching that all things spring from the heart's intention and thus the heart has to be kept faithful (faithful about what one strives and lusts after)? Or was it meant as a specific sexual-ethical instruction: that lustful thoughts are seriously sinful, in just the same way as adultery was, but daydreams about wealth and power (for example) are not?

The latter was certainly how the ascetical movement of the patristic age reinterpreted the logion, and that tradition has lasted to the present day in many forms of Christian ethics. The ascetical movement of the second century onward, especially gaining momentum in the fourth century and after (as bishops were then largely in the ranks of the ascetics and thus in charge of the canonical legislation of the church), is notable for applying this process of personalized internalization across the Christian tradition in a radical way.

***The Pauline and Pastoral Letters.*** The eschatological dimension that seems to have determined Jesus' teachings was still pressing in a lively way in the time of the apostle Paul. It determines most of his extant comments on sexual ethics. Like Jesus, these too are occasional in nature, though they are more specifically focused. In a very revealing section of his first letter to Corinth, he seems to be answering a list of questions that his new converts have posed to him (1 Cor 7:32-35). One of these is whether it is a good thing to get married or not. He replies by advocating the celibate unmarried state as the best. In trying to recreate the list of questions sent on to him from that list of answers he supplies in his letter, it seems that the particular question about marriage emanated from convert parents worrying whether they should go to all the trouble (and expense) of arranging the marriages of the sons and daughters. This can only mean "in the light of the impending end of things" that Paul had preached. If eschatology is to be understood as an imminent ending of this age and all its concerns, then what would be the point of arranging marriages (that could take many years for the planning to come to fruit)?

So we see here an eschatological sense very much related to "end times" understood in a terminal historicizing fashion. It would be comparable to a contemporary householder being informed that his house was undermined by erosion and would fall off a cliff in three months time. The question then arises: What would be the point of redecorating? Paul explains the rationale for his suggestion that marriage should be discontinued in this way: "I should like to see you free of all worries. The unmarried man is occupied with the Lord's affairs and concerned with pleasing the Lord. But the married man is occupied with the demands of this world and concerned with pleasing his wife. And that means he is divided." He tells the people of Corinth that he does not want to burden them, simply advise them for what is practically the best: "I go into these things with you for your own good. It is not that I want to place restrictions on you; but I do want to advance what is good, and what will help you devote yourselves entirely to the Lord."

This first time Paul theologizes about sexuality, therefore, is immensely significant. His words have a practical and immediate-temporal value. What I mean by this is that they are like the advice of the decorator to the person who owns the house on the cliff: why bother? Moreover, they are occasional. What happens after the second century, however, is that they are lifted out of this immediate and peculiar eschatological context and absolutized. Now they are given apostolic authority and referred to the relative value, *in abstractu*, of marriage compared to the single celibate state. A celibate, on this term, is better able to devote him- or herself to the Lord. Of course, what Paul had originally intended was to commend his own lifestyle as itinerant prophet/apostle.

Such a nomadic life demanded celibate commitment in ancient times. An ancient family could hardly be on the move, except for cases of immense wealth. Nevertheless, this occasional advice launches Christian thought on marriage and sexuality in a negative way. His final remarks to the Corinthians are something of a joke. By it he meant to release the young people who did not want to take his advice from any stricture. But the joke endured longer than it should have done: "But if they cannot control their sexual urges, they should get married, for it is better to be married than to burn." This is quite funny (in an ancient joke sort of way) because it uses the euphemism for sexual desire "burning" and reminds the listeners that immorality (sexual activity outside marriage, he implies) can lead them into the risk of judgment at the last day (burning in another fire). In its original context, a missive meant mainly for the older people of the church about the guidance of the young in matters of sexual relation, it is witty and liberal. It offers advice and allows individuals to make their own choices. Once it has become an "apostolic utterance" and given an absolutized status in the later centuries, however, it all amounts to making sexuality a weakness that less zealous Christians cannot manage to control, and marriage a barely tolerable thing permitted to those who are not strong enough to abstain from sexual behavior. This clearly falls into the larger pattern of the war between the spirit and the flesh that Paul talks about *in extenso*.

What a contrast we now have between Jesus, who elevates the joy of sexual loving communion in the symbol of marriage to a chief parable of the kingdom, and Paul, who robs it (however unintendedly) of its theological core values and reflects on it simply in terms of "necessities": the necessity of dealing with "urges" and the necessity of coping with children and households. The background to this thought disastrously excludes love, communion, and the greater fulfillment that pairing, companionships, and consolation can bring to human lives. In this it reveals itself as deeply Hellenistic in shape: for the long-standing ancient world's joking euphemistic slang for the male sexual organ was the *anangke* ("Mr. Necessity"), connoting the "urge that would not be ignored."[27] Paul has subconsciously shown in this passage that this is the horizon of interest (along with a particular form of eschatology) that determines his thought on sexuality and marriage.

It was not a good start. To this day Christian thought on love, marriage, and sex has limped along, lacking powerful theorists of the theology of love who were not celibate ascetics and who could theologize out of a positive and charged experience of loving communion. It goes without saying, also, that what is absolutely lacking here is any female perspective on love, sex, children, and family. There were equally no female theologians who could offer any alternative to the sophistic-ascetic medium in which this was all first put together.

Paul's attitude to homosexuality, as revealed in a few generic comments about sexual dissipation, is hostile. He seems to view habitual homosexual practice as a "pagan" identifier (a marker of Hellenistic culture belonging to those outside the church) and defines it as one of the behaviors that "will not inherit the kingdom" (1 Cor 6:9). His views, incorporated into the ethical-legislative mindset of early Christianity, were taken up by the patristic age and rendered into canonical observance: making homosexual practice something that debarred the Christian from reception of the Eucharist, along with other (numerous) excommunicable ethical offenses such as seeking abortion, adultery, or fornication. The deeper issues of human bonding are not discussed in the formative literature: it is heavily dependent on the legislative strictures of Leviticus, and added to that is the rationale of the "natural law," which determines that sexual activity must be, to make it moral, directly related to procreation.

---

[27]The Latin Antique term for the female sexual organ, *vagina*, is equally revelatory of pre-Christian ideas: it means the sheath or scabbard (for a sword).

Paul describes homosexuality, accordingly, as *contra naturam*, literally "against the natural purpose," but soon to be largely interpreted as meaning "unnatural." The legacy of this very partial and undeveloped thinking also remains with us to this day. It is no exaggeration to say that serious Christian reflection on the wider ethics of homosexuality, and more particularly the church's pastoral attitude to homosexual Christians (which it has clearly known for a very long time to be in its midst), began only in the mid-twentieth century.[28] Before that, most sexual theology, of any type at all was, in the face of an absolute refusal to acknowledge anything other than married hetersosexual engagement, a matter of "don't ask, don't tell." All the while, however, canonical sexual legislations grew ever more determinative, while a rational revisiting of the concept of sexual relationship was left to theorists outside the church.

***The patristic era: The triumph of renunciation theory.*** Clement of Alexandria reviews the Gnostics' positions on marriage and sex throughout book three of his *Stromata*. Their ideas, he says, range from extreme dislike of sexual union to permissive laxity. He wants to set out the Christian approach in contrast and is thus driven from that review to try to make a systematic approach from his own ecclesial resources. Here Clement finds himself poised in a triangulation: between an apologetic effort to counter Gnostic arguments on one side, a desire to marshal evidence from the evangelical and Old Testament evidences on another, and third between an overarching desire to set it all systematically in the light of contemporary "philosophic" ideals, namely, that the "wise person" should leave behind sex and attachments and move toward detachment as the purer goal of spiritual ascent.

So here we have an apologetic and sophistic biblicism driving his agenda. It is no surprise that his approach is a bewildering one: a synthesis of great schemes of earlier approaches not fully realized. In the main, Clement (philosopher that he is) follows the late antique Stoic ideas of sexuality being a distraction from ultimate realities and needing to be rationalized (by utility in the form of procreation) to make it ethically significant.[29] His synthetic alliance of biblicism and the sophistic philosophical agenda was to have a strong influence over the later patristic tradition, not least as it was repeated with greater substance by Origen of Alexandria, whose magisterial systematic and exegetical works became the reference library for generations to follow.

Origen was the intellectual who most fully synthesized the sophistic ascetic and biblical traditions for the later Christian ages; and in so doing, in terms of sexual theory, he architected an uneasy set of compromises. His works were highly valued by the ascetical movement of the fourth century onward. It soon came to be the

---

[28] As evidenced by the regular references to homosexual practice in its penitential literature across many centuries.
[29] See further J. Laporte, *The Role of Women in Early Christianity* (New York: Mellen, 1982), 30-40.

case that almost every instance of Christian reflection on sex was penned by ascetics who had vowed themselves to a virginal celibate lifestyle. Their devotion to a nonsexual lifestyle, paradoxically, makes their attentiveness to sexual thoughts and desires even more acute. The passage from the spiritual advice of Hesychius the Priest, a Palestinian ascetic of the sixth century, is clearly demonstrative of this, and the theme is a major one in the ascetical literature: read and reproduced extensively by ascetic monks and nuns for a thousand years to come precisely because it was relevant to their needs.[30] No one, at least no caucus of literati, was performing the same textual function for those (majority) Christians who were combining their discipleship with an active sexual life, and as a result the literature is like a stereo music system where one loudspeaker is unwired—fundamentally unbalanced in both its output and reception.

The sentiments we saw expressed earlier by the pagan Stoic Musonius are almost entirely reproduced by the Christian philosopher-theologian Firmianus Lactantius, one of the political advisers (and former tutor) of Constantine, in his *Divine Institutes* and went on to become a standard Christian ethic of marital sexuality for centuries to come.[31] His position was relaxed in Roman Catholic sexual ethics only in the late nineteenth century, but the same philosophy of entirely relating sexual pleasure to procreative reproduction (sex is only licit when precisely aimed at conception) is still at the root of the current Vatican policy to forbid the use of contraceptive devices and the application of the theory of "natural law" as the dominant matrix for sexual ethics.

Augustine is largely responsible for this in terms of Latin ecclesial tradition. It was his works that dominated the Latin imagination of the early and high Middle Ages. In fifth-century Africa the now-ascetic Bishop Augustine felt it necessary to compose a treatise on the good of married life titled *De Bono conjugali*. He knew he needed to offer his married parishioners practical advice that went beyond the strict prohibitions of any sexual expression that were commonplace for the monks and nuns. In this treatise he argues that in a lawful marriage intercourse engaged in with the intention of begetting children is perfect and not sinful in any way. Augustine regards the pleasure accompanying intercourse as an ancillary of the good (procreative instinct) and says it can be desired along with the good that that it supports, but that it can never be ethically desired in and for itself.[32] Here he is heavily following Aristotle's ideas on the logic of pleasure, and an overarching Stoic ethical

---

[30]The text is given in the short reader at the end of chapter.
[31]Lactantius, *Divine Institutes* 6.23. The passage is excerpted in the reader at the end of this chapter.
[32]Augustine, *De bono conjugali* 11.24.

approach (mediated to him through his reading of Cicero).[33] He argues, from Stoic bases, that sexuality enjoyed for the sake of the intrinsic delight it effects is a "disordered" act (and thus sinful) insofar as it contradicts the "natural law."[34]

But since such lustful sex (acts that are dominated by concupiscence and the will for independence) still occurs within lawful marriage, it is to be considered a relatively minor sin. Even such desire-centered sexuality has a good (and redeeming) end, which is the fostering of marital harmony and fidelity.[35] Lawfulness of marriage is preserved by avoiding criminal acts of violence such as abortion, which can turn even a lawful marriage back into a state of prostitution.[36] With regard to sexual desire, Augustine thinks that eventually age and the demands of married life, and all life's attendant difficulties, will calm down married people's lustful ways so that they settle into a more desire-controlled manner of living. He sees this as God's providential plan to redirect human weakness to his own ends.[37]

Jean Laporte finds the best thing to say about this whole approach is that couples going to discuss problems with their bishop in Hippo (did ancient couples ever do such a thing?) would find a more sympathetic ear with Augustine rather than with Pelagius, "who was less understanding of human weakness."[38] It does not say much! In next to none of the patristic materials, so dominated as they are by the contexts of ancient philosophical sophisms that regarded sexual abstinence as the mark of the truly wise person, is there any understanding of sexual energy as a psychic force that can and does serve the development of love and wisdom in a human being. The emphasis is entirely on production (procreation of children), law (being "in bondage to the flesh"), and resistance of instinct. One suspects that the nonliterate, nonsophistic Christians of the day, the 95 percent of all the church, who were married, living in ordinary families, and getting on with life in a nonelitist ascetical manner, probably let all of this pulpit talk pass by, as much as did an Irish Catholic congregation in the nineteenth century. But there is the historical problem, yet again, in a nutshell. We only have the textual evidence: the voice of the 5 percent of (marginal) ascetics. No one in the ancient church would have thought to record the day-to-day voices of parents who felt tenderness and vulnerability to spouses and children, let alone any details of their intimate lives.

---

[33] Aristotle, *Nicomachean Ethics* 7.11.
[34] Augustine, *De bono conjugali* 6.
[35] Augustine, *De Continentia* 12.
[36] Augustine, *De nuptiis et concupiscentia* 1.15-17. The use of abortofacient herbs in antiquity was widespread, usually with little effect. There were also physically intrusive methods, which were frequently imposed on the woman by the authority of the husband and could easily prove fatal.
[37] Augustine, *De Continentia* 11.26; 12.27.
[38] Laporte, *Role of Women in Early Christianity*, 46.

Augustine's friend and correspondent the poet Paulinus of Nola (353–431) was a wealthy nobleman who, with his wife, the Spanish aristocrat Therasia, was converted to Christianity in 389, much influenced by the ascetic St. Martin of Tours and Martin's disciple, historian Sulpicius Severus. After the death of their only child, they retired to live an ascetical life (married but separately chaste lifestyles), with him serving as the superintending priest of the shrine of St. Felix and her distributing very large amounts of largesse to the poor from her fortune.[39] Paulinus, as a newly minted Christian ascetic, decided to renounce the composition of secular poetry, a move that alarmed his famous teacher of literature, the court poet Ausonius. Paulinus remained nevertheless one of the greatest of all Christian poets, but he took his conversion seriously. He is the only ecclesiastical writer of ancient times to offer a Christian *Epithalamium*, the traditional song celebrating the erotic joys of a marriage.[40] Other Christian poets would indeed try that genre, but they simply reverted to pagan themes (Venus, Cupid's bow, and dancing nymphs).[41] Paulinus tried to remake the genre in a thoroughgoing ecclesial manner. He dispensed with all the pagan imagery and symbols and wrote the poem to celebrate the marriage of his friend Julian (later bishop of Eclanum), another Christian intellectual and littérateur. In Paulinus's version Christ stands blessing the union of a Christian brother and sister, encouraging them to live a chaste life together in harmony. So the one and only example of Christian marriage song is hesitant even to mention sex at all and comes from a married priest living as a celibate.

The accumulating message of the patristic ascetical literature, therefore, although it is all of one piece and fairly obvious by now, is by no means the whole story. Christians lauded virginity to the skies (as their ascetic heroes had instructed them) but chiefly allowed others to practice it on their behalf as a symbolic form of displacement. They agreed publicly with their bishops when they issued severe restrictions about what was or was not permissible about sexual relations but went on at full pace, nonetheless, marrying, singing bawdy songs at weddings (despite all their bishops' prohibitions), living out the majority of Christian experience in the nurturing matrix of family, and having a robust sexual life from those days and down the path of centuries; but all the while observing the rhetorical delicacies and not really talking about it—until twentieth-century psychology threw the Stoic handbook out of the window and made the couch,

---

[39]He was elected bishop some time between 403 and 413.
[40]Paulinus, *Carmen* 25. Text in P. G. Walsh, trans., *Poems of St. Paulinus of Nola*, Ancient Christian Writers 40 (Washington, DC: Newman Press, 1975).
[41]Dracontius (*Carmina* 6-7), Ennodius (book 1, *carmen* 4), and Venantius Fortunatus (book 6, *carmen* 1).

Viennese style, a place for incessant talk.[42] The surviving literature, therefore, is an encomium of the sophistic virtues of asceticism. The reality was very different, one suspects: it just did not make it into textuality, and chiefly, I think, because ancient society before the gospel had made textuality concerned with sexual matters solely a matter of pornography, and this the church steered well clear of in its own literary tradition, governed as it was mainly by clerics.

## A SHORT READER

***Wisdom of Solomon 7.1-8.*** I also am mortal, like all men, a descendant of the first-formed child of earth; and in the womb of a mother I was molded into flesh within the period of ten months, compacted with blood, from the seed of a man and the pleasure of marriage. And when I was born, I began to breathe the common air, and fell on the kindred earth, and my first sound was a cry, like that of all. I was nursed with care in swaddling clothes. For no king has ever had a different beginning of existence; there is for all humankind one entrance into life, and a common departure from it. Therefore I prayed, and understanding was given me; I called on God, and the spirit of wisdom came to me. I preferred her to scepters and thrones, and I accounted wealth as nothing in comparison with her.

***Song of Songs 1:1-5.*** The Song of Songs, which is Solomon's. O that you would kiss me with the kisses of your mouth! For your love is better than wine, your anointing oils are fragrant, your name is oil poured out; therefore the maidens love you. Draw me after you, let us make haste. The king has brought me into his chambers. We will exult and rejoice in you; we will extoll your love more than wine; rightly do they love you. I am very dark, but comely, O daughters of Jerusalem, like the tents of Kedar, like the curtains of Solomon.

***Gospel of Matthew.***

*Matthew 2:3.* The kingdom of heaven may be compared to a king who gave a marriage feast for his son, and sent his servants to call those who were invited to the marriage feast, but they would not come.

*Matthew 19:3-12.* And some Pharisees came up to him to test him by asking, "Is it in accordance with the law to divorce one's wife for any cause?" He answered, "Have you not read that he who made them from the beginning made them male and female, and said that for this reason a man shall leave his father and mother

---

[42]In the end, being unable to stop it, the bishops canonically forbade the clergy to attend on wedding festivals "once the music started."

and be joined to his wife, and the two shall become one flesh? And so, they are no longer two but one flesh. Therefore, what God has joined together, man should not set apart." But they answered him: "So why did Moses command us to give a certificate of divorce and to put the woman away?" And he said to them, "Because of your hardness of heart Moses allowed you to divorce your wives. But from the beginning it was not like this. And I tell you this: whoever divorces his wife, except for unchastity, and marries another, commits adultery." The disciples then said to him, "If this is how things are between a man and his wife, it would be better not to marry." But he said to them, "Not everyone can take this saying, only those to whom it has been given. For there are eunuchs who have been that way from birth, and there are eunuchs who have been made eunuchs by men, and there are eunuchs who have made themselves eunuchs for the sake of the kingdom of heaven. Whoever is able to take this, let him take it."

*Matthew 22:23-30.* Some Sadducees came to him, who argue that there is no resurrection, and they asked him a question, saying, "Rabbi, Moses said that if a man dies and has no children, his brother must marry the widow so as to raise up children for his brother. Now there were seven brothers among us; the first married, and died, and as he had no children he left his wife to his brother. So too the second and third, down to the seventh. After them all, the woman herself died. In the resurrection, therefore, to which of these seven will she be a wife, since they all possessed her?" But Jesus answered them, "How wrong you are. For you do not understand either the power of the Scriptures or the power of God. For in the resurrection they neither marry nor are they given in marriage, for they are like the angels in heaven."

**1 Corinthians 7:32-35.** I should like to see you free of all worries. The unmarried man is occupied with the Lord's affairs and concerned with pleasing the Lord. But the married man is occupied with the demands of this world and concerned with pleasing his wife. And that means he is divided. The virgin, indeed any unmarried woman, is concerned with the things of the Lord, pursuing holiness in body as well as spirit. The married woman, on the other hand, has all the cares of this world to keep her busy, and she is concerned with pleasing her husband. I go into these things with you for your own good. It is not that I want to place restrictions on you, but I do want to advance what is good and what will help you devote yourselves entirely to the Lord.

**Tertullian, To His Wife 2.9.** Where could we find sufficient words to describe the happiness of that marriage that the church binds together, that the oblation confirms, and the blessing signs and seals? Angels carry news of it back to heaven, and the Father regards it as ratified. Is it not the case that even on earth children would not legally and properly marry without their father's consent? What manner of bonding is it when two believers marry, who share the same hope, the same desire, the same discipline, the selfsame service? Both are fellow Christians, both serving in no difference of spirit or flesh. True to say they are two in one flesh. Because where the flesh is one, the spirit is also one. They pray together, prostrate together, fast together, teach and exhort and support one another. They are found together equally in the church of God, equally at the banquet of the Lord, equally in all troubles, persecutions or happiness. There is no need to hide anything between themselves; neither avoids the other or causes trouble. The sick can freely be visited, and the poor aided. Alms can be given out without fear of causing a row; worship can be attended without anxiety; our daily duties can be fulfilled diligently. There is no need for quiet sighs, no need to tremble in giving the greeting, or utter the blessing under the breath. Psalms and hymns echo back between the two, and they serve as mutual challenges as to which one shall better sing to the Lord. When Christ look down and hears this, it gladdens him. He sends his own peace down on them. Where such a two are present, there too he is in their midst. Wherever he is, the evil one is not.

**Clement of Alexandria,** **Stromata 6.12.** [The true Gnostic] will never prefer children or marriage or parents to the love of God and righteousness in this life. Such a man will hold his wife, after she has conceived, to be as a sister and regard her as if a daughter of the same father; she will only remember her husband when she looks on the children, considering her destiny is to be truly a sister once she has put off the flesh that divides and limits the gnosis of those who are spiritual because of the peculiar characteristics of the sexes. Souls in themselves, of course, are equal. Souls are neither male nor female when they "no longer marry or are given in marriage." Is not a woman then translated into man, when she has become equally defeminine, manly, and perfected?

**Firmianus Lactantius.**

Divine Institutes *6.23.1-5, 8, 16-18*. I treat now of the pleasure that is derived from touch sensation, which is something that pertains to the whole body. I think I will not deal with peripheral aspects but solely with sexual pleasure, since that which is most harmful stands most in need of being regulated. When God planned the system of two sexes he gave to them mutual desire and delight in conjunction, and so he added a very burning desire in the bodies of each of their souls, so that they might be led on strongly by such feelings and for this reason our race might be propagated and extended. We find that this desire and appetite is extraordinarily alive and active in the human species. This may be because God wished there to be an ever-greater number of gymankind, or because he gave virtue to humanity alone, so that praise and glory could be discovered in controlling our pleasures and in our abstinence. But our enemy, knowing the great power of this desire within us, which indeed some have called a necessity, perverted it from the right and good, to the evil and the depraved. So he sent on us illicit desires. . . . With such obscenities he pulled down into the sewer those souls that had been born for holiness. He extinguished modesty; he flung our sense of shame to the ground. Men related sexually to men, and he devised illicit sexual relations contrary to nature and to God's ordinances. In this way he spread the stain among humankind and armed us for every form of wickedness. . . . So now, whoever has been mired in the filth must learn to forget the filth. One's body is cleansed of filth fairly quickly, but a mind is not so easily rendered clean from the contagion of an immodest body; it takes a long time, and the application of many good deeds, so as to be purged by the cleaning power they contain. A person must understand, therefore, that the sexual congress of two sexes has been given to us for the purposes of procreation, and a law is placed within our very desire that it might effect reproduction. Just as God did not gives us eyes for looking around and seeking out pleasures, but rather that we might see to help us do those things that are necessary to support life, so too he gave us the genital part of our body (as the name itself teaches us) for no other reason at all except for generating children.

Divine Institutes *6.23. 23-25, 34*. I have not yet finished with all the aspects of chastity. For God is not only concerned with what we do in private, but even what we do in bed. So whoever has a wife must never have a slave girl or freedwoman as well. He must keep faith with his marriage. With us it is not as it is in the case of public law, where only a woman can be accounted an adulterer when she has another man; but even the man who has several others is not reckoned an adulterer. On the contrary, the divine law has bound these two in matrimony, that is, in a single body, with an equal prescript, so that either one who strays into an alien physical relationship is equally guilty of adultery. So not only the act of adultery must be avoided, but even the very thought of it. So let no man even look at another woman or desire her in his heart.

**John Chrysostom.**

Homily *20 (on Ephesians 5:22)*. From the beginning God seems to have made provision for the union of man and woman, speaking of the two even as one (Gen 1:27), for there is no relationship between a man and a woman so close as that between a man and wife, if they are joined together as they should be.... In truth this love is more dominant than any other dominating force. Other passions may indeed be strong, but this passion is not only strong; it shall never fade. For there is a certain love that is deeply rooted in our nature, that weaves together these bodies of ours, imperceptibly even to ourselves. So from the very beginning woman sprang from man, and afterward from woman and man sprang both woman and man. Can you not see how close is the bond and connection?

Homily *20 (on Ephesians 5:25)*. You must never chain down with menaces or fear the mother of your children, the foundation of your every joy, but bind her to you rather by love and good-naturedness. What kind of union would that be where a wife trembles before her husband? What kind of pleasure would the husband derive if he lives with his wife as if she were a slave, not a free woman? So, even if you suffer things on her account, do not shout at her. For neither did Christ act like this.

**Hesychius the Priest, On Watchfulness and Holiness *104, 112, 113*.** A heart that is constantly guarded, and is not allowed to receive the forms, images, and fantasies of the dark and evil spirits, is conditioned from nature to give birth within itself only to thoughts that are full of light. Just as a coal engenders flame, and a flame will light a candle, so will God, who after baptism dwells within our hearts, kindle the light of contemplation in our minds when he finds them free of the winds of evil and protected by the guarding of the intellect.... To cut off evil thoughts from the heart, as the gospel commands, contributes much more to purity of soul than injunctions about putting out a neighbor's eye or knocking out his teeth. It likewise contributes much more than any other bodily discipline or ascetic practice (such as fasting, sexual continence, sleeping on the ground, standing and long vigils, and the like), which are related to the body and prevent that aspect of the body that is vulnerable to passions from committing sinful deeds.... If we preserve, as we should, that purity of heart and watch and guard our intellect, this will not only uproot all passions and evils from our hearts; it will also introduce joy, hopefulness, compassion, sorrow, tears, an understanding of ourselves and of our sins, mindfulness of death, true humility, unlimited love for God, and an intense and heartfelt longing for the divine.

## FURTHER READING

Aries, P., ed. *Western Sexuality. Practice and Precept in Past and Modern Times.* Oxford: Blackwell, 1985.

Baer, R. A. *Philo's Use of the Categories Male and Female.* Leiden: Brill, 1994.

Bailey, D. S. *Sexual Relation in Christian Thought.* New York: Harper & Bros., 1959.

Boyarin, D. "Are There Any Jews in 'The History of Sexuality'?" *Journal of the History of Sexuality* 5 (1995): 333-55.

Brooten, B. J. *Love Between Women: Early Christian Responses to Female Homo-eroticism.* Chicago: University of Chicago Press, 1996.

Brown, P. "Bodies and Minds: Sexuality and Renunciation in Early Christianity." In *Before Sexuality: The Construction of Erotic Experience in the Ancient Greek World*, ed. D. M. Halperin, 479-93. Princeton, NJ: Princeton University Press, 1990.

———. *The Body and Society: Men, Women, and Sexual Renunciation in Early Christianity.* New York: Columbia University Press, 1988.

———. "The Notion of Virginity in the Early Church." In *Christian Spirituality: Origins to the Twelfth Century*, ed. B. McGinn and J. Leclerq, 427-43. World Spirituality 16. New York: Crossroad, 1985.

Cameron, A. "Virginity as Metaphor: Women and the Rhetoric of Early Christianity." In *History as Text: The Writing of Ancient History*, ed. A. Cameron, 181-205. Chapel Hill: University of North Carolina Press, 1989.

Clark, E. A. "Anti-familial Tendencies in Ancient Christianity." *Journal of the History of Sexuality* 5 (1995): 356-80.

———. "Ascetic Renunciation and Feminine Advancement: A Paradox of Late Ancient Christianity." *Anglican Theological Review* 63 (1981): 240-57.

———. "Foucault, the Fathers, and Sex." *Journal of the American Academy of Religion* 56 (1988): 619-41.

Dean-Jones, L. *Women's Bodies in Classical Greek Science.* Oxford: Clarendon, 1994.

Foucault, M. *The History of Sexuality.* Vol. 1, *An Introduction.* Vol. 2, *The Use of Pleasures.* Vol. 3, *The Care of the Self.* New York: Vintage Books, 1978, 1985, 1986.

Fuchs, E. *Sexual Desire and Love: Origins and History of the Christian Ethic of Sexuality and Marriage.* Cambridge: Lutterworth, 1979.

Goldhill, S. *Foucault's Virginity: Ancient Erotic Fiction and the History of Sexuality.* Cambridge: Cambridge University Press, 1995.

Hadot, P. *Exercices spirituels et philosophie antique.* Paris: Etudes Augustiniennes, 1981.

Halperin, D., ed. *Before Sexuality: The Construction of Erotic Experience in the Ancient Greek World.* Princeton, NJ: Princeton University Press, 1990.

Laeuchli, S. *Power and Sexuality: The Emergence of Canon Law at the Synod of Elvira (4th C).* Philadelphia: Temple University Press, 1971.

Levin, Eve. *Sex and Society in the World of the Orthodox Slavs: 900–1700.* London: Cornell University Press, 1989.

Lloyd, G. E. R. "The Hot and the Cold, the Dry and the Wet in Greek Philosophy." *Journal of Hellenic Studies* 84 (1964): 92-106.

Oort, J. van. *Augustine and Mani on Concupiscentia Sexualis.* Augustiniana Traiectina. Paris: Brepols, 1987, 137-52.

Pinault, J. R. "The Medical Case for Virginity in the Early 2nd Century CE: Soranus of Ephesus' Gynecology." *Helios* 19 (1992): 1-2, 123-39.

Radford-Ruether, R. "Misogynism and Virginal Feminism in the Fathers of the Church." In *Religion and Sexism: Images of Women in the Jewish and Christian Traditions*, ed. R. Radford-Ruether, 150-83. New York: Simon and Schuster, 1975.

Rouselle, Aline. *Porneia: On Desire and The Body in Late Antiquity.* New York: Blackwell, 1988.

Shaw, Theresa. *The Burden of the Flesh: Fasting and Sexuality in Early Christianity.* Minneapolis: Fortress, 1998.

———. "Sex and Sexual Renunciation." In *The Early Christian World*, ed. P. Esler, 401-21. London: Routledge, 2000.

Van Eijk, T. H. C. "Marriage and Virginity, Death and Immortality." In *Epektasis: mélanges patristiques offerts au cardinal Jean Daniélou*, ed. J. Fontaine and C. Kannengiesser, 209-35. Paris: Beauchesne, 1972.

Wiesner-Hanks, M. *Christianity and Sexuality in the Early Modern World.* New York: Routledge, 1999.

Wimbush, V., ed. *Ascetic Behaviour in Graeco-Roman Antiquity: A Sourcebook.* Minneapolis: Fortress, 1990.

Wimbush, V. L., and R. Valantasis, eds. *Asceticism.* New York: Oxford University Press, 1995.

# A BRIEF ACCOUNT OF ANCIENT CHRISTIAN ART

### EARLY CHRISTIAN EGYPT AND THE ORIGINS OF THE ICON

Roman Egypt begins with the fall of Antony and Cleopatra after the battle of Actium in 31 BC. In the following year, when Octavian sailed to capture the capital, the couple committed suicide, and all Egypt as well as the city fell to Rome without further resistance. Even before this, from the founding of Alexandria three hundred years earlier, the Ptolemaic heirs of Alexander had been trying to graft an internationalized Greek identity onto the ancient stock of Pharaonic Egypt. To an extent their efforts had been successful. The coastal littoral was well aware of the international *Koine* of Greek religion, letters, and civilization.[1] The capital at Alexandria was one of the greatest hubs of Greek literature and philosophy in the Greco-Roman world of the time, outshone only by the Greek rhetorical schools in Antioch of Syria.

What Alexandria lacked in rhetoricians, however, it made up for in littérateurs and philosophers. Alexandria was the largest center of Jewish intellectual life in the ancient world, followed by Rome, Antioch, and then Palestine. It boasted the Great Library, where a world literary database was first attempted, and where pride of place was given to the collation and interpretation of sacred literature.[2] For the Hellenistic sages this largely meant the Homeric and poetic canon; for Jewish philosophers such as Philo, it meant the Hebrew Scriptures; and for Christians such as Origen, the greatest Alexandrian philosopher of the third century, it meant the gospel.[3]

---

[1] See further R. S. Bagnall, *Egypt in Late Antiquity* (Princeton, NJ: Princeton University Press, 1996).
[2] J. H. Ellens, *The Ancient Library of Alexandria and Early Christian Theological Development*, Occasional Papers of the Institute for Antiquity and Christianity 27 (Claremont, CA: Institute for Antiquity and Christianity, 1993).
[3] See J. A. McGuckin, "Origen as Literary Critic in the Alexandrian Tradition," in *Origeniana Octava*, ed. L. Perrone (Leuven: Peeters, 2004), 121-35.

After the absorption of Egypt into the empire, it became one of the largest, and certainly one of the richest and most powerful, provinces. In Alexandria the international flow of Hellenic civilization was remarkable, even for us who think we understand the concept of global culture better than most previous societies. Even so, Egypt was distinctive. The further one left the littoral, and especially the institutions of Alexandria, and deviated from the Nile, the more one returned to a heartland that owed much less intellectual allegiance to Hellenistic ideals. This would remain true of Egyptian life for centuries to come. In antiquity, as today, when one left the Mediterranean littoral to pass into Upper Egypt (through that central lifeline of the Nile), time seemed to shift gears, and the wheels of change turned to different rhythms, and in different tongues, for Greek flourished only along the Nile and in the capital itself, apart from some outposts of Christian monastics in the desert.

The Christians were present in the Jewish towns of the Mediterranean littoral around Alexandria from the very beginning of the church. The city was a cradle of Christian civilization and a foundational force in the earliest articulation of the gospel message. There are several indications that the Fourth Gospel text originated in Egypt, and if so, most likely in the Jewish quarter of Alexandria, where the Jewish Wisdom literature (so marked an influence on the text of John) had also first made its way into the Bible, bearing with it that seminal term of Sophia-Logos (the Wisdom of God). The Fourth Gospel's first exemplars can be traced to late second- or early third-century Egyptian papyrus fragments found in Egypt, which are immensely strong origin indicators, being so early in date for so "late" a Gospel record (early second century). At times it evoked the Isis liturgy (Jn 17:5), and its self-organization around the concept of *zoe* (life) (which was better known to the Egyptians as *ankh*) made it a Gospel that was especially rich in resonance for Egyptians, long used to the cult of immortality, and ready for an evangelical message wherein the doctrine of resurrection was subordinated to the symbol of immortal life.

Responsive to the overwhelming importance of the Fourth Gospel, the Alexandrian church developed a theological tradition that would eventually dominate the whole of Christianity, setting agendas for the doctrine of the Trinity, the incarnation of the divine Logos, and the deity of the Holy Spirit. Egyptian theologians such as Clement, Origen, Dionysius, Peter, Alexander, Athanasius, Theophilus, and Cyril, from the early third to the fifth centuries, made the thought of Christian Alexandria into the dogmatic tradition of the entire world, their theology becoming synonymous with that of the ecumenical councils.

But after the divisions consequent on the Council of Chalcedon in 451, Egyptian Christian affairs would develop more and more strongly in a Coptic direction, separated from the larger and more internationalized cultures of Christian Byzantium and Rome. The Arab invasions and setting up of the Islamic caliphate in Egypt further divided Egyptian Christianity from the rest of the *oikoumene* and had the effect of turning the church inward, intent on keeping its traditions intact under "tolerantly oppressive" regimes. Its pace of life slowed inevitably, and it entered a more "enclosed" state of mind, using Arabic in preference to Greek.

As Alexandria's role as university city and cauldron of theological change ended for the Christians, the icon stepped forward, as it were, to continue to resist both the old religion (pagan cultic statues), and the new (Islam).[4] Mutely, the Egyptian church continued to show its deep devotion to Christ, the Theotokos, and its martyred saintly fellahin in the quiet reverence given in the churches to the holy icons. This very slow state of development from the eighth century onward, allied with the peculiarly dry climate of Egypt, conspired to make Egypt a veritable treasure house when it comes to preserving ancient Christian artifacts. Unlike Rome, where other ancient art examples exist because of the unbroken continuity of the church there, most of the Eastern Christian churches suffered relentless and heavy attrition in the second millennium, with concomitant massive losses of fabric. It is not surprising, then, that it is in Egypt that most of the oldest surviving portable icon panels survive.

## EARLIEST CHRISTIAN ART THEORY

In the patristic era there was much going on in the cultural life of the Alexandrian church that would give an intellectual foundation for a theory of Christian iconography. In the first quarter of the fourth century not only was the Egyptian church wonder-struck by the declaration of the Constantinian peace, but also it began to be electrified by the rise of the new ascetical movement (early monasticism), which raised up common folk (fellahin) as popular heroes of the faith.[5] Their exploits and sayings soon reached an international audience. Not much is known about the attitudes of the earliest monks to iconography, but after the fifth century they certainly emerge as the great defenders of the icons and the fervent supporters of the *cultus* of the Virgin Mother of God (Theotokos).

---

[4] *Eikon* is the Greek word meaning "image." Christian iconography is the practice of painting religious images for use in domestic prayers or liturgical service in church.

[5] The Egyptian church had suffered a particularly hard passage through the era of persecutions. See further D. Chitty, *The Desert a City* (Oxford: Blackwell, 1995); J. E. Goehring, *Ascetics, Society, and the Desert: Studies in Egyptian Monasticism*, Studies in Antiquity and Christianity (Harrisburg, PA: Trinity Press International, 1999); D. Burton-Christie, *The Word in the Desert: Scripture and the Quest for Holiness in Early Christian Monasticism* (Oxford: Oxford University Press, 1993); W. Harmless, *Desert Christians* (Oxford: Oxford University Press, 2004).

The figure of Mary the Virgin was ideally suited as a patron of monastic celibates. Her title of *Theotokos*, propagated by Cyril the patriarch of Alexandria at the Council of Ephesus in 431, led to a remarkable upsurge in devotion to her across the Christian world.[6] The title itself originated in Egypt. It was stolen by the Christians from Isis (the "mother of the god" Horus) to serve as a missionary tactic to wean away devotees of the old religion and habituate them to the new religion of Christ.[7]

In terms of the intellectual traditions of Egyptian Christian thought, Origen is the key figure at the heart of most of it. It is with Origen that we can chart the origins of Christian art theory. Although the earliest records of Christian theologians show a reserved, if not hostile, attitude to Christian art, there is no doubt that the practice of depicting Christ and the Virgin was more widespread by the third century than has hitherto been thought, and Christian art seems to have taken its origins not so much from the example or speculations of the learned, the literati, but rather from the practices of popular piety that were "displacing," with Christian forms, the domestic cultic rites of the old gods.[8] Tom Mathews's book *The Clash of Gods* argues that Christian iconography did not, as had often been presumed, take its origins from imperial art (applied after the Constantinian peace to Christ as the reigning monarch of the world dressed as emperor), but rather from the smaller domestic wooden panels of the old gods that were venerated in the lobbies of town and village houses that were now giving way (in Christian homes) to domestic shrine images of Jesus and the Virgin Mary.

These very early and primitive wood panels of the domestic gods share some resemblances with the earliest forms of Christian art. They feature the hero god, the benign pastor, the enthroned mother, all of which are themes that Christians shared in common with their pagan neighbors. The good Shepherd with the lamb over his shoulders could (and did) supplant popular images of Heracles. The image of Mary sitting with the young child enthroned on her lap could (and did) supplant icons of Isis mother of the god Horus. This religious folk art had special popularity in Egypt. It is thought by some to be tied in to the practice (in the Fayyum area of Egypt) of the images of the recently deceased (the so-called Fayyumic mummy portraits). One would pay for a self-portrait and keep it in the house until one's death, when it was

---

[6] See J. A. McGuckin, *St. Cyril of Alexandria and the Christological Controversy: Its History, Theology, and Texts* (Leiden: Brill, 1994); "The Paradox of the Virgin-Theotokos: Evangelism and Imperial Politics in the 5th Century Byzantine World," *Maria* 3 (Autumn 2001): 5-23.

[7] J. A. McGuckin, "The Influence of the Isis Cult on St. Cyril of Alexandria's Christology," *StPatr* 24 (1992): 191-199.

[8] P. C. Finney, *The Invisible God: The Earliest Christians on Art* (Oxford: Oxford University Press, 1994); T. F. Mathews, *The Clash of Gods: A Reinterpretation of Early Christian Art* (Princeton, NJ: Princeton University Press, 1993).

used as the facial covering for a cheap form of mummy coffin. Some of these remarkably lifelike paintings have survived and can be seen in the collections of the Metropolitan Museum of New York City or the Cairo Museum of Antiquities. The realistic life mask, and the technique of encaustic (painting by spreading pure pigment on wooden boards through a hot wax medium), is something these Fayyum portraits have in common with the earliest icons from the sixth century now preserved at St. Catherine's monastery, Sinai.

The earliest surviving examples of Christian art from this time (late second century), such as the Roman catacombs, the Dura Europos house church baptistery, or the Cleveland Jonah carvings, are wonders not just on the level of antiquity and craft—but simply in the fact that they survived at all.[9] The second-century house church at Dura Europos, on the ancient Roman-Persian border, which was discovered after the First World War, shows Christian worship rooms were already decorated with frescoes. Those in the baptistery showed the three Maries at the tomb. They are now at the Yale University museum. Further down the same lane at the ancient town of Dura Europos, the discovery of the massively decorated second-century synagogue (wall frescoes of biblical figures) made it no longer possible for scholars to speak of a "blanket avoidance" of art in late antique Jewish and Christian worship centers. New discoveries of small panel Christian icons in Egypt suggest that the practice was well established by the time the more numerous examples were preserved, that is, from the sixth century.

The prevalence of predominantly biblically themed frescos from the early third century Roman catacombs show an understanding of art that was, from earliest times, tied to the concept of scriptural narrative and interpretation. The earliest level of pastoral imagery (Christ the good Shepherd, lambs, fish, and vine) gave way to the second, more elaborated stage of eschatological art: Christ the judge and king (Pantocrator icons).[10] It was in the age of Justinian, in the following century, that we first begin to have the earliest of the surviving icons: many of the portable panels among them are at St. Catherine's monastery, Sinai, chief among which are magnificent icons

---

[9]See further M. Peppard, *The World's Oldest Church: Bible, Art, and Ritual at Dura-Europos, Syria* (New Haven, CT: Yale University Press, 2016); R. Cormack, *Byzantine Art* (Oxford: Oxford University Press, 2000).

[10]Christ the good Shepherd was a dominant motif of the Roman catacombs. Tertullian notes, in passing, how the image of the shepherd was drawn on the Communion chalice used in his church, *De Pudicitia* 7.10. Dean Stanley says, "As ages passed on, the Good Shepherd faded away from the mind of the Christian world, and other emblems of the Christian faith have taken his place. Instead of the gracious and gentle Pastor, there came the Omnipotent Judge or the Crucified Sufferer, or the Infant in his Mother's arms, or the Master in his Parting Supper, or the figures of innumerable saints and angels, or the elaborate expositions of the various forms of theological controversy." A. P. Stanley, *Lectures on the History of the Eastern Church* (London: J. M. Dent, 1924), 283.

of Christ Pantocrator, and various saints, among which the St. Peter stands out as a masterpiece.[11] There are also numerous other sixth-century church mosaics that survive, especially apsidal images of the Virgin Mother and child.

The great paucity of evidence about ancient Christian art has all too often been taken as evidence (echoing the literary critics of early and modern times) that the earliest Christians universally had "Jewish" nonrepresentational approaches to cult. This was a thesis highly favored by Protestant church historians, who used it as part of their post-Reformation apologia against Catholic medieval practices in church cult: arguing that the aniconic, biblical purity of the earliest Christians had been degraded at Rome. But the material remnants cannot stand as evidence for this, even though many theological writers still woodenly repeat the old prejudices. Art seems to have been an element in Christian cult almost from the beginning, even though many voices in the church knew that it was something of a paradox. Nowhere was that expressed so brilliantly and succinctly as in the apophthegm from the writer of the epistle to the Colossians: "[Christ] is the icon of the invisible God" (Col 1:15).

What art existed in Christian communes of the first few centuries would most probably have been folk art or domestic productions (cemetery art, such as that in the catacombs, or simple frescos on domestic walls), and this level of folk product just did not survive the ravages of the transmission process through history. It would have only been in the second century onward that art could be expected to have migrated to the church buildings themselves, as these start becoming more "fixed" as Christian buildings (as distinct from house churches of community members). Once the early house churches were in the second or third generation, decoration would have been a natural result.

One of the first elements of specific Christian architecture would have been the baptistery. The Dura Europos baptistery is already by the second century showing the three Maries approaching the tomb of Jesus in what is clearly a reference to baptismal theology—the entrance into the death of Christ by means of the baptismal waters (e.g., Rom 6:3). The second developmental step was most probably the creation of a low wooden or stone screen to mark off the altar area and protect the clergy from the pressing in of the congregation. This, the embryonic iconostasis, or chancel screen, was soon after decorated with curtains and pictures. It assumed the name *iconostasis* from the custom of first standing icon panels on it, which after the ninth century grew to become the main feature of a high altar screen that was more

---

[11]K. Weitzmann, *The Monastery of St. Catherine at Sinai: The Icons* (Princeton, NJ: Princeton University Press, 1976); R. Cormack, "The Icon of Saint Peter," Barbican Art Gallery (London: Barbican Centre, 1983).

or less covered with icons and partly obscured the view of the sanctuary: a thing that had not happened in the earliest Christian churches.

Soon the typical arrangement of the *iconostasis* was to have Christ the Lord to the right of the altar gates (royal doors) as one looked east, with the Virgin Mother to the left of the doors, and the forerunner (*prodromos*, John the Baptist) and local saints and angels added on either side. In the altar apse there would typically be a great mosaic or fresco icon of the Mother of God, either enthroned with the Christ child or with raised hands, praying for the world (*orans*).[12] Later pictorial sanctuary schemes would expand to include liturgical doctors ranged around the altar (those Eastern fathers who had written liturgies, such as James, Chrysostom, Basil, and Gregory of Nazianzus) and even scenes of the "Mystical Banquet" (known in the West as the Last Supper). In the later Byzantine churches, increasingly built around the shape of an equal-armed cross with a central dome, the roof of the transept in the nave was reserved for a bust of Christ in judgment (Pantocrator).

In any case, before the move to the churches occurred, Christian art was probably propelled forward by lay patronage, either in cemetery devotion or domestic ritual. Mathews has only recently drawn up from the dusty basements of museums firm evidences that ancient cults (both Christian and pagan) did indeed have domestic art; but it was material that had usually survived in such a condition that it could not command attention from a (modern) viewing public and had largely escaped the notice of historians.[13] Even if folk piety was really the advance edge of Christian art, the intelligentsia of the church had made important advances by the third century and set foundations for much of what was to come later in terms of Christian art theory. Alexandria, once again, played a leading role.

Origen, in his *Commentary on Exodus* 8, made the distinction between an idol (which was a "nonexistent phantasm"—following Paul in 1 Cor 8:4) and an image. He was intent on refuting the notion that the ancient Israelites had "idols" in their cultic system and (following from this) intended to denounce the Gnostic theory that it was not such a terrible thing for Christians to bow down before pagan idols, if they were only "pretending" to venerate them (since Paul had taught they were "nothing" anyway). Origen himself believed that the cult of images was not particularly helpful to the ascent of a soul to the divine vision, since the only "true image" (*eikon*) of God was the rational spirit-intellect (*nous*) of the believer.

Even so, Origen's application of the terms of Platonic mimesis theory was noted by later theologians and he had an (accidental) influence far larger than he would

---

[12]See R. Cormack, "The Mother of God in Apse Mosaics," in *Mother of God: Representations of the Virgin in Byzantine Art*, ed. M. Vassilaki (Athens: Abbeville, 2000), 91-106.
[13]Mathews, *Clash of Gods*.

ever have imagined. Even the ninth-century iconodules cite his arguments.[14] By the time of Athanasius of Alexandria in the fourth century, the comparison of Christ's incarnation to the act of an iconographer restoring a worn portrait had entered into the mainstream.[15] Athanasius's theological reflections (and those of Christian Egypt after him) revolved around the notion of the "restoration of the divine icon" as the central paradigm of how the human incarnation of the Logos-Creator had effected salvation in the world and in the race.

Plato's basic epistemological theory that "only like knows like" entered deeply into Origen's and Athanasius's systems of explaining how the soul was destined to rise to the divine presence in an ever-deepening process of deification, and this macrotheory also went on to become axiomatic for most of the Alexandrian theologies of redemption. The incarnation of God was thus seen as the ontological restoration of the icon of God in humankind. Plato had also sketched out the basic terminology for a philosophical reflection on image and reality (something that was also a fundamental matter for his epistemology). Origen took those ideas further and wedded them to the christological discourse, a process by which, after the time of Athanasius, they came into the specific domain of an argument about Christian icons per se.

The issue here turned on the relation of an image to its archetype. Plato's basic notion was that a good image was one that had reproduced the archetype the most closely. The earliest Greco-Roman art theories harp incessantly on "good art" being the lifelike reproduction of the outside world. Deeper thinkers, of course, recognized that art could only be "good" on these terms by being a clever illusion. Christians were highly conscious of (and partly agreed with) the Platonic complaint that material reality itself was an illusion: not a good copy of the "Ideal" realm and thus far from being a sure guide to reality. In its Christian guise, in the Alexandrian theologians, this devolved into the argument that the eternal Logos was the archetype of all true being and had patterned the human soul on that matrix such that it became the living icon of God on earth and could share in the divine destiny of heavenly communion and immortality (*theopoiesis*—deification).[16]

This idea of Jesus' body as the divine sacrament bearing within it life-giving light is a theme that dominates much of Greek patristic writing and flows over into the mystical treatises of the later Byzantine monks (Hesychasm). It also has a direct reference to

---

[14]See, for example, Nicephorus, *Refutation* (PG 100.277B). *Iconodules* is the Greek term for "venerators of the icons": the oppositional party to the iconoclasts—largely drawn from the monastic classes.

[15]Athanasius, *De Incarnatione* 14.

[16]See further J. Gross, *The Divinization of the Christian According to the Greek Fathers*, trans. P. Onica (Anaheim, CA: A&C, 2002).

iconic theory in the Eastern church.[17] Indeed, the theology of the icon is best understood as an extension of christological theory. As St. John of Damascus summed it up: Christ's body was deified, and deifying, and in an analogous way the icon can become a material sacrament of a divine presence: a window in prayer to the grace of God in the present moment. For the Damascene, hostility to the principle of icons serving as sacramental forms was theologically suspect in that it was possibly a manifestation an aversion to the fundamental principle of "God enfleshed."[18]

Thus, icon veneration was not really an "indifferent" matter, for John of Damascus, but actually central to the Christian faith in the incarnation. The possibility, indeed necessity, of Christian art as a cultic factor was elevated by the Greek church, then, as a basic defense of the reality of the incarnation as a present and empowering reality in the church. This was why the icon was canonized at the seventh ecumenical council (Nicaea 787), one of the last in a long series of christologically focused councils dealing with the issue of the divine revelation within the cosmos.

This christological-iconic theory is based on the notion that the Logos was the archetype to which all earthly icons of Christ related directly, as vehicles of the transmission of reverence. When one venerated an image of Christ, the Virgin, or a saint, therefore, this was substantially different from the earlier cult of idols. Their gods had no "substantive reality," at least as far as the theologians were concerned.[19] Christ, however, was the earthly "icon of the invisible deity" (Col 1:15). His image was charged with his own dynamic holiness. Using the later christological terminology—the icon of Christ was not substantively (*kat' ousian*) related to him (it was not an idol of a god, leading a worshiper to mistake the divine for a material illusion of the divine), but rather it was hypostatically, or subjectively (*kath' hypostasin*), related to him, in the sense that it personally represented the Lord's presence and could serve as a focus of veneration addressed to the Lord (a medium of worship, that is, not the goal of it). This hypostatic theory of Christian art is also the reason why the Byzantine Christian tradition afforded a quasi-sacramental status to the icons.

## SYMBOLS AND PRACTICES IN EARLY CHRISTIAN ART

An icon is usually painted onto a wooden panel, still today the process is followed in accordance with ancient techniques of Greco-Roman art established in the early

---

[17] M. Barasche, *Icon: Studies in the History of an Idea* (Crestwood, NY: St. Vladimir's Seminary Press, 1995).

[18] A. Louth, trans., *Three Treatises on the Divine Images. St. John of Damascus* (Crestwood, NY: St. Vladimir's Seminary Press, 2003).

[19] Though in more popular levels of the church icon reverence and superstitious practices were more common, perhaps.

centuries of the Christian movement. Frescoes (from the Italian word for "fresh"—as in painting onto freshly laid damp plaster, which absorbs the paint deep into its core as it dries) also show iconic figures (they are often found decorating the walls of Orthodox churches). These too are in a real sense icons—but the word *icon* is today normally reserved for portable panel paintings. These can be small in size (as used in Eastern Christian private houses, where each home has its eastern-facing corner fitted with an icon shelf, the so-called *krasniy*, or "red/beautiful," corner) or large (sometimes six feet or more in height), which are the type of icons found on iconostases (the large icon screen dividing the altar area from the nave in Orthodox churches) and used as public icons for the faithful in cathedrals or large parishes.

Icons depict a carefully maintained canon of subjects (Christ, the Virgin, the apostles, and saints) that was established by church rules by about the ninth century and increasingly regulated after that point. The figures in icons are perennially serene (even in icons of the crucifixion), as they depict history from the perspective of the next age, which is not tormented by the doubts and sufferings of the present order. To connote this the normal rules of naturalistic perspectival painting are reversed: there is no vanishing point within the image. The vanishing point stands outside where the observer is, within the transience of history. The world, as it were, bends to the presence of the Lord. Iconic mountains and trees often show this quite literally, bending in to the central figures of the drama of salvation. All things celebrate the dynamism of God. In nativity icons, the winter trees give fruit; animals stand attentively. In icons of the ministry of Jesus, all details of the scene are drawn around the focal point of the Lord.

While the historical origins of the icon are complex, as we have seen, popular traditions among the Christians pushed it back to the formative generation, insisting that the first great icon painter was no less than St. Luke the Evangelist, who accompanied the Virgin Mary (known in the East as Theotokos, Mother of God, or Panagia, All-Holy One), and drew her first portrait, which became the archetype of all other images of the Virgin. It is a pious tale without strong historical foundation. A more antique oral tradition relates the origin of the icon cult to Syria and tells the story of King Agbar of Edessa, who is said to have sent a portrait artist to Jesus during the time of his ministry so that an image could be brought back to the royal court, since the king was suffering from leprosy and could not travel to experience the cures about which he had heard rumors. The story goes that Jesus pressed his face onto a cloth and sent this back. When the cloth was unfolded in Edessa, the icon of Jesus was imprinted on it. The cloth cured the king and was responsible for the conversion of the Edessan nation (Syriac-speaking Christianity). The cloth image was called the *mandylion* (holy napkin) and also known as the *acheiropoetos* (image not made by human hands) and became the basis for a whole type of the icon of Christ's holy face (the Crusader Veronica legend is a mutation of this Agbar tradition).

Colors and forms used in the Christian icons are heavily stylized. The icons use a language of their own, employing many hidden symbolic values in terms of colors and gestures. The notion of ascent is important to the overall sense that the one who prays before an icon is meant to be drawn into a "spiritual ascent" to the presence of God. Earth colors (browns and greens) signify the lower levels of the process of ascent to God. Black and brown also tend to symbolize the ascetical struggle: simplicity of clothes and lifestyle. Green also signifies the simplifying and calming grace of the Holy Spirit. Christ is always drawn in blue and purple. Blue symbolizes divine presence; the purple symbolizes imperial status. Red symbolizes dedication and also martyrdom. Background gilding or gold on the nimbus signifies the awesome light of the next or eighth age (the kingdom of God).[20]

A cross in the hand of a saint is the symbol of a martyr. A bishop always is dressed in liturgical robes and holds the Gospel book closed. Christ, depicted as a child, holds the Gospel text in a closed scroll format, to demonstrate the preaching has not yet been delivered. Apostles also hold the Gospel in the form of a scroll, to signify their role as the first evangelists. Only Christ holds the Gospel book open, as it is his own doctrine (though sometimes he holds it closed too when it is a symbol of the end time, and the Gospel stands as charter of the judgment of Christ). Yet, even in icons of the judgment the Gospel book is sometimes open at a "comforting" text, such as, "Come to me, all you who labor and are heavy burdened," or else it is a text that explains the significance of Christ within that particular icon (a favored text for Pantocrator icons is "I am the Light of the World"). The merciful message of the open text and the hand raised in blessing offset the severe face and regal posture of the Christ sitting in judgment on the throne. Christ always holds his right hand out in blessing. The fingers spell out the symbolism of the divine name (Jesus the Christ, in Greek: *IC XC*), while the letters around the nimbus spell out in Greek the sacred

---

[20]Nimbus: A bright circle (also known as a halo) around the head of Christ, Virgin, or saint. It derived from the ancient Roman manner of signifying the emperor in early Roman imperial art. In Christian art it symbolizes the haloed figure is possessed of the light of the next age, that of the "glorified body" of the eighth day (the eschaton). The iconic halo is normally made in reflective gold, which shimmers in the light of votive candles to suggest the emission of light from "within" the icon, rather than the reception of light from the present world by the icon. When the halo is drawn around the whole figure of Christ, it is often rendered in blue (signifying the power of the divinity), with cherubic and seraphic (angelic) figures wheeling around within it. The halo covering the whole figure of Christ is usually drawn in an oval shape and is known as the *mandorla*. Examples of the *mandorla* are often found in icons of the resurrection of Christ or the *koimesis* (dormition) of the Mother of God.

tetragrammaton, "He Who Is."[21] The icons of the Pantocrator always occupy the main place on the church's iconostasis, or else are placed in the interior of the central dome of the church, so that those who look up to them are rendered in an uncomfortable position, evocative of judgment.[22]

The Virgin does not bless but always holds the source of blessing: the Christ child. Alternately, she holds the Christ within a roundel (*clypeus*) on her bosom to designate the unborn child, and she raises her hands in prayer to invoke mercy on the church.[23] If standing by the throne of Christ, she holds out her hands in intercession for mercy over the church at the judgment. This style of icon is known as the *deisis* (intercession), and she is depicted in it alongside John the Baptist, who mirrors her petitionary posture at the left side of the throne. The most common images of the Theotokos, however, are the variations on her icon as *hodegitria*, a word that means "pointer of the Way." The "Way" himself is the Christ, who sits on her lap. Mary is shown with the ancient "aristocratic gaze," usually not engaging the onlooker at all but (originally) looking out into space, contemplating the mystery she manifests and witnessed by pointing to her divine Son.[24] In later times this gaze was often redirected to the Christ and sometimes filled by the medieval artists with a sense of deep sorrow as she prophetically foresees the mystery of suffering redemption. One touching variant of this (the *eleousa* icon), introduced in the thirteenth century, describes the child reaching out his hand to his mother's neck, as if to comfort his mother's sorrow for what he knows she can foresee.

The Virgin is customarily drawn wearing imperial robes, reminiscent of the vesture of the queen as described in Psalm 45: "The queen at your side is dressed in golden robes all-glorious," a text that is used in the Byzantine eucharistic liturgy to commemorate the Mother of God. On her iconic robes she wears the three stars: one on the top of her headdress (*maphorion*) and one on each shoulder. These symbolize her threefold virginity: that before, during, and after the birth of the Christ. The church teaches the threefold doctrine in her ecumenical dogma, but to show that the *in partu* virginity must not be understood to introduce any element that takes away from the "naturalness" of the Lord's birth or his human nature, the third star in icons is always obscured by the very physical body of the child. Icons thus can teach things that logical discourse finds too paradoxical. It is the child who is the center of the

---

[21] Originally the four Hebrew letters of the name of God: I am who am—but in Greek, *Ho On*.
[22] Craning the neck to see: thus evoking the "uncomfortable" position one might be in at the actual throne of Christ at the end of time.
[23] This icon type is known as *blachernitissa*. In the Russian tradition it is known as the Virgin of the sign.
[24] R. Cormack, "The Eyes of the Mother of God," in *Images of the Mother of God: Perceptions of the Theotokos in Byzantium*, ed. M. Vassilaki (Aldershot, UK: Variorum, 2005), 167-73.

scene, as indicated by his mother's prophetic gesture of pointing, showing him as "the way, the truth, and the life" (Jn 14:6). He sits, old beyond his years, as the ancient of days (Dan 7:22)—a real child, but one seemingly possessed of the wisdom of all ages. As he has not yet begun to preach, the scroll of his Gospel is still sealed and carried in his left hand, while he blesses his mother with his right hand, foreshadowing the blessing he will bring to all through his saving passion and resurrection.

Saints in icons usually hold their hands forward in sign of greeting, or to accept the kiss of reverence from the one who prays before the icon. Sometimes bishops or priests are also depicted in the act of bestowing a blessing with their own fingers forming the Greek letters outlining the name of Jesus.[25] Icons of saints are reduced to theological basics. There is little expansiveness in form, though in later times the life of the saint began to be painted in small scenes around the central panel. These so-called vita icons were anxious to tell the whole tale of the (textually based) hagiography and often needed someone who knew the story to interpret the details for the viewer. The earlier icons of the saints reduced them to their basic elements of their Christian "witness" (*martyria*). Ascetics are drawn preternaturally long and thin: their asceticism has made them tall and "great" in God's eye, and their fasting has initiated, even on earth, their transfiguration into men and women of the Spirit. Their mouths are extraordinarily small, for in the kingdom we will speak not with the lips but from "heart to heart." They are endowed with transcendent serenity. Hierarchs (bishop-saints), of whom the chief Russian example was that medieval "supersaint" Nicholas, are always vested, for they celebrate the unending liturgy in the kingdom of God, and they carry the Gospel book (closed), which is the symbol of their ministry on earth and the root of their heavenly glory, since they preached it and put it into effect while they were alive.

The saint blesses and waits for the veneration of the observer, who would customarily kiss the upraised hand or the book of the Gospels. St. Nicholas is often shown surrounded by smaller figures of Jesus and Mary, recalling a detail from his hagiography when they both appeared to him, giving him signs of his future ministry as bishop. Martyrs are painted carrying a cross in one hand and frequently with the instruments of their passion, by which they can be recognized (Catherine with the wheel, Isaiah with a saw, and so forth). Founders of monastic houses will be represented with their monasteries in the background. Soldier saints are shown in a remarkable combination of vigor and peacefulness. Saints such as George the Megalomartyr kill

---

[25] Still today the ritual form that Orthodox priests use in the Divine Liturgy to confer a blessing. The thumb of the right hand crosses over the third finger (making a Greek X). The forefinger is held straight (a Greek I) while the middle finger and small finger are bent (the Greek S). All in all the hand makes up *IC XC*: Jesus the Christ.

the dragon with the grace of a dancer and the elegance of an athlete. It is a heavenly sign that in the next age all conflict and suffering will be resolved, while in the present age the church can count on the assistance of its great heroes of faith who have gone beforehand into glory yet still care for their troubled community on earth. Time is deliberately elided here. The Baptist (John the forerunner), with his head on his shoulders, also simultaneously holds his own head in a dish; the infant Christ is depicted in nativity icons as simultaneously in the manger and in the bottom corner of the same panel being washed by the midwives. As depictions of the eighth day, of the eschatological kingdom, icons are not subject to chronological time.

## ICONOCLASTIC OPPOSITION TO SACRED ART

In the eighth-century Eastern empire the growing popularity of icons, now not only in private homes but also well and truly established as a very prominent part of church decoration, was checked by the rise of the iconoclastic movement. *Iconoclasm* derives from the Greek term for "the smashing of images." It refers to a major disruption of the life of the Byzantine Christian world in two periods. The first iconoclastic era was instituted by the Syrian imperial dynasty (Leo III, and his son Constantine V, Copronymus) and lasted from 726 to the accession of his son Leo IV (775–780), when it began to abate.[26] After Leo's death, his wife, Irene, became regent for their son (Constantine VI), and in the face of much court opposition she began to reverse the iconoclastic policy, culminating in her arrangement of the Council of Nicaea II (the seventh ecumenical council) in the time of Patriarch Tarasius, which she summoned at Constantinople in 786 and then transferred to Nicaea in the following year.

This set out a dogmatic statement explaining the legitimacy and necessity of the veneration of icons of Christ, the Virgin, and the saints, whose images served as channels to transmit the veneration of the church to the "prototypes" represented by those icons. Adoration and worship of God (*latreia*) was strongly distinguished from all veneration of saints and holy things (*proskynesis, douleia*). Though the latter too were decreed as fitting recipients of Christian respect and veneration (*proskynesis*), worship and adoration (*latreia*) was only to be given to God, never to the icon. All veneration that was afforded the icon was to serve as a vehicle to transmit true adoration to God alone. Icons thus functioned as media of worship: one reverenced them as symbols in order to physically give adoration to the invisible and spiritual Godhead alone.

---

[26]*Copronymus* means "named for a turd"—clearly an expression of popular sentiment about his rule! Some scholars think that this Syrian military dynasty, coming from the far eastern provinces of Byzantium, had been influenced by Islamic attitudes to graphic religious art and was quite shocked when they came into the imperial city and found the practice of religious iconography so prevalent in the churches there.

Unfortunately, neither Latin nor English was able to have as much flexibility as Greek in relation to the key terms used in the theology of worship; and as a result this very precise doctrine of the Second Council of Nicaea is not well understood in the Western churches today, and the ancient and later Eastern Christian approach to icon veneration is also not well understood. Ill-informed commentators confuse it with idolatrous image worship. This confusion between the Latin and Greek traditions began almost from the time of the council of 787. The Latin translators of Charlemagne's court made such a poor job of the technical translations between *adoration* and *veneration* that they actually presented the council as teaching the necessity of idolatry.

At Nicaea II, which the ancient churches of East and West regard as the last of the common ecumenical councils of the church, the works of John of Damascus (*In Defense of the Holy Images*) and Patriarch Germanos, the chief anti-iconoclastic theologians, were afforded patristic status. John outlined the chief arguments against the iconoclastic claim that icon veneration was idolatrous and unbiblical by clarifying the distinction between idol worship and the Christian honor given to the Savior, through the medium of his icon in churches. He also demonstrated from the Scriptures the amount of times God commanded images to be made for the Jewish process of worship (the imagery on the ark of the covenant, or temple curtains, for example), and made the point that it was idolatry that was forbidden, not image making per se. In an unenlightened age the two might have been seen as synonymous, he argues, but in the time after the advent of God in the flesh, the icon is a suitable theological medium for expressing belief in the sacramentality of matter. As Christ's body was deified, and deifying, in an analogous way the icon can become a material sacrament of a divine presence: a window in prayer to the grace of God. For John, hostility to the principle of icons serving as sacramental forms manifested an aversion to the fundamental principles involved in the authentic revelation of God enfleshed. Thus icon veneration was not really an "indifferent" or peripheral matter but actually central to the orthodox faith. Iconoclasm was, therefore, not merely a form of puritanism, he said, but more precisely a christological heresy.

The second period of iconoclasm was revived by Emperor Leo V of the Byzantine Armenian dynasty and lasted from 814 to 842. The second phase of the attack against icons and their supporters (the "iconodules") was again centered in the court and the army and again resisted by the monks. In the second period of iconoclasm the leading theologians representing the legitimacy of icon veneration were Theodore the Studite and Patriarch Nicephorus. Second-phase iconoclasm was probably more violent than the first wave. It ended with the death of the emperor Theophilus in 842 and the institution of a great festival called the "Restoration of Orthodoxy" to coincide with the first Sunday of Lent. This involved the street procession of the sacred images of Byzantium, and it has remained an important feast in the Eastern church ever since.

## CONFLICTED ATTITUDES TO CHRISTIAN ART

Icons functioned as sacramental and innately sacred forms for the Byzantine Christians, and they continue in this same role today in most of the Eastern Christian (Orthodox) environments—that is, as the means of consecrating and enlivening prayer. They are not hung in churches or homes for decorative reasons but to serve as media of prayer. For this reason they are always placed where the faithful can access them to kiss them (*aspasia*). Old icons can often be seen with the hands "kissed away" by constant usage. Reverence given to the icons (the deep bow known as *proskynesis*, or the offering of incense by family members), following the teaching of John Damascene, Theodore Studite, and the Second Council of Nicaea, is understood to pass directly to the figure depicted. They are *never* worshiped; they are venerated, out of respect for the figure hypostatically depicted in the icon. Eastern Orthodox believers, today, when entering a church will first go to the icon of the saint to whom the church is dedicated (usually kept in the porch or narthex of the church) and then make straight for the altar area, where they venerate all the icons on the iconostasis, beginning with Christ and the Virgin and then passing to the other saints. In liturgical services in church, only the priest or deacon incenses the icons, and they do so before the people themselves are duly incensed (to designate that the faithful too serve an iconic function as images of Christ to one another).

In the Western churches iconography is gaining ground once more from the mid-twentieth century onward. In part this was because of Stalin's sale of many confiscated icons from the churches to aid his war effort. Icons came onto the art market in the late '50s and grew incrementally in popularity from that point onward until it is a common thing now to see icons in Western Catholic and even Protestant churches. Western traditions, however, are still dominated by the Reformation-era apologetics. Radical Reformed traditions often still tend to avoid the use of Christian art in any sacramental or cultic aspect, and even the Catholic traditions of the West today tend to relegate Christian art to a less sacramental role in the modern era, using them as didactic illustrations (as in stained-glass windows) of Christian hagiographic or biblical stories. When art is thus used in a didactic manner, it can be displayed rather than reverenced. It is for looking at, not for kissing. The location and function of how sacred art is placed in a contemporary church will reveal the theology behind the larger construct in a matter of seconds.

## A SHORT READER

***Epiphanius of Salamis (c. 310–403),* Letter to the Emperor Theodosios.** Which of the ancient fathers ever painted an image of Christ or deposited it in a church or in a private house? Which ancient bishop ever dishonored Christ by painting him on door curtains?[27] Which of them ever made an example and a spectacle of Abraham, Isaac, Jacob, Moses, and the other prophets and patriarchs; or of Peter, Andrew, James, John, Paul, and the other apostles, by painting them on curtains or walls? . . . Do you not see, most God-loving emperor, that this state of affairs is not agreeable to God? And so I petition you . . . that the curtains that bear images of apostles or prophets or of the Lord Christ himself, in this spurious style, should be collected from out of the churches, baptisteries, houses, and martyr shrines, and that you should order them to be given over as suitable for the burial shrouds of the paupers. As for images on the walls, direct that they be whitewashed. With regards to those already made in mosaic, since their removal would be difficult, you know best what to order in the wisdom God has given you. If it is possible to remove them, well and good. If not, then what has already be made can stand, but let no one else decorate in this manner from this time onward. For our fathers pictured nothing except the salutary sign of Christ[28] both on their doors and everywhere else.

***St. Nilus of Sinai (d. 430),* Letter to the Prefect Olympiodorus.** Since you are about to start building a large church in honor of the holy martyrs, you have inquired of me in writing whether or not it is appropriate to set up their icons in the sanctuary, seeing that they have offered witness to Christ by their martyrs' accomplishments, toils, and sweat. Should you fill the walls, on right and left, with all manner of animal hunts so that one could look at snares stretched out on the ground, animals like gazelles, hares and the like in full flight, with eager hunters pursuing them with their hounds, and nets being

---

[27] As recounted in Jerome's *Letter* 51, Epiphanius had visited a church that displayed an expensive, royal gift of a decorated curtain, containing an image of Christ or a saint (he says he cannot rightly remember) with a lamp in front of it, which he tore down. Complaints about his behavior were made to the presiding bishop, John of Jerusalem, and Epiphanius was forced to pay for a replacement. He had to spend a lot of time in the aftermath justifying himself to Bishop John (who found nothing objectionable in the local priest's arrangement), and this letter to the emperor is part of that "apologia." It is clear, despite Epiphanius's bluster, that the practice of decorating the churches with iconic curtains, frescoes, votive lamps, and mosaics was far more common than he was letting on; but the letter also reveals why some bishops, like him, thought it an innovatory thing in the churches. What had been a more private devotional form was now becoming institutionalized.

[28] The image of the cross.

lowered into the sea, and all kinds of fish being caught with fishermen carrying them to shore? Should you exhibit different kinds of stucco work so as to delight the eye in the house of God? Should you set up in the nave a thousand crosses along with pictures of different birds, beats, reptiles, and plants? In answer to your queries I would say that it would be a childish and infantile thing to so distract the eyes of the faithful with such a scheme. On the other hand, it would be the sign of a firm and virile mind to depict a single cross in the sanctuary, that is, at the eastern part of the most holy church, for it is by virtue of the single saving cross that humanity is in the process of salvation, and hope is preached everywhere to the hopeless. And I would fill the holy church on both sides with pictures derived from the Old and New Testaments, executed by the best of painters, so that the illiterate who are unable to read the Holy Scriptures may look at the pictures and be made mindful of the manly deeds of those who have so genuinely served the true God, and even be roused to imitate those glorious and celebrated achievements. . . . As for the nave, I would think it sufficient that a venerable cross ought to be set up in each bay. Whatever is not needful ought to be omitted.

**St. John of Damascus (c. 675–749), On the Orthodox Faith 4.16.** Some people find fault with us for reverencing and honoring the images (icons) of the Savior, the Virgin, or other saints and servants of Christ. But they ought to pay attention to the text that in the beginning God made man in his own image (Gen 1:26). And if we were not made in God's own image, why would we revere one another so? The God-inspired Basil, who was learned in divine things, says this: "The honor shown to the image is passed on to the prototype."[29] The prototype means the subject represented from which the derivative (*paragogon*) is made. Why is it that the people of Moses so venerated the tabernacle, which contained the image and pattern (*typos*) of heavenly things, indeed the whole of creation? God said to Moses: "See that you make everything after the pattern shown to you on the mountain" (Ex 25:40).[30] And the cherubim that overshadowed the mercy seat (Ex 25:18), were they too not made by human hands? What of the renowned temple in Jerusalem? Was it not constructed by human hand and skill? Divine Scripture thus condemns those who worshiped carved artifacts and also sacrificed to

---

[29]St. Basil the Great (c. 330–379), *On the Holy Spirit* 17.44.
[30]John is making an argument more generally that the Old Testament, far from prohibiting the veneration of images (the Greek word is the same for icons), is full of the direct commands of God to venerate holy things connected with the true cult of God. Its prohibitions, on the contrary, are directed to things (idols) that are not part of the worship of the one true God.

demons.[31] Both pagans and Jews offered sacrifice, but whereas pagans sacrificed to demons, Jews sacrificed to God. The sacrifice of the pagans was thus rejected and condemned, while that of the righteous was acceptable to God. . . . This is also why the carved idols of the pagan are rejected and prohibited, because they stand in place of demons. Moreover, who could ever make a likeness of God, who is invisible, incorporeal, uncircumscribable, and formless?[32] It is an act of extreme foolishness and impiety to depict God in a figure. This is why the use of icons was not practiced in the Old Testament. But since God, out of his essential mercy, became true man for the sake of our salvation (not as he had formerly been "seen" as a man by Abraham and the prophets, but truly a man in substance), who lived on the earth, spoke with humans, worked miracles, suffered and was crucified, rose from the dead and was carried up into heaven, well, since all those things really happened . . . they were written down for the memory and instruction of those of us who were not present at the time. . . . But since not everyone knows how to read, or has leisure for reading, the Fathers saw fit that these things, his deeds of renown, should be represented in icons, so as to serve as succinct reminders.[33] For example, when we are not thinking of the Lord's passion, sometimes we see the icon of the crucifixion, and being reminded of that salutary suffering, we fall to our knees and offer reverence—not to the matter of the thing but rather to the One represented there. In the same way, we do not adore the Gospel book as a thing, or the fabric of a cross—but rather that which is represented[34] by them. Surely there is no difference between a cross that does not bear the Lord's image[35] and one that does?[36] And the same applies to images of the Mother of God: since the honor that is done to her transfers to him who took on our flesh from out of her.

***Epitome* (Ekthesis) *of the Definition of the iconoclastic council (Conciliabulum) of Constantinople, AD 754.*** The holy and ecumenical synod, which by the grace of God and most pious command of the God-beloved and orthodox

---

[31]The early church considered all the gods of the Old Testament period as well as the Hellenistic era to be satanic demons hiding behind the myths in their temples, so as to seduce men and women from the worship of the one God.

[32]John here takes a line from the eucharistic liturgy of the Byzantine church describing God the Father.

[33]Scenes derived from the life and ministry of Christ.

[34]"Typified"—*ektypoma*.

[35]*Ektypoma*.

[36]The Conciliabulum of Constantinople (below) clearly shows how the iconoclasts found the unfigured cross acceptable for reverencing, but one with a figure of Christ on it unacceptable.

emperors Constantine and Leo, now assembled in the imperial city of Constantinople, in the temple of the holy and inviolate Mother of God and Virgin Mary, surnamed in Blachernae, have decreed as follows:[37]

Satan misguided men, so that they worshiped the creature instead of the Creator. The Mosaic law and the prophets cooperated to undo this ruin; but in order to save humankind thoroughly, God sent his own Son, who turned us away from error and from the worshiping of idols and taught us the worship of God in spirit and in truth. As messengers of his saving doctrine, he left us his apostles and disciples, and these adorned the church, which is his bride, with his glorious doctrines. The holy Fathers and the six ecumenical councils have preserved this ornament of the church inviolate. But the aforementioned spirit of wickedness could not endure the sight of this adornment and gradually brought back idolatry under the guise of Christianity. But just as formerly Christ armed his apostles against the ancient idolatry with the power of the Holy Spirit and sent them out into all the world, so now he has again awakened against the new idolatry his servants, our faithful emperors, and endowed them with the same wisdom of the Holy Spirit. Impelled by the Holy Spirit, they could no longer be witnesses to the church being laid waste by the deception of demons, and so they summoned the sanctified assembly of the God-beloved bishops, that they might institute at a synod a scriptural examination into the deceitful art of coloring pictures,[38] which pulls down the spirit of humanity from the lofty adoration (*latreia*) of God to the low and material adoration (*latreia*) of the creature, and so that under divine guidance, the bishops might express their view on the subject.... And so we, the 338 members of this our holy synod here assembled, follow the ancient synodal decrees, and accept and joyfully proclaim the dogmas handed down, principally those of the six holy ecumenical synods. In the first place the holy and ecumenical great synod assembled at Nicaea.... After we had carefully examined their decrees under the guidance of the Holy Spirit, we found that the unlawful art of painting living creatures blasphemed the fundamental doctrine of our salvation, namely, the incarnation of Christ, and contradicted the teaching of the six holy synods. These had condemned Nestorius because he divided the one Son and Word of God into two sons; and had condemned Arius, Dioscorus, Eutyches, and Severus, because on their part they maintained an indiscriminate mixture of the two natures of the one Christ. And so we thought it appropriate to

---

[37]Constantine and Leo were iconoclastic emperors. Blachernae was the imperial palace church.
[38]Literally "likenesses": *homoiomaton*.

demonstrate most accurately, in this our present definition, the error of those who make and venerate icons. For it is the unanimous doctrine of all the holy Fathers, and of the six ecumenical synods, that no one is allowed to envisage any kind of separation or mingling in regard to the unsearchable, unspeakable, and incomprehensible union of the two natures in the one hypostasis or person. What use, then, is this folly of the icon painter, who depicts that which should never be depicted at all out of sinful love for money? With defiled hands these painters try to fashion that which should only be believed in the heart and confessed with the mouth. They make an icon and call it Christ. But the name *Christ* signifies both God and man. Consequently it is an icon of God and man, and consequently he has in his foolish mind, in his representation of the created flesh, so it follows that in his foolishness this painter's image of the created flesh has depicted the Godhead, which of course cannot be represented, and so has made a mixture of what must never be mixed up. In this way a painter is guilty of a double blasphemy, first in making an icon of the Godhead, and then by mixing together Godhead and humanity.

Those who venerate icons fall into the same blasphemy and suffer the same lamentable fate, because they make the same heretical error as Arius, Dioscorus, Eutyches, and the Acephali.[39] If they are accused of having illegitimately depicted the divine nature of Christ, they adopt the excuse: No, we are only representing the flesh of Christ, which "we have seen and handled" (1 Jn 1:1). But that is the error of Nestorius. For we ought to think that that flesh was the very flesh of God the Word, inseparable from the Word, perfectly assumed by the divine nature and made wholly divine. So how can the flesh now be considered separate and represented distinctly? . . . And so, whoever makes an icon of Christ either depicts the Godhead, which cannot be depicted, and mixes it up with the manhood (like the Monophysites), or he represents the body of Christ as not having been divinized but still separate and as a person apart, as the Nestorians do. The only permissible figure of the humanity of Christ, however, is bread and wine in the holy supper. He himself has chosen this, and no other form, and no other type, to represent his incarnation. He ordered bread to be brought forward, and not any image of the human form, so that no idolatry might occur. And just as the body of Christ is made divine, so also this bread, this figure of the body of Christ, is made divine by the descent of the Holy Spirit and so becomes the divine body of Christ by the mediation of the priest, who separates the oblation from that which is profane and sanctifies it. . . .

---

[39] A Byzantine term referring to the Monophysite party (Severus, as mentioned earlier).

Christianity has rejected the whole of paganism, not merely pagan sacrifices, but also the pagan worship of images. The saints live on eternally with God, although they have died. If anyone thinks to call them back again to life by the dead art [of painting] invented by the pagans, he makes himself guilty of blasphemy. And who would dare attempt with such pagan art to paint the Mother of God, she who is exalted above all heavens and all the saints? It is not permitted to Christians, who have the hope of the resurrection, to imitate the customs of demon worshipers and to insult the saints, who shine in so great glory, by this means of common dead matter. Whoever in the future dares to make such an image, or venerate it, or set it up in a church, or in a private house, or possesses it in secret, shall be deposed if he is a bishop, presbyter, or deacon; and a monk or layman shall be anathematized, and will become liable to be tried by the secular laws as an adversary of God and an enemy of the doctrines handed down by the Fathers.

**St. Theodore Studite (759–826), Epistle to Plato.** Some people do not seem to know the difference between the concept of reverence (*proskynesis*) and adoration (*latreia*). We reverence saints but do not adore them. . . . What is more, people should understand that even this, our reverence, is not directed toward the material of the icon . . . but rather toward Christ, who is revered in his icon. . . . The case of a mirror is an appropriate example of this. A spectator's face is represented in a mirror, but the core likeness is something that remains outside the materiality of the mirror. When a person moves away from the mirror the reflection is likewise removed, since it has nothing in common with the material of the mirror itself. The same thing applies to the materiality of the icon. If ever the likeness that is visible on it (and toward which the reverence is directed) should be deleted, then the material itself would remain without any veneration, since it no longer has any intrinsic connection with the likeness. . . . I base myself upon the holy Fathers, as far as I know, and this is the way our veneration of the icons of Christ is to be understood. If we undermine this reverence, then we undermine Christ's incarnation. If we refuse to reverence the icon, we likewise destroy our reverence of Christ.[40]

**Decree of the Second Council of Nicaea (787).** The holy, great, and ecumenical synod, which was gathered together for the second time, by the grace of God and the will of the reverent and Christ-loving emperors, Constantine and Irene, his mother, at Nicaea the illustrious metropolis of the

---

[40]PG 99.500.

Bithynia province, in the holy church of God called the Divine Wisdom, having followed the tradition of the church catholic, makes the following definitions: Christ our Lord, who has given us the light of knowledge about himself and has redeemed us from the darkness of the frenzy of idolatry, took as his own bride the holy catholic church, which is without blemish or defect.[41] He promised that he would keep her thus and gave his word to this effect when he said to the holy disciples: "Behold, I am with you always, even to the end of the age." He made this promise not only to them but to us also who would believe in his name through their word. But there are those who have not respected this gift. They have become fickle through the temptation of the crafty enemy and have fallen away from correct faith. They have withdrawn from the traditions of the catholic church, they have lapsed from the truth, and as the proverb puts it: "The reapers have gone astray in their own harvesting and have gathered emptiness into their hands," and this because certain priests, priests in name only but not in fact, have dared to speak against the God-approved decoration of the sacred monuments. About these, God cries aloud through his prophet, "Many shepherds have corrupted my vineyard and have defiled my portion." Following after profane men, they have been led astray by their base instincts.[42] They have calumniated the church of Christ our God, which he espoused to himself, and failed to distinguish between what is holy and profane; for they called the icons of our Lord and his saints with the same title as the statues of the satanic idols. But the Lord who looked on this, who never wants his people to be corrupted by such plagues, exercised his kindness by calling us, his chief priests, together from every quarter, impelled by divine zeal and brought here by the will of our princes, Constantine and Irene, for this purpose: that the traditions of the catholic church may be stabilized by our common decree. And so, after making a thorough and diligent examination and analysis, following where the truth led us, we take away nothing, we add nothing, but instead we preserve unchanged all things that pertain to the catholic church. Following the six ecumenical synods, especially the one that met in this illustrious metropolis of Nicaea,

---

[41] The first meeting of the council was held in the upper galleries of Hagia Sophia church in Constantinople but was broken up by the protesting military. Empress Irene reassigned the officers and garrisons still loyal to the memory of the preceding iconoclastic emperor to distant frontiers and reconvoked the council to the symbolic city of Nicaea the following year.

[42] The synodical decree attacks the iconoclast bishops who put the two preceding emperors' policies ("profane men") into effect ecclesiastically.

as also that which was afterwards gathered together in the God-protected royal city, we confess: We believe in one God[43] ...

To keep our confession short, we guard unchanged all the ecclesiastical traditions handed down to us, whether in writing or orally, one of which is the making of pictorial representations that are in accordance with the history of the preaching of the gospel. This is in many ways a useful tradition, but especially so in this regard, that by this means the incarnation of the Word of God is shown forth as something real and no mere fantasy. For these matters have mutual relation and shared significance. And so, following the royal highway[44] and the divinely inspired authority of our holy Fathers[45] and the traditions of the catholic church (for, as we all know, the Holy Spirit indwells her), we thus define with all certitude and accuracy that just as is the case with the sign of the precious and life-giving cross, so it should be also with the holy icons: these should be set out in the holy churches of God in painted form and mosaic (or other appropriate materials) and placed on the sacred vessels and on vestments and on hangings and in pictures, both in houses and by the wayside. These icons will be of the figure of our Lord God and Savior Jesus Christ, of our spotless Lady, the Mother of God, of the honorable angels, of all saints and righteous people. For the more these are seen in artistic representations, so much more will believers be lifted up to the memory of their prototypes and be taught to long after them. To these icons appropriate salutation and honorable reverence should be given,[46] certainly not that true adoration of faith that pertains to the divine nature alone;[47] but certainly incense and votive lights made be added to the icons, just as is done with the figure of the precious and life-giving cross, and with the book of the Gospels and with other holy objects, in accordance with the ancient reverent custom. For the honor that is paid to the icon passes directly to that which the icon represents, and so whoever reveres the icon reveres within it the subject it represents. This is the teaching of our holy Fathers; this is the tradition of the catholic church, which from one end of the earth to the other has received the gospel, and so it shall be strengthened. In this we follow Paul, who spoke in Christ, and the whole divine apostolic company along with the holy Fathers, and we hold fast the traditions we have received. So it

---

[43]The synodical fathers state the creed deriving from Nicaea 1 and Constantinople 1.
[44]Scripture as guide to Christian faith.
[45]Patristic tradition as a guide to the "mind of the saints."
[46]*Aspasmon kai timetiken proskynesin*. Literally "veneration of an honorable kissing."
[47]*Latreia*: "adoration."

is we sing prophetically the triumphal hymns of the church, "Rejoice greatly, daughter of Zion; Shout, you daughter of Jerusalem. Rejoice and be glad with all your heart. The Lord has taken away from you the oppression of your enemies; you are redeemed from the hand of your foes. The Lord is king in your midst; you shall no longer look upon evil any more. Peace will be yours forever." But as for those who dare to think or teach other than this, those who as wicked heretics choose to spurn the traditions of the church and invent novelties, or else reject some of those things that the church has received (such as venerating the book of the Gospels, or the image of the cross, or the pictorial icons, or the holy relics of a martyr), or those who wickedly and violently devise things that are subversive of the lawful traditions of the catholic church, or to turn to secular usage the sacred vessels or the venerable monasteries, if they be bishops or clerics, we command that they be deposed from office; if they are monks or laity, that they be cut off from communion.

**FURTHER READING**

Andreopoulos, A. *Metamorphosis: The Transfiguration in Byzantine Theology and Iconography.* Crestwood, NY: St. Vladimir's Seminary Press, 2005.

Bagnall, R. S. *Egypt in Late Antiquity.* Princeton, NJ: Princeton University Press, 1996.

Barasche, M. *Icon: Studies in the History of an Idea.* Crestwood, NY: St. Vladimir's Seminary Press, 1995.

Beckwith, J. *Early Christian and Byzantine Art.* 2nd ed. New York: Penguin Books, 1979.

Bryer, A. M., and J. Herrin. *Iconoclasm.* New York: Birmingham University Centre for Byzantine Studies, 2001.

Cormack, R. *Byzantine Art.* Oxford: Oxford University Press, 2000.

———. "The Eyes of the Mother of God." In *Images of the Mother of God: Perceptions of the Theotokos in Byzantium*, ed. M. Vassilaki, 167-73. Aldershot, UK: Variorum, 2005.

———. "The Icon of Saint Peter." Barbican Art Gallery. London: Barbican Centre, 1983.

———. "The Mother of God in Apse Mosaics." In *Mother of God: Representations of the Virgin in Byzantine Art*, ed. M. Vassilaki, 91-106. Athens: Abbeville, 2000.

Du Bourguet, P. *Early Christian Art.* Translated by T. Burton. New York: Reynal, 1971.

Ellens, J. H. *The Ancient Library of Alexandria and Early Christian Theological Development.* Occasional Papers of the Institute for Antiquity and Christianity 27. Claremont, CA: Claremont Institute for Antiquity and Christianity, 1993.

Finney, P. C. *The Invisible God: The Earliest Christians on Art.* Oxford: Oxford University Press, 1994.

Goehring, J. E. *Ascetics, Society, and the Desert: Studies in Egyptian Monasticism.* Studies in Antiquity and Christianity. Harrisburg, PA: Trinity Press International, 1999.

Grabar, A. *Early Christian Art: From the Rise of Christianity to the Death of Theodosius.* Translated by S. Gilbart and J. Emmons. New York: Odyssey, 1969.

Griggs, W. *Early Egyptian Christianity from Its Origins to 451 C.E.* Coptic Studies 2. New York: Brill, 1990.

Gross, J. *The Divinization of the Christian According to the Greek Fathers.* Translated by P. Onica. Anaheim, CA: A&C, 2002.

Haas, C. *Alexandria in Late Antiquity: Topography and Social Conflict.* Baltimore: Johns Hopkins University Press, 1997.

Harmless, W. *Desert Christians.* Oxford: Oxford University Press, 2004.

Hyvernat, H. *Les Actes des Martyrs de l'Egypte: tirés des manuscrits coptes de la Bibliothèque Vaticane et du Musée Borgia: texte copte et traduction française avec introduction et commentaires.* Paris: Georg Olms Verlag, 1886.

Hussey, J. M. *The Orthodox Church in the Byzantine Empire.* Oxford: Oxford University Press, 1986, 30-68.

Jensen, R. M. *Baptismal Imagery in Early Christianity: Ritual, Visual, and Theological Dimensions.* Grand Rapids: Baker Academic, 2012.

———. *Face to Face: Portraits of the Divine in Early Christianity.* Minneapolis: Fortress, 2005.

———. *The Substance of Things Seen: Art, Faith, and the Christian Community.* Grand Rapids: Eerdmans, 2004.

———. *Understanding Early Christian Art.* New York: Routledge, 2000.

Louth, A., trans. *Three Treatises on the Divine Images. St. John of Damascus.* Crestwood, NY: St. Vladimir's Seminary Press, 2003.

Lowden, J. *Early Christian and Byzantine Art.* London: Phaidon, 1997.

Mathews, T. F. *The Clash of Gods: A Reinterpretation of Early Christian Art.* Princeton, NJ: Princeton University Press, 1993.

McGuckin, J. A. "The Influence of the Isis Cult on St. Cyril of Alexandria's Christology." *StPatr* 24 (1992): 191-99.

———. "Origen as Literary Critic in the Alexandrian Tradition." In *Origeniana Octava*, ed. L. Perrone, 121-35. Leuven: Peeters, 2004.

———. "The Paradox of the Virgin-Theotokos: Evangelism and Imperial Politics in the 5th Century Byzantine World." *Maria* 3 (Autumn 2001): 5-23.

———. *St. Cyril of Alexandria and the Christological Controversy.* Leiden: Brill, 1994. Reprint, Crestwood, NY: St. Vladimir's Seminary Press, 2004.

———. "The Theology of Images and the Legitimation of Power in Eighth Century Byzantium." *St. Vladimir's Theological Quarterly* 37, no. 1 (1993): 39-58.

———. *The Transfiguration of Christ in Scripture and Tradition.* Lewiston, NY: Mellen, 1987.

Meinardus, O. F. A. *Christian Egypt: Ancient and Modern.* Cairo: Cahiers d'histoire Egyptienne, 1965.

Mondésert, C. *Alexandrina: Hellénisme, Judaïsme et Christianisme à Alexandrie.* Mélanges offerts au P. C. Mondésert. Paris: du Cerf, 1987.

Ouspensky, L. *Theology of the Icon.* Vols. 1-2. Crestwood, NY: St. Vladimir's Seminary Press, 1992.

Rice, D. T. *The Beginnings of Christian Art*. London: Hodder & Stoughton, 1957.
Roth, C. P., trans. *On the Holy Icon: St. Theodore the Studite*. Crestwood, NY: St. Vladimir's Seminary Press, 1981.
Smith, B. E. *Early Christian Iconography and a School of Ivory Carvers in Provence*. Princeton, NJ: Princeton University Press, 1918.
Spier, J., ed. *Picturing the Bible: The Earliest Christian Art*. New Haven, CT: Yale University Press, 2007.
Van der Meer, F. *Early Christian Art*. Translated by P. Brown. London: University of Chicago Press, 1967.
Volbach, W. F. *Early Christian Art*. Translated by C. Ligota. New York: Abrams, 1962.
Webber, F. R. *Church Symbolism: An Explanation of the More Important Symbols of the Old and New Testament, the Primitive, the Mediaeval and the Modern Church*. 2nd ed. Cleveland: J. H. Jansen, 1938.
Weitzmann, K, ed. *Age of Spirituality: Late Antique and Early Christian Art, Third to Seventh Century*. Catalogue of the exhibition at the Metropolitan Museum of Art, November 1977–February 1978. New York: Metropolitan Museum of Art, 1979.
———. *The Monastery of St. Catherine at Sinai: The Icons*. Princeton, NJ: Princeton University Press, 1976.
Westenholtz, J. G., ed. *Images of Inspiration: The Old Testament in Early Christian Art*. Jerusalem: Bible Lands Museum Jerusalem, 2000.

# EPILOGUE

A thousand years is a long time to look over. Even then we finish our story with yet another thousand years distancing us between that time and ours. We have come through a lengthy journey of reading and reflecting in this one-volume history. At times it has been like speaking to antique peoples we can partly understand. At other times the language barrier of time and different interest has made communication strained, as if they were alien folk from a foreign planet. The book has, in part, been an attempt to translate them, and in so doing present the heritage, and the lineage, of the Christian tradition. It has been offered in two parts—one synchronous, or linear history, the other diachronic, or taking a sideways view of themes across Christian history—in order to try to offer a binocular vision that can offer some depth of perspective. It has been a history trying to communicate the truth of origins, not simply to offer moral examples that require simplification and abstraction according to preset agendas.

The story is a deep one, generally a bewildering and complex one, sometimes scandalous in its details but just as often deeply moving and inspirational in its import. It is a tale that has villains and heroes, saints and sinners: much like the present generation of the Christian church. The story has been told here with a view to laying open, for those who hold dear the Christian religion, the mechanisms of the church's early development. It has been told, therefore, with a view to historiography as well as doctrinal significances: a dual prospectus that is not always mirrored in available treatments of Christian origins, but that is necessary for the history of this eschatological movement, which is at once a *cultus* of prayer, a philosophy, a way of life, and a sociological and political force. One cannot be simply an historian in telling such a tale, nor merely a theologian. I hope I have got the balance of historicity and theology about right, and that accordingly this book might serve as a reliable doorway to the foundations of that enduring mystery that is the Christian church.

Appendix 1

# THE SEVEN ECUMENICAL COUNCILS

A Brief Guide

## THE FIRST COUNCIL OF NICAEA (325)

Held in Constantine the Great's palace at Nicaea in AD 325. Mainly Eastern bishops in attendance. The detailed acts of the council have not survived, but references to it can be found in contemporary writers: cf. the *De Synodis* of Athanasius. The central argument was over the status of the Word of God or Logos. Both sides (Athanasius and Arius) accepted that the Logos was incarnated in Jesus Christ. But was the Logos God from God, true God from true God (the Nicene Creed), or merely a supremely powerful agent of God's revelation to earth—something that could be called divine in a real and meaningful sense, but not something that could be called "God" in an unqualified way, without fatally compromising the sense of divine unity the church had received from its biblical heritage?

The argument was a critically serious matter that brought into question the whole tradition of Christian worship (if the Son of God was not "truly" God, then to worship him as divine would be idolatrous) and its whole tradition of interpreting its Scriptures. If the scriptural evidence was not crystal clear on the issue of the Son's divinity (some texts could easily be marshaled to defend it; other texts could easily be arranged to argue against it), then was it not better to begin to define Christian dogma on the basis of technical philosophical terms rather than the vague formulations of the Scriptures? Many contemporary bishops found this problem worried them most. Even those who had no doubts as to the divine status of the Son felt that the use of philosophy in defining dogma was an illegitimate step.

Suggested primary reading: Athanasius of Alexandria, *Contra Arianos* or *De Synodis*.

## THE COUNCIL OF CONSTANTINOPLE 381

Held in the Church of Divine Peace (St. Eirene: the present church of the same name marks the site, now in the Topkapi palace Istanbul) at Constantinople in 381. It was held to signal the definitive proscription of Arianism when Theodosius I took possession of his capital in 381 and exiled the remaining Arian bishops from the city. This council was led by Gregory of Nazianzus and Gregory of Nyssa (Cappadocian fathers). Their work definitively crowned the theology of Athanasius but also took matters a step further by explaining the relationship of the Nicene Christology to the doctrine of God, which, by implication, it pointed to. From the time of this council the doctrine of the Trinity has been one of the cardinal points of Christian theological architecture: there are three persons in the oneness of God. Each of the three, Father, Son, and Holy Spirit, are distinct in their identities (hypostatically distinct as persons) but one and the same in their essence and related as three into one because of their timeless origination from the Father, who is the sole originator (*arche*) of Godhead (the Father of the Son, and the issuer of the Spirit), the latter who in their own ways both represent the invisible God to the creation: the Son as the image and mediator, the Spirit as the sanctifier and reconciler.

Suggested primary reading: Gregory of Nazianzus, *Orations 27-31* (his renowned "Five Theological Orations"). For a modern English (part) translation, cf. E. R. Hardy, *The Christology of the Later Fathers* (Philadelphia: Westminster, 1954), or for the full text and commentary see F. W. Norris, *Faith Gives Fullness to Reason: The Five Theological Orations of St. Gregory Nazianzen* (Leiden: Brill, 1990). Gregory's autobiographical poem *De Vita Sua* (trans. C. White, *Gregory of Nazianzus: Autobiographical Poems* [Cambridge: Cambridge University Press, 1996]) gives a personal (and caustic) account of events at the council during his presidency of it. Official conciliar texts in N. P. Tanner, *Decrees of the Ecumenical Councils* (London: Sheed & Ward, 1989), 1:21-35.

## THE COUNCIL OF EPHESUS 431

Held in the magnificent city of Ephesus, Asia Minor. The ruins of the city are still a wonder of the ancient world. It was occasioned by the dispute that arose between the churches of Constantinople and Alexandria. The archbishop of Constantinople (Nestorius) held to an Antiochene type of Christology (he was an Antiochene monk by origin), which laid stress on the humanness of Jesus and the separateness of the human Jesus (and all his relevant human characteristics) from the divine Logos, who inhabited or indwelt the man Jesus. At its extreme form the Antiochene christology (as taught by Diodore of Tarsus or Theodore Mopsuestia in the generation before Nestorius) had even suggested a distinction between the Logos and the man Jesus.

Many felt this to be a revisiting of the ancient heresy of adoptionism (the divinity inhabiting the man for a short time).

Cyril of Alexandria found Nestorius was propagating his doctrine all over the Middle East and reacted against it. Cyril followed in the tradition of Athanasius and was himself archbishop of the city of Alexandria. He taught a Christology that saw the divine Logos as so intimately united with the human condition that even the body of Jesus was in a real sense "divinized": it was still a real human body that could (and did) die, but it was also a body that proved life-giving by its divine touch (miracles, etc.). He delighted in stressing the paradoxical element of Christian thought: God's death, God's flesh, and so on. This more paradoxical Christology was evidently mystical in tone and inspiration, whereas that of Nestorius was dominated by logical concerns.

The argument between the two hierarchs took on an international aspect, and the emperor (Theodosius II) called an ecumenical council to settle it. The controversy fixed on some technical terms: one of the most famous was the issue of the Theotokos, or "Mother of God." Nestorius had vetoed this as being at best silly and at worst heretical. In his opinion, if one meant to imply that God issued from a human mother, then God would have had a beginning in time, and thus would not be God. Christians, he argued, must say instead that Mary was the mother of the Christ, or the mother of Jesus, but not the mother of God; because, strictly speaking, it was not God who was born from her but Jesus the Christ.

Cyril countered by arguing that if Mary was not, strictly speaking, the mother of God, then the one who was born from her (Jesus) was not, strictly speaking, God. Thus he accused Nestorius of denying the divinity of Jesus. This was a new argument, because Nicaea had not clarified the relationship of Jesus to the divine—only the relation of the Logos to the divine. Cyril maintained that the Logos assumed a human body perfect in every regard, although it was not a distinct human person in its own right. In other words, there were not two persons in the Christ—one the person of the divine Logos, the other the human person Jesus of Nazareth—rather one single person. This was the divine and eternal person of God the Word, who in a specific time and place had assumed to himself a human body, and lived as a man by means of that body, for a specific purpose—to communicate with his human creation.

When Nestorius said that this was a silly view, Cyril countered by saying that it was an incomprehensible view, but clearly God's chosen plan of providential salvation and ought not to be mocked because it did not fit with the "wisdom of the world." For his part, Nestorius taught that Jesus of Nazareth was a servant, a human being, who emptied himself out in the service of God the Logos, who inhabited him. This is largely what he thought, but he did not wish to fall into the trap of agreeing to Cyril's arguments that this meant he had resurrected adoptionism. Nestorius did not agree with adoptionism, but it might be fair to say that he did not have a really good argument to explain to his opponents why his views were different from adoptionism.

As a result, his theology was obscure and less focused than Cyril's. He fell from grace at the council of Ephesus, and after several years of further protests, the emperor condemned him to lifelong exile in the Sahara desert. The council was so stormy and bad-tempered that for years afterwards the Syrian and Alexandrian churches would not speak with one another. In an an attempt to patch up the quarrel, an attempt that went badly wrong, another council was held at Ephesus in 449—during which the archbishop of Constantinople (Flavian) was beaten senseless by monks and died from his injuries. The resulting scandal led to the disregarding of its decisions and the summoning of another council at Chalcedon.

Suggested reading: Official conciliar texts in N. P. Tanner, *Decrees of the Ecumenical Councils* (London: Sheed & Ward, 1989), 1:37-74. Primary texts and historical context in J. A. McGuckin, *St. Cyril of Alexandria and the Christological Controversy* (Leiden: Brill, 1994; repr., Crestwood, NY: St. Vladimir's Seminary Press, 2004); *St. Cyril of Alexandria: That the Christ Is One* (Crestwood, NY: St. Vladimir's Seminary Press, 1995).

## THE COUNCIL OF CHALCEDON 451

Held immediately after the death of Theodosius II, in an imperial palace at Chalcedon, a suburb of Constantiniople, in 451. It was a serious effort to reconcile the divisions that had continued to plague the church after Ephesus I, particularly in terms of the rifts that had continued between the Syrian churches (Antiochene patriarchate) and Alexandria. In the lifetime of Cyril, Rome had been very much on the side of Alexandria, but after his death his successor Dioscorus had alienated feeling by his methods and one-sided way of reading his predecessor. The Roman church had come to agree with the Syrians that a decided stress on the two-natured reality of Christ was called for: that is, that the Christ had a divine nature and also a human nature. The Alexandrians and many other Easterners felt that this created an intolerably divided and artificial view of Christ.

The Council of Chalcedon studied the works of Cyril and also a letter sent in by Pope Leo (Leo's *Tome*), which set out the doctrine of two natures. Cyril had preferred the concept of two natures (God and man) before the union (the union that took place within the incarnation) but only one composite nature after the union (otherwise it should not be called a union). But by the time of Chalcedon, Cyril had been dead for seven years. The majority of bishops at the council wished to be loyal to his tradition but were also pressed heavily by the emperor (Marcian) to represent the Roman and Syrian views insofar as these could be reconciled.

Eventually a compromise was worked out that met the terms of the Roman letter but was also in harmony with the doctrine of Ephesus: Christ had two natures, one divine and one human, but he only had one person. This person was wholly and utterly divine and preexistent, and it was this person who adopted a human nature from the womb of Mary. There was thus, strictly speaking, no human person in Jesus: only a divine person made flesh. This definitive rejection of adoptionism stated that at no time could Jesus be regarded as "merely a man" or "simply a man": for from his birth he was the divine Word appearing in a human body. This has been the standard of christological orthodoxy up until the twentieth century, when it has again been much controverted.

Ostensibly the council was called to settle the Monophysite heresy (those who maintained Jesus only had one divine nature). In reality it was called to reconcile the differing traditions of Rome/Syria and Alexandria. While adopting the *Tome* of Leo as an orthodox text, the council fathers clearly stated all their theology in phrases borrowed from Cyril's writings, and they anathematized leading members of the Syrian tradition who were now dead, repeating the condemnation of Nestorius. The resentments left smoldering at Chalcedon were bound to flare into life again.

Suggested reading: Official conciliar texts in: N. P. Tanner, *Decrees of the Ecumenical Councils* (London: Sheed & Ward, 1989), 1:75-103. Primary texts in E. R. Hardy, *Christology of the Later Fathers* (Philadelphia: Westminster, 1964). Context in R. V. Sellers, *The Council of Chalcedon: A Historical and Doctrinal Survey* (London: SPCK, 1953); A. Grillmeier, *Christ in Christian Tradition*, 2nd ed. (London: Mowbray, 1975), 1:520-57.

## THE COUNCIL OF CONSTANTINOPLE 553

Held in the capital in 553, under the presidency of the Emperor Justinian. The christological divisions between Chalcedonians and Monophysites had ripped the Eastern church apart. Justinian was determined to resolve the conflict. The terms of this council largely veered away from the unsatisfactory compromise of Chalcedon and returned to the restatement of Ephesus 431. It was always unpopular in the West because of its implied snub to Pope Leo. In the course of its deliberations, the Roman pope (Vigilius) was dragged by the emperor to Constantinople to take part and bullied into subservience. For such reasons the West took many years to recognize it as an ecumenical council. It eventually did so, but in Western church history most textbooks continued to stop their accounts at Chalcedon and often still continue to regard Chalcedon as the end of the story—whereas Constantinople II is a significant readjustment of the argument. At Constantinople II the Syrian tradition was severely repressed, and the Cyrilline doctrine of the single divine personhood of Christ was proclaimed as the definitive theology of the church.

Suggested reading: Official conciliar texts in N. P. Tanner, *Decrees of the Ecumenical Councils* (London: Sheed & Ward, 1989), 1:105-122. Contexts in P. T. R. Gray, *The Defence of Chalcedon in the East, 451–553* (Leiden: Brill, 1979); A. Grillmeier, *Christ in Christian Tradition*, vol. 2, part 2 (London: Mowbray, 1995).

## CONSTANTINOPLE 681

This council was the last of the seven to be concerned wholly with christological doctrine. It was in a sense a reopening of the Monophysite dispute. The Monophysites were radical and uncompromising followers of Cyril who regarded the adjustments he made in his later and mature work as the lapses of a senile old man—in fact, they were important adjustments he made to his doctrine in the light of Syrian and Roman criticisms. By reverting to Cyril's early teaching, the Monophysites uttlerly rejected Chalcedon. Even after Constantinople II they felt the point of the divinization of Christ's body, by virtue of its divine inhabitation, had been neglected. Their opponents felt that they in turn had underestimated the genuineness of the human condition of Jesus.

The precise argument at this council was whether Christ had one will or two. That is—did he have one psychic center to his personality or two (i.e., one divine will [*thelema*] and one human)? If he had two, this would explain how he could be tempted and also how he could make genuinely human choices and entertain genuinely human feelings. If he only had one (presumably divine?), then how could he be a real man? On the other hand, if he had two psychic centers, then surely he was not one person but two: a God and a man stuck in the same shell. The one-will party was designated the Monothelites. The two-will party had the name Dyothelites.

The argument was settled in favor of the Dyothelites. This was declared the position closest to the spirit of the previous councils. Christ had to have two wills, otherwise he would not have possession of a perfect human nature. The earlier councils had defined that he had two natures: perfect manhood and perfect deity. On the other, hand the council of Constantinople II insisted that these two wills only existed in theoretical distinction. In actuality they were wholly united. In other words, just as Christ's humanity had never existed independently of the divine Word (there was no human being Jesus of Nazareth who had a separate life before the Logos took him over, but in fact the humanity only came into existence from the moment the Logos entered into the Virgin's womb and made for itself a human nature to represent it), so too the human will of Jesus (which was a fundamental part of that humanity) never had a separate existence from the divine will. It was a testimony to the perfect moral goodness of Jesus that the human will always and at every moment served and was subservient to the will of God.

Theologians argued much about the biblical text "Not my will but thine be done." But the ultimate point was that the existence of two wills, always bound together in perfect harmony at each and every single moment, was a way of reaffirming Jesus' genuine humanity, while at the same time maintaining the Ephesine doctrine of 431 that there was only one divine person present in the incarnate Logos, not a divine person alongside a human person. This was a little-known council that has not attracted much study despite its importance in terms of the difficulties of elaborating a Christian anthropology.

Suggested reading: Official conciliar texts in N. P. Tanner, *Decrees of the Ecumenical Councils* (London: Sheed & Ward, 1989), 1:124-30.

## THE COUNCIL OF NICAEA 787

Called in the basilica church at Nicaea (still standing, though in ruins, at Iznik, modern Turkey) in 787. Its fundamental point of argument was whether the Christ could be legitimately pictured in artistic forms or not, and whether icons were idolatrous. Those in favor of icons were called iconodules ("icon venerators"), those against iconoclasts ("icon smashers"). It is a complicated council. In some ways its argumentation is christological; in other ways it represented the closest the Byzantine church ever came to an experience similar to that of the Reformation in the West. The arguments ranged over a whole generation.

In the end the Eastern church proclaimed that icons were a sacramental form of representing not only the image of Christ, not merely a didactic aspect of the Gospel in art, but also in some mysterious sense were channels for actively representing his presence to his people who stood before him in prayer. The Western church concurred with the doctrine and the practice of using icons in worship, praying over the relics of the saints (which was closely related to it in the argument of the council), and the understanding of the sacraments (e.g., the Eucharist) as representing a real presence of Christ (not just a symbolic presence) were elements descriptive of both the Eastern and Western churches until, in the West, the Reformation divided attitudes profoundly on all three issues of church life and worship.

Eastern churches to this day still regard the place of icons in Christian prayer and worship as a test of faith: that is, a matter of serious import in a person's understanding of the incarnation, of the sacraments, and so on. By the time of the later medieval West iconography was understood in a significantly diminished fashion, and certainly in the Western churches after the Reformation, this more sacramentalized understanding (of Nicaea II) largely faded away both in the Protestant and Catholic churches. There are still significant remnants of it in the diffferent sacramental doctrines of the various churches, and to that extent Nicaea II is still an important council whose relevance goes beyond the mere surface argument over art and relics—to fundamental matters of the relationship of spirit and matter, and how material forms can be genuine vehicles of divine grace.

Suggested reading: Official conciliar texts in N. P. Tanner, *Decrees of the Ecumenical Councils* (London: Sheed & Ward, 1989), 1:132-56. Contexts in L. Ouspensky, *The Theology of the Icon* (Crestwood, NY: St. Vladimir's Seminary Press, 1978); A. Bryer and J. Herrin, eds., *Iconoclasm*, Papers Given at the Ninth Symposium of Byzantine Studies, University of Birmingham (Birmingham: Centre for Byzantine Studies, 1975).

Overall, the seven ecumenical councils not only stand as a historical chart of Christianity's intellectual and moral progress in the postbiblical era; they also represent the corpus of classical orthodoxy in Christian doctrine, especially in terms of its doctrine of God and its Christology. After the division of the Eastern and Western churches (beginning with Charlemagne's declaration of a separate Western empire under himself as Holy Roman Emperor in AD 800, and culminating with more formal divisions after the events of 1054 and 1204), the Latin church continued to hold "ecumenical" councils (councils of the worldwide church having worldwide authority), the most recent being Vatican II in the '60s of the present century. The Eastern churches only regard the first seven as having genuine ecumenical authority for the unbroken Christian ecumene. The Anglican Church tends to follow that view but historically has some ambivalence toward the seventh council and generally does not hold the same view as Orthodox and Catholic theologians, overall, on the infallibly inspired nature of councils. Protestant churches have widely differing views but generally do not afford the councils any particularly authoritative role in the contemporary church, beyond their historic and time-bound contribution to the theology of the era.

## FURTHER GENERAL READING

Davis, L. *The Seven Oecumenical Councils*. Wilmington, DE: M. Glazier, 1987.
Luibheid, C. *The Council of Nicaea*. Galway, UK: Galway University Press, 1982.
McGuckin, J. A. *St. Cyril of Alexandria and the Christological Controversy*. Leiden: Brill, 1994. Reprint, Crestwood, NY: St. Vladimir's Seminary Press, 2004.
Sellers, R. V. *The Council of Chalcedon*. London: SPCK, 1953.
Tanner, N. P. *The Councils of the Church: A Short History*. New York: Crossroad, 2001.
Trostyanskiy, S. *Seven Icons of Christ: An Introduction to the Oikoumenical Councils*. Piscataway, NJ: Gorgias Press, 2016.

# Appendix 2

# LIST OF THE ROMAN POPES TO 1054 AND THE PATRIARCHS OF CONSTANTINOPLE TO 1453

**ROMAN POPES**

| | |
|---|---|
| Peter (67) | (traditionally listed as first of popes; martyred in Rome under Nero) |
| Linus (67–76) | |
| Anacletus (Cletus) (76–88) | |
| Clement I (88–97) | |
| Evaristus (97–105) | |
| Alexander I (105–115) | |
| Sixtus I (115–125) or Xystus | |
| Telesphorus (125–136) | |
| Hyginus (136–140) | |
| Pius I (140–155) | |
| Aniketos (155–166) | |
| Soter (166–175) | |
| Eleutherius (175–189) | |
| Victor I (189–199) | |
| Zephyrinus (199–217) | |
| Callistus I (217–22) | Callistus and the following three popes were opposed by Hippolytus, theologian and martyr, who claimed the throne (217–236) |
| Urban I (222–30) | |
| Pontanus (230–35) | |
| Anterus (235–36) | |
| Fabian (236–50) | |
| Cornelius (251–53) | Opposed by Novatian, who claimed the throne (251) |
| Lucius I (253–54) | |
| Stephen I (254–257) | |

| | |
|---|---|
| Sixtus II (257–258) | |
| Dionysius (260–268) | |
| Felix I (269–274) | |
| Eutychian (275–283) | |
| Caius (283–296) or Gaius | |
| Marcellinus (296–304) | |
| Marcellus I (308–309) | |
| Eusebius (309 or 310) | |
| Miltiades (311–314) | |
| Sylvester I (314–335) | At the time of Constantine the Great |
| Marcus (336) | |
| Julius I (337–352) | |
| Liberius (352–366) | Opposed by Felix II, who claimed the throne (355–365) |
| Damasus I (366–383) | Opposed by Ursicinus, who claimed the throne (366–367) |
| Siricius (384–399) | |
| Anastasius I (399–401) | |
| Innocent I (401–417) | |
| Zosimus (417–418) | |
| Boniface I (418–422) | Opposed by Eulalius, who claimed the throne (418–419) |
| Celestine I (422–432) | |
| Sixtus III (432–440) | |
| Leo I (the Great) (440–461) | |
| Hilarius (461–468) | |
| Simplicius (468–483) | |
| Felix III (II) (483–492) | |
| Gelasius I (492–496) | |
| Anastasius II (496–498) | |
| Symmachus (498–514) | Opposed by Laurentius, who claimed the throne (498–501) |
| Hormisdas (514–523) | |
| John I (523–526) | |
| Felix IV (III) (526–530) | |
| Boniface II (530–532) | Opposed by Dioscorus, who claimed the throne (530) |
| John II (533–535) | |
| Agapetus I (535–536) | |
| Silverius (536–537) | |
| Vigilius (537–555) | |
| Pelagius I (556–561) | |

| | |
|---|---|
| John III (561–574) | |
| Benedict I (575–579) | |
| Pelagius II (579–590) | |
| Gregory I (the Great) (590–604) | |
| Sabinian (604–606) | |
| Boniface III (607) | |
| Boniface IV (608–615) | |
| Deusdedit I or Adeodatus (615–618) | |
| Boniface V (619–625) | |
| Honorius I (625–638) | |
| Severinus (640) | |
| John IV (640–642) | |
| Theodore I (642–649) | |
| Martin I (649–655) | |
| Eugene I (655–657) | |
| Vitalian (657–672) | |
| Adeodatus (II) (672–676) | |
| Donus (676–678) | |
| Agatho (678–681) | |
| Leo II (682–683) | |
| Benedict II (684–685) | |
| John V (685–686) | |
| Conon (686–687) | |
| Sergius I (687–701) | Opposed by Theodore and Paschal, who also claimed the throne (687) |
| John VI (701–705) | |
| John VII (705–707) | |
| Sisinnius (708) | |
| Constantine (708–715) | |
| Gregory II (715–731) | |
| Gregory III (731–741) | |
| Zachary (741–752) | |
| Stephen II (752) | Died before being consecrated |
| Stephen III (752–757) | |
| Paul I (757–767) | |
| Stephen IV (767–772) | Opposed by Constantine II (767) and Philip (768), who claimed the throne |
| Adrian I (772–795) | |
| Leo III (795–816) | |

| | |
|---|---|
| Stephen V (816–817) | |
| Paschal I (817–824) | |
| Eugene II (824–827) | |
| Valentine (827) | |
| Gregory IV (827–844) | |
| Sergius II (844–847) | Opposed by John, who claimed the throne (855) |
| Leo IV (847–855) | |
| Benedict III (855–858) | Opposed by Anastasius, who claimed the throne (855) |
| Nicholas I (858–867) | |
| Adrian II (867–872) | |
| John VIII (872–882) | |
| Marinus I (882–884) | |
| Adrian III (884–885) | |
| Stephen VI (885–891) | |
| Formosus (891–896) | |
| Boniface VI (896) | |
| Stephen VII (896–897) | |
| Romanus (897) | |
| Theodore II (897) | |
| John IX (898–900) | |
| Benedict IV (900–903) | |
| Leo V (903) | Opposed by Christopher, who claimed the throne (903–904) |
| Sergius III (904–911) | |
| Anastasius III (911–913) | |
| Lando (913–914) | |
| John X (914–928) | |
| Leo VI (928) | |
| Stephen VIII (929–931) | |
| John XI (931–935) | |
| Leo VII (936–939) | |
| Stephen IX (939–942) | |
| Marinus II (942–946) | |
| Agapetus II (946–955) | |
| John XII (955–963) | |
| Leo VIII (963–964) | |
| Benedict V (964) | |
| John XIII (965–972) | |

| | |
|---|---|
| Benedict VI (973–974) | |
| Benedict VII (974–983) | Opposed by Boniface VII, who claimed the throne (974; 984–985) |
| John XIV (983–984) | Opposed by Boniface VII, who claimed the throne (974; 984–985) |
| John XV (985–996) | |
| Gregory V (996–999) | Opposed by John XVI, who claimed the throne (997–998) |
| Sylvester II (999–1003) | |
| John XVII (1003) | |
| John XVIII (1003–1009) | |
| Sergius IV (1009–1012) | |
| Benedict VIII (1012–1024) | Opposed by Gregory, who claimed the throne (1012) |
| John XIX (1024–1032) | |
| Benedict IX (1032–1045) | Deposed 1045 |
| Sylvester III (1045) | Elected by a faction to replace Benedict IX; often considered illegitimate |
| Benedict IX (1045) | Restored after his 1045 deposition |
| Gregory VI (1045–1046) | |
| Clement II (1046–1047) | |
| Benedict IX (1047–1048) | Restored after second deposition in 1045 |
| Damasus II (1048) | |
| Leo IX (1049–1054) | Traditional date of the Great Schism with the Greek Eastern church |
| The rupture initiated by the papal legate after the pope's death. | |

## PATRIARCHS OF CONSTANTINOPLE TO 1453

| |
|---|
| Andrew the Apostle (Traditional apostolic founder of the see at Byzantium) |
| *See of Byzantium: Patriarchal territory of Antioch* |
| Stachys (38–54) |
| Onesimus (54–68) |
| Polycarpus I (69–89) |
| Plutarch (89–105) |
| Sedecion (105–114) |
| Diogenes (114–129) |
| Eleutherius (129–136) |
| Felix (136–141) |
| Polycarpus II (141–144) |
| Athenodorus (144–148) |
| Euzois (148–154) |
| Laurence (154–166) |
| Alypius (166–169) |

| |
|---|
| Pertinax (169–187) |
| Olympianus (187–198) |
| Mark I (198–211) |
| Philadelphus (211–217) |
| Cyriacus I (217–230) |
| Castinus (230–237) |
| Eugenius I (237–242) |
| Titus (242–272) |
| Dometius (272–284) |
| Rufinus I (284–293) |
| Probus (293–306) |
| Metrophanes (306–314) |
| Alexander (314–337) |
| *See of refounded capital: Bishops and archbishops of Christian Constantinople* |
| Paul I (337–339) |
| Eusebius of Nicomedia (339–341) |
| Paul I (341–342), second time |
| Macedonius I (342–346) |
| Paul I (346–351), third time |
| Macedonius I (351–360), second time |
| Eudoxius of Antioch (360–370) |
| Demophilus (370–379) |
| Evagrius (370 or 379) |
| Maximus (380) |
| Gregory the Theologian (379–381) |
| Nectarius (381–397) |
| John I Chrysostom (398–404) |
| Arsacius of Tarsus (404–405) |
| Atticus (406–425) |
| Sisinnius I (426–427) |
| Nestorius (428–431) |
| Maximianus (431–434) |
| Proclus (434–446) |
| Flavian (446–449) |
| Anatolius (449–458) |
| Gennadius I (458–471) |
| Acacius (471–488) |

| |
|---|
| Phrabitas or Fravitta (488–489) |
| Euphemius (489–495) |
| Macedonius II (495–511) |
| Timothy I (511–518) |
| John II the Cappadocian (518–520) |
| Epiphanius (520–535) |
| Anthimus I (535–536) |
| Menas (536–552) |
| Eutychius (552–565) |
| John III Scholasticus (565–577) |
| Eutychius (577–582), second time |
| John IV the Faster (582–595) |
| Cyriacus (596–606) |
| Thomas I (607–610) |
| Sergius I (610–638) |
| Pyrrhus I (638–641) |
| Paul II (641–653) |
| Peter (654–666) |
| Thomas II (667–669) |
| John V (669–675) |
| Constantine I (675–677) |
| Theodore I (677–679) |
| George I (679–686) |
| Paul III (687–693) |
| Callinicus I (693–705) |
| Cyrus (705–711) |
| John VI (712–715) |
| Germanus I (715–730) |
| Anastasius (730–754) |
| Constantine II (754–766) |
| Nicetas (766–780) |
| Paul IV (780–784) |
| Tarasius (784–806) |
| Nicephorus I (806–815) |
| Theodotos I Kassiteras (815–821) |
| Antony I (821–836) |
| John VII Grammaticus (836–843) |

- Methodius I (843–847)
- Ignatius I (847—December 25, 858)
- Photius I the Great (858—867)
- Ignatius I (867—October 23, 877), second time
- Photius I (877–886), second time
- Stephen I (886–893)
- Antony II Kauleas (893–901)
- Nicholas I Mystikos (901–907, 912–925)
- Euthymius I Synkellos (907–912)
- Stephen II of Amasea (925–928)
- Tryphon (928–931)
- Theophylactus (Lecapenus) (933–956)
- Polyeuctus (956–970)
- Basil I Scamandrenus (970–974)
- Antony III Studites (974–980)
- Nicholas II Chrysoberges (984–996)
- Sisinnius II (996–998)
- Sergius II (999–1019)
- Eustathius (1019–1025)
- Alexius I Studites (1025–1043)
- Michael I Cerularius (1043–1058)
- Constantine III Leichoudes (1059–1063)
- John VIII Xiphilinos (1064–1075)
- Cosmas I (1075–1081)
- Eustratius Garidas (1081–1084)
- Nicholas III Grammaticus (1084–1111)
- John IX Agapetus (1111–1134)
- Leo Styppis (1134–1143)
- Michael II Kourkouas (1143–1146)
- Cosmas II Atticus (1146–1147)
- Nicholas IV Muzalon (1147–1151)
- Theodotus II (1151–1153)
- Neophytos I (1153)
- Constantine IV Chliarenus (1154–1156)
- Luke Chrysoberges (1156–1169)
- Michael III of Anchialus (1170–1177)
- Chariton (1177–1178)

| |
|---|
| Theodosius I Borradiotes (1179–1183) |
| Basil II Camateros (1183–1186) |
| Nicetas II Muntanes (1186–1189) |
| Leon Theotokites (1189–1190) |
| Dositheus (1190–1191) |
| George II Xiphilinos (1191–1198) |
| John X Camaterus (1198–1206) |
| Michael IV Autoreianus (1207–1213) |
| Theodore II Eirenicus (1213–1215) |
| Maximus II (1215) |
| Manuel I Charitopoulos (1215–1222) |
| Germanus II (1222–1240) |
| Methodius II (1240) |
| See vacant (1240–1244) |
| Manuel II (1244–1255) |
| Arsenius Autoreianus (1255–1259) |
| Nicephorus II (1260–1261) |
| Arsenius Autoreianus (1261–1267), second time |
| Germanus III (1267) |
| Joseph I Galesiotes (1267–1275) |
| John XI Bekkos (1275–1282) |
| Gregory II of Cyprus (1283–1289) |
| Athanasius I (1289–1293) |
| John XII (1294–1303) |
| Athanasius I (1303–1309), second time |
| Niphon I (1310–1314) |
| John XIII Glykys (1315–1320) |
| Gerasimos I (1320–1321) |
| Isaias I (1323–1334) |
| John XIV Kalekas (1334–1347) |
| Isidore I (1347–1350) |
| Callistus I (1350–1354) |
| Philotheus Kokkinos (1354–1355) |
| Callistus I (1355–1363), second time |
| Philotheos Kokkinos (1364–1376), second time |
| Macarius (1376–1379) |
| Nilus Kerameus (1379–1388) |

| |
|---|
| Antony IV (1389–1390) |
| Macarius (1390–1391), second time |
| Antony IV (1391–1397), second time |
| Callistus II Xanothopoulos (1397) |
| Matthew I (1397–1410) |
| Euthymius II (1410–1416) |
| Joseph II (1416–1439) |
| Metrophanes II (1440–1443) |
| Gregory III Mammas (1443–1450) |
| Athanasius II (1450–1453) |

# Appendix 3

# LIST OF THE ROMAN EMPERORS TO 1453

## THE UNITED ROMAN EMPIRE

| Augustus Caesar | 31–14 |
| --- | --- |
| Tiberius | 14–37 |
| Gaius (Caligula) | 37–41 |
| Claudius | 41–54 |
| Nero | 54–68 |
| Caius Iulius Vindex | 68 |
| Lucius Clodius Macer | 68 |
| Caius Nymphidius Sabinus | 68 |
| Galba | 68–69 |
| Otho | 69 |
| Vitellius | 69 |
| Vespasian | 69–79 |
| Titus | 79–81 |
| Domitian | 81–96 |
| Lucius Antonius Saturninus | 89 |
| Nerva | 96–98 |
| Trajan | 98–117 |
| Hadrian | 117–138 |
| Antoninus Pius | 138–161 |
| Marcus Aurelius | 161–180 |
| L. Verus | 161–166 |
| Avidius Cassius | 175 |
| Commodus | 180–192 |
| Pertinax | 192–193 |
| Didius Julianus | 193 |

# LIST OF ROMAN EMPERORS TO 1453 | 1169

| | |
|---|---|
| Septimius Severus | 193–211 |
| Pescennius Niger | 193–194 |
| Clodius Albinus | 193–197 |
| Antoninus (Caracalla) | 198–211 (with Severus); 209–(February) 211 (with Severus and Geta); 211(February–December) (with Geta); 211–217 (alone) |
| Geta | 209–211 (with Severus and Caracalla) |
| Macrinus | 217–218 |
| Diadumenianus | 218 |
| Elagabalus | 218–222 |
| Seleucus | 221 |
| Uranius | (uncertain dates) |
| Gellius Maximus | 219 |
| Verus | 219 |
| Alexander Severus | 222–235 |
| Lucius Seius Sallustius | 225–227 |
| Taurinus | 232 |
| Maximinus Thrax | 235–238 |
| Magnus | 235 |
| Quartinus | 235 |
| Gordian I | 238 |
| Gordian II | 238 |
| Pupienus (Maximus) | 238 |
| Balbinus | 238 |
| Gordian III | 238–244 |
| Sabinianus | 240 |
| Philip the Arab | 244–249 |
| Pacatianus | 248 |
| Iotapianus | 248 |
| Silbannacus | 248? |
| Sponsianus | 248? |
| Philip Iunior | 247–249 |
| Decius | 249–251 |
| Terentius Julius Priscus | 250 |
| Iulius Valens Licinianus | 250 |
| Herennius Etruscus | 251 |
| Hostilian | 251 |
| Trebonianus Gallus | 251–253 |

| | |
|---|---|
| Volusianus | 251–253 |
| Uranius Antoninus | 253 |
| Aemilius Aemilianus | 253 |
| Valerian | 253–260 |
| Mareades | 252/253? |
| Gallienus | 253–268 |
| Ingenuus | 260 |
| Regalianus | 260 |
| Macrianus Senior | 260–261 |
| Macrianus Iunior | 260–261 |
| Quietus | 260–261 |
| Piso | 261 |
| Valens | 261 |
| Ballista | 261 |
| Mussius Aemilianus | 261 |
| Memor | 262 |
| Aureolus | 262, 268 |
| Claudius II Gothicus | 268–270 |
| Censorinus | 269–70 |
| Quintillus | 270 |
| Aurelian | 270–275 |
| Domitianus | 271–272 |
| Urbanus | 271–272 |
| Septimius | 271–272 |
| Firmus | 273 |
| Felicissimus | 270–271? |
| Vaballathus | 272 |
| Postumus | 260–269 |
| Laelianus | 269 |
| Marius | 269 |
| Victorinus | 269–270 |
| Tetricus I | 271–274 |
| Tetricus II | 273?–274 |
| Faustinus | 274 |
| Tacitus | 275–276 |
| Florianus | 276 |
| Probus | 276–282 |

| | |
|---|---|
| Bonosus | 280 |
| Proculus | 280–281 |
| Saturninus | 281 |
| Carus | 282–283 |
| Numerianus | 283–284 |
| Carinus | 283–285 |
| Diocletian | 284–305 |
| Lucius Domitius Domitianus | 297 (296?) |
| Aurelius Achilleus | 297–298? |
| Eugenius | 303? |
| Maximianus Herculius | 285–c. 310 |
| Amandus | 285 or 286 |
| Aelianus | 285 or 286 |
| Iulianus | c. 286–293 |
| Carausius | 286/7–293 |
| Allectus | 293–296/7 |
| Constantius I Chlorus | 293–306 |
| Galerius | 293–311 |
| Maximinus Daia | 305–313 |
| Severus II | 305–307 |
| Maxentius | 306–312 |
| Lucius Domitius Alexander | 308–309 |
| Licinius | 308–324 |
| Valens | 314 (316?) |
| Martinianus | 324 |
| Constantine I | 306–337 |
| Calocaerus | 333/334 |
| Constantine II | 337–340 |
| Constans I | 337–350 |
| Constantius II | 337–361 |
| Magnentius | 350–353 |
| Nepotian | 350 |
| Vetranio | 350 |
| Silvanus | 355 |
| Julian | 361–363 |
| Jovian | 363–364 |
| Valentinian I | 364–375 |

| Firmus | 372?–374 or 375 |
| --- | --- |
| Valens | 364–378 |
| Procopius | 365–366 |
| Marcellus | 366 |
| Gratian | 367–383 |
| Valentinian II | 375–392 |
| Theodosius I the Great | 378–395 |
| Magnus Maximus | 383–388 |
| Flavius Victor | 384–388 |
| Eugenius | 392–394 |

## 395: PARTITION OF THE WESTERN EMPIRE

| Honorius | 393–423 |
| --- | --- |
| Marcus | 406–407 |
| Gratian | 407 |
| Constantine III | 407–411 |
| Constans II | 409–411 |
| Maximus | 409–411 |
| Priscus Attalus | 409–410, 414–415 |
| Jovinus | 411–413 |
| Sebastianus | 412–413 |
| Constantius III | 421 |
| Johannes | 423–425 |
| Valentinian III | 425–455 |
| Petronius Maximus | 455 |
| Avitus | 455–456 |
| Majorian | 457–461 |
| Libius Severus | 461–465 |
| Anthemius | 467–472 |
| Arvandus | 468 |
| Romanus | 470 |
| Olybrius | 472 |
| Glycerius | 473–474 |
| Julius Nepos (last Western emperor recognized by the East) | 474–475 |
| Romulus Augustulus (last Western emperor) | 475–476 |

## 395: PARTITION OF THE EASTERN EMPIRE

| *Dynasty of Theodosius 395–457* | |
|---|---|
| Arcadius | 395–408 |
| Theodosius II | 408–450 |
| Marcian (m. Pulcheria, granddaughter of Theodosius I) | 450–457 |
| *Dynasty of Leo 457–518* | |
| Leo I | 457–474 |
| Leo II | 474 |
| Zeno | 474–491 |
| Basiliskos | 475–476 |
| Leontios | 484–488 |
| Anastasios | 491–518 |
| *Dynasty of Justinian 518–602* | |
| Justin | 518–527 |
| Justinian I | 527–565 |
| Justin II | 565–578 |
| Tiberius Constantine | 578–582 |
| Maurice | 582–602 |
| Phocas | 602–610 |
| *Dynasty of Heraclius 610–695* | |
| Heraclius | 610–641 |
| Heraclonas | 641 |
| Constantine III | 641 |
| Constans II | 641–668 |
| Gregory | 646–647 |
| Olympios | 649–653 |
| Mezezios | 669 |
| Constantine IV | 668–685 |
| Justinian II | 685–695 |
| *The Twenty-Year Anarchy 695–717* | |
| Leontios | 695–698 |
| Tiberius III | 698–705 |
| Justinian II (restored) | 705–711 |
| Bardanes | 711–713 |
| Anastasius II | 713–716 |
| Theodosius III | 716–717 |

| *Isaurian Dynasty 717–802* | |
|---|---|
| Leo III | 717–741 |
| Constantine V Copronymus | 741–775 |
| Artabasdos | 742–743 |
| Leo IV | 775–780 |
| Constantine VI | 780–797 |
| Irene | 797–802 |
| *Nikiphorian Dynasty 802–813* | |
| Nikiphoros I | 802–811 |
| Straurakios | 811 |
| Michael I | 811–813 |
| Leo V | 813–820 |
| *Amorian dynasty 820–867* | |
| Michael II | 820–829 |
| Thomas | 821–823 |
| Theophilos | 829–842 |
| Michael III | 842–867 |
| *Macedonian dynasty 867–1056* | |
| Basil I | 867–886 |
| Constantine | 869–879 |
| Leo VI | 887–912 |
| Alexander | 912–913 |
| Constantine VII Porphyrogenitos | 913–959 |
| Romanus I Lecapenos | 920–944 |
| Christopher | 921–931 |
| Stephen | 924–945 |
| Romanus II | 959–963 |
| Nicephorus II Phocas | 963–969 |
| John I Tzimiskes | 969–976 |
| Basil II | 976–1025 |
| Constantine VIII | 1025–1028 |
| Romanus III Argyros | 1028–1034 |
| Michael IV the Paphlagonian | 1034–1041 |
| Michael V Calaphates | 1041–1042 |
| Zoe and Theodora | 1042 |
| Constantine IX Monomachos | 1042–1055 |
| Theodora (alone) | 1055–1056 |
| Michael VI Bringas Stratiotikos | 1056–1057 |

# List of Roman Emperors to 1453 | 1175

| *Komnenan dynastic prelude* | |
|---|---|
| Isaac I Comnenus | 1057–1059 |
| *Doukid dynasty 1059–1081* | |
| Constantine X Doukas | 1059–1067 |
| Romanos IV Diogenes | 1068–1071 |
| Michael VII Doukas | 1071–1078 |
| Nicephorus III Botaniates | 1078–1081 |
| Nicephoros Melissenos | 1080–1081 |
| *Komnenan dynasty 1081–1185* | |
| Alexius I Comnenus | 1081–1118 |
| John II Comnenus | 1118–1143 |
| Manuel I | 1143–1180 |
| Alexios II | 1180–1183 |
| Andronikos I | 1183–1185 |
| [Isaac, Emperor of Cyprus] | 1183–1191 |
| *Angelid dynasty 1185–1204* | |
| Isaac II | 1185–1195 |
| Alexios III | 1195–1203 |
| Isaac II (restored) with Alexios IV | 1203–1204 |
| Alexios V Dukas Murtzuphlos | 1204 |
| *Lascarid dynasty removed to Nicaea* | |
| Theodore I Lascaris | 1204–1222 |
| John III Dukas Vatatzes | 1222–1254 |
| Theodore II Lascaris | 1254–1258 |
| John IV Lascaris | 1258–1261 |
| *Palaeologan dynasty at Constantinople 1259–1453* | |
| Michael VIII Paleologos | 1259–1282 |
| Andronikos II | 1282–1328 |
| Andronikos III | 1328–1341 |
| John V | 1341–1391 |
| John VI Cantakuzenos | 1347–1354 |
| Andronikos IV | 1376–1379 |
| John V (restored) | 1379–1391 |
| John VII | 1390 |
| Manuel II | 1391–1425 |
| John VIII | 1425–1448 |
| Constantine XI Dragases | 1449–1453 |
| Fall of Constantinople to the Ottomans. End of the Roman Empire. | |

# INDEX OF PERSONS AND PLACES

Aachen, 673-74
Aaron, 9, 651, 809, 1011
Abraham, monk, 914
Abraham, patriarch, 68, 351, 513, 521, 584, 651, 653-54, 778, 783, 963, 1051, 1077, 1137, 1139
Abraham bar Daschandad, 489
Abrahamse, D., 1017
Acacius of Constantinople, 464, 522, 565-67, 1163
Acacius the One-Eyed, 260, 328
Adalhard of Corbie, 675
Adam, 6, 36, 45, 96, 101, 144, 170-71, 188, 443, 454, 550, 628, 702, 718, 854, 917, 920, 932, 1054, 1086
Addai (Thaddeus), 168, 486-88, 497, 694, 714, 840-41
Addai the Manichee, 168
Adeodatus, 441
Adonis (Attis), 163-66, 1021
Adrian II, pope, 644
Adrian III, pope, 643
Aedan MacGabrain, 413
Aedesius, 504
Aelius Donatus, 456
Aelius Gellus, 612
Aelred of Rievaulx, 1095

Aesculapius, 154, 923-24
Aetius of Antioch, 218, 291, 312-14, 317, 321, 327-28, 351, 826
Afghanistan, 156, 168
Africa, 20, 22, 55, 93-96, 126, 129, 142-43, 157, 162, 167-68, 185, 195-99, 218, 219, 221, 243-45, 280, 285, 297-99, 305, 311, 428, 431, 436-42, 445, 450, 453-55, 467, 469, 481, 487, 490, 496, 501-4, 521-22, 606, 619, 627-28, 695, 701, 709-12, 715, 798, 811, 824, 902, 904, 908, 975, 999, 1023, 1046, 1052, 1063, 1069-70, 1111
Agabus, prophet, 19, 972
Agamemnon, 202
Agathias of Myrina, 426, 571
Agatho, pope, 629, 648, 1160
Agathopus of Antioch, 995
Agbar V, king, 487, 497, 1130-31
Agbar VIII, king, 40
Agincourt, 794
Agrippa, king, 970
Ahbel-Rappe, S., 576
Ahondokpe, A. Z., 144

Aion, 154, 960
Aix la Chapelle, 664
Aksum, 504
Alaric, 340-41, 430, 445
Alaric II, 431
Alberic, 680
Albert the Great, 577
Albinus, 231, 264, 268
Alcaeus, 827
Alcibiades of Apamea, 13, 19
Alcuin, 89, 673-75, 685, 687
Alexander, S. S., 619
Alexander II, pope, 712
Alexander of Alexandria, 259-60, 282-93, 295, 299-304, 343, 348-49, 1122
Alexander of Aphrodisias, 572
Alexander of Constantinople, 500
Alexander of Jerusalem, 225, 235, 244, 260
Alexander of Lycopolis, 167-68
Alexander Severus, emperor, 126, 241, 278
Alexander the Great, 397, 482, 790, 795, 1121
Alexandria, 12, 32-33, 40, 49, 69, 72, 98, 126, 146, 156, 159-60, 174, 177, 180-82, 191, 193, 223-59, 260, 268, 282, 285-86, 288-94, 299-300, 302-13, 320, 327, 330-31, 341, 347, 386, 394, 396, 398, 402, 427-28, 458, 460, 463, 487-88, 495, 501-4, 521-28, 530-34, 538-46, 552-60, 562, 564, 567, 571, 573-74, 593-94, 615, 623, 626, 648, 678-79, 694, 706, 714-16, 741, 777-78, 780, 824, 836, 892, 911, 923, 929-30, 942, 979-80, 983, 992, 997, 1013, 1042, 1046, 1102, 1121-23, 1127-28, 1151-54
Alexius I, emperor, 947, 1175
Alexius the Studite, 740
Allberry, C. R. C., 206
Allen, P., 340, 890
Allies, M. H., 655
Al-Mahidi, 489
Al-Muna, 397
Alp Arslan, 680, 748
Alwa (Alodia), 502
Amalek, king, 253, 764, 793-94
Ambrose of Alexandria, 148, 230, 239, 242, 244
Ambrose of Milan, 99, 303, 341, 377,

432, 434-35, 441, 458, 531, 643, 696, 710-11, 711, 802, 821, 823, 826, 845-48, 900, 990, 1000, 1074, 1086
Ambrosiaster, 979
Amiable Child, the, 1097
Ammonas of Skete, 886
Ammonius of Nitria, 396
Ammonius of Thmuis, 231
Ammonius Saccas, 230-31, 244, 572
Ammonius the Arian, 291
Amphilocius of Cyzicus, 643
Amphilocius of Iconium, 1050
Anacletus, pope, 55, 1158
Anastasius I, emperor, 465, 567, 604, 1159
Anastasius II, pope, 465, 535, 1159
Anastasius of Kiev, 656
Anastasius the Syrian, 544
Anatolius of Constantinople, 559-60
Ancyra, 305, 311-12, 347, 364-68, 370, 1000-1001
Andrew, apostle, 499, 505, 523, 967, 1035, 1137, 1162
Andrew of Crete, 577, 817, 832
Andrew of Jerusalem, 832
Aniketos of Rome, pope, 20, 24-25, 65
Anna Komnena, 748-49, 947
Anna Porphyrogenita, 645, 657

Annesoi, 316
Anselm de Bec, 376, 379-81, 383
Antioch, 8, 16, 32, 49, 58-59, 72, 127, 130, 167, 174, 194, 214, 218, 220, 244, 259, 283, 286, 300, 303, 311-12, 319, 322, 327-29, 331, 334, 389-90, 393-94, 456-58, 460, 482, 487-90, 494-95, 498, 500-501, 521-31, 533, 538-60, 562, 564, 567, 648, 672-79, 694, 704, 714-16, 741, 743-44, 780, 829-30, 946, 970, 972, 977, 980, 984, 990, 994-95, 997, 1001, 1072, 1086, 1121, 1151, 1153, 1162
Antoninus Pius, emperor, 40, 90, 186, 1168
Antonova, S., 896, 899
Antony and Cleopatra, 1121
Antony of Egypt, 307, 394-97, 399, 661, 874, 886, 926, 1092
Antony of Pechersk, 505
Antony the Studite, 730, 1165
Aphrahat the Persian, 177, 389-90, 484-85, 877-78
Aphrodite, 156, 651, 654
Apollinaris of Hierapolis, 16-19, 21, 90
Apollinaris of Laodicea, 10, 184, 303, 321, 323, 325, 457, 460, 540, 541, 543, 545, 547, 550,

558, 616-17, 626, 648, 827
Apollo, 339, 1012
Apollonius, 19
Apollophanes, 241
Apollos, apostle, 179
Apuleius of Madaura, 158, 1015
Aquila, apostle, 896
Aquila of Alexandria, 892
Arabia, 234, 239, 242-43, 260, 393, 482, 491-94, 521, 622, 631-32, 981
Ararat, Mount, 497
Arcadius, emperor, 529, 1173
Arcadius Charisius, 612
Archego, 172
Archidonus of Rome, 305
Aretaeus, 891-92
Aristides, 90
Aristo, 90
Aristophanes, 937
Aristotle, 5, 231, 241, 263, 265, 267-69, 271, 384, 464, 476, 494, 574-75, 596, 599, 790, 820, 916, 924, 1028-29, 1059, 1075, 1111-12
Aristulf the Lombard, 669
Arius of Alexandria, 43, 282-96, 299, 301, 310-11, 314, 342-43, 347-48, 585, 599, 709, 825-26, 1140, 1141, 1150
Armenia, 53, 99, 202, 258, 404, 482, 495-500, 502, 511, 522, 570, 623-24, 637, 639, 642, 694, 714, 912, 994, 1135
Arnold, D., 385
Artemis, 152, 156, 162, 1014
Artemon of Rome, 74

Asclepiades, 88
Asia Minor, 4, 14-16, 19, 20-22, 24-25, 44, 48, 58, 65, 67, 82, 94, 106, 143, 162, 184, 190, 196, 211, 401, 432, 481-82, 522, 524-25, 533, 616, 676, 708, 712, 729, 731, 733, 764, 819-20, 826, 898, 973, 975, 977, 979, 987, 1062, 1079, 1151
Astarte, 156
Aswan, 502
Athanaric the Goth, 429
Athanasius of Alexandria, 70, 72, 133, 184, 216, 258-60, 289, 292-93, 295, 300, 302-13, 319, 327-29, 331, 334, 336, 342-43, 350, 363, 382, 394-95, 401, 432-33, 480, 504, 533, 540, 543, 550, 649, 716, 770, 772, 775, 779, 784, 826, 902, 926, 932, 942, 989-90, 997, 1013, 1092, 1122, 1128, 1150-52
Athanasius the Arian, 291
Athanassakis, A., 819-20
Athenagoras, 90, 147, 189-91, 202
Athenodorus, 240
Athens, 94, 104, 184, 189, 195, 233, 243, 262, 269, 316, 320, 426-27, 521, 570-71, 573-74, 577, 616
Augustine of Canterbury, 663-64, 1070-72, 1074, 1086-87, 1111, 1113
Augustine of Hippo, 6, 11, 92, 96, 134, 139, 146, 148,

# Index of Persons and Places | 1179

166-68, 171-73, 195, 197, 217, 222, 255, 267, 299, 341, 370-71, 375, 377, 379, 381, 411, 417, 430, 432, 436, 438-56, 458, 463, 470-71, 480, 559, 643, 668, 696, 701, 703, 710, 777, 787-88, 791, 803-4, 810, 812-13, 822, 846, 848, 908, 962-63, 979, 999, 1012-13, 1016-17, 1052, 1069-72, 1074, 1086-87, 1111, 1113
Augustus (imperial title), 130, 279-81, 407, 425, 430, 470, 593, 673, 685, 902, 904
Augustus (Octavian), 134-35, 143, 191, 238, 260, 1168
Aune, D. E., 972
Aurelius of Carthage, 439
Auxentius of Cappadocia, 711
Auxentius of Milan, 407, 433-34, 710-11
Avars, 431, 620
Avitus, count, 408
Babcock, W., 454
Babylas of Antioch, 127, 214, 244
Babylon, 176, 182, 482, 511, 686, 791, 793, 808, 813, 917, 1020, 1079, 1087
Bacchylides, 819
Bach, J. S., 855
Bacha, C., 633
Bagatti, B., 493
Bagnall, R., 397, 1121, 1145
Bagnani, G., 973
Bahat, D., 621
Bainton, R. H., 791
Baishan, 206
Bakhuizen, J. N., 969

Barasche, M., 1129
Bar Kokhba, Simon, 13, 69, 90
Barb, A. A., 1012
Barbara, martyr, 902
Bardas, regent, 640
Bardas Phocas, 731
Bardesanes, 30, 32, 39-40, 484, 487-88, 824-25, 839, 841
Bardy, G., 283
Barnabas, apostle, 54, 67-70, 179, 1072
Barr, J., 765-66
Barsanuphius of Gaza, 402-3, 417
Barsauma, 490
Bartholomew, apostle, 491, 496
Bartlett, J. V., 980
Bartolomeo de la Casas, 1059
Basil, chamberlain, 730
Basil, Pseudo-, 951
Basil II, emperor, 730-32, 737, 1174
Basil of Ancyra, 1000
Basil the Great, 85, 221, 227, 268, 303, 309-10, 314-24, 327, 351, 353, 370, 401, 408, 433, 460, 480, 498-99, 527, 530-31, 533, 658, 661, 663-64, 682, 694, 707, 713, 715-16, 735, 751, 770, 773, 777, 786, 801-2, 805, 812, 900, 906-8, 929, 931-32, 963, 989, 1043-44, 1047-48, 1050, 1065, 1081, 1127, 1138
Basil the Macedonian, emperor, 642
Basilides, 30, 32, 40-41, 49
Basiliscus, emperor, 464, 565, 1173
Bauckham, R., 966

Beauteous, J., 199
Beck, R., 150
Bede of Jarrow, 413
Behm, J., 865
Beirut, 240, 310, 521, 607-8, 610, 614
Belisarius, 663, 669
Bell, D. N., 402, 1154-55
Bellan-Boyer, L., 893
Beneden, P. van, 981
Benedict of Aniane, 675, 688
Benedict of Nursia, 393, 400-402, 405, 409-10, 661-66, 669, 673, 676, 681-82
Benson, E. W., 816
Berardino, A. di, 13, 62, 493, 869
Berno of Cluny, 665
Beron, 84
Beruni, al-, 167
Beryllus of Bostra, 74, 242-43, 491-92
Bethzatha, 924
Bettenson, H., 327, 329
Bevenot, M., 216-17, 221, 275
Bingaman, B., 873
Bithynia, 124, 297, 310, 347, 593, 736, 823, 991, 1015, 1018, 1143
Blandina of Lyons, 1070
Blenkinsopp, J., 963
Blosser, B., 250
Blowers, P. M., 181
Bluhme, F., 609
Blumenthal, U. R., 671
Bobbio, 414
Boehringer, F., 232
Boethius, 467-68, 475-76, 574
Bogomils, 6, 39, 167, 736
Bonaventure, 577
Boniface, count, 448-49, 804

Boniface, saint, 664
Bonner, C., 190, 1012, 1023
Borchardt, F. A., 432
Bordo, S., 1091
Bosphorus, 281, 297, 523, 642, 946
Botte, B., 978
Bowman, P., 278
Bradley, K. R., 1063
Brennecke, H. C., 283
Brent, A., 99
Bride, king, 413
Britain, 280, 285, 296, 305, 411, 413, 673, 686, 713
Brock, S. P., 391, 393, 435, 483, 876-78, 882-84, 886, 888
Brooks, E. W., 646
Brown, P., 385, 393, 441
Brown, R., 966
Brown, R. M., 447
Browne, C. G., 982
Bryennios, P., 67-68, 70
Buddha, 168, 171
Bullough, V. L., 915
Bultmann, R., 700
Burkitt, F. C., 824
Burns, J. Patout, 453
Burns, P. C., 432
Burns, S., 878
Burrus, V., 895
Burton-Christie, D., 871, 1123
Butler, C., 493, 663
Butterworth, R., 9
Byzantium, 87, 131, 177-78, 267, 269, 281, 338, 342, 388, 392-93, 403, 463, 465-67, 483, 486, 488, 498-99, 501, 523-24, 532, 544, 563, 604-57, 667, 669, 671-72, 681, 713-15, 728, 732, 737, 741, 743, 748-49, 753, 778, 791, 797, 805, 817,

820, 823, 880, 882,
    911, 940, 945, 1028,
    1098, 1123, 1132,
    1134, 1136
Cadoux, C. J., 791
Caecilian of
    Carthage, 297-98,
    436-38
Caecilius of Carthage,
    213
Caecilius of Numidia,
    124, 198-99
Caecilius Thascius.
    *See* Cyprian of
    Carthage
Caelestius, 454-55
Caesarea
    (Cappadocia),
    316-18, 321, 405,
    497, 527, 907, 929,
    942, 1043-44, 1047
Caesarea (Maritima),
    12, 13, 64, 149, 177,
    181, 206-7, 223, 225,
    227-28, 231, 235-45,
    259-61, 280, 311, 328,
    492, 521, 526, 533,
    966-67, 996, 998
Caesarius of Arles,
    371, 401-2
Caesarius of
    Nazianzus, 929
Caleb, king, 504
Callixtus, pope, 13,
    20, 74, 85, 95-97,
    99, 101, 197, 1070,
    1071
Candidianus, count,
    555
Cappadocia, 227, 235,
    240, 242, 268, 289,
    303, 309-10, 314-16,
    318-20, 322-24, 335,
    370, 382, 388, 399,
    401, 405, 497, 522,
    524, 550, 694,
    772-73, 777, 812,
    844, 878, 907-9, 929,
    936, 942, 997, 1047,
    1062, 1065, 1151
Caracalla, emperor,
    234, 1169

Cardman, F., 901
Carpocrates, 49
Carr, D., 1101
Carthage, 92-93, 96,
    126-28, 162, 195, 197,
    199, 212, 214-17, 219,
    222, 225, 271,
    297-98, 362, 364,
    436-37, 439, 441,
    454, 619, 627, 703,
    705-6, 803, 902,
    975, 987
Casel, O., 822
Castel San Angelo,
    Rome, 667
Castelli, E., 894
Catherine of
    Alexandria, 402,
    1125, 1126, 1133
Cautes, 152
Cautopates, 152
Cavafy, C. P., 1017
Celestine I, pope, 411,
    522-23, 558, 593,
    1159
Celestine monks, 665
Celsus, 11, 46, 125,
    146-50, 180, 183,
    202, 248, 799, 801,
    803, 807, 926
Cerdo, 44, 49
Ceres, 154
Cerinthus, 8, 49
Cerularius, Michael,
    738-41, 743, 745,
    751-54
Chabot, J. B., 483
Chadwick, H., 5, 441
Chaeremon, 241
Chalcedon, 323, 331,
    336, 393, 401, 404,
    406, 460-61, 463,
    467, 484, 489, 494,
    498, 500, 502-3,
    505, 521-22, 526-27,
    530, 535-36, 539,
    555, 560-70, 593,
    597, 600, 604,
    615-18, 623-27,
    630-31, 633, 637,
    641, 646, 649, 656,
    678, 714-16, 740,

913, 966, 992-93,
    1053, 1072, 1122,
    1153-55, 1157
Chamberlain, C., 737
Chariton of
    Jerusalem, 501
Charlemagne, 428,
    640, 664, 670-74,
    685, 747, 856, 1135,
    1157
Charles V, emperor,
    1059
Charles Martel, 670
Charles the Bald, 675
Charlesworth, J., 825,
    838
Chatfield, A., 816
Chenoboskion, 27,
    399, 400
Chenu, B., 902
Chersonesus, 644,
    656-57
Chich-p'an, 167
Childeric, 430, 670
Childeric III, 670
China, 168, 481,
    489-91, 714, 716
Chitty, D., 874, 1123
Chloe, 896
Christ, 7, 10-12, 14, 22,
    25, 35, 38-40, 42,
    44, 47, 48, 50, 52,
    53, 57-60, 65-67,
    69-70, 78, 83-84, 86,
    87-89, 91, 93, 95-96,
    98-104, 107-11,
    120-21, 124, 132-33,
    141, 146-47, 149, 157,
    165-66, 168, 172,
    187-88, 190-91,
    194-95, 197,
    200-201, 205, 210,
    216-18, 220, 224,
    235, 237, 245, 250,
    258, 266-67, 272-73,
    280, 284, 290, 295,
    309, 321-22, 325-28,
    339, 344, 347, 349,
    357-63, 369, 378,
    380-81, 409, 411,
    413, 420-21, 433-34,
    439, 442, 457,

462-64, 471-74, 486,
    492, 497, 505,
    525-27, 530-31,
    533-35, 537, 539,
    557, 560, 564, 566,
    568-71, 576-84, 588,
    598, 600-619, 622,
    636-38, 665-66,
    674, 678-80, 682,
    684, 691, 695,
    697-98, 701-2,
    705-8, 711, 717-19,
    722, 724, 728,
    738-42, 744, 749-50,
    752, 758, 771-72,
    778, 784, 787-88,
    790, 792-94,
    797-99, 801-5, 809,
    818, 820, 826-27,
    829, 831, 834, 836,
    842-45, 847-51,
    853-58, 861-64,
    866-68, 870-71,
    877-78, 888, 893,
    897, 899-900, 903,
    907, 909, 918, 920,
    924, 931, 936,
    939-40, 946, 948,
    951-54, 956-57,
    960-62, 964-65,
    967, 970-73, 980-83,
    985, 987, 990,
    991-92, 998-99,
    1002-4, 1008, 1010,
    1012, 1016, 1019-21,
    1025, 1032-34, 1036,
    1038, 1043, 1051,
    1060, 1063, 1065-68,
    1072, 1086, 1092,
    1097-1100, 1104,
    1106, 1121, 1133, 1136,
    1138, 1143-47,
    1149-54, 1156-64,
    1166, 1170, 1172-76
Christ, W., 816
Christensen, M., 382,
    550, 844
Chronius, 241
Chrysippus, 865
Chrysopolis, 627, 732
Church, F. F., 817, 838
Cicero, 140, 142, 198,

441, 446, 457, 802-3, 812, 827, 1026, 1064, 1112
Citeaux, 665
Clark, E. A., 388, 904, 909
Claudianus of Vienne, 712
Clement of Alexandria, 6, 7, 29, 33, 38, 40, 46, 51, 69, 96, 101, 188, 191-95, 211, 225, 229, 231, 270, 798, 809, 820, 822, 825, 835-37, 899, 904, 942, 1001, 1042-43, 1046, 1068, 1069, 1110, 1116, 1122
Clement of Rome, pope, 54-58, 61-62, 64-65, 68, 107, 109, 123, 360, 386, 656, 691, 693, 796, 866, 977, 983-84, 995, 997, 1017, 1067, 1092, 1104, 1158
Cleomenes, 74, 82, 84
Cloke, G., 899
Clovis, 430
Clugnet, L., 914
Cluny, 665
Coelius Sedulius, 829
Coltrane, J., 359
Columba (Colm Cille), 412-13
Columbanus, 409, 412-13, 422, 713
Commodian, emperor, 184
Commodus, emperor, 146, 189, 202, 495, 1168
Connolly, R. H., 980
Constans I, emperor, 305-6, 339, 1171
Constans II, emperor, 627, 1173
Constantelos, D., 939-40, 942, 947
Constantine I, emperor, 122,
129-30, 132, 135, 153, 212, 271, 279-82, 296-305, 310-11, 329, 336-39, 341, 344, 347, 357, 364, 369, 425, 428, 430, 437, 449, 462, 483, 497, 499, 523, 594, 609, 620-21, 627-29, 637, 639, 644, 648-49, 671-72, 677, 697, 706, 713, 727, 733, 741, 743, 790, 795, 797, 799-800, 810-11, 828, 864, 955, 990, 1062, 1111, 1150, 1159, 1171
Constantine III, emperor, 627, 1165, 1172, 1173
Constantine IV, emperor, 629, 1165, 1173
Constantine V, emperor, 637, 639, 1134, 1174
Constantine VI, emperor, 637
Constantine IX, emperor, 735, 738, 740, 757
Constantine X, emperor, 735
Constantine Leichoudes, 735, 738, 745
Constantine Porphyrogenitos, 946
Constantineanu, C., 357
Constantinople, 54, 70, 72, 87, 102, 177, 182, 281, 297, 303, 310-17, 319, 322-23, 325, 327, 329-30, 332, 334-35, 338, 341, 371, 376, 388, 390-91, 393-94, 396, 403, 406, 410, 425, 427-30, 434, 457-58, 460-67, 469, 480-81,
483-84, 488, 499-500, 522-31, 535, 538-39, 542-44, 547, 552, 554-60, 563-70, 573, 577, 591, 593-95, 605-8, 610, 613-17, 619-23, 625, 627-30, 633, 636-45, 648-49, 656, 658, 664, 666-72, 674, 676, 678-80, 694, 707, 710, 713-15, 727-29, 733-35, 737-41, 743-46, 748-49, 752-53, 778, 780, 806, 826, 829-33, 850, 855, 908, 910, 929, 940, 942, 945-46, 948, 963-64, 984, 990, 992-94, 997, 1018, 1051, 1062, 1068, 1072, 1086, 1134, 1139-40, 1143-44, 1151, 1153-55, 1162-67, 1175
Constantius II, emperor, 305-8, 312, 339, 341, 406-7, 432-33, 504, 1171
Constantius Chlorus, emperor, 129, 279-80, 812, 1171
Copleston, F., 262
Corinth, 25, 56, 359, 361, 806, 983-84, 1031, 1045, 1107-8
Cormack, R., 1126-27, 1132
Cornelius, pope, 102, 216-18, 220, 224, 255, 1158
Cornutus, 241
Coroticus, 412
Cos, 924-25
Cosmas and Damian, 930
Cosmas Indicopleustes, 495
Cosmas of Maiouma, 832-33
Cotter, W., 896
Cratinus of Constantinople, 610
Cremer, H., 957-58
Crescens the Cynic, 90, 185-87
Crimea, 58
Croinin, D. A., 411
Cross, L., 390, 890
Crouzel, H., 227, 229, 232, 239
Cul Drebene, 413
Cumont, F., 150
Cunliffe, B., 1009
Cybele, 156, 162-66, 340
Cyprian of Carthage, 92, 127-28, 133, 184, 195, 199, 212-22, 255-56, 271-72, 275, 364, 377, 381, 439, 442, 699, 706, 710, 718, 798, 926, 975, 983, 999, 1017, 1069, 1086
Cyprus, 33, 167, 627, 1166, 1175
Cyril and Methodius, 505, 644
Cyril of Alexandria, 156-57, 159-61, 177, 259, 382, 390, 463-64, 498, 530, 539, 541-66, 568, 570, 580, 582, 586, 591, 593-94, 600, 615, 617-18, 624, 628-29, 646-47, 649-50, 698, 716, 772, 780, 924, 930, 1013, 1122, 1124, 1152-57
Cyril of Jerusalem, 43, 223, 331, 694, 701, 718-20, 963
Cyril of Scythopolis, 404, 536, 912-13
Cyrus of Alexandria, 160-61, 623, 648, 930
Cyrus of Phasis, 623, 648

D'Alès, A., 140-41
Dalriada, 413
Daly, R. J., 227, 814
Damascius the
 Syrian, 426-27, 571,
 573-77
Damascus, 491, 574,
 634, 970
Damasus I, pope, 319,
 322, 432, 457,
 459-60, 463, 469,
 473, 525, 643,
 676-77, 1159
D'Angelo, M. R., 894,
 895
Daniel, prophet, 98,
 132, 244, 473, 795,
 808, 959
Daniel the Stylite,
 394
Daniélou, J., 182, 932
David, king, 8, 53, 60,
 106, 353, 416, 511,
 513, 521, 584-86,
 619, 648, 720-21,
 778, 800, 811, 813,
 827, 867, 920
David of Basra, 496
David of Georgia,
 500
Davies, S., 904
Davis, H., 777
De Lange, N., 181
De Mille, C. B., 369
Decapolis, 8, 10, 966
Decius, emperor,
 127-28, 199, 214-15,
 228-29, 244-45,
 254-55, 824, 1169
Demeter, 156, 162
Demetrius,
 megalomartyr, 930
Demetrius of
 Alexandria, 225,
 228-29, 232-34, 533,
 984
Demophilus, 322,
 329, 331, 333, 1163
Demosthenes, 131,
 320, 935, 938, 941
Denzey, N., 897
Deone, H. A., 791

Devreesse, R., 493
Dhu Nuwas, king,
 504
Diadochus of
 Photike, 869,
 874-75, 880, 887
Didymus (Thomas),
 495, 840
Didymus the Blind,
 533-34, 716, 963
Dio Cassius, 56
Diocletian, emperor,
 128-29, 135, 165, 168,
 184, 199, 206,
 278-80, 296-97, 336,
 345, 369, 607,
 609-10, 800, 811-12,
 1171
Diodore of Tarsus,
 331, 334, 488, 528,
 539-43, 556, 561,
 564, 646, 777, 780,
 1151
Diogenes Laertes,
 865
Diogenes of Babylon,
 865
Diognetus, 54, 72-73,
 132, 146
Dionysius
 Gothofredus, 615
Dionysius of
 Alexandria, 85, 127,
 218, 257-58, 290,
 370
Dionysius of Corinth,
 56
Dionysius of Rome,
 pope, 258
Dionysius the
 Areopagite, 263,
 267, 570-72, 574-79,
 627, 887
Dioscorus of
 Alexandria, 463,
 557-60, 616, 1140-41,
 1153
Dives (and Lazarus),
 939
Divjak, H., 449
Dix, G., 981
Dnieper river, 505

Dodd, C. H., 765
Dodgeon, M. H., 620
Dolger, F., 1023
Domitian, emperor,
 55-56, 61, 122-23,
 159, 796, 1168
Domitilla, 123
Domnus of Antioch,
 557, 559
Donaldson, J., 981
Donatus, 298, 436-40
Dongola, 502
Doran, R., 394, 492
Dorival, G., 254
Dorotheus of Gaza,
 263, 367, 403, 607
Downey, G., 935
Druim Cett, 413
Dudden, F. H., 434
Duffy, J. M., 737
Duffy, S., 453
Dunn, D. G., 1016
Dura Europos, 126,
 1125-26
Durrow, 413
Duthoy, R., 164
Dvin, council of, 498
Ebionites, 7-14, 49,
 69, 102, 180
Edessa, 32, 40, 128,
 168, 389, 483-88,
 494, 539, 568, 1130
Edwards, M. J., 287,
 573, 791
Egbert of York, 673,
 685-86
Egypt, 7, 9, 54, 70,
 130, 147, 150-51,
 156-58, 161, 167, 191,
 202, 228-29, 232-34,
 239, 305-7, 311,
 315-16, 331, 347-49,
 378, 387, 390-91,
 394-404, 406,
 409-11, 455-57,
 463-65, 479, 486,
 498, 502, 522, 524,
 527, 530, 532,
 534-35, 543, 552,
 556-57, 559-66,
 569-70, 585, 604,
 607, 616-19, 622-23,

625, 631, 664, 716,
 749, 791, 794, 808,
 825, 839, 866,
 869-71, 874, 876,
 878, 882, 886, 900,
 903, 911, 913, 930,
 942, 963, 979, 995,
 999, 1005, 1011,
 1013-14, 1019, 1021,
 1023, 1121-25, 1128,
 1145
Ehrman, B., 896
Einhard, historian,
 673, 675, 685
Eisen, U., 975
Eleutherius,
 patriarch, 1162
Eleutherius, pope, 48,
 1158
Elijah, 923
Ellens, J. H., 1121
Elm, S., 908
Elvira, 369, 1071
Elymas, 1008
Emmaus, 90, 186,
 695, 698
Encratites, 4-7, 49,
 180
Ephesus, 25, 58, 90,
 152, 157, 186, 344,
 391, 411, 460,
 463-64, 483, 488,
 498, 502, 537, 546,
 548, 552-63, 565,
 569-70, 591-93, 600,
 616, 618, 656, 714,
 878, 1008, 1014,
 1124, 1151, 1153-54
Ephrem of Nisibis
 (Syrus), 39, 167, 177,
 484-85, 487-88,
 498, 825-26, 830,
 832, 842, 848-80,
 876, 880-81, 998,
 1085
Epidaurus, 924
Epigonus, 74, 82, 84
Epiphanius of
 Salamis, 6-14, 22,
 33, 38, 43, 58, 85-88,
 98, 167, 187, 189,
 228, 233, 242, 391,

### Index of Persons and Places | 1183

457, 534, 975-76, 978, 985, 987, 1137
Etchmiadzin, 497
Ethiopia, 258, 501, 503-4, 512, 514, 615, 631, 716, 967, 1012
Ethiopian eunuch, 481
Euboulos, 152
Eudoxia, empress, 530-31
Eudoxia II, empress, 619
Eulamius of Phrygia, 571
Eunomius of Cyzicus, 268, 312-15, 317-19, 321, 324, 327, 331, 599, 826
Euphrates, 194, 483
Eusebius of Caesarea, 6, 7, 9, 12, 13, 14, 15, 1-19, 21-25, 33, 40, 48-49, 53, 55-56, 59, 65, 67, 70, 85-88, 97, 102, 122-23, 125-29, 133, 147-48, 184, 187, 190-91, 194, 206, 227-32, 234-35, 237, 239-45, 254, 259-61, 266, 270, 280, 284, 286, 290-91, 299-304, 310-12, 318, 322, 327-28, 331, 334, 337-38, 344, 346, 348, 387-88, 433, 456, 458, 487, 491-92, 495-96, 523, 533, 557, 559, 711, 799-801, 811, 892, 926, 963, 967, 974-75, 985, 997
Eusebius of Cappadocia, 318
Eusebius of Dorylaeum, 557
Eusebius of Nicomedia, 284, 286, 291, 299, 301-4, 310-11, 327, 348, 523, 1163

Eusebius of Samosata, 303, 310, 322, 334
Eustathius of Antioch, 303, 309-11, 533, 539, 989
Eustathius of Cappadocia, 929
Eustathius of Marseilles, 712
Eustathius of Sebaste, 316, 319, 322, 369, 401, 906-7, 1044, 1062
Euthymius of Palestine, 404-6
Eutyches, patriarch, 667
Eutyches of Constantinople, 557-58, 562, 566, 594, 596, 599, 617, 1140-41
Eutychius of Constantinople, 568, 1164
Evagrius, historian, 522
Evagrius of Pontus, 262, 264, 267, 323-24, 331, 367, 396, 398, 403, 410, 532-38, 569, 869, 871, 875, 880-82, 885, 908
Evans, E., 43
Eve, 36, 56, 65, 116, 164, 191, 936-37, 1074
Evergetinos monastery, 403, 727
Fabian, pope, 97, 127, 214-16, 244, 1158
Facundus of Hermiane, 467
Family of Jesus, 8, 123
Fars, 502
Fayyum, 394-96, 1124-25
Felicity and Perpetua, 20, 126, 902-4, 917-19, 926
Felix, martyr, 851-52, 1113

Felix, procurator, 970
Felix III, pope, 463-65, 1159
Fellini, F., 369
Ferguson, E., 133, 363
Ferguson, J., 939
Ferrari, L., 370
Ferreira, J., 840
Fiensy, D. A., 981
Finian, 413
Finney, P. L., 1124
Firmicus Maternus, 339, 370
Firmilian of Cappadocia, 235, 242
Fitzgerald, A., 371, 440, 453
Flanagan, J. W., 357
Flavian, magistrate, 206
Flavian of Constantinople, 463, 528, 557, 559-60, 594, 649, 1153, 1163
Flavius Clemens, 56, 123, 191
Forbes, C. A., 340
Fortunatus of Carthage, 216, 219
Foster, J., 490
Francis, J. A., 385
Francis of Assisi, 742, 1026, 1045
Francis Xavier, 491
Fredouille, J. C., 140
Frega, 338
Frend, W. H. C., 299, 563, 1070
Friedrich, G., 941, 957
Fritigern the Goth, 429
Friuli, 669
Froidefond, C., 156
Fronto, Marcus Cornelius, 125, 183, 198
Frumentius of Ethiopia, 504
Fulgentius of Ruspe, 467

Gager, J., 1009
Gaius Cassius, 1067
Galerius, emperor, 128-30, 132, 279-80, 337, 345, 800, 1171
Galerius Maximus, 222
Galli (priests), 163
Gallienus, emperor, 128, 1170
Gallinara, 407
Gallus, Caesar, 312-13
Gallus, emperor, 127, 218, 228, 245
Gandhi, Mahatma, 792
Gangra, 369, 401, 754, 906, 1044, 1062-63
Gasparro, S., 6
Gaul, 19, 25, 49, 278, 305, 371, 402, 428, 430, 433-34, 456, 664, 670, 695, 710, 829
Gautier, P., 736
Geanokoplos, D., 753
Gebremedhin, E., 157, 382
Gelasius I, pope, 1159
Gelasius of Caesarea, 260
Gelasius of Cyzicus, 347
Genghis Khan, 490
Gennadius of Marseilles, 540, 710, 712
Genseric, 431
George, megalomartyr, 902, 946, 1133
George Cedrenos, 946
George Hamartolos, 830
George of Bostra, 651
George of Constantinople, 629
George of Paphlagonia. See Symeon the New

Theologian
George of Pisidia, 737
George of the Arabs (Giwargi), 494
Georgia, 99, 498-501, 511-12, 628, 715
Germanus of Constantinople, 638, 1135
Germanus of Valamo, 505
Germany, 106, 412, 664, 675
Germigny des Prés, 674
Germinius the Arian, 328
Gerontius of Jerusalem, 909
Gerson, L., 844
Geta, emperor, 234, 902, 1169
Ghassanids, 492
Gibbon, E., 294, 340, 801
Glei, R., 633
Goehring, J. E., 402, 1123
Gondophares I, king, 496
Gordian dynasty, 126, 243, 1169
Gorgonia of Cappadocia, 909-10
Goths, 127, 329-30, 429-31, 456, 467-68, 606, 686
Gottschalk, 675-76
Graf, G., 493
Gratian, emperor, 340, 425, 430, 469-70, 1172
Gregg, R. C., 432
Gregory I, pope, 376-77, 379, 429, 444-45, 450, 525, 577, 662-64, 666-69, 677, 682-84, 696, 710, 715, 777, 804, 982, 991, 1000, 1160
Gregory III, pope, 670, 1160
Gregory VII, pope, 747
Gregory Nazianzen, elder, 321-22, 909
Gregory of Khandzta, 500-501
Gregory of Narek, 511
Gregory of Nazianzus, 22, 131, 154, 184, 191, 238, 248, 251, 263, 303, 309, 314-16, 319-21, 323, 330, 331-36, 339, 352, 371, 376, 382, 387, 407, 429, 442, 457, 460, 480, 488-89, 527, 541, 577-78, 626-27, 635, 641, 650, 655, 703, 716, 724, 735, 739, 770-71, 785, 820, 823, 826, 829-30, 843-44, 904, 907, 909, 919, 928, 935-36, 950, 963, 982, 1000, 1004, 1043, 1064, 1070, 1075, 1081, 1151, 1163
Gregory of Nyssa, 263, 267-68, 303, 309, 319, 323-26, 331, 353, 379, 382, 392, 457, 550, 577-78, 834, 878, 906-7, 926, 929, 931-32, 963, 994, 997-98, 1044, 1062, 1065, 1070, 1075, 1081-84, 1088, 1151
Gregory of Tours, 49, 409, 712, 802
Gregory Palamas, 932
Gregory Thaumaturgos, 227, 240, 926
Gregory the Illuminator, 497
Grey, Viscount, 431
Griffith, S. H., 493, 633
Grillmeier, A., 402
Gross, J., 1128
Grtila, council of, 500
Guillaumont, A., 397
Gulic, C. B., 938
Gundispur, 168
Gwynn, J., 390
Hadot, P., 385
Hadrian, emperor, 40, 69, 124, 135, 184, 609, 667, 974, 1168
Hadrian, pope (Adrian), 671, 1160-61
Hagg, T., 820
Hagia Sophia, cathedral, 544, 568, 605, 728, 743, 850, 946, 1143
Hagman, P., 391
Halleux, A. de, 888
Halperin, D., 1093
Hanke, L., 1059
Hankinson, R. J., 1098
Hannah, 867
Hannibal, 162
Hanson, R. P. C., 357
Harmless, W., 1123
Harmonius the Syrian, 824-25
Harnack, A. von, 31, 44, 69, 104, 791, 1014
Harrassowitz, O., 172
Harris, J. R., 824
Harris-Cowper, B., 483-84
Harrison, C., 339
Hartgar of Liege, 856
Harvey, S., 176, 389, 394, 435, 515, 876
Hastings, A., 382
Hathor, 156
Hauser, A., 768
Hausherr, I., 371, 878
Hay, D., 747
Hector of Troy, 202
Hegesippus, 123, 984, 985
Heine, R., 15
Hekster, O., 278
Helen of Troy, 202
Helena, empress, 129, 281, 620-21
Helgeland, J., 791
Heliodorus, 474
Helios, 152-54
Helix, 84
Henanisho, patriarch, 489
Henry II, king, 747
Henry IV, emperor, 745
Heraclas of Alexandria, 225, 231, 233, 244, 254
Heracleon, 33, 37-38, 777, 987
Heraclius, emperor, 498, 619-24, 626-27, 632-33, 651, 946, 1173
Herais of Alexandria, 892
Herbert, R., 939
Hermas of Rome, 54, 61-65, 108, 123, 362, 386, 703, 705, 897, 971, 973-75, 980, 995, 1068, 1071, 1104
Hermas the Manichee, 168
Hermes Criophorus, 1013
Hermes of Phoenicia, 426, 571
Hermes Toth, 1021-22
Hermes Trismegistus, 151
Hermogenes, 32, 95, 194, 197
Hermolaos, 930
Herod Antipas, 1038
Herod of Idumea, 8, 1101
Herodotus, 737
Hesychios of Sinai, 889
Hilary of Poitiers, 303, 310, 328, 407-8, 432-34, 712, 826
Hildebert of Tours,

377
Hinchcliff, P., 216
Hincmar of Rheims, 679-80
Hippocrates, 924-25
Hippodrome, 605, 1095
Hippolytus, 6, 9,12-13, 33, 38, 41, 64, 67, 71, 74, 82-85, 87-88, 9-91, 95-102, 110, 126, 132, 197, 211, 234-35, 241, 691, 699, 801, 809, 926, 963, 975, 978, 997, 1071, 1080, 1158
Hoffman, R. J., 42
Holman, S., 936, 1043
Holte, R., 186
Holy Land, 178, 185, 238, 242, 494, 632, 642, 832, 1013
Honoré, T., 60
Honorius, emperor, 299, 439, 453, 1172
Honorius, pope, 623-24, 626-27, 631, 648, 1160
Horace, 852
Hormisdas, pope, 465, 567, 1159
Hornus, A. M., 791
Horus (Harpocrates), 156-57, 159, 229, 1013-14, 1124
Hoschaia Rabba, 236
Hosius of Cordoba, 260, 299-302, 304-5, 310, 334, 345, 1062
Houts, M., 900
Hubertus Candidus (Humbertus de Candida Silva), 712, 743-44, 752-55
Hunain ibn Ishaq, 494
Hunseric, king, 467
Hunt, H. M., 389
Hunter, D. G., 176, 435
Hyginus, 44, 1158

Hyldahl, N., 984
Hypatia of Alexandria, 892
Ibas of Edessa, 467, 484, 539, 568, 600
Iberia (Georgia), 499-501
Iberia (Spain), 430
Ignatius of Antioch, 16, 52, 54, 56-60, 65, 67, 72, 108, 218, 220, 695, 902, 974, 977-78, 980, 983-84, 992, 997, 1000-1001, 1067-68
Ignatius of Constantinople, 640, 642, 1165
India, 150, 168, 481, 489-91, 495-97, 502-3, 716
Indians (American), 456, 1059
Inman, T., 925
Inner Mountain, 394
Ioane III, patriarch, 500
Iona, 413
Ioullos, patriarch, 236
Irenaeus of Lyons, 6-12, 19, 24-30, 33, 38, 40, 43-44, 46, 48-53, 55, 60, 65-67, 72, 74, 83, 90-91, 95, 97, 101-2, 105-6, 110, 132, 186-87, 193-94, 196-97, 211, 218-19, 261, 295, 382, 498, 697, 712, 774-75, 926, 975, 980, 985-89
Isaac, patriarch, 99, 513, 653, 778, 883, 1137
Isaac (Sahak) the Great, 497
Isaac I Komnenos, emperor, 736, 739-40, 745, 1175
Isaac of Nineveh, 391-93, 484, 508-9,

513, 869, 877, 881-84
Isidore of Gaza, 426, 571
Isidore of Pelusium, 716
Isidore of Seville, 679, 716
Isis (Aset), 156-61, 166, 229, 340, 923-24, 930, 1013-14, 1122, 1124
Isochristoi, 538
Isocrates, 938
Italy, 102, 117, 139, 151, 153, 182, 191, 280, 305, 347, 406-7, 412, 414, 430-31, 434, 467-69, 606, 613-14, 662, 666, 669-71, 676, 680, 710, 716, 742-44, 747, 751, 753
Iznik (Nicaea), 281, 300, 1156
Jacob, patriarch, 99, 511, 513, 521, 783, 1137
Jacob Baradeus, 565
Jacob of Edessa, 494
Jacob of Serug, 488
Jacobs, A. S., 176
Jahn, A., 539
James, M. R., 8, 840
James, son of Zebedee, 1035
James of Jerusalem, 8-9, 13, 20, 34, 58, 121, 473, 499, 815, 926, 949, 964, 970, 977, 1031, 1045, 1127, 1137
James of Nisibis, 484
Janin, R., 488, 946
Jenkins, P., 490
Jerome, 10-11, 93, 97, 102, 123, 184, 190, 194-95, 213, 228-29, 234, 242, 245, 303, 329, 331, 375, 401-2, 435, 444, 450, 455-59, 474, 480,

491, 496, 523, 534, 557, 696, 710, 827-28, 900, 908, 910-12, 926, 962, 979, 983, 1000, 1066, 1086, 1137
Jerusalem, 4, 7-10, 12-13, 43, 67-70, 94, 104, 121, 160, 166, 180, 196, 223, 225, 235, 242, 244, 260, 301, 404, 453, 458, 475, 487, 491, 498-99, 501, 503-4, 526-27, 534, 536, 616, 619-23, 625, 679, 686, 694, 709, 714-15, 719, 741, 778, 781, 793, 806, 832, 864, 873, 898, 901, 909, 911-14, 924, 946, 949, 966, 970, 972, 979, 984, 990, 997, 1031, 1034, 1038-39, 1042, 1044, 1087, 1114, 1138, 1145
Jesse, 8-9
Jesus, 4, 8-11, 13, 17, 31-33, 35, 37, 39, 41-42, 44-47, 50-54, 57, 59-60, 64, 66, 68-69, 73, 75, 86-89, 91, 100, 104-11, 123, 125, 148-49, 151, 153, 155, 157-58, 166, 168, 171-72, 174-75, 177-80, 183, 185-87, 192, 201, 205, 211, 215, 219, 232, 236, 241-43, 248, 255, 270, 273, 285-86, 289, 293, 295-96, 300, 303, 307-8, 325, 333, 337, 344, 349, 358, 380-81, 395, 404, 421, 460, 464, 480-84, 486-87, 496, 514-15, 532-33, 537, 540-42, 544-47, 549, 551, 558, 563, 582-85, 587-90, 592,

595-600, 617, 621, 625-26, 632, 636, 646, 648-52, 692-93, 696, 698-700, 704, 708, 718, 720, 724, 728, 751, 764, 768-69, 773-74, 778, 782-84, 792, 794-96, 802, 804, 809, 818-19, 821, 830, 835-36, 843, 846, 850, 860, 863-64, 868, 873, 875, 878, 887-89, 894-95, 898-99, 919, 923-25, 933, 939-42, 949-50, 956, 958-60, 965-70, 972, 985-87, 996, 1001, 1005, 1016-17, 1027, 1031, 1034-41, 1053, 1073, 1076-78, 1102-7, 1109, 1115, 1124, 1128, 1130-31, 1133, 1144, 1150-52, 1154-56
Jews, 7, 11, 13, 18, 24, 35, 45, 54, 68-69, 96, 132, 145, 150, 155, 174-82, 201, 238, 250, 260, 266, 322, 393, 426, 447, 452, 482, 491, 529, 571, 584, 589, 632, 634, 652, 699, 742, 751, 785, 862-63, 925, 1009, 1011, 1016, 1018, 1077, 1139
Jezebel, 530, 972
Joanna, wife of Chuza, 1038
John, apostle/ evangelist, 65, 123, 187, 211, 227, 236, 251, 259, 285, 472, 587, 773, 923, 961, 1040, 1137
John, son of Zebedee, 1035
John and Cyrus, martyrs, 160-61, 930

John VI Katakouzenos, emperor, 636
John VIII, patriarch, 738
John VIII, pope, 642
John IX, pope, 680
John X, pope, 712
John XII, pope, 680
John Cassian, 367, 401-2, 409-11, 420, 450, 453, 456, 663, 682
John Chrysostom, 127, 177, 319, 411, 483, 527-31, 535, 539-40, 694, 703, 713-15, 722-23, 735, 780, 829, 850-51, 900, 910, 920, 929-30, 932, 943, 963, 979, 982, 994, 996, 1000, 1005, 1013, 1051, 1062, 1070, 1072, 1075, 1086, 1118
John Climacus, 402-5, 874
John Comnenus, emperor, 947
John Italus, 737, 739
John Malalas, 426
John Mauropous, 733-35, 740
John Moschus, 912-13
John of Alexandria, 160, 930
John of Antioch, 553, 556-57, 618
John of Apamea, 886
John of Cappadocia, 465
John of Damascus, 269, 634, 638-39, 651, 654-55, 817, 832, 932, 1129, 1135, 1138-39
John of Ephesus, 502, 616
John of Gaza, 402-3, 417
John of Jerusalem,

453, 457, 534, 979, 1137
John of Palestine, 912
John of Ravenna, 679-80
John of Talaia, 464
John of Trani, 742-43, 751
John Philoponus, 575
John Scotus Eriugena, 577, 676
John the Baptist, 8, 35, 60, 699, 719, 724, 813, 1127, 1132, 1134
John the Faster, 522
John the Monk, 887
John the Spaniard, 755
John Tzimisces, emperor, 729, 946
John Xiphilinus, 735-38
Jonah, prophet, 778, 1125
Jonas, H., 31
Jones, A. H. M., 278
Jordan, 7, 13, 87, 556, 621, 631, 693, 708, 912, 966
Joseph, patriarch, 808
Joseph of Nazareth, 9, 584
Joseph the Hymnographer, 817, 832
Josephus, 175, 179-80, 1016
Jovian, emperor, 308, 425, 826, 1171
Juan Ginès de Sepulveda, 1059
Judas (Jude, Thaddeus), 496, 840
Judas Iscariot, 970, 1040
Judas Maccabeus, 686
Judea, 7, 175, 199, 404, 912, 1101
Julian of Eclanum, 1113

Julian of Halicarnassus, 617
Julian the Apostate, emperor, 69, 130-31, 148, 184, 308, 313, 320, 339, 341, 406, 407, 425, 821, 929, 1017, 1171
Juliana the Virgin, 242
Julianus of Constantinople, 614
Julius, deacon, 293
Julius, martyr, 812
Julius I, pope, 305, 1159
Julius Africanus, 243-44
Junia, apostle, 895, 978
Junius Rusticus, 90
Justin I, emperor, 465, 1173
Justin II, emperor, 614, 946, 1173
Justin Martyr, 10-11, 43, 49, 74, 89-92, 95-96, 125, 147, 151, 180, 185-87, 270, 694, 697, 699, 717, 806, 926, 941, 989, 1016-17
Justinian I, emperor, 156, 177, 402, 406, 426-28, 431, 466-67, 469, 502, 526, 533, 536, 538, 565, 567-71, 574, 604-16, 619, 628, 645, 658, 663, 666-67, 669, 676, 830, 946, 990, 1068, 1094-95, 1125, 1154, 1173
Juvencus, 827, 829
Kadel, A., 893
Kandak of Ethiopia, the, 481, 503
Kannengiesser, C., 181, 768
Karpozilos, A., 733-34

Kassia, hymnographer, 833
Katherine, megalomartyr (Catherine of Alexandria), 402, 902, 1125-26, 1133
Keane, M. H., 904
Keble, J., 816
Kellia, 396-98
Kenny, J. F., 411
Kerouac, J., 862
Khavadh II, shah, 620
Khosrau I, shah, 426
Khosrau II, shah, 620
Khoury, A., 633
Kiev, 505, 644-45, 656
King, H., 892
King, K., 31, 51, 133
Kirion II, catholicos, 500
Kirk, K. E., 981
Kittel, G., 941, 957, 865
Klein, R., 144
Klijn, A. F. J., 13
Klingshirn, W. E., 402
Koch, G. A., 12
Koch, H., 5
Koder, J., 750
Komjathy, L. J., 873
Kore, 154, 1021-22
Kosmas of Maiouma, 832
Kramer, R. S., 894
Krausmuller, D., 635
Labriolle, P. de, 21
Lactantius, 90, 92, 122, 129, 132, 134, 139, 146, 184, 195, 198-99, 270-71, 338, 381, 425, 797, 800, 810-11, 827, 1017, 1111, 1116
Ladoga, lake, 505
Lagarde, P. de, 12-13
Lakhmids, 492
Lalibela, king, 504, 526

Lallemand, L., 938
Lamertin, H., 150
Lampadia, deaconess, 994
Lang, D. M., 512
Langener, L., 157
Laporte, J., 21, 1110, 1112
Lash, E., 831
Leo, deacon, 305
Leo, historian, 946
Leo I, emperor, 393, 1173
Leo I, pope, 410-11, 460, 463-64, 467, 521, 552, 558-59, 561-64, 566, 568-70, 594, 616, 624, 633, 637, 642, 647, 649-50, 1153-54, 1159
Leo II, pope, 1160
Leo III, emperor, 633, 637, 672, 1134, 1160, 1174
Leo III, pope, 672, 685, 1160
Leo IV, emperor 637
Leo V, emperor, 639, 1135, 1140
Leo VI, emperor, 642
Leo IX, pope, 743-45, 752, 754, 1162
Leo of Constantinople, 70
Leo of Ohrid, 742, 751, 753
Leo Tornikios, 734
Leonides of Alexandria, 229-30
Leontius of Byzantium, 269
Libanius, 528, 540
Libya, 85, 257, 293, 301, 306, 347, 397, 481
Licinius, emperor, 130, 280-82, 296, 299, 310, 337, 345, 364, 1171
Liderbach, D., 816
Lienhard, J. T., 305

Lieu, J., 894
Lieu, S., 620
Ligier, L., 371
Linus, pope, 55, 1158
Livanos, C., 734
Lombards, 431, 666, 669, 671
Longinus, 241
Lorenz, S., 937
Lothair I, emperor, 856
Louth, A., 1129
Lucian of Antioch, 130, 283, 286, 310
Lucian of Samosata, 183, 973, 1016
Lucifer, 845-46
Lucifer of Cagliari, 303
Luck, G., 941
Luibheid, C., 354, 402, 874, 887, 1157
Luna, 154
Lyons, 25-26, 33, 48-49, 57, 65, 110, 138, 218, 902, 1070
Lyons, martyrs of, 48, 125, 138, 902, 1070
Macarius, Pseudo-, 263, 391-93, 399, 489, 507, 848, 869, 878-81, 883, 963, 1165
Macarius of Alexandria, 398
Macarius of Antioch, 629-31, 648
Macarius the Great, 398-99, 878
Maccabees, 122, 132, 794, 934
Macedonius of Constantinople, 334, 599, 1163
MacMullen, R., 1009
Macrina, 316, 324, 388, 894, 900, 906-9, 994, 997-98, 1044, 1062
Madaba, 494
Madigan, K., 975-76
Magnesia, 58, 984

Magoulias, H. J., 1017
Makurrah (Makuria), 502
Malachi, 249, 473
Maloney, G., 391, 733, 879
Mamre, oak of, 513
Mani, 35, 43, 167-69, 171-74
Manicheans, 5-6, 14, 43, 45, 48, 166-67, 170-74, 205-6, 343, 400, 441-42, 446, 450, 482, 753, 785, 841
Manuel I, emperor, 635, 1175
Manuel II, emperor, 636, 1175
Mar Saba Monastery, 405, 832, 882
Mar Sabas, 404-6, 500-501, 536
Marcella of Alexandria, 892
Marcellinus of Rome, 803
Marcellus of Ancyra, 305-6, 311
Marcian, emperor, 560
Marcion, Marcionites, 19, 35, 38, 41-48, 52, 66, 95, 140, 173, 194, 197, 599, 773, 780, 824-25, 828
Marcus, Gnostic writer, 38
Marcus, patriarch, 490
Marcus Aurelius, emperor, 72, 90, 125, 131, 146, 148, 183-84, 186, 189, 190-91, 194, 198, 202, 212, 1015, 1168
Marcus Cornelius Fronto, 125, 183, 198
Mareotis, 9, 255
Marinos/Marina, saint, 914-16

## 1188 | Index of Persons and Places

Marinus, pope, 642
Marius Victorinus, 267
Markschies, C., 33, 34
Markus, R. A., 299, 777
Marozia, 680
Martens, P. W., 563
Martin, H., 937
Martin, R., 357
Martin I, pope, 628-29, 1160
Martin of Tours, 406-11, 413, 420-21, 434, 1113
Martyrios, Abba, 484, 508, 869, 887-88
Mary, Blessed Virgin, 8-9, 11-12, 38, 59, 111, 147, 157-58, 164, 171, 350, 488-99, 509-10, 512-14, 544, 551-52, 555, 584-85, 594-97, 600, 632, 649, 651, 688, 724, 829, 831-32, 838, 854-55, 888, 895, 1014, 1085, 1124, 1130, 1132, 1140, 1152, 1154
Mary, niece of Abraham, 914
Mary, sister of Moses, 651
Mary Magdalene, 895, 899
Mary of Bethany, 669
Mary of Egypt, 911-14
Maryam, mother of Mani, 167
Mathews, T. F., 1124, 1127
Matteo Ricci, 491
Matthew, evangelist, 249, 967
Matthias, apostle, 41
Maur, saint, 675
Maxentius, emperor, 130, 280, 1171
Maximian, emperor, 129, 279-80, 345, 812

Maximian of Constantinople, 556, 1163
Maximian of Syracuse, 683
Maximilian, martyr, 811-12
Maximilla, 15, 19, 22, 974
Maximinus Daia, emperor, 129-30, 279-81, 364, 1171
Maximinus Thrax, emperor, 126, 241, 1169
Maximus, emperor, 408, 1172
Maximus Confessor, 267, 269, 577, 579, 625-30, 887, 932
May, G., 43
Mazzucchi, C. M., 575
McCullough, W. S., 389
McDonald, M., 896
McElwain, H. T., 791
McGowan, A., 125
McGuckin, J. A., 20, 64, 133, 135, 153, 156-57, 160, 181, 192, 216, 227, 238, 254, 300, 304, 314, 320, 363, 370, 376, 379-80, 382, 390, 514, 543-44, 550, 554, 563, 567, 618, 635, 709, 728, 764, 772-73, 799-800, 802, 816, 818, 820, 822, 830, 834, 843-45, 864, 869, 873-74, 880, 822, 830, 834, 844-45, 864, 869, 873-74, 880, 885, 892, 902, 924, 928, 930, 936, 955, 970, 1026, 1039, 1043, 1064, 1105, 1121, 1124, 1153, 1016
McKenzie, J. L., 357
McKitterick, R., 675

McLynn, N., 339, 434, 799
McVey, K., 876, 881
Mehment II, sultan, 636-37
Mehmet Sokollu Pasha, 330
Meier, J. P., 1016
Meijering, E. P., 43, 432
Meister Eckhart, 577
Melania the Elder, 388, 908
Melania the Younger, 388, 457, 534, 803, 894, 901, 908, 909, 997
Melchizidek, 9, 88, 963
Meletius of Antioch, 319, 322, 329, 331, 334, 460, 528
Meletius of Lycopolis, 348-49
Melito of Sardis, 90, 123, 190-91, 708, 764, 781
Memnon of Ephesus, 533, 555-56
Menander, 49
Menouthi, 156, 159, 161, 923-24, 930
Mercier, J., 1012
Mercury, 154
Merobaudes, 823
Merovingians, 409, 670, 829
Merton, T., 862
Mesrob Mashtots, 497
Messalians, 6, 167, 391-92, 878
Messiah, 12, 178-79, 212, 360, 634, 701, 941, 1016, 1040-41
Methodius and Cyril, 644
Methodius of Constantinople, 639
Meyendorff, J., 392
Meyers, I., 857
Michael III, emperor, 640, 642

Michael IV, emperor, 740
Michael V, emperor, 738
Michael VI, emperor, 736, 745
Michael VII, emperor, 736
Michael Cerularius, 738-41, 743, 745, 751-54
Migne, J. P., xix, 577
Milan, 130, 279, 281, 303, 338, 341, 407, 425, 433, 434-35, 441-42, 569, 676, 695-96, 701, 710-11, 713-14, 802, 821, 826, 845-48, 990
Miller, D., 391, 876, 881, 883-84
Miller, T. S., 791
Miltiades, apologist, 90, 95
Miltiades, pope, 19, 90, 95, 298, 437, 1159
Milvian Bridge, Rome, 280-81, 338
Mingana, A., 489
Minucius Felix, 90, 124-25, 146, 151, 157, 185, 197-99, 1015
Mirecki, P., 1012
Mirian I, king, 499
Mithras, 150-55, 161, 163
Moderatus, 241
Monceaux, P., 199
Monica of Thagaste, 441-42
Monnier, A., 939
Montanists, 14, 17-18, 21, 48, 706, 980, 987
Montanus, 14-19, 974
Monte Cassino, 409, 662-63
Morgan Library, the, 622
Moscow, 505-6
Moses, 41, 68, 99, 145, 148, 188, 324, 422,

494, 511, 651-52, 751, 809, 1011, 1105, 1137-38
Muhammad, 631-32, 634-36, 651, 654
Mulry, J. T., 817, 838
Munz, P., 402
Murdar, Isa al-, 633
Murphy, F. X., 908
Murray, R., 876
Musaeus of Marseilles, 712
Musonius the Stoic, 1102-3
Musurillo, H., 812
Nablus, 89, 185
Nadim, an-, 167
Nag Hammadi, 27-28, 31, 34, 50, 400-401
Nana of Georgia, queen, 512
Nautin, P., 62, 227
Nazarenes, 7-12, 69, 753
Neale, J. M., 816-17
Nectarius, 371, 529, 707, 1163
Nedungatt, G., 389
Nemesius of Emesa, 1098
Nero, 56, 122, 132, 138, 143, 199-200, 269, 677, 892, 1015, 1027, 1063, 1158, 1168
Nestorius, 411, 464, 483, 488, 532, 539, 542-61, 566, 568-69, 580, 582, 586, 591-94, 596-97, 599-600, 649, 714, 778, 1140-41, 1151-54
Neusner, J., 176, 390
Neville, G., 982
Newman, J. H., 816
Nicaea, town, 282, 297, 300, 347
Nicaea I, council of, 23, 260, 261, 281, 282, 289, 294,
296-97, 300, 302-3, 306, 308-12, 347, 315, 318, 329, 331, 335, 344, 347, 364, 366, 368, 437, 464, 500, 519-20, 523, 528, 547, 554, 563, 566, 569, 594, 648, 678, 708, 709, 902, 987-88, 992-99, 1001, 1129, 1140, 1143-44, 1150
Nicaea II, council of, 637-39, 656, 674, 1134-36, 1142, 1156-57
Nicephorus Phocas, emperor, 729, 1174
Nicephorus Xanthopoulos, 883
Niceta of Remesiana, 822
Nicetas of Nicomedia, 745
Nicholas I, pope, 640-42, 679-80
Nicholas Chrysoberges, 731
Nicholas of Myra, 709, 1133
Nicholas of Sion, 709
Nichomachus, 241
Nicolaites, 49, 753
Nicomedia, 129-30, 239, 242, 279-81, 297, 310, 714, 731, 810
Niebuhr, R., 447
Nikephorus of Constantinople, 639, 1128, 1135, 1164
Niketas Byzantios, 635
Niketas Stethatos, 750
Nile river, 156, 394, 396, 399-401, 501-2, 521, 999, 1046, 1122, 1155
Nino the Illuminator, 499, 511-12
Nobatia, 502
Noetus of Smyrna, 74, 82-84, 99-100
Nola, A. M. di, 866
Norris, F. W., 314, 321, 1151
Norris, R. A., 777
North Africa, 20, 94-95, 126, 129, 142, 157, 167-68, 185, 195-99, 212, 214, 218, 298-99, 428, 431, 436-38, 440-54, 487, 606, 619, 627, 695, 701, 709-10, 712, 715, 798, 811, 902, 908, 975, 1023, 1052, 1069
Novatian, 74, 90, 101-4, 216, 218-19, 221, 225, 255, 706, 1158
Novatus, 213, 216
Nubia, 402, 481, 495, 501-2, 521
Nu'man III, king, 492
Numenius, 147, 231, 241, 572
Numidia, 198, 298, 436-38, 448
Obolensky, D., 643
Oceanus, 155, 228
Oden, T., 781
Odoacer, king, 430, 466, 468
Oedipus, 935
O'Leary, J., 181
Olympias of Constantinople, 894, 900, 910, 993, 997
Olympiodoros, 428
Olympius, 159
Omar, caliph, 633
O'Meara, D. J., 737
Optatus of Milevis, 298, 440, 471, 710
Origen of Alexandria, 11-13, 29, 37-38, 40-41, 46, 49, 51, 55, 56, 58, 61, 67, 83, 91, 96-99, 101, 104, 125-27, 133, 146-50,
157, 180-84, 188, 191-93, 195, 199, 202, 205, 211, 216, 225-54, 256, 259-60, 263-64, 266-68, 270, 273-74, 283, 286-90, 292, 301, 309, 316, 319-21, 323-24, 362-63, 375, 377-79, 381, 386-87, 396, 398, 403-6, 410, 433-35, 441, 456-58, 492, 528, 530, 532-40, 550, 569, 571-72, 577-78, 599, 615, 627, 696, 698, 764, 767, 770, 772-73, 776-78, 780, 782, 798-800, 807, 834, 877, 892, 897, 902, 908, 926, 932, 942, 962-63, 981, 996, 998, 1013, 1046, 1110, 1121-22, 1124, 1127-28
Oropeza, B. J., 1016
Orpheus, 820
Osiek, C., 975-76, 995
Osiris, 156, 157, 198, 229, 866
Pachomius, 27, 339-401, 409, 414, 663-64, 999
Palaiologina, poet, 833
Palamon, 399-400
Palestine, 9-11, 13, 61, 69, 126, 129, 174-75, 181, 191, 206, 232, 234-36, 238, 401, 403-5, 482, 491-92, 499-500, 521, 524, 526, 534-36, 569-72, 619-20, 622, 625, 627, 634, 636, 715, 908, 912, 926, 958, 981, 991, 996, 1102, 1105, 1121
Palladius, 242, 399, 401, 411, 534, 901
Palmer, G., 728, 751, 874

Palut of Edessa, 487
Pammachius, 228
Pamphilus of
 Caesarea, 227, 228,
 260, 290, 533
Panagopoulos, J., 768
Pangloss, 933
Pantaenus of
 Alexandria, 195,
 225, 495
Panteleimon, 930
Paor, L. de, 411
Papias, 49, 54, 67
Papinianus, jurist,
 612
Pappalardo, C., 493
Paranikas, M., 816,
 822, 836
Parascheva, 902
Paredi, A., 434
Paris, 433, 670, 747,
 816
Parthia, 167, 481, 496,
 839
Paschasius
 Radbertus, 675
Patik, 167
Patmos, 123
Patricius of Thagaste,
 441
Patrick, 409, 411-12
Patripassians, 76, 79,
 82
Patrophilus of Pityus,
 500
Paul, apostle, 7, 9-10,
 12, 19, 34, 38, 42-47,
 52, 55-56, 59, 61, 68,
 84, 121-22, 149, 168,
 172-73, 175, 177-79,
 182, 188-89, 227,
 230, 233, 236,
 251-52, 259, 265,
 270, 272, 274, 326,
 357-61, 377-79, 386,
 451-52, 454, 458,
 473, 475, 482, 486,
 491, 507, 509, 511,
 537, 548, 570, 577,
 583, 585-86, 677,
 696, 699, 702, 704,
 720, 764, 770,
 772-73, 778, 780,
 787, 796, 815, 818,
 834-35, 867-68,
 895-99, 904, 916,
 920, 926, 950, 962,
 964, 968-73, 982,
 987, 991, 996-97,
 1001, 1005, 1008,
 1016, 1031, 1036,
 1042, 1045, 1054,
 1059, 1065-68,
 1072-74, 1076-77,
 1079, 1086, 1094,
 1102-3, 1107-10, 1127,
 1137, 1144
Paul II, patriarch,
 648
Paul of
 Constantinople,
 524
Paul of Evergetinos,
 403
Paul of Samosata,
 74-75, 87-88, 289,
 294, 551, 989
Paul of Thebes, 912
Paul the Sophist, 565
Paula, 457, 900, 1000
Paulicians, 498, 643
Paulina, Anconia
 Fabia, 164
Paulinus of Antioch,
 331, 334, 457, 460
Paulinus of Aquileia,
 675
Paulinus of Nola,
 666, 823, 827-29,
 851-52, 1113
Paulinus the Arian,
 291
Paulus, jurist, 140,
 141, 612, 614
Pavel, F. van de, 371
Pbow, 400
Pearson, B. A., 402
Pedianus Secundus,
 1067
Pelagia of Jerusalem,
 914-15
Pelagius, 96, 197, 443,
 450-56, 458, 538,
 1112
Pelagius II, pope, 663,
 666-67, 1160
Pelagius of
 Constantinople, 538
Pella, 7, 10, 12
Pelliot, P., 490
Peltomaa, L. M., 832
Pepin (Pippin) the
 Short, 428, 670-71
Peppard, M., 1125
Pepuza, 17-18, 21-22
Percival, H. R., 308
Peregrinus Proteus,
 183, 973, 1016
Perler, O., 190
Perpetua and Felicity,
 20, 126, 902-4,
 917-19, 926
Perrone, L., 226, 254,
 1121
Peter, apostle, 13, 41,
 55-56, 58, 67,
 121-22, 217-18,
 220-22, 272, 338,
 351, 459, 462, 469,
 473, 482, 521, 525,
 587, 594, 622, 641,
 671-72, 677-80, 720,
 743, 796, 809, 846,
 967, 970, 976, 1001,
 1012, 1016
Peter I, of Alexandria,
 130, 259, 322, 331,
 466, 469, 533, 1122
Peter III, of Antioch,
 743
Peter Mongus, 567
Peter of Amalfi, 752
Peter of
 Constantinople, 648
Peter of Sebaste, 906
Petrus Siculus, 643
Pettis, J., 22, 159
Phantasiasts, 498
Pharisees, 175, 704,
 864, 873, 1105, 1114
Philadelphia, 16, 58,
 974, 1000
Philemon, 473, 1065,
 1067, 1079
Philemon, Apa, 887
Philip, apostle, 19, 34,
 481, 503, 825,
 967-68, 974, 996,
 1001
Philip, asiarch, 201
Philip, governor, 201
Philip of Macedon,
 938
Philip the Arab,
 emperor, 126-27,
 214, 243-44, 797,
 1169
Philippi, 56, 65-66,
 322, 473, 695, 979,
 982, 995
Philippopolis, 306
Philo, deacon, 1015
Philo Judaeus, 9, 192,
 196, 201, 212, 229,
 273, 1122, 1141
Philostorgius, 304
Philoxenus of
 Mabbug, 484, 617,
 1053
Philoxenus of Rome,
 305
Phocas, emperor, 619,
 1173
Photinus of Sirmium,
 87-88
Photius, 101, 192, 228,
 640-44, 655, 680,
 713, 740, 1165
Phrygia, 7, 14-15,
 17-19, 22, 152,
 162-64, 426, 432-71,
 917
Picasso, G., 374
Pindar, 819, 827
Pisidia, 7, 737
Pispir, 394, 886
Pistus of Libya, 293
Pitra, J. B., cardinal,
 816
Plato, 28, 30, 32, 36,
 40, 52, 89, 91, 147,
 151, 185, 225, 230-31,
 240-41, 244, 246,
 252, 256, 262-68,
 270-71, 287, 385,
 387, 426-27, 444,
 469, 476-77, 570-79,
 599, 616, 652, 734,

736-37, 739, 767, 820, 830, 865, 905, 907, 932, 937, 941, 957-58, 998, 1009, 1011, 1016, 1029, 1059, 1093, 1095-96
Pliny the Younger, 124, 131, 143, 823, 991, 1015
Plotinus, 28-29, 230-31, 244, 262, 266, 468, 572-74, 576-77
Plutarch of Alexandria, 231
Plutarch of Athens, 573
Plutarch of Chaeronea, 156, 734, 937
Polycarp of Smyrna, 24-25, 48, 54, 58-59, 65-67, 109, 125, 180, 200-202, 902, 977-78, 995, 997, 1068
Polycrates, 25, 190
Pontianus, pope, 99, 126, 228, 241, 533
Pontius, deacon, 213
Pontius Pilate, 11, 111, 179, 199
Porphyry of Gaza, 151-52, 183, 231, 240-41, 244, 266, 572-73, 576, 1016
Porziuncula of Assisi, 1045
Possidius of Hippo, 432, 444
Potamiaena of Alexandria, 892
Pothinus, 48, 712
Praetextatus, Vettius, 164
Praxeas, 20, 74, 79, 82, 95, 197
Preisendanz, K., 1010, 1019
Price, R. M., 390, 404, 536, 912
Prisca, apostle, 896

Prisca, prophetess, 15, 19, 22, 974
Priscian of Lydia, 426, 571
Priscillian, 408
Pritz, R. A., 9-10
Prochorius the Iberian, 501
Prochorus, 967
Proclus Lycaeus, 266, 427, 468, 573-75, 577
Proclus of Constantinople, 832, 984, 1163
Procopius, historian, 426, 604, 606
Procopius, martyr, 206
Prosper of Aquitaine, 411, 444, 668
Protoctetus of Caesarea, 242
Protoktistoi, 538
Prudentius, 164, 823, 827-29, 852-53
Psellus, Michael, 733-35, 737-40, 745, 755
Ptolemy the Gnostic, 32, 38
Pulcheria, empress, 325, 544, 552, 560-61, 997, 1173
Pyrrhus, patriarch, 627, 648, 1164
Pythagoreans, 5, 89, 147, 185, 241, 387
Qasr Ibrim, 502
Quadratus, 90, 184, 974
Quintilla, 22
Quintus Mucius Scaevola, 612
Ra, 176, 866
Rabanus Maurus, 675
Rabban Shabur, 881
Rabbula of Edessa, 43, 484
Ramelli, H., 40, 1089
Ratramnus of Corbie, 688
Ravenna, 409, 428,

430-31, 468, 604, 669-70, 679, 710, 714, 1000
Reiling, J., 971
Rhine, river, 329, 675
Rhoda, 61, 897
Ricci, Matteo, 491
Ripon, 526
Roberts, M. J., 435, 829
Robinson, A. W., 357
Romanianus of Thagaste, 441
Romanos the Melodist, 488, 728, 831-33, 853-55
Romanus IV, emperor, 681, 736, 748, 1175
Romanus Argyrus, emperor, 946
Rome, 13-14, 19-20, 23-26, 32-33, 41, 43-44, 46, 48-49, 54-56, 58, 61, 63-65, 71-74, 79, 82, 84-85, 87, 90, 93, 95-99, 101-2, 107, 110, 122-23, 125-26, 128, 130-32, 134-35, 138-39, 141-42, 144, 146, 149, 159, 159, 162-65, 167-68, 174, 177, 179, 182, 186-87, 189-90, 194-95, 197-99, 212-22, 223-25, 228-29, 232-35, 238, 241-45, 255, 257-60, 262, 278-82, 296-99, 303-5, 308, 315, 330-31, 336, 338, 340-41, 360, 364-66, 369, 371, 374-75, 388, 390, 410, 425-28, 428-32, 434, 437, 439, 441-43, 445-46, 448, 450-53, 455-66, 468, 473, 480-84, 487, 491, 506, 521-27, 531, 533-35, 540, 542, 544, 546,

552-54, 557-58, 560, 562, 564, 567, 572, 594, 609, 695-98, 703, 706, 708, 710-11, 713-14, 741-45, 752-53, 791-92, 796, 798-99, 801, 803, 806, 808, 809, 812, 824, 828, 862, 892, 896-97, 902, 908, 959, 964, 970, 974, 977, 980, 983-85, 987, 990, 992, 1001, 1015, 1027-29, 1061-68, 1071, 1079, 1086, 1088, 1101, 1121, 1123, 1126, 1153-54, 1158
Rose, E., 172
Roth, C. P., 639
Rouselle, A., 229
Rousseau, P., 402
Rudolph, K., 31
Ruether, R. R., 899
Rufinus of Aquileia, 70, 228, 304, 399, 456-57, 499-500, 504, 534, 908
Runciman, S., 746
Ryan, E., 791
Sabellius, 74-75, 82, 85-87, 99, 257, 317, 343
Sadhona, Abba, 484, 508, 869, 888
Sagnard, F. M., 33
Saint-Roch, P., 374
Sainte Chapelle, 622
San Apollinare, 409, 1000
Sanders, T., 816
Santa Maria Capua Vetere, 153
Sappho of Lesbos, 892, 1096
Sardinia, 97, 126, 301, 431, 467
Satahas, K. N., 737
Satan, 59, 66, 121, 132, 161, 203, 253, 282, 359, 648, 764, 794, 809, 831, 863, 903, 1023, 1084, 1139,

1140, 1143
Satornil, 49
Saturn, 338
Saturnus of Carthage, 917
Saul, king, 586, 619
Saxons, 338, 372, 374
Scete (Skete), 159, 396, 398, 410
Schaff, P., 440
Scher, A., 167
Schlusser-Fiorenza, E., 894, 899
Schottroff, L., 894
Scillitan martyrs, 142-43
Scipio Africanus, 800
Scorpio, 152, 154
Scott, A., 240
Secundus of Ptolemais, 293, 301, 348
Sedulius, poet, 823, 856
Sedulius Scotus, 412, 827, 852, 856-57
Seleucia (Asia Minor), 322, 330, 433
Seleucia-Ctesiphon, 167
Seneca, 198, 269-70, 1026, 1028, 1064
Serapeum of Alexandria, 342
Serapion of Antioch, 487
Serapion of Thmuis, 167, 310, 694, 716
Serapis, 151, 198, 342
Serdica, 305-6, 350
Sergius, patriarch, 623-24, 626-27, 631, 648, 832
Sergius II, Manuelites, 731
Sergius III, pope, 680, 1161
Sergius and Bacchus, martyrs, 605
Sergius of Radonezh, 505

Sergius of Reshaina, 484
Sergius of Valamo, 505
Seti, 156-57
Severan dynasty, 98, 125-26, 137, 228-29, 234, 241, 252, 278, 892, 902, 1169
Severus, Gnostic leader, 7
Severus II, emperor, 279-80
Severus of Antioch, 167, 577, 617, 646, 648, 1140, 1141
Sewter, E. R. A., 737
Shapur I, shah, 168
Sharastani, al-, 167
Sheba, queen of, 503
Shenoute of Atripe, 400-402
Sherrard, P., 728, 751, 874
Sibyl, 61, 162, 262, 977
Sicily, 431, 666, 1053
Sidonius Apollinaris, 712
Simeon Metaphrastes, 709
Simeon of Bulgaria, Tsar, 644
Simon, apostle, 1035
Simon Magus, 43-44, 49, 753, 967, 1011
Simon of Cyrene, 40-41
Simonetti, M., 33, 768
Simonides, 827
Simplicianus of Milan, 441, 711, 813
Sinai, 64, 67, 251, 338, 403, 491, 500, 513, 522, 526, 652, 834, 868, 874, 880, 888, 897, 1125-26, 1137
Sinope, 41, 43
Sixtus II, pope, 255, 1159
Smyrna, 24, 48, 58-59, 60, 65-66, 74, 82-83, 99, 109, 125, 201-2, 695, 902, 978, 995, 1042
Smyth, H. W., 938
Socrates, philosopher, 262, 324, 906-7
Socrates Scholasticus, 102, 228, 239, 328, 347, 504, 534, 1017
Sol Invictus, 153
Solomon, king, 473, 503, 513, 606, 719, 824-26, 837-38, 867, 1003, 1032, 1038, 1080, 1114
Sophronius of Jerusalem, 159-60, 624-27, 629-30, 911-14, 924
Soter, pope, 56
Soumakis, F., 1016
Sozomen, historian, 504, 534, 906
Spain, 56, 218, 305, 369, 428, 469, 499, 606, 674, 695, 710-12, 828, 852, 992, 1059, 1071
Stancliffe, C., 409
Stander, H. K., 971
Stanley, A. P., 1125
Stark, R., 337, 894
Statius Quadratus, 66
Ste-Croix, G. E. M. de, 1068, 1072-74, 1076
Stephen, protomartyr, 66, 121, 902, 967-68
Stephen I, pope, 212, 220-22, 255, 1158
Stephen II, pope, 670, 1160
Stephen of Alexina, 731-32
Stevenson, W. R., 791
Stewart, C., 389, 415, 878, 879
Stewart-Sykes, A., 190
Stylianopoulos, T., 768

Subiaco, 662
Suetonius, 369, 1010, 1015
Sullivan, F. A., 540
Sulpicius Severus, 409, 420, 1113
Susanna, 98, 244
Suzuki, D. T., 862
Sviatoslav of Kiev, 645
Swain, S., 791
Swift, L. J., 791
Symeon of Mesopotamia, 391, 399, 878
Symeon Stylites, 393-94, 492
Symeon Stylites the Younger, 394
Symeon the New Theologian, 403, 489, 727-33, 737, 743, 749, 758-59, 826, 833-34, 880
Symeon the Studite, 729-30
Symmachus, pope, 465-66, 1159
Symmachus, senator, 148, 340-41
Symmachus the Ebionite, 12, 242
Syncletica of Alexandria, 894, 997
Synesius of Cyrene, 716, 820, 829-30
Syragius, general, 430-31
Syria, 5-7, 10, 24-25, 32, 39-40, 43-44, 70-71, 90, 99, 126, 167-68, 177, 187-89, 191, 194, 258, 269, 281, 305, 316, 334, 369, 386-87, 389-93, 397, 399, 406, 426-27, 435, 456, 463, 481-500, 504, 506-9, 515-16, 521-22, 524, 527-29, 531, 539-44, 546-47, 549, 552-53, 555-56,

560, 562-67, 568-71, 573-74, 577, 604, 615, 617-20, 622-26, 633-34, 637, 646, 693-94, 702, 714, 716, 749, 777-78, 780, 791, 816-17, 824-25, 830-32, 837, 839-42, 848-49, 854, 869, 876-78, 880-89, 899, 912, 915, 941, 980, 994-95, 997-99, 1005, 1053, 1085, 1098, 1121, 1130, 1134, 1153-55
Tabernee, W., 15
Tabitha (Dorcas), 895
Tacitus, 131-32, 199
Tall Brothers, the, 396, 403, 530, 532, 535
Tanner, N. P., 344, 1151, 1153-57
Tao Klarjeti, 500
Tatian, 6, 8, 49, 90, 186-89, 485, 798, 806
Taurus, 152
Tekla Haymanot, 504
Tertullian, 12-13, 20-22, 33, 43-46, 48, 55, 63, 73-79, 81-82, 86, 90, 92-98, 101-4, 122-23, 126, 131-33, 136-46, 151, 184-85, 190, 194-97, 199, 203, 211, 213-14, 217, 219, 225, 257, 269-70, 362, 371, 377, 381, 386, 422, 463, 559, 695, 706, 775, 798, 806-8, 813, 824, 848, 899, 903-4, 917, 955, 963, 975, 978, 980, 987, 989, 999, 1001, 1017, 1031, 1070, 1115, 1125
Thais, 914
Thebes, 399-400
Thecla (Thekla), poet, 833
Thekla, megalomartyr, 902
Theoctist of Caesarea, 225, 235, 260
Theodora, empress, 502, 604-5, 639, 658, 736, 745, 946
Theodore, disciple of Origen, 150, 227, 240
Theodore, general, 622, 902
Theodore Abu Qurra, 633
Theodore Balsamon, 744
Theodore Bar Konai, 167
Theodore Mopsuestia, 467, 488, 523, 528, 539-43, 556, 564, 568, 596-97, 599-600, 696, 701, 777-80, 979, 1151
Theodore of Canterbury, 427
Theodore of Paran, 648
Theodore Prodromos, 833
Theodore the Studite, 402, 639, 664, 832, 1135-36, 1142
Theodore the Tyro, 501, 902
Theodoret of Cyrrh, 43, 291, 347, 350, 390-91, 467, 486, 504, 539, 556, 568, 600, 643, 696, 929, 1085
Theodoric, king, 430, 467-68
Theodosius I, emperor, 165, 303, 310, 315, 322-23, 325, 330-31, 335, 341-42, 376, 425, 429-30, 436, 460-61, 469, 525, 531, 797, 828, 904, 990, 1094, 1137, 1151, 1172
Theodosius II, emperor, 393, 521, 529, 544, 552, 555-56, 560, 607, 609-10, 727, 997, 1152-53, 1173
Theodosius of Pechersk, 505
Theodotus the Arian, 291
Theodotus the Tanner, 20, 32, 38, 74, 87-88, 193
Theodulf of Orleans, 674
Theognostos of Alexandria, 259
Theonas of Marmorica, 293, 301, 348
Theophanes, hymnographer, 832
Theophanes the Confessor, 634
Theophilus, emperor, 639, 1135
Theophilus of Alexandria, 259, 410, 530, 532, 534-35, 543, 607, 716, 1122
Theophilus of Antioch, 49, 90, 100, 102, 146, 194-95
Theophilus of Constantinople, 607, 610, 614
Theophylact of Tusculum, 680
Theotokos, 157, 513, 544-46, 555, 562, 582, 590, 594-95, 724, 824, 943, 1014, 1123-24, 1130, 1132, 1152
See also Mary, Blessed Virgin
Therasia of Nola, 1113
Third Messenger, the, 170
Thomas, apostle, 7, 39, 168, 386, 389, 484-87, 489, 495-96, 506, 599, 838-42, 899-900, 941
Thomas Aquinas, 269, 781
Thomas of Cana, 496
Thomas the Manichee, 168
Thomson, H. J., 853
Thor, 338
Thrace, 305, 329-30, 429, 524-25, 715
Three Hierarchs, the, 527
Thucydides, 737
Thyatira, 972
Tiberius II, emperor, 614, 1173
Timothy, apostle, 471, 583, 834, 916, 982, 995, 1078
Timothy I, of Baghdad, 489, 509
Timothy Aelurus, 565, 617
Timothy of Alexandria, 716
Tinh, V. T., 157
Tissot, Y., 7
Titus, apostle, 360, 473, 941, 1067
Titus, emperor, 159, 168
Titus Flavius Clemens, 56, 123
Titus of Bosra, 167
Tiw, 328
Tollinton, R. B., 239
Tomlin, R. S. O., 1009
Topping, E. C., 833
Torjesen, K., 254
Totila, king, 663
Toulouse, 431, 747
Trajan, emperor, 55, 58, 124-25, 143, 159, 183, 823, 991, 1015, 1168
Trakatellis, D., 768
Tralles, 58
Trastevere, 58
Tripolitis, A., 833
Trostyanskiy, S., 300

Trypanis, C., 817
Trypho, 11, 90-91, 180, 186, 926, 941, 1017
Tsung-Chien, 167
Turner, D. L., 357
Twelftree, G., 700, 924, 1016
Twomey, D. V., 153
Tychicus of Byzantium, 427
Tyre, 130, 245, 311, 314
Ubina, J. F., 791
Ulpianus, 140-41, 612, 614
Vagharhapat, 497
Vahtang, king, 500
Valamo, 505
Valantasis, R., 385
Valens, emperor, 303, 310, 318, 322, 324, 329, 331, 425, 429-30, 1044, 1172
Valens the Arian, 328-29, 899
Valentinian I, emperor, 459, 1171
Valentinian II, emperor, 165, 330, 340-41, 435-36, 1172
Valentinian III, emperor, 469, 593, 1172
Valentinus, Valentinianism, 6, 26, 30, 32-38, 40, 43, 49-50, 84, 94, 109, 193, 230, 343, 777, 824-25, 987
Valeria Proba, 827-28
Valerian, emperor, 128, 222, 229, 245, 824, 1170
Valerius of Thagaste, 442
Vassilaki, M., 1127, 1132
Vatican, 97, 122, 338, 462, 622, 677, 1013, 1111, 1157
Venantius Fortunatus, 829, 1113
Venerius of Marseilles, 712
Vermander, J. M., 146
Vespasian, emperor, 159, 179, 1168
Veyne, P., 1028
Victor I, pope, 24-25, 48, 87-88, 676, 708, 987, 1158
Victor II, pope, 745
Victor of Vita, 710
Vigilius, pope, 466, 538, 568-69, 628, 1154, 1159
Vincent of Lerins, 82, 93, 770
Vladimir of Kiev, 505, 645, 656-58
Voconius of Castellanum, 710
Vogel, C., 371, 374
Volusianus, emperor, 127, 1170
Volusianus of Carthage, 803
Von Campenhausen, H., 969
Voobus, A., 6, 26, 494
Waddell, H., 687, 874
Waddington, W. H., 493
Wadi al Ya'qub, 167
Wadi el Natroun, 398
Walalis, R. T., 575
Walsh, J. E., 122
Walsh, P. G., 852, 1113
Ward, B., 159, 914
Ware, K., 728, 751, 874
Watson, A., 611
Watson, D., 768
Weitzmann, K., 1126
West, C., 359
Westerink, L. G., 736
Whitby, M., 791
White, C., 335
William II, king, 379
Williams, D. H., 434
Williams, M., 31
Williams, R., 355
Willibrord, 664
Wilson, S. G., 176
Wilson-Kastner, P., 908
Witt, R. E., 156, 159
Wittgenstein, L., 313
Wittung, J., 382, 550, 844
Wodin, 338
Wolfson, H. A., 262
Wood, D., 64, 181, 192, 216, 902
Woods, V. C., 906
Woodward, G. E., 829
Wortley, J., 913
Wuzong, emperor, 490
Xavier, Francis, 491
Xenophon, 937-38, 1028
Xian, 490
Yahya ibn Adi, 494
Yahya ibn Yahya, 493-94
Yarmuk, battle of, 622
Yaropolk of Kiev, 645
Yeostre, 224, 338
Zeno, emperor, 430, 464-65, 468, 500, 565-67, 1173
Zeno, philosopher, 269
Zephyrinus, pope, 84-85, 88, 97, 234, 1158
Zoroaster, 168, 171, 622
Zosimas, presbyter, 912-13
Zosimus, pope, 455, 1159

# INDEX OF SUBJECTS

abortion, 34, 899, 1094, 1109, 1112
Acts of Thomas, 7, 39, 389, 485, 496, 506, 839-42, 941
adoptionism, 75, 86, 8-89, 102-3
adultery, 63, 217, 363, 654, 674, 703, 705, 823, 1071, 1092, 1104, 1107, 1109, 1115, 1117
aeons, 34-36, 40, 169-70, 246
afterlife, 32, 38, 46, 153-54
agape meal, 72, 358
Albigensians, 39, 167
allegory, 32-33, 38, 63, 68, 98-99, 829
almsgiving, 17, 109, 214, 363, 705, 1034, 1040
altar, 122, 160, 224, 321, 340-41, 359, 363, 365-66, 415, 435, 462, 514, 685-86, 688, 694-97, 703-5, 716, 720, 744, 753-54, 801-2, 805, 818, 863, 865, 877-78, 910, 927, 931, 943, 979, 992-96, 1005, 1126-27, 1130, 1136
*anakephalaiosis*, 52, 101
angels, 40, 61, 64, 68, 108-9, 110, 187, 201, 216, 234, 246-47, 250, 275, 294, 333, 377-78, 388, 421, 470-71, 508, 513, 579, 582, 655, 723, 725, 750, 753, 784, 834-35, 844, 850-51, 862, 879, 883, 888, 903, 911, 916, 933, 951, 959, 961, 993, 1023, 1104, 1106, 1115, 1125, 1127, 1144
anointing, 111, 224, 362, 701-2, 926-27, 931, 944, 950, 994, 1114
antichrist, 66-67, 72, 98, 433, 651
apocalypticism, 13, 16, 19-21, 31, 37, 61, 67-68, 121, 131, 139, 144, 161, 167, 174, 178-79, 264, 270, 369, 386, 388, 395, 482-86, 504, 779, 795, 800, 869, 878, 882, 959, 970-75, 997, 1036, 1039, 1101-4
Apocrypha, 6-8, 53, 57-58, 493, 496, 632, 826, 840, 895-96
*apokatastasis*, 324, 533
apologetics, 28-29, 33, 41, 49-50, 68, 82, 92-94, 125, 136, 166-67, 175-76, 183-206, 261, 323, 443, 458, 484, 493, 543, 617, 736, 803, 817, 834, 976, 1010-19, 1076, 1110, 1136
apostles, 45, 49, 53-54, 56-58, 65, 70-71, 103, 108, 218-20, 272-73, 472-73, 496, 768, 773, 828, 884, 894-96, 965-71, 978, 985-88
apostolic fathers, 54-72
apostolicity, 3, 46, 49, 52-53, 62, 65, 67, 71, 95, 97, 106, 196, 202, 210, 219-20, 236, 251, 273-74, 344, 348-49, 360, 519, 656-57, 678-79, 769, 774-76, 936, 966, 973, 985-89
Arianism, 26, 85, 88, 282-335, 376-78, 668, 837
art, 1121-45
asceticism, 4-6, 62, 206, 232, 237, 320, 324-25, 373, 385-91, 402, 406, 410, 485-86, 536, 666, 876, 894, 899, 904, 908, 914, 945, 1090, 1093, 1102, 1114, 1133
astrology, 13, 38-39, 167, 170, 187, 370, 450, 1009
atonement, 166, 314, 375-83, 422, 818
authority, 14, 23, 54-57, 59, 65, 71
baptism, 6, 13, 38, 59, 63, 71-72, 80-81, 88, 91, 99, 102, 106, 110, 127, 152, 161, 164, 166, 86-187, 197, 213-19, 221, 225, 240, 255-56, 272, 286, 301, 307, 320, 326, 330, 333, 361-66, 371, 389, 391, 407, 421, 439, 441-42, 451, 454, 472, 474, 485, 503, 506, 528, 578, 599, 606, 616, 635, 645, 656-58, 692-95, 698-706, 711, 717, 719-20, 764, 796-97, 808-9, 819-20, 835-36, 840, 860, 863, 878, 889, 967, 972, 976-78, 982, 994, 998, 1023, 1034, 1085, 1118, 1126
basilica, 122, 312, 338, 459, 462, 605, 663, 672, 677, 794, 1045, 1156
bishops, 14-17, 19-21, 26, 29, 32, 44-49, 51-54, 56, 59-60, 65, 67, 70, 72, 80-81, 91, 99, 106-8, 130, 161, 172, 180, 190, 193, 210-12, 214, 218-26, 228, 233, 235, 238, 242, 244, 258-61, 281, 284, 294, 296-312, 317, 319, 325, 327-31, 334, 340, 345, 347-49, 361, 364-71, 387, 392, 400-401, 408, 412, 414, 426, 432-34, 437-38, 440-42, 448-50, 457, 461-67, 473, 487, 492, 494, 497, 500-503, 506, 519, 529-69, 578, 592, 595, 612, 615, 627, 629, 640, 642, 649, 651, 656, 666-67, 672, 676-80, 694,

696-98, 701, 703, 709, 711-12, 721, 724, 746, 751-57, 774-76, 796, 801, 806-8, 812, 826, 829, 878, 901, 906, 927, 929, 936-39, 963-65, 974, 976-79, 981-98, 1002, 1006, 1044, 1056, 1059, 1062-65, 1069-73, 1094, 1107, 1113-14, 1133, 1140, 1143, 1150-57
burial, 621, 719, 833, 866, 896, 912, 1041, 1137
canonicity, 3-4, 20, 26, 39, 42, 44, 46-49, 51, 53-55, 61-62, 67, 70, 74, 84, 97, 106, 173, 221, 238, 253, 256, 303, 306, 313, 349, 361, 364-76, 409, 412, 442, 446, 458-62, 462, 465, 473, 485, 489, 493, 503, 520, 525-26, 531, 552, 593, 606, 612, 630, 641-42, 667, 706-8, 734, 754, 765-69, 773, 775, 778, 787-88, 790, 801-5, 812, 815, 826, 894, 897, 902, 904-10, 928, 968, 970, 972, 981, 985-87, 999-1011, 1059-60, 1062, 1067, 1077, 1080, 1107, 1109-10
capital punishment, 124, 142, 792, 1067-68
catacombs, 126, 153, 1125-26
catechumen, 6, 72, 172, 219, 223-24, 366, 371, 485, 515, 700-701, 818, 978, 998
catholicism, 26-27, 32, 49, 51, 81-82, 95,
105-6, 443, 450, 456, 643, 668, 989
celibacy, 6, 230, 233, 320, 369, 386, 389, 471, 485, 743, 753, 840, 842, 996, 998-99, 1036, 1095, 1102-4
Chalcedon (council of), 323, 331, 336, 393, 401, 404, 406, 460-61, 463-64, 467, 484, 489, 494, 498, 500-503, 521-22, 525-27, 530-36, 560-70, 597, 600, 602, 604, 615-18, 623-27, 630-33, 637, 641, 646, 649, 656, 678, 714-16, 740, 913, 966, 992-93, 1053, 1072, 1122, 1153-57
charism, 14, 47, 54-55, 62, 65, 102-3, 149, 211-12, 219-20, 225, 232, 486, 520, 563, 638, 698, 702, 767, 771-72, 775, 926-27, 942, 963-64, 967, 971-74, 979, 982, 1001
chastity, 6, 104, 189, 369, 419, 486, 674, 724, 846, 869, 871, 894, 898, 920, 1027, 1035-36, 1053, 1092, 1115, 1117
Cherubim, 687, 721-23, 850-51, 943, 1023, 1138
chiliasm, 67
church, 4-5, 9, 14, 16, 19, 23, 25, 28-29, 33-34, 43, 48-50, 53, 57, 61-63, 73, 90-91, 95, 98, 102, 104, 106, 110, 121, 132, 147, 175-78, 196-97, 210-12, 217, 219-22, 224, 226, 235, 237, 246, 256, 272, 337,
360, 363, 448-49, 464-66, 945-47, 956-91
class (social), 119-24, 126, 128, 137, 141, 145-47, 155, 185, 189, 213, 222, 229, 261, 336-40, 358, 369-70, 407, 429, 449, 523, 604, 823, 862, 897, 905-7, 909, 916, 928, 948, 996, 1009-10
clerical orders, 956-93
commentary (biblical), 33, 38, 40, 643, 667, 765, 776-81, 1103
confession (sacrament), 703-7
confessor (martyr), 19, 58, 60, 133, 206, 216, 273, 297, 363-64, 373, 707
cosmology, 28, 36, 40, 52, 233-34, 270, 579
councils, 296-309, 327-35, 553-69, 1150-57
creation, 52, 69, 73, 76, 78, 84, 98, 100-101, 117, 144, 194, 234, 246-47, 252, 267, 314, 319, 442, 533, 578, 655, 695, 927, 932, 1081-82
creed, 26, 36, 51-53, 62, 102, 105-6, 110-11, 174, 196, 219-20, 285, 303, 344, 593, 594, 819, 835, 961, 986
cremation, 122
cross, 40, 66, 68, 82, 89, 153, 166, 179, 223, 280-81, 300, 322, 326, 342, 381-83, 395, 486, 490, 512, 526, 545, 620-22, 632, 653,
688, 692, 700, 718, 778, 794, 800, 831-32, 907, 911, 934, 962, 1012-13, 1018, 1131, 1138-39
*daimones*, 36, 38, 45, 109-10, 360, 700
deacon, 40, 56, 72, 124, 991-93
decalogue, 69
deification (by grace), 52, 333, 382-83, 550, 559, 578-79, 618, 628, 830, 844, 1128
demiurge, 34-35, 36, 38, 40, 45-47, 169, 287, 572
denominationalism, 81, 763, 768
descent into hades, (harrowing of hell), 378, 830
Didache, 19, 54, 62, 68-72, 106-7, 386, 691, 699, 705, 961, 971, 973, 1068
Didascalia, 71, 714, 980-81, 993, 995-96
*didaskalos*, 28, 32, 44, 53, 80-82, 89, 189, 193, 225
divorce, 376, 815, 904, 1105, 1114-15
docetism, 32, 39, 41, 44, 48, 59-60, 66, 102, 172
doxology, 66, 592, 826, 944, 961, 1032
dualism, 6, 31, 34, 36-37, 39, 45, 173-74, 399, 446, 643, 828, 867
economy (of salvation), 77-78, 83-84, 100-104, 194, 256, 289, 314, 327, 332, 584, 594-95, 715, 779
ecstasy, 17-18, 21, 884
eighth day, 117, 1131, 1134
*eirenika*, 65, 520, 697

## Index of Subjects | 1197

*epiclesis*, 699, 711, 714-15, 888
*epinoiai*, 79, 247, 249
episcopos. *See* bishops
eschatology, 17, 20-21, 67, 96, 98, 118, 120-21, 193, 695, 779, 1034-35, 1107-9
Eucharist, 25, 47, 59, 60, 66, 71-72, 82, 91, 99, 106-7, 124, 133, 157, 165, 174, 186-87, 189, 215, 220-21, 224, 239, 249, 256, 273, 307, 358-59, 361-63, 366-68, 371, 378, 382, 397, 507, 531, 549, 578, 663, 675, 691-717, 731, 742, 780, 797, 802, 805, 812, 815, 821, 823, 842-44, 850-51, 860, 877, 899, 902, 910, 912-13, 927, 930, 943, 963, 966, 972-79, 981-83, 986, 991-93, 1010, 1014, 1031, 1045, 1071, 1109, 1132, 1139, 1156
eunuchs, 729, 850-51, 1104, 1106, 1115
excommunication, 25, 63, 83, 359, 372, 412, 567, 704, 743-44, 753, 801, 1071
exegesis, 21, 32, 37, 41-42, 44, 46, 67-68, 90-91
   *See also*
      commentary (biblical)
exorcism, 13, 89, 223, 442, 481, 699-700, 924-25, 930, 958-60, 978, 1002, 1008-9, 1016, 1020, 1023
Fall, the, 30, 34, 45, 53, 63, 168, 187, 249-52, 332, 357, 386, 399, 454-56, 548, 590, 628, 698,
813, 846, 862, 874, 880, 882, 1073
fasting, 17, 24, 63, 72, 96, 109, 230, 362-63, 373, 386, 398, 410, 416, 451, 705-7, 742, 871, 882, 912, 1034, 1118, 1133
fatalism, 39, 635, 1025
*filioque*, 379, 640-41, 643, 674, 679, 740, 752, 754
freedom, 34, 47, 92-94, 120, 123, 131-32, 138-39, 141, 146, 193, 358, 388, 395, 408, 420, 425, 455-56, 538, 578, 628, 630, 886, 896, 905, 914, 937, 957, 1048, 1056-57, 1061-62, 1072, 1074-75, 1077, 1081, 1083-84, 1098
Gentiles, 58, 71, 91, 107, 176, 178-79, 181, 186, 322, 686, 699, 708, 806, 818, 821, 885, 898, 960, 967-68, 1037, 1076
*glossolalia*, 17, 491
Gnosticism, 13, 18, 26-41, 44-45, 48-54, 66, 79-82, 89, 91, 95, 97-98, 104, 167, 192
Gospels, the, 8, 28, 67, 104-5, 109, 148, 151, 167, 172-74, 175, 178, 180, 187-88, 191, 193, 197, 210, 219, 226, 233, 251, 261, 266, 294, 345, 376, 457, 473, 589, 591, 754, 773, 783, 787, 826, 868, 895-96, 923, 925, 958, 965-67, 969, 985-86, 1034, 1038, 1040, 1047, 1144-45
grace, 45-46, 66, 86-88, 96, 101-3, 110, 132-33, 140, 149, 201,
205, 217, 221-22, 249, 255-58, 274, 291, 296, 298, 307, 333, 382, 393, 411, 420, 438-39, 443, 447, 450-51, 453-56, 462, 466, 471, 507, 511, 548, 550-51, 558-59, 579, 586, 588, 593-96, 637-38, 668, 704, 719, 722, 782-83, 830, 838, 847, 875, 880, 886, 933, 943-44, 950, 972, 1003, 1018, 1129, 1131, 1157
Great Father, the, 169-71
Great Mother, the, 152, 154, 156, 162-66
Great Spirit, the, 169-70
Hades, 46, 132, 154, 378, 588, 825, 830-31, 866, 948-49, 1021
hagiography, 313, 387, 394, 409, 533, 736, 909-10, 914, 930, 1000, 1017, 1133
healing, 923-51
heaven, 17, 22, 31, 35-36, 40, 46, 52, 61, 69, 88, 92, 102, 110-11, 118, 132-33, 154-58, 162, 164, 168-70, 200-201, 204-7, 213, 216, 236, 245-46, 251, 271-74, 296-97, 307, 326, 344-47, 350, 359, 363, 369, 376-77, 399-400, 403, 416, 433, 436, 442-43, 446-47, 474-75, 507-9, 512-15, 549, 556, 558, 578-80, 586, 588, 590, 595-96, 638, 650-52, 657, 668, 671, 677, 682, 687, 691, 693, 710, 720, 721-25,
750, 783-84, 786, 792, 794, 810, 825, 832, 835-37, 841, 843-44, 850-51, 853, 856, 877, 879, 883-88, 899, 902, 916-19, 943-44, 951, 959-61, 967, 996, 1012-14, 1023, 1037, 1040, 1044, 1047, 1052, 1067-68, 1078, 1087, 1101, 1106, 1114-16, 1128, 1133-34, 1138-39, 1142
*Henoticon*, 500
heresy, 12-14, 19, 25, 27-28, 43-44, 73-75, 79, 81-83, 85, 87-88, 104-6, 210, 219, 257, 286, 327, 348, 408, 436, 439, 455, 533-34, 545, 547, 551-52, 557, 595, 600, 627-28, 634, 636, 639, 641, 648, 651, 679, 739, 741, 775, 785, 1070, 1135, 1152, 1154
*Hexapla*, 12, 181, 236, 252
hierarchy, 19, 36, 41, 57, 172, 199, 298, 401, 408, 438-39, 552, 564, 578-79, 612, 616, 665, 732, 746, 1045
high priest, 110
Holy Spirit, xviii, 4, 10, 12, 16, 19, 21, 38, 41, 64, 66, 75, 77-78, 82-83, 85-88, 95, 100-103, 107, 109, 111, 132, 197, 201, 203-4, 213, 215, 222, 224, 231, 248, 255-57, 272-74, 287, 289, 294, 312, 314, 319, 321-22, 324, 332-35, 344, 349-50, 352-54, 363, 379, 392, 395, 399, 434,

442, 460, 470, 489, 506-7, 509, 513, 515, 585-87, 589-90, 592, 594-96, 599, 632, 638, 640-41, 643, 649, 651, 653, 655-56, 674, 688, 692, 698-99, 701-2, 714-15, 717, 719, 721-24, 740, 754, 770-72, 775, 782-84, 806, 820, 827, 834-35, 837-38, 841-43, 845-48, 868, 874-75, 879-80, 882, 888, 904, 906, 918, 942, 944, 950, 967, 970, 972-73, 988, 990, 995, 1001, 1003-5, 1077, 1122, 1131, 1133, 1140-41, 1144, 1151
Holy Week, 24, 371, 711, 833
*homoousion*, 85, 260, 281, 289-90, 303-6, 308-12, 317-18, 321-22, 324, 327-28, 330-32, 334-35, 343, 351, 432-33, 460, 533, 626, 906
hymns, 47, 108, 815-56
hypostasis, 86, 105, 256-57, 293, 314, 344, 350, 434, 547, 549, 562, 565, 590, 595-98, 617-18, 625, 630, 638, 646, 650, 655, 1141
icons, 136, 274, 337, 339, 637-39, 654, 674, 732, 850, 934-35, 945, 990, 993, 1012-13, 1065, 1123-47
impassibility, 354, 549, 584, 732
incarnation, 39, 52-53, 59, 69, 84, 95, 101, 104, 147, 171, 187, 197, 237, 241,

245, 265-67, 285, 295-96, 307-8, 321, 325-26, 351, 382, 411, 434, 513, 540-43, 545-54, 559, 563, 565-66, 583, 616-18, 625, 628, 634, 638, 648, 650, 715, 770, 779-84, 825-26, 829, 841, 854-55, 932, 940-42, 997, 1085, 1122, 1128-29, 1140-44, 1153, 1156
Ireland, 409, 411-13, 615, 664, 713
Jewish law, 4, 11-13, 70-71, 96, 104, 751, 958
Judaism, 31, 37, 44, 68-69, 73, 91, 95-96, 123, 126, 146, 161, 176, 179-81, 183, 253, 289, 390, 595, 634, 651, 693, 793, 799, 894, 1090, 1102
*kenosis*, 104, 321-22, 486, 549, 551, 934, 936, 940-42, 947, 960, 962, 966
*kerygma*, 31, 41, 46, 110, 360, 482, 700, 704, 768, 769, 774, 835, 896, 924, 926, 970
lapsed (lapsi), 87, 96, 118, 127, 129, 176, 197, 215-16, 218, 250, 255, 272-73, 362, 365-66, 438-39, 560, 635, 703, 705, 846, 854, 1143
*lavra*, 394, 404-6, 501, 505, 536, 538
law, 119, 123, 134-46
Lent, 24, 63, 223, 240, 442, 639, 700-701, 708-9, 712, 715, 854, 885, 912, 1136
*lex spiritalis*, 75
liturgy, 23, 26, 39, 47, 72, 74-79, 80, 99,

106, 691-724
Logos, 12, 36, 39-40, 50, 52, 54, 64, 73-79, 84-85, 89-104, 131, 144, 146-47, 149-50, 186-87, 192-94, 196-97, 234-35, 241-70, 283-96, 303-4, 307-15, 321, 324-28, 335, 339, 350-52, 380-82, 386-87, 433, 492, 533, 537, 540, 572-79, 624, 628, 635-36, 655, 728, 770, 773, 820, 834, 841, 848, 854, 875, 891, 923, 941-42, 1099, 1122, 1128-29, 1150-52, 1155-56
magic, 1088-22
Manicheanism, 14, 31, 42, 45, 48, 165-73
Marcionites, 19, 35, 38, 40, 52, 95, 113, 173, 194, 599, 773, 780, 824-25, 828
marriage, 5, 7, 17, 42, 46, 59, 63, 97, 188, 229, 245, 359, 369, 376, 441, 444, 458-59, 560-61, 591, 613, 645, 693, 754, 815, 838, 842, 850, 893-94, 904-7, 978, 994, 999, 1000, 1070, 1093, 1101-3, 1105-17
martyr cult, 15, 17, 56, 59-60, 117-34
martyrdom, 15, 18, 20, 58, 60, 66, 92-93, 103, 109, 117-18, 120
Matthew, Gospel of, 8, 9, 12, 67, 178, 181, 231-33, 248, 433, 458, 473, 482, 495-96, 675, 677, 704, 751, 764, 778, 885, 942-43, 958,

1008, 1038, 1041, 1076, 1103, 1106, 1114-15
Messalianism, 6, 391-92, 515, 878
Middle Platonism, 36, 40, 147, 185, 231, 264, 268, 941
*See also* Plato
missionaries, 14-16, 71, 172, 175, 178-79, 375, 384, 409, 467, 489, 490-91, 499, 504-5, 641, 643-44, 714, 716, 896, 968-69, 1038, 1044
Mithraism, 150-55
modalism, 75, 86, 95, 197, 257
Monarchianism, 48, 64, 73-88, 94-95, 97, 99, 102, 197, 257
monasticism, 10, 27, 316, 383-421, 444, 486, 500, 505, 661-64, 669, 673, 716, 727-28, 870, 880, 914-15, 929, 1044, 1047, 1062, 1075, 1123
monotheism, 73-74, 76, 83, 91, 199, 256, 258, 266, 281, 293, 631, 635, 797, 820, 1011
Montanism, 14-22, 48, 79, 92, 94, 164, 195-96, 211
morality, 6, 21, 42, 46, 55, 68, 71, 90, 123, 142, 145, 165, 191, 194, 247, 271, 360, 446, 448, 793, 804, 1103-13
Muratorian Canon, 61
mysteries, 32, 38, 91, 95, 97, 150-55, 165, 202, 224, 234, 237, 247, 250, 274, 366, 371, 383, 539, 668, 693-95, 698-99, 702,

718, 755, 769-70, 782, 831, 849-51, 877, 887-88, 930, 940, 944-45, 971, 1004, 1017, 1019
mysticism, 26, 32, 37, 106, 263, 314, 384, 406, 573, 728-29, 825, 861, 873, 885
Nag Hammadi, 27-28, 31, 34, 50, 113, 400-401
natural law, 96, 140, 144-45, 269, 646, 952, 1083, 1109, 1111-12
nature, 39, 84, 88-89, 95, 101-4, 139-40, 158, 187, 193-94, 197, 235, 257-58, 263, 266-69, 274-75, 289, 292, 295, 302, 307, 317, 322, 325-26, 342, 351-52, 377, 381-82, 404, 444, 454-55, 463-64, 469, 476, 498, 510, 528, 532, 540-43, 545-51, 556-68, 572-75, 580-95, 597-98, 616-18, 623, 626, 631, 646-50, 655, 675, 725, 750, 756-57, 781, 784, 786, 810, 842, 844, 883-84, 887, 889, 906, 913, 916, 931-33, 943, 1059, 1069, 1074, 1078, 1081-84, 1087, 1091, 1094, 1096, 1098, 1118, 1132, 1140-41, 1153-55, 1157
Neoplatonism, 157, 231, 240, 244, 256, 266-67, 427, 468, 571-79, 602, 616, 737, 739, 830, 1016
New Testament, 3-4, 8-11, 15, 17, 19, 31, 44-47, 53-54, 61, 64, 76, 88-89, 106, 123, 154, 173-79, 182, 189, 210, 214, 236, 241, 249-51, 256-57, 282, 288, 338, 343, 357, 360, 364, 367, 372, 375, 380, 386, 451, 491, 521, 571, 651, 682, 691-93, 697, 699-700, 768, 774, 778-79, 787, 796, 804, 816-19, 826, 834-35, 854, 867-69, 873, 895, 897, 903, 923, 930, 934, 936, 941, 947, 956-62, 965-66, 970, 972, 975, 977, 979, 982-83, 985, 988, 995-96, 1008, 1016, 1032, 1034-35, 1041-42, 1058, 1060, 1065, 1068, 1073, 1092, 1103-9, 1138
Nicaea I, council of, 23, 260-61, 281-82, 289, 294, 296, 300, 302-12, 315, 318, 327, 329, 331, 335, 344, 347-48, 351, 354-55, 364, 366, 368, 437, 464, 500, 519-20, 523, 526, 528, 542, 554, 563, 566, 569, 593-94, 648, 708-9, 902, 987-88, 992, 999, 1001, 1140, 1150, 1152
Nicaea II, council of, 637-39, 656, 674, 1129, 1134-36, 1142-44, 1156, 1157
North Africa, 20, 92-96, 195-98, 212-13, 223-58, 394-403, 436-99
*nous*, 34, 40-41, 246, 252, 263, 572, 576, 865-66, 871-75, 880-81, 883, 885, 1127
Nubia, 402, 481, 495, 501-2, 517, 521
Oak, synod of the, 410, 530, 535
Ogdoad, 34, 36, 41
Old Testament, 7, 11, 17, 32, 35, 42, 44-47, 52-53, 57, 68, 76-77, 90-91, 96, 105, 173, 177, 182, 185-86, 191, 236, 249, 250-51, 253, 266, 285, 295, 361, 375, 473, 619, 632, 691-93, 696, 765, 774, 778-81, 791, 793, 795, 799, 807, 809-10, 817-19, 824, 860, 865-67, 926-27, 932, 956, 958, 962-63, 969, 971, 976, 983, 995, 1011, 1031-32, 1057-58, 1073, 1083, 1092, 1110, 1138-39, 1147
ordination, 3-4, 6, 99, 102, 228, 231-32, 256, 298, 319, 405, 437-38, 442, 505, 640, 693, 736, 927, 965-93, 996, 1002-3
original sin, 96, 197, 443, 445, 454-55
orthodoxy, 7, 13, 25, 33, 39, 49, 51, 81-82, 85, 89, 95, 104-6, 197, 228, 242, 248, 305, 310, 318, 325, 426, 433, 459-60, 465, 467, 487, 492, 498, 524, 533, 539, 554, 566-68, 586, 611, 639, 644, 674, 712, 732, 741, 753, 831, 985, 989, 1135, 1154, 1157
papacy, 13, 20, 24-26, 48, 55-56, 61, 65, 74, 84-85, 87-88, 95-97, 101-2, 123, 126, 165, 197, 212, 214-18, 220-21, 228, 234, 241, 244, 251, 255, 257, 260, 298, 303, 305, 310, 319, 322, 329, 331, 338, 374, 376-79, 383, 410-41, 414, 429, 432, 435, 437, 439, 444-45, 450, 455, 457, 459-60, 462-68, 473, 480-81, 490-91, 521-22, 525-27, 533-35, 538, 552-53, 558, 563, 567-69, 577, 606, 615, 623-24, 626, 628-29, 631, 640-44, 648-49, 662-63, 665-68, 670-73, 676-80, 682, 689, 691, 697, 708, 712, 715, 740-45, 751-52, 759, 777, 804, 806, 862, 988, 991-92, 1000, 1070-71, 1153-54, 1158-62
Paraclete, 15-16, 79, 103, 168, 353, 632
*paradosis*. See tradition
Pascha, 23-26, 65, 97, 127, 160, 180, 190, 223-24, 259, 333, 338, 349, 374, 675-76, 683, 688, 694, 700-701, 708, 751, 764, 781, 829, 831, 977
Patripassians, 76, 79, 82
penance, 357-60, 371-74, 413-14, 703-7
peripatetics, 89, 185
persecution, 15, 17-18, 27, 40, 48, 51, 56, 59, 61-62, 72, 87, 92-93, 96-98, 117-46, 122-34, 180, 183-84, 188, 191, 195, 199, 206-7, 211-18, 222, 226, 228-29, 233, 237, 239, 242, 244-45, 252, 254-55, 272, 280-81, 283,

297-98, 300, 304, 336-38, 341, 360-67, 370, 384, 388, 425, 436, 438-39, 499, 677, 701, 703, 705, 716, 794, 796, 798-800, 811, 824-25, 836-37, 892, 898, 901-2, 909, 927, 955, 969, 983, 1027, 1068, 1073, 1080, 1116, 1123
philosophy, xvii, 30, 40, 45, 80, 90, 93, 96-99, 104, 125, 131, 136, 139, 145, 147, 150, 181, 185-88, 191-93, 231, 238, 240-41, 261-62, 265-70, 282, 286, 288, 294, 317, 320, 355, 385, 389, 405, 411, 426-27, 434, 444, 468-69, 475-76, 494, 571, 573-74, 576-77, 608, 615, 625, 627-28, 736-39, 757, 765, 801-3, 815, 827-28, 834, 844, 875, 924, 927, 935-36, 940, 948, 975, 1016, 1029, 1038, 1047, 1053, 1056, 1058, 1064, 1075-76, 1090-92, 1098, 1102, 1111, 1121, 1149-50
Photinianism, 87, 89
pilgrimage, xviii, 190, 374-75, 396, 404, 440, 663, 897, 912, 927, 933, 946, 966
Pleroma, 34
pneumatology, 18, 21, 48, 64, 102-3, 289, 434, 443, 880, 906
poetry, 39, 48, 261, 264, 282, 323, 412-14, 435, 478, 488, 575, 733-34, 736, 816-17, 819-22, 827-33, 842-43, 849,

852-53, 959, 1096, 1101, 1113
polytheism, 78
pope. *See* papacy
possession (Spirit), 17, 18, 108, 223, 700, 925, 930
prayer, 20, 21, 24, 26, 34, 53, 55, 66, 71-73, 75, 99, 106, 109, 133, 145, 153, 156, 158-60, 188, 201, 211, 214, 216, 223-24, 226, 230, 239, 240, 263, 285, 324, 345, 349, 362, 364-66, 373, 377-78, 384, 389-96, 398-400, 404, 406, 410, 414-16, 418, 444, 452, 454, 465, 472, 474, 481, 483-86, 509, 511, 514-15, 529, 536, 538, 544, 577, 628, 657, 663, 666, 669, 672, 674, 686, 691-95, 697-99, 701-2, 704-6, 708, 710-19, 720-22, 724, 728, 749, 770, 780, 795, 797, 815, 818, 820-22, 824, 828, 832-33, 838, 843-44, 846-48, 856, 860-90, 897, 910, 912, 916, 927, 931, 933, 943-45, 950, 954, 963, 973-74, 981-82, 986, 993, 995-96, 998, 1003, 1005, 1009, 1011-12, 1023, 1034, 1039, 1051, 1055, 1085, 1129, 1132, 1135-36, 1149, 1156
preaching, 4, 13-15, 19, 21, 53, 62, 78, 86, 91, 110, 121, 179-80, 190, 211, 227, 239-40, 243, 255, 257, 285, 306, 314, 322-24, 330-31, 343,

378, 408, 422, 435, 452, 482, 488, 492, 497, 505, 529, 532, 542-43, 550, 577, 583, 628, 632, 668-69, 696, 700, 763-65, 770, 774, 776-77, 779-82, 897, 916, 924, 958, 966-70, 978-81, 1035, 1037-38, 1044, 1059, 1103-6, 1131, 1144
See also *kerygma*
preexistence, 12, 30, 64, 194, 264, 537, 882, 1154
presbyter (priest), 14, 15, 21, 40, 44, 56, 65-66, 72, 82-83, 96, 99, 102, 111, 114, 150, 191, 195, 210, 211, 213-16, 219-20, 223-25, 231, 233, 238-39, 255, 260-61, 273, 291, 311, 322, 361-62, 365, 367, 370, 372, 387, 419, 442, 473, 519, 697-98, 700-701, 706, 712, 720, 754, 825, 900, 926-27, 950, 963, 965, 971, 974-84, 987, 990-93, 996, 999-1006, 1046, 1142
Primordial Man, the, 169-70
Prince of Darkness, the, 169-70
Prince of this world, the, 45, 120, 154, 174, 959
prophets, 10-22, 35, 41, 47, 53, 58, 60, 62-64, 70-71, 87, 96, 110, 162, 164, 168, 173, 178, 184, 188, 190, 193-94, 202, 204, 210, 225, 234, 236, 247, 251, 262,

335, 342-43, 350, 362, 402, 416, 458, 473, 486, 494, 511, 551, 579, 586, 591, 595, 631-32, 634, 636, 649, 651-53, 656, 658, 683, 699, 703, 706, 721, 724, 730, 764, 773, 778-79, 783, 794-95, 824-25, 838, 850, 863-64, 873, 894, 897-98, 903, 923, 926, 935, 950, 956, 958-59, 964-74, 988, 991, 996, 1003, 1007, 1008, 1011, 1030, 1033-34, 1037-38, 1042, 1079, 1103, 1105, 1108, 1132-33, 1137, 1139-40, 1143, 1145
providence, 40, 55, 138-39, 198-99, 239-40, 317, 337, 442-43, 469-70, 476, 620, 683, 697, 736-37, 787, 791, 793-94, 798, 811, 828, 932, 1037, 1039, 1050
Psalter, 47, 398, 416, 861, 885, 1047
Psilanthropism, 13, 87-88
purgatory, 376-79, 668
purification, 58, 63, 253, 357, 363, 369, 376-77, 382, 387, 578, 627, 668, 805, 877, 883, 1014, 1037
Pythagoreans, 5, 89, 147, 185, 231, 241, 387
Quartodecimans, 22-26, 65, 113, 190, 349, 676, 708, 987
Quinisext Synod, 630
rabbis, 8, 175, 180-81, 236, 1102-3
repentance, 13, 17, 41,

INDEX OF SUBJECTS | 1201

57, 61-63, 99, 108, 110, 139, 218, 223, 247, 249, 357, 359, 363, 365, 370, 373, 386-87, 416, 422, 451-52, 635, 663, 699, 704-6, 726, 729, 833, 844, 867, 882, 912, 917, 925, 931, 943, 969, 1035-37
resurrection, 10, 18, 22, 24, 46, 53, 60, 66, 87, 89, 95, 107, 110-11, 132, 148, 153, 155, 163-65, 173, 175, 187, 189-90, 197, 201, 223, 234, 237, 267, 272, 275, 285, 326, 330, 362, 378, 383, 386, 532-33, 535, 582-83, 588, 599, 620-22, 692, 695-96, 704, 719, 723-24, 749, 778, 807, 831, 835, 846, 896, 926, 930, 932, 934, 970, 972, 985, 1084, 1104, 1106, 1115, 1122, 1131, 1133, 1142
Revelation, book of, 16, 20-21, 98, 117, 123, 190, 249, 458, 693, 796, 972, 973, 996, 1079
Roman household code, 6, 15, 57, 92, 184, 360, 902, 1067-68
Roman religions, 150-73
rule of faith (*regula fidei*), 53, 105, 985, 986
sacrament, 6-7, 15, 36, 48, 52, 59-60, 74, 99, 106, 151, 153-54, 217, 221, 223-24, 245, 249-53, 255-56, 267, 272, 289, 295, 298, 307,

327, 333, 358-59, 361-62, 364-66, 368, 373-74, 382, 435, 437-39, 442, 501, 579, 633, 637-39, 675, 688, 690-93, 695-96, 698, 701-2, 704-5, 707, 710-12, 741, 767, 770-71, 835, 860, 879, 883, 910, 926-27, 933, 978, 981, 983, 986, 1008, 1010-12, 1065, 1105, 1128-29, 1135-36, 1156
sacrifice, 24, 53, 60, 90, 96, 107, 109, 117-18, 120, 127, 129, 137, 152, 164-66, 176, 186, 201-2, 206-7, 214-15, 218, 222, 255, 296, 339, 341, 364-66, 379-82, 511, 513, 559, 585, 588, 590, 592, 653, 658, 688, 691, 693, 718, 721-22, 738, 753, 778, 808-9, 812, 818-19, 863-65, 877-78, 888, 901, 940, 949, 963, 973, 983, 1004, 1020, 1039, 1138-39, 1142
salvation, 29-32, 35-38, 41, 53, 78-79, 83-84, 89, 92, 101, 103-5, 110, 120, 150, 153, 155, 168, 170-71, 173, 177, 183, 187-88, 190, 193, 195, 205, 208, 217, 222, 226, 237, 241, 245-47, 252, 256, 272-73, 284-85, 292-93, 295-96, 307-8, 313-14, 322-25, 327, 332-33, 344, 351, 354, 357, 359, 379, 382, 386-87, 439, 443, 451, 453, 512-13, 533, 541, 549-50, 565, 579, 581, 586,

595, 624, 628, 630, 649-50, 662, 686, 692, 697-98, 717-19, 724, 737, 751-52, 769, 773, 787, 821, 837, 841, 867-68, 870, 934, 942-43, 985, 1043, 1128, 1130, 1138-40, 1152
Savior, 24, 30-32, 35, 46, 57, 59, 73, 110, 130, 153, 155, 171, 184, 188, 200, 266, 274, 345-46, 350, 488, 507, 515, 540, 546, 578, 588-89, 593, 600, 627, 638, 650, 692, 697, 718-19, 722-25, 783, 785, 825, 836, 925, 935, 940, 950, 1079, 1135, 1138, 1144
schism, 25, 102, 216-17, 219-21, 255-56, 297-98, 349, 383, 390, 436, 438, 440, 442, 457, 459, 463-66, 483, 565, 567, 569, 615-16, 619, 623, 629, 633, 641-42, 671, 705, 739, 741, 744-46, 759, 806, 972, 1069, 1070, 1162
seraphim, 687, 721-24, 851, 888, 943, 1023
sexuality, 1090-120
Sheol, 377
sin, 30, 45, 60, 62-63, 71, 96, 102, 108, 400, 442, 746
slavery, 1056-89
Song of Songs, 99, 236-37, 243, 272, 324, 473, 718, 778-79, 824, 842, 998, 1101, 1114
Sophia (divine wisdom), 30, 32, 34, 187, 289, 825, 842, 866, 1105, 1122

Sophia (Gnostic aeon), 34, 40, 899
spirituality, 860-88
Stoics, 40, 55, 89, 92, 140, 145, 185, 198, 225, 241, 262, 269-70, 360, 384, 455, 468, 572-73, 575, 803, 865, 901, 957, 1026, 1028, 1059, 1081, 1091, 1094, 1097-99, 1102-4, 1110-13
subordinationism, 74, 91, 103, 302, 311-12, 327, 534
substance (*ousia*), 77-79, 85-86, 103, 257-58, 287, 289-94, 301-2, 308-9, 311-18, 332-33, 344, 350-51, 355, 433-34, 469, 565, 595, 598, 617-18, 625, 675, 688, 1010, 1031, 1129
synod, 14-15, 21, 24-26, 49, 62, 211, 218-20, 233, 239, 242-43, 257, 260, 292-93, 296, 298-300, 302-6, 308, 311, 314-16, 327-29, 334-35, 343-44, 347-48, 350, 361, 364-65, 368-71, 389, 400-401, 410, 414, 432, 437-38, 454-55, 462, 464-65, 473, 489, 491-92, 519-21, 526, 530-31, 533, 535-36, 538-39, 552, 559-62, 567-70, 580, 583, 586, 592-95, 597, 599-602, 612, 615, 628, 630, 637, 639-42, 648-49, 656, 678-80, 732, 740-43, 753-55, 801, 826, 906, 964-65, 981, 984, 987-90, 992, 999, 1013-14,

1044, 1062-63, 1068, 1071, 1119, 1139-44, 1150
syzygy, 34, 36
Talmud, 10, 236
*tauroctony*, 152
temple (of Jerusalem), 4, 10, 61, 68-69, 176, 251, 513, 583, 616, 686, 691, 693, 704, 793, 818, 860, 863-64, 873, 963, 977, 1039-40, 1071, 1138
theosophy, 27, 29, 36, 47, 52-53
tradition, 3, 12, 14, 16-17, 20, 23-26, 30-33, 35, 40-42, 46, 49-50, 52-55, 59, 67, 69-71, 73-74, 80-82, 88, 93, 97-99, 101-2, 106, 110, 120, 123, 125, 127, 130-31, 133-35, 147-51, 155, 162, 168, 176, 181, 183-84, 186-88, 192, 194-95, 198, 211, 214-15, 218, 222, 225-27, 231, 236, 240-41, 254, 258-60, 267, 270-71, 273, 278, 283, 285-86, 288, 290, 292-95, 300, 302, 304, 307, 309, 315-16, 320, 327, 337-38, 369, 375-79, 381-83, 385-86, 389-92, 394, 396-99, 401-4, 406, 410, 412, 414, 426, 435-36, 439-40, 444, 445-46, 448, 453-56, 458, 462, 466-69, 481-89, 491, 494-99, 502, 504-6, 513, 521-26, 528, 531-32, 538-40, 543, 545-47, 550, 554, 557-59, 561-63,
569-70, 573-75, 577-78, 583, 585, 598, 603, 608, 611, 615, 618, 621, 624, 628, 630-32, 635, 637, 641, 644-45, 651, 656, 668, 672, 677-79, 692-95, 699, 703, 710, 711-16, 727-28, 736-37, 739-42, 748, 758, 763, 765-66, 769-71, 773-75, 777-80, 790, 792-93, 801, 809, 816, 819, 825-27, 830, 833-34, 840, 844, 849, 861-62, 865-69, 873, 876-80, 882-90, 893, 899, 911-12, 916, 924, 926, 928, 930, 934, 941, 957, 962, 968-70, 972-73, 975-77, 985-88, 1012, 1014, 1022, 1027, 1030-35, 1041-42, 1046, 1053-54, 1065, 1067, 1080, 1094-95, 1097-98, 1101-7, 1110-14, 1122-24, 1129, 1130-32, 1135-36, 1143-45, 1149-50, 1152-54
transmigration (of souls), 41, 737
Trinity, 53, 64, 74, 77, 78-79, 82, 92, 95, 101-3, 197, 256-59, 270, 287, 289, 293-94, 310, 319, 321, 323, 332-33, 352-54, 379, 381, 397, 432, 434, 443, 469-70, 508, 513, 537, 540, 548-49, 554, 595-97, 599, 632, 634, 640, 643, 648-50, 655-56, 698, 701, 723, 752,
779, 830, 842, 850, 887, 1151
two ways, the, 5, 70-71, 386
typology, 46, 68, 182, 210, 263, 513, 696, 719-20, 764, 778-79, 781, 793-94, 899, 963, 983, 1004, 1134, 1138, 1141, 1144
unity (of God), 10, 36, 51, 74, 76-79, 83-84, 86, 102-3, 257, 289, 314, 318, 323, 415, 433, 545, 546, 550, 573, 576, 581, 587, 596, 641, 643
*See also* monotheism
vegetarianism, 5, 8, 172
virgin birth, 9, 12, 60, 87, 1132
virginity, 7, 103-4, 324, 369, 386, 435, 458, 471, 560, 826, 832, 840, 842, 876, 894, 904-5, 907-8, 932, 996, 998-1000, 1013, 1119-20, 1132
visions, 16, 20-22, 61-63, 98, 112, 158-60, 201, 280-81, 387, 392, 395, 400, 407-9, 421, 496-97, 507-9, 573, 634, 636, 667, 730, 758, 772, 778, 810, 842, 854, 882-84, 897, 903-4, 918, 924, 951, 967-68, 970-71, 974, 1021, 1127
war, 790-97
widows, 449, 846, 900, 905, 940, 966, 976, 991, 994-96, 1000, 1005-7, 1034, 1044
Wisdom of God. *See* Sophia
women (and Christianity), 891-920
wonderworker (*thaumaturg*), 14, 227, 240, 309, 395, 412, 926, 1016
Word of God, 42, 107, 178, 206, 236, 237, 295, 308, 311, 418, 510, 513, 540, 542, 544-45, 551, 581, 582, 586-87, 591-92, 596-97, 617, 631, 649-51, 653, 718, 780, 784-85, 852, 976, 1002, 1140, 1144, 1150
worship, 6, 8, 17, 21, 35, 62, 68-69, 73, 75, 78, 89, 92-93, 95, 98-99, 105, 120, 122-25, 132, 136-40, 148-49, 154-55, 158, 160-62, 164-65, 171, 174, 182, 185, 196, 201, 203, 211, 223, 284-85, 287, 293, 335, 342, 361, 363, 366-67, 380, 395, 397, 425, 4435, 470, 490, 511-12, 520, 544, 588, 592, 598, 616, 633, 638-39, 645, 651, 654, 687, 691-93, 697-99, 713, 723-25, 767, 769, 780, 782, 797, 808, 815, 817-25, 830, 840, 843, 855, 858-60, 862-64, 875, 896, 923, 935-36, 943, 958, 963, 975-76, 986, 988, 990, 1008, 1010-11, 1015, 1039, 1041, 1066, 1070, 1116, 1125, 1129, 1134-36, 1138-40, 1142, 1150, 1156

# INDEX OF BIBLICAL CITATIONS

**OLD TESTAMENT**
**Genesis**
1:1, *786*
1:3, *188*
1:10, *52*
1:26, *1083, 1088, 1138*
1:27, *1118*
13:15, *513*
13:18, *513*
14:14, *300*
14:18-20, *963*
16:8, *651*
22, *883*
22:6, *653*
22:13, *513*
28:12, *513*
41:8, *1011*
41:24, *1011*

**Exodus**
3:6, *83*
3:22, *150*
7:11-12, *1011*
8:18-19, *1011*
12, *190*
15:1-18, *818*
17:6, *513*
17:13-16, *794*
19:5-6, *963*
20:3, *83*
21:2, *1058*
21:20-21, *1058*
21:24, *375*
21:32, *1058*
22:22, *995*
25:18, *1138*
25:40, *1138*
33:19, *658*
33:20, *1004*

**Leviticus**
18:22, *1094*
19:26, *1011*
19:31, *1011*
20:6, *1011*
20:13, *1094*
25:39-40, *1058*

**Numbers**
6:1-21, *1102*

**Deuteronomy**
5:2, *513*
10:18, *995*
21:18-21, *976*
23:15-16, *1058*
23:17-18, *1101*

**Joshua**
14:8, *867*

**Judges**
5:3-5, *818*
5:16, *866*

**1 Samuel**
1:13, *867*
12:20, *866*
12:24, *866*
16:7, *867*
24:5, *867*
28:3-25, *239*

**2 Samuel**
2:22-24, *386*
24, *513*

**1 Kings**
3:9, *867*
3:12, *866*
4:29, *867*
8:11, *513*
8:17, *866*
8:27, *785*
17:22-24, *926*
18:38, *877*
21:8-12, *976*

**2 Kings**
5:1-14, *926*
11:3-4, *1003*
17:13, *386*
20:7, *514*
21:21-22, *386*
22:1, *1003*
24:13-14, *793*

**1 Chronicles**
21:26, *877*
24:31, *521*
27:22, *521*
29:12, *1032*

**2 Chronicles**
1:12, *1032*
23:20, *521*
24:1, *1003*
34:17, *107*

**Ezra**
7:10, *866*

**Job**
1:21, *1053*
5:9-16, *818*
7:15, *685*
9:13, *685*
11:13, *866*
12:13-25, *818*
34:10, *866*

**Psalms**
1:1-2, *386*
1:6, *386*
20:3, *863*
21:2-4, *957*
22:15, *1004*
27:1, *870*
34:18, *867*
36:9, *353*
40:6, *1004*
41:6, *867*
42:5, *205*
42:11, *205*
44:21, *867*
45:3, *841*
45:10-17, *841*
46:4, *470*
48:1, *470*
49:1-17, *1033*
49:5-6, *1033*
49:20, *1033*
50:5, *863*
50:16, *242*
51:7, *864*
58, *867*
66:13-15, *863*
72, *511*
73:7, *867*
87:3, *470*
88:15, *950*
94:18, *1004*
101:4-5, *867*
103:6, *867*
106:28-29, *863*
106:37-42, *863*
109:3, *344*
110:3, *344*
112:1-3, *1032*
112:8, *867*
115:4-8, *342*

# 1204 | Index of Biblical Citations

119:171, *1004*
137:6, *1004*
137:9, *253, 764*
140:2, *877*
141:2, *878*
147:8, *513*

**Proverbs**
3:5, *866*
6:18, *867*
8:22, *285, 784*
10:31, *841*
13:8, *1047*
15:19, *386*
18:15, *866*
19:8, *866*
19:17, *1050*
21:8, *386*
23:7, *867*
28:14, *867*
31:10, *841*
31:26, *841*

**Ecclesiastes**
2:7, *1083*
3:2, *719*
5:19, *1033*

**Song of Solomon**
4:4, *841*
5:3, *718*
6:9, *272*
7:4, *841*

**Isaiah**
1:11-17, *864*
5:20, *1050*
6, *850*
6:1, *647*
6:2-3, *721*
6:3, *236*
6:10, *205*
10:7, *866*
29:18, *658*
38:1-20, *926*
40:9, *353*
42:10-12, *818*
44:6, *83*
45:7, *45*
45:20, *342*
51:7, *205*
52:7, *841*

52:9-10, *818*
54:1, *57*
56:7, *1039*
61:6, *963*
65:8, *390*
66:2, *1003*

**Jeremiah**
7:11, *1039*
11:20, *866*
17:9, *87*
23:20, *866*
32:40, *866*

**Ezekiel**
1:4-2:1, *507*
13:18-20, *1011*
16:12, *1004*

**Daniel**
2:30, *866*
4:27, *959*
7:22, *1133*

**Hosea**
8:4, *683*
12:6, *951*

**Zechariah**
2:10, *785*
7:10, *867*
11:5, *1033*

**Malachi**
1:10, *107*
1:10-11, *877*
4:2, *779*

**APOCRYPHA**
**Baruch**
3:37, *785*

**2 Maccabees**
6:22, *934*
9:27, *934*
12:38-45, *377*
14:9, *934*

**3 Maccabees**
3:15, *934*

**4 Maccabees**
5:12, *934*

**Sirach**
3:11, *920*
24, *187, 834, 842*
39:14-35, *818*
42:15-43:33, *818*

**Tobit**
2:13, *958*

**Wisdom of Solomon**
7, *1114*

**NEW TESTAMENT**
**Matthew**
1:22, *971*
2:1, *1008*
2:3, *1114*
2:17, *971*
4:14, *971*
4:15-20, *386*
5:2-10, *819*
5:2-12, *764, 1048*
5:3, *11, 1038, 1048*
5:5, *1003*
5:7, *1003*
5:8, *109, 868, 1003*
5:10-12, *205*
5:14, *204, 507*
5:23-24, *864*
5:27-28, *1104*
5:28, *1092*
5:38-41, *792*
6:5-8, *864*
6:5-15, *885*
6:6, *877*
6:6-8, *860*
6:7-8, *821*
6:7-13, *1037*
6:9-13, *864*
6:14-15, *792*
6:19-21, *1040*
6:21, *204, 1045*
6:24, *1039*
6:25-30, *1038*
6:31-33, *1037*
7:13-14, *386, 1047*
7:14, *681*
7:15, *17*
7:16, *1050*

7:29, *960*
8:9, *960*
8:20, *1038*
8:21-22, *1035*
9:6, *960*
9:13, *864*
9:15, *1105*
10:1, *959, 960*
10:1-16, *969*
10:5-6, *178*
10:5-8, *969*
10:9-10, *1046, 1047*
10:14-15, *178*
10:18, *970*
10:23, *215, 255, 436*
12:6, *864*
12:34, *868*
12:36, *1002*
12:37, *1002*
13:15, *205, 868*
13:19, *868*
13:24-30, *439*
16:18, *132*
16:18-19, *218, 220, 272, 677*
16:26, *1084*
17:1-2, *204*
18:15-18, *704*
18:19-20, *231*
18:20, *648*
18:35, *868*
19:3-11, *1105*
19:3-12, *1114*
19:12, *232, 233, 996, 1104, 1106*
19:15, *977*
19:17, *109*
19:21, *394*
19:21-23, *1035*
19:24, *1038*
19:28, *969*
20:25, *958, 962*
20:25-28, *1076*
21:12, *1039*
21:12-13, *864*
21:22, *864*
22:2, *795*
22:2-14, *1105*
22:7, *795*
22:9, *439*
22:23-30, *1106, 1115*
22:30, *916, 1104*

# Index of Biblical Citations | 1205

22:37, *870*
23:6-7, *683*
23:34, *18*
23:37, *837*
24:30-31, *792*
25:27, *1040*
25:36-40, *1041*
26:26-28, *860*
26:34, *792*
26:38, *205*
26:52, *795, 809*
26:52-53, *792*
26:64-65, *967*
28:18, *960, 961*
28:19, *482, 699*

**Mark**
1:16-20, *1035*
1:18, *837*
1:29-34, *923*
1:35, *692*
1:40–2:12, *923*
2:11, *925*
2:24-26, *958*
3:1-6, *923*
3:4, *958*
3:15, *959*
4:1-20, *386*
4:13-17, *122*
4:18-19, *1027*
4:19, *1037*
5:21-43, *923*
5:23, *977*
6:5, *977*
6:7, *959*
6:18, *958*
6:30-44, *923*
6:46, *692*
6:53-56, *923*
7:21, *868*
7:24-37, *923*
7:33-35, *700*
8:22, *351*
8:22-26, *923*
8:23-25, *977*
8:36, *795*
9, *773*
9:1-8, *248*
10:2, *958*
10:17, *121*
10:25, *1038*
10:39, *121*

10:42, *960*
10:42-45, *792*
10:46-52, *873, 923*
11:15-18, *1039*
12:30, *868*
12:32-34, *864*
13, *61*
13:7-8, *795*
14:3-11, *1040*
14:26, *818*
15:39, *796*

**Luke**
1:23, *1041*
1:28, *854*
1:35, *888*
1:46-55, *816, 819*
1:51, *868*
1:53, *1041*
1:68-79, *819*
2:19, *831*
2:29-32, *816, 819*
2:35, *868*
4:36, *959*
6:20, *1038, 1048*
6:20-26, *819*
6:23, *205*
6:24, *1041*
7:1-10, *796*
7:36-50, *833*
8:3, *1038*
8:15, *868*
9:1, *959*
9:47, *868*
10:16, *681*
10:17, *692*
10:40-42, *669*
11:9-13, *864*
12:13-15, *1036*
12:18-20, *1041*
12:49, *877*
13:1-5, *949*
13:31, *175*
14:11, *1003*
14:13, *1038, 1044*
14:16-24, *1069*
14:31, *1038*
15:11-32, *864, 1036*
16:15, *868*
16:19-26, *1041*
16:19-31, *939*
17:21, *883*

18:9-14, *704*
18:10-14, *864, 873*
18:18-24, *1041*
18:22, *1053*
18:23, *1041*
18:25, *1038*
21:1-3, *1041*
22, *960*
22:19, *695*
23:24, *792*
23:43, *853*
24:13-35, *698*
24:25, *868*
24:32, *90, 186*
24:35, *695*
24:38, *868*

**John**
1:1, *942, 961*
1:1-3, *288*
1:1-16, *842*
1:1-18, *818*
1:5, *153, 942*
1:9, *353*
1:14, *36, 147, 785*
1:16, *1048*
3:14, *924*
4, *966*
4:2, *699*
4:22, *178*
5:1-18, *924*
5:27, *961*
5:30, *961*
6:38, *681*
7:17-18, *961*
8:28, *961*
8:40, *87*
8:44, *85*
8:58, *351*
10:15, *941*
11:34, *351*
12:3-8, *1040*
12:20-28, *967*
12:40, *868*
12:49, *961*
13:2, *868*
13:23-26, *773*
13:29, *1034*
14:2, *1044*
14:6, *1133*
14:10, *961*
14:26, *16, 353*

15:13-17, *941*
15:17-21, *121*
15:26, *314, 332*
16:7, *16*
16:13, *961*
16:14, *350*
16:15, *1048*
16:28, *344*
17:5, *1122*
17:17, *841*
17:19, *841*
18:11, *809*
18:36, *792*
20:17, *84*
20:21, *272*
20:22-23, *704*
21:1-7, *1035*
21:15, *272*
21:20, *773*

**Acts**
1:8, *507*
1:16-26, *970*
1:21-22, *970*
2:1-3, *507*
2:11, *491*
2:29, *521*
2:36, *785*
2:42, *695*
2:43, *926*
3:1-10, *926*
3:6-10, *926*
3:12, *691*
4:8, *972*
4:32, *682*
5:3, *868*
5:12-16, *926*
5:34, *175*
5:41, *205*
6, *991*
6–8, *968*
6:1, *966*
6:1-3, *1034*
6:1-6, *966*
6:6, *991*
7:2-4, *967*
7:8-9, *521*
7:23, *868*
7:55-57, *967*
7:60, *121*
8:5, *967*
8:17, *977*

**1206** | Index of Biblical Citations

8:20, *1011*
8:22, *868*
8:26-39, *503*
8:27-39, *481*
9:3-7, *970*
9:17, *977*
9:32-35, *926*
9:36-39, *895*
9:36-42, *926*
10, *796*
11:23, *868*
11:28, *972*
12:2-3, *121*
13:8-12, *1008*
14:3, *926*
14:8-18, *926*
14:23, *977*
15:5, *175*
15:9, *868*
15:29, *973*
16:14, *868*
16:25, *818*
17:10-13, *121*
18, *896*
18:2, *895*
18:18, *895*
18:26, *895*
19:6, *977*
19:11-20, *1008*
19:23-28, *1014*
20:7-11, *694*
20:17, *977, 983*
20:28, *107, 977, 983*
20:34, *1086*
21:8-9, *19*
21:8-11, *825*
21:9, *974, 996*
21:10-12, *972*
23:6-9, *175*
24–26, *970*
26:5, *175*
28:27, *205*

**Romans**
1:3, *920*
2:15, *868*
4:24–5:1, *322*
5:5, *868*
5:6-11, *357*
5:10, *357*
5:11, *357*
6:3, *1126*

6:13, *1004*
6:22, *1066*
7, *454*
7:22, *867*
8:9, *771*
8:9-11, *972*
8:11, *83*
8:29, *351*
10:12, *1042*
11:11, *179*
11:15, *357*
11:26, *178, 182*
11:28, *178*
11:29, *1083*
11:36, *344*
12:1, *1004*
13:12, *796*
16:1, *991, 993*
16:3-5, *896*
16:4, *897*
16:7, *895, 976*
16:14, *61*

**1 Corinthians**
1:11, *896*
1:18-23, *486*
1:20-25, *782*
1:23-24, *322*
1:25, *93, 149*
2:1-5, *782*
2:3-16, *772*
2:4, *926*
2:12-13, *771*
2:16, *770, 772, 783*
3:11-15, *377*
3:16-17, *704*
3:19, *486*
4:5, *868*
5:1-2, *359*
5:1-5, *704*
5:6, *359*
5:11-13, *704*
6:2, *204*
6:5-8, *1031*
6:9, *1094, 1109*
6:15-18, *361*
6:18-20, *704*
6:19, *972*
7:5, *188*
7:5-9, *233*
7:7-9, *1036*
7:17-24, *1077*

7:20-23, *1066*
7:25-31, *996*
7:28, *997*
7:29-31, *1103*
7:32-35, *1107, 1115*
7:37, *868*
8:4, *1127*
8:4-9, *973*
8:6, *64*
9:1-2, *971*
9:19, *1066*
10:12, *361*
10:21, *704*
11:2-14, *897*
11:18-22, *358*
11:18-34, *815, 1045*
11:20, *358*
11:22, *358*
11:26-29, *704*
11:26-34, *1031*
11:27, *358*
11:30, *358*
12:3, *875*
12:4-11, *972*
12:9, *926*
12:12-13, *1063*
12:13-17, *1077*
12:28, *971*
13:12, *951*
14:1, *507*
14:2, *1004*
14:33-36, *897*
14:34, *976*
15:24, *961*
15:49, *722*
16:19, *896*
16:20, *720*

**2 Corinthians**
1:3-6, *933*
1:22, *868*
2:5-11, *704*
2:15, *204*
4:7, *782*
5, *357*
5:4, *1005*
5:8, *205*
5:18, *357*
5:19, *357*
5:20, *357*
6:10, *1042*
6:14-18, *704*

6:16, *722*
8:9, *1048*
9:7, *682, 868*
10:3-4, *796*
11:2, *360*
12:1-6, *971*
12:2, *236*
12:2-4, *970*
12:12, *926*

**Galatians**
1:8-9, *47*
1:15-17, *491*
3:27-29, *1077*
3:28, *898, 916, 1063*
4:6, *868*
4:6-7, *1077*
5:1, *204*

**Ephesians**
1:10, *110*
1:17-18, *771*
1:18-23, *960*
1:21, *961*
2, *357*
2:4, *1042*
2:16, *322, 357*
3:10, *961*
3:17, *868*
4:4, *272*
4:22, *718*
4:30, *203*
5:3, *204*
5:5, *360*
5:8, *204*
5:19-20, *818*
5:22, *1118*
5:25, *1118*
5:32, *920*
6, *1066*
6:4, *1003*
6:4-12, *1077*
6:5-9, *1067*
6:10-17, *796*
6:12, *110, 961*
6:22, *868*

**Philippians**
1:1, *982, 992*
1:10, *360*
1:27, *770*
2:5, *205, 770, 783,*

INDEX OF BIBLICAL CITATIONS | 1207

*962*
2:5-11, *816, 818*
2:6-11, *486*
2:7, *350*
2:10, *835*
2:10-11, *110*
3:6-11, *835*
3:10-12, *933*
3:14-16, *770*
3:20, *691*
4:7, *205*

**Colossians**
1:11-20, *961*
1:11–4:6, *357*
1:15, *1126, 1129*
1:15-16, *288*
1:15-20, *818*
1:16, *961*
1:19-20, *288*
1:20, *357*
1:20-23, *359*
1:22, *357*
1:24, *933*
2:10, *961*
2:15, *961*
3:5-15, *1078*
3:9, *718*
3:10-13, *936*
3:16, *818*
3:22, *898*
3:22–4:1, *1078*
4:8, *868*

**1 Thessalonians**
2:4, *868*
4:8, *972*
4:13, *378*
5:8, *796*

**1 Timothy**
1:20, *704*

2:8-15, *916*
3:1-7, *982*
3:2, *1003*
3:4, *1003*
3:6, *1003*
3:8, *992*
3:16, *816, 819, 834*
4:14, *977*
5:8, *1087*
5:9-10, *995*
5:22, *977*
6:1-8, *1078*
6:1, *1067*
6:7, *1054*
6:10, *1052*

**2 Timothy**
1:6, *977*
2:3, *796*
4:7, *386*

**Titus**
1:4–2:13, *360*
1:5-7, *977, 983*
1:7, *982*
2:1-10, *360*
2:9, *1079*
3:4-8, *941, 950*

**Philemon**
10–20, *1079*

**Hebrews**
1:2, *343*
1:4, *784*
1:14, *691*
2:9-10, *933*
2:9-11, *934*
2:14, *959*
3:1, *784*
4:12, *868*
5:6, *88*

6:2, *977*
7, *963*
7:4, *521*
7:12, *963*
7:27, *963*
8:6, *691*
8:10, *868*
10:11-12, *963*
10:16, *868*
10:22, *868*

**James**
1:9-11, *1031*
1:27, *360, 995*
1:27–2:9, *1031*
2:1-7, *815, 1045*
2:5, *11*
2:14-18, *949*
5:1-6, *1031*
5:13-16, *949*
5:14, *977*
5:14-16, *926*

**1 Peter**
2:5, *983*
2:9-10, *963*
2:9-11, *360*
2:18-25, *1065*
2:25, *982*
3:15, *720*
3:22, *961*
4:1, *351*
4:7, *704*
5:1-4, *977, 983*

**2 Peter**
1:19, *868*
2:20-22, *704*

**1 John**
1:1, *1141*
1:6–2:17, *361*

1:8-10, *705*
2:18-19, *282*
2:19, *218*
3:3-8, *360*
3:4-6, *704*
4:1-3, *973*
4:18, *395*
5:15-17, *705*

**2 John**
7, *282*
9-11, *282*

**Jude**
4, *282*
19, *282*

**Revelation**
1:3, *972*
1:11, *190*
2:9, *1042*
2:13, *123*
2:20, *973*
2:23, *868*
3:1, *190*
3:4, *190*
3:17, *1042*
10:11, *972*
13:1-10, *121*
14:4, *996*
14:13, *378*
15:3-4, *818*
17:17, *868*
18:10-14, *1079*
19:1-3, *816, 818*
19:7-8, *360*
20:4, *123*
21:1, *1101*
21:1-10, *17*
22:7, *972*
22:10, *972*
22:18, *972*

# Finding the Textbook You Need

The IVP Academic Textbook Selector
is an online tool for instantly finding the IVP books
suitable for over 250 courses across 24 disciplines.

**ivpacademic.com**